WORLD
CHAMBER OF COMMERCE
DIRECTORY

2017
Published Annually in January

D1736487

W

World Chamber of Commerce Directory

2017 edition

P.O. Box 1029
Loveland, CO 80539 U.S.A
(970) 663-3231
info@chamberdirectoryonline.com
www.chamberdirectoryonline.com

ISBN -13: 978-0-943581-30-9
ISBN -10: 0-943581-30-3
ISSN: 1048-2849

CONTENTS

Directory Listings

U.S. Government Information

If you have any changes to your listing, please contact us at any time: (888) 883-3231 or info@ChamberDirectoryOnline.com

Sample Listing

1	Name of City
2	Name of Organization
3	County
4	Population of the Area Served
5	Membership of Organization
6	Ambassador Program

① **②** **⑥** **③** **④**

⑤

Loveland • *Loveland C/C* • Mindy Moree; Pres./CEO; 5400 Stone Creek Circle; 80538; Larimer; P 77,000; M 700; (970) 667-6311; Fax (970) 667-5211; info@ loveland.org; www.loveland.org*

LOVELAND VALENTINE RE-MAILING PROGRAM AND SWEETHEART CITY ACTIVITIES, FEBRUARY 1-14; BUSINESS EXPO AND TRADE SHOW, APRIL; OLD FASHIONED CORN ROAST FESTIVAL, AUGUST; SCULPTURE IN THE PARK, 2ND WEEKEND IN AUGUST-LARGEST SCULPTURE SHOW WEST OF THE MISSISSIPPI.

Legend

C/C	Chamber of Commerce
P	Population of the Area Served
M	Membership
*	Ambassador Program

Note: Every effort has been made to enter the e-mail and internet address as they were provided to us. There is an assumed "http://" at the beginning of each internet (web site) address. If you have problems with a particular e-mail or internet address, please contact the appropriate chamber. Also note that many area codes are changing. If you experience difficulty reaching a number, please check with Directory Assistance.

NOTES

UNITED STATES CHAMBER OF COMMERCE

1615 H Street, N.W. • Washington, D.C. • 20062-2000 • (202) 659-6000 • www.uschamber.com

Chairman of the Board
John L. Hopkins • (202) 463-5761

Vice Chairman of the Board
Thomas J. Wilson • (202) 463-5761

Executive Staff

President & CEO
Thomas J. Donohue • (202) 463-5300

Senior V.P., Development
Agnes Warfield • (202) 463-5702

COO & Exec. V.P.
Shannon DiBari • (202) 463-5391

Senior Exec. V.P.
Suzanne Clark • (202) 463-5761

CFO & CIO
Stan Harrell • (202) 463-5531

Chief of Staff
Christopher Roberti • (202) 463-5449

Exec. V.P. Government Affairs
R. Bruce Josten • (202) 463-5310

Department Heads

Center for Advanced Technology & Innovation
Amanda Engstrom Eversole • (202) 463-5904

Environment, Technology & Regulatory Affairs
William L. Kovacs • (202) 463-5457

Center for Capital Markets Competitiveness
David Hirschmann • (202) 463-5609

Institute for 21st Century Energy
Karen Alderman Harbert • (202) 463-5636

Chief Economist
Dr. Martin A. Regalia • (202) 463-5620

Institute for Legal Reform
Lisa Rickard • (202) 463-3107

Chief Legal Office & General Counsel
Lily Fu Claffee • (202) 463-5921

International Affairs
Myron Brilliant • (202) 463-5489

Communications & Strategy
Thomas Collamore • (202) 463-5686

Labor, Immigration & Employee Benefits
Randy Johnson • (202) 463-5448

Congressional & Public Affairs
Jack Howard • (202) 463-5683

Political Affairs, Federation Relations & National Political Director
Rob Engstrom • (202) 463-3178

STATE CHAMBERS OF COMMERCE

Alabama

Bus. Cncl. of Alabama • William J. Canary; Pres./CEO; 2 N. Jackson St., Ste. 501 P.O. Box 76, AL; 36,101; Montgomery, P 4,849,377; M 4,500; (334) 834-6000; (800) 665-9647; Fax (334) 241-5984; info@bcatoday.org; http://www.bcatoday.org

Alaska

Alaska Chamber • Curtis Thayer; Pres./CEO; 471 W. 36th Ave. Ste. 201; Anchorage; 99503; Anchorage; P 735,601; M 700; (907) 278-2739; cthayer@alaskachamber.com; www.alaskachamber.com

Arizona

Arizona C of C & Ind. • Glenn Hamer; Pres./CEO; 3200 N. Central Ave. Ste. 1125; Phoenix; 85012; Maricopa; P 6,700,000; M 500; (602) 248-9172; Fax (602) 391-2498; info@azchamber.com; www.azchamber.com

Arkansas

Arkansas State C of C • Randy Zook; Pres./CEO; 1200 W. Capitol Ave.; Little Rock; 72201; Pulaski; P 2,949,131; M 1,300; (501) 372-2222; Fax (501) 372-2722; jthatcher@arkansasstatechamber.com; www.arkansasstatechamber.com

California

California C of C • Allan Zaremberg; Pres./CEO; 1215 K St. Ste. 1400; P.O. Box 1736; Sacramento; 95812; Sacramento; P 39,200,000; M 1,400; (916) 444-6670; Fax (916) 325-1272; hrcalifornia.service@calchamber.com; www.calchamber.com

Colorado

Colorado Assn. of Comm. & Ind. • Chuck Berry; Pres.; 1600 Broadway Ste. 1000; Denver; 80202; Denver; P 5,187,582; M 500; (303) 831-7411; Fax (303) 860-1439; info@cochamber.com; www.cochamber.com

Connecticut

Connecticut Bus. & Ind. Assn. • Joseph Brennan; Pres./CEO; 350 Church St.; Hartford; 06103; Hartford; P 3,600,000; M 10,000; (860) 244-1900; Fax (860) 278-8562; joseph.brennan@cbia.com; www.cbia.com

Delaware

Delaware State C of C • A. Richard Heffron; Pres.; 1201 N. Orange St. Ste. 200; P.O. Box 671; Wilmington; 19899; New Castle; P 917,092; M 2,800; (302) 655-7221; (800) 292-9507; Fax (302) 654-0691; dscc@dscc.com; www.dscc.com*

District of Columbia

No State Chamber

Florida

Florida C of C • Mark A. Wilson; Pres./CEO; 136 S. Bronough St.; P.O. Box 11309; Tallahassee; 32302; Leon; P 19,893,000; M 7,000; (850) 521-1200; vplymel@flchamber.com; www.flchamber.com*

Georgia

Georgia C of C • Chris Clark; Pres./CEO; 270 Peachtree St. N.W. Ste. 2200; Atlanta; 30303; Fulton; P 10,098,000; M 4,000; (404) 223-2264; Fax (404) 223-2290; choltzclaw@gachamber.com; www.gachamber.com

Hawaii

C of C of Hawaii • Sherry Menor-McNamara; Pres./CEO; 1132 Bishop St. Ste. 2105; Honolulu; 96813; Honolulu; P 1,420,000; M 1,100; (808) 545-4300; Fax (808) 545-4369; smenor-mcnamara@cochawaii.org; www.cochawaii.org*

Idaho

Idaho Chamber Alliance • c/o Boise Metro C/C; P.O. Box 2368; Boise; 83701; Ada; P 1,635,000; (208) 733-3974; contact@idahochamberalliance.com; www.idahochamberalliance.com

Illinois

Illinois C of C • Todd Maisch; Pres./CEO; 300 S. Wacker Dr. Ste. 1600; Chicago; 60606; Cook; P 12,875,255; M 4,000; (312) 983-7100; Fax (312) 983-7101; info@ilchamber.org; ilchamber.org

Indiana

Indiana C of C • Kevin Brinegar; Pres.; 115 W. Washington St. Ste. 850S; Indianapolis; 46204; Marion; P 6,597,000; M 4,900; (317) 264-3110; Fax (317) 264-6855; info@indianachamber.com; www.indianachamber.com

Iowa

Iowa Assn. of Bus. & Ind. • Michael Ralston; Pres.; 400 E. Court Ave. Ste. 100; Des Moines; 50309; Polk & Warren; P 3,074,186; M 1,400; (515) 280-8000; (800) 383-4224; Fax (515) 244-3285; abi@iowaabi.org; www.iowaabi.org

Kansas

Kansas C of C • Mike O'Neal; Pres./CEO; 835 S.W. Topeka Blvd.; Topeka; 66612; Shawnee; P 2,904,021; M 10,000; (785) 357-6321; Fax (785) 357-4732; president@kansaschamber.org; www.kansaschamber.org

Kentucky

Kentucky C of C • David Adkisson; Pres./CEO; 464 Chenault Rd.; Frankfort; 40601; Franklin; P 4,413,457; M 2,700; (502) 695-4700; Fax (502) 695-5051; kcc@kychamber.com; www.kychamber.com

Louisiana

Louisiana Assn. of Bus. & Ind. • Stephen Waguespack; Pres.; 3113 Valley Creek Dr.; P.O. Box 80258; Baton Rouge; 70898; East Baton Rouge; P 4,650,000; M 3,000; (225) 928-5388; Fax (225) 929-6054; clairek@labi.org; labi.org

Maine

Maine State C of C • Dana F. Connors; Pres.; 125 Community Dr. Ste. 101; Augusta; 04330; Kennebec; P 1,329,192; M 1,200; (207) 623-4568; Fax (207) 622-7723; melanieb@mainechamber.org; www.mainechamber.org

Maryland

Maryland C of C • Christine Ross; Pres./CEO; 60 West St. Ste. 100; Annapolis; 21401; Anne Arundel; P 5,884,563; M 850; (410) 269-0642; (301) 261-2858; Fax (410) 269-5247; mcc@mdchamber.org; www.mdchamber.org*

Massachusetts

No State Chamber

Michigan

Michigan C of C • Richard K. Studley; Pres./CEO; 600 S. Walnut St.; Lansing; 48933; Ingham; P 9,883,360; M 6,800; (517) 371-2100; (800) 748-0266; Fax (517) 371-7224; bmcnerney@michamber.com; www.michamber.com

Minnesota

Minnesota C of C • Doug Loon; Pres.; 400 Robert St. N. Ste. 1500; St. Paul; 55101; Ramsey; P 5,457,200; M 2,400; (651) 292-4650; (800) 821-2230; Fax (651) 292-4656; cpeterson@mnchamber.com; www.mnchamber.com

Mississippi

Mississippi Eco. Cncl. • Blake Wilson; Pres./CEO; 248 E. Capitol St. Ste. 940; P.O. Box 23276; Jackson; 39225; Hinds; P 2,994,100; M 8,000; (601) 969-0022; (800) 748-7626; Fax (601) 353-0247; cnorthington@mec.ms; www.mec.ms

Missouri

Missouri C of C & Ind. • Daniel P. Mehan; Pres./CEO; 428 E. Capitol Ave.; P.O. Box 149; Jefferson City; 65102; Cole; P 6,021,988; M 4,000; (573) 634-3511; Fax (573) 634-8855; dmehan@mochamber.com; www.mochamber.com

Montana

Montana C of C • Webb Brown CAE; Pres./CEO; 900 Gibbon St.; P.O. Box 1730; Helena; 59624; Lewis & Clark; P 1,005,141; M 1,500; (406) 442-2405; Fax (406) 442-2409; stacye@montanachamber.com; www.montanachamber.com

Nebraska

Nebraska C of C & Ind. • Barry L. Kennedy CAE IOM; Pres.; 1320 Lincoln Mall Ste. 201; P.O. Box 95128; Lincoln; 68509; Lancaster; P 1,855,525; M 2,000; (402) 474-4422; Fax (402) 474-5681; nechamber@nechamber.com; www.nechamber.com

Nevada

Women's Chamber of Commerce of Nevada • June Beland; Founder Pres./CEO; 2300 W. Sahara Ave. Ste. 800; Financial Center Bldg.; Las Vegas; 89102; Clark; P 2,758,931; M 550; (702) 733-3955; Fax (702) 926-9270; wccnv2@womenschamberofnevada.org; www.womenschamberofnevada.org*

New Hampshire

Bus. & Ind. Assn. of N.H. • Jim Roche; Pres.; 122 N. Main St.; Concord; 03301; Merrimack; P 1,320,718; M 400; (603) 224-5388; Fax (603) 224-2872; sstreeter@biaofnh.com; www.biaofnh.com

New Jersey

New Jersey C of C • Thomas Bracken; Pres./CEO; 216 W. State St.; Trenton; 08608; Mercer; P 8,864,590; M 1,600; (609) 989-7888; Fax (609) 989-9696; scott.goldstein@njchamber.com; www.njchamber.com

New Mexico

Assn. of Commerce & Ind. of New Mexico • Jason Espinoza; Pres./CEO; 2201 Buena Vista Dr. S.E. Ste. 410; P.O. Box 9706; Albuquerque; 87119; Bernalillo; P 2,085,572; M 1,300; (505) 842-0644; Fax (505) 842-0734; info@nmaci.org; www.nmaci.org

New York

No State Chamber

North Carolina

North Carolina Chamber • S. Lewis Ebert; Pres./CEO; 701 Corporate Center Dr. Ste. 400; Raleigh; 27607; Wake; P 9,752,073; M 1,900; (919) 836-1400; Fax (919) 836-1425; info@ncchamber.net; www.ncchamber.net

North Dakota

Greater North Dakota Chamber • Andy Peterson; Pres./CEO; 2000 Schafer St.; P.O. Box 2639; Bismarck; 58502; Burleigh; P 699,628; M 1,100; (701) 222-0929; Fax (701) 222-1611; susan@ndchamber.com; www.ndchamber.com

Ohio

Ohio C of C • Andrew Doehrel; Pres./CEO; 230 E. Town St.; P.O. Box 15159; Columbus; 43215; Franklin; P 11,544,225; M 4,000; (614) 228-4201; (800) 622-1893; Fax (614) 228-6403; occ@ohiochamber.com; www.ohiochamber.com

Oklahoma

State Chamber of Oklahoma • Fred S. Morgan; Pres./CEO; 330 N.E. 10th St.; P.O. Box 53217; Oklahoma City; 73152; Oklahoma; P 3,752,000; M 3,000; (405) 235-3669; Fax (405) 235-3670; fmorgan@okstatechamber.com; www.okstatechamber.com

Oregon

Oregon State C of C • Alison Hart; Exec. Dir.; 867 Liberty St.; P.O. Box 3344; Salem; 97301; Linn; P 3,930,000; M 71; (503) 363-7984; alisonh@pacounsel.org; www.oregonchamber.org

Pennsylvania

The Pennsylvania Chamber of Bus. & Ind. • Gene Barr; Pres./CEO; 417 Walnut St.; Harrisburg; 17101; Cumberland Dauphin & Perry; P 12,763,536; M 9,000; (717) 255-3252; (800) 225-7224; Fax (717) 255-3298; info@pachamber.org; www.pachamber.org

Rhode Island

No State Chamber

South Carolina

South Carolina C of C • Otis Rawl; Pres./CEO; 1301 Gervais St. Ste. 1100; Columbia; 29201; Richland; P 4,723,723; M 2,000; (803) 799-4601; Fax (803) 779-6043; grassroots@scchamber.net; www.scchamber.net

South Dakota

South Dakota C of C & Ind. • David Owen; Pres.; 222 E. Capital Ste. 15; P.O. Box 190; Pierre; 57501; Hughes; P 883,354; M 450; (605) 224-6161; Fax (605) 224-7198; davido@sdchamber.biz; www.sdchamber.biz

Tennessee

Tennessee C of C & Ind. • Catherine Glover; Pres.; 414 Union St. Ste. 107; Nashville; 37219; Davidson; P 6,456,243; M 600; (615) 256-5141; Fax (615) 256-6726; info@tnchamber.org; www.tnchamber.org

Texas

Texas Assn. of Bus. • Bill Hammond; CEO; 1209 Nueces St.; Austin; 78701; Travis; P 26,059,203; M 5,000; (512) 477-6721; Fax (512) 477-0836; info@txbiz.org; www.txbiz.org

Utah

Utah State C of C • Heidi Walker; Exec. Admin.; 175 E. Univ. Blvd. (400 S.) Ste. 600; Salt Lake City; 84111; Salt Lake; P 2,855,287; M 15,500; (801) 328-5081; Fax (801) 328-5098; hwalker@slchamber.com; utahstatechamber.org

Vermont

Vermont C of C • Betsy Bishop; Pres.; P.O. Box 37; Montpelier; 05601; Washington; P 626,011; M 1,500; (802) 223-3443; Fax (802) 223-4257; info@vtchamber.com; www.vtchamber.com*

Virginia

Virginia C of C • Barry E. DuVal; Pres./CEO; 919 E. Main St. Ste. 900; Richmond; 23219; Richmond City; P 8,185,867; M 1,000; (804) 644-1607; Fax (804) 783-6112; b.duval@vachamber.com; www.vachamber.com

Washington

Assn. of Washington Bus. • Kristofer T. Johnson; Pres./CEO; 1414 Cherry St. S.E.; P.O. Box 658; Olympia; 98507; Thurston; P 700,000; M 7,000; (360) 943-1600; (800) 521-9325; Fax (360) 943-5811; krisj@awb.org; www.awb.org

West Virginia

West Virginia C of C • Steve Roberts; Pres.; 1624 Kanawha Blvd. E.; Charleston; 25311; Kanawha; P 1,855,413; M 1,850; (304) 342-1115; Fax (304) 342-1130; mhutchinson@wvchamber.com; www.wvchamber.com

Wisconsin

Wisconsin Manufacturers & Commerce • Kurt Bauer; Pres./CEO; 501 E. Washington Ave.; P.O. Box 352; Madison; 53701; Dane; P 5,726,398; M 3,500; (608) 258-3400; Fax (608) 258-3413; wmc@wmc.org; www.wmc.org

Wyoming

No State Chamber

UNITED STATES CHAMBERS OF COMMERCE

If the area that interests you is not listed in this section, please refer to the Economic Development Councils section. Many Economic Development Councils double as Chambers for their area.

Alabama

Bus. Cncl. of Alabama • William J. Canary; Pres./CEO; 2 N. Jackson St., Ste. 501; P.O. Box 76; Montgomery; 36101; Montgomery; P 4,849,377; M 4,500; (334) 834-6000; (800) 665-9647; Fax (334) 241-5984; info@bcatoday.org; www.bcatoday.org

Chamber of Commerce Assn. of Alabama • Jeremy Arthur IOM; Pres./CEO; 2 N. Jackson St., Ste. 603; Montgomery; 36104; Montgomery; P 4,822,023; M 150; (334) 264-2112; Fax (334) 264-2113; kimt@bcatoday.org; alabamachambers.org

Abbeville • *Abbeville C/C* • Ronnie Marshall; Pres.; 300 Kirkland St.; P.O. Box 202; 36310; Henry; P 3,000; M 119; (334) 585-2273; Fax (334) 585-2273; abbevillechamber@centurytel.net; www.abbevillecoc.com

Alabaster • *see Pelham*

Albertville • *Albertville C/C* • Jennifer Palmer; Pres.; 316 E. Sand Mountain Dr.; P.O. Box 1457; 35950; Marshall; P 24,156; M 502; (256) 878-3821; (800) 878-3821; Fax (256) 878-3822; albertvillechamber@charter.net; www.albertvillechamberofcommerce.com*

Alexander City • *Alexander City C/C* • Ann Rye; Pres./CEO; 120 Tallapoosa St.; P.O. Box 926; 35011; Tallapoosa; P 15,000; M 400; (256) 234-3461; Fax (256) 234-0094; ann.rye@alexandercitychamber.com; www.alexandercitychamber.com*

Aliceville • *Aliceville Area C/C* • Debbie Fason; Mgr.; 419 Memorial Pkwy. N.E., Ste. A; P.O. Drawer A; 35442; Pickens; P 3,009; M 200; (205) 373-2820; Fax (205) 373-8692; acc@nctv.com; www.cityofaliceville.com

Andalusia • *Andalusia Area C/C* • Ashley Eiland; Exec. V.P.; 700 River Falls St.; P.O. Box 667; 36420; Covington; P 9,000; M 387; (334) 222-2030; Fax (334) 222-7844; ashley@andalusiachamber.com; www.andalusiachamber.com

Anniston • *Calhoun County C/C* • Linda Hearn; Chamber Mgr.; 1330 Quintard Ave.; P.O. Box 1087; 36202; Calhoun; P 117,296; M 772; (256) 237-3536; (800) 489-1087; Fax (256) 237-0126; lindah@calhounchamber.com; www.calhounchamber.com*

Ardmore • *see Ardmore, TN*

Arab • *Arab C/C* • Wes Kitchens; Pres.; P.O. Box 626; 35016; Marshall; P 9,000; M 320; (256) 586-3138; (888) 403-2722; Fax (256) 586-0233; info@arab-chamber.org; www.arab-chamber.org*

Ashford • *Ashford Area C/C* • Denise Fowler; Pres.; P.O. Box 463; 36312; Houston; P 2,200; M 75; (334) 899-3366; ashfordalchamber@gmail.com; www.cityofashford.com

Athens • *Greater Limestone County C/C* • Jennifer Williamson; Pres.; 101 S. Beaty St.; 35611; Limestone; P 82,782; M 511; (256) 232-2600; Fax (256) 232-2609; jennifer@tourathens.com; www.tourathens.com*

Atmore • *Atmore Area C/C* • Sheryl Vickery; Exec. Dir.; 137 N. Main St.; 36502; Escambia; P 8,000; M 267; (251) 368-3305; Fax (251) 368-0800; director@atmorechamber.com; www.atmorechamber.com*

Auburn • *Auburn C/C* • Lolly Steiner; Pres.; 714 E. Glenn Ave.; P.O. Box 1370; 36831; Lee; P 53,400; M 850; (334) 887-7011; Fax (334) 821-5500; lolly@auburnchamber.com; www.auburnchamber.com

Bay Minette • *North Baldwin C/C* • Ashley Jones; Exec. Dir.; 301 McMeans Ave.; P.O. Box 310; 36507; Baldwin; P 20,000; M 265; (251) 937-5665; Fax (251) 937-5670; ashley@northbaldwinchamber.com; www.northbaldwinchamber.com*

Bayou La Batre • *Bayou La Batre Area C/C* • Dena Pigg; Pres.; 13640 N. Wintzell Ave.; P.O. Box 486; 36509; Mobile; P 6,000; M 100; (251) 824-4088; Fax (251) 824-1840; bayouareachamber@hotmail.org; bayoulabatreareachamber.org

Bessemer • *Bessemer Area C/C* • LaTasha Cook; Pres.; 321 18th St. N.; 35020; Jefferson; P 31,000; M 300; (205) 425-3253; (888) 423-7736; bessemerchamber@bellsouth.net; www.bessemerchamber.com*

Birmingham • *Birmingham Bus. Alliance* • Brian Hilson; Pres./CEO; 505 20th St. N., Ste. 200; 35203; Jefferson; P 1,100,000; M 4,200; (205) 324-2100; Fax (205) 324-2560; kroy@birminghambusinessalliance.com; www.birminghambusinessalliance.com

Boaz • *Boaz Area C/C* • Peggie Haney; Dir.; 100 E. Bartlett Ave.; P.O. Box 563; 35957; Marshall; P 8,000; M 400; (256) 593-8154; Fax (256) 593-1233; peggie@boazchamberofcommerce.com; www.boazchamberofcommerce.com*

Brewton • *Greater Brewton Area C/C* • Judy Crane; Exec. Dir.; 1010-B Douglas Ave.; 36426; Escambia; P 9,000; M 225; (251) 867-3224; Fax (251) 809-1793; jcrane@brewtonchamber.com; www.brewtonchamber.com

Butler • *Choctaw County C/C & Comm. Dev. Found.* • Cynthia McIlwain; Exec. Dir.; P.O. Box 180; 36904; Choctaw; P 15,855; M 170; (205) 459-3459; (205) 604-8085; Fax (205) 459-2511; choctawchamber@tds.net

Camden • *Wilcox Area C/C* • Hunter Hines; Chmn. of the Bd.; 1001 Earl Hilliard Rd.; 36726; Wilcox; P 10,400; M 160; (334) 682-4929; (334) 456-1055; Fax (334) 682-4929; wilcoxdev@pinebelt.net; www.wilcoxareachamber.com*

Centre • *Cherokee County C/C* • Thereasa Hulgan; Exec. Dir.; 801 Cedar Bluff Rd., Bldg. A; 35960; Cherokee; P 25,000; M 375; (256) 927-8455; Fax (256) 927-2768; thulgan@cherokee-chamber.org; www.cherokee-chamber.org*

Centreville • *Bibb County C/C* • Tracey Mitchell; Exec. Dir.; 835 Walnut St.; P.O. Box 25; 35042; Bibb; P 23,000; M 100; (205) 926-5222; bibbchamber@gmail.com; www.bibbchamber.org*

Chelsea • *see Columbiana*

Chickasaw • *Chickasaw C/C* • Cecilia Ann Dailey; Exec. Secy.; P.O. Box 11421; 36671; Mobile; P 6,100; M 78; (251) 452-8623; (251) 457-2707; www.chickasawchamber.com

Childersburg • *Childersburg C/C* • Peter Storey; Pres./CEO; 805 Third St. S.W.; P.O. Box 527; 35044; Shelby & Talladega; P 5,000; M 225; (256) 378-5482; (256) 510-0027; Fax (256) 378-5833; pbstorey@childersburg.com; www.childersburg.com*

Clanton • *Chilton County C/C* • Janice Hull; Dir.; 500 5th Ave. N.; P.O. Box 66; 35046; Chilton; P 43,819; M 350; (205) 755-2400; Fax (205) 755-8444; info@chiltonchamberonline.com; chiltonchamberonline.com*

Clay • *Clay-Pinson C/C* • Becky Johnson; Pres.; P.O. Box 26; 35048; Jefferson; P 8,500; M 100; (205) 680-6445; (205) 680-2757; www.claypinsonchamber.com

Columbiana • *South Shelby C/C* • April Stone; Exec. Dir.; 208 E. College St.; P.O. Box 396; 35051; Shelby; P 106,000; M 450; (205) 669-9075; director@southshelbychamber.com; www.southshelbychamber.com*

Cullman • *Cullman Area C/C* • Leah Bolin; Pres./CEO; 301 2nd Ave. S.W.; P.O. Box 1104; 35056; Cullman; P 80,000; M 842; (256) 734-0454; Fax (256) 737-7443; info@cullmanchamber.org; www.cullmanchamber.org*

Dadeville • *Dadeville Area C/C* • Linda Andrews; Exec. Admin; 345 E. LaFayette St., Ste. 102; 36853; Tallapoosa; P 4,000; M 165; (256) 825-4019; Fax (256) 825-0547; chamber@dadeville.com; www.dadeville.com

Daleville • *Daleville Area C/C* • Nancy Garner; Exec. Dir.; 750 S. Daleville Ave.; P.O. Box 688; 36322; Alabama; P 5,500; M 76; (334) 598-6331; Fax (334) 598-2333; chamber@dalevilleal.com; www.dalevillechamber.com

Daphne • *Eastern Shore C/C* • Casey Williams; 29750 Larry Dee Cawyer Dr.; P.O. Box 310; 36526; Baldwin; P 76,544; M 1,000; (251) 621-8222; office@eschamber.com; www.eschamber.com*

Dauphin Island • *Dauphin Island C/C* • Tricia Kerr; Pres.; P.O. Box 5; 36528; Mobile; P 1,240; M 62; (251) 861-5524; (877) 532-8744; contact@dauphinislandchamber.com; www.dauphinislandchamber.com

Decatur • *Decatur-Morgan County C/C* • John Seymour; Pres./CEO; 515 6th Ave. N.E.; P.O. Box 2003; 35602; Morgan; P 120,000; M 900; (256) 353-5312; Fax (256) 353-2384; john@dcc.org; www.dcc.org*

Demopolis • *Demopolis Area C/C* • Jenn Tate; Exec. Dir.; 102 E. Washington St.; P.O. Box 667; 36732; Marengo; P 30,000; M 175; (334) 289-0270; (334) 289-0216; Fax (334) 289-1382; demopchamber@yahoo.com; www.demopolischamber.com

Dora • *see Sumiton*

Dothan • *Dothan Area C/C* • Matt Parker; Pres.; 102 Jamestown Blvd.; P.O. Box 638; 36302; Houston; P 105,000; M 1,045; (334) 792-5138; (800) 221-1027; Fax (334) 794-4796; chamber@dothan.com; www.dothan.com*

Elba • *Elba C/C* • Kaye Whitworth; Exec. Dir.; 329 Putnam St.; 36323; Coffee; P 4,185; M 130; (334) 897-3125; Fax (334) 897-1762; elbachamber@yahoo.com; www.elbaalabama.net

Enterprise • *Enterprise C/C* • Erin Grantham; Pres.; 553 Glover Ave.; P.O. Box 310577; 36331; Coffee; P 29,903; M 620; (334) 347-0581; (800) 235-4730; Fax (334) 393-8204; chamber@enterprisealabama.com; www.enterprisealabama.com*

Eufaula • *Eufaula-Barbour County C/C* • Sallie Garrison; Exec. Dir.; 333 E. Broad St.; 36027; Barbour; P 28,000; M 350; (334) 687-6664; (800) 524-7529; Fax (334) 687-5240; kwright@eufaulachamber.com; www.eufaulachamber.com*

Eutaw • *Eutaw Area C/C* • Beverly Gordon; Pres.; 111 Main St.; P.O. Box 31; 35462; Greene; P 11,000; M 40; (205) 372-9002; Fax (205) 372-1393; eutawchamber@bellsouth.net; www.eutawchamber.com

Evergreen • *Evergreen/Conecuh County Area C/C* • Robert Humphrey; Pres.; 100 Depot Sq.; 36401; Conecuh; P 14,000; M 100; (251) 578-1707; evergreen.conecuh@yahoo.com; www.evergreenchamberofcommerce.org

Fairhope • *Eastern Shore C/C - Fairhope Ofc.* • Heiko Einfeld; Pres./CEO; 327 Fairhope Ave.; 36532; Baldwin; P 65,000; M 900; (251) 928-6387; office@eschamber.com; www.eschamber.com*

Fayette • *Fayette Area C/C* • Daniel B. White; Exec. Dir.; 102 2nd Ave.; P.O. Box 247; 35555; Fayette; P 5,000; M 165; (205) 932-4587; Fax (205) 932-8788; fcoc@cyberjoes.com; www.fayetteareachamber.org

Flomaton • *Flomaton C/C* • Wanda Vanlandingham; Pres.; P.O. Box 636; 36441; Escambia; P 7,000; M 50; (251) 296-1110; Fax (251) 296-1110; flomatoncoc@att.net; www.flomaton.com

Florala • *Tri-Cities C/C* • James O. Waldrop Jr.; Pres.; 1135 4th St.; 36442; Covington; P 4,000; M 45; (334) 858-6252; floralatricity@yahoo.com; www.tricitieschamberofcommerce.com

Florence • *Shoals C/C* • Barbara Hunt; Senior V.P.; 20 Hightower Pl.; P.O. Box 1331; 35631; Lauderdale; P 147,137; M 1,005; (256) 764-4661; Fax (256) 766-9017; shoals@shoalschamber.com; www.shoalschamber.com*

Foley • *South Baldwin C/C* • Donna Watts; Pres./CEO; 112 W. Laurel Ave.; P.O. Box 1117; 36536; Baldwin; P 50,300; M 715; (251) 943-3291; (877) 461-3712; Fax (251) 943-6810; infodesk@southbaldwinchamber.com; www.southbaldwinchamber.com*

Fort Deposit • *Fort Deposit C/C* • Erick Ellis; Pres.; P.O. Box 162; 36032; Lowndes; P 1,519; M 30; (334) 227-4411; www.fortdeposit.info

Fort Payne • *Fort Payne C/C* • Carol Beddingfield; Exec. Dir.; 300 Gault Ave. N.; 35968; DeKalb; P 15,000; M 310; (256) 845-2741; Fax (256) 845-5849; info@fortpaynechamber.com; www.fortpaynechamber.com

Gadsden • *The Chamber, Gadsden/Etowah County* • Heather New; Pres.; One Commerce Sq.; P.O. Box 185; 35902; Etowah; P 103,000; M 1,200; (256) 543-3472; Fax (256) 543-9887; kerri@gadsdenchamber.com; www.gadsdenchamber.com*

Gardendale • *Greater Gardendale C/C* • Amee Donald; Dir.; 2109 Moncrief Rd., Ste. 115; P.O. Box 26; 35071; Jefferson; P 13,000; M 300; (205) 631-9195; Fax (205) 631-9034; info@gardendalechamberofcommerce.com; www.gardendalechamber.com*

Geneva • *Greater Geneva Area C/C* • Alice Faye Smith; Dir.; 406 S. Commerce St.; 36340; Geneva; P 5,000; M 95; (334) 684-6582; genevacountychamber@centurylink.net; www.genevacounty.us

Gordo • *Gordo Area C/C* • Rusty Adams; Pres.; P.O. Box 33; 35466; Pickens; P 1,800; M 75; (205) 364-7870; Fax (205) 364-7870; gordococ@gmail.com

Grant • *Grant C/C* • Josh Barnes; Pres.; P.O. Box 221; 35747; Marshall; P 665; M 80; (256) 728-8800; Fax (256) 728-2777; grant@nehp.net; www.grantchamberofcommerce.com

Greenville • *Greenville Area C/C* • Francine Wasden; Exec. Dir.; One Depot Sq.; 36037; Butler; P 22,000; M 330; (334) 382-3251; Fax (334) 382-3181; chamber@greenville-alabama.com; www. greenvillealchamber.com*

Grove Hill • *Grove Hill Area C/C* • Cheryl Horton; Exec. Dir.; 104 N. Jackson St.; P.O. Box 567; 36451; Clarke; P 1,490; M 75; (251) 275-4188; Fax (251) 275-2278; grovehillcoc@tds.net; www.grovehillal.com

Gulf Shores • *Coastal Alabama Bus. Chamber* • Ed Rodriguez; Pres./CEO; 3150 Gulf Shores Pkwy.; P.O. Drawer 3869; 36547; Baldwin; P 40,000; M 1,000; (251) 968-7200; Fax (251) 968-5332; info@mygulfcoastchamber.com; www.mygulfcoastchamber.com*

Guntersville • *Lake Guntersville C/C* • Morri Yancy; Pres.; 200 Gunter Ave.; P.O. Box 577; 35976; Marshall; P 8,700; M 600; (256) 582-3612; (800) 869-LAKE; Fax (256) 582-3682; gcc@lakeguntersville.org; www. lakeguntersville.org*

Haleyville • *Haleyville Area C/C* • Natalie Boykin; Exec. Admin. Asst.; P.O. Box 634; 35565; Winston; P 4,200; M 75; (205) 486-4611; Fax (205) 486-5074; haleyvillechamberofcommerce@gmail.com; www. haleyvillechamber.org

Hamilton • *Hamilton Area C/C* • Dana Scott; Pres.; P.O. Box 1168; 35570; Marion; P 7,000; M 175; (205) 921-7786; Fax (205) 921-2220; hacoc@hamiltonchamberofcommerce.org; www. hamiltonchamberofcommerce.org

Harpersville • *see Columbiana*

Hartselle • *Hartselle Area C/C* • Susan Hines; Pres.; 110 Railroad St. S.W.; P.O. Box 817; 35640; Morgan; P 14,539; M 300; (256) 773-4370; (800) 294-0692; Fax (256) 773-4379; hartsell@hiwaay.net; www. hartsellechamber.com*

Headland • *Headland Area C/C* • Rhonda Harrison; Exec. Dir.; 25 Grove St.; P.O. Box 236; 36345; Henry; P 5,000; M 125; (334) 693-3303; Fax (334) 785-5020; headlandalchamber@gmail.com; www. headlandal.com

Heflin • *Cleburne County C/C* • Emily Brown; Exec. Dir.; P.O. Box 413; 36264; Cleburne; P 15,000; M 100; (256) 463-2222; Fax (256) 463-4668; emily@cleburnecountychamber.com; cleburnecountychamber. com

Homewood • *Homewood C/C* • Tricia Ford; Exec. Dir.; 1721 Oxmoor Rd.; P.O. Box 59494; 35259; Jefferson; P 25,500; M 480; (205) 871-5631; Fax (205) 871-5632; director@homewoodchamber.org; www. homewoodchamber.org

Hoover • *Hoover Area C/C* • Bill Powell; Exec. Dir.; 1694 Montgomery Hwy., Ste. 108; P.O. Box 36005; 35236; Jefferson-Shelby; P 87,000; M 1,100; (205) 988-5672; admin@hooverchamber.org; www. hooverchamber.org*

Hueytown • *Hueytown Area C/C* • Rebecca Williams; Exec. Dir.; 1320 Hueytown Rd.; P.O. Box 3650; 35023; Jefferson; P 16,000; M 221; (205) 491-8039; Fax (205) 491-7961; hueyoed@bellsouth.net; www. hueytownchamber.com*

Huntsville • *C of C of Huntsville/Madison County* • Chip Cherry CCE; Pres./CEO; 225 Church St.; 35801; Madison; P 343,080; M 2,500; (256) 535-2000; Fax (256) 535-2015; alocke@hsvchamber.org; www. hsvchamber.org*

Irondale • *Greater Irondale C/C* • Melanie Lyons; Exec. Dir.; 1912 1st Ave. S.; 35210; Jefferson; P 11,000; M 100; (205) 956-3104; caboose500@aol.com; www.greaterirondalechamber.com*

Jackson • *Jackson C/C* • LaShaunda Holly; Exec. Dir.; 500 Commerce St.; 36545; Clarke; P 5,600; M 150; (251) 246-3251; Fax (251) 246-3213; jacksonchamber@bellsouth.net; www.jacksonalabama.org

Jasper • *C/C of Walker County* • Linda Lewis; Pres.; 204 19th St. E., Ste. 101; P.O. Box 972; 35502; Walker; P 67,000; M 350; (205) 384-4571; Fax (205) 384-4901; linda@walkerchamber.us; www. walkerchamber.us*

Lafayette • *see Lanett*

Lanett • *Greater Valley Area C/C* • Ashley M. Crane; Exec./Tourism Dir.; 2102 S. Broad Ave.; P.O. Box 205; 36863; Chambers; P 40,000; M 225; (334) 642-1411; Fax (334) 642-1410; chamber@greatervalleyarea.com; www.greatervalleyarea.com*

Leeds • *Leeds Area C/C* • Sandra McGuire; Exec. Dir.; 7901 Pkwy. Dr.; P.O. Box 900; 35094; Jefferson; P 11,500; M 200; (205) 699-5001; Fax (205) 699-1777; sandra@leedsareachamber.com; www. leedsareachamber.com*

Lincoln • *Greater Talladega/Lincoln Area C/C* • Jason Daves; Exec. Dir.; 150 Magnolia St.; 35096; Talladega; P 21,170; M 300; (256) 362-9075; info@talladegachamber.com; www.talladegachamber.com*

Lineville • *Clay County C/C* • Mary Patchunka-Smith; Exec. Dir.; 88855 Hwy. 9; P.O. Box 85; 36266; Clay; P 13,900; M 130; (256) 396-2828; claychamber@centurytel.net; www.claycochamber.com

Lockhart • *see Florala*

Luverne • *Crenshaw County C/C* • Carol Staller; Secy./Treas.; 3 S. Forest Ave.; P.O. Box 4; 36049; Crenshaw; P 13,000; M 80; (334) 335-4468; Fax (334) 335-4469; crenshawco.chamber@yahoo.com; www. crenshawcochamber.com*

Madison • *Madison C/C* • Pam Honeycutt; Exec. Dir.; 130 Park Square Ln.; 35758; Madison; P 47,000; M 500; (256) 325-8317; director@madisonalchamber.com; www.madisonalchamber.com*

Marion • *Perry County C/C* • John L. Martin; Exec. Dir.; 1293 Washington St.; 36756; Perry; P 9,871; M 35; (334) 683-9622; Fax (334) 683-4561; perrycountychamb@bellsouth.net; www. perrycountyalabamachamber.com

Millbrook • *Millbrook Area C/C* • Marietta Kouns; Exec. Dir.; 3453 A Main St.; P.O. Box 353; 36054; Elmore; P 14,639; M 175; (334) 285-0085; Fax (334) 285-9854; info@millbrookareachamber.com; www. millbrookareachamber.com*

Mobile • *Mobile Area C/C* • Bill Sisson; Pres./CEO; 451 Government St.; 36602; Mobile; P 412,992; M 2,400; (251) 433-6951; Fax (251) 432-1143; info@mobilechamber.com; www.mobilechamber.com*

Monroeville • *Monroeville/Monroe County C/C* • Sandy Smith; Exec. Dir.; 86 N. Alabama Ave.; P.O. Box 214; 36461; Monroe; P 25,000; M 235; (251) 743-2879; Fax (251) 743-2189; sandy@monroecountyal. com; www.monroecountyal.com*

Montevallo • *Montevallo C/C* • Steve Gilbert; Exec. Dir.; 845 Valley St.; 35115; Shelby; P 6,000; M 100; (205) 665-1519; montevallochamber@gmail.com; montevallocc.com

Montgomery • *Montgomery Area C/C* • Randall L. George CEcD; Pres.; 41 Commerce St.; P.O. Box 79; 36101; Montgomery; P 230,000; M 1,900; (334) 834-5200; Fax (334) 265-4745; macc@montgomerychamber.com; www.montgomerychamber.com*

Montrose • *see Daphne*

Moody • *Moody Area C/C* • Andrea Machen; Exec. Dir.; 670 Park Ave.; 35004; St. Clair; P 13,859; M 140; (205) 640-6262; Fax (205) 640-2996; chamber@moodyalabama.gov; www.moodyalchamber.com*

Moulton • *Lawrence County C/C* • Kim Hood; Exec. Dir.; 12467 Alabama Hwy. 157; 35650; Lawrence; P 35,000; M 320; (256) 974-1658; Fax (256) 974-2400; lawrence@lawrencealabama.com; lawrencealabama.com

Mountain Brook • *Mountain Brook C/C* • Suzan Doidge; Exec. Dir.; 101 Hoyt Ln.; 35213; Jefferson; P 21,000; M 350; (205) 871-3779; Fax (205) 871-6678; suzan@welcometomountainbrook.com; www.welcometomountainbrook.com

Mt. Laurel • *see Columbiana*

Munford • *see Talladega*

Oneonta • *Blount County-Oneonta C/C* • Donny B. Ray; Exec. Dir.; 225 2nd Ave. E.; P.O. Box 1487; 35121; Blount; P 57,826; M 375; (205) 274-2153; Fax (205) 274-2099; info@blountoneontachamber.org; www.blountoneontachamber.org

Opelika • *Opelika C/C* • Barbara Patton; Pres.; 601 Ave. A; P.O. Box 2366; 36803; Lee; P 27,000; M 670; (334) 745-4861; Fax (334) 749-4740; coc@opelikachamber.com; www.opelikachamber.com*

Opp • *Opp & Covington County Area C/C* • Emilee Gage; Ofc. Admin.; 101 E. Ida Ave.; P.O. Box 148; 36467; Covington; P 7,000; M 250; (334) 493-3070; (800) 239-8054; Fax (334) 493-1060; chamber@oppcatv.com

Oxford • *see Anniston*

Ozark • *Ozark Area C/C* • Tanya T. Roberts; Exec. Dir.; 294 Painter Ave.; 36360; Dale; P 15,000; M 280; (334) 774-9321; Fax (334) 774-8736; info@ozarkalchamber.com; www.ozarkalchamber.com*

Pelham • *Greater Shelby County C/C* • Kirk R. Mancer IOM CCE; Pres./CEO; 1301 County Services Dr.; 35124; Shelby; P 200,000; M 1,000; (205) 663-4542; Fax (205) 663-4524; kirk@shelbychamber.org; www.shelbychamber.org*

Pell City • *Greater Pell City C/C* • Kelsey Bain; Exec. Dir.; 1000 Bruce Etheredge Pkwy., Ste. 105; P.O. Box 1561; 35125; St. Clair; P 14,000; M 354; (205) 338-3377; Fax (205) 338-1913; kelseybain@pellcitychamber.com; www.pellcitychamber.com

Phenix City • *Phenix City-Russell County C/C* • Victor W. Cross; Pres./CEO; 1107 Broad St.; P.O. Box 1326; 36868; Russell; P 53,000; M 435; (334) 298-3639; (800) 892-2248; Fax (334) 298-3846; pcrccham@ldl.net; pc-rcchamber.com*

Point Clear • *see Daphne*

Prattville • *Prattville Area C/C* • Patty VanderWal; Pres.; 131 N. Court St.; 36067; Autauga; P 60,000; M 700; (334) 365-7392; (800) 588-2796; Fax (334) 361-1314; pvanderwal@prattvillechamber.com; www.prattvillechamber.com*

Prichard • *see Mobile*

Rainsville • *Rainsville C/C* • Tim Eberhart; Exec. Dir.; P.O. Box 396; 35986; DeKalb; P 5,000; M 110; (256) 638-7800; timeberhart@farmerstel.com; www.rainsvillealabama.com

Roanoke • *Randolph County C/C* • Dorothy B. Tidwell; Exec. Dir.; P.O. Box 431; 36274; Randolph; P 23,253; M 175; (334) 863-6612; (800) 863-6612; Fax (334) 863-7280; rancococ@teleclipse.net; www.randolphcountyal.com

Robertsdale • *Central Baldwin C/C* • Gail Quezada; Exec. Dir.; 23150 Hwy. 59; P.O. Box 587; 36567; Baldwin; P 4,000; M 300; (251) 947-2626; Fax (251) 947-4809; gquezada@centralbaldwin.com; www.centralbaldwin.com*

Russellville • *Franklin County C/C* • Cassie Medley; Exec. Dir.; 103 N. Jackson Ave.; P.O. Box 44; 35653; Franklin; P 31,500; M 200; (256) 332-1760; Fax (256) 332-1740; director@franklincountychamber.org; www.franklincountychamber.org

Saraland • *Saraland Area C/C* • Pamela Burnham; Exec. Dir.; 939 Hwy. 43 S.; 36571; Mobile; P 15,000; M 200; (251) 675-4444; Fax (251) 675-2307; info@saralandcoc.com; www.saralandcoc.com*

Scottsboro • *Greater Jackson County C/C* • Rick Roden; Pres./CEO; 407 E. Willow St.; P.O. Box 973; 35768; Jackson; P 55,000; M 500; (256) 259-5500; (800) 259-5508; Fax (256) 259-4447; chamber@scottsboro.org; www.jacksoncountychamber.com*

Selma • *Selma & Dallas County C/C* • Sheryl Smedley; Exec. Dir.; 912 Selma Ave.; 36701; Dallas; P 43,820; M 325; (334) 875-7241; Fax (334) 875-7142; info@SelmaAlabama.com; www.SelmaAlabama.com

Spanish Fort • *see Daphne*

Springville • *Springville Area C/C* • Betty Wisner; Secy.; 6496 U.S. Hwy. 11; 35146; St. Clair; P 5,000; M 60; (205) 467-2339; bwisner@springvillealabama.org; www.springvillealabama.org

Sumiton • *East Walker County C/C* • Chee-Vee Whitfield; Dir.; 2510 Hwy. 78 W.; P.O. Box 188; 35148; Walker; P 12,000; M 80; (205) 255-0202; Fax (205) 255-0202; chee-vee@eastwalkerchamber.com; www.eastwalkerchamber.com*

Sylacauga • *Sylacauga C/C* • Carol A. Emlich-Bates; Exec. Dir.; 17 W. Fort Williams St.; P.O. Box 185; 35150; Talladega; P 14,000; M 442; (256) 249-0308; Fax (256) 249-0315; chamber@sylacauga.net; www.sylacaugachamber.com*

Talladega • *Greater Talladega/Lincoln Area C/C* • Jason Daves; Exec. Dir.; 210 East St. S.; P.O. Drawer A; 35160; Talladega; P 21,170; M 300; (256) 362-9075; Fax (256) 362-9093; info@talladegachamber.com; www.talladegachamber.com*

Tallassee • *Tallassee C/C* • Jeanna W. Kervin; Exec. Dir.; 650 Gilmer Ave.; 36078; Elmore; P 5,000; M 250; (334) 283-5151; (334) 850-2056; Fax (334) 252-0774; chamber@tallasseechamber.com; www.tallasseechamber.com*

Thomasville • *Thomasville Alabama C/C* • Amy Prescott; Exec. Dir.; 138 Wilson Ave.; P.O. Box 44; 36784; Clarke; P 5,500; M 150; (334) 636-1542; Fax (334) 636-6624; director@thomasvillealchamber.com; www.thomasvillealchamber.com

Tillman's Corner • *Tillman's Corner C/C* • Tina Poiroux; Dir.; 5055 Carol Plantation Rd.; 36619; Mobile; P 16,000; M 160; (251) 666-2488; (251) 666-2846; Fax (251) 666-2813; tillmanscornerco@bellsouth.net; www.tillmanscornerchamber.com

Troy • *Pike County C/C* • Kathleen Sauer; Pres.; 101A E. Church St.; P.O. Box 249; 36081; Pike; P 32,900; M 450; (334) 566-2294; Fax (334) 566-2298; pikecoc@troycable.net; www.pikecoc.com

Trussville • *Trussville Area C/C* • Diane Poole; Exec. Dir.; 400 Main St.; 35173; Jefferson; P 20,000; M 420; (205) 655-7535; Fax (205) 655-3705; info@trussvillechamber.com; www.trussvillechamber.com*

Tuscaloosa • *C/C of West Alabama* • Jim M. Page CCE; Pres./CEO; 2201 Jack Warner Pkwy.; P.O. Box 020410; 35402; Tuscaloosa; P 400,000; M 1,350; (205) 758-7588; (205) 391-0562; Fax (205) 391-0565; info@tuscaloosachamber.com; www.tuscaloosachamber.com*

Tuskegee • Tuskegee Area C/C • Lutalo K. Aryee; Exec. Dir.; 121 S. Main St.; P.O. Box 831034; 36083; Macon; P 10,000; M 110; (334) 727-6619; Fax (334) 725-1801; lutalo@tuskegeeareachamber.org; www.tuskegeeareachamber.org*

Union Springs • Union Springs-Bullock County C/C • Evelyn Smart; Pres.; P.O. Box 5006; 36089; Bullock; P 11,000; M 503; (334) 738-2424; info@usacoc.com; www.usacoc.com

Valley • see Lanett

Vernon • Vernon C/C • Ray Reeves; Pres.; P.O. Box 336; 35592; Lamar; P 2,000; M 60; (205) 695-7718; Fax (205) 695-1006

Vestavia Hills • Vestavia Hills C/C • Karen Odle; Exec. Dir.; 1975 Merryvale Rd.; 35216; Jefferson; P 32,000; M 950; (205) 823-5011; Fax (205) 823-8974; chamber@vestaviahills.org; www.vestaviahills.org*

Vincent • see Columbiana

Westover • see Columbiana

Wetumpka • Wetumpka Area C/C • Vanessa Lynch; Exec. Dir.; 110 E. Bridge St.; 36092; Elmore; P 15,000; M 400; (334) 567-4811; Fax (334) 567-1811; vlynch@wetumpkachamber.org; www.wetumpkachamber.com*

Wilsonville • see Columbiana

Winfield • Winfield C/C • Mike Nolen; Pres.; P.O. Box 916; 35594; Fayette; P 5,000; M 85; (205) 487-8841; Fax (205) 487-8841; chamber@winfieldcity.com; www.winfieldcity.org

Alaska

Alaska Chamber • Curtis Thayer; Pres./CEO; 471 W. 36th Ave., Ste. 201; Anchorage; 99503; Anchorage; P 735,601; M 700; (907) 278-2739; cthayer@alaskachamber.com; www.alaskachamber.com

Anchor Point • Anchor Point C/C • John Cox; Pres.; P.O. Box 610; 99556; Kenai Peninsula; P 2,400; M 150; (907) 235-2600; Fax (907) 235-2600; info@anchorpointchamber.org; www.anchorpointchamber.org

Anchorage • Anchorage C/C • Bruce Bustamante; Pres.; 1016 W. 6th Ave., Ste. 303; 99501; Anchorage; P 300,000; M 900; (907) 272-2401; Fax (907) 272-4117; caleb@anchoragechamber.org; www.anchoragechamber.org*

Barrow • City of Barrow • Bertha Akpik; City Clerk; P.O. Box 629; 99723; North Slope; P 4,600; (907) 852-5211; Fax (907) 852-5871; bertha.akpik@cityofbarrow.org; www.cityofbarrow.org

Bethel • Bethel C/C • Bonnie Bradbury; Admin. Asst.; P.O. Box 329; 99559; Bethel; P 6,100; M 74; (907) 543-2911; Fax (907) 543-2255; bethelchamber1@alaska.com; www.bethelakchamber.org

Big Lake • Big Lake C/C • Ina Mueller; Pres.; P.O. Box 520067; 99652; Matanuska-Susitna; P 3,700; M 115; (907) 892-6109; Fax (907) 892-6120; nancielinley@yahoo.com; www.biglakechamber.org

Chugiak • see Eagle River

Cooper Landing • Cooper Landing C/C • Jen Harpe; Pres.; P.O. Box 809; 99572; Kenai Peninsula; P 300; M 60; (907) 595-8888; Fax (907) 595-8888; info@cooperlandingchamber.com; www.cooperlandingchamber.com

Cordova • Cordova C/C • Martin Moe; Exec. Dir.; 404 First St.; P.O. Box 99; 99574; Valdez Cordova; P 2,000; M 150; (907) 424-7260; Fax (907) 424-7259; visitcordova@ak.net; www.cordovachamber.com

Delta Junction • Delta C/C & Visitor Center • Janet Hawi; Exec. Dir.; P.O. Box 987; 99737; SE Fairbanks; P 5,700; M 200; (907) 895-5068; Fax (907) 895-5141; deltacc@deltachamber.org; www.deltachamber.org

Dillingham • Dillingham C/C • Chris Napoli; Pres.; P.O. Box 889; 99576; Dillingham; P 2,400; M 70; (907) 842-4323; (907) 842-5212; dillinghamchamberofcommerce@gmail.com; www.dillinghamchamberofcommerce.org

Eagle River • Chugiak-Eagle River C/C • Susan Gorski; Exec. Dir.; Chugiak-Eagle River Town Center, 12001 Business Blvd., Ste. 108; P.O. Box 770353; 99577; Anchorage; P 35,000; M 325; (907) 694-4702; Fax (907) 694-1205; info@cer.org; www.cer.org*

Fairbanks • Greater Fairbanks C/C • Lisa Herbert; Exec. Dir.; 100 Cushman St., Ste. 102; 99701; Fairbanks North Star; P 97,970; M 750; (907) 452-1105; Fax (907) 456-6968; info@fairbankschamber.org; www.fairbankschamber.org*

Glennallen • Greater Copper Valley C/C • P.O. Box 469; 99588; Valdez Cordova; P 3,500; M 185; (907) 822-5555; Fax (907) 822-5559; chamber@coppervalley.org; www.coppervalleychamber.com

Haines • Greater Haines C/C • Debra Schnabel; Exec. Dir.; 219 Main St., Ste. 14; P.O. Box 1449; 99827; Haines; P 3,800; M 143; (907) 766-2202; Fax (907) 766-2271; chamber@haineschamber.org; www.haineschamber.org

Healy • Denali C/C • Kindahl Guhrt; Dir.; Mile .6 Healy Spur Rd.; P.O. Box 437; 99743; Denali; P 2,000; M 120; (907) 683-4636; denali.chamber@gmail.com; www.denalichamber.com

Homer • Homer C/C & Visitor Center • Karen Zak; Exec. Dir.; 201 Sterling Hwy.; 99603; Kenai Peninsula; P 5,000; M 529; (907) 235-7740; Fax (907) 235-8766; info@homeralaska.org; www.homeralaska.org*

Houston • Houston C/C • P.O. Box 940356; 99694; Matanuska-Susitna; P 2,100; M 50; (907) 892-6812; houstonakchamber@hotmail.com; houstonakchamber.tripod.com

Hyder • Stewart-Hyder Intl. C/C • Gwen McKay; Mgr.; P.O. Box 149; 99923; Prince of Wales-Hyder; P 100; M 70; (250) 636-9224; Fax (250) 636-2199; stewartchamber@gmail.com

Juneau • Juneau C/C • Cathie Roemmich; CEO; 3100 Channel Dr., Ste. 300; 99801; Juneau; P 32,000; M 400; (907) 463-3488; Fax (907) 463-3489; juneauchamber@gci.net; www.juneauchamber.com*

Kenai • Kenai C/C & Visitor Center • Johna Beech; Pres./COO; 11471 Kenai Spur Hwy.; 99611; Kenai; P 7,000; M 371; (907) 283-1991; Fax (907) 283-2230; johna@kenaichamber.org; www.kenaichamber.org

Ketchikan • Greater Ketchikan C/C • Chelsea Goucher; Bus. Mgr.; 2417 Tongass Ave., Ste. 223A; P.O. Box 5957; 99901; Gateway; P 13,000; M 225; (907) 225-3184; Fax (907) 225-3187; info@ketchikanchamber.com; www.ketchikanchamber.com

Klawock • Prince of Wales C/C • Wendy Hamilton; Ofc. Mgr.; 6488 Klawock-Hollis Hwy., Ste. 7; P.O. Box 490; 99925; Prince of Wales-Hyder; P 5,000; M 270; (907) 755-2626; Fax (907) 755-2627; info@princeofwalescoc.org; www.princeofwalescoc.org

Kodiak • Kodiak C/C • Trevor Brown; Exec. Dir.; 100 E. Marine Way, Ste. 300; 99615; Kodiak; P 14,000; M 350; (907) 486-5557; Fax (907) 486-7605; chamber@kodiak.org; www.kodiak.org

Kotzebue • *City of Kotzebue* • Nathan Kotch; Mayor; 258A 3rd Ave.; P.O. Box 46; 99752; NW Arctic; P 3,200; (907) 442-3401; Fax (907) 442-3742; nkotch@maniilaq.org; www.cityofkotzebue.com

Ninilchik • *Ninilchik C/C* • P.O. Box 39164; 99639; Kenai Peninsula; P 1,000; M 50; (907) 567-3571; ninilchik@alaska.com; www.ninilchikchamber.com

Nome • *Nome C/C* • Barb Nichols; Dir.; P.O. Box 250; 99762; Nome; P 3,500; M 60; (907) 443-3879; director@nomechamber.com; www.visitnomealaska.com

North Pole • *North Pole Comm. C/C & Visitor Center* • Sharon Hedding; 125 Saint Nicholas Dr.; P.O. Box 55071; 99705; Fairbanks North Star; P 2,130; M 100; (907) 488-2242; (907) 488-6296; Fax (907) 488-3002; info@northpolechamber.us; www.northpolechamber.us

Palmer • *Greater Palmer C/C* • Ralph Renzi; Exec. Dir.; 550 S. Alaska St., Ste. 101; P.O. Box 45; 99645; Matanuska-Susitna; P 5,940; M 320; (907) 745-2880; Fax (907) 746-4164; director@palmerchamber.org; www.palmerchamber.org

Petersburg • *Petersburg C/C* • Sally Dwyer; Exec. Dir.; 19 Fram St.; P.O. Box 649; 99833; Petersburg; P 3,000; M 140; (907) 772-3646; (907) 772-4636; Fax (907) 772-2453; pcoc@alaska.com; www.petersburg.org

Seldovia • *Seldovia C/C* • Jenny Chissus; Pres.; P.O. Drawer F; 99663; Kenai Peninsula; P 300; M 60; (907) 234-7612; president@seldoviachamber.org; www.seldoviachamber.org

Seward • *Seward C/C & CVB* • Cindy Clock; Exec. Dir.; 2001 Seward Hwy.; P.O. Box 749; 99664; Kenai Peninsula; P 3,200; M 300; (907) 224-8051; Fax (907) 224-5353; visitseward@seward.net; www.seward.com

Sitka • *Greater Sitka C/C* • Rachel Roy; Exec. Dir.; 104 Lake St.; P.O. Box 638; 99835; Sitka; P 9,046; M 175; (907) 747-8604; Info@sitkachamber.com; www.sitkachamber.com

Skagway • *Skagway C/C* • Jackie Schaefer; Pres.; P.O. Box 194; 99840; Skagway; P 950; M 115; (907) 983-1898; Fax (907) 983-2031; chamber@aptalaska.net; www.skagwaychamber.org

Soldotna • *Greater Soldotna C/C & Visitor Info. Center* • Michelle Glaves; Exec. Dir.; 44790 Sterling Hwy.; 99669; Kenai Peninsula; P 5,000; M 530; (907) 262-9814; Fax (907) 262-3566; info@soldotnachamber.com; www.visitsoldotna.com

Soldotna • *Funny River C/C* • Clark Meyer; Pres.; 35850 Pioneer Access Rd.; 99669; Kenai Peninsula; P 950; M 160; (907) 262-0879; www.ci.soldotna.ak.us

Talkeetna • *Talkeetna C/C* • Beth Valentine; Pres.; P.O. Box 334; 99676; Matanuska-Susitna; P 1,200; M 152; info@talkeetnachamber.org; www.talkeetnachamber.org

Tok • *Tok C/C* • P.O. Box 389; 99780; S.E. Fairbanks; P 1,258; M 43; (907) 883-5775; info@tokalaskainfo.com; www.tokalaskainfo.com

Wasilla • *Greater Wasilla C/C* • Ina Mueller; Exec. Dir.; 415 E. Railroad Ave.; 99654; Matanuska-Susitna; P 9,000; M 702; (907) 376-1299; Fax (907) 373-2560; contact@wasillachamber.org; www.wasillachamber.org*

Whittier • *Greater Whittier C/C* • P.O. Box 607; 99693; Valdez-Cordova; P 221; M 65; (907) 529-0235; whittiercoc@gmail.com; www.whittieralaskachamber.org

Willow • *Willow C/C* • Jim Huston; Pres.; P.O. Box 183; 99688; Matanuska-Susitna; P 3,000; M 50; (907) 495-6800; Fax (907) 495-6800; mail@willowchamber.org; www.willowchamber.org

Wrangell • *Wrangell C/C* • John Taylor; Pres.; P.O. Box 49; 99929; Wrangell; P 2,000; M 100; (907) 874-3901; Fax (907) 874-3905; wrangellchamber@gmail.com; www.wrangellchamber.org

Arizona

Arizona C of C & Ind. • Glenn Hamer; Pres./CEO; 3200 N. Central Ave., Ste. 1125; Phoenix; 85012; Maricopa; P 6,700,000; M 500; (602) 248-9172; Fax (602) 391-2498; info@azchamber.com; www.azchamber.com

Ajo • *Ajo Dist. C/C & Visitor Center* • Bety Allen; Exec. Dir.; 1 W. Plaza St.; 85321; Pima; P 4,000; M 63; (520) 387-7742; Fax (520) 387-3641; ajocofc@ajochamber.com; www.ajochamber.com

Alpine • *Alpine Area C/C* • Anne MacGregor; Pres.; P.O. Box 410; 85920; Apache; P 600; M 80; (928) 339-4330; thechamber@alpinearizona.com; www.alpinearizona.com

Apache Junction • *Apache Junction C/C* • Larry Johnson; Pres./CEO; 567 W. Apache Trl.; 85120; Pinal; P 36,600; M 500; (480) 982-3141; Fax (480) 982-3234; darcie@ajchamber.com; www.ajchamber.com*

Arizona City • *Arizona City C/C* • Nancy Hawkins; Treas.; 13640 S. Sunland Gin Rd., Ste. 106; P.O. Box 5; 85123; Pinal; P 6,000; M 125; (520) 466-5141; Fax (520) 466-8204; info@arizonacitychamber.com; www.arizonacitychamber.com

Avondale • *see Goodyear*

Benson • *Benson-San Pedro Valley C/C* • Lupe Diaz; Pres.; 168 E. 4th St.; 85602; Cochise; P 12,000; M 140; (520) 265-8031; Fax (520) 265-8031; president@bensonchamberaz.com; www.bensonchamberaz.org

Bisbee • *Bisbee C/C* • Jen Luria & Julie Epperson; Assoc. Dir.; 48 Main St.; P.O. Box 944; 85603; Cochise; P 4,400; M 150; (520) 432-5421; chamber@bisbeearizona.com; www.bisbeearizona.com

Black Canyon City • *Black Canyon City C/C* • Gloria Rogers; Pres.; 34301 S. Old Black Canyon Hwy., Ste. 3; P.O. Box 1919; 85324; Yavapai; P 4,800; M 64; (623) 374-9797; bcchamber_az@q.com; blackcanyonaz.com

Bouse • *Bouse C/C* • Norm Simpson; Pres.; P.O. Box 817; 85325; La Paz; P 850; M 50; (928) 851-2509; bousecofc@yahoo.com; www.bousechamber.com

Bowie • *Bowie C/C* • Nancy-Jean Welker; Pres.; P.O. Box 287; 85605; Cochise; P 706; M 50; (520) 253-0930; Fax (520) 847-2603; b2caz@vtc.net; www.bowiechamber.com

Buckeye • *Buckeye Valley C/C* • Deanna K. Kupcik; Pres./CEO; 508 E. Monroe Ave.; 85326; Maricopa; P 68,000; M 325; (623) 386-2727; Fax (623) 386-7527; info@buckeyevalleychamber.org; www.buckeyevalleychamber.org*

Bullhead City • *Bullhead Area C/C* • Chris Barton; Exec. Dir.; 1251 Hwy. 95; 86429; Mohave County; P 70,000; M 650; (928) 754-4121; info@bullheadchamber.com; www.bullheadareachamber.com*

Carefree • *Carefree Cave Creek C/C* • Patty Villeneuve; Exec. Dir.; 748 Easy St., Ste. 2; P.O. Box 734; 85377; Maricopa; P 8,100; M 300; (480) 488-3381; Fax (480) 488-0328; chamber@carefreecavecreek.org; www.carefreecavecreek.org*

Casa Grande • *Greater Casa Grande C/C* • Helen Neuharth; Pres./CEO; 575 N. Marshall St.; 85122; Pinal; P 52,000; M 505; (520) 836-2125; (800) 916-1515; Fax (520) 836-6233; info@casagrandechamber.org; www.casagrandechamber.org*

Chandler • *Chandler C/C* • Terri Kimble; Pres./CEO; 25 S. Arizona Pl., Ste. 201; 85225; Maricopa; P 250,000; M 1,568; (480) 963-4571; Fax (480) 963-0188; info@chandlerchamber.com; www.chandlerchamber.com*

Chino Valley • *Chino Valley Area C/C* • Tracie Schimikowsky; Pres./CEO; 175 E. Rd. 2 South; P.O. Box 419; 86323; Yavapai; P 10,000; M 300; (928) 636-2493; Fax (928) 636-4112; director@chinovalley.org; www.chinovalley.org*

Chloride • *Chloride C/C* • Allen Bercowetz; Pres.; 4940 Tennessee Ave.; P.O. Box 10; 86431; Mohave; P 300; M 22; (928) 565-4888; Fax (928) 565-9419; chloride_az@yahoo.com; www.chloridearizona.com

Coolidge • *Coolidge C/C* • Lynn Parsons; Exec. Dir.; 351 N. Arizona Blvd.,; 85128; Pinal; P 12,000; M 250; (520) 723-3009; Fax (520) 723-9410; info@coolidgechamber.org; www.coolidgechamber.org*

Cottonwood • *Cottonwood C/C* • Lana Tolleson; Pres./CEO; 1010 S. Main St.; 86326; Yavapai; P 11,300; M 530; (928) 634-7593; Fax (928) 634-7594; info@cottonwoodchamberaz.org; www.cottonwoodchamberaz.org*

Dolan Springs • *Dolan Springs C/C* • Lee MacWilliam; Pres.; P.O. Box 274; 86441; Mohave; P 2,000; M 170; (928) 767-4473; president@dolanspringschamberofcommerce.com; www.dolanspringschamberofcommerce.com

Douglas • *Greater Douglas C/C* • Susan Kramer; Pres.; 1129 N. G Ave.; 85607; Cochise; P 15,000; M 30; (520) 364-2477; president@douglasazchamber.com; www.douglasazchamber.com

Eagar • *see Springerville*

El Mirage • *see Surprise*

Eloy • *Eloy C/C* • Mark Benner; Exec. Dir.; 305 N. Stuart Blvd.; 85131; Pinal; P 16,000; M 100; (520) 466-3411; Fax (520) 466-4698; info@eloychamber.com; www.eloychamber.com

Flagstaff • *Greater Flagstaff C/C* • Julie Pastrick; Pres./CEO; 101 W. Rte. 66; 86001; Coconino; P 68,000; M 1,140; (928) 774-4505; Fax (928) 779-1209; info@flagstaffchamber.com; www.flagstaffchamber.com*

Florence • *Greater Florence C/C* • Lori Wood; Exec. Dir.; 24 W. Ruggles; P.O. Box 929; 85132; Pinal; P 9,433; M 190; (520) 868-9433; Fax (520) 868-5797; florencechamber@gmail.com; www.florenceazchamber.com

Fort Mohave • *see Mohave Valley*

Fountain Hills • *Fountain Hills C/C* • Scott Soldat-Valenzuela; Pres./CEO; 16837 E. Palisades Blvd.; P.O. Box 17598; 85269; Maricopa; P 23,000; M 500; (480) 837-1654; Fax (480) 837-3077; diane@fountainhillschamber.com; www.fountainhillschamber.com*

Fredonia • *see Kanab, UT*

Gila Bend • *Gila Bend C/C* • Chris Hubbard; Coord.; P.O. Box CC; 85337; Maricopa; P 1,700; M 45; (928) 420-1964; info@gilabendazchamber.com; www.gilabendazchamber.com*

Gilbert • *Gilbert C/C* • Kathy Tilque; Pres./CEO; 119 N. Gilbert Rd., Ste. 101; P.O. Box 527; 85234; Maricopa; P 227,598; M 630; (480) 892-0056; Fax (480) 892-1980; sarah@gilbertchamber.com; www.gilbertaz.com*

Glendale • *Glendale C/C* • Robert W. Heidt Jr.; Pres./CEO; 5800 W. Glenn Dr., Ste. 275; 85301; Maricopa; P 245,000; M 1,200; (623) 937-4754; Fax (623) 937-3333; info@glendaleazchamber.org; www.glendaleazchamber.org*

Globe • *Globe-Miami Reg. C/C & Eco. Dev. Corp.* • Ellen Kretsch; Dir.; 1360 N. Broad St.; 85501; Gila; P 17,000; M 300; (928) 425-4495; (800) 804-5623; Fax (928) 425-3410; visitorinfo@globemiamichamber.com; www.globemiamichamber.com

Golden Valley • *see Kingman*

Goodyear • *Southwest Valley C/C* • John Safin; Pres./CEO; 289 N. Litchfield Rd.; 85338; Maricopa; P 170,000; M 600; (623) 932-2260; Fax (623) 932-9057; info@southwestvalleychamber.org; www.southwestvalleychamber.org*

Grand Canyon • *Grand Canyon C/C & Visitors Bur.* • Josie Bustillos; Exec. Dir.; 469 Hwy. 64; P.O. Box 3007; 86023; Coconino; P 2,000; M 100; (928) 638-2901; (888) 472-2696; Fax (928) 638-4095; jbustillos@grandcanyonchamber.com; www.grandcanyonchamber.com

Green Valley • *Green Valley Sahuarita C/C & Visitor Center* • Jim Di Giacomo; Pres./CEO; 275 W. Continental Rd., Ste. 123; P.O. Box 566; 85622; Pima; P 75,000; M 600; (520) 625-7575; (520) 625-7594; Fax (520) 648-6154; info@greenvalleysahuarita.com; www.greenvalleysahuarita.com*

Hayden • *see Kearny*

Heber • *see Overgaard*

Holbrook • *Holbrook C/C* • Michael Nilsson; Exec. Dir.; 100 E. Arizona Ave.; 86025; Navajo; P 5,544; M 175; (928) 524-6558; (800) 524-2459; Fax (928) 524-2159; holbrookazchamberofcommerce@gmail.com; www.holbrookchamberofcommerce.com

Jerome • *Jerome C/C* • P.O. Box K; 86331; Yavapai; P 480; M 125; (928) 634-2900; staff@jeromechamber.com; www.jeromechamber.com

Kearny • *Copper Basin C/C* • Angela Hillan-Ramirez; Dir.; 355 Alden Rd.; P.O. Box 206; 85137; Gila & Pinal; P 3,500; M 42; (520) 363-7607; Fax (520) 363-9828; angela@copperbasinaz.com; www.copperbasinaz.com

Kingman • *Kingman Area C/C* • Gregg Martin; Pres./CEO; 3001 N. Stockton Hill Rd., Ste. 3; 86401; Mohave; P 44,000; M 400; (928) 753-6253; Fax (928) 753-1049; chamber@kingmanchamber.com; www.kingmanchamber.com*

Lake Havasu City • *Lake Havasu Area C/C* • Lisa Krueger IOM ACE; Pres./CEO; 314 London Bridge Rd.; 86403; Mohave; P 53,000; M 700; (928) 855-4115; Fax (928) 680-0010; lisak@havasuchamber.com; www.havasuchamber.com*

Lake Mead City • *see Meadview*

Lakeside • *see Pinetop*

Litchfield Park • *see Goodyear*

Marana • *Marana C/C* • Ed Stolmaker; Pres./CEO; 13881 N. Casa Grande Hwy.; 85653; Pima; P 36,800; M 500; (520) 682-4314; Fax (520) 682-2303; lizziekelley@maranachamber.com; www.maranachamber.com

Maricopa • *Maricopa C/C* • Sara Troyer; Exec. Dir.; 44480 W. Honeycutt Rd., Ste. 106; 85138; Pinal; P 48,000; M 301; (520) 568-9573; info@maricopachamber.org; www.maricopachamber.org*

Mayer • *Arizona Highway 69 C/C* • Ben Satran; Pres.; 12780 Central Ave., Unit 1; P.O. Box 141; 86333; Yavapai; P 6,700; M 65; (928) 632-4355; Fax (928) 632-4355; highway69chamber@gmail.com; www.arizonahighway69chamber.org*

Meadview • *Meadview Area C/C* • Jonathan Kiser; Pres.; 330 Meadview Blvd. E., Ste. D; P.O. Box 26; 86444; Mohave; P 1,300; M 45; (928) 564-2425; macc@meadviewchamber.com; www.meadviewchamber.com

Mesa • *Mesa C/C* • Sally Harrison; Pres./CEO; 40 N. Center St., Ste. 104; 85201; Maricopa; P 446,000; M 825; (480) 969-1307; Fax (480) 247-5414; bnelson@mesachamber.org; www.mesachamber.org*

Miami • *see Globe*

Mohave Valley • *Mohave C/C* • Ginny Clem; Pres.; Bentley Plaza South; 10225 Harbor Ave., Ste. 2; 86440; Mohave; P 16,000; M 85; (928) 768-2777; Fax (928) 768-6610; info@mohavevalleychamber.com; www.mohavevalleychamber.info

Nogales • *Nogales-Santa Cruz County C/C* • Olivia Ainza-Kramer; Pres./CEO; 123 W. Kino Park Way; 85621; Santa Cruz; P 42,000; M 300; (520) 287-3685; Fax (520) 287-3687; info@thenogaleschamber.org; www.thenogaleschamber.org

Oatman • *Oatman-Goldroad C/C* • Linda Woodard; P.O. Box 423; 86433; Mohave; P 135; M 12; (928) 768-6222; oatman@oatmangoldroad.org; www.oatmangoldroad.org

Overgaard • *Heber-Overgaard C/C* • June Call; Pres.; P.O. Box 1926; 85933; Navajo; P 2,500; M 160; (928) 535-5777; Fax (928) 535-3254; heberovergaard.coc@hotmail.com; www.heberovergaard.org

Page • *The Chamber Page Lake Powell* • Judy Franz; Exec. Dir.; 71 7th Ave., Ste. B; P.O. Box 727; 86040; Coconino; P 8,000; M 247; (928) 645-2741; Fax (928) 645-3181; chamber@pagechamber.com; www.pagechamber.com

Parker • *Parker Reg. C/C & Tourism* • Mary Hamilton; Exec. Dir.; 1217 California Ave.; 85344; La Paz; P 22,000; M 286; (928) 669-2174; Fax (928) 669-6304; info@parkeraz.org; www.parkeraz.org*

Payson • *Rim Country Reg. C/C* • Jaimee Hilgendorf; Ofc. Mgr.; 100 W. Main St.; P.O. Box 1380; 85547; Gila; P 15,000; M 300; (928) 474-4515; Fax (928) 474-8812; jaimee@rimcountrychamber.com; www.rimcountrychamber.com*

Pearce • *Pearce-Sunsites C/C* • Murray McClelland; Pres.; 301 N. Frontage Rd., Sunsites; P.O. Box 536; 85625; Cochise; P 2,000; M 75; (520) 826-3535; sunsitesazchamber@gmail.com; www.pearcesunsiteschamber.org

Peoria • *Peoria C/C* • Guy Erickson; Pres./CEO; 16165 N. 83rd Ave., Ste. 101; 85382; Maricopa & Yavapai; P 163,000; M 550; (623) 979-3601; Fax (623) 486-4729; support@peoriachamber.com; www.peoriachamber.com*

Phoenix Area

Ahwatukee Foothills C/C • Anne Gill; Pres./CEO; 4435 E. Chandler Blvd., Ste. 140; 85048; Maricopa; P 78,000; M 550; (480) 753-7676; Fax (480) 753-3898; paulette@ahwatukeechamber.com; www.ahwatukeechamber.com*

Arizona Hispanic C/C • Gonzalo De La Melena; Pres./CEO; 255 E. Osborn Rd., Ste. 201; 85012; Maricopa; P 1,488,000; M 425; (602) 279-1800; Fax (602) 279-8900; susettec@azhcc.com; www.azhcc.com

Asian C/C • Enrique Medina; Exec. Dir.; 1402 S. Central Ave., Bldg. A, Ste. C; 85004; Maricopa; P 6,553,000; M 410; info@asianchamber.org; www.asianchamber.org

Greater Phoenix Black C/C • Kerwin V. Brown; Pres./CEO; 201 E. Washington St., Ste. 350; 85004; Maricopa; P 1,488,000; M 350; (602) 307-5200; Fax (602) 307-5204; heather@phoenixblackchamber.com; www.phoenixblackchamber.com

Greater Phoenix C/C • Todd Sanders; Pres./CEO; 201 N. Central Ave., 27th Flr.; 85004; Maricopa; P 1,488,000; M 2,400; (602) 495-2195; (602) 495-6472; Fax (602) 495-8913; info@phoenixchamber.com; www.phoenixchamber.com

North Phoenix C/C • Jason Bressler; Exec. Dir.; 14001 N. 7th St., Bldg. C, Ste. 106; 85022; Maricopa; P 500,000; M 400; (602) 482-3344; Fax (602) 759-5781; jason@northphoenixchamber.com; www.northphoenixchamber.com*

Pinnacle Peak C/C • Kelly Wilson; Exec. Admin.; 2415 E. Camelback Rd., Ste. 700; 85016; Maricopa; (602) 381-2584; info@pinnaclepeakchamber.com; www.pinnaclepeakchamber.com

Pine • *see Payson*

Pinetop • *Pinetop-Lakeside C/C* • Crystal O'Donnell; Exec. Dir.; P.O. Box 4220; 85935; Navajo; P 5,000; M 350; (928) 367-4290; (800) 573-4031; Fax (928) 367-1247; malaina@pinetoplakesidechamber.com; www.pinetoplakesidechamber.com*

Prescott • *Prescott C/C & Visitor Info. Center* • David Maurer; CEO; 117 W. Goodwin St.; P.O. Box 1147; 86302; Yavapai; P 40,520; M 875; (928) 445-2000; (800) 266-7534; Fax (928) 445-0068; chamber@prescott.org; www.prescott.org*

Prescott Valley • *Prescott Valley C/C* • Marnie Uhl; Pres./CEO; 7120 E. Pav Way, Ste. 102; 86314; Yavapai; P 42,700; M 600; (928) 772-8857; Fax (928) 772-4267; gloria@pvchamber.org; www.pvchamber.org*

Quartzsite • *Quartzsite Area C/C & Tourism* • Phil Cushman; Bd. Pres.; 1240 W. Main St.; P.O. Box 640; 85346; La Paz; P 3,800; M 100; (928) 927-5200; quartzsitetourism@yahoo.com; www.quartzsitetourism.com

Queen Creek • *Queen Creek C/C* • Chris Clark; Pres./CEO; 22308 S. Ellsworth Rd.; P.O. Box 505; 85142; Pinal & Maricopa; P 31,000; M 200; (480) 888-1709; Fax (480) 289-4801; president@queencreekchamber.org; www.queencreekchamber.org*

Safford • *Graham County C/C* • Patrick O'Donnell; Exec. Dir.; 1111 Thatcher Blvd.; 85546; Graham; P 33,000; M 290; (928) 428-2511; (888) 837-1841; Fax (928) 428-0744; info@graham-chamber.com; www.graham-chamber.com

Salome • *McMullen Valley C/C* • P.O. Box 700; 85348; La Paz; P 4,000; M 120; (928) 859-3846; Fax (928) 859-4399; mcmullencoc@tds.net; www.azoutback.com*

Scottsdale • *Scottsdale Area C/C* • Mark Hiegel; Pres./CEO; 7501 E. McCormick Pkwy., Ste. 202-N; 85258; Maricopa; P 230,293; M 931; (480) 355-2700; (480) 949-2174; Fax (480) 355-2710; mhiegel@scottsdalechamber.com; www.scottsdalechamber.com*

Sedona • *Sedona C/C* • Jennifer Wesselhoff; Pres./CEO; 45 Sunset Dr.; 86336; Coconino & Yavapai; P 18,000; M 1,000; (928) 204-1123; (928) 282-7722; Fax (928) 204-1064; info@sedonachamber.com; www.sedonachamber.com*

Show Low • *Show Low C/C & Tourist Info. Center* • Lacey Ekberg; Exec. Dir.; 81 E. Deuce of Clubs; 85901; Navajo; P 12,000; M 320; (928) 537-2326; (888) SHOW-LOW; Fax (928) 532-7610; officem@showlowchamber.com; showlowchamber.com*

Sierra Vista • *Sierra Vista Area C/C* • Deanna La Velle; Exec. Dir.; 21 E. Wilcox Dr.; 85635; Cochise; P 50,000; M 650; (520) 458-6940; Fax (520) 452-0878; dlavelle@sierravistachamber.org/; www.sierravistachamber.org*

Snowflake • *Snowflake-Taylor C/C* • Charlotte Hatch; Exec. Dir.; 113 N. Main St., Ste. A; 85937; Navajo; P 9,500; M 300; (928) 536-4331; Fax (928) 536-5656; admin@snowflaketaylorchamber.org; www.snowflaketaylorchamber.org

Sonoita • *Sonoita-Elgin C/C* • Ron Izzo; Pres.; P.O. Box 607; 85637; Santa Cruz; P 1,420; M 75; (520) 455-5498; info@sonoitaelginchamber.org; www.sonoitaelginchamber.org

Springerville • *Springerville-Eagar Reg. C/C* • Becki Christensen; Exec. Dir.; 418 E. Main St.; P.O. Box 31; 85938; Apache; P 7,000; M 300; (928) 333-2123; Fax (928) 333-5690; director@sechamber.com; www.sechamber.com

Strawberry • *see Payson*

Sun City • *see Surprise*

Sun City West • *see Surprise*

Superior • *Superior C/C* • Pete Casillas; Pres.; 830 U.S Hwy. 60; P.O. Box 95; 85173; Pinal; P 3,000; M 112; (520) 689-0200; support@superiorarizonachamber.org; www.superiorarizonachamber.org*

Surprise • *Surprise Reg. C/C* • Diane McCarthy; Chrmn.; 16126 N. Civic Center Plaza; 85374; Maricopa; P 161,000; M 570; (623) 583-0692; Fax (623) 498-8387; chamber@surpriseregionalchamber.com; www.surpriseregionalchamber.com*

Taylor • *see Snowflake*

Tempe • *Tempe C/C* • Mary Ann Miller; Pres./CEO; 909 E. Apache Blvd.; P.O. Box 28500; 85285; Maricopa; P 166,840; M 1,000; (480) 967-7891; Fax (480) 966-5365; donna@tempechamber.org; www.tempechamber.org

Tolleson • *see Goodyear*

Tombstone • *Tombstone C/C* • Susan Wallace; Bd. Pres.; 109 S. 4th St.; P.O. Box 995; 85638; Cochise; P 1,700; M 100; (520) 457-9317; (888) 457-3929; Fax (520) 457-2458; info@tombstonechamber.com; www.tombstonechamber.com

Tonto Basin • *Tonto Basin C/C* • Ron Whitman; Pres.; 45675 N. Hwy. 188; P.O. Box 687; 85553; Gila; P 1,200; M 55; (520) 390-0207; swhitman@tontobasinchamber.org; www.tontobasinchamber.org

Tubac • *Tubac C/C* • Angela Kirkner; Exec. Dir.; P.O. Box 1866; 85646; Santa Cruz; P 1,200; M 120; (520) 398-2704; assistance@tubacaz.com; www.tubacaz.com

Tucson Area

Greater Oro Valley C/C • Dave Perry; Pres./CEO; 7435 N. Oracle Rd., Ste. 107; 85704; Pima; P 41,000; M 400; (520) 297-2191; Fax (520) 742-7960; dave@orovalleychamber.com; www.orovalleychamber.com*

Tucson Hispanic C/C • Lea Marquez Peterson; Pres./CEO; 823 E. Speedway Blvd., Ste. 101; 85719; Pima; P 524,300; M 900; (520) 620-0005; Fax (520) 844-7071; office@tucsonhispanicchamber.org; www.tucsonhispanicchamber.org*

Tucson Metro C/C • Michael V. Varney; Pres./CEO; 465 W. St. Mary's Rd.; P.O. Box 991; 85702; Pima; P 980,000; M 1,450; (520) 792-1212; (520) 792-2250; Fax (520) 882-5704; swilka@tucsonchamber.org; www.tucsonchamber.org*

Wickenburg • *Wickenburg C/C* • Julie Brooks; Exec. Dir.; 216 N. Frontier St.; 85390; Maricopa; P 10,000; M 579; (928) 684-5479; (928) 684-0977; Fax (928) 684-5470; events@wickenburgchamber.com; www.wickenburgchamber.com*

Willcox • *Willcox C/C & Ag.* • Alan Baker; Exec. Dir.; 1500 N. Circle I Rd.; 85643; Cochise; P 4,000; M 150; (520) 384-2995; (800) 200-2272; Fax (520) 384-0293; willcoxchamber@vtc.net; www.willcoxchamber.com

Williams • *Williams-Grand Canyon C/C* • Dr. Robert D. Argyelan; Pres./CEO; 200 W. Railroad Ave.; 86046; Coconino; P 5,000; M 225; (928) 635-0273; (800) 863-0546; Fax (928) 635-1417; info@williamschamber.com; www.williamschamber.org*

Winkelman • *see Kearny*

Winslow • *Winslow C/C & Visitors Center* • Bob Hall; Exec. Dir.; 523 W. 2nd St.; P.O. Box 460; 86047; Navajo; P 10,500; M 230; (928) 289-2434; Fax (928) 289-5660; winslowchamber@cableone.net; www.winslowarizona.org

Yarnell • *Yarnell-Peeples Valley C/C* • Vicki Velasquez; P.O. Box 275; 85362; Yavapai; P 1,500; M 50; (928) 277-6674; (928) 427-6262; visitus@y-pvchamber.com; www.y-pvchamber.com

Youngtown • *see Surprise*

Yuma • *Yuma County C/C* • John Courtis; Exec. Dir.; 180 W. First St., Ste. A; 85364; Yuma; P 200,000; M 900; (928) 782-2567; Fax (928) 247-6509; kelly@yumachamber.org; www.yumachamber.org*

Arkansas

Arkansas State C of C • Randy Zook; Pres./CEO; 1200 W. Capitol Ave.; Little Rock; 72201; Pulaski; P 2,949,131; M 1,300; (501) 372-2222; Fax (501) 372-2722; jthatcher@arkansasstatechamber.com; www.arkansasstatechamber.com

Altus • *Altus C/C* • Tom Sexton; Pres.; 125 W. Main; P.O. Box 404; 72821; Franklin; P 817; M 20; (479) 468-6891; (479) 468-4191

Arkadelphia • *Arkadelphia Area C/C* • Stephen Bell; Pres./CEO; 2401 Pine St., Ste. B; P.O. Box 400; 71923; Clark; P 22,750; M 300; (870) 246-5542; (870) 246-1460; Fax (870) 246-1462; tiffany@arkadelphiaalliance.com; www.arkadelphiaalliance.com*

Arkansas City • *Arkansas City C/C* • Carolyn Blissett; Pres.; P.O. Box 369; 71630; Desha; P 360; M 40; (870) 877-2306; Fax (870) 877-2306; www.arkansascityusa.com

Ash Flat • *see Highland*

Ashdown • *Little River C/C •* Jill Turner; Dir.; P.O. Box 160; 71822; Little River; P 14,000; M 130; (870) 898-2758; Fax (870) 898-6699; director@littlerivercounty.org; www.littlerivercounty.org

Augusta • *Augusta Area C/C •* Regina Burkett; Pres.; 115 S. 2nd St.; 72006; Woodruff; P 2,200; M 30; (870) 347-1802; (870) 347-3391; regina.burkett@arcare.net; www.augustaar.org

Bald Knob • *Bald Knob Area C/C •* 411 S. Elm; P.O. Box 338; 72010; White; P 3,500; M 110; (501) 724-3140; Fax (501) 724-3140; baldknobchamber@centurytel.net; www.baldknobchamber.com

Batesville • *Batesville Area C/C •* Crystal Johnson; Pres./CEO; 409 Vine St.; 72501; Independence; P 10,300; M 600; (870) 793-2378; Fax (870) 793-3061; crystal.johnson@mybatesville.org; www.mybatesville.org*

Beebe • *Beebe C/C •* Dr. Robert Beavers; Pres.; P.O. Box 724; 72012; White; P 7,600; M 105; (501) 882-8135; Fax (501) 882-8140; info@beebeark.org; www.beebenow.com

Benton • *Benton Area C/C •* Gary James; Pres./CEO; 607 N. Market St.; 72015; Saline; P 34,000; M 625; (501) 860-7002; reception@bentonchamber.com; www.bentonchamber.com*

Bentonville • *Bentonville/Bella Vista C/C •* Dana D. Davis IOM; Pres./CEO; 200 E. Central; P.O. Box 330; 72712; Benton; P 35,000; M 1,025; (479) 273-2841; Fax (479) 273-2180; tthurow@bbvchamber.com; www.bbvchamber.com*

Berryville • *Berryville C/C •* Chris Claybaker; Dir.; P.O. Box 402; 72616; Carroll; P 5,300; M 170; (870) 423-3704; berryvillechamber@windstream.net; www.berryvillear.com*

Blytheville • *Greater Blytheville Area C/C •* Elizabeth Smith IOM; Exec. Dir.; 300 W. Walnut; P.O. Box 485; 72316; Mississppi; P 15,500; M 317; (870) 762-2012; Fax (870) 762-0551; info@greaterblytheville.com; www.greaterblytheville.com

Booneville • *Booneville Dev. Corp./South Logan County C/C •* Trinity Damron; Exec. Dir.; 210 E. Main St.; P.O. Box 55; 72927; Logan; P 4,100; M 130; (479) 675-2666; information1@booneville.com; www.booneville.com

Bradley • *Bradley C/C •* Joe Middlebrooks; Pres.; P.O. Box 662; 71826; Lafayette; P 575; M 85; (870) 894-3935; Fax (870) 894-3554; deloisdm@yahoo.com

Brinkley • *Brinkley C/C •* Lynda Roche; Exec. Asst.; 217 W. Cypress; 72021; Monroe; P 3,000; M 95; (870) 734-2262; Fax (870) 589-2020; brinkleychamber@sbcglobal.net; www.brinkleychamber.com

Bryant • *Bryant C/C •* Rae Ann Fields; Exec. Dir.; P.O. Box 261; 72089; Saline; P 17,174; M 450; (501) 847-4702; Fax (501) 847-7576; bryant.chamber@bryant-ar.com; www.bryant-ar.com*

Bull Shoals • *Bull Shoals Lake/White River C/C •* 612 Central Blvd.; P.O. Box 354; 72619; Baxter & Marion; P 100,000; M 180; (870) 445-4443; director@bullshoals.org; www.bullshoals.org*

Cabot • *Cabot C/C •* Billye Everett; Exec. Dir.; 110 S. First St.; 72023; Lonoke; P 25,000; M 400; (501) 843-2136; chamber@cabotcc.org; www.cabotcc.org*

Calico Rock • *Calico Rock Area C/C •* Gloria Gushue; 104 Main St.; 72519; Izard; P 1,500; M 30; (870) 297-6100; calicorock@yahoo.com; www.calicorock.us

Camden • *Camden Area C/C •* Beth Osteen; Exec. Dir.; 314 S. Adams Ave.; P.O. Box 99; 71711; Ouachita; P 12,200; M 300; (870) 836-6426; Fax (870) 836-6400; bosteen@camdenareachamberofcommerce.org; www.teamcamden.com*

Cave City • *Cave City C/C •* John Beller; Pres.; P.O. Box 274; 72521; Independence & Sharp; P 1,900; M 40; (870) 283-5103; (870) 283-6132; laura@frontiercs.com; www.cavecityarkansas.info

Charleston • *Charleston C/C •* Donna Martin; Pres.; P.O. Box 456; 72933; Franklin; P 2,530; M 55; (479) 965-7654; Fax (479) 965-2205; charlestonarchamber@gmail.com; www.aboutcharleston.com

Cherokee Village • *see Highland*

Clarendon • *Clarendon C/C •* Susan Caplener; Secy.; P.O. Box 153; 72029; Monroe; P 1,700; M 28; (870) 747-5414; (870) 747-3802; scaplener@centurytel.net; www.clarendon-ar.com

Clarksville • *Clarksville-Johnson County C/C •* Travis Stephens; CEO; 101 N. Johnson; 72830; Johnson; P 9,178; M 240; (479) 754-2340; Fax (479) 754-4923; chamber@clarksvillear.org; www.clarksvillearchamber.com*

Clinton • *Clinton Area C/C •* Jayson Hayes; Pres.; 290 Main St.; P.O. Box 52; 72031; Van Buren; P 24,000; M 200; (501) 745-6500; cltchamber@artelco.com; www.clintonchamber.com

Conway • *Conway Area C/C •* Brad Lacy CCE IOM; Pres./CEO; 900 Oak St.; 72032; Faulkner; P 64,500; M 1,500; (501) 327-7788; Fax (501) 327-7790; getsmart@conwayarkansas.org; www.conwayarkansas.org*

Corning • *Corning Area C/C •* Barry Sellers; Dir.; 1621 W. Main St.; P.O. Box 93; 72422; Clay; P 3,600; M 100; (870) 857-3874; Fax (870) 857-3874; corning72422@hotmail.com; www.corningarchamber.org

Cotter • *Cotter-Gassville C/C •* Marcia Taylor; Pres.; P.O. Box 489; 72626; Baxter; P 2,400; M 120; (870) 321-1243; Fax (901) 490-4828; Cotter.Chamber@gmail.com; www.CotterGassville.com

Crossett • *Crossett Area C/C •* Pam Hipp; Exec. Dir.; 101 W. First Ave.; 71635; Ashley; P 12,000; M 190; (870) 364-6591; Fax (870) 364-7488; crossettchamber@windstream.net; www.crossettchamber.org

Danville • *Danville Area C/C •* David Fisher; P.O. Box 1140; 72833; Yell; P 2,400; M 70; (479) 495-3419; Fax (479) 495-3347; danark@danark.com; www.danark.com

Dardanelle • *Dardanelle C/C •* Andrea Pitts; Exec. Dir.; 2011 State Hwy. 22 W.; P.O. Box 208; 72834; Yell; P 4,228; M 100; (479) 229-3328; Fax (479) 229-5086; dardanellechamberofcommerce@gmail.com; www.dardanellechamber.com

Decatur • *Decatur C/C •* Shanna Tucker; Pres.; P.O. Box 247; 72722; Benton; P 1,700; M 30; (479) 752-3912

DeQueen • *DeQueen/Sevier County C/C •* Patty Sharp; Pres.; P.O. Box 67; 71832; Sevier; P 18,000; M 155; (870) 584-3225; Fax (870) 642-7959; dqscoc@ipa.net; www.dequeenchamberofcommerce.com

Dermott • *Dermott Area C/C •* Frank Henry Jr.; Exec. Dir.; P.O. Box 147; 71638; Chicot; P 4,000; M 100; (870) 538-5656; Fax (870) 538-5493; email@dermottchamber.com; www.dermottchamber.com

Des Arc • *Des Arc C/C •* Bob Childers; Pres.; P.O. Box 845; 72040; Prairie; P 1,800; M 45; (870) 256-4786; www.desarcchamber.com

DeWitt • *DeWitt C/C •* Gary Oltmann; Pres.; P.O. Box 366; 72042; Arkansas; P 3,300; M 40; (870) 946-3551; (870) 946-3506; www.dewittchamberofcommerce.com

Diamond City • *Diamond City Area C/C* • Mike Kansier; Pres.; P.O. Box 1406; 72630; Boone; P 700; M 15; (870) 422-7575; dchamber@diamondcity.net; www.diamondcitychamber.com

Dierks • *Dierks C/C* • Damon Mounts; Pres.; P.O. Box 292; 71833; Howard; P 1,300; M 40; (870) 286-2671; dierksarkansas.net

Dover • *Dover Area C/C* • Sandra Drittler; Bd. Member; P.O. Box 731; 72837; Pope; P 1,400; M 161; (479) 967-2838; Fax (479) 331-4151; drittler3@hotmail.com; doverchamber.net

Dumas • *Dumas C/C* • Judy Day; Exec. Dir.; 165 S. Main St.; P.O. Box 431; 71639; Desha; P 5,000; M 120; (870) 382-5447; Fax (870) 382-3031; dumaschamber@centurytel.net; www.dumasar.net

El Dorado • *El Dorado Union County C/C* • Jeremy Stratton; Pres./CEO; 111 W. Main St.; P.O. Box 10836; 71730; Union; P 20,000; M 560; (870) 863-6113; Fax (870) 864-6758; chamber@goeldorado.com; www.goeldorado.com*

Eureka Springs • *Greater Eureka Springs C/C* • Tammy Thurow; Pres./CEO; 516 Village Cir. Dr.; P.O. Box 551; 72632; Carroll; P 2,200; M 400; (479) 253-8737; Fax (479) 253-5037; president@eurekaspringschamber.com; www.eurekaspringschamber.com*

Fairfield Bay • *Fairfield Bay Area C/C* • Heather L. Dunn; Exec. Dir.; 110 Village Lane, Ste. 2C; P.O. Box 1159; 72088; Cleburne & Van Buren; P 2,388; M 200; (501) 884-3324; (888) 244-4386; Fax (501) 884-6250; ffbchamber@gmail.com; www.ffbchamber.com

Farmington • *Farmington C/C* • Joe Bailey; P.O. Box 1152; 72730; Washington; P 5,917; M 100; (479) 267-2368; facoc1@farmingtonchamberofcommerce.com; www.farmingtonchamberofcommerce.com

Fayetteville • *Fayetteville C/C* • Steve Clark; Pres./CEO; 123 W. Mountain St.; P.O. Box 4216; 72702; Washington; P 60,018; M 1,200; (479) 521-1710; Fax (479) 521-1791; chamber@fayettevillear.com; www.fayettevillear.com*

Flippin • *Flippin C/C* • Jennifer Cheek; Pres.; P.O. Box 118; 72634; Marion; P 1,355; M 40; (870) 405-4534; jcheek@goifb.com; www.flippinchamber.com

Fordyce • *Fordyce C/C* • Barbara Finley; Exec. Dir.; 119 W. 3rd St.; P.O. Box 588; 71742; Dallas; P 4,799; M 150; (870) 352-3520; Fax (870) 352-8090; fordyce@ipa.net

Forrest City • *Forrest City Area C/C* • Kirk Billingsley; Pres.; 203 N. Izard; 72335; St. Francis; P 15,000; M 200; (870) 633-1651; Fax (870) 633-9500; info@forrestcitychamber.com; www.forrestcitychamber.com*

Fort Smith • *Fort Smith Reg. C/C* • Tim Allen; Pres./CEO; 612 Garrison Ave.; 72901; Crawford, Franklin & Sebastian; P 290,000; M 1,100; (479) 783-3111; Fax (479) 783-6110; mdecora@fortsmithchamber.com; www.fortsmithchamber.com*

Gentry • *Gentry C/C - MainStreet* • Janie Parks; Dir.; P.O. Box 642; 72734; Benton; P 3,452; M 70; (479) 736-2358; info@gentrychamber.com; www.gentrychamber.com

Glenwood • *Glenwood Reg. C/C* • Ki Hartsfield; 73 Hwy. 70 E.; P.O. Box 2006; 71943; Pike; P 6,000; M 120; (870) 356-5266; Fax (870) 356-5266; cofcglenwoodar@windstream.net; www.glenwoodarkansaschamber.com

Gravette • *Greater Gravette C/C* • Dan Yates; Pres.; 205 Main St. S.E.; P.O. Box 112; 72736; Benton; P 2,500; M 68; (479) 787-6171; (479) 344-6464; gravetteinfo@gmail.com; www.gravettearkansas.com

Green Forest • *Green Forest C/C* • Ross Darby; Pres.; P.O. Box 376; 72638; Carroll; P 2,761; M 100; (870) 438-5568; greenforestchamber@hotmail.com; www.greenforestchamber.org

Greenbrier • *Greenbrier C/C* • Audreya Parks; Pres.; 89B N. Broadview, Ste. 3; P.O. Box 418; 72058; Faulkner; P 4,700; M 140; (501) 679-4009; info@greenbrierchamber.org; www.greenbrierchamber.org*

Greenwood • *Greenwood C/C* • Doris Tate; Exec. Dir.; P.O. Box 511; 72936; Sebastian; P 9,000; M 150; (479) 996-6357; Fax (479) 996-1162; info@greenwoodchamber.net; www.greenwoodarkansas.com

Greers Ferry • *Greers Ferry Area C/C* • Jo Ann Wanat; Pres.; 8101 Edgemont Rd., Ste. 4; P.O. Box 1354; 72067; Cleburne; P 2,000; M 115; (501) 825-7188; (888) 825-7199; info@greersferry.com; www.greersferry.com

Gurdon • *Gurdon C/C* • Clayton Franklin; Pres.; 207 E. Main St.; 71743; Clark; P 2,200; M 35; (870) 353-2661; (870) 353-5004

Hamburg • *Hamburg Area C/C* • Haley Chavis; Exec. Dir.; 403 C N. Main St.; P.O. Box 460; 71646; Ashley; P 3,000; M 100; (870) 853-8345; Fax (870) 853-8345; hamburgchamber@sbcglobal.net; www.hamburgark.com

Hardy • *see Highland*

Harrisburg • *Harrisburg Area C/C* • Melanie Mills; Dir. of Op.; 200 E. Jackson St.; 72432; Poinsett; P 5,500; M 137; (870) 578-4104; Fax (870) 578-9467; harrisburgchamber@pcsii.com; www.harrisburgchamber.com

Harrison • *Harrison Reg. C/C* • Patty Methvin; Pres./CEO; 621 E. Rush Ave.; 72601; Boone; P 37,000; M 475; (870) 741-2659; (800) 880-6265; Fax (870) 741-9059; cocinfo@harrison-chamber.com; www.harrison-chamber.com*

Hazen • *Hazen C/C* • Dee Black; P.O. Box 907; 72064; Prairie; P 1,470; M 25; (870) 255-3551; (870) 255-3144; Fax (870) 255-3970; hazenarchambercommerce@gmail.com; www.hazen.ws

Heber Springs • *Heber Springs Area C/C* • Julie Murray; Exec. Dir.; 1001 W. Main St.; 72543; Cleburne; P 26,000; M 400; (501) 362-2444; chamber@heber-springs.com; www.heber-springs.com*

Helena • *Phillips County C/C* • Chris Richey; Exec. Dir.; 111 Hickory Hills Dr.; PO Box 447; 72342; Phillips; P 22,000; M 250; (870) 338-8327; crichey@phillipscountychamber.org; www.phillipscountychamber.org

Highland • *Spring River Area C/C* • Laura Sackett-Clute; Pres.; 2423A Hwy. 62/412; 72542; Sharp; P 7,000; M 141; (870) 856-3210;; Fax (870) 856-3320; sracc@centurytel.net; www.sracc.com

Hope • *Hope-Hempstead County C/C* • Mark Keith; Dir.; 101 W. 2nd; P.O. Box 250; 71802; Hempstead; P 23,000; M 275; (870) 777-3640; Fax (870) 722-6154; hopemelonfest@yahoo.com; www.hopemelonfest.com*

Horseshoe Bend • *Horseshoe Bend Area C/C* • Brenda Doty; Pres.; 811 2nd St., Ste. 18; P.O. Box 4083; 72512; Fulton, Izard & Sharp; P 2,187; M 92; (870) 670-5433; horseshoebendarcc@yahoo.com; www.horseshoebendarcc.com

Hot Springs • *Greater Hot Springs C/C* • Jim Fram CCE CEcD FM; Pres./CEO; 659 Ouachita; P.O. Box 6090; 71902; Garland; P 97,000; M 920; (501) 321-1700; Fax (501) 321-3551; rita.koller@growinghotsprings.com; www.hotspringschamber.com*

Hot Springs Village • *Hot Springs Village Area C/C •* Michael Dollar; Exec. Dir.; 121 Cordoba Center Dr., Ste. 300; 71909; Garland; P 20,000; M 300; (501) 915-9940; (866) 984-9963; Fax (501) 984-9961; jill@hotspringsvillagechamber.com; www.hotspringsvillagechamber. com*

Huntsville • *Huntsville Area C/C •* David Pemberton; Exec. Dir.; 113 Main; P.O. Box 950; 72740; Madison; P 2,000; M 74; (479) 738-6000; Fax (479) 738-6000; chamber@madisoncounty.net; www. huntsvillearchamber.com

Jacksonville • *Jacksonville C/C •* Amy Mattison; CEO; 200 Dupree Dr.; 72076; Pulaski; P 30,900; M 400; (501) 982-1511; Fax (501) 982-1464; chamber@jacksonville-arkansas.com; www.jacksonville-arkansas.com

Jasper • *Newton County C/C •* Nancy Atkinson; Pres.; 204 N. Spring; P.O. Box 250; 72641; Newton; P 5,000; M 170; (870) 446-2455; Fax (870) 446-2477; chamber@ritternet.com; www.theozarkmountains. com

Jonesboro • *Jonesboro Reg. C/C •* Mark Young; Pres./CEO; 1709 E. Nettleton Ave.; P.O. Box 789; 72403; Craighead; P 69,000; M 1,200; (870) 932-6691; Fax (870) 933-5758; info@jonesborochamber.com; www.jonesborochamber.com*

Lake Village • *Lake Village C/C •* Connee Luttrell; Exec. Dir.; 111 Main St.; P.O. Box 752; 71653; Chicot; P 5,000; M 56; (870) 265-5997; Fax (870) 265-5254; lvccdirector@sbcglobal.net

Lincoln • *Lincoln Area C/C •* Bryan Snyder; Pres.; P.O. Box 942; 72744; Washington; P 2,200; M 56; (479) 824-0966; bs@bryke.com; lincolnareacofc.com

Little Rock • *Little Rock Reg. C/C •* Jay Chesshir CCE; Pres./ CEO; 1 Chamber Plaza; 72201; Faulkner, Pulaski & Saline; P 653,000; M 1,900; (501) 374-2001; Fax (501) 374-6018; chamber@ littlerockchamber.com; www.littlerockchamber.com*

Lonoke • *Lonoke Area C/C •* John Garner; Exec. Dir.; 102 N.W. Front St.; P.O. Box 294; 72086; Lonoke; P 4,500; M 167; (501) 676-4399; Fax (501) 676-4399; uni1mac55@sbcglobal.net; www.lonoke.com

Lowell • *see Rogers*

Magnolia • *Magnolia-Columbia County C/C •* Ellie Baker; Exec. Dir.; 211 W. Main St.; P.O. Box 866; 71754; Columbia; P 24,500; M 220; (870) 234-4352; Fax (870) 234-9291; ea@ccalliance.us; www. magnoliachamber.com

Malvern • *Malvern/Hot Spring County C/C •* Lance Howell; Exec. Dir.; 213 W. 3rd St.; P.O. Box 266; 72104; Hot Spring; P 33,000; M 300; (501) 332-2721; Fax (501) 332-8558; frontdesk@malvernchamber.com; www.malvernchamber.com

Mammoth Spring • *Mammoth Spring C/C •* Steve Russell; Pres.; P.O. Box 1; 72554; Fulton; P 1,000; M 43; (870) 625-7364; mammothspringchamber@gmail.com; www.mammothspringchamber. org

Marianna • *Marianna-Lee County C/C •* Tammie Miller; 67 W. Main St.; 72360; Lee; P 4,115; M 150; (870) 295-2469; chamcom@att.net; www.mariannaarkansas.org

Marked Tree • *Marked Tree C/C •* Sandee Teague; Pres.; 1 Elm St.; 72365; Poinsett; P 2,800; M 100; (870) 358-3000; (870) 358-3216; Fax (870) 358-2125; www.markedtreechamber.org

Marshall • *Greater Searcy County C/C •* Lee Walsh; Pres.; P.O. Box 1385; 72650; Searcy; P 7,800; M 130; (870) 448-2557; Fax (870) 448-4858; webmaster@searcycountyarkansas.org; searcycountyarkansas. org

Maumelle • *Maumelle Area C/C •* Julianne Cole; Exec. Dir.; 115 Audubon Dr., Ste. 14; P.O. Box 13099; 72113; Pulaski; P 25,000; M 330; (501) 851-9700; Fax (501) 851-6690; execdir@ maumellechamber.com; www.maumellechamber.com*

McGehee • *McGehee C/C •* Paula Mote; Secy./Ofc. Coord.; 901 Holly St.; P.O. Box 521; 71654; Desha; P 4,750; M 130; (870) 222-4451; Fax (870) 222-5729; admin@mcgeheechamber.com; www. mcgeheechamber.com

Mena • *Mena/Polk County C/C •* Paula Bailey; Exec. Dir.; 524 Sherwood Ave.; 71953; Polk; P 22,000; M 260; (479) 394-2912; secretary@menapolkchamber.com; menapolkchamber.com*

Monticello • *Monticello-Drew County C/C •* Glenda Nichols; Exec. Dir.; 335 E. Gaines; 71655; Drew; P 18,900; M 190; (870) 367-6741; monticellochamber@sbcglobal.net; www.montdrewchamber.com

Morrilton • *Morrilton Area C/C •* Jerry L. Smith; Pres./CEO; 115 E. Broadway; P.O. Box 589; 72110; Conway; P 6,700; M 325; (501) 354-2393; Fax (501) 354-8642; chamber@morrilton.com; www.morrilton. com

Mount Ida • *Mount Ida Area C/C •* Sherry Ellison; Pres.; 124 Hwy. 270 W.; P.O. Box 6; 71957; Montgomery; P 9,000; M 100; (870) 867-2723; Fax (870) 867-2723; director@mtidachamber.com; www.mtidachamber. com

Mountain Home • *Mountain Home Area C/C •* Eddie Majeste; Pres./ CEO; 1023 Hwy. 62 E.; P.O. Box 488; 72654; Baxter; P 12,500; M 600; (870) 425-5111; (800) 822-3536; Fax (870) 425-4446; emajeste@ EnjoyMountainHome.com; www.EnjoyMountainHome.com*

Mountain View • *Mountain View Area C/C •* Michalle Stevens; Exec. Dir.; 107 N. Peabody Ave.; P.O. Box 133; 72560; Stone; P 3,000; M 250; (870) 269-8068; Fax (870) 269-8748; mvchamber@mvtel.net; www.yourplaceinthemountains.com

Murfreesboro • *Murfreesboro C/C •* Zane Woodall; Pres.; P.O. Box 166; 71958; Pike; P 1,700; M 80; (870) 285-3131; (870) 200-0839; Fax (870) 285-3131; murfreesboro.chamber@yahoo.com; www. murfreesboroarkchamber.com

Nashville • *Nashville C/C •* Bonnie Hutto; Secy.; 107 S. Main St.; 71852; Howard; P 5,000; M 140; (870) 845-1262; Fax (870) 845-3443; nashvillecc@sbcglobal.net; www.nashvillear.com

Newark • *Newark Area C/C •* Ernie Pectol; P.O. Box 222; 72562; Independence; P 1,187; M 40; (870) 799-8888

Newport • *Newport Area C/C •* Julie Allen; Exec. Dir.; 201 Hazel St.; 72112; Jackson; P 7,879; M 300; (870) 523-3618; Fax (870) 523-1055; director@newportarchamber.org; www.newportarchamber.org

North Little Rock • *North Little Rock C/C •* John Owens; Pres./CEO; 100 Main St.; P.O. Box 5288; 72119; Pulaski; P 64,000; M 1,332; (501) 372-5959; Fax (501) 372-5955; jowens@nlrchamber.org; www. nlrchamber.org*

Osceola • *Osceola-South Mississippi County C/C •* Ammi Tucker; Exec. Dir.; 116 N. Maple; P.O. Box 174; 72370; Mississpppi; P 8,000; M 230; (870) 563-2281; Fax (870) 563-5385; osceolachamber@ sbcglobal.net; www.osceolasmcchamber.com

Ozark • *Ozark Area C/C* • Linda Millsap; Dir.; 300 W. Commercial St.; 72949; Franklin; P 3,700; M 200; (479) 667-2525; (479) 667-5750; ozarkareacoc@centurytel.net; www.ozarkareacoc.org

Paragould • *Paragould Reg. C/C* • Sue McGowan; Dir./CEO; 300 W. Court St.; P.O. Box 124; 72451; Greene; P 26,500; M 600; (870) 236-7684; Fax (870) 236-7142; ceo@paragould.org; www.paragould.org*

Paris • *Paris Area C/C* • Tonya Baumgartner; Exec. Dir.; 301 W. Walnut; 72855; Logan; P 3,800; M 158; (479) 963-2244; (479) 963-2244; Fax (479) 963-8321; pariscoc@gmail.com; www.parisarkansas.com*

Piggott • *Piggott Area C/C* • Jan Glover; Secy.; P.O. Box 96; 72454; Clay; P 3,849; M 71; (870) 598-3167; chamberpg@yahoo.com

Pine Bluff • *Pine Bluff Reg. C/C* • Ann Williams; Dir.; 510 Main St.; P.O. Box 5069; 71611; Jefferson; P 77,435; M 746; (870) 535-0110; Fax (870) 535-1643; awilliams@pinebluffchamber.com; www.pinebluffchamber.com*

Pocahontas • *Randolph County C/C* • Tim Scott; Exec. Dir.; 107 E. Everett St.; P.O. Box 466; 72455; Randolph; P 6,500; M 200; (870) 892-3956; Fax (870) 892-5399; chamber@randolphchamber.com; www.randolphchamber.com*

Prairie Grove • *Prairie Grove C/C* • Sandy Keeney; Secy./Treas.; P.O. Box 23; 72753; Washington; P 4,650; M 40; (479) 846-2197; info@pgchamber.com; www.pgchamber.com

Prescott • *Prescott-Nevada County C/C* • Jamie Hillery; Exec. Dir.; 116 E. 2nd St. S.; P.O. Box 307; 71857; Nevada; P 8,897; M 114; (870) 887-2101; Fax (870) 887-5317; jhillery@pnpartnership.org; www.pnpartnership.org

Rector • *Rector Area C/C* • Ron Kemp; Pres.; P.O. Box 307; 72461; Clay; P 1,977; M 60; (870) 595-2300; (870) 595-3035; jemanchester@yahoo.com; www.rectorarkansas.com

Rogers • *Rogers-Lowell Area C/C* • Raymond M. Burns CCE; Pres./CEO; 317 W. Walnut; 72756; Benton; P 63,000; M 2,000; (479) 636-1240; Fax (479) 636-5485; amanda@rogerslowell.com; www.rogerslowell.com*

Russellville • *Russellville Area C/C* • Stephanie Beerman; Exec. V.P.; 708 W. Main St.; 72801; Pope; P 90,000; M 917; (479) 968-2530; Fax (479) 968-5894; chamber@russellville.org; www.russellvillechamber.org*

Salem • *Salem C/C* • Holly Pate; Pres.; P.O. Box 649; 72576; Fulton; P 1,591; M 90; (870) 895-5565; salemar@centurytel.net; www.salemar.com

Searcy • *Searcy Reg. C/C* • Buck C. Layne Jr. CEcD PCED; Pres.; 2323 S. Main St.; 72143; White; P 55,000; M 700; (501) 268-2458; Fax (501) 268-9530; scc@searcychamber.com; www.searcychamber.com*

Sheridan • *Grant County C/C* • Becky Nichols; Exec. Dir.; 202 N. Oak St.; 72150; Grant; P 16,000; M 151; (870) 942-3021; Fax (870) 942-3378; gccc@windstream.net; www.grantcountychamber.com

Sherwood • *Sherwood C/C* • Marcia Cook; Exec. Dir.; 295 W. Kiehl Ave.; 72120; Pulaski; P 30,000; M 250; (501) 835-7600; Fax (501) 835-2326; shwdchamber@att.net; www.sherwoodchamber.net*

Siloam Springs • *Siloam Springs C/C* • O. Wayne Mays; Pres./CEO; 108 E. University St.; P.O. Box 476; 72761; Benton; P 15,438; M 450; (479) 524-6466; Fax (479) 549-3032; patti@siloamchamber.com; www.siloamchamber.com*

Smackover • *The Smackover C/C* • Lindsey Lawrence; Exec. Dir.; 710 Pershing Hwy.; P.O. Box 275; 71762; Union; P 1,929; M 85; (870) 725-3521; (870) 944-0221; Fax (870) 725-3521; smkovrcofc@sbcglobal.net; www.smackoverar.com

Springdale • *Springdale C/C* • Perry Webb CCE IOM; Pres./CEO; 202 W. Emma St.; P.O. Box 166; 72765; Benton & Washington; P 77,000; M 955; (479) 872-2222; (800) 972-7261; Fax (479) 751-4699; info@chamber.springdale.com; www.springdale.com*

Star City • *Star City C/C* • Shamby Donaldson; Secy.; P.O. Box 88; 71667; Lincoln; P 2,500; M 100; (870) 628-3100; Fax (870) 628-9943; starcitychamber@yahoo.com; www.stardazefestival.com

Stephens • *Stephens C/C* • Duncan Grayson; P.O. Box 572; 71764; Ouachita; P 900; M 34; (870) 786-5416

Stuttgart • *Stuttgart C/C* • Bethany Hodges; Exec. V.P.; 507 S. Main; P.O. Box 1500; 72160; Arkansas; P 10,000; M 270; (870) 673-1602; Fax (870) 673-1604; bethany@stuttgartchamber.com; www.stuttgartarkansas.org

Sulphur Springs • *Sulphur Springs Comm. C/C* • Shirley Barber; P.O. Box 115; 72768; Benton; P 500; M 5; (479) 298-3218

Texarkana • *see Texarkana, TX*

Trumann • *Trumann C/C* • Neal W. Vickers Ed.D.; Dir. of Eco. Dev.; 225 Hwy. 463 N.; P.O. Box 215; 72472; Poinsett; P 7,250; M 120; (870) 483-5424; Fax (870) 483-6833; director@trumannchamber.org; www.trumannchamber.org

Van Buren • *Van Buren C/C* • Jackie Krutsch; Exec. Dir.; 510 Main St.; 72956; Crawford; P 22,971; M 350; (479) 474-2761; Fax (479) 474-6259; janie@vanburenchamber.org; www.vanburenchamber.org*

Waldron • *Waldron Area C/C* • Jeff Brewer; Pres.; 323 Washington St.; P.O. Box 1985; 72958; Scott; P 10,900; M 125; (479) 637-2775; Fax (479) 637-0041; admin@waldronareachamberofcommerce.com; www.waldronchamberofcommerce.com

Walnut Ridge • *Lawrence County C/C* • Kathy Bradley; Exec. Secy.; 109 S.W. Front St.; P.O. Box 842; 72476; Lawrence; P 17,011; M 208; (870) 886-3232; Fax (870) 886-1736; lawrencecofc@suddenlinkmail.com; www.lawcochamber.org

Ward • *Ward C/C* • Sharon Roberts; Pres.; 80 S. 2nd St.; P.O. Box 106; 72176; Lonoke; P 2,500; M 90; (501) 843-6533; (501) 843-8348; wardchamber@gmail.com; www.wardchamber.com

Warren • *Bradley County C/C* • David King; Exec. Dir.; 104 N. Myrtle St.; 71671; Bradley; P 12,600; M 240; (870) 226-5225; Fax (870) 226-6285; bcc.warren@sbcglobal.net; www.bradleychamber.com

Watson • *Watson C/C* • Kelvin Fuller; Pres.; P.O. Box 16; 71674; Desha; P 288; M 48; (870) 866-7666; kelvinfuller0111@yahoo.com

West Memphis • *West Memphis Area C/C* • Holmes Hammett; Exec. Dir.; 108 W. Broadway; P.O. Box 594; 72303; Crittenden; P 30,000; M 548; (870) 735-1134; Fax (870) 735-6283; wmcoc@wmcoc.com; www.wmcoc.com*

White Hall • *White Hall C/C* • Steve Hood; Pres.; P.O. Box 20429; 71612; Jefferson; P 5,000; M 163; (870) 247-5502; whitehallchamber@gmail.com; whitehallarchamber.org

Wynne • *Cross County C/C* • Chris Clifton CED IOM; Pres./CEO; 1790 N. Falls Blvd., Ste. 2; P.O. Box 234; 72396; Cross; P 17,800; M 255; (870) 238-2601; Fax (870) 238-7844; jan@crosscountychamber.com; www.crosscountychamber.com*

Yellville • *Yellville Area C/C* • 414 W. 3rd; P.O. Box 369; 72687; Marion; P 1,300; M 125; (870) 449-4676; chamber@yellville.net; www. yellvillechamber.com

California

California C of C • Allan Zaremberg; Pres./CEO; 1215 K St., Ste. 1400; P.O. Box 1736; Sacramento; 95812; Sacramento; P 39,200,000; M 1,400; (916) 444-6670; Fax (916) 325-1272; hrcalifornia.service@ calchamber.com; www.calchamber.com

Acton • *Acton C/C* • Maureen Weston; Recording Secy.; P.O. Box 81; 93510; Los Angeles; P 12,000; M 200; (661) 269-5785; Fax (661) 269-4121; president@actoncoc.org; www.actoncoc.org

Adelanto • *Adelanto C/C* • M. Terri Ortega; Pres.; P.O. Box 712; 92301; San Bernardino; P 31,700; M 200; (760) 246-5711; office@ adelantochamber.com; www.adelantochamber.com

Agoura Hills • *see Westlake Village*

Agua Dulce • *see Santa Clarita*

Alameda • *Alameda C/C* • Mark Sorensen; Exec. Dir.; 2215-A S. Shore Center; P.O. Box 1530; 94501; Alameda; P 75,000; M 85; (510) 522-0414; Fax (510) 522-7677; connect@alamedachamber.com; www. alamedachamber.com*

Alamo • *see Danville*

Albany • *Albany C/C* • Winkie Campbell-Notar; Exec. Dir.; P.O. Box 6434; 94706; Alameda; P 25,000; M 150; (510) 525-1771; chamber@ albanychamber.org; www.albanychamber.org

Alhambra • *Alhambra C/C* • Sharon Gibbs; Exec. Dir.; 104 S. First St.; 91801; Los Angeles; P 90,000; M 500; (626) 282-8481; Fax (626) 282-5596; alhambrachamber@yahoo.com; www.alhambrachamber.org*

Alpine • *Alpine & Mountain Empire C/C* • Patricia Cannon; Pres./ CEO; 2157 Alpine Blvd.; 91901; San Diego; P 18,000; M 400; (619) 445-2722; Fax (619) 445-2871; info@alpinechamber.com; www. alpinechamber.com*

Altadena • *Altadena C/C* • Inger Miller; Pres.; 730 E. Altadena Dr.; 91001; Los Angeles; P 42,700; M 100; (626) 794-3988; Fax (626) 794-6015; office@altadenachamber.org; www.altadenachamber.org

Alturas • *Alturas C/C* • Rose Boulade; 600 S. Main St.; 96101; Modoc; P 3,000; M 150; (530) 233-3434; Fax (530) 233-5099; contactus@ alturaschamber.org; www.alturaschamber.org

Amador County • *see Jackson*

American Canyon • *American Canyon C/C* • James Cooper; Pres./ CEO; 3427 Broadway, Ste. F-3; 94503; Napa; P 19,500; M 170; (707) 552-3650; Fax (707) 552-9724; chamber@amcanchamber.org; www. amcanchamber.org*

Anaheim • *Anaheim C/C* • Sarah Bartzcak; Sr. V.P.; 2400 E. Katella Ave., Ste. 725; 92806; Orange; P 341,000; M 800; (714) 758-0222; Fax (714) 758-0468; info@anaheimchamber.org; www. anaheimchamber.org*

Anderson • *Anderson C/C* • Debe Hopkins; Mgr.; 2375 North St.; P.O. Box 1144; 96007; Shasta; P 10,000; M 350; (530) 365-8095; Fax (530) 365-4561; andersonchamberinfo@gmail.com; andersonchamberofcommerce.com*

Angels Camp • *see San Andreas*

Angwin • *Angwin Comm. Cncl.* • Kellie Lind; Pres.; P.O. Box 747; 94508; Napa; P 3,000; M 400; (707) 965-2867; president@ angwincouncil.org; www.angwincouncil.org

Antelope • *see Sacramento-North Sacramento C/C*

Antioch • *Antioch C/C* • Dr. Sean Wright; Pres./CEO; 101 H St., Ste. 4; 94509; Contra Costa; P 100,000; M 300; (925) 757-1800; Fax (925) 757-5286; martha@antiochchamber.com; www.antiochchamber.com*

Anza • *Anza Valley C/C* • Pamela Machado; Pres.; P.O. Box 391460; 92539; Riverside; P 12,000; M 80; (951) 290-2822; president@ anzavalleychamber.com; www.anzavalleychamber.com

Apple Valley • *Apple Valley C/C* • Janice Moore; Pres./CEO; 16010 Apple Valley Rd.; 92307; San Bernardino; P 70,000; M 450; (760) 242-2753; Fax (760) 242-0303; nyesha@avchamber.org; www.avchamber. org*

Aptos • *Aptos C/C* • Karen Hibble; Dir.; 7605-A Old Dominion Ct.; 95003; Santa Cruz; P 25,000; M 675; (831) 688-1467; Fax (831) 688-6961; info@aptoschamber.com; www.aptoschamber.com

Arcadia • *Arcadia C/C* • Karen Mac Nair; CEO; 388 W. Huntington Dr.; 91007; Los Angeles; P 56,400; M 500; (626) 447-2159; Fax (626) 445-0273; info@arcadiacachamber.org; www.arcadiacachamber.org

Arcata • *Arcata C/C* • Joellen Clark-Peterson; Exec. Dir.; 1635 Heindon Rd.; 95521; Humboldt; P 18,000; M 400; (707) 822-3619; Fax (707) 822-3515; arcata@arcatachamber.com; arcatachamber.com*

Arroyo Grande • *Arroyo Grande & Grover Beach C/C* • Judith Bean ACE; Pres./CEO; 800-A West Branch St.; 93420; San Luis Obispo; P 25,000; M 450; (805) 489-1488; Fax (805) 489-2239; info@ aggbchamber.com; www.aggbchamber.com*

Arvin • *Arvin C/C* • Randy Thompson; Secy./Mgr.; P.O. Box 645; 93203; Kern; P 16,000; M 60; (661) 854-2265; Fax (661) 854-2265; arvinchamberofcommerce@yahoo.com; www. arvinchamberofcommerce.com

Atascadero • *Atascadero C/C* • Linda Hendy; Pres./CEO; 6904 El Camino Real; 93422; San Luis Obispo; P 29,000; M 510; (805) 466-2044; linda@atascaderochamber.org; atascaderochamber.org*

Atwater • *also see Los Angeles-Atwater Village C/C*

Atwater • *Atwater C/C* • Kayla Moon; Dir. of Finance; 1181 Third St.; 95301; Merced; P 30,000; M 200; (209) 358-4251; Fax (209) 358-0934; chamber@atwaterchamberofcommerce.org; www. atwaterchamberofcommerce.org*

Auburn • *Auburn C/C* • Kevin Hanley; CEO; 1103 High St., Ste. 100; 95603; Placer; P 65,000; M 630; (530) 885-5616; Fax (530) 885-5854; info@auburnchamber.net; www.auburnchamber.net*

Avalon • *Catalina Island C/C & Visitors Bur.* • Jim Luttjohann; Pres./CEO; #1 Green Pleasure Pier; P.O. Box 217; 90704; Los Angeles; P 4,000; M 261; (310) 510-1520; Fax (310) 510-7606; info@ catalinachamber.com; www.catalinachamber.com

Azusa • *Azusa C/C* • Steve Castro; CEO; 240 W. Foothill Blvd.; 91702; Los Angeles; P 45,200; M 200; (626) 334-1507; Fax (626) 334-5217; info@azusachamber.org; www.azusachamber.org*

Badger • *see Miramonte*

Bakersfield Area

Greater Bakersfield C/C • Nicholas Ortiz; Pres./CEO; 1725 Eye St.; P.O. Box 1947; 93303; Kern; P 354,000; M 1,152; (661) 327-4421; Fax (661) 327-8751; info@bakersfieldchamber.org; www.bakersfieldchamber.org*

Kern County Bd. of Trade • Dave Hook; Exec. Dir.; 2101 Oak St.; 93301; Kern; P 750,000; (661) 868-5376; Fax (661) 861-2017; kerninfo@co.kern.ca.us; www.visitkern.com

North of the River C/C • Cathy Wolfe; Exec. Dir.; P.O. Box 5551; 93388; Kern; P 864,000; M 150; (661) 873-4709; info@norchamber.org; www.norchamber.org

Banning • Banning C/C • Don Robinson; Exec. Dir.; 60 E. Ramsey St.; P.O. Box 665; 92220; Riverside; P 30,000; M 350; (951) 849-4695; Fax (951) 849-9395; bcinfo1@verizon.net; www.banningchamber.net*

Barstow • Barstow Area C/C • Eugene Butticci; Exec. Dir.; 229 E. Main St.; 92311; San Bernardino; P 23,056; M 250; (760) 256-8617; Fax (760) 256-7675; bacc@barstowchamber.com; www.barstowchamber.com*

Bass Lake • Bass Lake C/C • P.O. Box 126; 93604; Madera; P 2,500; M 27; (559) 642-3676; chamber@basslakechamber.com; www.basslakechamber.com

Bay Point • *see Rio Vista-California Delta C of C & Visitors Bur.*

Baywood Park • *see Los Osos*

Beaumont • Beaumont C/C • Sheri Bogh; Exec. Dir.; 726 Beaumont Ave.; 92223; Riverside; P 40,000; M 390; (951) 845-9541; Fax (951) 769-9080; director@beaumontcachamber.com; www.beaumontcachamber.com*

Bell • Bell C/C • Gloria Medina; Exec. Dir.; 4401 E. Gage Ave.; P.O. Box 294; 90201-0294; Los Angeles; P 30,500; M 250; (323) 560-8755; Fax (323) 560-2060; bellchamber@sbcglobal.net; www.bellchamber.com

Bell Gardens • Bell Gardens C/C • Carlos Cruz; Exec. Dir.; 7535 Perry Rd.; 90201-0294; Los Angeles; P 45,000; M 150; (562) 806-2355; Fax (562) 806-1585; carlos@bellgardenschamber.org; www.bellgardenschamber.org

Bellflower • Bellflower C/C • Michele Moore; Chamber Mgr.; 16730 Bellflower Blvd., Ste. A; 90706; Los Angeles; P 75,000; M 275; (562) 867-1744; Fax (562) 866-7545; bellflowercoc@juno.com; www.bellflowerchamber.com

Belmont • Belmont C/C • George A. Burgess; Pres.; 1059A Alameda de las Pulgas; 94002; San Mateo; P 27,000; M 200; (650) 595-8696; execdirector@belmontchamber.org; www.belmontchamber.org*

Benicia • Benicia C/C • Stephanie L. Christiansen; Pres./CEO; 601 First St., Ste. 100; 94510; Solano; P 28,000; M 425; (707) 745-2120; Fax (707) 745-2275; info@beniciachamber.com; www.beniciachamber.com*

Berkeley • Berkeley C/C • Kirsten MacDonald; CEO/Operations; 1834 University Ave.; 94703; Alameda; P 121,000; M 375; (510) 549-7000; Fax (510) 549-1789; info@berkeleychamber.com; www.berkeleychamber.com*

Bethel Island • Bethel Island C/C • Dori Anderson; Pres.; P.O. Box 263; 94511; Contra Costa; P 2,300; M 150; (925) 684-3220; Fax (925) 684-9025; bicc@bethelisland-chamber.com; www.bethelisland-chamber.com

Beverly Hills • Beverly Hills C/C • Todd Johnson; Pres./CEO; 9400 S. Santa Monica Blvd., 2nd Flr.; 90210; Los Angeles; P 36,000; M 830; (310) 248-1000; Fax (310) 248-1020; info@beverlyhillschamber.com; www.beverlyhillschamber.com

Big Bear Lake • Big Bear C/C • Pamela Scannell; Exec. Dir.; 630 Bartlett Rd.; P.O. Box 2860; 92315; San Bernardino; P 21,000; M 438; (909) 866-4607; Fax (909) 866-5412; contact@bigbearchamber.com; www.bigbearchamber.com*

Big Bend • *see Burney*

Bird's Landing • *see Rio Vista-California Delta C of C & Visitors Bur.*

Bishop • Bishop Area C/C & Visitors Bur. • Tawni Tomson; Exec. Dir.; 690 N. Main St.; 93514; Inyo; P 14,000; M 300; (760) 873-8405; (888) 395-3952; Fax (760) 873-6999; info@bishopvisitor.com; www.bishopvisitor.com

Black Hawk • *see Danville*

Blue Lake • Blue Lake C/C • Mandi Kindred; P.O. Box 476; 95525; Humboldt; P 1,253; M 50; (707) 668-5655; bluelakecc@gmail.com; www.bluelakechamber.com

Blythe • Blythe Area C/C • Jim Shipley; COO; 145 N. Spring St., Ste. 605; 92225; Riverside; P 13,500; M 350; (760) 922-8166; Fax (760) 922-4010; blythecoc@yahoo.com; www.blytheareachamberofcommerce.com

Bolinas • *see Stinson Beach*

Boonville • Anderson Valley C/C • Dawn Emery Ballantine; P.O. Box 275; 95415; Mendocino; P 2,000; M 50; (707) 895-2379; info@andersonvalleychamber.com; www.andersonvalleychamber.com

Boron • Boron C/C • James Welling; Pres.; 26922-20 Mule Team Rd.; 93516; Kern; P 3,500; M 50; (760) 762-5810; Fax (760) 762-0012; chamber@boronchamber.com; www.boronchamber.com

Borrego Springs • Borrego Springs C/C & Visitors Bur. • Linda Haddock; Exec. Dir.; 786 Palm Canyon Dr.; P.O. Box 420; 92004; San Diego; P 3,000; M 210; (760) 767-5555; Fax (760) 767-5976; info@VisitBorrego.com; www.VisitBorrego.com*

Brawley • Brawley C/C • Jason Zara; Exec. Dir.; 204 S. Imperial Ave.; P.O. Box 218; 92227; Imperial; P 25,000; M 350; (760) 344-3160; Fax (760) 344-7611; jason@brawleychamber.com; www.brawleychamber.com*

Brea • Brea C/C • Heidi L. Gallegos; Pres./CEO; One Civic Center Cir., 2nd Flr.; 92821; Orange; P 42,000; M 400; (714) 529-3660; Fax (714) 529-3657; answers@breachamber.com; www.breachamber.com*

Brentwood • Brentwood C/C • Paul Kelly; Pres.; 8440 Brentwood Blvd., Ste. C; 94513; Contra Costa; P 52,000; M 350; (925) 634-3344; Fax (925) 634-3731; info@brentwoodchamber.com; www.brentwoodchamber.com*

Bridgeport • Bridgeport C/C • P.O. Box 541; 93517; Mono; P 800; M 65; (760) 932-7500; bridgeportcalifornia@bridgeportcalifornia.com; www.bridgeportcalifornia.com

Brisbane • *Brisbane C/C* • Mitch Bull; Pres./CEO; 50 Park Pl.; 94005; San Mateo; P 3,700; M 228; (415) 467-7283; Fax (415) 467-5421; mitch.bull@brisbanechamber.com; www.brisbanechamber.com

Buellton • *Buellton C/C* • Kathy Vreeland; Exec. Dir.; 597 Ave. of Flags, Ste. 101; P.O. Box 231; 93427; Santa Barbara; P 4,828; M 200; (805) 688-7829; (800) 324-3800; Fax (805) 688-5399; info@buellton.org; www.buellton.org

Buena Park • *West Orange County Reg. C/C* • Connie Pedenko; Pres./CEO; 8081 Stanton Ave., Ste. 306; 90620; Orange; P 85,000; M 250; (714) 484-1420; Fax (714) 484-1806; info@wocrcoc.org; www.wocrcoc.org*

Burbank • *Burbank C/C* • Tom Flavin; CEO; 200 W. Magnolia Blvd.; 91502; Los Angeles; P 105,400; M 1,000; (818) 846-3111; Fax (818) 846-0109; info@burbankchamber.org; www.burbankchamber.org

Burlingame • *Burlingame C/C* • Georgette Naylor; Pres./CEO; 417 California Dr.; 94010; San Mateo; P 29,000; M 450; (650) 344-1735; Fax (650) 344-1763; info@burlingamechamber.org; www.burlingamechamber.org

Burney • *Burney C/C* • Jill Barnett; Pres.; 36879 Main St.; P.O. Box 36; 96013; Shasta; P 3,500; M 120; (530) 335-2111; Fax (530) 335-2122; burneychamber@frontiernet.net; www.burneychamber.com

Buttonwillow • *Buttonwillow C/C & Ag.* • Gloria Selvidge; Secy./Mgr.; 104 W. 2nd St.; P.O. Box 251; 93206; Kern; P 1,266; M 112; (661) 764-5406; Fax (661) 764-5406; buttonwillowchamber@bak.rr.com; www.buttonwillowchamber.com

Byron • *see Rio Vista-California Delta C of C & Visitors Bur.*

Calabasas • *Calabasas C/C* • Bridget Karl; Pres./CEO; 23564 Calabasas Rd., Ste. 101; 91302; Los Angeles; P 23,000; M 375; (818) 222-5680; Fax (818) 222-5690; info@calabasaschamber.com; www.calabasaschamber.com*

Calaveras County • *see San Andreas*

Calexico • *Calexico C/C* • Hildy Carrillo; Exec. Dir.; 1100 Imperial Ave.; P.O. Box 948; 92231; Imperial; P 38,000; M 400; (760) 357-1166; Fax (760) 357-9043; hildy@calexicochamber.net; www.calexicochamber.net

California City • *California City C/C* • Karen Sanders; Pres.; 8001 California City Blvd.; P.O. Box 2008; 93504; Kern; P 14,100; M 150; (760) 373-8676; Fax (760) 373-1414; info@californiacitychamber.com; www.californiacitychamber.com*

Calimesa • *Calimesa C/C* • Monica Vollucci; Managing Dir.; 1007 Calimesa Blvd., Ste. D; P.O. Box 246; 92320; Riverside; P 8,500; M 135; (909) 795-7612; Fax (909) 795-2822; calimesachamber@cybertime.net; www.calimesachamber.org

Calistoga • *Calistoga C/C* • Chris Canning; Exec. Dir./CEO; 1133 Washington St.; 94515; Napa; P 5,200; M 330; (707) 942-6333; (866) 306-5588; Fax (707) 942-9287; chris@calistogachamber.net; www.calistogachamber.net*

Camarillo • *Camarillo C/C* • Gary Cushing; Pres./CEO; 2400 E. Ventura Blvd.; 93010; Ventura; P 65,000; M 550; (805) 484-4383; info@camarillochamber.org; www.camarillochamber.org*

Cambria • *Cambria C/C* • Mary Ann Carson; Exec. Dir.; 767 Main St.; 93428; San Luis Obispo; P 6,624; M 375; (805) 927-3624; Fax (805) 927-9426; info@cambriachamber.org; www.cambriachamber.org

Cameron Park • *see Shingle Springs*

Campbell • *Campbell C/C* • Christine Giusiana; CEO; 267 E. Campbell Ave., Ste. C; 95008; Santa Clara; P 41,000; M 700; (408) 378-6252; Fax (408) 378-0192; info@campbellchamber.net; www.campbellchamber.net*

Canoga Park • *Canoga Park/West Hills C/C* • Mark Neudorff; Pres.; 7248 Owensmouth Ave.; 91303; Los Angeles; P 92,000; M 200; (818) 884-4222; Fax (818) 884-4604; info@cpwhchamber.org; www.cpwhchamber.org

Canyon Country • *see Santa Clarita*

Canyon Lake • *Canyon Lake C/C* • Lee Clark; Exec. Dir.; 31640 Railroad Canyon Rd.; 92587; Riverside; P 10,800; M 194; (951) 244-6124; Fax (951) 244-0831; admin@canyonlakecoc.com; www.canyonlakecoc.com

Capitola • *Capitola-Soquel C/C* • Toni Castro; CEO; 716-G Capitola Ave.; 95010; Santa Cruz; P 15,000; M 500; (831) 475-6522; (800) 474-6522; Fax (831) 475-6530; capcham@capitolachamber.com; www.capitolachamber.com

Cardiff-By-The-Sea • *Cardiff 101 Main Street* • Tess Radmill; Program Mgr.; 124 Aberdeen Dr.; P.O. Box 552; 92007; San Diego; P 18,000; M 300; (760) 436-0431; Fax (760) 753-0144; cardiff101mainstreet@gmail.com; www.cardiff101.com

Carlsbad • *Carlsbad C/C* • Charles T. Owen; Pres./CEO; 5934 Priestly Dr.; 92008; San Diego; P 110,000; M 1,500; (760) 931-8400; Fax (760) 931-9153; towen@carlsbad.org; www.carlsbad.org*

Carmel • *Carmel C/C* • Monta Potter; CEO; P.O. Box 4444; 93921; Monterey; P 4,000; M 550; (831) 624-2522; (800) 550-4333; Fax (831) 624-1329; info@carmelcalifornia.org; www.carmelcalifornia.org

Carmel Mountain Ranch • *see San Diego-North San Diego Bus. Chamber*

Carmel Valley • *Carmel Valley C/C* • Elizabeth Suro; Managing Dir.; P.O. Box 288; 93924; Monterey; P 15,000; M 250; (831) 659-4000; Fax (831) 644-9476; elizabeth@carmelvalleychamber.com; www.carmelvalleychamber.com

Carmichael • *Carmichael C/C* • Linda Melody; Exec. Dir.; 6825 Fair Oaks Blvd., Ste. 100; 95608; Sacramento; P 62,000; M 200; (916) 481-1002; Fax (916) 481-1003; linda@carmichaelchamber.com; www.carmichaelchamber.com*

Carpinteria • *Carpinteria Valley C/C* • Joyce Donaldson IOM; Pres./CEO; 1056B Eugenia Pl.; P.O. Box 956; 93014; Santa Barbara; P 14,600; M 350; (805) 684-5479; Fax (805) 684-3477; info@carpinteriachamber.org; www.carpinteriachamber.org*

Carson • *Carson C/C* • John Wogan; Pres.; 530 E. Del Amo Blvd.; 90746; Los Angeles; P 100,000; M 600; (310) 217-4590; Fax (310) 217-4591; carsonchamber@carsonchamber.com; www.carsonchamber.com

Cassel • *see Burney*

Castaic • *see Santa Clarita*

Castro Valley • *Castro Valley/Eden Area C/C* • Roberta Rivet; Exec. Dir.; 3467 Castro Valley Blvd.; 94546; Alameda; P 60,000; M 400; (510) 537-5300; Fax (510) 537-5335; info@castrovalleychamber.com; www.edenareachamber.com*

Castroville • *North Monterey County C/C* • Denise Amerison; Exec. Dir.; 10700 Merritt St.; 95012; Monterey; P 13,000; M 200; (831) 633-2465; Fax (831) 633-0485; info@northmontereycountychamber.org; www.northmontereycountychamber.org

Catalina Island • *see Avalon*

Cathedral City • *Cathedral City C/C* • Lynn Mallotto; Exec. Dir.; 68733 Perez Rd., Ste. C8; 92234; Riverside; P 57,000; M 200; (760) 328-1213; Fax (760) 321-0659; admin@cathedralcitycc.com; www. cathedralcitycc.com*

Cayucos • *Cayucos C/C* • Tiffany Silva; Pres.; 41 S. Ocean Ave.; P.O. Box 346; 93430; San Luis Obispo; P 3,500; M 60; (805) 995-1200; cayucoschamber@charter.net; www.cayucoschamber.com

Cedarville • *Surprise Valley C/C* • Eric Antunez; Pres.; P.O. Box 518; 96104; Modoc; P 1,500; M 60; (530) 279-2001; Fax (530) 279-2012; contactsvc@surprisevalleychamber.com; www.surprisevalleychamber. com

Century City • *see Los Angeles-Century City C/C*

Ceres • *Ceres C/C* • Dovie Wilson; Ofc. Mgr.; 2904 4th St.; 95307; Stanislaus; P 48,000; M 200; (209) 537-2601; Fax (209) 537-2699; cereschamberboard@gmail.com; www.cereschamber.com*

Cerritos • *Cerritos Reg. C/C* • Scott Smith; Pres./CEO; 13259 E. South St.; 90703; Los Angeles; P 49,041; M 400; (562) 467-0800; Fax (562) 467-0840; scott@cerritos.org; www.cerritos.org*

Chatsworth • *Chatsworth/Porter Ranch C/C* • Rana Ghadban; Exec. Dir.; 10038 Old Depot Plaza Rd.; 91311; Los Angeles; P 90,000; M 300; (818) 341-2428; Fax (818) 341-4930; exec@chatsworthchamber.com; www.chatsworthchamber.com

Chester • *Chester-Lake Almanor C/C* • Susan Bryner; Exec. Dir.; 529 Main St.; P.O. Box 1198; 96020; Plumas; P 5,000; M 302; (530) 258-2426; (800) 350-4838; Fax (530) 258-2760; info@lakealmanorarea. com; www.lakealmanorarea.com*

Chico • *Chico C/C* • Kate Simmons; CEO; 441 Main St., Ste. 150; P.O. Box 3300; 95927; Butte; P 87,000; M 800; (530) 891-5556; (800) 852-8570; Fax (530) 891-3613; info@chicochamber.com; www. chicochamber.com*

Chino • *Chino Valley C/C* • Vickie Finklestein; Exec. Dir.; 13150 Seventh St.; 91710; San Bernardino; P 150,000; M 650; (909) 627-6177; Fax (909) 627-4180; info@chinovalleychamber.com; www. chinovalleychamber.com*

Chowchilla • *Chowchilla Dist. C/C* • Jacki Flanagan; Mgr.; P.O. Box 638; 93610; Madera; P 18,780; M 200; (559) 665-5603; Fax (559) 665-0896; chamberofcommerce@ci.chowchilla.ca.us; www.ci.chowchilla. ca.us

Chula Vista • *Chula Vista C/C* • Lisa Cohen; CEO; 233 Fourth Ave.; 91910; San Diego; P 230,000; M 950; (619) 420-6603; Fax (619) 420-1269; lisa@chulavistachamber.org; www.chulavistachamber.org

Citrus Heights • *Citrus Heights Reg. C/C* • Valerie Piotrowski; CEO; 7920 Alta Sunrise Blvd., Ste. 100; 95610; Sacramento; P 87,000; M 525; (916) 722-4545; Fax (916) 722-4543; chamber@chchamber. com; www.chchamber.com*

City of Industry • *Industry Manufacturers Cncl.* • Donald Sachs; Exec. Dir.; 15651 Stafford St.; 91744; Los Angeles; P 800; M 600; (626) 968-3737; Fax (626) 330-5060; chamber@cityofindustry.org; www. cityofindustry.org*

Clairemont Mesa • *see Del Mar-LaJolla Golden Triangle C/C*

Claremont • *Claremont C/C* • Maureen Aldridge; CEO; 205 Yale Ave.; 91711; Los Angeles; P 35,500; M 485; (909) 624-1681; Fax (909) 624-6629; contact@claremontchamber.org; www.claremontchamber.org*

Clarksburg • *see Rio Vista-California Delta C of C & Visitors Bur.*

Clearlake • *Clearlake C/C* • Jenn Jensen; Ofc. Mgr.; 3245 Bowers Rd.; P.O. Box 2886; 95422; Lake; P 14,000; M 215; (707) 994-3600; Fax (707) 994-3600; president@clearlakechamber.com; www. clearlakechamber.com

Clements • *see Lodi*

Cloverdale • *Cloverdale C/C* • Robin Wilkerson; Exec. Dir.; 126 N. Cloverdale Blvd.; 95425; Sonoma; P 8,400; M 200; (707) 894-4470; Fax (707) 894-9568; info@cloverdalechamber.com; www. cloverdalechamber.com*

Clovis • *Clovis C/C* • Mark Blackney; Pres./CEO; 325 Pollasky Ave.; 93612; Fresno; P 102,000; M 800; (559) 299-7363; Fax (559) 299-2969; mark@clovischamber.com; www.clovischamber.com*

Coachella • *Greater Coachella Valley C/C* • Joshua Bonner; CEO; 1258 Sixth St.; 92236; Riverside; P 40,000; M 1,300; (760) 398-8089; Fax (760) 398-8589; info@gcvcc.org; www.gcvcc.org*

Coalinga • *Coalinga Area C/C* • Katie Delano; Exec. Dir.; 380 Coalinga Plz.; 93210; Fresno; P 18,061; M 125; (559) 935-2948; exec@ coalingachamber.com; www.coalingachamber.org

Coleville • *see Topaz*

Colfax • *Colfax Area C/C* • Jenny Duncan; Exec. Dir.; P.O. Box 86; 95713; Placer; P 15,000; M 173; (530) 346-8888; Fax (530) 346-6788; contact@colfaxarea.com; www.colfaxarea.com*

Collinsville • *see Rio Vista-California Delta C of C & Visitors Bur.*

Colma • *see Daly City*

Colton • *Colton C/C* • Laura Morales; Exec. Dir.; 655 N. La Cadena Dr.; 92324; San Bernardino; P 52,400; M 275; (909) 825-2222; Fax (909) 824-1650; jane@coltonchamber.org; www.coltonchamber.org

Columbia • *Columbia C/C* • Gary Neubert; Pres.; P.O. Box 1824; 95310; Tuolumne; P 2,500; M 46; (209) 536-1672; info@ columbiacalifornia.com; www.columbiacalifornia.com

Colusa • *Colusa County C/C* • Ben Felt; Pres.; 2963 Davison Ct.; 95932; Colusa; P 22,000; M 240; (530) 458-5525; Fax (530) 458-8180; bfelt@colusachamber.org; www.colusachamber.org*

Commerce • *Commerce Ind. Cncl.-Chamber of Commerce* • Eddie Tafoya; Exec. Dir.; 6055 E. Washington Blvd., Ste. 120; 90040; Los Angeles; P 13,400; M 340; (323) 728-7222; Fax (323) 728-7565; eddie@industrialcouncil.org; www.industrialcouncil.org

Compton • *Compton C/C* • Dr. Lestean M. Johnson; Pres./CEO; 700 N. Bullis Rd., Ste. 6A; P.O. Box 4638; 90224; Los Angeles; P 100,000; M 300; (310) 631-8611; Fax (310) 631-2066; cptchamber@aol.com; www.comptonchamberofcommerce.com*

Concord • *Greater Concord C/C* • Marilyn Fowler; COO; 2280 Diamond Blvd., Ste. 200; 94520; Contra Costa; P 127,600; M 600; (925) 685-1181; Fax (925) 685-5623; smullin@concordchamber.com; www. concordchamber.com*

Corcoran • *Corcoran C/C* • Lisa Shaw; Exec. Dir.; 1040 Whitley Ave.; P.O. Box 459; 93212; Kings; P 14,000; M 180; (559) 992-4514; Fax (559) 992-2341; lisa@corcoranchamber.com; www. corcoranchamber.com

Corning • *Corning Dist. C/C* • Valanne Cardenas; Mgr.; 1110 Solano St.; 96021; Tehama; P 7,700; M 280; (530) 824-5550; Fax (530) 824-9499; info@corningcachamber.org; www.corningcachamber.org

Corona • *Corona C/C* • Bobby Spiegel; Pres./CEO; 904 E. Sixth St.; 92879; Riverside; P 160,000; M 800; (951) 737-3350; Fax (951) 737-3531; info@CORONAchamber.org; www.CORONAchamber.org*

Corona del Mar • *Corona del Mar C/C* • Linda Leonhard; Pres./CEO; 2855 E. Coast Hwy., Ste. 101; 92625; Orange; P 14,500; M 400; (949) 673-4050; Fax (949) 673-3940; info@cdmchamber.com; www.cdmchamber.com*

Coronado • *Coronado C/C* • Stephanie Rendon; Admin./Coord.; 1125 Tenth St.; 92118; San Diego; P 26,000; M 400; (619) 435-9260; Fax (619) 522-6577; lizzie@coronadochamber.com; www.coronadochamber.com*

Corte Madera • *Corte Madera C/C* • Julie Kritzberger; Exec. Dir.; 129 Corte Madera Town Center; 94925; Marin; P 9,700; M 214; (415) 924-0441; Fax (415) 924-1839; chamber@cortemadera.org; www.cortemadera.org*

Costa Mesa • *Costa Mesa C/C* • Ed Fawcett; Pres./CEO; 1700 Adams Ave., Ste. 101; 92626; Orange; P 106,000; M 410; (714) 885-9090; Fax (714) 885-9094; efawcett@costamesachamber.com; www.costamesachamber.com*

Costa Mesa • *Egyptian American Chamber of Commerce* • Nagui Tadros; Chrmn.; 575 Anton Blvd.; 92626; Orange; (949) 667-4999; info@eacham.com; *

Cotati • *Cotati C/C* • Suzanne Whipple; Exec. Dir.; 216 E. School St.; P.O. Box 592; 94931; Sonoma; P 8,000; M 160; (707) 795-5508; Fax (707) 795-5868; chamber@cotati.org; www.cotati.org

Cottonwood • *Cottonwood C/C* • Cheri Skudlarek; P.O. Box 584; 96022; Shasta; P 3,400; M 90; (530) 347-6800; Fax (530) 347-6800; cskudlarek@novb.com; www.cottonwoodcofc.org

Coulterville • *see Mariposa*

Courtland • *see Rio Vista-California Delta C of C & Visitors Bur.*

Covelo • *Round Valley C/C* • Pia McIsaac; Pres.; P.O. Box 458; 95428; Mendocino; P 3,000; M 150; rvcc@roundvalley.org; www.roundvalley.org

Covina • *Covina C/C* • Dawn Nelson; Pres./CEO; 935 W. Badillo, Ste. 100; 91722; Los Angeles; P 48,000; M 630; (626) 967-4191; Fax (626) 966-9660; chamber@covina.org; www.covina.org

Crenshaw • *see Los Angeles-Los Angeles Area C/C*

Crescent City • *Crescent City-Del Norte County C/C* • Jeff Parmer; Exec. Dir.; 1001 Front St.; 95531; Del Norte; P 27,212; M 350; (707) 464-3174; (800) 343-8300; Fax (707) 464-9676; chamber@delnorte.org; www.delnorte.org*

Crestline • *Crestline/Lake Gregory C/C* • Jody Glaviano; Pres.; 24385 Lake Dr.; P.O. Box 926; 92325; San Bernardino; P 11,000; M 115; (909) 338-2706; Fax (909) 338-6588; info@crestlinechamber.net; www.crestlinechamber.net

Crockett • *Crockett C/C* • Cole Adams; Pres.; 1214 A Pomona; P.O. Box 191; 94525; Contra Costa; P 3,800; M 110; (510) 787-1155; Fax (510) 787-1155; crockettchamber@aol.com; www.crockettcalifornia.com*

Cuddy Valley • *see Frazier Park*

Culver City • *Culver City C/C* • Steven J. Rose ACE; Pres./CEO; 6000 Sepulveda Blvd., Ste. 1260; 90230; Los Angeles; P 40,000; M 550; (310) 287-3850; Fax (310) 390-0395; ssssteve@culvercitychamber.com; www.culvercitychamber.com

Cupertino • *Cupertino C/C* • Paula Davis; Pres.; 20455 Silverado Ave.; 95014; Santa Clara; P 55,000; M 300; (408) 252-7054; Fax (408) 252-0638; info@cupertino-chamber.org; www.cupertino-chamber.org*

Cypress • *Cypress C/C* • Ed Munson; Pres./CEO; 5550 Cerritos Ave., Ste. B; 90630; Orange; P 49,300; M 260; (714) 827-2430; Fax (714) 827-1229; info@cypresschamber.org; www.cypresschamber.org

Daggett • *Daggett C/C* • P.O. Box 327; 92327; San Bernardino; P 900; M 4

Daly City • *Daly City-Colma C/C* • Georgette Sarles; Pres./CEO; 355 Gellert Blvd., Ste. 138; 94015; San Mateo; P 101,000; M 535; (650) 755-3900; Fax (650) 755-5160; staff@dalycity-colmachamber.org; www.dalycity-colmachamber.org

Dana Point • *Dana Point C/C* • Heather Johnston; Exec. Dir.; 24681 La Plaza, Ste. 115; 92629; Orange; P 33,000; M 330; (949) 496-1555; chamber@danapointchamber.com; www.danapointchamber.com*

Danville • *Danville Area C/C* • Shelley Despotakis; Pres.; 117-E Town & Country Dr.; 94526; Contra Costa; P 53,000; M 580; (925) 837-4400; Fax (925) 837-5709; office@danvilleareachamber.com; www.danvilleareachamber.com*

Davis • *Davis C/C* • Christina Blackman; CEO; 604 3rd St.; 95616; Yolo; P 64,000; M 500; (530) 756-5160; Fax (530) 756-5190; ceo@davischamber.com; www.davischamber.com*

Death Valley • *see Tecopa*

Del Mar • *La Jolla & Golden Triangle C/C* • George Schmall; Pres.; 1011 Camino Del Mar, Ste. 256; 92014; San Diego; P 200,000; M 100; (858) 350-1253; financialbodyguards@yahoo.com; www.ljgtcc.com*

Del Paso Heights • *see Sacramento-North Sacramento C/C*

Delano • *Delano C/C* • Janet Rabanal; Exec. Dir.; 931 High St.; 93215; Kern; P 53,000; M 216; (661) 725-2518; Fax (661) 725-4743; chamberofdelano@sbcglobal.net; www.chamberofdelano.org

Desert Hot Springs • *Desert Hot Springs C/C* • Heather Coladonato; Pres./CEO; 1408Palm Dr., Ste. D-422; 92240; Riverside; P 32,000; M 411; (760) 329-6403; (800) 346-3347; info@deserthotsprings.com; www.deserthotsprings.com*

Diablo • *see Danville*

Dinuba • *Dinuba C/C* • Sandra Sills; CEO; 210 North L St.; 93618; Tulare; P 23,000; M 150; (559) 591-2707; Fax (559) 591-2712; ssills@dinubachamber.com; www.dinubachamber.com*

Discovery Bay • *Discovery Bay C/C* • Christeen Era; Pres./CEO; P.O. Box 1332; 94505; Contra Costa; P 16,000; M 140; (925) 240-6600; (888) 832-3291; info@discoverybaychamber.com; www.discoverybaychamber.com*

Dixon • *Dixon Dist. C/C* • Carol Pruett; Chief Admin.; 220 N. Jefferson St.; P.O. Box 159; 95620; Solano; P 18,000; M 240; (707) 678-2650; Fax (707) 678-3654; info@dixonchamber.org; www.dixonchamber.org*

Dorris • *Butte Valley C/C* • Christine Baldwin; Pres.; P.O. Box 541; 96023; Siskiyou; P 2,000; M 90; (530) 397-2111; (530) 397-3472; buttevalleychamber@yahoo.com; www.buttevalleychamber.com

Downey • *Downey C/C* • Susan Nordin; Exec. Dir.; 11131 Brookshire Ave.; 90241; Los Angeles; P 112,000; M 425; (562) 923-2191; Fax (562) 869-0461; info@downeychamber.com; www.downeychamber.com*

Duarte • *Duarte C/C* • Jim Kirchner; Pres./CEO; 1634 Third St.; P.O. Box 1438; 91009; Los Angeles; P 22,000; M 300; (626) 357-3333; Fax (626) 357-3645; jim@duartechamber.com; www.duartechamber.com*

Dublin • *Dublin C/C* • Jim Telfer; Pres./CEO; 7080 Donlon Way, Ste. 110; 94568; Alameda; P 50,000; M 330; (925) 828-6200; Fax (925) 828-4247; info@dublinchamberofcommerce.org; www.dublinchamberofcommerce.org*

Dunlap • *see Miramonte*

Dunsmuir • *Dunsmuir C of C & Visitors Center* • Arlis "Missey" Steele; Exec. Dir.; 5915 Dunsmuir Ave., Ste. 100; 96025; Siskiyou; P 1,800; M 100; (530) 235-2177; (800) DUNSMUIR; Fax (530) 235-0911; chamber@dunsmuir.com; www.dunsmuir.com

Eagle Rock • *Eagle Rock C/C* • Michael A. Nogueira; Pres.; P.O. Box 41354; 90041; Los Angeles; P 39,000; M 120; (323) 257-2197; Fax (323) 257-4245; erccwebguy@aol.com; www.eaglerockchamberofcommerce.com

Eagleville • *see Cedarville*

East Los Angeles • *see Los Angeles-East Los Angeles C/C*

El Cajon • *San Diego East County C/C* • Eric Lund; Gen. Mgr.; 201 S. Magnolia Ave.; 92020; San Diego; P 104,000; M 700; (619) 440-6161; (800) 402-8765; Fax (619) 440-6164; info@eastcountychamber.org; www.eastcountychamber.org*

El Centro • *El Centro C/C & Visitors Bur.* • Darletta Willis; CEO; 1095 S. 4th St.; P.O. Box 3006; 92244; Imperial; P 44,000; M 500; (760) 352-3681; Fax (760) 352-3246; info@elcentrochamber.com; www.elcentrochamber.com*

El Cerrito • *El Cerrito C/C* • Mark L. Scott; Mgr.; 10296 San Pablo Ave.; P.O. Box 538; 94530; Contra Costa; P 24,000; M 220; (510) 705-1202; Fax (510) 705-1206; info@elcerritochamber.org; www.elcerritochamber.org

El Dorado Hills • *El Dorado Hills C/C* • Debbie Manning; Pres./CEO; 2085 Vine St., Ste. 105; P.O. Box 5055; 95762; El Dorado; P 43,000; M 550; (916) 933-1335; Fax (916) 933-5908; chamber@eldoradohillschamber.org; www.eldoradohillschamber.org*

El Monte • *El Monte/South El Monte C/C* • Ken Rausch; Exec. Dir.; 10505 Valley Blvd., Ste. 312; P.O. Box 5866; 91734; Los Angeles; P 135,000; M 500; (626) 443-0180; Fax (626) 443-0463; chamber@emsem.biz; www.emsem.biz*

El Segundo • *El Segundo C/C* • Marsha Hansen; Exec. Dir.; 427 Main St.; 90245; Los Angeles; P 16,000; M 380; (310) 322-1220; Fax (310) 322-6880; director@elsegundochamber.org; www.elsegundochamber.org

El Sobrante • *El Sobrante C/C* • Marie Carayanis; Pres.; 3769-B San Pablo Dam Rd.; 94803; Contra Costa; P 13,500; M 100; (510) 223-0757; mariecofces@yahoo.com; www.elsobrantecachamber.com

Elk Grove • *Elk Grove C/C* • Angela; Exec. Dir.; 9370 Studio Ct., Ste. 110; 95758; Sacramento; P 153,000; M 600; (916) 691-3760; Fax (916) 691-3810; chamber@elkgroveca.com; www.elkgroveca.com*

Emeryville • *Emeryville C/C* • Bob Canter; Pres./CEO; 3980 Harlan St.; 94608; Alameda; P 11,000; M 250; (510) 652-5223; Fax (510) 652-4223; info@emeryvillechamber.com; www.emeryvillechamber.com*

Encinitas • *Encinitas C/C* • Mimi Gattinella; 535 Encinitas Blvd., Ste. 116; 92024; San Diego; P 62,000; M 200; (760) 753-6041; Fax (760) 753-6270; info@encinitaschamber.com; www.encinitaschamber.com

Encino • *Encino C/C* • Diana Duenas; CEO; 4933 Balboa Blvd.; 91316; Los Angeles; P 41,905; M 450; (818) 789-4711; Fax (818) 789-2485; info@encinochamber.org; www.encinochamber.org*

Escalon • *Escalon C/C* • Pat Brown; Pres.; P.O. Box 222; 95320; San Joaquin; P 8,000; M 50; (209) 838-2793; escaloncofc@gmail.com; www.escalonchambersite.org

Escondido • *Escondido C/C* • Rorie Johnston; CEO; 720 N. Broadway; 92025; San Diego; P 151,500; M 500; (760) 745-2125; Fax (760) 745-1183; info@escondidochamber.org; www.escondidochamber.org*

Esparto • *Esparto Reg. C/C* • Monique Garcia; Exec. Dir.; 16856 Yolo Ave.; P.O. Box 194; 95627; Yolo; P 3,500; M 100; (530) 787-3242; Fax (530) 787-3373; espartonews@ymail.com; www.espartoregionalchamber.com*

Etna • *Scott Valley C/C* • Lorrie Bundy; Pres.; P.O. Box 374; 96027; Siskiyou; P 5,000; M 65; (530) 467-3355; mwseward@sisqtel.net; www.scottvalley.org

Eureka • *Greater Eureka C/C* • Don Smullin; Exec. Dir.; 2112 Broadway; 95501; Humboldt; P 45,000; M 650; (707) 442-3738; (800) 356-6381; Fax (707) 442-0079; chamber@eurekachamber.com; www.eurekachamber.com*

Exeter • *Exeter C/C* • Sandy Blankenship; Exec. Dir.; 101 W. Pine St.; 93221; Tulare; P 10,500; M 365; (559) 592-2919; Fax (559) 592-3720; chamber@exeterchamber.com; www.exeterchamber.com*

Fair Oaks • *Fair Oaks C/C* • Kimberley Pitillo; Exec. Dir.; 10014 Fair Oaks Blvd.; P.O. Box 352; 95628; Sacramento; P 50,000; M 325; (916) 967-2903; Fax (916) 967-8536; info@fairoakschamber.com; www.fairoakschamber.com*

Fairfax • *Fairfax C/C* • Rob Nye; Exec. Dir.; P.O. Box 1111; 94978; Marin; P 7,500; M 80; (415) 637-1978; rob@fairfaxchamberca.com; fairfaxchamberca.com

Fairfield • *Fairfield-Suisun C/C* • Debi Tavey; Pres./CEO; 1111 Webster St.; 94533; Solano; P 140,000; M 650; (707) 425-4625; Fax (707) 425-0826; melissa@fairfieldsuisunchamber.com; fairfieldsuisunchamber.com*

Fall River Mills • *Fall River Valley C/C* • Martha Fletcher; Pres.; P.O. Box 475; 96028; Shasta; P 650; M 94; (530) 336-5840; info@fallrivervalleycc.org; www.fallrivervalleycc.org

Fallbrook • *Greater Fallbrook Area C/C* • Richard Kennedy; CEO; 111 S. Main Ave.; 92028; San Diego; P 55,000; M 450; (760) 728-5845; Fax (760) 728-4031; kathie.richards@fallbrookchamberofcommerce.com; fallbrookchamberofcommerce.org*

Ferndale • *Ferndale C/C* • Karen Pingitore; P.O. Box 325; 95536; Humboldt; P 1,400; M 132; (707) 786-4477; Fax (707) 786-4477; info@victorianferndale.com; www.victorianferndale.com

Fillmore • *Fillmore C/C* • Irma Magana; Pres.; 246 Central Ave.; P.O. Box 815; 93016; Ventura; P 15,000; M 150; (805) 524-0351; Fax (805) 524-2555; fillmorechamberc@gmail.com; www.fillmorechamber.com

Folsom • *Folsom C/C* • Joseph P. Gagliardi; Pres./CEO; 200 Wool St.; 95630; Sacramento; P 73,000; M 1,050; (916) 985-2698; (916) 985-5555; Fax (916) 985-4117; cthompson@folsomchamber.com; www.folsomchamber.com*

Fontana • *Fontana C/C* • Elsie Hernandez; Ofc. Mgr.; 8491 Sierra Ave.; 92335; San Bernardino; P 190,000; M 400; (909) 822-4433; Fax (909) 822-6238; elsieh@fontanachamber.org; www.fontanachamber.org*

Foothill Farms • *see Sacramento-North Sacramento C/C*

Foresthill • *Foresthill Divide C/C* • 24470 Main St., Ste. B; P.O. Box 346; 95631; Placer; P 6,000; M 130; (530) 367-2474; Fax (530) 367-2474; foresthillchamber@sebastiancorp.net; www.foresthillchamber.org

Forestville • *Forestville C/C* • Robin Berardini; Pres.; P.O. Box 546; 95436; Sonoma; P 3,300; M 75; Fax (707) 887-0106; www.forestvillechamber.org

Fort Bragg • *Mendocino Coast C/C* • Debra De Graw; CEO; 217 S. Main St.; P.O. Box 1141; 95437; Mendocino; P 20,000; M 497; (707) 961-6300; Fax (707) 964-2056; chamber2@mcn.org; www.mendocinocoast.com*

Fortuna • *Fortuna C/C* • Erin Dunn; Dir.; 735 14th St.; P.O. Box 797; 95540; Humboldt; P 12,000; M 455; (707) 725-3959; Fax (707) 725-4766; erin@fortunachamber.com; fortunachamber.com*

Foster City • *Foster City C/C* • Joanne Bohigian; Pres./CEO; 100 Grand Ln., Ste. B; 94404; San Mateo; P 30,359; M 290; (650) 573-7600; Fax (650) 573-5201; info@fostercitychamber.com; www.fostercitychamber.com*

Fountain Valley • *Fountain Valley C/C* • Mary Parsons; Pres./CEO; 10055 Slater Ave., Ste.250; 92708; Orange; P 58,000; M 250; (714) 962-3822; Fax (714) 962-2045; info@fvchamber.com; www.fvchamber.com*

Fountain Valley • *Vietnamese American C/C of Orange County* • Dr. Tam Nguyen; Pres.; 16511 Brookhurst St., Ste. B; 92708; Orange; P 400,000; M 10,000; (714) 775-6050; Fax (888) 308-9730; info@vacoc.com; www.vacoc.com

Frazier Park • *Mountain Comm. C/C* • Rachel Unell; Pres.; P.O. Box 552; 93225; Kern; P 10,000; M 90; (661) 245-1212; board@mymountainchamber.com; www.mymountainchamber.com*

Freeport • *see Rio Vista-California Delta C of C & Visitors Bur.*

Fremont • *Fremont C/C* • Cindy Bonior; Pres./CEO; 39488 Stevenson Pl., Ste. 100; 94539; Alameda; P 224,922; M 1,000; (510) 795-2244; Fax (510) 795-2240; fmtcc@fremontbusiness.com; www.fremontbusiness.com*

French Camp • *see Rio Vista-California Delta C of C & Visitors Bur.*

Fresno • *Greater Fresno Area C/C* • Al Smith; Pres./CEO; 2331 Fresno St.; 93721; Fresno; P 917,517; M 2,000; (559) 495-4800; Fax (559) 495-4811; info@fresnochamber.com; www.fresnochamber.com*

Fresno • *Central Calif. Hispanic C/C* • John Hernandez; Exec. Dir.; 2331 Fresno St.; 93721; Fresno; P 1,200,000; M 600; (559) 495-4817; Fax (559) 495-4811; info@cchcc.net; www.cchcc.net

Fruitvale • *see Bakersfield-North of the River C/C*

Fullerton • *North Orange County Chamber* • Theresa Harvey; Pres./CEO; 444 N. Harbor Blvd., Ste. 200; P.O. Box 529; 92836-0529; Orange; P 250,000; M 1,000; (714) 871-3100; Fax (714) 871-2871; nocc@nocchamber.com; www.nocchamber.com*

Galt • *Galt Dist. C/C* • Vickie Hopkins; Ofc. Mgr.; 431 S. Lincoln Way; P.O. Box 1446; 95632; Sacramento; P 24,000; M 173; (209) 745-2529; Fax (209) 745-0840; info@galtchamber.com; www.galtchamber.com*

Garberville • *Garberville-Redway Area C/C* • Dee Way; Exec. Dir.; 782 Redwood Dr.; P.O. Box 445; 95542; Humboldt; P 15,000; M 220; (707) 923-2613; (800) 923-2613; Fax (707) 923-4789; chamber@garberville.org; www.garberville.org

Garden Grove • *Garden Grove C/C* • Cindy Spindle; Pres./CEO; 12866 Main St., Ste. 102; 92840; Orange; P 171,000; M 360; (714) 638-7950; Fax (714) 636-6672; ceo@gardengrovechamber.com; www.gardengrovechamber.com*

Gardena • *Gardena Valley C/C* • Wanda Love; Pres.; 1204 W. Gardena Blvd., Ste. E; 90247; Los Angeles; P 59,000; M 435; (310) 532-9905; Fax (310) 329-7307; info@gardenachamber.org; www.gardenachamber.org

Geyserville • *Geyserville C/C* • Joe Steward/Michael Villa; Officers; P.O. Box 276; 95441; Sonoma; P 1,650; M 250; (707) 276-6067; moreinfo@geyservillecc.com; www.geyservillecc.com

Gilroy • *Gilroy C/C* • Susan Valenta; Pres./CEO; 7471 Monterey St.; 95020; Santa Clara; P 55,000; M 700; (408) 842-6437; svalenta@gilroy.org; www.gilroy.org*

Glendale • *Glendale C/C* • Judith Kendall; Pres./CEO; 701 N. Brand Blvd., Ste. 120; 91203; Los Angeles; P 210,000; M 1,100; (818) 240-7870; Fax (818) 240-2872; info@glendalechamber.com; www.glendalechamber.com*

Glendora • *Glendora C/C* • Joe Cina; Pres./CEO; 224 N. Glendora Ave.; 91741; Los Angeles; P 55,000; M 420; (626) 963-4128; info@glendora-chamber.org; www.glendora-chamber.org*

Goleta • *Goleta Valley C/C* • Kristen Miller; Pres./CEO; 5662 Calle Real, Ste. 204; 93117; Santa Barbara; P 70,000; M 550; (805) 967-2500; (800) 646-5382; cortney@goletavalley.com; www.goletavalleychamber.com*

Gonzales • *Gonzales C/C* • Ismael Bucio; Pres.; P.O. Box 216; 93926; Monterey; P 8,200; M 55; (831) 675-9019; email@gonzaleschamber.org; www.gonzaleschamber.org

Gorman • *see Frazier Park*

Graeagle • *Eastern Plumas C/C* • Audrey Ellis; Exec. Dir.; 8989 Hwy. 89, Ste. 3; P.O. Box 1043; 96103; Plumas; P 8,000; M 290; (530) 836-6811; Fax (530) 836-6809; epcc@psln.com; www.easternplumaschamber.com

Granada Hills • *Granada Hills C/C* • Despina Crassa; Pres.; 17723 Chatsworth St.; 91344; Los Angeles; P 57,000; M 300; (818) 368-3235; Fax (818) 366-7425; email@granadachamber.com; www.granadachamber.com

Grand Terrace • *Grand Terrace Area C/C* • Sally McGuire; Pres.; 22365 Barton Rd., Ste. 101; 92313; San Bernardino; P 15,600; M 150; (909) 783-3581; Fax (909) 370-2906; office@gtchamber.com; www.gtchamber.com

Granite Bay • *see Roseville*

Grass Valley • *Greater Grass Valley C/C* • Robin Galvan-Davies; CEO; 128 E. Main St.; 95945; Nevada; P 12,000; M 550; (530) 273-4667; (800) 655-4667; Fax (530) 272-5440; rdavies@grassvalleychamber.com; www.grassvalleychamber.com*

Greenville • *Indian Valley C/C* • Lillian Basham; 408 Main St.; P.O. Box 516; 95947; Plumas; P 2,750; M 90; (530) 284-6633; Fax (530) 284-6907; indianvalleychamber@frontiernet.net; www.indianvalley.net

Gridley • *Gridley Area C/C* • Christine Cunningham; Mgr.; 613 Kentucky St.; 95948; Butte; P 7,500; M 80; (530) 846-3142; gridleychamber@hotmail.com; www.gridleyareachamber.com

Griffith Park • *see Los Angeles-Atwater Village C/C*

Groveland • Yosemite C/C • Carolyn Botell; Admin.; 11875 Ponderosa Way, Ste. A; P.O. Box 1263; 95321; Tuolumne; P 5,000; M 150; (209) 962-0429; (800) 449-9120; info@groveland.org; www.groveland.org

Grover Beach • see Arroyo Grande

Gualala • Redwood Coast C/C • Robert Juengling; Pres.; P.O. Box 199; 95445; Mendocino & Sonoma; P 6,000; M 125; (707) 884-1080; (800) 778-5252; info@redwoodcoastchamber.com; www.redwoodcoastchamber.com

Guerneville • Russian River C/C & Visitor Center • Kayte Guglielmino; Ofc. Mgr.; 16209 First St.; P.O. Box 331; 95446; Sonoma; P 7,000; M 250; (707) 869-9000; Fax (707) 869-9009; kayte@russianriver.com; www.russianriver.com*

Gustine • Gustine C/C • Judi Gandy; Exec. Dir.; 375 5th St.; P.O. Box 306; 95322; Merced; P 5,000; M 175; (209) 854-6975; Fax (209) 854-3511; gustinechamber@att.net; www.gustinechamberofcommerce.com

Half Moon Bay • Half Moon Bay Coastside C/C & Visitors Bur. • Charise McHugh; Pres./CEO; 235 Main St.; 94019; San Mateo; P 30,000; M 700; (650) 726-8380; Fax (650) 726-8389; cindy@hmbchamber.com; www.hmbchamber.com*

Hanford • Hanford C/C • Mike Bertaina; CEO; 113 Court St., Ste. 104; 93230; Kings; P 55,000; M 555; (559) 582-0483; Fax (559) 582-0960; hanfordchamber@comcast.net; www.hanfordchamber.com*

Happy Camp • Happy Camp C/C • Cathleen Searle; Pres.; P.O. Box 1188; 96039; Siskiyou; P 3,000; M 50; (530) 493-2900; info@happycampchamber.com; www.happycampchamber.com

Harbor City • Harbor City/Harbor Gateway C/C • Joeann Valle; Exec. Dir.; 1400 W. 240th St.; 90710; Los Angeles; P 55,000; M 200; (310) 534-3143; (310) 430-8658; Fax (310) 534-3178; hchgchamber@sbcglobal.net; www.hchgchamber.com*

Hat Creek • see Burney

Hawthorne • Hawthorne C/C • Patricia Feldman-Donaldson; Pres.; 12629 Crenshaw Blvd.; 90250; Los Angeles; P 85,000; M 230; (310) 676-1163; Fax (310) 676-7661; info@hawthorne-chamber.com; www.hawthorne-chamber.com*

Hayfork • see Trinity County

Hayward • Hayward C/C • Kim Huggett; Pres./CEO; 22561 Main St.; 94541; Alameda; P 153,000; M 750; (510) 537-2424; Fax (510) 537-2730; susanoc@hayward.org; www.hayward.org*

Healdsburg • Healdsburg C/C • Carla Howell; Exec. Dir.; 217 Healdsburg Ave.; 95448; Sonoma; P 11,000; M 650; (707) 433-6935; (800) 648-9922; Fax (707) 433-7562; carla@healdsburg.com; www.healdsburg.com*

Helendale • Helendale C/C • Mike McCoy; Pres.; P.O. Box 1449; 92342; San Bernardino; P 5,500; M 172; (760) 952-2231; Fax (760) 245-9908; info@helendalechamberofcommerce.com; www.helendalechamberofcommerce.com

Hemet • Hemet/San Jacinto Valley C/C • Andy Anderson; CEO; 615 N. San Jacinto St.; 92543; Riverside; P 150,000; M 500; (951) 658-3211; Fax (951) 766-5013; info@hsjvc.com; www.hsjvc.com*

Hercules • Hercules C/C • Sylvia Villa-Serrano; Exec. Dir.; P.O. Box 5283; 94547; Contra Costa; P 25,000; M 175; (510) 741-7945; Fax (510) 741-8965; sylvia@herculeschamber.com; www.herculeschamber.com*

Hermosa Beach • Hermosa Beach C/C • Maureen Hunt; Pres./CEO; 1007 Hermosa Ave.; 90254; Los Angeles; P 19,000; M 260; (310) 376-0951; info@hbchamber.net; www.hbchamber.net*

Hesperia • Hesperia C/C • Brad Letner; Pres./CEO; 14321 Main St.; 92345; San Bernardino; P 91,000; M 350; (760) 244-2135; chamber@hesperiacc.com; www.hesperiacc.com*

Highland • Highland C/C • Nanette Peykani; Exec. Dir.; 27255 Messina St.; P.O. Box 455; 92346; San Bernardino; P 53,000; M 295; (909) 864-4073; Fax (909) 864-4583; members@highlandchamber.org; www.highlandchamber.org

Hilmar • Hilmar C/C • Rob Mitchell; Pres.; P.O. Box 385; 95324; Merced; P 5,600; M 100; (209) 632-2028; info@hilmarchamber.com; www.hilmarchamber.com

Hollister • San Benito County C/C & Visitors Bur. • Juli Vieira; Pres./CEO; 243 Sixth St., Ste. 100; 95023; San Benito; P 63,000; M 385; (831) 637-5315; juli@sanbenitocountychamber.com; www.sanbenitocountychamber.com*

Hollywood • Hollywood C/C • Leron Gubler; Pres./CEO; 6255 Sunset Blvd., Ste. 150; 90028; Los Angeles; P 200,000; M 825; (323) 469-8311; Fax (323) 469-2805; leron@hollywoodchamber.net; www.hollywoodchamber.net

Holtville • Holtville C/C • Becky Miller; Chamber Mgr.; 101 W. 5th St.; 92250; Imperial; P 6,000; M 110; (760) 356-2923; Fax (760) 356-2925; becky@holtvillechamber.org; www.holtvillechamber.org

Hood • see Rio Vista-California Delta C of C & Visitors Bur.

Hopland • see Ukiah

Huntington Beach • Huntington Beach C/C • James O'Callaghan; Pres./CEO; 2134 Main St., Ste. 100; 92648; Orange; P 190,000; M 700; (714) 536-8888; hbchamber@hbcoc.com; www.hbchamber.com*

Huntington Park • Greater Huntington Park Area C/C • Dante D'Eramo; Exec. Dir./CEO; 6330 Pacific Blvd., Ste. 208; 90255; Los Angeles; P 60,000; M 250; (323) 585-1155; Fax (323) 585-2176; info@hpchamber1.com; www.hpchamber1.com

Imperial • Imperial C/C • Gregory Siota; CEO; 297 S. Imperial Ave.; 92251; Imperial; P 15,000; M 300; (760) 355-1609; Fax (760) 355-3920; ceo@imperialchamber.org; www.imperialchamber.org*

Imperial Beach • Imperial Beach C/C & Visitor's Bur. Inc. • Mike Osborne; Pres.; 805 Ocean Ln.; 91932; San Diego; P 26,000; M 170; (619) 424-3151; Fax (619) 424-3008; info@ib-chamber.com; www.ib-chamber.com

Independence • see Bishop

Indian Wells • Indian Wells C/C • Mike Avila; Dir.; 45-200 Club Dr,, Ste. B; 92210; Riverside; P 5,000; M 310; (760) 346-7095; Fax (760) 346-7605; info@indianwellschamber.com; www.indianwellschamber.com*

Indio • Greater Coachella Valley C/C • Joshua Bonner; CEO; 82-921 Indio Blvd.; 92201; Riverside; P 80,000; M 1,300; (760) 347-0676; Fax (760) 347-6069; info@gcvcc.org; www.gcvcc.org*

Inglewood • Inglewood/Airport Area C/C • Shannon R. Howe; Exec. V.P.; 330 E. Queen St.; 90301; Los Angeles; P 120,000; M 750; (310) 677-1121; (310) 677-1122; Fax (310) 677-1001; inglewoodchamber@sbcglobal.net; www.inglewoodchamber.org*

Irvine • *Orange County Bus. Cncl.* • Lucy Dunn; Pres./CEO; 2 Park Plaza, Ste. 100; 92614; Orange; P 3,000,000; M 250; (949) 476-2242; Fax (949) 476-9240; bmoulthrop@ocbc.org; www.ocbc.org

Irvine • *Irvine C/C* • Tallia Hart; Pres./CEO; 2485 McCabe Way, Ste. 150; 92614; Orange; P 209,000; M 800; (949) 660-9112; Fax (949) 660-0829; icc@irvinechamber.com; www.irvinechamber.com*

Irwindale • *Irwindale C/C* • Marlene Carney; Pres./CEO; 16102 Arrow Hwy.; P.O. Box 2307; 91706; Los Angeles; P 1,430; M 250; (626) 960-6606; Fax (626) 960-3868; info@irwindalechamber.org; www.irwindalechamber.org*

Isleton • *see Rio Vista-California Delta C of C & Visitors Bur.*

Jackson • *Amador County C/C & Visitors Bur.* • Jamie Barger; Managing Dir.; 115 Main St.; P.O. Box 596; 95642; Amador; P 40,000; M 596; (209) 223-0350; (800) 649-4988; Fax (209) 223-0508; chamber@amadorchamber.com; www.amadorchamber.com*

Johnson Park • *see Burney*

Joshua Tree • *Joshua Tree C/C* • Tera Lea Surratt; Exec. Dir.; 6448 Hallee Rd., Ste. 9; P.O. Box 600; 92252; San Bernardino; P 10,000; M 205; (760) 366-3723; Fax (760) 366-2573; info@joshuatreechamber.org; www.joshuatreechamber.org

Julian • *Julian C/C* • Michael Menghini; Pres.; 2129 Main St.; P.O. Box 1866; 92036; San Diego; P 3,000; M 280; (760) 765-1857; Fax (760) 765-2544; chamber@julianca.com; www.julianca.com

June Lake • *June Lake Loop C/C* • Don Morton; P.O. Box 2; 93529; Mono; P 630; M 48; (760) 648-4651; (800) 845-7922; don@junelakeaccommodations.com; www.visitjune.com

Jurupa Valley • *Jurupa Valley C/C* • Diana Leja; Pres.; 5754 Tilton Ave.; 92509; Riverside; P 92,000; M 250; (951) 681-9242; jurupachamber@gmail.com; www.jurupachamber.org

Kearny Mesa • *see Del Mar-LaJolla Golden Triangle C/C*

Kerman • *Kerman C/C* • Linda Geringer; Exec. Dir.; 783 S. Madera Ave.; 93630; Fresno; P 14,000; M 101; (559) 846-6343; Fax (559) 846-6344; info@kermanchamber.org; www.kermanchamber.org

Kernville • *Kernville C/C* • Cheryl Borthick; Pres.; 11447 Kernville Rd.; P.O. Box 397; 93238; Kern; P 10,000; M 155; (760) 376-2629; Fax (760) 379-4371; office@kernvillechamber.org; www.kernvillechamber.org

King City • *King City & Southern Monterey County C/C & Ag.* • Cindi B. Mora; Ofc. Mgr.; 200 Broadway, Ste. 40; 93930; Monterey; P 16,000; M 200; (831) 385-3814; Fax (831) 386-9462; kingcitychamber@sbcglobal.net; www.kingcitychamber.com

Kingsburg • *Kingsburg Dist. C/C* • Jess Chambers; Exec. Dir.; 1475 Draper St.; 93631; Fresno; P 11,382; M 230; (559) 897-1111; Fax (559) 897-4621; jessatkingsburg@aol.com; www.kingsburg-chamber-of-commerce.org

Klamath • *Klamath C/C* • Jan Crandall; Treas.; P.O. Box 476; 95548; Del Norte; P 1,200; M 70; (707) 482-7165; (800) 200-2335; janchinook@hughes.net; www.klamathcc.org

Knightsen • *see Rio Vista-California Delta C of C & Visitors Bur.*

La Canada Flintridge • *La Canada Flintridge C/C* • Patricia A. Anderson; Pres./CEO; 4529 Angeles Crest Hwy., Ste. 102; 91011; Los Angeles; P 20,000; M 650; (818) 790-4289; Fax (818) 790-8930; exec@lacanadaflintridge.com; www.lacanadaflintridge.com*

La Crescenta • *Crescenta Valley C/C* • Julia Rabago; Exec. Dir.; 3131 Foothill Blvd., Ste. D; 91214; Los Angeles; P 30,000; M 350; (818) 248-4957; Fax (818) 248-9625; crescentachamber@aol.com; www.crescentavalleychamber.org

La Habra • *La Habra Area C/C* • Mark Sturdevant; Pres./CEO; 321 E. La Habra Blvd.; 90631; Orange; P 63,000; M 410; (562) 697-1704; Fax (562) 697-8359; info@lahabrachamber.com; www.lahabrachamber.com*

La Jolla • *also see Del Mar-LaJolla Golden Triangle C/C*

La Jolla • *La Jolla Town Cncl. C/C* • Cindy Greatrex; CEO; 1150 Silverado St.; 92037; San Diego; P 42,000; M 500; (858) 454-1444; office@lajollatowncouncil.org; www.lajollatowncouncil.org*

La Mesa • *see El Cajon*

La Mirada • *La Mirada C/C* • 11900 La Mirada Blvd., Ste. 9; 90638; Los Angeles; P 50,000; M 250; (562) 902-1970; info@lmchamber.org; www.lmchamber.org

La Quinta • *Greater Coachella Valley C/C* • Joshua Bonner; Pres./CEO; 78-275 Calle Tampico, Ste. B; 92253; Riverside; P 42,000; M 1,300; (760) 564-3199; Fax ; info@gcvcc.org; www.gcvcc.org*

La Verne • *La Verne C/C* • Luis Cetina; Chrmn.; 2078 Bonita Ave.; 91750; Los Angeles; P 34,000; M 270; (909) 593-5265; annette@lavernechamber.org; www.lavernechamber.org*

Lafayette • *Lafayette C/C* • Jay Lifson; Exec. Dir.; 100 Lafayette Cir., Ste. 103; 94549; Contra Costa; P 24,000; M 683; (925) 284-7404; Fax (925) 284-3109; info@lafayettechamber.org; www.lafayettechamber.org*

Laguna Beach • *Laguna Beach C/C* • Kristine Thalman; Exec. Dir.; 357 Glenneyre; 92651; Orange; P 23,000; M 650; (949) 494-1018; Fax (949) 376-8916; info@lagunabeachchamber.org; www.lagunabeachchamber.org*

Laguna Niguel • *Laguna Niguel C/C* • Debbie Newman A.C.E.; CEO; 30111-A Crown Valley Pkwy.; 92677; Orange; P 65,000; M 350; (949) 363-0136; Fax (949) 363-9026; lncc@lnchamber.com; www.lnchamber.com*

Lake Almanor • *see Chester*

Lake Arrowhead • *Lake Arrowhead Comm. C/C* • Lewis Murray; Pres./CEO; P.O. Box 219; 92352; San Bernardino; P 15,000; M 500; (909) 337-3715; Fax (909) 336-1548; events@lakearrowhead.net; www.lakearrowhead.net

Lake City • *see Cedarville*

Lake County • *see Lakeport*

Lake Elsinore • *Lake Elsinore Valley C/C* • Kim Joseph Cousins; Pres./CEO; 132 W. Graham Ave.; 92530; Riverside; P 52,000; M 400; (951) 245-8848; Fax (951) 245-9127; kim@lakeelsinorechamber.com; www.lakeelsinorechamber.com*

Lake Forest • *Lake Forest C/C* • Brian Lau; Pres.; 22996 El Toro Rd., Ste. 116; 92630; Orange; P 80,000; M 165; (949) 583-9639; Fax (949) 596-0410; info@lakeforestcachamber.com; lakeforestcachamber.com

Lake Isabella • *Kern River Valley C/C* • Keri Swindle; Ofc. Mgr.; 6416 Lake Isabella Blvd., Ste. D; P.O. Box 567; 93240; Kern; P 10,000; M 194; (760) 379-5236; (866) 578-4386; Fax (760) 379-5457; office@kernrivervalley.com; www.kernrivervalley.com

Lake Los Angeles • *Lake Los Angeles C/C* • Maurice Kunkel; Treas.; P.O. Box 500071; 93550; Los Angeles; P 12,400; M 30; (661) 264-2786; info@lakelachamber.com; www.lakelachamber.com

Lake View Terrace • *see Tujunga*

Lakeport • *Lake County C/C* • Melissa Fulton; CEO; 875 Lakeport Blvd.; P.O. Box 295; 95453; Lake; P 68,000; M 600; (707) 263-5092; (866) 525-3767; Fax (707) 263-5104; ceo@lakecochamber.com; www.lakecochamber.com*

Lakeside • *Lakeside C/C* • Kathy Kassel; Exec. Dir.; 9924 Vine St.; 92040; San Diego; P 57,000; M 200; (619) 561-1031; Fax (619) 561-7951; info@lakesidechamber.org; www.lakesidechamber.org*

Lakewood • *Greater Lakewood C/C* • John Kelsall; Pres./CEO; 24 Lakewood Center Mall; 90712; Los Angeles; P 80,000; M 265; (562) 531-9733; Fax (562) 531-9737; info@lakewoodchamber.com; www.lakewoodchamber.com

Lamont • *Greater Lamont C/C* • J.R. Chagoya; Pres./CEO; 7517 Delight Ave.; P.O. Box 593; 93241; Kern; P 20,000; M 40; (661) 845-9211; (661) 706-1939; jrchagoya@sbcglobal.net; www.lamontchamber.com*

Lancaster • *Lancaster C/C* • Sandy Smith; COO; 554 W. Lancaster Blvd.; 93534; Los Angeles; P 160,000; M 530; (661) 948-4518; Fax (661) 949-1212; sandy.smith@lancasterchamber.org; www.lancasterchamber.org*

Larkspur • *see Corte Madera*

Lathrop • *Lathrop C/C* • Mary Kennedy-Bracken; Pres./CEO; 15040 Harlan Rd.; 95330; San Joaquin; P 19,000; M 200; (209) 858-4486; (209) 740-6503; Fax (209) 858-9572; lathropchamber@verizon.net; www.lathropchamber.org*

Lawndale • *Lawndale C/C* • Dyan Davis; Exec. Dir.; 14717 A Hawthorne Blvd.; 90260; Los Angeles; P 33,000; M 125; (310) 679-3306; (310) 738-8678; Fax (310) 679-3306; lawndalechamber@sbcglobal.net; www.lawndalechamber.org

Lebec • *see Frazier Park*

Lee Vining • *Lee Vining C/C* • P.O. Box 130; 93541; Mono; P 250; M 23; (760) 647-6629; Fax (760) 647-6377; info@leevining.com; www.leevining.com

Leggett • *Leggett Valley C/C* • Helen Ochoa; Pres.; P.O. Box 105; 95585; Mendocino; P 400; M 9; (707) 925-6385

Lemon Grove • *see El Cajon*

Lemoore • *Lemoore Dist. C/C* • Maureen Azevedo; CEO; 300 E St.; 93245; Kings; P 25,000; M 270; (559) 924-6401; Fax (559) 924-4520; manager@lemoorechamberofcommerce.com; www.lemoorechamberofcommerce.com

Leucadia • *see Encinitas*

Lewiston • *see Trinity County*

Lincoln • *Lincoln Area C/C* • 540 F St.; 95648; Placer; P 42,000; M 360; (916) 645-2035; Fax (916) 645-9455; terri@lincolnchamber.com; www.lincolnchamber.com*

Linda • *see Yuba City*

Linden • *Linden-Peters C/C* • P.O. Box 557; 95236; San Joaquin; P 2,500; M 145; (209) 547-3046; www.lindenchamber.net

Lindsay • *Lindsay C/C* • Virginia Loya; Exec. Dir.; 133 W. Honolulu, Ste. E; P.O. Box 989; 93247; Tulare; P 12,000; M 300; (559) 562-4929; Fax (559) 562-5219; lindsaychamber@lindsay.ca.us; www.thelindsaychamber.com*

Live Oak • *Live Oak Dist. C/C* • Annette Bertolini; Pres.; P.O. Box 391; 95953; Sutter; P 6,200; M 50; (530) 695-1519; liveoakchamber@syix.com; www.liveoakchamber.org

Livermore • *Livermore Valley C/C* • Dawn Argula; Pres./CEO; 2157 First St.; 94550; Alameda; P 85,000; M 700; (925) 447-1606; Fax (925) 447-1641; dargula@livermorechamber.org; www.livermorechamber.org*

Lockeford • *see Lodi*

Lodi • *Lodi Dist. C/C* • Pat Patrick; Pres./CEO; 35 S. School St.; 95240; San Joaquin; P 62,200; M 800; (209) 367-7840; Fax (209) 369-9344; frontdesk@lodichamber.com; www.lodichamber.com*

Loleta • *Loleta Comm. C/C* • Darlene Ricotta; Secy.; P.O. Box 327; 95551; Humboldt; P 800; M 50; (707) 498-0450; dr17usa@gmail.com

Loma Linda • *Loma Linda C/C* • Bill Arnold; CEO; 25541 Barton Rd., Ste. 4; P.O. Box 343; 92354; San Bernardino; P 23,300; M 290; (909) 799-2828; billarnold@lomalindachamber.org; www.lomalindachamber.org

Lomita • *Lomita C/C* • John Ballard; Exec. Dir.; 25332 Narbonne Ave., Ste. 250; P.O. Box 425; 90717; Los Angeles; P 20,700; M 250; (310) 326-6378; Fax (310) 326-2904; info@lomitacoc.com; www.lomitacoc.com

Lompoc • *Lompoc Valley C/C & Visitor Bur.* • Ken Ostini; Pres./CEO; 111 S. I St.; P.O. Box 626; 93438; Santa Barbara; P 60,000; M 432; (805) 736-4567; (800) 240-0999; Fax (805) 737-0453; chamber@lompoc.com; www.lompoc.com*

Lone Pine • *Lone Pine C/C* • Kathleen New; 120 S. Main St.; P.O. Box 749; 93545; Inyo; P 2,000; M 257; (760) 876-4444; Fax (760) 876-9675; info@lonepinechamber.org; www.lonepinechamber.org*

Long Beach • *Long Beach Area C/C* • Randy Gordon; Pres./CEO; One World Trade Center, Ste. 1650; 90831-0206; Los Angeles; P 470,000; M 1,500; (562) 436-1251; Fax (562) 436-7099; info@lbchamber.com; www.lbchamber.com

Long Beach • *Reg. Hispanic C/C* • Sandy Cajas; Pres./CEO; One World Trade Center; P.O. Box 32474; 90832; Los Angeles; P 470,000; M 300; (562) 212-2889; Fax (562) 685-0542; info@regionalhispaniccc.org; www.regionalhispaniccc.org*

Loomis • *Loomis Basin C/C* • Bob Ferreira; Pres.; 6090 Horseshoe Bar Rd.; 95650; Placer; P 6,300; M 310; (916) 652-7252; Fax (916) 652-7211; manager@loomischamber.com; www.loomischamber.com*

Los Alamitos • *Los Alamitos Area C/C* • Johnnie Strohmyer; CEO; 3231 Katella Ave.; 90720; Orange; P 30,000; M 300; (562) 598-6659; Fax (562) 598-7035; info@losalchamber.org; www.losalchamber.org

Los Altos • *Los Altos C/C* • Julie Rose; Pres.; 321 University Ave.; 94022; Santa Clara; P 36,000; M 500; (650) 948-1455; Fax (650) 948-6238; info@losaltoschamber.org; www.losaltoschamber.org*

Los Angeles Area

Atwater Village C/C • Andy Hasroun; Pres.; P.O. Box 39754; 90039; Los Angeles; P 30,000; M 70; (323) 251-3938; board@atwaterchamber.org; www.atwaterchamber.org

Black Business Assn. • Earl "Skip" Cooper II; Pres./CEO; P.O. Box 43159; 90043; Los Angeles; P 3,830,000; M 1,200; (323) 857-4600; Fax (323) 857-4610; mail@bbala.org; www.bbala.org

Boyle Heights C/C • Ralph Carmona; Coord.; 5271 E. Beverly Blvd.; 90022; Los Angeles; P 93,000; M 100; (323) 726-7734; bh.directory. ads@gmail.com; www.boyleheightschamber.com

Century City C/C • Susan Bursk; Pres./CEO; 2029 Century Park East; Concourse Level; 90067; Los Angeles; P 50,000; M 300; (310) 553-2222; Fax (310) 553-4623; contact@centurycitycc.com; www. centurycitycc.com

Crenshaw C/C • Michael Jones; Pres./CEO; P.O. Box 8193; 90008; Los Angeles; P 30,000; M 230; (323) 293-2900; crenshawchamber@ sbcglobal.net; www.crenshawchamber.com

East Los Angeles C/C • 4716 E. Cesar Chavez Ave.; 90022; Los Angeles; P 128,000; M 121; (323) 263-2005; Fax (323) 263-2006; elacoc@pacbell.net; www.elacoc.com

Japanese C/C of Southern Calif. • Jeff Yamazaki; Pres.; 244 San Pedro, Ste. 410; 90012; Los Angeles; M 157; (213) 626-3067; Fax (213) 626-3070; office@jccsc.com; www.jccsc.com

Lincoln Heights C/C • Antonietta Avila; Ofc. Secy.; 2716 N. Broadway, Ste. 210; 90031; Los Angeles; P 50,000; M 120; (323) 221-6571; Fax (323) 221-1513; lhcc_info@sbcglobal.net

Los Angeles Area C/C • Gary Toebben; Pres./CEO; 350 S. Bixel St., Ste. 201; 90017; Los Angeles; P 9,862,049; M 1,675; (213) 580-7500; Fax (213) 580-7510; gtoebben@lachamber.com; www.lachamber.com*

Los Angeles Latino C/C • Gilbert R. Vasquez; Chrmn.; 634 S. Spring St., Ste. 600; 90014; Los Angeles; P 10,200,000; M 1,000; (213) 347-0008; Fax (213) 347-0009; info@lalcc.org; www.lalcc.org

Silverlake C/C • Sarah McGowan; Pres.; 3531 W. Sunset Blvd.; 90026; Los Angeles; P 38,000; M 300; (323) 908-4086; Fax (323) 908-4086; secretary@silverlakechamber.com; www.silverlakechamber.com

West Los Angeles C/C • Roozbeh Farahanipour; Pres./CEO; 907 Westwood Blvd., Ste. 222; P.O. Box 64512; 90024; Los Angeles; P 1,300,000; M 500; (310) 4734763; (844) 699-5222; Fax (310) 477-8484; info@westlachamber.com; www.westlachamber.org*

Los Banos • **Los Banos C/C** • Bertha Faria; Exec. Dir.; 932 6th St.; 93635; Merced; P 37,000; M 400; (209) 826-2495; Fax (209) 826-9689; lbchamber@comcast.net; www.losbanos.com*

Los Gatos • **Town of Los Gatos C/C** • Catherine Somers; Exec. Dir.; 10 Station Way; 95030; Santa Clara; P 30,000; M 415; (408) 354-9300; Fax (408) 399-1594; chamber@losgatoschamber.com; www. losgatoschamber.com*

Los Molinos • **Los Molinos C/C** • Betty Joe Morales; Pres.; P.O. Box 334; 96055; Tehama; P 2,100; M 75; (530) 384-2251; Fax (530) 384-2284; losmo@theskybeam.com; www.losmochamber.com

Los Osos • **Los Osos/Baywood Park C/C** • Dawn Rodden; Exec. Dir.; 781 Los Osos Valley Rd.; P.O. Box 6282; 93412; San Luis Obispo; P 15,000; M 150; (805) 528-4884; Fax (805) 528-8401; info@ lobpchamber.org; www.lobpchamber.org

Lucerne Valley • **Lucerne Valley C/C** • Lorane Abercrombie; Pres.; 32750 Old Woman Springs Rd.; P.O. Box 491; 92356; San Bernardino; P 10,000; M 107; (760) 248-7215; Fax (760) 248-2096; crossrd@ lvchamber.net; http://lvchamber.net/

Lynwood • **Greater Lynwood C/C** • Edwin Hernandez; P.O. Box 713; 90262; Los Angeles; P 85,000; M 43; (310) 713-1428; (310) 603-0220; ehernandez@lynwood.ca.us; www.lynwood.ca.us

Madera • **Golden Valley C/C** • Virginia Vick; Ofc. Mgr.; 37167 Ave. 12, Ste. 5C; 93636; Madera; P 10,000; M 96; (559) 645-4001; Fax (559) 645-4002; goldenvalleychamber@yahoo.com

Madera • **Madera C/C** • Debi Bray; Pres./CEO; 120 North E St.; 93638; Madera; P 57,000; M 370; (559) 673-3563; Fax (559) 673-5009; dbray@maderachamber.com; www.maderachamber.com

Malibu • **Malibu C/C** • Mark Persson; Exec. Dir.; 23805 Stuart Ranch Rd., Ste. 105; 90265; Los Angeles; P 13,000; M 390; (310) 456-9025; Fax (310) 456-0195; info@malibu.org; www.malibu.org*

Mammoth Lakes • **Mammoth Lakes C/C** • Craig Schmidt; Dir.; 2520 Main St.; P.O. Box 3268; 93546; Mono; P 8,234; M 200; (760) 934-6717; Fax (760) 934-7066; info@mammothlakeschamber.org; www. mammothlakeschamber.org*

Manhattan Beach • **Manhattan Beach C/C** • James O'Callaghan; Pres./CEO; 425 15th St.; P.O. Box 3007; 90266; Los Angeles; P 34,000; M 750; (310) 545-5313; Fax (310) 545-7203; james@ manhattanbeachchamber.net; www.manhattanbeachchamber.com*

Manteca • **Manteca C/C** • Debby Moorhead; CEO; 183 W. North St., Ste. 6; 95336; San Joaquin; P 70,000; M 380; (209) 823-6121; Fax (209) 239-6131; chamber@manteca.org; www.manteca.org*

Marina • **Marina C/C** • Mike Mast; Pres.; P.O. Box 425; 93933; Monterey; P 20,000; M 200; (831) 594-1061; info@marinachamber. com; www.marinachamber.com

Marina del Rey • **see Westchester**

Mariposa • **Mariposa County C/C** • 5158 Hwy. 140; P.O. Box 425; 95338; Mariposa; P 20,000; M 300; (209) 966-2456; (209) 966-7081; Fax (209) 205-9161; admin@mariposachamber.org; www. mariposachamber.org*

Mark West • **see Santa Rosa-Mark West Area C/C**

Markleeville • **Alpine County C/C** • Teresa Burkhauser; Exec. Dir.; 3 Webster St.; P.O. Box 265; 96120; Alpine; P 1,200; M 100; (530) 694-2475; Fax (530) 694-2478; info@alpinecounty.com; www.alpinecounty. com

Martinez • **Martinez C/C** • Julie Johnston; Exec. Dir.; 603 Marina Vista; 94553; Contra Costa; P 36,000; M 300; (925) 228-2345; Fax (925) 228-2356; info@martinezchamber.com; www.martinezchamber.com*

Marysville • **see Yuba City**

McClellan Park • **see Sacramento-North Sacramento C/C**

McCloud • **McCloud C/C** • P.O. Box 372; 96057; Siskiyou; P 600; M 60; (530) 964-3113; contact@mccloudchamber.com; www. mccloudchamber.com

McKinleyville • **McKinleyville C/C** • Cindy Harrington; Exec. Dir.; 1640 Central Ave.; P.O. Box 2144; 95519; Humboldt; P 15,700; M 250; (707) 839-2449; executivedirector@mckinleyvillechamber.com; www. mckinleyvillechamber.com

Menifee • **Menifee Valley C/C** • Dorothy Wolons; Pres./CEO; 29683 New Hub Dr., Ste. C; 92586; Riverside; P 66,000; M 400; (951) 672-1991; Fax (951) 672-4022; ceo@menifeevalleychamber.com; www. menifeevalleychamber.com

Menlo Park • *Menlo Park C/C* • Fran Dehn; Pres./CEO; 1100 Merrill St.; 94025; San Mateo; P 33,309; M 270; (650) 325-2818; Fax (650) 325-0920; info@menloparkchamber.com; menloparkchamber.com*

Merced • *Greater Merced C/C* • Adam Cox; Pres./CEO; 1640 N St., Ste. 120; 95340; Merced; P 79,000; M 650; (209) 384-7092; Fax (209) 384-8472; brandy@mercedchamber.com; www.mercedchamber.com*

Mill Valley • *Mill Valley C/C & Visitor Center* • Jim Welte; Co-Dir.; 85 Throckmorton Ave.; 94941; Marin; P 13,810; M 325; (415) 388-9700; (415) 381-9727; info@millvalley.org; www.millvalley.org*

Millbrae • *Millbrae C/C* • Lorianne Richardson; Pres./CEO; 50 Victoria Ave., Ste. 103; 94030; San Mateo; P 22,000; M 200; (650) 697-7324; chamber@millbrae.com; www.millbrae.com*

Milpitas • *Milpitas C/C* • Liz Ainsworth; Pres.; 828 N. Hillview Dr.; 95035; Santa Clara; P 70,817; M 450; (408) 262-2613; Fax (408) 262-2823; info@milpitaschamber.com; www.milpitaschamber.com*

Mira Mesa • *see San Diego-North San Diego Bus. Chamber*

Miramar • *see San Diego-North San Diego Bus. Chamber*

Miramonte • *Central Sierra C/C* • Kasia Barr; Pres.; 54120 N. Hwy. 245; P.O. Box 65; 93641; Fresno; P 500; M 50; (559) 336-9577; sulfiati2@yahoo.com; www.centralsierrachamber.org

Modesto • *Modesto C/C* • Cecil Russell; Pres./CEO; 1114 J St.; 95354; Stanislaus; P 200,000; M 1,200; (209) 577-5757; Fax (209) 577-2673; crussell@modchamber.org; www.modchamber.org*

Monrovia • *Monrovia C/C* • Karin Crehan; Exec. Dir.; 620 S. Myrtle Ave.; 91016; Los Angeles; P 39,500; M 505; (626) 358-1159; Fax (626) 357-6036; chamber@monroviacc.com; www.monroviacc.com*

Montclair • *Montclair C/C* • Myra Kirscht; Pres./CEO; 8880 Benson Ave., Ste. 110; 91763; San Bernardino; P 35,000; M 200; (909) 985-5104; info@montclairchamber.com; www.montclairchamber.com*

Montebello • *Montebello C/C* • Pamela Wilkinson; Pres./CEO; 109 N. 19th St.; 90640; Los Angeles; P 63,000; M 500; (323) 721-1153; Fax (323) 721-7946; jacqueline@montebellochamber.org; www.montebellochamber.org

Monterey • *Monterey Peninsula C/C* • Jody Hansen; Pres./CEO; 30 Ragsdale Dr., Ste. 200; 93940; Monterey; P 54,000; M 1,000; (831) 648-5360; Fax (831) 649-3502; info@montereychamber.com; www.montereychamber.com*

Monterey Park • *Monterey Park C/C* • Mr. Vincent Chang; Pres.; 700 El Mercado Ave.; P.O. Box 387; 91754; Los Angeles; P 62,300; M 200; (626) 570-9429; Fax (626) 570-9491; mpccusa@yahoo.com; www.montereyparkchamber.org

Montgomery Creek • *see Burney*

Montrose • *Montrose-Verdugo City C/C* • Melinda Clarke; Exec. Dir.; 2424 Honolulu Ave., Ste. B; 91020; Los Angeles; P 6,500; M 270; (818) 249-7171; Fax (818) 249-8919; mvcc@montrosechamber.org; www.montrosechamber.org

Moorpark • *Moorpark C/C* • Valeria Auer; Mgr.; 18 E. High St.; 93021; Ventura; P 36,000; M 260; (805) 529-0322; Fax (805) 529-5304; info@moorparkchamber.com; www.moorparkchamber.com*

Moraga • *Moraga C/C* • Edy Schwartz; Pres.; 1480 Moraga Rd., Ste. I #254; 94556; Contra Costa; P 17,110; M 135; (925) 376-3779; edyschwartz@gmail.com; www.moragachamber.org

Moreno Valley • *Moreno Valley C/C* • Oscar Valdepena; Pres./CEO; 12625 Frederick St., Ste. E3; 92553; Riverside; P 193,400; M 225; (951) 697-4404; Fax (951) 697-0995; office@movalchamber.org; www.movalchamber.org*

Morgan Hill • *Morgan Hill C/C* • John Horner; Pres./CEO; 17485 Monterey Rd., Ste. 105; 95037; Santa Clara; P 44,000; M 500; (408) 779-9444; mhcoc@morganhill.org; www.morganhill.org*

Morro Bay • *Morro Bay C/C & Bus. Center* • Craig Schmidt; CEO; 695 Harbor St.; 93442; San Luis Obispo; P 11,000; M 410; (805) 772-4467; (800) 231-0592; Fax (805) 772-6038; craigschmidt@morrobay.org; www.morrobay.org*

Moss Landing • *Moss Landing C/C* • 8071 Moss Landing Rd.; P.O. Box 41; 95039; Monterey; P 266; M 50; (831) 633-4501; mosslandingcc@gmail.com; www.mosslandingchamber.com

Mount Shasta • *Mount Shasta C/C* • Jim Mullins; Exec. Dir.; 300 Pine St.; 96067; Siskiyou; P 3,500; M 360; (530) 926-3696; (800) 926-4865; Fax (530) 926-0976; info@mtshastachamber.com; www.mtshastachamber.com

Mountain View • *Mountain View C/C* • Oscar Garcia; Pres./CEO; 580 Castro St.; 94041; Santa Clara; P 75,000; M 600; (650) 968-8378; Fax (650) 968-5668; info@chambermv.org; www.chambermv.org*

Muir Beach • *see Stinson Beach*

Murrieta • *Murrieta C/C* • Patrick Ellis; Pres./CEO; 25125 Madison Ave., Ste. 108; 92562; Riverside; P 115,000; M 850; (951) 677-7916; Fax (951) 677-9976; pellis@murrietachamber.org; www.murrietachamber.org*

Napa • *Napa C/C* • Travis Stanley; Pres./CEO; 1556 First St.; 94559; Napa; P 78,000; M 1,150; (707) 226-7455; Fax (707) 226-1171; info@napachamber.com; www.napachamber.com*

National City • *National City C/C* • Jacqueline L. Reynoso; Pres./CEO; 901 National City Blvd.; 91950; San Diego; P 57,000; M 600; (619) 477-9339; Fax (619) 477-5018; thechamber@nationalcitychamber.org; www.nationalcitychamber.org

Needles • *Needles C/C* • Ed Horst; Pres.; 100 G St.; P.O. Box 705; 92363; San Bernardino; P 4,844; M 185; (760) 326-2050; Fax (760) 326-2194; needleschamber@frontier.com; www.needleschamber.com

Nevada City • *Nevada City C/C* • Cathy Whittlesey; Exec. Dir.; 132 Main St.; 95959; Nevada; P 3,001; M 390; (530) 265-2692; (800) 655-NJOY; Fax (530) 265-3892; info@nevadacitychamber.com; www.nevadacitychamber.com

Newark • *Newark C/C* • Valerie K. Boyle; Pres./CEO; 35501 Cedar Blvd.; 94560; Alameda; P 45,000; M 250; (510) 578-4500; Fax N/A; valerie@newark-chamber.com; www.newark-chamber.com*

Newberry Springs • *Newberry Springs C/C* • Sandra Brittian; Pres.; P.O. Box 116; 92365; San Bernardino; P 3,000; M 30; (760) 257-1072; Fax (760) 257-4107; newberryspringscoc@gmail.com; www.newberryspringscoc.com

Newbury Park • *see Westlake Village*

Newhall • *see Santa Clarita*

Newport Beach • *Newport Beach C/C* • Steve Rosansky; Pres./CEO; 1470 Jamboree Rd.; 92660; Orange; P 87,100; M 900; (949) 729-4400; Fax (949) 729-4417; psmith@newportbeach.com; www.newportbeach.com*

Niland • *Niland C/C* • Hollis Baker; Pres.; P.O. Box 97; 92257; Imperial; P 1,010; M 150; (760) 359-0870; hbaker@nilandchamber.org; www.nilandchamber.org

Nipomo • *Nipomo C/C* • Amber Wilson; Exec. Dir.; 239 W. Tefft St.; 93444; San Luis Obispo; P 16,700; M 220; (805) 929-1583; Fax (805) 929-5835; info@nipomochamber.org; www.nipomochamber.org*

Norco • *Norco Area C/C & Visitors Center* • Diane Collins; Pres./CEO; 3954 Old Hamner Rd., Ste. B; P.O. Box 844; 92860; Riverside; P 27,100; M 150; (951) 737-6222; info@norcoareachamber.org; www.norcoareachamber.org*

North Fork • *North Fork C/C* • Scott Marsh; Pres.; P.O. Box 426; 93643; Madera; P 3,500; M 40; (559) 877-2410; Fax (559) 877-2332; info@north-fork-chamber.com; www.north-fork-chamber.com

North Highlands • *see Sacramento-North Sacramento C/C*

North Hollywood • *Universal City North Hollywood C/C* • Michelle Gilstrap; Exec. Dir.; 6369 Bellingham Ave.; 91606; Los Angeles; P 160,000; M 170; (818) 508-5155; Fax (818) 508-5156; info@noho.org; www.noho.org

North Sacramento • *see Sacramento-North Sacramento C/C*

Northridge • *Northridge C/C* • Wayne Adelstein; Pres./CEO; 9401 Reseda Blvd., Ste. 100; 91324; Los Angeles; P 277,915; M 350; (818) 349-5676; Fax (818) 349-4343; wayne@nvrcc.com; www.nvrcc.com

Norwalk • *Norwalk C/C* • Caren Spilsbury; Exec. Dir.; 12040 Foster Rd.; 90650; Los Angeles; P 102,000; M 225; (562) 864-7785; Fax (562) 864-8539; ceo@norwalkchamber.com; www.norwalkchamber.com*

Novato • *Novato C/C* • Coy Smith; CEO; 807 DeLong Ave.; 94945; Marin; P 52,000; M 500; (415) 897-1164; Fax (415) 898-9097; kris@novatochamber.com; www.novatochamber.com*

Oakdale • *Oakdale Dist. C/C & Visitors Bur.* • Mary Guardiola; CEO; 590 N. Yosemite Ave.; 95361; Stanislaus; P 21,000; M 380; (209) 847-2244; Fax (209) 847-0826; info@oakdalechamber.com; www.oakdalechamber.com*

Oakhurst • *Oakhurst Area C/C* • Darin Soukup; Exec. Dir.; 40637 Hwy. 41; 93644; Madera; P 35,000; M 400; (559) 683-7766; Fax (559) 395-0903; chamber@oakhurstchamber.com; www.oakhurstchamber.com*

Oakland Area

Oakland African-American C/C • Crystal Mosley Cole; Pres./CEO; 333 Hegenberger Rd., Ste. 369; 94621; Alameda; P 419,300; M 480; (510) 268-1600; Fax (510) 268-1602; info@oaacc.org; www.oaacc.org

Oakland Chinatown C/C • Jennie Ong; Exec. Dir.; 388 Ninth St., Ste. 290; 94607; Alameda; P 26,000; M 275; (510) 893-8979; oaklandctchamber@aol.com; www.oaklandchinatownchamber.org

Oakland Metro C/C • Barbara Leslie; Pres./CEO; 475 14th St.; 94612; Alameda; P 419,300; M 1,000; (510) 874-4800; Fax (510) 839-8817; lana@oaklandchamber.com; www.oaklandchamber.com*

Oakley • *Oakley C/C* • Wendy Turner; Ofc. Mgr,; 3510 Main St.; P.O. Box 1340; 94561; Contra Costa; P 35,000; M 100; (925) 625-1035; Fax (925) 625-4051; office@oakleychamber.com; www.oakleychamber.com*

Oceanside • *Oceanside C/C* • David L. Nydegger; Pres./CEO; 928 N. Coast Hwy.; 92054; San Diego; P 169,000; M 660; (760) 722-1534; Fax (760) 722-8336; info@oceansidechamber.com; www.oceansidechamber.com*

Oildale • *see Bakersfield-North of the River C/C*

Ojai • *Ojai Valley C/C* • Scott Eicher; CEO; 206 N. Signal St., Ste. P; P.O. Box 1134; 93024; Ventura; P 28,000; M 220; (805) 646-8126; Fax (805) 309-2340; info@ojaichamber.org; www.ojaichamber.org

Old Station • *see Burney*

Olive Drive • *see Bakersfield-North of the River C/C*

Ontario • *Ontario C/C* • Peggi Hazlett; Pres./CEO; 3200 Inland Empire Blvd., Ste. 130; 91764; San Bernardino; P 174,000; M 350; (909) 984-2458; info@ontario.org; www.ontario.org*

Orange • *Orange C/C* • Charla Lenarth; Pres./CEO; 307 E. Chapman Ave.; 92866; Orange; P 136,500; M 650; (714) 538-3581; Fax (714) 532-1675; info@orangechamber.com; www.orangechamber.com*

Orangevale • *Orangevale C/C* • Lorae Oliver; Ofc. Mgr.; 9267 Greenback Ln., Ste. B91; 95662; Sacramento; P 27,000; M 120; (916) 988-0175; Fax (916) 988-1049; info@orangevalechamber.com; www.orangevalechamber.com*

Orick • *Orick C/C* • John Sutter; Pres.; P.O. Box 234; 95555; Humboldt; P 300; M 20; (707) 488-2885; (707) 488-2602; Fax (707) 488-5295; www.orick.net

Orinda • *Orinda C/C* • Candy Kattenburg; Exec. Dir.; 26 Orinda Way; P.O. Box 2271; 94563; Contra Costa; P 17,700; M 200; (925) 254-3909; Fax (925) 254-8312; info@orindachamber.org; www.orindachamber.org

Orland • *Orland Area C/C* • Candice Anderson; Ofc. Mgr.; 401 Walker St.; 95963; Glenn; P 7,600; M 200; (530) 865-2311; Fax (530) 865-8171; orlandchamber@sbcglobal.net; www.orland-chamber.com*

Oroville • *Oroville Area C/C* • Claudia Knaus; Pres./CEO; 1789 Montgomery St.; 95965; Butte; P 16,000; M 450; (530) 538-2542; (800) 655-GOLD; Fax (530) 538-2546; info@orovillechamber.net; www.orovillechamber.net*

Oxnard • *Oxnard C/C* • Nancy Lindholm; Pres./CEO; 400 E. Esplanade Dr., Ste. 302; 93036; Ventura; P 200,000; M 550; (805) 983-6118; Fax (805) 604-7331; info@oxnardchamber.org; www.oxnardchamber.org*

Pacific Grove • *Pacific Grove C/C* • Mr. Moe Ammar; Pres.; 584 Central Ave.; P.O. Box 167; 93950; Monterey; P 15,100; M 500; (831) 373-3304; Fax (831) 373-3317; chamber@pacificgrove.org; www.pacificgrove.org*

Pacific Palisades • *Pacific Palisades C/C* • Arnie Wishnick; CEO; 15330 Antioch St.; 90272; Los Angeles; P 27,000; M 375; (310) 459-7963; Fax (310) 459-9534; info@palisadeschamber.com; www.palisadeschamber.com*

Pacifica • *Pacifica C/C* • Courtney Conlon; CEO; 225 Rockaway Beach Blvd., Ste. 1; 94044; San Mateo; P 40,000; M 400; (650) 355-4122; Fax (650) 355-6949; debbie@pacificachamber.com; www.pacificachamber.com*

Palm Desert • *Palm Desert Area C/C* • Barbara deBoom IOM ACE; Pres./CEO; 72559 Hwy. 111; 92260; Riverside; P 48,500; M 1,400; (760) 346-6111; Fax (760) 346-3263; info@pdacc.org; www.pdacc.org*

Palm Springs • *Palm Springs C/C* • Nona Watson; CEO; 190 W. Amado Rd.; 92262; Riverside; P 50,000; M 950; (760) 325-1577; Fax (760) 400-0044; info@pschamber.org; www.pschamber.org*

Palmdale • *Antelope Valley Bd. of Trade* • Vicki Medina; Exec. Dir.; 41319 - 12th St. W., Ste. 104; 93551; Los Angeles; P 450,000; M 250; (661) 947-9033; Fax (661) 723-9279; info@avbot.org; www.avbot.org

Palmdale • *Palmdale C/C* • Caroline Bernal; Chrmn.; 817 E. Ave. Q-9; 93550; Los Angeles; P 150,000; M 500; (661) 273-3232; Fax (661) 273-8508; pcc@palmdalechamber.org; www.palmdalechamber.org*

Palo Alto • *Palo Alto C/C* • David MacKenzie; Pres./CEO; 400 Mitchell Ln.; 94301; Santa Clara; P 64,500; M 675; (650) 324-3121; Fax (650) 324-1215; david@paloaltochamber.com; www.paloaltochamber.com

Panorama City • *see Van Nuys*

Paradise • *Paradise Ridge C/C* • 5550 Skyway, Ste. 1; 95969; Butte; P 26,500; M 400; (530) 877-9356; (888) 845-2769; Fax (530) 877-1865; info@paradisechamber.com; www.paradisechamber.com*

Paramount • *Paramount C/C* • Peggy Lemons; Exec. Dir.; 15357 Paramount Blvd.; 90723; Los Angeles; P 60,000; M 319; (562) 634-3980; Fax (562) 634-0891; plemons@paramountchamber.com; www.paramountchamber.com*

Parlier • *Parlier C/C* • Israel Lara; Pres.; P.O. Box 453; 93648; Fresno; P 15,000; M 20; (559) 646-3837; Fax (559) 254-5115; www.parlier.ca.us

Pasadena • *Pasadena C/C & Civic Assn.* • Paul Little; Pres./CEO; 44 N. Mentor Ave.; 91106; Los Angeles; P 137,200; M 1,300; (626) 795-3355; Fax (626) 795-5603; linda@pasadena-chamber.org; www.pasadena-chamber.org*

Paso Robles • *Paso Robles C/C* • Sunni Mullinax; CEO; 1225 Park St.; 93446; San Luis Obispo; P 32,000; M 1,000; (805) 238-0506; Fax (805) 238-0527; sunni@pasorobleschamber.com; www.pasorobleschamber.com*

Patterson • *Patterson-Westley C/C* • Carolyn Harr; Pres.; P.O. Box 365; 95363; Stanislaus; P 21,000; M 175; (209) 895-8094; info@patterson-westleychamber.com; www.patterson-westleychamber.com*

Penn Valley • *Penn Valley Area C/C* • Mike Mastrodonato; Pres.; 11336 Pleasant Valley Rd.; P.O. Box 202; 95946; Nevada; P 14,000; M 140; (530) 432-1802; Fax (530) 432-7762; info@pennvalleycoc.org; www.pennvalleycoc.org

Perris • *Perris Valley C/C* • Ted Norton; CEO; 227 N. D St., Ste. A; 92570; Riverside; P 68,000; M 200; (951) 657-3555; Fax (951) 657-3085; pvcc@perrischamber.net; www.perrischamber.net*

Petaluma • *Petaluma Area C/C* • Onita Pellegrini; CEO; 6 Petaluma Blvd. N., Ste. A-2; 94952; Sonoma; P 59,000; M 750; (707) 762-2785; Fax (707) 762-4721; pacc@petalumachamber.com; www.petalumachamber.com*

Phelan • *Phelan C/C* • Alex Brandon; Exec. Dir.; P.O. Box 290010; 92329; San Bernardino; P 15,000; M 90; (760) 868-3291; Fax (760) 868-3291; phelanchamber@verizon.net; phelanchamber.org

Pico Rivera • *Pico Rivera C/C* • 5016 Passons Blvd.; 90660; Los Angeles; P 63,000; M 229; (562) 949-2477; nichole.arruda@picoriverachamber.org; www.picoriverachamber.org

Pine Mountain Club • *see Frazier Park*

Pinehurst • *see Miramonte*

Pinion Pines • *see Frazier Park*

Pinole • *Pinole C/C* • Deanna Million; Exec. Dir.; 647 Tennent Ave., Ste. 103; P.O. Box 1; 94564; Contra Costa; P 8,000; M 160; (510) 724-4484; Fax (510) 724-4408; pinolechamber@yahoo.com; www.pinolechamber.org*

Pinon Hills • *Pinon Hills C/C* • Nancy Cosgrove; Pres.; P.O. Box 720095; 92372; San Bernardino; P 7,000; M 75; (760) 868-5801; Fax (760) 868-5801; pinonhillschamber@verizon.net; www.pinonhillschamber.com

Pismo Beach • *Pismo Beach C/C & Visitors Info. Center* • Peter Candela; CEO; 581 Dolliver St.; 93449; San Luis Obispo; P 8,000; M 450; (805) 773-4382; (800) 443-7778; Fax (805) 773-6772; info@pismochamber.com; www.pismochamber.com*

Pittsburg • *Pittsburg C/C* • Harry York; CEO; 985 Railroad Ave.; 94565; Contra Costa; P 64,000; M 500; (925) 432-7301; Fax (925) 427-5555; chamber@pittsburgchamber.org; www.pittsburgchamber.org*

Placentia • *Placentia C/C* • Pam Tancordo; Ofc. Mgr.; 117 N. Main St.; 92870-5603; Orange; P 58,000; M 180; (714) 528-1873; Fax (714) 528-1879; placentiachamber@att.net; www.placentiachamber.com*

Placerville • *El Dorado County C/C* • Laurel Brent-Bumb; CEO; 542 Main St.; 95667; El Dorado; P 1,850,000; M 900; (530) 621-5885; (800) 457-6279; Fax (530) 642-1624; psi@eldoradocounty.org; www.eldoradocounty.org*

Pleasant Hill • *Pleasant Hill C/C* • Steve Van Dorn; Pres./CEO; 91 Gregory Ln., Ste. 11; 94523; Contra Costa; P 33,200; M 315; (925) 687-0700; Fax (925) 676-7422; tina@pleasanthillchamber.com; pleasanthillchamber.com*

Pleasanton • *Pleasanton C/C* • Scott Raty; Pres./CEO; 777 Peters Ave.; 94566; Alameda; P 70,000; M 800; (925) 846-5858; Fax (925) 846-9697; info@pleasanton.org; www.pleasanton.org*

Plumas Lake • *see Yuba City*

Point Reyes Station • *West Marin C/C* • Frank Borodic; Pres.; P.O. Box 1045; 94956; Marin; P 8,000; M 100; (415) 663-9232; info@pointreyes.org; www.pointreyes.org

Pomona • *Pomona C/C* • Frank Garcia; Exec. Dir.; 101 W. Mission Blvd., Ste 223; 91766; Los Angeles; P 175,000; M 450; (909) 622-8484; Fax (909) 620-5986; info@pomonachamber.org; www.pomonachamber.org*

Port Hueneme • *Hueneme C/C* • Tracy Sisson Phillips; Pres./CEO; 220 N. Market St.; 93041; Ventura; P 22,500; M 125; (805) 488-2023; Fax (805) 488-6993; chamberinfo@huenemechamber.com; www.huenemechamber.com*

Porterville • *Porterville C/C* • Deborah Sierra; Pres./CEO; 93 N. Main St., Ste. A; 93257; Tulare; P 54,000; M 850; (559) 784-7502; Fax (559) 784-0770; info@portervillechamber.org; www.portervillechamber.org*

Portola • *see Graeagle* • **Poway** • *Poway C/C* • Dolores Canizales; Pres./CEO; 14005-B Midland Rd.; P.O. Box 868; 92064; San Diego; P 50,000; M 550; (858) 748-0016; chamber@poway.com; www.poway.com

Prunedale • *see Castroville*

Quartz Hill • *Quartz Hill C/C* • Debbie Clark; Ofc. Mgr.; 42043 50th St. W.; 93536; Los Angeles; P 12,000; M 200; (661) 722-4811; Fax (661) 722-3235; info@qhchamber.org; www.qhchamber.org

Quincy • *Quincy C/C* • Kent Barrett; Pres.; 336 W. Main St.; P.O. Box 215; 95971; Plumas; P 5,000; M 220; quincychamber@yahoo.com; www.quincychamber.com

Ramona • *Ramona C/C* • Dr. Robert D. Argyelan; Exec. Dir.; 960 Main St.; 92065; San Diego; P 41,000; M 380; (760) 789-1311; Fax (760) 789-1317; rccstaff@ramonachamber.com; www.ramonachamber.com*

Rancho Bernardo • *see San Diego-North San Diego Bus. Chamber*

Rancho Cordova • *Rancho Cordova C/C* • Diann Rogers; Pres./CEO; 2729 Prospect Park Dr., Ste. 117; 95670; Sacramento; P 65,000; M 430; (916) 273-5700; Fax (916) 273-5727; reception@ranchocordova.org; www.ranchocordova.org*

Rancho Cucamonga • *Rancho Cucamonga C/C* • Maribel Brown; Pres./Chair; 9047 Arrow Rte., Ste. 180; 91730; San Bernardino; P 172,000; M 1,000; (909) 987-1012; Fax (909) 987-5917; info@ranchochamber.org; www.ranchochamber.org*

Rancho Mirage • *Rancho Mirage C/C* • Samantha Tweddell; Exec. Dir.; 71905 Hwy. 111, Ste. H; 92270; Riverside; P 17,200; M 300; (760) 568-9351; Fax (760) 779-9684; samantha@ranchomirage.org; www.ranchomiragechamber.com*

Rancho Penasquitos • *see San Diego-North San Diego Bus. Chamber*

Rancho Santa Fe • *see Del Mar-San Diego Coastal C/C*

Rancho Santa Margarita • *Rancho Santa Margarita C/C* • Suzanne Singh; Pres./CEO; 30162 Tomas, Ste. 202; 92688; Orange; P 48,000; M 200; (949) 242-3660; Fax (866) 728-0376; info@rsmchamber.com; www.rsmchamber.com*

Red Bluff • *Red Bluff-Tehama County C/C* • Dave Gowan; CEO; 100 Main St.; P.O. Box 850; 96080; Tehama; P 14,100; M 400; (530) 527-6220; (800) 655-6225; Fax (530) 527-2908; info@redbluffchamber.com; www.redbluffchamber.com

Redding • *Redding C/C* • Jake Mangas; Pres./CEO; 1321 Butte St., Ste. 100; 96001; Shasta; P 90,000; M 800; (530) 225-4433; Fax (530) 225-4398; info@reddingchamber.com; www.reddingchamber.com*

Redlands • *Redlands C/C* • Kathie Thurston; Exec. Dir.; 1 E. Redlands Blvd.; 92373; San Bernardino; P 70,000; M 610; (909) 793-2546; Fax (909) 335-6388; info@redlandschamber.org; www.redlandschamber.org*

Redondo Beach • *Redondo Beach C/C & Visitors Bur.* • Marna Smeltzer; Pres./CEO; 119 W. Torrance Blvd., Ste. 2; 90277; Los Angeles; P 68,000; M 600; (310) 376-6911; Fax (310) 374-7373; info@redondochamber.org; www.redondochamber.org   *

Redwood City • *Redwood City-San Mateo County C/C* • Laurence Buckmaster; Pres./CEO; 1450 Veterans Blvd., Ste. 125; 94063; San Mateo; P 75,000; M 1,100; (650) 364-1722; Fax (650) 364-1729; info@redwoodcitychamber.com; www.redwoodcitychamber.com*

Reedley • *Greater Reedley C/C* • Kimberly Hoff; CEO; 1633 11th St.; 93654; Fresno; P 25,000; M 120; (559) 638-3548; Fax (559) 638-8479; info@reedleychamberofcommerce.com; www.reedleychamberofcommerce.com

Rialto • *Rialto C/C* • Midge Zupanic; Interim Exec. Dir.; 120 N. Riverside Ave.; 92376; San Bernardino; P 103,200; M 300; (909) 875-5364; Fax (909) 875-6790; lisa@rialtochamber.org; www.rialtochamber.org*

Richmond • *Richmond C/C* • Ruth Vasquez-Jones; Pres./CEO; 3925 Macdonald Ave.; 94805; Contra Costa; P 103,000; M 500; (510) 234-3512; Fax (510) 234-3540; staff@rcoc.com; www.rcoc.com*

Ridgecrest • *Ridgecrest C/C* • Nathan Ahle; CEO; 128 E. California Ave., Ste. B; 93555; Kern; P 28,000; M 390; (760) 375-8331; Fax (760) 375-0365; chamber@ridgecrestchamber.com; www.ridgecrestchamber.com*

Rio Dell • *Rio Dell-Scotia C/C* • James Rich; Pres.; 406 Wildwood Ave.; 95562; Humboldt; P 4,150; M 80; (707) 506-5081; Fax (707) 506-5081; office@riodellscotiachamber.com; www.riodellscotiachamber.org

Rio Linda • *Rio Linda-Elverta C/C* • Lisa L. Morris; Pres.; P.O. Box 75; 95673; Sacramento; P 21,000; M 100; (916) 991-9344; Fax (916) 991-9344; rlechamberofcommerce@sbcglobal.net; www.rlechamber.org

Rio Vista • *Rio Vista C/C* • Karen James Smith; Exec. Dir.; 37 N. 2nd St.; 94571; Solano; P 10,000; M 150; (707) 374-2700; Fax (707) 374-2424; karen@riovista.org; www.riovista.org*

Rio Vista • *California Delta C of C & Visitors Bur.* • Bill Wells; Exec. Dir.; P.O. Box 1118; 94571; Sacramento & San Joaquin; P 500,000; M 300; (916) 777-4041; info@californiadelta.org; www.californiadelta.org

Ripon • *Ripon C/C* • Tamra Spade; Exec. Dir.; 929 W. Main St.; P.O. Box 327; 95366; San Joaquin; P 16,000; M 250; (209) 599-7519; Fax (888) 556-4944; tspade@riponchamber.org; www.riponchamber.org*

Riverbank • *Riverbank C/C* • Jerry Van Houten; Pres.; P.O. Box 340; 95367; Stanislaus; P 23,000; M 100; (209) 869-4541; info@riverbankchamber.org; www.riverbankchamber.org

Riverside • *Greater Riverside C/C* • Cindy Roth; Pres./CEO; 3985 University Ave.; 92501; Riverside; P 311,955; M 1,290; (951) 683-7100; Fax (951) 683-2670; rchamber@riverside-chamber.com; www.riverside-chamber.com*

Robla • *see Sacramento-North Sacramento C/C*

Rocklin • *Rocklin Area C/C* • Robin Trimble; CEO; 3700 Rocklin Rd.; 95677; Placer; P 57,000; M 650; (916) 624-2548; Fax (916) 624-5743; info@rocklinchamber.com; www.rocklinchamber.com*

Rodeo • *Rodeo C/C* • Mark Hughes; Bd. Member; P.O. Box 548; 94572; Contra Costa; P 12,000; M 60; (510) 245-4070; (510) 245-4400; rodeochamber@gmail.com; www.rodeoca.org

Rohnert Park • *Rohnert Park C/C* • Kelly Scullion; Dir.; 101 Golf Course Dr., Ste. C-7; 94928; Sonoma; P 41,000; M 250; (707) 584-1415; Fax (707) 584-2945; kelly@rohnertparkchamber.org; www.rohnertparkchamber.org*

Rolling Hills Estate • *Palos Verdes Peninsula C/C* • Eileen Hupp; Pres./CEO; 707 Silver Spur Rd., Ste. 100; 90274; Los Angeles; P 75,000; M 430; (310) 377-8111; Fax (310) 377-0614; office@palosverdeschamber.com; www.palosverdeschamber.com*

Rosamond • *Rosamond C/C* • Terry V. Landsiedel; Pres.; 2861 Diamond St.; P.O. Box 365; 93560; Kern; P 20,000; M 450; (661) 256-3248; Fax (661) 256-3249; visitrosamond@gmail.com; rosamondchamberofcommerce.com

Rosedale • *see Bakersfield-North of the River C/C*

Rosemead • *Rosemead C/C* • Min Hsien Wang; Exec. Dir.; 3953 Muscatel Ave.; 91770; Los Angeles; P 54,000; M 250; (626) 288-0811; Fax (626) 288-2514; office@rosemeadchamber.org; www.rosemeadchamber.org*

Roseville • *Roseville C/C* • Wendy Gerig; CEO; 650 Douglas Blvd.; 95678; Placer; P 121,000; M 1,380; (916) 783-8136; Fax (916) 783-5261; admin@rosevillechamber.com; www.rosevillechamber.com*

Rough and Ready • *Rough and Ready C/C* • Sheridan Loungway; Pres.; P.O. Box 801; 95975; Nevada; P 2,000; M 100; (530) 797-6729; info@roughandreadychamber.com; www.roughandreadychamber.com

Round Mountain • *see Burney*

Rowland Heights • *Reg. Chamber of Commerce-San Gabriel Valley* • Anthony Duarte; CEO; 1722 Desire Ave., Ste. 207; 91748; Los Angeles; P 200,000; M 365; (626) 810-8476; Fax (626) 810-8475; info@regionalchambersgv.com; www.regionalchambersgv.com*

Rubidoux • *see Jurupa Valley C/C*

Running Springs • *Running Springs Area C/C* • Kevin Somes; Pres.; P.O. Box 96; 92382; San Bernardino; P 6,000; M 155; (909) 867-2411; Fax (909) 867-2411; info@runningspringschamber.com; www.runningspringschamber.com

Sabre Springs • *see San Diego-North San Diego Bus. Chamber*

Sacramento Area

California Black C/C • Delores Thompson; V.P. of Op.; 1600 Sacramento Inn Way, Ste. 232; 95815; Sacramento; P 39,200,000; M 5,500; (916) 463-0178; Fax (916) 463-0190; cbcc@calbcc.org; www.calbcc.org

North Sacramento C/C • Franklin Burris; Exec. Dir.; P.O. Box 15468; 95851; Sacramento; P 50,000; M 118; (916) 275-4662; leadership@northsacramentochamber.org; www.northsacchamber.org

Sacramento Hispanic C/C • Cathy Rodriguez; Pres./CEO; 1451 River Park Dr. S., Ste. 220; 95815; Sacramento; P 2,400,000; M 800; (916) 486-7700; Fax (916) 486-7728; claudia@sachcc.org; www.sachcc.org*

Sacramento Metro Chamber • Peter Tateishi; Pres./CEO; One Capitol Mall, Ste. 300; 95814; Sacramento; P 2,400,000; M 2,200; (916) 552-6800; Fax (916) 443-2672; communications@metrochamber.org; www.metrochamber.org*

Saint Helena • *Saint Helena C/C* • Pam Simpson; Pres./CEO; 657 Main St.; 94574; Napa; P 143,000; M 500; (707) 963-4456; Fax (707) 963-5396; info@sthelena.com; www.sthelena.com*

Salinas • *Salinas Valley C/C* • Paul J. Farmer; Pres./CEO; 119 E. Alisal St.; 93901; Monterey; P 152,000; M 850; (831) 751-7725; Fax (831) 424-8639; info@salinaschamber.com; www.salinaschamber.com*

San Andreas • *Calaveras County C/C* • Staci Johnston; Exec. Dir.; 39 N. Main St.; P.O. Box 1075; 95249; Calaveras; P 46,000; M 410; (209) 754-5400; Fax (209)754-5401; chamber@calaveras.org; www.calaveras.org*

San Anselmo • *San Anselmo C/C* • Connie Rodgers; Pres./CEO; P.O. Box 2844; 94979; Marin; P 12,000; M 250; (415) 454-2510; Fax (415) 258-9458; info@sananselmochamber.org; www.sananselmochamber.org*

San Bernardino • *San Bernardino Area C/C* • Judi Penman; Pres./CEO; 546 W. Sixth St.; P.O. Box 658; 92402; San Bernardino; P 210,000; M 1,000; (909) 885-7515; Fax (909) 384-9979; sba.chamber@verizon.net; www.sbachamber.org*

San Bruno • *San Bruno C/C* • Jamie Monozon; CEO; 618 San Mateo Ave.; 94066; San Mateo; P 45,000; M 200; (650) 588-0180; Fax (650) 588-6473; office@sanbrunochamber.com; www.sanbrunochamber.com*

San Carlos • *San Carlos C/C* • David Bouchard; CEO; 610 Elm St., Ste. 206; 94070; San Mateo; P 29,000; M 750; (650) 593-1068; Fax (650) 593-9108; staff@sancarloschamber.org; www.sancarloschamber.org*

San Clemente • *San Clemente C/C* • Lynn Wood; Pres./CEO; 1231 Puerta Del Sol, Unit 200; 92673; Orange; P 72,000; M 500; (949) 492-1131; Fax (949) 492-3764; info@scchamber.com; www.scchamber.com*

San Diego Area

North San Diego Bus. Chamber • Debra Rosen; Pres./CEO; 10875 Rancho Bernardo Rd., Ste. 104; 92127; San Diego; P 240,000; M 700; (858) 487-1767; Fax (858) 487-8051; drosen@sdbusinesschamber.com; www.sdncc.com

Old Town San Diego C/C • Richard Stegner; Exec. Dir.; 2415 San Diego Ave., Ste. 104; 92110; San Diego; P 1,000,000; M 485; (619) 291-4903; Fax (619) 291-9383; otsd@aol.com; www.oldtownsandiego.org

Otay Mesa C/C • Alejandra Mier y Teran; Exec. Dir.; 9163 Siempre Viva Rd., Ste. I-2; 92154; San Diego; P 15,000; M 330; (619) 661-6111; Fax (619) 661-6178; hromero@otaymesa.org; www.otaymesa.org

San Diego County Hispanic C/C • Juan Carlos Hernandez; Chrmn. of the Bd.; 404 Euclid Ave., Ste. 200; P.O. Box 131548; 92114; San Diego; P 3,100,000; M 500; (858) 268-0790; info@sdchcc.org; www.sdchcc.org

San Diego Reg. C/C • Jerry Sanders; Pres./CEO; 402 W. Broadway, Ste. 1000; 92101; San Diego; P 3,187,729; M 3,110; (619) 544-1300; Fax (619) 744-7400; rlindell@sdchamber.org; www.sdchamber.org

San Dimas • *San Dimas C/C* • Autumn Washington; Op. & Events Mgr.; 246 E. Bonita Ave.; P.O. Box 175; 91773; Los Angeles; P 35,756; M 350; (909) 592-3818; Fax (909) 592-8178; info@sandimaschamber.com; www.sandimaschamber.com*

San Francisco Area

California-Asia Bus.Cncl. (Cal-Asia) • Ms. Jeremy W. Potash; Exec. Dir.; 525 Market St., 25th Flr.; 94105; San Francisco; P 37,700,000; M 100; (415) 986-8808; (510) 207-8990; Fax (415) 957-0108; alerts@calasia.org; www.calasia.org

San Francisco C/C • Bob Linscheid; Pres./CEO; 235 Montgomery St., Ste. 760; 94104; San Francisco; P 825,863; M 1,500; (415) 392-4520; Fax (415) 392-0485; info@sfchamber.com; www.sfchamber.com*

San Francisco Chinese C/C • Tony Fong; Pres.; 730 Sacramento St.; 94108; San Francisco; P 805,000; M 400; (415) 982-3000; Fax (415) 982-4720; chinesechambersf@yahoo.com

San Gabriel • *San Gabriel C/C* • Albert Hernandez; Pres.; 620 W. Santa Anita St.; 91776; Los Angeles; P 40,000; M 300; (626) 576-2525; Fax (626) 289-2901; rosco_sandy@yahoo.com; www.sangabrielchamber.org

San Jacinto • *see Hemet*

San Jose • *San Jose Silicon Valley C/C* • Matthew Mahood; Pres./CEO; 101 W. Santa Clara St.; 95113; Santa Clara; P 2,000,000; M 2,200; (408) 291-5250; Fax (408) 286-5019; info@sjchamber.com; www.sjchamber.com*

San Juan Bautista • *see Hollister*

San Juan Capistrano • *San Juan Capistrano C/C* • Mark Bodenhamer; CEO; 31421 La Matanza St.; P.O. Box 1878; 92675; Orange; P 37,000; M 350; (949) 493-4700; Fax (949) 489-2695; info@sanjuanchamber.com; www.sanjuanchamber.com*

San Leandro • *San Leandro C/C* • David Johnson; Pres./CEO; 120 Estudillo Ave.; 94577; Alameda; P 55,000; M 509; (510) 317-1400; Fax (510) 218-2644; info@sanleandrochamber.com; www.sanleandrochamber.com*

San Luis Obispo • *San Luis Obispo C/C* • Ermina Karim; Pres./CEO; 895 Monterey St.; 93401; San Luis Obispo; P 47,000; M 1,400; (805) 781-2670; Fax (805) 543-1255; aaron@slochamber.org; www.slochamber.org*

San Marcos • *San Marcos C/C* • Joan Priest; Pres./CEO; 904 W. San Marcos Blvd., Ste. 10; 92078; San Diego; P 90,000; M 625; (760) 744-1270; Fax (760) 744-5230; joan@sanmarcoschamber.com; www.sanmarcoschamber.com*

San Marino • *San Marino C/C* • Stewart Rogers; Pres.; 1800 Huntington Dr.; 91108; Los Angeles; P 13,000; M 200; (626) 286-1022; Fax (626) 286-7765; sanmarinochamber@att.net; www.sanmarinochamber.com

San Mateo County • *see Redwood City*

San Pablo • *San Pablo C/C* • William Erwin; Pres.; 13925 San Pablo Ave., Ste. 104; P.O. Box 6204; 94806; Contra Costa; P 32,000; M 100; (510) 234-2067; Fax (510) 234-0604; spchamber39@yahoo.com

San Pedro • *San Pedro C/C* • Camilla Townsend; Pres./CEO; 390 W. 7th St.; 90731; Los Angeles; P 81,000; M 460; (310) 832-7272; Fax (310) 832-0685; info@sanpedrochamber.com; www.sanpedrochamber.com*

San Rafael • *San Rafael C/C* • Joanne Webster; Pres./CEO; 817 Mission Ave.; 94901; Marin; P 58,500; M 650; (415) 454-4163; Fax (415) 454-7039; frontdesk@srchamber.com; www.srchamber.com*

San Rafael • *Hispanic C/C of Marin* • Cecilia Zamora; Pres.; P.O. Box 4423; 94913; Marin; P 265,000; M 225; (415) 721-9686; (415) 454-0102; Fax (415) 721-9686; hccmarin@um.att.com; www.hccmarin.com*

San Ramon • *San Ramon C/C* • Stewart L. Bambino; Pres./CEO; 2410 Camino Ramon, Ste. 125; Bishop Ranch 6; 94583; Contra Costa; P 80,000; M 400; (925) 242-0600; Fax (925) 242-0603; info@sanramon.org; www.sanramon.org*

San Simeon • *San Simeon C/C* • Michael Hanchett; Pres.; 250 San Simeon Ave., Ste. 3A; 93452; San Luis Obispo; P 500; M 50; (805) 927-3500; Fax (805) 927-6453; sansimeonchamber@yahoo.com; www.sansimeonchamber.com

San Ysidro • *San Ysidro C of C & Visitor Info. Center* • Jason M-B Wells; Exec. Dir.; 663 E. San Ysidro Blvd.; 92173; San Diego; P 40,000; M 200; (619) 428-1281; Fax (619) 428-1294; info@sanysidrochamber.org; www.sanysidrochamber.org

Sanger • *Sanger Dist. C/C & Visitors Center* • David Laurence Phillips; Pres./CEO; 1789 Jensen Ave., Ste. B; 93657; Fresno; P 26,000; M 200; (559) 875-4575; Fax (559) 875-0745; sangerchamber@gmail.com; www.sanger.org*

Santa Ana • *Orange County Hispanic C/C* • Reuben Franco; CEO; 2130 E. 4th St., Ste. 160; 92705; Orange; P 3,000,000; M 2,715; (714) 953-4289; Fax (714) 953-0273; mail@ochcc.com; ochcc.com*

Santa Ana • *Santa Ana C/C* • David Elliott; Pres./CEO; 1631 W. Sunflower Ave., Ste. C-35; 92704; Orange; P 329,400; M 749; (714) 541-5353; Fax (714) 541-2238; thatch@santaanachamber.com; www.santaanachamber.com*

Santa Barbara • *C/C of the Santa Barbara Region* • Ken Oplinger; Pres./CEO; 104 W. Anapamu St.; 93101; Santa Barbara; P 444,800; M 800; (805) 965-3023; Fax (805) 966-5954; info@sbchamber.org; www.sbchamber.org*

Santa Barbara • *Santa Barbara Hispanic C/C* • Lauro Ortiz; Exec. Dir.; P.O. Box 6592; 93160; Santa Barbara; P 90,000; M 350; (805) 233-3690; Fax (805) 233-3690; info@sbhcc.org; www.sbhcc.org

Santa Clara • *Santa Clara C/C & CVB* • Chris Horton; Pres./CEO; 1850 Warburton Ave.; 95050; Santa Clara; P 110,000; M 570; (408) 244-8244; tempest.early@santaclara.org; www.santaclarachamber.org*

Santa Clarita • *Santa Clarita Valley C/C* • Lois Bauccio; Pres./CEO; Santa Clarita City Hall; 23920 Valencia Blvd., Ste. 265; 91355; Los Angeles; P 213,178; M 1,200; (661) 702-6977; Fax (661) 702-6980; lbauccio@scvchamber.com; www.scvchamber.com*

Santa Cruz • *Santa Cruz Area C/C* • William Tysseling; Exec. Dir./CEO; 725 Front St., Ste. 401; 95060; Santa Cruz; P 62,000; M 750; (831) 457-3713; Fax (831) 423-1847; info@santacruzchamber.org; www.santacruzchamber.org

Santa Fe Springs • *Santa Fe Springs C/C* • Kathie Fink; CEO; 12016 E. Telegraph Rd., Ste. 100; 90670; Los Angeles; P 17,483; M 790; (562) 944-1616; Fax (562) 946-3976; mail@sfschamber.com; www.sfschamber.com*

Santa Maria • *Santa Maria Valley C/C* • Glenn D. Morris ACE; Pres./CEO; 614 S. Broadway; 93454; Santa Barbara; P 144,000; M 800; (805) 925-2403; (800) 331-3779; Fax (805) 928-7559; info@santamaria.com; www.santamaria.com*

Santa Monica • *Santa Monica C/C* • Laurel Rosen; Pres./CEO; 1234 6th St., Ste. 100; 90401; Los Angeles; P 93,000; M 900; (310) 393-9825; Fax (310) 394-1868; info@smchamber.com; www.smchamber.com

Santa Paula • *Santa Paula C/C* • Ken Brookes; Mgr.; 200 N. Tenth St.; P.O. Box 1; 93060; Ventura; P 29,000; M 260; (805) 525-5561; Fax (805) 525-8950; info@santapaulachamber.com; www.santapaulachamber.com

Santa Rosa Area

Hispanic C/C of Sonoma County • Lorena Barrera; Ofc. Mgr.; 3033 Cleveland Ave., Ste. 306; 95403; Sonoma; P 502,200; M 150; (707) 575-3648; Fax (707) 575-3693; hccadmin@hcc-sc.org; www.hcc-sc.org*

Mark West Area C/C & Visitors Center • Steve Plamann; Pres.; 4787 Old Redwood Hwy., Ste. 101; 95403; Sonoma; P 10,000; M 175; (707) 578-7975; office@markwest.org; www.markwest.org*

Santa Rosa C/C • Jonathan Coe; Pres./CEO; 50 Old Courthouse Sq., Ste. 110; 95404; Sonoma; P 175,000; M 900; (707) 545-1414; Fax (707) 545-6914; chamber@santarosachamber.com; www.santarosachamber.com*

Santee • *Santee C/C* • Sandy Schmitt; Pres./CEO; 10315 Mission Gorge Rd.; 92071; San Diego; P 58,000; M 290; (619) 449-6572; Fax (619) 562-7906; info@santeechamber.com; www.santeechamber.com*

Saratoga • *Saratoga C/C* • Judy Longacre; Ofc. Mgr.; 14460 Big Basin Way; 95070; Santa Clara; P 30,000; M 325; (408) 867-0753; Fax (408) 867-5213; info@saratogachamber.org; www.saratogachamber.org*

Saugus • *see Santa Clarita*

Sausalito • *Sausalito C/C* • Oonagh Kavanagh; CEO; 1913 Bridgeway; 94965; Marin; P 7,300; M 350; (415) 331-7262; Fax (415) 332-0323; chamber@sausalito.org; www.sausalito.org*

Scotts Valley • *Scotts Valley C/C* • Sharolynn Ullestad; Exec. Dir.; 360 Kings Village Rd.; 95066; Santa Cruz; P 12,000; M 300; (831) 438-1010; Fax (831) 438-6544; info@scottsvalleychamber.com; www.scottsvalleychamber.com*

Scripps Ranch • *see San Diego-North San Diego Bus. Chamber*

Seal Beach • *Seal Beach C/C* • Gina Phillips; Dir. of Op.; 201 8th St., Ste. 120; 90740; Orange; P 24,200; M 250; (562) 799-0179; Fax (562) 795-5637; director@sealbeachchamber.org; www.sealbeachchamber.org

Seaside • *Seaside, Sand City, Del Rey Oaks & Monterey C/C* • Jim Vossen; Gen. Mgr.; 505 Broadway Ave.; 93955; Monterey; P 70,000; M 250; (831) 394-6501; Fax (831) 393-0645; jim@thechamberoffice.org; www.thechamberoffice.org

Sebastopol • *Sebastopol Area C/C* • Teresa Ramondo; Exec. Dir./CEO; 265 S. Main St.; P.O. Box 178; 95473; Sonoma; P 35,000; M 350; (707) 823-3032; (877) 828-4748; Fax (707) 823-8439; chamber@sebastopol.org; www.sebastopol.org*

Selma • *Selma District C/C* • Bob Allen; Exec. Dir.; 1821 Tucker St.; 93662; Fresno; P 24,000; M 350; (559) 891-2235; Fax (559) 896-7075; chamberdirector@cityofselma.com; www.cityofselma.com/chamber*

Sepulveda • *see Van Nuys*

Shadow Hills • *see Tujunga*

Shafter • *Shafter C/C* • Jeff Martin; Pres.; 336 Pacific Ave.; 93263; Kern; P 16,208; M 75; (661) 746-2600; shafterchamber@shafter.com; www.shafter.com

Shasta Dam • *see Redding*

Shaver Lake • *Shaver Lake C/C* • P.O. Box 58; 93664; Fresno; P 800; M 150; (559) 841-3350; (866) 500-3350; Fax (559) 841-8645; info@shaverlakechamber.com; www.shaverlakechamber.com

Sherman Oaks • *Greater Sherman Oaks C/C* • Vicki Nussbaum; Exec. Dir.; 14827 Ventura Blvd., Ste. 207; 91403; Los Angeles; P 60,000; M 300; (818) 906-1951; Fax (818) 206-0288; info@shermanoakschamber.org; www.shermanoakschamber.org*

Sherman Oaks • *United Chambers of Commerce* • Marian E. Jocz; Exec. Dir.; 5121 Van Nuys Blvd., Ste. 203; 91403; Los Angeles; P 1,760,000; M 20,000; (818) 981-4491; Fax (818) 981-4256; marian@unitedchambers.org; www.unitedchambers.org

Shingle Springs • *Shingle Springs/Cameron Park C/C* • Linda Hopkins; Exec. Dir.; 4095 Cameron Park Dr.; P.O. Box 341; 95682; El Dorado; P 24,000; M 315; (530) 677-8000; Fax (530) 676-8313; info@sscpchamber.org; www.sscpchamber.org*

Sierra City • *Sierra County C/C* • P.O. Box 436; 96125; Sierra; P 3,300; M 71; (800) 200-4949; info@sierracountychamber.com; www.sierracountychamber.com

Sierra Madre • *Sierra Madre C/C* • Bill Coburn; Exec. Dir.; 20 W. Montecito Ave., Ste. C; 91024; Los Angeles; P 11,000; M 200; (626) 355-5111; Fax (626) 306-1150; info@sierramadrechamber.com; www.sierramadrechamber.com

Signal Hill • *Signal Hill C/C* • Terry Rogers; Pres.; 2201 E. Willow, Ste. D; PMB 138; 90755; Los Angeles; P 11,100; M 65; (562) 424-6489; admin@signalhillchamber.com; www.signalhillchamber.com*

Simi Valley • *Simi Valley C/C* • Rana Ghadban; Pres./CEO; 40 W. Cochran St., Ste. 100; 93065; Ventura; P 130,000; M 830; (805) 526-3900; Fax (805) 526-6234; info@simichamber.org; www.simichamber.org*

Slide Ranch • *see Stinson Beach*

Solana Beach • *Solana Beach C/C* • Carolyn Cohen; Pres.; 210 W. Plaza St.; P.O. Box 623; 92075; San Diego; P 13,000; M 325; (858) 755-4775; Fax (858) 755-4889; info@solanabeachchamber.com; www.solanabeachchamber.com*

Soledad • *Soledad Mission C/C* • Andria Brinson; Pres.; 641 Front St.; 93960; Monterey; P 16,000; M 100; (831) 678-3941; Fax (831) 678-3941; info@soledadchamber.com; www.soledådchamber.com*

Solvang • *Solvang C/C* • Linda Jackson; Exec. Dir.; 1693 Mission Dr., Ste. 201C; P.O. Box 465; 93464; Santa Barbara; P 5,500; M 300; (805) 688-0701; linda@solvangcc.org; www.solvangusa.com

Sonoma • *Sonoma Valley C/C* • Patricia Shults; Exec. Dir.; 651-A Broadway; 95476; Sonoma; P 11,000; M 720; (707) 996-1033; Fax (707) 996-9402; info@sonomachamber.com; www.sonomachamber.com*

Sonora • *Tuolumne County C/C* • A. Harrison; Exec. Dir.; 222 S. Shepherd St.; 95370; Tuolumne; P 53,000; M 300; (209) 532-4212; (877) 532-4212; Fax (209) 532-8068; info@tcchamber.com; www.tcchamber.com*

Soquel • *see Capitola*

Sorrento Mesa • *see San Diego-North San Diego Bus. Chamber*

Sorrento Valley • *see Del Mar-LaJolla Golden Triangle C/C*

South Gate • *South Gate C/C* • Everrette Hayes; Pres.; 3350 Tweedy Blvd.; 90280; Los Angeles; P 95,300; M 182; (323) 567-1203; Fax (323) 567-1204; southgatechamberofcommerce@gmail.com; sgatechamber.org*

South Lake Tahoe • *see Stateline, NV*

South San Francisco • *South San Francisco C/C* • Maria Martinucci; CEO; 213 Linden Ave.; 94080; San Mateo; P 64,000; M 600; (650) 588-1911; Fax (650) 588-2534; info@ssfchamber.com; www.ssfchamber.com*

Spring Valley • *Spring Valley C/C* • Tina Carlson; Exec. Dir.; 3322 Sweetwater Springs Blvd., Ste. 202; P.O. Box 1211; 91979; San Diego; P 30,000; M 300; (619) 670-9902; Fax (619) 670-9924; info@springvalleychamber.org; www.springvalleychamber.org

Springville • *Springville C/C* • Sandy Whaling; Pres.; 35680 Hwy. 190; P.O. Box 104; 93265; Tulare; P 6,500; M 125; (559) 539-0100; chamber@springville.ca.us; www.springville.ca.us

Squaw Valley • *see Miramonte*

Stinson Beach • *Stinson Beach Comm. Center* • Mary Greenwood; 32 Belvedere Ave.; P.O. Box 158; 94970; Marin; P 650; (415) 868-1444; Fax (415) 868-1904; info@stinsonbeachcommunitycenter.org; www.stinsonbeachcommunitycenter.org

Stockton • *Greater Stockton C/C* • Douglas W. Wilhoit Jr.; CEO; 445 W. Weber Ave., Ste. 220; 95203; San Joaquin; P 263,000; M 1,600; (209) 547-2770; Fax (209) 466-5271; schamber@stocktonchamber.org; www.stocktonchamber.org*

Studio City • *Studio City C/C* • Esther Walker; Exec. Dir.; 4024 Radford Ave., Ed. 2, Ste. F; 91604; Los Angeles; P 39,000; M 275; (818) 655-5916; Fax (818) 655-8392; admin@studiocitychamber.com; www.studiocitychamber.com

Suisun • *see Fairfield*

Sun Valley • *Sun Valley Area C/C* • Robert McAllister; Pres.; P.O. Box 308; 91353; Los Angeles; P 73,000; M 200; (818) 768-2014; Fax (818) 771-9793; info@svacc.com; www.svacc.com

Sunland • *see Tujunga*

Sunnyvale • *Sunnyvale C/C* • Don Eagleston; Pres./CEO; 260 S. Sunnyvale Ave., Ste. 4; 94086; Santa Clara; P 140,000; M 500; (408) 736-4971; Fax (408) 736-1919; communications@svcoc.org; www.svcoc.org*

Susanville • *Lassen County C/C* • Patricia Hagata; Exec. Dir.; 75 N. Weatherlow St.; P.O. Box 338; 96130; Lassen; P 35,000; M 300; (530) 257-4323; Fax (530) 251-2561; director@lassencountychamber.org; www.lassencountychamber.org

Sutter County • *see Yuba City*

Taft • *Taft District C/C* • Dr. Kathy Orrin; Exec. Dir.; 400 Kern St.; 93268; Kern; P 22,000; M 250; (661) 765-2165; (661) 765-2166; Fax (661) 765-6639; taftchamber@gmail.com; www.taftchamber.com*

Tahoe City • *North Lake Tahoe Chamber/CVB/Resort Assn.* • Sandy Evans Hall; Exec. Dir./CEO; 100 N. Lake Blvd.; P.O. Box 5459; 96145; Placer; P 15,000; M 500; (530) 581-6900; adminasst@gotahoenorth.com; www.nltra.org*

Tarzana • *see Woodland Hills*

Tecopa • *Death Valley C/C* • Old Spanish Trail Hwy.; P.O. Box 15; 92389; Inyo; P 20,000; M 35; (888) 600-1844; deathvalleychamber@gmail.com; www.deathvalleychamber.org

Tehachapi • *Greater Tehachapi C/C* • Ida Perkins; Pres.; 209 E. Tehachapi Blvd.; P.O. Box 401; 93581; Kern; P 38,000; M 500; (661) 822-4180; Fax (661) 822-9036; chamber@tehachapi.com; www.tehachapi.com*

Temecula • *Temecula Valley C/C* • Alice Sullivan; Pres./CEO; 26790 Ynez Ct., Ste. A; 92591; Riverside; P 108,000; M 1,020; (951) 676-5090; Fax (951) 694-0201; info@temecula.org; www.temecula.org*

Temple City • *Temple City C/C* • Peter Choi; Pres./CEO; 9050 Las Tunas Dr.; 91780; Los Angeles; P 39,000; M 400; (626) 286-3101; Fax (626) 286-2590; info@templecitychamber.org; www.templecitychamber.org

Templeton • *Templeton C/C* • Sarah Maggelet; Exec. Dir.; 321 Main St.; P.O. Box 701; 93465; San Luis Obispo; P 3,600; M 200; (805) 434-1789; info@templetonchamber.com; www.templetonchamber.com*

Terminous • *see Rio Vista-California Delta C of C & Visitors Bur.*

Thornton • *Thornton C/C* • Marlene Corbitt; Secy.; P.O. Box 37; 95686; San Joaquin; P 1,200; M 20; (209) 794-2255; Fax (209) 794-2355; mlcorbitt@att.net

Thousand Oaks • *see Westlake Village*

Thousand Palms • *Thousand Palms C/C* • Gail Heveron; Ofc. Mgr.; 72-715 La Canada Way; P.O. Box 365; 92276; Riverside; P 7,700; M 100; (760) 343-1988; info@thousandpalmscc.com; www.thousandpalmscc.com

Three Rivers • *Sequoia Foothills C/C* • Peter Sodhy; Pres.; 42268 Sierra Dr.; P.O. Box 818; 93271; Tulare; P 2,200; M 119; (559) 561-3300; (800) 530-3300; info@threerivers.com; www.threerivers.com

Tiburon • *Belvedere/Tiburon C/C* • Chris Koehler; Exec. Mgr.; 96-B Main St.; P.O. Box 563; 94920; Marin; P 9,000; M 225; (415) 435-5633; Fax (415) 435-1132; tibcc@sbcglobal.net; www.tiburonchamber.org

Toluca Lake • *Toluca Lake C/C* • Steve Hampar; Pres.; P.O. Box 2312; 91610; Los Angeles; P 17,000; M 125; (818) 761-6594; president@tolucalakechamber.com; www.tolucalakechamber.com

Topanga • *Topanga C/C* • Dianne Porchia; Pres.; P.O. Box 185; 90290; Los Angeles; P 8,500; M 200; (310) 455-0790; admin@topangachamber.org; www.topangachamber.org

Topaz • *Northern Mono C/C* • 115281 U.S. Hwy. 395; 96133; Mono; P 1,000; M 65; (530) 208-6078; info@northernmonochamber.com; www.northernmonochamber.com

Torrance • *Torrance Area C/C* • Donna Duperron; Pres./CEO; 3400 Torrance Blvd., Ste. 100; 90503; Los Angeles; P 147,400; M 1,000; (310) 540-5858; Fax (310) 540-7662; donna@torrancechamber.com; www.torrancechamber.com*

Torrey Highlands • *see San Diego-North San Diego Bus. Chamber*

Tracy • *Tracy C/C* • Sofia Valenzuela; Pres.; 223 E. 10th St.; 95376; San Joaquin; P 82,000; M 450; (209) 835-2131; Fax (209) 833-9526; svalenzuela@tracychamber.org; www.tracychamber.org*

Trinidad • *Greater Trinidad C/C* • Ashley Mobley; Exec. Dir.; P.O. Box 356; 95570; Humboldt; P 381; M 140; (707) 677-1610; ashleymobley@trinidadcalif.com; www.trinidadcalif.com

Trinity County • *Trinity County C/C* • Patricia Zugg; Pres.; P.O. Box 517, Weaverville; 96093; Trinity; P 14,200; M 200; (530) 623-6101; (800) 4TRINITY; Fax (530) 623-3753; trinitycoc@yahoo.com; www.trinitycounty.com

Truckee • *Truckee/Donner C/C* • Lynn Saunders; Pres./CEO; 10065 Donner Pass Rd.; 96161; Nevada; P 16,000; M 600; (530) 587-2757; (530) 587-8808; Fax (530) 587-2439; info@truckee.com; www.truckee.com*

Tujunga • *Sunland-Tujunga C/C* • Cindy Cleghorn; Pres.; 8250 Foothill Blvd., Ste. A; P.O. Box 571; 91043; Los Angeles; P 43,000; M 165; (818) 352-4433; Fax (818) 353-7551; stchamber91040@gmail.com; www.stchamber.com*

Tulare • *Tulare C/C* • Kathleen Johnson; CEO; 220 E. Tulare Ave.; P.O. Box 1435; 93275; Tulare; P 50,000; M 535; (559) 686-1547; Fax (559) 686-4915; info@tularechamber.org; www.tularechamber.org*

Tulelake • *Tulelake C/C* • Dave Misso; Pres.; P.O. Box 1152; 96134; Siskiyou; P 2,000; M 55; (530) 667-3276; Fax (530) 667-3277; tule@cot.net; www.visittulelake.com

Tuolumne County • *see Sonora*

Turlock • *Turlock C/C* • Karin M. Moss; Pres./CEO; 115 S. Golden State Blvd.; 95380; Stanislaus; P 69,000; M 445; (209) 632-2221; Fax (209) 632-5289; info@turlockchamber.com; www.turlockchamber.com*

Tustin • *Tustin C/C* • Sherri Munsey; Exec. Dir.; 700 W. First St., Ste. 7; 92780; Orange; P 70,000; M 300; (714) 544-5341; Fax (714) 544-2083; info@tustinchamber.org; www.tustinchamber.org*

Twain Harte • *Twain Harte Area C/C* • Pamela Jones; Pres.; 23000 Meadow Ln.; P.O. Box 404; 95383; Tuolumne; P 2,500; M 200; (209) 586-4482; Fax (209) 586-0360; info@twainhartecc.com; www.twainhartecc.com

Twentynine Palms • *Twentynine Palms C/C* • Ursula Gilmore; Exec. Dir.; 73484 Twentynine Palms Hwy.; 92277; San Bernardino; P 32,000; M 325; (760) 367-3445; Fax (760) 367-3366; 29chamber@29chamber.org; www.29chamber.org

Ukiah • *Greater Ukiah C/C* • Willow Anderson; Exec. Dir.; 200 S. School St.; 95482; Mendocino; P 17,000; M 500; (707) 462-4705; Fax (707) 462-5059; ukiahchamber@gmail.com; www.ukiahchamber.com*

Union City • *Union City C/C* • Rey M. Sison; Exec. Dir.; 3939 Smith St.; 94587; Alameda; P 69,500; M 70; (510) 952-9637; Fax (510) 952-9647; info@unioncitychamber.com; www.unioncitychamber.com*

Universal City • *see North Hollywood*

University City • *see Del Mar-La Jolla Golden Triangle C/C*

Upland • *Upland C/C* • Sonnie Faires; Pres./CEO; 215 N. 2nd Ave., Ste. D; 91786; San Bernardino; P 74,000; M 500; (909) 204-4465; Fax (909) 204-4464; realpeople@uplandchamber.org; www.uplandchamber.org

Vacaville • *Vacaville C/C* • Becky Craig; Pres./CEO; 300 Main St., Ste. A; 95688; Solano; P 95,000; M 600; (707) 448-6424; Fax (707) 448-0424; becky@vacavillechamber.com; www.vacavillechamber.com*

Val Verde • *see Santa Clarita*

Valencia • *see Santa Clarita*

Vallejo • *Vallejo C/C* • Rich Curtola; Pres./CEO; 425-A Virginia St.; 94590; Solano; P 121,300; M 500; (707) 644-5551; info@vallejochamber.com; www.vallejochamber.com*

Valley Center • *Valley Center C/C* • Mary Gordon; Exec. Dir.; 29115 Valley Center Rd., Ste. I-3; P.O. Box 8; 92082; San Diego; P 10,000; M 175; (760) 749-8472; Fax (760) 749-8483; info@vcchamber.com; www.vcchamber.com*

Van Nuys • *Greater San Fernando Valley C/C* • Nancy Hoffman Vanyek; CEO; 7120 Hayvenhurst, Ste. 114; 91406; Los Angeles; P 1,800,000; M 400; (818) 989-0300; Fax (818) 989-3836; info@sanfernandovalleychamber.com; www.sanfernandovalleychamber.com

Venice • *Venice C/C* • Donna Lasman; Exec. Dir.; P.O. Box 202; 90294; Los Angeles; P 40,000; M 375; (310) 822-5425; info@venicechamber.net; www.venicechamber.net*

Ventura • *Ventura C/C* • Stephanie Caldwell; Pres./CEO; 505 Poli St., 2nd Flr.; 93001; Ventura; P 109,000; M 800; (805) 643-7222; Fax (805) 653-8015; info@ventura-chamber.org; www.venturachamber.com*

Verdugo City • *see Verdugo City - see Montrose*

Vernon • *Vernon C/C* • Marisa Olguin; Pres./CEO; 3801 Santa Fe Ave.; 90058; Los Angeles; P 112; M 300; (323) 583-3313; Fax (323) 583-0704; info@vernonchamber.org; www.vernonchamber.org

Victorville • *Victor Valley C/C* • Michele Spears; Pres./CEO; 14174 Green Tree Blvd., Ste. A; P.O. Box 997; 92395; San Bernardino; P 122,300; M 500; (760) 245-6506; Fax (760) 245-6505; vvchamber@vvchamber.com; vvchamber.com*

Visalia • *Visalia C/C* • Gail Zurek; Pres./CEO; 222 N. Garden St., Ste. 300; 93291; Tulare; P 130,100; M 700; (559) 734-5876; Fax (559) 734-7479; info@visaliachamber.org; www.visaliachamber.org*

Vista • *Vista C/C* • Bret Schanzenbach; CEO; 127 Main St.; 92084; San Diego; P 98,100; M 600; (760) 726-1122; Fax (760) 726-8654; info@vistachamber.org; www.vistachamber.org*

Walnut • *see Rowland Heights*

Walnut Creek • *Walnut Creek C/C & Visitors Bur.* • Jay Hoyer; Pres./CEO; 1280 Civic Dr., Ste. 100; 94596; Contra Costa; P 80,000; M 800; (925) 934-2007; Fax (925) 934-2404; chamber@walnut-creek.com; www.walnut-creek.com*

Wasco • *Wasco C/C & Ag.* • Vickie Hight; Mgr.; P.O. Box 783; 93280; Kern; P 26,000; M 130; (661) 758-2746; Fax (661) 758-2900; vhight@ci.wasco.ca.us; www.ci.wasco.ca.us

Watsonville • *Pajaro Valley C/C & Ag.* • Katie Mahan; Chrmn.; 449 Union St.; P.O. Box 1748; 95077; Santa Cruz; P 50,000; M 450; (831) 724-3900; Fax (831) 728-5300; info@pajarovalleychamber.com; www.pajarovalleychamber.com*

Weaverville • *see Trinity County*

Weed • *Weed C/C & Visitor Center* • John Diehm; Pres.; 34 Main St.; 96094; Siskiyou; P 3,000; M 117; (530) 938-4624; (877) 938-4624; Fax (530) 938-1658; weedchamber@ncen.org; www.weedchamber.com

West Covina • *see Covina*

West Hollywood • *West Hollywood C/C* • Genevieve Morrill; Pres./CEO; 8272 Santa Monica Blvd.; 90046; Los Angeles; P 35,000; M 515; (323) 650-2688; Fax (323) 650-2689; info@wehochamber.com; www.wehochamber.com

West Sacramento • *West Sacramento C/C* • Verna Sulpizio; Pres./CEO; 1401 Halyard Dr., Ste. 120; 95691; Yolo; P 50,000; M 450; (916) 371-7042; Fax (916) 371-7007; wsinfo@westsacramentochamber.com; www.westsacramentochamber.com*

Westchester • *LAX Coastal Area C/C* • Christina Davis; Pres./CEO; 9100 S. Sepulveda, Ste. 210; 90045; Los Angeles; P 50,000; M 650; (310) 645-5151; Fax (310) 645-0130; info@laxcoastal.com; www.laxcoastal.com*

Westlake Village • *Greater Conejo Valley C/C* • Jill Lederer; Pres./CEO; 600 Hampshire Rd., Ste. 200; 91361; Los Angeles & Ventura; P 150,000; M 1,350; (805) 370-0035; Fax (805) 370-1083; chamber@conejochamber.org; www.conejochamber.org*

Westley • *see Patterson*

Westwood • *Westwood Area C/C* • Gail Brown; Exec. Secy.; 462-885 Third St.; P.O. Box 1247; 96137; Lassen; P 2,200; M 50; (530) 256-2456; wacc1@citlink.net; www.westwoodareachamber.com

Wheatland • *see Yuba City*

U.S. Chambers of Commerce

Whittier • Whittier Area C/C • Carol Crosby & Lyn Carty; Exec Dirs.; 8158 Painter Ave.; 90602; Los Angeles; P 89,000; M 600; (562) 698-9554; Fax (562) 693-2700; carol@whittierchamber.com; www.whittierchamber.com*

Wildomar • Wildomar C/C • Cheri Zamora; Mbrshp. Coord.; 33751 Mission Trl.; P.O. Box 885; 92595; Riverside; P 32,000; M 220; (951) 245-0437; Fax (951) 245-0427; admin@wildomarchamber.org; www.wildomarchamber.org*

Willits • Willits C/C • Lynn Kennelly; Exec. Dir.; 299 E. Commercial St.; 95490; Mendocino; P 15,000; M 230; (707) 459-7910; Fax (707) 459-7914; info@willits.org; www.willits.org*

Willow Creek • Willow Creek C/C • Cara Bussell; Pres.; P.O. Box 704; 95573; Humboldt; P 1,500; M 115; (530) 629-2693; (800) 628-5156; info@willowcreekchamber.com; www.willowcreekchamber.com

Willows • Willows C/C • Lisa Hill; Ofc. Mgr.; 118 W. Sycamore; 95988; Glenn; P 6,200; M 152; (530) 934-8150; willowschamber@sbcglobal.net; www.willowschamber.com*

Wilmington • Wilmington C/C • Daniel Hoffman; Exec. Dir.; 544 N. Avalon Blvd., Ste. 104; P.O. Box 90; 90748; Los Angeles; P 65,200; M 220; (310) 834-8586; Fax (310) 834-8887; info@wilmington-chamber.com; www.wilmington-chamber.com

Windsor • Windsor C/C & Visitors Center • Christine Tevini; Ofc. Mgr.; 9001 Windsor Rd.; P.O. Box 367; 95492; Sonoma; P 27,000; M 250; (707) 838-7285; Fax (707) 838-2778; info@windsorchamber.com; www.windsorchamber.com*

Winnetka • Winnetka C/C • Florine Goodman; 20122 Vanowen St.; 91306; Los Angeles; P 47,900; M 51; (818) 772-4838; florinegoodman5125@sbcglobal.net; www.winnetkachamberofcommerce.com

Winters • Winters Dist. C/C • Mike Sebastian; Exec. Dir.; 11 Main St.; 95694; Yolo; P 6,900; M 120; (530) 795-2329; Fax (530) 795-3202; info@winterschamber.com; www.winterschamber.com*

Woodland • Woodland C/C • Kristy W. Wright; CEO; 400 Court St.; 95695; Yolo; P 56,000; M 505; (530) 662-7327; Fax (530) 662-4086; kristyw@woodlandchamber.org; www.woodlandchamber.org*

Woodland Hills • West Valley-Warner Center C/C • Diana Williams; CEO; P.O. Box 1; 91365; Los Angeles; P 66,000; M 780; (818) 347-4737; Fax (818) 347-3321; felicia@woodlandhillscc.net; www.woodlandhillscc.net

Wrightwood • Wrightwood C/C • Carl Smith; Pres.; P.O. Box 416; 92397; San Bernardino; P 4,500; M 93; (760) 249-4320; Fax (760) 249-6822; info@wrightwoodchamber.org; www.wrightwoodchamber.org

Yorba Linda • Yorba Linda C/C • Susan Wan-Ross; Exec. Dir.; 17670 Yorba Linda Blvd.; 92886; Orange; P 69,000; M 360; (714) 993-9537; Fax (714) 993-7764; info@yorbalindachamber.com; www.yorbalindachamber.org*

Yountville • Yountville C/C • Cindy Sauserman; Exec. Dir.; P.O. Box 2064; 94599; Napa; P 3,200; M 270; (707) 944-0904; Fax (707) 944-4465; info@yountville.com; www.yountville.com*

Yreka • Yreka C/C • Karl Greiner; Exec. Dir.; 310 S. Broadway; 96097; Siskiyou; P 7,500; M 250; (530) 842-1649; Fax (530) 842-2670; yrekachamber117@gmail.com; www.yrekachamber.com*

Yuba City • Yuba-Sutter C/C • Kristy Santucci; CEO; 1300 Franklin Rd.; 95993; Sutter & Yuba; P 160,000; M 600; (530) 743-6501; chamber@yubasutterchamber.com; www.yubasutterchamber.com*

Yucaipa • Yucaipa Valley C/C • Pamela Emenger; Pres./CEO; 35139 Yucaipa Blvd.; 92399; San Bernardino; P 52,000; M 350; (909) 790-1841; Fax (909) 363-7373; info@yucaipachamber.org; www.yucaipachamber.org

Yucca Valley • Yucca Valley C/C • Cheryl Nankervis; Exec. Dir.; 56711 29 Palms Hwy.; 92284; San Bernardino; P 20,000; M 364; (760) 365-6323; Fax (760) 365-0763; chamber@yuccavalley.org; www.yuccavalley.org*

Colorado

Colorado Assn. of Comm. & Ind. • Chuck Berry; Pres.; 1600 Broadway, Ste. 1000; Denver; 80202; Denver; P 5,187,582; M 500; (303) 831-7411; Fax (303) 860-1439; info@cochamber.com; www.cochamber.com

Akron • Akron C/C • Annette Bowin; P.O. Box 233; 80720; Washington; P 1,800; M 50; (970) 345-2624; akrontown@centurytel.net; www.co.washington.co.us

Alamosa • Alamosa County C/C & EDC • Randy Wright; Exec. Dir.; 610 State Ave.; 81101; Alamosa; P 8,500; M 145; (719) 589-3681; (719) 589-6382; Fax (719) 589-6854; office@alamosa-chamber.com; www.alamosa.org

Alma • see Fairplay

Antonito • Conejos County C/C • P.O. Box 427; 81120; Conejos; P 8,200; M 50; (719) 376-2277; Fax (719) 376-2277; info@conejoschamber.org; www.conejoschamber.org

Arrowhead • see Vail

Arvada • Arvada C/C • Kami Welch; Pres.; 7305 Grandview Ave.; 80002; Jefferson; P 108,000; M 700; (303) 424-0313; Fax (303) 424-5370; denise@arvadachamber.org; www.arvadachamber.org*

Aspen • Aspen Chamber Resort Assn. • Debbie Braun; Pres./CEO; 425 Rio Grande Pl.; 81611; Pitkin; P 6,000; M 860; (970) 925-1940; (800) 670-0792; Fax (970) 920-1173; info@aspenchamber.org; www.aspenchamber.org

Aurora • Aurora C/C • Kevin Hougen; Pres./CEO; 14305 E. Alameda Ave., Ste. 300; 80012; Adams, Arapahoe & Douglas; P 450,000; M 1,200; (303) 344-1500; kevin.hougen@aurorachamber.org; www.aurorachamber.org*

Bailey • Platte Canyon Area C/C • Pat Davis; Pres.; P.O. Box 477; 80421; Park; P 10,000; M 150; (303) 838-9080; info@bailey-colorado.org; www.bailey-colorado.org

Basalt • Basalt Area C/C • Robin Waters; Pres./CEO; The Red Caboose, 101 Midland Ave.; P.O. Box 514; 81621; Eagle; P 3,500; M 460; (970) 927-4031; Fax (970) 927-2833; info@basaltchamber.com; www.basaltchamber.com*

Bayfield • Bayfield Area C/C & Visitor Info. Center • 41746 U.S. 160; P.O. Box 7; 81122; La Plata; P 2,100; M 100; (970) 884-7372; (866) 984-7372; Fax (970) 884-7372; pam@bayfieldchamber.org; www.bayfieldchamber.org

Bayfield • Vallecito Lake C/C • 17252 County Rd. 501; 81122; La Plata; P 400; M 45; (970) 247-1573; info@vallecitolakechamber.com; www.vallecitolakechamber.com

Beaver Creek • see Vail

Bennett • *I-70 Corridor C/C* • Ronny Marshall; Chamber Dir./Secy.; 401 S. First St.; 80102; Adams; P 6,000; M 101; (303) 644-4607; admin@i70ccoc.com; www.i70ccoc.com

Berthoud • *Berthoud Area C/C* • Deanne Mulvihill; Exec. Dir.; 428 Mountain Ave.; P.O. Box 1709; 80513; Larimer; P 5,700; M 294; (970) 532-4200; Fax (970) 532-7690; deanne@berthoudcolorado.com; www.berthoudcolorado.com*

Boulder • *Boulder C/C* • John Tayer; Pres./CEO; 2440 Pearl St.; 80302; Boulder; P 99,000; M 1,700; (303) 442-1044; Fax (303) 938-8837; frontdesk@boulderchamber.com; www.boulderchamber.com*

Breckenridge • *Breckenridge Resort C/C* • John McMahon; Pres.; 111 Ski Hill Rd.; P.O. Box 1909; 80424; Summit; P 3,406; M 450; (970) 453-2913; (970) 453-6018; Fax (970) 453-7238; gobreck@gobreck.com; www.gobreck.com

Breckenridge • *also see Summit County*

Brighton • *Brighton C/C* • Kami Welch; Exec. Dir.; 22 S. 4th Ave., Ste. 205; 80601; Adams; P 35,000; M 456; (303) 659-0223; Fax (303) 655-9251; kwelch@brightonchamber.com; www.brightonchamber.com*

Broomfield • *Broomfield C/C* • Jennifer Kerr; Pres./CEO; 2095 W. 6th Ave., Ste. 109; 80020; Broomfield; P 56,000; M 500; (303) 466-1775; Fax (303) 466-4481; info@broomfieldchamber.com; www.broomfieldchamber.com

Brush • *Brush Area C/C* • Melody Christensen; Exec. Dir.; 218 Clayton St.; 80723; Morgan; P 5,465; M 166; (970) 842-2666; (800) 354-8659; Fax (970) 842-3828; brush@brushchamber.org; www.brushchamber.org*

Buena Vista • *Buena Vista Area C/C & Visitors Center* • Kathrine Perry; Exec. Dir.; 343 Hwy. 24 S.; P.O. Box 2021; 81211; Chaffee; P 6,000; M 385; (719) 395-6612; (719) 395-8035; Fax (719) 395-8035; chamber@buenavistacolorado.org; www.buenavistacolorado.org*

Burlington • *Burlington C/C* • Jenna Zimbelman; Pres.; P.O. Box 62; 80807; Kit Carson; P 4,254; M 100; (719) 346-8070; Fax (719) 346-7169; www.burlingtoncolo.com

Byers • *see Bennett*

Canon City • *Canon City C/C* • Lisa Hyams; Exec. Dir.; 403 Royal Gorge Blvd.; 81212; Fremont; P 20,000; M 408; (719) 275-2331; Fax (719) 275-2332; chamber@canoncity.com; www.canoncity.com*

Carbondale • *Carbondale C/C* • Andrea Stewart; Exec. Dir.; 520 S. 3rd St., Ste. 3; P.O. Box 1645; 81623; Garfield; P 6,553; M 480; (970) 963-1890; Fax (970) 963-4719; andrea@carbondale.com; www.carbondale.com*

Castle Rock • *Castle Rock C/C & Visitors Center* • Pamela Ridler; Pres./CEO; 420 Jerry St.; 80104; Douglas; P 61,000; M 535; (303) 688-4597; (866) 441-8508; Fax (303) 688-2688; info@castlerock.org; www.castlerock.org*

Cedaredge • *Cedaredge Area C/C* • Carol Peterson; Admin.; 245 W. Main St.; P.O. Box 278; 81413; Delta; P 5,000; M 150; (970) 856-6961; Fax (970) 856-7292; info@cedaredgechamber.com; www.cedaredgechamber.com

Centennial • *South Metro Denver Chamber* • Robert Golden; Pres./CEO; 2154 E. Commons Ave., Ste. 342; 80122; Arapahoe; P 2,500,000; M 700; (303) 795-0142; Fax (303) 795-7520; rgolden@bestchamber.com; www.bestchamber.com*

Cherry Creek • *Cherry Creek C/C* • P.O. Box 6449; Denver; 80206; Denver; P 156,378; M 240; (303) 388-6022; Fax (303) 957-2327; staff@cherrycreekchamber.org; www.cherrycreekchamber.org*

Colorado City • *Greenhorn Valley C/C* • Jeannie Medina; P.O. Box 19429; 81019; Pueblo; P 5,000; M 90; (719) 676-3000; office@greenhornchamber.org; www.greenhornchamber.org

Colorado Springs • *Colorado Springs Reg. Bus. Alliance* • Dirk D. Draper; Pres./CEO; 102 S. Tejon St., Ste. 430; 80903; El Paso; P 676,597; M 1,000; (719) 471-8183; Fax (719) 471-9733; info@csrba.com; www.csrba.com*

Colorado Springs • *Southern Colorado Women's C/C* • Linda Mojer; Exec. Dir.; P.O. Box 49218; 80949; Pueblo; P 400,000; M 150; (719) 442-2007; info@scwcc.com; www.scwcc.com

Commerce City • *see Westminster*

Como • *see Fairplay*

Conifer • *Conifer Area C/C* • Melanie Swearengin; Exec. Dir.; P.O. Box 127; 80433; Jefferson; P 22,000; M 320; (303) 838-5711; director@goconifer.com; www.goconifer.com*

Copper Mountain • *see Summit County*

Cordillera • *see Vail*

Cortez • *Cortez Area C/C* • Dena Guttridge; Exec. Dir.; 31 W. Main St.; P.O. Box 968; 81321; Montezuma; P 25,000; M 416; (970) 565-3414; info@cortezchamber.com; www.cortezchamber.com*

Cowdrey • *see Walden*

Craig • *Craig C/C* • Christina Oxley; Dir.; 360 E. Victory Way; 81625; Moffat; P 10,000; M 325; (970) 824-5689; (800) 864-4405; Fax (970) 824-0231; info@craig-chamber.com; www.craig-chamber.com*

Crawford • *Crawford Area C/C* • P.O. Box 22; 81415; Delta; P 1,000; M 75; (970) 921-4000; info@crawfordcountry.org; www.crawfordcountry.org

Creede • *Creede-Mineral County C/C* • Brad Ayers; Exec. Dir.; 904 S. Main St.; P.O. Box 580; 81130; Mineral; P 850; M 120; (719) 658-2374; (800) 327-2102; Fax (719) 658-2717; office@creede.com; www.creede.com

Crested Butte • *Crested Butte/Mt. Crested Butte C/C* • David Ochs; Exec. Dir.; 601 Elk Ave.; P.O. Box 1288; 81224; Gunnison; P 2,500; M 350; (970) 349-6438; Fax (970) 349-1023; cbinfo@cbchamber.com; www.cbchamber.com

Cripple Creek • *Cripple Creek C/C* • Michael Shoaf; Pres.; P.O. Box 650; 80813; Teller; P 1,200; M 100; (719) 689-5877; info@cripple-creek.co.us; www.cripple-creek.co.us

Dacono • *see Westminster*

Deer Trail • *see Bennett*

Delta • *Delta Area C/C* • Kami Collins; Exec. Dir.; 301 Main St.; 81416; Delta; P 10,000; M 300; (970) 874-8616; Fax (970) 874-8618; director@deltacolorado.org; www.deltacolorado.org*

Denver Area

Colorado Black C/C • Lee Kathryn Gash-Maxey; Pres.; 924 W. Colfax Ave., Ste. 104-G; 80204; Denver; P 5,100,000; M 600; (303) 831-0720; staff@coloradoblackchamber.org; www.coloradoblackchamber.org

Colorado Women's C/C • Donna Evans; Pres.; 1350 17th St., Ste. 100; 80202; Denver; P 634,265; M 450; (303) 458-0220; Fax (303) 458-0222; info@cwcc.org; www.cwcc.org

Denver Metro C/C • Ms. Kelly Brough; Pres./CEO; 1445 Market St., 4th Flr.; 80202; Denver; P 2,800,000; M 3,000; (303) 534-8500; Fax (303) 534-3200; info@denverchamber.org; www.denverchamber.org

Hispanic C/C of Metro Denver • Diedra Garcia; Pres./CEO; 924 W. Colfax Ave., Ste. 201; 80204; Denver; P 2,800,000; M 2,600; (303) 534-7783; Fax (303) 595-8977; info@hispanicchamberdenver.org; www.hispanicchamberdenver.org

---

Dillon • see Summit County

Divide • Divide C/C • Lisa Lee; Pres.; P.O. Box 101; 80814; Teller; P 4,000; M 50; (719) 686-7605; (719) 686-7587; Fax (719) 686-9176; chamber@dividechamber.org; www.dividechamber.org

Dolores • Dolores C/C & Visitor Center • Rocky Moss; Dir.; 201 Railroad Ave.; P.O. Box 602; 81323; Montezuma; P 25,000; M 150; (970) 882-4018; info@doloreschamber.com; www.doloreschamber.com

Downieville • see Idaho Springs

Dumont • see Idaho Springs

Durango • Durango C/C • Jack Llewellyn; Exec. Dir.; 111 S. Camino del Rio; P.O. Box 2587; 81302; La Plata; P 50,000; M 820; (970) 247-0312; Fax (970) 385-7884; chamber@durangobusiness.org; www.durangobusiness.org*

Eads • Eads C/C • Dennis Pearson; P.O. Box 163; 81036; Kiowa; P 800; M 30; (719) 438-5590; dennis.pearson@state.co.us; www.kiowacountycolo.com

Eagle • Eagle Valley C/C • Michelle Morgan; Pres.; 100 Fairgrounds Rd.; P.O. Box 964; 81631; Eagle; P 5,000; M 300; (970) 328-5220; Fax (970) 328-1120; info@eaglevalleychamberofcommerce.org; www.eaglevalley.org

Eagle-Vail • see Vail

Edwards • see Vail

Elizabeth • Elizabeth Area C/C • Peg Kelley; Exec. Dir.; 166 Main St., Ste. E; P.O. Box 595; 80107; Elbert; P 1,700; M 187; (303) 646-4287; Fax (303) 646-2509; director@elizabethchamber.org; www.elizabethchamber.org*

Empire • see Idaho Springs

Englewood • Greater Englewood C/C • Colleen Mello; Exec. Dir.; 3501 S. Broadway, 2nd Flr.; 80113; Arapahoe; P 31,200; M 200; (303) 789-4473; Fax (303) 789-0098; colleen@myenglewoodchamber.com; www.myenglewoodchamber.com*

Englewood • also see Centennial

Erie • Erie C/C • Elle Cabbage; Exec. Dir.; 235 Wells St.; P.O. Box 97; 80516; Boulder & Weld; P 22,000; M 310; (303) 828-3440; Fax (303) 828-3330; erie@eriechamber.org; www.eriechamber.org*

Estes Park • see CVB Section

Evans • see Greeley

Evergreen • Evergreen Area C/C & Visitor Center • Betsy Hays; Pres.; 1524 Belford Ct.; 80439; Jefferson; P 44,000; M 500; (303) 674-3412; Fax (720) 361-2994; admin@evergreenchamber.org; www.evergreenchamber.org*

Fairplay • South Park C/C • Phil Brogan; Pres.; P.O. Box 312; 80440; Park; P 4,000; M 95; (719) 836-3410; (720) 205-0178; info@southparkchamber.com; www.southparkchamber.com

Federal Heights • see Westminster

Firestone • Carbon Valley C/C • Julia K. Davis; Exec. Dir.; 8308 Colorado Blvd., Ste. 203; 80504; Weld; P 20,000; M 260; (303) 833-5933; julia@carbonvalleychamber.com; www.carbonvalleychamber.com*

Florence • Florence C/C • Keith D Larsen; Pres.; 116 N. Pikes Peak Ave.; P.O. Box 145; 81226; Fremont; P 4,000; M 130; (719) 784-3544; florencecochamber@qwestoffice.net; www.FlorenceColoradoChamber.com*

Fort Collins • Fort Collins Area C/C • David May; Pres./CEO; 225 S. Meldrum St.; P.O. Drawer D; 80521; Larimer; P 144,000; M 1,050; (970) 482-3746; Fax (970) 482-3774; general@fcchamber.org; www.fortcollinschamber.org*

Fort Lupton • Fort Lupton C/C • Rachel Monroe; Exec. Dir.; 321 Denver Ave.; 80621; Weld; P 7,750; M 110; (303) 857-4474; fortluptonchamber@gmail.com; www.fortluptonchamber.org

Fort Morgan • Fort Morgan Area C/C • Robin Northrup; 300 Main St.; 80701; Morgan; P 27,000; M 280; (970) 867-6702; (800) 354-8660; Fax (970) 867-6121; fortmorganchamber@flci.net; www.fortmorganchamber.org

Fountain • Fountain Valley C/C • Carmen Shields; 116 S. Main St.; P.O. Box 201; 80817; El Paso; P 25,000; M 140; (719) 382-3190; Fax (719) 322-9395; info@fountainvalleychamber.com; www.fountainvalleychamber.com

Fowler • Fowler C/C • Brian Blackburn; Treas.; P.O. Box 172; 81039; Otero; P 1,200; M 45; (719) 263-4461; (719) 263-4914; www.fowlercolorado.com

Fraser Valley • see Winter Park

Frederick • see Firestone

Frisco • see Summit County

Fruita • Fruita Area C/C • Frank Ladd, IOM; Executive Director; 432 E. Aspen Ave.; 81521; Mesa; P 13,000; M 370; (970) 858-3894; Fax (970) 858-3121; info@fruitachamber.org; www.fruitachamber.org*

Georgetown • see Idaho Springs

Glendale • Greater Glendale C/C • Jeff Allen; COO; 950 S. Birch St.; 80246; Arapahoe; P 5,000; M 250; (303) 584-4180; Fax (303) 584-4183; info@ggchamber.com; www.ggchamber.com*

Glenwood Springs • Glenwood Springs Chamber Resort Assn. • Marianne Virgili IOM CCE; Pres./CEO; 802 Grand Ave.; P.O. Box 1238; 81602; Garfield; P 9,200; M 500; (970) 945-6589; Fax (970) 945-1531; info@glenwoodchamber.com; www.glenwoodchamber.com*

Golden • *Golden C/C & Visitors Center* • Gary L. Wink; Pres./CEO; 1010 Washington Ave.; 80401; Jefferson; P 18,000; M 500; (303) 279-3113; (800) 590-3113; Fax (303) 279-0332; info@goldencochamber.org; www.goldencochamber.org*

Gould • *see Walden*

Granby • *Greater Granby Area C/C* • Cathie Hook; Exec. Dir.; 475 E. Agate Ave.; P.O. Box 35; 80446; Grand; P 1,800; M 185; (970) 887-2311; (800) 325-1661; Fax (970) 887-3895; visitgrcoc@gmail.com; www.granbychamber.com

Grand Junction • *Grand Junction Area C/C* • Diane Schwenke; Pres./CEO; 360 Grand Ave.; 81501; Mesa; P 156,000; M 1,000; (970) 242-3214; Fax (970) 242-3694; info@gjchamber.org; www.gjchamber.org*

Grand Lake • *Grand Lake Area C/C* • Samantha Miller; Exec. Dir.; 14700 U.S. Hwy. 40; P.O. Box 429; 80447; Grand; P 500; M 160; (970) 627-3402; (800) 531-1019; Fax (970) 627-8007; glinfo@grandlakechamber.com; www.grandlakechamber.com

Greeley • *Evans Area C/C* • Michele Jones; Exec. Dir.; 2986 W. 29th St., Ste. 9; 80631; Weld; P 20,000; M 300; (970) 330-4204; ecc@evanschamber.org; www.evanschamber.org*

Greeley • *Greeley C/C* • Sarah L. MacQuiddy; Pres.; 902 7th Ave.; 80631; Weld; P 98,000; M 640; (970) 352-3566; Fax (970) 352-3572; info@greeleychamber.com; www.greeleychamber.com*

Greenwood Village • *DTC - Greenwood Village C/C* • John C. Herbers; Pres./CEO; 7600 Landmark Way, Ste. 1615 ; 80111; Arapahoe; P 14,454; M 350; (303) 290-9922; john@gvchamber.com; dtcchamber.com

Guffey • *see Fairplay*

Gunnison • *Gunnison Country C/C* • Eric Freson; Exec. Dir.; 500 E. Tomichi Ave.; 81230; Gunnison; P 7,700; M 368; (970) 641-1501; (800) 274-7580; info@gunnisonchamber.com; www.gunnisonchamber.com*

Hartsel • *see Fairplay*

Haxtun • *Haxtun C/C* • Barb Shafer; 145 S. Colorado; P.O. Box 535; 80731; Phillips; P 943; M 48; (970) 774-6104; Fax (970) 774-5875; haxtunco@pctelcom.coop; www.haxtunchamber.com

Heeny • *see Summit County*

Highlands Ranch • *C/C of Highlands Ranch* • Andrea LaRew; Pres.; 300 W. Plaza Dr., Ste. 225; 80129; Douglas; P 95,000; M 325; (303) 791-3500; Fax (303) 791-3522; christine@highlandsranchchamber.org; www.highlandsranchchamber.org*

Holyoke • *Holyoke C/C* • Elizabeth Hutches; Exec. Dir.; 212 S. Interocean; P.O. Box 134; 80734; Phillips; P 2,200; M 125; (970) 854-3517; director@holyokechamber.org; www.holyokechamber.org

Hotchkiss • *Hotchkiss Comm. C/C* • Nathan Sponseller; Pres.; P.O. Box 158; 81419; Delta; P 4,000; M 100; (970) 872-3226; chamberinfo@hotchkisschamber.com; www.hotchkisschamber.com

Idaho Springs • *Greater Idaho Springs C/C* • Debbie Lamberti; 1630 Miner St.; P.O. Box 1641; 80452; Clear Creek; P 9,000; M 60; (303) 567-4447; Fax (303) 567-9306; info@idahospringschambercommerce.com; www.idahospringschambercommerce.com

Jefferson County • *see Lakewood*

Johnstown • *Johnstown-Milliken C/C* • Ame Warren; Exec. Dir.; P.O. Box 501; 80534; Weld; P 11,500; M 180; (970) 587-7042; Fax (970) 587-8703; info@johnstownmillikenchamber.com; www.johnstownmillikenchamber.com*

Julesburg • *Sedgwick County C/C* • Richelle Schneider; Pres.; P.O. Box 222; 80737; Sedgwick; P 2,400; M 50; (970) 520-3821; Fax (970) 474-4008; sced@kci.net; www.sedgwickcountyco.com

Keenesburg • *Keenesburg Area C/C* • Patricia Cooke; Pres.; P.O. Box 44; 80643; Weld; P 1,100; M 40; (303) 732-4009; (303) 732-0131; Fax (303) 732-0137; webmaster@keenesburgco.org; www.keenesburgco.org

Kersey • *Kersey Area C/C* • Glenn McClain; Pres.; P.O. Box 397; 80644; Weld; P 1,500; M 35; (970) 330-3099; (970) 336-8500; kerseychamberofcommerce@gmail.com; www.kerseycochamber.com

Keystone • *see Summit County*

Kremmling • *Kremmling Area C/C* • Shannon Clark; Exec. Dir.; P.O. Box 471; 80459; Grand; P 3,000; M 120; (970) 724-3472; (877) 573-6654; Fax (970) 724-0397; director@kremmlingchamber.com; www.kremmlingchamber.com

La Junta • *La Junta C/C* • Angela Alaya; Mbrshp. Mgr.; 110 Santa Fe Ave.; 81050; Otero; P 7,100; M 165; (719) 384-7411; Fax (719) 384-2217; info@lajuntachamber.com; www.lajuntachamber.com*

La Veta • *La Veta/Cuchara C/C* • P.O. Box 32; 81055; Huerfano; P 1,765; M 115; (719) 742-3676; info@lavetacucharachamber.com; www.lavetacucharachamber.com

Lafayette • *Lafayette C/C* • Vicki Trumbo; Exec. Dir.; 1290 S. Public Rd.; P.O. Box 1018; 80026; Boulder; P 28,000; M 370; (303) 666-9555; Fax (303) 666-4392; info@lafayettecolorado.com; www.lafayettecolorado.com

Lake City • *Lake City/Hinsdale County C/C & Visitor Center* • Angela Hollingsworth; Dir.; 800 N. Gunnison Ave.; P.O. Box 430; 81235; Hinsdale; P 408; M 122; (800) 569-1874; (970) 944-2527; chamber@lakecity.com; www.lakecity.com

Lake County • *see Leadville*

Lakewood • *The West Chamber* • Dan Rodriguez; Pres./CEO; 1667 Cole Blvd., Ste. 400; 80401; Jefferson; P 530,000; M 800; (303) 233-5555; Fax (303) 237-7633; info@westchamber.org; www.westchamber.org*

Lamar • *Lamar C/C* • Vickie Dykes; Pres.; 109A E. Beech St.; 81052; Prowers; P 14,000; M 220; (719) 336-4379; Fax (719) 336-4370; lamarchamberofcommerce@gmail.com; www.lamarchamber.com*

Las Animas • *Las Animas-Bent County C/C* • Russell Smith; Exec. V.P.; 332 Amb. Thompson Blvd.; 81054; Bent; P 6,500; M 135; (719) 456-0453; Fax (719) 456-0455; russellatchamber@lycos.com; www.bentcounty.org

Lawson • *see Idaho Springs*

Leadville • *Leadville/Lake County C/C* • Heather Scanlon; Exec. Dir.; 809 Harrison Ave.; P.O. Box 861; 80461; Lake; P 8,800; M 120; (719) 486-3900; (888) 532-3845; Fax (719) 486-8478; leadville@leadvilleusa.com; www.leadvilleusa.com

Limon • *Limon C/C* • Lucille Reimer; Treas.; P.O. Box 101; 80828; Lincoln; P 1,900; M 90; (719) 775-9418; Fax (719) 775-8808; limonchamber@yahoo.com; www.limonchamber.com

Littleton • *see Centennial*

U.S. Chambers of Commerce

Logan County • see Sterling

Longmont • Longmont Area C/C • Bruce R. Partain; CEO; 528 Main St.; 80501; Boulder; P 90,000; M 700; (303) 776-5295; Fax (303) 776-5657; staff@longmontchamber.org; www.longmontchamber.org*

Louisville • Louisville C/C • Shelley Angell; Exec. Dir.; 901 Main St.; 80027; Boulder; P 19,500; M 425; (303) 666-5747; Fax (303) 666-4285; info@louisvillechamber.com; www.louisvillechamber.com

Loveland • Loveland C/C • Mindy McCloughan; Pres./CEO; 5400 Stone Creek Circle; 80538; Larimer; P 77,000; M 700; (970) 667-6311; Fax (970) 667-5211; mmccloughan@loveland.org; www.loveland.org*

LOVELAND VALENTINE RE-MAILING PROGRAM AND SWEETHEART CITY ACTIVITIES, FEBRUARY 1-14; OLD FASHIONED CORN ROAST FESTIVAL, AUGUST; SCULPTURE IN THE PARK 2ND WEEKEND IN AUGUST-LARGEST SCULPTURE SHOW WEST OF THE MISSISSIPPI.

Lyons • Lyons Area C/C • Tamara Haddad; P.O. Box 426; 80540; Boulder; P 2,000; M 165; (303) 823-5215; (877) LYONS-CO; admin@lyons-colorado.com; www.lyons-colorado.com

Mancos • Mancos Valley C/C • Marie Chiarizia; Dir.; 101 E. Bauer Ave.; P.O. Box 494; 81328; Montezuma; P 1,340; M 145; (970) 533-7434; chamber@mancosvalley.com; www.mancosvalley.com

Manitou Springs • Manitou Springs C/C, Visitors Bur. & Ofc. of Eco. Dev. • Leslie Lewis; Exec. Dir.; 354 Manitou Ave.; 80829; El Paso; P 5,200; M 250; (719) 685-5089; (800) 642-2567; Fax (719) 685-0355; manitou@pikes-peak.com; www.manitousprings.org

Meeker • Meeker C/C • P.O. Box 869; 81641; Rio Blanco; P 2,500; M 220; (970) 878-5510; Fax (970) 878-0271; director@meekerchamber.com; www.meekerchamber.com*

Mesa • see Collbran

Minturn • see Vail

Molina • see Collbran

Monte Vista • Monte Vista C/C • Linda Archuleta; Mgr.; 947 1st Ave.; 81144; Rio Grande; P 12,400; M 200; (719) 852-2731; Fax (719) 852-2731; chamber@monte-vista.org; www.monte-vista.org*

Montezuma • see Summit County

Montrose • Montrose C/C • Jenni Sopsic; Exec. Dir.; 1519 E. Main St.; 81401; Montrose; P 40,000; M 475; (970) 249-5000; Fax (970) 249-2907; information@MontroseChamber.com; www.MontroseChamber.com*

Monument • Tri-Lakes C/C & Visitor Center • Terri Hayes; Pres./CEO; 166 Second St.;; 80132; El Paso; P 35,000; M 450; (719) 481-3282; Fax (719) 481-1638; terri@trilakeschamber.com; www.trilakeschamber.com*

Naturita • Nucla-Naturita Area C/C • Paula Brown; P.O. Box 425; 81422; Montrose; P 1,400; M 50; (970) 865-2350; Fax (970) 865-2350; info@nucla-naturita.com; www.nucla-naturita.com

Nederland • Nederland Area C/C • Katrina Harms; Admin. Asst.; P.O. Box 85; 80466; Boulder; P 1,500; M 130; (303) 258-3936; info@nederlandchamber.org; www.nederlandchamber.org

New Castle • New Castle C/C • JoJo Godeski; Admin. Asst.; 386 W. Main St., Ste. 101; P.O. Box 983; 81647; Garfield; P 4,800; M 75; (970) 984-2897; info@newcastlechamber.org; www.newcastlechamber.org

Northglenn • see Westminster

Norwood • Norwood C/C • John Dobson; Pres.; P.O. Box 116; 81423; San Miguel; P 1,000; M 96; (970) 327-4982; (800) 282-5988; Fax (970) 327-4709; info@norwoodcolorado.com; www.norwoodcolorado.com

Nucla • see Naturita

Ordway • Crowley County C/C • Matthew Heimerick; Pres.; P.O. Box 332; 81063; Crowley; P 5,500; M 65; (719) 267-3845; chamber@crowleycounty.net; www.crowleycountychamber.com

Ouray • Ouray Chamber Resort Assn. • 1230 Main St.; P.O. Box 145; 81427; Ouray; P 850; M 230; (970) 325-4746; (800) 228-1876; Fax (970) 325-4868; ouray@ouraycolorado.com; www.ouraycolorado.com

Pagosa Springs • Pagosa Springs Area C/C • Clint Alley; Exec. Dir.; 105 Hot Springs Blvd.; P.O. Box 787; 81147; Archuleta; P 13,000; M 555; (970) 264-2360; Fax (970) 264-4625; info@pagosachamber.com; www.pagosachamber.com*

Palisade • Palisade C/C • Juliann Adams; Exec. Dir.; 305 Main St.; P.O. Box 729; 81526; Mesa; P 7,000; M 230; (970) 464-7458; Fax (970) 464-4757; juliann@palisadecoc.org; palisadecoc.com*

Paonia • Paonia C/C • Michael Drake; Pres.; 130 Grand Ave.; P.O. Box 366; 81428; Delta; P 1,451; M 120; (970) 527-3886; naturally@paoniachamber.com; www.paoniachamber.com

Parker • Parker C/C • Dennis Houston; Pres./CEO; 19590 E. Mainstreet, Ste. 100; 80138; Douglas; P 45,000; M 360; (303) 841-4268; Fax (303) 841-8061; reception@parkerchamber.com; www.parkerchamber.com*

Penrose • Penrose C/C • Calvin Sunderman; Exec. Dir.; P.O. Box 379; 81240; Fremont; P 5,000; M 100; (719) 372-3994; Fax (719) 372-3994; secretary@penrosechamber.com; www.penrosechamber.com

Plateau City • see Collbran

Pueblo • Greater Pueblo C/C • Rod Slyhoff; Pres./CEO; 302 N. Santa Fe Ave.; 81003; Pueblo; P 160,000; M 1,000; (719) 542-1704; (800) 233-3446; Fax (719) 542-1624; phylliss@pueblochamber.net; www.pueblochamber.org*

Rand • see Walden

Rangely • Rangely Area C/C • Konnie Billgren; Exec. Dir.; 255 E. Main St., Ste. A; 81648; Rio Blanco; P 2,500; M 100; (970) 675-5290; Fax (970) 675-5290; rangelychamber@gmail.com; www.rangelychamber.com

Ridgway • Ridgway C/C • Gale Ingram; Dir.; 150 Racecourse Rd.; 81432; Ouray; P 900; M 150; (970) 626-5181; Fax (970) 626-3681; racc@ridgwaycolorado.com; www.ridgwaycolorado.com

Rifle • Rifle Area C.C • Andrea Maddalone; Pres./CEO; 100 E. 11th St.; 81650; Garfield; P 10,000; M 330; (970) 625-2085; mail@riflechamber.com; www.riflechamber.com*

Rocky Ford • Rocky Ford C/C • Deborah Graffis; Pres.; 105 N. Main St.; 81067; Otero; P 4,300; M 85; (719) 254-7483; Fax (719) 254-7483; RFCinfo@rockyfordchamber.net; www.rockyfordchamber.net

Salida • *Heart of the Rockies C/C* • Lori Roberts; Exec. Dir.; 406 W. Hwy. 50; 81201; Chaffee; P 5,500; M 450; (719) 539-2068; (877) 772-5432; Fax (719) 539-7844; lori@salidachamber.org; www.salidachamber.org*

Sheridan • *see Centennial*

Silt • *see Rifle*

Silver Plume • *see Idaho Springs*

Silverthorne • *see Summit County* • **Silverton** • *Silverton Area C/C* • DeAnne Gallegos; Exec. Dir.; 414 Greene St.; P.O. Box 565; 81433; San Juan; P 640; M 150; (970) 387-5654; (800) 752-4494; Fax (970) 387-0282; info@silvertoncolorado.com; www.silvertoncolorado.com

South Fork • *South Fork C/C* • Todd Small; Pres.; 28 Silver Thread Ln.; P.O. Box 577; 81154; Rio Grande; P 750; M 100; (719) 873-5556; (800) 571-0881; info@southforkcoloradochamber.com; www.southforkcolorado.org

South Jeffco • *see Lakewood*

Springfield • *Springfield C/C* • James Bradley; Pres.; P.O. Box 12; 81073; Baca; P 1,500; M 55; (719) 523-4528; james.bradley@southeastcolorado.net; www.springfieldco.info

Sterling • *Logan County C/C* • Kimberly Sellers; Exec. Dir.; 109 N. Front St.; P.O. Box 1683; 80751; Logan; P 23,000; M 352; (970) 522-5070; (866) 522-5070; Fax (970) 522-4082; execdir@logancountychamber.com; www.logancountychamber.com*

Strasburg • *see Bennett*

Summit County • *Summit County C/C* • Cheri Ryan; Admin.; P.O. Box 5450, Frisco; 80443; Summit; P 29,600; M 500; (970) 668-2051; info@summitchamber.org; www.summitchamber.org*

Superior • *Superior C/C* • Heather Cracraft; Exec. Dir.; 124 E. Coal Creek Dr.; 80027; Boulder; P 12,400; M 250; (303) 554-0789; Fax (303) 499-1340; info@superiorchamber.com; www.superiorchamber.com*

Trinidad • *Trinidad & Las Animas County C/C* • Linda Barron; 136 W. Main St.; 81082; Las Animas; P 15,000; M 500; (719) 846-9285; Fax (719) 846-3545; info@tlacchamber.com; www.tlacchamber.com*

Trinidad • *Trinidad-Las Animas County Hispanic C/C* • Yolanda Romero; Pres.; 1804 N. Linden Ave.; P.O. Box 17; 81082; Las Animas; P 15,000; M 150; (719) 846-8234

Vail • *Vail Chamber & Bus. Assn.* • Rich Tenbraak; Exec. Dir.; 241 S. Frontage Rd. E., Ste. 2; 81657; Eagle; P 5,000; M 200; (970) 477-0075; (877) 477-0075; Fax (970) 477-0079; info@vailchamber.org; www.vailchamber.org

Vail • *Vail Valley Partnership* • Chris Romer; Exec. Dir.; P.O. Box 1130; 81658; Eagle; P 48,000; M 700; (970) 476-1000; (800) 525-3875; Fax (970) 476-6008; info@visitvailvalley.com; www.vailvalleypartnership.com

Walden • *North Park Area C/C* • James Carothers; Secy./Treas.; 467 Main St.; P.O. Box 92; 80480; Jackson; P 1,400; M 76; (970) 723-4600; (970) 819-4821; Fax (970) 723-8272; northparkchamber@centurytel.net; www.northparkchamber.net

Watkins • *see Bennett*

Wellington • *Wellington Area C/C* • Wendell Nelson; Chair; 4006 - B Cleveland Ave.; P.O. Box 1500; 80549; Larimer; P 8,000; M 122; (970) 568-4133; wellingtonareachamber@gmail.com; wellingtoncoloradochamber.com

Westcliffe • *Custer County C/C* • Rene Smith; Co-Dir.; 110 Rosita Ave; P.O. Box 81; 81252; Custer; P 4,200; M 150; (719) 783-9163; (877) 793-3170; Fax (719) 783-2724; info@custercountyco.com; www.custercountyco.com*

Westminster • *Metro North C/C* • Angela Habben; Pres./CEO; 1870 W. 122nd Ave., Ste. 300; 80234; Adams; P 500,000; M 1,000; (303) 288-1000; Fax (303) 227-1050; info@metronorthchamber.com; www.metronorthchamber.com*

Wheat Ridge • *see Lakewood*

Windsor • *Windsor C/C* • Michal Connors; Exec. Dir.; 421 Main St.; 80550; Weld; P 19,001; M 400; (970) 686-7189; Fax (970) 686-0352; information@windsorchamber.net; www.windsorchamber.net*

Winter Park • *Winter Park-Fraser Valley C/C* • Catherine Ross; Exec. Dir.; 78841 U.S. Hwy. 40; P.O. Box 3236; 80482; Grand; P 1,500; M 400; (970) 726-4118; (800) 903-7275; Fax (970) 726-9449; visitorcenter@playwinterpark.com; www.playwinterpark.com

Wolcott • *see Vail*

Woodland Park • *Greater Woodland Park C/C* • Debbie Miller IOM ACE; Pres.; 210 E. Midland Ave.; P.O. Box 9022; 80866; Teller; P 25,000; M 450; (719) 687-9885; (800) 551-7886; Fax (719) 687-8216; info@gwpcc.biz; www.woodlandparkchamber.com*

Wray • *Wray C/C* • Keith Lippoldt; Exec. Dir.; 110 E. 3rd St.; P.O. Box 101; 80758; Yuma; P 2,300; M 115; (970) 332-3484; (970) 630-4563; Fax (970) 332-3486; director@wraychamber.net; www.wraychamber.net

Yuma • *West Yuma County C/C* • Darlene Carpio; Dir.; 14 W. Second Ave.; 80759; Yuma; P 3,500; M 145; (970) 848-2704; Fax (970) 848-5700; director@westyumachamber.com; www.westyumachamber.com

Connecticut

Connecticut Bus. & Ind. Assn. • Joseph Brennan; Pres./CEO; 350 Church St.; Hartford; 06103; Hartford; P 3,600,000; M 10,000; (860) 244-1900; Fax (860) 278-8562; joseph.brennan@cbia.com; www.cbia.com

Amesville • *see Lakeville*

Andover • *see Vernon*

Ansonia • *see Shelton*

Avon • *Avon C/C* • Lisa Bohman; Exec. Dir.; 412 W. Avon Rd.; 06001; Hartford; P 17,000; M 310; (860) 675-4832; Fax (860) 675-0469; avonchamber@sbcglobal.net; www.avonchamber.com

Barkhamsted • *see Torrington*

Beacon Falls • *see Shelton*

Berlin • *Berlin C/C* • Katherine Fuechsel; Exec. Dir.; 40 Chamberlin Hwy.; 06037; Hartford; P 18,831; M 230; (860) 829-1033; Fax (860) 829-1243; director@berlinctchamber.org; www.berlinctchamber.org*

Bethel • *Bethel C/C* • Heather Hansen O'Neill; Pres./Exec. Dir.; 184 Greenwood Ave.; 06801; Fairfield; P 18,500; M 596; (203) 743-6500; Fax (203) 743-6500; heather@bethelchamber.com; www.bethelchamber.com*

Bolton • *see Vernon*

Branford • *Shoreline CT C/C* • Edward Lazarus; Pres.; 764 E. Main St.; 06405; New Haven; P 55,000; M 650; (203) 488-5500; Fax (203) 488-5046; info@shorelinechamberct.com; www.shorelinechamberct.com*

Bridgeport • *Bridgeport Reg. Bus. Cncl.* • Paul S. Timpanelli; Pres./CEO; 10 Middle St., 14th Flr.; 06604; Fairfield; P 250,000; M 1,000; (203) 335-3800; Fax (203) 366-0105; info@brbc.org; www.brbc.org

Bristol Area

Bloomfield C/C • Crista Morrone; Exec. Dir.; 200 Main St.; 06010; Hartford; P 20,000; M 150; (860) 242-3710; Fax (860) 584-4722; director@bloomfieldchamber.org; www.bloomfieldchamber.org

Central Conn. Chambers of Commerce • Cindy Scoville; Pres./CEO; 200 Main St.; 06010; Hartford; P 150,000; M 1,500; (860) 584-4718; Fax (860) 584-4722; info@centralctchambers.org; www.centralctchambers.org

Farmington C/C • Cindy Scoville; Exec. Dir.; 200 Main St.; 06010; Hartford; P 24,658; M 300; (860) 676-8490; Fax (860) 584-4718; marketing@farmingtonchamber.com; www.farmingtonchamber.com

Brooklyn • *see Danielson*

Burlington • *see Bristol Area*

Canaan • *see Torrington*

Canton • *Canton C/C* • Phil Worley; Exec. Dir.; 101 River Rd.; P.O. Box 704; 06019; Hartford; P 9,500; M 285; (860) 693-0405; Fax (860) 693-9105; phil@cantonchamberofcommerce.com; www.cantonchamberofcommerce.com

Cheshire • *Cheshire C/C* • Sheldon Dill; Pres.; 195 S. Main St.; 06410; New Haven; P 30,000; M 340; (203) 272-2345; Fax (203) 271-3044; sheldon@cheshirechamber.org; www.cheshirechamber.org

Clinton • *Clinton C/C* • Ellen Cavanagh; Exec. Dir.; 50 E. Main St.; P.O. Box 334; 06413; Middlesex; P 13,000; M 300; (860) 669-3889; Fax (860) 669-3889; chamber@clintonct; www.clintonct.com*

Colebrook • *see Torrington*

Columbia • *see Vernon*

Cornwall • *see Torrington*

Coventry • *see Vernon*

Danbury • *Greater Danbury C/C* • Stephen Bull; Pres.; 39 West St.; 06810; Fairfield; P 190,000; M 1,000; (203) 743-5565; Fax (203) 794-1439; info@danburychamber.com; www.danburychamber.com

Danielson • *Northeastern Connecticut C/C* • Elizabeth Kuszaj; Exec. Dir.; 3 Central St., Ste. 3; 06239; Windham; P 80,000; M 600; (860) 774-8001; Fax (860) 774-4299; info@nectchamber.com; www.nectchamber.com*

Darien • *Darien C/C* • Susan Cator; Pres.; 10 Corbin Dr.; 06820; Fairfield; P 20,700; M 300; (203) 655-3600; Fax (203) 655-2074; office@darienctchamber.com; www.darienctchamber.com*

Derby • *see Shelton*

East Berlin • *see Berlin*

East Granby • *Bradley Reg. C/C* • Jared Carillo; Pres.; P.O. Box 1335; 06026; Hartford; P 17,000; M 200; (860) 653-3833; Fax (860) 653-3855; admin@bradleyregionalchamber.org; www.bradleyregionalchamber.org*

East Hartford • *East Hartford C/C* • Timothy Coppage; Pres.; 1137 Main St.; 06108; Hartford; P 50,000; M 170; (860) 289-0239; Fax (860) 289-0230; ehchamber@easthartfordchamber.com; www.easthartfordchamber.com

East Haven • *East Haven C/C* • Mary W. Cacace; Pres.; 29 High St., 2nd Flr.; P.O. Box 120055; 06512; New Haven; P 29,200; M 165; (203) 467-4305; Fax (203) 469-2299; east.haven@sbcglobal.net; www.easthavenchamber.com

East Windsor • *see Enfield*

Ellington • *see Vernon*

Enfield • *North Central Connecticut C/C* • Debra A. Boronski; Exec. Dir.; P.O. Box 123; 06083; Hartford; P 85,000; M 280; (860) 741-3838; debra@ncccc.org; www.ncccc.org*

Fairfield • *Fairfield C/C* • Beverly A. Balaz; Pres.; 1597 Post Rd.; 06824; Fairfield; P 59,400; M 940; (203) 255-1011; Fax (203) 256-9990; beverly@fairfieldctchamber.com; www.fairfieldctchamber.com*

Falls Village • *see Torrington*

Glastonbury • *Glastonbury C/C* • Mary Ellen Dombrowski; Pres.; 2400 Main St., Ste. 2; 06033; Hartford; P 34,400; M 525; (860) 659-3587; Fax (860) 659-0102; heather@glastonburychamber.com; www.glastonburychamber.com*

Goshen • *see Torrington*

Granby • *Granby C/C* • John French; Exec. Dir.; 2 Park Pl.; P.O. Box 211; 06035; Hartford; P 12,000; M 165; (860) 653-5085; Fax (860) 844-8692; gcoc@granbycoc.org; www.granbycoc.org*

Greenwich • *Greenwich C/C* • Marcia O'Kane; Pres./CEO; 45 E. Putnam Ave., Ste. 121; 06830; Fairfield; P 62,000; M 525; (203) 869-3500; Fax (203) 869-3502; greenwichchamber@greenwichchamber.com; www.greenwichchamber.com

Guilford • *Guilford C/C* • Janet Testa; Exec. Dir.; 1300 Boston Post Rd.; 06437; New Haven; P 22,000; M 300; (203) 453-9677; Fax (203) 453-6022; chamber@guilfordct.com; www.guilfordct.com

Hamden • *Hamden C/C* • Nancy Dudchik; Pres.; 2969 Whitney Ave.; 06518; New Haven; P 60,000; M 400; (203) 288-6431; Fax (203) 288-4499; hcc@hamdenchamber.com; www.hamdenchamber.com*

Hartford • *Metro Hartford Alliance* • Oz Griebel; Pres./CEO; 31 Pratt St., 5th Flr.; 06103; Hartford; P 1,200,000; M 1,000; (860) 525-4451; Fax (860) 293-2592; krouthie@metrohartford.com; www.metrohartford.com

Harwinton • *see Torrington*

Hebron • *see Vernon*

Kensington • *see Berlin*

Kent • *Kent C/C* • Laura McLaughlin; Pres.; P.O. Box 124; 06757; Litchfield; P 3,000; M 150; (860) 355-2843; (203) 770-6186; president@kentct.com; www.kentct.com

Kent • *also see Torrington*

Killingly • *see Danielson*

Lakeville • *Tri-State C/C* • Susan Dickinson; Pres.; P.O. Box 386; 06039; Litchfield; P 4,500; M 200; (860) 435-0740; sdickinson@tristatechamber.com; www.tristatechamber.com

Lime Rock • *see Lakeville*

Litchfield • *see Torrington*

Lyme • *see Old Lyme*

Madison • *Madison C/C* • Eileen Banisch; Exec. Dir.; P.O. Box 706; 06443; New Haven; P 19,000; M 350; (203) 245-7394; chamber@madisonct.com; www.madisonct.com

Manchester • *Greater Manchester C/C* • April DiFalco; Pres.; 20 Hartford Rd.; 06040; Hartford; P 58,300; M 550; (860) 646-2223; Fax (860) 646-5871; staffgmcc@manchesterchamber.com; www.manchesterchamber.com*

Mansfield • *see Vernon*

Meriden • *Midstate C/C* • Séan W. Moore; Pres.; 3 Colony St., Ste. 301; 06450; New Haven; P 61,000; M 600; (203) 235-7901; Fax (203) 686-0172; info@midstatechamber.com; www.midstatechamber.com*

Middlebury • *see Southbury*

Middletown • *Middlesex County C/C* • Larry McHugh; Pres.; 393 Main St.; 06457; Middlesex; P 165,700; M 2,250; (860) 347-6924; Fax (860) 346-1043; info@middlesexchamber.com; www.middlesexchamber.com*

Milford • *Milford C/C* • Kathleen Alagno; Pres./CEO; 5 Broad St.; P.O. Box 389; 06460; New Haven; P 54,000; M 525; (203) 878-0681; Fax (203) 876-8517; chamber@milfordct.com; www.milfordct.com*

Monroe • *Monroe C/C* • Thomas P. Colville; Pres.; 458 Monroe Tpk.; 06468; Fairfield; P 20,000; M 125; (203) 268-6518; info@monroectchamber.com; monroectchamber.com

Morris • *see Torrington*

Mystic • *Greater Mystic C/C* • Tricia Walsh; Pres.; 2 Roosevelt Ave.; P.O. Box 143; 06355; New London; P 12,000; M 750; (860) 572-9578; (866) 572-9578; Fax (860) 572-9273; hannah@mysticchamber.org; www.mysticchamber.org

Naugatuck • *Naugatuck C/C* • Courtney Ligi; Dir.; 270 Church St.; 06770; New Haven; P 30,860; M 200; (203) 729-4511; Fax (203) 729-4512; cligi@waterburychamber.com; www.naugatuckchamber.com*

New Britain • *Greater New Britain C/C* • Timothy T. Stewart; Pres.; One Court St.; 06051; Hartford; P 74,000; M 450; (860) 229-1665; Fax (860) 223-8341; tim@greaternewbritinchamber.com; www.greaternewbritainchamber.com*

New Canaan • *New Canaan C/C* • Tucker Murphy; Exec. Dir.; 91 Elm St., 2nd Flr.; 06840; Fairfield; P 20,000; M 400; (203) 966-2004; Fax (203) 966-3810; tucker@newcanaanchamber.com; www.newcanaanchamber.com

New Haven • *Greater New Haven C/C* • Anthony P. Rescigno; Pres.; 900 Chapel St., 10th Flr.; 06510; New Haven; P 500,000; M 1,400; (203) 782-4300; Fax (203) 782-4329; pdaniel@gnhcc.com; www.gnhcc.com

New London • *see Waterford*

New Milford • *Greater New Milford C/C* • Denise Del Mastro; Exec. Dir.; 11 Railroad St.; 06776; Litchfield; P 30,000; M 325; (860) 354-6080; Fax (860) 354-8526; nmcc@newmilford-chamber.com; www.newmilford-chamber.com

Newington • *Newington C/C* • Gail Whitney; Exec. Dir.; 1046 Main St.; 06111; Hartford; P 30,000; M 320; (860) 666-2089; Fax (860) 665-7551; office@newingtonchamber.com; www.newingtonchamber.com*

Newtown • *C/C of Newtown Inc.* • Renia Marini; Interim Ofc. Mgr,; 45 Main St.; P.O. Box 314; 06470; Fairfield; P 26,000; M 200; (203) 426-2695; Fax (203) 426-2695; chamber@newtown-ct.com; www.newtown-ct.com

Norfolk • *see Torrington*

North Branford • *North Branford C/C* • Joanne Wentworth; P.O. Box 229; 06471; New Haven; P 13,000; M 110; (203) 484-1988; www.northbranfordchamber.com

North Canaan • *see Torrington*

North Haven • *see Wallingford*

Norwalk • *Greater Norwalk C/C* • Edward J. Musante Jr.; Pres.; 101 East Ave.; P.O. Box 668; 06852; Fairfield; P 85,000; M 1,000; (203) 866-2521; Fax (203) 852-0583; info@norwalkchamberofcommerce.com; www.norwalkchamberofcommerce.com*

Norwich • *Greater Norwich Area C/C* • Angela R. Adams; Dir. of Op.; 114 Main St.; 06360; New London; P 80,000; M 430; (860) 887-1647; Fax (860) 887-9238; membership@norwichchamber.com; www.norwichchamber.com*

Norwich • *see Waterford*

Oakville • *see Waterbury*

Old Lyme • *Lyme & Old Lyme C/C* • Cathy Frank; Pres.; P.O. Box 4152; 06371; New London; P 10,000; M 190; (888) 302-9246; email@lolcc.com; www.visitoldlyme.com

Old Saybrook • *Old Saybrook C/C* • Judy Sullivan; Exec. Dir.; One Main St.; P.O. Box 625; 06475; Middlesex; P 10,000; M 500; (860) 388-3266; Fax (860) 388-9433; info@oldsaybrookchamber.com; www.oldsaybrookchamber.com*

Orange • *Orange C/C* • Carol Smullen; Exec. Dir.; 605A Orange Center Rd.; 06477; New Haven; P 14,000; M 270; (203) 795-3328; Fax (203) 795-5926; linda@orangectchamber.com; www.orangectchamber.com

Oxford • *see Shelton*

Plainfield • *see Danielson*

Plainville • *Plainville C/C* • Maureen Saverick; Op. Mgr.; 1 Central Sq.; P.O. Box C; 06062; Hartford; P 19,000; M 230; (860) 747-6867; Fax (860) 793-1832; plvchamber@snet.net; www.plainvillechamber.com*

Plymouth • *see Bristol Area*

Portland • *see Middletown*

Prospect • *see Naugatuck*

Putnam • *see Danielson*

Ridgefield • *Ridgefield C/C* • Marion Roth; Exec. Dir.; 9 Bailey Ave.; 06877; Fairfield; P 25,000; M 410; (203) 438-5992; Fax (203) 438-9175; sbrennan@ridgefieldchamber.org; www.ridgefieldchamber.org*

Rockville • *see Vernon*

Rocky Hill • *Rocky Hill C/C* • Christina Palmer; Exec. Dir.; 2264 Silas Deane Hwy.; 06067; Hartford; P 20,000; M 181; (860) 258-7633; Fax (860) 258-7637; execdir@rhchamber.org; www.rhchamber.org

Salisbury • *see Lakeville*

Seymour • *see Shelton*

Sharon • *see Torrington*

Shelton • *Greater Valley C/C* • William Purcell CAE CCE; Pres.; 10 Progress Dr., 2nd Flr.; 06484; Fairfield; P 100,000; M 550; (203) 925-4981; Fax (203) 925-4984; info@greatervalleychamber.com; www.greatervalleychamber.com*

Simsbury • *Simsbury C/C* • Lisa Gray; Exec. Dir.; 749 Hopmeadow St.; P.O. Box 224; 06070; Hartford; P 23,400; M 330; (860) 651-7307; Fax (860) 651-1933; info@simsburycoc.org; www.simsburycoc.org*

Somers • *see Vernon*

Somers • *see Enfield*

South Windsor • *South Windsor C/C* • Shari Fiveash; Exec. Dir.; 22 Morgan Farms Dr.; 06074; Hartford; P 26,000; M 400; (860) 644-9442; Fax (860) 648-1911; info@southwindsorchamber.org; www.southwindsorchamber.org*

Southbury • *Greater Tribury C/C* • Dr. Jack Zazzaro; Pres.; P.O. Box 807; 06488; New Haven; P 35,000; M 250; (203) 267-4466; dklim@greatertriburychamber.org; www.greatertriburychamber.org

Southington • *Greater Southington C/C* • Elizabeth Francis; Exec. Dir.; 1 Factory Sq., Ste. 201; 06489; Hartford; P 43,100; M 515; (860) 628-8036; Fax (860) 276-9696; info@southingtonchamber.com; www.southingtonchamber.com*

Stafford • *see Vernon*

Stamford • *Bus. Cncl. of Fairfield County* • Christopher Bruhl; Pres./CEO; One Landmark Sq., Ste. 300; 06901; Fairfield; P 916,800; M 430; (203) 359-3220; Fax (203) 967-8294; rwoody@businessfairfield.com; www.businessfairfield.com

Stamford • *Stamford C/C* • John P. Condlin; Pres./CEO; 733 Summer St., Ste. 104; 06901; Fairfield; P 123,000; M 1,600; (203) 359-4761; Fax (203) 363-5069; stamfordchamber@stamfordchamber.com; www.stamfordchamber.com

Stratford • *see Bridgeport*

Suffield • *Suffield C/C* • Lisa Pepe; Pres.; P.O. Box 741; 06078; Hartford; P 11,370; M 150; (860) 668-4848; Fax (860) 668-4848; collichris@gmail.com; www.suffieldchamber.com

Suthington • *see Bristol Area*

Taconic • *see Lakeville*

Tolland • *see Vernon*

Torrington • *C/C of Northwest Connecticut* • JoAnn Ryan; Pres./CEO; 333 Kennedy Dr., Ste. R101; P.O. Box 59; 06790; Litchfield; P 190,000; M 750; (860) 482-6586; Fax (860) 489-8851; info@nwctchamberofcommerce.org; www.nwctchamberofcommerce.org*

Trumbull • *see Bridgeport*

Union • *see Vernon*

Vernon • *Tolland County C/C* • Candice Corcione; Exec. Dir.; 30 Lafayette Sq.; 06066; Tolland; P 170,000; M 400; (860) 872-0587; Fax (860) 872-0588; tccc@tollandcountychamber.org; www.tollandcountychamber.org*

Wallingford • *Quinnipiac C/C* • Dee Prior Nesti; Exec. Dir.; 50 N. Main St., 2nd Flr.; 06492; New Haven; P 80,000; M 600; (203) 269-9891; Fax (203) 269-1358; dee@quinncham.com; www.quinncham.com*

Warren • *see Torrington*

Washington • *see Torrington*

Waterbury • *Waterbury Reg. Chamber* • Lynn G. Ward; Pres./CEO; 83 Bank St.; P.O. Box 1469; 06721; New Haven; P 109,000; M 1,025; (203) 757-0701; Fax (203) 756-3507; info@waterburychamber.com; www.waterburychamber.com*

Waterford • *C/C of Eastern Connecticut* • Tony Sheridan; Pres./CEO; 914 Hartford Tpk.; 06385; New London; P 293,000; M 1,700; (860) 701-9113; Fax (860) 701-9902; info@chamberect.com; www.chamberect.com*

Watertown • *see Waterbury*

West Hartford • *West Hartford C/C* • Peter Lisi; Chrmn.; 948 Farmington Ave.; 06107; Hartford; P 63,600; M 650; (860) 521-2300; Fax (860) 521-1996; mmilio@WHChamber.com; www.WHChamber.com*

West Haven • *West Haven C/C* • Adonia Dontfraid; 355 Main St., City Hall; 06516; New Haven; P 55,600; M 450; (203) 933-1500; Fax (203) 931-1940; info@westhavenchamber.com; www.westhavenchamber.com*

Weston • *see Westport*

Westport • *Westport-Weston C/C* • Matthew Mandell; Exec. Dir./Pres.; 41 Riverside Ave.; 06880; Fairfield; P 27,000; M 300; (203) 227-9234; Fax (203) 454-4019; info@westportwestonchamber.com; www.westportwestonchamber.com

Wethersfield • *Wethersfield C/C* • Melanie Goodin; Exec. Dir.; 200 Main St., P.O. Box 290186; 06129; Hartford; P 27,000; M 205; (860) 721-6200; wethersfield@sbcglobal.net; www.wethersfieldchamber.com

Willimantic • *The Chamber of Commerce Inc. [Windham Region]* • Diane Nadeau; Pres./CEO; 1010 Main St.; 06226; New London, Tolland & Windham; P 100,000; M 400; (860) 423-6389; Fax (860) 423-8235; diane@windhamchamber.com; www.windhamchamber.com*

Willington • *see Vernon*

Wilton • *Wilton C/C* • Janeen Leppert; Exec. Dir.; 86 Old Ridgefield Rd.; P.O. Box 7094; 06897; Fairfield; P 19,000; M 350; (203) 762-0567; janeen@wiltonchamber.com; www.wiltonchamber.com*

Winchester • *see Torrington*

Windsor • *Windsor C/C* • Jane M. Garibay IOM; Exec. Dir.; 261 Broad St.; P.O. Box 9; 06095; Hartford; P 28,000; M 300; (860) 688-5165; Fax (860) 688-0809; jane@windsorcc.org; www.windsorcc.org*

Windsor Locks • *see East Granby*

Winsted • *see Torrington*

Wolcott • *see Bristol Area*

Woodbury • *see Southbury*

Delaware

Delaware State C of C • A. Richard Heffron; Pres.; 1201 N. Orange St., Ste. 200; P.O. Box 671; Wilmington; 19899; New Castle; P 917,092; M 2,800; (302) 655-7221; (800) 292-9507; Fax (302) 654-0691; dscc@dscc.com; www.dscc.com*

Bethany Beach • *see Fenwick Island*

Delmar • *Greater Delmar C/C* • P.O. Box 416; 19940; Sussex; P 4,600; M 80; (302) 846-3336; infochamber@comcast.net; delmar-chamberofcommerce.com

Dewey Beach • *see Rehoboth Beach*

Dover • *Central Delaware C/C* • Judith Diogo; Pres.; 435 N. DuPont Hwy.; 19901; Kent; P 146,000; M 870; (302) 734-7513; Fax (302) 678-0189; info@cdcc.net; www.cdcc.net*

Fenwick Island • *Bethany-Fenwick Area C/C* • Kristie Maravalli; Exec. Dir.; 36913 Coastal Hwy.; 19944; Sussex; P 3,000; M 800; (302) 539-2100; (800) 962-SURF; Fax (302) 539-9434; info@bethany-fenwick.org; www.bethany-fenwick.org*

Georgetown • *Greater Georgetown C/C* • Karen S. Duffield; Exec. Dir.; 827 E. Market St.; P.O. Box 1; 19947; Sussex; P 6,500; M 430; (302) 856-1544; Fax (302) 856-1577; info@georgetowncoc.com; www.georgetowncoc.com*

Laurel • *Laurel C/C* • Connie Lewis; Ofc. Mgr.; P.O. Box 696; 19956; Sussex; P 3,900; M 126; (302) 875-9319; Fax (302) 875-5908; info@laurelchamber.com; www.laurelchamber.com

Lewes • *Lewes C/C* • Betsy Reamer; Exec. Dir.; 120 Kings Hwy.; P.O. Box 1; 19958; Sussex; P 3,000; M 450; (302) 645-8073; (877) 465-3937; Fax (302) 645-8412; inquiry@leweschamber.com; www.leweschamber.com

Middletown • *Middletown Area C/C* • Roxane Ferguson; Exec. Dir.; 402 N. Cass St.; P.O. Box 1; 19709; New Castle; P 28,000; M 525; (302) 378-7545; Fax (302) 378-6260; info@maccde.com; www.maccde.com*

Milford • *C/C for Greater Milford Inc.* • Jo Schmeiser; Exec. Dir.; 411 N. Rehoboth Blvd.; 19963; Kent & Sussex; P 16,000; M 300; (302) 422-3344; Fax (302) 422-7503; milford@milfordchamber.com; www.milfordchamber.com*

Millsboro • *Greater Millsboro C/C* • Amy Simmons; Coord.; 322 Wilson Hwy.; P.O. Box 187; 19966; Sussex; P 4,000; M 175; (302) 934-6777; Fax (302) 934-6065; info@millsborochamber.com; www.millsborochamber.com

Milton • *Milton C/C* • Georgia Dalzell; Exec. Dir.; 707 Chestnut St.; P.O. Box 61; 19968; Sussex; P 2,600; M 125; (302) 684-1101; chamber@historicmilton.com; www.historicmilton.com

New Castle • *New Castle County C/C* • Mark Kleinschmidt; Pres.; 12 Penns Way; 19720; New Castle; P 538,479; M 1,400; (302) 737-4343; (302) 294-2051; Fax (302) 322-3593; info@ncccc.com; www.ncccc.com*

Rehoboth Beach • *Rehoboth Beach-Dewey Beach C/C* • Carol Everhart; Pres./CEO; 501 Rehoboth Ave.; P.O. Box 216; 19971; Sussex; P 168,000; M 1,200; (302) 227-2233; (800) 441-1329; Fax (302) 227-8351; carol@beach-fun.com; www.beach-fun.com*

Seaford • *Greater Seaford C/C* • Lynn Brocato; Exec. Dir.; 304A High St.; P.O. Box 26; 19973; Sussex; P 24,000; M 300; (302) 629-9690; Fax (302) 629-0281; admin@seafordchamber.com; www.seafordchamber.com*

District of Columbia

No State Chamber

D.C. C/C • Harry Wingo; Pres./CEO; 506 9th St. N.W.; 20004; District of Columbia; P 618,000; M 1,700; (202) 347-7201; Fax (202) 638-6762; info@dcchamber.org; www.dcchamber.org*

National Black C/C • Harry C. Alford Jr.; Pres./CEO; 4400 Jenifer St. N.W., Ste. 331; 20015; District of Columbia; (202) 466-6888; (202) 466-4918; Fax (202) 466-4918; info@nationalbcc.org; www.nationalbcc.org

United States C/C • Thomas J. Donohue; Pres./CEO; 1615 H St. N.W.; 20062; District of Columbia; P 300,000,000; (202) 659-6000; (800) 638-6582; custsvc@uschamber.com; www.uschamber.com

United States Hispanic C/C • Javier Palomarez; Pres./CEO; 1424 K St. N.W., Ste. 401; 20005; District of Columbia; M 200; (202) 842-1212; (800) USHCC86; Fax (202) 842-3221; dkutscher@ushcc.com; www.ushcc.com

U.S. Black Chambers Inc. • Ron Busby Sr.; Pres.; 1156 15th St. N.W., Ste. 1100; 20005; District of Columbia; P 314,000,000; M 115; (202) 463-8722; Fax (202) 872-8543; info@usblackchambers.org; www.usblackchambers.org

Florida

Florida C of C • Mark A. Wilson; Pres./CEO; 136 S. Bronough St.; P.O. Box 11309; Tallahassee; 32302; Leon; P 19,893,000; M 7,000; (850) 521-1200; vplymel@flchamber.com; www.flchamber.com*

Alachua • *Alachua C/C* • Robert Page; Secy.; P.O. Box 387; 32616; Alachua; P 8,000; M 151; (386) 462-3333; Fax (386) 462-3333; info@alachua.com; www.alachua.com

Altamonte Springs • *see Heathrow*

Amelia Island • *Amelia Island-Fernandina Beach-Yulee C/C* • Regina Duncan; Pres.; 961687 Gateway Blvd., Ste. 101G; 32034; Nassau; P 60,000; M 850; (904) 261-3248; Fax (904) 261-6997; regina@aifby.com; www.islandchamber.com*

Anna Maria Island • *see Holmes Beach*

Apalachicola • *Apalachicola Bay C/C* • Anita Gregory Grove; Exec. Dir.; 122 Commerce St.; 32320; Franklin; P 3,000; M 360; (850) 653-9419; info@apalachicolabay.org; www.apalachicolabay.org

Apollo Beach • *South Shore C/C* • Melanie Morrison; Exec. Dir.; 137 Harbor Village Ln.; 33572; Hillsborough; P 35,000; M 380; (813) 645-1366; Fax (813) 645-2099; accounts@southshorechamberofcommerce.org; www.southshorechamberofcommerce.org*

Apopka • *Apopka Area C/C* • Laura Heiselman; Pres.; 180 E. Main St.; 32703; Orange; P 45,000; M 475; (407) 886-1441; Fax (407) 886-1131; michelle@apopkachamber.org; www.apopkachamber.org*

Arcadia • *DeSoto County C/C* • Debbie Snyder; 16 S. Volusia Ave.; 34266; DeSoto; P 36,000; M 340; (863) 494-4033; Fax (863) 494-3312; chamber@desotochamberfl.com

Astor • *Astor Area C/C* • 23835 State Rd., Ste. A; P.O. Box 329; 32102; Lake & Volusia; P 2,000; M 75; (352) 759-2679; (352) 205-2581; Fax (352) 759-2679; info@astorchamber.com; www.astorareachamber.com

Auburndale • *Auburndale C/C* • Joy Pruitt; Exec. Dir.; 245 E. Lake Ave.; 33823; Polk; P 13,000; M 300; (863) 967-3400; Fax (863) 967-0880; auburndalechamber@live.com; myauburndalechamber.com

Avon Park • *Avon Park C/C* • Laura Wade; Exec. Dir.; 28 E. Main St.; 33825; Highlands; P 20,000; M 320; (863) 453-3350; avonparkchamberofcommerce@gmail.com; www.avonparkchamberofcommerce.com

Bartow • *Greater Bartow C/C* • Jeff Clark; Exec. Dir.; 510 N. Broadway Ave.; 33830; Polk; P 16,043; M 700; (863) 533-7125; Fax (863) 533-3793; virginia@bartowchamber.com; www.bartowchamber.com*

Bay Harbor Islands • *Florida Gold Coast C/C* • Peter Cohn; 9550 Bay Harbor Terr., Ste. 210; 33154; Miami-Dade; P 45,000; M 200; (305) 866-6020; Fax (305) 866-0635; www.bayharborislands.org

Bayonet Point • *see New Port Richey*

Belle Glade • *Belle Glade C/C* • Brenda Bunting; Exec. Dir.; 540 S. Main St.; 33430; Palm Beach; P 20,000; M 260; (561) 996-2745; Fax (561) 996-2252; bgchamber@aol.com; www.belleglade chamber.com

Belleair Beach • *see Saint Pete Beach*

Belleair Bluffs • *see Saint Pete Beach*

Belleair Shores • *see Saint Pete Beach*

Belleview • *Belleview-South Marion C/C* • Mariah Moody; Exec. Dir.; 5331 S.E. Abshier Blvd.; 34420; Marion; P 4,500; M 200; (352) 245-2178; Fax (352) 245-2178; belleviewchamber@gmail.com; www.belleviewsouthmarionchamber.org

Beverly Beach • *see Palm Coast*

Big Pine Key • *Lower Keys C/C* • Carole Stevens; Exec. Dir.; 31020 Overseas Hwy.; P.O. Box 430511; 33043; Monroe; P 16,000; M 225; (305) 872-2411; (800) 872-3722; Fax (305) 872-0752; officeassist@lowerkeyschamber.com; www.lowerkeyschamber.com

Blountstown • *Calhoun County C/C* • Kristy Terry; Exec. Dir.; 20816 Central Ave. E., Ste. 2; 32424; Calhoun; P 14,600; M 150; (850) 674-4519; Fax (850) 674-4962; chamber@calhounco.org; www.calhounco.org

Boca Grande • *Boca Grande Area C/C* • Lew Hastings; Exec. Dir.; 480 E. Railroad Ave.; P.O. Box 704; 33921; Lee; P 1,000; M 275; (941) 964-0568; Fax (941) 964-0620; info@bocagrandechamber.com; www.bocagrandechamber.com

Boca Raton • *Greater Boca Raton C/C* • Troy M. McLellan; Pres./CEO; 1800 N. Dixie Hwy.; 33432; Palm Beach; P 225,000; M 1,500; (561) 395-4433; Fax (561) 392-3780; info@bocaratonchamber.com; www.bocaratonchamber.com*

Bonifay • *Holmes County C/C* • Julia Bullington; Coord.; 106 E. Byrd Ave.; 32425; Holmes; P 19,900; M 129; (850) 547-4682; (850) 547-6155; Fax (850) 547-4206; juliabullington@gmail.com; www.holmescountyonline.com

Bonita Springs • *Bonita Springs Area C/C* • Tiffany Esposito; Pres./CEO; 25071 Chamber of Commerce Dr.; 34135; Lee; P 45,000; M 900; (239) 992-2943; Fax (239) 992-5011; info@bonitaspringschamber.com; www.bonitaspringschamber.com*

Boynton Beach • *Greater Boynton Beach C/C* • Jonathan Porges; Pres./CEO; 1880 N. Congress Ave., Ste. 214; 33426; Palm Beach; P 155,000; M 500; (561) 732-9501; Fax (561) 734-4304; jonathan@boyntonbeach.org; www.boyntonbeach.org*

Bradenton • *Manatee C/C* • Robert P. Bartz; Pres.; 222 10th St. W.; 4215 Concept Ct., Lakewood Ranch, 34211; 34205; Manatee; P 350,000; M 2,110; (941) 748-3411; Fax (941) 745-1877; info@manateechamber.com; www.manateechamber.com*

Brandon • *Greater Brandon C/C* • Christine Michaels; Exec. Dir.; 330 Pauls Dr., Ste. 100; 33511; Hillsborough; P 260,000; M 1,000; (813) 689-1221; Fax (813) 689-9440; info@brandonchamber.com; www.brandonchamber.com*

Bristol • *Liberty County C/C* • Michael Wright; Pres.; P.O. Box 523; 32321; Liberty; P 8,000; M 50; (850) 643-2359; Fax (850) 643-3334; info01@libertycountyflorida.com; www.libertycountyflorida.com

Brooksville • *Greater Hernando County C/C* • Patricia Crowley; Pres./CEO; 15588 Aviation Loop Dr.; 34604; Hernando; P 180,000; M 950; (352) 796-0697; Fax (352) 796-3704; info@hernandochamber.com; www.hernandochamber.com*

Bunnell • *see Palm Coast*

Bushnell • *see Lake Panasoffkee*

Callahan • *Greater Nassau County C/C* • Jana Sheffield; Exec. Dir.; P.O. Box 98; 32011; Nassau; P 56,843; M 200; (904) 879-1441; Fax (904) 879-4033; info@greaternassaucounty.com; www.greaternassaucounty.com*

Cape Canaveral • *see Cocoa Beach*

Cape Coral • *Chamber of Commerce of Cape Coral* • Donna Germain; Pres.; 2051 Cape Coral Pkwy. E.; P.O. Box 100747; 33904; Lee; P 165,000; M 750; (239) 549-6900; (800) 226-9609; Fax (239) 549-9609; info@capecoralchamber.com; www.capecoralchamber.com*

Cape Haze • *see Englewood*

Captiva Islands • *see Sanibel*

Carrabelle • *Carrabelle Area C/C* • Lisa Munson; Exec. Dir.; 105 St. James Ave.; P.O. Box DD; 32322; Franklin; P 1,300; M 120; (850) 697-2585; Fax (850) 697-4206; chamber@nettally.com; www.carrabelle.org

Casselberry • *Casselberry C/C* • Joan Kelly-Williamson; Pres.; P.O. Box 181130; 32718; Seminole; P 25,000; M 132; (407) 831-1231; Fax (407) 830-1781; casselberrychamber@gmail.com; www.casselberrychamber.com*

Cedar Key • *Cedar Key C/C* • Leslie Valen; Gen. Mgr.; 450 2nd St.; P.O. Box 610; 32625; Levy; P 800; M 170; (352) 543-5600; Fax (352) 543-5300; info@cedarkey.org; www.cedarkey.org

Celebration • *Greater Celebration C/C* • Alfred Valentino; Exec. Dir.; Sycamore 610, Ste. 110; P.O. Box 470593; 34747; P 11,000; M 100; (321) 285-9248; office@greatercelebrationchamber.com; www.greatercelebrationchamber.com

Center Hill • *see Lake Panasoffkee*

Century • *Century Area C/C* • Donald Ripley; Pres.; P.O. Box 857; 32535; Escambia; P 1,800; M 54; (850) 256-3155; Fax (850) 256-3155; centuryc@att.net

Chiefland • *Greater Chiefland Area C/C* • 23 S.E. 2nd Ave.; P.O. Box 1397; 32644; Levy; P 32,500; M 120; (352) 493-1849; Fax (352) 493-0282; info@chieflandchamber.com; www.chieflandchamber.com

Chipley • *Washington County C/C* • Ted Everett; Exec. Dir.; 672 5th St.; P.O. Box 457; 32428; Washington; P 29,000; M 300; (850) 638-4157; Fax (850) 638-8770; chris@washcomall.com; www.washcomall.com*

Chokoloskee • *see Everglades City*

Clay County • *see Orange Park*

Clearwater • *Clearwater Reg. C/C* • Bob Clifford; Pres./CEO; 401 Cleveland St.; 33755; Pinellas; P 125,000; M 1,100; (727) 461-0011; Fax (727) 449-2889; info@clearwaterflorida.org; www.clearwaterflorida.org*

Clearwater Beach • *Clearwater Beach C/C* • Darlene Kole; Pres./CEO; 333C S. Gulfview Blvd.; P.O. Box 3573; 33767; Pinellas; P 50,000; M 220; (727) 447-7600; (888) 799-3199; Fax (727) 443-7812; office@beachchamber.com; www.beachchamber.com*

Clermont • *South Lake C/C* • David Colby; Pres.; 620 W. Montrose St.; 34711; Lake; P 30,000; M 800; (352) 394-4191; Fax (352) 394-5799; office@southlakechamber-fl.com; www.southlakechamber-fl.com*

Clewiston • *Clewiston C/C* • Hillary M. Hyslope; Exec. Dir.; 109 Central Ave.; 33440; Hendry; P 7,100; M 350; (863) 983-7979; Fax (863) 983-7108; clewistonchamber@embarqmail.com; www.clewiston.org

Cocoa Beach • *Cocoa Beach Reg. C/C* • Linda Webster; CEO; 400 Fortenberry Rd.; Merritt Island; 32952; Brevard; P 250,000; M 1,500; (321) 459-2200; Fax (321) 459-2232; receptionist@cocoabeachchamber.com; www.cocoabeachchamber.com*

Coconut Grove • *Coconut Grove C/C* • Peter Laird; Pres.; 2889 McFarlane Rd.; 33133; Miami-Dade; P 20,000; M 275; (305) 444-7270; Fax (305) 444-2498; info@coconutgrove.com; www.coconutgrovechamber.com

Coleman • *see Lake Panasoffkee*

Cooper City • *see Davie*

Coral Gables • *Coral Gables C/C* • Mark Trowbridge; Pres./CEO; 224 Catalonia Ave.; 33134; Miami-Dade; P 43,000; M 1,500; (305) 446-1657; Fax (305) 446-9900; info@coralgableschamber.org; www.coralgableschamber.org*

Coral Springs • *Coral Springs C/C* • Cindy Brief; Pres.; 11805 Heron Bay Blvd.; 33076; Broward; P 126,500; M 500; (954) 752-4242; Fax (954) 827-0543; info@cschamber.com; www.cschamber.com*

Crawfordville • *Wakulla County C/C* • Petra Shuff; Ofc. Admin.; 23 High Dr.; P.O. Box 598; 32326; Wakulla; P 32,000; M 276; (850) 926-1848; Fax (850) 926-2050; info@wakullacountychamber.com; www.wakullacountychamber.com

Crescent City • *see Palatka*

Crestview • *Crestview Area C/C* • Wayne Harris; Exec. Dir.; 1447 Commerce Dr.; 32539; Okaloosa; P 75,000; M 600; (850) 682-3212; Fax (850) 682-7413; info@crestviewchamber.com; www.crestviewchamber.com*

Cross City • *Dixie County C/C* • Angie Bush; Secy.; P.O. Box 547; 32628; Dixie; P 18,000; M 108; (352) 498-5454; Fax (352) 498-7549; dixiechamber@usa.net; www.dixiechamber.com

Crystal River • *Citrus County C/C* • Josh Wooten; Pres./CEO; 915 N. Suncoast Blvd.; 34429; Citrus; P 140,000; M 1,000; (352) 795-3149; (352) 795-2187; Fax (352) 795-1921; reception@citruscountychamber.com; www.citruscountychamber.com*

Dade City • *Greater Dade City C/C* • Cliff Martin; Pres.; 14112 8th St.; 33525; Pasco; P 17,500; M 400; (352) 567-3769; Fax (352) 567-3770; info@dadecitychamber.org; www.dadecitychamber.org*

Dania Beach • *Greater Dania Beach C/C* • Randie Shane; Exec. Dir.; 102 W. Dania Beach Blvd.; 33004; Broward; P 30,000; M 207; (954) 926-2323; Fax (954) 926-2384; info@daniabeachchamber.org; www.daniabeachchamber.org*

Davenport • *see Haines City*

Davie • *Davie-Cooper City C/C* • Alice Harrington; Pres.; 4185 Davie Rd.; 33314; Broward; P 90,000; M 500; (954) 581-0790; Fax (954) 581-9684; dcch@davie-coopercity.org; www.davie-coopercity.org*

Daytona Beach • *Daytona Reg. C/C* • Nancy Keefer; Pres./CEO; 126 E. Orange Ave.; P.O. Box 2676; 32115; Volusia; P 68,000; M 1,200; (386) 255-0981; (800) 854-1234; Fax (386) 258-5104; info@daytonachamber.com; www.daytonachamber.com*

Daytona Beach Shores • *see Port Orange*

DeBary • *see DeLand*

Deerfield Beach • *Greater Deerfield Beach C/C* • Larry DeVille; Exec. Dir.; 1601 E. Hillsboro Blvd.; 33441; Broward; P 78,000; M 320; (954) 427-1050; Fax (954) 427-1056; director@deerfieldchamber.com; www.deerfieldchamber.com*

DeLand • *DeLand Area C/C* • Sally Updike; Interim Exec. Dir.; 120 S. Florida Ave., 2nd Flr.; 32720; Volusia; P 27,100; M 700; (386) 734-4331; Fax (386) 734-4333; contact@delandchamber.org; www.delandchamber.org*

Delray Beach • *Greater Delray Beach C/C* • Karen Granger; Pres./CEO; 140 N.E. 1st St.; 33444; Palm Beach; P 95,000; M 950; (561) 278-0424; Fax (561) 278-0555; chamber@delraybeach.com; www.delraybeach.com*

Deltona • *see DeLand*

Destin • *Destin Area C/C* • Shane Moody; Pres./CEO; 4484 Legendary Dr., Ste. A; 32541; Okaloosa; P 12,350; M 950; (850) 837-6241; Fax (850) 654-5612; mail@destinchamber.com; www.destinchamber.com*

Dover • *see Seffner*

Dundee • *Dundee Area C/C* • Lisa-Marie Brewer; Exec. Dir.; 310 E. Main St.; P.O. Box 241; 33838; Polk; P 3,500; M 200; (863) 439-3261; dundeechamber@hotmail.com; www.dundeechamberflorida.org

Dunedin • *Dunedin C/C* • Lynn Wargo; Pres./CEO; 301 Main St.; 34698; Pinellas; P 37,000; M 400; (727) 733-3197; Fax (727) 734-8942; chamber@dunedinfl.com; www.dunedinfl.com

Dunnellon • *Dunnellon Area C/C* • Beverly Leisure; Exec. Dir.; 20500 E. Pennsylvania Ave.; 34432; Marion; P 65,000; M 250; (352) 489-2320; Fax (352) 489-6846; dunnellonchamber@bellsouth.net; www.dunnellonchamber.org*

Edgewater • *see New Smyrna Beach*

Englewood • *Englewood Florida C/C* • Ed Hill; Exec. Dir.; 601 S. Indiana Ave.; 34223; Charlotte; P 54,000; M 550; (941) 474-5511; (800) 603-7198; Fax (941) 475-9257; business@englewoodchamber.com; www.englewoodchamber.com*

Estero • *Estero C/C* • Grace Fortuna; Exec. Dir.; P.O. Box 588; 33929; Lee; P 20,000; M 250; (239) 948-7990; Fax (239) 948-5072; info@esterochamber.com; www.esterochamber.com

Eustis • *Lake Eustis Area C/C* • Christie Bobbitt; Exec. Dir.; 1520 S. Bay St.; 32726; Lake; P 19,000; M 371; (352) 357-3434; Fax (352) 357-1392; info@eustischamber.org; www.eustischamber.org*

Everglades City • *Everglades Area C/C* • Kathryn Linder; Mgr.; 32016 Tamiami Trl. E.; P.O. Box 130; 34139; Collier; P 600; M 150; (239) 695-3941; (800) 914-6355; Fax (239) 695-2512; evergladeschamber@gmail.com; www.evergladeschamber.net

Fernandina Beach • *see Amelia Island*

Flagler Beach • *see Palm Coast*

Florida City • *see Homestead*

Fort Lauderdale • *Greater Fort Lauderdale C/C* • Dan Lindblade CAE; Pres./CEO; 512 N.E. Third Ave.; 33301; Broward; P 173,000; M 1,400; (954) 462-6000; Fax (954) 527-8766; info@ftlchamber.com; www.ftlchamber.com*

Fort Meade • *Fort Meade C/C* • Bill & Suzie Whitener; Co-Dir.; 214 W. Broadway, Ste. B; P.O. Box 91; 33841; Polk; P 5,800; M 100; (863) 285-8253; (863) 559-3318; Fax (863) 285-6968; fortmeadechamber@gmail.com; www.fortmeadechamber.iconosites.com*

Fort Myers Area

Chamber of Southwest Florida • David Miller; Exec. Dir.; 5237 Summerlin Commons Blvd., Ste. 114; 33907; Lee; P 700,000; M 125; (239) 275-2102; Fax (239) 275-2103; dave@chamberswfl.com; www.chamberswfl.com*

Greater Fort Myers C/C • Colleen DePasquale; Exec. Dir.; 2310 Edwards Dr.; P.O. Box 9289; 33902; Lee; P 618,754; M 1,000; (239) 332-3624; (800) 366-3622; Fax (239) 332-7276; fortmyers@fortmyers.org; www.fortmyers.org*

Southwest Florida Hispanic C/C • Veronica Culbertson; Pres./CEO; 1400 Colonial Blvd., Ste. 250; 33907; Lee; P 579,453; M 400; (239) 418-1441; Fax (239) 418-1475; info@hispanicchamberflorida.org; www.hispanicchamberflorida.org*

Fort Myers Beach • *Greater Fort Myers Beach C/C* • Fran (Bud) Nocera; Pres.; 1661 Estero Blvd., Ste. 8; 33931; Lee; P 6,700; M 432; (239) 454-7500; Fax (239) 454-7910; frontdesk@fmbchamber.com; www.fortmyersbeachchamber.org*

Fort Pierce • *St. Lucie County C/C* • Terissa Aronson; Pres./CEO; 2937 W. Midway Rd.; 34981; St. Lucie; P 283,900; M 800; (772) 595-9999; Fax (772) 595-9990; taronson@stluciechamber.org; www.stluciechamber.org*

Fort Walton Beach • *Greater Fort Walton Beach C/C* • Ted Corcoran; Pres./CEO; 34 Miracle Strip Pkwy. S.E.; P.O. Box 640; 32549; Okaloosa; P 125,000; M 1,945; (850) 244-8191; Fax (850) 244-1935; info@fwbchamber.org; www.fwbchamber.com*

Frostproof • *Frostproof Area C/C* • 15 E. Wall St.; P.O. Box 968; 33843; Polk; P 3,000; M 162; (863) 635-9112; Fax (863) 635-7222; info@frostproofchamber.com; www.frostproofchamber.com

Gainesville • *Gainesville Area C/C* • Susan Davenport; Pres./CEO; 300 E. University Ave., Ste. 100; 32601; Alachua; P 250,730; M 1,352; (352) 334-7100; Fax (352) 334-7141; info@gainesvillechamber.com; www.gainesvillechamber.com*

Goldenrod • *Goldenrod Area C/C* • Darlene Dangel; Exec. Dir.; 4755 Palmetto Ave.; P.O. Box 61; 32733; Orange; P 15,000; M 250; (407) 677-5980; Fax (407) 677-4928; director@goldenrodchamber.com; www.goldenrodchamber.com*

Green Cove Springs • *see Orange Park*

Groveland • *see Clermont*

Gulf Breeze • *Gulf Breeze Area C/C* • Kristen Loera; Pres./CEO; 409 Gulf Breeze Pkwy.; 32561; Santa Rosa; P 30,000; M 400; (850) 932-7888; Fax (850) 934-4601; ceo@gulfbreezechamber.com; www.gulfbreezechamber.com*

Haines City • *Haines City Area C/C* • Betsy Cleveland; Exec. Dir.; 35610 Hwy. 27; P.O. Box 986; 33845; Polk; P 32,000; M 385; (863) 422-3751; Fax (863) 422-4704; info@hainescitychamber.com; www.hainescitychamber.com*

Hallandale Beach • *Hallandale Beach Area C/C* • Norma Jules; CEO/Exec. Dir.; 400 S. Federal Hwy., Ste. 192; 33009; Broward; P 49,000; M 250; (954) 454-0541; Fax (866) 454 8399; info@hallandalebeachchamber.com; www.hallandalebeachchamber.com*

Harmony • *see Saint Cloud*

Hawthorne • *Hawthorne Area C/C* • Donna Boles; Pres.; 6800 S.E. U.S. Hwy. 301; P.O. Box 125; 32640; Alachua; P 2,500; M 65; (352) 363-5125; (352) 481-3534; Fax (352) 481-0839; hawthornechamber@hotmail.com; www.hawthorneareachamber.org

Heathrow • *Seminole County Reg. C/C* • Jason Brodeur; Pres.; 1055 AAA Dr., Ste. 153; 32746; Seminole; P 375,000; M 1,000; (407) 333-4748; Fax (407) 708-4615; info@seminolebusiness.org; www.seminolebusiness.org*

Hernando County • *see Brooksville*

Hialeah • *Hialeah C of C & Ind. [Latin C/C]* • Vivian Casals-Munoz; Exec. Dir.; 240 E. 1st Ave., Ste. 217; 33010; Miami-Dade; P 230,000; M 450; (305) 888-7780; Fax (305) 888-7804; info@hialeahchamber.org; www.hialeahchamber.org

High Springs • *High Springs C/C* • Wanda Kemp; Ofc. Coord.; 25 Railroad Ave.; P.O. Box 863; 32655; Alachua; P 5,350; M 130; (386) 454-3120; Fax (386) 454-5848; chamber@highsprings.com; www.highsprings.com

Hobe Sound • *Hobe Sound C/C* • Angela Hoffman; Exec. Dir.; 11954 S.E. Dixie Hwy.; P.O. Box 1507; 33475; Martin; P 22,000; M 425; (772) 546-4724; Fax (772) 546-9969; info@hobesound.org; www.hobesound.org*

Holiday • *see New Port Richey*

Holly Hill • *Holly Hill C/C* • Rose Schuhmacher; Exec. Dir.; 1066 Ridgewood Ave.; 32117; Volusia; P 15,000; M 300; (386) 255-7311; Fax (386) 267-0485; office@hollyhillchamber.com; www.hollyhillchamber.com*

Hollywood • *Greater Hollywood C/C* • Anne T. Hotte; Exec. Dir./CEO; 330 N. Federal Hwy.; 33020; Broward; P 139,000; M 900; (954) 923-4000; (800) 231-5562; Fax (954) 923-8737; information@hollywoodchamber.org; www.hollywoodchamber.org*

Holmes Beach • *Anna Maria Island C/C* • Deborah Wing; Pres.; 5313 Gulf Dr. N.; 34217; Manatee; P 8,500; M 600; (941) 778-1541; Fax (941) 778-9679; info@amichamber.org; www.amichamber.org

Homestead • *South Dade C/C •* Rosa Brito; Pres.; 455 N. Flagler Ave.; P.O. Box 901544; 33090; Miami-Dade; P 65,000; M 450; (305) 247-2332; info@chamberinaction.com; www.southdadechamber.org*

Homosassa Springs • *see Inverness*

Hudson • *see New Port Richey*

Immokalee • *Immokalee C/C •* Daniel Rosario; Exec. Dir.; 1390 N. 15th St.; 34142; Collier; P 30,000; M 200; (239) 657-3237; Fax (239) 657-5450; ecoc@comcast.net; www.immokaleechamber.com

Indialantic • *see Melbourne*

Indian Harbour Beach • *see Melbourne*

Indian Rocks Beach • *see Saint Pete Beach*

Indian Shores • *see Saint Pete Beach*

Indiantown • *Indiantown-Western Martin County C/C •* Allon R. Fish; Pres./CEO; 15935 S.W. Warfield Blvd.; P.O. Box 602; 34956; Martin; P 10,000; M 185; (772) 597-2184; Fax (772) 597-6063; itowncc@onearrow.net; www.indiantownfl.org

Inglis • *Withlacoochee Gulf Area C/C •* 167 Hwy. 40 W.; P.O. Box 427; 34449; Levy; P 2,100; M 45; (352) 447-3383; info@gmail.com; www.inglisyankeetown.org*

Inverness • *Citrus County C/C •* Josh Wooten; Pres./CEO; 106 W. Main St.; 34450; Citrus; P 140,000; M 1,100; (352) 726-2801; Fax (352) 637-6498; heather@citruscountychamber.com; www.citruscountychamber.com*

Islamorada • *Islamorada C/C •* Judy Hull; Exec. Dir.; 83224 Overseas Hwy.; P.O. Box 915; 33036; Monroe; P 8,000; M 500; (305) 664-4503; (800) 322-5397; Fax (305) 664-4289; director@islamoradachamber.com; www.islamoradachamber.com*

Jacksonville • *JAX Chamber •* Daniel Davis; Pres./CEO; 3 Independent Dr.; 32202; Duval; P 1,314,061; M 3,000; (904) 366-6600; Fax (904) 632-0617; info@myjaxchamber.com; www.myjaxchamber.com

Jacksonville Beach • *JAX Chamber - Beaches Div. •* John Bryan; Dir.; 1300 Marsh Landing Pkwy., Ste. 108; 32250; Duval; P 71,000; M 448; (904) 273-5366; Fax (904) 273-9361; beaches@myjaxchamber.com; www.myjaxchamber.com

Jasper • *Hamilton County C/C •* Monica Amerson; Admin. Asst.; 1153 U.S. Hwy 41 N.W., Ste. 9; P.O. Box 366; 32052; Hamilton; P 14,800; M 107; (386) 792-1300; Fax (386) 792-1300; hamcoc@windstream.net; www.hamiltoncountycoc.org

Jensen Beach • *Jensen Beach C/C •* Ronald Rose; Exec. Dir.; 1900 Ricou Terrace; P.O. Box 1536; 34958; Martin; P 12,000; M 500; (772) 334-3444; Fax (772) 334-0817; info@jensenbeachchamber.biz; www.jensenbeachchamber.biz*

Juno Beach • *see Palm Beach Gardens*

Jupiter • *see Palm Beach Gardens*

Jupiter Inlet Colony • *see Palm Beach Gardens*

Keaton Beach • *see Perry*

Kendall • *see South Miami*

Kennedy Space Center • *see Cocoa Beach*

Key Biscayne • *Key Biscayne C/C & Visitors Center •* Tatyana Chiocchetti; Exec. Dir.; 88 W. McIntyre St., Ste. 100; 33149; Miami-Dade; P 13,000; M 350; (305) 361-5207; Fax (305) 361-9411; info@keybiscaynechamber.org; www.keybiscaynechamber.org

Key Colony Beach • *Key Colony Beach Comm. Assn. •* Gail Cortelyou; Pres.; P.O. Box 510884; 33051; Monroe; P 2,500; M 500; (305) 289-1212; (305) 394-2480; gecortelyou@bellsouth.net; kcbca.org

Key Largo • *Key Largo C/C •* Lacey Ekberg; Exec. Dir.; 106000 Overseas Hwy.; 33037; Monroe; P 14,000; M 441; (305) 451-1414; (800) 822-1088; Fax (305) 451-4726; president@keylargochamber.org; www.keylargochamber.org*

Key West • *Key West C/C •* Virginia A. Panico; Exec. V.P.; 510 Greene St., 1st Flr.; 33040; Monroe; P 22,364; M 535; (305) 294-2587; (800) LAST-KEY; Fax (305) 294-7806; info@keywestchamber.org; www.keywestchamber.org

Keystone Heights • *see Starke*

Kissimmee • *Kissimmee/Osceola County C/C •* John Newstreet; Pres./CEO; 1425 E. Vine St.; 34744; Osceola; P 267,529; M 1,200; (407) 847-3174; Fax (407) 870-8607; info@kissimmeechamber.com; www.kissimmeechamber.com*

LaBelle • *Greater LaBelle C/C •* Joe Timm; Pres.; 125 E. Hickpochee Ave.; P.O. Box 456; 33975; Hendry; P 12,000; M 250; (863) 675-0125; Fax (863) 675-6160; lchamberofcomm@embarqmail.com; www.labellechamber.com

Lady Lake • *Lady Lake Area C/C •* Peggy Hayes; Exec. Dir.; 106 S. Hwy. 27/441; P.O. Box 1430; 32158; Lake; P 13,000; M 240; (352) 753-6029; Fax (352) 753-8029; info@ladylakechamber.com; www.ladylakechamber.com*

Lake Alfred • *Lake Alfred C/C •* Fran Beach; Exec. Dir.; 115 E. Pomelo St.; P.O. Box 956; 33850; Polk; P 4,000; M 181; (863) 875-7800; Fax (863) 875-7800; lachamber@lake-alfred.com; www.lake-alfred.com

Lake Butler • *see Starke*

Lake City • *Lake City-Columbia County C/C •* Dennille Decker; Exec. Dir.; 162 S. Marion Ave.; 32025; Columbia; P 70,354; M 678; (386) 752-3690; Fax (386) 755-7744; dennille@lakecitychamber.com; www.lakecitychamber.com*

Lake Mary • *see Heathrow*

Lake Panasoffkee • *Sumter County C/C •* Jessica Kelly; Chamber Admin.; 2031 County Rd. 470; P.O. Box 100 (Sumterville, FL 33585); 33538; Sumter; P 114,000; M 400; (352) 793-3099; Fax (352) 793-2120; sumter-coc@sumterchamber.org; www.sumterchamber.org*

Lake Park • *see Palm Beach Gardens*

Lake Placid • *Greater Lake Placid C/C •* Eileen M. May; Exec. Dir.; 18 N. Oak Ave.; 33852; Highlands; P 100,000; M 400; (863) 465-4331; Fax (863) 465-2588; chamber@lpfla.com; www.visitlakeplacidflorida.com*

Lake Wales • *Lake Wales Area C/C & EDC •* Kevin Kieft; Exec. Dir.; 340 W. Central Ave.; P.O. Box 191; 33859; Polk; P 40,000; M 400; (863) 676-3445; Fax (863) 676-3446; info@lakewaleschamber.com; www.lakewaleschamber.com*

Lake Worth • *Central Palm Beach County C/C •* Wayne Burns; CEO; 501 Lake Ave.; 33460; Palm Beach; P 400,000; M 1,200; (561) 582-4401; (800) 790-2364; Fax (561) 547-8300; amy@cpbchamber.com; www.cpbchamber.com*

Lake Worth • *Florida State Hispanic C/C* • Luana Goncalves; Program Mgr.; 8461 Lake Worth Rd., Ste. 210; 33467; Palm Beach; P 18,300,000; M 345,000; (561) 790-7501; Fax (480) 247-4578; luana@fshcc.com; www.fshcc.com

Lakeland • *Lakeland Area C/C* • Kathleen L. Munson; Pres.; 35 Lake Morton Dr.; P.O. Box 3607; 33802; Polk; P 237,000; M 1,700; (863) 688-8551; Fax (863) 683-7454; awiggins@lakelandchamber.com; www.lakelandchamber.com*

Land O'Lakes • *Central Pasco C/C* • 2810 Land O'Lakes Blvd.; P.O. Box 98; 34639; Pasco; P 40,000; M 620; (813) 909-2722; Fax (813) 909-0827; office@centralpascochamber.com; www.centralpascochamber.com*

Lantana • *Greater Lantana C/C* • Lynn M. Smith; Exec. Dir.; 212 Iris Ave.; 33462; Palm Beach; P 9,500; M 185; (561) 585-8664; Fax (561) 585-0644; lynn@lantanachamber.com; www.lantanachamber.com*

Largo • *Central Pinellas C/C* • Tom Morrissette; Pres.; 801 W. Bay Dr., Ste. 602; 33770; Pinellas; P 100,000; M 550; (727) 584-2321; Fax (727) 586-3112; info@centralchamber.biz; www.centralchamber.biz*

Lauderdale-By-The-Sea • *Lauderdale-By-The-Sea C/C* • Courtney Stanford; Pres.; 4201 Ocean Dr.; 33308; Broward; P 7,000; M 296; (954) 776-1000; Fax (954) 769-1560; info@lbts.com; www.lbts.com

Leesburg • *Leesburg Area C/C* • Sandi Moore; Exec. Dir.; 103 S. 6th St.; P.O. Box 490309; 34749; Lake; P 20,000; M 500; (352) 787-2131; Fax (352) 787-3985; sandi@leesburgchamber.com; www.leesburgchamber.com*

Lehigh Acres • *Greater Lehigh Acres C/C* • Inke Baker; Pres./CEO; 25 Homestead Rd. N., Ste. 41; P.O. Box 757; 33970; Lee; P 86,000; M 300; (239) 369-3322; Fax (239) 368-0500; info@lehighchamber.org; www.lehighacreschamber.org*

Live Oak • *Suwannee County C/C* • Jimmy Norris; Exec. Dir.; 212 N. Ohio Ave.; P.O. Drawer C; 32064; Suwannee; P 41,500; M 375; (386) 362-3071; Fax (386) 362-4758; staff@suwanneechamber.com; www.suwanneechamber.com

Longboat Key • *Longboat Key C/C* • Tom Aposporos; Pres.; 5570 Gulf of Mexico Dr.; 34228; Manatee; P 8,000; M 425; (941) 383-2466; Fax (941) 383-8217; info@longboatkeychamber.com; www.longboatkeychamber.com*

Loxahatchee • *Central Palm Beach County C/C* • Wayne Burns; CEO; 13901 Southern Blvd.; P.O. Box 1062; 33470; Palm Beach; P 400,000; M 1,200; (561) 790-6200; (800) 790-2364; Fax (561) 791-2069; amy@cpbchamber.com; www.cpbchamber.com*

Macclenny • *Baker County C/C* • Darryl Register; Exec. Dir.; 20 E. Macclenny Ave.; 32063; Baker; P 27,000; M 200; (904) 259-6433; Fax (904) 259-2737; dregister@bakerchamberfl.com; www.bakerchamberfl.com

Madeira Beach • *see Saint Pete Beach*

Madison • *Madison County C/C & Tourism* • P.O. Box 817; 32341; Madison; P 19,300; M 204; (850) 973-2788; Fax (850) 973-8864; chamber@madisonfl.org; www.madisonfl.org

Maitland • *Maitland Area C/C* • Jeff Aames; Exec. Dir.; 110 N. Maitland Ave.; 32751; Orange; P 17,600; M 180; (407) 644-0741; Fax (407) 539-2529; jeff@maitlandchamber.com; www.maitlandchamber.com*

Malabar • *see Palm Bay*

Mango • *see Seffner*

Mangonia Park • *see Palm Beach Gardens*

Marathon • *Greater Marathon C/C & Visitor Center* • Daniel Samess; CEO; 12222 Overseas Hwy.; 33050; Monroe; P 10,000; M 435; (305) 743-5417; (800) 262-7284; Fax (305) 289-0183; info@floridakeysmarathon.com; www.floridakeysmarathon.com*

Marco Island • *Marco Island Area C/C* • Sandi Riedemann-Lazarus; Exec. Dir.; 1102 N. Collier Blvd.; 34145; Collier; P 17,000; M 611; (239) 394-7549; (888) 330-1422; sandi@marcoislandchamber.org; www.marcoislandchamber.org*

Marianna • *Jackson County C/C* • Art Kimbrough; Pres.; 4318 Lafayette St.; P.O. Box 130; 32447; Jackson; P 50,000; M 400; (850) 482-8060; (850) 482-8061; Fax (850) 482-8002; info@jacksoncounty.com; www.jacksoncounty.com*

Marineland • *see Palm Coast*

Marion Oaks • *see Belleview*

Mascotte • *see Clermont*

Matlacha • *Greater Pine Island C/C* • Jennifer Jennings; Exec. Dir.; 3640 S.W. Pine Island Rd.; P.O. Box 325; 33993; Lee; P 15,000; M 300; (239) 283-0888; (239) 283-4842; Fax (239) 558-5647; info@pineislandchamber.org; www.pineislandchamber.org*

Mayo • *Lafayette County C/C* • Alton Scott; Pres.; P.O. Box 364; 32066; Lafayette; P 8,000; M 68; (386) 294-2705; Fax (386) 294-2445; lafayettechamber62@windstream.net; www.lafayettecountychamber.com

Melbourne • *Melbourne Reg. Chamber* • Christian D. Malesic MBA CAE IOM; Pres./CEO; 1005 E. Strawbridge Ave.; 32901; Brevard; P 500,000; M 1,200; (321) 724-5400; Fax (321) 725-2093; Christian@MelbourneRegionalChamber.com; www.MelbourneRegionalChamber.com*

Melbourne Beach • *see Melbourne*

Melbourne Village • *see Melbourne*

Merritt Island • *see Cocoa Beach*

Miami • *Greater Miami C/C* • Barry E. Johnson; Pres./CEO; 1601 Biscayne Blvd.; Ballroom Level; 33132; Miami-Dade; P 2,600,000; M 5,500; (305) 350-7700; Fax (305) 374-6902; info@miamichamber.com; www.miamichamber.com

Miami • *Miami-Dade C/C* • Gordon Eric Knowles; Pres./CEO; 100 S. Biscayne Blvd., Ste. 300; 33131; Miami-Dade; P 2,000,000; M 500; (305) 751-8648; Fax (305) 758-3839; mdc@m-dcc.org; www.m-dcc.org

Miami Beach • *Miami Beach C/C* • Jerry Libbin; Pres./CEO; 1920 Meridian Ave.; 33139; Miami-Dade; P 90,000; M 1,200; (305) 674-1300; Fax (305) 538-4336; info@miamibeachchamber.com; www.miamibeachchamber.com*

Miami Gardens • *North Dade Reg. C/C* • Joel Ransford; CEO; 1300 N.W. 167th St., Ste. 2; 33169; Dade; P 2,500,000; M 2,223; (305) 690-9123; Fax (305) 620-3002; susan@thechamber.cc; www.thechamber.cc

Miami Shores • *Greater Miami Shores C/C* • Jesse Walters; Exec. Dir.; 9701 N.E. 2nd Ave.; 33138; Miami-Dade; P 10,000; M 275; (305) 754-5466; Fax (305) 759-8872; jessewalters@miamishores.com; www.miamishores.com

Middleburg • *see Orange Park*

Milton • *Santa Rosa County C/C* • Donna Tucker; Exec. Dir.; 5247 Stewart St.; 32570; Santa Rosa; P 148,000; M 650; (850) 623-2339; membership@srcchamber.com; www.srcchamber.com*

Minneola • *see Clermont*

Miramar • *see Pembroke Pines*

Monticello • *Monticello-Jefferson County C/C* • Katrina Richardson; Exec. Dir.; 420 W. Washington St.; 32344; Jefferson; P 14,500; M 200; (850) 997-5552; Fax (850) 997-1020; info@monticellojeffersonfl.com; www.monticellojeffersonfl.com

Montverde • *see Clermont*

Mount Dora • *Mount Dora Area C/C* • Rob English; Pres.; 341 Alexander St.; P.O. Box 196; 32756; Lake; P 11,290; M 600; (352) 383-2165; Fax (352) 383-1668; chamber@mountdora.com; www.mountdora.com*

Mulberry • *Greater Mulberry C/C* • Monica DiNicolantonio; Exec. Dir.; 400 N. Church Ave.; P.O. Box 254; 33860; Polk; P 3,250; M 160; (863) 425-4414; Fax (863) 425-3837; chamber@mulberrychamber.org; www.mulberrychamber.org

Naples • *Greater Naples C/C* • Dudley Goodlette; Chrmn.; 2390 Tamiami Trl. N., Ste. 210; 34103; Collier; P 341,000; M 2,178; (239) 298-7932; Fax (239) 262-8374; lorilou@napleschamber.org; www.napleschamber.org*

Navarre • *Navarre Beach Area C/C* • Judy Morehead; Pres./CEO; 8543 Navarre Pkwy.; 32566; Santa Rosa; P 35,000; M 634; (850) 939-3267; Fax (850) 939-0085; exec@navarrechamber.com; www.navarrechamber.com*

New Port Richey • *West Pasco C/C* • Henry Wichmanowski; Pres.; 5443 Main St.; 34652; Pasco; P 476,000; M 936; (727) 842-7651; Fax (727) 848-0202; chamber@westpasco.com; www.westpasco.com*

New Smyrna Beach • *Southeast Volusia C/C* • Samantha Bishop; Exec. V.P.; 115 Canal St.; 32168; Volusia; P 45,000; M 601; (386) 428-2449; Fax (386) 423-3512; sevinfo@sevchamber.com; www.sevchamber.com*

Newberry • *Newberry-Jonesville C/C* • Blake Fletcher; Pres.; 25527 W. Newberry Rd.; P.O. Box 495; 32669; Alachua; P 5,000; M 110; (352) 472-6611; info@newberryjonesvillechamber.com; www.newberryjonesvillechamber.com*

Niceville • *Niceville Valparaiso C/C* • Tricia Brunson; Pres./CEO; 1055 E. John Sims Pkwy.; 32578; Okaloosa; P 35,000; M 650; (850) 678-2323; Fax (850) 678-2602; info@nicevillechamber.com; www.nicevillechamber.com*

North Fort Myers • *North Fort Myers C/C* • Christopher Jackson; Exec. Dir.; 2787 N. Tamiami Trl., Ste. 10; 33903; Lee; P 43,000; M 200; (239) 997-9111; Fax (239) 997-4026; info@nfmchamber.org; www.nfmchamber.org

North Miami • *Greater North Miami C/C* • Barry Vogel; Exec. Dir.; 13100 W. Dixie Hwy.; 33161; Miami-Dade; P 65,000; M 425; (305) 891-7811; info@northmiamichamber.com; www.northmiamichamber.com*

North Miami Beach • *Greater North Miami Beach C/C* • Zully Gonzalez; Exec. Dir.; 16901 N.E. 19th Ave.; 33162; Miami-Dade; P 43,000; M 500; (305) 944-8500; Fax (305) 944-8191; chamber@nmbchamber.com; www.nmbchamber.com*

North Palm Beach • *see Palm Beach Gardens*

North Port • *North Port Area C/C* • William Gunnin; Exec. Dir.; 15141 Tamiami Trl.; 34287; Sarasota; P 60,000; M 520; (941) 564-3040; Fax (941) 423-5042; info@northportareachamber.com; www.northportareachamber.com

North Redington Beach • *see Saint Pete Beach*

Oak Hill • *see New Smyrna Beach*

Oakland • *see Winter Garden*

Ocala • *Ocala/Marion County Chamber & Eco. Partnership* • Kevin T. Sheilley; Pres./CEO; 310 S.E. 3rd St.; 34471; Marion; P 335,000; M 1,400; (352) 629-8051; Fax (352) 629-7651; info@OcalaCEP.com; www.OcalaCEP.com*

Ochopee • *see Everglades City*

Ocoee • *see Winter Garden*

Okeechobee • *C/C of Okeechobee County* • Antoinette Rodriguez; Exec. Dir.; 55 S. Parrott Ave.; 34972; Okeechobee; P 37,481; M 350; (863) 763-6464; Fax (863) 763-3467; antoinette@okeechobeebusiness.com; www.okeechobeebusiness.com

Oklawaha • *Lake Weir C/C* • Richard Lillie; Pres.; 13125 S.E. Hwy. C-25; 32179; Marion; P 13,000; M 130; (352) 288-3751; Fax (352) 288-3980; lakeweirchamcom@juno.com; www.searchmelakeweir.com

Oldsmar • *Upper Tampa Bay C/C* • Jerry Peruzzi; Pres./CEO; 101 State St. W.; 34677; Hillsborough & Pinellas; P 14,000; M 500; (813) 855-4233; Fax (813) 854-1237; jperuzzi@utbchamber.com; www.utbchamber.com*

Opa Locka • *see Miami Gardens*

Orange City • *see DeLand*

Orange Park • *Clay County C/C* • Doug Conkey; Pres.; 1734 Kingsley Ave.; 32073; Clay; P 190,000; M 800; (904) 264-2651; Fax (904) 264-0070; kcollins@claychamber.com; www.claychamber.com*

Orlando • *Orlando Reg. C/C* • Jacob V. Stuart; Pres.; 75 S. Ivanhoe Blvd.; P.O. Box 1234; 32802; Orange; P 1,851,872; M 6,000; (407) 425-1234; Fax (407) 835-2500; info@orlando.org; www.orlando.org*

Orlando • *East Orlando C/C* • Nancy Hoehn; Mbrshp. Dir.; 3259 Progress Dr., Ste. 112; 32826; Orange; P 230,000; M 350; (407) 277-5951; Fax (407) 381-1720; eocc@eocc.org; www.eocc.org*

Ormond Beach • *Ormond Beach C/C* • Debbie Cotton; Pres./CEO; 165 W. Granada Blvd.; 32174; Volusia; P 38,000; M 870; (386) 677-3454; Fax (386) 677-4363; info@ormondchamber.com; www.ormondchamber.com*

Oviedo • *Oviedo-Winter Springs Reg. C/C* • Cory Skeates; Pres./CEO; 1511 E. State Rd. 434, Ste. 2001; P.O. Box 621236; 32762; Seminole; P 75,000; M 625; (407) 365-6500; Fax (407) 650-2712; staff@oviedowintersprings.org; www.oviedowintersprings.org*

Pahokee • *Pahokee C/C* • Regina Bohlen; Exec. Dir.; 115 E. Main St.; 33476; Palm Beach; P 7,000; M 200; (561) 924-5579; Fax (561) 924-5579; pahokeechamber@att.net; www.pahokee.com

Palatka • *Putnam County C/C* • Dana Jones; Pres.; 1100 Reid St.; 32177; Putnam; P 73,000; M 600; (386) 328-1503; Fax (386) 328-7076; chamber@pcccfl.org; www.putnamcountychamber.com

Palm Bay • *Greater Palm Bay C/C* • Victoria Northrup; Pres./CEO; 4100 Dixie Hwy. N.E.; 32905; Brevard; P 103,000; M 400; (321) 951-9998; (800) 276-9130; Fax (321) 473-8904; info@greaterpalmbaychamber.com; www.greaterpalmbaychamber.com*

Palm Beach • *Palm Beach C/C* • Laurel Baker; Exec. Dir.; 400 Royal Palm Way, Ste. 106; 33480; Palm Beach; P 10,500; M 550; (561) 655-3282; Fax (561) 655-7191; info@palmbeachchamber.com; www.palmbeachchamber.com*

Palm Beach Gardens • *Northern Palm Beach County C/C* • Beth Kigel; Pres./CEO; 5520 PGA Blvd., Ste. 200; 33418; Palm Beach; P 140,000; M 1,500; (561) 746-7111; Fax (561) 366-2396; info@npbchamber.com; www.npbchamber.com*

Palm Beach Shores/Singer Island • *see Palm Beach Gardens*

Palm City • *Palm City C/C* • Carolyn Davi; Exec. Dir.; 880 S.W. Martin Downs Blvd.; 34990; Martin; P 24,000; M 556; (772) 286-8121; (772) 214-4284; Fax (772) 286-3331; info@palmcitychamber.com; www.palmcitychamber.com*

Palm Coast • *Flagler County C/C* • Rebecca DeLorenzo; Pres.; 20 Airport Rd., Ste. C; 32164; Flagler; P 91,000; M 850; (386) 437-0106; (800) 881-1022; Fax (386) 437-5700; info@flaglerchamber.org; www.flaglerchamber.org*

Palm Harbor • *Greater Palm Harbor Area C/C* • Connie Davis; Pres./CEO; 1151 Nebraska Ave.; 34683; Pinellas; P 65,000; M 400; (727) 784-4287; Fax (727) 786-2336; phcc@palmharborcc.org; www.palmharborcc.org*

Palm Shores • *see Melbourne*

Palmetto Bay • *Palmetto Bay Office of the Chamber South* • Mary Scott Russell; Pres.; 900 Perrine Ave.; 33157; Miami-Dade; P 300,000; M 1,500; (305) 661-1621; Fax (305) 666-0508; info@chambersouth.com; www.chambersouth.com

Panama City • *Bay County C/C* • Carol Roberts; Pres./CEO; 235 W. 5th St.; 32401; Bay; P 169,854; M 1,011; (850) 785-5206; Fax (850) 763-6229; information@baychamberfl.com; www.panamacity.org*

Panama City Beach • *Panama City Beach C/C* • Lance Allison; Pres./CEO; 309 Richard Jackson Blvd., Ste. 101; 32407; Bay; P 105,000; M 875; (850) 235-1159; Fax (850) 235-2301; chamber@pcbeach.org; www.pcbeach.org*

Patrick Air Force Base • *see Cocoa Beach and Melbourne*

Paxton • *see Florala, AL*

Pembroke Pines • *Miramar-Pembroke Pines Reg. C/C* • Robert Goltz IOM; Pres./CEO; 9001-B Pembroke Rd.; 33025; Broward; P 247,000; M 620; (954) 432-9808; Fax (954) 432-9193; robert@miramarpembrokepines.org; www.miramarpembrokepines.org*

Pensacola • *Greater Pensacola Chamber* • Clay Ingram; Pres./CEO; 117 W. Garden St.; 32502; Escambia; P 550,000; M 1,300; (850) 438-4081; Fax (850) 438-6369; news@pensacolachamber.com; www.pensacolachamber.com*

Pensacola Beach • *Pensacola Beach C of C* • Nicole Stacey; Pres./CEO; 735 Pensacola Beach Blvd.; 32561; Escambia; P 153,000; M 200; (850) 932-1500; Fax (850) 932-1551; info@visitpensacolabeach.com; www.pensacolabeachchamber.com

Perdido Key • *Perdido Key Area C/C* • Tina Morrison; Dir.; 15500 Perdido Key Dr.; Pensacola; 32507; Escambia; P 50,000; M 300; (850) 492-4660; (850) 485-5624; Fax (850) 492-2932; director@perdidochamber.com; www.perdidochamber.com*

Perry • *Perry-Taylor County C/C* • Dawn Taylor; Pres./Exec. Dir.; 428 N. Jefferson St.; P.O. Box 892; 32348; Taylor; P 23,000; M 365; (850) 584-5366; Fax (850) 584-8030; taylorchamber@fairpoint.net; www.taylorcountychamber.com

CHAMBER SERVING THE TAYLOR COUNTY AREA WHICH INCLUDES STEINHATCHEE, KEATON BEACH, SALEM AND SHADY GROVE.

Pinellas Park • *Pinellas Park/Gateway C/C* • Jon Farris; Pres.; 5851 Park Blvd.; 33781; Pinellas; P 62,000; M 600; (727) 544-4777; Fax (727) 209-0837; office@pinellasparkchamber.com; www.pinellasparkchamber.com*

Plant City • *Greater Plant City C/C* • Christine Miller; Pres.; 106 N. Evers St.; P.O. Box CC; 33564; Hillsborough; P 37,000; M 680; (813) 754-3707; Fax (813) 752-8793; info@plantcity.org; www.plantcity.org*

Plantation • *Greater Plantation C/C* • Siobhan Edwards; Pres.; 7401 N.W. 4th St.; 33317; Broward; P 89,000; M 500; (954) 587-1410; Fax (954) 587-1886; info@plantationchamber.org; www.plantationchamber.org*

Pompano Beach • *Greater Pompano Beach C/C* • Ric Green; Pres./CEO; 2200 E. Atlantic Blvd.; 33062; Broward; P 85,000; M 650; (954) 941-2940; (888) 939-5711; Fax (954) 785-8358; info@pompanobeachchamber.com; www.pompanobeachchamber.com*

Ponte Vedra Beach • *Ponte Vedra Beach C/C & Visitor Center* • Sandy Kavanaugh; Dir.; 200 Solana Rd., Ste. B; 32082; St. Johns; P 200,000; M 1,100; (904) 285-2004; Fax (904) 285-8488; sandra.kavanaugh@sjcchamber.com; www.sjcchamber.com*

Port Charlotte • *Charlotte County C/C* • Julie Mathis; Exec. Dir.; 2702 Tamiami Trl.; 33952; Charlotte; P 162,000; M 1,100; (941) 627-2222; Fax (941) 627-9730; askus@charlottecountychamber.org; www.charlottecountychamber.org*

Port Orange • *Port Orange-South Daytona C/C* • Debbie Connors; Exec. Dir.; 3431 Ridgewood Ave.; 32129; Volusia; P 62,000; M 700; (386) 761-1601; Fax (386) 788-9165; info@pschamber.com; www.pschamber.com*

Port Richey • *see New Port Richey*

Port Saint Joe • *Gulf County C/C* • Roni Coppock; Exec. Dir.; 308 Reid Ave.; P.O. Box 964; 32456; Gulf; P 15,500; M 300; (850) 227-1223; (800) 239-9553; Fax (850) 227-9684; info@gulfchamber.org; www.gulfchamber.org

Punta Gorda • *Charlotte County C/C* • Julie Mathis; Exec. Dir.; 311 W. Retta Esplanade; 33950; Charlotte; P 162,000; M 1,100; (941) 639-2222; Fax (941) 639-6330; askus@charlottecountychamber.org; www.charlottecountychamber.org*

Quincy • *Gadsden County C/C* • David Gardner; Exec. Dir.; 208 N. Adams St.; P.O. Box 389; 32353; Gadsden; P 47,000; M 200; (850) 627-9231; Fax (850) 875-3299; gadsdencc@tds.net; www.gadsdencc.com

Redington Beach • *see Saint Pete Beach*

Redington Shores • *see Saint Pete Beach*

Ridge Manor • *see Brooksville*

Riverview • *Greater Riverview C/C* • Tanya Doran; Exec. Dir.; 10012 Water Works Ln.; 33578; Hillsborough; P 60,000; M 550; (813) 234-5944; Fax (813) 234-5945; info@riverviewchamber.com; www.riverviewchamber.com*

Riviera Beach • *see Palm Beach Gardens*

Rockledge • *see Cocoa Beach*

Royal Palm Beach • *see Loxahatchee*

Ruskin • *see Apollo Beach*

Safety Harbor • *Safety Harbor C/C* • Marie Padovich; 200 Main St.; 34695; Pinellas; P 18,000; M 250; (727) 726-2890; Fax (727) 726-2733; info@safetyharborchamber.com; www.safetyharborchamber.com*

Saint Augustine • *St. Johns County C/C* • Isabelle Rodriguez; Pres.; 1 Riberia St.; 32084; St. Johns; P 200,000; M 1,100; (904) 829-5681; Fax (904) 829-6477; isabelle.rodriguez@sjcchamber.com; www.sjcchamber.com*

Saint Cloud • *St. Cloud/Greater Osceola C/C* • Kari Whaley; Pres./CEO; 1200 New York Ave.; 34769; Osceola; P 45,000; M 600; (407) 892-3671; Fax (407) 892-5289; info@stcloudflchamber.com; www.stcloudflchamber.com*

Saint Pete Beach • *Tampa Bay Beaches C/C* • Robin A. Sollie; Pres./CEO; 6990 Gulf Blvd.; 33706; Pinellas; P 40,000; M 700; (727) 360-6957; Fax (727) 360-2233; info@tampabaybeaches.com; www.tampabaybeaches.com*

Sand Key • *see Saint Pete Beach*

Sanford • *Sanford Reg. C/C* • Frank S. Hale; Pres./CEO; 400 E. First St.; 32771; Seminole; P 58,000; M 2,900; (407) 322-2212; Fax (407) 322-8160; info@sanfordchamber.com; www.sanfordchamber.com*

Sanibel • *Sanibel & Captiva Islands C/C* • Ric Base; Pres.; 1159 Causeway Rd.; 33957; Lee; P 10,000; M 600; (239) 472-1080; Fax (239) 395-0783; services@sanibel-captiva.org; www.sanibel-captiva.org*

Santa Rosa Beach • *Walton Area C/C* • Kellie Jo Kilberg; Pres./CEO; 63 S. Centre Trl.; 32459; Walton; P 58,000; M 860; (850) 267-0683; Fax (850) 267-0603; kelliejo@waltonareachamber.com; www.waltonareachamber.com*

Santa Rosa Beach • *Walton Area C/C* • Kitty Whitney; Pres./CEO; 63 S. Centre Trl.; 32459; Walton; P 46,000; M 1,251; (850) 267-0683; Fax (850) 267-0603; info@waltonareachamber.com; www.waltonareachamber.com*

Santa Rosa County • *see Milton*

Sarasota • *Greater Sarasota C/C* • Stephen Queior; Pres.; 1945 Fruitville Rd.; 34236; Sarasota; P 500,000; M 1,640; (941) 955-8187; Fax (941) 366-5621; frontdesk@sarasotachamber.com; www.sarasotachamber.com*

Satellite Beach • *see Melbourne*

Sebastian • *Sebastian River Area C/C* • Beth Mitchell; Exec. Dir.; 700 Main St.; 32958; Indian River; P 23,000; M 450; (772) 589-5969; Fax (772) 589-5993; info@sebastianchamber.com; www.sebastianchamber.com*

Sebring • *Greater Sebring C/C* • Liz Barber; Pres./CEO; 227 U.S. Hwy. 27 N.; 33870; Highlands; P 100,000; M 700; (863) 385-8448; Fax (863) 385-8810; information@sebring.org; www.sebring.org*

Seffner • *Greater Seffner Area C/C* • Pat Magruder; Pres.; P.O. Box 1920; 33583; Hillsborough; P 10,000; M 158; (813) 627-8686; info@seffnerchamber.com; www.seffnerchamber.com

Seminole • *Greater Seminole Area C/C* • Roger Edelman; Pres.; 7985 113th St. N., Ste. 208; 33772; Pinellas; P 19,000; M 300; (727) 392-3245; Fax (727) 392-7753; rogere@myseminolechamber.com; www.seminolechamber.net

Seminole County • *see Heathrow*

Siesta Key • *Siesta Key C/C* • Shawna Frank; Interim Exec. Dir.; 5114 Ocean Blvd.; 34242; Sarasota; P 25,000; M 450; (941) 349-3800; Fax (941) 349-9699; ExecutiveDirector@siestakeychamber.com; www.siestakeychamber.com*

Sorrento • *East Lake County C/C* • BettyAnn Christian; Pres.; P.O. Box 774; 32776; Lake; P 19,000; M 187; (352) 383-8801; Fax (352) 383-9343; chamber@elcchamber.com; www.elcchamber.com

South Daytona • *see Port Orange*

South Miami • *Chamber South* • Mary Scott Russell; Pres.; 6410 S.W. 80th St.; 33143; Miami-Dade; P 300,000; M 1,500; (305) 661-1621; info@chambersouth.com; www.chambersouth.com*

Spring Hill • *see Brooksville*

St. Petersburg • *St. Petersburg Area C/C* • Chris Steinocher; Pres./CEO; 100 Second Ave. N., Ste. 150; 33701; Pinellas; P 245,000; M 1,000; (727) 821-4069; Fax (727) 895-6326; lcissna@stpete.com; www.stpete.com*

Starke • *North Florida Reg. C/C* • Pam Whittle; Pres./CEO; 100 E. Call St.; 32091; Bradford; P 44,000; M 200; (904) 964-5278; Fax (904) 964-2863; pam@northfloridachamber.com; www.northfloridachamber.com

Steinhatchee • *see Perry*

Stuart • *Stuart-Martin County C/C* • Joseph A. Catrambone; Pres./CEO; 1650 S. Kanner Hwy.; 34994; Martin; P 150,000; M 1,400; (772) 287-1088; info@stuartmartinchamber.org; www.stuartmartinchamber.org*

Sumterville • *see Lake Panasoffkee*

Sun City Center • *Sun City Center Area C/C* • Dana Dittmar; CEO; 1651 Sun City Center Plaza; 33573; Hillsborough; P 30,000; M 500; (813) 634-5111; Fax (813) 634-8438; dana@sccchamber.com; www.sccchamber.com*

Sunrise • *Greater Sunrise C/C* • Louis Feuer; Chrmn.; 6800 Sunset Strip; 33313; Broward; P 90,000; M 200; (954) 835-2428; Fax (954) 523-0607; suncc@sunrisechamber.org; www.sunrisechamber.org*

Suntree • *see Cocoa Beach and Melbourne*

Tallahassee • *Greater Tallahassee C/C* • Sue Dick; Pres.; P.O. Box 1639; 32302; Leon; P 265,714; M 1,600; (850) 224-8116; Fax (850) 561-3860; info@talchamber.com; www.talchamber.com*

Tamarac • *Tamarac C/C* • Vicki Reid; Exec. Dir.; 7525 Pine Island Rd.; 33321; Broward; P 60,000; M 200; (954) 722-1520; Fax (954) 721-2725; vicki@tamaracchamber.org; www.tamaracchamber.org*

U.S. Chambers of Commerce

Tampa Area

Greater Tampa C/C • Bob Rohrlack CCE; Pres./CEO; 201 N. Franklin St., Ste. 201; 33602; Hillsborough; P 1,118,988; M 1,300; (813) 228-7777; (800) 298-2672; Fax (813) 223-7899; laber@tampachamber.com; www.tampachamber.com*

North Tampa C/C • Carol Rehfelt; Exec. Dir.; P.O. Box 82043; 33682; Hillsborough; P 450,000; M 150; (813) 961-2420; Fax (813) 961-2903; contactNTCC@gmail.com; www.northtampachamber.com*

South Tampa C/C • Judy Gay; Exec. Dir.; 2113 S. Dale Mabry Hwy.; 33629; Hillsborough; P 100,000; M 540; (813) 637-0156; executivedirector@southtampachamber.org; www.southtampachamber.org*

Ybor City C/C • Wes Miller; Exec. Dir.; 1800 E. 9th Ave.; 33605; Hillsborough; P 500,000; M 365; (813) 248-3712; info@ybor.org; www.ybor.org

---

Tampa • **North Tampa C/C** • Carol Rehfelt; Exec. Dir.; P.O. Box 82043; 33682; Hillsborough; P 450,000; M 150; (813) 961-2420; Fax (813) 961-2903; contactNTCC@gmail.com; www.northtampachamber.com*

Tarpon Springs • **Tarpon Springs C/C** • Lacey Ekberg; Pres.; 1 N. Pinellas Ave., Ste. B; 34689; Pinellas; P 24,000; M 300; (727) 937-6109; Fax (727) 937-2879; reggie@tarponspringschamber.org; www.tarponspringschamber.com*

Tavares • **Tavares C/C** • J. Scott Berry; Exec. Dir.; 300 E. Main St.; 32778; Lake; P 14,000; M 360; (352) 343-2531; Fax (352) 343-7565; info@tavareschamber.com; www.tavareschamber.com*

Taylor County • *see Perry*

Temple Terrace • **Greater Temple Terrace C/C** • Barbara Sparks-McGlinchy; Exec. Dir.; 9385 N. 56th St.; 33617; Hillsborough; P 25,000; M 500; (813) 989-7004; Fax (813) 989-7005; bsparks@templeterracechamber.com; www.templeterracechamber.com*

Tequesta • *see Palm Beach Gardens*

Titusville • **Titusville Area C/C** • Marcia Gaedcke IOM; Pres.; 2000 S. Washington Ave.; 32780; Brevard; P 70,000; M 750; (321) 267-3036; Fax (321) 264-0127; info@titusville.org; www.titusville.org*

Treasure Island • *see Saint Pete Beach*

Trenton • **Gilchrist County C/C** • Pat Watson; Exec. Dir.; 220 S. Main St.; 32693; Gilchrist; P 17,106; M 279; (352) 463-3467; Fax (352) 463-3469; chamber@GilchristCounty.com; www.GilchristCounty.com

Umatilla • **Umatilla C/C** • Susan R. Martin; Exec. Dir.; 23 S. Central Ave.; P.O. Box 300; 32784; Lake; P 2,800; M 200; (352) 669-3511; Fax (352) 669-8900; umatilla@umatillachamber.org; www.umatillachamber.org*

Valparaiso • *see Niceville*

Valrico • *see Seffner*

Venice • **Venice Area C/C** • John G. Ryan; Pres./CEO; 597 Tamiami Trl. S.; 34285; Sarasota; P 30,000; M 1,100; (941) 488-2236; Fax (941) 484-5903; vchamber@venicechamber.com; www.venicechamber.com*

Vero Beach • **Indian River County C/C** • Penny Chandler; Pres./CEO; 1216 21st St.; P.O. Box 2947; 32961; Indian River; P 141,667; M 900; (772) 567-3491; Fax (772) 778-3181; info@indianriverchamber.com; www.indianriverchamber.com*

Viera • *see Melbourne*

Wakulla County • *see Crawfordville*

Wauchula • **Hardee County C/C** • Casey Dickson; Exec. Dir.; 107 E. Main St.; P.O. Box 683; 33873; Hardee; P 28,000; M 350; (863) 773-6967; Fax (863) 773-4915; casey@hardeecc.com; www.hardeecc.com

Webster • *see Lake Panasoffkee*

Weeki Wachee • *see Brooksville*

Wellington • **Wellington C/C** • Michela Perillo-Green; Exec. Dir.; 12230 Forest Hill Blvd., Ste. 183; 33414; Palm Beach; P 57,000; M 468; (561) 792-6525; Fax (561) 792-6200; info@wellingtonchamber.com; www.wellingtonchamber.com*

Wesley Chapel • **Greater Wesley Chapel C/C** • Hope Allen FCCP; Exec. Dir.; 6013 Wesley Grove Blvd., Ste. 105; 33544; Pasco; P 100,000; M 500; (813) 994-8534; Fax (813) 994-8154; hallen@wesleychapelchamber.com; www.wesleychapelchamber.com*

West Melbourne • *see Melbourne*

West Palm Beach • **C/C of the Palm Beaches** • Dennis Grady; CEO; 401 N. Flagler Dr.; 33401; Palm Beach; P 1,200,000; M 1,000; (561) 833-3711; Fax (561) 833-5582; chamber@palmbeaches.org; www.palmbeaches.org*

Wildwood • *see Lake Panasoffkee*

Williston • **Williston Area C/C** • Mary P. Kline; Exec. Dir.; 607 S.W. 1st Ave.; P.O. Box 369; 32696; Levy; P 2,400; M 130; (352) 528-5552; (866) 447-5537; wcoc@willistonfl.com; www.willistonfl.com

Windermere • *see Winter Garden*

Winter Garden • **West Orange C/C** • Stina D'Uva; Pres.; 12184 W. Colonial Dr.; 34787; Orange; P 240,000; M 1,000; (407) 656-1304; Fax (407) 656-0221; info@wochamber.com; www.wochamber.com*

Winter Haven • **Greater Winter Haven C/C** • Katie Worthington; Pres./CEO; 401 Ave. B N.W.; P.O. Box 1420; 33882; Polk; P 43,000; M 700; (863) 293-2138; Fax (863) 297-5818; info@winterhavenchamber.com; www.winterhavenchamber.com*

Winter Park • **Winter Park C/C** • Patrick Chapin; Pres./CEO; 151 W. Lyman Ave.; P.O. Box 280; 32790; Orange; P 28,000; M 1,800; (407) 644-8281; Fax (407) 644-7826; wpcc@winterpark.org; www.winterpark.org*

Winter Springs • *see Oviedo*

Ybor City • *see Tampa-Ybor City C/C*

Yulee • *see Amelia Island*

Zephyrhills • **Greater Zephyrhills C/C** • Rod Mayhew; Exec. Dir.; 38550 Fifth Ave.; 33542; Pasco; P 55,749; M 471; (813) 782-1913; Fax (813) 783-6060; info@zephyrhillschamber.org; www.zephyrhillschamber.org*

Georgia

Georgia C of C • Chris Clark; Pres./CEO; 270 Peachtree St. N.W., Ste. 2200; Atlanta; 30303; Fulton; P 10,098,000; M 4,000; (404) 223-2264; Fax (404) 223-2290; choltzclaw@gachamber.com; www.gachamber.com

Adel • **Adel-Cook County C/C** • Jerry Connell; Pres./CEO; 100 S. Hutchinson Ave.; 31620; Cook; P 17,332; M 275; (229) 896-2281; Fax (229) 896-8201; cookcochamber@windstream.net; www.adelcookchamber.org*

Alamo • **Wheeler County C/C & Dev. Auth.** • Gene Hopkins; Pres.; 6 W. Railroad Ave.; P.O. Box 654; 30411; Wheeler; P 7,400; M 120; (912) 568-7808; wchamber1@windstream.net; www.wheelercounty.org

Albany • **Albany Area C/C** • Chris Hardy IOM CCE; Pres./CEO; 225 W. Broad Ave.; 31701; Dougherty; P 94,000; M 1,150; (229) 434-8700; Fax (229) 434-8716; chamber@albanyga.com; www.albanyga.com*

Alma • **Alma-Bacon County C/C** • Cherry Rewis; Exec. Asst.; 504 N. Pierce St., Ste. 102; P.O. Box 450; 31510; Bacon; P 11,000; M 40; (912) 632-8643; Fax (912) 632-7710; abcchamber@accessatc.net; www.almagachamber.com

Alpharetta • **Greater North Fulton C/C** • Brandon Beach; Pres./CEO; 11605 Haynes Bridge Rd., Ste. 100; 30009; Fulton; P 350,000; M 1,800; (770) 993-8806; Fax (770) 594-1059; info@gnfcc.com; www.gnfcc.com*

Alpharetta • **Alpharetta C/C** • Hans Appen; Pres./CEO; 11175 Cicero Dr., Ste. 100; 30022; Fulton; P 61,981; M 133; (770) 817-7570; info@alpharettachamber.com; www.alpharettachamber.com

Americus • **Americus-Sumter County C/C** • Mrs. Angela H. Westra; Pres.; 409 Elm Ave., Ste. A; P.O. Box 724; 31709; Sumter; P 34,000; M 415; (229) 924-2646; Fax (229) 924-8784; info@americus-sumterchamber.com; www.americus-sumterchamber.com*

Ashburn • **Ashburn Turner County C/C** • Shelley Zorn; Pres./Eco. Dev.; 238 E. College Ave.; 31714; Turner; P 10,000; M 238; (229) 567-9696; (800) 471-9696; Fax (229) 567-2541; szorn@windstream.net; www.turnerchamber.com

Athens • **Athens Area C/C** • Doc Eldridge; Pres.; 246 W. Hancock Ave.; 30601; Clarke; P 116,700; M 1,100; (706) 549-6800; Fax (706) 549-5636; info@athensga.com; www.athensga.com*

Atlanta Area

Cobb C/C • David Connell; Pres./CEO; 240 Interstate N. Pkwy. S.E.; (P.O. Box 671868, Marietta, 30006); 30339; Cobb; P 707,442; M 2,500; (770) 980-2000; (770) 980-2008; Fax (770) 980-9510; info@cobbchamber.org; www.cobbchamber.org*

Metro Atlanta C/C • Hala Moddelmog; Pres./CEO; 235 Andrew Young Intl. Blvd. N.W.; 30303; Fulton; P 4,200,000; M 4,000; (404) 880-9000; Fax (404) 586-8416; president@macoc.com; www.metroatlantachamber.com

South Fulton C/C • Y. Dyan Matthews; Pres./CEO; 5155 Westpark Dr. S.W.; 30336; South Fulton; P 178,000; M 300; (770) 964-1984; Fax (404) 346-7393; office@southfultonchamber.com; www.southfultonchamber.com*

Augusta • **Augusta Metro C/C** • Sue Parr; Pres./CEO; 701 Greene St.; 30901; Augusta-Richmond; P 556,900; M 995; (706) 821-1300; (888) 639-8188; Fax (706) 821-1330; info@augustagausa.com; www.augustachamber.net*

Bainbridge • **Bainbridge-Decatur County C/C** • Diane Strickland; Pres.; P.O. Box 755; 39818; Decatur; P 28,823; M 462; (229) 246-4774; Fax (229) 243-7633; info@bainbridgegachamber.com; www.bainbridgegachamber.com*

Barnesville • **Barnesville-Lamar County C/C** • Marshall T. Hooks; Pres./CEO; 100 Commerce Pl.; P.O. Box 506; 30204; Lamar; P 18,300; M 250; (770) 358-5884; Fax (770) 358-5886; president@barnesville.org; www.barnesville.org

Baxley • **Baxley-Appling County C/C** • Keri Crosby; Exec. Dir.; 305 W. Parker St.; 31513; Appling; P 18,000; M 150; (912) 367-7731; Fax (912) 367-2073; chamberdirector@baxley.org; www.baxley.org

Blackshear • **Pierce County C/C** • Angela B. Manders; Exec. Dir.; 200 S.W. Central Ave.; P.O. Box 47; 31516; Pierce; P 18,800; M 300; (912) 449-7044; Fax (912) 449-7045; piercecountychamberofcommerce@gmail.com; pcgeorgia.com

Blairsville • **Blairsville-Union County C/C** • Regina Allison; Pres.; 129 Union County Recreation Rd.; P.O. Box 789; 30514; Union; P 22,000; M 580; (706) 745-5789; (877) 745-5789; admin@blairsvillechamber.com; www.visitblairsvillega.com*

Blakely • **Blakely-Early County C/C** • Kyle Kornegay; Pres./CEO; 214 Court Sq.; P.O. Box 189; 39823; Early; P 11,000; M 145; (229) 723-3741; Fax (229) 723-6876; kyle.earlychamber@gmail.com; www.blakelyearlycountychamber.com

Blue Ridge • **Fannin County C/C** • Jan Hackett; Pres.; 152 Orvin Lance Dr.; P.O. Box 1689; 30513; Fannin; P 24,000; M 800; (706) 632-5680; (800) 899-MTNS; Fax (706) 632-2241; fanninchamber@tds.net; www.blueridgemountains.com*

Brunswick • **Brunswick-Golden Isles C/C** • M.H. 'Woody' Woodside; Pres.; 1505 Richmond St., 2nd Flr.; 31520; Glynn; P 74,000; M 1,247; (912) 265-0620; Fax (912) 265-0629; info@brunswickgoldenisleschamber.com; www.brunswickgoldenisleschamber.com*

Buena Vista • **Buena Vista-Marion County C/C** • Janet Teele; Pres.; P.O. Box 471; 31803; Marion; P 8,800; M 40; (229) 649-2842; (800) 647-2842; bvmccoc@windstream.net; www.bvmccoc.com

Bulloch County • **see Statesboro**

Butler • **Taylor County C/C** • Amanda Haynie; Exec. Dir.; 21 E. Main St.; P.O. Box 443; 31006; Taylor; P 6,000; M 100; (478) 862-6022; taylorcountycofc@gmail.com; www.taylorcountycofc.com

Byromville • **see Vienna**

Cairo • **Cairo-Grady County C/C** • Chadd Mathis; Exec. Dir.; 961 N. Broad St.; P.O. Box 387; 39828; Grady; P 30,000; M 280; (229) 377-3663; Fax (229) 377-3901; cmathis@syrupcity.net; www.cairogachamber.com*

Calhoun • **Gordon County C/C** • Kathy B. Johnson; Pres.; 300 S. Wall St.; 30701; Gordon; P 56,000; M 430; (706) 625-3200; (800) 887-3811; Fax (706) 625-5062; kjohnson@gordonchamber.org; www.gordonchamber.org*

Camilla • **Camilla C/C** • Jennifer Burnum; Exec. Dir.; 212 E. Broad St.; P.O. Box 226; 31730; Mitchell; P 5,500; M 300; (229) 336-5255; Fax (229) 336-5256; chamber@camillageorgia.com; www.camillageorgia.com*

Canton • *Cherokee County C/C* • Pamela W. Carnes; Pres./CEO; 3605 Marietta Hwy.; P.O. Box 4998; 30114; Cherokee; P 235,000; M 900; (770) 345-0400; Fax (770) 345-0030; info@CherokeeChamber.com; www.CherokeeChamber.com*

Carnesville • *Franklin County C/C* • Aida Reynolds; Exec. Secy.; 165 Athens St.; P.O. Box 151; 30521; Franklin; P 22,100; M 200; (706) 384-4659; Fax (706) 384-3204; chamber@franklin-county.com; www.franklin-county.com

Carrollton • *Carroll County C/C* • Daniel Jackson; Pres./CEO; 200 Northside Dr.; 30117; Carroll; P 117,730; M 625; (770) 832-2446; Fax (770) 832-1300; daniel@carroll-ga.org; www.carroll-ga.org*

Cartersville • *Cartersville-Bartow County C/C* • Joe Frank Harris Jr.; Pres./CEO; 122 W. Main St.; P.O. Box 307; 30120; Bartow; P 100,100; M 850; (770) 382-1466; Fax (770) 382-2704; reception@cartersvillechamber.com; www.cartersvillechamber.com*

Chatsworth • *Chatsworth-Murray County C/C* • Dinah Rowe IOM GCCE; Pres./CEO; 126 N. 3rd Ave.; 30705; Murray; P 42,000; M 250; (706) 695-6060; (800) 969-9490; Fax (706) 517-0198; murraychamber@windstream.net; www.murraycountychamber.org*

Clarkesville • *see Cornelia*

Claxton • *Claxton-Evans County C/C* • Tammi Hall; Exec. Dir.; 4 N. Duval St.; 30417; Evans; P 11,000; M 225; (912) 739-1391; Fax (912) 739-3827; info@claxtonevanschamber.com; www.claxtonevanschamber.com*

Clayton • *Rabun County C/C* • Tony Allred; Pres.; 232 Hwy. 441 N.; P.O. Box 750; 30525; Rabun; P 18,000; M 300; (706) 782-4812; Fax (706) 782-4810; welcomecenter@gamountains.com; www.gamountains.com*

Cleveland • *White County C/C & Welcome Center* • Cindy Bailey; Pres.; 122 N. Main St.; 30528; White; P 28,000; M 485; (706) 865-5356; (800) 392-8279; cindy@whitecountychamber.org; www.whitecountychamber.org*

Cochran • *Cochran-Bleckley C/C* • Kathryn Fisher; Pres./CEO; 102 N. Second St., Ste. A; P.O. Box 305; 31014; Bleckley; P 12,448; M 109; (478) 934-2965; (478) 934-1766; Fax (478) 934-0353; cbchamber@comsouth.net; www.cochran-bleckleychamber.org

College Park • *see Jonesboro*

Colquitt • *Colquitt-Miller County C/C* • Veryl Garland-Cockey; Pres.; 302 E. College St.; 39837; Miller; P 8,300; M 185; (229) 758-2400; Fax (229) 758-8140; cmccoc@bellsouth.net; www.colquitt-georgia.com

Columbus • *Greater Columbus C/C* • Mike Gaymon; Pres./CEO; 1200 6th Ave.; P.O. Box 1200; 31902; Muscogee; P 290,000; M 1,500; (706) 327-1566; Fax (706) 327-7512; mgaymon@columbusgachamber.com; www.columbusgachamber.com*

Commerce • *see Jefferson*

Concord • *see Zebulon*

Conyers • *Conyers-Rockdale C/C* • Fred Boscarino GCCE; Pres./CEO; 1186 Scott St.; P.O. Box 483; 30012; Rockdale; P 80,000; M 538; (770) 483-7049; Fax (770) 922-8415; katy@conyers-rockdale.com; www.conyers-rockdale.com*

Cordele • *Cordele-Crisp C/C* • Monica Simmons; Pres.; 502 S. 2nd St.; P.O. Box 158; 31010; Crisp; P 22,000; M 485; (229) 273-1668; Fax (229) 273-5132; info@cordele-crisp-chamber.com; www.cordelecrispga.com*

Cornelia • *Habersham County C/C* • Judy Taylor PhD; Pres.; 668 Hwy. 441; P.O. Box 366; 30531; Habersham; P 43,000; M 725; (706) 778-4654; (800) 835-2559; Fax (706) 776-1416; taylorjudy@windstream.net; www.habershamchamber.com

Covington • *Covington/Newton County C/C* • Hunter Hall; Pres.; 2100 Washington St.; P.O. Box 168; 30015; Newton; P 98,000; M 540; (770) 786-7510; info@newtonchamber.com; www.newtonchamber.com*

Crawford • *Oglethorpe County C/C* • 1158 Athens Rd.; P.O. Box 56; 30630; Oglethorpe; P 15,000; M 140; (706) 743-3113; office@oglethorpecofc.org; www.countycommerce.org

Cumming • *Cumming-Forsyth County C/C* • James McCoy; Pres./CEO; 212 Kelly Mill Rd.; 30040; Forsyth; P 170,000; M 950; (770) 887-6461; cfccoc@cummingforsythchamber.org; www.cummingforsythchamber.org

Cuthbert • *Randolph County C/C* • Patricia Goodman; Pres.; 51 Court St.; P.O. Box 31; 39840; Randolph; P 7,500; M 100; (855) 782-6312; Fax (855) 782-6312; rcchamber@hotmail.com; www.randolphcountychamber.org

Dahlonega • *Dahlonega-Lumpkin County C/C & CVB* • Amy Booker; Pres./CEO; 13 Park St. S.; 30533; Lumpkin; P 32,000; M 580; (706) 864-3711; (800) 231-5543; Fax (706) 864-0139; info@dahlonega.org; www.dahlonega.org*

Dallas • *Paulding County C/C* • Carolyn S. Wright; Pres./CEO; 455 Jimmy Campbell Pkwy.; 30132; Paulding; P 142,000; M 800; (770) 445-6016; Fax (770) 445-3050; sbohannon@pauldingchamber.org; www.pauldingchamber.org

Dalton • *Greater Dalton C/C* • Brian Anderson; Pres./CEO; 100 South Hamilton St.; 30720; Whitfield; P 103,000; M 1,016; (706) 278-7373; Fax (706) 226-8739; info@daltonchamber.org; www.daltonchamber.org*

Danielsville • *Madison County C/C & Ind. Auth.* • Kasie Huffman; Chair; 101 Courthouse Sq., Ste. 1; P.O. Box 381; 30633; Madison; P 28,100; M 300; (706) 795-3473; Fax (706) 795-3262; mccc@madisoncountyga.org; www.madisoncountyga.org

Darien • *Darien-McIntosh County C/C & Visitor Center* • Wally Orrel; Pres.; 105 Fort King George Rd.; P.O. Box 1497; 31305; McIntosh; P 15,000; M 303; (912) 437-6684; Fax (912) 437-5251; info@mcintoshchamber.com; www.visitdarien.com

Dawson • *Terrell County C/C* • Gina Webb; Exec. Dir.; 211 W. Lee St.; P.O. Box 405; 39842; Terrell; P 94,000; M 110; (229) 995-2011; Fax (229) 995-3971; tccc@windstream.net; www.terrellcountygeorgia.org

Dawsonville • *Dawson County C/C* • Christie Haynes; Pres.; 44 Commerce Dr.; P.O. Box 299; 30534; Dawson; P 25,600; M 500; (706) 265-6278; Fax (706) 265-6279; info@dawson.org; www.dawson.org*

Decatur • *DeKalb C/C* • Leonardo McClarty; Pres./CEO; 125 Clairemont Ave., Ste. 235; 30030; DeKalb; P 715,000; M 600; (404) 378-8000; Fax (404) 378-3397; lmcclarty@dekalbchamber.org; www.dekalbchamber.org

Dillard • *see Clayton*

Donalsonville • *Donalsonville-Seminole County C/C* • Brenda Broome; Pres.; 122 E. Second St.; P.O. Box 713; 39845; Seminole; P 9,500; M 150; (229) 524-2588; Fax (229) 524-8406; dosemcc@windstream.net; www.donalsonvillega.com

Douglas • *Douglas-Coffee County C/C •* JoAnne Lewis; Pres.; 114 N. Peterson Ave., Ste. 205; 31533; Coffee; P 43,200; M 500; (912) 384-1873; Fax (912) 383-6304; jlewis@douglasga.org; www.douglasga.org*

Douglasville • *Douglas County C/C •* Kali Boatright; Pres./CEO; 6658 Church St.; 30134; Douglas; P 133,000; M 650; (770) 942-5022; Fax (770) 942-5876; info@douglascountygeorgia.com; www.douglascountygeorgia.com*

Dublin • *Dublin-Laurens County C/C •* Heath Taylor; Pres./CEO; 1200 Bellevue Ave.; P.O. Box 818; 31040; Laurens; P 48,000; M 500; (478) 272-5546; (478) 272-5547; Fax (478) 275-0811; chamber@dublin-georgia.com; www.dublin-georgia.com*

Duluth • *Gwinnett C/C •* Dan Kaufman; Pres./CEO; 6500 Sugarloaf Pkwy.; 30097; Gwinnett; P 805,300; M 2,700; (770) 232-3000; Fax (770) 232-8807; info@gwinnettchamber.org; www.gwinnettchamber.org*

Dunwoody • *Dunwoody Perimeter Chamber •* Stephanie Snodgrass; Exec. Dir.; 41 Perimeter Center East, Ste. 225; 30346; DeKalb; P 47,200; M 380; (678) 244-9700; info@dunwoodycommerce.org; www.dunwoodycommerce.org*

East Ellijay • *Gilmer County C/C •* Paige Green; Pres.; 696 First Ave.; P O Box 505, Ellijay; 30540; Gilmer; P 35,000; M 500; (706) 635-7400; Fax (706) 635-7410; paigeg@gilmerchamber.com; www.gilmerchamber.com*

Eastman • *Eastman/Dodge County C/C •* Judy Madden; Pres./CEO; 1646 College St.; P.O. Box 550; 31023; Dodge; P 20,000; M 250; (478) 374-4723; Fax (478) 374-4626; info@eastman-georgia.com; www.eastman-georgia.com

Eatonton • *Eatonton-Putnam C/C •* Roddie Anne Blackwell; Pres.; 305 N. Madison Ave.; P.O. Box 4088; 31024; Putnam; P 20,000; M 350; (706) 485-7701; Fax (706) 485-3277; epchamber@eatonton.com; www.eatonton.com*

Elberton • *Elbert County C/C •* Phyllis Brooks; Pres.; 104 Heard St.; P.O. Box 537; 30635; Elbert; P 21,000; M 340; (706) 283-5651; Fax (706) 283-5722; chamber@elbertga.com; www.elbertga.com

Ellaville • *Ellaville-Schley County C/C •* John T. Greene; P.O. Box 4; 31806; Schley; P 4,200; M 131; (229) 937-2262; Fax (229) 937-2262; ellavilleschley@windstream.net; www.ellavillega.com/chamber_of_commerce

Evans • *Columbia County C/C •* Tammy Shepherd; Pres./CEO; 4424 Evans to Locks Rd.; 30809; Columbia; P 124,000; M 700; (706) 651-0018; Fax (706) 651-0023; info@columbiacountychamber.com; www.columbiacountychamber.com*

Fannin County • *see Blue Ridge*

Fayetteville • *Fayette C/C •* Carlotta Ungaro; Pres./CEO; 600 W. Lanier Ave., Ste. 205; 30214; Fayette; P 107,000; M 800; (770) 461-9983; Fax (770) 461-9622; info@FayetteChamber.org; www.FayetteChamber.org*

Fitzgerald • *Fitzgerald-Ben Hill C/C •* Christi Schirack; Exec. Dir.; 121 E. Pine St.; P.O. Box 218; 31750; Ben Hill; P 18,000; M 300; (229) 423-9357; (800) 225-7899; Fax (229) 423-1052; cschirack@mediacombb.net; www.fitzgeraldchamber.org

Folkston • *Okefenokee C/C •* Dawn Malin; Exec. Dir.; 3795 Main St.; P.O. Box 756; 31537; Charlton; P 12,000; M 100; (912) 496-2536; Fax (912) 496-4601; director@folkston.com; www.folkston.com*

Forsyth • *Forsyth-Monroe County C/C •* Tiffany G. Andrews; Pres./CEO; 68 N. Lee St.; 31029; Monroe; P 27,000; M 300; (478) 994-9239; (888) 642-4628; Fax (478) 994-9240; tiffany@forsyth-monroechamber.com; www.forsyth-monroechamber.com*

Fort Gaines • *see Cuthbert*

Fort Oglethorpe • *see Ringgold*

Fort Valley • *Peach Reg. C/C •* Thomas Morrill; Chrmn. & Managing Dir.; 201 Oakland Hts. Pkwy.; 31030; Peach; P 27,000; M 267; (478) 825-3733; Fax (478) 825-2501; chamber@peachchamber.com; www.peachchamber.com*

Franklin • *Heard County C/C •* Kathy Knowles; Pres.; 121 S. Court Sq.; P.O. Box 368; 30217; Heard; P 12,000; M 130; (706) 675-0560; (888) 331-0560; Fax (706) 675-2129; info@heardchamber.com; www.heardchamber.com

Franklin Springs • *see Carnesville*

Gainesville • *Greater Hall C/C •* Kit Dunlap; Pres./CEO; 230 E.E. Butler Pkwy.; P.O. Box 374; 30503; Hall; P 180,000; M 2,900; (770) 532-6206; Fax (770) 535-8419; joy@ghcc.com; www.ghcc.com

Gray • *Jones County/Gray C/C •* Kathyjo Gordon; Exec. Dir.; 161 W. Clinton St.; P.O. Box 686; 31032; Jones; P 30,000; M 250; (478) 986-1123; Fax (478) 986-1022; info@jonescounty.org; www.jonescounty.org*

Greensboro • *Greene County C/C •* Becky Cronic; Pres.; 111 N. Main St.; P.O. Box 741; 30642; Greene; P 15,994; M 300; (706) 453-7592; Fax (706) 453-1430; chamber@greeneccoc.org; www.greeneccoc.org*

Griffin • *Griffin-Spalding C/C •* Bonnie Pfrogner; Exec. Dir.; 143 N. Hill St.; P.O. Box 73; 30224; Spalding; P 64,000; M 600; (770) 228-8200; (770) 227-3264; Fax (770) 228-8031; griffinchamber@cityofgriffin.com; www.griffinchamber.com*

Gwinnett • *see Duluth*

Habersham County • *see Cornelia*

Hamilton • *Harris County C/C •* Jayson Johnston; Pres.; 143 S. College St.; P.O. Box 426; 31811; Harris; P 32,024; M 389; (706) 628-0010; (888) 478-0010; Fax (706) 628-4429; info@harriscountychamber.org; www.harriscountychamber.org

Hapeville • *Airport Area C/C •* Ann Ray; Exec. Dir.; 600 S. Central Ave., Ste. 100; P.O. Box 82489; 30354; Fulton; P 30,000; M 250; (404) 209-0910; Fax (404) 389-0271; info@airportchamber.com; www.airportchamber.com

Hartwell • *Hart County C/C •* Nicki Meyer; Exec. Dir.; 31 E. Howell St.; P.O. Box 793; 30643; Hart; P 25,000; M 290; (706) 376-8590; Fax (706) 376-5177; hartchamber@hartcom.net; www.hart-chamber.org

Hawkinsville • *Hawkinsville-Pulaski County C/C •* Kim Brown; 46 Lumpkin St.; 31036; Pulaski; P 10,100; M 140; (478) 783-1717; Fax (478) 783-1700; kimberly@hawkinsvillechamber.org; www.hawkinsvillechamber.org

Hazlehurst • *Hazlehurst-Jeff Davis County C/C •* Bonnie Hulett; Exec. Dir.; 95 E. Jarman St.; P.O. Box 546; 31539; Jeff Davis; P 15,068; M 175; (912) 375-4543; Fax (912) 375-7948; hazjdcoc1@jeffdavisga.com; www.hazlehurstchamberofcommerce.com

Helen • *Greater Helen Area C/C •* Curtis Wade; P.O. Box 192; 30545; White; P 700; M 130; (706) 878-1908; Fax (706) 878-3064; office@helenchamber.com; www.helenchamber.com

Hiawassee • *Towns County C/C & Tourism Assn. •* Candace Lee; Pres.; 1411 Jack Dayton Cir.; Young Harris; 30582; Towns; P 10,000; M 295; (706) 896-4966; (800) 984-1543; info@mountaintopga.com; www.mountaintopga.com

Hinesville • *Liberty County C/C •* Leah Poole; Exec. Dir.; 425 W. Oglethorpe Hwy.; 31313; Liberty; P 64,000; M 400; (912) 368-4445; Fax (912) 368-4677; director@libertycounty.org; www.libertycounty.org

Hogansville • *see La Grange*

Homer • *Banks County Chamber CVB •* Brad Day; Exec. Dir.; P.O. Box 57; 30547; Banks; P 18,000; M 150; (706) 335-4866; (877) 389-2896; Fax (706) 677-2109; alicia@bankscountyga.info; www.bankscountyga.biz

Homerville • *Homerville-Clinch County C/C •* Phil Martin; Exec. V.P.; 23 W. Plant Ave.; 31634; Clinch; P 6,900; M 120; (912) 487-2360; Fax (912) 487-2384; clinchcountychamberofcommerce@windstream.net; www.clinchcountychamber.org

Irwinton • *Wilkinson County C/C •* Jonathan Jackson; Pres.; 100A Bacon St.; P.O. Box 413; 31042; Wilkinson; P 10,000; M 130; (478) 946-1122; Fax (478) 946-4394; jjackson@wilkinsoncounty.net; www.wilcodevauthority.com

Jackson • *Butts County C/C •* Melinda McLarnon; Exec. Dir.; 625 W. Third St., Ste. 6; P.O. Box 147; 30233; Butts; P 27,000; M 300; (770) 775-4839; Fax (770) 775-4868; mmclarnon102012@att.net; buttschamber.com

Jasper • *Pickens County C/C •* Gerry Nechvatal; Exec. & Eco. Dev. Dir.; 500 Stegall Dr.; 30143; Pickens; P 30,000; M 650; (706) 692-5600; Fax (706) 692-9453; info@pickenschamber.com; www.pickenschamber.com*

Jefferson • *Jackson County Area C/C •* Josh Fenn; Pres./CEO; 270 Athens St.; P.O. Box 629; 30549; Jackson; P 60,000; M 600; (706) 387-0300; Fax (706) 387-0304; info@jacksoncountyga.com; www.jacksoncountyga.com

Jeffersonville • *Twiggs County C/C •* Virginia Villatoro; Vice-Chair; P.O. Box 248; 31044; Twiggs; P 8,400; M 15; (478) 319-5461; chair@twiggschamber.com; www.twiggschamber.com

Jesup • *Jesup/Wayne County C/C •* John Riddle; Pres./CEO; 124 N.W. Broad St.; 31545; Wayne; P 29,000; M 335; (912) 427-2028; (888) 224-5983; Fax (912) 427-2778; chamberoffice@waynechamber.com; www.waynechamber.com*

Jonesboro • *Clayton County C/C •* Yulonda Darden Beauford; Pres./CEO; 2270 Mt. Zion Rd.; 30236; Clayton; P 260,000; M 600; (678) 610-4021; Fax (678) 610-4025; info@claytonchamber.org; www.claytonchamber.org

Kingsland • *Camden County C/C •* Amy M. Hendricks; Pres./CEO; 531 N. Lee St.; 31558; Camden; P 50,513; M 430; (912) 729-5840; Fax (912) 576-7924; president@camdenchamber.com; www.camdenchamber.com*

La Grange • *LaGrange-Troup County C/C •* Page Estes; Pres.; 111 Bull St.; P.O. Box 636; 30241; Troup; P 65,000; M 880; (706) 884-8671; Fax (706) 882-8012; pestes@lagrangechamber.com; www.lagrangechamber.com*

LaFayette • *see Rock Spring*

Lake City • *see Jonesboro*

Lake Park • *Lake Park Area C/C & Visitors Center •* Kathy Walker; Exec. Dir.; 5227 Mill Store Rd.; P.O. Box 278; 31636; Lowndes; P 8,500; M 170; (229) 559-5302; Fax (229) 559-0828; lpacocv@bellsouth.net; www.lakeparkga.com

Lakeland • *Lakeland-Lanier County C/C •* Sandy (J.H.) Sanders; Pres.; 8 S. Valdosta Rd.; P.O. Box 215; 31635; Lanier; P 10,000; M 120; (229) 482-9755; Fax (229) 588-2014; chamber@lakelandchamber.org; www.lakelandchamber.org

Lavonia • *Lavonia C/C •* Susan Poole; Pres.; 1222 E. Main St.; P.O. Box 763; 30553; Franklin; P 3,000; M 150; (706) 356-8202; lavoniacofc@gmail.com; www.thelavoniachamber.com

Lawrenceville • *see Duluth*

Leesburg • *Lee County C/C •* Winston A. Oxford CEcD; Exec. Dir.; 100 B. Starksville Ave. N.; 31763; Lee; P 33,000; M 400; (229) 759-2422; Fax (229) 759-9224; winstono@lee.ga.us; www.leechamber.net*

Lilly • *see Vienna*

Lincolnton • *Lincolnton-Lincoln County C/C •* Meagan Whitehead; Admin.; 112 N. Washington St.; P.O. Box 810; 30817; Lincoln; P 8,000; M 125; (706) 359-7970; Fax (706) 359-5477; chamber@lincolncountyga.com; lincolncountyga.org

Lithonia • *Greater Lithonia C/C •* Angela Garrett; Pres.; 3914 Button Gate Ct.; P.O. Box 57; 30058; DaKalb; P 10,000; M 40; (770) 482-1808; (770) 322-5543; Fax (770) 322-5543; angelagarrett57@aol.com; www.lithoniachamber.com

Louisville • *Jefferson County C/C •* Lillian Easterlin; Exec. Dir.; 302 E. Broad St.; P.O. Box 630; 30434; Jefferson; P 17,000; M 100; (478) 625-8134; (866) 527-2642; Fax (478) 625-9060; info@jeffersoncounty.org; www.jeffersoncounty.org

Lovejoy • *see Jonesboro*

Ludowici • *Long County C/C •* Don Melton; Pres.; P.O. Box 400; 31316; Long; P 15,150; M 80; (912) 545-2392; www.longcountychamberofcommerce.com

Lyons • *see Vidalia*

Macon • *Greater Macon C/C •* Mike Dyer; Pres./CEO; 305 Coliseum Dr.; P.O. Box 169; 31202; Bibb; P 150,000; M 980; (478) 621-2000; Fax (478) 621-2021; info@maconchamber.com; www.maconchamber.com*

Madison • *Madison-Morgan County C/C •* Bob Hughes; Pres.; 118 N. Main St.; 30650; Morgan; P 18,000; M 300; (706) 438-3120; sdaniel@madisonga.org; www.madisonga.org*

McDonough • *Henry County C/C •* David H. Gill; Pres./CEO; 1709 Highway 20 W.; Westridge Business Center; 30253; Henry; P 204,000; M 700; (770) 957-5786; Fax (770) 957-8030; memberservices@henrycounty.com; www.henrycounty.com*

McRae • *Telfair County C/C •* Paula Rogers; Pres.; 9 E. Oak St.; 31055; Telfair; P 16,500; M 130; (229) 868-6365; Fax (229) 868-7970; rogers@telfairco.org; www.telfairco.org

Meansville • *see Zebulon*

Metter • *Metter-Candler C/C •* Jaime Riggs; Exec. Dir.; 1210 S. Lewis St.; P.O. Box 497; 30439; Candler; P 11,000; M 150; (912) 685-2159; Fax (912) 685-2108; metterchamber@gmail.com; www.metter-candlercounty.com

Milledgeville • *Milledgeville-Baldwin County C/C* • Angie Martin; Pres./CEO; 130 S. Jefferson St.; P.O. Box 751; 31059; Baldwin; P 45,000; M 500; (478) 453-9311; Fax (478) 453-0051; chamber@milledgevillega.com; www.milledgevillega.com*

Millen • *Millen/Jenkins County C/C & Dev. Auth.* • Paula Herrington; Exec. Dir.; 548 Cotton Ave.; 30442; Jenkins; P 8,700; M 135; (478) 982-5595; Fax (478) 982-5512; pauladepot@bellsouth.net; www.jenkinscountyga.com

Molena • *see Zebulon*

Monroe • *Walton County C/C* • Teri H. Smiley; Pres.; 132 E. Spring St.; P.O. Box 89; 30655; Walton; P 85,000; M 600; (770) 267-6594; Fax (770) 267-0961; connie@waltonchamber.org; www.waltonchamber.org*

Monroe County • *see Forsyth*

Montezuma • *Macon County C/C & Dev. Auth.* • Jimmy Davis; Pres.; 109 N. Dooly St.; 31063; Macon; P 14,800; M 125; (478) 472-2391; Fax (478) 472-5186; info@maconcountyga.org; maconcountyga.org

Monticello • *Monticello-Jasper County C/C* • Pam Mayer; Pres.; 119 W. Washington St.; P.O. Box 133; 31064; Jasper; P 14,000; M 115; (706) 468-8994; Fax (706) 468-8043; jasperchamber@bellsouth.net; www.jaspercountycoc.com

Morrow • *see Jonesboro*

Moultrie • *Moultrie-Colquitt County C/C* • Darrell Moore; Pres.; 116 First Ave. S.E.; P.O. Box 487; 31776; Colquitt; P 48,000; M 510; (229) 985-2131; (888) 40-VISIT; Fax (229) 890-2638; contact@moultriechamber.com; www.moultriechamber.com*

Mountain City • *see Clayton*

Mountain Park • *see Alpharetta*

Nahunta • *Brantley County C/C* • P.O. Drawer B; 31553; Brantley; P 18,400; M 85; (912) 462-6282; info@brantleycountychamber.org; www.brantleycountychamber.org

Nashville • *Nashville-Berrien C/C* • Crissy Staley; Exec. Dir.; 201 N. Davis St.; P.O. Box 217; 31639; Berrien; P 19,000; M 300; (229) 686-5123; Fax (229) 686-1905; berrienchamber@windstream.net; www.berrienchamber.com

Newnan • *Newnan-Coweta Chamber* • Candace Boothby; Pres./CEO; 23 Bullsboro Dr.; 30263; Coweta; P 133,000; M 850; (770) 253-2270; Fax (770) 253-2271; info@newnancowetachamber.org; www.newnancowetachamber.org*

Ocilla • *Ocilla-Irwin C/C* • Hazel McCranie; Pres.; P.O. Box 104; 31774; Irwin; P 11,000; M 165; (229) 468-9114; Fax (229) 468-4452; irwinchamber@windstream.net; www.ocillachamber.net*

Peach County • *see Fort Valley*

Peachtree City • *see Fayetteville*

Pelham • *Pelham C/C* • Kent Holtzclaw; Exec. Dir.; 128 W. Railroad St.; P.O. Box 151; 31779; Mitchell; P 4,000; M 220; (229) 294-4924; Fax (229) 294-1583; pelhamchamber@pelhamga.org; www.pelhamchamber.org*

Pembroke • *North Bryan C/C Inc.* • Mary Warnell; Pres.; 18 E. Bacon St.; P.O. Box 916; 31321; Bryan; P 3,000; M 73; (912) 653-5655; (912) 653-4040; Fax (912) 653-5616; www.bryancounty.org

Perry • *Perry Area C/C* • Darlene McLendon; Pres./CEO; 101 General Courtney Hodges Blvd., Ste. B; 31069; Houston; P 17,000; M 400; (478) 987-1234; Fax (478) 988-1234; info@perrygachamber.com; www.perrygachamber.com*

Pine Mountain • *see Hamilton*

Pinehurst • *see Vienna*

Port Wentworth • *Port Wentworth C/C & Visitors Center* • Trisha M. Growe; Exec. Dir.; 7532 Hwy. 21; 31407; Chatham; P 5,500; M 120; (912) 965-1999; Fax (912) 965-1199; tgrowe@visitportwentworth.com; www.visitportwentworth.com

Quitman • *Quitman-Brooks County C/C* • 220 E. Screven St.; P.O. Box 151; 31643; Brooks; P 16,800; M 190; (229) 263-4841; Fax (229) 263-4822; lbasford@brookscoda.com; www.qbcchamber.com

Rabun County • *see Clayton*

Reidsville • *Greater Tattnall C/C & Dev. Auth.* • David Avery; Exec. Dir.; P.O. Box 759; 30453; Tattnall; P 25,500; M 400; (912) 557-6323; (912) 805-1177; Fax (912) 557-6088; davidavery61@yahoo.com; www.tattnall.com

Richmond Hill • *Richmond Hill-Bryan County C/C* • Brianne Yontz; Exec. Dir.; 2591 Hwy. 17, Ste. 100; 31324; Bryan; P 30,000; M 300; (912) 756-3444; (800) 834-3960; Fax (912) 756-4236; info@rhbcchamber.org; www.rhbcchamber.org*

Ringgold • *Catoosa County C/C* • Martha Eaker; Pres./CEO; 264 Catoosa Cir.; 30736; Catoosa; P 64,000; M 499; (706) 965-5201; (877) 965-5201; tmullis@catoosachamberofcommerce.com; www.catoosachamberofcommerce.com*

Riverdale • *see Jonesboro*

Roberta • *Roberta-Crawford County C/C* • Patti Temple; Dir.; 39 Wright Ave.; P.O. Box 417; 31078; Crawford; P 14,000; M 104; (478) 836-3825; (478) 412-0042; Fax (478) 836-3825; rcccoc@pstel.net; www.robertacrawfordchamber.org

Rock Spring • *Walker County C/C* • Lacey Wilson; Pres.; 10052 Hwy. 27 N.; P.O. Box 430; 30739; Walker; P 69,000; M 276; (706) 375-7702; Fax (706) 375-7797; info@walkercochamber.com; www.walkercochamber.com*

Rockmart • *Polk County C/C* • Tamaka Hudson; Exec. Dir.; 133 S. Marble St.; 30153; Polk; P 44,000; M 300; (770) 684-8760; Fax (770) 224-5320; info@polkgeorgia.com; www.polkgeorgia.com*

Rome • *Greater Rome C/C* • Al Hodge; Pres./CEO; 1 Riverside Pkwy.; 30161; Floyd; P 97,000; M 1,200; (706) 291-ROME; Fax (706) 232-5755; grcc@romega.com; www.romega.com*

Roswell • *see Alpharetta*

Royston • *see Carnesville*

Saint Simons Island • *see Brunswick*

Sandersville • *Washington County C/C* • Christy Hinton; Pres.; 131 W. Haynes St., Ste. B; 31082; Washington; P 21,100; M 220; (478) 552-3288; Fax (478) 552-1449; chamber@washingtoncountyga.com; www.washingtoncountyga.com

Sandy Springs • *see Alpharetta*

U.S. Chambers of Commerce

Savannah • *Savannah Area C/C* • William W. Hubbard; Pres./CEO; 101 E. Bay St.; P.O. Box 1628; 31402; Chatham; P 304,000; M 2,200; (912) 644-6400; Fax (912) 644-6499; info@savannahchamber.com; www.savannahchamber.com*

Sky Valley • *see Clayton*

Smyrna • *see Atlanta-Cobb C/C*

Soperton • *Soperton-Treutlen C/C* • Tammi Walraven; Secy.; 488 Second St.; P.O. Box 296; 30457; Treutlen; P 6,000; M 55; (912) 529-6868; Fax (912) 529-4385; sopertontreutlenchamber@hotmail.com

Springfield • *Effingham County C/C* • Rick Lott; Exec. Dir.; 520 W. Third St.; P.O. Box 1078; 31329; Effingham; P 56,000; M 350; (912) 754-3301; Fax (912) 754-1236; ricklott@effinghamcounty.com; www.effinghamcounty.com*

Statesboro • *Statesboro-Bulloch C/C* • Phyllis Thompson; Pres.; 102 S. Main St.; P.O. Box 303; 30459; Bulloch; P 70,000; M 700; (912) 764-6111; Fax (912) 489-3108; phyllis.thompson@statesboro-chamber.org; www.statesboro-chamber.org

Summerville • *Chattooga County C/C* • David Tidmore; Pres.; 44 Hwy. 48; P.O. Box 217; 30747; Chattooga; P 26,000; M 156; (706) 857-4033; Fax (706) 857-6963; dtidmore@windstream.net; chattoogachamber.us

Swainsboro • *Swainsboro-Emanuel County C/C* • Bill Rogers Jr.; Exec. Dir.; 102 S. Main St.; 30401; Emanuel; P 24,000; M 294; (478) 237-6426; Fax (478) 237-7460; swainsborochambr@bellsouth.net; www.emanuelchamber.org

Sylvania • *Screven County C/C* • Latasha Roberts; Exec. Dir.; 101 S. Main St.; 30467; Screven; P 15,000; M 170; (912) 564-7878; Fax (912) 564-7245; info@screvencounty.com; www.screvencounty.com

Sylvester • *Sylvester-Worth County C/C* • Karen M. Rackley; Exec. Dir./Pres.; 122 N. Main St.; P.O. Box 768; 31791; Worth; P 22,000; M 225; (229) 776-7718; (229) 776-6501; Fax (229) 776-7719; info@swcountychamber.com; www.swcountychamber.com*

Talbotton • *Talbot County C/C* • Pam Jordon; Exec. Dir.; P.O. Box 98; 31827; Talbot; P 6,900; M 100; (706) 665-8079; Fax (706) 665-8660; info@talbotcountychamber.org; www.talbotcountychamber.org

Tallulah Falls • *see Clayton*

Thomaston • *Thomaston-Upson C/C* • Lori Smith; Pres.; 110 W. Main St.; P.O. Box 827; 30286; Upson; P 27,000; M 320; (706) 647-9686; Fax (706) 647-1703; pam.white1@windstream.net; www.thomastongachamber.com*

Thomasville • *Thomasville-Thomas County C/C* • Lauren Basford; Exec. Dir.; 401 S. Broad St.; 31792; Thomas; P 45,000; M 500; (229) 226-9600; Fax (229) 226-9603; info@thomasvillechamber.com; www.thomasvillechamber.com*

Thomson • *Thomson-McDuffie County C/C* • Debbie Jones; Exec. Dir.; 149 Main St.; 30824; McDuffie; P 22,000; M 300; (706) 597-1000; Fax (706) 595-2143; debbie.jones@thomson-mcduffie.net; www.thomson-mcduffie.com*

Tifton • *Tifton-Tift County C/C* • Brian Marlowe; Pres./CEO; 100 Central Ave.; P.O. Box 165; 31793; Tift; P 47,000; M 600; (229) 382-6200; Fax (229) 386-2232; bmarlowe@tiftonchamber.org; www.tiftonchamber.org*

Tiger • *see Clayton*

Toccoa • *Toccoa-Stephens County C/C* • Wendi Bailey; Pres.; 160 N. Alexander St.; P.O. Box 577; 30577; Stephens; P 25,000; M 450; (706) 886-2132; wendi@taccoagachamber.com; www.toccoagachamber.com*

Towns County • *see Hiawassee*

Trenton • *Dade County C/C* • Debbie Tinker; Exec. Dir.; 111 Railway Ln.; P.O. Box 1014; 30752; Dade; P 16,100; M 130; (706) 657-4488; Fax (706) 657-7513; dcoc@tvn.net; www.dadechamber.com*

Tyrone • *see Fayetteville*

Unadilla • *see Vienna*

Valdosta • *Valdosta-Lowndes County C/C* • Myrna Ballard; Pres.; 416 N. Ashley St.; 31601; Lowndes; P 109,233; M 1,365; (229) 247-8100; Fax (229) 245-0071; chamber@valdostachamber.com; www.valdostachamber.com*

Vidalia • *Toombs-Montgomery C/C* • Bill Mitchell; Pres.; 2805 E. First St.; 30474; Toombs & Montgomery; P 35,000; M 500; (912) 537-4466; Fax (912) 537-1805; information@toombschamber.com; www.toombsmontgomerychamber.com

Vienna • *Dooly County C/C* • Rhonda Lamb-Heath; Exec. Dir.; 110 E. Union St.; P.O. Box 308; 31092; Dooly; P 11,566; M 150; (229) 268-8275; Fax (229) 268-8200; rhonda@bigpigjig.com; www.doolychamber.com

Waco • *Haralson County C/C* • Jennie English; Pres./CEO; 70 Murphy Campus Blvd.; 30182; Haralson; P 28,670; M 385; (770) 537-5594; Fax (770) 537-5873; hccoc@haralson.org; www.haralson.org*

Wadley • *see Louisville*

Ware County • *see Waycross*

Warm Springs • *Meriwether County C/C* • Carolyn McKinley; Pres.; 91 Broad St.; P.O. Box 9; 31830; Meriwether; P 22,800; M 214; (706) 655-2558; Fax (706) 655-2812; meriwetherchamber@windstream.net; www.meriwethercountychamberofcommerce.com

Warner Robins • *Robins Reg. C/C* • April Bragg; Pres./CEO; 1228 Watson Blvd.; 31093; Houston; P 125,000; M 900; (478) 922-8585; Fax (478) 328-7745; info@robinsregion.com; www.robinsregion.com*

Warrenton • *Warren County C/C* • Cindy Rivers; Pres.; 46 S. Norwood St.; P.O. Box 27; 30828; Warren; P 6,000; M 90; (706) 465-9604; Fax (706) 465-1789; chamber@warrencountyga.com; www.warrencountyga.com

Washington • *Washington-Wilkes C/C* • Jenny Clarke; Exec. Dir.; 22B West Sq.; P.O. Box 661; 30673; Wilkes; P 11,000; M 200; (706) 678-2013; (706) 678-5111; Fax (706) 678-2089; chamberdirectorwashingtonga@gmail.com; www.washingtonwilkes.org

Watkinsville • *Oconee County C/C* • Kay Keller; Pres.; 55 Nancy Dr.; P.O. Box 348; 30677; Oconee; P 32,800; M 346; (706) 769-7947; Fax (706) 769-7948; kkeller@oconeechamber.org; www.oconeechamber.org

Waycross • *Waycross-Ware County Chamber* • Eva Byrd; Exec. Dir.; 315 Plant Ave., Ste. B; 31501; Ware; P 36,312; M 450; (912) 283-3742; Fax (912) 283-0121; eva@waycrosschamber.org; www.waycrosschamber.org*

Waynesboro • *Burke County C/C* • Ashley Roberts; Exec. Dir.; 241 E. Sixth St.; 30830; Burke; P 23,100; M 200; (706) 554-5451; Fax (706) 554-7091; burkechamber@selectburke.com; www.burkechamber.org

West Point • *see Lanett, AL*

Williamson • *see Zebulon*

Winder • *Barrow County C/C* • Thomas R. Jennings; Pres./CEO; 6 Porter St.; P.O. Box 456; 30680; Barrow; P 75,000; M 430; (770) 867-9444; Fax (770) 867-6366; trjennings@barrowchamber.com; www.barrowchamber.com*

Woodbine • *see Kingsland*

Wrens • *see Louisville*

Wrightsville • *Wrightsville-Johnson County C/C* • Lynn Lamb; Admin.; 6745 E. College St.; P.O. Box 94; 31096; Johnson; P 9,500; M 95; (478) 864-7200; Fax (478) 864-7200; commerce@wrightsville-johnsoncounty.com; www.wrightsville-johnsoncounty.com

Young Harris • *see Hiawassee*

Zebulon • *Pike County C/C & Dev. Auth.* • Christy Hammons; Exec. Dir.; 416 Thomaston St.; P.O. Box 1147; 30295; Pike; P 18,000; M 302; (770) 567-2029; Fax (770) 567-7290; pikeida@pikecountygachamber.com; www.pikecountygachamber.com*

Guam

Guam C/C • David P. Leddy; Pres.; 173 Aspinall Ave., Ste. 101, Ada Plaza Center Bldg.; P.O. Box 283; Hagatna; 96932; P 182,111; M 396; (671) 472-6311; (671) 472-8001; Fax (671) 472-6202; info@guamchamber.com.gu; www.guamchamber.com.gu

Hawaii

C of C of Hawaii • Sherry Menor-McNamara; Pres./CEO; 1132 Bishop St., Ste. 2105; Honolulu; 96813; Honolulu; P 1,420,000; M 1,100; (808) 545-4300; Fax (808) 545-4369; smenor-mcnamara@cochawaii.org; www.cochawaii.org*

Haleiwa • *North Shore C/C* • Antya Miller; Exec. Dir.; 66-434 Kamehameha Hwy.; P.O. Box 878; 96712; Honolulu; P 18,300; M 160; (808) 637-4558; Fax (808) 637-4556; info@gonorthshore.org; www.gonorthshore.org

Hilo • *Hawaii Island C/C* • Miles Yoshioka; Exec. Officer; 117 Keawe St., Ste. 205; 96720; Hawaii; P 186,100; M 270; (808) 935-7178; Fax (808) 961-4435; admin@hicc.biz; www.hicc.biz

Honolulu • *Chinese C/C of Hawaii* • Wen Chung Lin; Exec. V.P.; 8 S. King St., Ste. 201; 96813; Honolulu; P 1,300,000; M 350; (808) 533-3181; Fax (808) 537-6767; info@chinesechamber.com; www.chinesechamber.com

Honolulu • *Filipino C/C* • Rosemarie Mendoza; Pres.; 1125 N. King St., Ste. 302; 96817; Honolulu; P 800,000; M 400; (808) 843-8838; info@filipinochamber.org; www.filipinochamber.org

Kailua • *Kailua (Oahu) C/C* • Puna Nam; Pres.; 600 Kailua Rd., Ste. 107; P.O. Box 1496; 96734; Honolulu; P 50,000; M 200; (808) 261-7997; (888) 261-7997; kcoc@kailuachamber.com; www.kailuachamber.com

Kailua-Kona • *Kona-Kohala C/C* • Kirstin Kahaloa; Exec. Dir.; 75-5737 Kuakini Hwy., Ste. 208; 96740; Hawaii; P 191,000; M 540; (808) 329-1758; Fax (808) 329-8564; info@kona-kohala.com; www.kona-kohala.com*

Kaunakakai • *Molokai C/C* • Robert Stephenson; Pres.; 40 Ala Malama St., Ste. 208; P.O. Box 515; 96748; Maui; P 7,000; M 50; (808) 646-0928; info@molokaichamber.org; www.molokaichamber.org

Lihue • *Kauai C/C* • Mark Perriello; Pres./CEO; 4268 Rice St., Ste. H; P.O. Box 1969; 96766; Kauai; P 67,100; M 450; (808) 245-7363; Fax (808) 245-8815; info@kauaichamber.org; www.kauaichamber.org

Ocean View • *Ka'u C/C* • Starina Leilani Libonati; Secy.; P.O. Box 6710; 96737; Hawaii; P 6,700; M 160; (808) 939-8449; (808) 937-2750; info@kauchamber.com; www.kauchamber.org

Wailuku • *Maui C/C* • Pamela Tumpap; Pres.; 95 Mahalani St., Ste. 22A; 96793; Maui; P 155,000; M 600; (808) 244-0081; Fax (808) 244-0083; info@mauichamber.com; www.mauichamber.com

Idaho

Idaho Chamber Alliance • c/o Boise Metro C/C; P.O. Box 2368; Boise; 83701; Ada; P 1,635,000; (208) 733-3974; contact@idahochamberalliance.com; www.idahochamberalliance.com

American Falls • *Greater American Falls C/C* • P.O. Box 207; 83211; Power; P 4,100; M 50; (208) 226-7214; amfallschamber@gmail.com; www.amfallschamber.com

Arco • *Butte County C/C* • Chad Cheyney; V.P.; P.O. Box 837; 83213; Butte; P 2,800; M 45; (208) 527-3060; (208) 527-3249; ccheyney@uidaho.edu; www.buttecountychamber.com

Ashton • *Ashton Area C/C* • Linda Janssen; Pres.; 714 Main St.; P.O. Box 351; 83420; Fremont; P 1,000; M 65; (208) 652-3355; info@ashtonidaho.com; www.ashtonidaho.com

Bayview • *Bayview C/C* • Marsha Ritzheimer; Pres.; P.O. Box 121; 83803; Kootenai; P 300; M 35; (208) 683-3276; peteritz@frontier.com; www.bayviewidaho.org

Blackfoot • *Greater Blackfoot Area C/C* • Jesica Smith; Comm. & Mktg. Mgr.; 130 N.W. Main St.; P.O. Box 801; 83221; Bingham; P 11,000; M 230; (208) 785-0510; Fax (208) 785-7974; chamber@blackfootchamber.org; www.blackfootchamber.org*

Boise • *Boise Metro C/C* • Bill Connors; Pres./CEO; 250 S. 5th St., Ste. 300; P.O. Box 2368; 83701; Ada; P 600,000; M 1,800; (208) 472-5205; Fax (208) 472-5201; bconnors@boisechamber.org; www.boisechamber.org*

Bonners Ferry • *Bonners Ferry C/C* • Rhea Verbanic; Pres.; 6373 Bonner St.; P.O. Box X; 83805; Boundary; P 2,600; M 7; (208) 267-5922; bonnersferrychamber@hotmail.com; www.bonnersferrychamber.com

Buhl • *Buhl C/C* • Michelle Olsen; Exec. Dir.; 716 Hwy. 30 E.; 83316; Twin Falls; P 4,122; M 180; (208) 543-6682; Fax (208) 543-2185; michelleo@buhlchamber.org; www.buhlchamber.org

Burley • *see Heyburn*

Caldwell • *Caldwell C/C* • Theresa Hardin IOM; Exec. Dir.; 704 Blaine St.; 83605; Canyon; P 60,000; M 380; (208) 459-7493; (866) 206-6944; Fax (208) 454-1284; thardin@caldwellchamber.org; www.caldwellchamber.org*

Cascade • *Cascade C/C* • Kathy Hull; P.O. Box 571; 83611; Valley; P 1,000; M 100; (208) 382-3833; info@cascadechamber.com; www.cascadechamber.com

Challis • *Challis Area C/C* • Melissa Perkins Fitzgerald; Exec. Dir.; 632 E. Main St.; P.O. Box 1130; 83226; Custer; P 1,000; M 70; (208) 879-2771; Fax (208) 879-5836; challischamber@custertel.net; www.challischamber.com

Coeur d'Alene • *Coeur d'Alene Area C/C* • Steve Wilson; Pres./CEO; 105 N. 1st St., Ste. 100; 83814; Kootenai; P 45,900; M 1,300; (208) 664-3194; Fax (208) 667-9338; info@cdachamber.com; www.cdachamber.com

Coolin • *Priest Lake C/C* • P.O. Box 174; 83821; Bonner; P 3,000; M 120; (208) 443-3191; (888) 774-3785; Fax (208) 443-3191; info@priestlake.org; www.priestlake.org

Cottonwood • *Cottonwood C/C* • Greg Wherry; Pres.; P.O. Box 15; 83522; Idaho; P 950; M 50; (208) 962-3851; www.cottonwoodidaho.org

Council • *Council C/C* • Ken Bell; Pres.; P.O. Box 527; 83612; Adams; P 815; M 100; (208) 253-6830; Fax (208) 253-6830; councilchamber@ctcweb.net; www.councilchamberofcommerce.com

Craigmont • *Greater Craigmont C/C* • Virginia Frazier; P.O. Box 365; 83523; Lewis; P 1,086; M 25; (208) 924-0050; (208) 924-5432; cm_frazier@wildblue.net; www.craigmontareachamber.com

Darlington • *see Arco*

Dixie • *see Elk City*

Donnelly • *Greater Donnelly Area C/C* • Cheryl Teed; P.O. Box 83; 83615; Valley; P 140; M 12; (208) 634-7137; cateed@cableone.net; www.donnellychamber.org

Downey • *Downey C/C* • Nancy Dalley; Pres.; P.O. Box 353; 83234; Bannock; P 650; M 30; (208) 897-5342; (208) 221-3028; Fax (208) 897-5677; cheri@srv.net; www.downeyidaho.com

Driggs • *Teton Valley C/C* • Jennie White; Chair; 57 S. Main St.; P.O. Box 250; 83422; Teton; P 10,000; M 200; (208) 354-2500; Fax (208) 354-2517; tvcc@tetonvalleychamber.com; www.tetonvalleychamber.com

Eagle • *Eagle C/C* • Gretchen Gilbert; Pres.; 148 N. Second St., Ste. 101; P.O. Box 1300; 83616; Ada; P 20,000; M 400; (208) 939-4222; Fax (208) 327-2139; information@eaglechamber.com; www.eaglechamber.com

Elk City • *Elk City Area Alliance* • Earl Sherrer; V.P.; P.O. Box 402; 83525; Idaho; P 265; M 60; (208) 842-2597; Fax (208) 842-2597; csherrer@yahoo.com; www.elkcityidaho.org

Emmett • *Gem County C/C* • Stephanie LaMore; Pres./CEO; 1022 S. Washington Ave.; P.O. Box 592; 83617; Gem; P 17,000; M 280; (208) 365-3485; Fax (208) 365-3220; chamber@emmettidaho.com; emmettidaho.com*

Garden Valley • *Greater Garden Valley Area C/C* • Diane Caughlin; Pres.; 609 S. Middlefork Rd.; P.O. Box 10; 83622; Boise; P 3,500; M 100; (208) 462-5003; (208) 462-4620; Fax (208) 462-3321; info@gvchamber.org; www.gvchamber.org

Glenns Ferry • *Glenns Ferry C/C & Visitors Center* • Jean Mulle; Dir.; 105 E. First Ave.; 83623; Elmore; P 1,400; M 80; (208) 366-7345; Fax (208) 366-2238; www.glennsferryidaho.org

Grace • *Grace C/C* • P.O. Box 214; 83241; Caribou; P 1,000; M 150; (208) 425-3912; Fax (208) 425-3912; info@graceidaho.com; www.graceidaho.com

Grangeville • *Grangeville C/C* • Melinda Hall; Pine & Hwy. 95 N.; P.O. Box 212; 83530; Idaho; P 3,300; M 135; (208) 983-0460; Fax (208) 983-1429; chamber@grangevilleidaho.com; www.grangevilleidaho.com

Hagerman • *Hagerman Valley C/C* • P.O. Box 599; 83332; Gooding; P 850; M 50; (208) 837-9131; info@hagermanvalleychamber.com; www.hagermanvalleychamber.com

Hailey • *Hailey C/C* • Debra Hall; Pres.; 781 S. Main; P.O. Box 100; 83333; Blaine; P 8,500; M 300; (208) 788-3484; Fax (208) 578-1595; info@haileyidaho.com; www.haileyidaho.com*

Hayden • *Hayden C/C* • Nancy Lowery; Pres.; P.O. Box 1210; 83835; Kootenai; P 14,000; M 184; (208) 762-1185; info@haydenchamber.org; www.haydenchamber.org

Heyburn • *Mini-Cassia C/C* • Kyla Sawyer; Pres./CEO; 1177 7th St.; P.O. Box 640; 83336; Cassia & Minidoka; P 80,000; M 400; (208) 679-4793; Fax (208) 679-4794; president@minicassiachamber.com; www.minicassiachamber.com*

Homedale • *Homedale C/C* • Gavin Parker; Pres.; P.O. Box 845; 83628; Owyhee; P 2,613; M 48; (208) 337-3271; Fax (208) 337-3272; www.cityofhomedale.com

Howe • *see Arco*

Idaho City • *Idaho City C/C* • Gary Secor; Pres.; 101 Main St.; P.O. Box 507; 83631; Boise; P 458; M 10; (208) 392-4159; www.idahocitychamber.com

Idaho Falls • *Greater Idaho Falls C/C* • Michelle Holt; CEO; 425 N. Capital Ave.; 83402; Bonneville; P 59,000; M 606; (208) 523-1010; Fax (208) 523-2255; ceo@idahofallschamber.com; www.idahofallschamber.com*

Island Park • *Island Park Area C/C* • Jay Bailey; Pres.; P.O. Box 83; 83429; Fremont; P 1,500; M 150; (208) 558-7755; ipchamber@yahoo.com; www.islandparkchamber.org

Jerome • *Jerome C/C* • Kathleen Hite; Exec. Dir.; 104 W. Main St.; P.O. Box 835; 83338; Jerome; P 10,000; M 200; (208) 324-2711; Fax (208) 416-6777; director@visitjeromeidaho.com; www.visitjeromeidaho.com*

Kamiah • *Kamiah C/C* • Robert Simmons; Pres.; 518 Main St.; P.O. Box 1124; 83536; Lewis; P 1,200; M 80; (208) 935-2290; info@kamiahchamber.com; www.kamiahchamber.com

Kellogg • *Historic Silver Valley C/C* • Colleen Rosson; Coord.; 10 Station Ave.; 83837; Shoshone; P 13,000; M 174; (208) 784-0821; Fax (208) 733-4343; director@silvervalleychamber.com; www.silvervalleychamber.com

Ketchum • *Visit Sun Valley* • 491 Sun Valley Rd.; P.O. Box 4934; 83340; Blaine; P 10,000; M 380; (208) 726-3423; (800) 634-3347; Fax (208) 726-2521; info@visitsunvalley.com; www.visitsunvalley.com

Kooskia • *Kooskia C/C* • Steve Summers; Pres.; P.O. Box 310; 83539; Idaho; P 625; M 20; (208) 926-4362; (208) 926-4109; Fax (208) 926-4362; kooskiachamber@qrowireless.com; www.kooskia.com

Kuna • *Kuna C/C* • 123 Swan Falls Rd.; P.O. Box 123; 83634; Ada; P 16,000; M 100; (208) 922-9254; information@kunachamber.com; www.kunachamber.com

Lava Hot Springs • *Greater Lava Hot Springs C/C* • Vicky Lyon; Pres.; 110 E. Main; P.O. Box 238; 83246; Bannock; P 550; M 85; (208) 776-5500; (208) 244-2570; findout@lavahotsprings.org; www.lavahotsprings.org

Leslie • *see Arco*

Lewiston • *see Clarkston, WA*

Mackay • *see Arco*

McCall • *McCall Area C/C* • Rick Certano; Pres.; 301 E. Lake St.; P.O. Box 350; 83638; Valley; P 3,500; M 250; (208) 634-7631; Fax (208) 634-7752; info@mccallchamber.org; www.mccallchamber.org

Meridian • *Meridian C/C* • Anne Little Roberts; Pres./CEO; 215 E. Franklin Rd.; P.O. Box 7; 83680; Ada; P 83,596; M 608; (208) 888-2817; Fax (208) 888-2682; info@meridianchamber.org; www.meridianchamber.org*

Middleton • *Middleton C/C* • Kassa Hartley; Pres.; P.O. Box 434; 83644; Canyon; P 5,000; M 80; (208) 713-5662; info@middletonchamber.org; www.middletonchamber.org*

Moore • *see Arco*

Moscow • *Moscow C/C* • Gina Taruscio; Exec. Dir.; 411 S. Main St.; P.O. Box 8936; 83843; Latah; P 21,000; M 650; (208) 882-1800; staff@moscowchamber.com; www.moscowchamber.com

Mountain Home • *Mountain Home C/C* • Renae Green; Exec. Dir.; 205 N. 3rd E.; 83647; Elmore; P 15,000; M 225; (208) 587-4334; chamber@mountainhomechamber.com; www.mountainhomechamber.com

Nampa • *Nampa C/C* • Debbie Kling; Pres./CEO; 315 11th Ave. S.; 83651; Canyon; P 91,000; M 490; (208) 466-4641; (208) 466-4626; Fax (208) 466-4677; info@nampa.com; www.nampa.com*

New Meadows • *Meadows Valley C/C* • Len Yancey; Pres.; P.O. Box 328; 83654; Adams; P 800; M 29; (208) 347 2421; (208) 347-4636; Fax (208) 347-4637; christinanelson@frontiernet.net; www.meadowsvalleychamber.org

New Plymouth • *New Plymouth C/C* • Janet Warnke; Bd. Member; P.O. Box 26; 83655; Payette; P 1,430; M 100; (208) 278-3696; www.npidaho.com

Orofino • *Orofino C/C* • Stephanie Deyo; Exec. Dir.; P.O. Box 2346; 83544; Clearwater; P 3,500; M 100; (208) 476-4335; Fax (208) 476-3634; director@orofino.com; www.orofino.com

Orogrande • *see Elk City*

Pierce • *see Weippe*

Pocatello • *Pocatello-Chubbuck C/C* • Matthew Hunter; Pres./CEO; 324 S. Main; P.O. Box 626; 83204; Bannock; P 69,000; M 800; (208) 233-1525; Fax (208) 233-1527; mhunter@pocatelloidaho.com; www.pocatelloidaho.com*

Post Falls • *Post Falls C/C* • Pam Houser; Pres./CEO; 201 E. 4th Ave.; 83854; Kootenai; P 80,000; M 480; (208) 773-5016; info@postfallschamber.com; www.postfallschamber.com*

Preston • *Greater Preston Bus. Assn.* • David Cox; Pres.; P.O. Box 552; 83263; Franklin; P 13,000; M 80; (208) 240-8296; www.prestonidaho.org

Priest River • *Priest River C/C* • Anne Sweetman; Secy.; 119 Main St., Ste. 203; P.O. Box 929; 83856; Bonner; P 1,500; M 120; (208) 448-2721; prchamber@conceptcable.com; www.priestriverchamber.com

Rathdrum • *Rathdrum Area C/C* • Shanie Campbell-Rountree; Mbrshp. & Events Dir.; 8184 W. Main St.; 83858; Kootenai; P 7,900; M 135; (208) 687-2866; Fax (208) 687-2866; office@rathdrumchamberofcommerce.com; rathdrumchamberofcommerce.com

Red River • *see Elk City*

Reubens • *see Craigmont*

Rexburg • *Rexburg Area C/C* • Ted Austin; Pres./CEO; 127 E. Main St.; 83440; Madison; P 25,000; M 400; (208) 356-5700; Fax (208) 356-5799; info@rexburgchamber.com; www.rexburgchamber.org

Riggins • *Salmon River C/C* • Carolyn Friend; P.O. Box 289; 83549; Idaho; P 438; M 100; (866) 221-3901; cfriend@frontiernet.net; www.rigginsidaho.com

Rupert • *see Heyburn*

Saint Anthony • *Greater Saint Anthony C/C* • Cathy Koon; Pres.; 420 N. Bridge St., Ste. C; 83445; Fremont; P 3,400; M 100; (208) 624-4870; sachamber@fretel.com; www.stanthonychamber.com

Saint Maries • *Saint Maries C/C* • Shirley Ackerman; Pres.; 906 Main Ave.; P.O. Box 162; 83861; Benewah; P 2,652; M 56; (208) 245-3563; manager@stmarieschamber.org; www.stmarieschamber.org

Salmon • *Salmon Valley C/C* • Debbie Ellis; Admin.; 200 Main St.; 83467; Lemhi; P 5,702; M 190; (208) 756-2100; (800) 727-2540; Fax (208) 756-2100; svcc1@centurytel.net; www.salmonchamber.com

Sandpoint • *Greater Sandpoint C/C* • Kate McAlister; Exec. Dir.; 1202 Hwy. 95 N.; P.O. Box 928; 83864; Bonner; P 8,000; M 550; (208) 263-2161; (800) 800-2106; Fax (208) 265-5289; info@sandpointchamber.com; www.sandpointchamber.com*

Soda Springs • *Soda Springs C/C* • Allen Skinner; 9 W. 2nd S.; 83276; Caribou; P 3,000; M 130; (208) 547-2600; sodacoc@sodachamber.com; www.sodachamber.com

Spirit Lake • *Spirit Lake C/C* • Tom Russell; Pres.; 32173 N. 5th; P.O. Box 772; 83869; Kootenai; P 1,600; M 94; (208) 623-3411; carol@spiritlakechamber.com; www.spiritlakechamber.com

Stanley • *Stanley-Sawtooth C/C* • Ellen Libertine; Coord.; Hwy. 21, Community Bldg.; P.O. Box 8; 83278; Custer; P 100; M 110; (208) 774-3411; (800) 878-7950; information@stanleycc.org; www.stanleycc.org

Tetonia • *see Driggs*

Twin Falls • *Twin Falls Area C/C* • Shawn Barigar; Pres./CEO; 2015 Neilsen Point Pl., Ste. 100; 83301; Twin Falls; P 200,000; M 830; (208) 733-3974; Fax (208) 733-9216; info@twinfallschamber.com; www.twinfallschamber.com*

Victor • *see Driggs*

Wallace • *Historic Wallace C/C* • Diane Reifer; Coord.; 10 River St., Exit 61; 83873; Shoshone; P 1,000; M 185; (208) 753-7151; Fax (208) 753-7151; director@wallaceidahochamber.com; www.wallaceidahochamber.com

Weippe • *Pierce-Weippe C/C* • Kim Cox; Pres.; 4116 Three Mile Rd.; P.O. Box 378; 83553; Clearwater; P 700; M 51; (208) 435-4406; Fax (208) 435-4556; info@pierce-weippechamber.com; www.pierce-weippechamber.com

U.S. Chambers of Commerce

**Weiser • *Weiser C/C •* Laurel Adams; Exec. Dir.; 309 State St.; 83672; Washington; P 5,500; M 275; (208) 414-0452; Fax (208) 414-0451; info@weiserchamber.com; www.weiserchamber.com

**Wilder • *Wilder C/C •* Tamara Patrick; Pres.; 20441 Patrick Ln.; 83676; Canyon; P 1,700; M 20; (208) 697-3571; tap@speedyquick.net; www.cityofwilder.org

**Winchester • *see Craigmont*

Illinois

Illinois C of C • Todd Maisch; Pres./CEO; 300 S. Wacker Dr., Ste. 1600; Chicago; 60606; Cook; P 12,875,255; M 4,000; (312) 983-7100; Fax (312) 983-7101; info@ilchamber.org; ilchamber.org

**Abingdon • *Abingdon C/C •* Bunny Dalton; 106 N. Monroe; 61410; Knox; P 3,600; M 54; (309) 462-2629

**Addison • *Addison C/C & Ind. •* Bernadette LaRocca; Exec. Dir.; 777 W. Army Trl. Rd., Ste. D; 60101; DuPage; P 37,000; M 287; (630) 543-4300; Fax (630) 543-4355; addisonchamber@sbcglobal.net; www.addisonchamber.org*

**Albion • *Albion Area C/C •* Susan Roethe; Pres.; P.O. Box 82; 62806; Edwards; P 2,000; M 80; (618) 445-2303; Fax (618) 445-2911; info@albionchamber.org; www.albionchamber.org

**Aledo • *Aledo Area C/C •* Diane Sharp; Exec. Asst.; P.O. Box 261; 61231; Mercer; P 4,000; M 120; (309) 582-5373; Fax (309) 582-5373; dsharp@aledochamber.org; www.aledochamber.org

**Algonquin • *Algonquin-Lake in the Hills C/C •* Katrina K. McGuire; Exec. Dir.; 2200 Harnish Dr.; 60102; Kane & McHenry; P 60,000; M 350; (847) 658-5300; Fax (847) 658-6546; info@alchamber.com; www.alchamber.com*

**Alsip • *Alsip C/C •* Mary Schmidt; Exec. Dir.; 12159 S. Pulaski Rd.; 60803; Cook; P 20,000; M 300; (708) 597-2668; (800) IN-ALSIP; Fax (708) 597-5962; info@alsipchamber.org; www.alsipchamber.org

**Altamont • *Altamont C/C •* Beth Smith; Admin. Asst.; P.O. Box 141; 62411; Effingham; P 2,300; M 70; (618) 483-5714; secretary@altamontchamber.com; www.altamontchamber.com

**Alton • *see Godfrey*

**Amboy • *Amboy Area C/C •* Dr. Colin Baker; Pres.; P.O. Box 163; 61310; Lee; P 3,000; M 100; (815) 857-2458; (815) 857-3814; amboychamber@gmail.com; www.amboychamber.com

**Anna • *Union County C/C •* Lindsey Sadler; Exec. Dir.; 330 S. Main St.; 62906; Union; P 18,293; M 155; (618) 833-6311; Fax (618) 833-1903; ucchamber@outlook.com; www.ucchamber.com

**Antioch • *Antioch C/C & Ind. •* Barbara Porch; Exec. Dir.; 882 Main St.; 60002; Lake; P 14,500; M 350; (847) 395-2233; Fax (847) 395-8954; office@antiochchamber.org; www.antiochchamber.org*

**Aptakisic • *see Lincolnshire*

**Arcola • *Arcola C/C •* Mark Spainhour; Exec. Dir.; P.O. Box 274; 61910; Douglas; P 3,000; M 90; (217) 268-4530; (800) 336-5456; Fax (217) 268-3690; staff@arcolachamber.com; www.arcolachamber.com

**Arlington Heights • *Arlington Heights C/C •* Jon S. Ridler; Exec. Dir.; 311 S. Arlington Heights Rd., Ste. 20; 60005; Cook & Lake; P 80,000; M 500; (847) 253-1703; Fax (847) 253-9133; info@arlingtonhcc.com; www.arlingtoncc.com

**Arthur • *Arthur Area Assn. of Commerce •* James Aikman; P.O. Box 42; 61911; Douglas & Moultrie; P 2,300; M 75; (217) 543-2999; randall@arthur.k12.il.us; www.arthurchamber.com

**Aurora • *Aurora Reg. C/C •* Joseph Henning IOM ACE; Pres./CEO; 43 W. Galena Blvd.; 60506; DuPage, Kane, Kendall & Will; P 182,000; M 800; (630) 256-3180; Fax (630) 256-3189; jhenning@aurorachamber.com; www.aurorachamber.com

**Bannockburn • *see Deerfield*

**Barrington • *Barrington Area C/C •* Suzanne Corr; Pres./CEO; 190 E. James St.; 60010; Lake; P 44,100; M 900; (847) 381-2525; Fax (847) 381-2540; email@barringtonchamber.com; www.barringtonchamber.com*

**Bartlett • *Bartlett C/C •* Amy Feeley; Pres./CEO; 138 S. Oak Ave.; 60103; Cook; P 70,000; M 350; (630) 830-0324; Fax (630) 830-9724; info@BartlettChamber.com; www.BartlettChamber.com*

**Batavia • *Batavia C/C •* Holly Deitchman; Exec. Dir.; 106 W. Wilson St.; 60510; Kane; P 27,000; M 300; (630) 879-7134; Fax (630) 879-7215; info@bataviachamber.org; www.bataviachamber.org*

**Beach Park • *see Gurnee*

**Beardstown • *Beardstown C/C •* Janice Jamison; Exec. Dir.; 101 W. 3rd St.; 62618; Cass; P 6,000; M 95; (217) 323-3271; Fax (217) 323-3271; info@beardstownil.org; www.beardstownil.org

**Bedford Park • *Burbank C/C •* Barbara Karcz; Exec. Secy.; P.O. Box 972; 60499; Cook; P 29,000; M 120; (708) 424-4668; Fax (708) 422-5805; burbankchamber@att.net; www.burbankilchamber.com

**Beecher • *Beecher C/C •* Patty Meyer; Exec. Dir.; P.O. Box 292; 60401; Will; P 4,400; M 100; (708) 946-6803; info@beecherchamber.com; www.beecherchamber.com

**Belleville • *Greater Belleville C/C •* John Lengerman; Exec. Dir.; 216 E. A St.; 62220; St. Clair; P 45,000; M 550; (618) 233-2015; Fax (618) 233-2077; info@bellevillechamber.org; www.bellevillechamber.org*

**Bellwood • *Bellwood C/C & Ind. •* Jacqueline Walton; Pres.; P.O. Box 86; 60104; Cook; P 21,000; M 100; (708) 397-6646; bellwoodchamber@gmail.com; www.bellwoodchamber.org

**Belvidere • *Belvidere Area C/C •* Thomas Lassandro; Exec. Dir.; 130 S. State St., Ste. 300; 61008; Boone; P 46,000; M 400; (815) 544-4357; Fax (815) 547-7654; tlassandro@belviderechamber.com; www.belviderechamber.com*

**Benld • *see Gillespie*

**Bensenville • *Bensenville C/C •* Peter Gallagher; Dir.; 161 N. Church Rd.; P.O. Box 905; 60106; DuPage; P 19,000; M 105; (630) 860-3800; Fax (630) 860-3814; board@bensenvillechamber.com; www.bensenvillechamber.com

**Benton • *Benton-West City Area C/C •* Steve Browning; Pres.; 211 N. Main St.; P.O. Box 574; 62812; Franklin; P 7,000; M 200; (618) 438-2121; (866) 536-8423; Fax (618) 438-8011; chamber@bentonwestcity.com; www.bentonwestcity.com

**Bethalto • *see Godfrey*

Bloomingdale • *Bloomingdale C/C* • Deborah S. Evans; Pres./CEO; 104 S. Bloomingdale Rd.; 60108; DuPage; P 20,000; M 250; (630) 980-9082; Fax (630) 980-9092; info@bloomingdalechamber.com; www.bloomingdalechamber.com*

Bloomington • *McLean County C/C* • Charlie Moore IOM CCE; Pres./CEO; 2203 E. Empire, Ste. B; P.O. Box 1586; 61702; McLean; P 170,000; M 1,000; (309) 829-6344; Fax (309) 827-3940; chamber@mcleancochamber.org; www.mcleancochamber.org*

Blue Island • *Blue Island Area C/C & Ind.* • Greg Lochow; Exec. Dir.; 2434 Vermont St.; 60406; Cook; P 22,600; M 150; (708) 388-1000; Fax (708) 388-1062; blueislandchamber@sbcglobal.net; www.blueislandchamber.org

Bolingbrook • *Bolingbrook Area C/C* • Kevin O'Keeffe; Exec. Dir.; 201-B Canterbury Ln.; 60440; DuPage; P 76,000; M 600; (630) 226-8420; Fax (630) 226-8426; info@bolingbrookchamber.org; www.bolingbrookchamber.org*

Bourbonnais • *see Kankakee*

Breese • *Breese C/C* • Emily Bruegge; Pres.; P.O. Box 132; 62230; Clinton; P 4,500; M 100; (618) 977-4995; (618) 526-7731; emilybruegge@gmail.com; www.breesechamber.org

Bridgeview • *Bridgeview C/C & Ind.* • Jerry Gresik; Pres.; 7300 W. 87th St.; Bridgeview Bank Bldg.; 60455; Cook; P 15,200; M 256; (708) 598-1700; Fax (708) 598-1709; info@bridgeviewchamber.com; www.bridgeviewchamber.com

Bridgeview • *The Hills C/C* • Donna Venezia; Exec. Dir./Secy.; P.O. Box 1164; 60455; Cook; P 30,000; M 175; (708) 364-7739; Fax (708) 364-7735; info@thehillschamber.com; www.thehillschamber.com

Brookfield • *Brookfield C/C* • Mike McNeily; Pres.; P.O. Box 38; 60513; Cook; P 19,000; M 90; (708) 268-8080; info@brookfieldchamber.net; www.brookfieldchamber.net

Bucktown • *see Chicago-Wicker Park & Bucktown C/C*

Buffalo Grove • *Buffalo Grove Lincolnshire C/C* • Lynne Schneider; Exec. Dir.; 50 1/2 Raupp Blvd.; P.O. Box 7124; 60089; Cook & Lake; P 44,000; M 310; (847) 541-7799; Fax (847) 541-7819; info@bgacc.org; bgacc.org*

Burr Ridge • *Willowbrook/Burr Ridge C/C & Ind.* • Cheryl Collins; Exec. Dir.; 8300 S. Madison; 60527; DuPage; P 18,600; M 250; (630) 654-0909; Fax (630) 654-0922; info@wbbrchamber.org; www.wbbrchamber.org*

Bushnell • *Bushnell C/C* • Don Swartzbaugh; Pres.; P.O. Box 111; 61422; McDonough; P 3,200; M 50; (309) 772-2171; chamber@bushnellchamber.com; www.bushnell.illinois.gov

Byron • *Byron Area C/C* • Deanna Mershon; Exec. Dir.; 232 W. 2nd St.; P.O. Box 405; 61010; Ogle; P 5,000; M 178; (815) 234-5500; Fax (815) 234-7114; byronchamber@gmail.com; www.byronchamber.com

Cahokia • *Cahokia Area C/C* • Richard Laux; Pres.; 103 Main St.; 62206; St. Clair; P 19,000; M 65; (618) 332-4258; Fax (618) 332-6690; cahokiachamber@gmail.com; www.cahokiachamber.org

Cairo • *Cairo C/C* • Monica Smith; 220 8th St.; 62914; Alexander; P 3,632; M 60; (618) 734-1840; cairo1@lazernetwireless.net

Calumet City • *Calumet City C/C* • Yolanda Lott; Pres.; 80 River Oaks Center; 60409; Cook; P 37,100; M 100; (708) 891-5888; Fax (708) 891-8877; info@calumetcitychamber.com; www.calumetcitychamber.com

Canton • *Canton Area C/C* • Amanda Atchley; Exec. Dir.; 45 East Side Sq., Ste. 303; 61520; Fulton; P 15,000; M 265; (309) 647-2677; Fax (309) 647-2712; aatchley@cantonillinois.org; www.cantonillinois.org*

Carbondale • *Carbondale C/C* • Les O'Dell; Exec. Dir.; 131 S. Illinois Ave.; 62903; Jackson; P 25,000; M 400; (618) 549-2146; Fax (618) 529-5063; info@carbondalechamber.com; www.carbondalechamber.com*

Carlinville • *Carlinville Comm. C/C* • Joyce Atteberry; Pres.; 112 North Side Sq.; 62626; Macoupin; P 5,851; M 150; (217) 854-2141; Fax (217) 854-8548; chambercarlinville@gmail.com; www.carlinvillechamber.com

Carmi • *Carmi C/C* • Glenn Coleman; Exec. Dir.; 225 E. Main St.; 62821; White; P 5,400; M 140; (618) 382-7606; Fax (618) 382-3458; chamber@cityofcarmi.com; www.cityofcarmi.com

Carol Stream • *Carol Stream C/C* • Luanne Newman; Exec. Dir.; 150 S. Gary Ave.; (inside the Holiday Inn & Suites); 60188; DuPage; P 41,000; M 280; (630) 665-3325; (630) 668-1900; Fax (630) 665-6965; info@carolstreamchamber.com; carolstreamchamber.com*

Carpentersville • *Northern Kane County C/C* • Melissa Hernandez; Exec. Dir.; 2429 Randall Rd., Ste. B; 60110; Kane; P 70,000; M 260; (847) 426-8565; Fax (847) 426-1098; melissa@nkcchamber.com; www.nkcchamber.com

Carriers Mills • *see Harrisburg*

Carrollton • *Carrollton C/C* • Marty Gross; Pres.; P.O. Box 69; 62016; Greene; P 2,000; M 35; (217) 942-3187; fieldsteve@hotmail.com

Carterville • *Carterville C/C* • Jan Campbell; Exec. Dir.; 120 N. Greenbriar; P.O. Box 262; 62918; Williamson; P 6,000; M 177; (618) 985-6942; (618) 713-6131; Fax (618) 985-6942; chamber@cartervillechamber.com; www.cartervillechamber.com*

Carthage • *Carthage Area C/C* • April Gavillet; Admin. Asst.; 8 S. Madison St.; P.O. Box 247; 62321; Hancock; P 3,000; M 100; (217) 357-3024; chamber@carthage-il.com; www.carthage-il.com

Cary • *Cary Grove Area C/C* • Lynn Caccavallo; Exec. Dir.; 445 Park Ave.; 60013; McHenry; P 27,000; M 500; (847) 639-2800; Fax (847) 639-2168; info@carygrovechamber.com; www.carygrovechamber.com*

Casey • *Casey C/C* • Karen Huddlestun; Pres.; P.O. Box 343; 62420; Clark & Cumberland; P 2,800; M 50; (217) 232-3430; caseyilchamber@aol.com; www.cityofcaseyil.org

Caseyville • *Caseyville C/C* • Chris Stewart; P.O. Box 470; 62232; St. Clair; P 4,300; M 50; www.caseyville.org

Centralia • *Greater Centralia C/C* • Bob Kelsheimer; Exec. Dir.; 130 S. Locust St.; 62801; Marion; P 20,500; M 375; (618) 532-6789; (888) 533-2600; Fax (618) 533-7305; gccoc@centraliail.com; www.centraliail.com*

Champaign • *Champaign County C/C* • Laura Weis IOM ACE; Pres./CEO; 303 W. Kirby Ave.; 61820; Champaign; P 180,000; M 1,400; (217) 359-1791; Fax (217) 359-1809; info@champaigncounty.org; www.ccchamber.org*

Channahon • *see Morris*

Charleston • *Charleston Area C/C* • Cynthia White; Pres./CEO; 501 Jackson Ave.; P.O. Box 77; 61920; Coles; P 31,000; M 280; (217) 345-7041; Fax (217) 345-7042; cacc@charlestonchamber.com; www.charlestonchamber.com*

Chatham • Chatham Area Chamber • Shannon McAuley; Pres.; 320 N. Main Plaza; 62629; Sangamon; P 12,000; M 210; (217) 483-6450; Fax (217) 483-6450; coordinator@chatham-il-chamber.com; www.chatham-il-chamber.com*

Chester • Chester C/C • Linda Sympson; Exec. Dir.; 10 Bridge By-Pass Rd.; P.O. Box 585; 62233; Randolph; P 8,600; M 135; (618) 826-2721; (618) 826-3171; chesteril@frontier.com; www.chesteril.org

Chicago Area

Albany Park C/C • Carla Agostinelli; Exec. Dir.; 3403 W. Lawrence Ave., Ste. 201; 60625; Cook; P 52,000; M 120; (773) 478-0202; Fax (773) 478-0282; cagostinelli@northrivercommission.org; www.albanyparkchamber.org

Bronzeville C/C • Johnnie Blair; Pres.; 4601 S. Cottage Grove; P.O. Box 53-634; 60653; Cook; P 125,000; M 275; (773) 268-1800; Fax (773) 442-0852; brvlchamber@aol.com; www.bronzevillechamber.com*

Business Partners, the Chamber for Uptown • John Blick; Dir. of Bus. Svcs.; 4753 N. Broadway, Ste. 822; 60640; Cook; P 57,000; M 150; (773) 878-1184; Fax (773) 878-3678; info@uptownbusinesspartners.com; www.exploreuptown.org

Chicagoland C/C • Theresa E. Mintle; Pres./CEO; The Wrigley Bldg.; 410 N. Michigan Ave., Ste. 900; 60611; Cook; P 7,500,000; M 1,000; (312) 494-6700; Fax (312) 861-0660; jgavin@chicagolandchamber.org; www.chicagolandchamber.org

Cosmopolitan C/C • Carnice Carey; Exec. Dir.; 30 E Adams St., Ste. 150; 60603; Cook; P 5,294,664; M 250; (312) 499-0611; chambers203@sbcglobal.net; www.cosmococ.org

East Side C/C • Yolanda DeAnda; Exec. Dir.; 3501 E. 106th St.; 60617; Cook; P 24,000; M 45; (773) 721-7948; Fax (773) 721-7446; eastsidechamber@sbcglobal.net; www.eastsidechamber.net

Edgebrook-Sauganash C/C • Bob Madiar; Exec. Dir.; 6440 N. Central Ave.; 60646; Cook; P 25,000; M 140; (773) 775-0378; Fax (773) 775-0371; edgebrookchamber@sbcglobal.net; www.edgebrookchamber.com

Edgewater C/C • Katrina Balog; Exec. Dir.; 1210 W. Rosedale; 60660; Clark; P 57,000; M 200; (773) 561-6000; Fax (773) 561-8584; info@edgewater.org; www.edgewater.org

Hyde Park C/C • Wallace Goode; Exec. Dir.; 1715 E. 55th St.; 60615; Cook; P 70,000; M 320; (773) 288-0124; Fax (773) 288-0464; contact@hydeparkchamberchicago.org; www.hydeparkchamberchicago.org

Jefferson Park C/C • Melissa Bukovatz; Exec. Dir.; 5214 W. Lawrence Ave., Ste. 5; 60630; Cook; P 26,000; M 100; (773) 736-6697; Fax (773) 736-3508; jeffparkcoc@sbcglobal.net; www.jeffersonpark.net

Lake View East C/C • Maureen Martino; Exec. Dir.; 3138 N. Broadway; 60657; Cook; P 68,000; M 335; (773) 348-8608; Fax (773) 348-7409; info@lakevieweast.com; www.lakevieweast.com

Lincoln Park C/C • Kim Schilf; Pres./CEO; 1925 N. Clybourn, Ste. 301; 60614; Cook; P 64,000; M 500; (773) 880-5200; Fax (773) 880-0266; info@lincolnparkchamber.com; www.lincolnparkchamber.com*

Mount Greenwood C/C • Darlene Myers; Exec. Dir.; 3052 W. 111 St.; 60655; Cook; P 12,000; M 260; (773) 238-6103; Fax (773) 238-6103; info@mtgcc.org; www.mtgcc.org

Portage Park C/C • Tividar (Ted) Szabo; Pres.; 5829 W. Irving Park Rd.; 60634; Cook; P 65,000; M 150; (773) 777-2020; Fax (773) 777-0202; info@portageparkchamber.org; www.portageparkchamber.org

Wicker Park & Bucktown C/C • Adam Burck; Exec. Dir.; 1414 N. Ashland Ave.; 60622; Cook; P 36,000; M 275; (773) 384-2672; Fax (773) 384-7525; info@wickerparkbucktown.com; www.wickerparkbucktown.com

Chillicothe • Chillicothe C/C • Nicholas Polyak; Pres.; 1028 N. 2nd St.; 61523; Peoria; P 6,100; M 100; (309) 274-4556; Fax (309) 274-3303; info@chillicothechamber.com; www.chillicothechamber.com*

Clinton • Clinton Area C/C • Marian Brisard; Exec. Dir.; 100 S. Center St., Ste. 101; 61727; DeWitt; P 7,150; M 170; (217) 935-3364; chamber@clintonilchamber.com; www.clintonilchamber.com

Collinsville • Collinsville C/C • Wendi Valenti; Exec. Dir.; 221 W. Main St.; 62234; Madison; P 26,100; M 376; (618) 344-2884; Fax (618) 344-7499; info@discovercollinsville.com; www.discovercollinsville.com*

Countryside • see LaGrange

Crete • Crete Area C/C • Patricia C. Herbert; Exec. Dir.; 1182 Main St.; P.O. Box 263; 60417; Will; P 25,000; M 75; (708) 672-9216; (708) 672-7600; Fax (708) 672-7640; cretechamber@sbcglobal.net; www.cretechamber.com

Crystal Lake • Crystal Lake C/C • Mary Margaret Maule; Pres.; 427 W. Virginia St.; 60014; McHenry; P 51,000; M 960; (815) 459-1300; Fax (815) 459-0243; info@clchamber.com; www.clchamber.com*

Danville • Vermilion Advantage-Chamber of Commerce Div. • Vicki Haugen; Pres./CEO; 28 W. North St.; 61832; Vermilion; P 85,000; M 415; (217) 442-6201; Fax (217) 442-6228; contact@vermilionadvantage.com; www.vermilionadvantage.com

Darien • Darien C/C • Clare Bongiovanni; Pres./CEO; 1702 Plainfield Rd.; 60561; DuPage; P 23,000; M 200; (630) 968-0004; Fax (630) 852-4709; info@darienchamber.com; www.darienchamber.com*

Decatur • Greater Decatur C/C • Mirinda Rothrock; Pres.; 101 S. Main St., Ste. 102; 62523; Macon; P 75,000; M 545; (217) 422-2200; Fax (217) 422-4576; customerservice@decaturchamber.com; www.decaturchamber.com*

Deerfield • Deerfield Bannockburn Riverwoods C/C • Victoria Street; Exec. Dir.; 601 Deerfield Rd., Ste. 200; 60015; Lake; P 24,000; M 460; (847) 945-4660; Fax (847) 940-0381; info@dbrchamber.com; www.dbrchamber.com

DeKalb • DeKalb C/C • Matt Duffy; Exec. Dir.; 164 E. Lincoln Hwy.; 60115; DeKalb; P 45,000; M 540; (815) 756-6306; Fax (815) 756-5164; chamber@dekalb.org; www.dekalb.org*

Des Plaines • Des Plaines C/C & Ind. • Jeffrey Rozovics; Pres.; 1401 E. Oakton St.; 60018; Cook; P 59,000; M 600; (847) 824-4200; Fax (847) 824-7932; info@dpchamber.com; www.dpchamber.com*

Dixon • Dixon Area C/C & Ind. • John R. Thompson; Pres./CEO; 101 W. Second St., Ste. 301; 61021; Lee; P 36,100; M 400; (815) 284-3361; Fax (815) 284-3675; john.thompson@dixoncc.com; www.dixonillinoischamber.com*

Dolton • Dolton C/C • Kurt Staehlin; Pres.; P.O. Box 510; 60419; Cook; P 24,000; M 52; (708) 849-4000; www.vodolton.org

Dorchester • see Gillespie

Downers Grove • *Chamber630 - Downers Grove Ofc.* • Laura Crawford; Pres./CEO; 2001 Butterfield Rd., Ste. 105; 60515; DuPage; P 80,000; M 800; (630) 968-4050; Fax (630) 968-8368; chamber@chamber630.com; www.chamber630.com

Du Quoin • *Du Quoin C/C* • Stacy Hirsch; Exec. Dir.; P.O. Box 57; 62832; Perry; P 6,020; M 125; (618) 542-9570; Fax (618) 542-8778; dqchamber@comcast.net; www.duquoin.org

Dwight • *Dwight Area C/C* • Phyllis Christensen; Admin. Asst.; 119 W. Main St.; 60420; Livingston; P 4,300; M 143; (815) 584-2091; dwightchamber@sbcglobal.net; www.dwightchamber.net

Eagarville • *see Gillespie*

East Alton • *see Godfrey*

East Dundee • *see Carpentersville*

East Gillespie • *see Gillespie*

East Moline • *see Moline*

East Peoria • *East Peoria C/C* • Rick Swan; Exec. Dir.; 2200 E. Washington St.; 61611; Peoria; P 24,000; M 475; (309) 699-6212; Fax (309) 699-6220; epcc@epcc.org; www.epcc.org*

Edwardsville • *Edwardsville/Glen Carbon C/C* • Desiree Bennyhoff; Pres./CEO; 1 N. Research Dr.; 62025; Madison; P 40,000; M 500; (618) 656-7600; Fax (618) 656-7611; dbennyhoff@edglenchamber.com; www.edglenchamber.com*

Effingham • *Effingham County C/C* • Norma Lansing; Pres./CEO; 903 N. Keller Dr.; P.O. Box 643; 62401; Effingham; P 13,000; M 565; (217) 342-4147; Fax (217) 342-4228; chamber@effinghamcountychamber.com; www.effinghamcountychamber.com*

El Paso • *El Paso C/C* • Lisa Barhum; Secy.; P.O. Box 196; 61738; Woodford; P 2,700; M 80; (309) 527-4400; lbarhum@hbtbank.com; www.elpasoilchamber.com

Eldorado • *see Harrisburg*

Elgin • *Elgin Area C/C* • Carol Gieske; Pres.; 31 S. Grove Ave.; P.O. Box 648; 60121; Cook & Kane; P 120,000; M 600; (847) 741-5660; Fax (847) 741-5677; info@elginchamber.com; www.elginchamber.com*

Elizabeth • *Elizabeth C/C* • P.O. Box 371; 61028; Jo Daviess; P 750; M 85; info@elizabeth-il.com; www.elizabeth-il.com

Elk Grove Village • *GOA Reg. Bus. Assn.* • Shirlanne Lemm; Pres.; P.O. Box 1516; 60009; Cook; P 4,000,000; M 800; (630) 773-2944; Fax (630) 773-2945; info@thegoa.com; www.thegoa.com*

Elmhurst • *Elmhurst C/C & Ind.* • John Quigley; Pres./CEO; 300 W. Lake St., Ste. 201; P.O. Box 752; 60126; DuPage; P 47,000; M 607; (630) 834-6060; Fax (630) 834-6002; info@elmhurstchamber.org; www.elmhurstchamber.org*

Elmwood Park • *Mont Clare-Elmwood Park C/C* • Ms. Lisa McManus; Exec. Dir.; 11 Conti Pkwy.; 60707; Cook; P 26,000; M 233; (708) 456-8000; Fax (708) 456-8680; mcepcoc@mcepchamber.org; www.mcepchamber.org

Elsah • *see Godfrey*

Evanston • *Evanston C/C* • Elaine Kemna-Irish; Exec. Dir.; 1609 Sherman Ave., Ste. 205; 60201; Cook; P 75,000; M 650; (847) 328-1500; Fax (847) 328-1510; info@evchamber.com; www.evchamber.com*

Evergreen Park • *Evergreen Park C/C* • Mike Dillon; Pres.; 9233 S. Homan; 60805; Cook; P 20,000; M 150; (708) 423-1118; Fax (708) 423-1859; epchamber@sbcglobal.net; www.evergreenparkchamber.org

Fairbury • *Fairbury C/C* • Becky Whitfill; Exec. Secy.; 101 E. Locust; P.O. Box 86; 61739; Livingston; P 3,800; M 130; (815) 692-3899; Fax (815) 692-4273; fairburychamberofcommerce@yahoo.com; www.fairburychamber.com

Fairfield • *Greater Fairfield Area C/C* • Carrie Halbert; Exec. Dir.; 121 E. Main St.; 62837; Wayne; P 5,100; M 125; (618) 842-6116; Fax (618) 842-4802; chamber@fairfieldwireless.net; www.fairfielddillinoischamber.com

Fairview Heights • *see Swansea*

Flora • *Flora C/C* • Heather Lucas; Exec. Asst.; 223 W. Railroad St.; 62839; Clay; P 5,100; M 138; (618) 662-5646; Fax (618) 662-5646; commerce@wabash.net; www.florachamber.com

Forest Park • *Forest Park C/C & Dev.* • Laurie Kokenes; Exec. Dir.; 7331 W. Roosevelt Rd.; 60130; Cook; P 14,200; M 200; (708) 366-2543; Fax (708) 366-3373; laurie@exploreforestpark.com; www.exploreforestpark.com

Fox Lake • *Fox Lake Area C/C & Ind.* • Linnea Pioro; Exec. Dir.; 71 N. Nippersink Blvd.; P.O. Box 203; 60020; Lake; P 10,000; M 230; (847) 587-7474; Fax (847) 587-1725; foxlakechamber@yahoo.com; www.discoverfoxlake.com

Fox River Grove • *see Cary*

Frankfort • *Frankfort C/C* • Karen Blake; Exec. Dir.; 123 Kansas St.; 60423; Will; P 18,000; M 540; (815) 469-3356; (877) 469-3356; Fax (815) 469-4352; office@frankfortchamber.com; www.frankfortchamber.com*

Franklin Park • *Franklin Park/Schiller Park C/C* • Kenneth Kollar; Pres.; P.O. Box 186; 60131; Cook; P 30,300; M 100; (708) 865-9510; Fax (708) 865-9520; info@chamberbyohare.org; www.chamberbyohare.org

Freeburg • *Freeburg C/C* • Peter Vogel; Pres.; P.O. Box 179; 62243; St. Clair; P 4,500; M 150; (618) 539-5613; Fax (618) 539-5613; secretary@freeburgchamberofcommerce.com; www.freeburgchamberofcommerce.com

Freeport • *Freeport Area C/C* • Mr. Kim Grimes; Pres./CEO; 27 W. Stephenson St.; 61032; Stephenson; P 26,000; M 500; (815) 233-1350; Fax (815) 233-3226; freeportareachamber@freeportilchamber.com; www.freeportilchamber.com

Fulton • *Fulton C/C* • Heather Bennett; Exec. Dir.; 415 11th Ave.; 61252; Whiteside; P 3,900; M 115; (815) 589-4545; Fax (815) 589-4421; chamber@cityoffulton.us; www.cityoffulton.us

Galatia • *see Harrisburg*

Galena • *Galena Area C/C* • Kathy Oberbroeckling; Exec. Dir.; 101 Bouthillier St.; 61036; Jo Daviess; P 3,600; M 325; (815) 777-9050; director@galenachamber.com; www.galenachamber.com*

Galesburg • *Galesburg Area C/C* • Jessica Linder; Exec. Dir.; 200 E. Main St., Ste. 200; P.O. Box 749; 61401; Knox; P 33,000; M 400; (309) 343-1194; Fax (309) 343-1195; chamber@galesburg.org; www.galesburg.org*

Galva • *Galva C/C* • Ron Rinkenberger; P.O. Box 112; 61434; Henry; P 2,600; M 65; (309) 932-2131; (309) 932-2555; chamber@gmail.com; www.galva.com

Geneseo • *Geneseo C/C* • Brian DeJohn; Exec. Dir.; 100 W. Main; 61254; Henry; P 6,500; M 180; (309) 944-2686; Fax (309) 944-2647; geneseo@geneseo.net; www.geneseo.org

Geneva • *Geneva C/C* • Jean Gaines; Pres.; 8 S. Third St., 2nd Flr.; P.O. Box 481; 60134; Kane; P 23,000; M 507; (630) 232-6060; (866) 4-GENEVA; Fax (630) 232-6083; chamberinfo@genevachamber.com; www.genevachamber.com

Genoa • *Genoa Area C/C* • Kristie M. Mulso; Exec. Dir.; 111 N. Sycamore St.; 60135; DeKalb; P 5,200; M 100; (815) 784-2212; Fax (815) 784-2212; genoachamber@gmail.com; genoaareachamber.com*

Gibson City • *Gibson Area C/C* • Amelie Beck; Secy./Treas.; 126 N. Sangamon Ave.; P.O. Box 294; 60936; Ford; P 3,400; M 140; (217) 784-5217; (217) 784-5872; gccoc@gibsoncityillinois.com; www.gibsoncityillinois.com

Gilberts • *see Carpentersville*

Gillespie • *Coal Country C/C* • Mickey Robinson; Exec. Dir.; 213 S. Macoupin; P.O. Box 57; 62033; Macoupin; P 10,000; M 69; (217) 710-5218; (217) 839-4888; mrer@madisontelco.com; www.coalcountrychamber.com*

Gilman • *Gilman Area C/C* • Ernie Potter; P.O. Box 13; 60938; Gilman; P 1,800; M 62; (815) 265-4818; Fax (815) 265-4961; www.gilmanil.com

Girard • *Girard C/C* • Debra Burnett; Secy.; P.O. Box 92; 62640; Macoupin; P 2,150; M 60; (217) 627-3512; Fax (217) 627-3656; cityclerk@royell.org; www.girardilusa.com*

Glen Carbon • *see Edwardsville*

Glen Ellyn • *Glen Ellyn C/C* • Dawn Smith; Exec. Dir.; 810 N. Main St.; 60137; DuPage; P 27,500; M 400; (630) 469-0907; Fax (630) 469-0426; director@glenellynchamber.com; www.glenellynchamber.com*

Glencoe • *Glencoe C/C* • Sally Sprowl; Exec. Dir.; P.O. Box 575; 60022; Cook; P 8,723; M 90; (847) 835-3333; glencoechamber@yahoo.com; www.glencoechamber.org

Glendale Heights • *Glendale Heights C/C* • Sharon Mennemeier; Prog. Coord.; P.O. Box 5054; 60139; DuPage; P 35,000; M 120; (630) 545-1099; Fax (630) 858-4418; questions@glendaleheightschamber.com; www.glendaleheightschamber.com

Glenview • *Glenview C/C* • Betsy Baer; Exec. Dir.; 2222 Chestnut, Ste. 100; 60025; Cook; P 47,000; M 469; (847) 724-0900; info@glenviewchamber.com; www.glenviewchamber.com*

Godfrey • *RiverBend Growth Assn.* • Monica Bristow; Pres.; 6722 Godfrey Rd. (Physical Address); 5800 Godfrey Rd. (Mailing Address); 62035; Madison; P 90,000; M 650; (618) 467-2280; Fax (618) 466-8289; info@growthassociation.com; www.growthassociation.com*

Golconda • *Golconda/Pope County C/C* • William Altman; Pres.; P.O. Box 688; 62938; Pope; P 4,300; M 12; (618) 683-9702; (618) 683-3341; www.popeco.net

Grafton • *see Godfrey*

Granite City • *Chamber of Commerce of Southwestern Madison County* • Rosemarie Brown; Exec. Dir.; 3600 Nameoki Rd., Ste. 101; P.O. Box 370; 62040; Madison; P 60,000; M 300; (618) 876-6400; Fax (618) 876-6448; chamber@chamberswmc.org; www.chamberswmadisoncounty.com*

Grant Park • *Grant Park C/C* • Scott Zizic; Pres.; P.O. Box 473; 60940; Kankakee; P 1,700; M 40; (815) 465-6531; Fax (815) 465-6611; president@grantparkchamber.org; www.grantparkchamber.org

Grayslake • *Grayslake Area C/C & Ind.* • Karen Christian-Smith IOM; Exec. Dir.; 10 S. Seymour St.; P.O. Box 167; 60030; Lake; P 25,000; M 250; (847) 223-6888; Fax (847) 223-6895; business@grayslakechamber.com; www.grayslakechamber.com

Grayville • *Grayville C/C* • Rick Conner; Dir.; P.O. Box 117; 62844; Edwards & White; P 1,660; M 50; (618) 375-7518; (618) 375-3671; www.cityofgrayville.com

Greenville • *Greenville C/C* • John Goldsmith; Exec. Dir.; P.O. Box 283; 62246; Bond; P 7,300; M 180; (618) 664-9272; (888) 862-8201; greenville@newwavecomm.net; www.greenvilleusa.org

Gurnee • *Lake County C/C* • Stewart Kerr; Exec. Dir.; 1313 N. Delany Rd., 2nd Flr.; 60031; Lake; P 703,500; M 400; (847) 249-3800; Fax (847) 249-3892; info@lakecountychamber.com; www.lakecountychamber.com*

Half Day • *see Lincolnshire*

Hampshire • *Hampshire Area C/C* • Mr. Lynn Acker; Pres.; 153 S. State St.; P.O. Box 157; 60140; Kane; P 6,000; M 175; (847) 683-1122; Fax (847) 683-1146; hampshirecc@fvi.net; www.hampshirechamber.org

Hanover Park • *Hanover Park C/C & Ind.* • Kevin Swan; Chair; 1981 E. Devon Ave.; 60133; Cook & DuPage; P 38,000; M 65; (630) 372-2009; Fax (630) 372-2052; staff@hanoverparkchamber.com; www.hanoverparkchamber.com*

Harrisburg • *Saline County C/C* • Lori Cox; Exec. Dir.; 2 E. Locust St., Ste. 200; 62946; Saline; P 25,000; M 125; (618) 252-4192; Fax (618) 252-0210; lori.cox@sic.edu; www.salinecountychamber.com

Hartford • *see Godfrey*

Harvard • *Harvard C/C & Ind.* • Crystal Musgrove; Exec. Dir.; 40 N. Ayer, Ste. 1; 60033; McHenry; P 9,000; M 200; (815) 943-4404; Fax (815) 943-4410; info@harvcc.net; www.harvcc.net

Havana • *Havana Area C/C* • Melanie Bleem; P.O. Box 116; 62644; Mason; P 3,300; M 115; (309) 543-3528; (888) 236-8406; havana@scenichavana.com; www.scenichavana.com

Henry • *Henry Area C/C* • Seth Chambers; P.O. Box 211; 61537; Marshall; P 3,000; M 90; (309) 364-3261; Fax (309) 364-3261; henrychamber@henrychamber.org; www.henrychamber.org

Herrin • *Herrin C/C* • Liz Lively; Exec. Dir.; 3 S. Park Ave.; 62948; Williamson; P 12,500; M 390; (618) 942-5163; (888) 942-5163; Fax (618) 942-3301; herrincc@herrinillinois.com; www.herrinillinois.com

Herscher • *Herscher C/C* • Julie Splear; Pres.; P.O. Box 437; 60941; Kankakee; P 1,600; M 100; (815) 474-0044; (815) 426-2131; juliesplear@sbherscher.com; www.herscher.net

Hickory Hills • *see Bridgeview-The Hills C/C*

Highland • *Highland C/C* • Jami Jansen; Exec. Dir.; 907 Main St.; 62249; Madison; P 9,500; M 300; (618) 654-3721; Fax (618) 654-8966; info@highlandillinois.com; www.highlandillinois.com

Highland Park • *Highland Park C/C* • Virginia Anzelmo Glasner; Pres./CEO; 508 Central Ave., Ste. 206; 60035; Lake; P 30,000; M 310; (847) 432-0284; Fax (847) 432-2802; info@chamberhp.com; www.chamberhp.com*

Highwood • *Highwood C/C* • Jennifer Ori; Pres.; P.O. Box 305; 60040; Lake; P 5,500; M 100; (847) 433-2100; Fax (847) 433-7959; info@highwoodchamberofcommerce.com; www.highwoodchamberofcommerce.com

Hillsboro • *Hillsboro C/C* • Lesley Pollard; Exec. Dir.; 447 S. Main St.; 62049; Montgomery; P 6,300; M 84; (217) 532-3711; Fax (217) 532-5567; hillsborochamber@consolidated.net; www.hillsborochamber.net

Hillside • *Hillside-Berkeley C/C* • Sue Hutsebaut; Exec. Secy.; 4850 Butterfield Rd.; P.O. Box 601; 60162; Cook; P 14,000; M 95; (708) 449-2449; Fax (708) 449-2442; hcochq@sbcglobal.net; www.hillsidechamberofcommerce.com

Hinsdale • *Hinsdale C/C* • Janet Anderson; Pres./CEO; 22 E. First St.; 60521; DuPage; P 18,000; M 265; (630) 323-3952; Fax (630) 323-3953; staff@hinsdalechamber.com; www.hinsdalechamber.com*

Hodgkins • *see LaGrange*

Hoffman Estates • *Hoffman Estates C/C & Ind.* • Tricia A. O'Brien; Pres.; 2200 W. Higgins Rd., Ste. 201; 60169; Cook; P 55,000; M 335; (847) 781-9100; Fax (847) 781-9172; tricia@hechamber.com; www.hechamber.com*

Homer Glen • *Homer Glen Area C/C* • Jane Bushong; Exec. Dir.; 15801 S. Bell Rd.; 60491; Will; P 25,000; M 300; (708) 301-8111; Fax (708) 301-2751; office@homerchamber.com; www.homerchamber.com*

Homewood • *Chicago Southland C/C* • David Hinderliter IOM ACE; Pres./CEO; 920 W. 175th St., Ste. 3; 60430; Cook; P 2,500,000; M 900; (708) 957-6950; Fax (708) 957-6968; info@chicagosouthlandchamber.com; www.chicagosouthlandchamber.com*

Homewood • *Homewood Area C/C* • Dennis Fares; Exec. Dir.; 1820 Ridge Rd., Ste. 200; 60430; Cook; P 22,000; M 200; (708) 206-3384; Fax (708) 206-3605; dennis@homewoodareachamber.com; www.homewoodareachamber.com*

Hoopeston • *Hoopeston C/C* • Valarie Hinkle; 301 W. Main St.; 60942; Vermilion; P 5,351; M 200; (217) 283-7873; Fax (217) 283-7873; hoopestonchambercommerce@gmail.com; www.hoopestonchamber.org

Huntley • *Huntley Area C/C & Ind.* • Rita Slawek; Pres./CEO; 11704 Coral St.; P.O. Box 399; 60142; Kane & McHenry; P 23,000; M 345; (847) 669-0166; Fax (847) 669-0170; info@huntleychamber.org; www.huntleychamber.org*

Indian Creek • *see Lincolnshire*

Indian Head Park • *see LaGrange*

Jacksonville • *Jacksonville Area C/C* • Lisa Musch; Pres.; 155 W. Morton; 62650; Morgan; P 33,000; M 600; (217) 245-2174; Fax (217) 245-0661; chamber@jacksonvilleareachamber.org; www.jacksonvilleareachamber.org*

Jerseyville • *Jersey County Bus. Assn.* • Mary Heitzig; CEO; 209 N. State St.; 62052; Jersey; P 20,000; M 250; (618) 639-5222; Fax (618) 498-3871; carrie@jcba-il.us; www.jcba-il.us*

Johnsburg • *see McHenry*

Joliet • *Joliet Region C/C & Ind.* • Russ Slinkard; Pres./CEO; 63 N. Chicago St.; P.O. Box 752; 60434; Will; P 170,000; M 1,500; (815) 727-5371; Fax (815) 727-5374; info@jolietchamber.com; www.jolietchamber.com*

Kankakee • *Kankakee County C/C* • Barbi Brewer-Watson; Pres./CEO; 200 E. Court St., Ste. 710; P. O. Box 154; 60901; Kankakee; P 113,449; M 470; (815) 351-9068; info@kankakeecountychamber.com; www.kankakeecountychamber.com*

Kewanee • *Kewanee C/C* • Mark Mikenas; Exec. V.P.; 113 E. 2nd St.; 61443; Henry; P 15,000; M 200; (309) 852-2175; Fax (309) 852-2175; chamber@kewanee-il.com; www.kewanee-il.com*

La Salle • *see Peru*

LaGrange • *West Suburban C/C & Ind.* • Kenneth Grunke; Exec. Dir.; 9440 Joliet Rd., Suite B (Hodgkins); P.O. Box 187; 60525; Cook; P 60,000; M 400; (708) 387-7550; Fax (708) 387-7556; info@wscci.org; www.wscci.org*

LaGrange Park • *see LaGrange*

Lake Bluff • *see Lake Forest*

Lake Forest • *Lake Forest/Lake Bluff C/C* • Joanna Rolek; Exec. Dir.; 272 E. Deerpath, Ste. 106; 60045; Lake; P 27,000; M 460; (847) 234-4282; Fax (847) 234-4297; info@LFLBchamber.com; www.LFLBchamber.com

Lake in the Hills • *see Algonquin*

Lake Villa • *Lindenhurst-Lake Villa C/C* • Connie Meadie; Exec. Dir.; 500 E. Grand Ave.; 60046; Lake; P 23,700; M 300; (847) 356-8446; Fax (847) 356-8561; llvchamber@sbcglobal.net; www.llvchamber.com

Lake Zurich • *Lake Zurich Area C/C* • Dale Perrin; Exec. Dir.; 444 S. Rand Rd., Ste. 308; 60047; Lake; P 33,000; M 500; (847) 438-5572; Fax (847) 438-5574; info@lzacc.com; www.lzacc.com*

Lansing • *Lansing Area C/C* • Dr. Renee N. Hale; Exec. Dir.; 3404 Lake St.; 60438; Cook; P 40,000; M 220; (708) 474-4170; Fax (708) 474-7393; director@chamberoflansing.com; www.chamberoflansing.com

Lawrenceville • *Lawrence County C/C* • Rachel Gard; Exec. Dir.; 619 12th St.; 62439; Lawrence; P 16,883; M 140; (618) 943-3516; Fax (618) 943-4748; lccc2@frontier.com; www.lawrencecountychamberofcommerce.com

Lebanon • *Lebanon C/C* • Joe Zimmerlee; Pres.; 221 W. St. Louis St.; 62254; St. Clair; P 4,000; M 93; (618) 537-8420; Fax (618) 537-8420; lebanonchamber@gmail.com; www.lebanonil.us

Lemont • *Lemont Area C/C* • Joanna Kmiec; Exec. Dir.; 101 Main St.; 60439; Cook; P 16,000; M 250; (630) 257-5997; Fax (630) 257-3238; info@lemontchamber.com; www.lemontchamber.com

Lewistown • *Lewistown C/C* • Becky Humphrey; Pres.; 119 S. Adams St.; 61542; Fulton; P 2,800; M 40; (309) 547-2501; (309) 547-4300; lewistownchamber.org

Libertyville • *Green Oaks/Libertyville/Mundelein/Vernon Hills C/C* • Ray Mullen; Exec. Dir.; 1123 S. Milwaukee Ave.; 60048; Lake; P 83,000; M 700; (847) 680-0750; Fax (847) 680-0760; info@glmvchamber.org; www.glmvchamber.org

Lincoln • *Lincoln/Logan County C/C* • Cathy Wilhite; Exec. Dir.; 110 N. Kickapoo St.; 62656; Logan; P 31,000; M 295; (217) 735-2385; Fax (217) 735-9205; chamber@lincolnillinois.com; www.lincolnillinois.com*

Lincoln Park • *see Chicago-Lincoln Park C/C*

Lincolnshire • *Greater Lincolnshire C/C* • Ida Butler; Exec. Dir.; One Marriott Drive; 60069; Lake; P 6,800; M 200; (847) 793-2409; Fax (847) 793-2405; executive.director@lincolnshirechamber.org; lincolnshirechamber.org*

Lincolnwood • *Lincolnwood C/C & Ind.* • J.K. Morley; Exec. Dir./Pres.; 4433 W. Touhy Ave.; 60712; Cook; P 12,000; M 125; (847) 679-5760; Fax (866) 660-8131; info@lincolnwoodchamber.org; www.lincolnwoodchamber.org*

Lisle • *Lisle Area C/C* • Jill Eidukas; Pres./CEO; 1111 Burlington Ave., Ste. 102; 60532; DuPage; P 23,000; M 400; (630) 964-0052; Fax (630) 964-2726; info@lislechamber.com; www.lislechamber.com*

Litchfield • *Litchfield C/C* • Rhea Weaver; Exec. Dir.; 311 N. Madison; P.O. Box 334; 62056; Montgomery; P 7,000; M 190; (217) 324-2533; Fax (217) 324-3559; info@litchfieldchamber.com; www.litchfieldchamber.com

Lockport • *Lockport C/C* • Lisa Kairis; Exec. Dir.; 921 S. State St.; 60441; Will; P 25,000; M 200; (815) 838-3357; Fax (815) 838-2653; office@lockportchamber.com; www.lockportchamber.com

Lombard • *Lombard Area C/C & Ind.* • Yvonne Invergo; Exec. Dir.; 10 Lilac Ln.; 60148; DuPage; P 44,000; M 250; (630) 627-5040; Fax (630) 627-5519; info@lombardchamber.com; www.lombardchamber.com*

Long Grove • *see Lincolnshire*

Loves Park • *Parks C/C* • Diana Johnson; Exec. Dir.; 100 Heart Blvd.; 61111; Winnebago; P 48,000; M 225; (815) 633-3999; Fax (815) 633-4057; diana@parkschamber.com; www.parkschamber.com

Lynwood • *Lynwood C/C* • Joseph Levy; Pres.; 21460 Lincoln Hwy.; 60411; Cook; P 9,000; M 65; (708) 474-2272; Fax (708) 474-2207; lynwoodchamber@yahoo.com; www.lynwoodchamber-lcc.com

Machesney Park • *see Loves Park*

Macomb • *Macomb Area C/C* • Alexandra Geisler; Pres./CEO; 214 N. Lafayette St.; P.O. Box 274; 61455; McDonough; P 20,000; M 400; (309) 837-4855; info@macombareachamber.com; www.macombareachamber.com*

Madison • *see Granite City*

Mahomet • *Mahomet Area C/C* • Ryan Heiser; Pres.; P.O. Box 1031; 61853; Champaign; P 7,300; M 122; (217) 586-3165; Fax (217) 586-3774; office@mahometchamberofcommerce.com; www.mahometchamberofcommerce.com

Manhattan • *Manhattan C/C* • Glenna Johnston; Exec. Dir.; P.O. Box 357; 60442; Will; P 7,400; M 89; (815) 478-3811; Fax (815) 478-7761; chamber@manhattan-il.com; www.manhattan-il.com

Manito • *Manito Area C/C* • Anthony Parkin; Pres.; P.O. Box 143; 61546; Mason; P 1,640; M 60; (309) 968-1113; www.manitoareachamberofcommerce.com

Manteno • *Manteno C/C* • Staci Wilken; Exec. Dir.; 211 Main St.; P.O. Box 574; 60950; Kankakee; P 9,000; M 100; (815) 468-6226; Fax (815) 468-6226; swilken@villageofmanteno.com; www.mantenochamber.com

Marengo • *Marengo-Union C/C* • Christine Wienke; Exec. Asst.; 116 S. State St.; 60152; McHenry; P 7,200; M 200; (815) 568-6680; Fax (815) 568-6879; chamber@marengo-union.com; www.marengo-union.com*

Marion • *Marion C/C* • Dalus Ben Avi; Exec. Dir.; 2305 W. Main St.; P.O. Box 307; 62959; Williamson; P 67,000; M 650; (618) 997-6311; (800) 699-1760; Fax (618) 997-4665; info@marionillinois.com; www.marionillinois.com*

Marseilles • *Illinois River Area C/C* • Ed Cavanaugh Jr.; Chrmn.; 135 Washington St.; 61341; LaSalle; P 8,000; M 120; (815) 795-2323; Fax (815) 795-4546; iracc@mtco.com; www.iracc.org

Marshall • *Marshall Area C/C* • Jennifer Bishop; Exec. Dir.; 708 Archer Ave.; 62441; Clark; P 4,000; M 85; (217) 826-2034; marshall.chamber@frontier.com; www.marshallilchamber.com

Martinsville • *Martinsville C/C* • Sheila Cribelar; Pres.; P.O. Box 429; 62442; Clark; P 1,300; M 50; (217) 382-4323; www.martinsvilleil.com

Maryville • *see Troy*

Mascoutah • *Mascoutah C/C* • Kathy Welker; Pres.; 200 E. Main St., Ste. 101; 62258; St. Clair; P 7,500; M 129; (618) 566-7355; Fax (618) 566-7355; info@mascoutahchamber.com; www.mascoutah.com

Matteson • *Matteson Business Assn.* • Laverne Murphy; Exec. Dir.; 4900 Village Commons Dr.; 60443; Cook; P 19,000; M 20; (708) 283-4765; Fax (708) 283-4951; mba@villageofmatteson.org; www.mattesonbusiness.com

Mattoon • *Mattoon C/C* • Edward P. Dowd; Exec. Dir.; 1518 Broadway Ave.; 61938; Coles; P 21,000; M 415; (217) 235-5661; matchamber@consolidated.net; www.mattoonchamber.com*

Maywood • *Maywood C/C* • Edwin H. Walker IV; Pres./CEO; 209 S. 3rd Ave.; 60153; Cook; P 26,000; M 98; (708) 345-7077; Fax (708) 345-9455; info@maywoodchamber.com; www.maywoodchamber.com

McHenry • *McHenry Area C/C* • Kay Rial Bates; Pres.; 1257 N. Green St.; 60050; McHenry; P 38,000; M 700; (815) 385-4300; Fax (815) 385-9142; info@mchenrychamber.com; www.mchenrychamber.com*

McLeansboro • *Hamilton County C/C* • Mark Epperson; P.O. Box 456; 62859; Hamilton; P 8,500; M 95; (618) 643-5424; info@hamcochamber.org; hamcochamber.org

Melrose Park • *Melrose Park C/C* • Richard A. Battaglia; Pres.; 900 N. 25th Ave.; 60160; Cook; P 25,000; M 200; (708) 338-1007; Fax (708) 338-9924; melroseparkchamber@att.net; www.melroseparkchamber.org

Mendota • *Mendota Area C/C* • Jesse Arellano; Exec. Dir.; 800 Washington St.; P.O. Box 620; 61342; LaSalle; P 7,300; M 240; (815) 539-6507; Fax (815) 539-6025; jarellano@mendotachamber.com; www.mendotachamber.com*

Metropolis • *Metropolis Area C/C, Tourism & Eco. Dev.* • Lisa Gower; Pres.; 516 Market St.; P.O. Box 188; 62960; Massac; P 7,200; M 225; (618) 524-2714; (800) 949-5740; Fax (618) 524-4780; office@metropolischamber.com; www.metropolischamber.com

Mettawa • *see Lincolnshire*

Midlothian • *Midlothian Area C/C* • Len Feil; Exec. Dir.; P.O. Box 909; 60445; Cook; P 15,000; M 160; (708) 389-0020; Fax (708) 577-5445; midlochamber@yahoo.com; www.midlochamber.com

Milan • *see Moline*

Minooka • *see Morris*

Mitchell • *see Granite City*

Mokena • *Mokena C/C* • Gail Bastas; Admin.; 19820D S. Wolf Rd.; 60448; Will; P 18,700; M 375; (708) 479-2468; Fax (708) 479-7144; chamber@mokena.com; www.mokena.com*

Moline • *Quad Cities C/C* • Tara Barney; Pres./CEO; 1601 River Dr., Ste. 310; 61265; Scott County, IA; Henry, Mercer & Rock Island, IL; P 400,000; M 2,000; (309) 757-5416; Fax (309) 757-5435; aespey@quadcitieschamber.com; www.quadcitieschamber.com*

Momence • *Momence C/C* • Veronica Smith; Pres.; P.O. Box 34; 60954; Kankakee; P 3,400; M 100; (815) 472-4620; Fax (815) 472-6453; membership@momence.net; www.momence.net

Monee • *Monee Area C/C* • Lee Boswell; Pres.; P.O. Box 177; 60449; Will; P 3,500; M 75; (708) 212-4133; Fax (708) 534-5320; info@moneechamber.org; www.moneechamber.org

Monmouth • *Monmouth Area C/C* • Angie McElwee; Exec. Dir.; 90 Public Sq.; 61462; Warren; P 9,500; M 230; (309) 734-3181; Fax (309) 734-6595; amm@monmouthilchamber.com; www.monmouthilchamber.com*

Mont Clare • *see Elmwood Park*

Montgomery • *Greater Montgomery Area C/C* • Pam Nagel; Exec. Admin.; 200 N. River St.; 60538; Kane & Kendall; P 14,500; M 144; (630) 897-8137; Fax (630) 897-6747; gmacc@montgomery-illinois.org; www.chamberofmontgomeryil.org

Monticello • *Monticello C/C* • Sue Gortner; Exec. Dir.; P.O. Box 313; 61856; Piatt; P 5,600; M 180; (217) 762-7921; (800) 952-3396; info@monticellochamber.org; www.monticellochamber.org

Morris • *Grundy County C/C & Ind.* • Christina Van Yperen; Exec. Dir.; 909 Liberty St.; 60450; Grundy; P 50,000; M 550; (815) 942-0113; info@grundychamber.com; www.grundychamber.com*

Morrison • *Morrison C/C* • Kimberly Ewoldsen; Exec. Dir.; 221 W. Main St.; P.O. Box 8; 61270; Whiteside; P 4,188; M 150; (815) 772-3757; Fax (815) 772-3757; morrisonchamber@morrisonil.org; www.morrisonchamber.com

Morton • *Morton C/C* • Jennifer Daly; Exec. Dir.; 415 W. Jefferson St.; 61550; Tazewell; P 16,300; M 320; (309) 263-2491; (888) 765-6588; Fax (309) 263-2401; jdaly@mortonillinois.org; www.mortonchamber.org*

Morton Grove • *Morton Grove C/C & Ind.* • Mark Matz; Exec. Dir.; 6101 Capulina Ave., Lower Level; 60053; Cook; P 23,500; M 255; (847) 965-0330; Fax (847) 965-0330; director@mgcci.org; www.mgcci.org

Mount Carmel • *Wabash County C/C* • Tanja Bingham; Exec. Dir.; 219 Market St., Ste. 1A; 62863; Wabash; P 12,000; M 140; (618) 262-5116; Fax (618) 262-2424; info@wabashcountychamber.com; www.wabashcountychamber.com

Mount Carroll • *Mount Carroll C/C* • Nancy Tobin; P.O. Box 94; 61053; Carroll; P 1,800; M 90; (800) 244-9594; info@mtcarrollil.org; www.mtcarrollil.org

Mount Clare • *see Gillespie*

Mount Prospect • *Mount Prospect C/C* • Dawn Fletcher Collins; Exec. Dir.; 107 S. Main St.; 60056; Cook; P 55,000; M 300; (847) 398-6616; Fax (847) 398-6780; dawn@mountprospect.com; www.mountprospectchamber.org*

Mount Vernon • *Jefferson County C/C* • Philip "Mike" Beard; Exec. Dir.; 200 Potomac Blvd.; 62864; Jefferson; P 38,800; M 600; (618) 242-5725; Fax (618) 242-5130; chamberexec@southernillinois.com; www.southernillinois.com*

Mount Zion • *Mount Zion C/C* • Judy Kaiser; Admin.; P.O. Box 84; 62549; Macon; P 8,000; M 185; (217) 864-2526; Fax (217) 864-6115; askjudy4@aol.com; www.mtzionchamber.org

Mundelein • *see Libertyville*

Murphysboro • *Murphysboro C/C* • Bruce Wallace; Exec. Dir.; 203 S. 13th St.; P.O. Box 606; 62966; Jackson; P 9,000; M 165; (618) 684-6421; Fax (618) 684-2010; director@murphysborochamber.com; www.murphysborochamber.com

Naperville • *Naperville Area C/C* • Nicki Anderson; Pres./CEO; 55 S. Main St., Ste. 351; 60540; DuPage; P 147,000; M 1,500; (630) 355-4141; Fax (630) 355-8335; nanderson@naperville.net; www.naperville.net*

Nashville • *Nashville C/C* • Doris Povolish; Dir.; 138 N.E. Court St.; 62263; Washington; P 3,300; M 111; (618) 327-3700; Fax (618) 464-0075; chamber@nashvilleilchamber.com; nashvilleilchamber.com

Nauvoo • *Nauvoo C/C* • Kim Orth; P.O. Box 41; 62354; Hancock; P 1,150; M 75; (217) 453-6648; Fax (217) 453-2348; vacation@beautifulnauvoo.com; www.beautifulnauvoo.com*

New Baden • *New Baden C/C* • Teri Crane; P.O. Box 22; 62265; Clinton; P 3,300; M 60; (618) 588-3813; www.newbadenchamber.com

New Lenox • *New Lenox C/C* • Debbera Hypke; CEO; 1 Veterans Pkwy., Ste. 104; P.O. Box 42; 60451; Will; P 28,000; M 400; (815) 485-4241; Fax (815) 485-5001; deb@newlenoxchamber.com; www.newlenoxchamber.com*

Newton • *Jasper County C/C* • Steve Hardwick; Exec. Dir.; 207 1/2 E. Jourdan St.; P.O. Box 21; 62448; Jasper; P 10,000; M 200; (618) 783-3399; Fax (618) 783-4556; jasperchamber@psbnewton.com; www.newtonillinois.com

Niles • *Niles C of C & Ind.* • Katie Schneider; Exec. Dir.; 8060 W. Oakton; 60714; Cook; P 30,000; M 478; (847) 268-8180; Fax (847) 268-8186; contactus@nileschamber.com; www.nileschamber.com*

Normal • *see Bloomington*

North Aurora • *see Aurora*

North Chicago • *North Chicago C/C* • Marvin Bembry; Pres.; P.O. Box 554; 60064; Lake; P 40,000; M 100; (847) 785-1912; Fax (847) 785-0109; info@northchicagochamber.org; northchicagochamber.org

Northbrook • *Northbrook C/C & Ind.* • Tensley Garris; Pres.; 2002 Walters Ave.; 60062; Cook; P 34,400; M 675; (847) 498-5555; Fax (847) 498-5510; info@northbrookchamber.org; www.northbrookchamber.org*

O'Fallon • *O'Fallon-Shiloh C/C* • Debbie Arell-Martinez; Exec. Dir.; 116 E. First St.; P.O. Box 371; 62269; St. Clair; P 27,000; M 420; (618) 632-3377; Fax (618) 632-8162; director@ofallonchamber.com; www.ofallonchamber.com*

Oak Brook • *Greater Oak Brook C/C* • Tracy Mulqueen; Pres./CEO; 619 Enterprise Dr., Ste. 100; 60523; Cook & DuPage; P 8,700; M 400; (630) 472-9377; Fax (630) 954-1327; info@obchamber.com; www.obchamber.com

Oak Forest • *Oak Forest-Crestwood Area C/C* • Kim Malecky-Iles; Exec. Dir.; 15440 S. Central Ave.; 60452; Cook; P 39,000; M 200; (708) 687-4600; Fax (708) 687-7878; info@oc-chamber.org; oc-chamber.org

Oak Lawn • *Oak Lawn C/C* • Julie Miller; Exec. Dir.; 5120 Museum Dr.; 60453; Cook; P 57,000; M 350; (708) 424-8300; Fax (708) 229-2236; office@oaklawnchamber.com; www.oaklawnchamber.com*

Oak Park • *see River Forest*

Oakland • *Oakland C/C* • Dan Krabel; Pres.; P.O. Box 283; 61943; Coles; P 900; M 40; (217) 346-2121; krabelfh@comcast.net

Oblong • *Oblong C/C* • Diane Houdasheldt; Pres.; P.O. Box 122; 62449; Crawford; P 1,600; M 100; info@theonlyoblong.com; www.theonlyoblong.com

Okawville • *Okawville C/C* • Jackie Bening; P.O. Box 345; 62271; Washington; P 1,420; M 65; (618) 243-5694; tourokaw@606front.net; www.okawvillecc.com

Olney • *Olney & the Greater Richland County C/C* • Amy Bissey-Murphy; Exec. Dir.; 216 E. Main St.; P.O. Box 575; 62450; Richland; P 16,000; M 200; (618) 392-2241; Fax (618) 392-4179; info@olneychamber.com; www.olneychamber.com*

Oregon • *Oregon Area C/C* • Debbie Dickson; Exec. Dir.; 124 N. Fourth St.; P.O. Box 69; 61061; Ogle; P 3,800; M 175; (815) 732-2100; Fax (815) 732-2177; ococ@oregonil.com; www.oregonil.com*

Orland Park • *Orland Park Area C/C* • Keloryn Putnam IOM; Exec. Dir.; 8799 W. 151st St.; 60462; Cook; P 57,000; M 600; (708) 349-2972; Fax (708) 349-7454; info@orlandparkchamber.org; www.orlandparkchamber.org*

Oswego • *Oswego C/C* • Angela Hibben; Pres./CEO; 73 W. Van Buren St.; 60543; Kendall; P 32,000; M 460; (630) 554-3505; (630) 608-3231; Fax (630) 554-0050; info@oswegochamber.org; www.oswegochamber.org*

Ottawa • *Ottawa Area C/C & Ind.* • Boyd Palmer; Exec. Dir.; 633 LaSalle St., Ste. 401; 61350; LaSalle; P 24,000; M 391; (815) 433-0084; Fax (815) 433-2405; info@ottawachamberillinois.com; www.ottawachamberillinois.com*

Palatine • *Palatine Area C/C* • Mindy Phillips; Dir.; 579 First Bank Dr., Ste. 205; 60067; Cook; P 70,000; M 450; (847) 359-7200; Fax (847) 359-7246; info@palatinechamber.com; www.palatinechamber.com*

Palestine • *Palestine C/C* • Vickie Perkins; Ofc. Mgr.; 103 S. Main St.; P.O. Box 155; 62451; Crawford; P 1,370; M 40; (618) 586-2222; Fax (618) 586-9477; palestinecofc@frontier.com; www.pioneercity.com

Palos Heights • *Palos Area C/C* • N. Pacetti; Admin.; P.O. Box 138; 60463; Cook; P 21,000; M 175; (708) 480-3025; info@palosareachamber.org; www.palosareachamber.org

Palos Hills • *see Bridgeview-The Hills C/C*

Pana • *Pana C/C* • Janet Blue; Exec. Dir.; 120 E. 3rd St.; 62557; Christian; P 7,500; M 125; (217) 562-4240; Fax (217) 562-3823; panachamber@consolidated.net; www.panachamber.com

Paris • *Paris Area C/C & Tourism* • Kathy Rhoads; Exec. Dir.; 105 N. Central Ave.; 61944; Edgar; P 19,000; M 275; (217) 465-4179; Fax (217) 465-4170; info@parisilchamber.com; www.parisilchamber.com*

Park Ridge • *Park Ridge C/C* • Ms. Gail Haller; Exec. Dir.; 720 Garden St.; 60068; Cook; P 37,000; M 420; (847) 825-3121; Fax (847) 825-3122; info@parkridgechamber.org; www.parkridgechamber.org*

Paxton • *Paxton Area C/C* • Diane Rasmus; Secy.; P.O. Box 75; 60957; Ford; P 4,500; M 145; (217) 379-4655; pacc@illicom.net; www.paxtonchamber.org

Pekin • *Pekin Area C/C* • Bill Fleming; Exec. Dir.; 402 Court St.; 61554; Tazewell; P 35,000; M 400; (309) 346-2106; Fax (309) 346-2104; info@pekinchamber.com; www.pekinchamber.com*

Peoria • *Peoria Area C/C* • Jeff Griffin; Pres.; 100 S.W. Water St.; 61602; Peoria; P 110,000; M 500; (309) 676-0755; Fax (309) 676-7534; jcole@peoriachamber.org; www.peoriachamber.org*

Peoria Heights • *Peoria Heights C/C* • Carolyn G. Catton; Pres.; 1203 E. Kingman Ave.; P.O. Box 9783; 61612; Peoria; P 6,200; M 82; (309) 685-4812; Fax (309) 685-4812; office@peoriaheightschamber.com; www.peoriaheightschamber.com

Peotone • *Peotone C/C* • Jody Thatcher; Exec. Dir.; P.O. Box 877; 60468; Will; P 3,500; M 60; (708) 258-9450; Fax (708) 258-0011; peotonechamber@gmail.com; www.peotonechamber.com

Peru • *Illinois Valley Area C/C & Eco. Dev.* • Joni Hunt PECD; Exec. Dir.; 1320 Peoria St.; 61354; Bureau, LaSalle & Putnam; P 50,000; M 400; (815) 223-0227; Fax (815) 223-4827; ivaced@ivaced.org; www.ivaced.org*

Petersburg • *Petersburg C/C* • Jacque Barbee; Secy.; 122 S. 6th St.; P.O. Box 452; 62675; Menard; P 4,000; M 100; (217) 415-4378; Fax (217) 632-3675; info@petersburgilchamber.com; www.petersburgilchamber.com

Pinckneyville • *Pinckneyville C/C* • Genevieve Brammeier; Exec. Dir.; 4 S. Walnut St.; P.O. Box 183; 62274; Perry; P 5,650; M 113; (618) 357-3243; Fax (618) 357-2688; pvillechamber.execdirector@gmail.com; www.pinckneyville.com*

Pittsfield • *Pike County C/C* • Kaye Iftner; Exec. Dir.; 224 W. Washington; P.O. Box 283; 62363; Pike; P 16,500; M 200; (217) 285-2971; Fax (217) 285-5251; info@pikeil.org; www.pikeil.org*

Plainfield • *Plainfield Area C/C* • Tasha Kitson; Exec. Dir.; 24047 W. Lockport St., Ste. 109; 60544; Will; P 100,000; M 525; (815) 436-4431; tkitson@plainfieldchamber.com; www.plainfieldchamber.com*

Plano • *Plano Area C/C* • Rich Healy; Exec. Dir.; 7050 Burroughs Ave.; 60545; Kendall; P 8,300; M 147; (630) 552-7272; Fax (630) 552-0165; director@planocommerce.org; www.planocommerce.org*

Polo • *Polo C/C* • Steve Frano; Pres.; 115 S. Franklin Ave.; 61064; Ogle; P 2,500; M 126; (815) 946-3131; Fax (815) 946-2004; polo@essex1.com; www.poloil.org

Pontiac • *Pontiac Area C/C* • Mindi Terrell; Exec. Dir.; 210 N. Plum St.; 61764; Livingston; P 12,000; M 245; (815) 844-5131; Fax (815) 844-2600; mterrell@pontiacchamber.org; www.pontiacchamber.org

Pontoon Beach • *see Granite City*

Prairie View • *see Lincolnshire*

Princeton • *Princeton Area C/C & Main Street* • Kim Frey; Exec. Dir.; 435 S. Main St.; 61356; Bureau; P 8,000; M 300; (815) 875-2616; (877) 730-4306; Fax (815) 875-1156; kfrey@princeton-il.com; www.princetonchamber-il.com*

Quincy • *Quincy Area C/C* • Amy Looten; Exec. Dir.; 300 Civic Center Plz., Ste. 245; 62301; Adams; P 60,000; M 650; (217) 222-7980; Fax (217) 222-3033; qacc@quincychamber.org; www.quincychamber.org*

Rantoul • *Rantoul Area C/C* • Kellie Wahl; Exec. Dir.; 601 S. Century Blvd., Ste. 1408; 61866; Champaign; P 15,000; M 210; (217) 893-3323; Fax (217) 893-3325; dir@rantoulchamber.com; www.rantoulchamber.com*

Red Bud • *Red Bud C/C* • Pres.; P.O. Box 66; 62278; Randolph; P 5,000; M 280; (618) 282-3505; redbudchamber@gmail.com; www.redbudchamber.com

Richmond • *Richmond/Spring Grove C/C •* Tom Henning; Exec. Dir.; 10906C Main St.; P.O. Box 475; 60071; McHenry; P 7,800; M 245; (815) 678-7742; info@rsgchamber.com; www.rsgchamber.com*

River Forest • *Oak Park-River Forest C/C •* Jim Doss; Exec. Dir.; 7727 Lake St.; 60305; Cook; P 64,000; M 500; (708) 771-5760; info@oprfchamber.org; www.oprfchamber.org

Riverdale • *Riverdale C/C •* 208 W. 144th St.; 60827; Cook; P 13,549; M 60; (708) 841-3311; Fax (708) 841-1805; rdpl2@earthlink.net; www.district148.net/rcoc

Riverside • *Riverside C/C •* David Moravecek; Pres.; P.O. Box 7; 60546; Cook; P 8,900; M 75; (708) 447-8510; Business@RiversideChamberofCommerce.com; www.riversidechamberofcommerce.com

Riverwoods • *see Deerfield*

Robinson • *Robinson C/C •* Mary Kindt; Admin.; 113 S. Court St.; P.O. Box 737; 62454; Crawford; P 8,000; M 150; (618) 546-1557; Fax (618) 546-0182; robinsonchamber@hotmail.com; www.robinsonchamber.org

Rochelle • *Rochelle Area C/C & Bus. Dev. •* Peggy Friday; Exec. Dir./CEO; 1221 Currency Ct.; P.O. Box 220; 61068; Ogle; P 10,000; M 250; (815) 562-4189; Fax (815) 562-4180; rochellechamber@gmail.com; www.rochellechamber.org*

Rock Falls • *Rock Falls C/C •* Bethany Bland; Pres./CEO; 601 W. 10th St.; 61071; Whiteside; P 9,600; M 400; (815) 625-4500; Fax (815) 625-4558; bland@rockfallschamber.com; www.rockfallschamber.com*

Rock Island • *see Moline*

Rockford • *Rockford C/C •* Einar K. Forsman; Pres./CEO; 308 W. State St., Ste. 190; 61101; Winnebago; P 153,000; M 1,300; (815) 987-8100; Fax (815) 987-8122; info@rockfordchamber.com; www.rockfordchamber.com*

Rockton • *Rockton C/C •* 330 E. Main St., Ste. 700; 61072; Winnebago; P 7,700; M 130; (815) 624-7625; Fax (815) 624-7385; info@rocktonchamber.com; www.rocktonchamber.com

Rolling Meadows • *Rolling Meadows C/C •* Linda Liles Ballantine; Exec. Dir.; 3601 Algonquin Rd., Ste. 322; 60008; Cook; P 26,000; M 200; (847) 398-3730; Fax (847) 398-3745; office@rmchamber.org; www.rmchamber.org

Romeoville • *Romeoville Area C/C •* Bridget Domberg; Exec. Dir.; 10 Montrose Dr.; 60446; Will; P 40,000; M 200; (815) 886-2076; Fax (815) 886-2096; info@romeovillechamber.org; www.romeovillechamber.org

Roscoe • *Roscoe Area C/C •* Mickey Heinzeroth; Exec. Dir.; 5310 Williams Dr.; 61073; Winnebago; P 17,000; M 280; (815) 623-9065; Fax (815) 623-1755; info@roscoechamber.com; roscoechamber.com*

Roselle • *Roselle C /C & Ind. •* Gail Croson; Exec. Dir.; 1350 W. Lake St., Ste. A; 60172; DuPage; P 23,300; M 200; (630) 894-3010; Fax (630) 894-3042; executivedirector@rosellechamber.com; www.rosellechamber.com

Rosemont • *Rosemont C/C •* Pam Hogan; Exec. Dir.; 9501 W. Devon Ave., Ste. 700; 60018; Cook; P 4,200; M 226; (847) 698-1190; Fax (847) 698-1195; info@rosemontchamber.com; www.rosemontchamber.com

Roseville • *Roseville Area C/C •* Ethel Logue; 145 S. Chamberlain; 61473; Warren; P 1,500; M 60; (309) 426-2134; www.roseville-il.org

Round Lake Beach • *Round Lake Area C/C & Ind. •* Shanna Coakley; Exec. Dir.; 2007 Civic Center Way; 60073; Lake; P 65,000; M 200; (847) 546-2002; Fax (847) 546-2254; info@rlchamber.org; www.rlchamber.org

Roxanna • *see Godfrey*

Saint Charles • *St. Charles C/C •* Stacey Ekstrom; Pres./CEO; 216 Riverside Ave.; 60174; DuPage & Kane; P 45,000; M 750; (630) 584-8384; Fax (630) 584-6065; info@stcharleschamber.com; www.stcharleschamber.com*

Salem • *Greater Salem C/C •* Leonard Ferguson; Exec. Dir.; 615 W. Main St.; 62881; Marion; P 7,800; M 280; (618) 548-3010; Fax (618) 548-3014; visitus@salemilchamber.com; www.salemilchamber.com

Sandwich • *Sandwich Area C/C •* Alethia Hummel; Exec. Dir.; 128 E. Railroad St.; P.O. Box 214; 60548; DeKalb; P 7,300; M 164; (815) 786-9075; Fax (815) 786-7855; info@sandwich-il.org; www.sandwich-il.org*

Savanna • *Savanna C/C •* Pam Brown; Exec. Dir.; 313 Main St.; P.O. Box 315; 61074; Carroll; P 3,200; M 100; (815) 273-2722; Fax (815) 273-2754; savchamber@grics.net; www.savanna-il.com

Sawyerville • *see Gillespie*

Schaumburg • *Schaumburg Bus. Assn. •* Kaili Harding; Pres.; 1501 E. Woodfield Rd., Ste. 115N; 60173; Cook; P 73,000; M 550; (847) 413-1010; Fax (847) 413-1414; kharding@schaumburgbusiness.com; www.schaumburgbusiness.com*

Schiller Park • *see Franklin Park*

Seneca • *see Marseilles*

Sesser • *Sesser Area C/C •* P.O. Box 367; 62884; Franklin; P 2,000; M 35; (618) 625-5566; Fax (618) 625-6291; sesser1904@gmail.com; www.sesserchamber.com

Shelbyville • *Greater Shelbyville C/C •* Vonda McConnell; Ofc. Mgr.; 143 E. Main St.; 62565; Shelby; P 5,000; M 165; (217) 774-2221; Fax (217) 774-2243; chamber01@consolidated.net; www.shelbyvillechamberofcommerce.com

Shorewood • *Shorewood Area C/C •* Carol Wagner; Pres.; 1 Towne Center Blvd., Ste. 103; 60404; Will; P 16,327; M 200; (815) 725-2900; Fax (815) 725-3573; president@shorewoodchamber.com; www.shorewoodchamber.com*

Silvis • *see Moline*

Skokie • *Skokie C/C •* Howard Meyer; Exec. Dir.; 5002 Oakton St.; P.O. Box 106; 60077; Cook; P 65,000; M 600; (847) 673-0240; Fax (847) 673-0249; info@skokiechamber.org; www.skokiechamber.org*

Sleepy Hollow • *see Carpentersville*

South Holland • *South Holland Business Assn. •* Blevian Moore; Exec. Dir.; P.O. Box 334; 60473; Cook; P 23,000; M 320; (708) 596-0065; Fax (708) 596-6696; info@shba.org; www.shba.org

South Roxanna • *see Godfrey*

Sparta • *Sparta Area C/C •* Christine Lochhead; Pres.; 1353B Sparta Center; P.O. Box 93; 62286; Randolph; P 7,000; M 95; (618) 317-7222; spartacc@spartailchamber.com; www.spartailchamber.com

Spring Grove • *see Richmond*

Springfield • *Illinois Assn. of C/C Execs.* • Lisa Weitzel; Pres.; P.O. Box 9436; 62791; Sangamon; P 12,900,000; M 140; (217) 585-2995; Fax (217) 522-5518; lisa@iacce.org; www.iacce.org

Springfield • *Greater Springfield C/C* • Chris Hembrough; Pres./CEO; 1011 S. 2nd St.; 62704; Sangamon; P 211,000; M 1,610; (217) 525-1173; Fax (217) 525-8768; info@gscc.org; www.gscc.org*

Staunton • *Staunton C/C* • Sue Campbell; P.O. Box 248; 62088; Macoupin; P 5,150; M 80; (618) 635-8356; Fax (618) 635-3644; chamber@stauntonil.com; www.stauntonil.com

Steeleville • *Steeleville C/C* • P.O. Box 177; 62288; Randolph; P 2,100; M 50; (618) 965-3134; steelevillechamber@gmail.com; www.steeleville.org

Sterling • *Sauk Valley Area C/C* • Kris Noble; Exec. Dir.; 211 Locust St.; 61081; Whiteside; P 65,000; M 370; (815) 625-2400; Fax (815) 625-9361; chamber@essex1.com; www.saukvalleyareachamber.com*

Stockton • *Stockton C/C* • Amy Laskye; Pres.; P.O. Box 3; 61085; Jo Daviess; P 2,000; M 145; (815) 947-2878; Fax (815) 947-2878; info@stocktonil.com; www.stocktonil.com

Streamwood • *Streamwood C/C* • Robin Lingle; Pres.; 22 W. Streamwood Blvd.; 60107; Cook; P 38,500; M 78; (630) 837-5200; Fax (630) 837-5251; contact@streamwoodchamber.com; www.streamwoodchamber.com

Streator • *Streator Area C/C* • Jack Dzuris; Exec. Dir.; 320 E. Main; P.O. Box 360; 61364; LaSalle; P 21,000; M 250; (815) 672-2921; Fax (815) 672-1768; sacci@mchsi.com; www.streatorchamber.com

Sugar Grove • *Sugar Grove C/C & Ind.* • Shari Baum; Exec. Dir.; 141 Main St.; P.O. Box 765; 60554; Kane; P 9,000; M 100; (630) 466-7895; Fax (630) 466-7825; info@sugargrovechamber.org; www.sugargrovechamber.org*

Sullivan • *Sullivan Chamber & Eco. Dev.* • Laurrie Minor; Admin.; 112 W. Harrison St.; 61951; Moultrie; P 4,600; M 200; (217) 728-4223; Fax (217) 728-4064; info@sullivanchamber.com; www.sullivanchamber.com

Swansea • *Metro-East Reg. C/C* • Tom Tyler; Exec. Dir.; 4387 N. Illinois St., Ste. 200; 62226; St. Clair; P 31,000; M 250; (618) 233-3938; chamber@metroeastchamber.org; metroeastchamber.org*

Sycamore • *Sycamore C/C* • Rosemarie M. Treml; Exec. Dir.; 407 W. State St., Ste. 10; 60178; DeKalb; P 17,200; M 450; (815) 895-3456; Fax (815) 895-0125; info@sycamorechamber.com; www.sycamorechamber.com*

Taylorville • *The Greater Taylorville C/C* • Patty Hornbuckle; CEO; 108 W. Market St., 2nd Flr.; 62568; Christian; P 35,372; M 296; (217) 824-4919; Fax (888) 824-3997; taylorvillechamber@gmail.com; www.taylorvillechamber.com*

Tinley Park • *Tinley Park C/C* • Bob Haustein; Pres.; 17316 S. Oak Park Ave.; 60477; Cook; P 60,000; M 500; (708) 532-5700; Fax (708) 532-1475; info@tinleychamber.org; www.tinleychamber.org

Trenton • *Trenton C/C* • Tim Deien; Pres.; P.O. Box 37; 62293; Clinton; P 3,200; M 86; (618) 224-9329; nhubert@gamesafeusa.com; www.trenton-ilchamber.com

Troy • *Troy/Maryville/St. Jacob Area C/C* • Dawn Mushill; Exec. Dir.; 647 E. U.S. Hwy. 40; 62294; Madison; P 18,600; M 380; (618) 667-8769; (888) 667-8769; Fax (618) 667-8759; info@troymaryvillecoc.com; www.troymaryvillecoc.com*

Tuscola • *Tuscola C/C* • Kara Kinney; Pres.; P.O. Box 434; 61953; Douglas; P 4,500; M 150; (217) 253-2112; info@tuscolachamber.org; www.tuscolachamber.org

Vandalia • *Vandalia C/C* • Ben Timmermann; Pres.; 1408 N. 5th St.; P.O. Box 238; 62471; Fayette; P 7,000; M 140; (618) 283-2728; Fax (618) 283-4439; vandaliachamber@swetlandcom.com; www.vandaliachamber.org*

Venice • *see Granite City*

Vernon Hills • *see Libertyville*

Vienna • *Johnson County C/C* • Kelly Groner; Exec. Dir.; P.O. Box 1361; 62995; Johnson; P 12,760; M 65; (618) 658-2063; jo.co.chamber@juno.com; www.jocochamber.com

Villa Park • *Villa Park C/C* • Alesia Bailey; Exec. Dir.; 10 W. Park Blvd.; 60181; DuPage; P 22,000; M 205; (630) 941-9133; Fax (630) 941-9134; vphamber@sbcglobal.net; www.villaparkchamber.org

Viola • *Viola C/C* • Jim Morrison; Pres.; P.O. Box 403; 61486; Mercer; P 950; M 21; (309) 596-2434; (309) 596-2513; www.villageofviola.org

Virden • *Virden Area C/C* • Tom Stoecker; Pres.; P.O. Box 252; 62690; Macoupin; P 3,500; M 61; (217) 965-4747; (217) 891-6514; Fax (217) 965-3737; www.virdenchamber.com

Walnut • *Walnut C/C* • Lori Wood; Dir.; 105 N. Main St.; P.O. Box 56; 61376; Bureau; P 1,500; M 140; (815) 379-2141; Fax (815) 379-9375; director@villageofwalnut.com; www.villageofwalnut.com

Warrenville • *see West Chicago*

Washington • *Washington C/C* • Chevie Ruder; Dir.; 114 Washington Sq.; 61571; Tazewell; P 14,728; M 250; (309) 444-9921; Fax (309) 444-9225; wcoc@mtco.com; www.washingtoncoc.com*

Waterloo • *Waterloo C/C* • Jenny Bullock; Exec. Dir.; 118 E. 3rd St.; P.O. Box 1; 62298; Monroe; P 13,000; M 250; (618) 939-5300; Fax (618) 939-1805; chamber@htc.net; www.enjoywaterloo.com

Watseka • *Watseka Area C/C* • Kendra Martin; Exec. Dir.; 110 S. 3rd St.; 60970; Iroquois; P 6,000; M 150; (815) 432-2416; Fax (815) 432-2762; wacc@att.net; www.watsekachamber.org

Wauconda • *Wauconda Area C/C* • Maria Weisbruch; Exec. Dir.; 100 N. Main St.; 60084; Lake; P 13,603; M 300; (847) 526-5580; Fax (847) 526-3059; info@waucondachamber.org; www.waucondaareachamber.org*

Waukegan • *see Gurnee*

West Chicago • *Western DuPage C/C* • David J. Sabathne IOM; Pres./CEO; 306 Main St.; 60185; DuPage; P 48,000; M 500; (630) 231-3003; Fax (630) 231-3009; team@westerndupagechamber.com; www.westerndupagechamber.com*

West Dundee • *see Carpentersville*

West Frankfort • *West Frankfort C/C* • Kathy Sikora; Exec. Dir.; 201 E. Nolen St.; 62896; West Frankfort; P 8,526; M 150; (618) 932-2181; Fax (618) 932-6330; wfchamber@frontier.com; www.westfrankfort-il.com

Westchester • *Westchester C/C* • Jeannie Helgesen; Pres.; P.O. Box 7309; 60154; Cook; P 16,800; M 130; (708) 240-8400; Fax (708) 240-8400; mary@westchesterchamber.org; www.westchesterchamber.org

Western Springs • *see LaGrange*

Westmont • *Westmont C/C & Tourism Bur.* • Larry Forssberg; Exec. Dir.; One S. Cass Ave., Ste. 101; Suite 101; 60559; DuPage; P 25,000; M 300; (630) 960-5553; Fax (630) 960-5554; wcctb@westmontchamber.com; www.westmontchamber.com*

Wheaton • *Wheaton C/C* • Kerry O'Brien; Exec. Dir.; 108 E. Wesley St.; 60187; DuPage; P 53,000; M 460; (630) 668-6464; kerry@wheatonchamber.com; www.wheatonchamber.com*

Wheeling • *Wheeling-Prospect Heights Area C/C & Ind.* • Catherine Powers; Exec. Dir.; 2 Community Blvd., Ste. 203; 60090; Cook; P 52,300; M 300; (847) 541-0170; Fax (847) 541-0296; info@wphchamber.com; wphchamber.com

Wicker Park • *see Chicago-Wicker Park & Bucktown C/C*

Willow Springs • *see LaGrange*

Willowbrook • *see Burr Ridge*

Wilmette • *Wilmette/Kenilworth C/C* • Nada Becker; Exec. Dir.; 1515 Sheridan Rd.; Plaza del Lago; 60091; Cook; P 30,164; M 450; (847) 251-3800; info@wilmettechamber.org; www.wilmettechamber.org*

Wilmington • *Wilmington C/C* • Eric Fisher; Pres.; 111 S. Water St.; P.O. Box 724; 60481; Will; P 5,600; M 100; (815) 476-5991; (815) 476-7966; Fax (815) 476-7002; eric.fisher@cbcast.com; www.wilmingtonilchamber.org

Wilsonville • *see Gillespie*

Winchester • *Winchester C/C* • Andy Moss; P.O. Box 201; 62694; Scott; P 1,600; M 65; (217) 742-3219

Winfield • *see West Chicago*

Winnetka • *Winnetka-Northfield C/C* • Teresa Dason; Exec. Dir.; 841 Spruce St., Ste. 204; 60093; Cook; P 18,000; M 350; (847) 446-4451; Fax (847) 446-4452; wcc@winnetkanorthfieldchamber.com; www.winnetkanorthfieldchamber.com*

Winthrop Harbor • *Winthrop Harbor C/C* • Karen Crane; Treas.; P.O. Box 347; 60096; Lake; P 7,000; M 40; (847) 872-3846; (847) 775-8364; www.cocwh.com

Wonder Lake • *Wonder Lake C/C* • Donna Sullivan; Exec. Dir.; 7602 Hancock Dr.; 60097; McHenry; P 1,500; M 120; (815) 728-0682; Fax (815) 653-6762; chamber@wonderlake.org; www.wonderlake.org

Wood Dale • *also see Elk Grove Village*

Wood Dale • *Wood Dale C/C* • Caterina Aiello; Pres.; P.O. Box 353; 60191; DuPage; P 14,000; M 150; (630) 595-0505; Fax (630) 595-0677; info@wooddalechamber.com; www.wooddalechamber.com

Wood River • *see Godfrey*

Woodridge • *Chamber630 - Woodridge Ofc.* • Laura Crawford; Pres./CEO; 5 Plaza Dr., Ste. 212; 60517; DuPage; P 80,000; M 800; (630) 960-7080; Fax (630) 852-2316; chamber@chamber630.com; www.chamber630.com*

Woodstock • *Woodstock C/C & Ind.* • Shari Gray; Exec. Dir.; 136 Cass St.; 60098; McHenry; P 22,500; M 300; (815) 338-2436; chamber@woodstockilchamber.com; www.woodstockilchamber.com

Wyoming • *Wyoming C/C* • Melody Anderson; Pres.; P.O. Box 157; 61491; Stark; P 1,500; M 40; (309) 695-9966; favoritethings11@yahoo.com; www.wyoming-chamber.org

Yorkville • *Yorkville Area C/C* • Sherri Farley; Exec. Dir.; 26 W. Countryside Pkwy.; 60560; Kendall; P 17,000; M 300; (630) 553-6853; Fax (630) 553-0702; sherri@yorkvillechamber.org; www.yorkvillechamber.org*

Zion • *Zion Area C/C* • Lorna Yates; Ofc. Admin.; 1300 Shiloh Blvd.; 60099; Lake; P 22,000; M 130; (847) 872-5405; info@zionchamber.com; www.zionchamber.com

Indiana

Indiana C of C • Kevin Brinegar; Pres.; 115 W. Washington St., Ste. 850S; Indianapolis; 46204; Marion; P 6,597,000; M 4,900; (317) 264-3110; Fax (317) 264-6855; info@indianachamber.com; www.indianachamber.com

Akron • *Akron C/C* • Kim Martin; P.O. Box 218; 46910; Fulton; P 1,200; M 35; (574) 893-4621; (574) 893-4121; www.akronindiana.com

Albion • *Albion C/C* • Chris Magnuson; Pres.; P.O. Box 63; 46701; Noble; P 2,350; M 120; (260) 403-1795; (260) 636-6200; Fax (260) 636-6255; chamber@albionin.org; www.albionin.org

Alexandria • *Alexandria-Monroe C/C* • John Dockrey; Exec. Dir.; 125 N. Wayne St.; 46001; Madison; P 6,400; M 130; (765) 724-3144; Fax (765) 683-3504; info@alexandriachamber.com; www.alexandriachamber.com

Anderson • *Madison County C/C* • Dennis Ashley; Pres./CEO; 1106 Meridian St., Ste. 109; 46016; Madison; P 132,000; M 500; (765) 642-0264; Fax (765) 642-0266; vanessa@getlinkedmadison.com; www.getlinkedmadison.com*

Angola • *Angola Area C/C* • Christina M. Koher; Exec. Dir.; 330 Intertech Pkwy., Ste. 251; 46703; Steuben; P 8,300; M 350; (260) 665-3512; Fax (260) 665-7418; info@angolachamber.org; www.angolachamber.org*

Arcadia • *see Cicero*

Ashley • *see Auburn*

Atlanta • *see Cicero*

Auburn • *DeKalb Chamber Partnership* • Shannon Carpenter; Exec. Dir.; 208 S. Jackson St.; 46706; DeKalb; P 47,000; M 203; (260) 925-2100; Fax (260) 925-2199; shannon@dekalbchamberpartnership.com; www.chamberinauburn.com*

Aurora • *see Lawrenceburg*

Avon • *Greater Avon C/C* • Tom Downard; Exec. Dir.; 8244 E. Hwy. 36, Ste. 140; 46123; Hendricks; P 12,500; M 220; (317) 272-4333; Fax (317) 272-7217; info@avonchamber.org; www.avonchamber.org

Batesville • *Batesville Area C/C* • Melissa Tucker; Exec. Dir.; 16 E. George St.; 47006; Franklin & Ripley; P 28,800; M 280; (812) 934-3101; Fax (812) 932-0202; chamber@batesvillein.com; www.batesvillein.com

Bedford • *Bedford Area C/C* • Blaine Parker; Interim Pres.; 1116 16th St.; 47421; Lawrence; P 15,000; M 500; (812) 275-4493; Fax (812) 279-5998; bedford@bedfordchamber.com; www.bedfordchamber.com

Berne • *Berne C/C* • Megan DeMoss; Exec. Dir.; 205 E. Main St.; 46711; Adams; P 5,000; M 180; (260) 589-8080; Fax (260) 589-8384; chamber@bernein.com; www.bernein.com

Beverly Shores • *see Chesterton*

Bloomington • *Greater Bloomington C/C* • Jeb Conrad; Pres./CEO; 400 W. 7th St., Ste. 102; 47404; Monroe; P 142,000; M 850; (812) 336-6381; info@chamberbloomington.org; www.chamberbloomington.org*

Bluffton • *Wells County C/C* • Erin Prible; Exec. Dir.; 211 W. Water St.; 46714; Wells; P 30,000; M 330; (260) 824-0510; Fax (260) 824-5871; eprible@wellscoc.com; www.wellscoc.com*

Boonville • *Warrick County C/C* • Shari Sherman; Exec. Dir.; 224 W. Main St., Ste. 203; P.O. Box 377; 47601; Warrick; P 64,000; M 270; (812) 897-2340; Fax (812) 897-2360; info@warrickchamber.org; www.warrickchamber.org*

Brazil • *Clay County C/C* • Molly Tipton; Secy./Ofc. Admin.; 535 E. National Ave.; P.O. Box 23; 47834; Clay; P 27,000; M 115; (812) 448-8457; Fax (812) 448-9957; info@claycountychamber.org; www.claycountychamber.org

Bremen • *Bremen C/C* • Bill Davis; Pres.; 104 W. Plymouth St.; P.O. Box 125; 46506; Marshall; P 5,000; M 100; (574) 546-2044; Fax (574) 546-5487; info@bremenchamberofcommerce.com; www.bremenchamberofcommerce.com

Brookville • *Franklin County C/C* • Kim Vonder Meulen; Exec. Dir.; 813 Main St.; P.O. Box 211; 47012; Franklin; P 5,000; M 250; (765) 647-3177; Fax (765) 647-4150; info@fcchamber.net; www.fcchamber.net*

Brownsburg • *Greater Brownsburg C/C* • Brian Rose; Exec. Dir.; 61 N. Green St.; P.O. Box 82; 46112; Hendricks; P 21,300; M 310; (317) 852-7885; Fax (317) 852-8688; chamber@brownsburg.com; www.brownsburg.com

Brownstown • *Brownstown C/C* • Maria Powell; Secy./Ofc. Mgr.; 119 W. Walnut St.; P.O. Box 334; 47220; Jackson; P 2,800; M 100; (812) 358-2930; Fax (812) 358-9321; secretary@brownstownchamber.org; www.brownstownchamber.org

Burns Harbor • *see Chesterton*

Butler • *see Auburn*

Carmel • *Carmel C/C* • Mo Merhoff; Pres.; 21 S. Rangeline Rd., Ste. 300A; 46032; Hamilton; P 80,000; M 760; (317) 846-1049; Fax (317) 844-6843; mm@carmelchamber.com; www.carmelchamber.com*

Cedar Lake • *Cedar Lake C/C* • Diane M. Jostes; Exec. Dir.; 7925 Lake Shore Dr.; P.O. Box 101; 46303; Lake; P 11,560; M 145; (219) 374-6157; Fax (219) 374-6157; cl-chamber@sbcglobal.net; www.cedarlakechamber.com*

Chesterton • *Chesterton/Duneland C/C* • Heather Ennis; Exec. Dir.; 220 Broadway; 46304; Porter; P 25,000; M 365; (219) 926-5513; Fax (219) 926-7593; hennis@chestertonchamber.org; www.chestertonchamber.org*

Chrisney • *see Rockport*

Churubusco • *Churubusco C/C* • Lee Prescott; Exec. Dir.; 9309 E. Commerce Dr., Ste. 5; 46723; Whitley; P 1,800; M 70; (260) 229-6766; Fax (260) 244-7165; churubusco.chamber@gmail.com

Cicero • *Northern Hamilton County C/C* • Catharine Heller; Exec. Dir.; 70 N. Byron St.; P.O. Box 466; 46034; Hamilton; P 6,500; M 200; (317) 984-4079; (317) 758-1311; catharine@northernhamiltoncountychamber.com; www.northernhamiltoncountychamber.com

Clay County • *see Brazil*

Clinton • *Greater Clinton C/C* • John E. Lang; Pres.; 407 S. Main St.; P.O. Box 7; 47842; Vermillion; P 16,000; M 51; (765) 832-3844; vermillionchamber@sbcglobal.net; www.greaterclintonchamber.org

Columbia City • *Whitley County C/C* • Doug Brown; Exec. Dir.; 518 Garland Ave., Ste. A; P.O. Box 166; 46725; Whitley; P 31,000; M 250; (260) 248-8131; Fax (260) 248-8162; doug@whitleychamber.com; www.whitleychamber.com*

Columbus • *Columbus Area C/C* • Cindy Frey; Pres.; 500 Franklin St.; 47201; Bartholomew; P 77,000; M 600; (812) 379-4457; kadams@columbusareachamber.com; www.columbusareachamber.com

Connersville • *Connersville/Fayette County C/C* • Katrina Bailey; Exec. Dir.; 504 Central Ave.; 47331; Fayette; P 24,277; M 212; (765) 825-2561; Fax (765) 825-4613; katrina@connersvillechamber.com; www.connersvillechamber.com*

Corydon • *C/C of Harrison County* • Lisa Long; Pres.; 111 W. Walnut St.; 47112; Harrison; P 39,200; M 300; (812) 738-0120; Fax (812) 738-0500; llong@harrisonchamber.org; www.harrisonchamber.org

Crawfordsville • *Crawfordsville-Montgomery County C/C* • Tom Utley; Exec. Dir.; 200 S. Washington St., Ste. 304; 47933; Montgomery; P 38,300; M 300; (765) 362-6800; Fax (765) 362-6900; anne.shaw@crawfordsvillechamber.com; www.crawfordsvillechamber.com*

Crown Point • *Crossroads Reg. C/C* • Sue Reed; Exec. Dir.; Old Court House Sq., Ste. 206; 46307; Lake; P 60,000; M 700; (219) 663-1800; Fax (219) 663-1989; geninq@crossroadschamber.org; www.crossroadschamber.org*

Culver • *Culver C/C* • Bobbie Ruhnow; Exec. Secy.; P.O. Box 129; 46511; Marshall; P 1,353; M 91; (574) 842-5253; (888) 252-5253; Fax (574) 842-5253; eruhnow@mediacombb.net; www.culverchamber.com

Dale • *see Rockport*

Danville • *Greater Danville C/C* • Marcia Lynch; Exec. Dir.; 49 N. Wayne St., Ste. 100; 46122; Hendricks; P 9,600; M 165; (317) 745-0670; Fax (317) 745-0682; shelby@danvillechamber.org; www.danvillechamber.org

Decatur • *Decatur C/C* • Craig Coshow; Exec. Dir.; 125 E. Monroe St.; 46733; Decatur; P 10,000; M 240; (260) 724-2604; Fax (260) 724-3104; info@decaturchamber.org; www.decaturchamber.org

Delphi • *Delphi C/C* • Dale R. Seward; Pres.; 113 S. Washington St.; P.O. Box 178; 46923; Carroll; P 3,000; M 75; (765) 564-3657; info@delphichamber.org; www.delphichamber.org

DeMotte • *DeMotte C/C* • Diva Rish; Exec. Dir.; 327 N. Halleck St.; P.O. Box 721; 46310; Jasper; P 3,800; M 155; (219) 987-5800; Fax (219) 987-5800; info@demottechamber.org; www.demottechamber.org

Dillsboro • *see Lawrenceburg*

Dune Acres • *see Chesterton*

Dunkirk • *see Portland*

Dyer • *Dyer C/C* • Suzy LaBarge; Pres.; P.O. Box 84; 46311; Lake; P 16,400; M 125; (219) 865-1045; Fax (219) 865-4233; chamber@dyerchamberofcommerce.com; www.dyerchamberofcommerce.com

East Chicago • *see Hammond*

Elkhart • *Greater Elkhart C/C* • Kyle Hannon IOM; Pres./CEO; 418 S. Main St.; 46516; Elkhart; P 197,000; M 900; (574) 293-1531; Fax (574) 294-1859; info@elkhart.org; www.elkhart.org*

Elwood • *Elwood C/C* • Marcy Fry; Exec. Dir.; 108 S. Anderson St.; 46036; Madison & Tipton; P 9,000; M 150; (765) 552-0180; Fax (765) 552-1277; elwoodchamber@sbcglobal.net; www.elwood-in.com

Evansville • *Southwest Indiana Chamber* • Christy Gillenwater CCE IOM; Pres./CEO; 318 Main St., Ste. 401; 47708; Vanderburgh; P 300,000; M 1,700; (812) 425-8147; Fax (812) 421-5883; cgillenwater@swinchamber.com; www.swinchamber.com*

Ferdinand • *Ferdinand C/C* • Chris James; Exec. Dir.; P.O. Box 101; 47532; Dubois; P 2,160; M 140; (812) 367-0550; Fax (812) 367-1303; cjames@ferdinandindiana.org; www.ferdinandindiana.org

Fishers • *Fishers C/C* • Dan Canan; Pres./CEO; 11601 Municipal Dr.; P.O. Box 353; 46038; Hamilton; P 70,000; M 750; (317) 578-0700; Fax (317) 578-1097; info@fisherschamber.com; www.fisherschamber.com*

Fort Wayne • *Greater Fort Wayne Inc.* • Eric Doden; CEO; 200 E. Main St., Ste. 800; 46802; Allen; P 370,000; M 1,800; (260) 420-6945; Fax (260) 426-0837; info@greaterfortwayneinc.com; www.greaterfortwayneinc.com

Fowler • *Benton County C/C* • Paul Jackson; Pres.; P.O. Box 163; 47944; Benton; P 8,700; M 51; (765) 884-2080; benton.co.chamber@gmail.com; www.bentoncountychamberin.com

Francesville • *see Winamac*

Frankfort • *Clinton County C/C* • Mr. Shan Sheridan; CEO; 301 E. Clinton St.; 46041; Clinton; P 33,300; M 250; (765) 654-5507; Fax (765) 654-9592; shan@ccinchamber.org; www.ccinchamber.org*

Franklin • *Franklin C/C* • Janice Bullman; Exec. Dir.; 120 E. Jefferson St.; 46131; Johnson; P 25,000; M 375; (317) 736-6334; Fax (317) 736-9553; franklincoc@franklincoc.org; www.franklincoc.org*

Fremont • *Fremont Area C/C* • Kathy Parsons; P.O. Box 462; 46737; Steuben; P 1,700; M 65; (260) 495-9010; fremontct@townoffremont.org; www.fremontchamber.org

French Lick • *French Lick-West Baden C/C* • Teresa Richardson; Exec. Secy.; 8594 W. State Rd. 56; P.O. Box 347; 47432; Orange; P 3,000; M 100; (812) 936-2405; Fax (812) 936-2904; trichardson@psci.net; www.frenchlickwestbadenchamber.com

Garrett • *Garrett C/C* • Amy Demske; Exec. Dir.; 111 W. Keyser St.; 46738; Dekalb; P 6,000; M 135; (260) 357-4600; Fax (260) 357-4600; garrettcoc@gmail.com; www.garrettchamber.org

Gary • *Gary C/C* • Charles Hughes; Exec. Dir.; 839 Broadway, Ste. S103; 46402; Lake; P 81,000; M 400; (219) 885-7407; Fax (219) 885-7408; info@garychamber.com; www.garychamber.com*

Gas City • *Gas City Area C/C* • Nancy L. Hoover; Exec. Dir.; 407 E. Main St.; 46933; Grant; P 6,000; M 215; (765) 674-7545; Fax (765) 674-1152; gascitychamber@indy.rr.com; www.gascity.com*

Gentryville • *see Rockport*

Goshen • *Goshen C/C* • David B. Daugherty; Pres.; 232 S. Main St.; 46526; Elkhart; P 32,000; M 500; (574) 533-2102; (800) 307-4204; Fax (574) 533-2103; goshenchamber@goshen.org; www.goshen.org*

Grabill • *Grabill C/C* • Jim Gerig; Pres.; 13717 First St.; P.O. Box 254; 46741; Allen; P 1,200; M 98; (260) 627-5227; gerig4@frontier.com; www.grabillchamberofcommerce.org

Grandview • *see Rockport*

Greencastle • *Greater Greencastle C/C* • Brian Cox; Exec. Dir.; 2 S. Jackson St.; P.O. Box 389; 46135; Putnam; P 38,000; M 340; (765) 653-4517; Fax (765) 848-1015; gchamber@gogreencastle.com; www.gogreencastle.com*

Greendale • *see Lawrenceburg*

Greenfield • *Greenfield Area C/C* • Retta Livengood; Pres.; One Courthouse Plaza; 46140; Hancock; P 20,600; M 450; (317) 477-4188; Fax (317) 477-4189; info@greenfieldcc.org; www.greenfieldcc.org*

Greensburg • *Greensburg/Decatur County C/C* • Jeff Emsweller; Exec. Dir.; 125 N. Broadway; 47240; Decatur; P 26,000; M 400; (812) 663-2832; Fax (812) 663-4275; info@greensburgchamber.com; www.greensburgchamber.com

Greenwood • *Greater Greenwood C/C* • Christian Maslowski; Pres./CEO; 65 Airport Pkwy., Ste. 140; 46143; Johnson; P 250,000; M 664; (317) 888-4856; Fax (317) 865-2609; info@greenwoodchamber.com; www.greenwoodchamber.com*

Griffith • *Griffith C/C* • Kathleen Reed; Pres.; P.O. Box 204; 46319; Lake; P 17,914; M 75; (219) 838-2661; Fax (219) 838-2401; griffithchamber1@hotmail.com; www.griffithchamberofcommerce.com

Hamilton • *Hamilton C/C* • Hester Stouder; Secy.; P.O. Box 66; 46742; Steuben; P 1,532; M 80; (260) 488-3607; Fax (260) 488-2577; hstouder@townofhamilton.org; www.hamiltonindiana.org

Hammond • *Lakeshore C/C* • Dave Ryan; Exec. Dir.; 5246 Hohman Ave.. Ste. 100; 46320; Lake; P 103,000; M 470; (219) 931-1000; Fax (219) 937-8778; info@lakeshorechamber.com; www.lakeshorechamber.com*

Harrison County • *see Corydon*

Hartford City • *Hartford City C/C* • Susan Gerard; Exec. Asst.; 121 N. High St.; Courthouse Annex; 47348; Blackford; P 6,000; M 100; (765) 348-1905; Fax (765) 348-4945; sgerard@blackfordcoedc.org; www.blackfordcounty.org

Hebron • *Hebron C/C* • Donna Paulk; Pres.; P.O. Box 672; 46341; Porter; P 3,610; M 40; (219) 996-5678; info@visithebron.org; www.hebronchamber.org

Highland • *HighlandGriffith C/C* • Mary Luptak; Exec. Dir.; 8536 Kennedy Ave.; 46322; Lake; P 23,727; M 315; (219) 923-3666; Fax (219) 923-3704; mary@highlandgriffithchamber.com; www.highlandgriffithchamber.com*

Hobart • *Hobart C/C* • Mike Adams; Exec. Dir.; 1001 Lillian St.; 46342; Lake; P 29,100; M 420; (219) 942-5774; Fax (219) 942-4928; info@hobartchamber.com; www.hobartchamber.com*

Hope • *Hope Area C/C & Welcome Center* • Donna Robertson; 613 Harrison St.; P.O. Box 131; 47246; Bartholomew; P 2,200; M 35; (812) 546-4673; donnar@advancs.com; www.hopechamber.com

Huntingburg • *Huntingburg C/C* • Nicholas D. Stevens; Exec. Dir.; 309 N. Geiger St.; 47542; Dubois; P 6,500; M 150; (812) 683-5699; chambersec@huntingburg-in.gov; www.huntingburgchamber.org

Huntington • *Huntington County C/C* • Steve Kimmel; Exec. Dir.; 305 Warren St.; 46750; Huntington; P 38,000; M 350; (260) 356-5300; Fax (260) 200-1222; info@huntington-chamber.com; www.huntington-chamber.com*

Indianapolis • *Indy Chamber* • Michael Huber; Pres./CEO; 111 Monument Circle, Ste. 1950; Chase Tower; 46204; Marion; P 1,756,000; M 3,000; (317) 464-2222; Fax (317) 464-2217; memberservices@indylink.org; www.indychamber.com*

Jasonville • *Shakamak Area C/C* • Andrea Pierce Duncan; Pres.; P.O. Box 101; 47438; Greene; P 2,300; M 65; (812) 665-3622; shakamakchamber.org

Jasper • *Jasper C/C* • Nancy Eckerle; Exec. Dir.; 302 W. 6th St.; P.O. Box 307; 47547; Dubois; P 15,038; M 400; (812) 482-6866; (812) 482-7716; Fax (812) 848-2015; chamber@jasperin.org; www.jasperin.org*

Jeffersonville • *see New Albany*

Jonesboro • *see Gas City*

Kendallville • *Kendallville Area C/C* • Lynette Leamon; Exec. Dir.; 122 S. Main St.; 46755; Noble; P 10,000; M 320; (260) 347-1554; Fax (260) 347-1575; lleamon@kendallvillechamber.com; www.kendallvillechamber.com*

Kentland • *Kentland Area C/C* • Rachel Riegle; P.O. Box 273; 47951; Newton; P 2,300; M 60; (219) 474-6050; Fax (219) 474-6097; novotnyins@centurylink.net; www.kentlandin.org

Knightstown • *Knightstown C/C* • Sally Conyers; Pres.; P.O. Box 44; 46148; Henry; P 2,200; M 75; (765) 345-5290; (800) 668-1895; info@knightstownchamber.org; www.knightstownchamber.org

Knox • *Starke County C/C* • Deborah J. Mix; Exec. Dir.; 400 N. Heaton St.; 46534; Starke; P 25,000; M 160; (574) 772-5548; Fax (574) 772-0867; info@starkecountychamber.com; www.starkecountychamber.com

Kokomo • *Greater Kokomo/Howard County C/C* • Charles E. Sparks; Pres./CEO; 325 N. Main St.; 46901; Howard; P 85,000; M 486; (765) 457-5301; Fax (765) 452-4564; csparks@greaterkokomo.com; www.greaterkokomo.com*

Lafayette • *Greater Lafayette Commerce* • Scott Walker; Pres./CEO; 337 Columbia St.; P.O. Box 348; 47901; Tippecanoe; P 173,000; M 1,000; (765) 742-4044; Fax (765) 742-6276; info@greaterlafayettecommerce.com; www.greaterlafayettecommerce.com*

LaGrange • *The Chamber of LaGrange County* • Beth Sherman; Exec. Dir.; 901 S. Detroit St., Ste. A; 46761; LaGrange; P 37,200; M 331; (260) 463-2443; (877) 735-0340; Fax (260) 463-2683; info@lagrangechamber.org; www.lagrangechamber.org*

Lake Station • *Lake Station C/C* • Bill Eaton; Pres.; P.O. Box 5191; 46405; Lake; P 12,600; M 45; (219) 962-1987; Fax (219) 962-1987; wmeaton_mphotog@msn.com; www.lakestationchamber.org*

Lake Township • *see Roselawn*

Lake Village • *see Roselawn*

Lamar • *see Rockport*

LaPorte • *Greater LaPorte C/C* • Michael B. Seitz; Pres.; 803 Washington St.; P.O. Box 486; 46352; LaPorte; P 23,000; M 310; (219) 362-3178; Fax (219) 324-7349; info@lpchamber.com; www.lpchamber.com*

Lawrence • *Greater Lawrence C/C* • Jessica Tower; Exec. Dir.; 9120 Otis Ave., Ste. 100; 46216; Marion; P 100,000; M 258; (317) 541-9876; Fax (317) 541-9875; info@lawrencechamberofcommerce.org; www.lawrencechamberofcommerce.org*

Lawrenceburg • *Dearborn County C/C* • Eric Kranz; Exec. Dir.; 320 Walnut St.; 47025; Dearborn; P 50,000; M 422; (812) 537-0814; (800) 322-8198; Fax (812) 537-0845; ekranz@dearborncountychamber.org; www.dearborncountychamber.org*

Leavenworth • *Crawford County C/C* • Don DuBois; Pres.; 6225 E. Industrial Ln.; 47137; Crawford; P 11,076; M 75; (888) 755-2282; Fax (812) 739-2246; don@crawfordcountychamber.com; www.crawfordcountychamber.com

Lebanon • *Boone County C/C* • Michelle Wiltermood; Exec. Dir.; 221 N. Lebanon St.; 46052; Boone; P 60,500; M 271; (765) 482-1320; Fax (765) 482-3114; info@boonechamber.org; www.boonechamber.org

Liberty • *Union County C/C* • Melissa Browning; Exec. Dir.; 5 W. High St.; 47353; Union; P 7,200; M 87; (765) 458-5976; Fax (765) 458-5976; unioncodc@frontier.com; www.ucdc.us

Ligonier • *Ligonier C/C* • Deb Imbody; Co-Secy.; P.O. Box 121; 46767; Noble; P 4,400; M 60; (260) 894-9909; (260) 894-3102; chamber@ligtel.com; www.ligonierindianachamber.org

Lincoln Township • *see Roselawn*

Linton • *Linton-Stockton C/C* • Lynette Shelton; Exec. Dir.; 159 N.W. 1st St.; P.O. Box 208; 47441; Greene; P 14,000; M 186; (812) 847-4846; Fax (812) 847-0246; lshelton@lintonchamber.org; www.lintonchamber.org

Logansport • *Logansport/Cass County C/C* • Bill Cuppy; Exec. Dir.; 311 S. 5th St.; 46947; Cass; P 39,000; M 325; (574) 753-6388; (800) 425-2071; Fax (574) 735-0909; info@logan-casschamber.com; www.logan-casschamber.com*

Loogootee • *Martin County C/C* • 210 N. Line St.; P.O. Box 257; 47553; Martin; P 10,400; M 100; (812) 295-4093; martincountychamberofcommerce@gmail.com; www.martincountyindianachamberofcommerce.org

Lowell • *Lowell C/C* • Laurie Hosmer; Pres.; 428 E. Commercial Ave.; 46356; Lake; P 8,400; M 74; (219) 696-0231; secretary@lowellinchamber.com; lowellinchamber.com

Madison • *Madison Chamber & Ind. Dev.* • Trevor Crafton; Exec. Dir.; 301 E. Main St.; 47250; Jefferson; P 33,000; M 401; (812) 265-3135; Fax (812) 265-9784; lbloos@madisonindiana.com; www.madisonindiana.com*

Marion • *Marion-Grant County C/C* • Kylie Jackson; Pres.; 217 S. Adams St.; 46952; Grant; P 70,000; M 400; (765) 664-5107; Fax (765) 668-5443; kylie@marionchamber.org; www.marionchamber.org*

Markle • *see Bluffton*

Martinsville • *Greater Martinsville C/C* • Jamie Thompson; Exec. Dir.; 109 E. Morgan St.; P.O. Box 1378; 46151; Morgan; P 12,000; M 200; (765) 342-8110; Fax (765) 342-5713; info@martinsvillechamber.com; www.martinsvillechamber.com

Medaryville • *see Winamac*

Mentone • *Mentone C/C* • Rita Simpson; Pres.; P.O. Box 366; 46539; Kosciusko; P 950; M 40; (574) 353-7417; valleyrs11@frontier.com; www.mentoneeggcity.com

Merrillville • *Crossroads Reg. C/C* • Sue Reed; Pres./CEO; 9101 Taft St.; 46410; Lake; P 60,000; M 700; (219) 769-8180; Fax (219) 736-6223; geninq@crossroadschamber.org; www.crossroadschamber.org*

Michigan City • *Michigan City Area C/C* • Ann Dahm; Pres.; 200 E. Michigan Blvd.; 46360; LaPorte; P 34,000; M 400; (219) 874-6221; info@mcachamber.com; www.michigancitychamber.com*

Middlebury • *Middlebury C/C* • Sam Pohl; Exec. Dir.; 201 E. Winslow St.; P.O. Box 243; 46540; Elkhart; P 3,420; M 160; (574) 825-4300; Fax (574) 358-0210; middleburychambersam@gmail.com; MiddleburyINChamber.com*

Mishawaka • *see South Bend*

Mitchell • *Greater Mitchell C/C* • 533 W. Main St.; P.O. Box 216; 47446; Lawrence; P 5,000; M 115; (812) 849-4441; mitchellchamber@frontier.com; www.mitchellchamberofcommerce.org

Monon • *Monon C/C* • Marshall Young; Pres.; P.O. Box 777; 47959; White; P 1,800; M 45; (219) 253-6441; www.monononline.com

Monterey • *see Winamac*

Monticello • *Greater Monticello C/C & White County Visitors Bur.* • Janet Ollman Dold; Exec. Dir.; 105 W. Broadway; P.O. Box 657; 47960; White; P 10,000; M 200; (574) 583-7220; Fax (574) 583-3399; info@monticelloin.com; www.monticelloin.com*

Moores Hill • *see Lawrenceburg*

Mooresville • *Greater Mooresville C/C* • Mindy Taylor; Exec. Dir.; 4 E. Harrison St.; P.O. Box 62; 46158; Morgan; P 10,000; M 270; (317) 831-6509; Fax (317) 831-9557; mindy@mooresvillechamber.com; www.mooresvillechamber.com*

Morocco • *see Roselawn*

Morristown • *Morristown Area C/C* • Elaine Goble Carlton; Secy.; P.O. Box 476; 46161; Shelby; P 1,220; M 70; (765) 763-6748; egcarlton@morristownin.us; morristownchamberin.com

Mount Ayr • *see Roselawn*

Mount Vernon • *Southwest Indiana Chamber/Posey County Ofc.* • Brittaney Johnson; Admin. Dir.; 915 E. Fourth St.; 47620; Posey; P 300,000; M 1,700; (812) 838-3639; Fax (812) 838-6358; bjohnson@swinchamber.com; www.swinchamber.com*

Muncie • *Muncie-Delaware County C/C* • Jay Julian; Pres./CEO; 401 S. High St.; P.O. Box 842; 47308; Delaware; P 181,000; M 700; (765) 288-6681; (800) 336-1373; Fax (765) 751-9151; eailstock@muncie.com; www.muncie.com*

Munster • *Munster C/C* • Wendy Mis; Exec. Dir.; 1040 Ridge Rd.; 46321; Lake; P 23,600; M 252; (219) 836-5549; Fax (219) 836-5551; wendy@chambermunster.org; www.chambermunster.org*

Nappanee • *Nappanee Area C/C* • Jeff Kitson; Exec. Dir.; 302 W. Market St.; 46550; Elkhart; P 6,678; M 190; (574) 773-7812; Fax (574) 773-4691; jeff@nappaneechamber.com; www.nappaneechamber.com

Nashville • *Brown County C/C* • Debbie Dunbar; Pres.; P.O. Box 164; 47448; Brown; P 15,000; M 180; (812) 988-0234; Fax (812) 988-1547; info@browncountychamber.org; www.browncountychamber.org

New Albany • *One Southern Indiana* • Wendy Dant Chesser; Pres./CEO; 4100 Charlestown Rd.; 47150; Clark & Floyd; P 183,000; M 900; (812) 945-0266; Fax (812) 948-4664; info@1si.org; www.1si.org*

New Castle • *New Castle-Henry County C/C* • Missy Modesitt; Exec. Dir.; 100 S. Main St., Ste. 108; 47362; Henry; P 49,500; M 300; (765) 529-5210; Fax (765) 521-7408; info@nchcchamber.com; www.nchcchamber.com*

New Haven • *New Haven C/C* • Vince Buchanan; Pres./CEO; 435 Ann St.; 46774; Allen; P 14,800; M 316; (260) 749-4484; Fax (260) 749-7900; info@newhavenindiana.org; www.newhavenindiana.org*

New Palestine • *New Palestine Area C/C* • Caralee Griffith; Exec. Dir.; 42 E. Main St.; P.O. Box 541; 46163; Hancock; P 2,000; M 170; (317) 861-2345; newpalchamber@att.net; www.newpalestinechamber.com*

New Paris • *New Paris C/C* • Bryan Perry; P.O. Box 402; 46553; Elkhart; P 1,200; M 50; (574) 831-7598; (574) 831-2176; www.newparis.net

Newtonville • *see Rockport*

Noblesville • *Noblesville C/C* • Bob DuBois; Pres./CEO; P.O.Box 2015; 46061; Hamilton; P 58,000; M 450; (317) 773-0086; Fax (317) 773-1966; info@noblesvillechamber.com; www.noblesvillechamber.com*

North Manchester • *North Manchester C/C* • Laura Rager; Exec. Dir.; 109 N. Market St.; 46962; Wabash; P 6,100; M 170; (260) 982-7644; Fax (260) 982-8718; nmcc@northmanchesterchamber.com; www.northmanchesterchamber.com

North Vernon • *Jennings County C/C Inc.* • Marie Shepherd; Exec. Dir.; 203 N. State St.; P.O. Box 340; 47265; Jennings; P 28,300; M 200; (812) 346-2339; Fax (812) 352-6023; mshepherd@jenningscountychamber.com; www.jenningscountychamber.com

North Webster • *North Webster-Tippecanoe Twp C/C* • Sue Ward; Pres.; P.O. Box 19; 46555; Kosciusko; P 6,661; M 120; (574) 834-7076; Fax (574) 834-2168; nwttchamber@gmail.com; www.northwebster.com

Orleans • *Orleans C/C* • Robert F. Henderson; Exec. Dir.; P.O. Box 9; 47452; Orleans; P 2,142; M 90; (812) 865-9930; Fax (812) 865-3413; historicorleans@netsurfusa.net; www.historicorleans.com

Ossian • *see Bluffton*

Paoli • *Paoli C/C* • Gretchen Anderson; Pres.; P.O. Box 22; 47454; Orange; P 4,200; M 100; (812) 723-4769; info@paolichamber.com; www.paolichamber.com

Pendleton • *see Anderson*

Peru • *Miami County C/C* • Sandy Chittum; Pres.; 13 E. Main St.; 46970; Miami; P 27,000; M 350; (765) 472-1923; Fax (765) 472-7099; info@miamicochamber.com; www.miamicochamber.com*

Petersburg • *Pike County C/C* • Leslie Tegmeyer; Exec. Dir.; 714 E. Main St.; P.O. Box 291; 47567; Pike; P 13,000; M 100; (812) 354-8155; Fax (812) 354-2335; chamber@frontier.com; www.pikecountyin.org

Plainfield • *Plainfield C/C* • Bradley DuBois; Exec. Dir.; 210 W. Main St.; P.O. Box 14; 46168; Hendricks; P 27,700; M 300; (317) 839-3800; Fax (317) 839-9670; chamber@town.plainfield.in.us; www.plainfield-in.com

Plymouth • *Plymouth Area C/C* • 120 N. Michigan St.; 46563; Marshall; P 10,000; M 400; (574) 936-2323; plychamber@plychamber.org; www.plychamber.org*

Poneto • *see Bluffton*

Portage • *Greater Portage C/C* • Terry Hufford; Exec. Dir.; 2642 Eleanor St.; 46368; Porter; P 40,000; M 410; (219) 762-3300; Fax (219) 763-2450; info@portageinchamber.com; www.portageinchamber.com

Porter • *see Chesterton*

Portland • *Jay County C/C* • Dean Saunders; Exec. Dir.; 118 S. Meridian St., Ste. A; 47371; Jay; P 22,000; M 280; (260) 726-4481; Fax (260) 726-3372; deansanders@jaycountychamber.com; www.jaycountychamber.com

Princeton • *Gibson County C/C* • James Stephens; Exec. Dir.; 202 E. Broadway; 47670; Gibson; P 33,600; M 300; (812) 385-2134; Fax (812) 385-2401; office@gibsoncountychamber.org; www.gibsoncountychamber.org*

Rensselaer • *Greater Rensselaer C/C Inc.* • Linda Comingore; Dir.; P.O. Box 73; 47978; Jasper; P 6,250; M 180; (219) 866-8223; Fax (219) 866-5884; info@rensselaerchamber.com; www.rensselaerchamber.com

Richmond • *Wayne County Area C/C* • Amy Holthouse; Pres./CEO; 33 S. 7th St., Ste. 2; 47374; Wayne; P 72,000; M 532; (765) 962-1511; Fax (765) 966-0882; amy@wcareachamber.org; www.wcareachamber.org

Roanoke • *Roanoke C/C* • Emily Hart; Pres.; P. O. Box 434; 46783; Huntington; P 1,722; M 65; (260) 672-2000; (260) 415-3500; emily@twoees.com; www.discoverroanoke.org

Rochester • *Fulton County C/C* • Amy Roe; Exec. Dir.; 822 Main St.; 46975; Fulton; P 21,000; M 250; (574) 224-2666; chamber@rtcol.com; www.fultoncountychamber.com

Rockport • *Spencer County Reg. C/C* • Kathy Reinke; Exec. Dir.; 2792 N. U.S. Hwy. 231; 47635; Spencer; P 21,000; M 160; (812) 649-2186; (812) 686-9208; scrcc@psci.net; www.spencercoin.org*

Rockville • *Parke County C/C* • Alan & Diane Ader; Co-Dirs.; 105 N. Market St., Ste. A; 47872; Parke; P 17,300; M 160; (765) 569-5565; Fax (765) 569-4271; parkecountychamber@sbcglobal.net; www.parkecountychamber.com*

Rome City • *Rome City C/C* • Roberta Stone; Pres.; P.O. Box 42; 46784; Noble; P 1,361; M 30; (260) 854-2412; Fax (260) 854-9270; romecitychamber.com

Roselawn • *North Newton Area C/C* • Debbie Rossiter; Pres.; P.O. Box 266; 46372; Jasper & Newton; P 4,200; M 35; (219) 345-2525; mail@northnewtonchamber.org; www.northnewtonchamber.org

Rushville • *Rush County C/C* • Sandy Fussner; Exec. Dir.; 315 N. Main St.; P.O. Box 476; 46173; Rush; P 18,000; M 165; (765) 932-2880; Fax (765) 932-5610; rushcountychamber@gmail.com; www.rushcounty.com

Saint John • *Saint John C/C* • Gina Fezler; Pres.; 9495 Keilman, Ste. 10; 46373; Lake; P 15,000; M 220; (219) 365-4686; Fax (219) 365-4602; office@stjohnchamber.com; www.stjohnchamber.com

Saint Leon • *see Lawrenceburg*

Salem • *Washington County C/C* • Anita Bush; Mktg. Dir.; 201 E. Market St., Ste. 104; 47167; Washington; P 28,300; M 215; (812) 883-4303; Fax (812) 883-1467; info@washingtoncountychamber.org; www.washingtoncountychamber.org

Santa Claus • *see Rockport*

Schererville • *Schererville C/C* • Evelyn Jones; Ofc. Admin.; 13 W. Joliet St.; 46375; Lake; P 29,300; M 320; (219) 322-5412; Fax (219) 322-0598; info@46375.org; www.46375.org

Scottsburg • *Greater Scott County C/C* • Kelly Dulaney; Exec. Dir.; 90 N. Main St., Ste. B; P.O. Box 404; 47170; Scott; P 24,000; M 300; (812) 752-4080; Fax (812) 752-4307; scottcom@c3bb.com; www.scottchamber.org*

Seymour • *Greater Seymour C/C* • Tricia E. Bechman; Pres.; 105 S. Chestnut St.; 47274; Jackson; P 20,000; M 402; (812) 522-3681; Fax (812) 524-1800; info@seymourchamber.com; www.seymourchamber.com

Shelbyville • *Shelby County C/C* • Julie Metz; Exec. Dir.; 501 N. Harrison St.; 46176; Shelby; P 45,000; M 450; (317) 398-6647; (800) 318-4083; Fax (317) 392-3901; chamberinfo@shelbychamber.net; www.shelbychamber.net*

Shipshewana • *see LaGrange*

South Bend • *St. Joseph County C/C* • Jeffrey Rea; Pres./CEO; 401 E. Colfax Ave., Ste. 310; 46617; St. Joseph; P 265,000; M 1,100; (574) 234-0051; info@sjchamber.org; www.sjchamber.org*

Spencer • *Owen County C/C & Eco. Dev. Corp.* • Denise Shaw; Exec. Dir.; 119 S. Main St.; P.O. Box 87; 47460; Owen; P 21,600; M 100; (812) 829-3245; Fax (812) 829-0936; info@owencountyindiana.org; www.owencountyindiana.org

Sullivan • *Sullivan County C/C* • Ken Bovenschen; Pres.; 25 S. Main St.; P.O. Box 325; 47882; Sullivan; P 20,501; M 150; (812) 905-0131; Fax (812) 905-0163; sullivanchamber@hotmail.com; www.sullivancountyin.com

Syracuse • *Syracuse-Wawasee C/C* • Andrea Keller; Exec. Dir.; 801 N. Huntington St., Ste. 4; P.O. Box 398; 46567; Indiana; P 3,000; M 205; (574) 457-5637; Fax (574) 457-5052; info@swchamber.com; www.swchamber.com*

Tell City • *Perry County C/C* • Lagina D. Gogel; Exec. Dir.; 601 Main St., Ste. A; P.O. Box 82; 47586; Perry; P 20,000; M 350; (812) 547-2385; Fax (812) 547-8378; perrychamber@psci.net; www.perrycountychamber.com*

Terre Haute • *Terre Haute C/C* • David Haynes; Pres./CEO; 630 Wabash Ave., Ste. 105; 47807; Vigo; P 108,000; M 920; (812) 232-2391; Fax (812) 232-2905; bedwards@terrehautechamber.com; www.terrehautechamber.com*

Thayer • *see Roselawn*

Tipton • *Tipton County C/C* • Vicki Warner; Exec. Dir.; 114 S. Main St.; 46072; Tipton; P 16,000; M 185; (765) 675-7533; vwarner@tiptonchamber.org; www.tiptonchamber.org

Union City • *Union City C/C* • Carla A. Benge; Exec. Dir.; 227 W. Oak St.; P.O. Box 424; 47390; Randolph; P 3,600; M 140; (765) 964-5409; Fax (765) 964-5409; ucchamber@embarqmail.com; www.myunioncity.com

Uniondale • *see Bluffton*

Upland • *Upland C/C* • Patty Hart; Pres.; P.O. Box 157; 46989; Grant; P 3,700; M 60; (765) 998-7439; (765) 998-2512; www.uplandin.org

Valparaiso • *Greater Valparaiso C/C* • Rex Richards; Pres.; 162 W. Lincolnway; 46383; Porter; P 40,000; M 815; (219) 462-1105; Fax (219) 462-5710; info@valpochamber.org; www.valpochamber.org*

Vera Cruz • *see Bluffton*

Versailles • *Ripley County C/C* • Amy Thomas; Exec. Dir.; 220 E. U.S. 50, Ste. A; P.O. Box 576; 47042; Ripley; P 28,000; M 700; (812) 689-6654; ripleycc@ripleycountychamber.org; www.ripleycountychamber.org

Vincennes • *Knox County C/C* • Marc A. McNeece; Pres./CEO; 316 Main St.; P.O. Box 553; 47591; Knox; P 38,500; M 375; (812) 882-6440; Fax (812) 882-6441; patti@knoxcountychamber.com; www.knoxcountychamber.com

Wabash • *Wabash County C/C* • 210 S. Wabash St.; 46992; Wabash; P 32,888; M 305; (260) 563-1168; Fax (260) 563-6920; info@wabashchamber.org; www.wabashchamber.org

Wakarusa • *Wakarusa C/C* • Deb Shively; Exec. Secy.; 100 W. Waterford St.; P.O. Box 291; 46573; Elkhart; P 1,750; M 100; (574) 862-4344; Fax (574) 862-2245; chamber@wakarusachamber.com; www.wakarusachamber.com

Walkerton • *Walkerton Area C/C* • John Small Jr.; Pres.; 612 Roosevelt Rd.; 46574; St. Joseph; P 2,200; M 100; (574) 586-3100; Fax (574) 586-3469; chamber@walkerton.org; www.walkerton.org

Warren • *Warren Area C/C* • Jill Houston; Pres.; P.O. Box 40; 46792; Huntington; P 2,000; M 55; (260) 375-3175; www.warrenindiana.com

Warrick County • *see Boonville*

Warsaw • *Kosciusko C/C* • Michelle Goble; Op. Mgr.; 523 S. Buffalo St.; 46580; Kosciusko; P 77,300; M 570; (574) 267-6311; Fax (574) 267-7762; info@kchamber.com; www.kchamber.com*

Washington • *Daviess County C/C* • Samantha Bobbitt; Exec. Dir.; One Train Depot St.; 47501; Daviess; P 32,000; M 319; (812) 254-5262; (800) 449-5262; Fax (812) 254-4003; sbobbitt@dcchamber.com; www.daviesscountychamber.com*

West Baden • *see French Lick*

West Harrison • *see Lawrenceburg*

West Lafayette • *see Lafayette*

Westfield • *Westfield C/C* • Julie Sole; Exec. Dir.; 130 Penn St.; P.O. Box 534; 46074; Hamilton; P 38,000; M 400; (317) 804-3030; Fax (317) 804-3035; info@westfield-chamber.org; www.westfield-chamber.org*

Westville • *Westville Area C/C* • Tom Fath; Pres.; P.O. Box 215; 46391; LaPorte; P 5,956; M 50; (219) 379-7918; westvillechamber@csinet.net; www.westvillechamber.org

Whiting • *Whiting-Robertsdale C/C* • Sarah Hildebranski; Exec. Dir.; 1417 119th St.; 46394; Lake; P 11,000; M 170; (219) 659-0292; Fax (219) 659-5851; sarah@wrchamber.com; www.whitingindiana.com

Winamac • *Pulaski County C/C* • Angela Anspach; Coord.; 102 N. Monticello St.; 46996; Pulaski; P 13,400; M 200; (574) 946-7600; Fax (574) 946-7617; chamber@pulaskionline.org; www.pulaskionline.org*

Winchester • *Winchester Area C/C* • Sandie Rowe; Exec. Dir.; 112 W. Washington St.; 47394; Randolph; P 27,066; M 175; (765) 584-3731; Fax (765) 584-5544; chamber@globalsite.net; www.winchesterareachamber.org

Zionsville • *Zionsville C/C* • Julie Johns-Cole; Exec. Dir.; 135 S. Elm St.; P.O. Box 148; 46077; Boone; P 14,760; M 350; (317) 873-3836; jcole@zionsvillechamber.org; www.zionsvillechamber.org

Iowa

Iowa Assn. of Bus. & Ind. • Michael Ralston; Pres.; 400 E. Court Ave., Ste. 100; Des Moines; 50309; Polk & Warren; P 3,074,186; M 1,400; (515) 280-8000; (800) 383-4224; Fax (515) 244-3285; abi@iowaabi.org; www.iowaabi.org

Ackley • *Ackley C/C* • Korey DeBerg; Pres.; P.O. Box 82; 50601; Franklin & Hardin; P 1,600; M 67; (515) 290-2158; (641) 847-3332; www.ackleyiowa.net

Adel • *Adel Partners C/C* • Deb Bengtson; Dir.; 301 S. 10th St.; P.O. Box 73; 50003; Dallas; P 4,000; M 154; (515) 993-5472; Fax (515) 993-3384; chamber@adelpartners.org; www.adelpartners.org

Albia • *Albia Area C/C* • Laura Teno; Exec. Dir.; 18 S. Main St.; 52531; Monroe; P 3,800; M 180; (641) 932-5108; albiachamber@albiachamber.org; www.albiachamber.org*

Algona • *Algona Area C/C* • Vicki Mallory; Exec. Dir.; 123 E. State St.; 50511; Kossuth; P 15,000; M 275; (515) 295-7201; Fax (515) 295-5920; vmallory@algona.org; www.algona.org*

Allerton • *see Corydon*

Altoona • *Altoona Area C/C* • Melissa Horton; Exec. V.P.; 119 2nd St. S.E., Ste. A; 50009; Polk; P 15,000; M 370; (515) 967-3366; Fax (515) 967-3346; info@altoonachamber.org; www.altoonachamber.org*

Ames • *Ames C/C* • Dan Culhane; Pres./CEO; 304 Main St.; 50010; Story; P 61,000; M 500; (515) 232-2310; Fax (515) 233-3203; info@ameschamber.com; www.ameschamber.com*

Anamosa • *Anamosa C/C* • Carla Burge; Admin.; 124 E. Main St.; 52205; Jones; P 5,000; M 120; (319) 462-4879; director@anamosachamber.org; www.anamosachamber.org*

Ankeny • *Ankeny Area C/C* • Julie C. Todtz; Pres./CEO; 1631 S.W. Main St., Ste. 204/205; 50023; Polk; P 50,000; M 845; (515) 964-0685; Fax (515) 964-0487; info@ankeny.org; www.ankeny.org*

Arnolds Park • *Iowa Great Lakes Area C/C* • Tom Kuhlman; Exec. V.P.; 243 W. Broadway; P.O. Box 9; 51331; Dickinson; P 16,424; M 400; (712) 332-2107; (800) 839-9987; Fax (712) 332-7714; tom@okobojichamber.com; www.vacationokoboji.com

Atlantic • *Atlantic Area C/C* • Ouida Hargens; Exec. Dir.; 102 Chestnut St.; 50022; Cass; P 7,500; M 220; (877) 283-2124; (712) 243-3017; Fax (712) 243-4404; chamber@atlanticiowa.com; www.atlanticiowa.com*

Audubon • *Audubon C/C* • Barbara Smith; Secy.; 302 Broadway; P.O. Box 66; 50025; Audubon; P 2,176; M 153; (712) 563-3780; Fax (712) 563-3780; audchmbr@iowatelecom.net; www.auduboniowa.org

Bedford • *Bedford Area C/C* • Doug Mullen; Dir.; 601 Madison Ave.; 50833; Taylor; P 1,450; M 60; (712) 523-3637; bedfordareachamber@gmail.com; www.bedfordia.org

Bellevue • *Bellevue Area C/C* • Tonia Thola; Dir.; 210 N. Riverview St.; P.O. Box 12; 52031; Jackson; P 2,300; M 210; (563) 872-5830; Fax (563) 872-3611; chamber@bellevueia.com; www.bellevueia.com

Belmond • *Belmond Area C/C* • Linda Thiele; Exec. Dir./Secy.; 223 E. Main St.; 50421; Wright; P 2,376; M 90; (641) 444-3937; Fax (641) 444-3937; belmondareachamberofcommerce@gmail.com; www.belmondiowa.com

Bettendorf • *see Davenport*

Bloomfield • *Bloomfield Area C/C* • Dana Day; Ofc. Asst.; 111 S. Washington; 52537; Davis; P 9,500; M 80; (641) 664-1726; dana@daviscounty.org; www.daviscounty.org

Boone • *Boone Area C/C* • Kurt R. Phillips; Exec. Dir.; 903 Story St.; 50036; Boone; P 13,000; M 285; (515) 432-3342; (800) 266-6312; Fax (515) 432-3343; director@booneiowa.us; www.booneiowa.us*

Britt • *Britt C/C* • P.O. Box 63; 50423; Hancock; P 2,200; M 82; (641) 843-3867; brittcoc@wctatel.net; www.brittiowa.com

Brooklyn • *Brooklyn Eco. Dev. Group* • 138 Jackson St.; P.O. Box 187; 52211; Poweshiek; P 1,468; (641) 522-5300; Fax (641) 522-5584; brkchmbr@netins.net; www.brooklyniowa.com

Burlington • *Greater Burlington Partnership* • Jason Hutcheson; Pres./CEO; 610 N. 4th St., Ste. 200; 52601; Des Moines; P 41,000; M 700; (319) 752-6365; Fax (319) 752-6454; jhutcheson@greaterburlington.com; www.greaterburlington.com*

Carroll • *Carroll C/C* • Shannon Landauer; Exec. Dir.; 407 W. 5th St.; P.O. Box 307; 51401; Carroll; P 21,000; M 370; (712) 792-4383; Fax (712) 792-4384; chamber@carrolliowa.com; www.carrolliowa.com

Cedar Rapids • *Cedar Rapids Metro Eco. Alliance* • Doug Neumann; Interim Pres./CEO; 501 First St. S.E.; 52401; Linn; P 259,000; M 1,100; (319) 398-5317; Fax (319) 398-5228; economicalliance@cedarrapids.org; www.cedarrapids.org*

Centerville • *Centerville-Rathbun Area C/C* • Joyce Bieber; Exec. Dir.; 128 N. 12th St.; 52544; Appanoose; P 14,000; M 250; (641) 437-4102; (800) 611-3800; Fax (641) 437-0527; chamber@centervilleia.com; www.centervilleia.com*

Chariton • *Chariton Area Chamber/Main Street* • Shantel Dow; Exec. Dir.; 104 N. Grand St.; P.O. Box 735; 50049; Lucas; P 4,321; M 200; (641) 774-4059; Fax (641) 774-2801; ccdc@iowatelecom.net; www.charitonareachambermainstreet.com*

Charles City • *Charles City Area C/C* • Mark Wicks; Dir.; 401 N. Main St.; 50616; Floyd; P 7,700; M 265; (641) 228-4234; Fax (641) 228-4744; info@charlescitychamber.com; www.charlescitychamber.com*

Cherokee • *Cherokee C/C* • Julie Hering Kent; Exec. Dir.; 201 W. Main St.; 51012; Cherokee; P 5,253; M 200; (712) 225-6414; Fax (712) 225-1991; info@cherokeeiowachamber.com; www.cherokeeiowachamber.com

Clarinda • *Clarinda C/C* • Elaine Farwell; Exec. Dir.; 115 E. Main St.; 51632; Page; P 5,700; M 175; (712) 542-2166; Fax (712) 542-4113; efarwell@clarinda.org; www.clarinda.org*

Clarion • *Clarion Chamber & Dev.* • Ali Disney; Exec. Dir.; 302 S. Main; P.O. Box 6; 50525; Wright; P 2,850; M 200; (515) 532-2256; chamber@clarioniowa.com; www.clarioniowa.com*

Clear Lake • *Clear Lake Area C/C* • Tim Coffey; CEO; 205 Main Ave.; P.O. Box 188; 50428; Cerro Gordo; P 8,200; M 437; (641) 357-2159; (800) 285-5338; Fax (641) 357-8141; info@clearlakeiowa.com; www.clearlakeiowa.com*

Clinton • *Clinton Area C/C* • Maureen Miller; Pres./CEO; 721 S. 2nd St.; P.O. Box 1024; 52733; Clinton; P 54,000; M 530; (563) 242-5702; Fax (563) 242-5803; chamber@clintonia.com; www.clintonia.com*

Clive • *see Des Moines*

Colfax • *Colfax Main Street* • 1 E. Howard St.; P.O. Box 62; 50054; Jasper; P 2,100; M 40; (515) 674-9071; Fax (515) 674-9072; colfaxmainstreet@gmail.com; www.colfaxmainstreet.com

Conrad • *Conrad Chamber-Main Street Inc.* • Darla Ubben; Exec. Dir.; 204 E. Center St.; P.O. Box 414; 50621; Grundy; P 1,108; (641) 366-2108; Fax (641) 366-2109; cmspd@heartofiowa.net; www.conrad.govoffice.com

Corning • *Adams Community C/C* • Ouida Wymer; Exec. Dir.; 710 Davis Ave.; 50841; Adams; P 1,600; M 150; (641) 322-3243; Fax (641) 322-4387; adamschamber@frontiernet.net; adamscountyiowa.com*

Corydon • *Chamber of Commerce Corydon & Allerton* • P.O. Box 253; 50060; Wayne; P 2,160; M 75; (641) 872-1338; www.cityofcorydoniowa.com

Council Bluffs • *Council Bluffs Area C/C* • Bob L. Mundt; Pres./CEO; 149 W. Broadway; P.O. Box 1565; 51502; Pottawattamie; P 62,300; M 768; (712) 325-1000; Fax (712) 322-5698; info@councilbluffsiowa.com; www.councilbluffsiowa.com*

Cresco • *Cresco Area C/C* • Jason Passmore; Exec. Dir.; 101 2nd Ave. S.W.; 52136; Howard; P 9,600; M 200; (563) 547-3434; crescochamber@yahoo.com; www.crescochamber.com

Creston • *Creston C/C* • Ellen Gerharz; Exec. Dir.; 208 W. Taylor St.; P.O. Box 471; 50801; Union; P 8,400; M 252; (641) 782-7021; Fax (641) 782-9927; chamber@crestoniowachamber.com; www.crestoniowachamber.com*

Dakota City • *see Humboldt*

Davenport • *Quad Cities C/C* • Tara Barney; Pres./CEO; 331 W. 3rd St., Ste. 100; 52801; Scott County, IA; Henry, Mercer & Rock Island, IL; P 400,000; M 2,000; (563) 322-1706; Fax (563) 322-7804; www.quadcitieschamber.com*

Decorah • *Decorah Area C/C* • Nikki Brevig IOM; Exec. Dir.; 507 W. Water St.; 52101; Winneshiek; P 8,200; M 401; (563) 382-3990; (800) 463-4692; Fax (563) 382-5515; director@decorahareachamber.com; www.decorahareachamber.com*

Denison • *Chamber & Dev. Cncl. of Crawford County* • Evan Blakley; Exec. Dir.; 18 S. Main St.; 51442; Crawford; P 17,000; M 200; (712) 263-5621; Fax (712) 263-4789; info@cdcia.org; www.cdcia.org*

Des Moines • *Greater Des Moines Partnership* • Jay Byers; CEO; 700 Locust St., Ste. 100; 50309; Polk, Dallas, Warren, Madison, Marshall, Jasper; P 600,000; M 5,800; (515) 286-4950; (800) 376-9059; Fax (515) 286-4902; info@desmoinesmetro.com; www.desmoinesmetro.com

DeWitt • *DeWitt Chamber & Dev. Co.* • Angela Rheingans; Exec. Dir.; 1010 6th Ave.; 52742; Clinton; P 5,200; M 200; (563) 659-8500; Fax (563) 659-2410; info@dewittiowa.org; www.dewittiowa.org*

Dubuque • *Dubuque Area C/C* • Molly Grover; Pres./CEO; 300 Main St., Ste. 200; 52001; Dubuque; P 95,100; M 1,450; (563) 557-9200; (800) 798-4748; Fax (563) 557-1591; office@dubuquechamber.com; www.dubuquechamber.com*

Durant • *Durant C/C* • Linda Titus; Pres.; P.O. Box 1111; 52747; Cedar, Muscatine & Scott; P 1,832; M 100; (563) 343-3680; www.durantchamber.com

Dyersville • *Dyersville Area C/C* • Karla Thompson; Exec. Dir.; 1100 16th Ave. Ct. S.E.; 52040; Dubuque; P 4,000; M 297; (563) 875-2311; (866) DYERSVILLE; Fax (563) 875-8391; dyersvillechamber@dyersville.org; www.dyersville.org*

Eagle Grove • *Eagle Grove Area C/C* • Lisa Knigge; Exec. Dir.; 212 W. Broadway; P.O. Box 2; 50533; Wright; P 3,500; M 120; (515) 448-4821; Fax (515) 603-6119; chamber@eaglegrove.com; www.eaglegrove.com*

Eldora • *Greater Eldora C/C Inc.* • 1442 Washington St.; 50627; Hardin; P 3,038; M 57; (641) 939-2393; president@eldorachamber.com; www.eldorachamber.com

Eldridge • *Eldridge-North Scott C/C* • Carolyn Scheibe; Exec. Dir.; 220 W. Davenport St.; 52748; Scott; P 9,000; M 190; (563) 285-9965; Fax (563) 285-9964; info@northscottchamber.com; www.northscottchamber.com*

Elkader • *Elkader Area C/C* • Christa Fosse; Coord. Dir.; 207 N. Main St.; P.O. Box 599; 52043; Clayton; P 1,300; M 80; (563) 245-2857; elkader@alpinecom.net; www.elkader-iowa.com

Emmetsburg • *Emmetsburg C/C* • Deb Hite; Exec. Dir.; 1121 Broadway; 50536; Palo Alto; P 4,000; M 150; (712) 852-2283; Fax (712) 852-2156; information@emmetsburg.com; www.emmetsburg.com

Essex • *Essex Comm. Club* • Dana Wenstrand; Exec. Dir.; P.O. Box 334; 51638; Page; P 800; M 175; (712) 586-4541; dana@essexiowa.com; www.essexiowa.com

Estherville • *Estherville Area C/C* • Lexie Ruter; Exec. Dir.; 620 First Ave. S.; 51334; Emmet; P 6,360; M 170; (712) 362-3541; Fax (712) 362-7742; echamberdirector@gmail.com; www.estherville.org

Fairfield • *Fairfield Area C/C* • Detra Dettmann; Exec. Dir.; 204 W. Broadway Ave.; 52556; Jefferson; P 16,000; M 325; (641) 472-2111; Fax (641) 472-6510; chamber@fairfieldiowa.com; www.fairfieldiowa.com*

Fayette • *Fayette Chamber Betterment Found.* • Delores Phom; 708 W. Water; 52142; Fayette; P 1,351; M 25; (563) 425-4410; delores@iowatelecom.net; www.fayetteia.com

Forest City • *Forest City C/C* • Kathy Rollefson; Exec. Dir.; 145 S. Clark St.; P.O. Box 306; 50436; Hancock & Winnebago; P 4,300; M 135; (641) 585-2092; (877) 585-2092; Fax (641) 585-2687; info@forestcityia.com; www.forestcityia.com*

Fort Dodge • *Greater Fort Dodge Growth Alliance/Chamber* • Dennis Plautz; CEO; 24 N. 9th St., Ste. A; 50501; Webster; P 39,000; M 500; (515) 955-5500; Fax (515) 955-3245; info@greaterfortdodge.com; www.greaterfortdodge.com*

Fort Madison • *Fort Madison Area C/C* • Mio Santiago; Pres.; 614 9th St.; P.O. Box 277; 52627; Lee; P 11,500; M 284; (319) 372-5471; Fax (319) 372-6404; info@fortmadison.com; www.fortmadison.com

Garner • *Garner C/C* • Lisa Formanek; Exec. Dir.; 485 State St.; 50438; Hancock; P 3,000; M 140; (641) 923-3993; Fax (641) 923-3993; chamber@comm1net.net; www.garneriachamber.com

George • *George C/C* • Kathy Bonestroo; Secy.; P.O. Box 51; 51237; Lyon; P 1,080; M 65; (712) 475-3271; help@george-iowa.com; www.georgeiowa.com

Glenwood • *Glenwood Area C/C* • Linda Washburn; Exec. Dir.; 5 N. Vine St.; 51534; Mills; P 15,500; M 225; (712) 527-3298; tana@glenwoodia.com; www.glenwoodia.com

Greenfield • *Greenfield Chamber/Main Street* • Ginny Kuhfus; Exec. Dir.; 215 S. First St.; P.O. Box 61; 50849; Adair; P 2,100; M 135; (641) 743-8444; Fax (641) 743-8205; grfld_cc_ms_dev@iowatelecom.net; www.greenfieldiowa.com

Grimes • *Grimes Chamber & Eco. Dev.* • Brian Buethe; Exec. Dir.; 404 S.E. 2nd St., Ste. 200; 50111; Dallas & Polk; P 1,100; M 250; (515) 986-5770; Fax (515) 986-5776; brianb@grimesiowa.com; www.grimesiowa.com*

Grinnell • *Grinnell Area C/C* • Rachael Kinnick; Exec. Dir.; 833 4th Ave.; P.O. Box 538; 50112; Poweshiek; P 9,300; M 300; (641) 236-6555; admin@getintogrinnell.com; www.getintogrinnell.com

Grundy Center • *Grundy Center Chamber & Dev.* • Kelly Riskedahl; Dir.; 705 F Ave.; 50638; Grundy; P 2,700; M 150; (319) 825-3838; Fax (319) 825-6471; chamber@gcmuni.net; www.grundycenter.com

Guthrie Center • *Guthrie Center C/C* • Becky Benton; Secy./Treas.; P.O. Box 193; 50115; Guthrie; P 1,713; M 85; (641) 332-2218; Fax (641) 332-2693; statestreetins@netins.net; www.guthriecenter.com

Guttenberg • *Guttenberg C/C* • Emily Sadewasser; Dir.; 323 S. River Park Dr.; P.O. Box 536; 52052; Clayton; P 1,900; M 90; (563) 252-2323; (877) 252-2323; Fax (563) 252-2378; guttenberg@alpinecom.net; www.guttenbergiowa.net

Hampton • *Greater Franklin County C/C* • Newton Grotzinger; Exec. Dir.; 5 1st St. S.W.; 50441; Franklin; P 4,500; M 300; (641) 456-5668; communications@hamptoniowa.org; www.hamptoniowa.org*

Harlan • *Shelby County C/C* • Dawn Cundiff; Dir.; 1101 7th St.; 51537; Shelby; P 13,000; M 195; (712) 755-2114; (888) 876-1774; Fax (712) 755-2115; info@exploreshelbycounty.com; www.exploreshelbycounty.com

Hartley • *Hartley C/C* • Andy Schierholz; Pres.; 56 2nd St. S.E.; P.O. Box 146; 51346; O'Brien; P 1,670; M 70; (712) 928-4278; (712) 928-2240; hartleychamber@tcaexpress.net; www.hartleyiowa.com

Hawarden • *Hawarden Chamber & Eco. Dev. Inc.* • Cathie Brown; Dir.; 1150 Central Ave.; 51023; Sioux; P 2,500; M 106; (712) 551-4433; Fax (712) 551-4439; chamber@cityofhawarden.com; www.cityofhawarden.com/chamber

Holstein • *Holstein C/C* • 119 S. Main St.; 51025; Ida; P 1,500; M 60; (712) 368-4898; holstein@netllc.net; www.holsteinchamber.com

Hudson • *Hudson C/C* • Blake Colwell; Pres.; P.O. Box 493; 50643; Black Hawk; P 2,300; M 53; (319) 988-4217; (319) 988-3600; info@hudsoniachamber.org; www.hudsoniachamber.org

Humboldt • *Humboldt-Dakota City C/C* • Jeff Goodell; Pres.; 29 5th St. S.; P.O. Box 247; 50548; Humboldt; P 5,000; M 126; (515) 332-1481; Fax (515) 332-1453; chamber@hdcchamber.com; www.ci.humboldt.ia.us

Ida Grove • *Ida Grove C/C* • J.D. Parks; Pres.; 407 Main St.; P.O. Box 252; 51445; Ida; P 2,050; M 100; (712) 364-3404; idagrovechamber@gmail.com; www.idagrovechamber.org

Independence • *Independence Area C/C* • Alissa Westphal; Exec. Dir.; 112 1st St. E.; P.O. Box 104; 50644; Buchanan; P 5,966; M 250; (319) 334-7178; (319) 334-0241; Fax (319) 334-7394; indycommerce@indytel.com; www.indeecommerce.com*

Indianola • *Indianola C/C* • Brenda Easter; Pres./CEO; 104 N. Howard St.; 50125; Warren; P 15,000; M 295; (515) 961-6269; Fax (515) 961-9753; chamber@indianolachamber.com; www.indianolachamber.com*

Iowa City • *Iowa City Area C/C* • Kim Casko; Pres.; 325 E. Washington St., Ste. 100; 52240; Johnson; P 131,000; M 1,000; (319) 337-9637; Fax (319) 338-9958; info@iowacityarea.com; www.iowacityarea.com

Iowa Falls • *Iowa Falls Chamber/Main Street* • Diana Thies; Exec. Dir.; 520 Rocksylvania Ave.; 50126; Hardin; P 5,193; M 150; (641) 648-5549; (641) 648-3432; Fax (641) 648-3702; chamber@iowafallschamber.com; www.iowafallschamber.com*

Jefferson • *Greene County Chamber & Dev.* • Ken Paxton; Exec. Dir.; 220 N. Chestnut St.; 50129; Greene; P 9,800; M 175; (515) 386-2155; Fax (515) 386-2156; info@greenecountyiowa.com; www.greenecountyiowa.com

Jesup • *Jesup C/C* • Todd Rohlfsen; Pres.; P.O. Box 592; 50648; Black Hawk & Buchanan; P 2,520; M 62; (319) 827-1522; Fax (319) 827-3510; jesup@jtt.net; www.jesupiowa.com

Johnston • *Johnston C/C* • Heather Goodwin; Admin.; 8711 Windsor Pkwy., Ste. 2; 50131; Polk; P 15,000; M 260; (515) 276-9064; Fax (515) 309-0144; heather@johnstonchamber.com; www.johnstonchamber.com*

Kalona • *Kalona Area C/C* • Renea Pickard; Events & Ofc. Coord.; 514 B Ave.; P.O. Box 615; 52247; Washington; P 3,900; M 85; (319) 656-2660; chamber@kctc.net; www.kalonachamber.com

Keokuk • *Keokuk Area C/C* • Shelley Oltmans; Exec. Dir.; 329 Main St.; 52632; Lee; P 30,000; M 250; (319) 524-5055; Fax (319) 524-5016; director@keokukchamber.com; www.keokukchamber.com*

Knoxville • *Knoxville C/C* • Mary Spurgeon; Ofc. Mgr.; 217 S. Second St.; 50138; Marion; P 8,000; M 275; (641) 828-7555; Fax (641) 828-7978; chamber@winwithknoxville.com; www.winwithknoxville.com*

La Motte • *see Bellevue*

La Porte City • *La Porte City C/C* • P.O. Box 82; 50651; Black Hawk; P 2,300; M 35; (319) 342-3396; lpcia.com

Lake City • *Lake City Betterment Assn.* • Leah Rosado; Dir.; 105 N. Center St.; P.O. Box 72; 51449; Calhoun; P 1,700; M 97; (712) 464-7611; bettterment@lakecityiowa.com; www.lakecityiowa.com

Lake Mills • *Lake Mills Chamber Dev. Corp.* • Cassie Johnson; Exec. Dir.; 203 N. 1st Ave. W.; P.O. Box 182; 50450; Winnebago; P 2,140; M 120; (641) 592-5253; Fax (641) 592-5252; lmcdc@wctatel.net; www.lakemillsia.org

Laurens • *Laurens C/C* • Connie Dallenbach; Secy.; P.O. Box 33; 50554; Pocahontas; P 1,500; M 50; (712) 841-2222; Fax (712) 841-5555; info@laurensiachamber.com; www.laurensiachamber.com

Le Claire • *Le Claire C/C* • Laura Ernster; Secy.; P.O. Box 35; 52753; Scott; P 3,800; M 135; (563) 289-9970; jackie@leclairechamber.com; www.leclairechamber.com*

Le Mars • *Le Mars Area C/C* • Neal Adler; Exec. Dir.; 50 Central Ave. S.E.; 51031; Plymouth; P 9,800; M 240; (712) 546-8821; Fax (712) 546-7218; info@lemarschamber.org; www.lemarsiowa.com*

Lenox • *Lenox Area C/C* • Michelle Tullberg; Coord.; 200 1/2 S. Main St.; 50851; Taylor; P 1,400; M 90; (641) 333-4272; lenoxchamber@lenoxia.com; www.lenoxia.com*

Leon • *Leon C/C* • Shane Akers; Pres.; c/o Leon City Hall; 50144; Decatur; P 2,000; M 70; info@leonchamber.org; www.leonchamber.org

Lisbon • *see Mount Vernon*

Logan • *Logan C/C* • Nikki Allen & Bill DeWitt; Co-Chairs; P.O. Box 113; 51546; Harrison; P 1,500; M 50; (712) 644-2113; Fax (712) 644-2114; www.loganiowa.com

Manchester • *Manchester Area C/C* • Jessica Pape; Exec. Dir.; 200 E. Main St.; 52057; Delaware; P 5,300; M 200; (563) 927-4141; Fax (563) 927-2958; macc@manchesteriowa.org; www.manchesteriowa.org*

Manning • *Manning C/C* • Kirk Huehn; Pres.; P.O. Box 345; 51455; Carroll; P 1,500; M 74; (712) 655-3541; Fax (712) 655-2478; chamber@mmctsu.com; www.manningia.com

Manson • *Manson Eco. Dev. Corp. & C/C* • Pat Essing; Secy.; P.O. Box 561; 50563; Calhoun; P 2,000; M 35; (712) 469-3311; Fax (877) 803-7633; www.mansoniowa.com

Mapleton • *Maple Valley C/C* • John Babl; Pres.; P.O. Box 164; 51034; Monona; P 1,300; M 60; (712) 881-1351; (712) 881-1451; www.mapleton.com

Maquoketa • *Maquoketa C/C* • Matt Notz; Exec. Dir.; 124 S. Main St., Ste. 2; 52060; Jackson; P 6,100; M 245; (563) 652-4602; (800) 989-4602; Fax (563) 652-3020; cheryl@maquoketachamber.com; www.maquoketachamber.com*

Marengo • *Marengo C/C* • Garth Grafft & Kim Nelson; Co-Chairs; 100 W. Main St.; 52301; Iowa; P 2,500; M 50; (319) 642-5411; knelson@grinnellbank.com; www.marengoiowa.com

Marion • *Marion C/C* • Jill Ackerman; Pres.; 1225 6th Ave., Ste. 100; 52302; Iowa; P 34,750; M 250; (319) 377-6316; Fax (319) 377-1576; jill@marioncc.org; www.marioncc.org*

Marquette • *see McGregor*

Marshalltown • *Marshalltown Area C/C* • Lynn Olberding; Exec. Dir.; 709 S. Center St.; P.O. Box 1000; 50158; Marshall; P 41,500; M 470; (641) 753-6645; Fax (641) 752-8373; info@marshalltown.org; www.marshalltown.org*

Mason City • *Mason City C/C* • Robin Anderson; Pres./CEO; 9 N. Federal Ave.; NI Reg. Commerce Center; 50401; Cerro Gordo; P 40,000; M 650; (641) 423-5724; Fax (641) 423-5725; chamber@masoncityia.com; www.masoncityia.com*

Massena • *Massena C/C* • Phyllis Stakey; 401 Main St.; 50853; Cass; P 380; M 30; (712) 779-3361; pstakey@aol.com

McGregor • *McGregor-Marquette C/C* • Carolyn Gallagher; Exec. Dir.; 146 Main St.; P.O. Box 105; 52157; Clayton; P 1,000; M 125; (563) 873-2186; Fax ; mcgregormarquettechamber@gmail.com; www.mcgreg-marq.org*

Milford • *see Arnolds Park*

Missouri Valley • *Missouri Valley C/C* • Annette Deakins; Exec. Dir.; 100 S. 4th St.; 51555; Harrison; P 3,000; M 120; (712) 642-2553; Fax (712) 642-3771; director@missourivalleychamber.com; www.missourivalleychamber.com

Monticello • *Monticello Area C/C* • Mary Phelan; Exec. Dir.; 204 E. 1st St.; 52310; Jones; P 3,700; M 145; (319) 465-5626; Fax (319) 465-3527; chamber@macc-ia.us; www.macc-ia.us*

Mount Ayr • *Mount Ayr C/C* • Sheila Shafer; Secy.; 117 S. Fillmore; P.O. Box 445; 50854; Ringgold; P 1,700; M 100; (641) 464-3704; mountayrchamber@gmail.com; www.mountayriowa.org

Mount Pleasant • *Mount Pleasant Area Chamber Alliance* • Kristy Ray; Exec. V.P.; 124 S. Main St.; 52641; Henry; P 8,000; M 351; (319) 385-3101; (877) 385-3103; Fax (319) 385-3012; mpaca@mountpleasantiowa.org; www.mountpleasantiowa.org*

Mount Vernon • *Mount Vernon-Lisbon Comm. Dev. Group* • Joe Jennison; Dir.; P.O. Box 31; 52314; Linn; P 6,000; M 135; (319) 895-8214; director@visitmvl.com; www.visitmvl.com

Muscatine • *Greater Muscatine C/C & Ind.* • Greg Jenkins; Pres./CEO; 102 Walnut St.; 52761; Muscatine; P 40,000; M 360; (563) 263-8895; Fax (563) 263-7662; chamber@muscatine.com; www.muscatine.com

Nevada • *Nevada C/C* • Lynn Scarlett; Exec. Dir.; 1015 6th St.; 50201; Story; P 6,800; M 155; (515) 382-6538; (800) 558-2288; chamber@midiowa.net; www.nevadaiowa.org*

New Hampton • *New Horizons C/C* • Whitney Mitvalsky; Exec. Dir.; 15 W. Main; 50659; Chickasaw; P 3,800; M 250; (641) 394-2021; nhcnewhampton@gmail.com; www.discovernewhampton.com

New London • *New London C/C* • Arlo Walljasper; Pres.; 213 W. Main St.; 52645; Henry; P 1,897; M 40; (319) 367-2573; (319) 217-0097; www.newlondoniowa.org

Newton • *Greater Newton Area C/C* • Amanda Price; Exec. Dir.; 113 First Ave. W.; 50208; Jasper; P 15,254; M 215; (641) 792-5545; Fax (641) 791-0879; info@experiencenewton.com; www.experiencenewton.com*

Northwood • *Northwood Area C/C* • P.O. Box 71; 50459; Worth; P 1,989; M 85; (641) 324-1075; info@northwoodchamber.org; www.northwoodchamber.org*

Norwalk • *Norwalk Area C/C* • Deb Mineart; Exec. Dir.; P.O. Box 173; 50211; Polk & Warren; P 8,549; M 125; (515) 981-0619; norwalkchamber@msn.com; www.norwalkchamber.org

Oelwein • *Oelwein Chamber & Area Dev.* • Deb Howard; Chamber Coord.; 25 W. Charles St.; 50662; Fayette; P 6,415; M 300; (319) 283-1105; ocad@oelwein.com; www.oelwein.com

Okoboji • *see Arnolds Park*

Onawa • *Onawa C/C* • Jenn Collison; Dir.; 707 Iowa Ave.; 51040; Monona; P 3,000; M 130; (712) 423-1801; Fax (712) 433-4622; chamber@onawa.com; www.onawachamber.com*

Orange City • *Orange City C/C* • Mike Hofman; Exec. Dir.; 509 8th St. S.E.; P.O. Box 36; 51041; Sioux; P 6,200; M 260; (712) 707-4510; Fax (712) 707-4523; occhmbr@gmail.com; www.orangecityiowa.com

Osage • *Osage C/C* • Wendy Heuton; Exec. Dir.; 808 Main St.; 50461; Mitchell; P 3,600; M 134; (641) 732-3163; Fax (641) 732-3163; chamber@osage.net; www.osagechamber.com

Osceola • *Osceola Chamber-Main Street* • Brian Evans; Pres.; 115 E. Washington; P.O. Box 425; 50213; Clarke; P 4,700; M 155; (641) 342-4200; Fax (641) 342-6353; ocms@iowatelecom.net; osceolachamber.com

Oskaloosa • *Oskaloosa Area Chamber & Dev. Group* • 222 1st Ave. E.; 52577; Mahaska; P 22,381; M 330; (641) 672-2591; Fax (641) 672-2047; oskycofc@oacdg.org; www.oskaloosachamber.org*

Ottumwa • *Ottumwa Area C/C* • Connie Hammersley-Wilson; Exec. Dir.; 217 E. Main St.; P.O. Box 308; 52501; Wapello; P 25,000; M 363; (641) 682-3465; (641) 814-5901; Fax (641) 682-3466; conniewilson@ottumwaiowa.com; www.ottumwachamber.org*

Panora • *Panora C/C* • Julie Dent-Zajicek; P.O. Box 73; 50216; Guthrie; P 1,200; M 120; (641) 755-3300; juliez@panorastatebank.com; www.panora.org

Parkersburg • *Parkersburg C/C* • Tracy Aswegen; Treas.; P.O. Box 550; 50665; Butler; P 1,900; M 76; (319) 346-1645; parkersburgchamber@gmail.com

Pella • *Pella C/C* • Karen Eischen IOM; Exec. Dir.; 818 Washington St.; 50219; Marion; P 10,000; M 300; (641) 628-2626; (888) 746-3882; Fax (641) 628-9697; pellacoc@pella.org; www.pella.org*

Perry • *Perry Area C/C* • Bob Wilson; Exec. Dir.; 1102 Willis Ave.; 50220; Dallas; P 8,000; M 178; (515) 465-4601; (515) 465-4602; Fax (515) 465-2256; perrychamber@perryia.org; www.perryia.org*

Pleasant Hill • *Pleasant Hill C/C* • Cathy Jensen; Exec. Dir.; 5160 Maple Dr., Ste. C; 50327; Polk; P 7,000; M 200; (515) 261-0466; Fax (515) 261-0467; phillchamber@qwestoffice.net; www.pleasanthillchamber.org*

Pleasantville • *Pleasantville C/C* • Brandon Bingham; Dir.; 102 E. Monroe St.; P.O. Box 672; 50225; Marion; P 1,700; M 50; (515) 848-3903; pleasantvillechamber@gmail.com; www.discoverpleasantville.com

Pocahontas • *Pocahontas C/C* • Christian Lynch; Exec. Dir.; P.O. Box 124; 50574; Pocahontas; P 1,732; M 100; (712) 358-0987; (712) 335-4841; pocahontaschamber@gmail.com; www.pocahontaschamber.com

Postville • *Postville C/C* • Jason Meyer; P.O. Box 776; 52162; Allamakee & Clayton; P 2,227; M 50; (563) 864-3333; (563) 864-7454; www.cityofpostville.com

Rathbun • *see Centerville*

Red Oak • *Red Oak Chamber & Ind. Assn.* • Paul M. Griffen; Exec. Dir.; 307 E. Reed St.; 51566; Montgomery; P 6,000; M 235; (712) 623-4821; (712) 623-4822; Fax (712) 623-4822; execdir@redoakiowa.com; www.redoakiowa.com*

Remsen • *Remsen C/C* • Karen Harnack; Secy./Treas.; P.O. Box 225; 51050; Plymouth; P 1,700; M 100; (712) 786-2416; (712) 786-2136; chamber@remseniowa.net; www.remseniowa.net

Rock Rapids • *Rock Rapids C/C* • Angie Jager; Exec. Dir.; 411 1st Ave.; P.O. Box 403; 51246; Lyon; P 2,500; M 150; (712) 472-3456; Fax (712) 472-2764; chamber@rockrapids.com; www.rockrapids.com

Rock Valley • *Rock Valley C/C* • Keith Sietstra; Exec. Dir.; P.O. Box 89; 51247; Sioux; P 3,580; M 94; (712) 476-9300; (712) 476-5707; Fax (712) 476-9116; www.rockvalleychamber.com

Rockwell • *Rockwell C/C* • c/o P.O. Box 446; 50469; Cerro Gordo; P 1,000; M 19; (641) 822-4906; www.rockwell-ia.org

Rockwell City • *Rockwell City Chamber & Dev.* • Theresa Hildreth; Admin. Dir.; 1219 High St.; 50579; Calhoun; P 2,100; M 81; (712) 297-8874; Fax (712) 297-8648; chamber@rockwellcity.com; www.rockwellcity.com

Rolfe • *Rolfe Betterment Inc.* • Jennifer Prenary; Pres.; 319 Garfield St.; 50581; Pocahontas; P 584; M 50; (712) 848-3124; Fax (712) 848-3128; rbi50581@gmail.com; www.rolfeiowa.com

Sac City • *Chamber-Main Street Sac City* • Brandy Ripley; Prog. Dir.; 615 W. Main St.; 50583; Sac; P 2,220; M 150; (712) 662-7316; saccitymainstreet@prairieinet.net; www.saccity.org

Saint Ansgar • *Saint Ansgar Comm. C/C* • Kathy Falk; Pres.; P.O. Box 133; 50472; Mitchell; P 1,120; M 150; (641) 736-4444; stansgarchamber@gmail.com; www.stansgar.org

Saint Donatus • *see Bellevue*

Schaller • *Schaller C/C* • Curt Rininger; P.O. Box 129; 51053; Sac; P 760; M 50; (712) 275-4236; (712) 275-4742

Sheldon • *Sheldon Chamber & Dev. Corp.* • Mark Gaul; Exec. Dir.; 416 9th St.; P.O. Box 276; 51201; O'Brien & Sioux; P 5,000; M 208; (712) 324-2813; Fax (712) 324-4602; mgaul@sheldoniowa.com; www.sheldoniowa.com

Shenandoah • *Shenandoah Chamber & Ind. Org.* • Gregg Connell; Exec. Dir.; 619 W. Sheridan Ave.; 51601; Page; P 5,500; M 300; (712) 246-3455; Fax (712) 246-3456; chamber@shenandoahiowa.net; www.shenandoahiowa.net

Sibley • *Sibley C/C* • Sheryl Peters; Exec. Dir.; 310 9th St.; 51249; Osceola; P 2,500; M 90; (712) 754-3212; Fax (712) 754-3212; chamber@hickorytech.net; www.sibleyiowa.net

Sioux Center • *Sioux Center C/C* • Ardith Lein; Exec. Dir.; 303 N. Main Ave.; 51250; Sioux; P 30,000; M 205; (712) 722-3457; Fax (712) 722-3465; scchambr@mtcnet.net; www.siouxcenterchamber.com

Sioux City • *Siouxland C/C* • Christopher J. McGowan; Pres.; 101 Pierce St.; 51101; Plymouth & Woodbury; P 143,000; M 1,000; (712) 255-7903; Fax (712) 258-7578; chamber@siouxlandchamber.com; www.siouxlandchamber.com

Spencer • *Spencer C/C* • Bill Campbell; Exec. Dir.; 1805 Highway Blvd.; 51301; Clay; P 11,350; M 500; (712) 262-5680; Fax (712) 262-5747; programs@spenceriowachamber.org; www.spenceriowachamber.org*

SPENCER, IOWA - WHERE THERE ARE GRAND EXPERIENCES EVERYDAY; HOME OF THE "WORLD'S GREATEST COUNTY FAIR"; THE CLAY COUNTY FAIR EACH SEPTEMBER AND ANNUAL FLAGFEST CELEBRATION EACH JUNE AND THE HOME OF "DEWEY" THE SMALL TOWN CAT THAT TOUCHED THE WORLD.

Spirit Lake • *Spirit Lake C/C* • Blain Andera; Exec. Dir.; 1710 Lincoln Ave., Ste. D; P.O. Box 155; 51360; Dickinson; P 5,000; M 180; (712) 336-4978; chamber@spiritlakecc.com; www.spiritlakecc.com

Storm Lake • *Storm Lake United* • Gary Lalone; Exec. Dir.; 119 W. 6th St.; P.O. Box 584; 50588; Buena Vista; P 10,000; M 275; (712) 732-3780; (888) 572-4692; Fax (712) 732-1511; angelique@stormlakeunited.com; www.visitstormlake.com*

Story City • *Story City Greater Chamber Connection* • John Hall; Exec. Dir.; 524 Broad St.; P.O. Box 39; 50248; Story; P 3,300; (515) 733-4214; Fax (515) 733-4504; director@storycitygcc.com; www.storycity.net

Strawberry Point • *Strawberry Point C/C* • Abbie Thompson; Pres.; P.O. Box 404; 52076; Clayton; P 1,220; M 80; (563) 933-4417; chamber@strawberrypt.com; www.strawberrychamber.com

Stuart • *Stuart C/C* • P.O. Box 425; 50250; Adair & Guthrie; P 1,700; M 52; (515) 523-1262; (515) 523-1455; stuartchamber@aol.com; www.stuartia.com

Sumner • *SEO Sumner* • Wendy Maifield; Pres.; P.O. Box 262; 50674; Bremer; P 2,028; M 80; (563) 578-5564; www.mysumneriowa.com

Tama • *see Toledo*

Tipton • *Tipton C/C* • Linda Beck; P.O. Box 5; 52772; Cedar; P 3,221; M 80; (563) 886-6350; tiptoniowachamber@gmail.com; www.tiptoniowa.org

Toledo • *Tama-Toledo Area C/C* • Cassie Sokol; Coord.; 103 S. Church St.; P.O. Box 367; 52342; Tama; P 5,000; M 134; (641) 484-6661; tama.toledochamber@yahoo.com; chamber.tamatoledo.org

Traer • *Traer C/C* • Gwen Seda; Pres.; P.O. Box 431; 50675; Tama; P 1,700; M 40; (319) 478-8949; traerchamber@hotmail.com; www.traer.com

Tripoli • *Tripoli Comm. Club* • Eric J. Sommermeyer; Pres.; 1275 Larrabee Ave.; 50676; Bremer; P 1,310; M 40; (319) 882-3595; ejsommermeyer@hotmail.com; tripoliiowa.com

Urbandale • *Urbandale C/C* • Tiffany Menke IOM; Pres.; 2830 100th St., Ste. 110; 50322; Dallas & Polk; P 35,904; M 710; (515) 331-6855; Fax (515) 331-2987; info@urbandalechamber.com; www.uniquelyurbandale.com

Villisca • *Villisca Comm. Betterment Assn.* • Mr. Gayle Heard; Treas.; 601 S. 3rd Ave.; 50864; Montgomery; P 1,250; M 40; (712) 826-5222; (712) 826-2282; www.villisca.com

Vinton • *Vinton Unlimited* • Melissa Schwan; Dir.; 310 A Ave.; 52349; Benton; P 5,200; M 220; (319) 472-3955; melissa@vintonia.org; www.vintonia.org*

Washington • *Washington C/C* • Michelle Redlinger; Exec. Dir.; 205 W. Main St.; 52353; Washington; P 7,300; M 240; (319) 653-3272; Fax (319) 653-5805; chamber@washingtoniowa.org; www.washingtoniowa.org*

Waterloo • *Greater Cedar Valley Alliance & Chamber* • Steve Dust CEcD; Pres./CEO; 10 W. Fourth St., Ste. 310; 50701; Black Hawk; P 236,000; M 800; (319) 232-1156; Fax (319) 233-4580; info@cedarvalleyalliance.com; www.cedarvalleyalliance.com*

Waukee • *Waukee Area C/C* • Melinda Behn; Exec. Dir.; 236 W. Hickman Rd.; P.O. Box 23; 50263; Dallas; P 20,000; M 280; (515) 978-7115; Fax (515) 987-1845; info@waukeechamber.com; www.waukeechamber.com*

Waukon • *Waukon C/C* • Stephanie Dugan; Exec. Dir.; 101 W. Main St.; 52172; Allamakee; P 4,200; M 165; (563) 568-4110; Fax (563) 568-6990; waukoncc@mchsi.com; www.waukon.org

Waverly • *Waverly C/C* • Travis Toliver; Exec. Dir.; 118 E. Bremer Ave.; 50677; Bremer; P 10,000; M 255; (319) 352-4526; waverly@waverlychamber.com; www.waverlychamber.com*

Webster City • *Webster City Area Dev. & C/C* • Deb Brown; Exec. Dir.; 628 2nd St.; P.O. Box 310; 50595; Hamilton; P 8,000; M 175; (515) 832-2564; Fax (515) 832-5130; info@webstercity-iowa.com; www.visitwebstercityiowa.com

West Bend • *West Bend C/C* • Marilyn Schutz; P.O. Box 366; 50597; Kossuth & Palo Alto; P 834; M 45; (515) 887-2181; chamber@westbendiowa.com; www.westbendiowa.com

West Des Moines • *West Des Moines C/C* • Ed Wallace; Pres./CEO; 650 S. Prairie View Dr., Ste. 110; P.O. Box 65320; 50265; Dallas, Polk & Warren; P 61,000; M 650; (515) 225-6009; Fax (515) 225-7129; info@wdmchamber.org; www.wdmchamber.org*

West Liberty • *West Liberty C/C* • Victor Oyervides; Dir.; 112 E. Third St.; 52776; Muscatine; P 3,800; M 130; (319) 627-4876; wlchambr@lcom.net; www.westlibertyiowa.com

West Union • *West Union C/C* • Brandy Burgin; Dir.; 101 N. Vine St.; 52175; Fayette; P 2,500; M 100; (563) 422-3070; Fax (563) 422-6322; chamber@westunion.com; www.westunion.com

Williamsburg • *Williamsburg C/C* • Barb Hopp; Exec. Asst.; 208 W. State St.; P.O. Box 982; 52361; Iowa; P 2,700; M 100; (319) 668-1500; Fax (319) 668-9112; wburgchamber@gmail.com; www.williamsburgiowa.org

Wilton • *Wilton C/C* • Eva Belitz; Exec. V.P.; 118 W. 4th St.; P.O. Box 280; 52778; Muscatine; P 2,820; M 110; (563) 732-2330; Fax (563) 732-2332; wiltoncc@netwtc.net; www.wiltoniowa.org*

Winfield • *Winfield C/C* • Klay Edwards; Pres.; P.O. Box 243; 52659; Henry; P 1,200; M 30; (319) 257-3305; www.winfieldiowa.com

Winterset • *Madison County C/C* • Heather Riley; Exec. Dir.; 73 Jefferson St.; 50273; Madison; P 20,000; M 160; (515) 462-1185; (800) 298-6119; Fax (515) 462-1393; chamber@madisoncounty.com; www.madisoncounty.com

Woodbine • *Woodbine Main Street C/C* • Deb Sprecker; Program Dir.; 313 Walker; 51579; Harrison; P 1,800; (712) 647-3434; woodbinechamber@iowatelecom.net; www.woodbineia.org

Kansas

Kansas C of C • Mike O'Neal; Pres./CEO; 835 S.W. Topeka Blvd.; Topeka; 66612; Shawnee; P 2,904,021; M 10,000; (785) 357-6321; Fax (785) 357-4732; president@kansaschamber.org; www.kansaschamber.org

Abilene • *Abilene C/C* • Torey Berndt; Exec. Dir.; 201 N.W. Second St.; 67410; Dickinson; P 6,844; M 146; (785) 263-1770; Fax (785) 263-4125; chamber@abileneks.net; www.abileneks.net

Alma • *Alma C/C* • Trish Ringel; Secy.; P.O. Box 234; 66401; Wabaunsee; P 850; M 45; (785) 765-3311; (785) 765-3922; Fax (785) 765-3584; www.cityofalma-kansas.net

Alta Vista • *Alta Vista C/C* • Pam McDiffett; P.O. Box 44; 66834; Wabaunsee; P 444; M 20; (785) 499-6620

Andover • *Andover Area C/C* • Becky Wolfe; Pres./Exec. Dir.; 1951 N. Andover Rd.; P.O. Box 339; 67002; Butler; P 12,000; M 110; (316) 733-0648; (316) 733-8808; info@andoverchamber.com; www.andoverchamber.com*

Anthony • *Anthony C/C* • Gwen Warner; Exec. Dir.; 227 W. Main; P.O. Box 354; 67003; Harper; P 2,240; M 160; (620) 842-5456; Fax (620) 842-3929; info@anthonychamber.com; www.anthonychamber.com

Arkansas City • *Arkansas City Area C/C* • Sydney Bland; CEO; 106 S. Summit; 67005; Cowley; P 18,000; M 400; (620) 442-0230; Fax (620) 441-0048; ceo@arkcitychamber.org; www.arkcitychamber.org*

Ashland • *Ashland Area C/C* • P.O. Box 37; 67831; Clark; P 1,032; M 50; (620) 635-0427; (620) 635-2531; aac@ashlandks.com; www.ashlandks.com

Atchison • *Atchison Area C/C* • Jacque Pregont; Pres.; 200 S. 10th St.; P.O. Box 126; 66002; Atchison; P 11,000; M 300; (913) 367-2427; (800) 234-1854; Fax (913) 367-2485; president@atchisonkansas.net; www.atchisonkansas.net*

Atwood • *Atwood C/C* • Sandy Mulligan; Exec. Dir.; 119 S. 4th St.; P.O. Box 152; 67730; Rawlins; P 1,200; M 82; (785) 626-9630; atwoodchamber@rawlinscounty.info; www.atwoodchamber.com

Augusta • *Augusta C/C* • Kent Overaker; Exec. Dir.; 112 E. 6th Ave.; 67010; Butler; P 9,300; M 250; (316) 775-6339; Fax (316) 775-1307; augustacoc@sbcglobal.net; www.chamberofaugusta.org*

Baldwin City • *Baldwin City C/C* • Kimberly Wolff; Ofc. Mgr.; 720 High St.; P.O. Box 501; 66006; Douglas; P 4,230; M 170; (785) 594-3200; info@baldwincitychamber.com; www.baldwincitychamber.com

Basehor • *Basehor C/C* • Blake Waters; Pres.; P.O. Box 35; 66007; Leavenworth; P 5,000; M 81; (913) 724-9000; (913) 845-5134; info@basehorchamber.org; www.basehorchamber.org

Baxter Springs • *Baxter Springs C/C* • Chris Zimmerman; Pres.; 1004 Military Ave.; 66713; Cherokee; P 4,500; M 85; (620) 856-3131; chamberinfo@baxtersprings.us; www.baxtersprings.us

Belle Plaine • *Belle Plaine Area C/C* • Julie Gooch; Pres.; P.O. Box 721; 67013; Sumner; P 1,700; M 36; (620) 488-2808; Fax (620) 488-3517; belleplainechamber@gmail.com; www.belleplainechamber.com

Belleville • *Belleville Chamber & Main Street* • Melinda Pierson; Dir.; 1205 18th St.; P.O. Box 261; 66935; Republic; P 2,000; M 120; (785) 527-5524; mainstreet@nckcn.com; www.bellevilleks.org

Beloit • *Beloit Area C/C* • Gina Broeckelman; Dir.; 123 N. Mill; P.O. Box 582; 67420; Mitchell; P 3,800; M 140; (785) 738-2717; beloitchamber@nckcn.com; www.beloitchamber.com

Blue Rapids • *Blue Rapids C/C* • P.O. Box 253; 66411; Marshall; P 1,400; M 65; (785) 363-7991; bluerapidschamberofcommerce@yahoo.com; skyways.lib.ks.us/towns/BlueRapids

Bonner Springs • *Bonner Springs-Edwardsville Area C/C* • Regina Utter; Exec. Dir.; 309 Oak St.; P.O. Box 548; 66012; Wyandotte; P 12,000; M 100; (913) 422-5044; info@bsedwchamber.org; www.bsedwchamber.org*

Burlingame • *Burlingame Area C/C* • Jeanne Riggs; Pres.; P.O. Box 102; 66413; Osage; P 1,000; M 40; (785) 654-3555; jeanneriggs@burlingamekschamber.com; www.burlingamekschamber.com

Burlington • *Coffey County C/C* • Kelli Higgins; Exec. Dir./CEO; 305A Neosho St.; 66839; Coffey; P 8,601; M 135; (620) 364-2002; (877) 364-2002; Fax (620) 364-3048; executivedirector@coffeycountychamber.com; www.coffeycountychamber.com

Caldwell • *Caldwell Area C/C* • Lu Ann Jamison; Exec. Dir.; 24 N. Main; P.O. Box 42; 67022; Sumner; P 1,200; M 60; (620) 845-6666; (620) 845-6444; Fax (620) 845-2444; caldwell@kanokla.net; www.caldwellkansas.com

Caney • *Caney C/C* • Jackie Freisberg; Pres.; P.O. Box 211; 67333; Montgomery; P 2,800; M 45; (620) 879-5131; Fax (620) 879-5131; caneycoc@caneycoc.kscoxmail.com; www.caney.com

Cedar Vale • *Cedar Vale C/C* • Faye Melton; P.O. Box 112; 67024; Chautauqua; P 565; M 30; (620) 758-2244; www.cedarvalekansas.com

Chanute • *Chanute Area C/C & Ofc. of Tourism* • Jane Brophy; Exec. Dir.; 21 N. Lincoln Ave.; P.O. Box 747; 66720; Neosho; P 10,000; M 182; (620) 431-3350; Fax (620) 431-7770; information@chanutechamber.com; www.chanutechamber.com*

Cheney • *Cheney C/C* • Joe Cowell; Pres.; P.O. Box 716; 67025; Sedgwick; P 2,094; M 80; (316) 540-3622; cheneychamber@gmail.com; www.cheneyks.org

Cherryvale • *Cherryvale C/C* • Tina Cunningham; Exec. Dir.; P.O. Box 112; 67335; Montgomery; P 2,400; M 50; (620) 891-0072; Fax (620) 922-3683; tina.cunningham@communitynational.net; www.cherryvaleusa.com/chamber

Chetopa • *Chetopa C/C* • Kathy Foss; Pres.; P.O. Box 182; 67336; Labette; P 1,230; M 45; (620) 236-7511; chetopachamber@chetopachamber.org; www.chetopachamber.org

Cimarron • *Cimarron Area C/C* • Patty Duncan; Secy./Treas.; P.O. Box 602; 67835; Gray; P 2,200; M 50; (620) 855-2507; (620) 855-2215; www.cimarronks.org

Clay Center • *Clay Center Area C/C* • Renee Langvardt; Pres./CEO; 517 Court St.; 67432; Clay; P 8,500; M 135; (785) 632-5674; ccchamber@eaglecom.net

Clearwater • *Clearwater Area C/C* • Joe Eash; P.O. Box 134; 67026; Sedgwick; P 2,481; M 139; (620) 584-3366; Fax (620) 584-5004; chamber@sktc.net; www.clearwaterschamber.org

Clyde • *Clyde Comm. C/C* • Karla Danielson; Pres.; P.O. Box 5; 66938; Cloud; P 750; M 45; (785) 446-3547; www.clydekansas.org

Coffeyville • *Coffeyville Area C/C* • Yvonne Hull; Exec. Dir.; 807 Walnut; P.O. Box 457; 67337; Montgomery; P 10,250; M 256; (620) 251-2550; Fax (620) 251-5448; chamber@coffeyville.com; www.coffeyvillechamber.org*

Colby • *Colby/Thomas County C/C* • Brette Hankin; Exec. Dir.; 350 S. Range Ave., Ste. 10; 67701; Thomas; P 7,900; M 220; (785) 460-3401; Fax (785) 460-4509; colbychamber@thomascounty.com; www.oasisontheplains.com*

Coldwater • *Coldwater C/C* • Johnita Stalcup; Treas.; P.O. Box 333; 67029; Comanche; P 850; M 30; (620) 582-2859; www.coldwaterkansas.com

Columbus • *Columbus C/C* • Jean Pritchett; Dir.; 320 E. Maple St.; 66725; Cherokee; P 3,500; M 180; (620) 429-1492; columbuschamber@columbus-ks.com; www.chamberofcolumbus.com*

Concordia • *Concordia Area C/C* • Roberta Lowrey; Pres.; 606 Washington; 66901; Cloud; P 6,000; M 170; (785) 243-4290; Fax (785) 243-2014; chamber@concordiakansas.org; www.concordiakansas.org

Conway Springs • *Conway Springs C/C* • P.O. Box 392; 67031; Sumner; P 1,300; M 33; (620) 456-2345; www.conwayspringsks.com

Cottonwood Falls • *Chase County C/C* • Jennifer Laird; Dir. of Eco. Dev.; 318 Broadway; P.O. Box 362; 66845; Chase; P 3,000; M 95; (620) 273-8469; (800) 431-6344; chasechamber@sbcglobal.net; www.chasecountychamber.org

Council Grove • *Council Grove/Morris County Chamber & Tourism* • Diane Wolfe; Exec. Dir.; 207 W. Main St.; 66846; Morris; P 2,300; M 141; (620) 767-5413; Fax (620) 767-5553; chamber@tctelco.net; www.councilgrove.com

Derby • *Derby C/C* • Mark Staats; Pres./CEO; 611 N. Mulberry St., Ste. 200; P.O. Box 544; 67037; Sedgwick; P 24,000; M 375; (316) 788-3421; info@derbychamber.com; www.derbychamber.com*

Desoto • *Desoto C/C* • Sara Ritter IOM; Exec. Dir.; P.O. Box 70; 66018; Johnson; P 5,400; M 190; (913) 583-1585; (877) 585-1821; Fax (913) 585-1821; sritter@desotoks.org; www.desotoks.org*

Dighton • *Lane County Area C/C* • Chelle Anderson; Secy.; 147 E. Long; P.O. Box 942; 67839; Lane; P 1,750; M 71; (620) 397-2211; Fax (620) 397-2416; lcacc@st-tel.net; www.dightonkansas.com

Dodge City • *Dodge City Area C/C* • Gary Johnson; Interim Pres.; 311 W. Spruce; P.O. Box 939; 67801; Ford; P 30,000; M 393; (620) 227-3119; Fax (620) 227-2957; info@dodgechamber.com; www.dodgechamber.com*

Downs • *Downs C/C* • Mandy Burda; Pres.; P.O. Box 172; 67437; Osborne; P 900; M 45; (785) 454-6670; aburda@ruraltel.net; www.downschamber.com

El Dorado • *El Dorado C/C* • Susie Carson; CEO; 201 E. Central; 67042; Butler; P 13,000; M 260; (316) 321-3150; Fax (316) 321-5419; reception@eldoradochamber.com; www.eldoradochamber.com*

Elkhart • *Elkhart Area C/C* • Brent McKinley; 546 Morton; P.O. Box 696; 67950; Morton; P 2,500; M 125; (620) 697-4600; www.ci.elkhart.ks.us

Ellinwood • *Ellinwood C/C* • Nancy Baird; Admin.; 110 1/2 N. Main St.; P.O. Box 482; 67526; Barton; P 2,200; M 155; (620) 566-7353; ellinwoodchamber@hotmail.com; www.ellinwoodchamber.com

Ellis • *Ellis C/C* • Dena Patee; Dir.; 820 Washington; 67637; Ellis; P 2,000; M 85; (785) 726-2660; Fax (785) 726-2661; ellischamber@eaglecom.net; www.ellischamberofcommerce.com

Ellsworth • *Ellsworth Area C/C* • Angela Schepmann; Dir.; 114 1/2 N. Douglas; P.O. Box 315; 67439; Ellsworth; P 3,500; M 150; (785) 472-4071; Fax (785) 472-5668; ecofc@eaglecom.net; goellsworth.com*

Emporia • *Emporia Area C/C* • Jeanine McKenna; Pres./CEO; 719 Commercial St.; 66801; Lyon; P 34,000; M 400; (620) 342-1600; Fax (620) 342-3223; jmckenna@emporiakschamber.org; www.emporiakschamber.org*

Eskridge • *Eskridge C/C* • Bret Kemble; P.O. Box 313; 66423; Wabaunsee; P 530; M 40; (785) 449-2555; (785) 449-2621; www.eskridgeks.org

Eudora • *Eudora C/C* • Theresa Noll-Thompson; Proj. Coord.; P.O. Box 725; 66025; Douglas; P 6,200; M 62; (785) 542-1212; eudorachamber@yahoo.com; www.cityofeudoraks.gov

Eureka • *Eureka Area C/C* • Lucas Mullins; Exec. Dir.; Memorial Hall Bldg.; P.O. Box 563; 67045; Greenwood; P 2,800; M 50; (620) 583-5452; Fax (620) 583-5452; welcomecenter@eurekakansas.com; www.eurekakansas.com

Everest • *Everest C/C* • Michael Wilburn; P.O. Box 6; 66424; Brown; P 285; M 30; (785) 548-7521

Fairway • *see Mission*

Florence • *Florence C/C* • 511 Main; 66851; Marion; P 450; M 30; (620) 878-4296; www.florenceks.com

Fort Scott • *Fort Scott Area C/C* • Lindsay Madison; Exec. Dir.; 231 E. Wall St.; 66701; Bourbon; P 15,733; M 400; (620) 223-3566; (800) 245-3678; Fax (620) 223-3574; fschamber@fortscott.com; www.fortscott.com

Fredonia • *Fredonia C/C* • Carey Spoon; Exec. Dir.; 716 Madison; P.O. Box 449; 66736; Wilson; P 2,500; M 100; (620) 378-3221; Fax (620) 378-4833; fredoniakschamber@centurylink.net; www.fredoniachamber.com

Galena • *Galena C/C* • Kathleen Anderson; Pres.; P.O. Box 465; 66739; Cherokee; P 3,000; M 50; (620) 783-5265

Garden City • *Garden City Area C/C* • Steve Dyer; Pres.; 1511 E. Fulton Terrace; 67846; Finney; P 40,000; M 450; (620) 276-3264; Fax (620) 276-3290; chamber@gardencitychamber.net; www.gardencitychamber.net*

Gardner • *Gardner Area C/C* • Steve Devore; Pres.; 109 E. Main; P.O. Box 402; 66030; Johnson; P 18,000; M 260; (913) 856-6464; Fax (913) 856-5274; devore@gardnerchamber.com; www.gardnerchamber.com*

Garnett • *Garnett Area C/C* • Helen Norman; Pres.; 131 W. 5th Ave.; P.O. Box H; 66032; Anderson; P 3,200; M 90; (785) 448-6767; Fax (785) 448-5555; director@garnettchamber.org; www.garnettchamber.org*

Girard • *Girard Area C/C* • Julie Smith; Exec. Dir.; 118 N. Ozark; P.O. Box 41; 66743; Crawford; P 2,800; M 85; (620) 724-4715; girardchamber@ckt.net; www.girardchamber.com

Glasco • *Glasco Chamber Pride* • Claude Haarwood; Secy.; 405 E. Spaulding Ave.; P.O. Box 572; 67445; Cloud; P 550; M 20; (785) 568-0120; jnothern334@usd334.org; www.glascokansas.org

Glen Elder • *Glen Elder Community Club* • Jessica Cunningham; Pres.; 316 N. High; 67446; Mitchell; P 440; M 75; (785) 545-3000; jessica_l_cunningham@yahoo.com; www.glenelder.com

Goodland • *Goodland Area C/C* • Suzanne McClure; Dir.; 204 W. 11th St.; 67735; Sherman; P 5,000; M 100; (785) 899-7130; suzanne.mcclure@cityofgoodland.org; www.goodlandchamber.com*

JOIN US FOR OUR ANNUAL EVENTS: FREEDOM FEST-JULY, SHERMAN COUNTY FREE FAIR-AUG, PRO BULL RIDERS/THUNDER ON THE PLAINS-AUG, FLATLANDERS FALL FEST-SEPT. HUNTERS ALWAYS WELCOME!

Great Bend • *Great Bend C/C & Eco. Dev.* • Jan Peters; Pres./CEO; 1125 Williams St.; 67530; Barton; P 16,000; M 930; (620) 792-2401; gbcc@greatbend.org; www.greatbend.org*

Greensburg • *Kiowa County C/C* • Dee Chandler; Dir.; 101 S. Main St., Ste. 103; 67054; Kiowa; P 2,300; M 52; (620) 723-3188; Fax (620) 723-3129; kiowadevelopment@gmail.com; www.kiowacountychamber.com

Halstead • *Halstead C/C* • Susie Bryant; Secy./Treas.; P.O. Box 328; 67056; Harvey; P 2,000; M 100; (316) 303-4174; chamber@discoverhalstead.com; www.discoverhalstead.com

Hanover • *Hanover C/C* • Carol Turner; Secy./Treas.; P.O. Box 283; 66945; Washington; P 652; M 45; (785) 337-2114

Harper • *Harper C/C* • Dee Short; P.O. Box 337; 67058; Harper; P 1,480; M 30; (620) 896-2511; www.cityofharper.com

Havensville • *see Onaga*

Hays • *Hays Area C/C* • Tammy Wellbrock; Exec. Dir.; 2700 Vine St.; 67601; Ellis; P 21,000; M 600; (785) 628-8201; hayscc@discoverhays.com; www.discoverhays.com*

Haysville • *Haysville C/C* • Tim Massey; Pres.; 150 Stewart; P.O. Box 372; 67060; Sedgwick; P 10,000; M 150; (316) 529-2461; Fax (316) 554-2342; haysvillechamber@gmail.com; www.haysvillechamber.com*

Hesston • *Hesston C/C* • Becky Galloway; Exec. Dir.; 115 E. Smith; P.O. Box 669; 67062; Harvey; P 3,900; M 125; (620) 327-4102; Fax (620) 327-4595; chamber@hesstonks.org; www.hesstonks.org

Hiawatha • *Hiawatha C/C* • Deidra Leander; Admin.; 611 Utah St.; 66434; Brown; P 3,500; M 80; (785) 742-7136; hiawathachamber@rainbowtel.net; www.hiawathachamber.com

Hill City • *Hill City Area C/C* • Diana Crouch; Exec. Dir.; 801 W. Main St.; P.O. Box 155; 67642; Graham; P 2,600; M 90; (785) 421-5621; Fax (785) 421-5620; hcchamber@ruraltel.net; www.discovergrahamcountyks.com

Hillsboro • *Hillsboro C/C* • Lena Hall; Ofc. Mgr.; 120 N. Main St.; 67063; Marion; P 3,000; M 185; (620) 947-3506; Fax (620) 947-2585; www.hillsborokschamber.com

Hoisington • *Hoisington C/C* • Kristi Lovett; Exec. V.P.; 123 N. Main St.; 67544; Barton; P 2,700; M 130; (620) 653-4311; Fax (620) 653-4311; hoisingtoncofc@embarqmail.com; www.hoisingtonkansas.com*

Holton • *Holton Jackson County C/C* • Carolyn McKee; Exec. Dir.; 104 W. 5th St., Ste. 10; 66436; Jackson; P 13,500; M 200; (785) 364-3963; chamber@exploreholton.com; www.exploreholton.com

Horton • *Horton C/C* • Rita Higley; Treas.; P.O. Box 105; 66439; Brown; P 2,000; M 70; (785) 486-3321; Fax (785) 486-3321; hortonchamber@rainbowtel.net; www.hortonkansas.org

Howard • *Howard C/C* • Nadine Baumgartel; Treas.; P.O. Box 545; 67349; Elk; P 850; M 80; (620) 374-2172; (620) 374-2321; Fax (620) 374-2173; howardchamber@gmail.com

Hugoton • *Hugoton Area C/C* • Alisha Owens; Exec. Dir.; 630 S. Main St.; 67951; Stevens; P 5,260; M 100; (620) 544-4305; hchamber@pld.com; www.stevenscountyks.com

Humboldt • *Humboldt C/C* • Chris Bauer; Pres.; P.O. Box 133; 66748; Allen; P 1,930; M 67; (620) 473-3011; www.humboldtks.net

Hutchinson • *Hutchinson/Reno County C/C* • Jason Ball; Pres./CEO; 117 N. Walnut St.; P.O. Box 519; 67504; Reno; P 64,000; M 850; (620) 662-3391; Fax (620) 662-2168; info@hutchchamber.com; www.hutchchamber.com*

Independence • *Independence C/C* • Lisa Wilson; Pres./CEO; 616 N. Pennsylvania Ave.; P.O. Box 386; 67301; Montgomery; P 9,400; M 240; (620) 331-1890; (800) 882-3606; Fax (620) 331-1899; chamber@indkschamber.org; www.indkschamber.org*

Inman • *Inman C/C* • Lori Bengston; P.O. Box 511; 67546; McPherson; P 1,377; M 65; (620) 585-2063; city@inmanks.net; www.inmanks.org

Iola • *Iola Area C/C & Ofc. of Tourism* • Shelia Lampe; Exec. Dir.; 208 W. Madison; 66749; Allen; P 5,613; M 110; (620) 365-5252; Fax (620) 365-8078; chamber@iolachamber.org; www.iolachamber.org*

Jewell • *Jewell C/C* • Becky Loomis; P.O. Box 235; 66949; Jewell; P 450; M 40; (785) 428-3600; (785) 428-3296; Fax (785) 428-3600; skyways.lib.ks.us/towns/Jewell/

Johnson • *Stanton County C/C* • Karla Dimmitt; Exec. Dir.; 206 S. Main St.; P.O. Box 9; 67855; Stanton; P 2,100; M 150; (620) 492-6606; stchamb@pld.com

Junction City • *Junction City Area C/C* • Tom Weigand; Pres./CEO; 222 W. 6th St.; P.O. Box 26; 66441; Geary; P 39,000; M 310; (785) 762-2632; Fax (785) 762-3353; junctioncitychamber@junctioncitychamber.org; www.junctioncitychamber.org*

Kanopolis • *see Ellsworth*

Kansas City • *Kansas City Kansas Area C/C* • Daniel Silva; Exec. Dir.; 727 Minnesota Ave.; 66101; Wyandotte; P 160,000; M 615; (913) 371-3070; Fax (913) 371-3732; gabrielle@kckchamber.com; www.kckchamber.com*

Kansas City • *Women's Chamber of Commerce of KCK* • Arlana J. Coleman; Pres.; P.O. Box 12611; 66112; Wyandotte; P 145,800; M 100; (913) 522-7526; Fax (913) 299-1748; kckwcc@gmail.com; www.womenschamberkck.org

Kingman • *Kingman Area C/C* • Wanda Kelsey; Exec. Dir.; 322 N. Main; 67068; Kingman; P 3,200; M 107; (620) 532-1853; kingmanareachamber@gmail.com; www.kingmancc.com

Kinsley • *Edwards County C/C* • Connie Oliphant; Pres.; 108 E. 6th; P.O. Box 161; 67547; Edwards; P 3,100; M 50; (620) 659-2711; Fax (620) 659-3304; ecedc@sbcglobal.net; www.edwardscounty.org

Kiowa • *Kiowa C/C* • Bob Hays; Pres.; 625 Main; P.O. Box 272; 67070; Barber; P 1,026; M 70; (620) 825-4636; www.kiowaks.org

LaCrosse • *Rush County C/C* • Linda Kinion; Pres.; P.O. Box 716; 67548; Rush; P 3,200; M 60; (785) 222-2639; Fax (785) 222-2639; rcnlinda@gbta.net; www.rushcounty.org

Lansing • *see Leavenworth*

Larned • *Larned Area C/C* • Lauren Long; Exec. Dir.; 502 Broadway; 67550; Pawnee; P 4,000; M 200; (620) 285-6916; (800) 747-6919; Fax (620) 285-6917; larnedcofc@gbta.net; www.larnedks.org*

Lawrence • *Lawrence C/C* • Larry McElwain; CEO; 646 Vermont St., Ste. 200; 66044; Douglas; P 90,000; M 1,300; (785) 865-4411; Fax (785) 865-4400; dlantz@lawrencechamber.com; www.lawrencechamber.com

Leavenworth • *Leavenworth-Lansing Area C/C* • Jennifer Daly; Pres.; 518 Shawnee St.; 66048; Leavenworth; P 35,251; M 500; (913) 682-4112; Fax (913) 682-8170; jennifer@llchamber.com; www.llchamber.com*

Leawood • *Leawood C/C* • Kevin Jeffries; Pres./CEO; 13451 Briar, Ste. 201; 66209; Johnson; P 32,000; M 470; (913) 498-1514; Fax (913) 491-0134; chamber@leawoodchamber.org; www.leawoodchamber.org*

Lebanon • *Lebanon Hub Club* • Lori Ladow; Pres.; P.O. Box 125; 66952; Smith; P 200; M 16; (785) 389-3261; (785) 389-1141

Lenexa • *Lenexa C/C* • Blake Schreck CED; Pres.; 11180 Lackman Rd.; 66219; Johnson; P 48,000; M 700; (913) 888-1414; Fax (913) 888-3770; staff@lenexa.org; www.lenexa.org*

Lenora • *Lenora C/C* • Gayle James; 125 E. Washington; Box 331; 67645; Norton; P 250; M 15; (785) 567-4860; www.discovernorton.com

Liberal • *Liberal Area C/C* • Rozelle Webb; CEO; 4 Rock Island Rd.; P.O. Box 676; 67905; Seward; P 20,500; M 400; (620) 624-3855; Fax (620) 624-8851; rozelle@liberalkschamber.com; www.liberalkschamber.com*

Lincoln • *Lincoln Area C/C* • Tammy Voeltz; Exec. Dir.; 144 E. Lincoln Ave.; 67455; Lincoln; P 3,200; M 100; (785) 524-4934; Fax (785) 524-4934; lcoc137@sbcglobal.net; www.lincolnkansaschamber.com

Louisburg • *Louisburg C/C* • Becky Bowes; Exec. Dir.; 16 S. Broadway; P.O. Box 245; 66053; Miami; P 4,800; M 110; (913) 837-2826; chamber@louisburgkansas.com; www.louisburgkansas.com*

Lucas • *Lucas Area C/C* • Connie Dougherty; Dir.; 201 S. Main; P.O. Box 186; 67648; Russell; P 406; M 45; (785) 525-6288; lucascoc@wtciweb.com; www.lucaskansas.com

Lyons • *Lyons C/C* • Shannon Young; Dir.; 116 E. Ave. S.; P.O. Box 127; 67554; Rice; P 3,700; M 100; (620) 257-2842; (866) 257-2842; Fax (620) 257-3426; lyonscc@lyons-chamber.com; www.lyons-chamber.com

Madison • *Madison Area C/C* • Rachael Ballard; P.O. Box 58; 66860; Greenwood; P 700; M 30; (620) 437-3463; (620) 437-2031; www.madisonkschamber.org

Manhattan • *Manhattan Area C/C* • Lyle Butler; Pres./CEO; 501 Poyntz Ave.; 66502; Riley; P 60,000; M 800; (785) 776-8829; Fax (785) 776-0679; chamber@manhattan.org; www.manhattan.org*

Mankato • *Mankato C/C* • Jason Ortman; Pres.; 117 E. Jefferson; 66956; Jewell; P 850; M 57; (785) 378-3212; www.mankatoks.com

Marion • *Marion C/C* • Margo Yates; Exec. Secy.; 203 N. 3rd; 66861; Marion; P 2,110; M 125; (620) 382-3425; Fax (620) 382-3993; chinga@eaglecom.net; www.marionks.com

Marysville • *Marysville C/C* • Brenda Staggenborg; Exec. Secy.; 101 N. 10th St.; P.O. Box 16; 66508; Marshall; P 3,280; M 182; (785) 562-3101; (800) 752-3965; Fax (785) 562-3101; info@marysvillekansaschamber.org; www.marysvillekansaschamber.org*

McPherson • *McPherson C/C* • Jennifer Burch; Exec. Dir.; 306 N. Main St.; P.O. Box 616; 67460; McPherson; P 14,000; M 380; (620) 241-3303; (620) 241-3304; Fax (620) 241-8708; chamber@mcphersonks.org; www.mcphersonchamber.org*

Meade • *Meade C/C* • Erin Boggs; Pres.; P.O. Box 576; 67864; Meade; P 1,721; M 48; (620) 873-2091; (620) 873-2359; www.meadechamber.com

Medicine Lodge • *Medicine Lodge Area C/C* • Cindy Brungardt; Dir.; 102 N. Main; P.O. Box 274; 67104; Barber; P 2,200; M 76; (620) 886-3417; mlchamber@sctelcom.net; www.medicinelodgechamber.com

Merriam • *see Mission*

Miltonvale • *Miltonvale C/C* • Carl Kennedy; P.O. Box 98; 67466; Cloud; P 530; M 25; (785) 427-3372; (785) 427-3160; www.miltonvaleks.com

Minneapolis • *Minneapolis Area C/C* • Hope Spano; Exec. Dir.; 200 W. Second St.; 67467; Ottawa; P 2,200; M 95; (785) 392-3068; mplschamber@eaglecom.net; www.minneapoliskansas.org

Mission • *Northeast Johnson County C/C* • Deb Settle; Pres./CEO; 5800 Foxridge Dr., Ste. 100; 66202; Johnson; P 100,000; M 350; (913) 262-2141; info@nejcchamber.com; www.nejcchamber.com*

Mission Hills • *see Mission*

Mission Woods • *see Mission*

Moline • *Moline C/C* • Stephanie Bogdahn; Pres.; P.O. Box 253; 67353; Elk; P 420; M 31; (620) 647-3665; Fax (620) 647-8152; molinecity@sktc.net; www.molinekansas.com

Mound City • *Mound City C/C* • Al Hurt; Pres.; P.O. Box A; 66056; Linn; P 682; M 65; (913) 795-2220; (913) 795-2050; www.moundcity.org

Moundridge • *Moundridge Area C/C* • Liz Johnson; Exec. Dir.; Box 312; 67107; McPherson; P 1,740; M 50; (620) 345-6300; cityinfo@moundridge.com; www.moundridge.com*

Mulvane • *Mulvane C/C* • Mike Robinson; Pres.; P.O. Box 67; 67110; Sedgwick & Sumner; P 6,100; M 75; (316) 777-4850; (316) 737-0534; mulvanechamber@gmail.com; www.mulvanechamber.com

Neodesha • *Neodesha C/C* • Karen Porter; Exec. Dir.; First & Main; P.O. Box 266; 66757; Wilson; P 3,000; M 110; (620) 325-2055; karen@neodeshachamber.com; www.neodeshachamber.com

Ness City • *Ness County C/C* • Cinda Flax; Exec. Dir.; 102 W. Main St.; P.O. Box 262; 67560; Ness; P 1,500; M 66; (785) 798-2413; nccofc@gbta.net; www.nesscountychamber.com

Newton • *Newton Area C/C* • Pam Stevens; Exec. Dir.; 500 N. Main, Ste. 101; 67114; Harvey; P 20,000; M 389; (316) 283-2560; (800) 868-2560; Fax (316) 283-8732; pam@thenewtonchamber.org; www.newtonchamberks.org*

Nickerson • *Nickerson C/C* • Sissy Thimesch; Pres.; 15 N. Nickerson St.; P.O. Box 3; 67561; Reno; P 1,060; M 40; (620) 200-5718; sissythimesch@gmail.com; www.nickersonks.org

North Overland Park • *see Mission*

Norton • *Norton Area C/C* • Darla Beasley; Exec. Dir.; 205 S. State St.; 67654; Norton; P 5,560; M 150; (785) 877-2501; Fax (785) 877-3300; nortoncc@ruraltel.net; www.discovernorton.com*

Oakley • *Oakley Area C/C* • Shannon Plummer; Exec. Dir.; 222 Center Ave.; 67748; Logan; P 2,000; M 77; (785) 672-4862; oakleycc@st-tel.net; www.discoveroakley.com*

Oberlin • *Decatur County Area C/C* • Carrie Morford & Heather McDougal; Co. Mgrs.; 104 S. Penn Ave.; 67749; Decatur; P 4,000; M 75; (785) 475-3441;; dcacc@eaglecom.net; www.oberlinks.com

Olathe • *Olathe C/C* • Tim McKee; CEO; 18001 W. 106th St., Ste. 160; 66061; Johnson; P 130,000; M 1,200; (913) 764-1050; Fax (913) 782-4636; chamber@olathe.org; www.olathe.org*

Onaga • *Onaga Area C/C* • Annette Cline; P.O. Box 278; 66521; Pottawatomie; P 706; M 35; (785) 889-4770; (785) 889-4456; www.cityofonaga.com

Osage City • *Osage City C/C* • Dr. Elton Taylor; Pres.; P.O. Box 56; 66523; Osage; P 3,400; M 60; (785) 528-3515; chamber@osagecity.com; www.osagecity.com

Osawatomie • *Osawatomie C/C* • Diana Neal; Exec. Dir.; 628 Main St.; P.O. Box 63; 66064; Miami; P 4,700; M 100; (913) 755-4114; chamber@osawatomiechamber.org; www.osawatomiechamber.org

Osborne • *Osborne Area C/C* • Kenny Ubelaker; Pres.; P.O. Box 275; 67473; Osborne; P 1,500; M 60; (785) 346-2670; (866) 346-2670; Fax (785) 346-2522; osborneed@ruraltel.net; www.discoverosborne.com

Oswego • *Oswego C/C* • Shawn Carter; P.O. Box 8; 67356; Labette; P 2,100; M 100; (620) 820-3402; cityinfo@oswegokansas.com; www.oswegokschamber.com

Ottawa • *Ottawa Area C/C* • John Coen; Pres./CEO; 109 E. 2nd St.; P.O. Box 580; 66067; Franklin; P 28,000; M 360; (785) 242-1000; (913) 980-3007; Fax (785) 242-4792; chamber@ottawakansas.org; www.ottawakansas.org*

Overland Park • *Overland Park C/C* • Tracey Osborne CCE; Pres.; 9001 W. 110th St., Ste. 150; 66210; Johnson; P 175,000; M 900; (913) 491-3600; Fax (913) 491-0393; opcc@opchamber.org; www.opchamber.org

Oxford • *Oxford C/C* • Betty Oliver; 115 S. Sumner St.; P.O. Box 337; 67119; Sumner; P 1,081; M 25; (620) 455-2223; cityofoxford@sutv.com; www.oxfordks.org

Paola • *Paola C/C* • Jason E. Camis; Exec. Dir.; 6 W. Peoria St.; 66071; Miami; P 5,600; M 240; (913) 294-4335; Fax (913) 294-4336; info@paolachamber.org; www.paolachamber.org*

Park City • *Park City C/C* • Al Taylor; Pres.; 6110 N. Hydraulic St.; 67219; Sedgwick; P 8,000; M 120; (316) 744-2026; pckschamber@gmail.com; www.parkcitykschamber.com

Parsons • *Parsons C/C* • Jonna Gabbert; Exec. Dir./CEO; 506 E. Main St.; 67357; Labette; P 11,000; M 250; (620) 421-6500; (800) 280-6401; Fax (620) 421-6501; chamber@parsonschamber.org; www.parsonschamber.org*

Phillipsburg • *Phillipsburg Chamber & Main Street* • Angie Wells; Exec. Dir.; 205 F St., Ste. 100; P.O. Box 326; 67661; Phillips; P 2,500; M 133; (785) 543-2321; pburgcham@ruraltel.net; www.phillipsburgareachamber.com

Pittsburg • *Pittsburg Area C/C* • Blake Benson; Pres.; 117 W. 4th St.; P.O. Box 1115; 66762; Crawford; P 20,276; M 525; (620) 231-1000; Fax (620) 231-3178; info@pittsburgareachamber.com; www.pittsburgareachamber.com

Pleasanton • *Pleasanton C/C* • Rocky Beltz; Pres.; P.O. Box 268; 66075; Linn; P 1,125; M 40; (913) 352-6235; (913) 352-8258; www.linncountyks.com

Prairie Village • *see Mission*

Pratt • *Pratt Area C/C* • Kimberly DeClue; Exec. Dir.; 114 N. Main St.; 67124; Pratt; P 9,656; M 250; (620) 672-5501; (888) 886-1164; Fax (620) 672-5502; info@prattkansas.org; www.prattkansas.org

Quinter • *Quinter Area C/C* • Carolyn Tuttle; Secy.; P.O. Box 35; 67752; Gove; P 2,500; M 60; (785) 754-3608

Roeland Park • *see Mission*

Rose Hill • *Rose Hill C/C* • Jason Jones; Pres.; P.O. Box 375; 67133; Butler; P 4,500; M 60; (316) 776-0900; (316) 776-2712; rosehillchamber@gmail.com; www.cityofrosehill.com

Russell • *Russell Area C/C* • Julie Counts; Exec. Dir.; 507 N. Main St.; P.O. Box 58; 67665; Russell; P 4,481; M 182; (785) 483-6960; Fax (785) 483-4535; director@russellchamber.com; russellchamber.com*

Sabetha • *Sabetha C/C* • Gina Murchison; Exec. Dir.; 805 Main St.; 66534; Nemaha; P 2,500; M 100; (785) 285-2139; Fax (785) 285-2139; sabethachamber@gmail.com; www.cityofsabetha.com

Saint Marys • *Saint Marys C/C* • Helen Pauly; Exec. Dir.; 702 W. Bertrand; 66536; Pottawatomie; P 2,500; M 120; (785) 437-2077; chamber@saintmarys.com; www.saintmarys.com

Salina • *Salina Area C/C* • Don Weiser; Pres./CEO; 120 W. Ash St.; P.O. Box 586; 67402; Saline; P 55,000; M 1,121; (785) 827-9301; (785) 493-8944; Fax (785) 827-9758; dweiser@salinakansas.org; www.salinakansas.org*

Satanta • *Satanta C/C* • Erika Alexander; Secy.; P.O. Box 98; 67870; Haskell; P 1,280; M 100; (620) 649-3602; satantachamber@gmail.com; www.satanta.org

Scott City • *Scott City Area C/C & EDC* • Katie Eisenhour; Exec. Dir.; 113 E. 5th; 67871; Scott; P 5,000; M 190; (620) 872-3525; Fax (620) 872-2242; sccc@wbsnet.org; www.scottcityks.org

Sedan • *Sedan Area C/C* • Kim Jones; Pres.; P.O. Box 182; 67361; Chautauqua; P 1,100; M 50; (620) 288-1100; sedanchamber@att.net; www.cityofsedan.com

Seneca • *Seneca Area Chamber & Downtown Impact* • Kylee Luckeroth; Exec. Dir.; 523 Main St.; P.O. Box 135; 66538; Nemaha; P 2,000; M 110; (785) 336-1313; senecaimpact@gmail.com; www.seneca-kansas.com/chamber

Shawnee • *Shawnee C/C* • Linda Leeper; Pres./CEO; 15100 W. 67th St., Ste. 202; 66217; Johnson; P 62,000; M 650; (913) 631-6545; Fax (913) 631-9628; info@shawneekschamber.com; www.shawneekschamber.com*

Smith Center • *Smith Center C/C* • Diane Peterson; Dir.; 219 S. Main; 66967; Smith; P 1,700; M 110; (785) 282-3895; scchamber@smithcenter.net; www.smithcenterks.com

Spring Hill • *Spring Hill C/C* • Sharon Mitchell; Pres./CEO; P.O. Box 15; 66083; Johnson & Miami; P 5,000; M 180; (913) 592-3893; Fax (913) 592-3876; chamber@springhillks.org; www.springhillks.org

St. Francis • *Bird City Comm. Club* • Rod Klepper; Pres.; P.O. Box 1138; 67756; Cheyenne; P 447; M 30; (785) 332-8452; (785) 332-3142; www.birdcity.com

Stafford • *Stafford C/C* • Janet Bronson; Secy./Treas.; 130 S. Main St.; P.O. Box 24; 67578; Stafford; P 1,350; M 40; (620) 234-5614; sfcofc@att.net; www.cityofstafford.net

Sterling • *Sterling C/C* • Cheryl Buckman; Secy./Treas.; 112 S. Broadway Ave.; P.O. Box 56; 67579; Rice; P 2,600; M 72; (620) 278-3360; lcbuckman@cm.kscoxmail.com; www.sterlingkschamber.com

Stockton • *Stockton C/C* • Denae Denio-Odle; Pres.; 115 S. Walnut; P.O. Box 1; 67669; Rooks; P 1,211; M 55; (785) 425-6703; Fax (785) 425-6424; stocktonchamber@hotmail.com; www.stocktonkansas.net

Syracuse • *Syracuse-Hamilton County C/C* • Steve Phillips; Pres.; 118 N. Main St.; P.O. Box 678; 67878; Hamilton; P 2,690; M 110; (620) 384-5459; (620) 384-7317; syracusechamber@wbsnet.org; www.syracuseks.gov/chamber

Tonganoxie • *Tonganoxie C/C* • Susan Freemyer; Exec. Dir.; 330 S. Delaware St.; 66086; Leavenworth; P 5,000; M 95; (913) 845-9244; tonganoxichamber@gmail.com; www.tonganoxiechamber.org

Topeka • *Greater Topeka C/C* • Douglas S. Kinsinger; Pres./CEO; 120 S.E. 6th Ave., Ste. 110; 66603; Shawnee; P 200,000; M 1,200; (785) 234-2644; Fax (785) 234-8656; topekainfo@topekachamber.org; www.topekachamber.org*

Troy • *Doniphan County C/C* • Lawrence Mays; Exec. Dir.; County Courthouse; P.O. Box 250; 66087; Doniphan; P 8,000; M 120; (785) 985-2235; Fax (785) 985-2215; lmaysdoniphancounty@yahoo.com; www.dpcountyks.com

Ulysses • *Grant County C/C & Tourism* • Marieta Hauser; Dir.; 113 B S. Main St.; 67880; Grant; P 7,829; M 169; (620) 356-4700; Fax (620) 424-2437; uchamber@pld.com; www.ulysseschamber.org*

Valley Center • *Valley Center C/C* • Marshella Peterson; Dir.; 200 W. Main St.; P.O. Box 382; 67147; Sedgwick; P 8,000; M 111; (316) 755-7340; Fax (316) 755-7341; vccc67147@yahoo.com; www.vckschamber.com

Valley Falls • *Valley Falls C/C* • Leslee Bowers; P.O. Box 162; 66088; Jefferson; P 1,250; M 55; (785) 945-3245; (785) 945-6612; Fax (785) 945-6269; www.valleyfalls.org

Wamego • *Wamego C/C & Mainstreet* • Mary Lyn Barnett; Exec. Dir.; 529 Lincoln Ave.; 66547; Pottawatomie; P 4,500; M 150; (785) 456-7849; Fax (785) 456-7427; wchamber@wamego.net; www.wamegochamber.com*

Waterville • *Waterville C/C* • Sandy Harding; P.O. Box 301; 66548; Marshall; P 681; M 85; (785) 363-2515; secretary@watervillekansas.com; www.watervillekansas.com

Wellington • *Wellington Area C/C & CVB* • Annarose White; Exec. Dir.; 208 N. Washington Ave., Upper Level; P.O. Box 686; 67152; Sumner; P 8,200; M 372; (620) 326-7466; Fax (620) 326-7467; wellingtonkschamber@gmail.com; www.wellingtonkschamber.com*

Wellsville • *Wellsville C/C* • Nicole Vlcek; Pres.; P.O. Box 472; 66092; Franklin; P 1,857; M 80; (785) 883-2296; wellsvillechamberofcommerce@hotmail.com; www.wellsvillechamber.com

Westwood • *see Mission*

Westwood Hills • *see Mission*

Wheaton • *see Onaga*

Wichita • *Wichita Metro C/C* • Gary Plummer; Pres./CEO; 350 W. Douglas Ave.; 67202; Sedgwick; P 638,000; M 1,800; (316) 265-7771; Fax (316) 265-7502; jbaggett@wichitachamber.org; www.wichitachamber.org

Wilson • *Wilson C/C* • Jerry Florian; Pres.; 2407 Ave. E; P.O. Box 328; 67490; Ellsworth; P 800; M 50; (785) 658-2211; wilsoncoc@wilsoncom.us; www.wilsonks.com

Winfield • *Winfield Area C/C* • Sarah Werner; CEO; 123 E. 9th Ave.; P.O. Box 640; 67156; Cowley; P 12,000; M 290; (620) 221-2420; Fax (620) 221-2958; win@winfieldchamber.org; www.winfieldchamber.org*

Winona • *Winona C/C* • Julie Arnberger; Treas.; P.O. Box 54; 67764; Logan; P 230; M 30; (785) 846-7480

Yates Center • *Woodson County C/C* • Carla Green; Exec. Dir.; 110 N. Main St.; P.O. Box 233; 66783; Woodson; P 3,350; M 80; (620) 625-3235; Fax (620) 625-2416; info@woodsoncountychamber.com; www.woodsoncountychamber.com

Kentucky

Kentucky C of C • David Adkisson; Pres./CEO; 464 Chenault Rd.; Frankfort; 40601; Franklin; P 4,413,457; M 2,700; (502) 695-4700; Fax (502) 695-5051; kcc@kychamber.com; www.kychamber.com

Adairville • *Adairville-South Logan C/C* • Sarah Shoulders; Treas.; P.O. Box 266; 42202; Logan; P 2,500; M 50; (270) 539-2080; (270) 539-6731; www.visitlogancounty.net

Ashland • *Ashland Alliance* • Tim Gibbs; Pres./CEO; 1730 Winchester Ave.; P.O. Box 830; 41105; Boyd & Greenup; P 86,000; M 550; (606) 324-5111; Fax (606) 325-4607; paula@ashlandalliance.com; www.ashlandalliance.com*

Barbourville • *Knox County C/C* • Claudia Greenwood; P.O. Box 1809; 40906; Knox; P 31,900; M 73; (606) 546-4300; (606) 546-9515; cgreenwo@barbourville.com; www.knoxcochamber.com*

Bardstown • *Bardstown-Nelson County C/C* • Samantha Brady; Exec. Dir.; One Court Square; 40004; Nelson; P 43,500; M 550; (502) 348-9545; Fax (502) 348-6478; chamber@bardstownchamber.com; www.bardstownchamber.com*

Barren County • *see Glasgow*

Beattyville • *Beattyville/Lee County C/C* • Carole Kincaid; Pres.; P.O. Box 676; 41311; Lee; P 7,500; M 60; (606) 464-2696; (606) 464-5007; www.beattyville.org

Benton • *Kentucky Lake C/C in Marshall County* • Debbie Buchanan; Exec. Dir.; 17 U.S. Hwy. 68 W.; 42025; Marshall; P 31,997; M 260; (270) 527-7665; chamber@marshallcounty.net; www.marshallcounty.net

Berea • *Berea C/C* • David Rowlette; Exec. Dir.; 204 N. Broadway, Ste. 1; 40403; Madison; P 15,000; M 275; (859) 986-9760; Fax (859) 986-2501; david@bereachamber.com; www.bereachamber.com*

Boone County • *see Fort Mitchell*

Bowling Green • *Bowling Green Area C/C* • Ron Bunch; Pres./CEO; 710 College St.; P.O. Box 51; 42102; Warren; P 122,900; M 1,300; (270) 781-3200; (866) 330-2422; info@bgchamber.com; www.bgchamber.com*

Brandenburg • *Meade County Area C/C* • Carole Logsdon; Dir.; 79 Broadway; P.O. Box 483; 40108; Meade; P 29,200; M 187; (270) 422-3626; Fax (270) 422-1389; clogsdon@meadekychamber.org; www.meadekychamber.org*

Brooksville • *Bracken County C/C* • Perry Poe; Pres.; P.O. Box 7; 41004; Bracken; P 8,500; M 65; (606) 735-3474; Fax (606) 735-3103; ppoe@windstream.net; www.augustaky.com

Buechel • *see Louisville-Fern Creek Comm. Assn. & C/C*

Burkesville • *Burkesville-Cumberland County C/C* • Stephen Poindexter; P.O. Box 312; 42717; Cumberland; P 7,000; M 200; (270) 864-5890; chamber@burkesville.com; www.burkesville.com/chamber

Cadiz • *Trigg County C/C* • Connie Allen; Dir.; 5748 Hopkinsville Rd.; P.O. Box 647; 42211; Trigg; P 15,000; M 250; (270) 522-0259; Fax (270) 522-6343; info@triggchamber.com; www.triggchamber.com*

Calhoun • *McLean County C/C* • Dinky Hicks; Pres.; 297 Main St.; P.O. Box 303; 42327; McLean; P 10,000; M 110; (270) 273-9760; mcleancountychamber@connectgradd.net

Campbell County • *see Fort Mitchell*

Campbellsville • *Campbellsville/Taylor County C/C* • Judy R. Cox; Exec. Dir.; 107 W. Broadway; P.O. Box 116; 42718; Taylor; P 23,000; M 345; (270) 465-8601; Fax (270) 465-0607; chamber@teamtaylorcounty.com; www.campbellsvillechamber.com*

Carrollton • *Carroll County C/C* • 511 Highland Ave.; 41008; Carroll; P 11,000; M 135; (502) 732-7034; (502) 732-7035; Fax (502) 732-7028; b.calhoun@carrollcountyky.com; www.carrollcountyky.com

Cave City • *Cave City C/C* • Carol DeGroft; Exec. Secy.; 418 Mammoth Cave St.; P.O. Box 460; 42127; Barren; P 2,300; M 101; (270) 773-5159; Fax (270) 773-7446; ccchamber@scrtc.com; www.cavecitychamber.com

Central City • *Greater Muhlenberg C/C* • Dorothy Walker; Exec. Secy.; 214 N. 1st St.; P.O. Box 671; 42330; Muhlenberg; P 31,200; M 200; (270) 754-2360; Fax (270) 754-2365; dorothy@greatermuhlenbergchamber.com; www.greatermuhlenbergchamber.com

Clinton • *Hickman County C/C* • Deena Pittman; Pres.; P.O. Box 152; 42031; Hickman; P 5,000; M 60; (270) 653-4301; deena.pittman@fcbwky.com; www.clintonhickmancountychamber.com

Columbia • *Columbia-Adair County C/C* • Sue C. Stivers; Exec. Dir.; 201 Burkesville St.; P.O. Box 116; 42728; Adair; P 18,196; M 247; (270) 384-6020; (270) 384-4401; Fax (270) 384-2056; coladair@duo-county.com; www.columbia-adaircounty.com

Corbin • *Southern Kentucky C/C* • Bruce Carpenter; Exec. Dir.; 101 N. Depot St.; 40701; Knox & Whitley; P 60,000; M 325; (606) 528-6390; Fax (606) 523-6538; info@southernkychamber.org; www.southernkychamber.org

Covington • *see Fort Mitchell*

Cumberland • *Tri-City C/C & Cumberland Tourist & Conv. Comm.* • W. Bruce Ayers; Exec. Dir.; 506 W. Main St.; 40823; Harlan; P 4,500; M 50; (606) 589-5812; Fax (606) 589-5812; tricitychamber@windstream.net; www.harlancountytourism.com

Cynthiana • *Cynthiana-Harrison County C/C* • Patricia Grenier; Exec. Dir.; 201 S. Main St.; 41031; Harrison; P 18,800; M 200; (859) 234-5236; Fax (859) 234-6647; cynchamber@setel.com; www.cynthianaky.com

Danville • *Danville-Boyle County C/C* • Paula Fowler; Exec. Dir.; 105 E. Walnut St.; 40422; Boyle; P 30,000; M 330; (859) 236-2361; Fax (844) 270-2252; info@danvilleboylechamber.com; www.danvilleboylechamber.com*

Dawson Springs • *Dawson Springs C/C* • Melissa Heflin; Coord.; 301 W. Arcadia Ave; P.O. Box 345; 42408; Hopkins; P 2,900; M 50; (270) 797-4248; Fax (270) 797-2221; dawsonspringsmains@att.net; www.dawsonspringsky.com

Eddyville • *Lake Barkley C/C* • Cheryl Johnston; Exec. Dir.; 629 Trade Ave.; P.O. Box 453; 42038; Lyon; P 6,500; M 154; (270) 388-4769; Fax (270) 388-5301; lakebarkleychamber1@gmail.com; lakebarkleychamber.com

Edmonton • *Edmonton-Metcalfe County C/C* • Gaye Shaw; Exec. Dir.; P.O. Box 42; 42129; Metcalfe; P 10,100; M 353; (270) 432-3222; Fax (270) 432-3224; metchamb@scrtc.com; www.metcalfechamber.com

Elizabethtown • *Elizabethtown-Hardin County C/C* • Brad Richardson; Pres./CEO; 111 W. Dixie Ave.; 42701; Hardin; P 108,000; M 750; (270) 765-4334; (270) 769-2391; Fax (270) 737-0690; helen@hardinchamber.com; www.hardinchamber.com*

Falmouth • *Pendleton County C/C* • Amanda Moore; Ofc. Supervisor; 230 Main St.; P.O. Box 213; 41040; Pendleton; P 14,900; M 160; (859) 654-6937; pccoc@fuse.net; www.pendletoncountychamber.org

Flatwoods • *see Ashland*

Flemingsburg • *Fleming County C/C* • Crystal L. Ruark; Exec. Dir.; 165 W. Water St.; P.O. Box 24; 41041; Fleming; P 13,000; M 225; (606) 845-1223; Fax (606) 845-1213; crystal@flemingkychamber.com; www.flemingkychamber.com

Fort Mitchell • *Northern Kentucky C/C* • Trey Grayson; Pres./CEO; 300 Buttermilk Pike, Ste. 330; P.O. Box 17416; 41017; Kenton; P 355,000; M 2,000; (859) 578-8800; Fax (859) 578-8802; info@nkychamber.com; www.nkychamber.com*

Frankfort • *Frankfort Area C/C* • Carmen Inman; Pres./CEO; 100 Capital Ave., 2nd Flr.; 40601; Franklin; P 47,000; M 705; (502) 223-8261; Fax (502) 223-5942; chamber@frankfortky.info; www.frankfortky.info*

Franklin • *Franklin-Simpson C/C* • Steve Thurmond; Exec. Dir.; 201 S. Main St.; P.O. Box 513; 42135; Simpson; P 18,000; M 375; (270) 586-7609; Fax (270) 586-5438; cfreese@f-schamber.com; www.f-schamber.com

Frenchburg • *Frenchburg/Menifee County C/C & Tourism* • Lola Thomas; Exec. Dir.; 46 Back St.; P.O. Box 333; 40322; Menifee; P 6,500; M 97; (606) 768-9000; Fax (606) 768-9000; fchamber@mrtc.com; www.frenchburgmenifee.org

Fulton • *see South Fulton, TN*

Georgetown • *Georgetown-Scott County C/C* • John Conner; Exec. Dir.; 160 E. Main St.; 40324; Scott; P 50,000; M 550; (502) 863-5424; Fax (502) 863-5756; laura@gtown.org; www.gtown.org*

Glasgow • *Glasgow-Barren County C/C* • Ernie Myers; Exec. V.P.; 118 E. Public Sq.; 42141; Barren; P 42,100; M 471; (270) 651-3161; (800) 264-3161; Fax (270) 651-3122; chamber@glasgow-ky.com; www.glasgowbarrenchamber.com*

Grand Rivers • *Grand Rivers C of C & Tourism Comm.* • P.O. Box 181; 42045; Livingston; P 380; M 65; (270) 362-0152; (888) 493-0152; info@grandrivers.org; www.grandrivers.org

Grayson • *Grayson Area C/C* • Pat Collier; Coord.; 302 E. Main St.; P.O. Box 612; 41143; Carter; P 4,100; M 150; (606) 474-4401; graysonchamber41143@windstream.net; www.graysonchamber.org

Greensburg • *Greensburg-Green County C/C* • Ivy Stanley; 110 W. Court St.; 42743; Green; P 11,000; M 80; (270) 932-4298; Fax (270) 932-7778; i.stanley@greensburgonline.com; www.greensburgonline.com

Greenville • *Greater Muhlenberg C/C* • Dorothy Walker; Exec. Secy.; 100 E. Main Cross; P.O. Box 313; 42345; Muhlenberg; P 31,200; M 200; (270) 338-5422; Fax (270) 338-5440; dorothy@greatermuhlenbergchamber.com; www.greatermuhlenbergchamber.com*

Hardinsburg • *Breckinridge County C/C* • Sherry D. Stith; Exec. Dir.; 224 S. Main St.; P.O. Box 725; 40143; Breckinridge; P 20,056; M 185; (270) 756-0268; Fax (270) 580-4783; chamber@breckinridgecountychamberky.com; www.breckinridgecountychamberky.com

Harlan • *Harlan County C/C* • Aimee Blanton; Pres.; P.O. Box 268; 40831; Harlan; P 29,300; M 80; (606) 573-4717; Fax (606) 573-4717; doitbest.aimee@bellsouth.net; www.harlancountychamber.com

Harrison County • *see Cynthiana*

Harrodsburg • *Mercer County C/C* • Jill Cutler; Exec. Dir.; 1150 Danville Rd., Ste. 100; 40330; Mercer; P 21,300; M 260; (859) 734-2365; info@mercerchamber.com; www.mercerchamber.com

Hartford • *Ohio County C/C* • Judy Law; Exec. Ofc. Admin.; P.O. Box 3; 42347; Ohio; P 23,000; M 200; (270) 298-3551; Fax (270) 298-3331; chamber@ohiocounty.com; www.ohiocounty.com

Hawesville • *Hancock County C/C* • Edna Rice; Exec. Dir.; P.O. Box 404; 42348; Hancock; P 8,600; M 160; (270) 927-8223; Fax (270) 927-8223; erice@hancockky.us; www.hancockky.us

Hazard • *Hazard-Perry County C/C* • Betsy Clemons; Exec. Dir.; 601 Main St.; 41701; Perry; P 28,700; M 140; (606) 439-2659; Fax (606) 436-6074; hazardcoc@cityofhazard.com; www.hazardperrychamber.com

Henderson • *Kyndle* • Tony Iriti; CEO; 136 2nd St., Ste. 500; 42420; Henderson; P 46,400; M 635; (270) 826-7505; Fax (270) 826-4471; info@kyndle.us; www.kyndle.us*

Hickman • *Hickman C/C* • Bonnie Poynor; Exec. Dir.; P.O. Box 166; 42050; Fulton; P 2,000; M 75; (270) 236-2902; hickmanchamber@att.net; www.hickmanchamber.com

Highview • *see Louisville-Fern Creek Comm. Assn. & C/C*

Hodgenville • *LaRue County C/C* • Krista Levee; Exec. Dir.; 60 Lincoln Sq.; P.O. Box 176; 42748; LaRue; P 14,200; M 150; (270) 358-3411; Fax (270) 358-3411; info@laruecountychamber.org; www.laruecountychamber.org*

Hopkinsville • *Christian County C/C* • Marian Mason; Pres./CEO; 2800 Fort Campbell Blvd.; 42240; Christian; P 102,525; M 881; (270) 885-9096; (800) 842-9959; Fax (270) 886-2059; chamber@christiancountychamber.com; www.christiancountychamber.com*

Irvine • *Estill Dev. Alliance* • Joe Crawford; Exec. Dir.; 177 Broadway; P.O. Box 421; 40336; Estill; P 15,000; M 58; (606) 723-2450; info@estillcountyky.net; www.estillcountyky.net

Jeffersontown • *The Chamber Jeffersontown* • Denise Wills; Mbrshp. Dev. Dir.; 10434 Watterson Trl.; 40299; Jefferson; P 26,000; M 830; (502) 267-1674; Fax (502) 267-2070; info@jtownchamber.com; www.jtownchamber.com

Kenton County • *see Fort Mitchell*

Kuttawa • *see Eddyville*

La Center • *Ballard County C/C* • Myra J. Hook; Exec. Dir.; 325 E. Kentucky Dr.; P.O. Box 322; 42056; Ballard; P 8,900; M 123; (270) 665-8277; Fax (270) 665-8277; bcchamberinfo@brtc.net; www.ballardcountychamber.org*

LaGrange • *Oldham County C/C* • Deana Epperly Karem; Exec. Dir.; 412 E. Main St.; 40031; Oldham; P 58,000; M 420; (502) 222-1635; Fax (502) 222-3159; dekarem@oldhamcountychamber.com; www.oldhamcountychamber.com*

Lancaster • *Garrard County C/C* • Dewayne Holland; Exec. Dir.; 308 W. Maple St., Ste. 1; P.O. Box 462; 40444; Garrard; P 17,092; M 105; (859) 792-2282; Fax (859) 792-2282; garrardchamber@gmail.com; www.garrardchamber.com*

Lawrenceburg • *Anderson County C/C* • Pamela Brough; Exec. Dir.; 1090 Glensboro Rd., Ste. 6A; 40342; Anderson; P 20,000; M 188; (502) 839-5564; (502) 680-1268; accoc@andersonchamberky.org; www.andersonchamberky.org*

Lebanon • *Marion County C/C* • Greg Gribbin; Exec. Dir.; 239 N. Spalding Ave., Ste. 201; 40033; Marion; P 19,820; M 254; (270) 692-9594; Fax (270) 692-2661; director@marioncountykychamber.com; www.marioncountykychamber.com*

Leitchfield • *Grayson County C/C* • Caryn Lewis; Exec. Dir.; 425 S. Main St.; 42754; Grayson; P 26,000; M 260; (270) 259-5587; (800) 667-5934; Fax (270) 230-0615; info@graysoncountychamber.com; www.graysoncountychamber.com

Lexington • *Commerce Lexington Inc.* • Robert L. Quick; Pres./CEO; 330 E. Main St., Ste. 100; 40507; Fayette; P 300,000; M 1,900; (859) 254-4447; Fax (859) 233-3304; dwilson@commercelexington.com; www.commercelexington.com*

Liberty • *Liberty-Casey County C/C* • Nicki Johnson; Secy./Treas.; P.O. Box 278; 42539; Casey; P 16,000; M 101; (606) 706-9694; Fax (606) 787-0146; chamber@libertykentucky.org; www.libertykentucky.org/chamber.html

London • *London/Laurel County C/C* • Deanna Herrmann; Exec. Dir.; 409 S. Main St.; 40741; Laurel; P 59,000; M 500; (606) 864-4789; Fax (606) 864-7300; info@londonlaurelchamber.com; www.londonlaurelchamber.com*

Louisville Area

Fern Creek Comm. Assn. & C/C • Jean Henle; Coord.; P.O. Box 91564; 40291; Jefferson; P 30,000; M 200; (502) 239-7550; Fax (502) 239-7650; info@ferncreek.org; www.ferncreek.org

Greater Louisville Inc./The Metro Chamber • Kent Oyler; Pres./CEO; 614 W. Main St., Ste. 6000; 40202; Jefferson; P 1,200,000; M 2,900; (502) 625-0000; Fax (502) 625-0010; support@greaterlouisville.com; www.greaterlouisville.com*

St. Matthews Area C/C • Glenn Knight; Exec. Dir.; 3940 Grandview Ave., Ste. 216; 40207; Jefferson; P 253,100; M 780; (502) 899-2523; Fax (502) 899-2520; chamber@stmatthewschamber.com; www.stmatthewschamber.com*

Madisonville • *Madisonville-Hopkins County C/C* • Lee S. Lingo; Pres.; 15 E. Center St.; 42431; Hopkins; P 47,000; M 487; (270) 821-3435; Fax (270) 821-9190; chamber@madisonville-hopkinschamber.com; www.madisonville-hopkinschamber.com*

Manchester • *Manchester/Clay County C/C* • Corbett Hensley; Pres.; P.O. Box 1284; 40962; Clay; P 21,400; M 50; (606) 598-8150; www.claycounty.ky.gov

Marion • *Crittenden County C/C* • Susan Alexander; Exec. Dir.; P.O. Box 164; 42064; Crittenden; P 9,400; M 138; (270) 965-5015; Fax (270) 965-0058; susan@crittendenchamber.org; www.crittendenchamber.org

Mayfield • *Mayfield Graves County C/C* • Denise Leath; Pres.; 201 E. College St.; 42066; Graves; P 47,000; M 320; (270) 247-6101; Fax (270) 247-6110; info@mayfieldgraveschamber.com; www.mayfieldgraveschamber.com*

Maysville • *Maysville-Mason County Area C/C* • Vicki Steigleder; Exec. Dir.; 201 E. Third St.; 41056; Mason; P 17,500; M 235; (606) 564-5534; Fax (606) 564-5535; chamber@maysvilleky.net; www.maysvillekentucky.com

Middlesboro • *Bell County C/C* • Candice Jones; Exec. Dir.; N. 20th St.; P.O. Box 788; 40965; Bell; P 30,000; M 210; (606) 248-1075; Fax (606) 248-8851; chamber@bellcountychamber.com; www.bellcountychamber.com*

Middletown • *Louisville East-Middletown C/C* • David Eggleston; Pres.; 133 Evergreen Rd., Ste. 203; 40243; Jefferson; P 50,000; M 150; (502) 400-8519; Fax (502) 244-0185; dave@middletownchamber.com; www.middletownchamber.com*

Monticello • *Monticello-Wayne County C/C* • Charles Peters; Pres.; 120 S. Main St., Ste. 3, City Hall; P.O. Box 566; 42633; Wayne; P 20,800; M 110; (606) 348-3064; (866) 348-3064; Fax (606) 348-3064; info@monticellokychamber.com; www.monticellokychamber.com

Morehead • *Morehead-Rowan County C/C* • Tracy Williams; Exec. Dir.; 150 E. 1st St.; 40351; Rowan; P 24,000; M 380; (606) 784-6221; Fax (606) 783-1373; tcwilliams@moreheadchamber.com; www.moreheadchamber.com

Morganfield • *Morganfield C/C* • Becky Greenwell; Admin. Asst.; 1295 U.S. Hwy. 60 W.; P.O. Box 66; 42437; Union; P 3,000; M 70; (270) 389-9777; mfieldchamber@bellsouth.net; www.morganfieldchamber.org

Morgantown • *Morgantown-Butler County C/C* • Donna Morris; Secy.; 112 S. Main; P.O. Box 408; 42261; Butler; P 13,010; M 100; (270) 526-6827; Fax (270) 526-6830; bcchamber07@bellsouth.net; www.morgantown-ky.com

Mount Sterling • *Mt. Sterling-Montgomery County C/C & Ind. Auth.* • Sandy C. Romenesko; Exec. Dir.; 126 W. Main St.; 40353; Montgomery; P 26,500; M 400; (859) 498-5343; Fax (859) 498-3947; sandy@mtsterlingchamber.com; www.mtsterlingchamber.com

Munfordville • *Hart County C/C* • Virginia Davis; Exec. Dir.; 119 E. Union St.; P.O. Box 688; 42765; Hart; P 18,199; M 230; (270) 524-2892; hart_co@scrtc.com; www.hartcountyky.org*

Murray • *Murray-Calloway County C/C* • Aaron Dail; Pres./CEO; 805 N. 12th St.; P.O. Box 190; 42071; Calloway; P 37,000; M 692; (270) 753-5171; (800) 900-5171; Fax (270) 753-0948; chamber@mymurray.com; www.mymurray.com*

New Castle • *Henry County C/C* • Pat Wallace; Exec. Dir.; 11 N. Main; P.O. Box 355; 40050; Henry; P 15,400; M 178; (502) 845-0806; Fax (502) 845-5313; henrychamber@insightbb.com; chamber.henrycountyky.com*

Nicholasville • *Jessamine County C/C* • Amy Cloud; Exec. Dir.; 508 N. Main St., Ste. A; 40356; Jessamine; P 50,000; M 400; (859) 887-4351; info@jessaminechamber.com; www.jessaminechamber.com*

Olive Hill • *Olive Hill Area C/C* • Jonathan Lewis; Secy./Treas.; P.O. Box 1570; 41164; Carter; P 2,500; M 150; (606) 286-6115; (606) 286-5533; johnsgarage@windstream.net

Owensboro • *Greater Owensboro C/C* • Candance Brake; Pres./CEO; 200 E. 3rd St.; P.O. Box 825; 42303; Daviess; P 100,000; M 1,000; (270) 926-1860; Fax (270) 926-3364; lnunez@owensboro.com; chamber.owensboro.com*

Owingsville • *Owingsville-Bath County C/C* • Kelly Wilson; P.O. Box 360; 40360; Bath; P 11,740; M 60; (606) 674-8830; info@bathchamber.com; www.bathchamber.com

Paducah • *Paducah Area C/C* • Sandra Wilson; Pres.; 300 S. 3rd St.; P.O. Box 810; 42002; McCracken; P 65,000; M 1,050; (270) 443-1746; Fax (270) 442-9152; info@paducahchamber.org; www.paducahchamber.org*

Paintsville • *Paintsville/Johnson County C/C* • Fran Jarrell; Exec. Dir.; 228 Main St., Ste. 201; P.O. Box 629; 41240; Johnson; P 24,000; M 120; (606) 789-5688; franjarrell@pjcchamber.com; www.pjcchamber.com*

Paris • *Paris-Bourbon County C/C* • Lucy Cooper; Exec. Dir.; 720 High St.; 40361; Bourbon; P 20,000; M 200; (859) 987-3205; Fax (859) 987-4640; lcooper@parisky.com; www.parisky.com*

Pikeville • *Southeast Kentucky C/C* • Jared Arnett; Pres./CEO; 178 College St.; 41501; Pike; P 217,700; M 499; (606) 432-5504; Fax (606) 432-7295; info@sekchamber.com; www.sekchamber.com*

Prestonsburg • *Floyd County C/C* • Kathy King Allen; Exec. Dir.; 313 Westminster, Ste. 210; P.O. Box 1508; 41653; Floyd; P 39,500; M 225; (606) 886-0364; Fax (606) 889-6574; floydcounty@setel.com; www.floydcountykentucky.com

Princeton • *Princeton-Caldwell County C/C* • Shea Hughes; Exec. Dir.; P.O. Box 47; 42445; Caldwell; P 13,000; M 200; (270) 963-0644; princetonkychamber@gmail.com; www.princetonkychamber.org

Radcliff • *Radcliff-Hardin County C/C* • Brad Richardson; Pres./CEO; 306 N. Wilson Rd.; 40160; Hardin; P 108,000; M 750; (270) 351-4450; Fax (270) 352-4449; brenda@hardinchamber.com; www.hardinchamber.com*

Richmond • *Richmond C/C* • Mendi Goble; Exec. Dir.; 201 E. Main St.; 40475; Madison; P 33,400; M 650; (859) 623-1720; Fax (859) 623-0839; events@richmondchamber.com; www.richmondchamber.com*

Russell Springs • *Russell County C/C* • Lindsey Westerfield; Ofc. Mgr.; 650 S. Hwy. 127; P.O. Box 64; 42642; Russell; P 17,000; M 250; (270) 866-4333; chamber@duo-county.com; www.russellcountyky.com

Russellville • *Logan County C/C* • Lisa Browning; Exec. Dir.; 116 S. Main St.; 42276; Logan; P 26,000; M 300; (270) 726-2206; Fax (270) 726-2237; info@loganchamber.com; www.loganchamber.com*

Scottsville • *Scottsville-Allen County C/C* • Beth Herrington; Exec. Dir.; 110 S. Court St.; 42164; Allen; P 25,000; M 265; (270) 237-4782; Fax (270) 237-5498; chamber@scottsvilleky.info; www.scottsvilleky.info*

Sebree • *Sebree C/C* • Bruce Wiggins; Pres.; P.O. Box 326; 42455; Webster; P 2,000; M 50; (270) 835-0330; bwiggins72@yahoo.com

Shelbyville • *Shelby County C/C* • John Wieland; Exec. Dir.; 316 Main St.; P.O. Box 335; 40066; Shelby; P 43,000; M 332; (502) 633-1636; Fax (502) 633-7501; info@shelbycountykychamber.com; www.shelbycountykychamber.com*

Shepherdsville • *Bullitt County C/C* • Alex Wimsatt; Exec. Dir.; 162 S. Buckman St.; P.O. Box 1656; 40165; Bullitt; P 75,000; M 375; (502) 543-6727; Fax (502) 543-1765; cindy@bullittchamber.org; www.bullittchamber.org*

Somerset • *Somerset-Pulaski County C/C* • Bobby Clue; Exec. Dir.; 445 S. Hwy. 27, Ste. 101; 42501; Pulaski; P 64,000; M 650; (606) 679-7323; Fax (606) 679-1744; jessica.carlton@somersetpulaskichamber.com; www.somersetpulaskichamber.com*

Springfield • *Springfield-Washington County C/C* • Olivia Thompson; Exec. Dir.; 124 W. Main St., Ste. 3; 40069; Washington; P 11,000; M 85; (859) 336-3810; Fax (859) 336-9410; administrator@springfieldkychamber.com; www.springfieldkychamber.com

Stanford • *Lincoln County C/C* • Andrea Miller; Exec. Dir.; 201 E. Main St., Ste. 5; 40484; Lincoln; P 24,700; M 180; (606) 365-4118; Fax (606) 365-4118; director@lincolncountychamber.com; www.lincolncountychamber.com

Sturgis • *Sturgis C/C* • Lisa Jones; Ofc. Mgr.; 513 N. Main St.; P.O. Box 125; 42459; Union; P 2,200; M 73; (270) 333-9316; (270) 952-1568; Fax (270) 333-9319; sturgischamber@att.net; www.sturgischamberofcommerce.com

Taylorsville • *Spencer County-Taylorsville C/C* • Jan Kehne; Pres.; 19 E. Main St.; P.O. Box 555; 40071; Spencer; P 17,740; M 65; (502) 477-8369; president@spencercountykychamber.com; www.spencercountykychamber.com

Tompkinsville • *Tompkinsville/Monroe County C/C & Eco. Dev.* • Patti Richardson; Coord.; 202 N. Magnolia St.; 42167; Monroe; P 11,750; M 100; (270) 487-1314; Fax (270) 487-0975; monroecountycc@hotmail.com; www.monroecountykychamber.com

Versailles • *Woodford County C/C* • Don Vizi; Exec. Dir.; 141 N. Main St.; 40383; Woodford; P 25,500; M 270; (859) 873-5122; Fax (877) 817-6585; woodforddirector@gmail.com; www.woodfordcountyinfo.com

Warsaw • *Gallatin County C/C* • Rena Mylor; Pres.; P.O. Box 1029; 41095; Gallatin; P 8,000; M 40; (859) 992-2300; rena@gallatinkychamber.com; www.gallatinkychamber.com

West Liberty • *Morgan County C/C* • Hank Allen; Pres.; 565 Main St.; 41472; Morgan; P 14,000; M 50; (606) 743-2300; Fax (606) 743-2202; wliberty@mrtc.com; www.cityofwestliberty.com

West Point • *see Radcliff*

Whitesburg • *Letcher County C/C* • Joe DePriest; Pres.; P.O. Box 127; 41858; Letcher; P 24,500; M 60; (606) 634-4441; jbdep@yahoo.com; www.letchercountychamber.com

Whitley City • *McCreary County C/C* • Greg Burdine; Pres.; P.O. Box 548; 42653; McCreary; P 18,300; M 110; (606) 376-5004; Fax (606) 376-9060; chamber7@highland.net; www.mccrearychamber.com

Williamsburg • *see Corbin*

Williamstown • *Grant County C/C & Eco. Dev.* • Jamie S. Baker; Dir.; P.O. Box 365; 41097; Grant; P 25,000; M 225; (859) 824-3322; (800) 824-2858; Fax (859) 824-7082; jbaker@grantcommerce.com; www.grantcommerce.com*

Winchester • *Winchester-Clark County C/C* • Cindy Banks; Exec. Dir.; 2 S. Maple St.; 40391; Clark; P 36,000; M 365; (859) 744-6420; (859) 744-9616; Fax (859) 744-9229; cindybanks@winchesterkychamber.com; www.winchesterkychamber.com*

Louisiana

Louisiana Assn. of Bus. & Ind. • Stephen Waguespack; Pres.; 3113 Valley Creek Dr.; P.O. Box 80258; Baton Rouge; 70898; East Baton Rouge; P 4,650,000; M 3,000; (225) 928-5388; Fax (225) 929-6054; clairek@labi.org; labi.org

Abbeville • *Greater Abbeville-Vermilion C/C* • Lynn Guillory; Exec. Dir.; 1907 Veterans Memorial Dr.; 70510; Vermilion; P 52,000; M 240; (337) 893-2491; Fax (337) 893-1807; abbevillechamber@abbevillechamber.com; www.abbevillechamber.com

Abita Springs • *see Covington*

Addis • *West Baton Rouge C/C* • Jamie Hanks; Exec. Dir.; 7520 Hwy. 1 S.; P.O. Box 448; 70710; West Baton Rouge; P 25,000; M 360; (225) 383-3140; Fax (225) 685-1044; jamie@wbrchamber.org; www.wbrchamber.org*

Alexandria • *Central Louisiana C/C* • Deborah Randolph; Pres.; 1118 Third St.; P.O. Box 992; 71309; Rapides; P 400,000; M 850; (318) 442-6671; Fax (318) 442-6734; info@cenlachamber.org; www.cenlachamber.org*

Amite • *Amite C/C* • Alissa Cannon; Pres.; 101 S.E. Central Ave.; 70422; Tangipahoa; P 5,000; M 115; (985) 748-5537; Fax (985) 748-5537; amitecoc@att.net; www.townofamitecity.com

Arcadia • *Bienville Parish C/C* • Virginia Becker; Ofc. Mgr.; 2440 Hazel St.; P.O. Box 587; 71001; Bienville; P 14,000; M 174; (318) 263-9897; Fax (318) 263-9897; arcadiachamber@bellsouth.net

Arnaudville • *Arnaudville Area C/C* • Lorna Wells; Pres.; 292 Front St.; P.O. Box 125; 70512; Saint Landry; P 1,100; M 125; (337) 754-5316; Fax (337) 754-5316; arnaudvillechamber@aol.com; www.arnaudvillechamber.org

Ascension • *Ascension C/C* • Sherrie Despino; Pres./CEO; 1006 W. Hwy. 30; P.O. Box 1204, Gonzales; 70707; Ascension; P 100,000; M 500; (225) 647-7487; Fax (225) 647-5124; info@ascensionchamber.com; www.ascensionchamber.com*

Baker • *Baker Area C/C* • LaTania Anderson; Exec. Dir.; 3439 Groom Rd.; 70714; East Baton Rouge; P 14,000; M 160; (225) 775-3547; Fax (225) 775-8060; bakercoc@bellsouth.net; www.bakercoc.com

Bastrop • *Bastrop-Morehouse C/C* • Dorothy Ford; Exec. Dir.; 110 N. Franklin St.; P.O. Box 1175; 71221; Morehouse; P 30,000; M 200; (318) 281-3794; Fax (318) 281-3781; director@bastroplacoc.org; www.bastroplacoc.org

Baton Rouge • *Baton Rouge Area C/C* • Adam Knapp; Pres./CEO; 564 Laurel St.; 70801; East Baton Rouge; P 850,000; M 1,500; (225) 381-7125; Fax (225) 336-4306; info@brac.org; www.brac.org

Bogalusa • *Bogalusa C/C* • Marilyn Bateman; Exec. Dir.; 608 Willis Ave.; 70427; Washington Parish; P 14,000; M 200; (985) 735-5731; bogalusachamber@bellsouth.net; bogalusachamber.cc

Bossier City • *Bossier C/C* • Lisa Johnson; Pres.; 710 Benton Rd.; 71111; Bossier; P 113,000; M 900; (318) 746-0252; Fax (318) 746-0357; info@bossierchamber.com; www.bossierchamber.com*

Breaux Bridge • *Breaux Bridge Area C/C* • Tina Begnaud; Exec. Dir.; 314 E. Bridge St.; P.O. Box 88; 70517; Saint Martin; P 8,200; M 230; (337) 332-5406; Fax (337) 332-5424; info@breauxbridgelive.com; www.gov.breauxbridgelive.com

Bunkie • *Bunkie C/C* • Roxann Gautreaux; Dir.; 110 N.W. Main St.; P.O. Box 70; 71322; Avoyelles; P 5,000; M 100; (318) 346-2575; Fax (318) 346-2576; bunkiechamber@bellsouth.net; www.bunkiechamber.net

Central • *City of Central C/C* • Ron Erickson; Pres.; 13013 Hooper Rd.; 70818; East Baton Rouge; P 27,000; M 240; (225) 261-5818; Fax (225) 261-5122; chamber@cityofcentralchamber.com; www.cityofcentralchamber.com*

Claiborne • *see Homer*

Colfax • *Grant Parish C/C* • Bo Vets; Pres.; P.O. Box 32; 71417; Grant; P 20,000; M 100; (318) 627-2211; info@grantcoc.org; www.grantcoc.org

Columbia • *Caldwell Parish C/C* • Beth Hefner; Pres.; P.O. Box 726; 71418; Caldwell; P 10,200; M 85; (318) 649-0726; Fax (318) 649-0509; cpchamber60@yahoo.com; www.caldwellparishchamberofcommerce.com

Coushatta • *Red River C/C* • Martha Gates; Exec. Asst.; 2010 Red Oak Rd.; P.O. Box 333; 71019; Red River; P 9,600; M 126; (318) 932-3289; Fax (318) 932-6919; redriverchamber@bellsouth.net; coushattaredriverchamberofcommerce.com

Covington • *St. Tammany West C/C* • Lacey O. Toledano; Pres./CEO; 610 Hollycrest Blvd.; 70433; Saint Tammany; P 140,000; M 1,080; (985) 892-3216; Fax (985) 893-4244; info@sttammanychamber.org; www.sttammanychamber.org*

Crowley • *Crowley C/C* • Amy S. Thibodeaux; Pres./CEO; 11 N. Parkerson Ave., Ste. B; P.O. Box 2125; 70527; Acadia; P 64,000; M 300; (337) 788-0177; info@crowleychamber.com; www.crowleychamber.com*

Cut Off • *see Larose*

Denham Springs • *Livingston Parish C/C* • April Wehrs; Pres./CEO; 248 Veterans Blvd.; 70726; Livingston; P 120,000; M 520; (225) 665-8155; Fax (225) 665-2411; staff@livingstonparishchamber.org; www.livingstonparishchamber.org*

DeQuincy • *DeQuincy C/C* • Lillian Karr; 218 E. 4th St.; P.O. Box 625; 70633; Calcasieu; P 3,600; M 60; (337) 786-6451; Fax (337) 786-2173; karrlillian@yahoo.com

DeRidder • *Greater Beauregard C/C* • Cynthia Congleton; Exec. V.P./Dir.; 111 N. Washington St.; 70634; Beauregard; P 36,000; M 350; (337) 463-5533; Fax (337) 463-2244; deridder@bellsouth.net; www.beauchamber.org

Donaldsonville • *Donaldsonville Area C/C* • Juanita C. Pearley; Exec. Dir.; 714 Railroad Ave.; 70346; Ascension; P 8,300; M 165; (225) 473-4814; Fax (225) 473-4817; dvillecoc@bellsouth.net; www.donaldsonvillecoc.org

Dutchtown • *see Ascension*

Eunice • *Eunice C/C* • Francine Hughes; Exec. Dir.; 200 S. C.C. Duson St.; P.O. Box 508; 70535; Saint Landry; P 12,000; M 200; (337) 457-2565; Fax (337) 546-0278; director@eunicechamber.net; www.eunicechamber.com

Farmerville • *Union Parish C/C* • Jerry W. Taylor; Pres./CEO; 116 N. Main St.; 71241; Union; P 24,000; M 155; (318) 368-3947; Fax (318) 368-3945; upcoc@att.net; www.unionparishchamber.org

Ferriday • *see Vidalia*

Folsom • *see Covington*

Franklin • *St. Mary C/C* • Donna F. Meyer; Pres.; 600 Main St.; 70538; Saint Mary; P 52,000; M 580; (337) 828-5608; Fax (337) 828-5606; info@stmarychamber.com; www.stmarychamber.com*

Franklinton • *Franklinton C/C* • Linda E. Crain; Exec. Dir.; 211 11th Ave.; 70438; Washington; P 3,745; M 150; (985) 839-5822; Fax (985) 335-1050; franklintonchamber@franklinton.net; www.franklintonlouisiana.org

Geismar • *see Ascension*

Gonzales • *see Ascension*

Grambling • *Greater Grambling C/C* • Barbara McIntyre; Pres.; 323 Main; P.O. Box 703; 71245; Lincoln Parish; P 4,940; M 35; (318) 243-1858; greatergramblingchamber@yahoo.com

Gueydan • *Gueydan C/C* • Beverly Baker; P.O. Box 562; 70542; Vermilion; P 1,400; M 120; (337) 536-6232; (337) 536-9223; www.gueydan.org

Hammond • *Hammond C/C* • Christopher Brannon; Pres./CEO; 400 N.W. Railroad Ave.; P.O. Box 1458; 70404; Tangipahoa; P 25,000; M 600; (985) 345-4457; Fax (985) 345-4749; cbrannon@hammondchamber.org; www.hammondchamber.org*

Homer • *Claiborne C/C* • Paige Reeder; Exec. Dir.; P.O. Box 484; 71040; Claiborne; P 16,000; M 100; (318) 927-3271; Fax (318) 927-3271; execdir_ccoc@bellsouth.net; www.claibornechamber.org

Houma • *Houma-Terrebonne C/C* • Suzanne Nolfo Carlos; Pres./CEO; 6133 Hwy. 311; 70360; Terrebonne; P 115,000; M 730; (985) 876-5600; Fax (985) 876-5611; info@houmachamber.com; www.houmachamber.com*

Jackson • *East Feliciana C/C & Tourism* • Audrey Faciane; Exec. Dir.; 1752 High St.; P.O. Box 667; 70748; East Feliciana; P 22,000; M 120; (225) 634-7155; Fax (225) 634-7154; tourism1@bellsouth.net; www.eastfelicianachamber.org

Jeanerette • *Jeanerette C/C* • Jeremy Stockstill; Pres.; 1503 Main St.; P.O. Box 31; 70544; Iberia; P 9,000; M 75; (337) 335-0721; Fax (337) 276-5911; jeanerettechamber@gmail.com; www.jeanerettechamber.org

Jennings • *Jeff Davis C/C* • Marion Fox; Pres./CEO; 100 Rue de l'Acadie; P.O. Box 1209; 70546; Jefferson Davis; P 32,000; M 430; (337) 824-0933; Fax (337) 824-5536; chamber@jeffdavis.org; www.jeffdavis.org

Jonesboro • *Jackson Parish C/C* • Wilda Smith; Dir.; 102 Fourth St.; 71251; Jackson; P 15,000; M 171; (318) 259-4693; Fax (318) 395-8539; jacksonparishcoc@aol.com; www.jacksonparishchamber.org

Kaplan • *Kaplan Area C/C* • Kathy Boudreaux; Event Planner/Corresp. Agent; 701 N. Cushing Ave.; 70548; Vermilion; P 5,000; M 102; (337) 643-2400; Fax (337) 643-2400; chamberkaplan@yahoo.com; www.kaplanchamber.com

Kinder • *Kinder C/C* • Barbara Savant; Exec. Dir.; P.O. Box 853; 70648; Allen; P 2,800; M 150; (337) 738-5945; Fax (337) 738-5681; kindercc@centurytel.net; www.kinderchamber.org

Lafayette • *One Acadiana* • Jason El Koubi; Pres./CEO; 804 E. St. Mary Blvd.; P.O. Box 51307; 70505; Lafayette; P 152,893; M 1,400; (337) 233-2705; Fax (337) 234-8671; info@lafchamber.org; www.oneacadiana.org*

Lake Charles • *The Chamber Southwest Louisiana* • George Swift; Pres./CEO; 4310 Ryan St., 3rd Flr.; P.O. Box 3110; 70602; Calcasieu; P 287,001; M 1,500; (337) 433-3632; Fax (337) 436-3727; gswift@allianceswla.org; www.allianceswla.org*

LaPlace • *River Region C/C* • Chassity McComack; Exec. Dir.; 390 Belle Terre Blvd.; 70068; St. John the Baptist; P 118,140; M 373; (985) 359-9777; Fax (985) 359-9778; chassity@riverregionchamber.org; www.riverregionchamber.org

Larose • *Lafourche C/C* • Lin Kiger; Pres./CEO; 107 W. 26th St.; P.O. Box 1462; 70373; Lafourche; P 100,000; M 400; (985) 693-6700; Fax (985) 693-6702; admin@lafourchechamber.com; www.lafourchechamber.com*

Leesville • *Vernon Parish C/C* • Anne T. Causey; Exec. Dir.; 1309 N. 5th St.; P.O. Box 1228; 71496; Vernon; P 52,334; M 260; (337) 238-0349; Fax (337) 238-0340; chambervernonparish@hotmail.com; www.chambervernonparish.com

Logansport • *Logansport C/C* • 606 Main St.; P.O. Box 320; 71049; DeSoto; P 1,700; M 35; (318) 697-0076; (318) 697-5359; logansportchamberofcommerce@yahoo.com; www.townoflogansport.com

Madisonville • *Greater Madisonville Area C/C* • Steven Marcus; Pres.; P.O. Box 746; 70447; Saint Tammany; P 4,000; M 100; (985) 845-9824; president@madisonvillechamber.org; www.madisonvillechamber.org

Mandeville • *see Covington*

Mansfield • *DeSoto Parish C/C* • Brenda Hall; Exec. Dir.; 115 N. Washington Ave.; 71052; DeSoto; P 27,100; M 200; (318) 872-1310; Fax (318) 871-1875; chamber75@bellsouth.net; www.desotoparishchamber.net

Mansura • *Mansura C/C* • Al Lemoine; Pres.; P.O. Box 536; 71350; Avoyelles; P 2,000; M 150; (318) 964-2771

Many • *Sabine Parish C/C* • Garland Anthony; Exec. Dir.; 1125 W. Mississippi Ave., Ste. F; 71449; Sabine; P 24,000; M 300; (318) 256-3523; Fax (318) 256-4137; spchamber@cp-tel.net; www.sabineparishchamber.com

Marksville • *Marksville C/C* • Allison Augustine; Pres.; 113 N. Main St.; P.O. Box 767; 71351; Avoyelles; P 5,500; M 300; (318) 253-8599; Fax (318) 625-0616; marksvillechamber@gmail.com; www.marksvillechamberofcommerce.com

Metairie • *Jefferson C/C* • Todd P. Murphy; Pres./CEO; 3421 N. Causeway Blvd., Ste. 203; 70002; Jefferson; P 433,000; M 1,000; (504) 835-3880; Fax (504) 835-3828; todd@jeffersonchamber.org; www.jeffersonchamber.org*

Minden • *Minden-South Webster C/C* • Stephanie Barnette; Pres./CEO; 110 Sibley Rd.; 71055; Webster; P 14,000; M 300; (318) 377-4240; Fax (318) 377-4215; president@mindenchamber.com; www.mindenchamber.com

Monroe • *Monroe C/C* • Susan Nicholson; Pres./CEO; 212 Walnut St., Ste. 100; 71201; Ouachita; P 250,000; M 800; (318) 323-3461; (888) 531-9535; Fax (318) 322-7594; snicholson@monroe.org; www.monroe.org*

Morgan City • *St. Mary C/C* • Donna F. Meyer; Pres.; 727 Myrtle St.; P.O. Box 2606; 70381; St. Mary Parish; P 54,650; M 560; (985) 384-3830; Fax (985) 384-0771; admin@stmarychamber.com; www.stmarychamber.com*

Napoleonville • *Assumption Area C/C* • Becky Thibodaux; Exec. Dir.; 5010 Hwy. 1; P.O. Box 718; 70390; Assumption; P 24,000; M 180; (985) 369-2816; Fax (985) 369-4461; assumption@bellsouth.net; www.assumptionchamber.org

Natchitoches • *Natchitoches Area C/C* • Tony Davis; Pres./CEO; 560 Second St.; P.O. Box 3; 71457; Natchitoches; P 39,777; M 410; (318) 352-6894; Fax (318) 352-5385; chamber@natchitoches.net; www.natchitocheschamber.com*

New Iberia • *Greater Iberia C/C* • Janet Faulk; Pres./CEO; 111 W. Main St.; 70560; Iberia; P 75,000; M 400; (337) 364-1836; Fax (337) 367-7405; info@iberiachamber.org; www.iberiachamber.org

New Orleans • *New Orleans C/C* • G. Ben Johnson; Pres./CEO; 1515 Poydras St., Ste. 1010; 70112; Orleans; P 380,000; M 1,200; (504) 799-4260; Fax (504) 799-4259; info@neworleanschamber.org; www.neworleanschamber.org*

New Roads • *Greater Pointe Coupee C/C* • Alecisa Matte; Pres.; 2506 False River Dr.; P.O. Box 555; 70760; Pointe Coupee; P 22,000; M 150; (225) 638-3500; Fax (225) 638-9858; pointecoupeechamber@yahoo.com; www.pcchamber.org

Oak Grove • *West Carroll C/C* • Ruth Horton; Pres.; P.O. Box 1336; 71263; West Carroll; P 2,000; M 63; (318) 428-8283; westcarrollchamber@gmail.com; www.westcarrollchamber.com

Oakdale • *Oakdale Area C/C* • Brenda Fontenot; Ofc. Mgr.; 107 S. 12th St.; P.O. Box 1138; 71463; Allen; P 8,200; M 109; (318) 335-1729; oakdaleareachamb@bellsouth.net

Opelousas • *Opelousas-Saint Landry C/C* • Ms. Frankie Bertrand; Pres./CEO; 109 W. Vine St.; 70570; St. Landry; P 120,000; M 490; (337) 942-2683; Fax (337) 942-2684; opelousaschamber@opelousaschamber.com; www.opelousaschamber.org

Plaquemine • *Iberville C/C* • Hank Grace; Exec. Dir.; 23520 Eden St.; P.O. Box 248; 70765; Iberville; P 33,400; M 275; (225) 687-3560; Fax (225) 687-3575; hgrace@ibervillechamber.com; www.ibervillechamber.com

Ponchatoula • *Ponchatoula C/C* • Liz Anderson; Ofc. Assoc.; 105 W. Pine St.; P.O. Box 306; 70454; Tangipahoa Parish; P 7,000; M 275; (985) 386-2536; (985) 386-2533; Fax (985) 386-2537; chamber@ponchatoulachamber.com; www.ponchatoulachamber.com

Prairieville • *see Ascension*

Raceland • *see Larose*

Rayne • *Rayne C/C & Ag.* • Fran Bihm; Exec. Dir.; 107 Oak St.; 70578; Acadia; P 8,578; M 125; (337) 334-2332; Fax (337) 334-8341; raynechamber1@bellsouth.net; www.raynechamber.com

Ruston • *Ruston-Lincoln C/C* • Judy Copeland; Pres./CEO; 2111 N. Trenton St.; 71270; Lincoln Parish; P 43,000; M 550; (318) 255-2031; (318) 232-7981; Fax (318) 255-3481; jcopeland@rustonlincoln.org; www.rustonlincoln.org*

Sabine Parish • *see Many*

Saint Amant • *see Ascension*

Saint Francisville • *Greater St. Francisville C/C* • Linda Osterberger; Dir.; 11936 Ferdinand St.; P.O. Box 545; 70775; West Feliciana; P 15,111; M 200; (225) 635-6717; Fax (225) 635-6717; sfchamber@bellsouth.net; www.stfrancisvillechamber.com

Saint Landry • *see Opelousas*

Saint Martinville • *Saint Martinville C/C* • Nicole Allen; Exec. Dir.; P.O. Box 436; 70582; Saint Martin; P 7,800; M 90; (337) 394-7578; Fax (337) 394-4497; ctpnicolea@aol.com; www.stmartinvillechamber.com

Shreveport • *Greater Shreveport C/C* • Richard H. Bremer; Pres.; 400 Edwards St.; 71101; Caddo; P 400,000; M 1,920; (318) 677-2500; (800) 448-5432; Fax (318) 677-2541; info@shreveportchamber.org; www.shreveportchamber.org

Slidell • *East St. Tammany C/C* • Dawn Sharpe; CEO; 1808 Front St.; 70458; Saint Tammany; P 100,000; M 1,100; (985) 643-5678; (800) 471-3758; Fax (985) 649-2460; info@estchamber.com; www.estchamber.com*

Sorrento • *see Ascension*

South Webster Parish • *see Minden*

Springhill • *Springhill North Webster C/C* • Ronda Taylor; Mgr.; 400 N. Giles St.; 71075; Webster; P 12,000; M 200; (318) 539-4717; Fax (318) 539-2500; manager@nwebsterchamber.com; www.springhilllouisiana.net

Sulphur • *West Calcasieu Assn. of Commerce* • Lena McArthur; Exec. Dir.; 500 N. Huntington St.; 70663; Calcasieu; P 30,239; M 350; (337) 313-1121; Fax (337) 527-4910; associationw@bellsouth.net; www.westcal.org

Tallulah • *Madison Parish C/C* • Terry Murphy; Pres.; P.O. Box 311; 71284; Madison; P 12,000; M 50; (318) 574-4820; Fax (318) 574-9147; pmurphy@ladelta.edu; www.tallulah-la.gov

Thibodaux • *Thibodaux C/C* • Kathy B. Benoit IOM; Pres./CEO; 318 E. Bayou Rd.; P.O. Box 467; 70302; Lafourche; P 15,000; M 600; (985) 446-1187; Fax (985) 446-1191; kathy@thibodauxchamber.com; www.thibodauxchamber.com*

Vernon • *see Leesville*

Vidalia • *Concordia C/C* • Jamie K. Wiley; Exec. Dir.; 1401 Carter St.; 71373; Concordia; P 5,000; M 225; (318) 336-8223; jamieburley@att.net; www.concordiapchamber.com*

Ville Platte • *Ville Platte C/C* • Camille L. Fontenot; Exec. Dir.; 306 W. Main St.; P.O. Box 331; 70586; Evangeline; P 9,000; M 160; (337) 363-1878; Fax (337) 363-1894; villep001@centurytel.net; www.vpla.com

Vinton • *see Sulphur*

Vivian • *Vivian C/C* • Betty Matthews; Pres.; 100 Front St.; P.O. Box 182; 71082; Caddo; P 4,031; M 40; (318) 375-5300; Fax (318) 375-5300; chamberofcom@centurytel.net; www.vivian.la.us

West Baton Rouge • *see Addis*

West Monroe • *West Monroe-West Ouachita C/C* • Courtney Hornsby; Pres.; 112 Professional Dr.; 71291; Ouachita; P 15,000; M 500; (318) 325-1961; Fax (318) 325-4296; info@westmonroechamber.org; westmonroechamber.org

Westlake • *see Sulphur*

Winnfield • *Winn C/C* • June Melton; Secy.; 499 E. Main St.; P.O. Box 565; 71483; Winn; P 17,714; M 150; (318) 628-4461; Fax (318) 628-2551; winnchamber@bellsouth.net; www.winnchamberofcommerce.com

Winnsboro • *Winnsboro-Franklin Parish C/C* • Zach Johnson; Pres.; 513 Prairie St.; P.O. Box 1574; 71295; Franklin; P 24,000; M 160; (318) 435-4488; Fax (318) 435-5398; winnsborochamber@bellsouth.net; www.winnsborochamber.com

Zachary • *Zachary C/C* • Greg McDougall; Exec. Dir.; 4633 Main St.; 70791; East Baton Rouge; P 16,000; M 275; (225) 654-6777; Fax (225) 654-3957; cefferson@zacharychamber.com; www.zacharychamber.com

Maine

Maine State C of C • Dana F. Connors; Pres.; 125 Community Dr., Ste. 101; Augusta; 04330; Kennebec; P 1,329,192; M 1,200; (207) 623-4568; Fax (207) 622-7723; melanieb@mainechamber.org; www.mainechamber.org

Appleton • *see Union*

Ashland • *see Presque Isle*

Auburn • *see Lewiston*

Augusta • *Kennebec Valley C/C* • Ross H. Cunningham; Pres./CEO; 269 Western Ave.; 04330; Kennebec; P 70,000; M 750; (207) 623-4559; Fax (207) 626-9342; drc@kennebecvalleychamber.com; www.kennebecvalleychamber.com

Bangor • *Bangor Region C/C* • Deb Neuman; Pres./CEO; 20 South St.; 04401; Penobscot; P 154,000; M 800; (207) 947-0307; Fax (207) 990-1427; admin@bangorregion.com; www.bangorregion.com

Bar Harbor • *Bar Harbor C/C* • Mr. Chris Fogg; Exec. Dir.; P.O. Box 158; 04609; Hancock; P 4,500; M 450; (207) 664-2940; (800) 288-5103; Fax (207) 667-9080; visitors@barharborinfo.com; www.barharborinfo.com

Bath • *see Brunswick*

Belfast • *Belfast Area C/C* • Michaelene Achorn; Exec. Dir.; 14 Main St.; P.O. Box 58; 04915; Waldo; P 6,700; M 400; (207) 338-5900; Fax (207) 338-5823; belfastchamber@gmail.com; www.belfastmaine.org

Benedicta • *see Houlton*

Bethel • *Bethel Area C/C* • Robin Zinchuk; Exec. Dir.; 8 Station Pl.; P.O. Box 1247; 04217; Oxford; P 6,000; M 235; (207) 824-2282; (800) 442-5826; Fax (207) 824-7123; info@bethelmaine.com; www.bethelmaine.com

Biddeford • *see Saco*

Bingham • *Upper Kennebec Valley C/C* • Barbara Lord; Secy.; 356 Main St.; P.O. Box 491; 04920; Somerset; P 5,000; M 85; (207) 672-4100; info@upperkennebecvalleychamber.com; upperkennebecvalleychamber.com

Blaine • *see Presque Isle*

Blue Hill • *Blue Hill Peninsula C/C* • Lori Sitzabee; Exec. Dir.; 16B South St.; P.O. Box 520; 04614; Hancock; P 3,245; M 267; (207) 374-3242; chamber@bluehillpeninsula.org; www.bluehillpeninsula.org

Boothbay • *Boothbay Region Info. Center & C/C* • David Dudley; Pres.; 323 Adams Pond Rd.; P.O. Box 187; 04537; Lincoln; P 5,000; M 190; (207) 633-4743; (207) 633-3933; info@boothbay.org; www.boothbay.org

Boothbay Harbor • *Boothbay Harbor Region C/C* • Tony Cameron; Exec. Dir.; 192 Townsend Ave.; P.O. Box 356; 04538; Lincoln; P 34,000; M 385; (207) 633-2353; Fax (207) 633-7448; seamaine@boothbayharbor.com; www.boothbayharbor.com*

Bowdoinham • *see Brunswick*

Bridgton • *Greater Bridgton Lakes Region C/C* • Susan Mercer; Exec. Dir.; 101 Portland Rd.; P.O. Box 236; 04009; Cumberland & Oxford; P 35,000; M 290; (207) 647-3472; Fax (207) 647-8372; info@mainelakeschamber.com; www.mainelakeschamber.com

Brighton • *see Bingham*

Brooklin • *see Blue Hill*

Brooksville • *see Blue Hill*

Brunswick • *Southern Midcoast Maine C/C* • Carolyn Farkas-Noe; Interim Exec. Dir.; 8 Venture Ave., Brunswick Landing; P.O. Box 33; 04011; Cumberland; P 70,222; M 720; (207) 725-8797;; Fax ; info@midcoastmaine.com; www.midcoastmaine.com*

Bucksport • *Bucksport Bay Area C/C* • Leslie M. Wombacher; Exec. Dir.; 52 Main St.; P.O. Box 1676; 04416; Hancock; P 5,000; M 200; (207) 469-6818; visit@bucksportbaychamber.com; www.bucksportbaychamber.com

Burlington • *see Lincoln*

Calais • *St. Croix Valley C/C* • Amy Jeanroy; Exec. Dir.; 39 Union St.; 04619; Washington; P 4,000; M 100; (207) 454-2308; (888) 422-3112; Fax (207) 454-2308; visitstcroixvalley@gmail.com; www.visitstcroixvalley.com

Camden • *Penobscot Bay Reg. C/C* • Dan Bookham; Exec. Dir.; 2 Public Landing; P.O. Box 919; 04843; Knox; P 20,000; M 1,010; (207) 236-4404; (800) 223-5459; Fax (207) 236-4315; info@penbaychamber.com; www.penbaychamber.com

Caratunk • *see Bingham*

Caribou • *Caribou Area C/C* • Jenny Coon; Exec. Dir.; 657 Main St., Ste. 1; 04736; Aroostook; P 8,800; M 244; (207) 498-6156; info@cariboumaine.net; www.cariboumaine.net

Carroll • *see Lincoln*

Casco • *see Windham*

Castine • *see Blue Hill*

Castle Hill • *see Presque Isle*

Chapman • *see Presque Isle*

Chester • *see Lincoln*

Corinna • *see Newport*

Crystal/Golden Ridge • *see Houlton*

Danforth • *Greater East Grand Lake C/C* • Heather Zakupowsky; Chrmn.; P.O. Box 159; 04424; Washington; P 600; M 50; info@eastgrandlake.net; www.eastgrandlake.net

Deer Isle • *Deer Isle-Stonington C/C* • Henry Borntraeger; Pres.; P.O. Box 490; 04627; Hancock; P 3,000; M 175; (207) 348-6124; deerisle@deerisle.com; www.deerislemaine.com

Detroit • *see Newport*

Dexter • *see Newport*

Dover-Foxcroft • *Piscataquis C/C* • Denise M. Buzzelli; Exec. Dir.; 1033 South St.; 04426; Piscataquis; P 17,419; M 210; (207) 564-7533; exdir@piscataquischamber.com; www.piscataquischamber.com

Durham • *see Lewiston*

Dyer Brook • *see Houlton*

East Boothbay • *see Boothbay Harbor*

East Millinocket • *see Millinocket*

East Wilson • *see Farmington*

Easton • *see Presque Isle*

Eastport • *Eastport Area C/C* • Meg Keay; Exec. Dir.; 141 Water St., Ste. 3; P.O. Box 254; 04631; Washington; P 1,300; M 140; (207) 853-4644; Fax (207) 853-4644; info@eastportchamber.net; www.eastportchamber.net

Edgecomb • *see Boothbay Harbor*

Eliot • *see York*

Ellsworth • *Ellsworth Area C/C* • Susan Farley; Exec. Dir.; 163 High St.; 04605; Hancock; P 7,700; M 630; (207) 667-5584; Fax (207) 667-2617; info@ellsworthchamber.org; www.ellsworthchamber.org

Enfield • *see Lincoln*

Etna • *see Newport*

Exeter • *see Newport*

Farmington • *Franklin County C/C* • Penny Meservier; Exec. Dir.; 615 Wilton Rd.; P.O. Box 123; 04938; Franklin; P 31,000; M 200; (207) 778-4215; Fax (207) 778-2438; director@franklincountymaine.org; www.franklincountymaine.org

Farmington Falls • *see Farmington*

Fort Fairfield • *Fort Fairfield C/C* • Tim Goff; Exec. Dir.; 18 Community Center Dr.; 04742; Aroostook; P 3,500; M 85; (207) 472-3802; Fax (207) 472-3810; tgoff@fortfairfield.org; www.fortfairfield.org

Fort Kent • *Greater Fort Kent Area C/C* • Dona Saucier; Exec. Dir.; 291 W. Main St.; P.O. Box 430; 04743; Aroostook; P 5,000; M 170; (207) 834-5354; seefkme@fairpoint.net; www.fortkentchamber.com

Franklin • *see Winter Harbor*

Freeport • *Freeport USA* • Myra Hopkins; Exec. Dir.; 23 Depot St.; P.O. Box 452; 04032; Cumberland; P 8,200; M 170; (207) 865-1212; (800) 865-1994; Fax (207) 865-0881; info@freeportusa.com; www.freeportusa.com*

Gouldsboro • *see Winter Harbor*

Gray • *see Windham*

Greene • *see Lewiston*

Greenville • *Moosehead Lake C/C* • Angela S. Arno; Exec. Dir.; 480 Moosehead Lake Rd.; P.O. Box 581; 04441; Piscataquis; P 1,778; M 135; (207) 695-2702; (888) 876-2778; info@mooseheadlake.org; www.mooseheadlake.org

Hallowell • *Hallowell Area Bd. of Trade* • P.O. Box 246; 04347; Kennebec; P 2,532; M 90; (207) 620-7477; info@hallowell.org; www.hallowell.org

Harpswell • *see Brunswick*

Harrison • *see South Paris*

Hartland • *see Newport*

Hebron • *see South Paris*

Hersey • *see Houlton*

Hope • *see Union*

Houlton • *Greater Houlton C/C* • Jane Reed Torres; Exec. Dir.; 109 Main St.; 04730; Aroostook; P 8,000; M 236; (207) 532-4216; Fax (207) 532-4961; director@greaterhoulton.com; www.greaterhoulton.com

Howland • *see Lincoln*

Industry • *see Farmington*

Island Falls • *see Houlton*

Jackman • *Jackman Moose River Region C/C* • P.O. Box 368; 04945; Somerset; P 800; M 60; (207) 668-4171; (888) 633-5225; mooserus@jackmanmaine.org; www.jackmanmaine.org

Kennebunk • *Kennebunk-Kennebunkport-Arundel C/C* • Laura Dolce; Exec. Dir.; 16 Water St.; P.O. Box 740; 04043; York; P 18,500; M 450; (207) 967-0857; Fax (207) 967-2867; director@gokennebunks.com; www.gokennebunks.com*

Kittery • *see York*

Lakeville • *see Lincoln*

Lee • *see Lincoln*

Leeds • *see Lewiston*

Lewiston • *Lewiston Auburn Metropolitan C/C* • Matt J. Leonard; Pres./CEO; 415 Lisbon St.; 04240; Androscoggin; P 110,000; M 1,375; (207) 783-2249; Fax (207) 783-4481; rachel@lametrochamber.com; lametrochamber.com*

Limestone • *Limestone C/C* • Michelle Albert; Pres.; 93 Main St.; 04750; Aroostook; P 2,500; M 45; (207) 325-4704; Fax (207) 325-3330; chamber@limestonemaine.org; www.limestonemaine.org

Lincoln • *Lincoln Lakes Region C/C* • Traci Gauthier; Exec. Dir.; 256 W. Broadway; P.O. Box 164; 04457; Penobscot; P 5,800; M 115; (207) 794-8065; Fax (207) 794-8065; llrcc@myfairpoint.net; www.lincolnmechamber.org

Lincolnville • *see Camden*

Lisbon • *see Lewiston*

Livermore • *see Lewiston*

Livermore Falls • *see Lewiston*

Machias • *Machias Bay Area C/C* • Kathy Howell; Exec. Dir.; 85 Main St., Ste. 2; P.O. Box 606; 04654; Washington; P 2,800; M 211; (207) 255-4402; Fax (207) 255-4402; info@machiaschamber.org; www.machiaschamber.org

Madawaska • *Greater Madawaska C/C* • Roger Thibodeau; Exec. Dir.; 356 Main St.; P.O. Box 144; 04756; Aroostook; P 4,000; M 115; (207) 728-7000; Fax (207) 728-4696; chamber@townofmadawaska.net; www.greatermadawaskachamber.com

Magalloway • *see Errol, NH*

Mapleton • *see Presque Isle*

Mars Hill • *see Presque Isle*

Masardis • *see Presque Isle*

Mattamiscontis • *see Lincoln*

Mattawamkeag • *see Lincoln*

Mayfield • *see Bingham*

Mechanic Falls • *see Lewiston*

Medway • *see Millinocket*

Merrill • *see Houlton*

Millinocket • *Katahdin Area C/C* • Jean Boddy; Ofc. Coord.; 1029 Central St.; 04462; Penobscot; P 5,000; M 130; (207) 723-4443; info@katahdinmaine.com; www.katahdinmaine.com

Minot • *see Lewiston*

Monada/Silver Ridge • *see Houlton*

Moro Plantation • *see Houlton*

Moscow • *see Bingham*

Mount Chase/Shin Pond • *see Houlton*

Naples • *see Windham*

New Sharon • *see Farmington*

New Vineyard • *see Farmington*

Newcastle • *Damariscotta Region C/C* • Toni L. Crouch; Exec. Dir.; 67A Main Street; (P.O. Box 13, Damariscotta, ME 04543); 04553; Lincoln; P 2,061; M 279; (207) 563-8340; info@damariscottaregion.com; www.damariscottaregion.com

Newport • *Sebasticook Valley C/C* • Nicole Robison; Exec. Dir.; P.O. Box 464; 04953; Somerset; P 20,000; M 250; (207) 368-4698; Fax (207) 368-5312; info@ourchamber.org; www.ourchamber.org*

Norridgewock • *Norridgewock Area C/C* • Denise Delorie; Pres.; P.O. Box 184; 04957; Somerset; P 3,400; M 103; (207) 692-7384; denise@delorie.com; www.norridgewockareachamber.com

Northeast Harbor • *Mount Desert C/C* • Khristina Landers; Exec. Dir.; 18 Harbor Dr.; P.O. Box 675; 04662; Hancock; P 2,000; M 125; (207) 276-5040; info@mountdesertchamber.org; www.mountdesertchamber.org

Norway • *see South Paris*

Oakfield • *see Houlton*

Ogunquit • *Ogunquit C/C* • Karen Marie Arel; Pres.; 36 Main St.; P.O. Box 2289; 03907; York; P 1,300; M 425; (207) 646-2939; Fax (207) 641-0856; director@ogunquit.org; www.ogunquit.org*

Old Orchard Beach • *Old Orchard Beach C/C* • James Harmon; Pres./CEO; 11 First St.; 04064; York; P 9,000; M 250; (207) 934-2500; Fax (207) 934-4994; info@oldorchardbeachmaine.com; www.oldorchardbeachmaine.com

Orland • *see Bucksport*

Otisfield • *see South Paris*

Oxbow • *see Presque Isle*

Oxford • *see South Paris*

Palmyra • *see Newport*

Paris • *see South Paris*

Passadumkeag • *see Lincoln*

Patten • *see Houlton*

Penobscot • *see Blue Hill*

Pittsfield • *see Newport*

Plymouth • *see Newport*

Poland • *see Lewiston*

Portage • *see Presque Isle*

Portland • *Portland Reg. C/C* • Christopher Hall; CEO; 443 Congress St.; 04101; Cumberland; P 250,000; M 1,350; (207) 772-2811; Fax (207) 772-1179; chamber@portlandregion.com; www.portlandregion.com

Prentis • *see Lincoln*

Presque Isle • *Central Aroostook C/C* • Theresa Fowler; Exec. Dir.; 3 Houlton Rd.; 04769; Aroostook; P 20,283; M 325; (207) 764-6561; Fax (207) 764-1583; info@centralaroostookchamber.com; www.centralaroostookchamber.com

Rangeley • *Rangeley Lakes Region C/C* • Gail Spaulding; Ofc. Mgr.; 6 Park Rd.; P.O. Box 317; 04970; Franklin; P 1,600; M 200; (207) 864-5571; (800) 685-2537; Fax (207) 864-5366; info@rangeleymaine.com; www.rangeleymaine.com

Raymond • *see Windham*

Rockland • *Penobscot Bay Reg. C/C* • Dan Bookham; Exec. Dir.; P.O. Box 508; 04841; Knox; P 20,000; M 1,010; (207) 596-0376; (800) 562-2529; Fax (207) 596-6549; info@penbaychamber.com; www.penbaychamber.com

Rockport • *see Camden*

Rumford • *River Valley C/C* • Cheryl A. G. Dickson; Admin.; 10 Bridge St.; 04276; Oxford; P 17,000; M 200; (207) 364-3241; info@rivervalleychamber.com; www.rivervalleychamber.com

Sabattus • *see Lewiston*

Saco • *Biddeford-Saco C/C & Ind.* • Craig Pendleton; Dir.; 138 Main St., Ste. 101; 04072; York; P 45,000; M 500; (207) 282-1567; Fax (207) 282-3149; info@biddefordsacochamber.org; www.biddefordsacochamber.org*

Saint Albans • *see Newport*

Saint Francis • *Saint Francis C/C* • Gerald Jandreau; Pres.; Main St.; P.O. Box 13; 04774; Aroostook; P 550; M 12; (207) 398-3102; jouelet@roadrunner.com

Saint John • *see Saint Francis*

Sanford • *Sanford/Springvale C/C* • Richard Stanley; Pres.; 917 Main St., Ste. B; 04073; York; P 22,000; M 350; (207) 324-4280; Fax (207) 324-8290; ricks@metrocast.net; www.sanfordchamber.org*

Sebago Lake • *see Windham*

Seboeis • *see Lincoln*

Sedgwick • *see Blue Hill*

Sherman Mills • *see Houlton*

Skowhegan • *Skowhegan Area C/C* • Mr. Jason S. Gayne; Exec. Dir.; 23 Commercial St.; 04976; Somerset; P 10,000; M 225; (207) 474-3621; Fax (207) 474-3306; exdir@skowheganchamber.com; www.skowheganareachamber.com*

Smyrna Mills • *see Houlton*

Solon • *see Bingham*

Sorrento • *see Winter Harbor*

South Berwick • *see York*

South Paris • *Oxford Hills C/C* • John Williams; Exec. Dir.; 4 Western Ave.; 04281; Oxford; P 22,000; M 390; (207) 743-2281; Fax (207) 743-0687; info@oxfordhillsmaine.com; www.oxfordhillsmaine.com*

Southport • *see Boothbay Harbor*

Southwest Harbor • *Southwest Harbor & Tremont C/C •* Cynthia Crow; Gen. Mgr,; 329 Main St.; P.O. Box 1143; 04679; Hancock; P 1,800; M 145; (207) 244-9264; office@acadiachamber.com; www.acadiachamber.com

Springvale • *see Sanford*

Stacyville • *see Houlton*

Standish • *see Windham*

Stetson • *see Newport*

Stonington • *see Deer Isle*

Sullivan • *see Winter Harbor*

Thomaston • *see Rockland*

Topsfield • *see Lincoln*

Trenton • *see Ellsworth*

Turner • *see Lewiston*

Union • *Union Area C/C •* Erica Morton; Pres.; P.O. Box 603; 04862; Knox; P 12,000; M 90; (207) 785-3300; uacoc@tidewater.net; www.unionareachamber.org

Upton • *see Errol, NH*

Van Buren • *Greater Van Buren C/C •* Tony Martin; Exec. Dir.; 51 Main St., Ste. 101; 04785; Aroostook; P 2,200; M 52; (207) 868-5059; vbchamber@gmail.com; www.vanburenmaine.com

Verona • *see Bucksport*

Wales • *see Lewiston*

Warren • *see Rockland*

Washburn • *see Presque Isle*

Washington • *see Union*

Waterford • *see South Paris*

Waterville • *Mid-Maine C/C •* Kimberly N. Lindlof; Pres./CEO; 50 Elm St.; 04901; Kennebec; P 50,000; M 715; (207) 873-3315; Fax (207) 877-0087; info@midmainechamber.com; www.midmainechamber.com*

Webster Plantation • *see Lincoln*

Weeks Mills • *China Area C/C •* Marlene Reed; 128 Weeks Mills Rd.; 04358; Kennebec; P 4,100; (207) 445-3183

Wellington • *see Bingham*

Wells • *Wells C/C •* Eleanor Vadenais; Exec. Dir.; 136 Post Rd.; P.O. Box 356; 04090; York; P 10,000; M 330; (207) 646-2451; Fax (207) 646-8104; wellschamber@wellschamber.org; www.wellschamber.org

West Enfield • *see Lincoln*

West Forks • *The Forks Area C/C •* Pam Christopher; Exec. Dir.; P.O. Box 1; 04985; Somerset; P 2,150; M 40; (207) 663-2121; Fax (207) 663-2122; info@forksarea.com; www.forksarea.com

West Paris • *see South Paris*

Westfield • *see Presque Isle*

Whiting • *Cobscook Bay Area C/C •* P.O. Box 42; 04691; Washington; P 7,000; M 80; (207) 733-2201; info@cobscookbay.com; www.cobscookbay.com

Wilsons Mills • *see Errol, NH*

Wilton • *see Farmington*

Windham • *Sebago Lakes Region C/C •* Aimee Senatore; Exec. Dir.; 747 Roosevelt Trl.-Rte. 302; P.O. Box 1015; 04062; Cumberland; P 55,000; M 370; (207) 892-8265; Fax (207) 893-0110; info@sebagolakeschamber.com; www.sebagolakeschamber.com*

Winn • *see Lincoln*

Winter Harbor • *Schoodic Area C/C •* Linda Elliott; P.O. Box 381; 04693; Hancock; P 3,000; M 60; (207) 546-2960; lelliott@mainesavings.com; www.acadia-schoodic.org*

Winthrop • *Winthrop Area C/C •* Sarah Fuller; Pres.; P.O. Box 51; 04364; Kennebec; P 6,300; M 100; (207) 377-8020; Fax (207) 377-2767; info@winthropchamber.org; www.winthropchamber.org

Yarmouth • *Yarmouth C/C •* Carolyn Schuster; Mgr. Dir.; 162 Main St.; 04096; Cumberland; P 8,600; M 210; (207) 846-3984; Fax (207) 846-5419; info@yarmouthmaine.org; www.yarmouthmaine.org

York • *York Region C/C •* Holly Roberts; Exec. Dir.; 1 Stonewall Ln.; 03909; York; P 37,000; M 650; (207) 363-4422; Fax (207) 363-7320; info@yorkme.org; www.gatewaytomaine.org

Maryland

Maryland C of C • Christine Ross; Pres./CEO; 60 West St., Ste. 100; Annapolis; 21401; Anne Arundel; P 5,884,563; M 850; (410) 269-0642; (301) 261-2858; Fax (410) 269-5247; mcc@mdchamber.org; www.mdchamber.org*

Aberdeen • *Aberdeen C/C •* Jeanette K. Lucas; Dir.; 117 S. Philadelphia Blvd. Rte. 40; 21001; Harford; P 15,000; M 250; (410) 272-2580; Fax (410) 272-9357; jlucas@aberdeencc.org; www.aberdeencc.org

Annapolis • *Annapolis & Anne Arundel County C/C •* Robert Burdon; Pres./CEO; 134 Holiday Ct., Ste. 316; P.O. Box 346; 21401; Anne Arundel; P 537,700; M 900; (410) 266-3960; Fax (410) 266-8270; info@aaaccc.org; www.annearundelchamber.org*

Annapolis Junction • *see Laurel*

Anne Arundel County • *see Annapolis and Laurel*

Baltimore Area

Baltimore City C/C • Charles Owens; Pres.; P.O. Box 4483; 21223; Baltimore; P 640,000; M 400; (410) 837-7101; Fax (410) 837-7104; charlieo@baltimorecitychamber.org; www.baltimorecitychamber.org*

Chesapeake Gateway C/C • Sharon Kihn; Exec. Dir.; 405 Williams Ct., Ste. 108; 21220; Baltimore; P 74,000; M 150; (443) 317-8763; Fax (443) 317-8772; info@chesapeakechamber.org; www.chesapeakechamber.org*

Maryland Hispanic C/C • Natalie Villabon-Martz; Exec. Dir.; 3601 E. Joppa Rd.; 21234; Montgomery; P 5,700,000; (410) 933-3457; Fax (410) 931-8111; customerservice@mdhcc.org; www.mdhcc.org*

U.S. Chambers of Commerce

Bel Air • *Harford County C/C •* Pam Klahr; Pres./CEO; 108 S. Bond St.; 21014; Harford; P 248,322; M 720; (410) 838-2020; Fax (410) 893-4715; ceo@harfordchamber.org; www.harfordchamber.org*

Beltsville • *see Laurel*

Berlin • *Ocean Pines Area C/C •* Ginger Fleming; Exec. Dir.; 11031 Cathell Rd.; 21811; Worcester; P 20,000; M 300; (410) 641-5306; Fax (410) 641-6176; info@oceanpineschamber.org; www.oceanpineschamber.org*

Berlin • *Berlin C/C •* Olive Mawyer; Exec. Dir.; P.O. Box 212; 21811; Worcester; P 3,500; M 200; (410) 641-4775; Fax (410) 641-3118; chamberinfo@berlinchamber.org; www.berlinchamber.org

Berwyn Heights • *see Lanham*

Bethesda • *Greater Bethesda-Chevy Chase C/C •* Ginanne M. Italiano; Pres.; 7910 Woodmont Ave., Ste. 1204; 20814; Montgomery; P 1,000,000; M 750; (301) 652-4900; Fax (301) 657-1973; staff@bccchamber.org; www.bccchamber.org*

Bladensburg • *see Lanham*

Bowie • *also see Lanham*

Bowie • *Greater Bowie C/C •* David Emanuel; Exec. Dir.; 2614 Kenhill Dr., Ste. 117; 20715; Prince George's; P 58,000; M 255; (301) 262-0920; Fax (301) 262-0921; david@bowiechamber.org; www.bowiechamber.org*

Brentwood • *see Lanham*

Burtonsville • *see Laurel*

BWI Airport • *see Laurel*

California • *St. Mary's County C/C •* William E. Scarafia; Pres./CEO; 44200 Airport Rd.; 20619; St. Mary's; P 109,000; M 525; (301) 737-3001; Fax (301) 737-0089; info@smcchamber.com; www.smcchamber.com*

Cambridge • *Dorchester County C/C •* Deborah Divins; Exec. Dir.; 528 Poplar St.; 21613; Dorchester; P 33,000; M 500; (410) 228-3575; Fax (410) 228-6848; info@dorchesterchamber.org; www.dorchesterchamber.org*

Capitol Heights • *see Lanham*

Catonsville • *Greater Catonsville C/C •* Teal Cary; Exec. Dir.; 924 Frederick Rd.; 21228; Baltimore; P 40,000; M 375; (410) 719-9609; Fax (410) 744-6127; chamber@catonsville.org; www.catonsville.org

Chester • *Queen Anne's County C/C •* Linda Friday; Pres.; 1561 Postal Rd.; P.O. Box 511; 21619; Queen Anne's; P 47,800; M 550; (410) 643-8530; Fax (410) 643-8477; business@qacchamber.com; www.qacchamber.com*

Chestertown • *Kent County C/C •* Loretta M. Lodge; Exec. Dir.; 122 N. Cross St.; P.O. Box 146; 21620; Kent; P 20,000; M 300; (410) 810-2968; Fax (410) 778-1406; kentchamber@verizon.net; www.kentchamber.org

Cheverly • *see Lanham*

Chevy Chase • *see Bethesda*

Churchton • *Southern Anne Arundel C/C •* Carla Catterton; Exec. Dir.; 5503 Muddy Creek Rd.; 20733; Southern Anne Arundel; P 30,000; M 260; (410) 867-3129; Fax (410) 867-3556; southcounty@toad.net; www.southcounty.org*

College Park • *see Lanham and Laurel*

Colmar Manor • *see Lanham*

Columbia • *also see Laurel*

Columbia • *Howard County C/C •* Leonardo McClarty; Pres./CEO; 5560 Sterrett Pl., Ste. 105; 21044; Howard; P 287,000; M 700; (410) 730-4111; Fax (410) 730-4584; info@howardchamber.com; www.howardchamber.com*

Cottage City • *see Lanham*

Crisfield • *Crisfield Area C/C •* Valerie Howard; Exec. Dir.; 906 W. Main St.; P.O. Box 292; 21817; Somerset; P 2,800; M 135; (410) 968-2500; (800) 782-3913; Fax (410) 968-0524; info@crisfieldchamber.com; www.crisfieldchamber.com

Crofton • *Greater Crofton C/C •* Thomas Locke; Pres.; P.O. Box 4146; 21114; Anne Arundel; P 27,500; M 185; (410) 721-9131; Fax (410) 721-0785; info@croftonchamber.com; www.croftonchamber.com

Cumberland • *Allegany County C/C •* Stuart Czapski; Exec. Dir.; Bell Tower Bldg.; 24 Frederick St.; 21502; Allegany; P 72,532; M 425; (301) 722-2820; Fax (301) 722-5995; info@alleganycountychamber.com; www.alleganycountychamber.com*

Delmar • *see Delmar, DE*

District Heights • *see Lanham*

Dundalk • *see Towson*

Eagle Harbor • *see Lanham*

East Baltimore • *see Towson*

Easton • *Talbot County C/C •* Alan I. Silverstein IOM; Pres./CEO; 101 Marlboro Ave., Ste. 53; P.O. Box 1366; 21601; Talbot; P 36,000; M 800; (410) 822-4653; Fax (410) 822-7922; info@talbotchamber.org; www.talbotchamber.org*

Edgemere • *see Towson*

Edmonston • *see Lanham*

Elkridge • *see Laurel*

Elkton • *Elkton Chamber & Alliance •* Mary Jo Jablonski; Exec. Dir.; 101 E. Main St.; 21921; Cecil; P 15,000; M 105; (410) 398-5076; Fax (410) 398-4971; maryjo@elktonalliance.org; www.elktonalliance.org

Elkton • *Cecil County C/C •* Laura Mayse; Exec. Dir.; 106 E. Main St., Ste. 101A; 21921; Cecil; P 101,000; M 640; (410) 392-3833; Fax (410) 392-6225; info@cecilchamber.com; www.cecilchamber.com*

Essex • *see Baltimore*

Fairmont Heights • *see Lanham*

Forest Heights • *see Lanham*

Fort Meade • *see Laurel*

Frederick • *Frederick County C/C •* Elizabeth Cromwell; Pres./CEO; 8420-B Gas House Pike; 21701; Frederick; P 200,000; M 913; (301) 662-4164; Fax (301) 846-4427; info@frederickchamber.org; www.frederickchamber.org*

Gaithersburg • *Gaithersburg-Germantown C/C* • Marilyn Balcombe; Pres.; 910 Clopper Rd., Ste. 205N; 20878; Montgomery; P 150,000; M 400; (301) 840-1400; Fax (301) 963-3918; mbalcombe@ggchamber.org; www.ggchamber.org*

Germantown • *Mid-Atlantic Hispanic C/C* • Jorge Ribas; Pres./CEO; P.O. Box 910; 20875; Montgomery; P 28,500,000; M 350; (301) 404-1946; mahcc1947@gmail.com; www.mahcc.org

Germantown • *see Gaithersburg*

Glen Burnie • *Northern Anne Arundel County C/C* • Frances Schmidt; CEO; 7439 Baltimore-Annapolis Blvd.; 21061; Anne Arundel; P 500,000; M 400; (410) 766-8282; Fax (410) 766-5722; info@naaccc.com; www.naaccc.com*

Glenarden • *see Lanham*

Glyndon • *see Reisterstown*

Greenbelt • *see Lanham and Laurel*

Hagerstown • *Hagerstown-Washington County C/C* • Paul Frey; Pres.; 28 W. Washington St., Ste. 200; 21740; Washington; P 149,000; M 550; (301) 739-2015; Fax (301) 739-1278; chamber@hagerstown.org; www.hagerstown.org*

Hancock • *Hancock C/C* • Angie Hager; Treas.; 126 W. High St.; 21750; Washington; P 1,752; M 70; (301) 678-5900; info@hancockmd.com; www.hancockmd.com

Hanover • *see Laurel*

Harford County • *see Bel Air*

Havre de Grace • *Havre de Grace C/C* • Cathy Vincenti; Exec. Dir.; 450 Pennington Ave.; 21078; Harford; P 13,000; M 270; (410) 939-3303; (800) 851-7756; Fax (410) 939-3490; hdegchamber1@comcast.net; www.hdgchamber.com

Howard County • *see Columbia and Laurel*

Hyattsville • *see Lanham*

Jessup • *see Laurel*

Kingsville • *see Towson*

La Plata • *Charles County C/C* • Betsy Burian; Pres./CEO; 101 Centennial St., Ste. A; 20646; Charles; P 146,546; M 550; (301) 932-6500; Fax (301) 932-3945; info@charlescountychamber.org; www.charlescountychamber.org

Landover Hills • *see Lanham*

Lanham • *Prince George's C/C* • David Harrington; Pres./CEO; 4640 Forbes Blvd., Ste. 130; 20706; Prince George's; P 890,000; M 900; (301) 731-5000; (301) 731-5009; Fax (301) 731-8015; dstaples@pgcoc.org; www.pgcoc.org*

Laurel • *also see Lanham*

Laurel • *Baltimore Washington Corridor Chamber* • H. Walter Townshend III; Pres./CEO; 312 Marshall Ave., Ste. 104; 20707; Anne Arundel, Howard, Montgomery & Prince George; P 2,200,000; M 550; (301) 725-4000; (410) 792-9714; Fax (301) 725-0776; bwcc@bwcc.org; www.bwcc.org

Maryland City • *see Laurel*

McHenry • *Garrett County C/C & Visitors Center* • Nicole Christian; Pres./CEO; 15 Visitors Center Dr.; 21541; Garrett; P 30,100; M 600; (301) 387-4386; (301) 387-6171; Fax (301) 387-2080; info@garrettchamber.com; www.visitdeepcreek.com*

Montgomery County • *see Laurel and Rockville*

Morningside • *see Lanham*

Mount Airy • *Greater Mount Airy C/C* • Linda Koons; Pres.; P.O. Box 741; 21771; Carroll & Frederick; P 8,500; M 300; (301) 829-5426; inquiries@mtairybusiness.com; www.mtairybusiness.com

Mount Rainier • *see Lanham*

North East • *North East C/C* • Keith Moore; Pres.; 20 Merganser Ct.; 21901; Cecil; P 20,000; M 100; info@northeastchamber.org; www.northeastchamber.org

Oakland • *see McHenry*

Ocean City • *Greater Ocean City C/C* • Melanie Pursel; Exec. Dir.; 12320 Ocean Gateway; 21842; Worcester; P 8,400; M 850; (410) 213-0552; Fax (410) 213-7521; info@oceancity.org; www.oceancity.org*

Odenton • *West Anne Arundel County C/C* • Claire Louder; Pres./CEO; 8385 Piney Orchard Pkwy.; 21113; Anne Arundel; P 100,000; M 350; (410) 672-3422; Fax (410) 672-3475; info@westcountychamber.org; www.waaccc.org*

Olney • *Olney C/C* • Jon Hulsizer; Exec. Dir.; 3460 Olney-Laytonsville Rd.. Ste. 211; P.O. Box 550; 20830; Montgomery; P 37,000; M 225; (301) 774-7117; Fax (301) 774-4944; chamber@olneymd.org; www.olneymd.org

Owings Mills • *see Reisterstown*

Oxford • *see Easton*

Parkville • *see Towson*

Perry Hall • *see Towson*

Pikesville • *Pikesville C/C* • Jessica Normington; Exec. Dir.; 7 Church Ln., Ste. 6; 21208; Baltimore; P 31,000; M 350; (410) 484-2337; Fax (410) 484-4151; info@pikesvillechamber.org; www.pikesvillechamber.org*

Pocomoke City • *Pocomoke Area C/C* • Debbie Godwin Brown; Exec. Dir.; 6 Market St.; P.O. Box 356; 21851; Worcester; P 4,500; M 150; (410) 957-1919; Fax (410) 957-4784; pocomokechamber@gmail.com; www.pocomoke.com*

Poolesville • *Poolesville Area C/C* • Maggie Nightingale; Exec. Secy.; P.O. Box 256; 20837; Montgomery; P 5,674; M 140; (301) 349-5753; (301) 972-8896; info@poolesvillechamber.com; www.poolesvillechamber.com

Potomac • *Potomac C/C* • Jennifer Matheson; Dir. of Op.; 10220 River Rd., Ste. 300; P.O. Box 59160; 20859; Montgomery; P 44,822; M 106; (301) 299-2170; Fax (301) 983-9700; pcc@potomacchamber.org; www.potomacchamber.org

Prince Frederick • *Calvert County C/C* • William R. Chambers; Pres./CEO; 120 Dares Beach Rd.; P.O. Box 9; 20678; Calvert; P 90,000; M 500; (410) 535-2577; Fax (443) 295-7213; calvertchamber@calvertchamber.org; www.calvertchamber.org*

Prince George County • *see Lanham and Laurel*

Princess Anne • *Princess Anne C/C* • Mr. Williams; Pres.; P.O. Box 642; 21853; Somerset; P 3,300; M 80; (410) 651-2118; (410) 651-2961; Fax (410) 651-3836; princessannechamberofcommerce@gmail.com; www.princessannebusiness.org

Queen Anne's County • *see Chester*

Reisterstown • *Reisterstown-Owings Mills-Glyndon C/C* • Colleen Brady; Pres.; P.O. Box 336; 21136; Baltimore; P 80,000; M 200; (410) 702-7073; Fax (410) 702-7075; romg@romgchamber.com; www.romgchamber.com*

Rockville • *Montgomery County C/C* • Georgette Godwin; Pres./CEO; 51 Monroe St., Ste. 1800; 20850; Montgomery; P 757,000; M 500; (301) 738-0015; Fax (301) 738-8792; ggodwin@mcccmd.com; www.mcccmd.com

Rockville • *Rockville C/C* • Michelle F. Day; Pres./CEO; 1 Research Ct., Ste. 450; 20850; Montgomery; P 65,000; M 300; (301) 424-9300; Fax (301) 762-7599; rockville@rockvillechamber.org; www.rockvillechamber.org

Rosedale • *see Towson*

Rossville • *see Towson*

Saint Michaels • *see Easton*

Salisbury • *Salisbury Area C/C* • Ernie Colburn; CEO; 144 E. Main St.; P.O. Box 510; 21803; Wicomico; P 100,000; M 850; (410) 749-0144; Fax (410) 860-9925; chamber@salisburyarea.com; www.salisburyarea.com*

Sandy Spring • *see Laurel*

Savage • *see Laurel*

Severna Park • *Greater Severna Park & Arnold C/C* • Linda S. Zahn; CEO; 1 Holly Ave.; 21146; Anne Arundel; P 40,000; M 650; (410) 647-3900; Fax (410) 647-3999; info@severnaparkchamber.com; www.severnaparkchamber.com*

Silver Spring • *Greater Silver Spring C/C* • Jane Redicker; Pres.; 8601 Georgia Ave., Ste. 203; 20910; Montgomery; P 235,000; M 400; (301) 565-3777; Fax (301) 565-3377; info@gsscc.org; www.gsscc.org*

Snow Hill • *Snow Hill C/C* • Lee Chisholm; Pres.; P.O. Box 176; 21863; Worcester; P 5,100; M 55; (410) 632-0809; (410) 632-1700; blaws@taylorbank.com; www.snowhillmd.com

Talbot County • *see Easton*

Taneytown • *Taneytown C/C* • 24 E. Baltimore St.; P.O. Box 18; 21787; Carroll; P 7,000; M 90; (410) 756-4234; Fax (410) 756-4234; biz@taneytownchamber.org; www.taneytownchamber.org

Tilghman Island • *see Easton*

Towson • *Baltimore County C/C* • Keith Scott; Pres./CEO; 102 W. Pennsylvania Ave., Ste. 101; 21204; Baltimore; P 800,000; M 700; (410) 825-6200; Fax (410) 821-9901; mball@baltcountychamber.com; www.baltcountycc.com

Upper Marlboro • *see Lanham*

Westminster • *Carroll County C/C* • Mike McMullin; Pres.; 9 E. Main St., Ste. 105; P.O. Box 871; 21158; Carroll; P 168,000; M 500; (410) 848-9050; Fax (410) 876-1023; info@carrollcountychamber.org; www.carrollcountychamber.org*

Wheaton • *Wheaton-Kensington C/C* • William Moore; Pres.; 2401 Blueridge Ave., Ste. 101; 20902; Montgomery; P 153,000; M 150; (301) 949-0080; Fax (301) 949-0081; wkchamber@wkchamber.org; www.wkchamber.org

White Marsh • *see Baltimore*

Massachusetts

No State Chamber

Abington • *see Brockton*

Acton • *Middlesex West C/C* • Kathleen McDonald; Exec. Dir.; 179 Great Rd., Ste. 104B; 01720; Middlesex; P 92,000; M 290; (978) 263-0010; Fax (978) 264-0303; info@mwcoc.com; www.mwcoc.com*

Adams • *see North Adams*

Agawam • *see Springfield*

Agawam • *also see West Springfield*

Alford • *see Great Barrington*

Amesbury • *Amesbury C/C & Ind. Found. Inc.* • Melissa Cerasulo; Exec. Dir.; 5 Market Sq.; 01913; Essex; P 18,000; M 300; (978) 388-3178; Fax (978) 388-4952; melissa@amesburychamber.com; www.amesburychamber.com

Amherst • *Amherst Area C/C* • Don Courtemanche; Exec. Dir.; 28 Amity St.; 01002; Hampshire; P 37,000; M 600; (413) 253-0700; Fax (413) 256-0771; info@amherstarea.com; www.amherstarea.com*

Arlington • *Arlington C/C* • Jennifer Tripp; Exec. Dir.; 611 Massachusetts Ave.; 02474; Middlesex; P 42,389; M 258; (781) 643-4600; Fax (781) 646-5581; info@arlcc.org; www.arlcc.org

Ashburnham • *see North Central Mass.*

Ashby • *see North Central Mass.*

Ashland • *see Framingham*

Ashley Falls • *see Lakeville, CT*

Athol • *North Quabbin Chamber & Visitors Bur.* • Mark Wright; Exec. Dir.; 251 Exchange St.; 01331; Worcester; P 100,000; M 200; (978) 249-3849; info@northquabbinchamber.com; www.northquabbinchamber.com*

Attleboro • *United Reg. C/C* • Jack Lank; Pres./CEO; 42 Union St.; 02703; Bristol; P 120,000; M 700; (508) 222-0801; Fax (508) 222-1498; jack@unitedregionalchamber.org; www.unitedregionalchamber.org*

Avon • *see Brockton*

Ayer • *see Devens*

Barnstable • *see Hyannis*

Barre • *see Gardner*

Becket • *see Great Barrington*

Bedford • *Bedford C/C* • Maureen Sullivan; Exec. Dir.; 12 Mudge Way; 01730; Middlesex; P 13,000; M 200; (781) 275-8503; bcoc@bedfordchamber.org; www.bedfordchamber.org*

Bellingham • *see Milford*

Belmont • *see Watertown*

Berkley • *see Taunton*

Berlin • *see Hudson*

Beverly • *Beverly C/C* • John M. Somes; Exec. Dir.; 100 Cummings St., Ste. 107K; 01915; Essex; P 60,000; M 400; (978) 232-9559; Fax (978) 232-9372; jsomes@beverlychamber.com; www.beverlychamber.com*

Billerica • *Billerica Comm. Alliance* • Pat Zapert; Exec. Dir.; 12 Andover Rd., Ste. 1; 01821; Middlesex; P 40,243; M 120; (978) 667-4174; Fax (978) 528-4343; info@billerica-alliance.org; www.billerica-alliance.org

Blackstone • *see Franklin*

Bolton • *see Hudson*

Boston • *Greater Boston C/C* • Paul Guzzi; Pres./CEO; 265 Franklin St., 12th Flr.; 02110; Suffolk; P 6,016,425; M 1,700; (617) 227-4500; Fax (617) 227-7505; info@bostonchamber.com; www.bostonchamber.com

Boston • *Mass. Chamber of Bus. & Ind.* • Debra A. Boronski; Pres.; 60 State St.; 02109; Suffolk; P 6,500,000; M 780; (617) 512-9667; (413) 525-2506; Fax (888) 649-7077; president@massachusettschamberofcommerce.com; www.massachusettschamberofcommerce.com

Bourne • *see Cape Cod Canal*

Boylston • *see North Central Mass.*

Braintree • *see Rockland*

Brewster • *Brewster C/C* • Kyle Hinkle; Exec. Dir.; P.O. Box 1241; 02631; Barnstable; P 9,500; M 200; (508) 896-3500; Fax (508) 896-1086; info@brewster-capecod.com; www.brewster-capecod.com

Bridgewater • *see Brockton and Middleborough*

Brimfield • *see Sturbridge*

Brockton • *Metro South C/C* • Christopher Cooney CCE; Pres./CEO; Sixty School St.; 02301; Plymouth; P 285,000; M 850; (508) 586-0500; Fax (508) 587-1340; chris@metrosouthchamber.com; www.metrosouthchamber.com*

Brookline • *Brookline C/C* • Harry Robinson; Exec. Dir.; 251 Harvard St., Ste. 1; 02446; Norfolk; P 57,107; M 230; (617) 739-1330; Fax (617) 739-1200; info@brooklinechamber.com; www.brooklinechamber.com

Buzzards Bay • *Cape Cod Canal Region C/C* • Marie Oliva; Pres./CEO; 70 Main St.; 02532; Barnstable; P 22,000; M 650; (508) 759-6000; Fax (508) 759-6965; info@capecodcanalchamber.org; www.capecodcanalchamber.org*

Cambridge • *Cambridge C/C* • Kelly Thompson Clark; Pres./CEO; 859 Massachusetts Ave.; 02139; Middlesex; P 105,000; M 1,540; (617) 876-4100; ccinfo@cambridgechamber.org; www.cambridgechamber.org*

Canton • *see Brockton and Norwood*

Cape Cod • *Cape Cod C of C & CVB* • Wendy K. Northcross; CEO; 5 Patti Page Way; Centerville; 02632; Barnstable; P 214,000; M 1,329; (508) 362-3225; (888) 33-CAPECOD; Fax (508) 362-3698; info@capecodchamber.org; www.capecodchamber.org

Carver • *see Middleborough*

Charlton • *see Sturbridge*

Chatham • *Chatham C/C* • Lisa Franz; Exec. Dir.; 2377 Main St.; P.O. Box 793; 02633; Barnstable; P 6,500; M 360; (508) 945-5199; Fax (508) 430-7919; info@chathaminfo.com; www.chathaminfo.com

Chathamport • *see Chatham*

Chelmsford • *see Lowell*

Chelsea • *Chelsea C/C* • Donald Harney; Exec. Dir.; 308 Broadway; 02150; Suffolk; P 37,000; M 180; (617) 884-4877; Fax (617) 884-4878; dharney@chelseachamber.org; www.chelseachamber.org

Chicopee • *Greater Chicopee C/C* • Eileen Drumm; Pres.; 264 Exchange St.; 01013; Hampden; P 55,000; M 380; (413) 594-2101; Fax (413) 594-2103; eileendrumm@chicopeechamber.org; www.chicopeechamber.org*

Clinton • *see North Central Mass.*

Cohasset • *Cohasset C/C* • Darilynn Evans; Pres.; P.O. Box 336; 02025; Norfolk; P 7,500; M 100; (781) 383-1010; info@cohassetchamber.org; www.cohassetchamber.org

Concord • *Concord C/C* • Jane Obbagy; Exec. Dir.; 15 Walden St., Ste. 7; 01742; Middlesex; P 17,700; M 275; (978) 369-3120; Fax (978) 369-1515; director@concordchamberofcommerce.org; www.concordchamberofcommerce.org

Cotuit • *see Hyannis*

Danvers • *North Shore C/C* • Robert G. Bradford; Pres.; 5 Cherry Hill Dr., Ste. 100; 01923; Essex; P 300,000; M 1,000; (978) 774-8565; Fax (978) 774-3418; rachel@northshorechamber.org; www.northshorechamber.org

Dedham • *see Norwood*

Deerfield • *see Greenfield*

Dighton • *see Taunton*

Dracut • *see Lowell*

Dudley • *see Worcester*

East Boston • *C/C of East Boston* • Joe Sinatra; Ofc. Coord.; 175 McClellan Hwy., Ste. 1; 02128; Suffolk; P 32,000; M 300; (617) 569-5000; Fax (617) 569-1945; contact@eastbostonchamber.com; www.eastbostonchamber.org

East Bridgewater • *see Brockton*

East Longmeadow • *Massachusetts C/C* • Debra A. Boronski; Pres.; 143 Shaker Rd.; P.O. Box 414; 01028; Suffolk; P 6,500,000; M 780; (413) 426-3850; (617) 512-9667; Fax (888) 649-7077; president@massachusettschamberofcommerce.com; www.massachusettschamberofcommerce.com

East Longmeadow • *also see Springfield*

Eastham • *Eastham C/C* • Jim Russo; Exec. Dir.; 4730 State Hwy.; P.O. Box 1329; 02642; Barnstable; P 5,500; M 265; (508) 240-7211; Fax (774) 561-2101; info@easthamchamber.com; www.easthamchamber.com

Easthampton • *Greater Easthampton C/C* • Maureen Belliveau; Exec. Dir.; 33 Union St.; 01027; Hampshire; P 17,000; M 250; (413) 527-9414; Fax (413) 527-1445; info@easthamptonchamber.org; www.easthamptonchamber.org

Easton • *see Brockton*

Everett • *Everett C/C* • Cheryl Smith; Exec. Dir.; 467 Broadway; 02149; Middlesex; P 35,701; M 300; (617) 387-9100; Fax (617) 389-6655; info@everettmachamber.com; www.everettmachamber.com

Fall River • *Fall River Area C/C & Ind.* • Robert Mellion Esq.; Pres./CEO; 200 Pocasset St.; 02721; Bristol; P 90,000; M 700; (508) 676-8226; Fax (508) 675-5932; info@fallriverchamber.com; www.fallriverchamber.com

Falmouth • *Falmouth C/C* • Michael Kasparian; Pres./CEO; 20 Academy Ln.; 02540; Barnstable; P 32,000; M 670; (508) 548-8500; (800) 526-8532; Fax (508) 548-8521; info@falmouthchamber.com; www.falmouthchamber.com*

Fitchburg • *see North Central Mass.*

Foxborough • *see Mansfield*

Framingham • *MetroWest C/C* • Bonnie Biocchi; Pres./CEO; 1671 Worcester Rd., Ste. 301; 01701; Middlesex; P 325,000; M 600; (508) 879-5600; Fax (508) 875-9325; chamber@metrowest.org; www.metrowest.org

Franklin • *United Reg. C/C* • Jack Lank; Pres./CEO; 4 West St.; 02038; Norfolk; P 120,000; M 700; (508) 528-2800; Fax (508) 528-7864; jack@unitedregionalchamber.org; www.unitedregionalchamber.org*

Gardner • *Greater Gardner C/C* • James Bellina; Pres./CEO; 210 Main St.; 01440; Worcester; P 50,000; M 450; (978) 632-1780; Fax (978) 630-1767; jbellina@garderma.com; www.gardnerma.com*

Gloucester • *Cape Ann C/C* • Ken Riehl; CEO; 33 Commercial St.; 01930; Essex; P 45,000; M 1,000; (978) 283-1601; Fax (978) 283-4740; info@capeannchamber.com; capeannchamber.com*

Granby • *see South Hadley*

Great Barrington • *Southern Berkshire C/C* • Christine B. Ludwiszewski; Exec. Dir.; 40 Railroad St., Ste. 2; P.O. Box 810; 01230; Berkshire; P 16,027; M 350; (413) 528-4284; Fax (413) 528-2200; info@southernberkshirechamber.com; www.southernberkshirechamber.com

Greenfield • *Franklin County C/C* • Ann L. Hamilton; Pres.; 395 Main St.; P.O. Box 898; 01302; Franklin; P 78,000; M 500; (413) 773-5463; Fax (413) 773-7008; fccc@franklincc.org; www.franklincc.org*

Groton • *see North Central Mass.*

Halifax • *see Brockton and Middleborough*

Hamilton • *see Danvers*

Hampden • *see Springfield*

Hanover • *Hanover C/C* • Francie Donohue; Exec. Secy.; P.O. Box 68; 02339; Plymouth; P 15,000; M 185; (781) 826-8865; Fax (781) 826-7721; chamber@hanovermachamber.com; www.hanovermachamber.com

Hanson • *see Brockton*

Harvard • *see North Central Mass.*

Harwich Port • *Harwich C/C* • Jeremy Gingras; Exec. Dir.; One Schoolhouse Rd., Rte. 28; 02646; Barnstable; P 14,000; M 325; (508) 430-1165; (800) 4-HARWICH; Fax (508) 430-2105; info@harwichcc.com; www.harwichcc.com*

Haverhill • *Greater Haverhill C/C* • Stacey Bruzzese; Pres.; 80 Merrimack St.; 01830; Essex; P 65,000; M 700; (978) 373-5663; Fax (978) 373-8060; info@haverhillchamber.com; www.haverhillchamber.com*

Holbrook • *see Brockton*

Holden • *Holden Area C/C* • Jennifer Stanovich; Exec. Dir.; 1174 Main St.; 01520; Worcester; P 30,000; M 170; (508) 829-9220; info@holdenareachamber.org; www.holdenareachamber.org

Holland • *see Sturbridge*

Holliston • *see Framingham and Milford*

Holyoke • *Greater Holyoke C/C* • Kathleen Anderson; Pres.; 177 High St.; 01040; Hampden; P 50,000; M 500; (413) 534-3376; Fax (413) 534-3385; info@holyokechamber.com; www.holyokechamber.com*

Hopedale • *see Milford*

Hopkinton • *see Framingham and Milford*

Housatonic • *see Great Barrington*

Hubbardston • *see Gardner*

Hudson • *Assabet Valley C/C* • Sarah B. Cressy; Pres./CEO; 18 Church St.; P.O. Box 578; 01749; Middlesex; P 34,000; M 460; (978) 568-0360; Fax (978) 562-4118; info@assabetvalleychamber.org; www.assabetvalleychamber.org

Hull • *Hull/Nantasket Beach C/C* • Patricia Abbate; Pres.; P.O. Box 140; 02045; Plymouth; P 11,000; M 100; (781) 925-9980; info@hullchamber.com; www.hullchamber.com

Hyannis • *Hyannis Area C/C* • Jessica Sylver; Pres./CEO; 397 Main St.; P.O. Box 100; 02601; Barnstable; P 20,000; M 650; (508) 775-7778; Fax (508) 775-7131; guidebook@hyannis.com; www.hyannis.com

Ipswich • *Ipswich C/C* • Bob McNeil; Pres.; P.O. Box 94; 01938; Essex; P 13,500; M 260; (978) 356-9055; Fax (978) 356-5239; info@ipswichchamber.org; www.ipswichchamber.org

Lakeville • *see Middleborough*

Lancaster • *see North Central Mass.*

Lawrence • *Merrimack Valley C/C* • Joseph J. Bevilacqua; Pres./CEO; 264 Essex St.; 01840; Essex; P 200,000; M 1,200; (978) 686-0900; Fax (978) 794-9953; office@merrimackvalleychamber.com; www.merrimackvalleychamber.com*

Lee • *Lee C/C* • Colleen A. Henry; Exec. Dir.; P.O. Box 345; 01238; Berkshire; P 6,000; M 150; (413) 243-1705; director@leechamber.org; www.leechamber.org

Lenox • *Lenox C/C* • Ralph Petillo; Dir.; 12 Housatonic St.; P.O. Box 646; 01240; Berkshire; P 5,800; M 200; (413) 637-3646; Fax (413) 637-3626; info@lenox.org; www.lenox.org

Leominster • *see North Central Mass.*

Lexington • *Lexington C/C* • Mary Jo Bohart; Exec. Dir.; 1875 Massachusetts Ave.; 02420; Middlesex; P 31,000; M 300; (781) 862-2480; Fax (781) 862-5995; jterhune@lexingtonchamber.org; www.lexingtonchamber.org

Lincoln • *see Waltham*

Lowell • *Greater Lowell C/C* • Danielle Bergeron; Pres./CEO; 131 Merrimack St.; 01852; Middlesex; P 200,000; M 1,000; (978) 459-8154; Fax (978) 452-4145; info@greaterlowellchamber.org; www.glcc.biz*

Ludlow • *see Springfield*

Lunenburg • *see North Central Mass.*

Lynn • *Lynn Area C/C* • Leslie Gould; Pres./CEO; 583 Chestnut St., Ste. 8; 01904; Essex; P 90,000; M 450; (781) 592-2900; Fax (781) 592-2903; info@lynnareachamber.com; www.lynnareachamber.com*

Lynnfield • *see Danvers and Lynn*

Malden • *Malden C/C* • Jenna Coccimiglio; Exec. Dir.; Malden Government Center; 200 Pleasant St., Ste. 416; 02148; Middlesex; P 56,000; M 400; (781) 322-4500; Fax (781) 322-4866; jcoccimiglio@maldenchamber.org; www.maldenchamber.org

Mansfield • *Tri-Town C/C* • Kara J. Griffin; Exec. Dir.; 280 School St., Ste. L100; Mansfield Crossing; 02048; Bristol; P 50,000; M 325; (508) 339-5655; Fax (508) 339-8333; office@tri-townchamber.org; www.tri-townchamber.org*

SERVING FOXBOROUGH, MANSFIELD AND NORTON. HOME TO GILLETTE STADIUM, PATRIOT PLACE, TPC BOSTON, DEUTSCHE BANK CHAMPIONSHIP, XFINITY CENTER. STRIVING TO IMPROVE THE ECONOMIC DEVELOPMENT IN ALL OUR COMMUNITIES.

Marblehead • *Marblehead C/C* • Deb Pesanti Payson; Exec. Dir.; 62 Pleasant St.; 01945; Essex; P 20,000; M 450; (781) 631-2868; Fax (781) 639-8582; deb@marbleheadchamber.org; www.marbleheadchamber.org

Marlborough • *Marlborough Reg. C/C* • Susanne Morreale-Leeber CCE IOM; Pres./CEO; 11 Florence St.; 01752; Middlesex; P 40,000; M 550; (508) 485-7746; Fax (508) 481-1819; marlcham@marlboroughchamber.org; www.marlboroughchamber.org*

Marshfield • *Marshfield C/C* • Ashley Stanford; Exec. Dir.; P.O. Box 238; 02050; Plymouth; P 25,200; M 130; (781) 834-6262; office@marshfieldchamberofcommerce.com; www.marshfieldchamberofcommerce.com

Marstons Mills • *see Hyannis*

Martha's Vineyard • *see Vineyard Haven*

Mashpee • *Mashpee C/C* • Mary Lou Palumbo; Exec. Dir.; 520 Main St.; P.O. Box 1245; 02649; Barnstable; P 15,000; M 302; (508) 477-0792; Fax (508) 477-5541; info@mashpeechamber.com; www.mashpeechamber.com

Maynard • *see Hudson*

Medfield • *see Norwood*

Medford • *Medford C/C* • Janet Donnelly; Exec. Dir.; 1 Shipyard Way, Ste. 302; 02155; Middlesex; P 70,000; M 285; (781) 396-1277; Fax (781) 396-1278; director@medfordchamberma.com; www.medfordchamberma.com

Medway • *see Milford*

Melrose • *Melrose C/C* • Lauren Grymek; Exec. Dir.; One W. Foster St.; 02176; Middlesex; P 27,000; M 300; (781) 665-3033; Fax (781) 665-5595; info@melrosechamber.org; www.melrosechamber.org

Mendon • *see Milford*

Middleborough • *Cranberry Country C/C* • Valerie Glynn; Pres.; 40 N. Main St., Ste. F-1; 02346; Plymouth; P 125,000; M 260; (508) 947-1499; Fax (508) 947-1446; info@cranberrycountry.org; www.cranberrycountry.org*

Milford • *Milford Area C/C* • Siobhan Bohnson; Pres./CEO; 258 Main St., Ste. 306; P.O. Box 621; 01757; Middlesex; P 150,000; M 700; (508) 473-6700; Fax (508) 473-8467; sbohnson@milfordchamber.org; www.milfordchamber.org*

Millis • *see Milford*

Monterey • *see Great Barrington*

Mount Washington • *see Great Barrington*

Nahunt • *see Lynn*

Nantucket • *Nantucket Island C/C* • P.J. Smith; Exec. Dir.; Zero Main St., 2nd Flr.; 02554; Nantucket; P 12,000; M 600; (508) 228-3643; Fax (508) 325-4925; info@nantucketchamber.org; www.nantucketchamber.org

Natick • *see Framingham*

Needham • *see Newton*

New Bedford • *New Bedford Area C/C* • Rick Kidder; Pres./CEO; 794 Purchase St.; P.O. Box 8827; 02742; Bristol & Plymouth; P 250,000; M 1,000; (508) 999-5231; Fax (508) 999-5237; info@newbedfordchamber.com; www.newbedfordchamber.com*

Newburyport • *Greater Newburyport C/C* • Ann Ormond; Pres.; 38R Merrimac St.; 01950; Essex; P 17,000; M 800; (978) 462-6680; Fax (978) 465-4145; info@newburyportchamber.org; www.newburyportchamber.org

Newton • *Newton-Needham C/C* • Bob Halpin; Pres.; 281 Needham St.; Upper Level; 02464; Middlesex; P 112,000; M 700; (617) 244-5300; Fax (617) 244-5302; lbest@nnchamber.com; www.nnchamber.com*

Norfolk • *see Franklin*

North Adams • *North Adams C/C* • Ricco Fruccio; Prog. Coord.; P.O. Box 344; 01247; Berkshire; P 13,600; M 50; (413) 441-4528; ricco@explorenorthadams.com; www.explorenorthadams.com

North Attleboro • *see Attleboro*

North Central Mass. • *North Central Massachusetts C/C* • Roy Nascimento IOM; Pres./CEO; 860 South St.; Fitchburg; 01420; Worcester; P 269,000; M 1,000; (978) 353-7600; Fax (978) 353-4896; chamber@northcentralmass.com; northcentralmass.com*

North Chatham • *see Chatham*

North Easton • *see Brockton*

North Egremont • *see Great Barrington*

North Reading • *see Reading*

North Truro • *Truro C/C* • Jane Peters; Exec. Secy./Treas.; P.O. Box 26; 02652; Barnstable; P 2,087; (508) 487-1288; info@trurochamberofcommerce.com; www.trurochamberofcommerce.com

Northampton • *Greater Northampton C/C* • Suzanne Beck; Exec. Dir.; 99 Pleasant St.; 01060; Hampshire; P 30,000; M 750; (413) 584-1900; Fax (413) 584-1934; suzanne@explorenorthampton.com; www.explorenorthampton.com

Northborough • *see Westborough*

Northfield • *see Greenfield*

Norton • *see Mansfield*

Norwell • *Norwell C/C* • Reiko Beach; Pres.; P.O. Box 322; 02061; Plymouth; P 10,000; M 100; info@norwellchamberofcommerce.com; www.norwellchamberofcommerce.com

Norwood • *Neponset Valley C/C* • Thomas O'Rourke; Pres./CEO; 520 Providence Hwy., Ste. 4; 02062; Norfolk; P 180,000; M 550; (781) 769-1126; Fax (781) 769-0808; tom@nvcc.com; www.nvcc.com*

Orleans • *Orleans C/C* • Noelle Pina; Exec. Dir.; 44 Main St.; P.O. Box 153; 02653; Barnstable; P 6,800; M 300; (508) 255-1386; Fax (508) 255-2774; info@orleanscapecod.org; www.orleanscapecod.org

Otis • *see Great Barrington*

Oxbury • *see Worcester*

Palmer • *Quaboag Hills C/C* • Lenny Weake; Pres.; 3 Converse St., Ste. 103; 01069; Hampden; P 85,000; M 300; (413) 283-2418; Fax (413) 289-1355; info@qhma.com; www.qhma.com

Peabody • *Peabody Area C/C* • Deanne Healey; Exec. Dir.; 24 Main St.; 01960; Essex; P 49,000; M 400; (978) 531-0384; Fax (978) 532-7227; execdir@peabodychamber.com; www.peabodychamber.com

Pepperell • *see North Central Mass.*

Pittsfield • *Berkshire C/C* • Jonathan Butler; Pres./CEO; 66 Allen St.; 01201; Berkshire; P 135,150; M 1,200; (413) 499-4000; Fax (413) 447-9641; info@berkshirechamber.com; www.berkshirechamber.com*

Plainville • *see Attleboro*

Plymouth • *Plymouth Area C/C* • Mark Carey; Exec. Dir.; 134 Court St.; 02360; Plymouth; P 580,000; M 800; (508) 830-1620; Fax (508) 830-1621; info@plymouthchamber.com; www.plymouthchamber.com

Plympton • *see Middleborough*

Princeton • *see North Central Mass.*

Provincetown • *Provincetown C/C* • Candice Collins-Boden; Exec. Dir.; 307 Commerical St.; P.O. Box 1017; 02657; Barnstable; P 3,500; M 300; (508) 487-3424; Fax (508) 487-8966; info@ptownchamber.com; www.ptownchamber.com

Quincy • *see Rockland*

Randolph • *Randolph C/C* • Linda F. Werman; Pres.; 1 Credit Union Way; 02368; Norfolk; P 31,000; M 200; (781) 963-6862; Fax (781) 963-5252; office@randolphchamberofcommerce.org; www.randolphchamberofcommerce.org*

Raynham • *see Taunton*

Reading • *Reading-North Reading C/C* • Janet Wolbrom; Exec. Dir.; P.O. Box 771; 01867; Middlesex; P 37,000; M 265; (978) 664-5060; Fax (781) 944-6125; rnrchambercom@aol.com; www.readingnreadingchamber.org

Rehoboth • *see Taunton*

Revere • *Revere C/C* • Kerri Abrams; Pres.; 108 Beach St.; 02151; Suffolk; P 60,204; M 200; (781) 289-8009; Fax (781) 289-2166; info@reverechamber.org; www.reverechamber.org

Rochester • *see Middleborough*

Rockland • *South Shore C/C* • Peter Forman; Pres./CEO; 1050 Hingham St.; 02370; Plymouth; P 133,000; M 2,461; (781) 421-3900; Fax (617) 479-9274; info@southshorechamber.org; www.southshorechamber.org*

Rockport • *see Gloucester*

Salem • *Salem C/C* • Rinus Oosthoek; Exec. Dir.; 265 Essex St.; 01970; Essex; P 42,000; M 650; (978) 744-0004; Fax (978) 745-3855; info@salem-chamber.org; www.salem-chamber.org*

Salisbury • *Salisbury C/C* • Maria Miles; Pres.; P.O. Box 1000; 01952; Essex; P 10,000; M 100; (978) 465-3581; salisburychamber@aol.com; www.salisburychamber.com

Sandisfield • *see Great Barrington*

Sandwich • *see Cape Cod Canal*

Saugus • *Saugus C/C* • Sean Grant; Pres.; Marleah E. Graves Bldg.; 54-58 Essex St.; 01906; Essex; P 27,000; M 300; (781) 233-8407; Fax (781) 231-1145; sauguschamber@verizon.net

Scituate • *Scituate C/C* • Dr. Nico Afanasenko; Pres.; P.O. Box 401; 02066; Plymouth; P 18,779; M 125; (781) 545-4000; info@scituatechamber.org; www.scituatechamber.org

Sheffield • *see Great Barrington*

Sheffield • *see Lakeville, CT*

Shelburne • *see Greenfield*

Sherborn • *see Framingham*

Shirley • *see North Central Mass.*

Shirley • *Nashoba Valley C/C* • Melissa Fetterhoff; Pres./CEO; 2 Shaker Rd., Ste. B200; 01464; Middlesex & Worcester; P 30,000; M 550; (978) 425-5761; Fax (978) 425-5764; director@nvcoc.com; www.nvcoc.com*

Shrewsbury • *see Westborough*

Somerville • *Somerville C/C* • Stephen V. Mackey; Pres./CEO; 2 Alpine St.; P.O. Box 440343; 02144; Middlesex; P 78,000; M 325; (617) 776-4100; smackey@somervillechamber.org; www.somervillechamber.org

South Chatham • *see Chatham*

South Egremont • *see Great Barrington*

South Hadley • *South Hadley & Granby C/C* • Susan Stockman; Exec. Dir.; 116 Main St., Ste. 4; 01075; Hampshire; P 20,000; M 125; (413) 532-6451; mail@shchamber.com; www.southhadleygranbychamber.com

South Yarmouth • *Yarmouth C/C* • Mary Vilbon; Exec. Dir.; P.O. Box 479; 02664; Barnstable; P 25,300; M 400; (508) 778-1008; (800) 732-1008; Fax (508) 778-5114; director@yarmouthcapecod.com; www.yarmouthcapecod.com

Southborough • *see Framingham and Westborough*

Southbridge • *see Sturbridge*

Spencer • *see Sturbridge*

Springfield • *Springfield Reg. Chamber* • Nancy Creed; Pres.; 1441 Main St.; 01103; Hampden; P 250,000; M 700; (413) 787-1555; Fax (413) 755-1322; cavanaugh@springfieldregionalchamber.com; www.springfieldregionalchamber.com*

Sterling • *see North Central Mass.*

Stockbridge • *Stockbridge C/C* • Barbara J. Zanetti; Exec. Dir.; 50 Main St.; P.O. Box 224; 01262; Berkshire; P 2,500; M 100; (413) 298-5200; Fax (413) 931-3128; info@stockbridgechamber.org; www.stockbridgechamber.org

Stoneham • *Stoneham C/C* • Sharon Iovanni; Exec. Dir.; 271 Main St., Ste. L-02; 02180; Middlesex; P 24,000; M 275; (781) 438-0001; Fax (781) 438-0007; info@stonehamchamber.org; www.stonehamchamber.org

Stoughton • *Stoughton C/C* • Terry Schneider; Exec. Dir.; P.O. Box 41; 02072; Norfolk; P 30,000; M 175; (781) 297-7450; chamber@stoughtonma.com; www.stoughtonma.com

Stow • *see Hudson*

Sturbridge • *Central Mass. South C/C* • Alexandra McNitt; Exec. Dir.; 46 Hall Rd.; 01566; Worcester; P 60,000; M 380; (508) 347-2761; (800) 628-8379; Fax (508) 347-5218; info@cmschamber.org; www.cmschamber.org

Sudbury • *see Framingham*

Swampscott • *see Lynn*

Taunton • *Taunton Area C/C* • Kerrie Babin; Pres./CEO; 6 Pleasant St., Ste. A; 02780; Bristol; P 70,000; M 450; (508) 824-4068; Fax (508) 884-8222; info@tauntonareachamber.org; www.tauntonareachamber.org*

Templeton • *see Gardner*

Tewksbury • *see Wilmington*

Three Rivers • *Three Rivers C/C* • Fred Orszulak; Pres.; P.O. Box 147; 01080; Hampden; P 3,300; M 45; (413) 283-5620; www.threeriverschamber.org

Townsend • *see North Central Mass.*

Truro • *see North Truro*

Tyngsboro • *see Lowell*

Upton • *see Milford*

Vineyard Haven • *Martha's Vineyard C/C* • Nancy Gardella; Exec. Dir.; 24 Beach Rd.; P.O. Box 1698; 02568; Dukes; P 15,000; M 1,050; (508) 693-0085; (800) 505-4815; Fax (508) 693-7589; info@mvy.com; www.mvy.com*

Wakefield • *Wakefield C/C* • Kendall Inglese; Exec. Dir.; 467 Main St.; P.O. Box 585; 01880; Middlesex; P 25,000; M 300; (781) 245-0741; wakefieldchamberofcommerce@gmail.com; www.wakefieldschamber.org

Wales • *see Sturbridge*

Walpole • *Walpole C/C* • Dick Power; Secy.; P.O. Box 361; 02081; Norfolk; P 24,000; M 200; (508) 668-0081; office@walpolechamber.com; walpolechamber.com

Waltham • *Waltham West Suburban C/C* • John Peacock; Exec. Dir.; 84 South St.; 02453; Middlesex; P 60,000; M 500; (781) 894-4700; Fax (781) 894-1708; jpeacock@walthamchamber.com; www.walthamchamber.com

Wareham • *see Cape Cod Canal and Middleborough*

Watertown • *Watertown-Belmont C/C* • Brenda Fanara; Exec. Dir.; 182 Main St.; P.O. Box 45; 02471; Middlesex; P 56,000; M 450; (617) 926-1017; Fax (617) 926-2322; info@wbcc.org; www.wbcc.org*

Wayland • *see Framingham*

Webster • *see Worcester*

Wellesley • *Wellesley C/C* • Maura O'Brien; Pres./CEO; One Hollis St., Ste. 232; 02482; Norfolk; P 26,615; M 250; (781) 235-2446; Fax (781) 235-7326; sconlon@wellesleychamber.org; www.wellesleychamber.org

Wellfleet • *Wellfleet C/C* • Marcia Sexton; Exec. Secy.; Off Rte. 6; P.O. Box 571; 02667; Barnstable; P 3,000; M 230; (508) 349-2510; Fax (508) 349-3740; info@wellfleetchamber.com; www.wellfleetchamber.com

Wenham • *see Danvers*

West Barnstable • *see Hyannis*

West Boylston • *see North Central Mass.*

West Chatham • *see Chatham*

West Dennis • *Dennis C/C* • Spyro Mitrokostas; Exec. Dir.; 238 Swan River Rd.; P.O. Box 1001; 02670; Barnstable; P 14,000; M 400; (508) 398-3568; Fax (508) 760-5212; info@dennischamber.com; www.dennischamber.com

West Springfield • *West of the River C/C* • Noelle Myers; P.O. Box 48; 01090; Hampden; P 28,391; M 260; (413) 426-3880; Fax (888) 649-7077; info@westoftheriverchamber.com; ourwrc.com

West Stockbridge • *see Great Barrington*

West Yarmouth • *see South Yarmouth*

Westborough • *Corridor Nine Area C/C* • Karen Chapman; Pres.; 30 Lyman St., Ste. 6; P.O. Box 1555; 01581; Worcester; P 73,000; M 540; (508) 836-4444; Fax (508) 836-2652; events@corridornine.org; www.corridornine.org*

Westborough • *also see Framingham*

Westfield • *see Springfield*

U.S. Chambers of Commerce

Westfield • *Greater Westfield C/C* • Kate Phelon; Exec. Dir.; 53 Court St.; 01085; Hampden; P 60,195; M 210; (413) 568-1618; kphelon@westfieldbiz.org; www.westfieldbiz.org

Westford • *see Lowell*

Westminster • *see North Central Mass.*

Weston • *see Waltham*

Westwood • *see Norwood*

Weymouth • *see Rockland*

Whitinsville • *Blackstone Valley C/C* • Jeannie Hebert; Pres./CEO; 670 Linwood Ave., Bldg. A, Ste. 5; 01588; Worcester; P 95,000; M 500; (508) 234-9090; Fax (508) 234-5152; administrator@blackstonevalley.org; www.blackstonevalley.org*

Whitman • *see Brockton*

Wilbraham • *see Springfield*

Williamstown • *Williamstown C/C* • Jennifer Civello; Exec. Dir.; 7 Denison Park Dr.; P.O. Box 357; 01267; Berkshire; P 8,500; M 135; (413) 458-9077; (800) 214-3799; Fax (413) 458-2666; info@williamstownchamber.com; www.williamstownchamber.com

Wilmington • *Wilmington/Tewksbury C/C* • Nancy Vallee; Exec. Dir.; 226 Lowell St., Ste. B-4-A; P.O. Box 463; 01887; Middlesex; P 22,000; M 200; (978) 657-7211; Fax (978) 657-0139; director@wilmingtontewksburychamberofcommerce.org; www.wilmingtontewksburychamberofcommerce.org

Winchendon • *see Gardner*

Winchester • *Winchester C/C* • Catherine S. Alexander; Exec. Dir.; 25 Waterfield Rd.; 01890; Middlesex; P 21,000; M 210; (781) 729-8870; Fax (781) 729-8884; info@winchesterchamber.com; www.winchesterchamber.com

Winthrop • *Winthrop C/C* • Betsy Shane; Exec. Dir.; 207 Hagman Rd.; 02152; Suffolk; P 18,000; M 425; (617) 846-9898; Fax (617) 846-9922; info@winthropchamber.com; www.winthropchamber.com*

Woburn • *North Suburban C/C* • Maureen A. Rogers; Pres.; 76R Winn St., Ste. 3-D; 01801; Middlesex; P 100,000; M 407; (781) 933-3499; Fax (781) 933-1071; info@northsuburbanchamber.com; www.northsuburbanchamber.com*

Worcester • *Worcester Reg. C/C* • Timothy P. Murray; Pres./CEO; 446 Main St., Ste. 200; 01608; Worcester; P 181,000; M 3,000; (508) 753-2924; Fax (508) 754-8560; tmurray@worcesterchamber.org; www.worcesterchamber.org*

Wrentham • *see Franklin*

Yarmouth • *see South Yarmouth*

Michigan

Michigan C of C • Richard K. Studley; Pres./CEO; 600 S. Walnut St.; Lansing; 48933; Ingham; P 9,883,360; M 6,800; (517) 371-2100; (800) 748-0266; Fax (517) 371-7224; bmcnerney@michamber.com; www.michamber.com

Adrian • *Adrian Area C/C* • John R. Bartoszewicz; Pres./CEO; 137 N. Main St.; 49221; Lenawee; P 22,000; M 480; (517) 265-2320; Fax (517) 265-2432; info@adrianareachamber.com; www.adrianareachamber.com*

Albion • *Greater Albion C/C & Visitors Bur.* • Amy Robertson; Pres./CEO; 310 S. Superior St.; P.O. Box 238; 49224; Calhoun; P 9,200; M 150; (517) 629-5533; Fax (517) 629-4284; president@greateralbionchamber.org; www.greateralbionchamber.org*

Algonac • *Greater Algonac C/C* • Bob Weisenbaugh; 7215 Dyke Rd.; 48001; St. Clair; P 1,000; M 25; (586) 725-1279; Fax (866) 643-0023; execdirector@algonacchamber.com

Allegan • *Allegan Area C/C* • Sara Decker; Exec. Dir.; 221 Trowbridge St., Ste. B; 49010; Allegan; P 10,000; M 153; (269) 673-2479; Fax (269) 673-7190; mail@alleganchamber.com; www.alleganchamber.com

Allen Park • *Allen Park C/C* • Jim Beri; Dir. of Bus. Dev.; 6543 Allen Rd.; 48101; Wayne; P 28,200; M 146; (313) 382-7303; Fax (313) 382-4409; info@allenparkchamber.org; www.allenparkchamber.org

Allendale • *Allendale Area C/C* • Janessa Smit; Exec. Dir.; 6181 Lake Michigan Dr., #167; 49401; Ottawa; P 17,000; M 200; (616) 892-2632; aacc@allendalechamber.org; www.allendalechamber.org

Alma • *Gratiot Area C/C* • Jayne Norris; Exec. Dir.; 110 W. Superior St.; P.O. Box 516; 48801; Gratiot; P 39,000; M 380; (989) 463-5525; Fax (989) 463-6588; chamber@gratiot.org; www.gratiot.org

Alpena • *Alpena Area C/C* • Jaclynn A. Krawczak; Pres./CEO; 235 W. Chisholm St.; 49707; Alpena; P 30,000; M 490; (989) 354-4181; (800) 4-ALPENA; Fax (989) 356-3999; info@alpenachamber.com; www.alpenachamber.com*

Ann Arbor • *Ann Arbor/Ypsilanti Reg. C/C* • Diane Keller; Pres./CEO; 115 W. Huron St., 3rd Flr.; 48104; Washtenaw; P 134,000; M 1,300; (734) 665-4433; Fax (734) 665-4191; diane@a2ychamber.org; www.a2ychamber.org*

Armada • *see Romeo*

Ashley • *see Alma*

Atlanta • *Atlanta C/C* • Phil LaMore; Pres.; P.O. Box 410; 49709; Montmorency; P 2,500; M 200; (989) 785-3400; Fax (989) 785-3400; info@atlantamichigan.com; www.atlantamichigan.com

Au Gres • *Au Gres Area C/C* • Sandy Metzger; Pres.; P.O. Box 455; 48703; Arenac; P 800; M 73; (989) 876-6688; staff@augreschamber.com; www.augreschamber.com

Au Sable • *see Oscoda*

Auburn • *Auburn Area C/C* • Renee Gradowski; Pres.; P.O. Box 215; 48611; Bay; P 3,000; M 65; (989) 662-4001; Fax (989) 662-3333; contact@auburnchambermi.org; www.auburnchambermi.org

Auburn Hills • *Auburn Hills C/C* • Denise Asker; Exec. Dir.; 3395A Auburn Rd.; P.O. Box 214083; 48321; Oakland; P 21,400; M 300; (248) 853-7862; info@auburnhillschamber.com; www.auburnhillschamber.com*

Bad Axe • *Bad Axe C/C* • Laurel Brickel; Pres.; P.O. Box 87; 48413; Huron; P 4,000; M 120; (989) 269-6936; Fax (989) 269-8756; badaxemich@yahoo.com; www.badaxemich.com

Baldwin • *Lake County C/C & Tourist Center* • Rick Delamater; Pres.; 911 Michigan Ave.; P.O. Box 130; 49304; Lake; P 10,000; M 200; (231) 745-4331; (800) 245-3240; info@lakecountymichigan.com; www.lakecountymichigan.com

Bannister • *see Alma*

Battle Creek • *Battle Creek Area C/C* • Kara Beer; Exec. Dir.; One Riverwalk Centre; 34 W. Jackson St., Ste. 3A; 49017; Calhoun; P 60,000; M 600; (269) 962-4076; Fax (269) 962-6309; info@battlecreek.org; www.battlecreek.org*

Bay City • *Bay Area C/C* • Michael Seward; Pres./CEO; 901 Saginaw St.; 48708; Bay; P 110,000; M 800; (989) 893-4567; Fax (989) 895-5594; chamber@baycityarea.com; www.baycityarea.com*

Beaver Island • *Beaver Island C/C* • Steve West; Exec. Dir.; P.O. Box 5; 49782; Charlevoix; P 2,000; M 120; (231) 448-2505; chamber@beaverisland.org; www.beaverisland.org

Belding • *Belding Area C/C* • Michelle Francisco; Pres.; 120 Covered Village Mall; 48809; Ionia; P 6,000; M 80; (616) 794-9890; Fax (616) 794-1915; info@beldingchamber.org; www.beldingchamber.org

Bellaire • *Bellaire Area C/C* • Patricia Savant; Exec. Dir.; 308 E. Cayuga; P.O. Box 205; 49615; Antrim; P 1,250; M 160; (231) 533-6023; Fax (231) 533-8764; info@bellairechamber.org; www.bellairechamber.org

Belleville • *Belleville Area C/C* • Paul W. Henning; Exec. Dir.; 248 Main St.; 48111; Wayne; P 44,000; M 248; (734) 697-7151; Fax (734) 697-1415; info@bellevilleareachamber.org; www.bellevilleareachamber.org

Benton Harbor • *Cornerstone C/C* • Chris Heugal; Pres.; 38 W. Wall St.; 49022; Berrien; P 157,000; M 700; (269) 932-4042; Fax (269) 925-4471; pmuellen@cornerstonechamber.com; www.cornerstonechamber.com*

Benzonia • *Benzie County C/C* • Mary Carroll; Pres.; 826 Michigan Ave.; P.O. Box 204; 49616; Benzie; P 17,000; M 440; (231) 882-5801; Fax (231) 882-9249; director@benzie.org; www.benzie.org

Bergland • *Lake Gogebic Area C/C* • Mary Lou Driesenga; Secy.; P.O. Box 114; 49910; Gogebic & Ontonagon; P 600; M 81; (888) 464-3242; info@lakegogebicarea.com; www.lakegogebicarea.com

Berkley • *Berkley Area C/C* • Darlene Rothman; Exec. Dir.; P.O. Box 72-1253; 48072; Oakland; P 14,970; M 148; (248) 414-9157; membership@berkleychamber.com; www.berkleychamber.com*

Berrien Springs • *see Benton Harbor*

Bessemer • *Bessemer C/C* • Candice Snyder; Secy.; P.O. Box 243; 49911; Gogebic; P 1,920; M 110; (906) 663-0026; glen@pavlovichfamily.net; www.bessemerchamber.org

Big Rapids • *Mecosta County Area C/C* • Jennifer Heinzman; Exec. Dir.; 246 N. State St.; 49307; Mecosta; P 43,000; M 400; (231) 796-7649; Fax (231) 796-1625; director@mecostacounty.com; www.mecostacounty.com*

Birch Run • *Birch Run/Bridgeport Area C/C & CVB* • Mike Szukhent; Pres./CEO; 7971 Main St.; P.O. Box 153; 48415; Saginaw; P 11,000; M 222; (989) 624-9193; (888) 624-9193; Fax (989) 624-5337; info@birchrun.org; www.BirchRun.org*

Birmingham • *Birmingham-Bloomfield C/C* • Joe Bauman; Pres.; 725 S. Adams Rd., Ste. 130; 48009; Oakland; P 75,000; M 650; (248) 644-1700; Fax (248) 644-0286; thechamber@bbcc.com; www.bbcc.com*

Boyne City • *Boyne Area C/C* • Ashley Cousens; Exec. Dir.; 28 S. Lake St.; 49712; Charlevoix; P 3,800; M 350; (231) 582-6222; Fax (231) 582-6963; info@boynechamber.com; www.boynechamber.com

Breckenridge • *see Alma*

Bridgeport • *Bridgeport Area C/C* • Jan Crane; Exec. Secy.; P.O. Box 564; 48722; Saginaw; P 11,000; M 107; (989) 777-1801; Fax (989) 777-2223; execsecbridgeportcoc@yahoo.com; bridgeportchambermi.org

Brighton • *Greater Brighton Area C/C* • Pamela McConeghy IOM; Pres./CEO; 218 E. Grand River; 48116; Livingston; P 150,000; M 950; (810) 227-5086; pamm@brightoncoc.org; www.brightoncoc.org*

Bronson • *see Coldwater*

Brooklyn • *Brooklyn-Irish Hills C/C* • Cindy Hubbell; Exec. Dir.; 124 S. Main St., Ste. A; P.O. Box 805; 49230; Jackson; P 25,000; M 302; (517) 592-8907; Fax (517) 592-8907; info@brooklynmi.com; www.brooklynmi.com*

Bruce Township • *see Romeo*

Buchanan • *Buchanan Area C/C* • Randy Hendrixson; Exec. Dir.; 324 E. Dewey St., Ste. 109; P.O. Box 127; 49107; Berrien; P 5,000; M 200; (269) 695-3291; Fax (269) 695-3813; bacc@buchanan.mi.us; www.buchanan.mi.us

Burr Oak • *see Sturgis*

Cadillac • *Cadillac Area C/C* • William Tencza IOM; Pres.; 222 Lake St.; 49601; Wexford; P 35,000; M 420; (231) 775-9776; Fax (231) 775-1440; info@cadillac.org; www.cadillac.org*

Canton • *Canton C/C* • Thomas Paden; Exec. Dir.; 45525 Hanford Rd.; 48187; Wayne; P 90,200; M 520; (734) 453-4040; Fax (734) 453-4503; tpaden@cantonchamber.com; www.cantonchamber.com*

Capac • *Capac Area C/C* • Samantha Ramirez; Pres.; P.O. Box 386; 48014; St. Clair; P 2,100; M 50; (810) 395-8350; capacchamber@hotmail.com; www.villageofcapac.com

Caro • *Caro C/C* • Brenda Caruthers; Exec. Dir.; 429 N. State St., Ste. 101; 48723; Tuscola; P 4,200; M 200; (989) 673-5211; Fax (989) 673-2517; executivedirector@carochamber.org; www.carochamber.org

Caseville • *Caseville Area C/C* • Debbie Fulgham; Coord.; 6632 Main St.; P.O. Box 122; 48725; Huron; P 2,700; M 170; (989) 856-3818; (800) 606-1347; Fax (989) 856-2596; ccofc@avci.net; www.casevillechamber.com

Cass City • *Cass City C/C* • Carla Cifka; Admin.; 6506 Main St.; 48726; Tuscola; P 6,200; M 120; (989) 872-4618; (989) 551-7274; Fax (989) 872-4855; ccc@casscitychamber.com; www.casscitychamber.com

Cedarville • *Les Cheneaux Islands C/C* • Amy Polk; Coord.; P.O. Box 10; 49719; Mackinac; P 2,200; M 117; (906) 484-3935; (888) 364-7526; Fax (906) 484-9941; lcichamber@lescheneaux.net; www.lescheneaux.net

Center Line • *see Mount Clemens*

Central Lake • *Central Lake Area C/C* • 2587 N. M-88 Hwy.; P.O. Box 428; 49622; Antrim; P 1,000; M 90; (231) 599-3250; clcc@torchlake.com; www.central-lake.com

Charlevoix • *Charlevoix Area C/C* • Alison Hubbard; Pres.; 109 Mason St.; 49720; Charlevoix; P 20,000; M 500; (231) 547-2101; Fax (231) 547-6633; info@charlevoix.org; www.charlevoix.org

Charlotte • *Charlotte C/C* • Grace Boehmer; Exec. Dir.; 126 N. Bostwick St.; P.O. Box 356; 48813; Eaton; P 10,000; M 240; (517) 543-0400; charlottechamberofcommerce@gmail.com; www.micharlotte.org*

Cheboygan • *Cheboygan Area C/C* • Matthew Friday; Mgr.; 124 N. Main St.; 49721; Cheboygan; P 29,000; M 312; (231) 627-7183; (800) 968-3302; Fax (231) 627-2770; info@cheboygan.com; www.cheboygan.com*

Chelsea • *Chelsea Area C/C* • Bob Pierce; Exec. Dir.; 310 N. Main St., Ste. 120; 48118; Washtenaw; P 6,000; M 300; (734) 475-1145; Fax (734) 475-6102; bpierce@chelseamichamber.org; www.chelseamichamber.org*

Chesaning • *Chesaning C/C* • Randy Stoddard; Pres.; 218 N. Front St.; P.O. Box 83; 48616; Saginaw; P 4,900; M 150; (989) 845-3055; Fax (989) 845-6006; info@chesaningchamber.org; www.chesaningchamber.org

Chesterfield Twp • *see Mount Clemens and New Baltimore*

Clare • *Clare Area C/C* • Pam O'Laughlin; Mgr.; 202 W. Fifth St.; 48617; Clare; P 3,050; M 200; (989) 386-2442; Fax (989) 386-3173; manager@claremichigan.com; www.claremichigan.com*

Clarkston • *Clarkston Area C/C* • Janelle Best; Exec. Dir.; 5856 S. Main St.; 48346; Oakland; P 32,000; M 600; (248) 625-8055; Fax (248) 625-8041; info@clarkston.org; www.clarkston.org*

Clarksville • *see Lake Odessa*

Clawson • *Clawson C/C* • Mary L. Sames; Exec. Dir.; 425 N. Main St.; P.O. Box 217; 48017; Oakland; P 12,000; M 200; (248) 435-6500; Fax (248) 435-6868; clawsonchamber@gmail.com; www.clawsonchamber.com*

Clinton Township • *see Mount Clemens*

Clinton Township • *Multicultural C/C* • Dr. Shakil A. Khan; Pres.; 41800 Hayes Rd., Ste. 116; 48038; Macomb; M 50; (586) 573-7300; (248) 822-6000; info@multiculturalchamber.org; www.multiculturalchamber.org

Clio • *Clio Area C/C* • Craig Nelson; Dir.; 192 W. Vienna St.; P.O. Box 543; 48420; Genesee; P 24,000; M 260; (810) 686-4480; Fax (810) 564-0635; info@cliochamber.com; www.cliochamber.com

Coldwater • *Branch County Area C/C* • Jamie Bracy; Exec. Admin.; 20 Division St.; 49036; Branch; P 45,000; M 500; (517) 278-5985; Fax (517) 278-8369; info@branchareachamber.com; www.branchareachamber.com*

Coloma • *Coloma-Watervliet Area C/C* • Chana Kniebes; 142 Badt Dr.; P.O. Box 418; 49038; Berrien; P 12,000; M 149; (269) 468-4430; Fax (269) 468-7088; info@coloma-watervliet.org; www.coloma-watervliet.org*

Commerce Twp. • *see Walled Lake*

Coopersville • *Coopersville Area C/C* • Rose Zainea-Wieten; Exec. Dir.; 289 Danforth St.; 49404; Ottawa; P 4,000; M 250; (616) 997-5164; Fax (616) 997-6679; rwieten@coopersville.com; www.coopersville.com*

Corunna • *see Owosso*

Curtis • *Curtis C/C* • Bud Chamberlin; Pres.; N9687 H33; P.O. Box 477; 49820; Mackinac; P 1,100; M 150; (906) 586-3700; curtiscofc@sbcglobal.net; www.curtischamber.com

Davison • *Davison Area C/C* • LaDawn Hastings; Exec. Dir.; 410 W. Flint Street; 48423; Genesee; P 32,000; M 250; (810) 653-6266; Fax (810) 653-0669; DavisonChamber@gmail.com; www.davisonchamberofcommerce.com*

Dearborn • *Dearborn Area C/C* • Jackie Lovejoy; Pres.; 22100 Michigan Ave.; 48124; Wayne; P 96,500; M 600; (313) 584-6100; Fax (313) 584-9818; info@dearbornareachamber.org; www.dearbornareachamber.org*

Dearborn Heights • *see Dearborn*

Decatur • *Greater Decatur C/C* • David Moormann; Pres.; P.O. Box 211; 49045; Van Buren; P 1,900; M 60; (269) 423-2411; Fax (269) 423-2411; info@decaturmi.org; www.decaturmi.org

Delton • *see Hastings*

Detroit • *Detroit Reg. Chamber* • Sandy K. Baruah; Pres./CEO; One Woodward Ave., Ste. 1900; P.O. Box 33840; 48232; Wayne; P 5,200,000; M 20,000; (313) 964-4000; Fax (313) 964-0183; members@detroitchamber.com; www.detroitchamber.com*

Dexter • *Dexter Area C/C* • Joe Schultz; Pres.; 3074 Baker Rd.; 48130; Washtenaw; P 4,000; M 215; (734) 426-0887; Fax (734) 426-5069; info@dexterchamber.org; www.dexterchamber.org*

Dowagiac • *Greater Dowagiac C/C* • Vickie Phillipson; Prog. Dir.; 200 Depot Dr.; 49047; Cass; P 5,200; M 150; (269) 782-8212; vphillipson@dowagiac.org; www.dowagiacchamber.com

Durand • *Greater Durand Area C/C* • Vicki Fuja; Exec. Dir.; 109 N. Saginaw St.; 48429; Shiawassee; P 4,000; M 116; (989) 288-3715; Fax (989) 288-5177; durandchamberofcommerce@yahoo.com; www.durandchamberofcommerce.com*

East Jordan • *East Jordan Area C/C* • Mary H. Faculak; Pres.; 100 Main St., Ste. B; P.O. Box 137; 49727; Charlevoix; P 3,500; M 290; (231) 536-7351; Fax (231) 536-0966; info@ejchamber.org; www.ejchamber.org*

Eastpointe • *Eastpointe-Roseville C/C* • Linda Weishaupt; Exec. Dir.; 23320 Gratiot Ave.; 48021; Macomb; P 36,000; M 250; (586) 776-5520; Fax (586) 776-7808; director@erchamber.com; erchamber.com*

Eaton Rapids • *Eaton Rapids Area C/C* • Donald Wyckoff; Exec. Dir.; Union Street Center; P.O. Box 420; 48827; Eaton; P 5,330; M 85; (517) 663-6480; info@eatonrapidschamber.com; www.eatonrapidschamber.com

Eau Claire • *see Benton Harbor*

Edmore • *Edmore Area C/C* • Rich Adgate; Pres.; P.O. Box 102; 48829; Montcalm; P 1,300; M 60; (989) 506-1402; edmore@edmorechamber.com; www.edmorechamber.com

Edwardsburg • *Edwardsburg Area C/C* • Karen Sinkiewicz; Admin.; 26225 U.S. 12; P.O. Box 575; 49112; Cass; P 5,200; M 70; (574) 343-3721; (269) 663-2244; administration@edwardsburg.biz; www.edwardsburg.biz

Elk Rapids • *Elk Rapids Area C/C* • Tom Kern; Exec. Dir.; 305 U.S. - 31 N.; P.O. Box 854; 49629; Antrim; P 2,500; M 260; (231) 264-8202;; Fax (231) 264-6591; info@elkrapidschamber.org; www.elkrapidschamber.org

Elwell • *see Alma*

Escanaba • *Delta County Area C/C* • Vickie Micheau; Dir.; 230 Ludington St.; 49829; Delta; P 37,780; M 700; (906) 786-2192; (888) DELTA-MI; Fax (906) 786-8830; info@deltami.org; www.deltami.org*

Evart • *Evart Area C/C* • Jan Booher; Secy.; P.O. Box 688; 49631; Osceola; P 1,745; M 75; (231) 734-9799; Fax (231) 734-9799; jabooher102@yahoo.com; www.evart.org

Fair Haven • *see Algonac*

Farmington Hills • *Greater Farmington Area C/C •* Dan Irvin; Exec. Dir.; 33425 Grand River Ave., Ste. 101; 48335; Oakland; P 80,000; M 600; (248) 919-6917; Fax (248) 919-6921; info@gfachamber.com; www.gfachamber.com*

Farwell • *Farwell Area C/C •* Mike Fetzer; Chrmn. of the Bd.; 221 W. Main; P.O. Box 771; 48622; Clare; P 4,000; M 95; (989) 588-0580; Fax (989) 588-0580; facc@farwellareachamber.com; www.farwellareachamber.com

Fennville • *Greater Fennville C/C •* Erica Ramos; Pres.; P.O. Box 484; 49408; Allegan; P 1,500; M 91; (269) 639-9533; treasurer@greaterfennville.com; www.greaterfennville.com

Fenton • *Fenton Reg. C/C •* Shelly Day; Exec. Dir.; 104 S. Adelaide St.; 48430; Genesee; P 33,000; M 490; (810) 629-5447; Fax (810) 629-6608; info@fentonchamber.com; www.fentonchamber.com*

Ferndale • *Ferndale Area C/C •* Ashleigh Laabs; Exec. Dir.; 407 E. Nine Mile Rd.; 48220; Oakland; P 20,000; M 275; (248) 542-2160; Fax (248) 542-8979; info@ferndalechamber.com; www.ferndaleareachamber.com

Ferrysburg • *see Grand Haven*

Fife Lake • *Fife Lake C/C •* Bob Sturdavant; Pres.; P.O. Box 283; 49633; Grand Traverse; P 468; M 40; (231) 577-1737; president@fifelakechamber.com; www.fifelakechamber.com

Flint • *Flint & Genesee C/C •* Tim Herman; CEO; 519 S. Saginaw St., Ste. 200; 48502; Genesee; P 425,800; M 1,100; (810) 600-1404; Fax (810) 600-1461; info@flintandgenesee.org; www.flintandgenesee.org*

Flushing • *Flushing Area C/C •* Susan Little; Exec. Dir.; 309 E. Main St.; P.O. Box 44; 48433; Genesee; P 32,000; M 250; (810) 659-4141; Fax (810) 659-6964; info@flushingchamber.com; www.flushingchamber.com*

Frankenmuth • *Frankenmuth C/C •* Jamie Furbush; Pres./CEO; 635 S. Main St.; 48734; Saginaw; P 4,400; M 401; (989) 652-6106; (800) 386-8696; Fax (989) 652-3841; chamber@frankenmuth.org; www.frankenmuth.org*

Frankfort • *Frankfort-Elberta Area C/C •* Joanne Bartley; Exec. Dir.; 517 Main St.; P.O. Box 566; 49635; Benzie; P 1,401; M 210; (231) 352-7251; Fax (231) 352-6750; fcofc@frankfort-elberta.com; www.frankfort-elberta.com

Fraser • *see Mount Clemens*

Freeport • *see Hastings & Lake Odessa*

Fremont • *Fremont Area C/C •* Karen Baird; Exec. Dir.; 7 E. Main St.; 49412; Newaygo; P 12,000; M 300; (231) 924-0770; Fax (231) 924-9248; info@fremontcommerce.com; www.fremontcommerce.com*

Garden City • *see Westland*

Gaylord • *Gaylord Area C/C •* Paul Beachnau; Exec. Dir.; 101 W. Main St.; P.O. Box 513; 49734; Otsego; P 26,000; M 500; (989) 732-6333; Fax (989) 732-7990; info@gaylordchamber.com; www.gaylordchamber.com*

Gladwin • *Gladwin County C/C •* Tom Tucholski; Exec. Dir.; 608 W. Cedar Ave.; P.O. Box 209; 48624; Gladwin; P 25,692; M 168; (989) 426-5451; chamber@ejourney.com; www.gladwincountychamber.com

Glen Arbor • *Glen Lake C/C •* Raquel Jackson; Mktg. Dir.; P.O. Box 217; 49636; Leelanau; P 1,200; M 145; (231) 334-3238; Fax (231) 334-3238; info@visitglenarbor.com; www.visitglenarbor.com

Grand Beach • *see New Buffalo*

Grand Blanc • *Grand Blanc C/C •* Jet Kilmer; Pres.; 512 E. Grand Blanc Rd.; 48439; Genesee; P 45,000; M 450; (810) 695-4222; Fax (810) 695-0053; gbcc@grandblancchamber.com; www.grandblancchamber.com*

Grand Haven • *The Chamber-Grand Haven, Spring Lake, Ferrysburg •* Joy A. Gaasch; Pres.; One S. Harbor Dr.; 49417; Ottawa; P 49,000; M 700; (616) 842-4910; Fax (616) 842-0379; areainfo@grandhavenchamber.org; www.grandhavenchamber.org*

Grand Ledge • *Grand Ledge Area C/C •* Jill Russell; Exec. Dir.; 220 S. Bridge St.; 48837; Eaton; P 8,000; M 130; (517) 627-2383; glaccgl@gmail.com; www.grandledgechambercom

Grand Marais • *Grand Marais C/C •* Aleta Hubbard; Pres.; P.O. Box 139; 49839; Elger; P 400; M 36; (906) 494-2447; president@grandmaraismichigan.com; www.grandmaraismichigan.com

Grand Rapids • *Grand Rapids Area C/C •* Rick Baker; Pres./CEO; 111 Pearl St. N.W.; 49503; Kent; P 547,000; M 2,800; (616) 771-0300; Fax (616) 771-0318; info@grandrapids.org; www.grandrapids.org*

Grandville • *Grandville-Jenison C/C •* Sandy LeBlanc; Exec. Dir.; 2939 Wilson, Ste. 106; 49418; Kent & Ottawa; P 63,000; M 500; (616) 531-8890; Fax (616) 531-8896; sandy@grandjen.com; www.grandvillejenisonchamber.com*

Grayling • *Grayling Reg. C/C •* Traci Cook; Exec. Dir.; 213 N. James St.; P.O. Box 406; 49738; Crawford; P 17,000; M 225; (989) 348-2921; Fax (989) 348-7315; executivedirector@graylingchamber.com; www.graylingchamber.com*

Greenbush • *Greenbush C/C •* Nebbie Kushmaul; Dir.; 4115 S. U.S. 23; 48738; Alcona; P 1,373; M 200; (989) 739-7635; (989) 739-9812

Greenville • *Greenville Area C/C •* Candy Kerschen; Exec. Dir.; 210 S. Lafayette St.; 48838; Montcalm; P 12,000; M 300; (616) 754-5697; Fax (616) 754-4710; info@greenvillechamber.net; www.greenvillechamber.net

Grosse Pointe • *see Mount Clemens*

Grosse Pointe Farms • *Grosse Pointe C/C •* Jennifer Palms Boettcher; Pres./CEO; 63 Kercheval, Ste. 16; 48236; Wayne; P 40,000; M 650; (313) 881-4722; Fax (313) 881-4723; info@grossepointechamber.com; www.grossepointechamber.com

Gwinn • *Gwinn-Sawyer Area C/C •* Jeanette Maki; Pres.; 248 Wellington Dr.; 49841; Marquette; P 8,000; M 145; (906) 346-9666; (888) 346-4946; Fax (906) 346-9695; gccdir@gwinnmi.com; www.gwinnmi.com

Hamburg • *see Brighton*

Harbert • *see New Buffalo*

Harbor Beach • *Harbor Beach C/C •* Julie Purdy; Pres.; P.O. Box 113; 48441; Huron; P 1,700; M 100; (989) 479-6477; (800) HB-MICH-5; Fax (989) 479-6477; visitor@harborbeachchamber.com; www.harborbeachchamber.com

Harbor Springs • *Harbor Springs Area C/C •* Daniel DeWindt; Exec. Dir.; 368 E. Main St.; 49740; Emmet; P 1,100; M 400; (231) 526-7999; Fax (231) 526-5593; info@harborspringschamber.com; www.harborspringschamber.com*

Harper Woods • *see Mount Clemens*

Harrison • *Harrison C/C* • Michelle Grant; Pres.; 809 N. First St.; P.O. Box 682; 48625; Clare; P 2,114; M 170; (989) 539-6011; (989) 630-8311; Fax (989) 539-6099; harrisonchamber@sbcglobal.net; www.harrisonchamber.com

Harrison Twp • *see Mount Clemens*

Harrisville • *Alcona County C/C* • Judie Labadie; Pres.; 410 E. Main St.; P.O. Box 581; 48740; Alcona; P 11,000; M 120; (989) 724-5107; (800) 432-2823; Fax (989) 724-6656; alconacountychamber@gmail.com; www.alconacountychamberofcommerce.com

Harsens Island • *see Algonac*

Hart • *Silver Lake Sand Dunes Area C/C* • Lisa Fleury; 2388 N. Comfort Dr.; 49420; Oceana; P 10,000; M 190; (231) 873-2247; (231) 873-1683; director@thinkdunes.com; www.thinkdunes.com*

Hartland • *Hartland Area C/C* • Katie Chuba; Exec. Dir.; 3508 Avon St.; P.O. Box 427; 48353; Livingston; P 14,588; M 195; (810) 632-9130; Fax (866) 970-4508; info@hartlandchamber.org; www.hartlandchamber.org*

Hastings • *Barry County C/C* • David Hatfield; Interim Pres.; 221 W. State St.; 49058; Barry; P 59,000; M 438; (269) 945-2454; Fax (269) 945-3839; dave@mibarry.com; www.mibarry.com*

Hazel Park • *see Madison Heights*

Hesperia • *Hesperia Area C/C* • Rick Roberson; Pres.; P.O. Box 32; 49421; Oceana; P 900; M 70; (231) 854-3695; jean@hesperiachamberofcommerce.org; www.hesperiachamberofcommerce.org

Hessel • *see Cedarville*

Highland • *see Milford*

Hillman • *Hillman Area C/C* • James Stoddard; Pres.; P.O. Box 506; 49746; Alpena & Montmorency; P 3,000; M 120; (989) 742-3739; hillmanchamber.org

Hillsdale • *Hillsdale County C/C* • Christine Bowman; Exec. Dir.; 44 N. Howell St.; P.O. Box 842; 49242; Hillsdale; P 46,000; M 300; (517) 439-4341; Fax (517) 439-4111; info@hillsdalecountychamber.com; www.hillsdalecountychamber.com*

Holland • *Michigan West Coast C/C* • Jane Clark; Pres.; 272 E. 8th St.; 49423; Ottawa; P 100,000; M 1,200; (616) 392-2389; Fax (616) 392-7379; info@westcoastchamber.org; www.westcoastchamber.org*

Holly • *Holly Area C/C* • Andrea Silvis; Exec. Dir.; 300 East St.; 48442; Oakland; P 6,000; M 80; (248) 215-7099; thehollychamber@gmail.com; www.hollychamber.com*

Houghton • *Keweenaw C/C* • Cheryl Fahrner; Exec. Dir.; 902 College Ave.; P.O. Box 336; 49931; Houghton; P 38,000; M 450; (906) 482-5240; (866) 304-5722; Fax (906) 482-5241; info@keweenaw.org; www.keweenaw.org*

Houghton Lake • *Houghton Lake C/C* • Linda Tuck; Exec. Dir.; 1625 W. Houghton Lake Dr.; 48629; Roscommon; M 150; (989) 366-5644; (800) 248-5253; Fax (989) 366-9472; hlcc@houghtonlakechamber.org; www.houghtonlakechamber.net

Howard City • *Montcalm County Panhandle Area C/C* • Marianne VanBennekom; Exec. Dir.; P.O. Box 474; 49329; Montcalm; P 10,000; M 110; (231) 937-5681; panhandlechamber@hotmail.com; www.panhandlechamber.com

Howell • *Howell Area C/C* • Pat Convery; Pres.; 123 E. Washington St.; 48843; Livingston; P 40,000; M 674; (517) 546-3920; Fax (517) 546-4115; chamber@howell.org; howell.org*

Hudson • *Hudson Area C/C* • Joann Crater; Pres.; P.O. Box 45; 49247; Lenawee; P 2,300; M 40; (517) 448-3801; Fax (517) 448-5095; hudsonchamber@gmail.com; www.hudsonmich.com

Hudsonville • *Hudsonville Area C/C* • Michelle Fare; Exec. Dir.; 3275 Central Blvd.; 49426; Ottawa; P 8,000; M 160; (616) 662-0900; Fax (616) 669-2330; director@hudsonvillechamber.com; www.hudsonvillechamber.com*

Imlay City • *Imlay City Area C/C* • Ann Hintz; Exec. Dir.; 150 N. Main St.; 48444; Lapeer; P 4,000; M 140; (810) 724-1361; Fax (810) 724-8821; executivedirector@imlaycitymich.com; www.imlaycitymich.com

Indian River • *Indian River Resort Reg. C/C* • Dawn Bodnar; Exec. Dir.; 3435 S. Straits Hwy.; P.O. Box 57; 49749; Cheboygan; P 4,500; M 300; (231) 238-9325; (800) EXIT-310; Fax (231) 238-0949; info@irchamber.com; www.irchamber.com*

Interlochen • *Interlochen Area C/C* • Tom Ingold; Pres.; 2120 M-137 S.; P.O. Box 13; 49643; Grand Traverse; P 3,200; M 90; (231) 276-7141; interlochenchamber@juno.com; www.interlochenchamber.org

Ionia • *Ionia Area C/C* • Tina Conner Wellman; Exec. Dir.; 439 W. Main St.; 48846; Ionia; P 10,500; M 300; (616) 527-2560; Fax (616) 527-0894; info@ioniachamber.net; www.ioniachamber.org*

Ira Twp • *see New Baltimore*

Iron Mountain • *Dickinson Area Chamber Alliance* • Lynda Zanon; Chamber Dir.; 600 S. Stephenson Ave.; 49801; Dickinson; P 26,100; M 395; (906) 774-2002; (906) 828-3389; Fax (906) 774-2004; lzanon@dickinsonchamber.com; www.dickinsonchamber.com*

Iron River • *Iron County Eco. Chamber Alliance* • Erika Lindwall; Chamber Dir.; 50 E. Genesee St.; 49935; Iron; P 3,000; M 230; (906) 265-3822; (888)879-4766; Fax (906) 265-5605; info@iron.org; www.iron.org

Ironwood • *Ironwood Area C/C* • Peter J. Grewe; Pres.; P.O. Box 45; 49938; Gogebic; P 5,500; M 130; (906) 932-1122; Fax (906) 932-2756; chamber@ironwoodchamber.org; www.ironwoodchamber.org

Ithaca • *see Alma*

Jackson • *Jackson County C/C* • Mindy Bradish-Orta; Pres./Exec. Dir.; 141 S. Jackson St.; 49201; Jackson; P 162,400; M 725; (517) 782-8221; Fax (517) 780-3688; mindy@jacksonchamber.org; www.jacksonchamber.org*

Jenison • *see Grandville*

Kalamazoo • *Southwest Michigan First* • Keith Kehlbeck; Pres.; 241 E. Michigan Ave.; P.O. Box 50827; 49005; Kalamazoo; P 241,000; M 500; (269) 553-9588; Fax (269) 553-6897; kkehlbeck@southwestmichiganfirst.com; www.southwestmichiganfirst.com*

Kalkaska • *see Traverse City*

Kentwood • *see Wyoming*

L'Anse • *Baraga County C/C* • Debbie Stouffer; V.P.; P.O. Box 122; 49946; Baraga; P 7,500; M 97; (906) 353-8808; baragacountychamber@gmail.com; www.baragacounty.org

Lake City • *Lake City Area C/C* • Kim Mosher; Admin. Asst.; 107 S. Main St.; P.O. Box H; 49651; Missaukee; P 14,000; M 209; (231) 839-4969; Fax (231) 839-5991; lakecitymich@centurylink.net; www.lakecitymich.com*

Lake Odessa • *Lakewood Area C/C* • Marnie Thomas; Exec. Dir.; Page Memorial Bldg.; 839 4th Ave.; 48849; Berry, Eaton & Ionia; P 2,300; M 72; (616) 374-0766; director@lakewoodareacoc.org; www.lakewoodareacoc.org

Lake Orion • *Orion Area C/C* • Alaina Campbell; Exec. Dir.; P.O. Box 484; 48361; Oakland; P 33,000; M 350; (248) 693-6300; Fax (248) 693-9227; info@orionareachamber.com; www.orionareachamber.com*

Lakeland • *see Brighton*

Lakeside • *see New Buffalo*

Lansing • *Lansing Reg. C/C* • Tim Daman; Pres./CEO; 500 E. Michigan Ave., Ste. 200; 48912; Clinton, Eaton & Ingham; P 447,728; M 1,275; (517) 487-6340; Fax (517) 484-6910; tdaman@lansingchamber.org; www.lansingchamber.org*

Lapeer • *Lapeer Area C/C* • Neda Payne; Exec. Dir.; 108 W. Park St.; 48446; Lapeer; P 90,000; M 400; (810) 664-6641; (810) 441-1491; Fax (810) 664-4349; neda@lapeerareachamber.org; www.lapeerareachamber.org*

Leelanau Peninsula • *see Suttons Bay*

Lenox Twp • *see New Baltimore*

Les Cheneaux • *see Cedarville*

Leslie • *Leslie Area C/C* • Ted Urban; Pres.; P.O. Box 214; 49251; Ingham; P 1,900; M 125; (517) 589-5078; (517) 589-8236; leslieareachamber@gmail.com; www.leslieareachamber.com

Lewiston • *Lewiston Area C/C* • Elaine Dixon; Chrmn. of the Bd.; 2946 Kneeland St.; P.O. Box 656; 49756; Montmorency; P 4,000; M 180; (989) 786-2293; Fax (989) 786-4515; lewistonchamber@i2k.com; www.lewistonchamber.com

Lexington • *Greater Croswell-Lexington C/C* • Jane Lehman; Pres.; P.O. Box 142; 48450; Sanilac; P 6,500; M 170; (810) 359-2262; croslex@greatlakes.net; www.cros-lex-chamber.com

Lincoln Park • *Lincoln Park C/C* • Karen Maniaci; Exec. Dir.; 1650 Champaign; P.O. Box 382; 48146; Wayne; P 39,000; M 100; (313) 386-0140; Fax (313) 386-0140; info@lpchamber.org; www.lpchamber.org

Linden • *see Fenton*

Linwood • *see Pinconning*

Litchfield • *Litchfield C/C* • P.O. Box 236; 49252; Hillsdale; P 1,483; M 50; (517) 542-2921; Fax (517) 542-2491; clerk@cityoflitchfield.org; www.cityoflitchfield.org

Livonia • *Livonia C/C* • Dan West; Pres.; 33233 Five Mile Rd.; 48154; Wayne; P 97,000; M 880; (734) 427-2122; Fax (734) 427-6055; dwest@livonia.org; www.livonia.org*

Lowell • *Lowell Area C/C* • Liz Baker; Exec. Dir.; 113 Riverwalk Plaza; P.O. Box 224; 49331; Kent; P 4,000; M 342; (616) 897-9161; Fax (616) 897-9101; info@lowellchamber.org; www.discoverlowell.org*

Ludington • *Ludington & Scottville Area C/C* • Kathryn Maclean; Pres./CEO; 5300 W. U.S. 10; 49431; Mason; P 30,000; M 450; (231) 845-0324; Fax (231) 845-6857; chamberinfo@ludington.org; www.ludington.org

Mackinaw City • *Mackinaw City C/C* • Kelly Vieau; Admin.; 580 S. Nicolet St., 2nd Flr.; P.O. Box 856; 49701; Cheboygan & Emmet; P 850; M 206; (231) 436-5574; (888) 455-8100; info@mackinawchamber.com; www.mackinawchamber.com*

Macomb Twp • *see Mount Clemens*

Madison Heights • *Madison Heights-Hazel Park C/C* • Keri Valmassei; Exec. Dir.; 939 E. 12 Mile Rd.; 48071; Oakland; P 47,700; M 300; (248) 542-5010; Fax (248) 542-6821; intern@madisonheightschamber.com; www.madisonheightschamber.com*

Mancelona • *Mancelona Area C/C* • Joanie Moore; Exec. Dir.; P.O. Box 558; 49659; Antrim; P 1,400; M 100; (231) 587-5500; mancelonachamber.org

Manchester • *Manchester Area C/C* • Janet Larson; Pres.; P.O. Box 521; 48158; Washtenaw; P 2,000; M 116; (734) 476-4565; president@manchestermi.org; www.manchestermi.org

Manistee • *Manistee Area C/C* • Stacie Bytwork; Exec. Dir.; 11 Cypress St.; 49660; Manistee; P 24,450; M 350; (231) 723-2575; (800) 288-2286; Fax (231) 723-1515; contact@manisteechamber.com; www.manisteechamber.com*

Manistique • *Schoolcraft County C/C* • Connie Diller; Exec. Dir.; 1000 W. Lakeshore Dr.; P.O. Box 301; 49854; Schoolcraft; P 8,576; M 247; (906) 341-5010; (888) 819-7420; Fax (906) 341-1549; cadillerchamber@hotmail.com; www.schoolcraftcountychamber.org*

Manton • *Manton C/C* • Chuck Brandt; Pres.; P.O. Box 313; 49663; Wexford; P 1,300; M 115; (231) 824-4158; Fax (231) 824-3664; info@mantonmichigan.org; www.mantonmichigan.org

Maple Valley • *see Howard City*

Marine City • *Marine City Area C/C* • Erika DeLange; Exec. Dir.; 201-A Broadway; 48039; St. Clair; P 4,500; M 141; (810) 765-4501; chamber@visitmarinecity.com; www.visitmarinecity.com

Marion • *Marion Area C/C* • Anndrea McCrimmon; Pres.; P.O. Box 294; 49665; Osceola; P 816; M 40; (231) 743-2461; Fax (231) 743-2461; chambermarionmi@gmail.com; www.marionmichigan.com

Marlette • *Marlette Area C/C* • Sarah Kady; Secy./Treas.; P.O. Box 222; 48453; Sanilac; P 1,875; M 70; (989) 635-7448; cityofmarlette.com

Marquette • *Marquette Area C/C-Lake Superior Comm. Partnership* • Amy Clickner; CEO; 501 S. Front St.; 49855; Marquette; P 311,361; M 900; (906) 226-6591; (888) 57-UNITY; Fax (906) 226-2099; lscp@marquette.org; www.marquette.org

Marshall • *Marshall Area C/C* • Monica Anderson; Pres./CEO; 424 E. Michigan Ave.; 49068; Calhoun; P 15,000; M 350; (269) 781-5163; (800) 877-5163; Fax (269) 781-6570; info@marshallmi.org; www.marshallmi.org*

Marysville • *see Port Huron*

Mason • *Mason Area C/C* • Douglas J. Klein APR CTA; Exec. Dir.; 148 E. Ash St.; 48854; Ingham; P 15,000; M 300; (517) 676-1046; (517) 676-4816; Fax (517) 676-8504; masonchamber@masonchamber.org; www.masonchamber.org*

Mears • *see Hart*

Memphis • *Memphis C/C* • Rodona Soles; Secy.; P.O. Box 41006; 48041; Macomb & St. Clair; P 1,200; M 20; (586) 295-3157; (810) 531-7376; www.memphischamber.webs.com

Menominee • *see Marinette, WI*

Metamora • *Metamora Area C/C* • Wes Wickham; Pres.; P.O. Box 16; 48455; Lapeer; P 600; M 90; (810) 678-6222; info@metamorachamber.org; www.metamorachamber.org

Michiana • *see New Buffalo*

Middleton • *see Alma*

Middleville • *see Hastings*

Midland • *Midland Area C/C* • Bill Allen; Pres./CEO; 300 Rodd St., Ste. 101; 48640; Midland; P 80,000; M 950; (989) 839-9901; Fax (989) 835-3701; chamber@macc.org; www.macc.org*

Milan • *Milan Area C/C* • Carrie Ritchie; Pres.; 153 E. Main; P.O. Box 164; 48160; Monroe & Washtenaw; P 5,700; M 137; (734) 439-7932; Fax (734) 241-3520; info@milanchamber.org; www.milanchamber.org

Milford • *Huron Valley C/C* • Joell Beether; Exec. Dir.; 317 Union St., Ste. F; 48381; Oakland; P 60,000; M 415; (248) 685-7129; Fax (248) 685-9047; info@huronvcc.com; www.huronvcc.com*

Mio • *C/C for Oscoda County* • Ann Galbraith; 201 Morenci Ave.; P.O. Box 670; 48647; Oscoda; P 9,000; M 160; (989) 826-3331; (800) 800-6133; chamber@oscodacountymi.org; oscodacountymi.org

Monroe • *Monroe County C/C* • Michelle Dugan; Exec. Dir.; P.O. Box 626; 48161; Monroe; P 150,000; M 364; (734) 384-3366; Fax (734) 384-3367; chamber@monroecountychamber.com; www.monroecountychamber.com*

Montague • *see Whitehall*

Montrose • *Montrose Area C/C* • 48457; Genesee; P 8,400; M 20; (810) 639-6168; info@montrosemichamber.com; www.cityofmontrose.us

Mount Clemens • *Macomb County Chamber* • Grace M. Shore; CEO; 28 First St., Ste. B; 48043; Macomb; P 865,000; M 1,000; (586) 493-7600; Fax (586) 493-7602; charnita@macombcountychamber.com; www.macombcountychamber.com*

Mount Pleasant • *Mt. Pleasant Area C/C* • Bret Hyble; Pres./CEO; 113 W. Broadway St., Ste. 180; 48858; Isabella; P 26,111; M 500; (989) 772-2396; Fax (989) 773-2656; chamber@mt-pleasant.net; www.mt-pleasant.net*

Munising • *Alger County C/C* • Katherine A. Reynolds; Exec. Dir.; 129 E. Munising Ave.; 49862; Alger; P 9,600; M 200; (906) 387-2138; Fax (906) 387-1858; info@algercounty.org; www.algercounty.org

Muskegon • *Muskegon Lakeshore C/C* • Cindy Larsen; Pres.; 380 W. Western Ave., Ste. 202; 49440; Muskegon; P 173,000; M 1,150; (231) 722-3751; Fax (231) 728-7251; mlcc@muskegon.org; www.muskegon.org*

Napoleon • *Napoleon C/C* • P.O. Box 224; 49261; Jackson; P 1,300; M 46; (517) 536-0547; info@napoleonmichigan.com; www.napoleonmichigan.com

Nashville • *see Hastings*

New Baltimore • *also see Mount Clemens*

New Baltimore • *Anchor Bay C/C* • Brian Powers; Chrmn. of the Bd.; 51180 Bedford St.; 48047; Macomb; P 45,000; M 200; (586) 725-5148; Fax (708) 778-6011; anchorbaychamber@yahoo.com; www.anchorbaychamber.com*

New Haven • *see New Baltimore*

New Haven Center • *see Alma*

Newaygo • *River Country C/C of Newaygo County* • Colleen Lynema; Exec. Dir.; 1 State Rd.; P.O. Box 181; 49337; Newaygo; P 16,500; M 126; (231) 652-3068; Fax (231) 652-9489; info@rivercountrychamber.com; www.rivercountrychamber.com

Newberry • *Newberry Area C/C* • Jomay Bomber; Dir.; 4947 E. County Rd. 460; P.O. Box 308; 49868; Luce; P 8,000; M 130; (906) 293-5562; Fax (906) 293-5739; newberry@lighthouse.net; www.newberrychamber.net

Niles • *Four Flags Area C/C Inc.* • Tyanna Weller; Pres./CEO; 321 E. Main St.; P.O. Box 10; 49120; Berrien; P 37,200; M 500; (269) 683-3720; Fax (269) 683-3722; chamber@nilesmi.com; www.nilesmi.com*

Northstar • *see Alma*

Northville • *Northville C/C* • Jody Humphries; Exec. Dir.; 195 S. Main St.; 48167; Oakland & Wayne; P 32,000; M 360; (248) 349-7640; Fax (248) 349-8730; tracisincock@northville.org; www.northville.org*

Novi • *Novi C/C* • Sheryl Romzek; Exec. Dir.; 41875 W. 11 Mile Rd., Ste. 201; 48375; Oakland; P 55,200; M 550; (248) 349-3743; Fax (248) 349-9719; info@novichamber.com; www.novichamber.com*

Oakland County • *see Detroit*

Onaway • *Onaway Area C/C* • Carol Northcott; Exec. Dir.; 20774 State St.; 49765; Presque Isle; P 900; M 100; (989) 733-2874; (800) 711-3685; Fax (989) 733-2874; info@onawaychamber.com; www.onawaychamber.com

Ontonagon • *Ontonagon County C/C* • Dave Bishop; Pres.; P.O. Box 266; 49953; Ontonagon; P 7,918; M 100; (906) 884-4735; ontcofc@up.net; www.ontonagonmi.org

Ortonville • *Greater Ortonville Area C/C* • Jennifer Whitwell; Ofc. Mgr.; P.O. Box 152; 48462; Oakland; P 13,000; M 84; (248) 627-8079; Fax (248) 627-8079; bjwhitwell@juno.com; www.ortonvillechamber.com

Oscoda • *Oscoda-Au Sable C/C* • Leisa Sutton; Exec. Dir.; 4440 N. U.S. 23; 48750; Iosco; P 9,000; M 234; (989) 739-7322; (800) 235-4625; Fax (989) 739-9195; director@oscodachamber.com; www.oscodachamber.com

Otsego • *Otsego C/C* • Misty Bottorff; Exec. Dir.; 135 E. Allegan St.; 49078; Allegan; P 4,000; M 110; (269) 694-6880; info@otsegochamber.org; www.otsegochamber.org

Owosso • *Shiawassee Reg. C/C* • Jeff Deason; Pres./CEO; 215 N. Water St.; 48867; Shiawassee; P 71,000; M 600; (989) 723-5149; Fax (989) 723-8353; customerservice@shiawasseechamber.org; www.shiawasseechamber.org*

Oxford • *Oxford Area C/C* • Holly Bills; Exec. Dir.; P.O. Box 142; 48371; Oakland; P 20,500; M 210; (248) 628-0410; Fax (248) 628-0430; info@oxfordchamberofcommerce.com; www.oxfordchamber.net

Paradise • *Paradise C/C* • P.O. Box 82; 49768; Chippewa; P 1,000; M 50; (906) 492-3219; paradisecoc@jamadots.com; www.paradisemichigan.org

Paw Paw • *Greater Paw Paw Area C/C* • Mary E. H. Springer; Exec. Dir.; 129 S. Kalamazoo St.; 49079; Van Buren; P 7,174; M 245; (269) 657-5395; Fax (269) 655-8755; ppccdda@btc-bci.com; www.pawpawchamber.com*

Pearl Beach • *see Algonac*

Pentwater • *Pentwater C/C* • Eva Gregwer; Exec. Dir.; 324 S. Hancock St.; P.O. Box 614; 49449; Oceana; P 1,300; M 225; (231) 869-4150; travelinfo@pentwater.org; www.pentwater.org

Perrinton • *see Alma*

Petoskey • *Petoskey Reg. C/C* • Carlin Smith; Pres.; 401 E. Mitchell St.; 49770; Emmet; P 35,000; M 780; (231) 347-4150; Fax (231) 348-1810; chamber@petoskey.com; www.petoskey.com

Pierson • *see Howard City*

Pigeon • *Pigeon C/C* • Jodi Hurren; Pres.; P.O. Box 618; 48755; Huron; P 1,200; M 100; (989) 453-7400; pgncofc@avci.net; www.pigeonchamber.com

Pinckney • *see Brighton*

Pinconning • *Pinconning & Linwood Area C/C* • Ellen Charlebois; Pres.; 200 N. Mable St.; P.O. Box 856; 48650; Bay; P 5,000; M 125; (989) 879-2816; chamber@pinconninglinwood.com; www.pinconninglinwood.com

Plymouth • *Plymouth Comm. C/C* • G. Wesley Graff; Pres.; 850 W. Ann Arbor Trl.; 48170; Wayne; P 38,000; M 750; (734) 453-1540; Fax (734) 453-1724; chamber@plymouthmich.org; www.plymouthmich.org*

Pontiac • *Pontiac Reg. Chamber* • Dawnaree Demrose; Pres.; 402 N. Telegraph Rd.; 48341; Oakland; P 71,000; M 400; (248) 335-9600; Fax (248) 335-9601; info@pontiacchamber.com; www.pontiacchamber.com

Port Austin • *Greater Port Austin Area C/C* • Joyce Stanek; Exec. Dir.; 2 W. Spring St.; P.O. Box 274; 48467; Huron; P 1,747; M 110; (989) 738-7600; pacofc@airadvantage.net; www.portaustinarea.com

Port Huron • *Blue Water Area C/C* • Thelma Castillo; Pres./CEO; 512 McMorran Blvd.; 48060; St. Clair; P 162,000; M 480; (810) 985-7101; (800) 361-0526; Fax (810) 985-7311; info@bluewaterchamber.com; www.bluewaterchamber.com*

Portland • *Portland Area C/C* • Lynne Paradiso; Pres.; P.O. Box 303; 48875; Ionia; P 4,000; M 100; (517) 647-2100; Fax (517) 647-2100; info@portlandareachamber.com; www.portlandareachamber.com

Potterville • *Potterville Area Chamber of Businesses* • P.O. Box 76; 48876; Eaton; P 2,300; M 40; (517) 645-2313; Fax (517) 645-7889; info@gizzardfest.com; www.pottervillechamber.org

Quincy • *Quincy C/C* • P.O. Box 132; 49082; Branch; P 4,411; M 65; (517) 639-8369; info@branchareachamber.com; www.branchareachamber.com

Ravenna • *Ravenna C/C* • Larry D. Gardiner; Pres.; P.O. Box 332; 49451; Muskegon; P 1,800; M 50; (231) 853-2360; www.ravennami.com

Ray Township • *see Romeo*

Redford • *Redford Twp. C/C* • Marti Swek; Exec. Dir.; 26050 Five Mile; 48239; Wayne; P 51,622; M 325; (313) 535-0960; (313) 535-0974; Fax (313) 535-6356; marti@redfordchamber.org; www.redfordchamber.org*

Reed City • *Reed City Area C/C* • Suzie Williams; Exec. Dir.; 200 N. Chestnut; P.O. Box 27; 49677; Osceola; P 2,400; M 250; (231) 832-5431; (877) 832-7332; Fax (231) 832-5431; suzie@reedcity.org; www.reedcity.org*

Reese • *Reese Area C/C* • Kay Bierlein; Acting Secy.; P.O. Box 113; 48757; Tuscola; P 1,400; M 65; (989) 868-4291; Fax (989) 868-4407; kabierlein@gmail.com; www.villageofreese.net

Reynolds • *see Howard City*

Richmond • *Richmond Area C/C* • 68371 Oak St.; 48062; Macomb; P 25,000; M 164; (586) 727-3266; Fax (586) 727-3635; executive@robn.org; www.robn.org

Riverdale • *see Alma*

Rochester • *Rochester Reg. C/C* • Sheri L. Heiney; Pres.; 71 Walnut Blvd., Ste. 110; 48307; Oakland; P 100,000; M 1,200; (248) 651-6700; Fax (248) 651-5270; info@rrc-mi.com; www.rrc-mi.com*

Rockford • *Rockford C/C* • Linda Southwick; Exec. Dir.; 17 S. Monroe St.; P.O. Box 520; 49341; Kent; P 30,000; M 295; (616) 866-2000; Fax (616) 866-2141; execdir@rockfordmichamber.com; www.rockfordmichamber.com*

Rogers City • *Rogers City Area C/C* • Alexa Donakowski; Exec. Dir.; 292 S. Bradley Hwy.; 49779; Presque Isle; P 2,800; M 205; (989) 734-2535; Fax (989) 734-4656; alexa@rogerscityareachamber.com; www.rogerscityareachamber.com*

Romeo • *Greater Romeo-Washington C/C* • Kelley Stephens; Exec. Dir.; 228 N. Main, Ste. D; P.O. Box 175; 48065; Macomb; P 42,000; M 300; (586) 752-4436; Fax (586) 752-2835; contact@rwchamber.com; www.rwchamber.com*

Romulus • *Greater Romulus C/C* • Betsey J. Krampitz; Exec. Dir.; 11189 Shook St., Ste. 200; 48174; Wayne; P 24,000; M 190; (734) 893-0695; Fax (734) 893-0696; info@romuluschamber.com; www.romuluschamber.org

Roscommon • *Higgins Lake-Roscommon C/C* • Cathy Boyle; Exec. Dir.; 709 Lake St.; P.O. Box 486; 48653; Roscommon; P 24,500; M 200; (989) 275-8760; Fax (989) 275-2029; info@hlrcc.com; www.hlrcc.com*

Roseville • *see Mount Clemens*

Royal Oak • *Greater Royal Oak C/C* • Shelly Kemp; Exec. Dir.; 200 S. Washington Ave.; 48067; Oakland; P 60,000; M 700; (248) 547-4000; Fax (248) 547-0504; shellyk@royaloakchamber.com; www.royaloakchamber.com

Saginaw • *Saginaw County C/C* • Bob Van Deventer; Pres./CEO; 515 N. Washington Ave.; 48607; Saginaw; P 200,169; M 900; (989) 752-7161; Fax (989) 752-9055; info@saginawchamber.org; www.saginawchamber.org*

Saint Charles • *Saint Charles Area C/C* • P.O. Box 26; 48655; Saginaw; P 2,100; M 75; (989) 865-8289; Fax (989) 865-6480; www.stcmi.com

Saint Clair Shores • *see Mount Clemens*

Saint Helen • *Saint Helen C/C* • Jan Waltz; P.O. Box 642; 48656; Roscommon; P 3,500; M 100; (989) 389-3725; sainthelen_chamber@yahoo.com; www.sainthelenchamber.net

Saint Johns • *Clinton County C/C* • Brenda Terpening; Exec. Dir.; 1013 S. U.S. 27; P.O. Box 61; 48879; Clinton; P 68,000; M 260; (989) 224-7248; Fax (989) 224-7667; ccchamber@4wbi.net; www.clintoncountychamber.org*

Saline • *Saline Area C/C* • Art Trapp; Exec. Dir.; 141 E. Michigan Ave., Ste. B; 48176; Washtenaw; P 75,000; M 450; (734) 429-4494; Fax (734) 944-6835; office@salinechamber.org; www.salinechamber.org*

Sandusky • *Sandusky C/C* • Sandy Miller; Co-Pres.; 105 E. Sanilac Ave., Ste. 4; 48471; Sanilac; P 2,800; M 150; (810) 648-4445; Fax (810) 648-3332; sanduskychamber.mi@gmail.com; www.sanduskychamber.us

Sanford • *Sanford Area C/C* • Mr. Pat Wortley; P.O. Box 98; 48657; Midland; P 1,000; M 21; (989) 687-2800; (989) 687-5000; info@sanfordmi.com; sanfordmi.com/chamber

Sault Sainte Marie • *Sault Sainte Marie C/C* • Tony Haller; Exec. Dir.; 2581 I-75 Business Spur; 49783; Chippewa; P 14,500; M 315; (906) 632-3301; Fax (906) 632-2331; info@saultstemarie.org; www.saultstemarie.org*

Sawyer • *see Gwinn*

Scottville • *see Ludington*

Sebewaing • *Sebewaing C/C* • Doug Deming; Pres.; P.O. Box 622; 48759; Huron; P 2,000; M 60; (989) 883-2150; www.sebewaingchamber.com

Shelby Township • *see Sterling Heights*

Shepherd • *Shepherd Area C/C* • Gina Gross; Pres.; P.O. Box 111; 48883; Isabella; P 1,515; M 53; (989) 828-5278; clerk@villageofshepherd.org; www.villageofshepherd.org

Silver Lake • *see Hart*

South Haven • *Greater South Haven Area C/C* • Kathy Wagaman; Exec. Dir.; 606 Phillips St.; 49090; Van Buren; P 20,000; M 400; (269) 637-5171; Fax (269) 639-1570; cofc@southhavenmi.com; www.southhavenmi.com*

South Lyon • *C/C for the South Lyon Area* • Kim Thompson; Exec. Dir.; 127 N. Lafayette; 48178; Oakland; P 45,000; M 300; (248) 437-3257; Fax (248) 437-4116; kimthompson@southlyonchamber.com; www.southlyonchamber.com*

Southfield • *Southfield Area C/C* • Tanya Markos-Vanno; Exec. Dir.; 20300 Civic Center Dr., Ste. 1102; 48076; Oakland; P 78,000; M 320; (248) 557-6661; info@southfieldchamber.com; www.southfieldchamber.com*

Sparta • *Sparta C/C* • Elizabeth Gorski; Exec. Dir.; 156 E. Division St.; P.O. Box 142; 49345; Kent; P 8,000; M 135; (616) 887-2454; ddadirector@spartami.org; www.spartachamber.com

Spring Lake • *see Grand Haven*

St. Clair • *St. Clair C/C* • Jodi Skonieczny; Exec. V.P.; 201 N. Riverside Ave.; P.O. Box 121; 48079; St. Clair; P 5,600; M 200; (810) 329-2962; Fax (810) 329-2422; info@stclairchamber.com; www.stclairchamber.com

St. Ignace • *St. Ignace C/C* • Janet Peterson; Exec. Dir.; 560 N. State St.; 49781; Mackinac; P 2,600; M 220; (906) 643-8717; (800) 970-8717; Fax (906) 643-9380; director@saintignace.org; www.saintignace.org*

St. Joseph • *see Benton Harbor*

St. Louis • *see Alma*

Standish • *Standish Area C/C* • Stephen Kolaja; Pres.; P.O. Box 458; 48658; Arenac; P 1,500; M 100; (989) 846-7867; contact@standishchamber.com; www.standishchamber.com

Sterling Heights • *also see Mount Clemens*

Sterling Heights • *Sterling Heights Reg. C/C & Ind.* • Wayne Oehmke; Pres.; 12900 Hall Rd., Ste. 100; 48313; Macomb; P 230,000; M 1,350; (586) 731-5400; Fax (586) 731-3521; Woehmke@shrcci.com; www.shrcci.com*

Stevensville • *Lakeshore C/C* • Stacy Loar-Porter; Pres.; 4290 Red Arrow Hwy.; P.O. Box 93; 49127; Berrien; P 15,465; M 165; (269) 429-1170; Fax (269) 429-8882; lakeshore.chamber@gmail.com; www.lakeshorechamber.org

Sturgis • *Sturgis Area C/C* • Cathi Abbs; Exec. Dir.; 306 W. Chicago Rd.; 49091; St. Joseph; P 25,000; M 350; (269) 651-5758; Fax (269) 651-4124; info@sturgischamber.com; www.sturgischamber.com*

Sumner • *see Alma*

Sumpter Township • *see Belleville*

Sunfield • *see Lake Odessa*

Suttons Bay • *Suttons Bay C/C* • Karen Pontius; Pres.; P.O. Box 46; 49682; Leelanau; P 20,000; M 150; (231) 271-5077; www.suttonsbayarea.com

Suttons Bay • *Leelanau Peninsula C/C* • Sally Guzowski; Exec. Dir.; 5046 S. West Bayshore Dr., Ste. G; 49682; Leelanau; P 20,000; M 475; (231) 271-9895; (800) 980-9895; Fax (231) 271-9896; info@leelanauchamber.com; www.leelanauchamber.com*

Swartz Creek • *see Flint*

Tawas City • *Tawas Area C/C* • Tonia Brenk; Mgr.; 402 E. Lake St.; P.O. Box 608; 48764; Iosco; P 8,000; M 300; (989) 362-8643; (800) 55-TAWAS; Fax (989) 362-7880; director@tawas.com; www.tawas.com

Taylor • *Southern Wayne County Reg. C/C* • Saundra Mull; Pres.; 20904 Northline Rd.; 48180; Wayne; P 400,000; M 675; (734) 284-6000; Fax (734) 284-0198; info@swcrc.com; www.swcrc.com*

Tecumseh • *Tecumseh Area C/C* • Vicki Philo; Exec. Dir.; 132 W. Chicago Blvd.; 49286; Lenawee; P 10,000; M 175; (517) 423-3740; (888) 261-3367; Fax (517) 423-5748; chamber@tecumsehchamber.org; www.tecumsehchamber.org*

Tekoncha • *see Coldwater*

Three Oaks • *Harbor Country C/C* • Viki Gudas; Exec. Dir.; 15311 Three Oaks Rd.; 49128; Berrien; P 16,000; M 502; (269) 469-5409; (800) 362-7251; Fax (269) 469-2257; request@harborcountry.org; www.harborcountry.org*

Three Oaks • *see New Buffalo*

Three Rivers • *Three Rivers Area C/C* • 57 N. Main St.; 49093; St. Joseph; P 21,000; M 300; (269) 278-8193; Fax (269) 273-1751; info@trchamber.com; www.trchamber.com*

Traverse City • *Traverse City Area C/C* • Douglas Luciani; Pres./CEO; 202 E. Grandview Pkwy.; 49684; Grand Traverse; P 91,700; M 2,100; (231) 947-5075; Fax (231) 946-2565; galbraith@tcchamber.org; www.tcchamber.org*

Troy • *Troy C/C* • Ara Topouzian; Pres./CEO; 4555 Investment Dr., Ste. 300; 48098; Oakland; P 81,000; M 720; (248) 641-8151; Fax (248) 641-0545; sheila@troychamber.com; www.troychamber.com*

Trufant • *Trufant Area C/C* • Ralph Krantz; Pres.; P.O. Box 129; 49347; Montcalm; P 500; M 87; (616) 984-2555; (616) 984-2396; Fax (616) 984-6311

Union Pier • *see New Buffalo*

Utica • *see Sterling Heights*

VanBuren Township • *see Belleville*

Vassar • *Vassar C/C* • Betty Burley; Dir.; 122 S. Main St.; P.O. Box 126; 48768; Tuscola; P 3,500; M 96; (989) 823-2601; office@vassarchamber.com; www.vassarchamber.com

Wakefield • *Wakefield C/C* • Dennis Ferson; Pres.; 499 Lakeshore Dr.; P.O. Box 93; 49968; Gogebic; P 1,800; M 45; (906) 224-2222; wakefieldcoc@ioitwx.com; wakefieldmi.org

Walled Lake • *Lakes Area C/C* • Jo Alley; Exec. Dir.; 305 N. Pontiac Trl., Ste. A; 48390; Oakland; P 137,900; M 500; (248) 624-2826; Fax (248) 624-2892; info@lakesareachamber.com; www.lakesareachamber.com*

Warren • *see Mount Clemens*

Washington Township • *see Romeo*

Waterford • *Waterford C/C* • Marie Hauswirth; Exec. Dir.; 2309 Airport Rd.; 48327; Oakland; P 74,000; M 570; (248) 666-8600; Fax (248) 666-3325; info@waterfordchamber.org; www.waterfordchamber.org*

Waterford Twp. • *see Walled Lake*

Wayland • *Wayland Area C/C* • Denise Behm; Exec. Dir.; 117 S. Main St., Ste. 6; 49348; Allegan; P 4,500; M 200; (269) 792-9246; Fax (269) 509-4512; info@waylandchamber.org; www.waylandchamber.org*

Wayne • *Wayne C/C* • Sherrie Brindley; Exec. Dir.; 34844 W. Michigan Ave.; 48184; Wayne; P 17,600; M 170; (734) 721-0100; Fax (734) 721-3070; susan@waynechamber.net; www.waynechamber.net*

West Bloomfield • *West Bloomfield C/C* • Jules Haapala; Exec. Dir.; 6668 Orchard Lake Rd., Ste. 207; 48322; Oakland; P 66,920; M 187; (248) 626-3636; Fax (248) 626-4218; info@westbloomfieldchamber.com; www.westbloomfieldchamber.com*

West Branch • *West Branch Area C/C* • Heather Johnson; Exec. Dir.; 422 W. Houghton Ave.; 48661; Ogemaw; P 30,000; M 250; (989) 345-2821; (800) 755-9091; Fax (989) 345-9075; president@wbacc.com; www.wbacc.com*

Westland • *Westland C/C* • Brookellen Swope; Pres./CEO; 36900 Ford Rd.; 48185; Wayne; P 84,100; M 400; (734) 326-7222; Fax (734) 326-6040; info@westlandchamber.com; www.westlandchamber.com

Wheeler • *see Alma*

White Cloud • *see Newaygo*

White Lake Twp. • *see Walled Lake*

Whitehall • *White Lake Area C/C* • Amy VanLoon; Exec. Dir.; 124 W. Hanson St.; 49461; Muskegon; P 18,000; M 334; (231) 893-4585; (800) 879-9702; Fax (231) 893-0914; info@whitelake.org; www.whitelake.org*

Whitmore Lake • *see Brighton*

Whittemore • *Whittemore Area C/C* • Paula Engle; Secy.; P.O. Box 178; 48770; Losco; P 460; M 20; (989) 756-5231; (989) 756-3011

Williamston • *Williamston Area C/C* • Barbara Burke; Exec. Dir.; 369 W. Grand River Ave.; P.O. Box 53; 48895; Ingham; P 5,000; M 170; (517) 655-1549; Fax (517) 655-8859; info@williamston.org; www.williamston.org*

Winfield • *see Howard City*

Wixom • *see Walled Lake*

Wolverine Village • *see Walled Lake*

Woodland • *see Hastings & Lake Odessa*

Wyoming • *Wyoming-Kentwood Area C/C* • Ken Malik; Pres./CEO; 921 47th St. S.W.; 49509; Kent; P 118,000; M 400; (616) 531-5990; Fax (616) 531-0252; ken@southkent.org; www.southkent.org*

Yale • *Yale C/C* • Barb Stasik; Pres.; P.O. Box 59; 48097; St. Clair; P 2,000; M 100; (810) 387-9253; president@yalechamber.com; www.yalechamber.com

Ypsilanti • *Ann Arbor/Ypsilanti Reg. C/C* • Diane Keller; Pres./CEO; 215 W. Michigan Ave.; SPARK East; 48197; Washtenaw; P 134,000; M 1,300; (734) 665-4433; Fax (734) 665-4191; diane@a2ychamber.org; www.a2ychamber.org*

Zeeland • *Zeeland C/C* • James Schoettle; Pres.; 149 Main Pl.; 49464; Ottawa; P 23,000; M 400; (616) 772-2494; Fax (616) 772-0065; zchamber@zeelandchamber.org; www.zeelandchamber.org*

Minnesota

Minnesota C of C • Doug Loon; Pres.; 400 Robert St. N., Ste. 1500; St. Paul; 55101; Ramsey; P 5,457,200; M 2,400; (651) 292-4650; (800) 821-2230; Fax (651) 292-4656; cpeterson@mnchamber.com; www.mnchamber.com

Ada • *Ada C/C* • Lee Ann Hall; Secy./Treas.; P.O. Box 1; 56510; Norman; P 1,700; M 73; (218) 784-3542; Fax (218) 784-3890; leeannko@loretel.net; www.adamnchamber.com

Aitkin • *Aitkin Area C/C* • Amanda MacDonald; Exec. Dir.; 10 3rd St. N.E.; P.O. Box 127; 56431; Aitkin; P 2,000; M 200; (218) 927-2316; upnorth@aitkin.com; www.aitkin.com

Albany • *Albany C/C* • Susan Iverson; Exec. Secy.; P.O. Box 634; 56307; Stearns; P 23,000; M 115; (320) 845-7777; Fax (320) 845-2346; albanycc@albanytel.com; www.albanymnchamber.com

Albert Lea • *Albert Lea-Freeborn County C/C* • Randy Kehr; Exec. Dir.; 1725 W. Main St.; 56007; Freeborn; P 30,927; M 500; (507) 373-3938; Fax (507) 373-0344; alfccoc@albertlea.org; www.albertlea.org*

Albertville • *see Rogers*

Aldrich • *see Staples*

Alexandria • *Alexandria Lakes Area C/C* • Tara Bitzan; Exec. Dir.; 206 Broadway; 56308; Douglas; P 25,000; M 570; (320) 763-3161; Fax (320) 763-6857; info@alexandriamn.org; www.alexandriamn.org*

Andover • *see Anoka*

Angle Inlet • *see Baudette*

Annandale • *Annandale Area C/C* • Jeremy Wheeler; Pres.; P.O. Box 417; 55302; Wright; P 3,200; M 125; (320) 274-2474; www.annandalechamber.org*

Anoka • *Anoka Area C/C* • Peter Turok; Pres.; 12 Bridge Sq.; 55303; Anoka; P 100,000; M 650; (763) 421-7130; Fax (763) 421-0577; mail@anokaareachamber.com; www.anokaareachamber.com*

Apple Valley • *Apple Valley C/C & CVB* • Edward Kearney; Pres.; 14800 Galaxie Ave., Ste. 101; 55124; Dakota; P 51,300; M 350; (952) 432-8422; (800) 301-9435; Fax (952) 432-7964; info@applevalleychamber.com; www.applevalleychamber.com*

Appleton • *Appleton Area C/C* • Emma Haugen; Dir.; 127 W. Sorenson; P.O. Box 98; 56208; Swift; P 2,800; M 60; (320) 289-1527; appletonmn@mchsi.com; www.appletonmn.com

Arden Hills • *see Saint Paul*

Arlington • *Arlington Area C/C* • James Haviland; Pres.; P.O. Box 543; 55307; Sibley; P 2,100; M 70; (612) 454-9972; president@arlingtonmnchamber.com; www.arlingtonmnchamber.com

Atwater • *Atwater C/C* • Goldie Smith; 322 Atlantic Ave.; P.O. Box 59; 56209; Kandiyohi; P 1,133; M 50; (320) 974-8760; Fax (320) 974-8760; atwaterchamber@yahoo.com; www.atwaterchamber.com

Austin • *Austin Area C/C* • Sandy Forstner; Exec. Dir.; 329 N. Main St., Ste. 102; 55912; Mower; P 24,000; M 400; (507) 437-4561; (888) 319-5655; Fax (507) 437-4561; sandy@austincoc.com; www.austincoc.com*

Avon • *Avon Area C/C* • Shelly Pierson; Pres.; P.O. Box 293; 56310; Stearns; P 1,400; M 75; (320) 217-4792; info@avonmnchamber.com; www.avonmnchamber.com

Barnesville • *Barnesville Main Street Program* • Ryan Tonsfledt; Pres.; 202 Front St. N.; P.O. Box 550; 56514; Clay; P 2,200; M 152; (218) 354-2479; mainstreet@bvillemn.net; www.barnesvillemn.com

Baudette • *Baudette-Lake of the Woods Area C/C* • 930 W. Main; P.O. Box 659; 56623; Lake of the Woods; P 4,000; M 100; (218) 634-1174; (800) 382-3474; Fax (218) 634-2915; info@lakeofthewoodsmn.com; www.lakeofthewoodsmn.com

Bay Lake • *see Crosby*

Becker • *Becker Area C/C* • Lynette Brannan; Ofc. Mgr.; 12060 Sherburne Ave.; P.O. Box 313; 55308; Sherburne; P 4,800; M 75; (763) 262-2420; chamber@beckerchamber.org; www.beckerchamber.org*

Belle Plaine • *Belle Plaine C/C* • Carrie Traxler; Exec. Dir.; 204 N. Meridian St.; 56011; Scott; P 5,200; M 90; (952) 873-4295; Fax (952) 873-4142; bellepln@frontiernet.net; www.belleplainemn.com*

Bemidji • *Bemidji Area C/C* • Lori Paris; Pres.; 300 Bemidji Ave.; 56601; Beltrami; P 25,000; M 450; (218) 444-3541; (800) 458-2223; lori@bemidji.org; www.bemidji.org*

Benson • *Benson Area C/C* • MaryBeth Thayer; Chamber Mgr.; 1228 Atlantic Ave.; 56215; Swift; P 3,240; M 60; (320) 843-3618; Fax (320) 843-3618; bensonchamber@embarqmail.com; www.bensonareachamber.com*

Bethel • *see Blaine*

Big Lake • *Big Lake C/C* • Corrie Scott; Pres.; 160 N. Lake St.; P.O. Box 241; 55309; Sherburne; P 20,000; M 120; (763) 263-7800; (877) 363-0549; Fax (763) 263-7668; info@biglakechamber.com; www.biglakechamber.com

Birchdale • *see Baudette*

Birchwood Village • *see White Bear Lake*

Blaine • *MetroNorth C/C* • Lori Higgins; Exec. Dir.; 9380 Central Ave., Ste. 320; 55434; Anoka; P 350,000; M 800; (763) 783-3553; Fax (763) 783-3557; chamber@metronorthchamber.org; www.metronorthchamber.org*

Blooming Prairie • *Blooming Prairie C/C* • Becky Noble; Exec. Dir.; 138 Hwy. 218 S.; P.O. Box 805; 55917; Steele; P 2,000; M 120; (507) 583-4472; Fax (507) 583-4520; bpcofc@frontiernet.net; www.bloomingprairie.com*

Bloomington • *Bloomington C/C* • Maureen Scallen Failor; Exec. Dir.; 9633 Lyndale Ave. S., Ste. 200; 55420; Hennepin; P 88,700; M 1,000; (952) 888-8818; Fax (952) 888-0508; info@bloomingtonchamber.org; www.minneapolischamber.org*

Blue Earth • *Blue Earth Area C/C* • Cindy Lyon; Exec. Dir.; 113 S. Nicollet St.; 56013; Faribault; P 3,500; M 135; (507) 526-2916; chamber@bevcomm.net; www.blueearthchamber.com*

Brainerd • *Brainerd Lakes C/C* • Matt Kilian; CEO; 124 N. 6th St.; 56401; Crow Wing; P 22,000; M 1,200; (218) 829-2838; (800) 450-2838; Fax (218) 829-8199; mkilian@explorebrainerdlakes.com; www.explorebrainerdlakes.com*

Breckenridge • *see Wahpeton, ND*

Breezy Point • *see Pequot Lakes*

Brooklyn Center • *see Plymouth - TwinWest C/C*

Brooklyn Park • *see Osseo*

Buffalo • *Buffalo Area C/C* • Sally Custer; Pres.; 205 Central Ave.; 55313; Wright; P 17,000; M 240; (763) 682-4902; Fax (763) 682-5677; sally@buffalochamber.org; www.buffalochamber.org*

Burnsville • *Burnsville C/C* • Bill Corby; Pres.; 350 W. Burnsville Pkwy., Ste. 425; 55337; Dakota; P 60,300; M 360; (952) 435-6000; Fax (952) 435-6972; chamber@burnsvillechamber.com; www.burnsvillechamber.com

Caledonia • *Caledonia Area C/C & Tourism Center* • Eric Halverson; Pres.; 120 S. Kingston St.; 55921; Houston; P 2,965; M 69; (507) 725-5477; (877) 439-4893; caledoniacoc@gmail.com; www.caledoniamn.gov

Cambridge • *see Isanti*

Canby • *Canby Area C/C* • Tony Ourada; P.O. Box 115; 56220; Yellow Medicine; P 1,800; M 70; (507) 223-7775; www.canbychamber.com

Cannon Falls • *Cannon Falls Area C/C* • Patricia A. Anderson; Pres.; 103 N. 4th St.; P.O. Box 2; 55009; Goodhue; P 4,000; M 180; (507) 263-2289; tourism@cannonfalls.org; www.cannonfalls.org

Carver • *see Chanhassen*

Cass Lake • *Cass Lake Area C/C* • Terri Vail; Dir.; P.O. Box 548; 56633; Cass; P 1,000; M 100; (218) 987-2299; info@casslake.com; www.casslake.com

Center City • *see Lindstrom*

Centerville • *see Circle Pines*

Champlin • *see Anoka*

Chanhassen • *SouthWest Metro C/C* • Lori Anderson; Pres.; 7925 Stone Creek Dr., Ste. 130; 55317; Carver; P 58,000; M 450; (952) 474-3233; Fax (952) 474-3408; info@swmetrochamber.com; www.swmetrochamber.com*

Chaska • *see Chanhassen*

Chatfield • *Chatfield Commerical Club* • Pam Bluhm; 220 S. Main St.; 55923; Fillmore & Olmsted; P 2,500; M 75; (507) 867-3870; www.ci.chatfield.mn.us

Chisago City • *see Lindstrom*

Chisholm • *Chisholm Area C/C* • Shannon Kishel-Roche; Exec. Dir.; 223 W. Lake St.; 55719; St. Louis; P 5,000; M 140; (218) 254-7930; (800) 422-0806; Fax (218) 254-7932; info@chisholmchamber.com; www.chisholmchamber.com*

Circle Pines • *Quad Area C/C* • P.O. Box 430; 55014; Anoka; P 40,000; M 50; (651) 815-2750; annamwicks@msn.com; www.quadchamber.org*

Claremont • *Claremont Area C/C* • Dean Schuette; Pres./CEO; P.O. Box 236; 55924; Dodge; P 670; M 40; (507) 456-3899; Fax (507) 528-2126; schuette@myclearwave.net; www.claremontmn.com

Clarissa • *Clarissa Comm. Club* • Becky Pratt; Pres.; 20251 400th St.; 56440; Todd; P 668; M 40; (218) 756-2125; cityofclarissa.weebly.com

Clementson • *see Baudette*

Cloquet • *Cloquet Area C/C & Ofc. of Tourism* • 225 Sunnyside Dr.; 55720; Carlton; P 12,000; M 285; (218) 879-1551; (800) 554-4350; Fax (218) 878-0223; chamber@cloquet.com; www.cloquet.com*

Cokato • *Cokato C/C* • Louann Worden; Secy.; 255 Broadway Ave. S.; P.O. Box 819; 55321; Wright; P 2,700; M 60; (320) 286-5505; Fax (320) 286-5876; depclerk@cokato.mn.us; www.cokato.mn.us

Cold Spring • *Cold Spring Area C/C* • 20 Red River Ave. S., Ste. 110; 56320; Stearns; P 4,000; M 108; (320) 685-4186; Fax (320) 685-4186; info@coldspringmn.com; www.coldspringmn.com*

Columbia Heights • *see New Brighton*

Cook • *Cook Area C/C* • Lisa Ojanen; P.O. Box 296; 55723; St. Louis; P 800; M 75; (218) 666-6093; (877) 526-6562; chamber@cookminnesota.com; www.cookminnesota.com

Coon Rapids • *see Blaine*

Corcoran • *see Rogers*

Cottage Grove • *Cottage Grove Area C/C* • Colleen Stelmach; Ofc. Mgr.; 7516 80th St. S., Ste. E; P.O. Box 16; 55016; Washington; P 35,000; M 150; (651) 458-8334; Fax (651) 458-8383; office@cottagegrovechamber.org; www.cottagegrovechamber.org*

Crookston • *Crookston Area C/C* • Amanda Lien; Exec. Dir.; 107 W. 2nd St.; P.O. Box 115; 56716; Polk; P 8,000; M 200; (218) 281-4320; (800) 809-5997; Fax (218) 281-4349; info@visitcrookston.com; www.visitcrookston.com*

Crosby • *Cuyuna Lakes C/C* • Jessica Holmvig; Exec. Dir.; P.O. Box 23; 56441; Crow Wing; P 2,400; M 200; (218) 546-8131; Fax (218) 546-2618; info@cuyunalakes.com; www.cuyunalakes.com*

Crosslake • *Brainerd Lakes C/C - Crosslake Ofc.* • Cindy Myogeto; Dir.; P.O. Box 315; 56442; Crow Wing; P 2,100; M 900; (218) 692-4027; (800) 450-2838; cmyogeto@explorebrainerdlakes.com; www.explorebrainerdlakes.com*

Crystal • *see Plymouth - TwinWest C/C*

Cuyuna • *see Crosby*

Dawson • *Dawson Area C/C* • Jesi Martinson; Chamber Asst.; 579 Pine St.; P.O. Box 382; 56232; Lac qui Parle; P 1,700; M 100; (320) 769-2981; dawsonchamber@frontiernet.net; www.dawsonchamber.com

Dayton • *see Anoka and Rogers*

Deer River • *Deer River C/C* • Mike Kane; Pres.; 208 2nd St. S.E.; P.O. Box 505; 56636; Itasca; P 1,000; M 105; (218) 246-8055; (888) 701-2226; drchamb@deerriver.org; www.deerriver.org

Deerwood • *see Crosby*

Delano • *Delano Area C/C* • Ryan Gueningsman; Exec. Dir.; P.O. Box 27; 55328; Wright; P 5,000; M 130; (763) 972-6756; dacc@delanochamber.com; www.delanochamber.com*

Dellwood • *see White Bear Lake*

Detroit Lakes • *Detroit Lakes Reg. C/C* • Carrie Johnston; Pres.; 700 Summit Ave.; P.O. Box 348; 56502; Becker; P 10,000; M 450; (218) 847-9202; (800) 542-3992; Fax (218) 847-9082; carrie@visitdetroitlakes.com; www.visitdetroitlakes.com*

Duluth • *Duluth Area C/C* • David Ross; Pres./CEO; 5 W. First St., Ste. 101; 55802; St. Louis; P 84,167; M 1,150; (218) 722-5501; Fax (218) 722-3223; inquiry@duluthchamber.com; www.duluthchamber.com*

Eagan • *Dakota County Reg. C/C* • Vicki Stute; Pres.; 3352 Sherman Ct., Ste. 201; 55121; Dakota; P 150,000; M 500; (651) 452-9872; Fax (651) 452-8978; vstute@dcrchamber.com; www.dcrchamber.com*

East Bethel • *see Blaine*

East Grand Forks • *The Chamber Grand Forks - East Grand Forks* • Barry Wilfahrt; Pres./CEO; 202 N. 3rd St.; P.O. Box 315; 56721; Grand Forks; P 75,000; M 1,100; (701) 772-7271; Fax (701) 772-9238; info@gochamber.org; www.gochamber.org*

Eden Prairie • *Eden Prairie C/C* • Pat MulQueeny; Pres.; 11455 Viking Dr., Ste. 270; 55344; Hennepin; P 58,000; M 510; (952) 944-2830; Fax (952) 944-0229; adminj@epchamber.org; www.epchamber.org*

Eden Valley • *Eden Valley C/C* • Dave Currens; P.O. Box 557; 55329; Meeker; P 1,033; M 45; (320) 453-2000; (320) 453-5251; www.edenvalley.govoffice.com

Edina • *Edina C/C* • Lori Syverson; Pres.; 3300 Edinborough Way, Ste. 150; 55435; Hennepin; P 47,000; M 400; (952) 806-9060; Fax (952) 806-9065; chamber@edina.org; www.edinachamber.com*

Elbow Lake • *Elbow Lake C/C* • Edie Johnson; Managing Dir.; P.O. Box 1083; 56531; Grant; P 1,275; M 120; (218) 685-5380; chamber@runestone.net; www.elbowlakechamber.com

Elk River • *Elk River Area C/C* • Debbi Rydberg; Exec. Dir.; 509 Hwy. 10; 55330; Sherburne; P 24,000; M 350; (763) 441-3110; Fax (763) 441-3409; eracc@elkriverchamber.org; www.elkriverchamber.org*

Ely • *Ely C/C* • Linda Fryer; Admin. Dir.; 1600 E. Sheridan St.; 55731; St. Louis; P 3,700; M 300; (218) 365-6123; (800) 777-7281; Fax (218) 365-5929; fun@ely.org; www.ely.org

Elysian • *Elysian Area C/C* • Mike Meyer; Pres.; P.O. Box 95; 56028; Le Sueur; P 652; M 80; (507) 267-4708; (507) 267-4040; Fax (507) 267-4750; pnusbaum@myclearwave.net; www.elysianmn.com

Eveleth • *see Virginia*

Excelsior • *Excelsior-Lake Minnetonka C/C* • Laura Hotvet; Exec. Dir.; 37 Water St.; 55331; Hennepin; P 16,000; M 220; (952) 474-6461; Fax (952) 474-3139; director@excelsior-lakeminnetonkachamber.com; www.excelsior-lakeminnetonkachamber.com*

Fairfax • *Fairfax Civic & Commerce* • Craig Buboltz; P.O. Box 114; 55332; Renville; P 1,205; M 60; (507) 426-7255; www.cityoffairfax-mn.gov

Fairmont • *Fairmont Area C/C* • Margaret Dillard; Pres.; 323 E. Blue Earth Ave.; P.O. Box 826; 56031; Martin; P 11,000; M 277; (507) 235-5547; Fax (507) 235-8411; info@fairmontchamber.org; www.fairmontchamber.org*

Falcon Heights • *see Saint Paul*

Faribault • *Faribault Area C/C* • Kymn Anderson; Pres.; 530 Wilson Ave.; P.O. Box 434; 55021; Rice; P 28,000; M 490; (507) 334-4381; (800) 658-2354; Fax (507) 334-1003; chamber@faribaultmn.org; www.faribaultmn.org*

Farmington • *see Eagan*

Fergus Falls • *Fergus Falls Area C/C* • Lisa Workman; Exec. Dir.; 202 S. Court St.; 56537; Otter Tail; P 14,000; M 300; (218) 736-6951; chamber@prtel.com; www.fergusfalls.com*

Flag Island • *see Baudette*

Floodwood • *Floodwood Bus./Comm. Partnership* • Jessica Rich; Pres.; P.O. Box 337; 55736; St. Louis; P 500; M 45; (218) 476-2751; fbcp55736@yahoo.com; www.floodwoodbusinesses.com

Forest Lake • *Forest Lake Area C/C* • Colleen Eddy; Pres.; The State Farm Building, 568 S. Lake St.; P.O. Box 474; 55025; Washington; P 45,000; M 275; (651) 464-3200; Fax (651) 464-3201; colleen@flacc.org; www.flacc.org*

Frankfort Twp. • *see Rogers*

Fridley • *see New Brighton*

Gaylord • *Gaylord C/C* • Vickie Holtz; Pres.; P.O. Box 987; 55334; Sibley; P 2,300; M 50; (507) 237-2338; Fax (507) 237-5121; www.exploregaylord.org

Gem Lake • *see White Bear Lake*

Gilbert • *see Virginia*

Glencoe • *Glencoe Area C/C* • Myranda VanDamme; 1107 11th St. E., Ste. 104; 55336; McLeod; P 5,700; M 150; (320) 864-3650; mvandamme@ci.glencoe.mn.us; www.glencoemn.org

Glenwood • *Glenwood Lakes Area Chamber & Welcome Center* • Scott A. Formo; Exec. Dir.; 7 1st St. N.W.; 56334; Pope; P 12,000; M 325; (320) 634-3636; Fax (320) 634-3637; chamber@glenwoodlakesarea.org; www.glenwoodlakesarea.org*

Golden Valley • *see Plymouth - TwinWest C/C*

Grand Marais • *Greater Grand Marais C/C* • Bev Wolke; Exec. Dir.; P.O. Box 805; 55604; Cook; P 2,200; M 100; (218) 370-8904; gmcc@boreal.org; www.grandmaraismn.com

Grand Rapids • *Grand Rapids Area C/C* • Bud Stone; Pres./CEO; One N.W. Third St.; 55744; Itasca; P 40,000; M 600; (218) 326-6619; (800) 472-6366; Fax (218) 326-4825; info@grandmn.com; www.grandmn.com*

Granite Falls • *Granite Falls Area C/C* • Mary Gillespie; Exec. Dir.; 807 Prentice St.; 56241; Yellow Medicine; P 3,000; M 125; (320) 564-4039; Fax (320) 564-3843; gfchamber@mvtvwireless.com; www.granitefallschamber.com

Greenfield • *see Rogers*

Hackensack • *Hackensack C/C* • Jean Dawson; Coord.; 100 Fleisher Ave. S.; P.O. Box 373; 56452; Cass; P 275; M 100; (218) 675-6135; (800) 279-6932; chamber@hackensackchamber.com; www.hackensackchamber.com

Ham Lake • *Ham Lake Area C/C* • Kim Hogdal; Exec. Dir.; 1207 Constance Blvd. N.E.; 55304; Anoka; P 50,000; M 100; (763) 434-3011; Fax (763) 434-6668; admin@hamlakecc.org; www.hamlakecc.org

Hamel • *see Rogers*

Hanover • *see Rogers*

Hassan Twp. • *see Rogers*

Hastings • *Hastings Area C/C & Tourism Bur.* • Kristy Barse; Pres.; 314 Vermillion St., Ste. 100; 55033; Dakota; P 22,000; M 300; (651) 437-6775; Fax (651) 437-2697; info@hastingsmn.org; www.hastingsmn.org*

Hayfield • *Hayfield C/C* • Rich Rieken; Secy.; P.O. Box 1113; 55940; Dodge; P 1,340; M 65; (507) 477-2000; (507) 477-3535; rich@semnrealty.com; www.hayfieldchamber.com

Hermantown • *Hermantown Area C/C* • Michael Lundstrom; Exec. Dir.; 5094 Miller Trunk Hwy., Ste. 600; 55811; St. Louis; P 9,760; M 350; (218) 729-6843; Fax (218) 729-7132; info@hermantownchamber.com; www.hermantownchamber.com*

Hibbing • *Hibbing Area C/C* • Lory Fedo; Pres./CEO; 211 E. Howard St.; P.O. Box 727; 55746; St. Louis; P 35,000; M 400; (218) 262-3895; (800) 4-HIBBING; Fax (218) 262-3897; hibbcofc@hibbing.org; www.hibbing.org*

Hilltop • *see Blaine*

Hinckley • *Hinckley Area C/C* • Charlene Gafkjen; Dir.; 208 Fire Monument Rd.; P.O. Box 189; 55037; Pine; P 1,400; M 80; (320) 384-7837; info@hinckleychamber.com; www.hinckleychamber.com

Hopkins • *see Plymouth - TwinWest C/C*

Houston • *Houston Area C/C* • Kristie Treptow; Secy.; P.O. Box 3; 55943; Houston; P 979; M 50; (507) 896-4668; (507) 896-3234; HoustonMNChamber@gmail.com; www.houstonmnchamber.com

Hoyt Lakes • *Hoyt Lakes C/C* • Robert Bartholomew; Pres.; P.O. Box 429; 55750; St. Louis; P 2,700; M 100; (218) 225-2787; info@hoytlakes.com; www.hoytlakes.com

Hugo • *see White Bear Lake*

Hutchinson • *Hutchinson Area C/C & Tourism* • Mary Hodson; Pres.; 2 Main St. S.; 55350; McLeod; P 14,600; M 330; (320) 587-5252; (800) 572-6689; Fax (320) 587-4752; info@explorehutchinson.com; www.explorehutchinson.com*

International Falls • *International Falls Area C/C* • Faye Whitbeck; Pres.; 301 2nd Ave.; 56649; Koochiching; P 7,000; M 210; (218) 283-9400; Fax (218) 283-3572; chamber@Intlfalls.org; www.ifallschamber.com*

Inver Grove Heights • *River Heights C/C •* Jennifer Gale; Pres.; 5782 Blackshire Path; 55076; Dakota; P 53,470; M 350; (651) 451-2266; Fax (651) 451-0846; jennifer@riverheights.com; www.riverheights.com*

Ironton • *see Crosby*

Isanti • *North 65 C/C •* Melissa Bettendorf; Exec. Dir.; 2 Enterprise Ave. N.E., Ste. C4; P.O. Box 343; 55040; Isanti; P 36,000; M 250; (763) 689-2505; Fax (763) 552-2505; info@north65chamber.com; www.north65chamber.com*

Jackson • *Jackson Area C/C •* Sharon Henning; Dir.; 114 3rd St., Ste. B; 56143; Jackson; P 4,000; M 161; (507) 847-3867; Fax (507) 847-3869; chamber@jacksonmn.com; www.jacksonmn.com

Janesville • *Janesville C/C •* Paul Pfenning; Pres.; P.O. Box O; 56048; Waseca; P 2,200; M 30; (507) 234-5110; Fax (507) 234-5236; janesville.govoffice.com

Jordan • *Jordan Area C/C •* Shelly Tolonen; Exec. Dir.; 212 Second St. E., Ste. 104; P.O. Box 102; 55352; Scott; P 5,500; M 100; (952) 492-2355; info@jordanchamber.org; www.jordanchamber.org*

Kasson • *Kasson C/C •* Cathy Pletta; P.O. Box 326; 55944; Dodge; P 5,200; M 100; (507) 634-7618; kassonchamber@kmtel.com; www.kassonchamber.org

Kimball • *Kimball Area C/C •* Tammy Konz; Pres.; P.O. Box 214; 55353; Stearns; P 762; M 52; (320) 398-5011; (320) 398-5013; tkonz@meltel.net; www.kimballareachamber.com

La Crescent • *La Crescent C/C •* Eileen Krenz; Exec. Dir.; 109 S. Walnut St., Ste. B; 55947; Houston; P 5,000; M 140; (507) 895-2800; (800) 926-9480; Fax (507) 895-2619; lacrescent.chamber@acegroup.cc; www.lacrescentmn.com

Lake Benton • *Lake Benton Area C/C & CVB •* 110 S. Center St.; P.O. Box 205; 56149; Lincoln; P 700; M 55; (507) 368-9577; lbenton@itctel.com; www.lakebentonminnesota.com

Lake City • *Lake City Area C/C •* Andrea Hamilton; Exec. Dir.; 101 W. Center St.; 55041; Wabasha; P 5,000; M 200; (651) 345-4123; Fax (651) 345-4195; lcchamber@lakecity.org; www.lakecity.org*

Lake Crystal • *Lake Crystal Area C/C •* Julie Reed; Exec. Dir.; 113 S. Main; P.O. Box 27; 56055; Blue Earth; P 2,500; M 100; (507) 726-6088; lcchambr@hickorytech.net; www.lakecrystalchamber.com

Lake Lillian • *Lake Lillian Civic & Commerce •* Wendy Lund; P.O. Box 205; 56253; Kandiyohi; P 238; M 20; (320) 664-4597; (320) 664-4440; www.lakelillian.govoffice.com

Lakeville • *Lakeville Area C/C •* Tim Roche; Pres.; 19950 Dodd Blvd., Ste. 101; 55044; Dakota; P 50,000; M 450; (952) 469-2020; Fax (952) 469-2028; info@lakevillechambercvb.org; www.lakevillechamber.org*

Lamberton • *Lamberton Comm. Club •* Mike Bent; Pres.; P.O. Box 35; 56152; Redwood; P 825; M 55; (507) 752-7020; (507) 752-7601; www.lambertonmn.com

Lanesboro • *Lanesboro Area C/C •* Dee Slinde; Exec. Dir.; 100 Milwaukee Rd.; P.O. Box 348; 55949; Fillmore; P 754; M 134; (507) 467-2696; director@lanesboro.com; www.lanesboro.com

Lauderdale • *see Saint Paul*

Le Center • *Le Center Area C/C •* Don Hayden; Exec. Dir.; 10 W. Tyrone St.; P.O. Box 54; 56057; Le Sueur; P 2,200; M 100; (507) 357-6737; Fax (507) 357-6888; donlc@frontiernet.net; www.cityoflecenter.com

Le Sueur • *Le Sueur Area C/C •* Julie Boyland; Exec. Dir.; 500 N. Main St.; 56058; Le Sueur; P 4,300; M 185; (507) 665-2501; Fax (507) 665-4372; julieb@lesueurchamber.org; www.lesueurchamber.org*

Lewiston • *Lewiston Area C/C & Civic Group •* Holly Jacobs; Pres.; P.O. Box 423; 55952; Winona; P 1,600; M 70; (507) 523-2691; (507) 523-2300; www.lewistonmn.org

Lexington • *see Circle Pines*

Lilydale • *see Eagan*

Lindstrom • *Chisago Lakes Area C/C •* Wendy Redland; Exec. Dir.; 30525 Linden St.; P.O. Box 283; 55045; Chisago; P 15,000; M 200; (651) 257-1177; Fax (651) 257-1770; clacc@frontiernet.net; www.chisagolakeschamber.com

Lino Lakes • *see Circle Pines*

Litchfield • *Litchfield C/C •* Dee Schutte; Exec. Dir.; 219 Sibley Ave. N.; 55355; Meeker; P 6,500; M 300; (320) 693-8184; Fax (320) 593-8184; litch@litch.com; www.litch.com*

Little Canada • *see Saint Paul*

Little Falls • *Little Falls Area C/C •* Debora K. Boelz; Pres./CEO; 200 First St. N.W.; 56345; Morrison; P 33,000; M 360; (320) 632-5155; Fax (320) 632-2122; assistance@littlefallsmnchamber.com; www.littlefallsmnchamber.com*

Long Lake • *Long Lake Area C/C •* Sutton McGraw; Pres.; P.O. Box 662; 55356; Hennepin; P 1,803; M 75; (952) 491-0813; info@longlakechamber.com; www.longlakeareachamber.com*

Long Prairie • *Long Prairie Area C/C •* Karin Nauber; Exec. Dir.; 42 N. 3rd St.; 56347; Todd; P 3,500; M 100; (320) 732-2514; chamber@longprairie.org; www.longprairie.org*

Longville • *Longville C/C •* Dawn Gilsrud; Secy.; P.O. Box 33; 56655; Cass; P 300; M 90; (218) 363-2630; (800) 756-7583; chamber@longville.com; www.longville.com

Lonsdale • *Lonsdale C/C •* Shanna Gutzke-Kupp; Exec. Dir.; 102 N. Main St., Ste. 2; P.O. Box 37; 55046; Rice; P 3,900; M 75; (507) 744-4962; Fax (507) 744-4963; lacc@lonstel.com; www.lonsdalechamber.com

Loretto • *see Rogers*

Luverne • *Luverne Area Chamber •* Jane Wildung Lanphere; Exec. Dir.; 213 E. Luverne St.; Rock County Courthouse Square; 56156; Rock; P 5,000; M 190; (888) 283-4061; (507) 283-1884; Fax (507) 283-4061; luvernechamber@co.rock.mn.us; www.luvernechamber.com*

Madelia • *Madelia Area C/C & Visitor Bur. •* Karla Grev; Exec. Dir.; 127 W. Main St.; P.O. Box 171; 56062; Watonwan; P 2,400; M 100; (507) 642-8822; (888) 941-7283; Fax (507) 642-8832; chamber@madeliamn.com; www.visitmadelia.com

Madison • *Madison Area C/C •* Maynard R. Meyer; Coord.; 623 W. 3rd St.; P.O. Box 70; 56256; Lac qui Parle; P 2,000; M 100; (320) 598-7301; Fax (320) 598-7955; klqpfm@farmerstel.net; www.madisonmn.info

Mahnomen • *Mahnomen County C/C •* City Hall; P.O. Box 250; 56557; Mahnomen; P 5,250; M 65; (218) 935-2573; www.mahnomen.govoffice.com

Mahtomedi • *see White Bear Lake*

Mankato • *Greater Mankato Growth Inc.* • Jonathan Zierdt; Pres./CEO; 1961 Premier Dr., Ste. 100; 56001; Blue Earth; P 99,000; M 915; (507) 385-6640; (800) 697-0652; Fax (507) 345-4451; info@greatermankato.com; www.greatermankato.com*

Maple Grove • *see Osseo*

Mapleton • *Mapleton Area C/C* • Stacie Mattison; Coord.; P.O. Box 288; 56065; Blue Earth; P 2,000; M 75; (507) 524-4756; mapletonchamber@gmail.com; www.mapletonchamber.com

Maplewood • *see Saint Paul*

Marshall • *Marshall Area C/C* • Cal Brink; Exec. Dir.; 118 W. College Dr.; 56258; Lyon; P 13,700; M 512; (507) 532-4484; Fax (507) 532-4485; chamber@marshall-mn.org; www.marshall-mn.org*

McGregor • *McGregor Area C/C* • Nicole Eld; Dir.; P.O. Box 68; 55760; Aitkin; P 500; M 85; (218) 768-3692; chamber@mcgregormn.com; www.mcgregormn.com

Medicine Lake • *see Plymouth - TwinWest C/C*

Medina • *see Rogers*

Melrose • *Melrose Area C/C* • Sara Hoffner; Exec. Dir.; 223 E. Main St.; 56352; Stearns; P 3,293; M 90; (320) 256-7174; Fax (320) 256-7177; chamber@meltel.net; www.melrosemn.org*

Mendota Heights • *see Eagan*

Milaca • *Milaca Area C/C* • Rich Melvin; Exec. Dir.; 255 1st St. E.; P.O. Box 155; 56353; Mille Lacs; P 3,000; M 100; (320) 983-3140; Fax (320) 983-3142; info@milacachamber.com; www.milacachamber.com

Minneapolis • *Minneapolis Reg. C/C* • Jonathan Weinhagen; Pres./CEO; 81 S. 9th St., Ste. 200; 55402; Hennepin; P 2,968,806; M 1,000; (612) 370-9100; Fax (612) 370-9195; landerson@minneapolischamber.org; www.minneapolischamber.org*

Minneapolis • *Northeast Minneapolis C/C* • Christine Levens; Exec. Dir.; 2329 Central Ave. N.E.; 55418; Hennepin; P 37,000; M 1,000; (612) 378-0050; Fax (612) 378-8870; clevens@northeastminneapolischamber.org; www.minneapolischamber.org*

Minnetonka • *see Plymouth - TwinWest C/C*

Montevideo • *Montevideo Area C/C* • Emily Sumner; Exec. Dir.; 301 N. 1st St.; 56265; Chippewa; P 5,500; M 250; (320) 269-5527; (800) 269-5527; Fax (320) 269-5696; generalinfo@montechamber.com; www.montechamber.com*

Monticello • *Monticello C/C* • Marcy Anderson; Dir.; 205 Pine St.; P.O. Box 192; 55362; Wright; P 12,000; M 330; (763) 295-2700; Fax (763) 295-2705; info@monticellocci.com; www.monticellocci.com*

Montrose • *Montrose-Waverly C/C* • Jim Tourville; P.O. Box 421; 55363; Wright; P 2,700; M 40; (612) 508-6474; jamest55363@msn.com; www.montrosewaverlychamber.com*

Moorhead • *Fargo Moorhead West Fargo C/C* • Craig Whitney; Pres./CEO; 202 1st Ave. N.; P.O. Box 2443, Fargo, ND 58108; 56560; Clay, MN & Cass, ND; P 233,000; M 2,000; (218) 233-1100; Fax (218) 233-1200; info@fmwfchamber.com; www.fmwfchamber.com*

Moose Lake • *Moose Lake Area C/C* • Dusty Wilson; Exec. Dir.; 4524 S. Arrowhead Ln.; P.O. Box 110; 55767; Carlton; P 3,700; M 180; (218) 485-4145; (800) 365-3680; mooselakechamber@gmail.com; www.mooselakechamber.com*

Mora • *Mora Area C/C* • 16 N. Lake St.; 55051; Kanabec; P 15,000; M 125; (800) 291-5792; karen@moramn.com; www.moramn.com

Morris • *Morris Area C/C* • Carolyn Peterson; Admin. Dir.; 215 Atlantic Ave.; 56267; Stevens; P 5,000; M 200; (320) 589-1242; Fax (320) 585-4814; morrismnchamber@gmail.com; www.morrismnchamber.org*

Morton • *Morton Area C/C & Tourism Bur.* • Shirley Dove; P.O. Box 0127; 56270; Renville; P 448; M 30; (507) 697-6912; mortoncityhall@mchsi.com; www.mortonmnchamber.com

Motley • *see Staples*

Mounds View • *see New Brighton*

Mountain Iron • *see Virginia*

Mountain Lake • *Mountain Lake C/C* • Rob Anderson; Dir.; 930 Third Ave.; P.O. Drawer C; 56159; Cottonwood; P 2,100; M 70; (507) 427-2999; Fax (507) 427-3327; eda@mountainlake.govoffice.com; www.mountainlakemn.com

Nashwauk • *Nashwauk Area C/C* • Mike Olson; Pres.; P.O. Box 156; 55769; Itasca; P 1,000; M 100; (218) 969-3538; (218) 969-1234; www.nashwaukchamber.com

New Brighton • *Twin Cities North C/C* • Todd Kruse; Pres./CEO; 525 Main St., Ste. 200; 55112; Ramsey; P 87,000; M 700; (763) 571-9781; info@twincitiesnorth.org; www.twincitiesnorth.org*

New Hope • *see Plymouth - TwinWest C/C*

New London • *see Willmar*

New Prague • *New Prague C/C* • Debbie Kalousek; Exec. Dir.; 101 E. Main St.; 56071; Le Sueur & Scott; P 6,200; M 220; (952) 758-4360; Fax (952) 758-5396; info@newprague.com; www.newprague.com*

New Ulm • *New Ulm Area C/C* • Audra Shaneman; Pres./CEO; 1 N. Minnesota St.; P.O. Box 384; 56073; Brown; P 15,000; M 340; (507) 233-4300; (888) 4-NEWULM; Fax (507) 354-1504; chamber@newulm.com; www.newulm.com*

New York Mills • *New York Mills Civic & Commerce Assn.* • Nathan Welte; Pres.; P.O. Box 176; 56567; Otter Tail; P 1,200; M 60; (218) 385-3100; info@explorenewyorkmills.com; www.explorenewyorkmills.com

Nisswa • *Nisswa C/C* • Amanda Luepke; CEO; 25336 Smiley Rd.; P.O. Box 185; 56468; Crow Wing; P 2,000; M 300; (218) 963-2620; (800) 950-9610; guest@nisswa.com; www.nisswa.com

North Branch • *North Branch Area C/C* • Kathy Lindo; Exec. Dir.; 6063 Main St.; P.O. Box 577; 55056; Chisago; P 10,000; M 300; (651) 674-4077; Fax (651) 674-2600; nbachamber@izoom.net; northbranchchamber.com

North Maplewood • *see White Bear Lake*

North Oaks • *see Saint Paul and White Bear Lake*

North Saint Paul • *see Saint Paul*

Northfield • *Northfield Area C/C & Tourism* • Todd Bornhauser; Pres.; 205 Third St. W., Ste. B; 55057; Rice; P 20,000; M 260; (507) 645-5604; (800) 658-2548; Fax (507) 663-7782; info@northfieldchamber.com; www.northfieldchamber.com*

Norwood Young America • *Norwood Young America C/C* • Chris Lund; Pres.; P.O. Box 292; 55368; Carver; P 4,000; M 80; (952) 467-4003; info@nyachamber.org; www.nyachamber.org

Oak Grove • see Blaine

Oakdale • see Saint Paul

Olivia • *Olivia Area C/C* • Nancy Standfuss; Exec. Dir.; 909 W. DePue Ave.; P.O. Box 37; 56277; Renville; P 2,600; M 100; (320) 523-1350; Fax (320) 523-1514; oliviachamber@tds.net; www.oliviachamber.org

Orr • *Orr C/C* • P.O. Box 64; 55771; St. Louis; P 300; M 30; (218) 757-3288; info@orrchamber.com; www.orrchamber.com

Ortonville • *Big Stone Lake Area C/C* • Mary Hillman; Exec. Dir.; 987 U.S. Hwy. 12; 56278; Big Stone; P 2,000; M 195; (320) 839-3284; Fax (320) 839-2621; chamber@bigstonelake.com; www.bigstonelake.com

Osakis • *Osakis C/C & Info. Center* • Laura Backes; Pres.; P.O. Box 399; 56360; Douglas & Todd; P 1,615; M 80; (320) 859-3777; cityhall@cityofosakis.com; www.visitosakis.com

Osseo • *North Hennepin Area C/C* • Stephen E. Erickson; Exec. Dir.; 229 1st Ave. N.E.; 55369; Hennepin; P 120,000; M 450; (763) 424-6744; Fax (763) 424-6927; steve@nhachamber.com; www.nhachamber.com*

Otsego • see Rogers

Owatonna • *Owatonna Area C/C & Tourism* • Jennifer Libby; Pres./CEO; 320 Hoffman Dr.; 55060; Steele; P 26,000; M 570; (507) 451-7970; Fax (507) 451-7972; oacct@owatonna.org; www.owatonna.org*

Park Rapids • *Park Rapids Lakes Area C/C* • Katharine B. Magozzi; Exec. Dir.; 1204 Park Ave. S.; P.O. Box 249; 56470; Hubbard; P 25,000; M 400; (218) 732-4111; (800) 247-0054; Fax (218) 732-4112; katie@parkrapids.com; www.parkrapids.com*

Paynesville • *Paynesville Area C/C* • P.O. Box 4; 56362; Stearns; P 2,267; M 125; (320) 243-3233; (800) 547-9034; chamber@lakedalelink.net; www.paynesvillechamber.org

Pelican Rapids • *Pelican Rapids Area C/C* • 25 N. Broadway; P.O. Box 206; 56572; Otter Tail; P 2,500; M 100; (218) 863-1221; Fax (218) 863-4606; tourism@loretel.net; www.pelicanrapidschamber.com*

Pequot Lakes • *Brainerd Lakes C/C - Pequot Lakes Ofc.* • Jenna Crawford; Dir.; P.O. Box 208; 56472; Crow Wing; P 1,802; M 1,100; (218) 568-8911; (800) 950-0291; Fax (218) 568-8910; jcrawford@explorebrainerdlakes.com; www.explorebrainerdlakes.com*

Perham • *Perham Area C/C* • Don Schroeder; Exec. Dir.; 185 E. Main St.; 56573; Otter Tail; P 12,000; M 262; (218) 346-7710; (800) 634-6112; Fax (218) 346-7712; chamber@perham.com; www.perham.com*

Pillager • see Staples

Pine City • *Pine City Area C/C* • Becky Schueller; Exec. Dir.; 315 Main St. S., Ste. 155; 55063; Pine; P 3,400; M 191; (320) 322-4040; info@pinecitychamber.com; www.pinecitychamber.com

Pine River • *Pine River C/C* • John Wetrosky; Dir.; P.O. Box 131; 56474; Cass; P 4,000; M 125; (218) 587-4000; (800) 728-6926; Fax (218) 587-4096; prcofc@uslink.net; www.pinerivermn.com*

Pipestone • *Pipestone Area C/C* • Erica Volkir; Exec. Dir.; 117 8th Ave. S.E.; P.O. Box 8; 56164; Pipestone; P 4,317; M 150; (507) 825-3316; (800) 336-6125; Fax (507) 825-3317; pipecham@pipestoneminnesota.com; PipestoneMinnesota.com

Plymouth • also see Rogers

Plymouth • *TwinWest C/C* • Deb McMillan; Interim Pres.; 10700 Old County Rd. 15, Ste. 170; 55441; Hennepin; P 250,000; M 1,000; (763) 450-2220; Fax (763) 450-2221; deb@twinwest.com; www.twinwest.com*

Princeton • *Princeton Area C/C* • Karen Michels; Exec. Dir.; 705 2nd St. N.; 55371; Mille-Lacs & Sherburne; P 4,700; M 180; (763) 389-1764; Fax (763) 631-1764; pacc@sherbtel.net; www.princetonmnchamber.org*

Prior Lake • *Prior Lake Area C/C* • Sandi Fleck; Pres.; 4785 Dakota St. S.E.; P.O. Box 114; 55372; Scott; P 22,000; M 425; (952) 440-1000; Fax (952) 440-1611; sandi@priorlakechamber.com; www.priorlakechamber.com*

Proctor • *Proctor Area C/C* • Rich Borg; P.O. Box 1016; 55810; St. Louis; P 2,900; M 100; (218) 624-4136; info@proctorchamber.com; www.proctorchamber.com*

Ramsey • see Anoka

Raymond • *Raymond Civic & Commerce* • Larry Macht; P.O. Box 353; 56282; Kandiyohi; P 800; M 60; (320) 967-4439; Fax (320) 967-4439; raymondminnesota@yahoo.com; www.raymondminnesota.com

Red Wing • *Red Wing Area C/C* • Patty Brown; Exec. Dir./Pres.; 439 Main St.; 55066; Goodhue; P 16,000; M 360; (651) 388-4719; frontdesk@redwingchamber.com; www.redwingchamber.com*

Redwood Falls • *Redwood Area Chamber & Tourism* • Anne Johnson; Exec. Dir.; 200 S. Mill St.; 56283; Redwood; P 16,815; M 176; (507) 637-2828; Fax (507) 637-5202; chamber@redwoodfalls.org; www.redwoodfalls.org*

Remer • *Remer Area C/C* • Bob Stoekel; Pres.; P.O. Box 101; 56672; Cass; P 342; M 70; (800) 831-4070; info@remerchamber.com; www.remerchamber.com

Rice • *Rice C/C* • Brian Laverdiere; Pres.; P.O. Box 22; 56367; Benton; P 1,300; M 80; (320) 393-2280; 320 281-9323; chamber@riceminnesota.com; www.riceminnesota.com

Richfield • *Richfield C/C* • Lori Nelson; Pres.; 6601 Lyndale Ave. S., Ste. 110; 55423; Hennepin; P 35,000; M 180; (612) 866-5100; Fax (612) 861-8302; lori@richfieldmnchamber.org; richfieldmnchamber.org*

Richmond • *Richmond Civic & Commerce* • Patti Plantenberg; Pres.; P.O. Box 355; 56368; Stearns; P 1,200; M 75; (320) 597-5300; richmondmn@hotmail.com; www.richmondmn.com

Riverton • see Crosby

Robbinsdale • *Robbinsdale C/C* • Dave Kiser; Secy.; P.O. Box 22646; 55422; Hennepin; P 14,500; M 68; (763) 531-1279; dkiser@twelve.tv; www.robbinsdalemn.com/chamber.htm

Rochester • *Rochester Area C/C* • Rob Miller; Pres./CEO; 220 S. Broadway, Ste. 100; 55904; Olmsted; P 120,000; M 1,260; (507) 288-1122; chamber@rochestermnchamber.com; www.rochestermnchamber.com*

Rockford • see Rogers

Rogers • *I-94 West C/C* • Donna J. Hartley; Pres.; 21370 John Milless Dr.; P.O. Box 95; 55374; Hennepin & Wright; P 35,000; M 650; (763) 428-2921; Fax (763) 428-9068; requests@i94westchamber.org; www.i94westchamber.org*

Roosevelt • see Baudette

Roseau • *Roseau Civic & Commerce* • Lyle Grindy; P.O. Box 304; 56751; Roseau; P 4,000; M 128; (218) 463-0009; (800) 815-1824; Fax (218) 463-1252; roseaupromotions@mncable.net; www.goroseau.com

Rosemount • *see Eagan*

Roseville • *see Saint Paul*

Rush City • *Rush City Area C/C* • Jeana Mikyska; Exec. Dir.; P.O. Box 713; 55069; Chisago; P 3,000; M 92; (320) 358-4639; director@rushcitychamber.com; www.rushcitychamber.com*

Rushford • *Rushford Area C/C* • Doug Botcher; Pres.; P.O. Box 338; 55971; Fillmore; P 1,679; M 90; (507) 864-3338; chamber@rushfordchamber.com; www.rushfordchamber.com

Saint Anthony • *Saint Anthony C/C* • 3301 Silver Lake Rd.; 55418; Hennepin; P 8,000; M 76; (612) 782-3301; info@saintanthonychamber.org; www.saintanthonychamber.org

Saint Cloud • *Saint Cloud Area C/C* • Teresa Bohnen; Pres.; 1411 W. Saint Germain St., Ste. 101; P.O. Box 487; 56302; Stearns; P 100,000; M 1,000; (320) 251-2940; Fax (320) 251-0081; information@stcloudareachamber.com; www.stcloudareachamber.com*

Saint Francis • *see Anoka*

Saint James • *Saint James Area C/C* • Jennie Firchau; Exec. Dir.; 516 1st Ave. S.; 56081; Watonwan; P 4,900; M 125; (507) 375-3333; (888) 859-0813; director@stjameschamberofcommerce.com; stjameschamberofcommerce.com

Saint Joseph • *Saint Joseph C/C* • Mary McCarney; Staff; P.O. Box 696; 56374; Stearns; P 5,000; M 80; (320) 363-4173; sjchamber@charter.net; www.stjosephchamber.com

Saint Louis Park • *see Plymouth - TwinWest C/C*

Saint Michael • *see Rogers*

Saint Paul • *Saint Paul Area C/C* • Matt Kramer; Pres.; 401 Robert St. N., Ste. 150; 55101; Ramsey; P 3,200,000; M 1,500; (651) 223-5000; info@saintpaulchamber.com; www.saintpaulchamber.com*

Saint Peter • *Saint Peter Area C/C* • Ed Lee; Exec. Dir.; 101 S. Front St.; 56082; Nicollet; P 11,000; M 250; (507) 934-3400; (800) 473-3404; Fax (507) 934-8960; spchamb@hickorytech.net; www.stpeterchamber.com*

Sandstone • *Sandstone Area C/C* • 402 N. Main; P.O. Box 23; 55072; Pine; P 2,200; M 100; (320) 245-2271; info@sandstonechamber.com; www.sandstonechamber.com

Sartell • *Sartell Area C/C* • Juli Sieben; Sales & Events Mgr.; P.O. Box 82; 56377; Stearns; P 18,000; M 225; (320) 258-6061; info@sartellchamber.com; www.sartellchamber.com*

Sauk Centre • *Sauk Centre Area C/C* • Jennifer Nelson; Exec. Dir.; 308 Oak St., Ste. 101; 56378; Stearns; P 4,400; M 188; (320) 352-5201; Fax (320) 351-5202; jennifer@saukcentrechamber.com; www.saukcentrechamber.com

Savage • *Savage C/C* • Anne Masis; Pres.; 6050 McColl Dr.; 55378; Scott; P 25,000; M 225; (952) 894-8876; Fax (952) 894-9906; mail@savagechamber.com; www.savagechamber.com*

Shafer • *see Lindstrom*

Shakopee • *Shakopee Chamber & Visitors Bur.* • Angela Whitcomb; Pres.; 1801 E. Cty. Rd. 101; 55379; Scott; P 37,500; M 225; (952) 445-1660; Fax (952) 445-1669; awhitcomb@shakopee.org; www.shakopee.org*

Sherburn • *Sherburn Civic & Commerce Club* • Laura Ringnell; Pres.; P.O. Box 108; 56171; Martin; P 1,200; M 40; (507) 764-4311; (507) 764-3151; www.sherburn.govoffice.com

Shoreview • *see Saint Paul*

Silver Bay • *see Two Harbors*

Slayton • *Slayton Area C/C* • Karen Onken; Dir.; 2635 Broadway Ave.; 56172; Murray; P 2,153; M 95; (507) 836-6902; Fax (507) 836-6650; slaytoncham@iw.net; www.slaytonchamber.com

Sleepy Eye • *Sleepy Eye Area C/C & CVB* • Christina Andres; Exec. Dir.; 115 2nd Ave. N.E.; 56085; Brown; P 3,600; M 130; (507) 794-4731; (800) 290-0588; Fax (507) 794-4732; secofc@sleepyeyetel.net; www.sleepyeyechamber.com*

Soudan • *see Tower*

South Saint Paul • *see Inver Grove Heights*

Spring Lake Park • *see New Brighton*

Spring Valley • *Spring Valley Area C/C* • Andrea Hindt; Pres.; P.O. Box 13; 55975; Fillmore; P 2,600; M 42; (507) 346-1015; (507) 346-7367; info@springvalleychamberofcommerce.com; www.springvalleychamberofcommerce.com

Springfield • *Springfield Area C/C & CVB* • Katie Mueller; Exec. Dir.; 33 S. Cass; P.O. Box 134; 56087; Brown; P 2,152; M 128; (507) 723-3508; spfdchamber@newulmtel.net; www.springfieldmnchamber.org

Staples • *Staples-Motley Area C/C* • Barb Cline; Admin.; Staples Depot, 320 U.S. Hwy. 10; P.O. Box 133; 56479; Todd; P 4,000; M 120; (218) 894-3974; smchamber@arvig.net; www.staplesmotleychamber.org

Starbuck • *Starbuck Area C/C* • Breeana Zaic; Dir.; 508 N. Main St.; P.O. Box 234; 56381; Pope; P 1,300; M 100; (320) 239-4220; Fax (320) 239-4759; starbuckchamber@hcinet.net; www.starbuckmn.org*

Stewartville • *Stewartville Area C/C* • Kathleen Stier; Admin.; 417 S. Main St.; P.O. Box 52; 55976; Olmsted; P 6,000; M 98; (507) 533-6006; admin@stewartvillechamber.com; www.stewartvillechamber.com*

Stillwater • *Greater Stillwater C/C* • Robin Anthony; Dir.; 200 Chestnut St. E., Ste. 204; 55082; Washington; P 19,000; M 435; (651) 439-4001; Fax (651) 439-4035; director@greaterstillwaterchamber.com; www.greaterstillwaterchamber.com*

Sunfish Lake • *see Eagan*

Thief River Falls • *Thief River Falls C/C* • Rhonda Lofberg; Exec. Dir.; 102 Main Ave. N.; 56701; Pennington; P 8,600; M 250; (218) 681-3720; (800) 827-1629; Fax (218) 681-3739; rhonda.lofberg@trfchamber.com; www.trfchamber.com*

Tower • *Lake Vermilion Area C/C* • Troy Swanson; Exec. Dir.; Train Depot; P.O. Box 776; 55790; St. Louis; P 300; M 63; (218) 753-8909; troyswanson@hotmail.com; www.lakevermilioncommerce.com

Tracy • *Tracy Area C/C* • Missie Erbes; Dir.; 372 Morgan St.; 56175; Lyon; P 3,400; M 71; (507) 629-4021; tracychamber@iw.net; www.tracymn.org

Trimont • *Trimont Area C/C* • Mary Ebeling; Exec. Secy.; P.O. Box 278; 56176; Martin; P 750; M 50; (507) 639-3082; trimontchamber@hotmail.com

Trommald • *see Crosby*

Two Harbors • *Two Harbors Area C/C* • Gordy Anderson; Pres./CEO; 1313 Fairgrounds Rd.; 55616; Lake; P 3,630; M 260; (218) 834-2600; Fax (218) 834-2600; shell@twoharborschamber.com; www.twoharborschamber.com

Tyler • *Tyler Area Comm. Club* • Angie Dubbeldee; Secy./Treas.; P.O. Box 445; 56178; Lincoln; P 1,175; M 50; (507) 247-5556; (507) 247-5878; www.tyler.govoffice.com

Vadnais Heights • *see Saint Paul and White Bear Lake*

Victoria • *see Chaska*

Virginia • *Laurentian C/C* • Jim Currie; Pres./CEO; 403 1st St. North; 55792; St. Louis; P 15,000; M 275; (218) 741-2717; Fax (218) 749-4913; jcurrie@laurentianchamber.org; www.laurentianchamber.org*

Wabasha • *Wabasha-Kellogg Chamber/CVB* • 137 W. Main St.; P.O. Box 105; 55981; Wabasha; P 3,200; M 120; (651) 565-4158; (800) 565-4158; Fax (651) 565-2808; info@wabashamn.org; www.wabashamn.org*

Waconia • *Waconia Area C/C* • Kellie Sites; Pres.; 209 S. Vine St.; 55387; Carver; P 10,000; M 200; (952) 442-5812; Fax (952) 856-4476; ksites@destinationwaconia.org; www.destinationwaconia.org*

Wadena • *Wadena Area C/C* • Shirley Uselman; Dir.; 5 Aldrich Ave. S.E.; P.O. Box 107; 56482; Wadena; P 4,100; M 150; (218) 632-7704; (877) 631-7704; Fax (218) 632-7705; chamber@wadenacoc.com; www.wadenachamber.com*

Walker • *Leech Lake Area C/C* • Cindy Wannarka; Pres./CEO; 205 Minnesota Ave.; P.O. Box 1089; 56484; Cass; P 1,067; M 250; (218) 547-1313; (800) 833-1118; Fax (218) 547-1338; info@leech-lake.com; www.leech-lake.com*

Warren • *Warren C/C* • Jay Ulferts; 56762; Marshall; P 1,675; M 65; (218) 745-4535; Fax (218) 745-4444; www.warrenminnesota.com

Warroad • *Warroad Area C/C & CVB* • Donna LaDuke; Exec. Dir.; P.O. Box 551; 56763; Roseau; P 2,300; M 177; (218) 386-3543; (800) 328-4455; Fax (218) 386-3454; visitwarroad@gmail.com; www.warroad.org

Waseca • *Waseca Area C/C* • Kim Foels; Exec. Dir.; 111 N. State St.; 56093; Waseca; P 9,827; M 240; (507) 835-3260; (888) 9-WASECA; Fax (507) 835-3267; info@wasecachamber.com; www.wasecachamber.com*

Watertown • *Watertown Area C/C* • Heather Jarvis; Exec. Secy.; P.O. Box 994; 55388; Carver; P 4,300; M 68; (952) 955-5175; watertownchamber@gmail.com; www.watertown-chamber.com*

Waterville • *Waterville Area C/C* • Marlys Meskan; Exec. Secy.; 213 Blowers; 56096; Le Sueur; P 1,800; M 55; (507) 362-4968; (507) 362-4609; lmesk@frontiernet.net; www.watervillemn.com

Waverly • *see Montrose*

Wayzata • *Greater Wayzata Area C/C* • Becky Pierson; Pres.; 402 E. Lake St.; 55391; Hennepin; P 4,100; M 400; (952) 473-9595; Fax (952) 473-6266; info@wayzatachamber.com; www.wayzatachamber.com*

Wells • *Wells Area C/C* • Andrea Neubauer; Exec. Dir.; 28 S. Broadway; P.O. Box 134; 56097; Faribault; P 2,400; M 80; (507) 553-6450; (866) 553-6450; Fax (507) 553-6451; wellscc@bevcomm.net; www.cityofwells.net*

West Saint Paul • *see Eagan*

Wheaton • *Wheaton Area C/C* • P.O. Box 493; 56296; Traverse; P 1,600; M 60; (320) 563-4110; www.cityofwheaton.com

White Bear Lake • *White Bear Area C/C* • Tom Snell; Exec. Dir.; 4751 Hwy. 61; 55110; Ramsey; P 25,000; M 375; (651) 429-8593; Fax (651) 429-8592; maureen@whitebearchamber.com; www.whitebearchamber.com*

White Bear Lake Township • *see White Bear Lake*

Willernie • *see White Bear Lake*

Williams • *see Baudette*

Willmar • *Willmar Lakes Area C/C* • Ken Warner; Pres.; 2104 Hwy. 12 E.; 56201; Kandiyohi; P 20,000; M 573; (320) 235-0300; Fax (320) 231-1948; chamber@willmarareachamber.com; www.willmarareachamber.com*

Windom • *Windom Area C/C & CVB* • Alexandra Leland; Exec. Dir.; 303 9th St.; 56101; Cottonwood; P 4,646; M 150; (507) 831-2752; Fax (507) 831-2755; director@windomchamber.com; windomchamber.com*

Winnebago • *Winnebago C/C* • Scott Robertson; Pres.; P.O. Box 516; 56098; Faribault; P 1,500; M 40; bagocofc@bevcomm.net

Winona • *Winona Area C/C* • Della Schmidt; Pres./CEO; 902 E. 2nd St., Ste. 120; P.O. Box 870; 55987; Winona; P 27,069; M 450; (507) 452-2272; Fax (507) 454-8814; info@winonachamber.com; www.winonachamber.com*

Winsted • *Winsted Area C/C* • Jeff Campbell; Pres.; P.O. Box 352; 55395; McLeod; P 2,400; M 75; (320) 485-2366; info@winstedchamber.com; www.winstedchamber.com*

Winthrop • *Winthrop Area C/C* • Doug Hanson; Exec. Secy.; P.O. Box 594; 55396; Sibley; P 1,400; M 85; (507) 647-2627; (800) 647-9461; dwhanson24@hotmail.com; www.winthropminnesota.com

Woodbury • *Woodbury Area C/C* • Barbara Tuccitto Warren; Pres.; 700 Commerce Dr., Ste. 245; 55125; Washington; P 60,000; M 500; (651) 578-0722; chamber@woodburychamber.org; www.woodburychamber.org*

Worthington • *Worthington Area C/C* • Darlene Macklin; Exec. Dir.; 1121 Third Ave.; 56187; Nobles; P 12,724; M 380; (507) 372-2919; Fax (507) 372-2827; wcofc@worthingtonmnchamber.com; www.worthingtonmnchamber.com*

Zimmerman • *Greater Zimmerman Area C/C* • Meghann Morris; Comm. Rel. Dir.; 12980 Fremont Ave., Ste. C; 55398; Sherburne; P 11,282; M 94; (763) 856-4404; zimmchamber@izoom.net; www.zimmermanchamber.org*

Mississippi

Mississippi Eco. Cncl. • Blake Wilson; Pres./CEO; 248 E. Capitol St., Ste. 940; P.O. Box 23276; Jackson; 39225; Hinds; P 2,994,100; M 8,000; (601) 969-0022; (800) 748-7626; Fax (601) 353-0247; cnorthington@mec.ms; www.mec.ms

Aberdeen • *Monroe County C/C* • Skip Scaggs; Exec. Dir.; 124 W. Commerce St.; P.O. Box 727; 39730; Monroe; P 37,000; M 335; (662) 369-6488; Fax (662) 369-6489; skip@gomonroe.org; www.gomonroe.org

Amory • *Monroe County C/C* • Tony Green; Pres.; 1619 Hwy. 25 N.; 38821; Monroe; P 36,691; M 300; (662) 256-7194; Fax (662) 256-9671; chamber@gomonroe.org; www.gomonroe.org*

Baldwyn • *Baldwyn Main Street Chamber* • Lori Tucker; Exec. Dir.; 202 S. Second St.; 38824; Lee & Prentiss; P 3,400; M 85; (662) 365-1050; Fax (662) 365-2387; mainstreet@cityofbaldwyn.com; www.cityofbaldwyn.com*

Batesville • *Panola Partnership Inc.* • Sonny Simmons; CEO; 150A Public Sq.; 38606; Panola; P 35,000; M 265; (662) 563-3126; Fax (662) 563-0704; partnership@panolacounty.com; www.panolacounty.com*

Bay Saint Louis • *Hancock County C/C* • Tish Williams; Exec. Dir.; 100 S. Beach Blvd, Ste. A; 39520; Hancock; P 43,929; M 1,500; (228) 467-9048; Fax (228) 467-6033; linda@hancockchamber.org; www.hancockchamber.org*

Belzoni • *Belzoni-Humphreys Dev. Found.* • Mark Bellipanni; Pres.; 111 Magnolia St.; P.O. Box 145; 39038; Humphreys; P 9,500; M 60; (662) 247-4838; Fax (662) 247-4805; catfish@belzonicable.com; www.belzonims.com

Biloxi • *Biloxi Bay Area C/C* • Tina Ross-Seamans; Exec. Dir.; P.O. Box 889; 39533; Harrison; P 51,000; M 1,200; (228) 435-6149; Fax (228) 435-6327; info@biloxibayareachamber.org; www.biloxibayareachamber.org*

Bolivar County • *see Cleveland*

Booneville • *Booneville Area C/C* • Trudy Featherston; Dir.; 100 W. Church St.; P.O. Box 927; 38829; Prentiss; P 9,000; M 125; (662) 416-3375; (800) 300-9302; trudyfeatherston@yahoo.com

Brandon • *Rankin County C/C* • Mandi Arinder; Exec. Dir.; 101 Service Dr.; P.O. Box 428; 39043; Rankin; P 118,000; M 1,000; (601) 825-2268; Fax (601) 825-1977; info@rankinchamber.com; www.rankinchamber.com*

Brookhaven • *Brookhaven-Lincoln County C/C* • Garrick Combs; Exec. Dir.; 230 S. Whitworth Ave.; P.O. Box 978; 39602; Lincoln; P 35,000; M 600; (601) 833-1411; Fax (601) 833-1412; info@brookhavenchamber.com; www.brookhavenchamber.org*

Bruce • *Bruce C/C* • Carol Shoemaker; Secy.; P.O. Box 1013; 38915; Calhoun; P 2,200; M 49; (662) 983-2222; Fax (662) 983-7300; chamber@brucetelephone.com; www.cityofbruce.com

Burnsville • *Burnsville C/C* • P.O. Box 211; 38833; Tishomingo; P 940; M 40; (662) 427-9526; Fax (662) 427-0001; www.burnsvillems.com

Byhalia • *Byhalia Area C/C* • Sarah Sawyer; Exec. Dir.; 2452 Church St.; P.O. Box 910; 38611; Marshall; P 36,000; M 300; (662) 838-8127; Fax (662) 838-8128; byhaliachamber@aol.com

Calhoun City • *Calhoun City C/C* • Laura B. Edwards; Pres.; 138-B Public Sq.; P.O. Box 161; 38916; Calhoun; P 1,900; M 53; (662) 628-6990; Fax (662) 628-6990; calhouncitychamber@tds.net; www.calhouncitychamberofcommerce.com

Canton • *Canton C/C Main St. Assn.* • Jordan Hillman; Exec. Dir.; 100 Depot Dr.; 39046; Madison; P 12,000; M 200; (601) 859-5816; ccoc@canton-mississippi.com; www.canton-mississippi.com*

Carthage • *Leake County C/C* • Terri Neal; Exec. Dir.; 103 N. Pearl St.; P.O. Box 209; 39051; Leake; P 22,000; M 200; (601) 267-9231; Fax (601) 267-8123; director@leakems.com; www.leakems.com

Clarksdale • *Clarksdale-Coahoma County C/C & Ind. Found.* • Ronald E. Hudson; Exec. Dir.; 1540 DeSoto Ave.; P.O. Box 160; 38614; Coahoma; P 20,000; M 300; (662) 627-7337; Fax (662) 627-1313; chamberofcommerce@clarksdale-ms.com; www.clarksdale-ms.com

Cleveland • *Cleveland-Bolivar County C/C* • Judson Thigpen III; Exec. Dir.; 101 S. Bayou Ave.; P.O. Box 490; 38732; Bolivar; P 35,000; M 347; (662) 843-2712; Fax (662) 843-2718; info@clevelandmschamber.com; www.clevelandmschamber.com

Clinton • *Clinton C/C* • T.J. McSparrin; Exec. Dir.; 100 E. Leake; P.O. Box 143; 39060; Hinds; P 25,000; M 475; (601) 924-5912; (800) 611-9980; Fax (601) 925-4009; director@clintonchamber.org; www.clintonchamber.org*

Coffeeville • *Coffeeville Area C/C* • Beverly Freer; Treas.; P.O. Box 184; 38922; Yalobusha; P 1,000; M 20; (662) 675-8385; coffeeville@bellsouth.net; www.coffeevillems.com

Collins • *Covington County C/C* • Marie Shoemake; Exec. Dir.; 500 Komo St.; P.O. Box 1595; 39428; Covington; P 21,743; M 200; (601) 765-6012; Fax (601) 765-1740; ms@covingtonchamber.com; www.covingtonchamber.com*

Columbia • *Marion County Dev. Partnership* • Carolyn Burton; V.P. of Chamber; 412 Courthouse Sq.; P.O. Box 272; 39429; Marion; P 27,000; M 300; (601) 736-6385; Fax (601) 736-6392; info@mcdp.info; www.mcdp.info*

Columbus • *Golden Triangle Dev. LINK* • Joe Max Higgins Jr.; CEO; 1102 Main St.; P.O. Box 1328; 39703; Lowndes; P 63,000; M 680; (662) 328-8369; (800) 748-8882; Fax (662) 327-3417; jhiggins@gtrlink.org; www.gtrlink.org*

Como • *see Batesville*

Corinth • *The Alliance* • Gary Chandler; Pres.; 810 Tate St.; 38834; Alcorn; P 15,000; M 400; (662) 287-5269; info@corinthalliance.com; www.corinthalliance.com*

Courtland • *see Batesville*

Crenshaw • *see Batesville*

Crystal Springs • *Crystal Springs C/C* • Donna Y. Wells; Exec. Dir.; 210 E. Railroad Ave.; P.O. Box 519; 39059; Copiah; P 6,005; M 145; (601) 892-2711; Fax (601) 892-4870; crystalspringschamber@telepak.net; www.crystalspringsmiss.com

D'Iberville • *D'Iberville-St. Martin Area C/C* • Sharon Seymour; Exec. Dir.; P.O. Box 6054; 39540; Harrison; P 10,000; M 265; (228) 392-2293; Fax (228) 396-3216; dsmchamber@att.net; www.dsmchamber.com

Decatur • *Greater Decatur C/C* • Phil Sutphin; Pres.; P.O. Box 307; 39327; Newton; P 2,000; M 70; (601) 635-2761; www.decaturms.org

DeKalb • *Kemper County C/C & Eco. Dev.* • June Aust; Exec. Dir.; 14064 Hwy. 16 W.; P.O. Box 518; 39328; Kemper; P 10,456; M 55; (601) 743-2754; Fax (601) 743-2760; austjune@yahoo.com; www.kempercounty.com

Drew • *Drew C/C* • Penny Andrews; Mgr.; 129 Shaw Ave.; 38737; Sunflower; P 2,500; M 90; (662) 745-8975; www.drew-ms.gov

Flora • *see Ridgeland-Madison County C/C*

Forest • *Forest Area C/C* • Allyce Lott; Exec. Dir.; 120 S. Davis St.; P.O. Box 266; 39074; Scott; P 7,000; M 160; (601) 469-4332; Fax (601) 469-3224; forestareachamber@att.net; www.forestareachamber.com

Fulton • *Itawamba County Dev. Cncl.* • Greg Deakle; Exec. Dir.; 107 W. Wiygul St.; P.O. Box 577; 38843; Itawamba; P 23,229; M 320; (662) 862-4571; (800) 371-8642; Fax (662) 862-5637; icdc@itawamba.com; www.itawamba.com

Gautier • *see Pascagoula*

Greenville • *Washington County Eco. Alliance* • Cary Karlson; Exec. Dir.; 342 Washington Ave., Ste. 201; P.O. Box 933; 38702; Washington; P 34,000; M 483; (662) 378-3141; Fax (662) 378-3143; dwintory@wceams.com; www.wceams.com*

Greenwood • *Greenwood-Leflore County C/C* • Beth Stevens; Exec. Dir.; 402 Hwy. 82 W.; P.O. Box 848; 38935; Leflore; P 15,000; M 600; (662) 453-4152; Fax (662) 453-8003; info@greenwoodms.com; www.greenwoodmschamber.com*

Grenada • *Grenada Area C/C* • Tonja Ray Smith; Exec. Dir.; P.O. Box 628; 38902; Grenada; P 38,142; M 350; (662) 226-2571; Fax (662) 226-9745; info@grenadamississippi.com; www.grenadamississippi.com*

Gulfport • *Mississippi Gulf Coast C/C* • Kimberly Nastasi; CEO; 11975E Seaway Rd., Ste. B-120; 39503; Harrison; P 141,000; M 1,100; (228) 604-0014; Fax (228) 604-0105; info@mscoastchamber.com; www.mscoastchamber.com

Hattiesburg • *Area Dev. Partnership* • Chad Newell; Pres.; One Convention Center Plaza; 39401; Lamar; P 142,842; M 1,500; (601) 296-7500; (800) 238-HATT; Fax (601) 296-7505; adp@theadp.com; www.theadp.com

Hazlehurst • *Hazlehurst Area C/C* • Randall Day; Exec. Dir.; 138 N. Ragsdale Ave.; P.O. Box 446; 39083; Copiah; P 4,500; M 100; (601) 894-3752; Fax (601) 894-3752; hazlechamber@bellsouth.net; www.hazlechamber.com

Hernando • *Hernando Main Street Chamber of Commerce* • Susan Fernandez; Exec. Dir.; 2440 Hwy. 51 S.; 38632; DeSoto; P 15,000; M 350; (662) 429-9055; chamber@hernandoms.org; www.hernandoms.org*

Holly Springs • *Holly Springs C/C* • Rebecca Bourgeois; Exec. Dir.; 148 E. College Ave.; 38635; Marshall; P 8,000; M 200; (662) 252-2943; office@hschamber.org; www.hschamber.org

Horn Lake • *Horn Lake C/C* • Varina Hopper; Exec. Dir.; 3101 Goodman Rd. W.; 38637; DeSoto; P 26,000; M 220; (662) 393-9897; Fax (662) 342-3476; info@hornlakechamber.com; www.hornlakechamber.com*

Houston • *Chickasaw Dev. Found.* • Joyce East; Exec. Dir.; 635 Starkville Rd.; P.O. Box 505; 38851; Chickasaw; P 18,000; M 98; (662) 456-2321; Fax (662) 456-2595; jeastcdf@bellsouth.net; www.houstonms.org

Hurley • *see Pascagoula*

Indianola • *Indianola C/C* • Cherri Kirk; Exec. Dir.; 112 S. MLK Dr.; P.O. Box 151; 38751; Sunflower; P 13,500; M 250; (662) 887-4454; Fax (662) 887-4454; icoc@tecinfo.com; www.indianolams.org

Inverness • *Inverness C/C* • Jody Evans; Pres.; P.O. Box 13; 38753; Sunflower; P 972; M 105; (662) 265-5741; icc@in-ms.org; www.in-ms.org

Jackson • *Greater Jackson Chamber Partnership* • Duane A. O'Neill; Pres./CEO; 201 S. President St.; P.O. Box 22548; 39225; Hinds; P 540,000; M 2,200; (601) 948-7575; Fax (601) 948-1808; pjones@greaterjacksonpartnership.com; www.greaterjacksonpartnership.com*

Laurel • *Jones County C/C* • Larkin Simpson; Dir.; 153 Base Dr., Ste. 3; P.O. Box 527; 39441; Jones; P 67,761; M 450; (601) 428-0574; Fax (601) 428-2047; info@edajones.com; www.jonescounty.com*

Leland • *Leland C/C* • Melia Christensen; Exec. Dir.; P.O. Box 67; 38756; Washington; P 4,400; M 100; (662) 686-2687; (662) 379-3764; lelandcoc@gmail.com; www.lelandchamber.com

Lexington • *Holmes County C/C* • Jean Carson; Exec. Dir.; 104 W. China St., Ste. A; 39095; Holmes; P 18,200; M 65; (662) 834-3372; Fax (662) 834-3372; holmescountycoc@att.net; www.holmescountymississippi.com

Liberty • *Liberty Area C/C* • Melissa Jackson; Secy./Treas.; P.O. Box 18; 39645; Amite; P 1,900; M 65; (601) 657-8035

Long Beach • *see Gulfport*

Louisville • *Louisville-Winston County C/C* • Linda Skelton; Dir.; 311 W. Park St.; P.O. Box 551; 39339; Winston; P 20,160; M 200; (662) 773-3921; Fax (662) 773-8909; linda@winstoncounty.com; winstoncountyms.com*

Lucedale • *George County C/C* • Cheryl Balius; Pres.; 116 Beaver Dam Rd.; P.O. Box 441; 39452; George; P 22,578; M 110; (601) 947-2755; Fax (601) 947-2650; georgecountyedf@bellsouth.net

Lyman • *see Gulfport*

Macon • *Noxubee County Eco. & Comm. Dev. Alliance* • Ms. Marti Kauffman; 503 S. Washington St.; P.O. Box 308; 39341; Noxubee; P 11,800; M 100; (662) 726-4456; (800) 487-0165; Fax (662) 726-1041; noxubeems@yahoo.com; www.noxubeecountyms.com

Madison • *Madison the City C/C* • Pam Mahony; Exec. Dir.; 2023 Main St.; P.O. Box 544; 39130; Madison; P 24,000; M 801; (601) 856-7060; Fax (601) 856-4852; information@madisonthecitychamber.com; www.madisonthecitychamber.com*

Magee • *Magee C/C* • Doris Adcox; Exec. Dir.; 117 1st Ave. N.W.; 39111; Simpson; P 5,000; M 215; (601) 849-2517; Fax (601) 849-2517; commercechamber@bellsouth.net; www.mageechamberofcommerce.com

Magnolia • *South Pike Area C/C* • Jimmy Harris; Pres.; 175 E. Railroad Ave. N.; 39652; Pike; P 3,000; M 45; (601) 783-5267; www.cityofmagnoliams.com

McComb • *Pike County C/C* • Catherine Sanders; Exec. Dir.; 213 Main St.; P.O. Box 83; 39649; Pike; P 40,000; M 450; (601) 684-2291; Fax (601) 684-4899; csanders@pikeinfo.com; www.pikeinfo.com*

Meadville • *Franklin C/C* • Brad Jones; Pres.; P.O. Box 606; 39653; Franklin; P 8,000; M 120; (601) 384-2305; www.meadvillems.com

Mendenhall • *Mendenhall Area C/C* • Marsha Bratcher; Secy.; P.O. Box 635; 39114; Simpson; P 2,500; M 125; (601) 847-1725; mendenhallchamber@gmail.com; www.ci.mendenhall.ms.us

Meridian • *East Mississippi Bus. Dev. Corp.* • Bill Hannah; Pres./CEO; 1901 Front St., Ste. A; P.O. Box 790; 39302; Lauderdale; P 93,551; M 520; (601) 693-1306; Fax (601) 693-5638; dmathis@embdc.org; www.embdc.org*

Monticello • *Lawrence County C/C* • Bob Smira; Pres./CEO; 517 Broad St. E.; P.O. Box 996; 39654; Lawrence; P 13,000; M 80; (601) 587-3007; Fax (601) 587-0765; bsmira@lccda.org; www.lccda.org

Moorhead • *Moorhead C/C* • Joyce Walker; P.O. Box 177; 38761; Sunflower; P 2,400; M 22; (662) 246-5461

Morton • *Morton C/C* • Brenda M. McCaughn; Exec. Dir.; 91 W. 1st Ave.; P.O. Box 530; 39117; Scott; P 3,500; M 75; (601) 732-6135; Fax (601) 732-7188; mccaughn.brenda@yahoo.com; www.cityofmorton.com

Moss Point • *see Pascagoula*

Natchez • *Natchez-Adams County C/C* • Debbie Hudson; Pres./CEO; 211 Main St., Ste. A; P.O. Box 1403; 39121; Adams; P 33,000; M 400; (601) 445-4611; Fax (601) 445-9361; natchezchamber@natchezchamber.com; www.natchezchamber.com*

Newton • *Newton C/C* • Leigh Anne Whittle; Exec. Dir.; 128 S. Main St.; 39345; Newton; P 3,200; M 100; (601) 683-2201; Fax (601) 683-2201; chambernewton@bellsouth.net; www.newtonchamberofcommerce.com

Ocean Springs • *Ocean Springs C/C* • Margaret Miller; Exec. Dir.; 1000 Washington Ave.; 39564; Jackson; P 18,000; M 600; (228) 875-4424; Fax (228) 875-0332; mail@oceanspringschamber.com; www.oceanspringschamber.com*

Okolona • *Okolona Area C/C-Main Street Program* • Perry Grubbs; Exec. Dir.; 219 Main St.; P.O. Box 446; 38860; Chickasaw; P 3,500; M 150; (662) 447-5913; Fax (662) 447-0254; jperrygrubbs@hotmail.com; www.okolonams.org

Olive Branch • *Olive Branch C/C* • Vickie DuPree IOM; CEO/Exec. Dir.; 9123 Pigeon Roost; P.O. Box 608; 38654; DeSoto; P 35,000; M 572; (662) 895-2600; Fax (662) 895-2625; info@olivebranchms.com; www.olivebranchms.com*

Orange Grove • *see Gulfport*

Oxford • *Oxford-Lafayette County C/C* • Max D. Hipp CEcD; Pres./CEO; P.O. Box 147; 38655; Lafayette; P 50,000; M 500; (662) 234-4651; Fax (662) 234-4655; frontdesk@oxfordms.com; www.oxfordms.com*

Pascagoula • *Jackson County C/C* • Carla Todd IOM; Pres./CEO; 720 Krebs Ave.; P.O. Box 480; 39568; Jackson; P 135,000; M 800; (228) 762-3391; Fax (228) 769-1726; chamber@jcchamber.com; www.jcchamber.com*

Pass Christian • *see Gulfport*

Pearl • *Pearl C/C* • Kathy Deer; Exec. Dir.; 110 George Wallace Dr.; P.O. Box 54125; 39288; Rankin; P 26,000; M 450; (601) 939-3338; Fax (601) 936-5717; pearlchamberofcommerce@pearlms.org; www.pearlms.org*

Petal • *Petal Area C/C* • Deborah Reynolds; Exec. Dir.; 712 S. Main St., Ste. B; P.O. Box 421; 39465; Forrest; P 10,000; M 250; (601) 583-3306; Fax 583-3312; dacofc@aol.com; www.petalchamber.com

Philadelphia • *Community Dev. Partnership* • 256 W. Beacon St.; P.O. Box 330; 39350; Neshoba; P 30,000; M 220; (601) 656-1000; (877) 752-2643; Fax (601) 656-1066; karowell@bellsouth.net; www.neshoba.org

Picayune • *Greater Picayune Area C/C* • April Lovelace; Pres.; 201 Hwy. 11 N.; P.O. Box 448; 39466; Pearl River; P 12,000; M 465; (601) 798-3122; Fax (601) 798-6984; aprillovelace@picayunechamber.org; www.picayunechamber.org

Pontotoc • *Pontotoc County C/C & Mainstreet Assn.* • Ellen Russell; Mgr.; 109 N. Main; P.O. Box 530; 38863; Pontotoc; P 30,000; M 150; (662) 489-5042; Fax (662) 489-5263; chamber@pontotocchamber.com; www.pontotocchamber.com

Pope • *see Batesville*

Poplarville • *Poplarville Area C/C* • Michelle McBride; Pres.; 101 N. Main St.; P.O. Box 367; 39470; Pearl River; P 20,000; M 175; (601) 795-0578; poplarvillechamber@gmail.com; www.poplarville.org

Port Gibson • *Port Gibson-Claiborne County C/C* • Linda Ory; Dir.; 1601 Church St.; P.O. Box 491; 39150; Claiborne; P 2,000; M 46; (601) 437-4351; portgibsonchamber@att.net; www.portgibsonchamber.com

Prentiss • *Jefferson Davis County Chamber Partnership* • Jerleen White; Admin.; 1025 3rd St.; P.O. Box 342; 39474; Jefferson Davis; P 12,000; M 62; (601) 792-5903; Fax (601) 792-0291; www.jeffdavisms.com

Quitman • *Clarke County C/C* • 100 S. Railroad Ave.; P.O. Box 172; 39355; Clarke; P 17,000; M 125; (601) 776-5701; Fax (601) 776-5745; clarkechamber@att.net; www.clarkecountychamber.com

Raymond • *Raymond C/C* • DeAnna Dillard IOM; Chamber Consultant; P.O. Box 1162; 39154; Hinds; P 2,000; M 60; (601) 857-8942; raymondchamberofcommerce@gmail.com; www.raymondchamber.org

Ridgeland • *Madison County C/C* • Paige Petersen; Exec. Dir.; 618 Crescent Blvd., Ste. 101; 39157; Madison; P 90,000; M 525; (601) 605-2554; Fax (601) 605-2260; info@madisoncountychamber.com; www.madisoncountychamber.com*

Ridgeland • *City of Ridgeland C/C* • Linda T. Bynum; Exec. Dir.; 754 S. Pear Orchard Rd.; P.O. Box 194; 39158; Madison; P 24,047; M 950; (601) 991-9996; Fax (601) 991-9997; admin@ridgelandchamber.com; www.ridgelandchamber.com*

Ruleville • *Ruleville C/C* • Jo Frothingham; V.P.; P.O. Box 552; 38771; Sunflower; P 3,500; M 50; (662) 756-2249; Fax (662) 756-2249; jofroth@cableone.net; www.rulevillechamberofcommerce.com

Sardis • *Sardis C/C* • Penny Hart; Exec. Secy.; 304 S. Main St.; P.O. Box 377; 38666; Panola; P 1,900; M 75; (662) 609-7517; www.sardislake.com

Senatobia • *Tate County C/C, Eco. Dev. Found. & Main Street* • J.E. Mortimer; Exec. Dir.; 135 N. Front St.; 38668; Tate; P 29,000; M 260; (662) 562-8715; Fax (662) 562-5786; jemortimer@cityofsenatobia.com; www.tate-county.com*

Southaven • *Southaven C/C* • Carmen Kyle; Exec. Dir.; 8710 Northwest Dr.; P.O. Box 211; 38671; DeSoto; P 53,000; M 610; (662) 342-6114; (800) 272-6551; Fax (662) 342-6365; info@southavenchamber.com; www.southavenchamber.com*

Starkville • *Greater Starkville Dev. Partnership/Chamber* • Heath Barret; Interim CEO; 200 E. Main St.; 39759; Oktibbeha; P 50,000; M 530; (662) 323-3322; (800) 649-8687; Fax (662) 323-5815; hbarret@starkville.org; www.starkville.org*

Tunica • *Tunica County C/C* • Lyn Arnold; Pres./CEO; 1301 Main St.; P.O. Box 1888; 38676; Tunica; P 11,000; M 323; (662) 363-2865; Fax (662) 357-0378; larnold@tunicachamber.com; www.tunicachamber.com

Tupelo • *Comm. Dev. Found.* • David Rumbarger; Pres./CEO; 398 E. Main St.; P.O. Box A; 38802; Lee; P 39,000; M 1,400; (662) 842-4521; Fax (662) 841-0693; info@cdfms.org; www.cdfms.org*

Tylertown • **Walthall County C/C** • Doug Walker; Pres.; P.O. Box 227; 39667; Walthall; P 15,380; M 172; (601) 876-2680; Fax (601) 876-2680; walthallchamber@bellsouth.net; www.walthallchamber.com

Union • **Union C/C** • Joyce Holifield; Exec. Dir.; P.O. Box 90; 39365; Newton; P 2,000; M 10; (601) 774-9586; (601) 774-9422; unionchamberofcommerce@yahoo.com; www.unionmschamber.com

Vancleave • **see Pascagoula**

Vicksburg • **Vicksburg-Warren County C/C** • Jane Flowers; Exec. Dir.; 2020 Mission 66; 39180; Warren; P 48,800; M 400; (601) 636-1012; Fax (601) 636-4422; info@vicksburgchamber.org; www.vicksburgchamber.org*

Water Valley • **Water Valley Area C/C** • Zandra Walker; Ofc. Mgr.; 206 Main St.; P.O. Box 726; 38965; Yalobusha; P 3,500; M 75; (662) 473-1122; Fax (662) 473-1477; wvchamber@bellsouth.net; www.watervalleychamber.info*

Waynesboro • **Wayne County C/C** • Shirley Yates; Exec. Dir.; 707-A Azalea Dr.; P.O. Box 864; 39367; Wayne; P 21,000; M 100; (601) 735-3311; Fax (601) 735-3094; shirley.yates64@gmail.com; www.waynesboroinfo.com

Wesson • **Wesson C/C** • Melissa Meredith; Secy./Treas.; P.O. Box 557; 39191; Copiah; P 1,770; M 55; (601) 643-5000; Fax (601) 643-5000; wesson_chamber@yahoo.com; www.wessonms.org

Winston County • **see Louisville**

Yazoo City • **Yazoo County C/C** • Whitney Hurt; Exec. Dir.; P.O. Box 172; 39194; Yazoo; P 28,100; M 175; (662) 746-1273; ccyazoo@bellsouth.net; yazoochamber.com

Missouri

Missouri C of C & Ind. • Daniel P. Mehan; Pres./CEO; 428 E. Capitol Ave.; P.O. Box 149; Jefferson City; 65102; Cole; P 6,021,988; M 4,000; (573) 634-3511; Fax (573) 634-8855; dmehan@mochamber.com; www.mochamber.com

Affton • **Affton C/C** • Lisa Rackley; Exec. Dir.; 9815 Mackenzie Rd.; 63123; St. Louis; P 21,000; M 300; (314) 631-3100; Fax (314) 631-3102; info@afftonchamber.com; www.afftonchamber.com*

Albany • **Albany C/C** • Kathy Morgan; Pres.; 106 E. Clay St.; P.O. Box 231; 64402; Gentry; P 1,800; M 90; (660) 726-3935; ecodev@albanymo.net; www.albanymo.net*

Anderson • **see Pineville**

Arnold • **Arnold C/C** • Brandi Shufeldt; Exec. Dir.; 110 Richardson Crossing; 63010; Jefferson; P 22,000; M 274; (636) 296-1910; director@arnoldchamber.org; www.arnoldchamber.org*

Augusta • **Greater Augusta C/C** • Robin White; Pres.; 5577 Walnut St.; P.O. Box 41; 63332; St. Charles; P 250; M 50; (636) 228-4005; gacc.augusta@gmail.com; www.augusta-chamber.org

Aurora • **Aurora C/C** • Shannon Walker; Exec. Dir.; 121 E. Olive; P.O. Box 257; 65605; Lawrence; P 7,450; M 185; (417) 678-4150; Fax (417) 678-1387; auroracoc@mo-net.com; www.auroramochamber.com

Ava • **Ava Area C/C** • Judy Shields; Exec. Dir.; 810 S.W. 13th Ave.; P.O. Box 1103; 65608; Douglas; P 13,600; M 144; (417) 683-4594; Fax (417) 683-9464; director@avachamber.org; www.avachamber.org

Ballwin • **see Ellisville**

Belton • **Belton C/C** • Diane Huckshorn; Exec. Dir.; 323 Main St.; P.O. Box 350; 64012; Cass; P 24,000; M 400; (816) 331-2420; Fax (816) 331-8736; chamberbelton@gmail.com; www.beltonmochamber.org*

Bethany • **Bethany Area C/C** • Casey Campbell; Bd. Secy.; 116 N. 16th St.; 64424; Harrison; P 3,300; M 75; (660) 425-6358; (660) 425-3511; bchamber@grm.net; www.bethanymochamber.org

Blue Springs • **Blue Springs C/C** • Lara Vermillion; Pres.; 1000 W. Main St.; 64015; Jackson; P 53,000; M 456; (816) 229-8558; Fax (816) 229-1244; bschamberinfo@bluespringschamber.com; www.bluespringschamber.com*

Bolivar • **Bolivar Area C/C** • Linda Bunch; Exec. Dir.; 454 S. Springfield Ave.; P.O. Box 202; 65613; Polk; P 11,000; M 250; (417) 326-4118; Fax (417) 777-9080; info@bolivarchamber.com; www.bolivarchamber.com

Bonne Terre • **Bonne Terre C/C** • Ron Allen; Exec. Dir.; 30 N. Allen; P.O. Box 175; 63628; St. Francois; P 5,000; M 200; (573) 358-4000; Fax (573) 358-0071; btchamberofcommerce@yahoo.com; www.bonneterrechamber.com

Boonville • **Boonville Area C/C** • Laura Wax; Exec. Dir.; 320 1st St., Ste. A; 65233; Cooper; P 8,200; M 300; (660) 882-2721; Fax (660) 882-5660; boonvillemochamber@gmail.com; www.boonvillemochamber.com

Bowling Green • **Bowling Green C/C** • Sarah Patton; Exec. Dir.; 16A W. Church St.; P.O. Box 401; 63334; Pike; P 3,500; M 85; (573) 324-3733; bgmocc@att.net; www.bgchamber.org

Branson • **Branson/Lakes Area C/C & CVB** • Jeff Seifried; Pres./CEO; 269 State Hwy. 248; P.O. Box 1897; 65615; Taney; P 35,000; M 1,000; (417) 334-4084; (800) 214-3661; Fax (417) 334-4139; info@bransonchamber.com; www.bransonchamber.com*

Braymer • **Braymer C/C** • MaryLou Tuck; Secy./Treas.; 2nd & Main St.; P.O. Box 176; 64624; Caldwell; P 830; M 35; (660) 645-2802; (660) 645-2355; www.braymer.homestead.com

Breckenridge Hills • **see Saint Louis-Northwest C/C**

Brentwood • **Brentwood C/C** • Gina March; Exec. Dir.; 8754 Rosalie Ave.; 63144; St. Louis; P 8,100; M 200; (314) 963-9007; chamber@brentwoodmo.org; www.brentwoodmochamber.com*

Brookfield • **Brookfield Area C/C** • Paul W. Frey; Exec. Dir.; 207B N. Main St.; 64628; Linn; P 4,500; M 140; (660) 258-7255; Fax (660) 258-7255; chamber@brookfieldmochamber.com; www.brookfieldmochamber.com

Brunswick • **Brunswick Area C/C** • Roseanne Meyer; Pres.; P.O. Box 104; 65236; Chariton; P 847; M 54; (660) 548-3337; info@brunswickmo.com; www.brunswickmo.com

Buckner • **Buckner C/C** • Patrick Farrell; Pres.; P.O. Box 287; 64016; Jackson; P 3,076; M 50; (816) 650-5535; (816) 650-7019; sibleyorchards@hotmail.com

Buffalo • **Buffalo Area C/C** • Kathy Kesler-Strawsma; Exec. Dir.; 101 N. Maple St.; P.O. Box 258; 65622; Dallas; P 15,000; M 125; (417) 345-2852; Fax (417) 345-2852; chamber@buffalococ.com; www.buffalococ.com

Butler • **Butler C/C** • Lee Anna Schowengerdt; Exec. Dir.; 15 N. Main; 64730; Bates; P 4,500; M 176; (660) 679-3380; Fax (660) 679-0156; director@butlerchamber.com; www.butlerchamber.com

Cabool • **Cabool Area C/C** • Sarah Montgomery; P.O. Box 285; 65689; Texas; P 2,600; M 82; (417) 962-3002; Fax (417) 962-3002; info@caboolchamber.org; www.caboolmo.org

California • *California Area C/C* • Sandra Ratcliff; Exec. Secy.; 500 S. Oak St.; 65018; Moniteau; P 4,300; M 120; (573) 796-3040; Fax (573) 796-8309; office@calmo.com; www.calmo.com

Camdenton • *Camdenton Area C/C* • Trish Creach; Exec. Dir.; 739 W. U.S. Hwy. 54; P.O. Box 1375; 65020; Camden; P 15,000; M 390; (573) 346-2227; (800) 769-1004; Fax (573) 346-3496; info@camdentonchamber.com; www.camdentonchamber.com

Cameron • *Cameron Area C/C* • Mary Murdock; Exec. Dir.; 416 N. Walnut, Ste. A; 64429; Clinton & DeKalb; P 8,500; M 170; (816) 632-2005; Fax (816) 632-2005; office@cameronmochamber.com; www.cameronmochamber.com*

Canton • *Canton C/C* • Mark Fryer; Pres.; P.O. Box 141; 63435; Lewis; P 2,600; M 75; (573) 288-8300; staff@cantonmochamber.com; www.cantonmochamber.com

Cape Fair • *Cape Fair C/C* • Alan Kram; P.O. Box 104; 65624; Stone; P 600; M 45; (417) 538-2222; info@capefairchamber.com; www.capefairchamber.com

Cape Girardeau • *Cape Girardeau Area C/C* • John E. Mehner; Pres./CEO; 220 N. Fountain; 63701; Cape Girardeau; P 75,000; M 1,200; (573) 335-3312; Fax (573) 335-4686; info@capechamber.com; www.capechamber.com*

Carl Junction • *Carl Junction Area C/C* • Gary Stubblefield; Exec. Dir.; P.O. Box 301; 64834; Jasper; P 7,500; M 280; (417) 649-8846; cjchamberofcommerce@gmail.com; www.carljunctioncc.com

Carrollton • *Carrollton C/C* • Sharon Metz; Exec. Dir.; 111 N. Mason; 64633; Carroll; P 4,100; M 150; (660) 542-0922; Fax (660) 542-3489; director@carrolltonareachamber.org; www.carrolltonareachamber.org

Carthage • *Carthage C/C* • Sabrina Drackert; Pres./Eco. Dev. Dir.; 402 S. Garrison Ave.; 64836; Jasper; P 14,055; M 360; (417) 358-2373; Fax (417) 358-7479; sdrackert@carthagechamber.com; www.carthagechamber.com*

Caruthersville • *Caruthersville C/C* • Amanda Irvin; Coord.; 200 W. 3rd; P.O. Box 806; 63830; Pemiscot; P 6,200; M 200; (573) 333-1222; Fax (573) 333-4247; caruthersvillechamber@gmail.com; www.caruthersvillecity.com

Cassville • *Cassville Area C/C* • Mindi Artherton; Exec. Dir.; 504 Main St.; 65625; Barry; P 4,000; M 215; (417) 847-2814; chamber@cassville.com; www.cassville.com*

Centralia • *Centralia C/C* • Ginny Zoellers; Exec. Dir.; 101 W. Singleton; P.O. Box 235; 65240; Boone; P 4,027; M 91; (573) 682-2272; Fax (573) 682-1111; ginny@midamerica.net; www.centraliamochamber.com

Chaffee • *Chaffee C/C* • Ken Latham; Pres.; P.O. Box 35; 63740; Scott; P 2,955; M 60; (573) 887-3555; information@chaffeechamber.com; www.chaffeechamber.com

Charlack • *see Saint Louis-Northwest C/C*

Charleston • *Charleston C/C* • Karen Teeters; Exec. Dir.; 110 E. Commercial St.; P.O. Box 407; 63834; Mississippi; P 5,000; M 100; (573) 683-6509; Fax (573) 683-6799; chamber@charlestonmo.org; www.charlestonmo.org

Chesterfield • *Chesterfield C/C* • Nora Amato; Exec. Dir.; 101 Chesterfield Business Pkwy.; 63005; St. Louis; P 47,700; M 650; (636) 532-3399; (888) 242-4262; Fax (636) 532-7446; nora@chesterfieldmochamber.com; www.chesterfieldmochamber.com*

Chillicothe • *Chillicothe Area C/C* • Crystal Narr; Exec. Dir.; 514 Washington St.; P.O. Box 407; 64601; Livingston; P 9,500; M 300; (660) 646-4050; (877) 224-4554; Fax (660) 646-3309; chamber@chillicothemo.com; www.chillicothemo.com*

Clarksville • *Clarksville Comm. C/C* • Joanna Brock; Pres.; 301 N. Hwy 79; P.O. Box 162; 63336; Pike; P 500; M 20; (573) 242-3132; (573) 242-3945; Fax (573) 242-3450; clarksvillecommunitychamber@gmail.com; www.clarksvillemo.us

Clayton • *Clayton C/C* • Ellen Gale; Exec. Dir.; 225 S. Meramec Ave., Ste. 300; 63105; St. Louis; P 16,000; M 450; (314) 726-3033; Fax (314) 726-0637; mrosner@claytoncommerce.com; www.claytoncommerce.com*

Clinton • *Greater Clinton Area C/C* • Debby VanWinkle; Dir.; 200 S. Main St.; 64735; Henry; P 9,008; M 375; (660) 885-8166; (800) 222-5251; Fax (660) 885-8168; debby@clintonmo.com; www.clintonmo.com*

Cole Camp • *Cole Camp C/C* • Judy Silva; Ofc. Mgr.; P.O. Box 94; 65325; Benton; P 1,124; M 55; (660) 668-2295; chamber@colecampmo.com; www.colecampmo.com

Columbia • *Columbia C/C* • Matt McCormick; Pres.; 300 S. Providence Rd.; P.O. Box 1016; 65205; Boone; P 150,000; M 1,050; (573) 874-1132; Fax (573) 443-3986; admin@columbiamochamber.com; www.columbiamochamber.com*

Concord • *see South County*

Concordia • *Concordia Area C/C* • Cara Harris; Exec. Dir.; 802 S. Gordon; P.O. Box 143; 64020; Lafayette; P 2,400; M 100; (660) 463-2454; Fax (660) 463-2845; concordiachamber@centurytel.net; www.concordiamo.com

Creve Coeur • *Creve Coeur-Olivette C/C* • Nancy M. Gray; Exec. V.P.; 10950 Olive Blvd., Ste. 101; 63141; St. Louis; P 25,800; M 300; (314) 569-3536; Fax (314) 569-3073; info@ccochamber.com; www.ccochamber.com

Crocker • *Crocker Comm. C/C* • Dot Gilstrap; Pres.; P.O. Box 833; 65452; Pulaski; P 1,120; M 35; (573) 736-5922; Fax (573) 736-5922; www.cityofcrocker.net

Crystal City • *see Festus*

Cuba • *Cuba Area C/C & Visitor Center* • Norma Bretz; Secy.; 71 Hwy. P; P.O. Box 405; 65453; Crawford; P 3,500; M 195; (573) 885-2531; (877) 212-8429; Fax (573) 885-0988; cuba@misn.com; www.cubamochamber.com

Dardenne Prairie • *Lake Saint Louis Dardenne Prairie Area C/C* • Gena Breyne; Pres./CEO; 2032 Hanley Rd., Ste. 113; 63368; St. Charles; P 11,400; M 250; (636) 755-5335; info@lsldpchamber.com; www.lsldpchamber.com*

De Soto • *De Soto C/C* • Sarah Greenlee; Ofc. Coord.; 47 Jefferson Sq.; 63020; Jefferson; P 20,000; M 120; (636) 586-5591; Fax (636) 586-5591; desotomo_chamber@yahoo.com; www.desotomochamber.com

Des Peres • *see Kirkwood*

Desloge • *Desloge C/C* • Donna Masson; Exec. Dir.; 200 N. Lincoln; 63601; St. Francois; P 4,802; M 50; (573) 431-3006; deslogechamber@sbcglobal.net; www.deslogechamber.com

Dexter • *Dexter C/C* • Hillary Starnes; Exec. Dir.; 515B W. Market St.; P.O. Box 21; 63841; Stoddard; P 13,000; M 285; (573) 624-7458; (800) 332-8857; Fax (573) 624-7459; info@dexterchamber.com; www.dexterchamber.com

Doniphan • *Ripley County C/C* • April Black; Admin. Asst.; 209 W. Hwy. St.; P.O. Box 718; 63935; Ripley; P 12,000; M 150; (573) 996-2212; Fax (573) 351-1441; rcchamber@windstream.net; www.ripleycountymissouri.org

Earth City • *see Saint Louis-Northwest C/C*

East Prairie • *East Prairie C/C* • Cyndi Norton; Dir.; 106 S. Washington; 63845; Mississippi; P 3,713; M 100; (573) 649-5243; cyndi.norton@epmochamber.org; www.epmochamber.org

Edgerton • *Edgerton C/C* • Rick Roan; Pres.; P.O. Box 62; 64444; Platte; P 546; M 32; (785) 230-4605; (816) 790-3484; www.edgertonmo.org

Edina • *Knox County C/C* • Echo Menges; Pres.; P.O. Box 124; 63537; Knox; P 4,100; M 38; (660) 397-2226; www.knoxcountychamber.org

Edmundson • *see Saint Louis-Northwest C/C*

El Dorado Springs • *El Dorado Springs C/C* • W. Jackson Tough; Exec. Dir.; 1303 S. Hwy. 32; 64744; Cedar; P 4,000; M 125; (417) 876-4154; Fax (417) 876-4154; info@eldomo-cofc.org; www.eldomo-cofc.org

Eldon • *Eldon Area C/C* • Dee Spalding; Ofc. Asst.; 203 E. First St.; P.O. Box 209; 65026; Miller; P 10,000; M 200; (573) 392-3752; Fax (573) 392-0634; eldoninfo@eldonchamber.com; www.eldonchamber.com*

Ellington • *Ellington C/C* • Christy Roberts; Pres.; P.O. Box 515; 63638; Reynolds; P 1,000; M 55; (573) 663-7997; chamber@ellingtonmo.com; www.ellingtonmo.com

Ellisville • *West St. Louis County C/C* • Lori Kelling; Pres.; 15965 Manchester Rd., Ste. 102; 63011; St. Louis; P 200,000; M 384; (636) 230-9900; Fax (636) 230-9912; info@westcountychamber.com; www.westcountychamber.com*

Elvins • *see Park Hills*

Eminence • *Eminence Area C/C* • Crystal Layman; P.O. Box 415; 65466; Shannon; P 600; M 135; (573) 226-3318; chamber@eminencemo.com; www.eminencemo.com

Esther • *see Park Hills*

Eureka • *Eureka C/C* • Kelly Lubker; Exec. Dir.; 22 Dreyer Ave.; 63025; Jefferson & St. Louis; P 10,000; M 380; (636) 938-6062; Fax (636) 938-5202; kellylubker@eurekachamber.us; www.eurekachamber.org

Excelsior Springs • *Excelsior Springs Area C/C* • Bob Nance; Exec. Dir.; 461 S. Thompson Ave.; P.O. Box 632; 64024; Clay; P 12,000; M 245; (816) 630-6161; (816) 630-7500; Fax (816) 630-7500; info@exspgschamber.com; www.exspgschamber.com*

Fair Grove • *Fair Grove Area C/C* • Justin Loveday; P.O. Box 91; 65648; Greene; P 1,393; M 62; (417) 759-2807; info@fairgrove.org; www.fairgrovemo.org

Farmington • *Farmington C/C* • Doug McDermott; Pres./CEO; 302 N. Washington St.; P.O. Box 191; 63640; St. Francois; P 17,000; M 400; (573) 756-3615; Fax (573) 756-1003; chamber@growingfarmington.com; www.growingfarmington.com

Fayette • *Fayette Area C/C* • Kurt Himmelmann; Pres.; P.O. Box 414; 65248; Howard; P 4,000; M 50; (660) 248-2235; president@fayettemochamber.com; www.fayettemochamber.org

Fenton • *Fenton Area C/C* • Jeannie Braun; Exec. Dir.; 1400 S. Hwy. Dr., Ste. 99; 63026; St. Louis; P 65,000; M 440; (636) 717-0200; Fax (636) 717-0214; exdir@fentonmochamber.com; www.fentonmochamber.com*

Festus • *Twin City Area C/C* • Claudia Kirn; Admin.; 114 E. Main St.; 63028; Jefferson; P 20,000; M 360; (636) 931-7697; Fax (636) 937-0925; twincity.chamber@sbcglobal.net; www.twincity.org

Flat River • *see Park Hills*

Florissant • *Greater North County C/C* • Carolyn Marty; Pres.; 420 W. Washington St.; 63031; St. Louis; P 200,000; M 500; (314) 831-3500; Fax (314) 831-9682; jaime@greaternorthcountychamber.com; www.greaternorthcountychamber.com*

Forsyth • *Forsyth C/C* • Bill Bassett; Exec. Dir.; 16075 Hwy. 160; P.O. Box 777; 65653; Taney; P 2,500; M 150; (417) 546-2741; Fax (417) 546-4192; info@forsythmissouri.org; www.forsythmissouri.org*

Frontenac • *see Town & Country*

Fulton • *Callaway C/C* • Tamara Fitzpatrick; Exec. Dir.; 510 Market St.; 65251; Callaway; P 44,000; M 400; (573) 642-3055; (800) 257-3554; Fax (573) 642-5182; tamara@callawaychamber.com; www.callawaychamber.com*

Gainesville • *Ozark County C/C* • Lynn Bentele; Pres.; P.O. Box 605; 65655; Ozark; P 9,723; M 100; (417) 679-4913; info@ozarkcounty.net; www.ozarkcounty.net

Gerald • *Gerald Area C/C* • Jim Hackstedt; Pres.; P.O. Box 274; 63037; Franklin; P 1,300; M 105; (573) 764-4627; geraldch@fidnet.com; www.geraldchamber.com

Gladstone • *Gladstone Area C/C* • Amy Harlin; Pres.; 7001 N. Oak Trafficway, Ste. 101; 64118; Clay; P 28,000; M 420; (816) 436-4523; Fax (816) 436-4352; info@gladstonechamber.com; www.gladstonechamber.com*

Glasgow • *Glasgow C/C* • Scott Morris; Pres.; P.O. Box 192; 65254; Howard; P 1,120; M 50; (660) 338-2277; www.glasgowmo.com

Grain Valley • *Grain Valley C/C* • Zachary Pross; Exec. Dir.; 711 Main; 64029; Jackson; P 13,000; M 130; (816) 847-2627; Fax (816) 847-2555; director@grainvalleychamber.org; www.grainvalleychamber.org

Grandview • *Grandview C/C* • Kim Curtis; Pres.; 12500 S. 71 Hwy., Ste. 100; 64030; Jackson; P 25,300; M 282; (816) 761-6505; (816) 761-0500; Fax (816) 763-8460; ksc@grandview.org; www.grandview.org*

Grant City • *Grant City C/C* • Amber Monticue; V.P.; P.O. Box 134; 64456; Worth; P 1,000; M 25; (660) 564-4000; www.grantcity.us

Green City • *Green City C/C* • Travis Hall; 111 N. Sherman St.; 63545; Sullivan; P 657; M 20; (660) 874-4387; (660) 874-4219

Greenfield • *Greenfield C/C* • Kim Kinder; Pres.; P.O. Box 63; 65661; Dade; P 1,400; M 80; (417) 637-2040; info@greenfieldmochamber.com; www.greenfieldmochamber.com

Hannibal • *Hannibal Area C/C* • McKenzie Disselhorst; Exec. Dir.; 201 Broadway; P.O. Box 230; 63401; Marion; P 25,000; M 350; (573) 221-1101; Fax (573) 221-3389; director@hannibalchamber.org; www.hannibalchamber.org*

Harrisonville • *Harrisonville Area C/C* • Sara Craig; Program Dir.; 106 S. Independence; 64701; Cass; P 10,000; M 215; (816) 380-5271; Fax (816) 884-4291; info@harrisonvillechamber.com; www.harrisonvillechamber.com*

Hazelwood • *see Saint Louis-Northwest C/C*

Hermann • *Hermann Area C/C* • June Diebal; Mgr.; 312 Market St.; 65041; Gasconade; P 2,800; M 199; (573) 486-2313; Fax (573) 486-3066; hermannchamber@centurytel.net; www.visithermann.com

Higginsville • *Higginsville C/C* • Teri Ray; Exec. Dir.; 1813 N. Main St.; P.O. Box 164; 64037; Lafayette; P 4,682; M 200; (660) 584-3030; Fax (660) 584-3033; chamber@ctcis.net; www.higginsvillechamber.org*

High Ridge • *Northwest Jefferson County C/C* • Sharon Reineri; Pres.; 24 Gravois Station, House Springs, 63051; P.O. Box 371; 63049; Jefferson; P 45,000; M 90; (636) 671-8010; Fax (636) 671-8010; nwjcounty@gmail.com; www.nwchamberweb.org

Hillsboro • *Greater Hillsboro C/C* • Mandy Alley; Treas.; P.O. Box 225; 63050; Jefferson; P 2,100; M 75; (636) 789-4920; Fax (636) 789-4920; chamberoffice@sbcglobal.net; www.hillsboromo.org

Holden • *Holden C/C* • Linda Frazier; Pres.; 100 E. 2nd St.; P.O. Box 72; 64040; Johnson; P 2,500; M 67; (816) 732-6844; info@holdenchamber.org; www.holdenchamber.com

Hollister • *Hollister Area C/C* • D. Todd Aeschliman; Chrmn.; P.O. Box 674; 65673; Taney; P 4,426; M 190; (417) 334-3050; Fax (417) 334-5501; Info@HollisterChamber.net; www.HollisterChamber.net*

Houston • *Houston Area C/C* • Brenda Jarrett; Exec. Dir.; 501 E. Walnut; P.O. Box 374; 65483; Texas; P 3,000; M 200; (417) 967-2220; Fax (417) 967-2178; information@houstonmochamber.com; www.houstonmochamber.com*

Humansville • *Humansville C/C* • Clara Merrill; Pres.; P.O. Box 195; 65674; Polk; P 1,000; M 60; (417) 754-2251; humansvillecofc@hotmail.com; www.humansville.net

Independence • *Independence C/C* • Hap Graff; Pres./CEO; 210 W. Truman Rd.; P.O. Box 1077; 64051; Jackson; P 117,300; M 600; (816) 252-4745; Fax (816) 252-4917; info@ichamber.biz; ichamber.biz*

Ironton • *Arcadia Valley C/C* • Brian Parker; Pres.; P.O. Box 343; 63650; Iron; P 3,500; M 150; (573) 546-7117; Fax (573) 546-7117; avchamber@centurytel.net; www.arcadiavalley.biz

Jackson • *Jackson Area C/C* • Brian Gerau; Exec. Dir.; 125 E. Main; P.O. Box 352; 63755; Cape Girardeau; P 15,000; M 450; (573) 243-8131; (888) 501-8827; Fax (573) 243-0725; director@jacksonmochamber.org; www.jacksonmochamber.org*

Jamesport • *Jamesport Comm. Assn.* • Marshall Hopkins; Dir. of Tourism & Eco. Dev.; P.O. Box 215; 64648; Daviess; P 524; M 50; (660) 684-6146; (660) 973-2996; jamesportmo@yahoo.com; www.jamesportmissouri.org

Jefferson City • *Jefferson City Area C/C* • Randall Allen; Pres./CEO; 213 Adams St.; P.O. Box 776; 65102-0776; Cole; P 50,000; M 840; (573) 634-3616; Fax (573) 634-3805; info@jcchamber.org; www.jeffersoncitychamber.org*

Joplin • *Joplin Area C/C* • Rob O'Brian CEcD; Pres.; 320 E. 4th St.; 64801; Jasper; P 50,000; M 1,100; (417) 624-4150; Fax (417) 624-4303; info@joplincc.com; www.joplincc.com*

Kahoka • *Kahoka/Clark County C/C* • Tim Bertram; Pres.; 250 N. Morgan St.; 63445; Clark; P 7,000; M 90; (660) 727-2011; Fax (660) 727-3750

Kansas City Area

Greater Kansas City C/C • James Heeter; Pres./CEO; 30 W. Pershing Rd., Ste. 301; 64108; Jackson; P 1,800,000; M 8,000; (816) 221-2424; Fax (816) 221-7440; chamber@kcchamber.com; www.kcchamber.com

Northeast Kansas City C/C • Bobbi Baker; Pres.; 2657 Independence Ave.; P.O. Box 240392; 64124; Jackson; P 30,000; M 105; (816) 231-3312; Fax (816) 231-2101; nekcchamber@aol.com; www.nekcchamber.com

Northland Reg. C/C • Sheila Tracy; Pres.; 634 N.W. Englewood Rd.; 64118; Clay & Platte; P 296,000; M 700; (816) 455-9911; sheila@northlandchamber.com; www.northlandchamber.com*

South Kansas City C/C • Vickie Wolgast; Pres.; 406 E. Bannister Rd., Ste. F; 64131; Jackson; P 77,000; M 225; (816) 761-7660; Fax (816) 761-7340; vwolgast@southkcchamber.com; www.southkcchamber.com*

Kearney • *Kearney C/C* • Siouxsan Eisen; Exec. Dir.; P.O. Box 242; 64060; Clay; P 8,400; M 240; (816) 628-4229; Fax (816) 902-1234; info@kearneychamber.org; www.kearneychamber.org*

Kennett • *Kennett C/C* • Melissa Combs; Exec. Dir.; 1601 First St.; P.O. Box 61; 63857; Dunklin; P 10,900; M 300; (573) 888-5828; (866) 848-5828; Fax (573) 888-9802; info@kennettmo.com; www.kennettmo.com

Kimberling City • *Table Rock Lake C/C* • Sheila Thomas; Exec. Dir.; 14226 Hwy. 13; P.O. Box 495; 65686; Stone; P 32,200; M 350; (417) 739-2564; Fax (417) 739-2580; trlchamber@visittablerocklake.com; www.visittablerocklake.com*

Kirksville • *Kirksville Area C/C* • Sandra Williams; Exec. Dir.; 304 S. Franklin; P.O. Box 251; 63501; Adair; P 17,505; M 375; (660) 665-3766; Fax (660) 665-3767; info@kirksvillechamber.com; www.kirksvillechamber.com*

Kirkwood • *Kirkwood-Des Peres Area C/C* • Jim Wright; Pres./CEO; 108 W. Adams; 63122; St. Louis; P 50,000; M 613; (314) 821-4161; Fax (314) 821-5229; jim@thechamber.us; www.kirkwooddesperes.com*

Lake Ozark • *Lake Area C/C* • Wendy White; Exec. Dir.; 1 Willmore Ln.; P.O. Box 1570; 65049; Miller; P 5,300; M 930; (573) 964-1008; (800) 451-4117; Fax (573) 964-1010; info@lakeareachamber.com; www.lakeareachamber.com

Lamar • *Barton County C/C & CDC* • Astra Ferris; Exec. Dir.; 102 W. 10th St.; 64759; Barton; P 13,000; M 330; (417) 682-3595; Fax (417) 682-9566; astra@bartoncounty.com; www.bartoncounty.com*

Lebanon • *Lebanon Area C/C* • Darrell Pollock; Exec. Dir.; 186 N. Adams; P.O. Box 505; 65536; Laclede; P 14,000; M 400; (417) 588-3256; (888) 588-5710; Fax (417) 588-3251; darrell@lebanonmissouri.com; www.lebanonmissouri.com*

Lee's Summit • *Lee's Summit C/C* • Nancy K. Bruns CCE; Pres.; 220 S.E. Main; 64063; Jackson; P 93,000; M 1,000; (816) 524-2424; Fax (816) 524-5246; lscoc@lschamber.com; www.lschamber.com*

Lexington • *Lexington Area C/C* • Penny Grosso; Exec. Dir.; 1029 Franklin Ave.; 64067; Lafayette; P 4,726; M 200; (660) 259-3082; Fax (660) 259-7776; chamber@historiclexington.com; www.historiclexington.com

Liberty • *Liberty Area C/C •* Gayle Potter; Pres.; 1170 W. Kansas St., Ste. H; 64068; Clay; P 40,000; M 410; (816) 781-5200; Fax (816) 781-4901; info@libertychamber.com; www.libertychamber.com*

Licking • *Licking C/C •* Kyle Smith; Pres.; P.O. Box 89; 65542; Texas; P 3,100; M 50; (573) 674-2510; Fax (573) 674-2914; www.lickingmo.org

Lincoln • *Lincoln C/C •* Kathy Kreisler; Pres.; P.O. Box 246; 65338; Benton; P 1,100; M 50; (660) 547-2718; www.lincolnmissouri.com

Louisiana • *Louisiana C/C •* 221 Mansion St.; 63353; Pike; P 5,000; M 100; (573) 754-5921; lamochamber@gmail.com; www.louisiana-mo.com

Macon • *Macon Area C/C •* Sharon Scott; Exec. Dir.; 119 N. Rollins St.; 63552; Macon; P 2,900; M 220; (660) 385-2811; Fax (660) 385-6543; director@maconmochamber.com; www.maconmochamber.com

Malden • *Malden C/C •* Leah Rose; Pres.; 607 N. Douglass; 63863; Dunklin; P 5,000; M 105; (573) 276-4519; Fax (573) 276-4925; info@maldenchamber.com; www.maldenchamber.com

Manchester • *see Ellisville*

Mansfield • *Mansfield Area C/C •* Darrel Adamson; P.O. Box 322; 65704; Wright; P 2,500; M 70; (417) 924-3525; mansfieldcofc@gmail.com; www.mansfieldchamber.com

Maplewood • *Maplewood C/C •* Jeannine Beck; Exec. Dir.; 2915 Sutton Blvd.; 63143; St. Louis; P 8,100; M 167; (314) 781-8588; Fax (844) 701-5904; info@maplewood-chamber.com; www.maplewood-chamber.com*

Marceline • *Marceline C/C •* Albert Yocom; Pres.; 209 N. Main St.; P.O. Box 93; 64658; Chariton & Linn; P 2,300; M 70; (660) 376-3347; www.marceline.com

Marshall • *Marshall C/C •* Jill Murray; Exec. Dir.; 214 N. Lafayette; 65340; Saline; P 14,000; M 184; (660) 886-3324; Fax (660) 831-0349; jill@marshallmochamber.com; marshallmochamber.com*

Marshfield • *Marshfield Area C/C & Tourist Info. Center •* Sara Herren; Exec. Dir./Secy.; 1469 Spur Dr.; 65706; Webster; P 7,500; M 225; (417) 859-3925; Fax (417) 468-3944; mfldchamber1439@gmail.com; www.marshfieldmochamberofcommerce.com

Marthasville • *Marthasville Area C/C •* Trei Irwin; Pres.; P.O. Box 95; 63357; Warren; P 2,000; M 82; (636) 433-5242; rrichardson@marthasvillecoc.net; www.marthasvillemo.net

Maryland Heights • *Maryland Heights C/C •* Sherry Huibonhoa; Pres./CEO; 547 Westport Plaza; St. Louis; 63146; St. Louis; P 27,500; M 450; (314) 576-6603; Fax (314) 576-6855; sherry@mhcc.com; www.mhcc.com*

Maryville • *Greater Maryville C/C •* Lily E. White; Exec. Dir.; 408 N. Market St.; 64468; Nodaway; P 15,000; M 235; (660) 582-8643; chamber@maryvillechamber.com; www.maryvillechamber.com*

Maysville • *Maysville C/C •* Missy Meek; P.O. Box 521; 64469; DeKalb; P 1,114; M 40; (816) 449-5402

Mehlville • *see South County*

Mexico • *Mexico Area C/C •* Dana Keller; Exec. Dir.; 100 W. Jackson St.; 65265; Audrain; P 12,000; M 400; (573) 581-2765; (800) 581-2765; Fax (573) 581-6226; mexicochamber@mexico-chamber.org; www.mexico-chamber.org*

Moberly • *Moberly Area C/C •* Deborah Dean-Miller; Exec. Dir.; 211 W. Reed St.; 65270; Randolph; P 27,000; M 267; (660) 263-6070; Fax (660) 263-9443; chamber@moberly.com; www.moberlychamber.com*

Monett • *Monett C/C •* Jeff Meredith; Exec. Dir.; 200 E. Broadway; P.O. Box 47; 65708; Barry & Lawrence; P 8,862; M 275; (417) 235-7919; Fax (417) 235-4076; jeff@monett-mo.com; www.monett-mo.com

Monroe City • *Monroe City Area C/C •* Tara Thomas; 314 S. Main St.; P.O. Box 22; 63456; Marion, Monroe & Ralls; P 2,600; M 90; (573) 735-4391; mcchamber@centurytel.net; www.monroecitymo.org

Monroe City • *Mark Twain Lake C/C •* Doug Smith; Pres.; P.O. Box 182; 63456; Monroe & Ralls; P 20,000; M 35; (573) 565-2228; Fax (573) 565-2205; mtlcoc@socket.net; www.visitmarktwainlake.org

Montgomery City • *Montgomery City Area C/C •* Brad Arens; Pres.; P.O. Box 31; 63361; Montgomery; P 2,500; M 110; (573) 564-3941; Fax (573) 564-5134; president@mcchamber.org; www.montgomerycitymo.org

Mount Vernon • *Mount Vernon C/C •* Pam Dudley; Exec. Dir.; 425 E. Mt. Vernon Blvd.; P.O. Box 373; 65712; Lawrence; P 4,700; M 220; (417) 466-7654; Fax (417) 466-7654; mtvchamber@mchsi.com; www.mtvernonchamber.com

Mountain Grove • *Mountain Grove Area C/C •* Mary Armstrong; Exec. Dir.; 205 W. 3rd, Ste. 8; P.O. Box 434; 65711; Wright; P 4,500; M 200; (417) 926-4135; Fax (417) 926-5440; chamber@mountaingrovechamber.com; www.mountaingrovechamber.com

Mountain View • *Mountain View C/C •* Renee DePriest; Exec. Dir.; 125 E. 1st St.; P.O. Box 24; 65548; Howell; P 2,719; M 175; (417) 934-2794; Fax (417) 934-2882; mvcoc@centurytel.net; www.mountainviewmo.com

Neosho • *Neosho Area C/C •* Lauri Lyerla; Exec. Dir.; 216 W. Spring St.; P.O. Box 605; 64850; Newton; P 25,000; M 400; (417) 451-1925; Fax (417) 451-8097; lauri@neoshocc.com; www.neoshocc.com

Nevada • *Nevada/Vernon County C/C •* Jennifer Eaton; Exec. Dir.; 225 W. Austin, Ste. 200; 64772; Vernon; P 21,200; M 200; (417) 667-5300; Fax (417) 667-3492; chamber1@nevada-mo.com; www.nevada-mo.com*

New Haven • *New Haven Area C/C •* Luke Otten; Pres.; P.O. Box 201; 63068; Franklin; P 2,000; M 100; (573) 237-3830; info@newhavenmo.com; www.newhavenmo.com

New Madrid • *New Madrid C/C •* Christina McWaters; Dir.; 537 B Mott St.; P.O. Box 96; 63869; New Madrid; P 3,400; M 100; (573) 748-5300; (877) 748-5300; Fax (573) 748-5402; chambernm@yahoo.com; www.new-madrid.mo.us

New Melle • *New Melle C/C •* Harry Kishpaugh; Bd. Dir.; P.O. Box 212; 63365; St. Charles; P 300; M 100; (636) 828-5600; info@newmellechamber.com; www.newmellechamber.com

Nixa • *Nixa Area C/C •* Tammy Mast; Exec. Dir.; 106 Sherman Way, Ste. 6; P.O.Box 548; 65714; Christian; P 21,000; M 500; (417) 725-1545; Fax (417) 725-4532; info@nixachamber.com; www.nixachamber.com*

Oak Grove • *Oak Grove C/C •* 1212B S. Broadway; P.O. Box 586; 64075; Jackson; P 7,000; M 84; (816) 690-4147; Fax (816) 690-4147; oakgrovechamber@hotmail.com; www.oakgrovechamber.biz

Oakland • *see Kirkwood*

Oakville • *see South County*

Odessa • *Odessa C/C* • Kate Gosoroski; Exec. Dir.; 309A Park Ln.; 64076; Lafayette; P 4,700; M 78; (816) 633-4044; Fax (816) 633-4044; odessacoc@embarqmail.com; www.odessamochamber.com

OFallon • *O'Fallon C/C & Ind.* • Erin Williams; Pres./CEO; 2145 Bryan Valley Commercial Dr.; 63366; St. Charles; P 85,000; M 650; (636) 240-1818; info@ofallonchamber.org; www.ofallonchamber.org*

Olivette • *see Creve Coeur*

Osceola • *Osceola Comm. C/C* • Ron Hogan; Pres.; P.O. Box 422; 64776; St. Clair; P 947; M 50; (417) 646-2727; Fax (417) 646-5662; rhogan@osceolamochamber.com; www.osceolamochamber.com

Overland • *see Saint Louis-Northwest C/C*

Owensville • *Owensville C/C* • Bob Neibruegge; Exec. Dir.; P.O. Box 77; 65066; Gasconade; P 2,600; M 125; (573) 437-4270; Fax (573) 437-4299; chamber1@fidnet.com; www.owensvillemissouri.com

Ozark • *Ozark Area C/C* • Dori Grinder; Exec. Dir.; 191 N. 18th St.; P.O. Box 1450; 65721; Christian; P 17,800; M 260; (417) 581-6139; Fax (417) 581-0639; info@ozarkmissouri.com; www.ozarkchamber.com*

Pacific • *Pacific Area C/C* • Tiffany Wilson; Exec. Dir.; 333 Chamber Dr.; 63069; Franklin; P 7,300; M 200; (636) 271-6639; Fax (636) 257-2109; exdir@pacificchamber.com; www.pacificchamber.com*

Palmyra • *Palmyra C/C* • Michelle Merkel; Pres.; 417 S. Main; P.O. Box 446; 63461; Marion; P 3,500; M 90; (573) 769-0777; palmyrachamber@gmail.,com; www.showmepalmyra.com

Paris • *Paris Area C/C* • David Eales; Pres.; 208 N. Main St.; 65275; Monroe; P 1,200; M 100; (660) 327-4450; Fax (660) 327-1376; chamber@parismo.net; www.parismo.net

Park Hills • *Park Hills-Leadington C/C* • Tamara Coleman; Exec. Dir.; 12 Municipal Dr.; 63601; St. Francois; P 9,000; M 151; (573) 431-1051; Fax (573) 431-2327; info@phlcoc.net; www.phlcoc.net*

Peculiar • *Peculiar Area C/C* • Kim Duey; Pres.; P.O. Box 669; 64078; Cass; P 6,000; M 72; (816) 758-6900; info@peculiarchamber.com; www.peculiarchamber.com

Perryville • *Perryville Area C/C* • Melissa Hemmann; Exec. Dir.; 2 W. Ste. Maries St.; 63775; Perry; P 18,971; M 420; (573) 547-6062; Fax (573) 547-6071; Melissa@perryvillemo.com; www.perryvillemo.com

Piedmont • *Piedmont Area C/C* • Robert Gayle; Pres.; 215 S. Main St.; P.O. Box 101; 63957; Wayne; P 3,000; M 120; (573) 223-4046; Fax (573) 223-4046; contact@piedmontchamber.com; www.piedmontchamber.com

Pineville • *McDonald County C/C* • Billie Benson; Exec. Dir.; P.O. Box 593; 64856; McDonald; P 27,000; M 175; (417) 223-8888; Fax (417) 223-8889; info@mcdonaldcountychamber.org; www.mcdonaldcountychamber.org

Platte City • *Platte City Area C/C* • Angie Mutti; Exec. Dir.; 620 3rd St.; P.O. Box 650; 64079; Platte; P 10,000; M 250; (816) 858-5270; info@plattecitymo.com; www.plattecitymo.com*

Plattsburg • *Plattsburg C/C* • Bradley Lawrence; Pres.; P.O. Box 134; 64477; Clinton; P 2,500; M 80; (816) 539-2649; (816) 539-2148; Fax (816) 539-3530; chamber@plattsburgmo.com; www.plattsburgmo.com

Poplar Bluff • *Greater Poplar Bluff Area C/C* • Steve Halter; Pres.; 1111 W. Pine St.; 63901; Butler; P 17,000; M 720; (573) 785-7761; Fax (573) 785-1901; info@poplarbluffchamber.org; www.poplarbluffchamber.org*

Portageville • *Portageville C/C* • Ben Brown; Pres.; P.O. Box F; 63873; New Madrid & Pemiscot; P 3,228; M 40; (573) 379-5789; Fax (573) 379-3080; info@portagevillechamber.com

Potosi • *Potosi/Washington County C/C* • Kris Richards; P.O. Box 404; 63664; Washington; P 2,700; M 100; (573) 438-4517; Fax (573) 438-3676; www.potosichamber.com

Raymore • *Raymore C/C* • Cherie Turney; Ofc. Mgr.; 1000 W. Foxwood Dr.; 64083; Cass; P 19,200; M 175; (816) 322-0599; Fax (816) 322-7127; info@raymorechamber.com; www.raymorechamber.com*

Raytown • *Raytown Area C/C* • Vicki Turnbow; Pres.; 5909 Raytown Trafficway; 64133; Jackson; P 31,000; M 300; (816) 353-8500; Fax (816) 353-8525; staff@raytownchamber.com; www.raytownchamber.com

Republic • *Republic Area C/C* • Ron Peabody; Exec. Dir.; 113 W. Hwy. 174; 65738; Greene; P 14,751; M 200; (417) 732-5200; Fax (417) 732-2851; director@republicchamber.com; www.republicchamber.com*

Richmond • *Richmond Area C/C* • Natalie Lamar; Exec. Dir.; 104 W. North Main St.; 64085; Ray; P 5,800; M 204; (816) 776-6916; Fax (816) 776-6917; director@richmondchamber.org; www.richmondchamber.org

Richmond Heights • *Richmond Heights C/C* • Mr. Pat Croghan; Pres.; 7960 Clayton Rd.; 63117; St. Louis; P 10,000; M 50; (314) 645-4000; rsvp@rhchambercommerce.com; www.richmondheights.org

Rivermines • *see Park Hills*

Riverside • *Riverside Area C/C* • April Roberson; Exec. Dir.; 2950 N.W. Vivion Rd.; 64168; Platte; P 3,100; M 100; (816) 741-9985; info@riversidemochamber.com; www.riversidemochamber.com

Rock Port • *Rock Port C/C* • Amy Elam; P.O. Box 134; 64482; Atchison; P 1,318; M 45; (660) 744-6562; amy@palmtag.com; www.atchisoncounty.org

Rogersville • *Rogersville Area C/C* • Tami North; Exec. Dir.; 107 E. Center St.; P.O. Box 77; 65742; Christian, Greene & Webster; P 3,300; M 134; (417) 753-7538; Fax (417) 753-7538; info@rogersvillechamber.com; www.rogersvillechamber.com

Rolla • *Rolla Area C/C & Visitor Center* • Stevie Kearse; Exec. Dir.; 1311 Kingshighway; 65401; Phelps; P 19,500; M 450; (573) 364-3577; Fax (573) 364-5222; stevie@rollachamber.org; www.rollachamber.org*

Saint Ann • *see Saint Louis-Northwest C/C*

Saint Charles • *Greater Saint Charles County C/C* • Scott Tate; Pres./CEO; 2201 First Capitol Dr.; 63301; Saint Charles; P 380,000; M 750; (636) 946-0633; Fax (636) 946-0301; info@gstccc.com; www.gstccc.com*

Saint James • *Saint James C/C* • Jennie Miller; Dir.; 100 State Rte. B; P.O. Box 358; 65559; Phelps; P 4,216; M 178; (573) 265-6649; info@stjameschamber.net; www.stjameschamber.net

Saint Johns • *see Saint Louis-Northwest C/C*

Saint Joseph • *St. Joseph C/C* • R. Patt Lilly; Pres./CEO; 3003 Frederick Ave.; 64506; Buchanan; P 125,000; M 1,040; (816) 232-4461; Fax (816) 364-4873; chamber@saintjoseph.com; saintjoseph.com*

Saint Louis Area

Crestwood-Sunset Hills Area C/C • Mary Ann McWilliams; Exec. Dir.; 9058-A Watson Rd.; 63126; St. Louis; P 15,000; M 225; (314) 843-8545; Fax (314) 843-8526; info@ourchamber.com; www.ourchamber.com

Lemay C/C • Angela Lorenz; Exec. Dir.; P.O. Box 6642; 63125; St. Louis; P 20,000; M 250; (314) 631-2796; Fax (314) 638-9500; angela@lemaychamber.com; www.lemaychamber.com*

Northwest C/C • Brian Goldman; Pres./CEO; 8944 St. Charles Rock Rd., 3rd Flr.; 63114; St. Louis; P 50,000; M 570; (314) 291-2131; Fax (314) 291-2153; info@northwestchamber.com; www.northwestchamber.com*

St. Louis Reg. Chamber & Growth Assn. • Joseph F. Reagan; Pres./CEO; One Metropolitan Square, Ste. 1300; 63102; P 2,817,300; M 2,500; (314) 231-5555; Fax (314) 444-1122; mperez@stlregionalchamber.com; www.stlregionalchamber.com

---

Saint Mary • **Saint Mary C/C** • P.O. Box 38; 63673; St. Genevieve; P 360; M 16; (573) 543-2279; www.saintmarymo.com

Saint Peters • see Saint Charles

Salem • **Salem Area C/C** • Tabatha Utley; Dir.; 200 S. Main St.; 65560; Dent; P 5,000; M 200; (573) 729-6900; Fax (573) 729-6741; chamber@salemmo.com; www.salemmo.com

Salisbury • **Salisbury Area C/C** • Diana Morris; Pres.; P.O. Box 5; 65281; Chariton; P 1,618; M 52; (660) 388-6116; info@salisburymo.net; www.salisburymo.net

Sarcoxie • **Sarcoxie Area C/C** • Tory Velten; Pres.; P.O. Box 171; 64862; Jasper; P 1,400; M 97; (417) 548-6130; (417) 548-6390; j_hankins@mo-net.com; www.sarcoxiemo.com

Savannah • **Savannah Area C/C** • Mary Ingersoll; Exec. Dir.; 411 Court St.; P.O. Box 101; 64485; Andrew; P 5,100; M 135; (816) 324-3976; Fax (816) 324-5728; saccmo@gmail.com; www.savannahmochamber.com

Scott City • **Scott City Area C/C** • Chodra Mason; Treas.; P.O. Box 4101; 63780; Scott; P 4,600; M 40; (573) 264-2117; (573) 264-2157; www.scottcitymochamber.com

Sedalia • **Sedalia Area C/C** • Angie Thompson; Exec. Dir.; 600 E. Third St.; 65301; Pettis; P 22,000; M 300; (660) 826-2222; Fax (660) 826-2223; angie@sedaliamo.org; www.sedaliachamber.com*

Seligman • **Seligman Greater Area C/C** • David VanPetty; Pres.; P.O. Box 250; 65745; Barry; P 10,000; M 48; (417) 662-3611; info@seligmanchamber.com; www.seligmanchamber.com

Seneca • **Seneca C/C** • Josh Dodson; Pres.; P.O. Box 332; 64865; Newton; P 2,300; M 90; (417) 776-2100; chamberpresident@senecamochamber.com; www.senecamochamber.com

Seymour • **Greater Seymour Area C/C** • Heather Johns; Pres.; P.O. Box 700; 65746; Webster; P 2,000; M 35; (417) 935-9300; april@seymourmochamber.com; www.seymourmochamber.com

Shelbina • **Shelbina C/C** • Amanda Buckman; Pres.; P.O. Box 646; 63468; Shelby; P 1,800; M 75; (573) 588-4104; thadweekly@centurytel.net; www.cityofshelbina.com

Shell Knob • **Shell Knob C/C** • Twilia Harrison; Dir.; 25364 State Hwy. 39; P.O. Box 193; 65747; Barry; P 1,600; M 190; (417) 858-3300; Fax (417) 858-9428; info@shellknob.com; www.shellknob.com

Sikeston • **Sikeston Reg. C/C** • Barry Sellers; CEO/Exec. Dir.; 128 N. New Madrid St.; 63801; New Madrid & Scott; P 68,000; M 500; (573) 471-2498; Fax (573) 471-2499; chamber@sikeston.net; www.sikeston.net

Slater • **Slater C/C** • Jason Weiker; Secy./Treas.; P.O. Box 177; 65349; Saline; P 2,000; M 50; (660) 529-2271; (660) 529-2211; Fax (660) 529-2593; info@cityofslater.com; www.cityofslater.com

Smithville • **Smithville Area C/C** • Lia Jennings; Exec. Dir.; 105 W. Main; 64089; Clay; P 8,500; M 215; (816) 532-0946; smithvillechamber@sbcglobal.net; www.smithvillechamber.org

South County • **South County C/C** • Donna Abernathy/Schumann; Exec. Dir.; 4179 Crescent Dr., Ste. A; St. Louis; 63129; St. Louis; P 140,000; M 380; (314) 894-6800; Fax (314) 894-6888; dascounty@sbcglobal.net; socochamber.org*

Springfield • **Springfield Area C/C** • Matt Morrow; Pres.; 202 S. John Q. Hammons Pkwy.; P.O. Box 1687; 65801; Greene; P 448,744; M 1,800; (417) 862-5567; Fax (417) 862-1611; info@springfieldchamber.com; www.springfieldchamber.com*

St. Clair • **St. Clair Area C/C** • Charlene Saling; Exec. Dir.; 960 Plaza Dr., Ste. H; 63077; Frankin; P 5,000; M 149; (636) 629-1889; Fax (636) 629-5510; chamber@stclairmo.com; www.stclairmo.com*

St. Robert • **Waynesville-St. Robert Area C/C** • Cecilia Murray; Exec. Dir.; 137 St. Robert Blvd., Ste. B; 65584; Pulaski; P 9,100; M 424; (573) 336-5121; Fax (573) 336-5472; info@wsrchamber.com; www.waynesville-strobertchamber.com*

Ste. Genevieve • **Ste. Genevieve C/C** • Dena Kreitler; Exec. Dir.; 51 S. Third St.; 63670; Ste. Genevieve; P 18,500; M 320; (573) 883-3686; (573) 883-7020; Fax (573) 883-7092; info@stegenchamber.org; www.stegenchamber.org

Steele • **Steele C/C** • Leigh Ann Powell; c/o 122 E. Main; 63877; Pemiscot; P 2,200; M 80; (573) 695-4710; (573) 695-4732; www.cityofsteele.org

Steelville • **Steelville C/C** • Jeanne Locklear; Pres.; P.O. Box 956; 65565; Crawford; P 1,642; M 87; (573) 775-4721; (573)775-5533; Fax (573) 775-5521; chamber@misn.com; www.steelville.com

Stockton • **Stockton Area C/C** • Charlotte Haden; Exec. Dir.; P.O. Box 410; 65785; Cedar; P 2,000; M 135; (417) 276-5213; stocktonchamber@windstream.net; www.stocktonmochamber.com

Stover • **Stover C/C** • Vi Dale; Pres.; P.O. Box 370; 65078; Morgan; P 1,100; M 80; (573) 377-2303; (573) 377-4510; Fax (573) 377-2521

Strafford • **Strafford Area C/C** • Debbie Phillips; V.P.; P.O. Box 21; 65757; Greene; P 3,000; M 60; (417) 759-1175; info@straffordmo.org; www.straffordmo.org

Sullivan • **Sullivan Area C/C** • Lori Rego; Exec. Dir.; 2 W. Springfield Rd.; 63080; Franklin; P 7,500; M 247; (573) 468-3314; Fax (573) 860-2313; chamber@fidnet.com; www.sullivanmochamber.com

Summersville • **Summersville C/C** • Cathy Tuttle; Pres.; P.O. Box 251; 65571; Shannon & Texas; P 501; M 20; (417) 932-5373; Fax (417) 932-4791; catron@hotmail.com; www.summersvillemo.com

Sunrise Beach • *Lake of the Ozarks West C/C* • Paul Hooper; Exec. Dir.; P.O. Box 340; 65079; Camden & Morgan; P 16,000; M 455; (573) 374-5500; (877) 227-4086; Fax (573) 374-8576; info@lakewestchamber.com; www.lakewestchamber.com*

Sweet Springs • *Sweet Springs C/C* • Dee Friel; Pres.; P.O. Box 255; 65351; Saline; P 1,500; M 40; (660) 335-6321; Fax (660) 335-4592; deefriel@embarqmail.com; www.visitsweetsprings.com

Table Rock Lake • *see Kimberling City*

Tarkio • *Tarkio C/C* • Eryn Stepp; P.O. Box 222; 64491; Atchison; P 1,584; M 75; (660) 736-4821; tarkiochambercommerce@tarkio.net; www.tarkiomo.com

Thayer • *Thayer C/C* • LaRee Rees; Secy.; P.O. Box 14; 65791; Oregon; P 2,300; M 88; (417) 264-7324; info@thayerchamber.net; www.thayerchamber.net

Theodosia • *Theodosia Area C/C* • Cindy Korver; Pres.; P.O. Box 11; 65761; Ozark,Taney, Marion, Baxter, Boone; P 10,000; M 90; (417) 273-4245; theodosiachamber@yahoo.com; theodosiaareachamber.com

Tipton • *Tipton C/C* • Denny Higgins; Pres.; P.O. Box 307; 65081; Moniteau; P 3,500; M 85; (660) 433-6377; denny.higgins@commercebank.com; www.tiptonmo.com

Town & Country • *Town & Country/Frontenac C/C* • Tammy Wildman Baldanza; Exec. Dir.; 13443 Clayton Rd., Ste. 2; 63131; St. Louis; P 15,000; M 130; (314) 469-3335; tcfchamber@charter.net; www.tcfchamber.com

Trenton • *Trenton Area C/C* • Debbie Carman; Exec. Dir.; 617 Main St.; 64683; Grundy; P 6,000; M 138; (660) 359-4324; Fax (660) 359-4606; trentonchamber@att.net; www.trentonmochamber.com*

Union • *Union C/C* • Melissa Vogt; Exec. Dir.; 103 S. Oak St.; P.O. Box 168; 63084; Franklin; P 10,200; M 275; (636) 583-8979; Fax (636) 583-4001; director@unionmochamber.org; www.unionmochamber.org*

Van Buren • *Van Buren Area C/C Inc.* • Cathy Alford; P.O. Box 693; 63965; Carter; P 6,365; M 100; (573) 323-0800; (573) 429-9266; chamber@seevanburen.com; www.seevanburen.com

Vandalia • *Vandalia Area C/C* • Karen Shaw; City Clerk; 200 E. Park St.; 63382; Audrain & Ralls; P 2,800; M 70; (573) 594-6186; www.vandaliamochamber.com

Versailles • *Versailles Area C/C* • Mignon Dureka; Dir.; 109 N. Monroe; P.O. Box 256; 65084; Morgan; P 2,600; M 125; (573) 378-4401; Fax (573) 378-2499; vchamber@sbcglobal.net; www.versailleschamber.com

Vinita Park • *see Saint Louis-Northwest C/C*

Warrensburg • *Greater Warrensburg Area C/C* • Tammy Long; Pres.; 100 S. Holden St.; 64093; Johnson; P 23,300; M 436; (660) 747-3168; Fax (660) 429-5490; chamber@warrensburg.org; www.warrensburg.org*

Warrenton • *Warrenton Area C/C* • Jan Olearnick; Managing Dir.; P.O. Box 333; 63383; Warren; P 8,000; M 200; (636) 456-2530; Fax (636) 456-2542; warrentoncoc@socket.net; www.warrentoncoc.com

Warsaw • *Warsaw Area C/C* • Rachael Sherrer; Dir.; 818 E. Main St.; P.O. Box 264; 65355; Benton; P 2,127; M 200; (660) 438-5922; (800) 927-7294; Fax (660) 438-3493; warsawcc@embarqmail.com; www.warsawmo.org

Warson Woods • *see Kirkwood*

Washington • *Washington Area C/C* • Jennifer Giesike CFE; Pres./CEO; 323 W. Main St.; 63090; Franklin; P 14,000; M 580; (636) 239-2715; Fax (636) 239-1381; tsteffens@washmo.org; www.washmochamber.org*

Waynesville • *see St. Robert*

Webb City • *Webb City Area C/C* • Gwen Allen; Mbrshp. Dir.; 112 W. Broadway; P.O. Box 287; 64870; Jasper; P 12,000; M 215; (417) 673-1154; Fax (417) 673-2856; gwen@webbcitychamber.com; www.webbcitychamber.com*

Webster Groves • *Webster Groves/Shrewsbury/Rock Hill Area C/C* • Rebecca Now; Exec. Dir.; 357 Marshall Ave., Ste. 102; 63119; St. Louis; P 30,000; M 300; (314) 962-4142; Fax (314) 962-9398; chamberinfo@go-webster.com; www.webstershrewsburychamber.com*

Wentzville • *Wentzville C/C* • Tony Mathews; Pres./Ceo; P.O. Box 11; 63385; St. Charles; P 30,000; M 400; (636) 327-6914; Fax (636) 634-2760; info@wentzvillechamber.com; www.wentzvillechamber.com*

West Plains • *Greater West Plains Area C/C* • Joanne White; Executive Director; 401 Jefferson Ave.; 65775; Howell; P 12,000; M 432; (417) 256-4433; Fax (417) 256-8711; info@wpchamber.com; www.wpchamber.com*

Weston • *Weston C/C* • Jennifer Toy; Ofc. Mgr.; 526 Main St.; 64098; Platte; P 1,703; M 125; (816) 640-2909; Fax (816) 640-2909; westonmo@kc.rr.com; www.westonmo.com*

Westport • *see Maryland Heights*

Wildwood • *see Ellisville*

Willard • *Willard Area C/C* • Kendall Cook; Pres.; P.O. Box 384; 65781; Greene; P 4,700; M 100; (417) 742-2442; willardchamber@yahoo.com; http://willardmo.org/wacc/

Willow Springs • *Willow Springs Area C/C* • Patty Hocking; Secy.; 112 E. Main St.; 65793; Howell; P 2,200; M 95; (417) 469-5519; Fax (417) 469-3192; willowspringschamber@gmail.com; www.willowspringsmochamber.com

Winchester • *see Ellisville*

Windsor • *Windsor Area C/C* • Kevin Gnuschke; Pres.; 102 N. Main St.; 65360; Henry; P 3,000; M 120; (660) 647-2318; windsorm@iland.net; www.windsormo.org

Woodson Terrace • *see Saint Louis-Northwest C/C*

Wright City • *Wright City Area C/C* • Chris Gray; Pres.; P.O. Box 444; 63390; Warren; P 3,200; M 100; (636) 745-7855; wcchamber@wrightcitychamber.com; www.wrightcitychamber.com

Montana

Montana C of C • Webb Brown CAE; Pres./CEO; 900 Gibbon St.; P.O. Box 1730; Helena; 59624; Lewis & Clark; P 1,005,141; M 1,500; (406) 442-2405; Fax (406) 442-2409; stacye@montanachamber.com; www.montanachamber.com

Alder • *see Twin Bridges*

Anaconda • *Anaconda C/C* • Edith Fransen; Exec. Dir.; 306 E. Park Ave.; 59711; Deer Lodge; P 9,400; M 195; (406) 563-2400; Fax (406) 563-2400; anacondachamber@rfwave.net; www.discoveranaconda.com

Baker • *Baker C of C & Ag.* • Pat Ehret; Pres.; 121 S. Main St.; P.O. Box 849; 59313; Fallon; P 1,800; M 65; (866) 862-2537; (406) 778-2266; Fax (406) 778-2020; bakerchamberofcommerce@yahoo.com; www.bakermt.com

Belgrade • *Belgrade C/C* • Debra K. Youngberg; Exec. Dir.; 10 E. Main; 59714; Gallatin; P 16,000; M 340; (406) 388-1616; Fax (406) 388-2090; info@belgradechamber.org; www.belgradechamber.org*

Big Sandy • *Big Sandy C/C* • Wendy Kleinsasser; P.O. Box 411; 59520; Chouteau; P 700; M 40; (406) 378-2418; www.bigsandymt.org

Big Sky • *Big Sky C/C* • Marne Hayes; Exec. Dir.; 3091 Pine Dr.; P.O. Box 160100; 59716; Gallatin; P 2,200; M 410; (406) 995-3000; (800) 943-4111; Fax (406) 995-3054; info@bigskychamber.com; www.bigskychamber.com

Big Timber • *Sweet Grass County C/C & Visitor Info. Center* • Karen Ward; Exec. Admin.; 1350 Hwy. 10 W.; P.O. Box 1012; 59011; Sweet Grass; P 3,500; M 80; (406) 932-5131; info@bigtimber.com; www.bigtimber.com

Bigfork • *Bigfork Area C/C* • Gretchen Gates; Pres.; 8155 MT Hwy. 35; P.O. Box 237; 59911; Flathead; P 2,000; M 335; (406) 837-5888; Fax (406) 837-5808; chamber@bigfork.org; www.bigfork.org

Bigfork • *Swan Lake C/C* • Diane Kautzman; Pres.; P.O. Box 993; 59911; Flathead; P 300; M 118; (406) 886-2268; (406) 886-2152; www.swanlakemontana.org

Billings • *Billings C/C* • John Brewer CAE; Pres./CEO; 815 S. 27th St.; P.O. Box 31177; 59107; Yellowstone; P 150,000; M 1,100; (406) 245-4111; Fax (406) 245-7333; info@billingschamber.com; www.billingschamber.com*

Bozeman • *Bozeman Area C/C* • Daryl Schliem; Pres./CEO; 2000 Commerce Way; 59715; Gallatin; P 40,000; M 1,000; (406) 586-5421; Fax (406) 586-8286; info@bozemanchamber.com; www.bozemanchamber.com

Broadus • *Powder River C/C & Ag.* • Sheila Rasmussen; Exec. Secy.; P.O. Box 484; 59317; Powder River; P 468; M 80; (406) 436-2778; powderriverchamber@rangeweb.net; www.powderriverchamber.com

Browning • *Browning Area C/C* • P.O. Box 990; 59417; Glacier; P 1,200; M 20; (406) 338-4015; Fax (406) 338-2605; info@browningchamber.com; www.browningmontana.com

Butte • *Butte-Silver Bow C/C* • Marko Lucich; Exec. Dir.; 1000 George St.; 59701; Silver Bow; P 35,000; M 400; (406) 723-3177; Fax (406) 723-1215; bsbchamber@gmail.com; www.buttechamber.org*

Checkerboard • *see White Sulpher Springs*

Chester • *Liberty County C/C* • Lynda Vande Sandt; Coord.; 30 Main St.; P.O. Box 632; 59522; Liberty; P 2,100; M 105; (406) 759-4848; Fax (406) 759-4848; lynda@libertycountycc.com; www.libertycountycc.com

Chinook • *Chinook C/C* • Heather DePriest; Pres.; P.O. Box 744; 59523; Blaine; P 1,300; M 165; (406) 357-7483; info@chinookmontana.com; www.chinookmontana.com

Choteau • *Choteau C/C* • Laura Buck; Pres.; 815 Main Ave. N.; P.O. Box 897; 59422; Teton; P 1,400; M 90; (406) 466-5316; choteauchamber@choteaumontana.us; www.choteaumontana.us

Circle • *Circle C of C & Ag.* • Jana Hance; Secy.; P.O. Box 321; 59215; McCone; P 2,000; M 60; (406) 485-4782; Fax (406) 485-4786; chamber@circle-montana.com; www.circle-montana.com

Colstrip • *Colstrip C/C* • Terry Curries; Pres.; P.O. Box 1100; 59323; Rosebud; P 2,000; M 50; info@colstripchamber.com; www.colstripchamber.com

Columbia Falls • *Columbia Falls Area C/C* • Carol Pike; Exec. Dir.; P.O. Box 312; 59912; Flathead; P 4,400; M 200; (406) 892-2072; info@columbiafallschamber.org; www.columbiafallschamber.org*

Columbus • *Stillwater County C/C* • Tressie Goddard; Chamber Admin.; 565 N. 9th St. #50; P.O. Box 783; 59019; Stillwater; P 8,500; M 150; (406) 322-4505; Fax (406) 322-4505; admin@stillwatercountychamber.com; www.stillwatercountychamber.com

Conrad • *Conrad Area C/C* • Barbie Killion; Mgr.; 12 Fifth Ave. S.E.; 59425; Pondera; P 3,500; M 120; (406) 271-7791; chamber@3rivers.net; www.conradmt.com

Cooke City • *Colter Pass, Cooke City, Silver Gate C/C* • Donna Rowland; Exec. Dir.; 109 W. Main; P.O. Box 1071; 59020; Park; P 100; M 45; (406) 838-2495; Fax (406) 838-2495; info@cookecitychamber.org; www.cookecitychamber.org

Culbertson • *Culbertson C/C* • W. Bruce Houle; Pres.; P.O. Box 639; 59218; Roosevelt; P 1,000; M 40; (406) 787-6643; culbertsonmt@hotmail.com; www.culbertsonmt.com

Cut Bank • *Cut Bank Area C/C* • Amy Overstreet; Dir.; P.O. Box 1243; 59427; Glacier; P 3,400; M 150; (406) 873-4041; info@cutbankchamber.com; www.cutbankchamber.com

Deer Lodge • *Powell County C/C* • David Williams; Exec. Dir.; 1109 Main St.; 59722; Powell; P 7,200; M 80; (406) 846-2094; Fax (406) 846-2094; chamber@powellcountymontana.com; www.powellcountymontana.com

Dillon • *Beaverhead C/C & Ag.* • Claudia Conger; Pres.; 10 W. Reeder St.; P.O. Box 425; 59725; Beaverhead; P 4,000; M 230; (406) 683-5511; info@beaverheadchamber.org; www.beaverheadchamber.org

Drummond • *Drummond Comm. C/C* • Blaine Bradshaw; Acting Chair; P.O. Box 364; 59832; Granite; P 348; M 20; (406) 531-5846; Fax (406) 288-0223; bcbradshaw@yahoo.com; www.drummondmontana.com

East Glacier Park • *East Glacier C/C* • Terry Sherburne; Pres.; P.O. Box 260; 59434; Glacier; P 350; M 25; (406) 226-4403; terry@mtnpine.com; www.eastglacierpark.info

Ekalaka • *Carter County C/C* • Alisha Knapp; Secy.; P.O. Box 108; 59324; Carter; P 1,500; M 30; (406) 975-2222; cartercountychamberofcommerce@yahoo.com; www.cartercountychamberofcommerce.com

Ennis • *Ennis Area C/C* • Kenzi Clark; Exec. Dir.; P.O. Box 291; 59729; Madison; P 1,000; M 200; (406) 682-4388; info@ennischamber.com; www.ennischamber.com

Eureka • *Eureka Area C/C* • Randy McIntyre; Exec. Dir.; P.O. Box 186; 59917; Lincoln; P 4,000; M 152; (406) 889-4636; Fax (406) 297-7794; randy@welcome2eureka.com; www.welcome2eureka.com

Fairfield • *Fairfield C/C* • Marci Shaw; Pres.; P.O. Box 776; 59436; Teton; P 700; M 70; (406) 467-2531; info@fairfieldmt.com; www.fairfieldmt.com

Fairview • *Fairview C/C* • Ray Trumpower; Pres.; P.O. Box 374; 59221; Richland; P 800; M 60; (406) 742-5259; Fax (406) 742-5259; trumpwer@midrivers.com; www.midrivers.com/~fairview

Forsyth • *Forsyth Area C/C & Ag.* • Danielle Erickson; Pres.;
P.O. Box 448; 59327; Rosebud; P 1,777; M 80; (406) 347-5656;
forsythchamber@rangeweb.net; forsythmt.com

Fort Benton • *Fort Benton C/C & Info. Center* • Keith Ballantyne;
Pres.; P.O. Box 12; 59442; Chouteau; P 1,400; M 60; (406) 622-3864;
info@fortbentonchamber.org; www.fortbentonchamber.org

Gardiner • *Gardiner C/C* • Barbara Shesky; Exec. Dir.; 222 Park St.;
P.O. Box 81; 59030; Park; P 875; M 137; (406) 848-7971; Fax 855-828-
8706; info@gardinerchamber.com; www.gardinerchamber.com

Glasgow • *Glasgow Area C/C & Ag.* • Lisa A. Koski; Exec. Dir.;
313 Klein Ave.; P.O. Box 832; 59230; Valley; P 3,500; M 225;
(406) 228-2222; Fax (406) 228-2244; chamber@nemont.net;
www.glasgowchamber.net

Glendive • *Glendive C of C & Ag.* • Briana Daniels; Exec.
Dir.; 808 N. Merrill Ave.; 59330; Dawson; P 10,000; M 400;
(406) 377-5601; Fax (406) 377-5602; chamber@midrivers.com;
www.glendivechamber.com

Great Falls • *Great Falls Area C/C* • Percy "Steve" Malicott;
Pres./CEO; 100 1st Ave. N.; 59401; Cascade; P 75,000; M 675;
(406) 761-4434; Fax (406) 761-6129; info@greatfallschamber.org;
www.greatfallschamber.org*

Hamilton • *Bitterroot Valley C/C* • Al Mitchell; Exec. Dir.; 105 E. Main
St.; 59840; Ravalli; P 39,940; M 500; (406) 363-2400; Fax (406) 363-
2402; localinfo@bvchamber.com; www.bitterrootchamber.com*

Hardin • *Hardin Area C/C & Ag.* • Dorothy Stenerson; Secy.;
10 E. Railway; P.O. Box 446; 59034; Big Horn; P 3,000;
M 90; (406) 665-1672; (406) 665-3577; Fax (406) 665-3577;
info@thehardinchamber.org; www.thehardinchamber.org

Harlowton • *Wheatland County C/C & Ag.* • Erin Fisk; Dir.; P.O.
Box 694; 59036; Wheatland; P 1,000; M 80; (406) 632-4694;
chamber@harlowtonchamber.com; www.wheatlandchamber.com

Havre • *Havre Area C/C* • Debbie Vandeberg; Exec. Dir.; 130 5th Ave.;
P.O. Box 308; 59501; Hill; P 10,000; M 275; (406) 265-4383; Fax (406)
265-7748; chamber@havremt.net; www.havrechamber.com

Helena • *Helena Area C/C* • Cathy Burwell; Pres./CEO; 225 Cruse
Ave., Ste. A; 59601; Lewis & Clark; P 29,134; M 800; (406) 442-4120;
(800) 743-5362; Fax (406) 447-1532; info@helenachamber.com;
www.helenachamber.com

Hot Springs • *Hot Springs C/C* • Sandra Prongua; Secy.;
P.O. Box 627; 59845; Sanders; P 590; M 60; (406) 741-2662;
hscofc@hotspringsmt.net; www.hotspringsmtchamber.org

Hysham • *Hysham C/C* • Cora Marks; Secy.; P.O. Box 63;
59038; Treasure; P 800; M 25; (406) 342-5676; info@hysham.org;
www.hysham.org

Jordan • *Garfield County C/C & Ag.* • Jo Dee Watson; P.O. Box 370;
59337; Garfield; P 1,200; M 100; (406) 557-6158; Fax (406) 557-6158;
garfieldcountychamber@gmail.com; www.garfieldcounty.com

Kalispell • *Kalispell C/C & CVB* • Joe Unterreiner; Pres./CEO; 15
Depot Park; 59901; Flathead; P 90,928; M 700; (406) 758-2800;
(406) 758-2803; Fax (406) 758-2805; info@kalispellchamber.com;
www.kalispellchamber.com*

Lakeside • *Lakeside-Somers C/C* • Erin Duval; Secy.; 100 Bierney
Creek Rd.; P.O. Box 177; 59922; Flathead; P 2,400; M 100; (406) 844-
3715; info@lakesidesomers.org; www.lakesidesomers.org

Laurel • *Laurel C/C* • Joanne Flynn; Exec. Dir.; 108 E. Main
St.; 59044; Yellowstone; P 7,000; M 138; (406) 628-8105;
laurelchamber@rbbmt.org; www.laurelmontana.org

Laurin • *see Twin Bridges*

Lennep • *see White Sulpher Springs*

Lewistown • *Lewistown Area C/C* • Connie L. Fry; Exec. Dir.;
408 N.E. Main; 59457; Fergus; P 6,000; M 250; (406) 535-5436;
(866) 912-3980; Fax (406) 535-5437; lewchamb@midrivers.com;
www.lewistownchamber.com

Libby • *Libby Area C/C* • Pamela Peppenger; Exec. Dir.; 905 W.
9th St.; P.O. Box 704; 59923; Lincoln; P 10,000; M 217; (406) 293-
4167; Fax (406) 293-2197; executivedirector@libbychamber.org;
www.libbychamber.org*

Lincoln • *Lincoln Valley C/C* • Sue Howsmon; Secy.; P.O.
Box 985; 59639; Powell; P 1,500; M 50; (406) 362-4949;
lincolnmontana@linctel.net; www.lincolnmontana.com

Livingston • *Livingston Area C/C & CVB* • Lou Ann Nelson; Exec.
Dir.; 303 E. Park St.; 59047; Park; P 7,000; M 430; (406) 222-0850;
(406) 222-0851; Fax (406) 222-0852; info@livingston-chamber.com;
www.discoverlivingston.com

Malta • *Malta Area C/C* • Courtney Moles; 10 S. 4 E.; P.O. Box 1420;
59538; Phillips; P 3,000; M 125; (406) 654-1776; Fax (406) 654-1776;
malta@itstriangle.com; www.maltachamber.com

Manhattan • *Manhattan Area C/C* • Katie Hart; Exec. Secy./Ofc.
Mgr.; 112 S. Broadway; P.O. Box 606; 59741; Gallatin; P 1,600;
M 150; (406) 284-4162; manhattanmontana@yahoo.com;
www.manhattanareachamber.com

Martinsdale • *see White Sulpher Springs*

Miles City • *Miles City Area C/C* • John Laney; Exec. Dir.; 511
Pleasant St.; 59301; Custer; P 8,500; M 306; (406) 234-2890;
Fax (406) 234-6914; milescitychamber@milescitychamber.com;
www.milescitychamber.com

Missoula • *Missoula Area C/C* • Kim Latrielle; Pres./CEO; 825 E.
Front; P.O. Box 7577; 59807; Missoula; P 100,086; M 1,000; (406)
543-6623; Fax (406) 543-6625; korin@missoulachamber.com;
www.missoulachamber.com*

Philipsburg • *Philipsburg C/C* • Heidi Beck-Heser; Secy.;
P.O. Box 661; 59858; Granite; P 915; M 30; (406) 859-3388;
chamber@philipsburgmt.com; www.philipsburgmt.com

Plains • *Plains-Paradise C/C* • Sherry McCartney; Secy./Treas.;
P.O. Box 1531; 59859; Sanders; P 1,500; M 100; (406) 826-4700;
pln3686@blackfoot.net; www.plainsmtchamber.com

Plentywood • *Sheridan County C/C & Ag.* • Karla Aus; Bd. of Dir.;
108 N. Main St.; P.O. Box 104; 59254; Sheridan; P 4,000; M 80; (406)
765-8500; (406) 765-2810; chamberofcommerce34@gmail.com;
www.sheridancountychamber.org

Polson • *Polson C/C* • Tina M. Hanken; Ofc. Mgr.; 418 Main St.; P.O.
Box 667; 59860; Lake; P 6,000; M 293; (406) 883-5969; Fax (406) 883-
1716; chamber@polsonchamber.com; www.polsonchamber.com*

Red Lodge • *Red Lodge Area C/C* • Sherry Weamer; Exec. Dir.;
701 N. Broadway; P.O. Box 988; 59068; Carbon; P 2,500; M 230;
(406) 446-1718; (888) 281-0625; director@redlodgechamber.org;
www.redlodgechamber.org

Ringling • *see White Sulpher Springs*

Ronan • *Ronan C/C •* Ronna Walchuk; Exec. Dir.; P.O. Box 254; 59864; Lake; P 1,800; M 100; (406) 676-8300; info@ronanchamber.com; www.ronanchamber.com

Saco • *Saco C/C •* Carla Nelson; P.O. Box 75; 59261; Phillips; P 224; M 10; (406) 527-3434; (406) 527-3312; www.sacomontana.net

Saint Ignatius • *Saint Ignatius C/C •* Stuart Morton; Dir.; P.O. Box 396; 59865; Lake; P 1,000; M 40; (406) 745-2190; Fax (406) 745-2201; stignatiusinfo@stignatius.net; www.stignatiusmontana.com

Scobey • *Daniels County C/C & Ag. •* Jason Wolf; Pres.; 120 Main St.; P.O. Box 91; 59263; Daniels; P 1,082; M 43; (406) 487-2061; scobey@nemontel.net; www.scobeymt.com

Seeley Lake • *Seeley Lake Area C/C •* Cheryl Thompson; Exec. Dir.; 2920 Hwy. 83 N.; P.O. Box 516; 59868; Missoula; P 2,500; M 95; (406) 677-2880; Fax (406) 677-2880; slchamber@blackfoot.net; www.seeleylakechamber.com

Shelby • *Shelby Area C/C •* Audie Bancroft; Exec. Dir.; 100 Montana Ave.; P.O. Box 865; 59474; Toole; P 3,500; M 100; (406) 434-7184; Fax (406) 424-7234; shelbycoc@3rivers.net; www.shelbymtchamber.org

Sheridan • *see Twin Bridges*

Sidney • *Sidney Area C/C & Ag. •* Jessica Davies; Exec. Dir.; 909 S. Central Ave.; 59270; Richland; P 9,500; M 250; (406) 433-1916; Fax (406) 433-1127; schamber@midrivers.com; www.sidneymt.com*

Silver Gate • *see Cooke City*

Silver Star • *see Twin Bridges*

St. Regis • *see Superior*

Stanford • *Judith Basin C/C •* Kim Holzer; Pres.; P.O. Box 223; 59479; Judith Basin; P 2,000; M 35; info@jbchamber.com; www.jbchamber.com

Superior • *Mineral County C/C •* Anita Bailey; Pres.; 102 River St.; P.O. Box 483; 59872; Mineral; P 4,000; M 80; (406) 822-4891; chamber@montanarockies.org; www.montanarockies.org

Terry • *Prairie County C/C •* Dale Galland; P.O. Box 667; 59349; Prairie; P 1,200; M 50; (406) 635-4031; prairiecountycc@gmail.com; www.visitterrymontana.com

Thompson Falls • *Thompson Falls C/C & Visitor Center •* Mike Thilmony; Pres.; 1213 Main St.; P.O. Box 493; 59873; Sanders; P 10,227; M 135; (406) 827-4930; tfchamber@thompsonfallschamber.com; www.thompsonfallschamber.com

Three Forks • *Three Forks C/C & Visitor Center •* Val Aughney; Pres.; P.O. Box 1103; 59752; Gallatin; P 1,800; M 113; (406) 285-4753; (406) 285-3992; val.aughney@holcim.com; www.threeforksmontana.com

Townsend • *Townsend Area C/C •* M.A. Upton; Secy.; P.O. Box 947; 59644; Broadwater; P 5,000; M 80; (406) 266-4101; (877) 266-4101; Fax (406) 266-4042; townsendchamber@mt.net

Troy • *Troy C/C •* David Hall; Pres.; P.O. Box 3005; 59935; Lincoln; P 1,000; M 51; (406) 295-1064; secretary@troymtchamber.org; www.troymtchamber.org

Twin Bridges • *Greater Ruby Valley C/C •* Heather Puckett; P.O. Box 134; 59754; Madison; P 1,500; M 160; (406) 684-5678; info@rubyvalleychamber.com; www.rubyvalleychamber.com

Virginia City • *Virginia City Area C/C •* Pamela Kimmey; Exec. Dir.; P.O. Box 218; 59755; Madison; P 140; M 95; (406) 843-5555; (800) 829-2969; info@virginiacity.com; www.virginiacity.com

West Yellowstone • *West Yellowstone C/C & Visitors Center •* 30 Yellowstone Ave.; P.O. Box 458; 59758; Gallatin; P 1,020; M 250; (406) 646-7701; Fax (406) 646-9691; visitorservices@westyellowstonechamber.com; www.westyellowstonechamber.com

White Sulphur Springs • *Meagher County C/C •* Kelly Huffield; Pres.; P.O. Box 356; 59645; Meagher; P 1,000; M 50; (406) 547-2250; info@meagherchamber.com; www.meagherchamber.com

Whitefish • *Whitefish C/C •* Kevin O. Gartland; Exec. Dir.; 307 Spokane Ave., Ste. 103; P.O. Box 1120; 59937; Flathead; P 6,357; M 520; (406) 862-3501; Fax (406) 862-9494; visitus@whitefishchamber.org; www.whitefishchamber.org*

Whitehall • *Whitehall C/C •* 501 N. Whitehall St.; P.O. Box 72; 59759; Jefferson; P 1,200; M 80; (406) 287-2260; (406) 498-3807; Fax (866) 497-8982; whitehallmtchamber@gmail.com; www.whitehallchamberofcommerce.com

Wibaux • *Wibaux County C/C •* Michelle Hodges; Pres.; P.O. Box 159; 59353; Wibaux; P 1,500; M 100; (406) 796-2412

Wolf Point • *Wolf Point C of C & Ag. •* Jeff Presser; Pres.; 218 3rd Ave. S., Ste. B; 59201; Roosevelt; P 3,200; M 125; (406) 653-2012; wpchmber@nemont.net; www.ci.wolf-point.mt.us

Nebraska

Nebraska C of C & Ind. • Barry L. Kennedy CAE IOM; Pres.; 1320 Lincoln Mall, Ste. 201; P.O. Box 95128; Lincoln; 68509; Lancaster; P 1,855,525; M 2,000; (402) 474-4422; Fax (402) 474-5681; nechamber@nechamber.com; www.nechamber.com

Ainsworth • *Ainsworth Area C/C & North Central Dev. Center •* Lesley Holmes; Exec. Secy.; 335 N. Main St.; 69210; Brown; P 3,000; M 150; (402) 387-2740; ncdc@ainsworthlink.com; www.ainsworthchamber.com

Albion • *Albion C/C •* Lori Krohn; Pres.; 420 W. Market St.; 68620; Boone; P 1,700; M 115; (402) 395-6012; albionchamber@cityofalbion-ne.com; www.albionne.com

Alliance • *Alliance C/C •* Susan Unzicker; Exec. Dir.; 305 Box Butte Ave.; 69301; Box Butte; P 9,000; M 300; (308) 762-1520; (800) 738-0648; Fax (308) 762-4919; chamber@alliancechamber.com; www.alliancechamber.com*

Alma • *Alma C/C •* Teri Bach; Pres.; P.O. Box 52; 68920; Harlan; P 1,200; M 57; (308) 928-2992; almanechamberofcommerce@gmail.com; www.ci.alma.ne.us

Arapahoe • *Arapahoe C/C •* Tammie Middagh; Admin. Asst.; P.O. Box 624; 68922; Furnas; P 1,028; M 65; (308) 962-7777; chamber@arapahoe-ne.com; www.arapahoe-ne.com

Arnold • *Arnold C/C •* Becky Dailey; V.P.; P.O. Box 166; 69120; Custer; P 600; M 65; (308) 848-2522; (308) 848-2228; www.arnoldne.org

Arthur • *Arthur C/C •* Ron Jageler; Pres.; 103 N. Hwy. 61; 69121; Arthur; P 140; M 4; (308) 764-2367

Ashland • *Ashland C/C* • Patrick Liewer; Pres.; P.O. Box 5; 68003; Saunders; P 2,600; M 100; (402) 944-2050; Fax (402) 944-3205; www.historicashland.com

Atkinson • *Atkinson C/C* • Pam Winer; Pres.; P.O. Box 871; 68713; Holt; P 1,245; M 50; (402) 925-5313; louann.tooker@atkinsonne.com; www.atkinsonne.com

Auburn • *Auburn C/C* • Tonia Greiner; Exec. Dir.; 1101 J St.; 68305; Nemaha; P 3,500; M 200; (402) 274-3521; Fax (402) 274-4020; auburnchamberofcommerce@gmail.com; www.auburnnechamber.org*

Aurora • *Aurora Area Chamber & Dev. Corp.* • Barb Ernst; Exec. Dir.; 1604 L St.; P.O. Box 146; 68818; Hamilton; P 4,400; M 150; (402) 694-6911; christian.evans@auroranebraska.com; www.auroranebraska.com

Axtell • *Axtell Area C/C* • Jim Messer; P.O. Box 26; 68924; Kearney; P 730; M 75; (308) 743-2635; (308) 743-2437; www.axtellne.com

Bassett • *Bassett/Rock County C/C* • Bill Sanger; P.O. Box 537; 68714; Rock; P 1,700; M 73; (402) 684-3319; bassettcda@bassettnebr.com; www.bassettnebr.com

Beatrice • *Beatrice Area C/C & Tourism* • Lora Young; Exec. Dir.; 218 N. 5th St.; 68310; Gage; P 13,000; M 375; (402) 223-2338; Fax (402) 223-2339; lyoung@beatricechamber.com; www.beatricechamber.com*

Beaver City • *Beaver City C/C* • Linda Tomlinson; Coord.; P.O. Box 303; 68926; Furnas; P 680; M 40; (308) 268-9966; steveandlinda@frontiernet.net

Beaver Crossing • *Beaver Crossing C/C* • Mike Stutzman; Pres.; 800 Dimery Ave.; 68313; Seward; P 450; M 30; (402) 532-3925; chamber@beavercrossingne.com; www.beavercrossingne.com

Bellevue • *Bellevue C/C Inc.* • Jim Ristow; Pres./CEO; 1102 Galvin Rd. S.; 68005; Sarpy; P 77,000; M 430; (402) 898-3000; (402) 291-5216; Fax (402) 291-8729; president@bellevuenebraska.com; www.bellevuenebraska.com*

Benkelman • *Dundy County C/C & Dev.* • P.O. Box 661; 69021; Dundy; P 2,008; M 36; (308) 423-5210; benkchamber@bwtelcom.net; www.bwtelcom.net/dcccd

Bennington • *see Elkhorn*

Big Springs • *Big Springs C/C* • Ron Hendrickson; P.O. Box 436; 69122; Deuel; P 400; M 12; (308) 889-3681; www.ci.big-springs.ne.us

Blair • *Blair Area C/C* • Harriet Waite; Exec. Dir.; 1646 Washington St.; 68008; Washington; P 7,700; M 240; (402) 533-4455; Fax (402) 533-4456; mail@blairchamber.org; www.blairchamber.org*

Bloomfield • *Bloomfield Comm. Club* • Lu Jessen; P.O. Box 292; 68718; Knox; P 1,077; M 60; (402) 373-4343; www.bloomfieldnebraska.com

Blue Hill • *Blue Hill Comm. Club* • Ron Kuehner; Pres.; P.O. Box 63; 68930; Webster; P 936; M 30; (402) 756-3703; (402) 756-2056; www.bluehillne.com

Bridgeport • *Bridgeport C/C* • Andrew Plummer; 428 Main St.; P.O. Box 640; 69336; Morrill; P 1,600; M 100; (308) 262-1825; Fax (308) 262-0229; bridgeportchamber@gmail.com; www.bridgeport-ne.com

Broken Bow • *Broken Bow C/C* • Donnis Hueftle-Bullock; Exec. Dir.; 444 S. 8th Ave.; 68822; Custer; P 3,400; M 241; (308) 872-5691; Fax (308) 872-6137; info@brokenbow-ne.com; www.brokenbow-ne.com

Burwell • *Burwell C/C* • David Sawyer; Dir.; P.O. Box 131; 68823; Garfield; P 1,300; M 150; (308) 346-5210; Fax (308) 346-5121; burwellcondev@nctc.net; www.visitburwell.org

Callaway • *Callaway C/C* • Shirley Trout; Pres.; P.O. Box 414; 68825; Custer; P 650; M 65; (402) 310-9070; strout@teachablemoments.com; www.callaway-ne.com

Cambridge • *Cambridge C/C* • Vernita Saylor; Treas.; P.O. Box 8; 69022; Furnas; P 1,100; M 50; (308) 697-4344; (308) 697-3711; cambridgechamber1@gmail.com; www.cambridgene.org/chamberofcommerce

Campbell • *Campbell Area C/C* • William Pearson; P.O. Box 219; 68932; Franklin; P 400; M 100; (402) 756-8851; (402) 756-8121; www.campbellne.com

Central City • *Central City Area C/C* • Angie Cordsen; Exec. Dir.; 1532 17th Ave.; 68826; Merrick; P 3,000; M 200; (308) 946-3897; ccareachamber@gmail.com; www.cc-ne.com

Chadron • *Chadron C/C* • Brooke Smith; Exec. Dir.; 706 W. 3rd St.; 69337; Dawes; P 6,000; M 200; (308) 432-4401; Fax (308) 432-4757; director@chadron.com; www.chadron.com*

Chappell • *Chappell C/C* • P.O. Box 121; 69129; Deuel; P 980; M 50; (308) 874-9912; Fax (308) 874-2929; chamber69129@yahoo.com; www.chappellchamber.com

Clearwater • *Clearwater C/C* • Curt Thiele; Pres.; 85314 516th Ave.; 68726; Antelope; P 380; M 100; (402) 640-5734; curtthiele@hotmail.com; www.clearwaterne.com

Columbus • *Columbus Area C/C* • K.C. Belitz; Pres.; 753 33rd Ave.; P.O. Box 515; 68602; Platte; P 22,000; M 795; (402) 564-2769; Fax (402) 564-2026; chamber@megavision.com; www.thecolumbuspage.com*

Cozad • *Cozad Area C/C* • Sandra Bappe; Exec. Dir.; 135 W. 8th St.; 69130; Dawson; P 3,900; M 245; (308) 784-3930; Fax (308) 784-3026; cozadchamber@cozadtel.net; www.cozadchamber.com*

Crawford • *Crawford C/C* • Jamie Rivera Haas; Pres.; P.O. Box 145; 69339; Dawes; P 1,107; M 45; (308) 665-1817; (866) 665-1817; crawfordchamber@yahoo.com; www.crawfordnebraska.info

Creighton • *Creighton Area C/C* • Steve Morrill; P.O. Box 502; 68729; Knox; P 1,200; M 90; (402) 360-4148; creightonchamber@gpcom.net; www.creighton.org

Crete • *Crete C/C* • Dan McElravy; Exec. Dir.; P.O. Box 465; 68333; Saline; P 7,135; M 125; (402) 826-2136; Fax (402) 826-2136; cretechamber@neb.rr.com; www.cretechamber.com*

Crofton • *Crofton Comm. Club* • Doyle & Joyce Stevens; Pres.; P.O. Box 81; 68730; Knox; P 800; M 50; (402) 388-2477; (605) 661-5736; Fax (402) 388-2777; ccclub@gpcom.net; www.crofton-nebraska.com

Curtis • *Medicine Creek C/C* • P.O. Box 463; 69025; Frontier; P 800; M 30; (308) 367-4122; medcreekchamber@curtis-ne.com; www.curtis-ne.com/chamber.html

David City • *Butler County C/C* • Mandie Polivka; Exec. Dir.; 457 D St.; 68632; Butler; P 8,500; M 120; (402) 367-4238; director@buildbutlercounty.com; www.buildbutlercounty.com*

Deshler • *Deshler C/C* • P.O. Box 449; 68340; Thayer; P 747; M 50; (402) 365-4260; Fax (402) 365-4415; www.deshlerchamber.org

Elgin • *Elgin C/C* • Duane Esau; Pres.; P.O. Box 277; 68636; Antelope; P 735; M 50; (402) 843-5442; (402) 843-2411; www.elginne.com

Elkhorn • *Western Douglas County C/C* • Jenni Soukup; Pres.; 20801 Elkhorn Dr.; P.O. Box 202; 68022; Douglas; P 10,000; M 375; (402) 289-9560; Fax (402) 715-5888; wdccc@wdccc.org; www.wdccc.org*

Elm Creek • *Elm Creek C/C* • Jan Hinrichsen; Pres.; P.O. Box 103; 68836; Buffalo; P 930; M 40; (308) 856-0095; www.elmcreekne.com

Elwood • *Elwood C/C* • Charlotte Schwenninger; Village Clerk/Treas.; P.O. Box 92; 68937; Gosper; P 700; M 75; (308) 785-2480; Fax (308) 785-3316; elwoodchamber@hotmail.com; www.elwoodnebraska.com

Eustis • *Eustis C/C* • P.O. Box 372; 69028; Frontier; P 400; M 50; (308) 486-5515; www.eustisnebraska.com

Fairbury • *Fairbury C/C* • Sharon Priefert; Exec. Dir.; 518 E St.; P.O. Box 274; 68352; Jefferson; P 4,262; M 161; (402) 729-3000; Fax (402) 729-3076; fairburychamber@diodecom.net; www.fairburychamber.org*

Falls City • *Falls City Area C/C* • David Branch; Exec. Dir.; 1705 Stone St.; 68355; Richardson; P 5,000; M 200; (402) 245-4228; directorccms@sentco.net; www.fallscityareachamber.com*

Fremont • *Fremont Area C/C* • Tara Lea; Exec. Dir.; 128 E. Sixth St.; 68025; Dodge; P 26,500; M 620; (402) 721-2641; Fax (402) 721-9359; tara@fremontne.org; www.fremontne.org

Friend • *Friend C/C* • Vickie Himmelberg; 201 Maple St.; 68359; Saline; P 1,200; M 52; (402) 947-2143; (402) 947-2711; www.ci.friend.ne.us

Geneva • *Geneva C/C* • Jill Swartzendruber; Exec. Dir.; 145 N. 9th St.; P.O. Box 85; 68361; Fillmore; P 2,100; M 85; (402) 759-1155; chamber@cityofgeneva.org; www.cityofgeneva.org/chamber/

Genoa • *Genoa C/C* • Tony Mathis; Pres.; P.O. Box 40; 68640; Platte; P 1,000; M 20; (402) 993-2330; cgenoa@cablene.com; www.ci.genoa.ne.us

Gering • *see Scottsbluff*

Gibbon • *Gibbon C/C* • Bob Krier; Pres.; P.O. Box 56; 68840; Buffalo; P 1,759; M 60; (308) 468-6118; gibbonchamber@nctc.net; www.gibbonchamber.org

Gothenburg • *Gothenburg Area C/C* • Deb Egenberger; Ofc. Mgr.; 1001 Lake Ave.; 69138; Dawson; P 3,600; M 200; (308) 537-3505; (800) 482-5520; Fax (308) 537-2541; chamber@gothenburgdelivers.com; www.gothenburgdelivers.com*

Grand Island • *Grand Island Area C/C* • Cindy K. Johnson; Pres.; 309 W. 2nd St.; P.O. Box 1486; 68802; Hall; P 50,000; M 835; (308) 382-9210; (308) 391-9210; Fax (308) 382-1154; cjohnson@gichamber.com; www.gichamber.com*

Grant • *Perkins County C/C* • 223 Central Ave.; P.O. Box 767; 69140; Perkins; P 3,000; M 80; (308) 252-2100; chamber@gpcom.net; www.perkinscountychamber.com

Gretna • *Gretna Area C/C* • Kara Alexander; Admin.; 798 Village Sq.; 68028; Sarpy; P 5,000; M 241; (402) 332-3535; info@gretnachamber.com; www.gretnachamber.com*

Hartington • *Hartington C/C* • Karma Schulte; Pres.; 107 W. State St.; P.O. Box 742; 68739; Cedar; P 1,560; M 125; chamberpres@hartel.net; www.ci.hartington.ne.us

Hastings • *Hastings Area C/C* • Tom Hastings; Pres.; 301 S. Burlington Ave.; P.O. Box 1104; 68902; Adams; P 30,000; M 715; (402) 461-8400; Fax (402) 461-4400; info@hastingschamber.com; www.hastingschamber.com*

Hay Springs • *Hay Springs C/C* • Christi Hilliker; P.O. Box 264; 69347; Sheridan; P 570; M 50; (308) 638-4593; (308) 638-7132

Hebron • *Hebron C/C* • Tina Reed; Exec. Dir.; 216 Lincoln Ave.; 68370; Thayer; P 1,600; M 80; (402) 768-7156; Fax (402) 768-6176; hebronchamber@yahoo.com; www.hebronnebraska.us

Hemingford • *Hemingford C/C* • Amy Raben; Pres.; P.O. Box 51; 69348; Box Butte; P 803; M 40; (308) 487-5578; hemingfordtourism@bbc.net; www.ci.hemingford.ne.us

Henderson • *Henderson C/C* • Kelsey Bergen; Dir.; P.O. Box 225; 68371; York; P 1,000; M 90; (402) 723-4228; Fax (402) 723-5785; hchamber@mainstaycomm.net; www.cityofhenderson.org

Holdrege • *Holdrege Area C/C* • Carol Rapstine; Exec. Dir.; 701 4th Ave., Ste. 10; 68949; Phelps; P 8,000; M 225; (308) 995-4444; Fax (308) 995-4445; carol@justtheplacenebraska.com; www.justtheplacenebraska.com*

Humboldt • *Humboldt C/C* • Kathy Kanel; Secy.; P.O. Box 125; 68376; Richardson; P 880; M 70; (402) 862-2821; (402) 862-2171; www.ci.humboldt.ne.us

Hyannis • *Sandhills C/C* • Jeanne Davis; P.O. Box 271; 69350; Grant; P 300; M 25; (308) 458-2579; (308) 458-2625; jedavis@nebnet.net

Imperial • *Imperial C/C* • Merrilyn Leibbrandt; Pres.; P.O. Box 82; 69033; Chase; P 2,120; M 100; (308) 882-5444; Fax (308) 882-4319; events@imperialchamber.com; www.imperialchamber.com

Kearney • *Kearney Area C/C* • Max Kathol; Pres./CEO; 1007 2nd Ave.; P.O. Box 607; 68848; Buffalo; P 47,000; M 920; (308) 237-3101; Fax (308) 237-3103; erodgers@kearneycoc.org; www.kearneycoc.org*

Kimball • *Kimball-Banner County C/C* • Rod Horton; Exec. Dir.; 122 S. Chestnut St.; 69145; Kimball; P 3,500; M 202; (308) 235-3782; Fax (308) 235-3825; kbccc@megavision.com; www.kimballbannercountychamber.com*

Lexington • *Lexington Area C/C* • Tina Reil-Lux; Exec. Dir.; 1501 Plum Creek Pkwy., Ste. 2A; P.O. Box 97; 68850; Dawson; P 11,500; M 257; (308) 324-5504; (308) 324-5505; Fax (308) 324-5505; tina@lexcoc.com; www.lexcoc.com*

Lincoln • *Lincoln C/C* • Wendy Birdsall; Pres.; 3 Landmark Centre; 1128 Lincoln Mall, Ste. 100; 68508; Lancaster; P 250,000; M 1,700; (402) 436-2350; Fax (402) 436-2360; info@lcoc.com; www.lcoc.com*

Long Pine • *Long Pine C/C* • Ruth Goodrich; Secy.; P.O. Box 234; 69217; Brown; P 305; M 20; (402) 273-4120; www.cityoflongpine.org

Loup City • *Loup City Area C/C* • Eric Kowalski; Pres.; P.O. Box 24; 68853; Sherman; P 1,600; M 40; (308) 745-0430; lcchamber@cornhusker.net; www.loupcity

Madison • *Madison Area C/C* • Rebecca Higby; Exec. Dir.; 209 S. Lincoln St.; P.O. Box 287; 68748; Madison; P 2,500; M 110; (402) 454-2251; Fax (402) 454-2262; madisonchamber@telebeep.com; www.madison.ne.com

McCook • *McCook Area C/C* • Tacie Fawver; Exec. Dir.; 203 West 2nd; P.O. Box 337; 69001; Red Willow; P 8,000; M 200; (308) 345-3200; Fax (308) 345-3201; info@aboutmccook.com; www.aboutmccook.com*

Milford • *Milford C/C* • Marcie DeLong; Secy./Treas.; P.O. Box 174; 68405; Seward; P 2,000; M 75; (402) 761-3247; chamber@milford-ne.com; www.milfordnechamber.com

Minden • *Minden C/C* • Marcia Davis; Dir.; 325 N. Colorado Ave.; P.O. Box 375; 68959; Kearney; P 3,000; M 180; (308) 832-1811; Fax (308) 832-1811; mindenchamber@gtmc.net; www.mindenne.org*

Mitchell • *Mitchell Area C/C* • Shane Reinpold; Pres.; P.O. Box 72; 69357; Scottsbluff; P 1,831; M 31; (308) 623-2766; contact@mitchellareachamber.org; www.mitchellareachamber.org

Nebraska City • *Nebraska City Tourism & Commerce* • Rebecca Turner; Exec. Dir.; 806 1st Ave.; 68410; Otoe; P 7,000; M 250; (402) 873-6654; Fax (402) 873-6701; tourism@nebraskacity.com; www.nebraskacity.com*

Neligh • *Neligh C/C* • Carrie Pitzer; Pres.; 105 E. 2nd St.; 68756; Antelope; P 1,600; M 70; (402) 887-4447; Fax (402) 887-4399; nelighchamberofcommerce@gmail.com; www.nelighchamber.com

Norfolk • *Norfolk Area C/C* • Mark Zimmerer; Pres./CEO; 609 W. Norfolk Ave.; 68701; Madison; P 35,100; M 600; (402) 371-4862; Fax (402) 371-0182; info@norfolkareachamber.com; www.norfolkareachamber.com*

North Bend • *North Bend C/C* • Scott Aschoff; Pres.; P.O. Box 361; 68649; Dodge; P 1,200; M 82; (402) 652-8312; (402) 652-3584; www.northbendne.org

North Platte • *North Platte Area Chamber & Dev. Corp.* • Gary Person; Pres./CEO; 502 S. Dewey St.; 69101; Lincoln; P 30,000; M 630; (308) 532-4966; Fax (308) 532-4827; gary@nparea.com; www.nparea.com*

Oakland • *Oakland C/C* • Curt Hineline & Kelly Dortch; Co-Pres.; 217 N. Oakland Ave.; 68045; Burt; P 1,300; M 100; (402) 685-5624; curthineline@abbnebraska.com; www.ci.oakland.ne.us

Ogallala • *Ogallala/Keith County C/C* • Lori Wortman; Exec. Dir.; 119 E. 2nd St.; P.O. Box 628; 69153; Keith; P 10,000; M 400; (308) 284-4066; (800) 658-4390; Fax (308) 284-3126; lwortman@explorekeithcounty.com; www.explorekeithcounty.com*

Omaha • *Greater Omaha C/C* • David G. Brown; Pres./CEO; 1301 Harney St.; 68102; Douglas; P 941,165; M 3,100; (402) 346-5000; Fax (402) 346-7050; info@omahachamber.org; www.omahachamber.org*

Ord • *Ord Area C/C* • Kristina Foth; Asst. Dir.; 1514 K St.; 68862; Valley; P 2,100; M 200; (308) 728-7875; (877) 728-7875; Fax (308) 728-7691; kristinafoth@ordnebraska.com; www.ordnebraska.com*

Oshkosh • *Garden County C/C* • Buddy Paulsen; P.O. Box 91; 69154; Garden; P 1,900; M 80; (308) 772-4468; buddypaulsen@yahoo.com

O'Neill • *O'Neill Area C/C* • Lauri Havranek; Exec. Dir.; 125 S. 4th St.; 68763; Holt; P 3,000; M 230; (402) 336-2355; Fax (402) 336-4563; oneill@telebeep.com; www.oneillchamber.org*

Papillion • *Sarpy County C/C* • Wendy Richey; Pres.; 7775 Olson Dr., Ste. 207; 68046; Sarpy; P 147,000; M 670; (402) 339-3050; Fax (402) 339-9968; chamber@sarpychamber.org; www.sarpychamber.org*

Pawnee City • *Pawnee City C/C* • Nanette Hatfield; V.P.; P.O. Box 6; 68420; Pawnee; P 1,033; (402) 852-2405; lfsdanl@hotmail.com; www.pawneecity.com

Pender • *Pender Thurston C/C* • Connie Wichman; P.O. Box 250; 68047; Thurston; P 1,000; M 69; (402) 385-3200; www.penderthurston.com

Peru • *Peru C/C* • Ken Hastings; P.O. Box 246; 68421; Nemaha; P 800; M 20; (402) 872-6685

Pierce • *Pierce C/C* • Chuck Micek; Pres.; P.O. Box 82; 68767; Pierce; P 1,767; M 50; (402) 329-6879; cityadm@ptcnet.net; www.piercenebraska.com

Plainview • *Plainview C/C* • Amy Dummer; Secy.; 306 W. Park Ave.; P.O. Box 783; 68769; Pierce; P 1,246; M 65; (402) 582-7800; plainviewchamber@plvwtelco.net

Plattsmouth • *Plattsmouth C/C* • Max Kathol; Exec. Dir.; 918 Washington Ave.; 68048; Cass; P 7,023; M 200; (402) 296-6021; info@plattsmouthchamber.com; www.plattsmouthchamber.com

Ralston • *Ralston Area C/C* • Tara Lea; Pres.; 5505 Miller Ave.; 68127; Douglas; P 6,200; M 300; (402) 339-7737; Fax (402) 339-7954; info@ralstonareachamber.org; www.ralstonareachamber.org*

Ravenna • *Ravenna Area C/C* • Heidi Standage; Exec. Dir.; 318 Grand Ave.; 68869; Buffalo; P 1,400; M 70; (308) 452-3344; chamber@myravenna.com; www.myravenna.com

Red Cloud • *Red Cloud C/C* • Ken Van Wey; Co-Pres.; P.O. Box 327; 68970; Webster; P 1,131; M 40; (402) 746-3238; redcloudchamber@hotmail.com; www.redcloudguiderock.com

Schuyler • *Schuyler Area C/C* • Lora Johnson; Dir.; 1107 B St.; 68661; Colfax; P 6,211; M 182; (402) 352-5472; Fax (402) 352-2754; schuylerchamber@gmail.com; www.ci.schuyler.ne.us/chamber.asp

Scottsbluff • *Scottsbluff/Gering United C/C* • Karen S. Anderson; Exec. Dir.; 1517 Broadway, Ste. 104; 69361; Scotts Bluff; P 24,000; M 430; (308) 632-2133; Fax (308) 632-7128; office@scottsbluffgering.net; www.scottsbluffgering.net*

Seward • *Seward Area C/C* • Charles Lieske; Exec. Dir.; 616 Bradford St.; 68434; Seward; P 7,000; M 200; (402) 643-4189; Fax (402) 643-4713; sewcham@sewardne.com; www.sewardne.com*

Shelby • *Shelby C/C* • P.O. Box 27; 68662; Polk; P 714; M 60; (402) 527-5198; www.ci.shelby.ne.us

Sidney • *Cheyenne County Chamber* • Glenna Phelps-Aurich; Pres./CEO; 740 Illinois St.; 69162; Cheyenne; P 10,000; M 300; (308) 254-5851; (800) 421-4769; Fax (308) 254-3081; director@cheyennecountychamber.com; www.cheyennecountychamber.com*

South Sioux City • *South Sioux City Area C/C & Tourism* • Jim Steele; Pres.; 4401 Dakota Ave.; 68776; Dakota; P 13,500; M 382; (402) 494-1626; Fax (402) 494-5010; officemanager@southsiouxchamber.org; www.southsiouxchamber.org*

St. Paul • *St. Paul Area C/C* • Carolyn C. Scarborough; Mgr./Secy.; 619 Howard Ave.; 68873; Howard; P 2,500; M 140; (308) 754-5558; Fax (308) 754-5558; stpaulcham@qwestoffice.net; www.stpaulnebraska.com

Stamford • *Stamford C/C* • Rolena T. Novak; P.O. Box 34; 68977; Harlan; P 200; M 6; (308) 868-2401; rnovak@accessdirectwb.net

Stratton • *Stratton Area C/C* • P.O. Box 264; 69043; Hitchcock; P 343; M 24; (308) 276-2184; info@strattonnebraska.com; www.strattonnebraska.com

Superior • *Superior C/C* • Sherry Kniep; Mgr.; 354 N. Commercial Ave.; 68978; Nuckolls; P 1,957; M 135; (402) 879-3419; superiorcc@windstream.net; www.cityofsuperior.org*

Sutherland • *Sutherland C/C* • P.O. Box 81; 69165; Lincoln; P 1,200; M 36; (308) 386-4721; clerkvos@gpcom.net; www.ci.sutherland.ne.us

Syracuse • *Syracuse C/C* • Carolyn Gigstad; Exec. Dir.; P.O. Box J; 68446; Otoe; P 1,900; M 75; (402) 269-3242; chamber@gosyracusene.com; www.syracusene.com

Table Rock • *Table Rock Comm. Club* • 712 State; 68447; Pawnee; P 270; (402) 839-2180

Tecumseh • *Tecumseh C/C* • Eloise Bartels; Secy.; P.O. Box 126; 68450; Johnson; P 2,000; M 64; (402) 335-3400; (402) 335-3235; tecumsehchamber@windstream.net; www.tecumsehne.com

Tekamah • *Tekamah C/C* • Harriet Shafer; Secy./Treas.; P.O. Box 231; 68061; Burt; P 1,800; M 100; (402) 374-2020; (402) 850-9287; Fax (402) 374-1392; www.tekamahchamberofcommerce.com

Valentine • *Valentine C/C* • Dean Jacobs; Exec. Dir.; 239 S. Main St.; P.O. Box 201; 69201; Cherry; P 3,000; M 200; (402) 376-2969; (800) 658-4024; Fax (402) 376-2688; valentinecc@qwestoffice.net; www.visitvalentine.com

Valley • *see Elkhorn*

Wahoo • *Wahoo C/C* • Doug Watts; Exec. Dir.; 640 N. Broadway St.; 68066; Saunders; P 4,500; M 140; (402) 443-4001; Fax (402) 443-3077; watts@wahoo.ne.us; www.wahoo.ne.us

Waterloo • *see Elkhorn*

Waverly • *Waverly C/C* • Alex Hill; Secy.; P.O. Box 331; 68462; Lancaster; P 2,500; M 50; (402) 786-5111; ahill@phoenixwebgroup.com; www.waverlyne.com

Wayne • *Wayne Area Eco. Dev./Chamber/Main Street* • Irene Fletcher; Asst. Dir.; 108 W. 3rd St.; P.O. Box 275; 68787; Wayne; P 6,000; M 200; (402) 375-2240; (877) 929-6363; Fax (402) 375-2246; info@wayneworks.org; www.wayneworks.org*

Weeping Water • *Weeping Water C/C* • Tammy Cavanaugh; Pres.; P.O. Box 329; 68463; Cass; P 1,050; M 50; (402) 297-9723; (402) 267-5152; www.weepingwaternebraska.com

West Point • *West Point C/C* • Tina Biteghe Bi Ndong; Exec. Dir.; P.O. Box 125; 68788; Cuming; P 3,660; M 155; (402) 372-2981; Fax (402) 372-1105; info@westpointchamber.com; www.westpointchamber.com

Wilber • *Wilber Area C/C* • Sheryl Kastanek; Pres.; P.O. Box 1164; 68465; Saline; P 1,800; M 150; (402) 821-2732; (888) 494-5237; www.wilberchamberofcommerce.com

Winnetoon • *see Creighton*

Wisner • *Wisner Area C/C* • Jamie Parker; Pres.; P.O. Box 296; 68791; Cuming; P 1,300; M 56; wisnerchamber@yahoo.com; www.wisnerareachamberofcommerce.com

York • *Greater York Area C/C* • Todd Kirshenbaum; Exec. Dir.; 603 N. Lincoln Ave.; 68467; York; P 8,000; M 370; (402) 362-5531; Fax (402) 362-5953; toddk@yorkchamber.org; www.yorkchamber.org*

Nevada

Women's Chamber of Commerce of Nevada • June Beland; Founder, Pres./CEO; 2300 W. Sahara Ave., Ste. 800; Financial Center Bldg.; Las Vegas; 89102; Clark; P 2,758,931; M 550; (702) 733-3955; Fax (702) 926-9270; wccnv2@womenschamberofnevada.org; www.womenschamberofnevada.org*

Amargosa Valley • *Amargosa Valley C/C* • Jon Delee; Pres.; P.O. Box 2; 89020; Nye; P 1,400; M 12; (775) 372-1515; amargosachamber.org

Austin • *Austin C/C* • Frank Whitman; Pres.; 122 Main St.; P.O. Box 212; 89310; Lander; P 800; M 51; (775) 964-2200; Fax (775) 964-2200; chamber@austinnevada.com; www.austinnevada.com

Battle Mountain • *Battle Mountain C/C* • Sady S. Tingey; Exec. Dir.; 625 S. Broad St.; P.O. Box 333; 89820; Lander; P 5,000; M 150; (775) 635-8245; Fax (775) 635-8064; membership@battlemountainchamber.com; www.battlemountainchamber.com

Beatty • *Beatty C/C* • Ann Marchand; Bd. Pres.; P.O. Box 956; 89003; Nye; P 1,010; M 50; (775) 553-2424; Fax (775) 553-2424; beattychamber@sbcglobal.net; www.beattynevada.org

Boulder City • *Boulder City C/C* • Jill Lagan; CEO; 465 Nevada Way; 89005; Clark; P 15,000; M 420; (702) 293-2034; Fax (702) 293-0574; info@bouldercitychamber.com; www.bouldercitychamber.com*

Carson City • *Carson City Area C/C* • Ronni Hannaman; Exec. Dir.; 1900 S. Carson St.; 89701; Carson City; P 55,000; M 600; (775) 882-1565; Fax (775) 882-4179; manager@carsoncitychamber.com; www.carsoncitychamber.com

Crystal Bay • *see Tahoe City, CA*

Dayton • *Dayton Area C/C* • Jojo Myers; Pres.; P.O. Box 2408; 89403; Lyon; P 17,000; M 200; (775) 246-7909; Fax (775) 246-5838; info@daytonnvchamber.org; www.daytonnvchamber.org*

Elko • *Elko Area C/C* • Billie Crapo; CEO; 1405 Idaho St.; 89801; Elko; P 48,000; M 601; (775) 738-7135; (775) 778-3307; Fax (775) 738-7136; chamber@elkonevada.com; www.elkonevada.com*

Ely • *White Pine C/C* • Wayne Cameron; Exec. Dir.; 636 Aultman St.; 89301; White Pine; P 10,400; M 180; (775) 289-8877; Fax (775) 289-6144; wpcc@whitepinechamber.com; www.whitepinechamber.com

Fallon • *Fallon C/C* • Natalie Parrish; Exec. Dir.; 85 N. Taylor St.; 89406; Churchill; P 24,063; M 240; (775) 423-2544; Fax (775) 423-0540; info@fallonchamber.com; www.fallonchamber.com

Fernley • *Fernley C/C* • Pat Hon; Exec. Dir.; 70 N. West St.; 89408; Lyon; P 18,000; M 265; (775) 575-4459; info@fernleychamber.org; www.fernleychamber.org*

Gardnerville • *Carson Valley C/C & Visitors Auth.* • Bill Chernock; Exec. Dir.; 1477 Hwy. 395, Ste. A; 89410; Douglas; P 52,000; M 450; (775) 782-8144; (800) 727-7677; Fax (775) 782-1025; info@carsonvalleynv.org; www.carsonvalleynv.org*

Goldfield • *Goldfield C/C* • Lisa Farnsworth; Pres.; 165 E. Crook Ave.; P.O. Box 204; 89013; Esmeralda; P 400; M 35; (775) 485-3560; Fax (775) 485-3560; gfnvchamber@aol.com; goldfieldnevada.org

Hawthorne • *Mineral County C/C* • Roy Colbert; 822 5th St.; P.O. Box 2250; 89415; Mineral; P 4,700; M 60; (775) 945-2507; info@mineralcountychamber.com; www.mineralcountychamber.com

Henderson • *Henderson C/C* • Scott Muelrath; Pres./CEO; 590 S. Boulder Hwy.; 89015; Clark; P 260,000; M 1,500; (702) 565-8951; Fax (702) 565-3115; info@hendersonchamber.com; www.hendersonchamber.com*

Incline Village • *see Tahoe City, CA*

Lake Tahoe • *see Stateline*

Las Vegas • *Latin C/C* • Otto Merida; Pres./CEO; 300 N. 13th St.; 89101; Clark; M 1,200; (702) 385-7367; Fax (702) 385-2614; otto@lvlcc.com; www.lvlcc.com*

Las Vegas • *Las Vegas Metro C/C* • Kristin McMillan; Pres./CEO; 575 Symphony Park Ave., Ste. 100; 89106; Clark; P 2,000,000; M 3,000; (702) 641-5822; Fax (702) 735-0406; info@lvchamber.com; www.lvchamber.com*

Laughlin • *Laughlin C/C* • Connie Davis; Exec. Dir.; 1585 Casino Dr.; 89029; Clark; P 8,500; M 425; (702) 298-2214; (800) 227-5245; Fax (702) 298-5708; cdavis@laughlinchamber.com; www.laughlinchamber.com*

Lovelock • *Pershing County C/C* • Beth Reid; Mgr.; 1005 W. Broadway Ave.; P.O. Box 821; 89419; Pershing; P 7,700; M 120; (775) 273-7213; Fax (775) 273-1212; info@pershingcountynevada.com; www.pershingcountynevada.com

Mesquite • *Mesquite Area C/C* • Julie Stoltz; Pres./CEO; 12 W. Mesquite Blvd., Ste. 107; 89027; Clark; P 15,677; M 305; (702) 346-2902; Fax (702) 346-6138; info@mesquite-chamber.com; www.mesquite-chamber.com*

North Las Vegas • *see Las Vegas Metro C/C*

Overton • *Moapa Valley C/C* • Lois Hall; Pres.; P.O. Box 361; 89040; Clark; P 10,000; M 78; (702) 398-7160; chamber@moapavalley.com; www.moapavalley.com

Pahrump • *Pahrump Valley C/C* • Michael Dreyer; CEO; 1301 S. Hwy. 160, 2nd Flr.; P.O. Box 42; 89041; Nye; P 38,000; M 490; (775) 727-5800; Fax (775) 727-3909; info@pahrumpchamber.com; www.pahrumpchamber.com

Pioche • *Pioche C/C* • Mr. Shanks; P.O. Box 127; 89043; Lincoln; P 1,000; M 40; (775) 962-5544; (775) 962-5271; info@piochenevada.com; www.piochenevada.com

Reno • *The Chamber (Reno-Sparks-Northern Nevada)* • Ann Silver; CEO; 449 S. Virginia St., Ste 200; 89501; Washoe; P 316,600; M 1,500; (775) 636-9550; Fax (775) 337-3038; info@thechambernv.org; www.thechambernv.org*

Silver Springs • *Silver Springs Area C/C* • Bridget Perez; 1190 W. Hwy. 50, Ste. 1; P.O. Box 617; 89429; Lyon; P 6,700; M 25; (775) 577-4336; Fax (775) 577-4399; ssacc@att.net; www.silverspringsnevada.org*

Sparks • *see Reno*

Stateline • *TahoeChamber.org* • Betty Gorman; Pres./CEO; 169 U.S. Hwy. 50; P.O. Box 7139; 89449; Douglas & El Dorado; P 20,000; M 650; (775) 588-1728; (775) 588-5900; Fax (775) 588-1941; info@tahoechamber.org; www.tahoechamber.org*

Wells • *Wells C/C* • Yvonne Stuart; Pres.; 436 6th St.; P.O. Box 615; 89835; Elko; P 2,000; M 56; (775) 752-3540; wellschamber@wellsnevada.com; www.wellschamber.com

Winnemucca • *Humboldt County C/C* • Debbie Stone; Exec. Dir.; 30 W. Winnemucca Blvd.; 89445; Humboldt; P 18,000; M 300; (775) 623-2225; Fax (775) 623-6478; chamber@winnemucca.net; www.humboldtcountychamber.com*

Yerington • *Yerington C/C* • Shaline Montgomery; Pres.; 227 S. Main St.; PO Box 1692; 89447; Lyon; P 3,086; M 78; (775) 463-2245; Fax (775) 463-0030; yeringtonchamber@gmail.com; www.yeringtonchamber.org*

New Hampshire

Bus. & Ind. Assn. of N.H. • Jim Roche; Pres.; 122 N. Main St.; Concord; 03301; Merrimack; P 1,320,718; M 400; (603) 224-5388; Fax (603) 224-2872; sstreeter@biaofnh.com; www.biaofnh.com

Acworth • *see Bellows Falls, VT*

Amherst • *Souhegan Valley C/C* • May Balsama; Exec. Dir.; 69 Rte. 101A; 03031; Hillsborough; P 60,000; M 300; (603) 673-4360; Fax (603) 673-5018; may@souhegan.net; www.souhegan.net*

Berlin • *Androscoggin Valley C/C* • Paula Kinney; Exec. Coord.; 961 Main St.; 03570; Coos; P 17,000; M 175; (603) 752-6060; Fax (603) 752-1002; info@androscogginvalleychamber.com; www.androscogginvalleychamber.com

Bethlehem • *Bethlehem Visitors Center* • 2182 Main St.; P.O. Box 189; 03574; Grafton; P 2,000; M 40; (603) 869-3409; info@bethlehemwhitemtns.com; www.bethlehemwhitemtns.com

Brentwood • *see Exeter*

Bretton Woods • *see Twin Mountain*

Bristol • *see Plymouth*

Brookline • *see Amherst*

Cambridge • *see Errol*

Campton • *Waterville Valley Region C/C* • Joe Collie; Exec. Dir.; 12 Vintinner Rd.; 03223; Grafton; P 15,000; M 230; (603) 726-3804; Fax (603) 726-4058; info@watervillevalleyregion.com; www.nhchamber.com

Center Harbor • *see Meredith*

Center Ossipee • *Greater Ossipee Area C/C* • Joseph Ferreira; Pres.; P.O. Box 323; 03814; Carroll; P 12,000; M 150; (603) 539-6201; (866) 683-6295; Fax (603) 941-0133; info@ossipeevalley.org; www.ossipeevalley.org

Charlestown • *see Claremont*

Claremont • *Greater Claremont C/C* • Shelly Hudson; Exec. Dir.; 24 Opera House Sq., Ste. 100; 03743; Sullivan; P 13,902; M 250; (603) 543-1296; Fax (603) 542-1469; executive@claremontnhchamber.org; www.claremontnhchamber.org

Colebrook • *North Country C/C* • Kirsten Silfvenius; Exec. Dir.; 104 Main St., Ste. 206; P.O. Box 1; 03576; Coos; P 5,000; M 139; (603) 237-8939; (800) 698-8939; Fax (603) 237-4573; info@chamberofthenorthcountry.com; www.chamberofthenorthcountry.com

Concord • *Greater Concord C/C* • Timothy G. Sink CCE; Pres.; 49 S. Main St., Ste. 104; 03301; Merrrimack; P 43,000; M 900; (603) 224-2508; Fax (603) 224-8128; info@concordnhchamber.com; www.concordnhchamber.com*

Conway • *see North Conway*

Cornish • *see Windsor, VT*

Derry • *Greater Derry Londonderry C/C* • Will Stewart; Pres.; 29 W. Broadway; 03038; Rockingham; P 33,100; M 300; (603) 432-8205; Fax (603) 432-7938; info@gdlchamber.org; www.gdlchamber.org*

Dover • *Greater Dover C/C* • Molly Hodgson Smith; Exec. Dir.; 550 Central Ave.; 03820; Strafford; P 30,000; M 536; (603) 742-2218; info@dovernh.org; www.dovernh.org*

Dummer • *see Berlin*

East Kingston • *see Exeter*

Easton • *see Franconia*

Effingham • *see Center Ossipee*

Epping • *see Exeter*

Errol • *Umbagog Area C/C* • Christina Cote; P.O. Box 113; 03579; Coos; P 300; M 30; info@umbagogchamber.com; www.umbagogchamber.com

Exeter • *Exeter Area C/C* • Michael Schidlovsky; Pres.; 24 Front St., Ste. 101; P.O. Box 278; 03833; Rockingham; P 51,000; M 500; (603) 772-2411; Fax (603) 772-9965; info@exeterarea.org; www.exeterarea.org*

Franconia • *Franconia Notch C/C* • Greg Keeler; Interim Pres.; 421 Main St.; P.O. Box 780; 03580; Grafton; P 2,500; M 200; (603) 823-5661; info@franconianotch.org; www.franconianotch.org

Freedom • *see Center Ossipee*

Gorham • *see Berlin*

Greenfield • *see Amherst*

Greenville • *see Amherst*

Hampton • *Hampton Area C/C* • B.J. Noel; Pres.; 1 Lafayette Rd.; P.O. Box 790; 03843; Rockingham; P 16,000; M 425; (603) 926-8718; Fax (603) 926-9977; info@hamptonchamber.com; www.hamptonchamber.com

Hanover • *Hanover Area C/C* • Janet Rebman; Exec. Dir.; 53 S. Main St., Ste. 208; P.O. Box 5105; 03755; Grafton; P 11,000; M 370; (603) 643-3115; Fax (603) 643-5606; hacc@hanoverchamber.org; www.hanoverchamber.org*

Hillsborough • *Greater Hillsborough Area C/C* • Virginia Leiby; Exec. Dir.; 3 School St.; P.O. Box 541; 03244; Hillsborough; P 6,000; M 88; (603) 464-5858; info@hillsboroughnhchamber.org; www.hillsboroughnhchamber.org*

Hollis • *see Amherst*

Hudson • *Hudson C/C* • Brenda Collins; Exec. Dir.; 71 Lowell Rd.; 03051; Hillsborough; P 24,500; M 140; (603) 889-4731; Fax (603) 889-7939; info@hudsonchamber.com; www.hudsonchamber.com*

Jackson • *Jackson Area C/C* • Kathleen Driscoll; P.O. Box 304; 03846; Carroll; P 900; M 100; (603) 383-9356; Fax (603) 383-0931; info@jacksonnh.com; www.jacksonnh.com

Jaffrey • *Jaffrey C/C* • Becky Newton; Exec. Asst.; P.O. Box 2; 03452; Cheshire; P 5,700; M 210; (603) 532-4549; Fax (603) 532-8823; info@jaffreychamber.com; www.jaffreychamber.com*

Jefferson • *see Berlin*

Keene • *Greater Keene C/C* • Philip Suter; Pres.; 48 Central Sq.; 03431; Cheshire; P 23,000; M 443; (603) 352-1303; Fax (603) 358-5341; info@keenechamber.com; www.keenechamber.com*

Kensington • *see Exeter*

Kinston • *see Exeter*

Laconia • *Lakes Region C/C* • Karmen Gifford; Exec. Dir.; 383 S. Main St.; 03246; Belknap; P 18,000; M 500; (603) 524-5531; Fax (603) 524-5534; info@lakesregionchamber.org; www.lakesregionchamber.org*

Lake Sunapee • *see New London*

Lancaster • *Northern Gateway Reg. C/C* • Beth Cape; Admin. Asst.; 25 Park St.; P.O. Box 537; 03584; Coos; P 10,000; M 120; (603) 788-2530; northerngatewaychamber@gmail.com; www.northerngatewaychamber.org

Lebanon • *Lebanon Area C/C* • Rob Taylor; Exec. Dir.; 2 S. Park St.; P.O. Box 97; 03766; Grafton; P 13,500; M 341; (603) 448-1203; Fax (603) 448-6489; lebanonchamber@lebanonchamber.com; www.lebanonchamber.com

Lincoln • *Lincoln-Woodstock C/C* • Mark LaClair; Exec. Dir.; Rte. 112; P.O. Box 1017; 03251; Grafton; P 3,036; M 240; (603) 745-6621; Fax (603) 745-4908; info@lincolnwoodstock.com; www.lincolnwoodstock.com*

Littleton • *Littleton Area C/C* • Lauren Anderson; Exec. Dir.; 2 Union St.; P.O. Box 105; 03561; Grafton; P 6,200; M 300; (603) 444-6561; Fax (603) 444-2427; info@littletonareachamber.com; www.littletonareachamber.com

Londonderry • *see Manchester*

Lyndeborough • *see Amherst*

Madison • *see Center Ossipee*

Manchester • *Greater Manchester C/C* • Michael J. Skelton; Pres./CEO; 54 Hanover St.; 03101; Hillsborough; P 108,000; M 1,000; (603) 666-6600; Fax (603) 626-0910; info@Manchester-Chamber.org; www.Manchester-Chamber.org*

Mason • *see Amherst*

Meredith • *Meredith Area C/C* • Susan Cerutti; Exec. Dir.; P.O. Box 732; 03253; Belknap; P 20,000; M 340; (603) 279-6121; Fax (603) 279-4525; meredith@lr.net; www.meredithareachamber.com

Merrimack • *Merrimack C/C* • Dawn Shepherd; Pres.; 4 John Tyler St., Unit H; 03054; Hillsborough; P 27,000; M 200; (603) 424-3669; Fax (603) 429-4325; info@merrimackchamber.org; www.merrimackchamber.org*

Milan • *see Berlin*

Milford • *see Amherst*

Millsfield • *see Errol*

Mont Vernon • *see Amherst*

Moultonboro • *see Meredith*

Nashua • *Greater Nashua C/C* • Tracy S. Hatch; Pres./CEO; 142 Main St., 5th Flr.; 03060; Hillsborough; P 170,000; M 750; (603) 881-8333; Fax (603) 881-7323; cwilliams@nashuachamber.com; www.nashuachamber.com*

New Ipswich • *see Amherst*

New London • *Lake Sunapee Region C/C* • 328 Main St.; P.O. Box 532; 03257; Merrimack & Sullivan; P 15,000; M 240; (603) 526-6575; (877) 526-6575; chamberinfo@tds.net; www.LakeSunapeeNH.org

Newfields • *see Exeter*

Newmarket • *see Exeter*

Newport • *Newport Area C/C* • Ella M. Casey; Exec. Dir.; 2 N. Main St.; 03773; Sullivan; P 6,538; M 120; (603) 863-1510; Fax (603) 863-9486; chamber@newportnhchamber.org; www.newportnhchamber.org

North Conway • *Mount Washington Valley C/C* • Janice Crawford; Exec. Dir.; 2617 White Mountain Hwy.; P.O. Box 2300; 03860; Carroll; P 30,000; M 800; (603) 356-5701; (800) 367-3364; Fax (603) 356-7069; visitor@mtwashingtonvalley.org; www.mtwashingtonvalley.org

North Walpole • *see Bellows Falls, VT*

Ossipee • *see Center Ossipee*

Peterborough • *Greater Peterborough C/C* • Sean Ryan; Exec. Dir.; 10 Wilton Rd.; P.O. Box 401; 03458; Hillsborough; P 6,200; M 325; (603) 924-7234; Fax (603) 924-7235; info@peterboroughchamber.com; www.peterboroughchamber.com*

Plainfield • *see Windsor, VT*

Plymouth • *Plymouth Reg. C/C* • Scott Stephens; Exec. Dir.; 144 Rte. 175A, Holderness; P.O. Box 65; 03264; Grafton; P 12,000; M 230; (603) 536-1001; (800) 386-3678; info@plymouthnh.org; www.plymouthnh.org*

Portsmouth • *Greater Portsmouth C/C* • Douglas Bates; Pres.; 500 Market St., Unit 16A; P.O. Box 239; 03802; Rockingham; P 70,000; M 800; (603) 610-5510; Fax (603) 436-5118; president@portsmouthchamber.org; www.portsmouthchamber.org*

Randolph • *see Berlin*

Raymond • *see Exeter*

Rindge • *Rindge C/C* • Lisa Murray; Pres.; P.O. Box 911; 03461; Cheshire; P 6,000; M 83; (603) 899-5051; info@rindgechamber.org; www.rindgechamber.org

Rochester • *Greater Rochester C/C* • Laura Ring; Pres./CEO; 18 S. Main St.; 03867; Strafford; P 80,000; M 450; (603) 332-5080; Fax (603) 332-5216; info@rochesternh.org; www.rochesternh.org*

Salem • *Greater Salem C/C* • Donna Morris; Exec. Dir.; 81 Main St.; 03079; Rockingham; P 70,000; M 350; (603) 893-3177; Fax (603) 894-5158; donna@gschamber.com; www.gschamber.com*

Sandwich • *see Center Ossipee*

Shelburne • *see Berlin*

Somersworth • *Greater Somersworth C/C* • Sarah Potter; Exec. Dir.; 58 High St.; P.O. Box 615; 03878; Strafford; P 11,500; M 200; (603) 692-7175; Fax (603) 692-4501; info@somersworthchamber.com; www.somersworthchamber.com*

Stratham • *see Exeter*

Sugar Hill • *see Franconia*

Sunapee • *see New London*

Tamworth • *see Center Ossipee*

Temple • *see Amherst*

Twin Mountain • *Twin Mountain-Bretton Woods C/C* • P.O. Box 194; 03595; Coos; P 800; M 50; (800) 245-TWIN; info@twinmountain.org; www.twinmountain.org

Wakefield • *Greater Wakefield C/C* • Rod Cools; Pres.; P.O. Box 111; 03872; Carroll; P 5,900; M 100; (603) 522-6106; wakefieldchamberaa@gmail.com; www.greaterwakefieldchamber.com

Walpole • *see Bellows Falls, VT*

Waterville Valley • *see Campton*

Weirs Beach • *see Laconia*

West Ossipee • *see Center Ossipee*

Westmoreland • *see Bellows Falls, VT*

Wilton • *see Amherst*

Wolfeboro • *Wolfeboro Area C/C* • Mary DeVries; Exec. Dir.; 32 Central Ave.; P.O. Box 547; 03894; Carroll; P 6,300; M 350; (603) 569-2200; mary@wolfeborochamber.com; www.wolfeborochamber.com*

New Jersey

New Jersey C of C • Thomas Bracken; Pres./CEO; 216 W. State St.; Trenton; 08608; Mercer; P 8,864,590; M 1,600; (609) 989-7888; Fax (609) 989-9696; scott.goldstein@njchamber.com; www.njchamber.com

Aberdeen • *see Matawan*

Allumuchy • *see Phillipsburg*

Alpha • *see Phillipsburg*

Asbury Park • *Asbury Park C/C* • Sylvia Sylvia-Cioffi; Exec. Dir.; 1201 Springwood Ave., Unit 104; P.O. Box 649; 07712; Monmouth; P 16,200; M 275; (732) 775-7676; Fax (732) 775-7675; info@asburyparkchamber.com; www.asburyparkchamber.com

Atlantic City • *Greater Atlantic City Chamber* • Joseph Kelly; Pres.; 12 S. Virginia Ave.; 08401; Atlantic; P 275,000; M 700; (609) 345-4524; Fax (609) 345-1666; info@acchamber.com; www.acchamber.com*

Atlantic Highlands • *see Hazlet*

Avalon • *Avalon C/C* • John O'Dea; Pres.; 2989 Ocean Dr.; P.O. Box 22; 08202; Cape May; P 1,400; M 250; (609) 967-3936; Fax (609) 967-1815; chamber@avalonbeach.com; www.avalonbeach.com

Basking Ridge • *Bernards Twp. Reg. C/C* • Albert LiCata; Exec. Dir.; P.O. Box 11; 07920; Somerset; P 26,600; M 210; (908) 766-6755; Ren1co@aol.com; www.bernardstwpregionalchamber.org

Bay Head • *see Point Pleasant Beach*

Bayonne • *Bayonne C/C* • Matthew Dorans; Pres.; P.O. Box 266; 07002; Hudson; P 63,100; M 120; (201) 436-4333; Fax (201) 339-0305; pres@bayonnechamber.org; www.bayonnechamber.org

Bayville • *see Toms River*

Belford • *see Hazlet*

Belmar • *Belmar C/C* • Brenda Yarnold; Admin.; 700A 10th Ave.; 07719; Monmouth; P 7,000; M 35; (732) 894-9340; info@belmarchamber.org; www.belmarchamber.org

Belvidere • *see Phillipsburg*

Bergen • *see Hasbrouck Heights*

Berkeley Heights • *see Summit*

Bernardsville • *Bernardsville C/C* • Eileen Loughnane; Pres.; P.O. Box 672; 07924; Somerset; P 7,400; M 160; (908) 766-9900; Fax (908) 696-9771; nancymclurebcc@gmail.com; bvillechamber.com

Blairstown • *see Phillipsburg*

Bloomfield • *Suburban Essex C/C* • Nestor L. Arce; Pres.; 256 Broad St., Ste. 2F; 07003; Essex; P 150,000; M 200; (973) 748-2000; admin@suburbanessexchamber.com; www.suburbanessexchamber.com

Bloomingdale • *Tri-Boro Area C/C* • Jamie Certosimo; Pres.; P.O. Box 100; 07403; Passaic; P 29,000; M 80; (973) 838-5678; Fax (973) 838-5229; triborochamber@aol.com; www.triborochamber.org

Boonton • *Tri-Town C/C* • Maria Accardi; Exec. Dir.; P.O. Box 496; 07005; Morris; P 19,000; M 170; (973) 334-4117; Fax (973) 263-4164; info@tritownchamber.org; www.tritownchamber.org

Bordentown • *Northern Burlington Reg. C/C* • Bill Ryan; Pres.; P.O. Box 65; 08505; Burlington; P 10,000; M 140; (609) 298-7774; Fax (609) 291-5008; info@nbrchamber.org; www.nbrchamber.org

Brick • *Brick Township C/C* • Michele Eventoff; Exec. Dir.; 270 Chambers Bridge Rd., Ste. 6; 08723; Ocean; P 76,000; M 600; (732) 477-4949; Fax (732) 477-5788; info@brickchamber.com; www.brickchamber.com*

Bridgeton • *Bridgeton Area C/C* • Anthony Stanzione; Exec. Dir.; P.O. Box 1063; 08302; Cumberland; P 26,000; M 190; (856) 455-1312; Fax (856) 453-9795; bacc@baccnj.com; www.baccnj.com

Bridgewater • *Somerset County Bus. Partnership* • Michael Kerwin; Pres./CEO; 360 Grove St. at Rte. 22 E.; 08807; Somerset; P 324,600; M 650; (908) 218-4300; Fax (908) 722-7823; info@scbp.org; www.scbp.org*

Brielle • *Brielle C/C* • Heidi Wittenberg; Pres.; P.O. Box 162; 08730; Monmouth; P 4,800; M 100; (732) 528-0377; contactus@briellechamber.com; www.briellechamber.com

Brigantine Beach • *Brigantine Beach C/C* • Emmett Turner; Pres.; P.O. Box 484; 08203; Atlantic; P 10,000; M 115; (609) 266-3437; info@brigantinechamber.com; www.brigantinechamber.com

Broadway • *see Phillipsburg*

Budd Lake • *Mount Olive Area C/C* • Greg Stewart; Pres.; P.O. Box 192; 07828; Morris; P 28,200; M 130; (908) 509-1774; info@mountolivechambernj.com; mountolivechambernj.com

Burlington • *Greater Burlington C/C* • Sue Woolman; Secy.; P.O. Box 67; 08016; Burlington; P 23,000; M 55; (609) 387-4528; gbcoc1@gmail.com; www.greaterburlingtoncoc.com

Burlington County • *see Mount Laurel*

Butler • *see Bloomingdale and Wayne*

Caldwell • *see West Caldwell*

Camden • *see Cherry Hill*

Cape May • *C/C of Greater Cape May* • John Cooke; Pres.; P.O. Box 556; 08204; Cape May; P 5,000; M 300; (609) 884-5508; Fax (609) 884-2054; request@capemaychamber.com; www.capemaychamber.com

Cape May County • *Cape May County C/C* • Carol Sawyer; Pres.; P.O. Box 74; Cape May Court House; 08210; Cape May; P 98,000; M 965; (609) 465-7181; Fax (609) 465-5017; info@cmcchamber.com; www.capemaycountychamber.com*

Cape May Court House • *Middle Township C/C* • Bob Noel; Pres.; P.O. Box 6; 08210; Cape May; P 19,000; M 125; (609) 463-1655; info@mtcc4u.com; www.mtcc4u.com

Carneys Point • *see Salem*

Cedar Grove • *see West Caldwell*

Cedar Knolls • *see Florham Park*

Chatham • *Chatham Area C/C* • Carolyn Cherry; Exec. Dir.; P.O. Box 231; 07928; Morris; P 10,500; M 200; execdir@chathamchambernj.org; www.chathamchambernj.org

Cherry Hill • *Camden County Reg. C/C* • Arthur Campbell; Pres./CEO; 1060 Kings Hwy. N., Ste. 200; 08034; Camden; P 513,600; M 950; (856) 667-1600; Fax (856) 667-1464; info@camdencountychamber.com; www.camdencountychamber.com

Cliffside Park • *Cliffside Park C/C* • Lynne Nesbihal; Exec. Dir.; 645 Anderson Ave.; 07010; Bergen; P 24,000; (201) 941-9505; Fax (201) 941-8499; info@cliffsideparkchamber.org; www.cliffsideparkonline.com/chamber

Clifton • *North Jersey Reg. C/C* • Brian Tangora; Pres./CEO; 1033 Rte. 46 E., Ste. A103; 07013; Passaic; P 150,000; M 600; (973) 470-9300; Fax (973) 470-9245; staff@njrcc.org; www.njrcc.org

Clinton • *see Flemington*

Colts Neck • *see Freehold*

Columbia • *see Phillipsburg*

Cranford • *Cranford C/C* • Dottie Baniewicz; Exec. Dir.; 8 Springfield Ave.; P.O. Box 165; 07016; Union; P 25,000; M 200; (908) 272-6114; Fax (908) 272-3742; cranfordchamber@comcast.net; www.cranford.com/chamber

Dennis Township • *see Cape May*

Denville • *Denville C/C* • Kristin Pamperin; Pres.; P.O. Box 333; 07834; Morris; P 16,600; M 155; (973) 625-1171; moreinfo@denville-nj.com; www.denville-nj.com

Dover • *Dover Area C/C* • Susan Konight; Pres.; P.O. Box 506; 07802; Ocean; P 16,000; M 80; (973) 676-8725; Fax (973) 673-5828; email@doverareachamber.com; www.doverareachamber.com

Dumont • *Dumont C/C* • Michael Brown; P.O. Box 10; 07628; Bergen; P 18,000; M 30; (201) 280-4441; info@dumontchamber.org; www.dumontchamber.org

East Brunswick • *East Brunswick Reg. C/C* • P.O. Box 56; 08816; Middlesex; P 100,000; M 190; (732) 257-3009; Fax (732) 257-0949; office@ebchamber.org; www.ebchamber.org

East Hanover • *see Florham Park*

East Millstone • *see Franklin Twp.*

East Newark • *see Jersey City*

East Orange • *East Orange C/C* • Amir Hashemi; Pres.; P.O. Box 2418; 07019; Essex; P 80,000; M 50; (973) 674-0900; Fax (973) 673-5027; info@eastorangechamber.biz; www.eastorangechamber.biz

East Windsor • *see Mercerville*

Eatontown • *see Red Bank*

Edison • *Hanover Area C/C* • Rajeev Sharma; Pres./CEO; 3 Woodfern St.; 08820; Middlesex; P 25,000; M 100; (973) 884-3278; president@hanoverareachamber.org; www.hanoverareachamber.org

Edison • *Edison C/C* • Nathan Rudy; Pres./CEO; 1028 Amboy Ave.; Campus Plaza 6; 08837; Middlesex; P 100,000; M 325; (732) 738-9482; Fax (732) 738-9485; nathan@edisonchamber.com; www.edisonchamber.com*

Egg Harbor City • *Egg Harbor City Chamber* • James Schroeder; P.O. Box 129; 08215; Atlantic; P 4,545; M 50; (609) 270-7590; info@greatereggchamber.com; www.greatereggchamber.com

Elizabeth • *Gateway Reg. C/C* • James R. Coyle; Pres.; 135 Jefferson Ave.; P.O. Box 300; 07207; Union; P 504,000; M 1,800; (908) 352-0900; Fax (908) 352-0865; kateconroy@gatewaychamber.com; www.gatewaychamber.com

Elizabeth • *Greater Elizabeth C/C* • Gordon F. Haas; Pres./CEO; 456 N. Broad St., 2nd Flr.; 07208; Union; P 150,000; M 500; (908) 355-7600; Fax (908) 436-2054; ghaas.gecc@gmail.com; elizabethchamber.com*

Englewood • *Englewood C/C* • Carol Rauscher; Pres.; P.O. Box 8161; 07631; Bergen; P 30,000; M 250; (201) 567-2381; crauscher@englewoodnjchamber.com; www.englewoodnjchamber.com

Englewood Cliffs • *see Englewood*

Englishtown • *see Freehold*

Essex County • *see Wayne and West Caldwell*

Essex Fells • *see West Caldwell*

Ewing • *see Mercerville*

Fair Haven • *see Red Bank*

Fair Lawn • *Fair Lawn C/C* • Adele Badalamenti; Admin. Mgr.; 12-45 River Rd.; 07410; Bergen; P 33,000; M 280; (201) 796-7050; Fax (201) 475-0619; info@fairlawnchamber.org; www.fairlawnchamber.org*

Fairfield • *see Wayne and West Caldwell*

Flemington • *Hunterdon County C/C* • Christopher J. Phelan; Pres./CEO; 14 Mine St., 2nd Flr.; CenturyLink Bldg.; 08822; Hunterdon; P 121,000; M 600; (908) 782-7115; Fax (908) 782-7283; info@hunterdon-chamber.org; www.hunterdonchamber.org*

Florham Park • *Morris County C/C* • Paul Boudreau; Pres.; 325 Columbia Tpk., Ste. 101; 07932; Morris; P 492,300; M 840; (973) 539-3882; Fax (973) 377-0859; dina@morrischamber.org; www.morrischamber.org*

Fort Lee • *Fort Lee Reg. C/C* • Liz Crawford; Admin. Asst.; 210 Whiteman St.; 07024; Bergen; P 36,000; M 200; (201) 944-7575; Fax (201) 944-5168; assistant@fortleechamber.com; www.fortleechamber.com

Franklin Lakes • *Franklin Lakes C/C* • Jeff Allen; Pres.; P.O. Box 81; 07417; Bergen; P 11,100; M 50; (973) 891-8790; info@flcoc.org; www.flcoc.org

Franklin Twp. • *Franklin Twp. C/C* • Michael Harris; Pres.; 675 Franklin Blvd.; Somerset; 08873; Somerset; P 62,300; M 200; (732) 545-7044; www.franklinchamber.com

Freehold • *Greater Monmouth C/C* • Tony Howley; Exec. Dir.; 10 E. Main St., Ste. 1A; 07728; Monmouth; P 72,000; M 400; (732) 462-3030; Fax (732) 462-2123; admin@greatermonmouthchamber.com; www.greatermonmouthchamber.com*

Gibbstown • *see Cherry Hill*

Glassboro • *Gloucester County C/C* • Les Vail; Pres./CEO; 205 Rowan Blvd.; 08028; Gloucester; P 288,300; M 600; (856) 881-6560; lvail@gloucestercountychamber.com; www.gc-chamber.com*

Glen Rock • *Glen Rock C/C* • Pat Zengel; Treas.; 372 Franklin Ave.; 07481; Bergen; P 11,600; M 60; (201) 670-8700; sureselpat@aol.com; www.glenrocknj.net

Gloucester Twp. • *see Cherry Hill*

Great Meadows • *see Phillipsburg*

Griggstown • *see Franklin Twp.*

Guttenberg • *see Jersey City*

Hackensack • *Hackensack Reg. C/C* • Lauren Zisa Samulka; Exec. Dir.; 5 University Plaza Dr.; 07601; Bergen; P 42,000; M 250; (201) 489-3700; Fax (201) 489-1741; info@hackensackchamber.org; www.hackensackchamber.org*

Hackettstown • *see Phillipsburg*

Haddonfield • *see Voorhees*

Haledon • *see Wayne*

Hammonton • *Greater Hammonton C/C* • Michele Samanic; Exec. Dir.; 10 S. Egg Harbor Rd.; P.O. Box 554; 08037; Atlantic; P 14,800; M 125; (609) 561-9080; Fax (609) 561-9411; info@hammontonnj.us; www.hammontonnj.us

Hanover Twp. • *see Florham Park*

Hardwick • *see Phillipsburg*

Harrison • *see Jersey City*

Hasbrouck Heights • *Hasbrouck Heights C/C* • Ray Vorisek; Pres.; P.O. Box 1; 07604; Bergen; P 12,000; M 100; (201) 288-5464; heightsflowershoppe@verizon.net; www.hasbrouck-heights.org

Hawthorne • *Hawthorne C/C* • Joann Ciampa; Exec. Secy.; 471 Lafayette Ave.; P.O. Box 331; 07507; Passaic; P 18,800; M 230; (973) 427-5078; Fax (973) 427-6066; info@hawthornechamber.org; www.hawthornechamber.org

Hazlet • *Northern Monmouth C/C* • Terence Biggs II; Exec. Dir.; 1340 Hwy. 36, Ste. 22; P.O. Box 5007; 07730; Monmouth; P 90,000; M 350; (732) 203-0340; Fax (732) 203-0341; director@northernmonmouthchamber.com; www.northernmonmouthchamber.com

Highlands • *see Hazlet*

Hightstown • *see Mercerville*

Hillside • *Hillside C/C* • John Kruse; P.O. Box 965; 07205; Union; P 27,000; M 100; (908) 964-6659; Fax (908) 964-3781; information@hillsidechamber.com; www.hillsidechamber.com

Hoboken • *Hoboken C/C* • Michael Novak; Pres.; P.O. Box 349; 07030; Hudson; P 50,000; M 160; (201) 222-1100; hobchamber@aol.com; www.hobokenchamber.com

Hohokus • *Ho-Ho-kus C/C* • Steve Sager; Pres.; P.O. Box 115; 07423; Bergen; P 5,000; M 20; (201) 788-5588; (201) 652-4400; www.ho-ho-kusboro.com

Holmdel • *see Hazlet*

Hope • *Hope Area C/C* • Chris Maier; Pres.; P.O. Box 2; 07844; Warren; P 2,000; M 52; (908) 475-8322; chamberhope@yahoo.com; www.hopeareachamber.com

Hopewell Township • *see Mercerville*

Howell • *Howell C/C* • Susan Dominguez; Exec. Dir.; 103 W. 2nd St.; P.O. Box 196; 07731; Monmouth; P 51,100; M 246; (732) 363-4114; Fax (732) 363-8747; info@howellchamber.com; www.howellchamber.com

Irvington • *Irvington C/C* • Luz Carde; Exec. Dir.; P.O. Box 323; 07111; Essex; P 54,000; M 150; (973) 676-8725; Fax (973) 673-5828; email@irvington-nj.com; www.irvington-nj.com

Iselin • *see Woodbridge*

Jackson • *Jackson C/C* • Catherine Gross; Ofc. Mgr.; 1021 W. Commodore Blvd.; 08527; Ocean; P 54,400; M 245; (732) 833-0005; Fax (732) 833-7033; jcinfo@jacksonchamber.com; www.jacksonchamber.com

Jersey City • *Hudson County C/C* • Maria Nieves; Pres./CEO; 150 Hudson St., Ste. 100; 07311; Hudson; P 635,000; M 500; (201) 386-0699; Fax (201) 386-8480; info@hudsonchamber.org; www.hudsonchamber.org

Johnsonburg • *see Phillipsburg*

Keansburg • *see Hazlet*

Kearny • *see Jersey City*

Kingston • *see Franklin Twp.*

Kinnelon • *see Bloomingdale and Wayne*

Lake Hiawatha • *Parsippany Area C/C* • Craig Schlosser; Exec. Dir.; 12-14 N. Beverwyck Rd.; 07034; Morris; P 55,000; M 300; (973) 402-6400; craig@parsippanychamber.org; www.parsippanychamber.org

Lake Hopatcong • *Jefferson Twp. C/C* • Dr. Bret Hartman; Pres.; P.O. Box 64; 07849; Sussex; P 21,300; M 70; (973) 663-2240; jtccinfo@gmail.com; www.jeffersontownshipchamber.org

Lakewood • *Lakewood C/C* • Robert Gazic; Exec. Dir.; 681 River Ave., Ste. 2F; 08701; Ocean; P 92,800; M 490; (732) 363-0012; Fax (732) 367-4453; staff@mylakewoodchamber.com; www.mylakewoodchamber.com

Lambertville • *Delaware River Towns C/C* • David Morgan; Exec. Dir.; 77 Bridge St.; 08530; Hunterdon; P 4,300; M 350; (609) 397-0055; Fax (609) 397-7423; info@delawarerivertowns.com; www.delawarerivertowns.com*

Landing • *see Ledgewood*

Lavallette • *see Toms River*

Lawrenceville • *see Mercerville*

Lebanon • *see Flemington*

Ledgewood • *Roxbury Area C/C* • Pam Smith; Secy.; P.O. Box 436; 07852; Morris; P 24,000; M 120; (973) 770-0740; info@roxburynjchamber.org; www.roxburynjchamber.org

Leonardo • *see Hazlet*

Lincoln Park • *see Wayne*

Little Falls • *see Clifton, Wayne & West Caldwell*

Little Silver • *see Red Bank*

Livingston • *Livingston Area C/C* • Beth Lippman; Exec. Dir./Admin.; 25 S. Livingston Ave.; 2nd Flr., Ste. E; 07039; Essex; P 29,400; M 160; (973) 992-4343; Fax (888) 501-7023; info@livingstonchambernj.com; www.livingstonchambernj.com

Long Branch • *Greater Long Branch C/C* • Nancy Kleiberg; Exec. Dir.; 228 Broadway; P.O. Box 628; 07740; Monmouth; P 31,000; M 280; (732) 222-0400; Fax (732) 571-3385; info@longbranchchamber.org; www.longbranchchamber.org

Madison • *Madison Area C/C* • Mr. John Morris; Pres.; P.O. Box 152; 07940; Morris; P 16,000; M 180; (973) 377-7830; info@MadisonNJChamber.org; www.MadisonNJChamber.org

Mahwah • *Mahwah Reg. C/C* • Sharon Rounds; Exec. Dir.; 65 Ramapo Valley Rd., Ste. 211; 07430; Bergen; P 26,000; M 520; (201) 529-5566; Fax (201) 529-8122; sharon@mahwah.com; www.mahwah.com

Manahawkin • *see Ship Bottom*

Manalapan • *see Freehold*

Manasquan • *Manasquan C/C* • Bill Sepe; Pres.; 107 Main St.; 08736; Monmouth; P 6,000; M 135; (732) 223-8303; info@manasquanchamber.org; www.manasquanchamber.org

Manville • *see Franklin Twp.*

Maplewood • *Maplewood C/C* • Rene Conlon; Exec. Secy.; P.O. Box 423; 07040; Essex; P 24,000; M 150; contact11@mindspring.com; www.maplewoodchamber.org

Marlboro • *see Freehold*

Marlton • *see Mount Laurel*

Matawan • *Matawan-Aberdeen C/C* • Jeff Pantelas; Pres.; 201 Broad St.; P.O. Box 522; 07747; Monmouth; P 27,000; M 150; (732) 290-1125; Fax (888) 552-5892; info@macocnj.com; www.macocnj.com

Maywood • *Maywood C/C* • Dr. Timothy Eustace; Pres.; 140 W. Pleasant Ave.; 07607; Bergen; P 9,555; M 75; (201) 843-3111; teustace@aol.com; www.maywoodboro.org

Meadowlands • *see Rutherford-Meadowlands Reg. C/C*

Medford • *see Burlington*

Mercerville • *MIDJersey C/C* • Robert D. Prunetti; Pres./CEO; 1A Quakerbridge Plaza Dr., Ste. 2; 08619; Mercer; P 367,000; M 1,300; (609) 689-9960; Fax (609) 586-9989; amy@midjerseychamber.org; www.midjerseychamber.org

Metuchen • *Metuchen Area C/C* • Angela Sielski; Exec. Dir.; 323 Main St., Ste. B; 08840; Middlesex; P 13,100; M 300; (732) 548-2964; Fax (732) 548-4094; metuchen.chamber@verizon.net; www.metuchenchamberexchange.com

Middlesex County • *see New Brunswick*

Middletown • *see Hazlet*

Midland Park • *Midland Park C/C* • Lisa Plasse; Pres.; 47 Prospect St.; P.O. Box 267; 07432; Bergen; P 7,200; M 75; (201) 445-8780; flute76@aol.com; www.midlandparkchamber.com

Millburn • *Millburn-Short Hills C/C* • Roxanne Giacalone; Exec. Dir.; 343 Millburn Ave., Ste. 303; P.O. Box 651; 07041; Essex; P 20,200; M 250; (973) 379-1198; Fax (973) 376-5678; info@millburnshorthillschamber.org; www.millburnshorthillschamber.org

Millstone • *see Freehold*

Millville • *Greater Millville C/C* • Earl Sherrick; Exec. Dir.; 2 N. High St.; P.O. Box 831; 08332; Cumberland; P 28,000; M 200; (856) 825-2600; Fax (856) 776-5391; info@millville-nj.com; www.millville-nj.com

Monmouth Beach • *see Red Bank*

Montclair • *see West Caldwell*

Montville • *Montville Twp. C/C* • Tony Giordano; Pres.; 195 Changebridge Rd.; 07045; Morris; P 24,000; M 190; (973) 263-3310; Fax (973) 263-3453; info@montvillechamber.com; www.montvillechamber.com

Moorestown • *see Mount Laurel*

Mooresville • *see Mount Laurel*

Mount Freedom • *Randolph Area C/C* • Lou Nisivoccia; Pres.; P.O. Box 391; 07970; Morris; P 26,000; M 85; (973) 361-3462; Fax (973) 895-3297; www.randolphchamber.org

Mount Laurel • *Burlington County C/C* • Kristi Howell-Ikeda; Pres.; 100 Technology Way, Ste. 110; 08054; Burlington; P 448,700; M 425; (856) 439-2520; Fax (856) 439-2523; bccoc@bccoc.com; www.bccoc.com*

Mount Olive • *see Budd Lake*

Mountain Lakes • *see Boonton*

Mountainside • *see Elizabeth*

Navesink • *see Hazlet*

New Brunswick • *Middlesex County Reg. C/C* • Lina Llona; Pres.; 109 Church St.; 08901; Middlesex; P 810,000; M 750; (732) 745-8090; Fax (732) 745-8098; info@mcrcc.org; www.mcrcc.org

New Providence • *see Summit*

Newark • *Newark Reg. Bus. Partnership* • Chip Hallock; Pres./CEO; Military Park Bldg.; 60 Park Place, Ste. 1800; 07102; Essex; P 280,000; M 500; (973) 522-0099; Fax (973) 824-4587; ndrake@newarkrbp.org; www.newarkrbp.org

Newark • *Statewide Hispanic C/C of NJ* • Dr. Daniel H. Jara; Pres./CEO; 1 Gateway Center, Ste. 615; 07102; Essex; P 500,000; M 2,800; (201) 451-9512; Fax (866) 226-1828; chamber@shccnj.org; www.shccnj.org

Newton • *Sussex County C/C* • Tammie Horsfield; Pres.; 120 Hampton House Rd.; 07860; Sussex; P 149,200; M 700; (973) 579-1811; Fax (973) 579-3031; mail@sussexcountychamber.org; www.sussexcountychamber.org*

North Bergen • *see Jersey City*

North Caldwell • *see West Caldwell*

Northfield • *see Atlantic City*

Nutley • *Nutley C/C* • Barbara Chiarieri; Ofc. Mgr.; 172 Chestnut St.; 07110; Essex; P 28,400; M 200; (973) 667-5300; Fax (973) 667-5300; chamber@nutleychamber.com; www.nutleychamber.com

Oakhurst • *Greater Ocean Twp. C/C* • Kim Horn-Blanda; Exec. Dir.; 163 Monmouth Rd.; 07755; Monmouth; P 30,000; M 250; (732) 660-1888; Fax (732) 660-1688; gotcc@gotcc.org; gotcc.org

Ocean City • *Ocean City Reg. C/C* • Michele Gillian; Exec. Dir.; 16 E. 9th St.; 08226; Cape May; P 15,000; M 500; (609) 399-1412; (800) BEACH-NJ; Fax (609) 398-3932; info@oceancitychamber.com; www.oceancityvacation.com

Ocean County • *see Toms River*

Ocean Grove • *Ocean Grove Area C/C* • Rebecca Cavanaugh; Exec. Dir.; 45 Pilgrim Pathway; P.O. Box 415; 07756; Monmouth; P 7,500; M 122; (732) 774-1391; (800) 388-4768; Fax (732) 774-3799; info@oceangrovechamber.org; www.oceangrovenj.com

Ocean Twp. • *see Oakhurst*

Ocean View • *see Cape May*

Oceanport • *see Red Bank*

Old Bridge • *The C/C serving Old Bridge, Sayreville & South Amboy* • VIncent Blasi; Pres.; P.O. Box 5241; 08857; Middlesex; P 150,000; M 145; (732) 607-6340; Fax (732) 607-6341; officers@chamberofcommerceobssa.org; www.chamberofcommerceobssa.org

Oradell • *see River Edge*

Ortley Beach • *see Toms River*

Oxford • *see Phillipsburg*

Paramus • *Paramus Reg. C/C* • Fred Rohdieck; Pres.; 332 Rte. 4 East, South Lobby; P.O. Box 325; 07652; Bergen; P 26,000; M 350; (201) 261-3344; Fax (201) 261-3346; info@paramuschamber.org; www.paramuschamber.org

Parsippany • *see Lake Hiawatha*

Passaic • *see Clifton*

Passaic County • *see Wayne*

Paterson • *Greater Paterson C/C* • James Dykes II; Pres.; 199 Market St.; 07505; Passaic; P 150,000; M 650; (973) 881-7300; Fax (973) 881-8233; gladys@greaterpatersoncc.org; www.greaterpatersoncc.org

Paulsboro • *Greater Paulsboro C/C* • Virginia Scott; Secy.; P.O. Box 181; 08066; Gloucester; P 6,100; M 50; (856) 423-7600; president@paulsborochamber.com; www.paulsborochamber.com

Pennington • *see Mercerville*

Pequannock • *see Bloomingdale and Wayne*

Phillipsburg • *Greater Lehigh Valley C/C* • Alison Pickel; VP, Easton & Phillipsburg Initiatives; 445 Marshall St., Ste. 156; 08865; Warren; P 15,000; M 250; (610) 739-1512; Fax (610) 330-9177; alisonp@lehighvalleychamber.org; www.lehighvalleychamber.org*

Phillipsburg • *also see Bethlehem, PA*

Pine Beach • *see Toms River*

Plainfield • *Plainfield C/C •* 320 Park Ave.; 07060; Union; P 48,600; M 200; (908) 753-2296; Fax (908) 753-6609; chamber@positivelyplainfield.org; www.positivelyplainfield.org

Point Pleasant Beach • *Point Pleasant Beach C/C •* Carol Vaccaro; Exec. Dir.; 517A Arnold Ave.; 08742; Ocean; P 5,000; M 310; (732) 899-2424; (888) PPBFUN2; Fax (732) 899-0103; info@pointpleasantbeachnj.com; www.pointpleasantbeachnj.org

Pompton Lakes • *Pompton Lakes C/C •* Art Kaffka; Pres.; P.O. Box 129; 07442; Passaic; P 11,100; M 95; (973) 839-0187; Fax (973) 839-0187; info@pomptonchamber.com; www.pomptonlakeschamber.com

Port Murray • *see Phillipsburg*

Princeton • *Princeton Reg. C/C •* Peter Crowley; Pres./CEO; 182 Nassau St., Ste. 301; 08542; Mercer; P 150,000; M 745; (609) 924-1776; Fax (609) 924-5776; info@princetonchamber.org; www.princetonchamber.org

Princeton Junction • *see Princeton*

Randolph • *see Mount Freedom*

Readington • *see Flemington*

Red Bank • *Eastern Monmouth Area C/C •* Lynda Rose; Pres./COO; 8 Reckless Pl., Ste. 1; 07701; Monmouth; P 50,000; M 500; (732) 741-0055; lynda@emacc.org; www.emacc.org*

Ridgewood • *Ridgewood C/C •* Joan Groome; Exec. Dir.; 27 Chestnut St., Ste. 1B; 07450; Bergen; P 25,000; M 250; (201) 445-2600; Fax (201) 251-1958; info@ridgewoodchamber.com; www.ridgewoodchamber.com

Ringwood • *Ringwood C/C •* Penny Safane; Pres.; P.O. Box 62; 07456; Passaic; P 12,300; M 200; president@ringwoodchamber.com; www.ringwoodchamber.com

River Edge • *Greater River Dell C/C •* David Palmer & Frank Puglise; Co-Pres.; 800 Summit Ave.; 07661; Bergen; P 11,340; M 75; info@rccchamber.org; www.riverdellchamber.com

Riverdale • *see Bloomingdale and Wayne*

Rochelle Park • *see Paramus*

Roseland • *see West Caldwell*

Roxbury • *see Ledgewood*

Rumson • *see Red Bank*

Rutherford • *Rutherford C/C •* Alice Allen; Exec. Secy.; P.O. Box 216; 07070; Bergen; P 18,000; M 75; (201) 933-3633; Fax (201) 507-7077; info@rutherfordchamber.com; www.rutherfordchamber.com

Rutherford • *Meadowlands Reg. Chamber •* James Kirkos; Pres./CEO; 201 Route 17 N., 2nd Flr.; 07070; Bergen; P 1,000,000; M 800; (201) 939-0707; Fax (201) 939-0522; jkirkos@meadowlands.org; www.meadowlands.org*

Saddle Brook • *see Hackensack*

Salem • *Salem County C/C •* Jennifer A. Jones; Exec. Dir.; 174 E. Broadway, Rm. 109; P.O. Box 71; 08079; Salem; P 66,100; M 380; (856) 351-2245; (856) 351-2243; Fax (856) 935-0961; info@salemcountychamber.com; www.salemcountychamber.com*

Sandy Hook • *see Hazlet*

Sayreville • *see Old Bridge*

Scotch Plains • *see Westfield*

Sea Bright • *see Red Bank*

Sea Girt • *see Wall*

Sea Isle City • *Sea Isle City Chamber & Revitalization •* Christopher Glancey; Pres.; P.O. Box 635; 08243; Cape May; P 3,000; M 85; (609) 263-9090; Fax (609) 263-9090; sicccr@gmail.com; www.seaislechamber.com

Seaside Heights • *see Toms River*

Seaside Park • *see Toms River*

Secaucus • *see Jersey City*

Ship Bottom • *Southern Ocean County C/C •* Rick Reynolds; Exec. Dir.; 265 W. 9th St.; 08008; Ocean; P 50,000; M 700; (609) 494-7211; (800) 292-6372; Fax (609) 494-5807; info@visitlbiregion.com; www.visitlbiregion.com

Short Hills • *see Millburn*

Shrewsbury • *see Red Bank*

Somerset • *see Franklin Twp.*

Somerville • *see Bridgewater*

South Amboy • *see Old Bridge*

South Orange • *South Orange Village C/C •* Dave Lackey; Pres.; 31 Vose Ave.; 07079; Essex; P 17,000; M 60; (201) 213-5716; www.southorangenjchamber.com

Spring Lake • *Greater Spring Lake C/C •* Lynn Kegelman; Corresp. Secy.; 302 Washington Ave.; P.O. Box 694; 07762; Monmouth; P 8,000; M 140; (732) 449-0577; splk.cofc@verizon.net; www.springlake.org

Stewartsville • *see Phillipsburg*

Stone Harbor • *Stone Harbor C/C •* Madlyn Zurawski; P.O. Box 422; 08247; Cape May; P 1,000; M 200; (609) 368-6101; admin@stoneharborbeach.com; www.stoneharborbeach.com

Summit • *Suburban C/C •* Karen Hadley; Exec. Dir.; 71 Summit Ave.; 07901; Union; P 48,000; M 260; (908) 522-1700; Fax (908) 522-9252; info@suburbanchambers.org; www.suburbanchambers.org

Sussex County • *see Newton*

Teaneck • *Teaneck C/C •* Larry Bauer; Pres.; P.O. Box 224; 07666; Bergen; P 39,776; M 120; (201) 801-0012; Fax (201) 490-1808; info@teaneckchamber.org; www.teaneckchamber.org*

Tenafly • *Tenafly C/C •* Christine Evron; Pres.; P.O. Box 163; 07670; Bergen; P 14,600; M 70; (201) 805-6053; www.tenaflynjchamberofcommerce.org

Tinton Falls • *see Red Bank*

Toms River • *Greater Toms River C/C •* Noelle Lotano; Exec. Dir.; 1027 Hooper Ave.; Bldg. 1, 2nd Flr., Ste. 5; 08753; Ocean; P 91,000; M 500; (732) 349-0220; Fax (732) 349-1252; noelle@tomsriverchamber.com; www.tomsriverchamber.com*

Totowa • *see Clifton and Wayne*

Turnersville • *Washington Twp. C/C* • Thomas Fletcher; Pres.; 5001 Rte. 42, Ste. C; P.O. Box 734; 08012; Gloucester; P 48,600; M 175; (856) 227-1776; Fax (856) 227-1225; info@washingtontownshipchamber.org; www.washingtontownshipchamber.org

Union • *Twp. of Union C/C* • Jim Masterson; Exec. Dir.; 355 Chestnut St., 2nd Flr.; 07083; Union; P 56,600; M 200; (908) 688-2777; Fax (908) 688-0338; info@unionchamber.com; www.unionchamber.com

Union Beach • *see Hazlet*

Union City • *see Jersey City*

Vernon • *Vernon C/C* • Elmer Platz; Pres.; P.O. Box 308; 07462; Sussex; P 25,500; M 35; (973) 764-0764; info@vernonchamber.com; www.vernonchamber.com

Verona • *see West Caldwell*

Vineland • *Greater Vineland C/C* • Dawn Hunter; Exec. Dir.; 2115 S. Delsea Dr.; 08360; Cumberland; P 60,000; M 500; (856) 691-7400; Fax (856) 691-2113; info@vinelandchamber.org; www.vinelandchamber.org

Voorhees • *Chamber of Commerce Southern NJ* • Debra DiLorenzo; Pres./CEO; 4015 Main St.; 08043; Camden; P 2,500,000; M 2,000; (856) 424-7776; Fax (856) 424-8180; info@chambersnj.com; www.chambersnj.com

Wall • *Southern Monmouth C/C* • Evelyn Mars; Exec. Dir.; P.O. Box 1305; 07719; Monmouth; P 90,000; M 350; (732) 280-8800; Fax (732) 280-8505; info@smcconline.org; www.smcconline.org*

Washington Township • *see Turnersville*

Wayne • *Tri-County C/C* • Caryn Luberto; Pres.; P.O. Box 2420; 07474; Passaic; P 120,000; M 350; (862) 210-8328; Fax (973) 882-0464; caryn@tricounty.org; www.tricounty.org*

Weehawken • *see Jersey City*

West Caldwell • *North Essex C/C* • Betty Albanesius; Ofc. Mgr.; 3 Fairfield Ave.; 07006; Essex; P 52,000; M 650; (973) 226-5500; Fax (973) 403-9335; email@northessexchamber.com; www.northessexchamber.com

West Milford • *West Milford C/C* • Stu Feldman; Pres.; 1614-O Union Valley Rd.; 07480; Passaic; P 27,000; M 100; (973) 264-9622; info@westmilford.com; www.westmilford.com

West New York • *West New York C/C* • Dom Rounido; Pres.; 425 60th St.; 07093; Hudson; P 49,700; M 200; (201) 295-5065; wnychamber@gmail.com; www.westnewyorknj.org

West Orange • *West Orange C/C* • Brittany S. Chiles; Exec. Dir.; P.O. Box 83; 07052; Essex; P 45,000; M 190; (973) 731-0360; Fax (973) 736-3156; mail@westorangechamber.com; www.westorangechamber.com

West Patterson • *see Clifton and Wayne*

West Windsor • *see Mercerville*

Westfield • *Greater Westfield Area C/C* • Gene Jannotti; Exec. Dir.; 173 Elm St., 3rd Flr.; 07090; Union; P 100,000; M 360; (908) 233-3021; Fax (908) 654-8183; info@gwaccnj.com; www.gwaccnj.com

Whippany • *see Florham Park*

Wildwood • *Greater Wildwood C/C* • Tracey DuFault; Exec. Dir.; 3306 Pacific Ave.; 08260; Cape May; P 12,000; M 600; (609) 729-4000; Fax (609) 729-4003; info@gwcoc.org; www.gwcoc.com

Willingboro • *see Mount Laurel*

Woodbridge • *Woodbridge Metro C/C* • Karen Barnes; Pres.; 91 Main St.; 07095; Middlesex; P 100,000; M 480; (732) 636-4040; Fax (732) 636-3492; woodbridgechamber@comcast.net; www.woodbridgechamber.com*

Woodbury • *Greater Woodbury C/C* • John P. Campbell; Exec. Dir.; P.O. Box 363; 08096; Gloucester; P 10,500; M 300; (856) 845-4056; Fax (856) 848-4445; info@greaterwoodburychamber.com; www.greaterwoodburychamber.com*

Wyckoff • *Wyckoff C/C* • Howard Felixbrod; Pres.; P.O. Box 2; 07481; Bergen; P 3,000; M 150; (201) 468-1999; wyckoffchamber@gmail.com; www.wyckoffchamber.com

Zarepath • *see Franklin Twp.*

New Mexico

Assn. of Commerce & Ind. of New Mexico • Jason Espinoza; Pres./CEO; 2201 Buena Vista Dr. S.E., Ste. 410; P.O. Box 9706; Albuquerque; 87119; Bernalillo; P 2,085,572; M 1,300; (505) 842-0644; Fax (505) 842-0734; info@nmaci.org; www.nmaci.org

Alamogordo • *Alamogordo C/C* • Michael Espiritu; Pres./CEO; 1301 N. White Sands Blvd.; 88310; Otero; P 35,000; M 516; (575) 437-6120; (800) 826-0294; Fax (575) 437-6334; dir@alamogordo.com; www.alamogordo.com*

Albuquerque Area

Albuquerque Hispano C/C • Alex O. Romero; Pres./CEO; 1309 4th St. S.W.; 87102; Bernalillo; P 600,000; M 1,500; (505) 842-9003; (888) 451-7824; Fax (505) 764-9664; alex@ahcnm.org; www.ahcnm.org*

American Indian C/C of New Mexico • Theodore M. Pedro; Exec. Dir.; 2401 12th St. NW, Ste. 5-S; 87104; Bernalillo; P 1,900,000; M 375; (505) 766-9545; Fax (505) 766-9499; americanch@qwestoffice.net; www.aiccnm.com

Greater Albuquerque C/C • Mrs. Terri L. Cole CCE; Pres./CEO; 115 Gold Ave. S.W., Ste. 201; 87102; Bernalillo; P 850,000; M 5,600; (505) 764-3700; Fax (505) 764-3714; info@abqchamber.com; www.abqchamber.com*

Algodones • *see Rio Rancho*

Angel Fire • *Angel Fire C/C* • Jo Mixon; Exec. Dir.; 3407 Mountain View Blvd., Centro Plaza; P.O. Box 547; 87710; Colfax; P 1,200; M 200; (575) 377-6353; (800) 446-8117; Fax (575) 377-3034; manager@angelfirechamber.org; www.angelfirechamber.org*

Anthony • *Anthony C/C* • Theresa Fisher; Pres.; P.O. Box 1086; 88021; Dona Ana; P 15,000; M 50; (575) 882-5677; (915) 471-5115; anthonycofc@aol.com; www.anthonychamberofcommerce.com

Arenas Valley • *see Silver City*

Artesia • *Artesia C/C* • Hayley Klein; Exec. Dir.; 107 N. First St.; 88210; Eddy; P 12,000; M 552; (575) 746-2744; Fax (575) 746-2745; chamber@artesiachamber.com; www.artesiachamber.com

Aztec • *Aztec C/C* • Theresa Bailey; Exec. Dir.; 110 N. Ash St.; 87410; San Juan; P 6,800; M 124; (505) 334-7646; Fax (505) 334-7648; info@aztecchamber.com; www.aztecchamber.com

Belen • *Greater Belen C/C* • Rhona Baca Espinoza; Exec. Dir.; 712 Dalies Ave.; 87002; Valencia; P 7,000; M 300; (505) 864-8091; Fax (505) 864-7461; belenchamber@belenchamber.org; www.belenchamber.org

Bernalillo • *see Rio Rancho*

Bloomfield • *Bloomfield C/C* • Amy Garcia; Tourism Specialist; 224 W. Broadway; 87413; San Juan; P 7,800; M 175; (505) 632-0880; Fax (505) 634-1431; askus@bloomfieldchamber.info; www.bloomfieldchamber.info*

Bosque Farms • *see Los Lunas*

Carlsbad • *Carlsbad C/C* • Robert P. Defer; CEO; 302 S. Canal St.; P.O. Box 910; 88220; Eddy; P 55,000; M 515; (575) 887-6516; Fax (575) 885-1455; director@carlsbadchamber.com; www.carlsbadchamber.com*

Carrizozo • *Carrizozo C/C* • Pres.; P.O. Box 567; 88301; Lincoln; P 1,050; M 70; (575) 648-2732; zozoccc@tularosa.net; www.carrizozochamber.org

Chama • *Chama Valley C/C* • Rose Martinez; Exec. Dir.; P.O. Box 306-RB; 87520; Rio Arriba; P 1,400; M 182; (575) 756-2306; (800) 477-0149; Fax (575) 756-2892; info@chamavalley.com; www.chamavalley.com

Cimarron • *Cimarron C/C* • Candee Rinde; Exec. Secy.; 104 N. Lincoln Ave.; P.O. Box 604; 87714; Colfax; P 900; M 64; (575) 376-2417; cimarronnm@gmail.com; www.cimarronnm.com

Clayton • *Clayton-Union County C/C* • Judy Steen; Exec./Tourism Dir.; 1103 S. 1st St.; P.O. Box 476; 88415; Union; P 3,500; M 103; (575) 374-9253; Fax (575) 374-9250; cuchamber@plateautel.net; www.claytonnewmexico.org

Cloudcroft • *Cloudcroft C/C* • Lisa King; Dir.; P.O. Box 1290; 88317; Otero; P 768; M 185; (575) 682-2733; (866) 874-4447; Fax (575) 682-6028; cloudcroft@cloudcroft.net; www.cloudcroft.net

Clovis • *Clovis/Curry County C/C* • Ernie Kos; Exec. Dir.; 105 E. Grand Ave.; 88101; Curry; P 47,663; M 550; (575) 763-3435; Fax (575) 763-7266; events@clovisnm.org; www.clovisnm.org*

Cuba • *Cuba Area C/C* • Dan Delgado; Dir.; P.O. Box 1000; 87013; Sandoval; P 8,000; M 75; (575) 289-0302; info@cubanewmexico.com; www.cubanewmexico.com

Deming • *Deming-Luna County C/C* • Mary M. Galbraith; Exec. Dir.; 103 E. Pine St.; P.O. Box 8; 88031; Luna; P 27,000; M 300; (575) 546-2674; (800) 848-4955; Fax (575) 546-9569; executivedirector@demingchamber.com; www.demingchamber.com

Eagle Nest • *Eagle Nest C/C* • Richard Ellis; Pres.; 284 E. Therma Dr.; P.O. Box 322; 87718; Colfax; P 350; M 60; (575) 377-2420; Fax (575) 377-2697; info@eaglenestchamber.org; www.eaglenestchamber.org

Edgewood • *Edgewood C/C* • Madeline Heitzman; Exec. Dir.; 95 Hwy. 344, Ste. 3; P.O. Box 457; 87015; Santa Fe; P 14,000; M 120; (505) 286-2577; (505) 850-2523; info@edgewoodchambernm.com; www.edgewoodchambernm.com

Elephant Butte • *Elephant Butte C/C* • Judith Anderson or Toni Lindstedt; Visitor Ambassadors; 402 Butte Blvd., Ste. A; P.O. Box 1355; 87935; Sierra; P 1,400; M 150; (575) 744-4708; (877) 744-4900; Fax (575) 744-0044; chamber@ebcocnm.com; www.ebcocnm.com

Espanola • *Espanola Valley C/C* • Eric Vasquez; Exec. Dir.; 1 Calle de las Espanolas, Ste. F & G; P.O. Box 190; 87532; Rio Arriba; P 50,000; M 280; (505) 753-2831; Fax (505) 753-1252; director@espanolanmchamber.com; www.espanolanmchamber.com

Farmington • *Farmington C/C* • Audra Winters; Pres./CEO; 100 W. Broadway; 87401; San Juan; P 46,500; M 750; (505) 325-0279; (888) 325-0279; Fax (505) 327-7556; chamber@gofarmington.com; www.gofarmington.com*

Fort Sumner • *Fort Sumner/DeBaca County C/C* • Cindy King; Exec. Dir.; 707 N. 4th St.; P.O. Box 28; 88119; DeBaca; P 2,500; M 80; (575) 355-7705; fortsumnerchamber@hotmail.com; www.fortsumnerchamber.com

Gallup • *Gallup-McKinley County C/C* • Bill Lee; CEO; 106 W. Historic Hwy. 66; 87301; McKinley; P 72,000; M 450; (505) 722-2228; (800) 380-4989; Fax (505) 863-2280; gretchen@thegallupchamber.com; www.thegallupchamber.com

Grants • *Grants/Cibola County C/C* • Star Gonzales; Exec. Dir.; 100 N. Iron Ave.; P.O. Box 297; 87020; Cibola; P 26,595; M 200; (505) 287-4802; discover@grants.org; www.grants.org*

Hatch • *Hatch Valley C/C* • Robert Spence; Pres.; 530 E. Hall St.; P.O. Box 568; 87937; Dona Ana; P 1,667; M 70; (575) 519-4723; hatchchamber@gmail.com; www.hatchchilefest.com

Hobbs • *Hobbs C/C* • Patricia (Patty) Collins; Exec. Dir.; 400 N. Marland Blvd.; 88240; Lea; P 47,000; M 500; (575) 397-3202; Fax (575) 397-1689; executive@hobbschamber.org; www.hobbschamber.org*

Jal • *Jal C/C* • Amelia Trevino; P.O. Box 1205; 88252; Lea; P 2,089; M 125; (575) 395-2620; Fax (575) 395-2620; jalchamber@leaco.net; www.jalnm.com

Las Cruces • *Las Cruces Hispanic C/C* • Curtis Rosemond; Pres./CEO; 277 E. Amador Ave., Ste. 305; P.O. Box 1964; 88001; Dona Ana; P 209,233; M 350; (575) 524-8900; Fax (575) 532-9255; office@LasCrucesHispanicChamber.com; www.LasCrucesHispanicChamber.com*

Las Cruces • *Greater Las Cruces C/C* • Debbi Moore; Pres./CEO; 505 S. Main St., Ste. 134; 88001; Dona Ana; P 200,000; M 1,000; (575) 524-1968; Fax (575) 527-5546; dmoore@lascruces.org; www.lascruces.org

Las Vegas • *Las Vegas-San Miguel C/C* • Lavinia Fenzi; Exec. Dir.; 500 Railroad; P.O. Box 128; 87701; San Miguel; P 27,000; M 100; (505) 425-8631; lvexec@qwestoffice.net; www.lasvegasnewmexico.com

Logan • *Logan/Ute Lake C/C* • Bobby Dugger; Pres.; 6009 540 Loop; P.O. Box 277; 88426; Quay; P 1,000; M 31; (575) 403-6255; duggerdo@plateautel.net; www.utelakeloganchamber.com

Lordsburg • *Lordsburg-Hidalgo County C/C* • Marsha Hill; Dir.; 206 Main St.; P.O. Box 699; 88045; Hidalgo; P 5,000; M 65; (575) 542-9864; (575) 542-3421; lordsburgcoc@aznex.net; www.lordsburghidalgocounty.net

Los Alamos • *Los Alamos C/C* • Nancy Partridge; Mgr.; 109 Central Park Sq.; 87544; Los Alamos; P 18,000; M 305; (505) 661-4816; Fax (505) 662-0099; chamber@losalamos.org; losalamoschamber.com

Los Lunas • *Los Lunas C/C* • Stephanie Flynn; Exec. Dir.; 3447 Lambros Loop; P.O. Box 13; 87031; Valencia; P 14,000; M 300; (505) 352-3596; Fax (505) 352-3589; vcchamber@loslunasnm.gov; www.loslunaschamber.com

Lovington • *Lovington C/C* • Raelynn Dunlap; Exec. Dir.; 201 S. Main; 88260; Lea; P 11,600; M 180; (575) 396-5311; Fax (575) 396-2823; lovingtonchamber@hotmail.com; www.lovingtonchamber.org*

Magdalena • *Magdalena C/C* • ZW Farnsworth; Pres.; 902 W. First St.; P.O. Box 281; 87825; Socorro; P 970; M 60; (866) 854-3217; (575) 854-3310; info@magdalena-nm.com; www.magdalena-nm.com

Melrose • *Melrose C/C* • James Townson; Pres.; P.O. Box 216; 88124; Curry; P 645; M 74; (575) 253-4530; jftownson@hotmail.com

Mountainair • *Mountainair C/C* • Kevin Turner; Pres.; P.O. Box 595; 87036; Torrance; P 1,000; M 57; (505) 847-3490; (505) 847-2321; mountainairchamber@gmail.com; www.discovermountainairnm.com

Placitas • *see Rio Rancho*

Portales • *Roosevelt County C/C* • Karl Terry; Exec. Dir.; 100 S. Ave. A; 88130; Roosevelt; P 18,500; M 300; (575) 356-8541; (800) 635-8036; Fax (575) 356-8542; chamber@portales.com; www.portales.com*

Raton • *Raton C/C* • Paul Jenkins; Pres.; 100 Clayton Rd.; 87740; Colfax; P 6,187; M 40; (575) 445-3689; ratonchamber@ratonnm.us; www.raton.info*

Red River • *Red River C/C* • Rebecca Sanchez; Dir. of Chamber Svcs.; P.O. Box 870; 87558; Taos; P 500; M 176; (575) 754-2366; (800) 348-6444; Fax (575) 754-3104; rebecca@redriverchamber.org; www.redrivernewmex.com

Rio Rancho • *Rio Rancho Reg. C/C* • Jerry Schalow; Pres./CEO; 4001 Southern Blvd. S.E., Ste. B; 87124; Sandoval; P 94,000; M 430; (505) 892-1533; Fax (505) 892-6157; info@rrrcc.org; www.rrrcc.org*

Roswell • *Roswell C/C* • Dorrie Faubus-McCarty; Exec. Dir.; 131 W. Second St.; 88201; Chaves; P 53,000; M 550; (575) 623-5695; (877) 849-7679; Fax (575) 624-6870; information@roswellnm.org; www.roswellnm.org

Ruidoso • *Ruidoso Valley C/C & Visitors Center* • Becky Brooks; Pres.; 720 Sudderth Dr.; 88345; Lincoln; P 10,000; M 500; (575) 257-7395; (877) 784-3676; Fax (575) 257-4693; info@ruidosonow.com; www.ruidosonow.com*

San Miguel • *see Las Vegas*

Sandia Pueblo • *see Rio Rancho*

Santa Ana Pueblo • *see Rio Rancho*

Santa Fe • *Santa Fe C/C* • Simon Brackley; Pres./CEO; 1644 St. Michael's Dr.; P.O. Box 1928; 87504; Santa Fe; P 148,700; M 950; (505) 988-3279; Fax (505) 984-2205; info@santafechamber.com; www.santafechamber.com*

Silver City • *Silver City Grant County C/C* • Scott C. Terry; Pres./CEO; 500 18th St., Rm. 214; P.O. Box 1028; 88062; Grant; P 29,000; M 291; (575) 538-3785; (800) 548-9378; Fax (575) 597-3790; info@silvercity.org; www.silvercity.org

Socorro • *Socorro County C/C* • Deb Caldwell; Exec. Dir.; 101 Plaza; P.O. Box 743; 87801; Socorro; P 17,600; M 270; (575) 835-0424; Fax (575) 835-9744; socorrochamber@gmail.com; www.socorro-nm.com

Taos • *Taos County C/C* • Susan Cady; Ofc. Mgr.; 1139 Pasco del Pueblo Sur; 87571; Taos; P 30,000; M 500; (575) 751-8800; member@taoschamber.com; www.taoschamber.com

Tatum • *Tatum C/C* • Marilyn J. Burns; Pres.; P.O. Box 814; 88267; Lea; P 748; M 30; (575) 398-5455; Fax (575) 398-5455; mburns@leaco.net; www.townoftatum.org

Tijeras • *East Mountain C/C* • Nancy Carpenter; Pres.; P.O. Box 2436; 87059; Bernalillo; P 1,060; M 100; (505) 281-1999; info@eastmountainchamber.com; www.eastmountainchamber.com*

Truth or Consequences • *Truth or Consequences C/C* • Ed (Hans) Townsend; Pres.; 207 S. Foch St.; 87901; Sierra; P 13,000; M 75; (575) 894-3536; info@torcchamber.com; www.torcchamber.com

Tucumcari • *Tucumcari/Quay County C/C* • Patsy Gresham; Exec. Dir.; 404 W. Rte. 66 Blvd.; P.O. Drawer E; 88401; Quay; P 9,300; M 164; (575) 461-1694; Fax (575) 461-3884; chamber@tucumcarinm.com; www.tucumcarinm.com

White's City • *see Carlsbad*

New York

No State Chamber

Adams • *South Jeff C/C* • Connie Elliott; 14 E. Church St.; P.O. Box 167; 13605; Jefferson; P 10,000; M 200; (315) 232-4215; info@southjeffchamber.org; www.southjeffchamber.org

Adirondack Region • *see Glens Falls*

Albany • *Capital Region Chamber - Albany Office* • Mark N. Eagan; CEO; Five Computer Dr. S.; 12205; Albany; P 850,000; M 2,500; (518) 431-1400; info@capitalregionchamber.com; www.capitalregionchamber.com*

Alden • *Alden C/C* • Jenny Urbanski; Exec. Secy.; 13500 Broadway; P.O. Box 149; 14004; Erie; P 12,000; M 130; (716) 937-6177; Fax (716) 937-4106; secretary@aldenny.org; www.aldenny.org

Alexandria Bay • *Alexandria Bay C/C* • Susan Boyer; Exec. Dir.; 7 Market St.; 13607; Jefferson; P 2,000; M 250; (315) 482-9531; (800) 541-2110; Fax (315) 482-5434; info@alexbay.org; www.visitalexbay.org

Amenia • *see Lakeville, CT*

Amherst • *Amherst C/C* • Colleen DiPirro; Pres./CEO; 400 Essjay Rd., Ste. 150; Williamsville; 14221; Erie; P 116,000; M 3,000; (716) 632-6905; Fax (716) 632-0548; jvecchio@amherst.org; www.amherst.org

Amityville • *Amityville C/C* • Dina Shingleton; Pres.; P.O. Box 855; 11701; Suffolk; P 11,000; M 170; (631) 598-0695; (917) 776-6680; chamber@amityvillechamber.org; www.amityvillechamber.org

Angola • *Evans-Brant C/C* • Robert Biondi; Pres.; 70 N. Main St.; 14006; Erie; P 20,500; M 50; (716) 549-3221; Fax (716) 549-3475; robertbiondi@verizon.net; www.ebccny.org

Arcade • *Arcade Area C/C* • Kelly Schubert; Chamber Svcs. Dir.; 684 W. Main St.; 14009; Wyoming; P 7,000; M 350; (585) 492-2114; Fax (585) 492-5103; kelly@arcadechamber.org; www.arcadechamber.org

Athens • *see Coxsackie*

Auburn • *Cayuga County C/C* • Tracy Verrier; Exec. Dir.; 2 State St.; 13021; Cayuga; P 81,400; M 600; (315) 252-7291; Fax (315) 255-3077; admin@cayugacountychamber.com; www.cayugacountychamber.com*

Avoca • *see Bath*

Avon • *Avon C/C* • Mike Carroll; Pres.; 74 Genesee St.; 14414; Livingston; P 6,600; M 85; (585) 226-8080; www.avonny.org

Baldwin • *Baldwin C/C* • Ralph Rose & Erik Mahler; Co-Pres.; P.O. Box 804; 11510; Nassau; P 31,000; M 150; (516) 223-8080; Fax (516) 223-0090; info@baldwinchamber.com; www.baldwinchamber.com

Baldwinsville • *Greater Baldwinsville C/C* • Sharon Reiser; Exec. Dir.; 27 Water St., 2nd Flr.; 13027; Onondaga; P 8,000; M 300; (315) 638-0550; Fax (315) 638-2078; baldwinsvillechamber@gmail.com; www.baldwinsvillechamber.com*

Ballston Lake • *see Clifton Park*

Ballston Spa • *see Clifton Park*

Barcelona • *see Dunkirk*

Batavia • *Genesee County C/C* • Tom Turnbull; Pres.; 8276 Park Rd.; 14020; Genesee; P 61,000; M 1,000; (585) 343-7440; Fax (585) 343-7487; chamber@geneseeny.com; www.geneseeny.com

Bath • *Central Steuben C/C* • Nancy Latour; Ofc. & Events Coord.; 47 Liberty St.; P.O. Box 488; 14810; Steuben; P 47,600; M 250; (607) 776-7122; steubenchamber@gmail.com; www.centralsteubenchamber.com

Bay Shore • *C/C of Greater Bay Shore* • Donna Periconi; Pres.; 77 E. Main St.; P.O. Box 5110; 11706; Suffolk; P 27,000; M 300; (631) 665-7003; Fax (631) 665-5204; bayshorecofcbid@optonline.net; www.bayshorecommerce.com

Beacon • *see Poughkeepsie*

Bedford Hills • *Bedford Hills C/C* • Dr. Gregory J. Riley; Pres.; P.O. Box 162; 10507; Westchester; P 50,000; M 100; (914) 381-3356; (914) 241-8627; purpose396@gmail.com; www.bedfordhills.org

Bellmore • *Chamber of Commerce of the Bellmores* • Debby Izzo; Pres.; 2700 Pettit Ave.; 11710; Nassau; P 33,000; M 350; (516) 679-1875; Fax (516) 409-0544; info@bellmorechamber.com; www.bellmorechamber.com

Bellmore • *Nassau Cncl. of Chambers of Commerce* • Julie Marchesella; Pres.; P.O. Box 365; 11710; Nassau; P 1,400,000; M 49; (516) 248-1112; Fax (516) 663-6715; www.ncchambers.org

Bellport • *Bellport C/C* • Dianne Romano; Pres.; P.O. Box 246; 11713; Suffolk; P 2,400; M 110; (631) 776-9268; Fax (631) 286-7500; email@bellportchamber.com; www.bellportchamber.com

Belmont • *Greater Allegany County C/C Inc.* • Gretchen Hanchett; Exec. Dir.; 6087 State Rte. 19N, Ste. 120; 14813; Allegany; P 49,000; M 150; (585) 268-5500; (800) 836-1869; Fax (585) 268-7473; ghanchett@alleganychamber.org; www.alleganychamber.org*

Bethlehem • *see Delmar*

Binghamton • *Greater Binghamton C/C* • Jennifer Conway; Pres./CEO; 49 Court St., 2nd Flr.; P.O. Box 995; 13902; Broome; P 200,536; M 800; (607) 772-8860; (800) 836-6740; Fax (607) 722-4513; chamber@greaterbinghamtonchamber.com; www.greaterbinghamtonchamber.com

Blue Mountain Lake • *see Indian Lake*

Bolton Landing • *Bolton C/C Inc.* • Elaine Chiovarou-Brown; Pres.; 4928 Lakeshore Dr.; P.O. Box 368; 12814; Warren; P 2,117; M 150; (518) 644-3831; Fax (518) 644-5951; mail@boltonchamber.com; www.boltonchamber.com

Boonville • *Boonville Area C/C* • Bill Flack; Pres.; 122 Main St.; P.O. Box 163; 13309; Oneida; P 4,400; M 180; (315) 942-5112; Fax (315) 942-6823; info@boonvillechamber.com; www.boonvillechamber.com

Bradford • *see Bath*

Brant • *see Angola*

Brewerton • *Fort Brewerton/Greater Oneida Lake C/C* • Dr. Thomas Carroll; Pres.; P.O. Box 655; 13029; Oneida, Onondaga & Oswego; P 15,000; M 125; (315) 668-3408; info@oneidalakechamber.com; www.oneidalakechamber.com

Brewster • *Brewster C/C* • Rose Z. Aglieco; Exec. Dir.; 16 Mount Ebo Rd. S., Ste. 12A; 10509; Putnam; P 19,000; M 200; (845) 279-2477; info@brewsterchamber.com; www.brewsterchamber.com

Brockport • *Greater Brockport C/C* • Marie Bell; Pres.; P.O. Box 119; 14420; Monroe; P 40,000; M 110; bportchamber@gmail.com; www.brockportchamber.org

Bronx • *Bronx C/C* • Michelle Dolgow Cristofaro; Pres./CEO; 1200 Waters Pl., Ste. 106; 10461; New York; P 1,500,000; M 600; (718) 828-3900; Fax (718) 409-3748; michelle@bronxchamber.org; www.bronxchamber.org*

Bronxville • *Bronxville C/C* • Peggy Conway; Exec. Dir.; 81 Pondfield Rd., Ste. 7; 10708; Westchester; P 6,500; M 250; (914) 337-6040; Fax (914) 337-6040; director@bronxvillechamber.com; www.bronxvillechamber.com

Brooklyn • *Brooklyn C/C* • Carlo Scissura; Pres./CEO; 335 Adams St., Ste. 2700; 11201; Kings; P 2,500,000; M 1,200; (718) 875-1000; Fax (718) 237-4274; info@brooklynchamber.com; www.ibrooklyn.com*

Broome County • *see Binghamton*

Buffalo • *Buffalo Niagara Partnership* • Dottie Gallagher-Cohen; Pres./CEO; 665 Main St., Ste. 200; 14203; Erie; P 1,292,000; M 2,500; (716) 852-7100; (800) 241-0474; Fax (716) 852-2761; dgc@thepartnership.org; www.thepartnership.org

Burnt Hills • *see Clifton Park*

Cambria • *see Sanborn*

Camden • *Camden Area C/C* • Diane Miller; Pres.; P.O. Box 134; 13316; Oneida; P 6,200; M 130; (315) 245-5000; contact@camdennychamber.com; www.camdennychamber.com

Camillus • *Greater Camillus C/C* • Kathy Kitt; Exec. Dir.; P.O. Box 415; 13031; Onondaga; P 25,000; M 250; (315) 247-5992; kathykitt@gmail.com; www.camilluschamber.com

Campbell • *see Bath*

Canajoharie • *see Gloversville*

Canandaigua • *Canandaigua Area C/C* • Alison Grems; Pres./CEO; 113 S. Main St.; 14424; Ontario; P 22,000; M 650; (585) 394-4400; Fax (585) 394-4546; chamber@canandaiguachamber.com; www.canandaiguachamber.com*

Canastota • *Canastota C/C* • Winifred Hood; Exec. Secy.; 222 S. Peterboro St.; P.O. Box 206; 13032; Madison; P 4,700; M 80; (315) 697-3677; www.canastota.org

Candor • *Candor C/C* • David Astorina; Dir.; P.O. Box 32; 13743; Tioga; P 1,000; M 65; candorguy@hotmail.com; www.candornychamber.org

Canton • *St. Lawrence County C/C* • Brooke Rouse; Exec. Dir.; 101 Main St., 1st Flr.; 13617; St. Lawrence; P 111,000; M 500; (315) 386-4000; (877) 228-7810; Fax (315) 379-0134; info@slcchamber.org; www.northcountryguide.com

Canton • *Canton C/C* • Sally Hill; Exec. Dir.; P.O. Box 369; 13617; St. Lawrence; P 11,600; M 200; (315) 386-8255; Fax (315) 386-8255; cantoncc@northnet.org; www.cantonnychamber.org

Cape Vincent • *Cape Vincent C/C* • Shelley F. Higgins; Exec. Dir.; 173 N. James St.; P.O. Box 482; 13618; Jefferson; P 1,200; M 125; (315) 654-2481; Fax (315) 654-4141; thecape@tds.net; www.capevincent.org

Carmel • *Carmel-Kent C/C* • Bill Nulk; P.O. Box 447; 10512; Putnam; P 45,000; M 150; (845) 278-3004; Fax (845) 225-8420; info@carmelkentchamber.org; www.carmelkentchamber.org

Carthage • *Carthage Area C/C* • Lori Borland; Exec. Dir.; 120 S. Mechanic St.; 13619; Jefferson; P 10,000; M 200; (315) 493-3590; Fax (315) 519-3144; carthagechamber@centralny.twcbc.com; www.carthageny.com

Catskill • *Heart of Catskill Assn. - Catskill C/C* • Linda Overbaugh; Exec. Dir.; 327 Main St.; P.O. Box 248; 12414; Greene; P 49,000; (518) 943-0989; (800) 603-7737; Fax (518) 943-0989; catskillchamber@mhcable.com; greatnortherncatskillschamber.com

Catskill • *Great Northern Catskills C/C* • Kathleen McQuaid Packard; Chair; 327 Main St.; P.O. Box 248; 12414; Greene; P 49,000; M 600; (518) 943-4222; Fax (518) 943-1700; office@greatnortherncatskillschamber.com; greatnortherncatskillschamber.com

Cayuga County • *see Auburn*

Cazenovia • *Greater Cazenovia Area C/C* • Anna Marie Neuland; Exec. Dir.; 59 Albany St.; 13035; Madison; P 6,500; M 350; (315) 655-9243;; Fax (315) 655-9244; info@cazenovia.com; www.cazenoviachamber.com

Center Moriches • *Chamber of Commerce of the Moriches* • Julie Pratt; Pres.; P.O. Box 686; 11934; Suffolk; P 15,000; M 140; (631) 874-3849; correspondingsec@morischeschamber.org; www.morischeschamber.org

Centereach • *Greater Middle Country C/C* • Jeff Freund; Pres.; P.O. Box 65; 11720; Suffolk; P 65,000; M 150; (631) 681-8708; suggestions@middlecountrychamber.com; www.middlecountrychamber.com

Chaumont • *see Three Mile Bay*

Chautauqua • *see Mayville*

Cheektowaga • *Cheektowaga C/C* • Debra Liegl; Pres./CEO; 2875 Union Rd., Ste. 7A; 14227; Erie; P 80,000; M 692; (716) 684-5838; Fax (716) 684-5571; chamber@cheektowaga.org; www.cheektowaga.org

Chemung County • *see Elmira*

Cherry Valley • *Greater Cherry Valley C/C* • Jackie Hull; Pres.; P.O. Box 37; 13320; Otsego; P 2,000; M 90; (607) 264-3100; Fax (607) 264-3447; aroseisarose17@hotmail.com; www.cherryvalleychamber.org

Cicero • *see Mattydale*

Cicero • *Plank Road C/C* • Angela Tucciarone; Exec. Dir.; 5885 E. Circle Dr., Ste. 225; 13039; Onondaga; P 14,500; M 125; (315) 458-4181; info@plankroadchamber.com; www.plankroadchamber.com

Clarence • *Clarence C/C* • Judith Sirianni; Pres.; 8899 Main St., Ste. 4; P.O. Box 177; 14031; Erie; P 28,500; M 600; (716) 631-3888; Fax (716) 631-3946; info@clarence.org; www.clarence.org*

Clarkson • *see Brockport*

Clayton • *Clayton Area C/C* • Tricia Bannister; Exec. Dir.; 517 Riverside Dr.; 13624; Jefferson; P 4,500; M 350; (315) 686-3771; (800) 252-9806; Fax (315) 686-5564; info@1000islands-clayton.com; www.1000islands-clayton.com

Clifton Park • *The Chamber of Southern Saratoga County* • Pete Bardunias; Pres./CEO; 58 Clifton Country Rd., Ste. 102; 12065; Saratoga; P 109,804; M 1,069; (518) 371-7748; Fax (518) 371-5025; info@southernsaratoga.org; www.southernsaratoga.org*

Clifton Springs • *Clifton Springs Area C/C* • Jeff Criblear; Pres.; 2 E. Main St.; P.O. Box 86; 14432; Ontario; P 5,000; M 70; (315) 462-8200; info@cliftonspringschamber.com; www.cliftonspringschamber.com

Clinton • *Clinton C/C* • Jackie Walters; Exec. Dir.; 21 W. Park Row; P.O. Box 142; 13323; Oneida; P 10,000; M 170; (315) 853-1735; Fax (315) 853-1735; info@clintonnychamber.org; www.clintonnychamber.org

Clyde • *Clyde C/C* • John Robert; P.O. Box 69; 14433; Wayne; P 2,300; M 65; (315) 923-7364; (315) 923-3971; www.clydeny.com

Cohoes • *see Albany*

Cold Spring • *Cold Spring Area C/C* • Nat Prentice; Pres.; P.O. Box 36; 10516; Putnam; P 6,000; M 180; (845) 265-3200; chamber@gmail.com; www.coldspringchamber.com*

Colonie • *see Albany*

Conklin • *see Binghamton*

Cooperstown • *Cooperstown C/C* • Matt Hazzard; Exec. Dir.; 31 Chestnut St.; 13326; Otsego; P 2,000; M 420; (607) 547-9983; Fax (607) 547-6006; hanna@cooperstownchamber.org; www.cooperstownchamber.org

Copiague • *Copiague C/C* • Sharon Fattoruso; Pres.; P.O. Box 8; 11726; Suffolk; P 25,000; M 110; (631) 226-2956; info@copiaguechamber.org; www.copiaguechamber.org

Corning • *Corning Area C/C* • Denise Ackley IOM; Pres.; 1 W. Market St., Ste. 202; 14830; Steuben; P 30,000; M 325; (607) 936-4686; Fax (607) 936-4685; info@corningny.com; www.corningny.com*

Cortland • *Cortland County C/C* • Bob Haight; Exec. Dir.; 37 Church St.; 13045; Cortland; P 49,000; M 440; (607) 756-2814; Fax (607) 756-4698; info@cortlandchamber.com; www.cortlandchamber.com

Coxsackie • *Coxsackie Area C/C* • Laurel Mann; Pres.; P.O. Box 251; 12051; Greene; P 8,000; M 130; (518) 731-7300; info@coxsackieregionalchamber.com; www.coxsackieregionalchamber.com

Crompond • *see Yorktown Heights*

Croton-on-Hudson • *see Peekskill*

Cutchogue • *see Southold*

Dansville • *Dansville Area C/C* • William Bacon; Pres.; 126 Main St.; P.O. Box 105; 14437; Livingston; P 6,000; M 400; (585) 335-6920; (800) 949-0174; Fax (585) 335-6296; dansvillechamber@frontier.com; www.dansvilleny.net

Delhi • *Delaware County C/C* • Ray Pucci; Pres.; 5 1/2 Main St.; 13753; Delaware; P 47,000; M 400; (607) 746-2281; Fax (607) 746-3571; info@delawarecounty.org; www.delawarecounty.org

Delmar • *Bethlehem C/C* • Jennifer Kilcoyne; Pres.; 318 Delaware Ave., Ste. 11; 12054; Albany; P 33,000; M 480; (518) 439-0512; Fax (518) 475-0910; info@bethlehemchamber.com; www.bethlehemchamber.com

Depew • *see Lancaster*

Deposit • *Deposit C/C* • Nick Barone; Pres.; P.O. Box 222; 13754; Delaware; P 6,200; M 65; (607) 467-4161; www.depositchamber.com

Dunkirk • *Chautauqua County C/C* • Todd Tranum; Pres./CEO; 10785 Bennett Rd.; 14048; Chautauqua; P 135,000; M 1,200; (716) 366-6200; Fax (716) 366-4276; cccc@chautauquachamber.org; www.chautauquachamber.org

East Amherst • *see Amherst*

East Aurora • *Greater East Aurora C/C* • Gary D. Grote; Exec. Dir.; 652 Main St.; 14052; Erie; P 13,500; M 600; (716) 652-8444; Fax (716) 652-8384; eanycc@verizon.net; www.eanycc.com

East Fishkill • *see Poughkeepsie*

East Hampton • *East Hampton C/C* • Steven Ringel; Exec. Dir.; 42 Gingerbread Ln.; 11937; Suffolk; P 21,000; M 315; (631) 324-0362; Fax (631) 329-1642; info@easthamptonchamber.com; www.easthamptonchamber.com

East Islip • *East Islip Comm. Chamber Inc.* • Joe Gabriel; Pres.; P.O. Box 225; 11730; Suffolk; P 14,000; M 50; eichamber.com

East Meadow • *see Garden City*

East Moriches • *see Center Moriches*

East Quogue • *see Southampton*

East Setauket • *Three Village C/C* • David Woods; Exec. Dir.; P.O. Box 6; 11733; Suffolk; P 40,000; M 250; (631) 689-8838; info@3VChamber.com; www.threevillagechamber.com

East Williston • *see Williston Park*

East Yaphank • *East Yaphank C/C* • Michael Giacomaro; Pres.; 524 Birch Hollow Dr.; 11967; Suffolk; P 5,000; M 146; (631) 345-0805; Fax (631) 924-8193; eyaphankchamber@aol.com; www.eyaphankchamber.net

Eastport • *Eastport C/C* • Andrea Milano; Pres.; 447 Montauk Hwy.; 11941; Suffolk; P 12,000; M 90; (631) 325-5911

Eden • *Eden C/C* • Sharon Baur; Admin.; 8584 S. Main St.; 14057; Erie; P 8,300; M 200; (716) 992-4799; bercomm@gmail.com; www.edenny.org

Ellenville • *Ellenville-Wawarsing C/C* • Dr. Mark Craft; Pres.; 124 Canal St.; P.O. Box 227; 12428; Ulster; P 15,000; M 160; (845) 647-4620; info@ewcoc.com; www.ewcoc.com

Ellicottville • *Ellicottville C/C* • Brian McFadden; Exec. Dir.; 9 W. Washington St.; P.O. Box 456; 14731; Cattaraugus; P 1,700; M 350; (716) 699-5046; Fax (716) 699-5636; info@ellicottvilleny.com; www.ellicottvilleny.com

Elma • *see Lancaster*

Elmira • *Chemung County C/C* • Kevin D. Keeley; Pres./CEO; 400 E. Church St.; 14901; Chemung; P 89,000; M 600; (607) 734-5137; Fax (607) 734-4490; info@chemungchamber.org; www.chemungchamber.org*

Evans • *see Angola*

Fair Haven • *Fair Haven Area C/C* • Dan Larson; Pres.; P.O. Box 13; 13064; Cayuga; P 6,000; M 45; (315) 947-6037; fairhaveninfo@fairhavenny.com; www.fairhavenny.com

Farmington • *Farmington C/C* • John Malvaso; Pres.; P.O. Box 25001; 14425; Ontario; P 11,000; M 45; (585) 398-2861; jam@fsisys.com; www.farmingtoncofc.com

Farmingville • *Farmingville Hills C/C Inc.* • Michael Wentz; Pres.; P.O. Box 30; 11738; Suffolk; P 16,000; M 80; (631) 317-1738; info@farmingvillechamber.com; www.farmingvillechamber.com

Farnham • *see Angola*

Fayetteville • *The Greater Manlius C/C* • Jennifer Baum; Ofc. Admin.; 425 E. Genesee St.; 13066; Onondaga; P 32,000; M 250; (315) 637-4760; Fax (315) 637-4762; greatermanlius@windstream.net; www.manliuschamber.com*

Fire Island Pines • *Greater Fire Island Pines C/C* • Kenneth Stein; Pres.; P.O. Box 695; Sayville; 11782; Suffolk; P 3,000; M 51; (631) 597-3058; info@pineschamber.com; www.pineschamber.com

Fishkill • *see Poughkeepsie*

Floral Park • *Floral Park C/C* • Michael Jakob; Pres.; P.O. Box 20093; 11002; Nassau; P 16,000; M 210; (516) 641-1200; info@floralparkchamber.org; www.floralparkchamber.org

Flushing • *see Queens*

Fonda • *see Gloversville*

Forest Hills • *Forest Hills C/C* • Leslie Brown; Pres./Exec. Dir.; P.O. Box 751123; 11375; Queens; P 71,000; M 150; (718) 268-6565; fhchamber@aol.com; www.foresthillschamber.org

Fort Edward • *Fort Edward C/C* • Adam DeVoe; Pres.; P.O. Box 267; 12828; Washington; P 4,000; M 80; (518) 747-3000; chamber@fortedwardchamber.org; www.fortedwardchamber.org

Fort Plain • *see Gloversville*

Franklin • *Greater Franklin C/C* • Marc Burgin; Pres.; P.O. Box 814; 13775; Delaware; P 2,500; M 72; (607) 829-8500; franklinnychamber@yahoo.com; franklinny.org

Fredonia • *see Dunkirk*

Freeport • *Freeport C/C* • Maureen Mercogliano; Ofc. Mgr.; 300 Woodcleft Ave.; 11520; Nassau; P 44,000; M 213; (516) 223-8840; Fax (516) 223-1211; freeportchamber@juno.com; www.freeportchamberofcommerce.com

Fulton • *see Oswego*

Fulton County • *see Gloversville*

Fultonville • *see Gloversville*

Garden City • *Garden City C/C* • Althea Robinson; Exec. Dir.; 230 Seventh St.; 11530; Nassau; P 23,000; M 370; (516) 746-7724; Fax (516) 746-7725; gcchamber@gardencitychamber.org; www.gardencitychamber.org

Genesee County • *see Batavia*

Geneseo • *Livingston County C/C* • Laura Lane; Pres./CEO; 4635 Millennium Dr.; 14454; Livingston; P 65,000; M 1,200; (585) 243-2222; Fax (585) 243-4824; jkeane@livingstoncountychamber.com; www.livingstoncountychamber.com

Geneva • *Geneva Area C/C* • Spike Herzig; Pres./CEO; One Franklin Sq.; P.O. Box 587; 14456; Ontario; P 15,000; M 400; (315) 789-1776; (877) 5-GENEVA; Fax (315) 789-3993; info@genevany.com; www.genevany.com*

Getzville • *see Amherst*

Glen Cove • *Glen Cove C/C* • Phyllis Gorham; Exec. Dir.; 264 Glen St.; 11542; Nassau; P 27,000; M 255; (516) 676-6666; Fax (516) 676-5490; info@glencovechamber.org; www.glencovechamber.org

Glens Falls • *Adirondack Reg. C/C* • Peter Aust IOM; Pres./CEO; 136 Glen St., Ste. 3; 12801; Warren; P 145,600; M 1,100; (518) 798-1761; Fax (518) 792-4147; paust@adirondackchamber.org; www.adirondackchamber.org*

Gloversville • *Fulton Montgomery Reg. C/C* • Mark Kilmer; Pres./CEO; 2 N. Main St.; 12078; Fulton, Montgomery; P 104,800; M 1,000; (518) 725-0641; Fax (518) 725-0643; info@fultonmontgomeryny.org; www.fultonmontgomeryny.org*

Goshen • *Goshen C/C* • Terry Smallin; Exec. Dir.; 223 Main St.; 10924; Orange; P 13,500; M 300; (845) 294-7741; Fax (845) 294-7746; info@goshennychamber.com; www.goshennychamber.com*

Gouverneur • *Gouverneur C/C* • Donna M. Lawrence; Exec. Dir.; 214 E. Main St.; Lawrence Manor Bldg.; 13642; St. Lawrence; P 4,000; M 115; (315) 287-0331; Fax (315) 287-3694; www.gouverneurchamber.net

Gowanda • *Gowanda Area C/C* • Jennine Sauriol; 49 W. Main St.; P.O. Box 45; 14070; Cattaraugus; P 3,000; M 150; (716) 532-2834; Fax (716) 532-2834; GowandaUSA@yahoo.com; www.gowandanychamber.org

Grand Island • *Grand Island C/C* • Eric Fiebelkorn; Pres.; 2257 Grand Island Blvd.; 14072; Erie; P 20,000; M 300; (716) 773-3651; Fax (716) 773-3316; info@gichamber.org; www.gichamber.org*

Granville • *Granville Area C/C* • Denise Davies; Secy.; 1 Main St.; P.O. Box 13; 12832; Washington; P 6,000; M 125; (518) 642-2815; jcpeterson@roadrunner.com; www.granvillechamber.com

Great Neck • *Great Neck C/C* • Hooshang Nematzadeh; Pres.; P.O. Box 220432; 11022; Nassau; P 10,000; M 250; (516) 487-2000; greatneckinfo@gmail.com; www.greatneckchamber.org

Greece • *Greece C/C* • Sarah E. Lentini; Pres./CEO; 2402 W. Ridge Rd.; 14626; Monroe; P 100,000; M 800; (585) 227-7272; Fax (585) 227-7275; sarah@greecechamber.org; www.greecechamber.org*

Greene • *Greater Greene C/C* • Grace Benkovitz; Exec. Dir.; P.O. Box 441; 13778; Chenango; P 6,000; M 200; (607) 656-8225; info@greenenys.com; www.greenenys.com

Greenport • *see Southold*

Greenwich • *Greater Greenwich C/C* • Kathy Nichols-Tomkins; Secy./Ofc. Mgr.; 6 Academy St.; 12834; Washington; P 10,000; M 245; (518) 692-7979; Fax (518) 692-7979; info@greenwichchamber.org; www.greenwichchamber.org

Greenwich Village • *see New York-Greenwich Village-Chelsea C/C*

Guilderland • *Guilderland C/C* • Kathy Burbank; Pres.; 2050 Western Ave., Ste. 109; 12084; Albany; P 35,000; M 550; (518) 456-6611; Fax (518) 456-6690; egauthier@guilderlandchamber.com; www.guilderlandchamber.com*

Hague • *Hague-on-Lake George C/C* • P.O. Box 615; 12836; Warren; P 700; (518) 543-6353; haguechamberofcommerce@yahoo.com; www.visithague.com

Halfmoon • *see Clifton Park*

Hamburg • *Hamburg C/C* • Cyndi Matla; Exec. Dir.; 6122 South Park Ave.; P.O. Box 848; 14075; Erie; P 57,000; M 700; (716) 649-7917; (877) 322-6890; Fax (716) 649-6362; marktng@hamburg-chamber.org; www.hamburg-chamber.org

Hammond • *Black Lake C/C* • P.O. Box 12; 13646; St. Lawrence; P 1,300; M 60; (315) 375-8640; info@blacklakeny.com; www.blacklakeny.com

Hammondsport • *The Greater Hammondsport Area C/C* • Kenneth Corey; Pres.; 47 Shethar St.; P.O. Box 539; 14840; Steuben; P 3,300; M 165; (607) 569-2989; Fax (607) 569-2989; info@hammondsport.org; www.hammondsport.org

Hampton Bays • *Hampton Bays C/C* • Dot Capuano; Pres.; 140 W. Main St.; 11946; Suffolk; P 13,092; M 150; (631) 728-2211; Fax (631) 728-0308; info@hamptonbayschamber.com; www.hamptonbayschamber.com

Hancock • *Hancock Area C/C* • Bill Gross; Pres.; P.O. Box 525; 13783; Delaware; P 3,200; M 45; hancockchamber@hancock.net; www.hancockareachamber.com

Hanover • *see Dunkirk*

Harlem • *see New York-Greater Harlem C/C*

Harrison • *Harrison C/C* • Anthony D'Arpino; Pres./CEO; 1 Heineman Pl.; 10528; Westchester; P 27,470; M 140; (914) 835-0125; (914) 670-3000; harrisoncc04@yahoo.com; www.theharrisoncofc.org

Hartland • *see Sanborn*

Haverstraw • *Greater Haverstraw C/C* • Maria Rodd; Exec. Dir.; 4 Broadway; P.O. Box 159; 10927; Rockland; P 11,100; M 150; (845) 947-5646; director@haverstrawchamber.org; www.haverstrawchamber.org

Hempstead • *Hempstead C/C* • Max Rodriguez; Pres.; 1776 Denton Green Park; P.O. Box 4264; 11550; Nassau; P 56,000; M 125; (516) 489-3400; president@hempsteadchamber.com; www.hempsteadchamber.com

Henderson Harbor • *Henderson Harbor C/C* • Aileen Martin; Exec. Dir.; P.O. Box 468; 13651; Jefferson; P 1,500; M 160; (315) 938-5568; (888) 938-5568; thechambertreasurer@gmail.com; www.hendersonharborny.com

Herkimer • *Herkimer County C/C* • John Scarano; Exec. Dir.; 420 E. German St.; 13350; Herkimer; P 64,000; M 350; (315) 866-7820; (877) 984-4636; Fax (315) 866-7833; info@herkimercountychamber.com; www.herkimercountychamber.com

Hicksville • *Hicksville C/C* • Lionel J. Chitty; Pres.; 10 W. Marie St.; 11801; Nassau; P 41,000; M 274; (516) 931-7170; Fax (516) 931-8546; info@hicksvillechamber.com; www.hicksvillechamber.com

Highland • *Southern Ulster County C/C* • Juliana Burger; Pres.; 3553 Rte. 9W; P.O. Box 320; 12528; Ulster; P 40,000; M 130; (845) 691-6070; Fax (845) 691-9194; info@southernulsterchamber.org; www.southernulsterchamber.org

Hinsdale • *see Mattydale*

Holbrook • *Holbrook C/C* • Rick Ammirati; Pres.; P.O. Box 565; 11741; Suffolk; P 29,000; M 250; (631) 471-2725; Fax (631) 343-4816; admin@holbrookchamber.com; www.holbrookchamber.com

Holtsville • *see Farmingville*

Honeoye Falls • *Honeoye Falls Mendon C/C* • Pam Scully; P.O. Box 526; 14472; Ontario; P 9,152; M 500; (585) 234-2755; admin@hfmchamber.org; www.hfmchamber.org

Hopewell Junction • *see Poughkeepsie*

Hornell • *Hornell Area C/C* • James W. Griffin CEcD; Pres.; 40 Main St.; 14843; Steuben; P 11,000; M 450; (607) 324-0310; Fax (607) 324-3776; griff@hornellny.com; www.hornellny.com

Howes Cave • *Schoharie County C/C* • Georgia Van Dyke; Exec. Dir.; 143 Caverns Rd.; 12092; Schoharie; P 33,000; M 275; (518) 296-8820; Fax (518) 296-8825; info@schohariechamber.com; www.schohariechamber.com

Hudson • *Columbia County C/C* • Jeffrey C. Hunt CCE; Pres./CEO; 1 N. Front St.; 12534; Columbia; P 60,000; M 750; (518) 828-4417; Fax (518) 822-9539; mail@columbiachamber-ny.com; www.columbiachamber-ny.com*

Hunter • *Town of Hunter C/C* • Michael B. McCrary; P.O. Box 177; 12442; Greene; P 2,700; M 124; (518) 263-4900; Fax (518) 589-0117; chamberinfo@hunterchamber.org; www.hunterchamber.org

Huntington • *Huntington Twp. C/C* • Ellen O'Brien; Exec. Dir.; 164 Main St.; 11743; Suffolk; P 197,000; M 600; (631) 423-6100; Fax (631) 351-8276; ellen@huntingtonchamber.com; www.huntingtonchamber.com

Hyde Park • *Hyde Park C/C* • John Coppola; Pres.; 4389 Albany Post Rd.; P.O. Box 17; 12538; Dutchess; P 22,000; M 200; (845) 229-8612; Fax (845) 229-8638; info@hydeparkchamber.org; www.hydeparkchamber.org

Indian Lake • *Indian Lake C/C* • Kristina Eldridge; Admin. Asst.; 6301 NYS Rte. 30; P.O. Box 724; 12842; Hamilton; P 1,500; M 90; (518) 648-5112; (800) 328-LAKE; Fax (518) 648-5489; indianlakechamber@frontiernet.net; www.indian-lake.com

Inlet • *Inlet Info. Ofc.* • Adele Burnett; Tourism Dir.; 160 Rte. 28; P.O. Box 266; 13360; Hamilton; P 485; M 160; (315) 357-5501; (866) GO-INLET; Fax (315) 357-3570; info@inletny.com; www.inletny.com

Islip • *Islip C/C* • Cheryl Von Hassel; Secy.; P.O. Box 112; 11751; Suffolk; P 33,000; M 200; (631) 581-2720; Fax (631) 581-2720; info@islipchamberofcommerce.org; www.islipchamberofcommerce.org

Ithaca • *Tompkins County C/C* • Jennifer Tavares; Pres./CEO; 904 E. Shore Dr.; 14850; Tompkins; P 105,000; M 675; (607) 273-7080; Fax (607) 272-7617; info@tompkinschamber.org; tompkinschamber.org*

Jamaica • *Jamaica C/C* • Robert M. Richards; Pres.; 157-11 Rockaway Blvd.; 11434; Queens; P 500,000; M 500; (718) 657-4800; Fax (718) 413-2325; jamaicachamber@aol.com; www.JamaicaChamberOfCommerce.com

MEMBERSHIP, EXPORT DOCUMENTATION, CERTIFICATE OF ORIGIN

Jamestown • *Chautauqua County C/C* • Todd Tranum; Pres./CEO; 512 Falconer St.; 14701; Chautauqua; P 135,000; M 1,200; (716) 484-1101; Fax (716) 487-0785; cccc@chautauquachamber.org; www.chautauquachamber.org

Jefferson Valley • *see Yorktown Heights*

Jeffersonville • *Jeffersonville Area C/C* • P.O. Box 463; 12748; Sullivan; P 400; M 60; (845) 482-5688; info@jeffersonvilleny.com; www.jeffersonvilleny.com

Kanona • *see Bath*

Katonah • *Katonah C/C* • Alan Eifert & Anne Hanley; Co-Pres.; P.O. Box 389; 10536; Westchester; P 10,500; M 135; (914) 232-2668; info@katonahchamber.org; www.katonahchamber.org

Kenmore • *Kenmore-Town of Tonawanda C/C* • Tracey Lukasik-Hochfield; Exec. Dir.; 3411 Delaware Ave., Ste. 206; 14217; Erie; P 82,414; M 400; (716) 874-1202; Fax (716) 874-3151; info@ken-ton.org; www.ken-ton.org*

Kings Park • *Kings Park C/C* • Charles Gardner; Pres.; P.O. Box 322; 11754; Suffolk; P 19,000; M 140; (631) 269-7678; info@kingsparkli.com; www.kingsparkli.com

Kingston • *Ulster County Reg. C/C* • Ward Todd; Pres.; 214 Fair St.; 12401; Ulster; P 180,200; M 1,300; (845) 338-5100; Fax (845) 338-0968; info@ulsterchamber.org; www.ulsterchamber.org*

Lackawanna • *Lackawanna Area C/C* • Michael Sobaszek; Exec. Dir.; 638 Ridge Rd.; 14218; Erie; P 18,121; M 350; (716) 823-8841; Fax (716) 823-8848; info@lackawannachamber.com; www.lackawannachamber.com

Lake George • *Lake George Reg. C/C & CVB* • Michael Consuelo; Exec. Dir.; 2176 State Rte. 9; P.O. Box 272; 12845; Warren; P 3,900; M 400; (518) 668-5755; (800) 705-0059; Fax (518) 668-4286; info@lakegeorgechamber.com; www.lakegeorgechamber.com

Lake Pleasant • *see Speculator*

Lakewood • *see Jamestown*

Lancaster • *Lancaster Area C/C* • John Chmarney; Pres.; 11 W. Main St., Ste. 100; P.O. Box 284; 14086; Erie; P 50,000; M 500; (716) 681-9755; Fax (716) 684-3385; john@wnychamber.com; www.wnychamber.com*

Latham • *Colonie C/C* • Tom Nolte; Exec. Dir.; 950 New Loudon Rd.; 12110; Albany; P 78,000; M 550; (518) 785-6995; Fax (518) 785-7173; info@coloniechamber.org; www.coloniechamber.org

Levittown • *Levittown C/C* • Dean Baer; Pres.; P.O. Box 207; 11756; Nassau; P 53,000; M 150; (516) 520-8000; Fax (516) 520-8000; info@levittownchamber.com; www.levittownchamber.com

Liberty • *see Mongaup Valley*

U.S. Chambers of Commerce

Liverpool • *Greater Liverpool C/C* • Lucretia Hudzinski; Exec. Dir.; 314 2nd St.; 13088; Onondaga; P 36,000; M 420; (315) 457-3895; Fax (315) 234-3226; chamber@liverpoolchamber.com; www.liverpoolchamber.com*

Lockport • *see Sanborn*

Long Beach • *Long Beach C/C* • Michael J. Kerr; Pres.; 350 National Blvd.; 11561; Nassau; P 35,000; M 300; (516) 432-6000; Fax (516) 432-0273; info@thelongbeachchamber.com; www.thelongbeachchamber.com

Long Island City • *see Queens*

Long Island City • *Sunnyside C/C* • Luke Adams; Dir.; c/o La Guardia Comm. College,30-20 Thomson Ave., Ste. B221; P.O. Box 4399; 11104; Queens; P 24,999; M 145; (718) 784-8439; luke@sunnysidechamber.org; www.sunnysidechamber.org

Lowville • *Lewis County C/C* • Anne Merrill; Exec. Dir.; 7576 S. State St.; 13367; Lewis; P 26,157; M 460; (315) 376-2213; (800) 724-0242; Fax (315) 376-0326; anne@lewiscountychamber.org; www.lewiscountychamber.org

Lyme • *see Three Mile Bay*

Lynbrook • *Lynbrook C/C* • Bill Gaylor; Pres.; 11 Atlantic Ave.; 11563; Nassau; P 19,900; M 210; (516) 599-3436; info@lynbrookusa.com; www.lynbrookusa.com

Lyons • *Lyons C/C* • P.O. Box 39; 14489; Wayne; P 5,000; M 40; (315) 946-6691; www.lyonsny.com

Mahopac • *Greater Mahopac-Carmel C/C* • Terry Fokine; Ofc. Admin.; 953 S. Lake Blvd.; 10541; Putnam; P 31,886; M 460; (845) 628-5553; info@mahopaccarmelchamber.com; www.mahopaccarmelchamber.com

Malone • *Malone C/C* • Susan LeVitre; Exec. Dir.; 497 E. Main St.; 12953; Franklin; P 10,000; M 169; (518) 483-3760; director@malonechamberofcommerce.com; www.malonechamberofcommerce.com

Malta • *see Clifton Park*

Mamaroneck • *Mamaroneck C/C* • Jane Elkindeney; 430 Center Ave.; 10543; Westchester; P 19,100; M 120; (914) 698-4400; www.mamaroneckchamberofcommerce.org

Manhattan • *see New York-Manhattan C/C*

Manlius • *see Fayetteville*

Manorville • *Manorville C/C* • Karen Lee Dunne; Pres.; P.O. Box 232; 11949; Suffolk; P 13,745; M 75; info@manorvillechamber.org; www.manorvillechamber.org

Marcy • *Marcy C/C* • Mason Somerville; Treas.; P.O. Box 429; 13403; Oneida; P 9,000; M 120; (315) 534-2351; marcycofc@gmail.com; www.marcychamber.com

Margaretville • *Central Catskills C/C* • Carol O'Beirne; Exec. Dir.; 806 Main St.; P.O. Box 605; 12455; Delaware & Ulster; P 4,630; M 160; (845) 586-3300; Fax (845) 586-3161; chamber.admin@centralcatskills.com; www.centralcatskills.com

Massapequa • *C/C of the Massapequas Inc.* • Susan Martin; Pres.; 674 Broadway; 11758; Nassau; P 70,000; M 300; (516) 541-1443; Fax (516) 541-8625; masscoc@aol.com; www.massapequachamber.org

Massena • *Greater Massena C/C* • Michael Gleason; Exec. Dir.; 16 Church St.; 13662; St. Lawrence; P 11,000; M 300; (315) 769-3525; Fax (315) 769-5295; chamber@massenachamber.com; www.massenachamber.com*

Mastic • *Mastics-Shirley C/C* • Mark Smothergill; Pres.; P.O. Box 4; 11950; Suffolk; P 42,900; M 145; (631) 399-2228; president@masticshirleychamber.com; www.masticshirleychamber.com

Mattituck • *Mattituck C/C* • Donielle Cardinale; Pres.; P.O. Box 1056; 11952; Suffolk; P 4,900; M 170; (631) 734-8301; (631) 298-5757; info@mattituckchamber.org; www.mattituckchamber.org

Mattydale • *Greater North Syracuse C/C* • Terri Reilly; Treas.; 2621 Brewerton Rd.; 13211; Onondaga; P 14,500; M 125; (315) 458-4181; terrir@gnscc.org; www.gnscc.org

Mayville • *Mayville/Chautauqua Area C/C* • Deborah Marsala; Coord.; P.O. Box 22; 14757; Chautauqua; P 4,666; M 80; (716) 753-3113; Fax (716) 753-3113; info@mayvillechautauquachamber.org; www.mayvillechautauquachamber.org

Mechanicville • *Mechanicville-Stillwater Area C/C* • Barbara Corsale; Pres.; 312 N. 3rd Ave.; 12118; Saratoga; P 5,500; M 180; (518) 664-7791; Fax (518) 664-0826; mechanicvillestillwaterchamber@albany.twcbc.com; www.mechanicvilleareachamber.com

Medford • *Medford C/C* • Michael Gorton Jr.; Pres.; P.O. Box 926; 11763; Suffolk; P 24,700; M 65; (631) 475-3374; medfordchamberofcommerce@gmail.com; www.medfordchamberny.org

Medina • *Orleans County C/C* • Kathy Blackburn; Exec. Dir.; P.O. Box 501; 14103; Orleans; P 42,000; M 370; (585) 301-8464; Fax (585) 589-7326; sroskowski@orleanschamber.com; www.orleanschamber.com*

Melville • *Long Island Assn.* • Kevin S. Law; Pres./CEO; 300 Broadhollow Rd., Ste. 110W; 11747; Suffolk; P 7,500,000; (631) 493-3000; Fax (631) 499-2194; info@longislandassociation.org; www.longislandassociation.org

Mexico • *Greater Mexico C/C* • Adam Judware; Pres.; P.O. Box 158; 13114; Oswego; P 5,500; M 60; (315) 963-1042; president@mexico-cofc.org; www.mexicony.net

Miller Place • *see Mount Sinai*

Millerton • *see Lakeville, CT*

Mineola • *Mineola C/C* • Bill Greene; Pres.; P.O. Box 62; 11501; Nassau; P 18,900; M 225; (516) 746-5500; (516) 746-3944; www.mineolachamber.com

Minoa • *see Fayetteville*

Mohegan Lake • *see Yorktown Heights*

Montauk • *Montauk C/C* • Laraine Creegan; Exec. Dir.; 742 Montauk Hwy.; 11954; Suffolk; P 5,000; M 350; (631) 668-2428; Fax (631) 668-9363; info@montaukchamber.com; www.montaukchamber.com

Montgomery • *Orange County C/C* • Lynn Allen Cione; Pres.; 30 Scott's Corners Dr.; 12549; Orange; P 372,813; M 1,400; (845) 457-9700; Fax (845) 457-8799; info@orangeny.com; www.orangeny.com*

Montgomery • *Town of Montgomery C/C* • Riki Lent; V.P.; P.O. Box 662; 12549; Orange; P 20,000; M 150; (845) 213-4066; (845) 926-2727; info@townofmontgomerychamber.com; www.townofmontgomerychamber.net

Monticello • *Sullivan County C/C* • Cathy Paty; Pres./CEO; 196 Bridgville Rd., Ste. 7; P.O. Box 405; 12762; Sullivan; P 80,000; M 500; (845) 791-4200; Fax (845) 791-4220; chamber@catskills.com; www.catskills.com

Morehouse • *see Speculator*

Moriches • *see Center Moriches*

Mount Kisco • *Mount Kisco C/C* • Kathleen Mooney; Exec. Dir.; 3 N. Moger Ave.; 10549; Westchester; P 10,000; M 200; (914) 666-7525; Fax (914) 666-7663; director@mtkiscochamber.com; www.mtkiscochamber.com*

Mount Sinai • *North Brookhaven C/C* • Joel DeGregorio; Pres.; 5507-10 Nesconset Hwy., Ste. 410; 11766; Suffolk; P 13,000; M 200; (631) 821-1313; Fax (631) 331-0027; membership@northbrookhavenchamber.org; www.northbrookhavenchamber.org

Mount Vernon • *African American C/C* • Robin Douglas; Pres./CEO; P.O. Box 3730; 10553; Rockland & Westchester; M 250; (914) 699-9050; Fax (914) 699-6279; robinlisadouglas@cs.com; www.aaccnys.org

Nanuet • *Greater Nanuet C/C* • Risa Hoag; Pres.; 228 E. Rte. 59; Box 333; 10954; Rockland; P 17,882; M 150; (845) 436-3043; info@nanuetchamber.com; www.nanuetchamber.com

Narrowsburg • *Narrowsburg C/C* • Jane Luchsinger; P.O. Box 300; 12764; Sullivan; P 1,600; M 45; (845) 252-7234; janeluchsinger@frontiernet.net; www.narrowsburgchamber.org

New Baltimore • *see Coxsackie*

New City • *New City C/C* • Steven Weissblatt; Pres.; 65 N. Main St., 2nd Flr.; 10956; Rockland; P 35,000; M 120; Fax (845) 638-4636; info@newcitychamber.com; www.newcitychamber.com

New Hartford • *New Hartford C/C* • Mark Turnbull; Pres.; 48 Genesee St.; P.O. Box 372; 13413; Oneida; P 23,000; M 150; (315) 735-1974; Fax (315) 266-1231; info@newhartfordchamber.com; www.newhartfordchamber.com

New Hyde Park • *Greater New Hyde Park C/C* • Stewart Small; Pres.; P.O. Box 247; 11040; Nassau; P 39,000; M 225; (516) 647-5496; (888) 400-0311; info@nhpchamber.com; www.nhpchamber.com

New Paltz • *New Paltz Reg. C/C* • Peter Ingellis; Exec. Dir.; 257 Main St.; 12561; Ulster; P 12,830; M 600; (845) 255-0243; Fax (845) 255-5189; info@newpaltzchamber.org; www.newpaltzchamber.org*

New Rochelle • *New Rochelle C/C* • Bob Marrone; Exec. Dir.; 459 Main St., Ste. 204; P.O. Box 140; 10802; Westchester; P 69,500; M 250; (914) 632-5700; Fax (914) 632-0708; info@newrochamber.org; newrochellechamber.org

New Suffolk • *see Southold*

New York City Area

Greater Harlem C/C • Lloyd Williams; Pres./CEO; 200A W. 136th St.; 10030; New York; P 500,000; M 1,900; (212) 862-7200; Fax (212) 862-8745; ecausey@harlemdiscover.com; www.harlemdiscover.com

Greater New York C/C • Mark Jaffe; Pres./CEO; 20 W. 44th St., 4th Flr.; 10036; Manhattan; P 15,000,000; M 2,800; (212) CHAMBER; info@chamber.nyc; www.chamber.nyc*

Greenwich Village-Chelsea C/C • Maria Diaz; Exec. Dir.; 40 W. 27th St., 5th Flr.; 10001; New York; P 96,000; M 200; (646) 470-1773; maria@villagechelsea.com; www.villagechelsea.com

Manhattan C/C • Nancy Ploeger; Pres.; 1375 Broadway, 3rd Flr.; 10018; New York; P 1,600,000; M 1,500; (212) 479-7772; Fax (212) 473-8074; info@manhattancc.org; www.manhattancc.org*

West Manhattan C/C • Andrew Albert; Exec. Dir.; P.O. Box 1028; Planetarium Station; 10024; New York; P 250,000; M 400; (212) 787-1112; Fax (212) 787-1115; mail@westmanhattanchamber.org; www.westmanhattanchamber.org

Newark • *Greater Newark C/C* • John Tickner; Pres.; 199 Van Buren St.; 14513; Wayne; P 15,000; M 225; (315) 331-2705; Fax (315) 331-2705; newarkchamber@rochester.rr.com; www.newarknychamber.org

Newburgh • *see Montgomery*

Newfane • *see Sanborn*

Niagara Falls • *see Sanborn*

North Creek • *Gore Mountain Reg./North Creek C/C* • Dave Bulmer; P.O. Box 84; 12853; Warren; P 2,100; M 145; (518) 251-2612; Fax (518) 251-5317; info@gorechamber.com; www.gorechamber.com

North Tonawanda • *C/C of the Tonawandas* • Angela R. Johnson-Renda; Exec. Dir.; 254 Sweeney St.; 14120; Niagara; P 49,398; M 600; (716) 692-5120; Fax (716) 692-1867; Director@the-tonawandas.com; www.the-tonawandas.com

Northport • *Northport C/C* • Flemming Hansen; Pres.; P.O. Box 33; 11768; Suffolk; P 8,500; M 180; (631) 754-3905; Fax (631) 754-0670; nptchamberofcommerce@live.com; www.northportny.com

Norwich • *Commerce Chenango* • Steve Craig; Pres./CEO; 15 S. Broad St.; 13815; Chenango; P 49,500; M 300; (607) 334-1400; (877) CHENANGO; Fax (607) 336-6963; info@chenangony.org; www.chenangony.org

Nyack • *C/C of the Nyacks* • Scott Baird; Pres.; P.O. Box 677; 10960; Rockland; P 7,500; M 195; (845) 353-2221; Fax (845) 353-4204; carlo@nyackchamber.org; www.nyackchamber.org

Oceanside • *Oceanside C/C* • Gail Carlin; Pres.; P.O. Box 1; 11572; Nassau; P 33,000; M 175; (516) 763-9177; (516) 620-8006; info@oceansidechamber.org; www.oceansidechamber.org

Ogdensburg • *Greater Ogdensburg C/C* • Laura Pearson; Exec. Dir.; 1 Bridge Plz.; 13669; St. Lawrence; P 12,364; M 280; (315) 393-3620; Fax (315) 393-1380; chamber@gisco.net; www.ogdensburgny.com

Old Field • *see East Setauket*

Olean • *Greater Olean Area C/C* • Meme K. Yanetsko; COO; 301 N. Union St.; 14760; Cattaraugus; P 35,000; M 589; (716) 372-4433; Fax (716) 372-7912; info@oleanny.com; www.oleanny.com*

Oneida • *Greater Oneida C/C* • Royale Scuderi; Dir.; 136 Lenox Ave.; 13421; Madison; P 10,500; M 150; (315) 363-4300; Fax (315) 361-4558; office@oneidachamberny.org; oneidachamberny.org

Oneonta • *The Otsego County Chamber* • Rob Robinson; Pres./CEO; 189 Main St., Ste. 201; 13820; Otsego; P 62,200; M 550; (607) 432-4500; Fax (607) 432-4506; tocc@otsegocountychamber.com; www.otsegocountychamber.com

Ontario • *Ontario C/C •* Town of Ontario; P.O. Box 100; 14519; Wayne; P 10,200; M 120; (315) 524-5886; (585) 750-2277; Fax (315) 524-9709; jeswitz@rochester.rr.com; www.ontarionychamber.org

Orange County • *see Montgomery*

Orchard Park • *Orchard Park C/C •* Nancy L. Conley; Exec. Dir.; 4211 N. Buffalo St., Ste. 14; 14127; Erie; P 30,000; M 600; (716) 662-3366; Fax (716) 662-5946; opcc@orchardparkchamber.org; www.orchardparkchamber.org

Ossining • *Greater Ossining C/C •* Gayle Marchica; Pres.; 2 Church St.; 10562; Westchester; P 35,000; M 150; (914) 941-0009; Fax (914) 941-0812; info@ossiningchamber.org; www.ossiningchamber.org

Oswego • *Greater Oswego-Fulton C/C •* Jackie Zaborowski; Coord.; 44 E. Bridge St.; 13126; Oswego; P 30,000; M 510; (315) 343-7681; Fax (315) 342-0831; director@oswegofultonchamber.com; www.oswegofultonchamber.com*

Owego • *Tioga County C/C •* Gwen Kania; Pres./CEO; 80 North Ave.; 13827; Tioga; P 50,000; M 300; (607) 687-2020; Fax (607) 687-9028; info@tiogachamber.com; www.tiogachamber.com

Oxford • *Promote Oxford Now •* David Emerson; P.O. Box 11; 13830; Chenango; P 3,900; M 90; (607) 843-8722; www.oxfordny.com

Oyster Bay • *Oyster Bay/East Norwich C/C •* Alex Gallego; Pres.; P.O. Box 21; 11771; Nassau; P 11,906; M 200; (516) 922-6464; obenchamber@gmail.com; www.visitoysterbay.com

Painted Post • *see Corning*

Palatine Bridge • *see Gloversville*

Patchogue • *Greater Patchogue C/C •* David Kennedy; Exec. Dir.; 15 N. Ocean Ave.; 11772; Suffolk; P 20,000; M 450; (631) 207-1000; Fax (631) 475-1599; info@patchogue.com; www.patchogue.com

Patterson • *Patterson C/C •* Vince Murphy; Interim Pres.; P.O. Box 316; 12563; Putnam; P 7,500; M 75; (845) 363-6304; info@pcofc.org; www.pcofc.org

Pawling • *Pawling C/C •* Peter Cris; Pres.; Charles Colman Blvd.; P.O. Box 19; 12564; Dutchess; P 8,000; M 200; (845) 855-0500; petercris@aol.com; www.pawlingchamber.org

Pearl River • *Pearl River C/C •* Annie Paratore; Secy.; P.O. Box 829; 10965; Rockland; P 16,000; M 100; info@pearlriverny.org; www.pearlriverny.org

Peekskill • *Hudson Valley Gateway C/C •* Debbie Milone; Exec. Dir.; One S. Division St.; 10566; Westchester; P 57,000; M 425; (914) 737-3600; Fax (914) 737-0541; info@hvgatewaychamber.com; www.hvgatewaychamber.com*

Pelham • *Pelham C/C •* Shiv Dawadi; Pres.; P.O. Box 8354; 10803; Westchester; P 13,000; M 110; pelhamccny@gmail.com; www.pelhamchamberofcommerce.com

Pendleton • *see Sanborn*

Penn Yan • *Yates County C/C •* Michael Linehan; Pres./CEO; 2375 Route 14A; 14527; Yates; P 25,000; M 425; (315) 536-3111; (800) 868-9283; Fax (315) 536-3791; info@yatesny.com; www.yatesny.com

Perry • *Perry Area C/C •* Joseph Dally; Pres.; P.O. Box 35; 14530; Wyoming; P 3,620; M 85; (585) 237-5040; (585) 237-6310; www.villageofperry.com

Phelps • *Phelps C/C •* Bette Collier; Pres.; P.O. Box 1; 14532; Ontario; P 6,000; M 120; (315) 548-5481; pcoc@wmsmicro.com; www.phelpsny.com

Phoenix • *see Oswego*

Piseco • *see Speculator*

Plainview • *Plainview-Old Bethpage C/C •* Elan Wurtzel; Pres.; P.O. Box 577; 11803; Nassau; P 37,000; M 130; (516) 937-5646; chamber@pobcoc.com; www.pobcoc.com

Plattsburgh • *North Country C/C •* Garry Douglas; Pres./CEO; 7061 Rte. 9; P.O. Box 310; 12901; Clinton, Franklin, Essex, Hamilton, Warren; P 200,000; M 4,200; (518) 563-1000; Fax (518) 563-1028; info@northcountrychamber.com; www.northcountrychamber.com*

Pleasantville • *Pleasantville C/C •* Bill Flooks; Pres.; P.O. Box 94; 10570; Westchester; P 7,200; M 173; (914) 769-0001; Fax (914) 769-0037; info@pleasantville.com; www.pleasantville.com

Poquott • *see East Setauket*

Port Chester • *Port Chester-Rye Brook-Rye Town C/C •* Ken Manning; Pres.; 222 Grace Church St.; 10573; Westchester; P 50,000; M 300; (914) 939-1900; Fax (914) 437-7779; pcrbchamber@gmail.com; www.pcrbchamber.com

Port Jefferson • *Greater Port Jefferson C/C •* Suzanne Velazquez; Pres.; 118 W. Broadway; 11777; Suffolk; P 10,000; M 210; (631) 473-1414; info@portjeffchamber.com; www.portjeffchamber.com

Port Jervis • *Tri-State C/C •* Charlene Trotter; Exec. Dir.; P.O. Box 121; 12771; Orange; P 25,000; M 250; (845) 856-6694; Fax (845) 856-6695; info@tristatechamber.org; www.tristatechamber.org*

Port Washington • *Port Washington C/C •* Roberta Polay; Exec. Dir.; P.O. Box 121; 11050; Nassau; P 32,000; M 300; (516) 883-6566; Fax (516) 883-6591; office@pwcoc.org; www.pwguide.com

Potsdam • *Potsdam C/C •* Marylee Ballou; Exec. Dir.; 24 Market St.; P.O. Box 717; 13676; St. Lawrence; P 17,000; M 250; (315) 274-9000; Fax (315) 274-9222; potsdam@slic.com; www.potsdamchamber.com

Poughkeepsie • *Dutchess County Reg C/C •* Charles North; Pres./CEO; 1 Civic Center Plaza, Ste. 400; 12601; Dutchess; P 294,000; M 2,400; (845) 454-1700; Fax (845) 454-1702; office@dcrcoc.org; www.dcrcoc.org*

Prattsburg • *see Bath*

Pulaski • *Pulaski/Eastern Shore C/C •* Brian Leary; Pres.; 3044 State Rte. 13; P.O. Box 34; 13142; Oswego; P 3,000; M 110; (315) 298-2213; info@pulaskinychamber.com; www.pulaskinychamber.com*

Queens • *C/C of the Borough of Queens •* Jack Friedman; Exec. Dir.; 75-20 Astoria Blvd., Ste. 140; Jackson Heights; 11370; Queens; P 2,200,000; M 1,700; (718) 898-8500; Fax (718) 898-8599; info@queenschamber.org; www.queenschamber.org*

Red Hook • *Red Hook Area C/C •* Ed Pruitt; Pres.; P.O. Box 254; 12571; Dutchess; P 10,000; M 220; (845) 758-0824; info@redhookchamber.org; www.redhookchamber.org

Rensselaer County • *see Troy*

Rhinebeck • *Rhinebeck Area C/C •* Colleen Cruikshank; Exec. Dir.; 23F E. Market St.; P.O. Box 42; 12572; Dutchess; P 10,000; M 400; (845) 876-5904; Fax (845) 876-8624; info@rhinebeckchamber.com; www.rhinebeckchamber.com*

Richfield Springs • *Richfield Springs Area C/C* • Christine Corrigan; Pres.; P.O. Box 909; 13439; Otsego; P 1,300; M 80; (315) 858-0964; richfieldspringschamber@gmail.com; www.richfieldspringschamber.org

Riverhead • *Riverhead C/C* • Mary Hughes; Exec. Dir.; 59 E. Main St.; 11901; Suffolk; P 27,680; M 350; (631) 727-7600; Fax (631) 727-7946; info@riverheadchamber.com; www.riverheadchamber.com

Rochester • *Rochester Business Alliance* • Sandra Parker; CEO; 150 State St.; 14614; Monroe; P 1,062,420; M 2,400; (585) 244-1800; Fax (585) 263-3679; rballiance@rballiance.com; www.rochesterbusinessalliance.com

Rockville Centre • *Rockville Centre C/C* • Margarita Fox; Pres.; P.O. Box 226; 11571; Nassau; P 24,568; M 175; (516) 766-0666; Fax (516) 706-1550; mailbox@rvcchamber.org; www.rvcchamber.com

Rocky Point • *see Mount Sinai*

Rome • *Rome Area C/C* • William K. Guglielmo; Pres.; 139 W. Dominick St.; 13440; Oneida; P 32,600; M 550; (315) 337-1700; Fax (315) 337-1715; info@romechamber.com; www.romechamber.com*

Ronkonkoma • *Ronkonkoma C/C* • Denise Schwarz; Pres.; P.O. Box 2546; 11779; Suffolk; P 20,000; M 195; (631) 963-2796; president@ronkonkomachamber.com; www.ronkonkomachamber.com

Roscoe • *Roscoe-Rockland C/C* • Elaine Fettig; Pres.; P.O. Box 443; 12776; Sullivan; P 600; M 83; info@roscoeny.com; www.roscoeny.com

Round Lake • *see Clifton Park*

Royalton • *see Sanborn*

Rye • *Rye C/C* • Lisa Summa-Guarino; Pres.; P.O. Box 72; 10580; Westchester; P 15,000; M 173; (914) 925-6701; lisa.summa-guarino@ryechamberofcommerce.com; www.ryechamberofcommerce.com

Rye Brook • *see Port Chester*

Sabael • *see Indian Lake*

Sackets Harbor • *Sackets Harbor C/C* • Cheryl Payne; Pres.; P.O. Box 17; 13685; Jefferson; P 1,500; M 75; (315) 646-1700; info@visitsackets.com; www.sacketsharborchamberofcommerce.com

Sag Harbor • *Sag Harbor C/C* • Lisa Field; Pres.; The Windmill; P.O. Box 2810; 11963; Suffolk; P 5,000; M 200; (631) 725-0011; Fax (631) 919-1662; info@sagharborchamber.com; www.sagharborchamber.com

Saint James • *Saint James C/C* • Lawrence Glazer; Pres.; P.O. Box 286; 11780; Suffolk; P 15,000; M 125; (631) 584-8510; Fax (631) 862-9839; info@stjameschamber.org; www.stjameschamber.org

Salamanca • *Salamanca Area C/C* • Jenny Ingrao; 26 Main St.; 14779; Cattaraugus; P 6,000; M 125; (716) 945-2034; Fax (716) 945-9143; info@salamancachamber.org; www.salamancachamber.org

Sanborn • *Niagara USA Chamber* • Deanna Alterio Brennen; Pres./CEO; 6311 Inducon Corporate Dr.; 14132; Niagara; P 220,000; M 1,000; (716) 285-9141; Fax (716) 285-0941; dalteriobrennen@niagarachamber.org; www.niagarachamber.org

Saranac Lake • *Saranac Lake Area C/C* • Katy Van Anden; Exec. Dir.; 193 River St.; 12983; Essex & Franklin; P 5,000; M 490; (518) 891-1990; (800) 347-1992; Fax (518) 891-7042; info@saranaclake.com; www.saranaclake.com

Saratoga Springs • *Saratoga County C/C* • Todd L. Shimkus CCE; Pres.; 28 Clinton St.; 12866; Saratoga; P 226,300; M 2,600; (518) 584-3255; Fax (518) 587-0318; info@saratoga.org; www.saratoga.org*

Savona • *see Bath*

Sayville • *Greater Sayville C/C* • Richard Trpicovsky; Pres.; Lincoln Ave. & Montauk Hwy.; P.O. Box 235; 11782; Suffolk; P 18,024; M 200; (631) 567-5257; Fax (631) 218-0881; info@sayvillechamber.com; www.sayvillechamber.com

Scarsdale • *Scarsdale C/C* • Jen Flores; Secy.; P.O. Box 635; 10583; Westchester; P 18,000; M 93; mail@scarsdalechamber.org; www.scarsdalechamber.org

Schenectady • *Capital Region Chamber - Schenectady Office* • Mark N. Eagan; CEO; 306 State St.; 12305; Schenectady; P 850,000; M 2,500; (518) 372-5656; Fax (518) 370-3217; info@capitalregionchamber.com; www.capitalregionchamber.com*

Schroon Lake • *Schroon Lake Area C/C* • Tony Kostecki; Pres.; 1075 U.S. Rte. 9; P.O. Box 726; 12870; Essex; P 2,000; M 100; (518) 532-7675; Fax (518) 532-7675; chamber@schroonlakeregion.com; www.schroonlakeregion.com

Schuylerville • *Schuylerville Area C/C* • Dave Roberts; Pres.; 43 Spring St.; P.O. Box 80; 12871; Saratoga; P 25,000; M 100; (518) 424-9673; info@schuylervillechamber.org; www.schuylervillechamber.org

Seneca Falls • *Seneca County C/C* • Jeff Shipley; Exec. Dir.; 2020 Rtes. 5 & 20 W.; 13148; Seneca; P 34,000; M 400; (315) 568-2906; (800) 732-1848; Fax (315) 568-1730; info@senecachamber.org; www.senecachamber.org*

Setauket • *see East Setauket*

Shelter Island • *Shelter Island C/C* • P.O. Box 598; 11964; Suffolk; P 1,333; M 60; (877) 893-2290; info@shelterislandchamber.org; www.shelterislandchamber.org

Shirley • *see Mastic*

Shoreham • *see Wading River*

Shrub Oak • *see Yorktown Heights*

Sidney • *Sidney C/C* • Stephanie Taylor; Pres.; 85 Main St., Ste. 2; 13838; Delaware; P 4,000; M 130; (607) 561-2642; Fax (607) 561-2644; office@sidneychamber.org; www.sidneychamber.org

Skaneateles • *Skaneateles C/C* • Susan Dove; Exec. Dir.; 22 Jordan St.; P.O. Box 199; 13152; Onondaga; P 8,000; M 400; (315) 685-0552; Fax (315) 685-0552; info@skaneateles.com; www.skaneateles.com

Sleepy Hollow • *see Tarrytown*

Smithtown • *Smithtown C/C* • Barbara Franco; Exec. Dir.; P.O. Box 1216; 11787; Suffolk; P 14,000; M 375; (631) 979-8069; Fax (631) 979-2206; bfranco@smithtownchamber.com; www.smithtownchamber.com

Snyder • *see Amherst*

Sodus • *Sodus C/C* • Mary Jane Mumby; Secy.; P.O. Box 187; 14551; Wayne; P 10,000; M 115; (315) 576-3818; chamber14551@yahoo.com; www.sodusny.org

Somers • *Somers C/C* • Edward M. Liss; V.P.; P.O. Box 602; 10589; Westchester; P 20,434; M 100; (914) 276-3904; info@somerschamber.com; www.somerschamber.com

Somerset • *see Sanborn*

Sound Beach • *see Mount Sinai*

South Setauket • *see East Setauket*

Southampton • *Southampton C/C* • Karen Connolly; Exec. Dir.; 76 Main St.; 11968; Suffolk; P 50,000; M 475; (631) 283-0402; Fax (631) 283-8707; info@southamptonchamber.com; www.southamptonchamber.com

Southern Dutchess • *see Poughkeepsie*

Southold • *North Fork C/C* • Joseph Corso; Pres.; P.O. Box 1415; 11971; Suffolk; P 22,000; M 200; (631) 765-3161; (631) 477-1383; Fax (631) 765-3161; info@northforkchamber.org; www.northforkchamberofcommerce.org

Speculator • *Adirondacks Speculator Region C/C* • Donna Benkovich; Dir.; Rtes. 30 & 8; P.O. Box 184; 12164; Hamilton; P 1,000; M 170; (518) 548-4521; Fax (518) 548-4905; info@speculatorchamber.com; www.speculatorchamber.com

Sprakers • *see Gloversville*

Springville • *Springville Area C/C* • Jennifer Weber; Dir.; 23 N. Buffalo St.; P.O. Box 310; 14141; Erie; P 12,000; M 175; (716) 592-4746; Fax (716) 592-4746; assistant@springvillechamber.com; www.springvilleareachamber.com

St. Johnsville • *see Gloversville*

Staten Island • *Staten Island C/C* • Linda M. Baran; Pres./CEO; 130 Bay St.; 10301; Richmond; P 500,000; M 700; (718) 727-1900; Fax (718) 727-2295; lbaran@sichamber.com; www.sichamber.com

Stillwater • *see Mechanicville*

Stony Brook • *see East Setauket*

Suffern • *Suffern C/C* • Richard Gandon; Pres.; 71 Lafayette Ave.; P.O. Box 291; 10901; Rockland; P 10,000; M 125; (845) 357-8424; suffernchamberofcommerce@yahoo.com; www.suffernchamberofcommerce.com

Sugarloaf • *SugarLoaf C/C* • Kiki Rosner; P.O. Box 125; 10981; Orange; P 13,000; M 40; (848) 467-8427; sugarloafnewyork@gmail.com; www.sugarloafnewyork.com

Sweden • *see Brockport*

Syracuse • *CenterState CEO* • Rob Simpson; Pres./CEO; 115 W. Fayette St.; 13202; Onondaga; P 458,336; M 2,000; (315) 470-1800; Fax (315) 471-8545; ceo@centerstateceo.com; www.centerstateceo.com*

Tarrytown • *Sleepy Hollow Tarrytown C/C* • John Sardy; Exec. Dir.; 1 Neperan Rd.; 10591; Westchester; P 20,000; M 300; (914) 631-1705; Fax (914) 206-5115; info@sleepyhollowchamber.com; www.sleepyhollowchamber.com*

Terryville • *see Mount Sinai*

Three Mile Bay • *Chaumont-Three Mile Bay C/C* • P.O. Box 24; 13693; Jefferson; P 2,500; (315) 649-3404; chaumontchamber@yahoo.com; www.chaumontchamber.com

Ticonderoga • *Ticonderoga Area C/C* • Matthew J. Courtright; Exec. Dir.; 94 Montcalm St., Ste. 1; 12883; Essex, Warren & Washington; P 5,000; M 180; (518) 585-6619; Fax (518) 585-9184; chamberinfo@ticonderogany.com; www.ticonderogany.com*

Tioga County • *see Owego*

Tonawanda • *see North Tonawanda*

Troy • *Rensselaer County Reg. C/C* • Linda Hillman; Pres.; 90 Fourth St., Ste. 200; 12180; Rensselaer; P 160,000; M 1,200; (518) 274-7020; clovely@renscochamber.com; www.renscochamber.com*

Trumansburg • *Trumansburg Area C/C* • Mary Spicer; Secy.; P.O. Box 478; 14886; Tompkins; P 2,000; M 80; (607) 387-7331; mspicer@tompkinsins.com; www.trumansburgchamber.com

Tuckahoe • *Eastchester-Tuckahoe C/C* • Mairam Janusz; Village Hall; 65 Main St., Ste. 202; 10707; Westchester; P 32,000; M 120; (914) 779-7344; cetcoc@aol.com; www.eastchestertuckahoechamberofcommerce.com

Tupper Lake • *Tupper Lake C/C* • Sonny Young; Pres.; 121 Park St.; P.O. Box 987; 12986; Franklin; P 6,000; M 125; (518) 359-3328; Fax (518) 359-2434; info@tupperlake.com; tupperlake.com

Ulster County • *see Kingston*

Unadilla • *Unadilla C/C* • Jackie Carey; Co-Pres.; P.O. Box 275; 13849; Otsego; P 10,000; M 100; (607) 563-1104; unadillachamber@yahoo.com; www.unadillachamberofcommerce.org

Utica • *Mohawk Valley C/C* • Pamela G. Matt, Esq.; Exec. Dir.; 200 Genesee St.; 13502; Herkimer, Madison & Oneida; P 228,000; M 800; (315) 724-3151; Fax (315) 724-3177; info@mvchamber.org; www.mvchamber.org*

Valley Stream • *Valley Stream C/C* • Debbie Gyulay; Pres.; P.O. Box 1016; 11582; Nassau; P 36,300; M 200; (516) 825-1741; Fax (516) 825-1741; valleystreamcc@gmail.com; www.valleystreamchamber.org

Victor • *Victor C/C* • Mitch Donovan; Pres.; 37 E. Main St.; 14564; Ontario; P 16,000; M 350; (585) 742-1476; Fax (585) 857-6338; info@victorchamber.com; www.victorchamber.com*

Victory • *see Schuylerville*

Waddington • *Waddington C/C* • Jill Winters; Pres.; 38 Main St.; P.O. Box 291; 13694; St. Lawrence; P 2,000; M 67; (315) 388-4079; (315) 388-5967; waddingtonchamber@gmail.com; www.waddingtonny.com

Wading River • *Wading River-Shoreham C/C* • Walter Colleran & Millie Thomas; Co-Dirs.; P.O. Box 348; 11792; Suffolk; P 8,130; M 60; (631) 929-8201; info@wrschamber.org; www.wrschamber.org

Walden • *see Montgomery*

Walton • *Walton C/C* • Maureen Wacha; Pres.; 129 North St.; 13856; Delaware; P 6,000; M 125; (607) 865-6656; walton_chamber@yahoo.com; www.waltonchamber.com

Wantagh • *Wantagh C/C* • Linda Swanson; Exec. Dir.; P.O. Box 660; 11793; Nassau; P 19,400; M 215; (516) 679-0100; director@wantaghchamber.com; www.wantaghchamber.com

Warrensburg • *Warrensburg C/C* • Nancy Craig; Admin. Asst.; 3847 Main St.; 12885; Warren; P 4,000; M 100; (518) 623-2161; Fax (518) 623-2184; info@warrensburgchamber.com; www.warrensburgchamber.com

Warsaw • *Wyoming County C/C & Tourism* • Scott A. Gardner; Pres./CEO; 36 Center St., Ste. A; 14569; Wyoming; P 42,100; M 503; (585) 786-0307; Fax (585) 786-0009; info@wycochamber.org; www.wycochamber.org

Warsaw • *Greater Warsaw C/C* • Lori Standish; Pres.; P.O. Box 221; 14569; Wyoming; P 5,000; M 200; (585) 786-3981; (585) 786-2888; info@warsawchamber.com; www.warsawchamber.com

Warwick • *Warwick Valley C/C* • Michael A. Johndrow; Exec. Dir.; South St., 'Caboose'; P.O. Box 202; 10990; Orange; P 32,000; M 565; (845) 986-2720; Fax (845) 986-6982; info@warwickcc.org; www.warwickcc.org

Washingtonville • *Blooming Grove/Washingtonville C/C* • P.O. Box 454; 10992; Rockland; P 20,000; M 100; (845) 497-7717; bgwcc1@gmail.com; www.bgwcc.org

Waterford • *see Clifton Park*

Watertown • *Greater Watertown-North Country C/C* • Kylie Peck; Pres./CEO; 1241 Coffeen St.; 13601; Jefferson; P 146,208; M 841; (315) 788-4400; Fax (315) 788-3369; chamber@watertownny.com; www.watertownny.com*

Watkins Glen • *Watkins Glen Area C/C* • Rebekah LaMoreaux; Pres.; 214 N. Franklin St.; 14891; Schuyler; P 19,000; M 408; (607) 535-4300; (800) 607-4552; Fax (607) 535-6243; info@watkinsglenchamber.com; www.watkinsglenchamber.com*

Waverly • *Greater Valley C/C* • Greg Joseph; Pres.; 109 Chemung St.; 14892; Tioga; P 40,000; M 253; (607) 249-6192; Fax (607) 249-6193; gvcc@cqservices.com; www.greatervalleychamberofcommerce.com

Webster • *Webster C/C Inc.* • Barry Howard; Pres./CEO; 1110 Crosspointe Ln., Ste. C; 14580; Monroe; P 53,000; M 500; (585) 265-3960; Fax (585) 265-3702; websterchamber@gmail.com; www.websterchamber.com

Wells • *see Speculator*

Wellsville • *Wellsville Area C/C* • Steven Havey; Exec. Dir.; 114 N. Main St.; 14895; Allegheny; P 70,000; M 265; (585) 593-5080; Fax (585) 593-5088; s.havey@wellsvilleareachamber.com; www.wellsvilleareachamber.com

West Amherst • *see Amherst*

West Islip • *West Islip C/C* • Diane Fontana; Pres.; P.O. Box 58; 11795; Suffolk; P 29,000; M 400; (631) 661-3838; aperfectviewcwfi@aol.com; www.westislip.org

West Seneca • *West Seneca C/C* • Frank Calieri; Exec. Dir.; 950A Union Rd., Ste. 5; Southgate Plaza; 14224; Erie; P 47,000; M 300; (716) 674-4900; Fax (716) 674-5846; director@westseneca.org; www.westseneca.org

Westbury • *Westbury-Carle Place C/C* • MaryAnn DiGuiseppi; Exec. Dir.; P.O. Box 474; 11590; Nassau; P 20,300; M 150; (516) 997-3966; info@wcpchamber.com; www.wcpchamber.com

Westchester County • *Bus. Cncl. of Westchester* • Marsha Gordon; Pres./CEO; 108 Corporate Park Dr., Ste. 101; White Plains; 10604; Westchester; P 949,113; M 1,200; (914) 948-2110; Fax (914) 948-0122; hmillman@westchesterny.org; www.westchesterny.org*

Westfield • *see Dunkirk*

Westhampton Beach • *Greater Westhampton C/C* • JoAnn Rich; Prog. Admin.; 7 Glovers Ln.; P.O. Box 1228; 11978; Suffolk; P 8,246; M 204; (631) 288-3337; Fax (631) 288-3322; info@whbcc.org; www.whbcc.com

Westport • *Westport C/C* • P.O. Box 394; 12993; Essex; P 1,270; M 100; (518) 962-8383; Chamber@WestportNY.com; www.westportny.com

White Plains • *see Westchester County*

Whitehall • *Whitehall C/C* • Beth Reynolds; Pres.; P.O. Box 97; 12887; Washington; P 3,800; M 100; (518) 499-4435; whitehallthrives@aol.com; www.whitehall-chamber.org

Williamson • *Williamson C/C* • Vince Pilato; Pres.; P.O. Box 907; 14589; Wayne; P 7,000; M 70; (585) 697-4012; williamsoncofc@aol.com; www.williamsonchamberofcommerce.com

Williamsville • *see Amherst*

Williston Park • *C/C of the Willistons* • Lucille Walters; Exec. Dir.; P.O. Box 207; 11596; Nassau; P 7,500; M 100; (516) 739-1943; Fax (516) 294-1444; lamw50@optonline.net; www.chamberofthewillistons.org

Wilson • *see Sanborn*

Windham • *Windham C/C* • Graham Merk; P.O. Box 613; 12496; Greene; P 1,660; M 115; (518) 734-4419; windhamchamber1@me.com; www.windhamchamber.org

Woodstock • *Woodstock C/C* • Randy Conti; Pres.; P.O. Box 36; 12498; Ulster; P 2,300; M 260; (845) 679-6234; info@woodstockchamber.com; www.woodstockchamber.com

Yonkers • *Yonkers C/C* • Kevin T. Cacace; Pres.; 55 Main St., 2nd Flr.; 10701; Westchester; P 198,000; M 500; (914) 963-0332; Fax (914) 963-0455; info@yonkerschamber.com; www.yonkerschamber.com

Yorktown Heights • *Yorktown C/C* • Nancy Stingone; Exec. Dir.; P.O. Box 632; 10598; Westchester; P 38,000; M 400; (914) 245-4599; Fax (914) 734-7171; info@yorktownchamber.org; www.yorktownchamber.org

North Carolina

North Carolina Chamber • S. Lewis Ebert; Pres./CEO; 701 Corporate Center Dr., Ste. 400; Raleigh; 27607; Wake; P 9,752,073; M 1,900; (919) 836-1400; Fax (919) 836-1425; info@ncchamber.net; www.ncchamber.net

Ahoskie • *Ahoskie C/C Inc.* • W. Dan Joyner; Exec. V.P.; 310 S. Catherine Creek Rd.; P.O. Box 7; 27910; Hertford; P 15,000; M 145; (252) 332-2042; Fax (252) 332-8617; ahoskiechamber@ahoskie.net; www.ahoskiechamber.com

Albemarle • *Stanly County C/C* • Kathy Almond; Pres./CEO; 116 E. North St.; P.O. Box 909; 28002; Stanly; P 61,600; M 500; (704) 982-8116; Fax (704) 983-5000; mthompson@stanlychamber.org; www.stanlychamber.org*

Andrews • *Andrews C/C* • Margaret DeLuna; Pres.; 345 Locust St.; P.O. Box 800; 28901; Cherokee; P 1,760; M 150; (828) 321-3584; Fax (828) 321-3584; info@andrewschamber.com; www.andrewschamber.com

Angier • *Angier C/C* • Cindy Hunter; Exec. Dir.; 24 E.Depot St.; P.O. Box 47; 27501; Harnett; P 4,400; M 200; (919) 639-2500; Fax (919) 639-8826; angiercc@angierchamber.org; www.angierchamber.org*

Apex • *Apex C/C* • Shannon Flaherty; Exec. Dir.; 220 N. Salem St.; 27502; Wake; P 38,000; M 543; (919) 362-6456; (800) 345-4504; Fax (919) 362-9050; join@apexchamber.com; www.apexchamber.com*

Archdale • *Archdale-Trinity C/C* • Beverly M. Nelson; Pres.; 213 Balfour Dr.; P.O. Box 4634; 27263; Randolph; P 18,000; M 250; (336) 434-2073; Fax (336) 431-5845; beverly@archdaletrinitychamber.com; www.archdaletrinitychamber.com

Asheboro • *Asheboro/Randolph C/C* • Linda Brown; Pres.; 137 S. Fayetteville St.; 27203; Randolph; P 20,000; M 645; (336) 626-2626; Fax (336) 626-7077; chamber@asheboro.com; www.chamber.asheboro.com*

Asheville • *Asheville Area C/C* • Kit Cramer; Pres./CEO; 36 Montford Ave.; 28801; Buncombe; P 238,300; M 2,000; (828) 258-6114; Fax (828) 251-0926; member@ashevillechamber.org; www.ashevillechamber.org*

Aurora • *Aurora Richland Twp. C/C* • Gail Phelps; Pres.; P.O. Box 326; 27806; Beaufort; P 4,700; M 68; (252) 322-4405; aurorachamber@embarqmail.com; www.aurorarichlandchamber.net

Ayden • *Ayden C/C* • Laura Todd; Exec. Dir.; P.O. Box 31; 28513; Pitt; P 5,000; M 75; (252) 746-2266; Fax (252) 746-2266; chamber@ayden.com; www.aydenchamber.com

Banner Elk • *Avery County C/C* • Susan Freeman; Exec. Dir.; 4501 Tynecastle Hwy., Ste. 2; 28604; Avery; P 17,700; M 407; (828) 898-5605; (800) 972-2183; Fax (828) 898-8287; chamber@averycounty.com; www.averycounty.com

Bat Cave • *see Chimney Rock*

Beech Mountain • *Beech Mountain C/C* • Bernie Knepka; Pres.; 403-A Beech Mountain Pkwy.; 28604; Avery & Watauga; P 1,000; M 50; (828) 387-9283; chamber@beechmtn.com; www.beechmountainchamber.com*

Belhaven • *Belhaven Comm. C/C* • Diana Lambeth; Exec. Dir.; 125 W. Main St.; P.O. Box 147; 27810; Beaufort; P 2,000; M 124; (252) 943-3770; Fax (252) 943-3769; belhaveninfo@gotricounty.com; www.belhavenchamber.com

Belmont • *Montcross Area C/C* • Ted Hall; Pres.; 100 N. Main St.; P.O. Box 368; 28012; Gaston; P 30,000; M 322; (704) 825-5307; Fax (704) 825-5550; deborah.ray@montcrossareachamber.com; www.montcrossareachamber.com*

Benson • *Benson Area C/C* • Loretta Byrd; Exec. Dir.; 303 E. Church St.; P.O. Box 246; 27504; Johnston; P 3,300; M 350; (919) 894-3825; Fax (919) 894-1052; loretta@benson-chamber.com; www.benson-chamber.com*

Bessemer City • *Bessemer City Area C/C* • Robert Crouch; Pres.; P.O. Box 1342; 28016; Gaston; P 5,400; M 75; (704) 629-3900; bsmrctychamber@bellsouth.net; www.bessemercity.com

Black Mountain • *Black Mountain-Swannanoa C/C* • Bob McMurray; Exec. Dir.; 201 E. State St.; 28711; Buncombe; P 9,500; M 375; (828) 669-2300; (800) 669-2301; Fax (828) 669-1407; bmchamber@juno.com; www.exploreblackmountain.com

Blowing Rock • *Blowing Rock C/C* • Charles Hardin; Exec. Dir.; 132 Park Ave.; P.O. Box 406; 28605; Watauga; P 1,600; M 520; (828) 295-7851; (800) 295-7851; Fax (828) 295-7651; terri@blowingrock.com; www.blowingrock.com

Bolivia • *see Southport*

Boone • *Boone Area C/C* • Dan Meyer; Pres./CEO; 870 W. King St., Ste. A; 28607; Watauga; P 51,000; M 825; (828) 264-2225; Fax (828) 264-6644; ginnycampbell@boonechamber.com; www.boonechamber.com

Boonville • *see Yadkinville*

Brevard • *Brevard-Transylvania C/C* • Clark Lovelace; Exec. Dir.; 175 E. Main St.; 28712; Transylvania; P 33,100; M 500; (828) 883-3700; (800) 648-4523; Fax (828) 883-8550; sara@brevardncchamber.org; www.brevardncchamber.org*

Bryson City • *Swain County C/C* • Karen Wilmot; Exec. Dir.; 210 Main St.; P.O. Box 509; 28713; Swain; P 14,000; M 360; (828) 488-3681; (800) 867-9246; Fax (828) 488-6858; chamber@greatsmokies.com; www.greatsmokies.com

Burgaw • *Burgaw Area C/C* • Emily Baker; Exec. Dir.; 115 S. Dickerson St.; P.O. Box 1096; 28425; Pender; P 4,000; M 200; (910) 259-9817; info@burgawchamber.com; www.burgawchamber.com

Burlington • *Alamance County Area C/C* • Mac Williams; Pres.; 610 S. Lexington Ave.; P.O. Box 450; 27216; Alamance; P 153,900; M 850; (336) 228-1338; Fax (336) 228-1330; lisafoster@alamancechamber.com; www.alamancechamber.com*

Burnsville • *Yancey County/Burnsville C/C* • Ginger Johnson; Exec. Dir.; 106 W. Main St.; 28714; Yancey; P 17,600; M 346; (828) 682-7413; ginger@yanceychamber.com; www.yanceychamber.com

Cabarrus County • *see Kannapolis*

Canton • *see Waynesville*

Carolina Beach • *Pleasure Island C/C* • Greg Reynolds; Pres.; 1121 N. Lake Park Blvd.; 28428; New Hanover; P 8,000; M 415; (910) 458-8434; Fax (910) 458-7969; greg@pleasureislandnc.org; www.pleasureislandnc.org

Carrboro • *see Chapel Hill*

Carteret County • *see Morehead City*

Cary • *Cary C/C* • Howard S. Johnson; Pres.; 307 N. Academy St.; 27513; Wake; P 145,000; M 1,200; (919) 467-1016; (800) 919-2279; Fax (919) 469-2375; hjohnson@carychamber.com; www.carychamber.com

Cashiers • *Cashiers Area C/C* • Stephanie Edwards; Exec. Dir.; 202 Hwy. 64 West; P.O. Box 238; 28717; Jackson; P 2,500; M 400; (828) 743-5191; Fax (828) 743-9446; info@cashiersareachamber.com; www.cashiersareachamber.com

Catawba County • *see Hickory*

Chadbourn • *Greater Chadbourn C/C* • Virginia Cox; P.O. Box 200; 28431; Columbus; P 2,000; M 60; (910) 516-2004; (910) 654-4148; www.townofchadbourn.com

Chapel Hill • *Chapel Hill-Carrboro C/C* • Aaron Nelson IOM; Pres./CEO; 104 S. Estes Dr.; P.O. Box 2897; 27515; Orange; P 100,000; M 1,300; (919) 967-7075; Fax (919) 968-6874; jsimmons@carolinachamber.org; www.carolinachamber.org*

Charlotte • *Charlotte C/C* • Bob Morgan; Pres.; 330 S. Tryon St.; P.O. Box 32785; 28202; Mecklenburg; P 809,958; M 3,300; (704) 378-1300; Fax (704) 374-1903; chamber@charlottechamber.com; www.charlottechamber.com

Cherokee • *Cherokee C/C* • Amy Parker; Exec. Dir.; 1148 Tsali Blvd.; P.O. Box 1838; 28719; Swain; P 14,000; M 400; (828) 497-6700; (877) 433-6700; amy@cherokeesmokies.com; www.cherokeesmokies.com

Cherryville • *Cherryville C/C* • Richard Randall; Pres.; 220 E. Main St.; P.O. Box 305; 28021; Gaston; P 5,800; M 150; (704) 435-3451; Fax (704) 435-4200; mbtackett@cityofcherryville.com; www.cherryvillechamber.com

Chimney Rock • *The Chamber of Hickory Nut Gorge* • Tommy Hartzog; Exec. Dir.; 107 Arcade St., Lake Lure, 28746, NC;; P.O. Box 32; 28720; Rutherford; P 2,500; M 250; (828) 625-2725; (828) 429-9375; Fax (828) 625-9601; info@hickorynutchamber.org; www.hickorynutchamber.org*

Clayton • *Clayton C/C* • Mr. Jim Godfrey; Pres.; 301 E. Main St.; P.O. Box 246; 27528; Johnston; P 16,100; M 454; (919) 553-6352; Fax (919) 553-1758; jim@claytonchamber.com; www.claytonchamber.com*

Clinton • *Clinton-Sampson C/C* • Janna Bass; Exec. Dir.; 414 Warsaw Rd.; P.O. Box 467; 28329; Sampson; P 63,700; M 400; (910) 592-6177; info@clintonsampsonchamber.org; www.clintonsampsonchamber.org*

Coats • *Coats Area C/C* • Pat Godwin; Exec. Dir.; P.O. Box 667; 27521; Harnett; P 2,280; M 200; (910) 897-6213; Fax (910) 897-4672; chamber@coatschamber.com; www.coatschamber.com*

Columbus • *see Tryon*

Concord • *see Kannapolis*

Cornelius • *Lake Norman C/C* • W.E. 'Bill' Russell CCE IOM; Pres./CEO; 19900 W. Catawba Ave., Ste. 102; P.O. Box 760; 28031; Mecklenburg; P 150,000; M 1,000; (704) 892-1922; Fax (704) 892-5313; chamber@lakenorman.org; www.lakenormanchamber.org*

Cramerton • *see Belmont*

Currituck County • *see Kill Devil Hills*

Dare County • *see Kill Devil Hills*

Davidson • *see Cornelius*

Davie County • *see Mocksville*

Denton • *Denton Area C/C* • Dixie Kearns; P.O. Box 1268; 27239; Davidson; P 1,700; M 4; (336) 859-4556; (336) 859-4231; www.townofdenton.com

Dunn • *Dunn Area C/C* • Tammy Williams; Exec. V.P.; 209 W. Divine St.; P.O. Box 548; 28335; Harnett; P 10,000; M 420; (910) 892-4113; Fax (910) 892-4071; office@dunnchamber.com; www.dunnchamber.com*

Durham • *Greater Durham C/C* • Casey Steinbacher; Pres./CEO; 300 W. Morgan St., Ste. 1400; P.O. Box 3829; 27702; Durham; P 265,290; M 900; (919) 328-8700; Fax (919) 688-8351; info@durhamchamber.org; www.durhamchamber.org*

Eden • *Eden C/C* • Randy Hunt; Pres.; 678 S. Van Buren Rd.; 27288; Rockingham; P 15,500; M 325; (336) 623-3336; (336) 623-8800; Fax (336) 623-8800; info@edenchamber.com; www.edenchamber.com

Edenton • *Edenton-Chowan C/C* • Win Dale; Exec. Dir.; 101 W. Water St.; 27932; Chowan; P 14,800; M 200; (252) 482-3400; (800) 775-0111; Fax (252) 482-7093; win.dale@edenton.nc.gov; www.edentonchamber.org

Elizabeth City • *Elizabeth City Area C/C* • Mike Hindenach; Pres.; 502 E. Ehringhaus St.; 27909; Pasquotank; P 40,700; M 600; (252) 335-4365; Fax (252) 335-5732; dayna@elizabethcitychamber.org; www.elizabethcitychamber.org*

Elizabethtown • *Elizabethtown-White Lake Area C/C* • Dawn Maynard; Exec. Dir.; 805 W. Broad St.; P.O. Box 306; 28337; Bladen; P 4,200; M 266; (910) 862-4368; (910) 862-0285; Fax (910) 863-2317; tourism28337@embarqmail.com; www.elizabethtownwhitelake.com

Elkin • *Yadkin Valley C/C* • Myra D. Cook; Pres./CEO; 116 E. Market St.; P.O. Box 496; 28621; Surry; P 5,600; M 354; (336) 526-1111; Fax (336) 526-1879; mmatthews@yadkinvalley.org; www.yadkinvalley.org*

Erwin • *Erwin Area C/C* • Pamela S. Addison; Admin.; P.O. Box 655; 28339; Harnett; P 4,900; M 133; (910) 897-7300; Fax (910) 897-5543; contact@erwinchamber.org; www.erwinchamber.org*

Fair Bluff • *Fair Bluff C/C* • Karen Grainger; Pres.; P.O. Box 648; 28439; Columbus; P 1,100; M 35; (910) 649-7202; visitfairbluff@tds.net; www.fairbluff.com

Farmville • *Farmville C/C* • Maury LaFleur; Admin. & Events Coord.; P.O. Box 150; 27828; Pitt; P 4,650; M 77; (252) 753-4670; Fax (252) 753-7313; jhgreenefdp@embarqmail.com; www.farmvillencchamber.org

Fayetteville • *Greater Fayetteville Chamber* • Rodney O. Anderson; Pres./CEO; 159 Maxwell St.; 28301; Cumberland; P 330,000; M 1,400; (910) 484-4242; Fax (910) 483-0263; rodney@faybiz.com; www.faybiz.com*

Franklin • *Franklin C/C* • Linda Harbuck; Exec. Dir.; 425 Porter St.; 28734; Macon; P 35,000; M 550; (828) 524-3161; (800) 336-7829; Fax (828) 369-7516; facc@franklin-chamber.com; www.franklin-chamber.com*

Franklin County • *Franklin County C/C* • Brenda Fuller; Admin.; 112 E. Nash St.; P.O. Box 62, Louisburg; 27549; Franklin; P 75,000; M 200; (919) 496-3056; Fax (919) 496-0422; bfuller@franklin-chamber.org; www.franklin-chamber.org*

Fuquay-Varina • *Fuquay-Varina Area C/C* • Linda Frenette; Exec. Dir.; 121 N. Main St.; 27526; Wake; P 25,000; M 475; (919) 552-4947; Fax (919) 552-1029; director@fuquay-varina.com; www.fuquay-varina.com*

Garner • *Garner C/C* • Neal Padgett; Pres.; 401 Circle Dr.; 27529; Wake; P 27,000; M 580; (919) 772-6440; Fax (919) 772-6443; info@garnerchamber.com; www.garnerchamber.com*

Gastonia • *Gaston Reg. C/C* • Anissa Starnes; Pres./CEO; 601 W. Franklin Blvd.; 28052; Gaston; P 213,000; M 800; (704) 864-2621; Fax (704) 854-8723; enews@gastonchamber.com; www.gastonchamber.com*

Goldsboro • *Wayne County C/C* • Kate M. Daniels; Pres. & Exec. Dir.; 308 N. William St.; P.O. Box 1107; 27533; Wayne; P 123,000; M 535; (919) 734-2241; Fax (919) 734-2247; kated@waynecountychamber.com; www.waynecountychamber.com*

Grandy • *Currituck C/C* • Josh Bass; Pres.; 5798-A Caratoke Hwy., Poplar Branch; P.O. Box 1160; 27939; Currituck; (252) 453-9497; Fax (252) 453-2349; info@currituckchamber.org; www.currituckchamber.org

Grantsboro • *Pamlico County C/C* • Joyce Swimm; Exec. Dir.; P.O. Box 92; 28529; Pamlico; P 13,000; M 150; (252) 745-3008; Fax (252) 745-3090; pamlicochamber@embarqmail.com; www.pamlicochamber.com

Greensboro • *Greensboro C/C* • Brent Christensen; Pres./CEO; 111 W. February One Place; 27401; Guilford; P 269,700; M 1,900; (336) 387-8301; Fax (336) 275-9299; info@greensboro.org; www.greensboro.org

Greenville • *Greenville-Pitt County C/C* • Leo Corbin; Pres.; 302 S. Greene St.; 27834; Pitt; P 175,000; M 1,000; (252) 752-4101; Fax (252) 752-5934; chamber@greenvillenc.org; www.greenvillenc.org*

Hamlet • *Richmond County C/C* • Emily S. Tucker; Pres.; 2 Main St., Ste. 204; 28345; Richmond; P 46,627; M 400; (910) 895-9058; Fax (910) 895-9056; info@richmondcountychamber.com; www.richmondcountychamber.com*

Hampstead • *see Surf City*

Havelock • *Havelock C/C* • Tim Newton; Chrmn.; 201 Tourist Center Dr.; P.O. Box 21; 28532; Craven; P 23,000; M 250; (252) 447-1101; Fax (252) 447-0241; info1@havelockchamber.org; www.havelockchamber.org*

Hayesville • *Clay County C/C* • Pam Roman; Exec. Dir.; 388 Bus. Hwy. 64; 28904; Clay; P 10,853; M 305; (828) 389-3704; Fax (828) 389-1033; info@ncmtnchamber.com; www.ncmtnchamber.com*

Henderson • *Henderson-Vance County C/C* • Bill Edwards; Pres.; 414 S. Garnett St.; 27536; Vance; P 45,400; M 467; (252) 438-8414; Fax (252) 492-8989; chamber@hendersonvance.org; www.hendersonvance.org

Hendersonville • *Henderson County C/C* • Bob Williford; Pres.; 204 Kanuga Rd.; 28739; Henderson; P 106,000; M 1,000; (828) 692-1413; Fax (828) 693-8802; chamber@hendersoncountychamber.org; www.hendersoncountychamber.org*

Hertford • *Perquimans County C/C* • Sid Eley; Exec. Dir.; 118 W. Market St.; 27944; Perquimans; P 12,000; M 285; (252) 426-5657; Fax (252) 426-7542; chamber@visitperquimans.com; www.visitperquimans.com

Hickory • *Catawba County C/C* • G. Daniel Hearn CCE; Pres./CEO; 1055 Southgate Corp. Park S.W.; P.O. Box 1828; 28603; Catawba; P 154,400; M 900; (828) 328-6111; Fax (828) 328-1175; info@catawbachamber.org; www.catawbachamber.org*

High Point • *High Point C/C* • Patrick Chapin; CEO; 1634 N. Main St.; P.O. Box 5025; 27262; Guilford; P 104,400; M 1,100; (336) 882-5000; Fax (336) 889-9499; info@highpointchamber.org; www.highpointchamber.org*

Highlands • *Highlands Area C/C* • Bob Kieltyka; Exec. Dir.; 108 Main St.; P.O. Box 62; 28741; Macon; P 3,000; M 300; (828) 526-5841; (828) 526-2112; Fax (828) 526-5803; president@highlandschamber.org; www.highlandschamber.org*

Hillsborough • *Hillsborough/Orange County C/C* • Kim Tesoro; Interim CEO; 121 N. Churton St., Ste. 1C; 27278; Orange; P 6,500; M 325; (919) 732-8156; Fax (866) 306-3644; info@hillsboroughchamber.com; www.hillsboroughchamber.com*

Holly Springs • *Holly Springs C/C* • Chris "Scoop" Green; Exec. Dir.; 344 Raleigh St., Ste. 100; P.O. Box 695; 27540; Wake; P 22,000; M 311; (919) 567-1796; Fax (919) 567-1380; director@hollyspringschamber.org; www.hollyspringschamber.org

Hope Mills • *Hope Mills Area C/C* • Tiffany Aldridge; Exec. Dir.; 5546 Trade St.; P.O. Box 451; 28348; Cumberland; P 17,000; M 300; (910) 423-4314; Fax (910) 423-6796; hmacc@hopemillschamber.org; www.hopemillschamber.org*

Hot Springs • *see Mars Hill*

Huntersville • *see Cornelius*

Jackson • *Northampton County C/C* • Judy Collier; Exec. Dir.; 127 W. Jefferson St.; P.O. Box 1035; 27845; Northampton; P 22,000; M 125; (252) 534-1383; Fax (252) 534-1739; jcolliernhcoc@embarqmail.com; www.northamptonchamber.org

Jacksonville • *Jacksonville Onslow C/C* • Laurette Leagon; Pres.; 1099 Gum Branch Rd.; 28540; Onslow; P 177,700; M 876; (910) 347-3141; Fax (910) 347-4705; president@jacksonvilleonline.org; www.jacksonvilleonline.org*

Jonesville • *see Elkin*

Kannapolis • *Cabarrus Reg. C/C* • Barbi Jones; Exec. Dir.; 3003 Dale Earnhardt Blvd., Ste. 200; 28083; Cabarrus; P 187,000; M 700; (704) 782-4000; Fax (704) 782-4050; bjones@cabarrus.biz; www.cabarrus.biz*

Kenansville • *Kenansville Duplin County C/C* • Faith Cameron; Pres.; 406 S. Main St.; P.O. Box 358; 28349; Duplin; P 1,215; M 60; (910) 275-0323; kenansvilleareachamber@gmail.com; www.kenansville.org

Kenly • *Kenly Area C/C* • P.O. Box 190; 27542; Johnston; P 1,600; M 150; (919) 284-5510; Fax (919) 284-1179; kacc@embarqmail.com; www.kenlynorthcarolina.com

Kernersville • *Kernersville C/C* • Chris Corner; Pres./CEO; 136 E. Mountain St.; 27284; Forsyth; P 23,000; M 585; (336) 993-4521; Fax (336) 993-3756; kchamber@kernersvillenc.com; www.kernersvillenc.com*

Kill Devil Hills • *Outer Banks C/C* • Karen Brown; Pres./CEO; 101 Town Hall Dr.; P.O. Box 1757; 27948; Dare; P 46,000; M 1,100; (252) 441-8144; Fax (252) 441-0338; info@outerbankschamber.com; www.outerbankschamber.com*

King • *King C/C* • Deanne Moore; Exec. Dir.; 124 S. Main St.; P.O. Box 863; 27021; Stokes; P 20,000; M 200; (336) 983-9308; Fax (336) 983-9526; kcoc@windstream.net; www.kingnc.com

Kings Mountain • *Cleveland County C/C-Kings Mountain Ofc.* • Anna Lineberger; Ofc. Mgr.; 150 W. Mountain St.; 28086; Cleveland; P 20,000; M 575; (704) 739-4755; Fax (704) 480-5969; anna@clevelandchamber.org; www.clevelandchamber.org

Kinston • *Kinston-Lenoir County C/C* • Laura Lee Sylvester; Pres.; 301 N. Queen St.; P.O. Box 157; 28502; Lenoir; P 58,000; M 500; (252) 527-1131; Fax (252) 527-1914; info@kinstonchamber.com; www.kinstonchamber.com*

Kitty Hawk • *see Kill Devil Hills*

Knightdale • *Knightdale C/C* • Mary Yount IOM; Exec. Dir.; 207 Main St.; 27545; Wake; P 13,000; M 380; (919) 266-4603; (919) 266-8170; Fax (919) 794-8644; knightdalechamber@knightdalechamber.org; www.knightdalechamber.org*

LaGrange • *see Kinston*

Lake Gaston • *see Littleton*

Lake Lure • *see Chimney Rock*

Laurinburg • *Laurinburg/Scotland County Area C/C* • Janet C. Smith; Exec. Dir.; 606 S. Atkinson St.; 28352; Scotland; P 36,000; M 350; (910) 276-7420; Fax (910) 277-8785; janetsmith@laurinburgchamber.com; www.laurinburgchamber.com*

Leland • *North Brunswick C/C* • Dana Fisher; Exec. Dir.; 151 Poole Rd., Ste. 3; 28451; Brunswick; P 13,000; M 330; (910) 383-0553; (888) 383-0553; Fax (910) 383-1992; nbchamber@nbchamber.net; www.nbchamberofcommerce.com*

Lenoir • *Caldwell County C/C* • Ralph Prestwood; Exec. Dir.; 1909 Hickory Blvd. S.E.; 28645; Caldwell; P 83,100; M 500; (828) 726-0616; frontdesk@caldwellcochamber.org; www.caldwellcochamber.org*

Lexington • *Lexington Area C/C* • Burr Sullivan; Pres./CEO; 507 E. Center St.; P.O. Box C; 27293; Davidson; P 21,000; M 400; (336) 248-5929; Fax (336) 248-2161; chamber@lexingtonchamber.net; www.lexingtonchamber.net*

Liberty • *Liberty C/C* • Don Herndon; Pres.; 112 S. Greensboro; P.O. Box 986; 27298; Randolph; P 3,000; M 100; (336) 622-4937; libertychamber@rtelco.net

Lillington • *Lillington Area C/C* • Nancy Guy; Exec. Dir.; 24 W. Front St.; P.O. Box 967; 27546; Harnett; P 3,600; M 207; (910) 893-3751; Fax (910) 514-9797; contact@lillingtonchamber.org; www.lillingtonchamber.org*

Lincolnton • *Lincolnton-Lincoln County C/C* • Ken Kindley; Pres.; 101 E. Main St.; P.O. Box 1617; 28093; Lincoln; P 80,000; M 700; (704) 735-3096; Fax (704) 735-5449; lisa.ormsby@lincolnchambernc.org; www.lincolnchambernc.org*

Littleton • *Lake Gaston C/C & Visitors Center Inc.* • Almira Papierniak; Exec. Dir.; 2475 Eaton Ferry Rd.; 27850; Halifax; P 7,400; M 280; (252) 586-5711; Fax (252) 586-3152; lgcc@earthlink.net; www.lakegastonchamber.com

Louisburg • *see Franklin County*

Lowell • *see Belmont*

Lumberton • *Lumberton Area C/C* • Cindy S. Kern; Exec. Dir.; 800 N. Chestnut St.; P.O. Box 1008; 28359; Robeson; P 27,000; M 550; (910) 739-4750; Fax (910) 671-9722; lumbertonchamber@bellsouth.net; www.lumbertonchamber.com*

Madison • *Western Rockingham C/C* • 112 W. Murphy St.; 27025; Rockingham; P 10,000; M 225; (336) 548-6248; Fax (336) 548-4466; executivedirector@mywrcc.com; www.mywrcc.com

Maggie Valley • *Maggie Valley Area C/C* • Teresa D. Smith; Exec. Dir.; 2781 Soco Rd.; P.O. Box 279; 28751; Haywood; P 1,100; M 225; (828) 926-1686; (800) 624-4431; Fax ; cmaggie@maggievalley.org; www.maggievalley.org

Manteo • *see Kill Devil Hills*

Marion • *McDowell C/C* • Steve Bush; Exec. Dir.; 1170 W. Tate St.; 28752; McDowell; P 45,000; M 360; (828) 652-4240; Fax (828) 659-9620; mountains@mcdowellchamber.com; www.mcdowellchamber.com*

Mars Hill • *Madison County C/C* • O'Neil Shelton; Pres.; 56 S. Main St.; P.O. Box 1085; 28754; Madison; P 20,800; M 250; (828) 689-9351; (877) 2-MADISON; info@madisoncounty-nc.com; www.madisoncounty-nc.com

Marshall • *see Mars Hill*

Marshville • *Marshville C/C* • Richard Paschal; Pres.; P.O. Box 337; 28103; Union; P 2,500; M 60; (704) 624-3183; Fax (704) 624-2371; marshvillechamberofcommerce.com

Matthews • *Matthews C/C* • Kelly Barnhardt; Exec. Dir.; 210 Matthews Stations St.; P.O. Box 601; 28106; Mecklenburg; P 27,200; M 450; (704) 847-3649; chamberinfo@matthewschamber.org; www.matthewschamber.org*

Mayodan • *see Madison*

McAdenville • *see Belmont*

Mocksville • *Davie County C/C* • Carolyn McManamy; Pres.; 135 S. Salisbury St.; 27028; Davie; P 41,240; M 395; (336) 751-3304; Fax (336) 751-5697; chamber@daviecounty.com; www.daviechamber.com*

Monroe • *Union County C/C* • Pat Kahle; Pres.; 903 Skyway Dr.; P.O. Box 1789; 28111; Union; P 203,000; M 580; (704) 289-4567; Fax (704) 282-0122; pat@unioncountycoc.com; www.unioncountycoc.com*

Montgomery County • *see Troy*

Mooresville • *Mooresville-South Iredell C/C* • Kirk Ballard; Pres.; 149 E. Iredell Ave.; P.O. Box 628; 28115; Iredell; P 69,000; M 800; (704) 664-3898; Fax (704) 664-2549; info@mooresvillenc.org; www.mooresvillenc.org*

Morehead City • *Carteret County C/C* • Mike Wagoner; Pres.; 801 Arendell St., Ste. 1; 28557; Carteret; P 66,400; M 950; (252) 726-6350; (800) 622-6278; Fax (252) 726-3505; mike@nccoastchamber.com; www.nccoastchamber.com*

Morganton • *Burke County C/C* • Jerry Davis; Pres./CEO; 110 E. Meeting St.; 28655; Burke; P 90,000; M 450; (828) 437-3021; Fax (828) 437-1613; info@burkecounty.org; www.burkecounty.org*

Morrisville • *Morrisville C/C* • Sarah Gaskill; Pres.; 260 Town Hall Dr., Ste. A; 27560; Wake; P 17,000; M 350; (919) 463-7150; Fax (919) 439-0212; chamber@morrisvillechamber.org; www.morrisvillechamber.org*

Mount Airy • *Greater Mount Airy C/C* • Randy Collins; Pres./CEO; 200 N. Main St.; P.O. Box 913; 27030; Surry; P 11,000; M 500; (336) 786-6116; Fax (336) 786-1488; chambermembership@mtairyncchamber.org; www.mtairyncchamber.org*

Mount Holly • *see Belmont*

Mount Olive • *Mount Olive Area C/C* • Julie R. Beck; Pres.; 123 N. Center St.; 28365; Wayne; P 4,800; M 200; (919) 658-3113; Fax (866) 228-3235; president@mountolivechamber.com; www.mountolivechamber.com

Murfreesboro • *Murfreesboro C/C* • Judy Hachey; Exec. Dir.; 116 E. Main St.; P.O. Box 393; 27855; Hertford; P 3,000; M 90; (252) 398-4886; murfreesborochamber@gmail.com; www.murfreesboroncchamberofcommerce.org

Murphy • *Cherokee County C/C* • Meridith Jorgensen; Exec. Dir.; 805 W. U.S. 64; 28906; Cherokee; P 27,444; M 350; (828) 837-2242; info@cherokeecountychamber.com; www.cherokeecountychamber.com*

Nags Head • *see Kill Devil Hills*

Nashville • *Nashville C/C* • Dylan Bunch; Pres.; P.O. Box 1003; 27856; Nash; P 5,000; M 88; (252) 459-4050; nashvillencchamber@gmail.com; www.nashvillencchamber.org

New Bern • *New Bern Area C/C* • Kevin Roberts; Pres.; 316 S. Front St.; P.O. Drawer C; 28563; Craven; P 100,000; M 910; (252) 637-3111; Fax (252) 637-7541; nbchamber@newbernchamber.com; www.newbernchamber.com

North Wilkesboro • *Wilkes C/C* • Linda S. Cheek; Pres.; 717 Main St.; P.O. Box 727; 28659; Wilkes; P 68,000; M 635; (336) 838-8662; Fax (336) 838-3728; info@wilkesnc.org; www.wilkesnc.org*

Oak Island • *see Southport*

Ocracoke Island • *see Kill Devil Hills*

Old Fort • *Old Fort C/C* • Rick Acrivos; Mgr.; P.O. Box 1447; 28762; McDowell; P 980; M 50; (828) 668-7223; chamber@oldfortchamber.com; www.oldfortchamber.com

Outer Banks • *see Kill Devil Hills*

Oxford • *Granville County C/C* • Ginnie D. Currin; Exec. Dir.; 124 Hillsboro St.; P.O. Box 820; 27565; Granville; P 60,000; M 385; (919) 693-6125; Fax (919) 693-6126; wanda@granville-chamber.com; www.granville-chamber.com*

Pembroke • *Pembroke Area C/C* • Faline Locklear Dial; Pres.; 636 Prospect Rd.; P.O. Box 1978; 28372; Robeson; P 2,500; M 100; (910) 522-2162; pembrokechamber@gmail.com; www.pembrokechamber.com*

Pinehurst • *see Southern Pines*

Pittsboro • *see Siler City*

Plymouth • *Washington County C/C* • Jennifer Arnold; Exec. Dir.; 701 Washington St.; 27962; Washington; P 13,000; M 180; (252) 793-4804; Fax (252) 793-2143; chamber@washconc.org; www.chamberofwashingtoncounty.com

Poplar Branch • *see Grandy*

Raeford • *Raeford-Hoke C/C* • Jackie Lynch; Bus. Admin.; 101 N. Main St.; 28376; Hoke; P 37,000; M 200; (910) 875-5929; Fax (910) 875-1010; rae-hokchamber@embarqmail.com; www.raefordhokechamber.com

Raleigh • *Greater Raleigh C/C* • Tim Giuliani; Pres./CEO; 800 S. Salisbury St.; P.O. Box 2978; 27602; Wake; P 900,993; M 2,300; (919) 664-7000; Fax (919) 664-7097; info@raleighchamber.org; www.raleighchamber.org

Randleman • *Randleman C/C* • Mr. Jeff Freeman; Exec. Dir./CEO; 102 W. Naomi St.; P.O. Box 207; 27317; Randolph; P 18,000; M 125; (336) 495-1100; Fax (336) 495-1133; chamber43@northstate.net; www.randlemanchamber.com

Red Springs • *Red Springs C/C* • Fran Ray; Exec. Dir.; 225 S. Main; 28377; Robeson; P 4,500; M 160; (910) 843-5441; Fax (910) 843-2975; franrschamber@aol.com; www.redsprings.org

Reidsville • *Reidsville C/C & Visitor Center* • Diane Sawyer; Pres./CEO; 140 S. Scales St.; P.O. Box 1020; 27323; Rockingham; P 15,300; M 385; (336) 349-8481; Fax (336) 349-8495; info@reidsvillechamber.org; www.reidsvillechamber.org*

Roanoke Rapids • *Roanoke Valley C/C* • Ruby Gerald; Interim Exec. Dir.; 260 Premier Blvd.; P.O. Box 519; 27870; Halifax; P 75,000; M 700; (252) 537-3513; Fax (252) 535-5767; lhammack@rvchamber.com; www.rvchamber.com*

Robeson County • *see Lumberton*

Rocky Mount • *Rocky Mount Area C/C* • Theresa Pinto IOM; Pres.; 100 Coastline St., Ste. 200; 27804; Nash; P 165,000; M 635; (252) 446-0323; Fax (252) 446-5103; tpinto@rockymountchamber.org; www.rockymountchamber.org*

Roxboro • *Roxboro Area C/C* • Alicia Puryear; Pres./CEO; 211 N. Main St.; 27573; Person; P 39,276; M 350; (336) 599-8333; Fax (336) 599-8335; chamber@roxboronc.com; www.roxboronc.com*

Rutherfordton • *Rutherford County C/C* • Clark Poole; Exec. Dir.; 162 N. Main St.; 28139; Rutherford; P 67,000; M 400; (828) 287-3090; Fax (828) 287-0799; info@rutherfordcoc.org; www.rutherfordcoc.org*

Saint Pauls • *Saint Pauls C/C* • Libby Ferguson; Secy.; P.O. Box 243; 28384; Robeson; P 2,500; M 40; (910) 865-3890; dferguson36@nc.rr.com; www.stpaulsnc.gov

Salisbury • *Rowan County C/C* • Elaine Spalding IOM CCE; Pres.; 204 E. Innes St., Ste. 110; P.O. Box 559; 28144; Rowan; P 150,000; M 900; (704) 633-4221; Fax (704) 642-2011; info@rowanchamber.com; www.rowanchamber.com*

Sanford • *Sanford Area C/C* • Bob Joyce; Pres.; 143 Charlotte Ave.; P.O. Box 519; 27331; Lee; P 55,000; M 650; (919) 775-7341; Fax (919) 776-6244; info@sanford-nc.com; www.sanford-nc.com*

Selma • *see Smithfield*

Shallotte • *Brunswick County C/C* • Shannon Viera; Pres./CEO; 114 Wall St.; P.O. Box 1185; 28459; Brunswick; P 106,000; M 600; (910) 754-6644; (800) 426-6644; Fax (910) 754-6539; info@brunswickcountychamber.org; www.brunswickcountychamber.org*

Shelby • *Cleveland County C/C* • Bill Watson; Pres.; 200 S. Lafayette St.; 28150; Cleveland; P 20,000; M 575; (704) 487-8521; Fax (704) 487-7458; adrian@clevelandchamber.org; www.clevelandchamber.org*

Siler City • *Chatham C/C* • Cindy Poindexter IOM; Pres./CEO; 531 E. 3rd St.; 27344; Chatham; P 68,000; M 375; (919) 742-3333; Fax (919) 742-1333; info@ccucc.net; www.ccucc.net*

Smithfield • *Greater Smithfield-Selma Area C/C* • Richard W. Childrey; Pres.; 1115 Industrial Park Dr.; P.O. Box 467; 27577; Johnston; P 25,000; M 550; (919) 934-9166; Fax (919) 934-1337; rchildrey@smithfieldselma.com; www.smithfieldselma.com*

Snow Hill • *Greene County C/C* • Trudy B. Hardy; Exec. Dir.; 208 N. Greene St.; P.O. Box 364; 28580; Greene; P 22,000; M 110; (252) 747-8090; (252) 560-1411; greenechamberdirector@centurylink.net; www.greenechamber.com*

Southern Pines • *Moore County C/C* • Linda M. Parsons IOM CCEC; Pres./CEO; 10677 Hwy. 15-501; 28387; Moore; P 98,000; M 650; (910) 692-3926; Fax (910) 692-0619; info@moorecountychamber.com; www.moorecountychamber.com*

Southern Shores • *see Kill Devil Hills*

Southport • *Southport-Oak Island Area C/C* • Karen Sphar; Exec. V.P.; 4433 Long Beach Rd. S.E.; 28461; Brunswick; P 19,843; M 512; (910) 457-6964; (800) 457-6964; Fax (910) 457-0598; info@southport-oakisland.com; www.southport-oakisland.com*

Sparta • *Alleghany County C/C* • Ashley Weaver; Exec. Dir.; 58 S. Main St.; P.O. Box 1237; 28675; Alleghany; P 11,000; M 300; (336) 372-5473; (800) 372-5473; Fax (336) 245-9601; info@sparta-nc.com; www.sparta-nc.com

Spinedale • *see Rutherfordton*

Spring Hope • *Spring Hope Area C/C* • Jerry Breedlove; Pres.; P.O. Box 255; 27882; Nash; P 1,400; M 60; (252) 478-1919; jerry@breedloveinc.net; www.springhopechamber.com

Spring Lake • *Greater Spring Lake C/C* • Jeffrey C. Hunt; Pres./CEO; 300 Ruth St., Ste. 16; P.O. Box 333; 28390; Cumberland; P 41,000; M 143; (910) 497-8821; Fax (910) 497-1897; jchunt@springlakechamber.com; www.springlakechamber.com

Spruce Pine • *Mitchell County C/C* • Shirley Hise; Dir.; 79 Parkway Maintenance Rd.; P.O. Box 858; 28777; Mitchell; P 16,000; M 450; (828) 765-9033; (800) 227-3912; Fax (828) 765-9034; getinfo@mitchell-county.com; www.mitchell-county.com

Stanley • *see Belmont*

Statesville • *Greater Statesville C/C* • David Bradley; Pres./CEO; 121 N. Center St., Ste. 101; 28677; Iredell; P 25,000; M 750; (704) 873-2892; Fax (704) 871-1552; mandy@statesvillechamber.org; www.statesvillechamber.org*

Stoneville • *see Madison*

Surf City • *Greater Topsail Area C/C & Tourism* • Chuck Strickland; Exec. Dir.; P.O. Box 2486; 28445; Onslow; P 6,000; M 333; (910) 329-4446; (800) 626-2780; Fax (910) 329-4432; info@topsailcoc.com; www.topsailcoc.com*

Swan Quarter • *Greater Hyde County C/C* • Melissa Joyner; Exec. Dir.; 20646 U.S. Hwy. 264; 27885; Hyde; P 5,810; M 220; (252) 926-9171; (888) 493-3826; Fax (252) 926-9041; info@hydecountychamber.org; www.hydecountychamber.org

Sylva • *Jackson County C/C* • Julie Spiro; Exec. Dir.; 773 W. Main St.; 28779; Jackson; P 36,000; M 450; (828) 586-2155; (800) 962-1911; Fax (828) 586-4887; jctta@nc-mountains.com; www.mountainlovers.com*

Tabor City • *Tabor City C/C* • Cynthia Nelson; Exec. V.P.; 103-D E. Fifth St.; P.O. Box 446; 28463; Columbus; P 4,000; M 125; (910) 377-3012; (910) 840-0292; Fax (910) 377-3012; tccofc@yahoo.com; www.taborcitync.org

Tarboro • *Tarboro Edgecombe C/C* • Bobbie F. Martin; Pres.; 509 Trade St.; P.O. Drawer F; 27886; Edgecombe; P 30,000; M 200; (252) 823-7241; Fax (252) 823-1499; bmartin@tarborochamber.com; www.tarborochamber.com*

Thomasville • *Thomasville Area C/C* • Keith Tobin; Pres.; 941 Randolph St.; P.O. Box 1400; 27361; Davidson; P 27,000; M 300; (336) 475-6134; Fax (336) 475-4802; thomasvillechamber@thomasvillechamber.net; www.thomasvillechamber.net

Troy • *Market MontGOmery Chamber & Tourism* • Mark Scott; Exec. Dir.; 215 N. Main St.; 27371; Montgomery; P 30,000; M 200; (910) 572-4300; mscott@marketmontgomery.com; www.montgomery-county.com

Tryon • *Carolina Foothills C/C* • Janet W. Sciacca; Exec. Dir.; 2753 Lynn Rd., Ste. A; 28782; Polk, NC & Spartanburg, SC; P 23,000; M 365; (828) 859-6236; Fax (888) 296-0711; janet@carolinafoothillschamber.com; www.carolinafoothillschamber.com*

Wadesboro • *Anson County C/C* • Lynn Edwards; Exec. Dir.; 107-A E. Wade St.; P.O. Box 305; 28170; Anson; P 26,000; M 279; (704) 694-4181; Fax (704) 694-3830; ansonchamber@windstream.net; www.ansoncounty.org

Wake Forest • *Wake Forest Area C/C* • Ann Welton; Pres.; 350 S. White St.; 27587; Wake; P 27,000; M 686; (919) 556-1519; Fax (919) 556-8570; info@wakeforestchamber.org; www.wakeforestchamber.org*

Wallace • *Wallace C/C* • Lou Powell; Exec. Dir.; P.O. Box 427; 28466; Duplin; P 3,800; M 165; (910) 285-4044; lou@wallacechamber.com; www.wallacechamber.com

Warrenton • *C/C of Warren County* • Craig Hahn; Exec. Dir.; 130 N. Main St.; P.O. Box 826; 27589; Warren; P 20,300; M 165; (252) 257-2657; Fax (252) 257-2657; info@warren-chamber.org; www.warren-chamber.org

Warsaw • *Warsaw C/C* • Dennis Riley; Exec. Dir.; P.O. Box 585; 28398; Duplin; P 3,000; M 96; (910) 293-7804; Fax (910) 293-6773; warsawchamber@townofwarsawnc.com; townofwarsawnc.com

Washington • *Washington-Beaufort County C/C* • Catherine Glover; Exec. Dir.; 102 Stewart Pkwy.; P.O. Box 665; 27889; Beaufort; P 45,000; M 450; (252) 946-9168; Fax (252) 946-9169; cglover@wbcchamber.com; www.wbcchamber.com*

Waynesville • *Haywood County C/C* • CeCe Hipps IOM; Dir.; 28 Walnut St.; 28786; Haywood; P 60,000; M 600; (828) 456-3021; info@haywood-nc.com; www.haywood-nc.com

Wendell • *Wendell C/C* • Stacy Bradfield; Pres.; 115 N. Pine St.; P.O. Box 562; 27591; Wake; P 7,500; M 235; (919) 365-6318; wcoc@wendellchamber.com; www.wendellchamber.com*

West Jefferson • *Ashe County C/C & Visitor Center* • Cabot Hamilton; Exec. Dir.; 1 N. Jefferson Ave., Ste. C; P.O. Box 31; 28694; Ashe; P 27,500; M 375; (336) 846-9550; Fax (336) 846-8671; director@ashechamber.com; www.ashechamber.com

Whiteville • *Greater Whiteville C/C* • Jackie Ray; Pres.; 601 S. Madison St.; 28472; Columbus; P 5,400; M 385; (910) 642-3171; (888) 533-7196; Fax (910) 642-6047; whitevillechamber@centurylink.net; www.whitevillechamber.org

Wilkesboro • *see North Wilkesboro*

Williamston • *Martin County C/C* • David Whitley; Exec. Dir.; 415 E. Blvd.; 27892; Martin; P 24,000; M 275; (252) 792-4131; Fax (252) 792-0993; admin@martincountync.com; www.MartinCountyNC.com

Wilmington • *Wilmington and Beaches CVB* • Kim Hufham; Pres./CEO; 505 Nutt St., Unit A; 28401; New Hanover; P 206; (910) 341-4030; Fax (910) 341-4029; visit@wilmingtonandbeaches.com; www.WilmingtonAndBeaches.com

Wilmington • *Wilmington C/C* • Richard Blouse; Interim Pres./CEO; 1-Estell Lee Place; 28401; New Hanover; P 375,686; M 900; (910) 762-2611; Fax (910) 762-9765; info@wilmingtonchamber.org; www.wilmingtonchamber.org*

Wilson • *Wilson C/C* • Ryan Simons; Pres.; 200 Nash St. N.E.; 27893; Wilson; P 50,000; M 500; (252) 237-0165; Fax (252) 243-7931; tstewart@wilsonncchamber.com; www.wilsonncchamber.com*

Windsor • *Windsor/Bertie County C/C* • Collins Cooper; Exec. Dir.; 102 N. York St.; P.O. Box 572; 27983; Bertie; P 21,000; M 172; (252) 794-4277; Fax (252) 794-5070; windsorbertiechamber@gmail.com; www.windsorbertie.com

Winston-Salem • *Greater Winston-Salem C/C* • Gayle Anderson; Pres./CEO; 411 W. Fourth St., Ste. 211; 27101; Forsyth; P 338,774; M 1,800; (336) 728-9200; Fax (336) 721-2209; info@winstonsalem.com; www.winstonsalem.com*

Yadkinville • *Yadkin County C/C* • Bobby Todd; Exec. Dir.; 205 S. Jackson St.; P.O. Box 1840; 27055; Yadkin; P 39,000; M 230; (336) 679-2200; Fax (336) 679-3034; btodd@yadkinchamber.org; www.yadkinchamber.org

Yanceyville • *Caswell County C/C* • Sharon Sexton; Dir.; 142 Main St.; P.O. Box 29; 27379; Caswell; P 23,400; M 120; (336) 694-6106; sharon9.caswellchamber@gmail.com; www.caswellchamber.com

Zebulon • *Zebulon C/C* • Kim Valentine; Exec. Dir.; 815 N. Arendell Ave.; P.O. Box 546; 27597; Wake; P 4,700; M 260; (919) 269-6320; Fax (919) 269-6350; zebcoc@zebulonchamber.org; www.zebulonchamber.org*

North Dakota

Greater North Dakota Chamber • Andy Peterson; Pres./CEO; 2000 Schafer St.; P.O. Box 2639; Bismarck; 58502; Burleigh; P 699,628; M 1,100; (701) 222-0929; Fax (701) 222-1611; susan@ndchamber.com; www.ndchamber.com

Ashley • **Ashley C/C** • Marvel Haas; Pres.; 58413; McIntosh; P 750; M 30; (701) 288-3247; marvelheadshed@drtel.net; www.ashley-nd.com

Beach • **Beach Area C/C** • Vanessa Ueckert; Exec. Secy.; 22 Central Ave., Ste. 6; P.O. Box 757; 58621; Golden Valley; P 1,300; M 40; (701) 300-0256; Fax (701) 872-3125; beachnd@gmail.com; www.beachndchamber.com

Belfield • **Belfield Area C/C** • Susan Wolf; Secy.; 515 6th St. N.E.; P.O. Box 959; 58622; Stark; P 866; M 30; (701) 575-8135; susannw2@msn.com; www.belfieldnd.com

Beulah • **Beulah C/C** • Steffanie Boeckel; Exec. Dir.; 120 Central Ave. N.; P.O. Box 730; 58523; Mercer; P 3,200; M 125; (701) 873-4585; (800) 441-2649; Fax (701) 873-5361; chamber@westriv.com; www.beulahnd.org

Bismarck • **Bismarck-Mandan C/C** • Scott Meske; Pres.; 1640 Burnt Boat Dr.; P.O. Box 1675; 58502; Burleigh & Morton; P 117,000; M 1,250; (701) 223-5660; Fax (701) 255-6125; admin@bismancc.com.; www.bismarckmandan.com*

Bottineau • **Greater Bottineau Area C/C & CVB** • Clint Reinoehl; Exec. Dir.; 519 Main St.; 58318; Bottineau; P 2,400; M 175; (701) 228-3849; (800) 735-6932; Fax (701) 228-5130; bcc@utma.com; www.bottineau.org

Bowman • **Bowman Area C/C** • Emily Bostyan; Pres.; P.O. Box 1143; 58623; Bowman; P 1,800; M 150; (701) 523-5880; Fax (701) 523-3322; chamber@bowmannd.com; www.bowmannd.com

Cando • **Cando Area C/C** • Jamie Halverson; Pres.; 1310 4th Ave.; 58324; Towner; P 1,150; M 55; (701) 968-4535; (701) 968-3632; candochamber@candochamber.com; www.candochamber.com

Carrington • **Carrington Area C/C** • Laurie Dietz; Exec. Dir.; 871 Main St.; 58421; Foster; P 2,100; M 130; (701) 652-2524; (800) 641-9668; Fax (701) 652-2391; chambergal@daktel.com; www.cgtn-nd.com*

Cavalier • **Cavalier Area C/C** • Bryan McCoy; Exec. Dir.; 206 Division Ave. S.; P.O. Box 271; 58220; Pembina; P 1,540; M 110; (701) 265-8188; Fax (701) 265-8720; cacc@polarcomm.com; www.cavaliernd.com

Crosby • **Crosby C/C** • Doreen Schilke; Pres.; P.O. Box 635; 58730; Divide; P 1,200; M 80; (701) 965-5483; doreenschilke@hotmail.com; www.crosbynd.com

Devils Lake • **Devils Lake Area C/C** • Paula Vistad; Exec. Dir.; 208 Hwy. 2 W.; P.O. Box 879; 58301; Ramsey; P 7,100; M 600; (701) 662-4903; (800) 233-8048; Fax (701) 662-2147; chamber@gondtc.com; www.devilslakend.com*

Dickinson • **Dickinson Area C/C** • Cheryl Viola; Exec. Dir.; 314 3rd Ave. W.; P.O. Box C; 58602; Stark; P 32,000; M 470; (701) 225-5115; Fax (701) 225-5116; team@dickinsonchamber.org; www.dickinsonchamber.org*

Drayton • **Drayton Comm. C/C** • Larry Ritzo; P.O. Box 265; 58225; Pembina; P 824; M 53; (701) 454-3474; chamber@draytonnd.com; www.draytonnd.com

Fargo • **see Moorhead, MN**

Garrison • **Garrison C/C** • Amy Heger; Dir.; P.O. Box 274; 58540; McLean; P 1,460; M 80; (701) 463-2631; (800) 799-4242; Fax (701) 463-2634; garrisonchamber@restel.com; garrisonnd.com

Grafton • **Grafton Area C/C** • Todd Morgan; Exec. Dir.; 432 Hill Ave.; 58237; Walsh; P 5,000; M 160; (701) 352-0781; Fax (701) 352-3043; gracha@polarcomm.com; www.graftonevents.com*

Grand Forks • **The Chamber Grand Forks - East Grand Forks** • Barry Wilfahrt; Pres./CEO; 202 N. 3rd St.; 58203; Grand Forks; P 65,009; M 1,100; (701) 772-7271; Fax (701) 772-9238; info@gochamber.org; www.gochamber.org*

Harvey • **Harvey Area C/C** • Ann Adams; Exec. Dir.; 100 E. 8th St.; P.O. Box 112; 58341; Wells; P 6,000; M 107; (701) 324-2604; harveychamber@gondtc.com

Hazen • **Hazen C/C** • Kolie Kadrmas; Exec. Dir.; 146 E. Main; P.O. Box 423; 58545; Mercer; P 2,500; M 100; (701) 748-6848; (888) 464-2936; hazenchamber@westriv.com; www.hazennd.org

Hettinger • **Hettinger Area C/C** • Earleen Friez; Admin. Secy.; 120 S. Main St.; P.O. Box 1031; 58639; Adams; P 1,300; M 110; (701) 567-2531; adamschmbr@ndsupernet.com; www.hettingernd.com

Jamestown • **Jamestown Area C/C** • Becky Thatcher-Keller; Exec. Dir.; 120 2nd St. S.E.; P.O. Box 1530; 58402; Stutsman; P 18,000; M 475; (701) 252-4830; Fax (701) 952-4837; director@jamestownchamber.com; www.jamestownchamber.com*

Kenmare • **Kenmare Assn. of Commerce** • Penny Sigloh; Pres.; P.O. Box 324; 58746; Ward; P 1,200; M 75; (701) 385-3070; news@kenmarend.com; www.kenmarend.com

Langdon • **Langdon C/C** • Barb Mehlhoff; Exec. Dir.; 324 8th Ave.; P.O. Box 348; 58249; Cavalier; P 2,300; M 100; (701) 256-3079; Fax (701) 256-2156; langdonchamber@cityoflangdon.com; www.cityoflangdon.com

Lisbon • **Lisbon Civic & Comm.** • Sherri Lunneborg; Secy./Treas.; P.O. Box 812; 58054; Ransom; P 2,300; M 120; (701) 683-5680; Fax (701) 683-5680; lisbonnd@drtel.net; www.lisbonnd.com

Mandan • **see Bismarck**

Medora • **Medora C/C** • Jodi Johnson; Pres.; P.O. Box 186; 58645; Billings; P 112; M 40; (701) 623-4910; chamber@medorandchamber.com; www.medorandchamber.com

Minot • **Minot Area C/C** • L. John MacMartin; President; 1020 20th Ave. S.W.; P.O. Box 940; 58702; Ward; P 50,000; M 750; (701) 852-6000; Fax (701) 838-2488; chamber@minotchamber.org; www.minotchamber.org*

New England • **New England Commercial Club** • Lyle Hochhalter; Pres.; P.O. Box 151; 58647; Hettinger; P 600; M 30; (701) 579-8001; (701) 579-4496; Fax (701) 579-8033; nendcc@hotmail.com; www.newenglandcommercialclub.com

New Rockford • **New Rockford Area C/C** • Jessica Dillon; Chair; P.O. Box 67; 58356; Eddy; P 1,400; M 42; (701) 947-2211; www.cityofnewrockford.com

New Town • **New Town C/C** • Jenna Estvold; Pres.; P.O. Box 422; 58763; Mountrail; P 1,900; M 91; (701) 627-4812; (701) 627-3500; Fax (701) 627-4316; ntchamb@rtc.coop; www.newtownchamber.com

Oakes • *Oakes Area C/C* • Audrey O'Brien; Ofc. Mgr.; 412 Main Ave.; 58474; Dickey; P 4,500; M 100; (701) 742-3508; Fax (701) 742-3139; oakesnd@drtel.net; www.oakesnd.com

Ray • *Ray C/C* • Mary Schmitt; Pres.; P.O. Box 153; 58849; Williams; P 800; M 23; (701) 568-3321; rfdchief@nccray.net; www.raynd.com

Rolla • *Rolla C/C* • Jason Nordmark; Pres.; P.O. Box 712; 58367; Rolette; P 1,300; M 84; (701) 477-3610; chamber@utma.com; rolla.nd.utma.com

Rugby • *Geographical Center C/C* • Shelley Block; Exec. Dir.; 224 Hwy 2 S.W.; 58368; Pierce; P 2,950; M 200; (701) 776-5846; Fax (701) 776-6390; rugbychamber@gondtc.com; www.rugbynorthdakota.com*

Stanley • *Stanley Commercial Club* • Kelly Jones; Secy./Treas.; Box 974; 58784; Mountrail; P 1,300; M 67; (701) 628-2225; Fax (701) 628-2232; commercialclub@midstatetel.com; www.stanleynd.com

Tioga • *Tioga C/C* • P.O. Box 52; 58852; Williams; P 1,265; M 60; (701) 664-2807; Fax (701) 664-2543; tiogachamber@nccray.com; tiogand.net

Valley City • *Valley City Area C/C & CVB* • Kay Vinje; Exec. V.P.; 250 Main St. W.; P.O. Box 724; 58072; Barnes; P 7,000; M 250; (701) 845-1891; (888) 288-1891; Fax (701) 845-1892; chamber@hellovalley.com; www.valleycitynd.com*

Velva • *Velva Assn. of Commerce* • Mr. Cory Schmaltz; Pres.; P.O. Box 334; 58790; McHenry; P 1,049; M 44; (701) 338-2816; www.velva.net

Wahpeton • *Wahpeton Breckenridge Area C/C* • Tessa Tschakert; Exec. V.P.; 118 N. 6th St.; 58075; Richland; P 13,000; M 300; (701) 642-8744; (800) 892-6673; Fax (701) 642-8745; tessa@wahpetonbreckenridgechamber.com; www.wahpetonbreckenridgechamber.com*

Walhalla • *Walhalla Area C/C* • Liann Zeller; Exec. Dir.; 1105 Central Ave.; P.O. Box 34; 58282; Pembina; P 1,000; M 98; (701) 549-3939; Fax (701) 549-2410; walchmbr@utma.com; www.walhalland.org

Watford City • *Watford City Area C/C* • Mary Gumke; Chamber Coord.; P.O. Box 458; 58854; McKenzie; P 6,000; M 300; (701) 570-5084; wcchamber@ruggedwest.com; watfordcitychamber.com*

West Fargo • *see Moorhead, MN*

Williston • *Williston Area C/C* • Janna Lutz; Pres.; 10 Main St.; P.O. Box G; 58802; Williams; P 30,000; M 500; (701) 577-6000; Fax (701) 577-8591; wchamber@willistonchamber.com; www.willistonchamber.com*

Ohio

Ohio C of C • Andrew Doehrel; Pres./CEO; 230 E. Town St.; P.O. Box 15159; Columbus; 43215; Franklin; P 11,544,225; M 4,000; (614) 228-4201; (800) 622-1893; Fax (614) 228-6403; occ@ohiochamber.com; www.ohiochamber.com

Ada • *Ada Area C/C* • Deb Curlis; Pres.; P.O. Box 225; 45810; Hardin; P 6,000; M 75; (419) 788-9459; www.adachamber.org

Akron • *Greater Akron C/C* • Daniel C. Colantone; Pres./CEO; One Cascade Plaza, 17th Flr.; 44308; Summit; P 900,000; M 2,000; (330) 376-5550; (800) 621-8001; Fax (330) 379-3164; info@greaterakronchamber.org; www.greaterakronchamber.org*

Alliance • *Alliance Area C/C* • R. Mark Locke; Pres.; 210 E. Main St.; 44601; Stark; P 24,000; M 450; (330) 823-6260; Fax (330) 823-4434; info@allianceohiochamber.org; www.allianceohiochamber.org

Andover • *Andover Area C/C* • Pamela Harting; Pres.; P.O. Box 503; 44003; Ashtabula; P 2,000; M 75; (440) 293-5895; info@andoverohio.com; www.andoverohio.com

Antwerp • *Antwerp C/C* • Mike Renno; Pres.; P.O. Box 1111; 45813; Paulding; P 1,740; M 65; (419) 258-1722; www.antwerpohio.com

Archbold • *Archbold Area C/C* • Amy Krueger; Exec. Dir.; 300 N. Defiance St.; P.O. Box 102; 43502; Fulton; P 4,200; M 200; (419) 445-2222; Fax (419) 445-0205; info@archboldchamber.com; www.archboldchamber.com

Ashland • *Ashland Area C/C* • Barbara A. Lange; Pres./CEO; 211 Claremont Ave.; 44805; Ashland; P 60,000; M 563; (419) 281-4584; Fax (419) 281-4585; chamber@ashlandoh.com; www.ashlandoh.com*

Ashtabula • *Ashtabula Area C/C* • Jessica Forsythe; Pres./CEO; 4536 Main Ave.; 44004; Ashtabula; P 101,500; M 375; (440) 998-6998; Fax (440) 992-8216; lori@ashtabulachamber.net; www.ashtabulachamber.net

Athens • *Athens Area C/C* • Wendy W. Jakmas; Pres.; 449 E. State St.; 45701; Athens; P 64,700; M 500; (740) 594-2251; Fax (740) 594-2252; wendy@athenschamber.com; www.athenschamber.com*

Aurora • *Aurora Area C/C* • Laura Holman; Exec. Dir.; 9 E. Garfield Rd., Ste. 101; 44202; Portage; P 15,000; M 200; (330) 562-3355; Fax (330) 995-9052; director@allaboutaurora.com; www.allaboutaurora.com

Avon • *see Avon Lake*

Avon Lake • *North Coast C/C* • John Sobolewski; Exec. Dir.; P.O. Box 275; 44012; Lorain; P 40,000; M 200; (440) 933-9311; contact@northcoastchamber.com; www.northcoastchamber.com

Baltimore • *Baltimore Area C/C* • Kasey Farmer; Pres.; P.O. Box 193; 43105; Fairfield; P 5,000; M 85; (740) 438-0837; president@baltimoreareachamber.com; www.baltimoreareachamber.com

Barberton • *South Summit C/C* • Tom Jackson; CEO; 503 W. Park Ave.; 44203; Summit; P 48,800; M 315; (330) 745-3141; Fax (330) 777-0597; tomjackson@southsummitchamber.org; www.southsummitchamber.org

Barnesville • *Barnesville Area C/C* • Derek Deal; Ofc. Mgr.; 130 W. Main St.; P.O. Box 462; 43713; Belmont; P 4,193; M 154; (740) 425-4300; Fax (740) 425-1048; bacc@barnesvilleohiochamber.com; www.barnesvilleohiochamber.com

Beachwood • *Beachwood C/C* • Cindy Caldwell; Exec. Dir.; 24000 Mercantile Rd., Ste. 3; 44122; Cuyahoga; P 12,000; M 500; (216) 831-0003; Fax (216) 831-1209; cindy@beachwood.org; www.beachwood.org*

Beavercreek • *Beavercreek C/C* • Ranna Patel; Pres./CEO; 3210 Beaver-Vu Dr.; 45434; Greene; P 60,000; M 650; (937) 426-2202; Fax (937) 426-2204; ranna@beavercreekchamber.org; www.beavercreekchamber.org*

Bedford • *Bedford C/C* • Gina Pieragostine; Ofc. Mgr.; 33 S. Park St.; 44146; Cuyahoga; P 13,100; M 130; (440) 232-0115; Fax (440) 232-0521; bedfordchamberoh@sbcglobal.net; www.bedfordchamberoh.org

Bedford Heights • *Bedford Heights C/C* • 24816 Aurora Rd., Ste. C; 44146; Cuyahoga; P 11,000; M 100; (440) 232-3369; Fax (440) 232-4862; bedfordhtscofc@aol.com; www.bedfordheightschamber.com

Belden • *see Jackson Twp.*

Bellaire • *Bellaire Area C/C* • Lou Ann Bennett; Pres.; 3287 Belmont St.; P.O. Box 428; 43906; Belmont; P 4,300; M 70; (740) 676-9723; Fax (740) 676-8005; belleairechamber@yahoo.com; www.bellairechamber.net

Bellbrook • *Bellbrook-Sugarcreek Area C/C* • Chris Ewing; Exec. Dir.; 41 W. Franklin St.; 45305; Greene; P 15,000; M 195; (937) 848-4930; Fax (937) 848-4930; info@bellbrooksugarcreekchamber.com; www.bellbrooksugarcreekchamber.com*

Bellefontaine • *Logan County Area C/C* • Paul Benedetti; Pres./CEO; 100 S. Main St.; 43311; Logan; P 46,000; M 400; (937) 599-5121; Fax (937) 599-2411; info@logancountyohio.com; www.logancountyohio.com*

Bellevue • *Bellevue Area C/C* • Pamela E. Verhoff; Exec. Dir.; 110 W. Main St.; 44811; Sandusky; P 8,900; M 135; (419) 483-2182; Fax (419) 483-4259; pam@bellevuechamberofcommerce.org; www.bellevuechamberofcommerce.org*

Bellville • *Clear Fork C/C* • Sheryl Smith; Pres.; P.O. Box 336; 44813; Richland; P 2,000; M 35; (419) 883-3291; Fax (419) 883-3682; ssmith@richlandbank.com; www.bellvilleohio.net

Belpre • *Belpre Area C/C* • Karen Waller; Exec. Dir.; 713 Park Dr.; 45714; Washington; P 7,000; M 150; (740) 423-8934; Fax (740) 423-6616; info@belprechamber.com; belprechamber.com

Berea • *Berea C/C* • Megan Baechle; Exec. Dir.; 173 Front St.; 44017; Cuyahoga; P 19,500; M 175; (440) 243-8415; chamber@bereaohio.com; www.bereaohio.com

Beverly • *Beverly-Waterford Area C/C* • Elizabeth Stephens; Pres.; P.O. Box 908; 45715; Washington; P 2,300; M 76; (704) 984-8259; (704) 984-2381; estephens@thecitizens.com; www.bwchamber.org

Beverly • *Muskingum Valley Area C/C* • Glen Miller; Chrmn.; P.O. Box 837; 45715; Washington; P 61,000; M 150; (740) 984-8259; www.mvacc.com

Bexley • *Bexley Area C/C* • Colleen Krupp; Pres.; 2770 E. Main St., Ste. 5; 43209; Franklin; P 13,000; M 220; (614) 236-4500; info@bexleyareachamber.org; www.bexleyareachamber.org

Blanchester • *Blanchester Area C/C* • Chris Owens; Pres.; P.O. Box 274; 45107; Clinton; P 4,500; M 60; (937) 783-3601; owensch@oplin.org; www.blanchesterchamber.com

Bluffton • *Bluffton Area C/C* • Fred Steiner; CEO; P.O. Box 142; 45817; Allen & Hancock; P 4,100; M 169; (419) 369-2985; blufftonchamber@gmail.com; www.explorebluffton.com

Bowling Green • *Bowling Green C/C* • Earlene Kilpatrick; Exec. Dir.; 163 N. Main St.; P.O. Box 31; 43402; Wood; P 30,000; M 500; (419) 353-7945; Fax (419) 353-3693; chamber@bgchamber.net; www.bgchamber.net

Brecksville • *Brecksville C/C* • Rachel Torchia; Pres.; 49 Public Sq.; 44141; Cuyahoga; P 15,000; M 120; (440) 526-7350; Fax (440) 526-7889; chamber@brecksvillechamber.com; www.brecksvillechamber.com

Bremen • *Bremen C/C* • Connie S. Moyer; Pres.; P.O. Box 45; 43107; Fairfield; P 3,500; M 60; (740) 569-9150; bremencoc@gmail.com; www.bremenvillage.com

Bridgeport • *Bridgeport Area C/C* • Ann Gallagher; Exec. Dir.; P.O. Box 86; 43912; Belmont; P 1,850; M 60; (740) 635-3377; (740) 635-1244

Brimfield • *see Kent*

Broadview Heights • *Broadview Heights C/C* • Cheryle Costa; P.O. Box 470211; 44147; Cuyahoga; P 19,400; M 140; (440) 838-4510; office@broadviewhts.org; www.broadviewhts.org*

Brook Park • *Brook Park C/C* • Sharon Zimmer; Exec. Dir.; 17400 Holland Rd.; 44142; Cuyahoga; P 19,200; M 95; (216) 898-9755; Fax (216) 898-9755; bpchamber@sbcglobal.net; www.bpcoc.com

Brooklyn Heights • *see Independence*

Brookville • *Brookville Area C/C* • Rene Chase; Pres.; 245 Sycamore St.; P.O. Box 84; 45309; Montgomery; P 5,900; M 140; (937) 833-2375; Fax (937) 833-2375; admin@brookvilleareachamber.org; www.brookvilleareachamber.org

Brunswick • *Brunswick Area C/C* • Melissa Krebs; Pres./CEO; 1324 Pearl Rd. M2; 44212; Medina; P 35,000; M 270; (330) 225-8411; Fax (330) 273-8172; info@brunswickareachamber.org; www.brunswickareachamber.org*

Bryan • *Bryan Area C/C* • Daniel Yahraus; Exec. Dir.; 138 S. Lynn St.; 43506; Williams; P 8,500; M 325; (419) 636-2247; Fax (419) 636-5556; info@bryanchamber.org; www.bryanchamber.org*

Buckeye Lake • *The Buckeye Lake Region C/C* • Jodi Miller; P.O. Box 5; 43008; Fairfield, Licking & Perry; P 3,000; M 142; (740) 348-6293; jmiller@buckeyelakecc.com; www.buckeyelakecc.com

Bucyrus • *Bucyrus Area C/C* • Deb Pinion IOM; Exec. Dir.; 122 W. Rensselaer St.; 44820; Crawford; P 13,500; M 300; (419) 562-4811; Fax (419) 562-9966; bacc@bucyrusohio.com; www.bucyrusohio.com

Burton • *Burton C/C* • Brian Brockway; V.P.; P.O. Box 537; 44021; Geauga; P 4,500; M 200; (440) 834-4204; info@burtonchamberofcommerce.org; www.burtonchamberofcommerce.org

Butler • *see Vandalia*

Calcutta • *St. Clair Twp. C/C* • Debra Miller; Exec. Dir.; 15442 Pugh Rd.; 43920; Columbiana; P 10,000; M 72; (330) 386-6060; Fax (330) 386-6060; chamber@stclairtwp.com

Caldwell • *Noble County C/C & Tourism Bur.* • Jill R. McCartney IOM CCEO-AP; Exec. Dir.; 508 Main St.; P.O. Box 41; 43724; Noble; P 14,058; M 120; (740) 732-7715; Fax (740) 732-7646; jill@noblecountychamber.com; www.noblecountychamber.com

Cambridge • *Cambridge Area C/C* • Joanne Sexton; Pres.; 607 Wheeling Ave.; 43725; Guernsey; P 40,000; M 350; (740) 439-6688; Fax (740) 439-6689; info@cambridgeohiochamber.com; www.cambridgesupersite.com

Canal Fulton • *Canal Fulton Area C/C* • Kelly Gosiewski; Exec. Dir.; 116 N. Canal St.; P.O. Box 636; 44614; Stark; P 6,000; M 100; (330) 854-9095; Fax (330) 854-9095; cfcc@sssnet.com; www.canalfultonchamber.com

Canal Winchester • *Canal Winchester Area C/C* • Amanda Lemke; Pres.; 57 W. Waterloo St.; 43110; Fairfield & Franklin; P 8,000; M 300; (614) 837-1556; Fax (614) 837-9901; chamber@canalwinchester.com; www.canalwinchester.com*

Canal Winchester • *Southeastern Franklin County C/C* • Heather Bolin; Exec. Dir.; 6198 Meriden Ct.; 43110; Franklin; M 200; (614) 834-7700; Fax (614) 834-9185; chambersefc@gmail.com; www.chambersefc.com

Canton • *Canton Reg. C/C* • Dennis P. Saunier; Pres.; 222 Market Ave. N.W.; 44702; Stark; P 379,000; M 1,580; (330) 456-7253; (800) 533-4302; Fax (330) 452-7786; dennys@cantonchamber.org; www.cantonchamber.org

Carey • *Carey Area C/C* • Cassie Carlson; Exec. Dir.; 132 W. Findlay St.; P.O. Box 94; 43316; Wyandot; P 3,600; M 120; (419) 396-7856; director@careychamber.com; www.careychamber.com*

Carrollton • *Carroll County C/C & Eco. Dev.* • Amy Rutledge; Exec. Dir.; 61 N. Lisbon St.; P.O. Box 277; 44615; Carroll; P 28,800; M 227; (330) 627-4811; (800) 956-4684; Fax (330) 627-3647; carrollchamber@eohio.net; www.carrollohchamber.com

Celina • *Celina-Mercer County C/C* • Pam Buschur; Exec. Dir.; 226 N. Main St.; 45822; Mercer; P 40,471; M 390; (419) 586-2219; Fax (419) 586-8645; info@celinamercer.com; www.celinamercer.com*

Chagrin Falls • *Chagrin Valley C/C* • Darci Spilman; Exec. Dir.; 83 N. Main St.; 44022; Cuyahoga; P 15,000; M 430; (440) 247-6607; darci@cvcc.org; www.cvcc.org

Chardon • *Chardon Area C/C* • Erna Leagan-Mabel; Exec. Secy.; 111 South St.; 44024; Geauga; P 10,000; M 200; (440) 285-9050; Fax (440) 286-8964; emabel@chardonchamber.com; www.chardonchamber.com

Chesterland • *Chesterland C/C* • Melanie Reda; Co-Dir.; 8430 Mayfield Rd., Ste. 100; 44026; Geauga; P 11,100; M 225; (440) 729-7297; Fax (440) 729-2690; ccoc@chesterlandchamber.com; www.chesterlandchamber.com

Chillicothe • *Chillicothe Ross C/C* • Randy Davies; Pres./CEO; 45 E. Main St.; 45601; Ross; P 74,000; M 664; (740) 702-2722; Fax (740) 702-2727; rdavies@chillicotheohio.com; www.chillicotheohio.com*

Cincinnati Area

African American C/C - Greater Cincinnati & Northern KY • Sean Rugless; Pres./CEO; 2945 Gilbert Ave.; 45206; Hamilton; P 2,100,000; M 350; (513) 751-9900; Fax (513) 751-9100; info@african-americanchamber.com; african-americanchamber.com

Anderson Area C/C • Eric Miller; Exec. Dir.; 7850 Five Mile Rd.; 45230; Hamilton; P 44,000; M 500; (513) 474-4802; Fax (513) 474-4857; info@andersonareachamber.org; www.andersonareachamber.org

Cincinnati USA Reg. Chamber • Brian Carley; Pres./CEO; 441 Vine St., Ste. 300, Carew Tower; 45202; Hamilton; P 2,100,000; M 6,000; (513) 579-3100; Fax (513) 579-3101; info@cincinnatichamber.com; www.cincinnatichamber.com

Clermont C/C • Matthew Van Sant; Pres./CEO; 4355 Ferguson Dr., Ste. 150; 45245; Clermont; P 197,400; M 1,100; (513) 576-5000; Fax (513) 576-5001; chamber@clermontchamber.com; www.clermontchamber.com*

Hamilton County C/C • J. Gruber; Exec. Dir.; P.O. Drawer 42250; 45242; Hamilton; P 1,700,000; M 1,200; (513) 984-6555; Fax (513) 793-1063; hccc@fuse.net

Over-the-Rhine C/C • Brian Tiffany; Pres.; 111 E. 13th St.; 45202; Hamilton; P 7,000; M 260; (513) 241-2690; Fax (513) 241-6770; otrchamber@zoomtown.com; www.otrchamber.com

Circleville • *Pickaway County C/C* • Amy Elsea; Pres./CEO; 325 W. Main St.; 43113; Pickaway; P 53,000; M 300; (740) 474-4923; Fax (740) 477-6800; chamber@pickaway.com; www.pickaway.com*

Clermont County • *see Cincinnati-Clermont C/C*

Cleveland • *Greater Cleveland Partnership* • Joe Roman; Pres./CEO; 1240 Huron Rd. E., Ste. 300; 44115; Cuyahoga; P 2,871,000; M 16,000; (216) 621-3300; (888) 304-GROW; Fax (216) 621-6013; customerservice@gcpartnership.com; www.gcpartnership.com

Cleveland • *Greater Cleveland African American C/C* • Shirley A. Stevens; Pres./Exec. Dir.; 3775 E. 131st St., Unit 3; 44120; Cuyahoga; P 2,871,000; M 500; (216) 624-5119; estevensii@aol.com; www.gcaaccs.com

Coldwater • *Coldwater Area C/C* • Deb Post; Pres.; P.O. Box 57; 45828; Mercer; P 4,427; M 150; (419) 678-4882; info@coldwaterchamberofcommerce.com; www.coldwaterchamberofcommerce.com

Columbiana • *Columbiana Area C/C* • David Barbee; V.P.; 328 N. Main St.; 44408; Columbiana; P 6,400; M 199; (330) 482-3822; Fax (330) 482-3960; info@columbianachamber.com; www.columbianachamber.com

Columbus Area

Clintonville Area C/C • Jenny Smith; Pres.; 11 W. Cooke Rd., Ste. 5; 43214; Franklin; P 30,000; M 300; (614) 262-2790; Fax (614) 262-2791; jenny@clintonvillechamber.com; www.clintonvillechamber.com

Grandview Area Chamber • Michelle Wilson; Exec. Dir.; 1305 Holly Ave.; 43212; Franklin; P 7,000; M 300; (614) 486-0196; mwilson@grandviewchamber.org; www.grandviewchamber.org*

Greater Columbus C/C • Michael Dalby CCE; Pres./CEO; 150 S. Front St., Ste. 200; 43215; Franklin; P 1,160,000; M 2,300; (614) 221-1321; Fax (614) 221-1408; tracy_bloom@columbus.org; www.columbus.org*

Columbus Grove • *Columbus Grove Area C/C* • Alicia Langhals; Pres.; 424 E. Sycamore, Ste. 6; 45830; Putnam; P 2,200; M 65; (419) 302-2258; (419) 235-1196; www.columbusgrove.org

Conneaut • *Conneaut Area C/C* • Wendy M. DuBey; Exec. Dir.; 235 Main St.; 44030; Ashtabula; P 12,000; M 200; (440) 593-2402; Fax (440) 599-1514; conneautchamber@suite224.net; www.conneautchamber.org

Coshocton • *Coshocton County C/C* • Amy Stockdale; Exec. Dir.; 200 N. Whitewoman St.; 43812; Coshocton; P 37,000; M 300; (740) 622-5411; amystockdale@coshoctonchamber.com; www.coshoctonchamber.com

Covington • *Covington Area C/C* • Esther Alspaugh; Pres.; P.O. Box 183; 45318; Miami; P 2,600; M 90; covingtonchambersecretary@gmail.com; www.covingtonohiochamber.com

Crestline • *see Galion*

Cuyahoga Falls • *Cuyahoga Falls C/C* • Laura A. Petrella; CEO; 151 Portage Trl., Ste. 1; 44221; P 50,000; M 300; (330) 929-6756; Fax (330) 929-4278; info@cfchamber.com; www.cfchamber.com

Dalton • *Dalton Area C/C* • Dan Hostetler; Pres.; P.O. Box 168; 44618; Wayne; P 2,000; M 76; (330) 201-1438; daltonohchamber@gmail.com; www.daltonohchamber.com

Dayton • *Dayton Area C/C* • Phillip L. Parker CAE CCE; Pres./CEO; 22 E. Fifth St., Chamber Plaza; 45402; Montgomery; P 970,000; M 2,600; (937) 226-1444; Fax (937) 226-8254; mbostick@dacc.org; www.daytonchamber.org*

Dayton • *South Metro Reg. C/C* • Julia Maxton; Pres.; 683 Miamisburg Centerville Rd., Ste. 210; 45449; Montgomery; P 30,000; M 850; (937) 433-2032; Fax (937) 433-6881; info@smrcoc.org; www.smrcoc.org

Defiance • *Defiance Area C/C* • Isaac Lee; Pres.; 325 Clinton St.; 43512; Defiance; P 40,000; M 450; (419) 782-7946; Fax (419) 782-0111; isaaclee@defiancechamber.com; www.defiancechamber.com*

Delaware • *Delaware Area C/C* • Holly Quaine; Pres.; 32 S. Sandusky St.; 43015; Delaware; P 110,000; M 420; (740) 369-6221; Fax (740) 369-4817; dachamber@delawareareachamber.com; www.delawareareachamber.com*

Delphos • *Delphos Area C/C* • Tara Krendl; Exec. Dir.; 310 N. Main St.; 45833; Allen & Van Wert; P 7,000; M 225; (419) 695-1771; Fax (419) 692-1751; info@delphoschamber.com; www.delphoschamber.com*

Delta • *Delta C/C* • Lindsay Willman; Admin. Asst.; P.O. Box 96; 43515; Fulton; P 3,000; M 65; (419) 822-3089; Fax (419) 822-3089; deltachambercommerce@gmail.com

Dennison • *see Uhrichsville*

Deshler • *Deshler C/C* • Deb Jackson; Secy./Treas.; P.O. Box 123; 43516; Henry; P 1,800; M 95; (419) 601-2255; inforequest@deshlerohiochamber.com; www.deshlerohiochamber.com

Dublin • *Dublin C/C* • Margery S. Amorose; Exec. Dir.; 129 S. High St.; 43017; Franklin; P 40,000; M 1,200; (614) 889-2001; Fax (614) 889-2888; info@dublinchamber.org; www.dublinchamber.org*

East Liverpool • *Southern Columbiana County Reg. Chamber* • Leigh Ann Alexander; Exec. Dir.; 529 Market St.; P.O. Box 94; 43920; Columbiana; P 12,500; M 125; (330) 385-0845; Fax (330) 385-0581; office@sccregionalchamber.org; www.sccregionalchamber.org

East Palestine • *East Palestine Area C/C* • Tim Weigle; Pres.; 15 S. Market St.; P.O. Box 329; 44413; Columbiana; P 4,750; M 89; (330) 426-2128; contactme@eastpalestinechamber.com; www.eastpalestinechamber.com

East Toledo • *see Oregon*

Eastlake • *see Willoughby*

Eaton • *Preble County C/C* • Matt Owen; Exec. Dir.; 122 W. Decatur St.; P.O. Box 303; 45320; Preble; P 43,000; M 240; (937) 456-4949; Fax (937) 456-4949; chamberoffices@preblecountyohio.com; www.preblecountyohio.com

Edgerton • *Edgerton C/C* • Susan Herman; Pres.; c/o 113 N. Michigan Ave.; 43517; Williams; P 2,000; M 75; (419) 298-0100; edgertonohchamber@gmail.com; www.edgerton-ohio.com

Edon • *Edon Area C/C* • Jim Whitman; P.O. Box 19; 43518; Williams; P 700; M 45; (419) 272-2331; www.edon-ohio.com

Elyria • *Lorain County C/C* • Tony Gallo; Pres.; 226 Middle Ave., 5th Flr.; 44035; Lorain; P 301,400; M 600; (440) 328-2550; Fax (440) 328-2557; agallo@loraincountychamber.com; www.loraincountychamber.com

Englewood • *Northmont Area C/C* • Cathy Hutton; CEO; 9 W. National Rd.; P.O. Box 62; 45322; Montgomery; P 35,000; M 250; (937) 836-2550; Fax (937) 836-2485; cathy@northmontchamber.com; www.northmontchamber.com

Euclid • *Euclid C/C* • Sheila Gibbons; Exec. Dir.; P.O. Box 32611; 44132; Cuyahoga; P 49,000; M 200; (216) 731-9322; Fax (216) 865-4925; info@euclidchamber.com; www.euclidchamber.com

Fairborn • *Fairborn Area C/C* • Paul Newman Jr.; Exec. Dir.; 12 N. Central Ave.; 45324; Greene; P 33,000; M 428; (937) 878-3191; (937) 546-3191; Fax (937) 878-3197; chamber@fairborn.com; www.fairborn.com*

Fairfield • *Fairfield C/C* • Kert Radel; Pres./CEO; 670 Wessel Dr.; 45014; Butler; P 42,600; M 504; (513) 881-5500; Fax (513) 881-5503; president@fairfieldchamber.com; www.fairfieldchamber.com*

Fairlawn • *Fairlawn Area C/C* • Polly Riffle; Exec. Dir.; P.O. Box 13388; 44334; Summit; P 7,450; M 350; (330) 777-0032; Fax (330) 777-0032; info@fairlawnareachamber.org; www.fairlawnareachamber.org

Fayette • *Fayette Area C/C* • Tom Spiess; P.O. Box 8; 43521; Fulton; P 1,300; M 45; (419) 237-2116; www.villageoffayette.com

Findlay • *Findlay-Hancock County C/C* • Dionne K. Neubauer IOM; Dir.; 123 E. Main Cross St.; 45840; Hancock; P 75,000; M 650; (419) 422-3313; Fax (419) 422-9508; info@findlayhancockchamber.com; www.findlayhancockchamber.com*

Fort Recovery • *Fort Recovery C/C* • Roberta Staugler; Treas.; P.O. Box 671; 45846; Mercer; P 1,430; M 75; (419) 375-1056; Fax (419) 375-4709; frinfo@fortrecovery.org; www.fortrecovery.org

Fostoria • *Fostoria Area C/C* • Pamela Smith; Dir.; 121 N. Main St.; 44830; Seneca; P 14,000; M 275; (419) 435-0486; Fax (419) 435-0936; chamberfost@aol.com; www.fostoriachamber.com*

Franklin • *Franklin Area C/C* • Peggy Darragh-Jeromos; Exec. Dir.; 1200 E. Second St., Ste. B; P.O. Box 721; 45005; Warren; P 27,800; M 220; (937) 746-8457; chamber45005@gmail.com; www.chamber45005.org

Fremont • *C/C of Sandusky County* • Jill Simpson; Pres./CEO; 215 Croghan St.; 43420; Sandusky; P 61,000; M 350; (419) 332-1591; Fax (419) 332-8666; info@scchamber.org; www.scchamber.org*

Gahanna • *Gahanna Area C/C* • Leslee Blake; Pres.; 81 Mill St., Ste. 300; 43230; Franklin; P 34,000; M 410; (614) 471-0451; Fax (614) 471-5122; info@gahannaareachamber.com; www.gahannaareachamber.com*

Galion • *Galion-Crestline Area C/C* • Joe Kleinknecht; Pres./CEO; 138 Harding Way W.; 44833; Crawford; P 12,000; M 300; (419) 468-7737; Fax (419) 462-5487; ceo@galion-crestlinechamber.org; www.galion-crestlinechamber.org*

Gallipolis • *Gallia County C/C* • Michelle Miller; Exec. Dir.; 16 State St.; P.O. Box 465; 45631; Gallia; P 30,000; M 193; (740) 446-0596; Fax (740) 446-7031; mmiller@galliacounty.org; www.galliacounty.org

Garfield Heights • *Garfield Heights C/C* • Gabriella Huszarik; Exec. Dir.; 5522 Turney Rd.; 44125; Cuyahoga; P 31,000; M 211; (216) 475-7775; Fax (216) 475-2237; info@garfieldchamber.com; www.garfieldchamber.com

Garrettsville • *Garrettsville Area C/C* • Hallie Higgins; 8309 Center St.; P.O. Box 1; 44231; Portage; P 3,000; M 132; (330) 527-2411; patricks@apk.net; www.garrettsvillearea.com

Geneva • *Geneva Area C/C* • Sue Ellen Foote; Exec. Dir.; 866 E. Main St.; P.O. Box 84; 44041; Ashtabula; P 26,000; M 300; (440) 466-8694; Fax (440) 466-0823; info@genevachamber.org; www.genevachamber.org

Geneva-on-the-Lake • *Geneva-on-the-Lake C/ C & CVB* • Tim Mills; Pres. of Bd.; 5540 Lake Rd.; 44041; Ashtabula; P 1,600; M 100; (440) 466-8600; (800) 862-9948; Fax (440) 466-8911; penny@visitgenevaonthelake.com; www.visitgenevaonthelake.com

Genoa • *Genoa Area C/C* • Timothy A. Davies; P.O. Box 141; 43430; Ottawa; P 3,000; M 175; (419) 855-7761; media@genoachamber.com; www.genoachamber.com

Georgetown • *Brown County C/C* • Brian Elliott; Pres.; P.O. Box 21606; 45121; Brown; P 45,000; M 183; (937) 378-4784; Fax (937) 378-1634; brchcom@gmail.com; www.browncountyohiochamber.com*

Germantown • *Germantown C/C* • Jeff Fannin; Pres.; P.O. Box 212; 45327; Montgomery; P 8,500; M 50; (937) 855-3471; germantownchamber@gmail.com; www.germantown.oh.us

Girard • *Greater Girard Area C/C* • Jeff Kay; Pres.; 16 W. Liberty; 44420; Trumble; P 10,000; M 75; (330) 545-8108; www.cityofgirard.com

Grand Rapids • *Grand Rapids Area C/C* • P.O. Box 391; 43522; Wood; P 1,200; M 50; (419) 832-1106; Fax (419) 832-1106; information@grandrapidsohio.com; www.grandrapidsohio.com

Granville • *Granville Area C/C* • Steve Matheny; Exec. Dir.; 125 E. Broadway; P.O. Box 603; 43023; Licking; P 5,000; M 250; (740) 587-4490; Fax (740) 587-4490; chamber@granvilleoh.com; www.granvilleoh.com

Greentown • *see Hartville*

Greenville • *Darke County C/C* • Sharon Deschambeau; Pres.; 209 E. Fourth St.; 45331; Darke; P 53,309; M 300; (937) 548-2102; Fax (937) 548-5608; info@darkecountyohio.com; www.darkecountyohio.com*

Greenwich • *see Willard*

Grove City • *Grove City Area C/C* • Shawn Conrad; Exec. Dir.; 4069 Broadway; 43123; Franklin; P 35,000; M 550; (614) 875-9762; (877) 870-5393; Fax (614) 875-1510; e.dir@gcchamber.org; www.gcchamber.org*

Hamilton • *Greater Hamilton C/C* • Scott Ellsworth; Interim Pres./CEO; 201 Dayton St.; 45011; Butler; P 62,500; M 600; (513) 844-1500; Fax (513) 844-1999; www.hamilton-ohio.com*

Hartville • *Lake Township C/C* • Christa Kozy; Pres./CEO; P.O. Box 1207; 44632; Stark; P 25,000; M 175; (330) 877-5500; Fax (330) 877-2149; president@lakechamber.com; www.lakechamber.com

Hicksville • *Hicksville Area C/C* • Angie Freese; Pres.; P.O. Box 244; 43526; Defiance; P 3,500; M 94; (419) 542-6912; Fax (419) 542-8046; chamber@hicksvillechamber.org; www.hicksvillechamber.org

Highland Hills • *see Warrensville Heights*

Hilliard • *Hilliard Area C/C* • Libby Gierach; Pres./CEO; 4081 Main St.; 43026; Franklin; P 25,000; M 400; (614) 876-7666; Fax (614) 876-3113; info@hilliardchamber.org; www.hilliardchamber.org*

Hillsboro • *Highland County C/C* • Terry Mull; Exec. Dir.; 1575 N. High St., Ste. 400; 45133; Highland; P 43,600; M 350; (937) 393-1111; Fax (937) 393-9604; info@highlandcountychamberoh.com; www.highlandcountychamber.com*

Hinckley • *Hinckley C/C* • Martha Catherwood; P.O. Box 354; 44233; Medina; P 6,600; M 35; (330) 278-2066; (330) 416-3629; Fax (330) 225-0239; www.hinckleyohchamber.com

Holland • *Holland/Springfield C/C* • Pat Hicks; Pres./CEO; 7350 Airport Hwy., Ste. 10; 43528; Lucas; P 26,000; M 280; (419) 865-2110; Fax (419) 865-3740; info@hollandspringfieldcoc.org; www.hollandspringfieldcoc.org*

Hubbard • *Hubbard Area C/C* • Beverly Scott; Admin. Asst.; 105 N. Main St.; P.O. Box 177; 44425; Trumbull; P 16,700; M 70; (330) 534-5120; hubbardcofc@yahoo.com; www.hubbardchamber.org

Huber Heights • *Huber Heights C/C* • Mark Burns; Exec. Dir.; 4707 Brandt Pike; P.O. Box 24006; 45424; Greene, Miami & Montgomery; P 40,000; M 300; (937) 233-5700; Fax (937) 233-5769; chamber.director@hubercc.com; huberheightschamber.com*

Hudson • *Hudson Area C/C* • Carolyn Konefal; Exec. Dir.; 245 N. Main St., Ste. 100; 44236; Summit; P 22,300; M 300; (330) 650-0621; Fax (330) 656-1646; info@hudsoncoc.org; www.explorehudson.com

Huron • *Huron C/C* • Sheila Ehrhardt; Dir.; 509 Huron St.; P.O. Box 43; 44839; Erie; P 10,000; M 285; (419) 433-5700; Fax (419) 433-5700; chamber@huron.net; www.huron.net*

Independence • *Cuyahoga Valley C/C* • April Acuna; Exec. Dir.; P.O. Box 31326; 44131; Cuyahoga; P 39,600; M 200; (216) 573-2707; info@cuyahogavalleychamber.com; www.cuyahogavalleychamber.com

Ironton • *see South Point*

Jackson • *Jackson Area C/C* • Randy Heath; Exec. Dir.; 234 Broadway St.; 45640; Jackson; P 6,400; M 275; (740) 286-2722; Fax (740) 286-8443; rheath@zoomnet.net; www.jacksonohio.org

Jackson Twp. • *Jackson-Belden C/C* • Steven M. Meeks; Pres.; 5735 Wales Ave. N.W.; 44646; Stark; P 42,500; M 800; (330) 833-4400; Fax (330) 833-4456; info@jbcc.org; www.jbcc.org*

Jamestown • *Jamestown Area C/C* • Jim Saner; Pres.; P.O. Box 66; 45335; Greene; P 3,700; M 60; (937) 675-7292; jim@jtchamber.com; www.jtchamber.com

Jefferson • *Jefferson Area C/C* • Pat Bradek; Pres.; P.O. Box 100; 44047; Ashtabula; P 3,600; M 120; (440) 576-0133; Fax (440) 576-4352; membership@jeffersonchamber.com; www.jeffersonchamber.com

Jerusalem • *see Oregon*

Kelleys Island • *Kelleys Island C/C* • Cindy Holmes; Co-Director; 240 E. Lakeshore Dr.; P.O. Box 783; 43438; Erie; P 2,000; M 130; (419) 746-2360; info@kelleysislandchamber.com; www.kelleysislandchamber.com

Kent • *Kent Area C/C* • Lori Wemhoff; Exec. Dir.; 176 E. Main St., Ste. 303; 44240; Portage; P 29,000; M 294; (330) 673-9855; lwemhoff@kentbiz.com; www.kentbiz.com

Kent • *Brimfield Area C/C* • Dee Pamer; Pres.; P.O. Box 1613; 44240; Portage; P 10,400; M 86; (330) 673-2170; windowbox7248@sbcglobal.net; www.brimfieldchamber.com

Kenton • *Hardin County Chamber & Bus. Alliance* • Jon Cross; Pres.; 225 S. Detroit St.; 43326; Hardin; P 31,000; M 320; (419) 673-4131; Fax (419) 674-4876; alliance@hccba.com; www.hccba.com*

Kettering • *Kettering-Moraine-Oakwood C/C* • Ann-Lisa Rucker; Pres.; 2977 Far Hills Ave.; 45419; Greene & Montgomery; P 80,000; M 875; (937) 299-3852; Fax (937) 299-3851; info@kmo-coc.org; www.kmo-coc.org

Lakewood • *Lakewood C/C* • Patricia L. Ryan; Pres./CEO; 16017 Detroit Ave.; 44107; Cuyahoga; P 56,000; M 350; (216) 226-2900; Fax (216) 226-1340; pryan@lakewoodchamber.org; www.lakewoodchamber.org

Lancaster • *Lancaster Fairfield County C/C* • Travis Markwood; Pres.; 109 N. Broad St., Ste. 100; P.O. Box 2450; 43130; Fairfield; P 136,000; M 625; (740) 653-8251; Fax (740) 653-7074; alicia@lancoc.org; www.lancoc.org*

Lawrence County • *see South Point*

Lebanon • *Lebanon Area C/C* • Sara Arseneau; Exec. Dir.; 212 N. Broadway, Ste. 2; 45036; Warren; P 24,000; M 400; (513) 932-1100; Fax (513) 932-9050; info@lebanonchamber.org; www.lebanonchamber.org*

Leipsic • *Leipsic Area C/C* • Roberta Howard; Pres.; 142 E. Main St.; 45856; Putnam; P 2,300; M 60; (419) 943-2009; rhoward@fairpoint.net; www.leipsic.net

Lewisburg • *Lewisburg Area C/C* • P.O. Box 436; 45338; P 2,000; M 25; (937) 962-4377; info@lewisburg.net; www.lewisburg.net

Lexington • *see Mansfield*

Lima • *Lima/Allen County C/C* • Jed E. Metzger; Pres./CEO; 144 S. Main St., Ste. 100; 45801; Allen; P 121,832; M 1,023; (419) 222-6045; Fax (419) 229-0266; chamber@limachamber.com; www.limachamber.com*

Lisbon • *Lisbon Area C/C* • Marilyn McCullough; Exec. Dir.; 120 N. Market St.; 44432; Columbiana; P 3,000; M 86; (330) 424-1803; Fax (330) 424-9003; lacoc2@sbcglobal.net; www.lisbonareachamber.com

Lodi • *Lodi Area C/C* • Cecelia Sivard; Pres.; P.O. Box 6; 44254; Medina; P 3,000; M 95; (330) 948-8047; info@lodiohiochamber.com; www.lodiohiochamber.com

Logan • *Logan-Hocking C/C* • Bill Rienhart; Exec. Dir.; 4 E. Hunter St.; P.O. Box 838; 43138; Hocking; P 29,000; M 250; (740) 385-6836; (800) 414-6731; Fax (740) 385-7259; lo-hockchamber@hocking.net; www.logan-hockingchamber.com

Logan County • *see Bellefontaine*

London • *Madison County C/C* • Sean Hughes; Exec. Dir.; 730 Keny Blvd.; 43140; Madison; P 44,000; M 300; (740) 852-2250; Fax (740) 852-5133; sean@madisoncountychamber.org; www.madisoncountychamber.org*

Lorain • *see Elyria*

Loudonville • *Loudonville-Mohican C/C* • Jeanne Leckrone; Ofc. Mgr.; 131 W. Main St.; 44842; Ashland; P 2,900; M 130; (419) 994-4789; Fax (419) 994-5950; jeanne@loudonville-mohican.com; www.loudonvillechamber.com

Louisville • *Louisville Area C/C* • Laura Krstevski; Chrmn.; P.O. Box 67; 44641; Stark; P 9,000; M 82; (330) 875-7371; Fax (330) 875-3839; louisvilleareachamber@gmail.com; www.louisvilleohchamber.org

Loveland • *Little Miami River Chamber Alliance* • CeeCee Collins; Pres./CEO; 123 S. Second St.; 45140; Clermont, Hamilton & Warren; P 20,000; M 275; (513) 683-1544; Fax (513) 683-5449; info@lmrchamberalliance.org; www.lmrchamberalliance.org*

Lyndhurst • *see Beachwood*

Madison • *Madison-Perry Area C/C* • Alice Cable; Pres.; 5965 N. Ridge Rd.; P.O. Box 4; 44057; Lake; P 35,000; M 300; (440) 428-3760; Fax (440) 428-6668; exec@mpacc.org; www.mpacc.org

Mansfield • *Richland Area C/C* • Jodie A. Perry IOM; Pres.; 55 N. Mulberry St.; 44902; Richland; P 124,500; M 1,000; (419) 522-3211; Fax (419) 526-6853; info@richlandareachamber.com; www.richlandareachamber.com*

Marblehead • *Marblehead Peninsula C/C* • Judy Balsom; Exec. Dir.; 5681 E. Harbor Rd., Ste. C; 43440; Ottawa; P 800; M 188; (419) 734-9777; Fax (419) 960-7206; info@themarbleheadpeninsula.com; www.themarbleheadpeninsula.com

Marietta • *Marietta Area C/C* • Charlotte Keim; Pres./CEO; The Riverview Bldg.; 100 Front St., Ste. 200; 45750; Washington; P 61,000; M 590; (740) 373-5176; Fax (740) 373-7808; info@mariettachamber.com; www.mariettachamber.com*

Marion • *Marion Area C/C* • Pamela S. Hall; Pres.; 267 W. Center St., Ste. 200; 43302; Marion; P 67,000; M 600; (740) 382-2181; Fax (740) 387-7722; phall@marionareachamber.org; www.marionareachamber.org*

Martins Ferry • *Martins Ferry Area C/C* • Dorothy Powell; Exec. Dir.; 108 S. Zane Hwy.; 43935; Belmont; P 7,200; M 98; (740) 633-2565; Fax (740) 633-2641; m.chamber@comcast.net; www.martinsferrychamber.com

Marysville • *Union County C/C* • Tina Knotts; Exec. Dir.; 227 E. Fifth St.; 43040; Union; P 53,000; M 517; (937) 642-6279; (800) 642-0087; Fax (937) 644-0422; chamber@unioncounty.org; www.unioncounty.org*

Mason • *Mason Deerfield Chamber* • Sherry Taylor; Pres./CEO; 316 W. Main St.; 45040; Warren; P 70; M 600; (513)-336-0125; Fax (513) 398-6371; info@madechamber.org; www.madechamber.org*

Massillon • *Massillon WestStark C/C* • Ted Herncane; Pres.; 137 Lincoln Way E.; 44646; Stark; P 32,300; M 375; (330) 833-3146; Fax (330) 833-8944; info@massillonohchamber.com; www.massillonohchamber.com

Maumee • *Maumee C/C* • Brenda Clixby; Exec. Dir.; 605 Conant St.; 43537; Lucas; P 15,752; M 450; (419) 893-5805; Fax (419) 893-8699; info@maumeechamber.com; www.maumeechamber.com*

Mayfield Heights • *Mayfield Area C/C* • 1284 SOM Ctr. Rd., Ste. 308; 44124; Cuyahoga; P 55,000; M 153; (216) 556-4598; jasspring@aol.com; www.mayfieldareachamber.org

McArthur • *Vinton County C/C* • Caleb Appleman; Mktg. Dir.; 104 W. Main St.; P.O. Box 307; 45651; Vinton; P 13,500; M 110; (740) 596-5033; (800) 596-4459; Fax (740) 596-9262; info@vintoncounty.com; www.vintoncounty.com

McConnelsville • *Morgan County C/C* • Amy Grove; Bd. Member; 155 E. Main St., Rm. 147; P.O. Box 508; 43756; Morgan; P 15,100; M 130; (740) 962-3200; (740) 962-4854; Fax (740) 962-6508; info@morgancounty.org; www.morgancounty.org

Medina • *Greater Medina C/C* • Heather Taylor; Exec. Dir.; 145 N. Court St.; 44256; Medina; P 30,000; M 500; (330) 723-8773; info@medinaohchamber.com; www.medinaohchamber.com

Mentor • *Mentor Area C/C* • Kevin Malecek; Pres./CEO; 6972 Spinach Dr.; 44060; Lake; P 52,000; M 650; (440) 255-1616; Fax (440) 255-1717; info@mentorchamber.org; www.mentorchamber.org

Miami Twp. • *see Milford*

Middleburg Heights • *Middleburg Heights C/C* • Doris J. Wroble; Exec. Dir.; 16000 Bagley Rd.; P.O. Box 30161; 44130; Cuyahoga; P 15,790; M 210; (440) 243-5599; Fax (440) 243-8660; info@middleburgheightschamber.com; www.middleburgheightschamber.com

Middlefield • *Middlefield C/C* • Lynnette Bramley; Exec. Dir.; P.O. Box 801; 44062; Geauga; P 2,500; M 100; (440) 632-5705; Fax (440) 632-5705; mccinfo@middlefieldcc.com; www.middlefieldcc.com

Middletown • *The C/C serving Middletown, Monroe & Trenton* • Rick Pearce; Pres./CEO; 1500 Central Ave.; 45044; Butler & Warren; P 125,000; M 450; (513) 422-4551; Fax (513) 422-6831; info@thechamberofcommerce.org; www.thechamberofcommerce.org*

Milan • *Milan C/C* • Anne Basilone-Jones; Secy.; P.O. Box 544; 44846; Erie; P 1,500; M 200; (419) 499-4909; Fax (419) 499-9004; secretary@milanohio.com; www.milanohio.com

Milford • *Milford-Miami Twp. C/C* • Karen Wikoff; CEO; 745 Center St., Ste. 302; 45150; Clermont & Hamilton; P 52,000; M 285; (513) 831-2411; Fax (513) 831-3547; karen@milfordmiamitownship.com; www.milfordmiamitownship.com

Millersburg • *Holmes County C/C & Tourism Bur.* • Shasta Mast; Exec. Dir.; 6 W. Jackson St., Ste. A; 44654; Holmes; P 40,000; M 400; (330) 674-3975; Fax (330) 674-3976; andrea@holmescountychamber.com; www.holmescountychamber.com

Minerva • *Minerva Area C/C* • Denise R. Freeland; Exec. Dir.; 203 N. Market St.; 44657; Carroll & Stark; P 10,000; M 104; (330) 862-3323; (330) 868-7979; denise.freeland@minervachamber.org; www.minervachamber.org

Minster • *see New Bremen*

Monroe • *see Middletown*

Montpelier • *Montpelier Area C/C* • Ms. Terry L. Buntain; Exec. Dir.; 410 W. Main St.; 43543; Williams; P 4,200; M 129; (419) 485-4416; Fax (419) 485-4416; macofc@frontier.com; www.montpelierchamber.com

Moraine • *see Kettering*

Morrow • *Little Miami Area C/C* • Norma Rayl; Secy.; P.O. Box 164; 45152; Warren; P 4,300; M 76; (513) 932-3299; Fax (513) 932-3299; info@lmachamber.com; www.lmachamber.com

Mount Gilead • *Morrow County C/C & Visitors Bur.* • Ann Tittle; CEO; 17 1/2 W. High St.; P.O. Box 174; 43338; Morrow; P 34,000; M 120; (419) 946-2821; Fax (419) 946-3861; director@morrowchamber.org; www.morrowchamber.org*

Mount Vernon • *Knox County C/C* • Carol Grubaugh; Exec. Dir.; 400 S. Gay St.; 43050; Knox; P 60,900; M 360; (740) 393-1111; Fax (740) 393-1590; chamber@knoxchamber.com; www.knoxchamber.com*

Munroe Falls • *see Stow*

Napoleon • *Henry County C/C* • Joel Miller; Pres.; 611 N. Perry St.; 43545; Henry; P 29,893; M 330; (419) 592-1786; Fax (419) 592-4945; hcncoc@ohiohenrycounty.com; www.henrycountychamber.org

Nelsonville • *Nelsonville Area C/C* • Dave Loge; Pres.; P.O. Box 276; 45764; Athens; P 5,444; M 122; (740) 753-4346; info@nelsonvillechamber.com; www.nelsonvillechamber.com

New Albany • *New Albany C/C* • Courtney Orr; Exec. Dir.; 55 W. Main St.; P.O. Box 202; 43054; Franklin; P 8,000; M 500; (614) 855-4400; Fax (614) 855-4446; director@newalbanychamber.com; www.newalbanychamber.com

New Bremen • *Southwestern Auglaize County C/C* • Scott M. Frey; Exec. Dir.; 22 S. Water St.; P.O. Box 3; 45869; Auglaize; P 7,000; M 300; (419) 629-0313; Fax (419) 629-0411; info@auglaize.org; www.auglaize.org

New Carlisle • *New Carlisle Area C/C* • Linda Campbell; 131 S. Main St.; 45344; Clark; P 12,000; M 35; (937) 845-3911; www.newcarlisle.net

New Concord • *New Concord Area Bd. of Trade* • Jeremy Morrow; Dir.; 1 W. Main St.; 43762; Muskingum; P 3,000; M 150; (740) 826-7676; Fax (740) 826-4500; jmorrow@centurynationalbank.com; www.ncboardoftrade.com

New Lexington • *Perry County C/C* • John Ulmer; Exec. Dir.; 121 S. Main St.; 43764; Perry; P 36,058; M 175; (740) 342-3547; Fax (740) 342-9124; pcccofc@yahoo.com; www.perrycountyohiochamber.com

New Paris • *New Paris Area C/C* • Dale Hall; Pres.; P.O. Box 101; 45347; Preble; P 1,500; M 65; (937) 621-9533; info@newparisoh.com; www.newparisoh.com

New Philadelphia • *Tuscarawas County C/C* • Scott Robinson; Pres./CEO; 1323 Fourth St. N.W.; 44663; Tuscarawas; P 90,000; M 600; (330) 343-4474; Fax (330) 343-6526; info@tuschamber.com; www.tuschamber.com*

Newark • *Licking County C/C* • Cheri Hottinger; Pres.; 50 W. Locust St.; P.O. Box 702; 43058; Licking; P 154,000; M 725; (740) 345-9757; Fax (740) 345-5141; chottinger@lickingcountychamber.com; www.lickingcountychamber.com

Newcomerstown • *Newcomerstown C/C* • Gary Chaney; P.O. Box 456; 43832; Tuscarawas; P 7,800; M 100; (740) 498-7244; Fax (740) 498-6310; gjc@sota-oh.com; www.newcomerstownoh.com

Niles • *see Youngstown*

North Baltimore • *North Baltimore Area C/C* • Jaimye Bushey; Pres.; 124 E. Broadway; P.O. Box 284; 45872; Wood; P 4,200; M 55; (419) 257-3523; (419) 257-3514; Fax (419) 257-2107; info@nbacc.org; www.nbacc.org

North Canton • *North Canton Area C/C* • Doug Lane; Pres.; 121 S. Main St.; 44720; Stark; P 17,500; M 400; (330) 499-5100; Fax (330) 499-7181; info@northcantonchamber.org; www.northcantonchamber.org*

North Olmsted • *North Olmsted C/C* • John Sobolewski; Exec. Dir.; 28938 Lorain Rd., Ste. 204; 44070; Cuyahoga; P 32,800; M 250; (440) 777-3368; Fax (440) 777-9361; nocc@nolmstedchamber.org; www.nolmstedchamber.org

North Randall • *see Warrensville Heights*

North Ridgeville • *North Ridgeville C/C* • Dayle Noll; Pres./CEO; 34845 Lorain Rd.; 44039; Lorain; P 32,000; M 200; (440) 327-3737; Fax (440) 327-1474; nrcoc@nrchamber.com; www.nrchamber.com*

North Royalton • *North Royalton C/C* • Maria Magnelli; Exec. Dir.; 13737 State Rd.; P.O. Box 33122; 44133; Cuyahoga; P 30,400; M 220; (440) 237-6180; Fax (440) 237-6181; rrnews@aol.com; www.nroyaltonchamber.com

Northfield • *Nordonia Hills C/C* • Laura Sparano; Exec. Dir.; P.O. Box 34; 44067; Summit; P 25,000; M 310; (330) 467-8956; Fax (330) 468-4901; laura@nordoniahillschamber.org; www.nordoniahillschamber.org*

Northwood • *see Oregon*

Norwalk • *Huron County C/C* • Melissa James; Exec. Dir.; 10 W. Main St.; 44857; Huron; P 60,000; M 480; (419) 668-4155; Fax (419) 663-6173; chamber@huroncountyohio.com; www.huroncountychamber.com

Norwood • *Norwood C/C* • Kathy Walters; Exec. Dir.; P.O. Box 12144; 45212; Hamilton; P 19,200; M 110; (513) 956-7935; Fax (513) 741-8778; kathy@norwoodchamberofcommerce.org; www.norwoodchamberofcommerce.org

Oak Harbor • *Oak Harbor Area C/C* • Valerie Winterfield; Exec. Dir.; 161 W. Water St., Ste. A; 43449; Ottawa; P 3,000; M 158; (419) 898-0479; Fax (419) 898-2429; chamber@oakharborohio.net; www.oakharborohio.net

Oak Hill • *Oak Hill Area C/C* • Kurtis Strickland; Pres.; P.O. Box 354; 45656; Jackson; P 2,700; M 100; (740) 682-3021; info@oakhillchamber.org; www.oakhillchamber.org

Oakwood • *see Kettering*

Oberlin • *Oberlin Bus. Partnership* • Janet K. Haar; Exec. Dir.; 23 E. College St.; 44074; Lorain; P 8,000; M 110; (440) 774-6262; Fax (888) 812-8419; director@oberlin.org; www.oberlin.org

Olmsted Falls • *Olmsted C/C* • Mark Hannah; Pres.; 25630 Bagley Road; P.O. Box 38043; 44138; Cuyahoga; P 9,000; M 82; (440) 235-0032; director@olmstedchamber.org; www.olmstedchamber.org

Oregon • *Eastern Maumee Bay C/C* • Yvonne Thoma-Patton; Exec. Dir.; 4350 Navarre Ave., Ste. C; 43616; Lucas; P 43,616; M 200; (419) 693-5580; director@embchamber.org; www.embchamber.org

Orrville • *Orrville Area C/C* • Lori Reinbolt; Pres.; 132 S. Main St.; 44667; Wayne; P 8,500; M 260; (330) 682-8881; Fax (330) 682-8383; chamberoffice@orrvillechamber.com; www.orrvillechamber.com

Orwell • *Orwell-Grand Valley Area C/C* • Gary Hunter; P.O. Box 261; 44076; Ashtabula; P 4,800; M 75; (440) 437-5782; orwellgv@fairpoint.net; www.orwellgvchamber.org

Ottawa • *Ottawa Area C/C* • Amy Sealts; Exec. Dir.; 129 Court St.; P.O. Box 68; 45875; Putnam; P 4,460; M 270; (419) 523-3141; Fax (419) 523-5860; ottawachamber@earthlink.net; ottawachamber.org

Ottoville • *Ottoville Area C/C* • P.O. Box 275; 45876; Putnam; P 900; M 69; (419) 453-3636; ottoville@villageofottoville.org; ottovillechamber.com

Oxford • *Oxford C/C* • Kelli Riggs; Pres.; 30 W. Park Pl., 2nd Flr.; 45056; Butler; P 26,000; M 230; (513) 523-5200; Fax (513) 523-2308; president@oxfordchamber.org; www.oxfordchamber.org

Painesville • *Painesville Area C/C* • Linda Reed; Exec. Dir.; One Victoria Sq., Ste. 265A; 44077; Lake; P 50,000; M 420; (440) 357-7572; Fax (440) 357-8752; office@painesvilleohchamber.org; www.painesvilleohchamber.org

Pandora • *Pandora Area C/C* • Stan Schneck; Secy./Village Admin.; P.O. Box 193; 45877; Putnam; P 1,188; M 20; (419) 384-7600; villageadministrator@bright.net; www.pandoraoh.com

Parma • *Parma Area C/C* • David Nedrich; Pres./CEO; 5790 Ridge Rd.; 44129; Cuyahoga; P 120,000; M 400; (440) 886-1700; Fax (440) 886-1770; chamber@parmaareachamber.org; www.parmaareachamber.org

Parma Heights • *see Parma*

Pataskala • *Pataskala Area C/C* • Diane Grove; Ofc. Admin.; P.O. Box 132; 43062; Licking; P 15,000; M 200; (740) 964-6100; PACC132@embarqmail.com; www.pataskalachamber.com

Paulding • *Paulding C/C* • Peggy Emerson; Exec. Dir.; 220 N. Main St., Lower Level; P.O. Box 237; 45879; Paulding; P 20,000; M 128; (419) 399-5215; pauldingchamber@gmail.com; www.pauldingchamber.com

Perrysburg • *Perrysburg Area C/C* • Sandy Latchem; Exec. Dir.; 105 W. Indiana Ave.; 43551; Wood; P 28,000; M 300; (419) 874-9147; Fax (419) 872-9347; director@perrysburgchamber.com; www.perrysburgchamber.com

Picaway County • *see Circleville*

Pickerington • *Pickerington Area C/C* • Helen Mayle; Pres.; 13 W. Columbus St.; 43147; Fairfield; P 30,000; M 425; (614) 837-1958; Fax (614) 837-6420; president@pickeringtonchamber.com; www.pickeringtonchamber.com*

Pioneer • *Pioneer Area C/C* • Jim Fee; P.O. Box 633; 43554; Williams; P 1,500; M 80; (419) 737-2614; Fax (419) 737-2066; pioneerchamber@hotmail.com; www.pioneerchamber.com

Piqua • *Piqua Area C/C* • Kathy Sherman; Pres.; 326 N. Main; P.O. Box 1142; 45356; Miami; P 22,000; M 400; (937) 773-2765; Fax (937) 773-8553; k.sherman@piquaareachamber.com; www.piquaareachamber.com*

Plymouth • *see Willard*

Pomeroy • *Meigs County C/C* • Luke Ortman; Exec. Dir.; 238 W. Main St.; 45769; Megis; P 23,700; M 160; (740) 992-5005; Fax (740) 992-7922; luke@meigscountychamber.com; www.meigscountychamber.com

Port Clinton • *Port Clinton Area C/C* • Laura Schlachter; Pres./CEO; 110 Madison St.; 43452; Ottawa; P 6,300; M 464; (419) 734-5503; Fax (419) 734-4768; admin@portclintonchamber.com; www.portclintonchamber.com*

Portsmouth • *Portsmouth Area C/C* • Lisa Carver; Exec. Dir.; 342 2nd St.; P.O. Box 509; 45662; Scioto; P 89,000; M 475; (740) 353-7647; Fax (740) 353-5824; lcarver@portsmouth.org; www.portsmouth.org

Powell • *Greater Powell Area C/C* • Nancy Buckley; Exec. Dir.; 50 S. Liberty St., Ste. 170; 43065; Delaware; P 20,000; M 250; (614) 888-1090; Fax (614) 888-4803; admin@powellchamber.com; www.powellchamber.com

Put-In-Bay • *Put-In-Bay C/C & Visitors Bur.* • Maggie Beckford; Exec. Dir.; 148 Delaware Ave.; P.O. Box 250; 43456; Ottawa; P 550; M 185; (419) 285-2832; maggie@visitputinbay.com; visitputinbay.com

Ravenna • *Ravenna Area C/C* • Jack Ferguson; Exec. Dir.; 135 E. Main St.; 44266; Portage; P 12,000; M 150; (330) 296-3886; Fax (330) 296-6986; ravennachamber@att.net; www.ravennaareachamber.com

Reading • *Reading C/C* • Kathy Walters; Admin. Dir.; P.O. Box 15164; 45215; Hamilton; P 10,500; M 100; (513) 741-7951; (513) 786-7274; Fax (513) 741-8778; mkwalters@cinci.rr.com; www.readingohiochamber.org

Reynoldsburg • *Reynoldsburg Area C/C* • Jan Hills; Pres./CEO; 1580 Brice Rd.; 43068; Fairfield, Franklin & Licking; P 35,000; M 335; (614) 866-4753; Fax (614) 866-7313; jan@reynoldsburgchamber.com; www.reynoldsburgchamber.com*

Richland • *see Mansfield*

Richmond Heights • *see Beachwood*

Rittman • *Rittman Area C/C* • Tina Gienger; Exec. Dir.; 12 N. Main St., Ste. 2; 44270; Wayne; P 6,500; M 95; (330) 925-4828; Fax (330) 925-4828; rittmanchamber@ohio.net; www.rittmanchamber.com

Riverside • *Riverside Area C/C* • Brett Domescik; Chrmn.; 5100 Springfield Pk., Ste. 105; 45431; Montgomery; P 35,000; M 50; (937) 253-5674; Fax (937) 253-7693; chairman@riversidechamber.com; www.riversidechamber.com

Rockford • *Rockford C/C* • Jane Cozad; Pres.; P.O. Box 175; 45882; Mercer; P 1,120; M 75; (419) 363-3032; www.rockfordalive.com

Rocky River • *Rocky River C/C* • Liz Manning; Exec. Dir.; 19543 Center Ridge Rd.; 44116; Cuyahoga; P 20,500; M 400; (440) 331-1140; Fax (440) 331-3485; info@rockyriverchamber.com; www.rockyriverchamber.com*

Rootstown • *Rootstown Area C/C* • P.O. Box 254; 44272; Portage; P 7,200; M 107; president@rootstownchamber.org; www.rootstownchamber.org

Russells Point • *Indian Lake Area C/C* • Pam Miller; Exec. Dir.; 8200 State Rte. 366, Ste. D; P.O. Box 717; 43348; Logan; P 14,500; M 425; (937) 843-5392; Fax (937) 843-9051; office@indianlakechamber.org; www.indianlakechamber.org

Saint Bernard • *Saint Bernard C/C* • Bob Sawtell; Pres.; 110 Washington Ave.; 45217; Hamilton; P 4,600; M 2; (513) 242-7770; Fax (513) 641-1840; www.cityofstbernard.org

Saint Clairsville • *St. Clairsville Area C/C* • Jennifer Woollard; Exec. Dir.; 133 E. Main St.; 43950; Belmont; P 12,600; M 375; (740) 695-9623; Fax (740) 695-4280; info@stcchamber.com; www.stcchamber.com

Salem • *Salem Area C/C* • Audrey C. Null; Exec. Dir.; 713 E. State St.; 44460; Columbiana; P 16,000; M 365; (330) 337-3473; Fax (330) 337-3474; acnull@salemohiochamber.org; www.salemohiochamber.org*

Sandusky • *Erie County C/C* • Pamela Smith; Pres.; 604 W. Washington St.; 44870; Erie; P 75,000; M 490; (419) 625-6421; Fax (419) 625-7914; marjie@eriecountychamber.com; www.eriecountychamber.com*

Seven Hills • *see Parma*

Seville • *Seville Area C/C* • Velvet Eby; Pres.; P.O. Box 471; 44273; Medina; P 2,500; M 70; (330) 769-1522; sevilleareaohiochamber@gmail.com; www.sevilleareachamberofcommerce.com

Shadyside • *Shadyside Area C/C* • Bobbie Jo Kenimond; P.O. Box 115; 43947; Belmont; P 3,700; M 50; (740) 676-3202; (740) 671-8982

Shaker Heights • *see Beachwood*

Shaker Heights • *Shaker Heights C/C* • Debra Hegler; Pres.; P.O.Box 201193; 44120; Cuyahoga; P 26,000; M 50; (216) 392-8688; 781-81MYBIZ (69249); info@shakerheightschamber.org; www.shakerheightschamber.org

Sharonville • *Sharonville C/C* • Richard Arnold; Pres.; 2704 E. Kemper Rd.; 45241; Butler & Hamilton; P 14,000; M 300; (513) 554-1722; Fax (513) 554-1307; info@sharonvillechamber.com; www.sharonvillechamber.com*

Sheffield Lake • *see Avon Lake*

Sheffield Village • *see Avon Lake*

Shelby • *see Mansfield*

Sidney • *Sidney-Shelby County C/C* • Jeff Raible; Pres.; 101 S. Ohio Ave., Flr. 2; 45365; Shelby; P 49,000; M 530; (937) 492-9122; Fax (937) 498-2472; info3@sidneyshelbychamber.com; www.sidneyshelbychamber.com

Solon • *Solon C/C* • Jennifer Natale; Pres./CEO; 6240 SOM Center Rd., Ste. 110; 44139; Cuyahoga; P 24,000; M 550; (440) 248-5080; Fax (440) 248-9121; staff@solonchamber.com; www.solonchamber.com

South Euclid • *Heights-Hillcrest Reg. C/C* • Angie Pohlman; Exec. Dir.; 4320 Mayfield Rd., Ste. 212; 44121; Cuyahoga; P 155,000; M 350; (216) 397-7322; Fax (216) 397-7353; info@hrcc.org; www.hrcc.org

South Point • *Lawrence County C/C* • Bob Smith; Exec. Dir.; 216 Collins Ave.; 45680; Lawrence; P 62,450; M 350; (740) 377-4550; Fax (740) 377-2091; bobsmith@lawrencecountyohio.org; www.lawrencecountyohio.org*

Spencerville • *Spencerville C/C* • Shanna Holland; Pres.; 108 S. Broadway; 45887; Allen; P 2,300; M 75; (419) 647-2020; spencervillechamber@yahoo.com; www.spencervillechamber.com

Spring Valley • *Spring Valley Area C/C* • Judy Madden; Pres.; P.O. Box 396; 45370; Greene; P 2,000; M 80; (937) 862-4110; www.springvalleyoh.com

Springboro • *Springboro C/C* • Carol Hughes; Exec. Dir.; 325 S. Main St.; 45066; Warren; P 18,600; M 525; (937) 748-0074; Fax (937) 748-0525; chamber@SpringboroOhio.org; www.SpringboroOhio.org*

Springdale • *Springdale C/C* • Julie Matheny; Exec. Dir.; 11700 Springfield Pike; 45246; Hamilton; P 11,200; M 126; (513) 346-5712; julie@springdalechamber.org; www.springdalechamber.org

Springfield • *The Chamber of Greater Springfield* • Michael McDorman; Pres./CEO; 20 S. Limestone St., Ste. 100; 45502; Clark; P 136,000; M 800; (937) 325-7621; Fax (937) 325-8765; info@greaterspringfield.com; www.greaterspringfield.com*

St. Marys • *St. Marys Area C/C* • Tim Dicke; Exec. Dir.; 301 E. Spring St.; 45885; Auglaize; P 8,500; M 250; (419) 300-4611; Fax (419) 300-6202; info@stmarysohio.org; www.stmarysohio.org

Steubenville • *Jefferson County C/C* • Rich Deluca; Pres.; 630 Market St.; 43952; Jefferson; P 68,000; M 498; (740) 282-6226; Fax (740) 282-6285; president@jeffersoncountychamber.com; www.jeffersoncountychamber.com*

Stow • *Stow-Munroe Falls C/C* • Doris Stewart; Exec. Dir.; 4301 Darrow Rd., Ste. 2450; 44224; Summit; P 44,000; M 360; (330) 688-1579; Fax (330) 688-6234; smfcc@smfcc.com; www.smfcc.com

Streetsboro • *Streetsboro Area C/C* • Valerie Fiala; Exec. Dir.; 9205 State Rte. 43, Ste. 202; 44241; Portage; P 16,000; M 200; (330) 626-4769; Fax (330) 422-1118; sacc@streetsborochamber.org; www.streetsborochamber.org

Strongsville • *Strongsville C/C* • Amy Ferree; Exec. Dir.; 18829 Royalton Rd.; 44136; Cuyahoga; P 44,700; M 600; (440) 238-3366; Fax (440) 238-7010; info@strongsvillechamber.com; www.strongsvillechamber.com

Stryker • *Stryker C/C* • Larry Soles; P.O. Box 58; 43557; Williams; P 1,335; M 75; (419) 682-1108; www.villageofstryker.com

Sunbury • *Sunbury/Big Walnut Area C/C* • Cindy Hall; Exec. Dir.; 45. S. Columbus St.; P.O. Box 451; 43074; Delaware; P 11,000; M 250; (740) 965-2860; Fax (740) 965-2860; chall@sunburybigwalnutchamber.com; www.sunburybigwalnutchamber.com

Swanton • *Swanton Area C/C* • Neil Toeppe; Pres./CEO; 100 Zeiter Way; 43558; Fulton & Lucas; P 14,000; M 120; (419) 826-1941; Fax (419) 826-3242; swantoncc@aol.com; www.swantonareacoc.com

Sylvania • *Sylvania Area C/C* • Ms. Pat Nowak; Exec. Dir.; 5632 N. Main St.; 43560; Lucas; P 25,000; M 550; (419) 882-2135; Fax (419) 885-7740; admin@sylvaniachamber.org; www.sylvaniachamber.org

Tallmadge • *Tallmadge C/C* • Mary Cea; Exec. Dir.; 80 Community Rd.; 44278; Portage & Summit; P 17,500; M 200; (330) 633-5417; Fax (330) 633-5415; tallmadgechamber@onecommail.com; www.tallmadge-chamber.com

Tiffin • *Seneca Reg. C/C & Visitor Svcs.* • John Detwiler; Pres./CEO; 19 W. Market St., Ste. C; 44883; Seneca; P 25,000; M 320; (419) 447-4141; Fax (419) 447-5141; info@tiffinchamber.com; tiffinchamber.com*

Tipp City • *Tipp City Area C/C* • Liz Sonnanstine; Exec. Dir.; 12 S. Third St.; 45371; Miami; P 11,000; M 212; (937) 667-8300; Fax (937) 667-8862; liz@tippcitychamber.com; www.tippcitychamber.org

Toledo • *Toledo Reg. C/C* • Wendy R.Gramza CCE; Pres.; 300 Madison Ave., Ste. 200; 43604; Lucas; P 658,000; M 1,800; (419) 243-8191; Fax (419) 241-8302; joinus@toledochamber.com; www.toledochamber.com

Toronto • *Toronto Ohio C/C* • P.O. Box 158; 43964; Jefferson; P 6,000; M 79; (740) 537-4355; Fax (740) 537-4355; info@torontoohiochamber.com; www.torontoohiochamber.com

Trenton • *see Middletown*

Trotwood • *Trotwood C/C* • Marie Battle CAP; Exec. Dir.; 5790 Denlinger Rd., Ste. 4011; 45426; Montgomery; P 27,400; M 80; (937) 837-1484; Fax (937) 837-1508; info@trotwoodchamber.org; www.trotwoodchamber.org

Troy • *Troy Area C/C* • J.C. Wallace; Pres.; 405 S.W. Public Sq., Ste. 330; 45373; Miami; P 26,000; M 400; (937) 339-8769; Fax (937) 339-4944; tacc@troyohiochamber.com; www.troyohiochamber.com*

Twinsburg • *Twinsburg C/C* • Abby Schroll-Fechter; Exec. Dir.; 9044 Church St.; 44087; Summit; P 18,000; M 285; (330) 963-6249; Fax (330) 963-6995; wvoelker@twinsburgchamber.com; www.twinsburgchamber.com

Uhrichsville • *Twin City C/C* • Teri Edwards; Exec. Dir.; P.O. Box 49; 44683; Tuscarawas; P 11,000; M 250; (740) 922-5623; Fax (740) 922-1371; twincityinfo@sbcglobal.net; www.twincitychamber.org

Union City • *see Union City, IN*

Uniontown • *see Hartville*

University Heights • *see Beachwood*

Upper Arlington • *Upper Arlington Area C/C* • Becky Hajost; Pres.; 2152 Tremont Center; 43221; Franklin; P 34,000; M 584; (614) 481-5710; Fax (614) 481-5711; admin@uachamber.org; www.uachamber.org*

Upper Sandusky • *Upper Sandusky/Wyandot County C/C* • Kathy Tolle-Grasz; Exec. Dir.; 108 E. Wyandot Ave.; P.O. Box 223; 43351; Wyandot; P 23,000; M 300; (419) 294-3349; (419) 674-6722; uppersanduskychamber@gmail.com; www.uppersanduskychamber.com*

Urbana • *Champaign County C/C & Visitors Bur.* • Sandi Arnold; Exec. Dir.; 107 N. Main St.; 43078; Champaign; P 40,100; M 295; (937) 653-5764; (877) 873-5764; Fax (937) 652-1599; info@champaignohio.com; www.champaignohio.com

Valley City • *Valley City C/C* • Linda Garrett; P.O. Box 304; 44280; Medina; P 4,600; M 109; (330) 483-1111; chamberofcommerce@valleycity.org; www.valleycity.org

Valley View • *see Independence*

Van Wert • *Van Wert Area C/C* • Erika Wise; Ofc. Mgr.; 118 N. Washington St.; 45891; Van Wert; P 28,000; M 300; (419) 238-4390; Fax (419) 238-4589; chamber@vanwertchamber.com; www.vanwertchamber.com

Vandalia • *Vandalia-Butler C/C* • Will Roberts; Exec. Dir.; 544 W. National Rd.; P.O. Box 224; 45377; Montgomery; P 25,000; M 400; (937) 898-5351; Fax (937) 898-5491; info@vandaliabutlerchamber.org; www.vandaliabutlerchamber.org*

Vermilion • *Vermilion C/C* • Sandy Grisel; Exec. Dir.; 5495 Liberty Ave.; 44089; Erie; P 11,000; M 250; (440) 967-4477; Fax (440) 967-2877; vermilionchamber@centurytel.net; www.vermilionohio.com

Wadsworth • *Wadsworth C/C* • Janie Parish; Exec. Dir.; 123 Broad St., Ste. C; 44281; Medina; P 25,000; M 336; (330) 336-6150; business@wadsworthchamber.com; www.wadsworthchamber.com

Walbridge • *see Oregon*

Walton Hills • *see Independence*

Wapakoneta • *Wapakoneta Area C/C* • Dan Graf; Exec. Dir.; 30 E. Auglaize St.; P.O. Box 208; 45895; Auglaize; P 15,000; M 285; (419) 738-2911; Fax (419) 738-2977; chamber@wapakoneta.com; www.wapakoneta.com

Warren • *see Youngstown*

Warrensville Heights • *Warrensville Heights Area C/C* • Steve Petti; Pres./CEO; P.O. Box 22098; 44122; Cuyahoga; P 23,000; M 135; (216) 454-0199; Fax (216) 378-7371; steve@whacc.org; www.whacc.org

Washington Court House • *Fayette County C/C* • Whitney L. Gentry; Pres./CEO; 101 E. East St.; 43160; Fayette; P 32,000; M 315; (740) 335-0761; (800) 479-7797; whitney@fayettecountyohio.com; www.fayettecountyohio.com*

Waterville • *Waterville Area C/C* • Corina Pfleghaar; Exec. Dir.; 122 Farnsworth Rd.; P.O. Box 74; 43566; Lucas; P 5,530; M 190; (419) 878-5188; Fax (419) 878-5199; admin@watervillechamber.com; www.watervillechamber.com*

Wauseon • *Wauseon C/C* • Debbie Nelson; Exec. Dir.; 115 N. Fulton St.; P.O. Box 217; 43567; Fulton; P 7,400; M 180; (419) 335-9966; Fax (419) 335-7693; debbie@wauseonchamber.com; www.wauseonchamber.com

Waverly • *Pike County C/C* • Shirley Bandy; Exec. Dir.; 12455 St. Rte. 104; P.O. Box 107; 45690; Pike; P 28,000; M 300; (740) 947-7715; Fax (740) 947-7716; pikechamber@yahoo.com; www.pikechamber.org

Waynesburg • *Waynesburg Area Bus. Assn.* • Steve Chandler; Pres.; P.O. Box 394; 44688; Stark; P 1,000; M 61; (330) 866-3435; Fax (330) 866-3488; stevechandler40@aol.com

Waynesville • *Waynesville Area C/C* • Dawn Schroeder; Exec. Dir.; 10B N. Main St.; P.O. Box 281; 45068; Warren; P 3,000; M 100; (513) 897-8855; Fax (513) 897-9833; dawn@waynesvilleohio.com; www.waynesvilleohio.com

Wellington • *Wellington Area C/C* • Virginia Haynes; Pres.; P.O. Box 42; 44090-0042; Lorain; P 4,700; M 70; (440) 647-2222; vskhaynes@yahoo.com; www.wellingtonchamberofcommerce.org

Wellston • *Wellston Area C/C* • Dan Lockard; 5 S. Ohio Ave.; 45692; Jackson; P 5,700; M 50; (740) 384-2720; (740) 384-3606; wellstonchamber.net

Wellsville • *Wellsville Area C/C* • Randy Allmon; Pres.; 439 Riverside Ave.; P.O. Box 636; 43968; Columbiana; P 4,000; M 85; (330) 843-3475; rallmon@hotmail.com; www.wellsvilleohiochamber.com

West Chester • *West Chester-Liberty Chamber Alliance* • Joseph A. Hinson IOM; Pres./CEO; 8922 Beckett Rd.; 45069; Butler; P 100,000; M 900; (513) 777-3600; Fax (513) 777-0188; info@thechamberalliance.com; www.thechamberalliance.com*

West Lafayette • *West Lafayette C/C* • Christy Patterson; Secy.; P.O. Box 113; 43845; Coshocton; P 2,300; M 60; (740) 545-7834; (740) 545-9773; www.westlafayettevillage.com

West Union • *Adams County C/C* • Deana Swayne; Exec. Dir.; 509 E. Main St.; P.O. Box 398; 45693; Adams; P 28,550; M 165; (937) 544-5454; Fax (937) 544-6957; deana@adamscountychamber.org; www.adamscountychamber.org

West Unity • *West Unity C/C* • Katie Baltosser; Secy.; P.O. Box 263; 43570; Williams; P 2,000; M 47; (419) 924-2952; westunitycoc@gmail.com; www.westunitycoc.com

Westerville • *Westerville Area C/C* • Janet Davis; Pres./CEO; 99 Commerce Park Dr.; 43082; Franklin & Delaware; P 40,000; M 600; (614) 882-8917; Fax (614) 882-2085; jdavis@westervillechamber.com; www.westervillechamber.com*

Westlake • *West Shore C/C* • John Sobolewski; Exec. Dir.; Westlake Holiday Inn; P.O. Box 45297; 44145; Cuyahoga; P 32,000; M 425; (440) 835-8787; Fax (440) 835-8798; powerofmorechambers@gmail.com; www.westshorechamber.org

Whitehall • *Whitehall Area C/C* • Shirley Walker Freeman; Pres.; 538 S. Yearling Rd.; 43213; Franklin; P 19,000; M 45; (614) 237-7792; (614) 633-9063; whitehallchamber@yahoo.com; whitehallareachamberofcommerce.org

Whitehouse • *Anthony Wayne Reg. C/C* • Josh Torres; Pres./CEO; 10802 Waterville St.; P.O. Box 2451; 43571; Lucas; P 4,500; M 345; (419) 877-2747; josh@awchamber.com; www.awchamber.com*

Willard • *Willard Area C/C* • Ricky Branham; Exec. Dir.; 16 S. Myrtle Ave.; P.O. Box 73; 44890; Huron; P 6,600; M 135; (419) 935-1888; willardareachamber@yahoo.com; www.willardchamber.com

Willoughby • *Willoughby Western Lake County C/C* • Karen W. Tercek; Pres./CEO; 28 Public Sq.; 44094; Lake; P 50,000; M 550; (440) 942-1632; Fax (440) 942-0586; ktercek@wwlcchamber.com; www.wwlcchamber.com

Willowick • *see Willoughby*

Wilmington • *Wilmington Clinton County C/C* • Mark Rembert; Dir.; 40 N. South St.; 45177; Clinton; P 4,200; M 250; (937) 382-2737; info@wccchamber.com; www.wccchamber.com

Woodsfield • *Monroe County C/C* • Myrna Morrison; Ofc. Mgr.; 117 N. Main St.; P.O. Box 643; 43793; Monroe; P 15,000; M 165; (740) 472-5499; Fax (740) 472-5499; monroechamber@gmn4u.com; www.monroecountyohiochamber.com

Wooster • *Wooster Area C/C* • Justin Starlin; Pres.; 377 W. Liberty St.; 44691; Wayne; P 28,000; M 780; (330) 262-5735; Fax (330) 262-5745; jstarlin@woosterchamber.com; www.woosterchamber.com*

Worthington • *Worthington Area C/C* • Kathryn Paugh; Pres./CEO; 25 W. New England Ave., Ste. 100; 43085; Franklin; P 48,000; M 700; (614) 888-3040; Fax (614) 841-4842; connect@worthingtonchamber.org; www.worthingtonchamber.org*

Xenia • *Xenia Area C/C* • Alan D. Liming; Pres./CEO; 334 W. Market St.; 45385; Greene; P 26,000; M 475; (937) 372-3591; Fax (937) 372-2192; carole@xacc.com; www.xacc.com*

Yellow Springs • *Yellow Springs C/C* • Karen Wintrow; Exec. Dir.; 101 Dayton St.; 45387; Greene; P 3,500; M 269; (937) 767-2686; Fax (937) 767-7876; info@yellowspringsohio.org; www.yellowspringsohio.org

Youngstown • *Youngstown/Warren Reg. C/C* • Thomas M. Humphries; Pres./CEO; 11 Central Sq., Ste. 1600; 44503; Mahoning; P 796,905; M 2,619; (330) 744-2131; Fax (330) 746-0330; shari@regionalchamber.com; www.regionalchamber.com*

Zanesville • *Zanesville-Muskingum County C/C* • Thomas C. Poorman; Pres.; 205 N. Fifth St.; 43701; Muskingum; P 83,388; M 835; (740) 455-8282; Fax (740) 454-2963; tpoorman@zmchamber.com; www.zmchamber.com

Oklahoma

***State Chamber of Oklahoma* •** Fred S. Morgan; Pres./CEO; 330 N.E. 10th St.; P.O. Box 53217; Oklahoma City; 73152; Oklahoma; P 3,752,000; M 3,000; (405) 235-3669; Fax (405) 235-3670; fmorgan@okstatechamber.com; www.okstatechamber.com

Ada • *Ada Area C/C* • Michael Southard; CEO; 209 W. Main; P.O. Box 248; 74821; Pontotoc; P 17,100; M 340; (580) 332-2506; Fax (580) 332-3265; adachamber@adachamber.com; www.adachamber.com*

Adair • *Adair Area C/C* • Donna Vickers; Secy.; P.O. Box 377; 74330; Mayes; P 850; M 65; (918) 785-4242; (918) 232-1293; info@adairok.com; www.adairok.com

Aline • *Aline C/C* • City of Aline; 415 N. Main St.; 73716; Alfalfa; P 209; M 25; (580) 463-2612

Allen • *Allen C/C* • Frank Bell; Pres.; P.O. Box 465; 74825; Hughes & Pontotoc; P 1,000; M 40; (580) 857-2687; allennews@aol.com; www.allenoklahoma.com

Altus • *Altus C/C* • Brian Bush; Pres./CEO; 301 W. Commerce St.; P.O. Box 518; 73521; Jackson; P 20,000; M 300; (580) 482-0210; Fax (580) 482-0223; altuschamber@altuschamber.com; www.altuschamber.com*

Alva • *Alva Area C/C* • Bryan Gragg; Exec. V.P.; 502 Oklahoma Blvd.; 73717; Woods; P 5,200; M 170; (580) 327-1647; Fax (580) 327-1647; chamber@alvaok.net; www.alvaok.net

Anadarko • *Anadarko C/C* • Carla Hall; Exec. Dir.; 106 E. Broadway, 2nd Flr.; P.O. Box 366; 73005; Caddo; P 6,700; M 145; (405) 247-6651; Fax (405) 247-6652; coc@anadarko.org; www.anadarko.org

Antlers • *Pushmataha County C/C* • Jo Ann Matthews; Pres.; P.O. Box 25; 74523; Pushmataha; P 5,500; M 80; (580) 298-2488; Fax (580) 298-5566; pushmatahachamber@gmail.com; www.pushchamber.com*

Apache • *Apache C/C* • Gladys Loflin; Pres.; P.O. Box 461; 73006; Caddo; P 1,800; M 100; (580) 588-3006; (580) 588-3505

Ardmore • *Ardmore C/C* • Mita A. Bates; Pres.; 410 W. Main St.; P.O. Box 1585; 73402; Carter; P 35,000; M 720; (580) 223-7765; Fax (580) 223-7825; mbates@ardmore.org; www.ardmore.org*

Atoka • *Atoka County C/C* • Jewell Darst; Dir.; 415 E. Court; P.O. Box 778; 74525; Atoka; P 15,000; M 183; (580) 889-2410; (580) 364-4753; Fax (580) 889-2410; chamber1atoka@sbcglobal.net; www.atokachamber.com*

Barnsdall • *Barnsdall C/C* • Claud Rosendale; Pres.; P.O. Box 443; 74002; Osage; P 1,400; M 50; (918) 847-2202; crosendale@windstream.net; www.barnsdallchamber.com

Bartlesville • *Bartlesville Reg. C/C* • Sherri Wilt; Pres.; 201 S.W. Keeler; 74003; Osage & Washington; P 36,000; M 700; (918) 336-8708; Fax (918) 337-0216; reception@bartlesville.com; www.bartlesville.com*

Beaver • *Beaver County C/C* • Sherry Parker; Secy./Mgr.; 33 W. 2nd St.; P.O. Box 81; 73932; Beaver; P 2,500; M 100; (580) 625-4726; Fax (580) 625-4726; bvrchamber@ptsi.net; www.beaverchamber.com

Beggs • *Beggs C/C* • Crystal Simmons; V.P.; P.O. Box 270; 74421; Okmulgee; P 1,500; M 35; (918) 267-4461; information@beggschamber.org; www.beggschamber.org

Bethany • *Northwest C/C* • Jill McCartney; Pres./CEO; 7440 N.W. 39th Expy.; P.O. Box 144; 73008; Oklahoma; P 22,000; M 300; (405) 789-1256; Fax (405) 789-2478; info@nwokc.com; www.nwokc.com*

Billings • *Billings Comm. C/C* • Lewain Learned; Pres.; P.O. Box 264; 74630; Noble; P 512; M 220; (580) 725-3610

Bixby • *Bixby Metro C/C* • Krystal Crockett; Pres./CEO; 10441 S. Regal Blvd., Ste. 104; P.O. Box 158; 74008; Tulsa; P 50,000; M 485; (918) 366-9445; info@bixbychamber.com; www.bixbychamber.com*

Blackwell • *Blackwell Area C/C* • John Robertson; Exec. Dir.; 120 S. Main St.; 74631; Kay; P 10,000; M 200; (580) 363-4195; Fax (580) 363-1704; johnr@blackwellchamber.org; www.blackwellchamber.org

Blanchard • *Blanchard C/C* • Laura Callaham; Exec. Dir.; 113 W. Broadway; P.O. Box 1190; 73010; McClain; P 8,000; M 150; (405) 485-8787; Fax (405) 485-8707; bchamber@pldi.net; www.blanchardchamber.com

Boley • *Boley C/C* • Dr. Francis Shelton; Pres.; P.O. Box 31; 74829; Okfuskee; P 1,117; M 30; (918) 667-3612; (918) 667-9790; www.boley-ok.com

Bristow • *Bristow C/C* • Jennifer Taylor; Exec. Dir.; One Railroad Pl.; P.O. Box 127; 74010; Creek; P 4,500; M 165; (918) 367-5151; director@bristowchamber.com; www.bristowchamber.com

Broken Arrow • *American Indian C/C of Oklahoma* • Boyd Miller; Pres.; P.O. Box 141424; 74014; Tulsa; (918) 624-9382; (800) 652-4226; Fax (918) 872-6382; chamber@aiccok.org; www.aiccok.org

Broken Arrow • *Broken Arrow Area C/C & EDC* • Wes Smithwick; Pres./CEO; 210 N. Main, Ste. C; 74012; Tulsa & Wagoner; P 102,815; M 850; (918) 251-1518; Fax (918) 251-1777; info@brokenarrowchamber.com; www.bachamber.com*

Broken Bow • *Broken Bow C/C* • Charity O'Donnell; Exec. Dir.; 113 W. Martin Luther King Dr.; 74728; McCurtain; P 4,247; M 290; (580) 584-3393; (800) 528-7337; Fax (580) 584-7698; bchamber@pine-net.com; www.brokenbowchamber.com

Buffalo • *Buffalo C/C* • James Leonard; P.O. Box 439; 73834; Harper; P 1,300; M 20; (580) 735-2521; buffalo@pldi.net; www.buffalooklahoma.com

Canton • *Canton C/C* • Erica Withers; P.O. Box 128; 73724; Blaine; P 650; M 50; (580) 886-2611; (580) 886-2212; cantonlake@gmail.com; www.cantonlakeoklahoma.com

Carnegie • *Carnegie C/C* • Paula Watson; Pres.; P.O. Box 615; 73015; Caddo; P 1,637; M 60; (580) 654-2121; www.carnegieok.com

Catoosa • *Catoosa C/C* • Glenna Scott; Exec. Dir.; 650 S. Cherokee, Ste. C; P.O. Box 297; 74015; Rogers; P 7,100; M 150; (918) 266-6042; Fax (918) 266-6314; catoosachamber@gmail.com; www.catoosachamber.org*

Chandler • *Chandler Area C/C* • Marilyn Emde; Exec. Dir.; 400 E. Route 66; 74834; Lincoln; P 3,500; M 140; (405) 258-0673; Fax (405) 258-0008; chandlerchamber@gmail.com; www.chandlerareachamberok.com

Checotah • *Checotah C/C* • Lloyd Jernigan; Exec. Dir.; 201 N. Broadway; 74426; McIntosh; P 20,600; M 120; (918) 473-2070; Fax (918) 473-1453; checotahchamber@windstream.net; www.checotah.com

Chelsea • *Chelsea Area C/C* • Rick Johnson; Pres.; P.O. Box 392; 74016; Rogers; P 2,100; M 60; (918) 789-2220; chelseaokchamber@earthlink.net; www.chelseaareachamber.com

Cherokee • *Cherokee Main Street & C/C* • Susie Koontz; Prog. Mgr.; 121 E. Main St.; 73728; Alfalfa; P 1,500; M 25; (580) 596-6111; Fax (580) 596-2464; mainstreet@akslc.net

Cheyenne • *Cheyenne-Roger Mills C/C* • Cindy Clift; Exec. V.P.; 101 S. L.L. Males Ave.; P.O. Box 57; 73628; Roger Mills; P 3,407; M 47; (580) 497-3318; cheyennecoc@gmail.com; www.cheyenneokchamberofcommerce.com

Chickasha • *Chickasha C/C* • Mark Rathe; Pres.; 221 Chickasha Ave.; P.O. Box 1717; 73023; Grady; P 17,000; M 420; (405) 224-0787; Fax (405) 222-3730; president@chickashachamber.com; www.chickashachamber.com*

Choctaw • *Choctaw C/C* • Tracy Mosley; Pres./CEO; 2437 Main St.; P.O. Box 1000; 73020; Oklahoma; P 11,500; M 340; (405) 390-3303; chocchamber@tds.net; www.choctawchamber.com

Chouteau • *Chouteau C/C* • Jeanne Neugin; Dir.; P.O. Box 332; 74337; Mayes; P 2,097; M 60; (918) 476-4100; jneugin@fairpoint.net; www.chouteauok.net

Claremore • *Claremore Area C/C* • Dell Davis; Pres./CEO; 419 W. Will Rogers Blvd.; 74017; Rogers; P 18,000; M 450; (918) 341-2818; Fax (918) 342-0663; chamber@claremore.org; www.claremore.org*

Cleveland • *Cleveland C/C* • Mary Johnson; Exec. Dir.; P.O. Box 240; 74020; Pawnee; P 3,282; M 93; (918) 358-2131; info@chamberofclevelandok.com; www.chamberofclevelandok.com

Clinton • *Clinton C/C* • Julie Menge; Pres.; 101 S. 4th St.; 73601; Custer & Washita; P 10,000; M 350; (580) 323-2222; Fax (580) 323-2931; office@clintonok.org; www.clintonok.org*

Coalgate • *Coal County C/C* • Pamela Looney; Exec. Dir.; P.O. Box 323; 74538; Coal; P 6,000; M 80; (580) 927-2119; coalcountychamber@yahoo.com; www.coalcountychamber.com

Colcord • *Colcord Area C/C* • Marsha Kirby; P.O. Box 265; 74338; Delaware; P 1,000; M 10; (918) 326-4563; (479) 238-5079; colcordchamber@yahoo.com; www.colcordok.com

Collinsville • *Collinsville C/C* • Melissa Carlson; Chamber Mgr.; 1126 W. Main St.; P.O. Box 245; 74021; Rogers & Tulsa; P 5,000; M 150; (918) 371-4703; Fax (918) 371-4262; cvillechamber3477@gmail.com; www.collinsvillechamber.org*

Cordell • *Cordell C/C* • Dirk Webb; Admin.; 114 N. Market; 73632; Washita; P 2,950; M 125; (580) 832-3538; (888) CORDELL; Fax (580) 832-5432; office@cordellchamber.org; cordellchamber.org

Coweta • *Coweta C/C* • Carrie Allamby; Exec. Dir.; 115 S. Broadway; P.O. Box 70; 74429; Wagoner; P 10,000; M 172; (918) 486-2513; Fax (888) 605-5698; info@cowetachamber.com; www.cowetachamber.com*

Crescent • *Crescent C/C* • Chad Johnson; P.O. Box 333; 73028; Logan; P 1,500; M 60; (405) 969-2814; www.crescentoklahoma.com

Cushing • *Cushing C of C & Ind.* • Tracy Caulfield; Exec. Dir.; 1301 E. Main St.; 74023; Payne; P 9,000; M 315; (918) 225-2400; 9182252400; Fax (918) 225-2903; secretary@cushingchamber.org; www.cushingchamber.org*

Davenport • *Davenport C/C* • Steve Guest; Secy.; P.O. Box 66; 74026; Lincoln; P 1,000; M 125; (918) 377-2241; Fax (918) 377-2506; davenportcoc@brightok.net; www.davenportok.org

Davis • *Davis C/C* • Janet Mathis; Exec. Dir.; 100 E. Main St.; P.O. Box 5; 73030; Murray; P 2,800; M 206; (580) 369-2402; (580) 247-5567; davischamber@sbcglobal.net; www.davisok.org

Del City • *Del City C/C* • Kay Bibens; Exec. Dir.; 4505 S.E. 15th St.; P.O. Box 15643; 73155; Oklahoma; P 22,000; M 130; (405) 677-1910; Fax (405) 672-5285; delcitychamber@sbcglobal.net; www.delcitychamber.com*

Drumright • *Drumright C/C* • Cleo Ramsey; Pres.; 103 E. Broadway; P.O. Box 828; 74030; Creek & Payne; P 3,000; M 110; (918) 352-2204; Fax (918) 352-2065; drumrightchamber@aol.com; www.cityofdrumright.org

Duncan • *Duncan C of C & Ind.* • Chris Deal; Pres./CEO; 911 W. Walnut; P.O. Box 699; 73534; Stephens; P 25,000; M 483; (580) 255-3644; Fax (580) 255-6482; duncancc@duncanchamber.com; www.duncanchamber.com*

Durant • *Durant Area C/C* • Janet Reed; Exec. Dir.; 215 N. 4th Ave.; 74701; Bryan; P 43,000; M 500; (580) 924-0848; (580) 924-0849; Fax (580) 924-0348; manager@durantchamber.org; www.durantchamber.org*

Edmond • *Edmond Area C/C* • Ken Moore; Pres.; 825 E. 2nd, Ste. 100; 73034; Oklahoma; P 83,259; M 1,100; (405) 341-2808; Fax (405) 340-5512; info@edmondchamber.com; www.edmondchamber.com*

El Reno • *El Reno C/C* • Karen Nance; Exec. Dir.; 206 N. Bickford Ave.; 73036; Canadian; P 16,700; M 200; (405) 262-1188; Fax (405) 262-1189; elrenochamber@coxinet.net; www.elrenochamber.com*

Elgin • *Elgin C/C* • Leslie Durham; Secy.; 8209 U.S. Hwy. 277, Ste. 7; P.O. Box 362; 73538; Comanche; P 2,500; M 120; (580) 678-7886; Fax (580) 492-6650; secretary@elginchamber.net; www.elginchamber.net

Elk City • *Elk City C/C* • Susie Cupp; Exec. Dir.; P.O. Box 972; 73648; Beckham; P 13,000; M 300; (580) 225-0207; Fax (580) 225-1008; elkcitychamber@itlnet.net; www.visitelkcity.com*

Enid • *Greater Enid C/C* • Jon Blankenship; Pres./CEO; 210 Kenwood Blvd.; P.O. Box 907; 73702; Garfield; P 60,000; M 520; (580) 237-2494; Fax (580) 237-2497; ralinda@enidchamber.com; www.enidchamber.com*

Erick • *Erick C/C* • Paula Harris; Pres.; P.O. Box 1232; 73645; Beckham; P 1,473; M 40; (580) 526-3332; erickchamber@yahoo.com; www.erickchamber.com

Eufaula • *Eufaula Area C/C* • Ms. Pam Rossi; Exec. Dir.; 321 N. Main St.; 74432; McIntosh; P 3,000; M 235; (918) 689-2791; Fax (918) 689-7746; chamber@eufaulachamberofcommerce.com; www.eufaulachamberofcommerce.com*

Fairfax • *Fairfax C/C* • Tina Steele; Pres.; P.O. Box 35; 74637; Osage; P 1,450; M 20; (918) 642-5266; (918) 642-5266; tsteele@hmccah.com; www.fairfaxchamber.com

Fairview • *Fairview C/C* • Jeannie Marlin; Exec. Dir.; 624 N. Main;; 73737; Major; P 2,700; M 145; (580) 227-2527; Fax ; fairviewchamber@att.net; www.fairviewokchamber.net*

Fort Gibson • *Fort Gibson C/C* • Sue Godwin; Exec. Dir.; 108 W. Poplar St.; P.O. Box 730; 74434; Cherokee & Muskogee; P 4,800; M 120; (918) 478-4780; Fax (918) 478-4780; fortgibson@sbcglobal.net; www.fortgibson.com

Fort Sill • *see Lawton*

Frederick • *Frederick C/C* • Haley Hoover; Exec. Dir.; 100 S. Main St.; 73542; Tillman; P 4,000; M 150; (580) 335-2126; Fax (580) 335-3767; frederickcc@pldi.net; www.frederickokchamber.org*

Freedom • *Freedom C/C* • Roger Gagnon; Pres.; P.O. Box 76; 73842; Woods; P 300; M 120; (580) 621-3276; Fax (580) 621-3275; www.freedomokla.com

Garber • *Garber Comm. Improvement Assn.* • Debbie Roggow; Pres.; P.O. Box 574; 73738; Garfield; P 830; M 10; (580) 863-2961

Geary • *Geary C/C* • Vonda Base; Pres.; P.O. Box 273; 73040; Blaine; P 1,290; M 30; (405) 884-2765

Glenpool • *Glenpool C/C* • Amy T. Rogers; Pres./CEO; 12205 S. Yukon Ave.; P.O. Box 767; 74033; Tulsa; P 10,800; M 210; (918) 322-3505; Fax (918) 322-3505; info@glenpoolchamber.org; www.glenpoolchamber.org*

Gore • *Gore C/C* • Linda Bighorse; Secy.; P.O. Box 943; 74435; Sequoyah; P 900; M 70; goreokchamber@yahoo.com; www.goreok.net

Grove • *Grove Area C/C* • Lisa Friden; Pres.; 9630 U.S. Hwy 59; 74344; Delaware; P 6,623; M 400; (918) 786-9079; Fax (918) 786-2909; grovecc@sbcglobal.net; www.groveok.org*

Guthrie • *Guthrie C/C* • Mary Coffin; Pres./CEO; 212 W. Oklahoma Ave.; 73044; Logan; P 38,000; M 358; (405) 282-1947; (800) 299-1889; Fax (405) 282-0061; info@guthrieok.com; www.guthrieok.com*

Guymon • *Guymon C/C* • Jada Breeden; Exec. Dir.; 711 S.E. Hwy. 3; Rte. 5, Box 120; 73942; Texas; P 14,000; M 150; (580) 338-3376; Fax (580) 338-0014; jada@guymonokchamber.com; www.guymonokchamber.com*

Harrah • *Harrah C/C* • Benita Peeler; Pres.; P.O. Box 907; 73045; Oklahoma; P 5,000; M 125; (405) 454-2190; benita@thepeelerosa.com; www.harrahchamberofcommerce.com

Hartshorne • *Hartshorne Area C/C* • 1018 Pennsylvania Ave.; 74547; Pittsburg; P 2,200; M 55; (918) 297-2055; www.hartshornechamberofcommerce.com

Henryetta • *Henryetta C/C* • Roy E. Madden; Exec. Dir.; 415 W. Main; 74437; Okmulgee; P 6,000; M 125; (918) 652-3331; henryettachamber@att.net; www.henryetta.org*

Hinton • *Hinton C/C* • Charles Jaques; Pres.; P.O. Box 48; 73047; Caddo; P 1,500; M 80; (405) 542-6428; www.hintonokchamber.com

Hobart • *Hobart C/C* • Nancy Ledford; Exec. Dir.; 106 W. 4th St.; 73651; Kiowa; P 3,800; M 110; (580) 726-2553; Fax (580) 726-2553; hobartchamber@att.net; www.hobartok.com*

Holdenville • *Holdenville C/C* • Roberta Davis; Exec. Dir.; 102 N. Broadway; P.O. Box 70; 74848; Hughes; P 5,600; M 100; (405) 379-3675; Fax ; chamber@holdenvillechamber.com; www.holdenvillechamber.com

Hominy • *Hominy C/C* • Jerry Stumpff; Pres.; P.O. Box 99; 74035; Osage; P 3,200; M 50; (918) 885-4939; Fax (918) 885-4049; hominychamberofcommerce@windstream.net; www.hominychamber.com

Hooker • *Hooker C/C* • Linda Martin; Pres.; P.O. Box 989; 73945; Texas; P 1,800; M 100; (580) 652-2809; hookerchamberofcommerce@hotmail.com; www.hookerchamber.com

Hugo • *Hugo Area C/C* • Sheila Salyer; Exec. Dir.; 200 S. Broadway; 74743; Choctaw; P 6,500; M 100; (580) 326-7511; Fax (580) 326-7512; hugo-chamber@sbcglobal.net; www.hugo2choctawcountyok.com*

Idabel • *Idabel C of C & Ag.* • Betty L. Johnson; Exec. Dir.; 7 S.W. Texas St.; 74745; McCurtain; P 7,000; M 214; (580) 286-3305; Fax (580) 286-6708; idabelchamber@yahoo.com; www.idabelchamberofcommerce.com

Jay • *Jay C/C* • Becki Farley; Pres.; P.O. Box 806; 74346; Delaware; P 2,482; M 62; (918) 253-8698; dchsmuseum@grand.net; www.jaychamber.org

Jenks • *Jenks C/C* • Josh Driskell; Pres.; 224 E. A St.; P.O. Box 902; 74037; Tulsa; P 17,000; M 350; (918) 299-5005; Fax (918) 299-5799; info@jenkschamber.com; www.jenkschamber.com*

Kingfisher • *Kingfisher C/C* • Judy Whipple; Mgr.; 123 W. Miles; 73750; Kingfisher; P 13,000; M 140; (405) 375-4445; Fax (405) 375-5304; chamber@pldi.net; www.kingfisher.org*

Kingston • *see Madill*

Konawa • *Konawa C/C* • Matthew Dean; Pres.; P.O. Box 112; 74849; Seminole; P 1,290; M 65; (580) 925-3254; (580) 925-3775

Langley • *South Grand Lake Area C/C* • Rusty Fleming; Exec. Dir.; P.O. Box 215; 74350; Mayes; P 25,000; M 210; (918) 782-3214; Fax (918) 782-3215; grandlakechamber@gmail.com; www.grandlakechamber.org

Laverne • *Laverne Area C/C* • Terri Wheeler; Exec. Dir.; 108 W. Jane Jayroe Blvd.; P.O. Box 634; 73848; Harper; P 1,250; M 40; (580) 921-3612; lvrnokcc@ptsi.net; www.laverneok.com

Lawton • *Lawton Fort Sill C/C* • Debra Welch IOM; Pres./CEO; 302 W. Gore Blvd.; P.O. Box 1376; 73502; Comanche; P 100,000; M 1,040; (580) 355-3541; (800) 872-4540; Fax (580) 357-3642; info@lawtonfortsillchamber.com; www.lawtonfortsillchamber.com*

Lindsay • *Lindsay C/C* • Paula Barker; Mgr.; 107 N. Main St.; P.O. Box 504; 73052; Garvin; P 3,000; M 123; (405) 756-4312; Fax (405) 756-8657; lchamber@oriok.net

Locust Grove • *Locust Grove C/C* • Wayne Pergo; Pres.; 109 E. Ross; P.O. Box 525; 74352; Mayes; P 1,600; M 20; (918) 479-6336; locustgroveokchamber@hotmail.com; www.lgchamber.com*

Madill • *Marshall County C/C* • Johnna Harding; Exec. Dir.; 11544 Hwy. 70; P.O. Box 542; 73446; Marshall; P 20,000; M 140; (580) 795-2431; (580) 795-5870; Fax (580) 795-5870; info@mccoconline.org; www.mccoconline.org

Mangum • *Greer County C/C* • Wayne Vaughn; Exec. Dir.; 119 E. Jefferson; 73554; Greer; P 6,095; M 165; (580) 782-2444; Fax (580) 782-2229; info@greercountychamber.com; www.greercountychamber.com

Mannford • *Mannford Area C/C* • Rita Bougher; P.O. Box 487; 74044; Creek, Pawnee & Tulsa; P 5,000; M 100; (918) 865-2000; (918) 809-8824; Fax (918) 865-3187; info@mannfordchamberofcommerce.com; www.mannfordchamberofcommerce.com

Marietta • *Love County C/C* • Gwen Wyatt; Secy.; P.O. Box 422; 73448; Love; P 3,000; M 100; (580) 276-3102; lovecountychamber@yahoo.com; www.lovecountyokla.org

Marlow • *Marlow C/C* • Debbe Ridley; Exec. Dir.; 223 W. Main; 73055; Stephens; P 4,592; M 230; (580) 658-2212; marlowchamber@cableone.net; www.marlowchamber.org

Maysville • *Maysville C/C* • Claudia Reeves; Pres.; P.O. Box 515; 73057; Garvin; P 1,250; M 20; (405) 867-5151

McAlester • *McAlester Area C/C & Ag.* • Jeff Warmuth; Pres./CEO; 119 E. Choctaw, Ste. 103; 74501; Pittsburg; P 20,000; M 400; (918) 423-2550; Fax (918) 423-1345; info@mcalester.org; www.mcalester.org*

McLoud • *McLoud C/C* • Victoria Mongold; Ofc. Mgr,; P.O. Box 254; 74851; Pottawatomie; P 3,548; M 63; (405) 964-6566; Fax (405) 964-6566; chamber@mcloudchamber.com; www.mcloudchamber.com

Miami • *Miami Reg. C/C* • Steve Gilbert; Pres.; 111 N. Main St.; 74354; Ottawa; P 30,000; M 300; (918) 542-4481; Fax (918) 540-1260; info@miamiokchamber.com; www.miamiokchamber.com*

Midwest City • *Midwest City C/C* • Bonnie Cheatwood; Exec. Dir.; 5905 Trosper Rd.; P.O. Box 10980; 73140; Oklahoma; P 55,000; M 560; (405) 733-3801; Fax (405) 733-5633; information@midwestcityok.com; www.mwcok.com*

Minco • *Minco C/C* • John Hacker; Pres.; P.O. Box 451; 73059; Grady; P 1,800; M 42; (405) 352-4382; (405) 352-4274

Moore • *Moore C/C* • Kathy Gillette; Pres./CEO; 305 W. Main ; P.O. Box 6305; 73153; Cleveland; P 60,000; M 723; (405) 794-3400; Fax (405) 794-8555; nmcdaniel@moorechamber.com; www.moorechamber.com*

Muldrow • *Muldrow C/C* • Katherine Jones; Mayor; 100 S. Main; P.O. Box 429; 74948; Sequoyah; P 4,700; M 10; (918) 427-3226

Muskogee • *Greater Muskogee Area C/C & Tourism* • Treasure McKenzie; Pres./CEO; 310 W. Broadway; P.O. Box 797; 74402; Muskogee; P 40,000; M 800; (918) 682-2401; (866) 381-6543; Fax (918) 682-2403; treasure@muskogeechamber.org; www.visitmuskogee.com*

Mustang • *Mustang C/C* • Becky Julian; Exec. Dir.; 1201 N. Mustang Rd.; P.O. Box 213; 73064; Canadian; P 17,000; M 291; (405) 376-2758; Fax (405) 376-4764; bjulian@mustangchamber.com; www.mustangchamber.com*

Newcastle • *Newcastle C/C* • Kim Brown; Exec. Dir.; P.O. Box 1006; 73065; McClain; P 7,685; M 180; (405) 387-3232; Fax (405) 387-3885; chamber@newcastleok.org; www.newcastleok.org*

Newkirk • *Newkirk C/C* • Glenna Blair; Exec. Secy.; 114 S. Main St.; 74647; Kay; P 2,400; M 115; (580) 362-2155; Fax (580) 362-3774; newkirkchamber@att.net; www.newkirkchamber.com*

Noble • *Noble C/C* • Daniela Newville; Exec. Dir.; 114 S. Main; P.O. Box 678; 73068; Cleveland; P 6,481; M 110; (405) 872-5535; Fax (405) 872-2020; info@nobleok.net; www.nobleok.net*

Norman • *Norman C/C* • John Woods; Pres./CEO; 115 E. Gray St.; 73069; Cleveland; P 111,000; M 1,350; (405) 321-7260; Fax (405) 360-4679; angie@normanchamber.com; www.normanchamber.com*

Nowata • *Nowata Area C/C* • Skyler Watters; Exec. Dir.; 126 S. Maple St.; P.O. Box 202; 74048; Nowata; P 14,000; M 125; (918) 273-2301; (918) 440-7652; nowatachamber@sbcglobal.net; www.nowata.com

Oilton • *Oilton C/C* • Dawna Johnson; Pres.; P.O. Box 624; 74052; Creek; P 1,400; M 35; (918) 862-1061; (918) 862-3202; www.cityofoilton.com

Okeene • *Okeene C/C* • Sherri Feely; Exec. Dir.; 116 W. E St.; P.O. Box 704; 73763; Blaine; P 1,200; M 75; (580) 822-3005; Fax (580) 822-3008; okchamber@pldi.net; www.okeene.com

Okemah • *Okemah C/C* • Alan Oatsvall; Pres.; 407 W. Broadway; P.O. Box 508; 74859; Okfuskee; P 3,600; M 235; (918) 623-2440; chamber@okemahok.org; www.okemahok.org

Oklahoma City • *Greater Oklahoma City C/C* • Roy H. Williams; Pres./CEO; 123 Park Ave.; 73102; Oklahoma; P 1,240,000; M 5,000; (405) 297-8900; Fax (405) 297-8986; jdeleon@okcchamber.com; www.okcchamber.com

Oklahoma City • *South Oklahoma City C/C* • Elaine Lyons; Pres./CEO; 701 S.W. 74th St.; 73139; Oklahoma; P 610,613; M 750; (405) 634-1436; Fax (405) 634-1462; info@southokc.com; www.southokc.com*

Okmulgee • *Okmulgee C/C* • Kay Rabbitt-Brower; Exec. Dir.; 112 N. Morton Ave.; 74447; Okmulgee; P 13,000; M 200; (918) 756-6172; Fax (918) 756-6441; okmulgeechamber74447@gmail.com; www.okmulgeeonline.com*

Oologah • *Oologah Area C/C* • Amos Berry; P.O. Box 109; 74053; Rogers; P 3,600; M 110; (918) 443-2790; Fax (918) 443-2790; chamber@oologah.org; www.oologah.org

Owasso • *Owasso C/C* • Gary W. Akin; Pres.; 315 S. Cedar; 74055; Rogers & Tulsa; P 45,000; M 450; (918) 272-2141; Fax (918) 272-8564; fayrene@owassochamber.com; www.owassochamber.com*

Pauls Valley • *Pauls Valley C/C* • Sherri Wing; Pres.; 112 E. Paul Ave.; P.O. Box 638; 73075; Garvin; P 6,900; M 270; (405) 238-6491; Fax (405) 238-2335; president@paulsvalleychamber.com; www.paulsvalleychamber.com

Pawhuska • *Pawhuska C/C* • Michael McCartney; Exec. Dir.; 210 W. Main; P.O. Box 5; 74056; Osage; P 3,825; M 150; (918) 287-1208; Fax (918) 287-3159; pawhuskachamber@sbcglobal.net; www.pawhuskachamber.com

Pawnee • *Pawnee Comm. C/C* • Tom Briggs; Mgr.; 613 Harrison St.; 74058; Pawnee; P 2,200; M 105; (918) 762-2108; (918) 399-5675; pawneeok@att.net; www.cityofpawnee.com

Perkins • *Perkins C/C* • Jeremy McCasland; Pres.; P.O. Box 502; 74059; Payne; P 2,600; M 88; (405) 747-6809; jacque_vassar@hotmail.com; www.cityofperkins.net

Perry • *Perry C/C* • Noel Black; Pres./CEO; 327 N. 7th St.; P.O. Box 426; 73077; Noble; P 11,500; M 300; (580) 336-4684; Fax (580) 336-3522; noel@perrychamber.net; www.perryokchamber.com*

Piedmont • *Piedmont Area C/C* • Lisa Gigstad; Exec. Dir.; 12 Monroe Ave. N.W.; P.O. Box 501; 73078; Canadian; P 6,000; M 125; (405) 373-2234; piedmontokchamber@gmail.com; www.piedmontokchamber.org

Ponca City • *Ponca City Area C/C* • Rich Cantillon; Pres./CEO; 420 E. Grand Ave.; P.O. Box 1109; 74602; Kay & Osage; P 25,300; M 565; (580) 765-4400; Fax (580) 765-2798; rich@poncacitychamber.com; www.poncacitychamber.com*

Poteau • *Poteau C/C* • Karen Wages; CEO; 501 S. Broadway; 74953; LeFlore; P 8,900; M 400; (918) 647-9178; Fax (918) 647-4099; poteauchamber@windstream.net; www.poteauchamber.com

Prague • *Prague C/C* • Maxine Dukes; Exec. Secy.; 820 Jim Thorpe Blvd.; P.O. Box 111; 74864; Lincoln; P 2,200; M 80; (405) 567-2616; Fax (405) 567-2616; praguecoc@windstream.net; www.pragueok.org

Pryor • *Pryor Area C/C* • Barbara Hawkins; Pres.; 100 E. Graham Ave.; P.O. Box 367; 74362; Mayes; P 9,500; M 310; (918) 825-0157; Fax (918) 825-0158; info@pryorchamber.com; www.pryorchamber.com*

Purcell • *Heart of Oklahoma C/C* • Justina Reaves; Exec. Dir.; 218 W. Main St.; 73080; McClain; P 7,500; M 200; (405) 527-3093; Fax (405) 527-4351; chamberoffice@theheartofok.com; www.theheartofok.com

Roland • *Roland C/C* • Dale Phelps II; Pres.; P.O. Box 492; 74954; Sequoyah; P 5,000; M 50; (918) 427-5551; info@rolandchamber.com; www.rolandchamber.com

Salina • *Salina Area C/C* • Tammie Halbach; Secy.; P.O. Box 422; 74365; Mayes; P 1,500; M 90; (918) 434-8181; salinachamber@sstelco.com; www.salinaoklahoma.org

Sallisaw • *Sallisaw C/C* • Judy Martens; Exec. Dir.; 301 E. Cherokee; P.O. Box 251; 74955; Sequoyah; P 10,000; M 220; (918) 775-2558; Fax (918) 775-4021; director@sallisawchamber.com; www.sallisawchamber.com

Sand Springs • *Sand Springs Area C/C* • Kristen Valentin; Pres.; 1 West 1st St.; 74063; Osage & Tulsa; P 19,000; M 330; (918) 245-3221; Fax (918) 245-2530; info@sandspringschamber.com; www.sandspringschamber.com*

Sapulpa • *Sapulpa C/C* • Suzanne Shirey; Pres.; 101 E. Dewey; 74066; Creek & Tulsa; P 20,000; M 331; (918) 224-0170; Fax (918) 224-0172; suzanne@sapulpachamber.com; www.sapulpachamber.com*

Sayre • *Sayre C/C* • Belinda Graham; Exec. Dir.; 117 N. 4th; P.O. Box 474; 73662; Beckham; P 4,400; M 115; (580) 928-3386; Fax (580) 928-8976; sayrechamber@att.net; www.sayrechamber.org*

Seiling • *Seiling C/C* • Charlotte Pittman; Pres.; P.O. Box 794; 73663; Dewey; P 1,200; M 41; (580) 922-3110; www.seilingchamber.com

Seminole • *Seminole C/C* • Amy Britt; Exec. Dir.; 326 E. Evans; P.O. Box 1190; 74818; Seminole; P 7,500; M 250; (405) 382-3640; Fax (405) 382-3529; seminolechamber@sbcglobal.net; www.seminoleokchamber.org*

Sentinel • *Sentinel C/C* • P.O. Box 131; 73664; Washita; P 900; M 60; (580) 393-4952

Shattuck • *Shattuck C/C* • McKenzie Pshigoda; Exec. Dir.; 115 S. Main St.; P.O. Box 400; 73858; Ellis; P 1,500; M 105; (580) 938-2818; (580) 331-7827; Fax (580) 938-2852; shattuckcc@pldi.net; www.shattuckchamber.org

Shawnee • *Greater Shawnee C/C* • Nancy Keith; Pres./CEO; 231 N. Bell; P.O. Box 1613; 74802; Pottawatomie; P 32,000; M 500; (405) 273-6092; Fax (405) 275-9851; nkeith@shawneechamber.com; www.shawneechamber.com*

Shidler • *Shidler Area C/C* • P.O. Box 281; 74652; Osage; P 441; M 21; (918) 793-4171; Fax (918) 793-4021; chamber@shidleroklahoma.com; www.shidleroklahoma.com

Skiatook • *Skiatook C/C* • Stephanie Upton; Exec. Dir.; 304 E. Rogers Blvd.; 74070; Osage & Tulsa; P 8,500; M 120; (918) 396-3702; Fax (918) 396-3577; info@skiatookchamber.com; www.skiatookchamber.com

Spencer • *Greater Spencer C/C* • Mary Hammon; P.O. Box 53; 73084; Oklahoma; P 3,550; M 87; (405) 771-9933; www.cityofspencer.us

Spiro • *Spiro Area C/C* • Glenda Stokes; Pres.; 210 S. Main St.; P.O. Box 401; 74959; Le Flore; P 2,300; M 100; (918) 962-3461; Fax (918) 962-5320

Stigler • *Stigler-Haskell County C/C* • Janice Williams; Exec. Dir.; 204 E. Main St.; 74462; Haskell; P 15,000; M 70; (918) 967-8681; Fax (918) 967-4319; chamber@tulsaconnect.com

Stillwater • *Stillwater C/C* • Lisa Navrkal; Pres./CEO; 409 S.Main St.; 74074; Payne; P 46,560; M 842; (405) 372-5573; Fax (405) 372-4316; info@stillwaterchamber.org; www.stillwaterchamber.org*

Stilwell • *Stilwell Area C/C* • Betty Barker; Secy.; P.O. Box 845; 74960; Adair; P 3,000; M 100; (918) 696-7845; achandga@windstream.net; www.strawberrycapital.com

Stratford • *Stratford C/C* • Jason O'Neal; Pres.; P.O. Box 491; 74872; Garvin; P 1,525; M 35; (580) 759-2116; www.stratfordok.org

Stroud • *Stroud C/C* • Tommy Smith; Pres.; 216 W. Main; 74079; Creek & Lincoln; P 2,755; M 145; (918) 968-3321; stroudch@brightok.net; www.stroudchamber.com

Sulphur • *Sulphur C/C* • Tori Bates; Exec. Dir.; 717 W. Broadway; 73086; Murray; P 5,000; M 245; (580) 622-2824; Fax (580) 622-4217; sulphur@brightok.net; www.sulphurokla.com

Tahlequah • *Tahlequah Area C/C* • David Moore; Exec. Dir.; 123 E. Delaware St.; 74464; Cherokee; P 46,000; M 500; (918) 456-3742; (800) 456-4860; Fax (918) 456-3751; tahlequahchamber@swbell.net; www.tahlequahchamber.com*

Talihina • *Talihina C/C* • Vera Nelson; Dir.; 201 First St.; 74571; Le Flore; P 1,300; M 100; (918) 567-3434; Fax (918) 567-3388; chamber@talihinacc.com; www.talihinacc.com

Tecumseh • *Tecumseh C/C* • Justin D. Stone; Exec. Dir.; 114 N. Broadway St.; 74873; Pottawatomie; P 6,200; M 105; (405) 598-8666; Fax (405) 598-6760; chambertecumseh@windstream.net; www.tecumsehchamber.com

Temple • *Temple C/C* • Virginia Dupler; Pres.; P.O. Box 58; 73568; Cotton; P 993; M 67; (580) 342-6991; (580) 342-6776

Thomas • *Thomas Area C/C* • Jennifer Billy; Exec. V.P.; 122 W. Broadway; P.O. Box 250; 73669; Custer; P 1,238; M 130; (580) 661-3685; (580) 661-3687; Fax (580) 661-3689; thomasacoc@pldi.net

Tipton • *Tipton C/C* • Mike Balderas; Pres.; P.O. Box 403; 73570; Tillman; P 993; M 100; (580) 649-8403; (580) 667-5211

Tishomingo • *Johnston County C/C* • Seigel Paul Heffington; Exec. Dir.; 106 W. Main; 73460; Johnston; P 10,500; M 150; (580) 371-2175; Fax (580) 371-2175; johnstoncochamber@yahoo.com; www.johnstoncountyok.org*

Tonkawa • *Tonkawa C/C* • Erin Burns; Pres.; 102 E. Grand Ave.; 74653; Kay; P 3,299; M 160; (580) 628-2220; Fax (580) 628-2221; info@tonkawachamber.org; www.tonkawachamber.org*

Tulsa • *Tulsa Reg. C/C* • Mike Neal; Pres./CEO; One W. Third St., Ste. 100; 74103; Osage, Rogers, Tulsa & Wagoner; P 920,000; M 3,100; (918) 585-1201; Fax (918) 585-6126; webmaster@tulsachamber.com; www.tulsachamber.com*

Tuttle • *Tuttle Area C/C* • Pat Cox; Dir.; Tuttle City Hall; P.O. Box 673; 73089; Grady; P 6,000; M 100; (405) 381-4600; (405) 816-4612; Fax (405) 381-4600; pat@tuttlechamber.org; www.tuttlechamber.org*

Vici • *Vici C/C* • Doug Peeks; Pres.; 107 E. Broadway; P.O. Box 2; 73859; Dewey; P 750; M 40; (580) 995-3425; Fax (580) 995-4987; vicichamber@vicihorizon.com; www.viciok.com

Vinita • *Vinita Area C/C* • B.J. Mooney; Dir.; 105 W. Delaware; P.O. Box 882; 74301; Craig; P 7,000; M 237; (918) 256-7133; Fax (918) 256-8261; chamber@vinita.com; www.vinita.com*

Wagoner • *Wagoner Area C/C* • Meredith Zehr; Exec. Dir.; 301 S. Grant; 74467; Wagoner; P 8,500; M 265; (918) 485-3414; Fax (918) 485-2523; chamber@thecityofwagoner.org; www.thecityofwagoner.org*

Walters • *Walters C/C* • Shirley Howard; Admin.; 116 N. Broadway; P.O. Box 352; 73572; Cotton; P 2,551; M 75; (580) 875-3335; Fax (580) 875-3652; walterschamber@att.net; www.waltersok.us

Warner • *Warner C/C* • Dale Wiggins; Pres.; P.O. Box 170; 74469; Muskogee; P 1,600; M 25; (918) 463-2696

Watonga • *Watonga C/C* • Mary Larson; Dir.; P.O. Box 537; 73772; Blaine; P 3,500; M 175; (580) 623-5452; Fax (580) 623-5428; cwatonga@pldi.net; www.watongachamber.com

Waurika • *Waurika C/C* • Jon Waid; Pres.; P.O. Box 366; 73573; Jefferson; P 1,900; M 100; (580) 228-2041; (580) 228-2326; jwaid@ffnbank.com; www.waurikachamber.com

Waynoka • *Waynoka C/C* • Wayne LaMunyon; Pres.; 1565 Main St.; P.O. Box 173; 73860; Woods; P 1,000; M 40; (580) 824-4741; waynokachamberofcommerce@gmail.com; www.waynokachamber.com

Weatherford • *Weatherford Area C/C* • Haley Kliewer; Exec. Dir.; 522 W. Rainey; P.O. Box 857; 73096; Custer; P 10,500; M 299; (580) 772-7744; Fax (580) 772-7751; welcome@weatherfordchamber.com; www.weatherfordchamber.com*

Westville • *Westville C/C* • Patsy Winn; Comm. Bldg.; P.O. Box 1020; 74965; Adair; P 1,640; M 25; (918) 723-3243; Fax (918) 723-4936; pswinn58@hotmail.com

Wetumka • *Wetumka C/C* • Vernon Stout; Ofc. Mgr.; 202 N. Main; 74883; Hughes; P 1,850; M 30; (405) 452-3237; wetumkacoc@hotmail.com

Wewoka • *Wewoka C/C* • Cindy Hall; Pres. of the Bd.; 101 W. Park; P.O. Box 719; 74884; Seminole; P 3,560; M 200; (405) 257-5485; Fax (405) 257-2662; wewokachamberofcommerce@gmail.com; www.wewokachamberofcommerce.org

Wilburton • *Wilburton C/C* • Mae Mings; 302 W. Main; 74578; Latimer; P 3,500; M 88; (918) 465-2759; Fax (918) 465-2759; wilburtonchamber@sbcglobal.net; www.wilburtonchamber.com

Woodward • *Woodward C/C* • CJ Montgomery; Pres.; 1006 Oklahoma Ave.; P.O. Box 1026; 73802; Woodward; P 15,000; M 400; (580) 256-7411; (800) 364-5352; Fax (580) 254-3585; wwchamber@sbcglobal.net; www.woodwardchamber.com

Wynnewood • *Wynnewood C/C* • Tabitha Hayes; Pres.; P.O. Box 616; 73098; Garvin; P 2,200; M 50; (405) 665-4466; secretary@wynnewoodchamber.com; www.wynnewoodchamber.com

Yale • *Yale C/C* • Cindy White; Pres.; P.O. Box 132; 74085; Payne; P 1,300; M 40; (918) 387-2406; (918) 387-2444; cwhite@ahb-ok.com; www.yaleok.org

Yukon • *Yukon C/C* • Paisley Hopkins; Exec. Dir.; 510 Elm Ave.; 73099; Canadian; P 25,000; M 400; (405) 354-3567; Fax (405) 354-3580; phopkins@yukoncc.com; www.yukoncc.com*

Oregon

Oregon State C of C • Alison Hart; Exec. Dir.; 867 Liberty St.; P.O. Box 3344; Salem; 97301; Linn; P 3,930,000; M 71; (503) 363-7984; alisonh@pacounsel.org; www.oregonchamber.org

Albany • *Albany Area C/C* • Janet Steele; Pres.; 435 1st Ave. W.; 97321; Benton & Linn; P 54,000; M 560; (541) 926-1517; Fax (541) 926-7064; info@albanychamber.com; www.albanychamber.com*

Ashland • *Ashland C/C* • Sandra Slattery; Exec. Dir.; 110 E. Main St.; P.O. Box 1360; 97520; Jackson; P 21,000; M 805; (541) 482-3486; Fax (541) 482-2350; katharine@ashlandchamber.com; www.ashlandchamber.com*

Astoria • *Astoria-Warrenton Area C/C* • Skip Hauke; Exec. Dir.; 111 W. Marine Dr.; P.O. Box 176; 97103; Clatsop; P 16,000; M 618; (503) 325-6311; (800) 875-6807; Fax (503) 325-9767; suzanne@oldoregon.com; www.oldoregon.com*

Baker City • *Baker County Chamber & Visitor Bur.* • Debi Bainter; Exec. Dir.; 490 Campbell St.; 97814; Baker; P 10,000; M 420; (541) 523-5855; (888)523-5855; Fax (541) 523-9187; debi@visitbaker.com; www.visitbaker.com

Bandon • *Bandon C/C* • Julie Miller; Exec. Dir.; 300 S.E. Second; P.O. Box 1515; 97411; Coos; P 3,000; M 369; (541) 347-9616; Fax (541) 347-7006; bandoncc@mycomspan.com; www.bandon.com*

Banks • *Banks C/C* • Ray Deeth; Pres.; P.O. Box 206; 97106; Washington; P 1,700; M 69; (503) 324-1081; www.oregonbankschamber.com

Beaver • see Cloverdale

Beaverton • *Beaverton Area C/C* • Lorraine Clarno; Pres.; 12600 S.W. Crescent St., Ste. 160; 97005; Washington; P 93,542; M 550; (503) 644-0123; Fax (503) 526-0349; info@beaverton.org; www.beaverton.org*

Bend • *Bend Chamber* • Sandy Stephenson; CFO/COO; 777 N.W. Wall St., Ste. 200; 97701; Deschutes; P 81,000; M 1,500; (541) 382-3221; (800) 905-BEND; Fax (541) 385-9929; info@bendchamber.org; www.bendchamber.org*

Blaine • see Cloverdale

Boardman • *Boardman C/C* • Julie A. Gisi; Exec. Dir.; 101 Olson Rd.; P.O. Box 1; 97818; Morrow; P 3,400; M 180; (541) 481-3014; Fax (541) 481-2733; info@boardmanchamber.org; www.boardmanchamber.org*

Boring • see Happy Valley

Brookings • *Brookings-Harbor C/C* • Arlis Steele; Pres./CEO; 16330 Lower Harbor Rd.; P.O. Box 940; 97415; Curry; P 14,000; M 300; (541) 469-3181; (800) 535-9469; Fax (541) 469-4094; arlis@brookingsor.com; www.brookingsharborchamber.com

Brownsville • *Brownsville Comm. C/C* • Mandy Cole & Sharon McCoy; Co-Pres.; P.O. Box 161; 97327; Linn; P 1,700; M 55; (541) 928-0831; events@historicbrownsville.com; www.historicbrownsville.com

Burns • *Harney County C/C* • Chelsea Harrison; Exec. Dir.; 484 N. Broadway; 97720; Harney; P 7,300; M 200; (541) 573-2636; Fax (541) 573-3408; info@harneycounty.com; www.harneycounty.com

Canby • *Canby Area C/C* • Bev Doolittle; Exec. Dir.; 191 S.E. 2nd Ave.; P.O. Box 35; 97013; Clackamas; P 15,000; M 300; (503) 266-4600; Fax (503) 266-4338; chamber@canby.com; www.canbyareachamber.org

Cannon Beach • *Cannon Beach C/C & Visitor Center* • 207 N. Spruce St.; P.O. Box 64; 97110; Clatsop; P 1,600; M 265; (503) 436-2623; Fax (503) 436-0910; chamber@cannonbeach.org; www.cannonbeach.org

Canyonville • *Canyonville C/C* • Debbie Hopkins; Secy.; P.O. Box 1028; 97417; Douglas; P 1,649; M 50; (541) 839-4232; webmaster@canyonvillechamber.org; www.canyonvillechamber.org

Cave Junction • *Illinois Valley C/C* • Dulcie Moore; Ofc. Mgr.; 201 Caves Hwy.; P.O. Box 312; 97523; Josephine; P 18,000; M 120; (541) 592-3326; ivchamberofcommerce@cavenet.com; www.cavejunctionoregon.com*

Central Point • *Central Point C/C* • Cindy Hudson; Exec. Dir.; 150 Manzanita St.; 97502; Jackson; P 17,890; M 168; (541) 664-5301; Fax (541) 664-3667; cpchamber@qwestoffice.net; www.centralpointchamber.org*

Christmas Valley • *Christmas Valley C/C* • Debbie Kirkland; Pres.; P.O. Box 65; 97641; Lake; P 3,000; M 110; (541) 576-3838; Fax (541) 576-2079; info@christmasvalleychamber.org; www.christmasvalleychamber.org

Clackamas • see Happy Valley

Clackamas • *African American C/C of Oregon* • Roy Jay; Pres./CEO; P.O. Box 2979; 97015; Clackamas; P 1,000,000; M 950; (503) 244-5794; Fax (503) 293-2094; roy@africanamericanchamberofcommerce.com; www.blackchamber.info

Clatskanie • *Clatskanie C/C* • Gina Dines; 155 W. Columbia River Hwy.; P.O. Box 635; 97016; Columbia; P 1,750; M 60; (503) 728-4321; (503) 728-2622; www.clatskaniechamber.org

Cloverdale • *Pacific City-Nestucca Valley C/C* • Jose Solano; V.P.; P.O. Box 75; 97112; Tillamook; P 1,027; M 150; (503) 392-4340; manager@pcnvchamber.org; www.pcnvchamber.org

Columbia City • *see St. Helens*

Condon • *Condon C/C* • Canda Rattray; Pres.; 307 S. Main St.; P.O. Box 315; 97823; Gilliam; P 650; M 107; (541) 384-7777; condonchamber@condonchamber.org; www.condonchamber.org

Coos Bay • *Bay Area C/C* • Timm Slater; Exec. Dir.; 145 Central Ave.; 97420; Coos; P 26,000; M 600; (541) 266-0868; Fax (541) 267-6704; timmslater@oregonsbayarea.org; www.oregonsbayarea.org*

Coquille • *Coquille C of C & Info. Center* • Dian Courtright; Exec. Dir.; 119 N. Birch St.; 97423; Coos; P 4,000; M 85; (541) 396-3414; Fax (541) 824-0138; coquillechamber@mycomspan.com; www.coquillechamber.net

Corvallis • *Corvallis C/C* • Marcy Eastham; Exec. Dir.; 420 N.W. 2nd St.; 97330; Benton; P 55,000; M 486; (541) 757-1505; info@corvallischamber.com; www.corvallischamber.com*

Cottage Grove • *Cottage Grove Area C/C* • Travis Palmer; Exec. Dir.; 700 E. Gibbs, Ste. C; 97424; Lane; P 9,745; M 200; (541) 942-2411; Fax (888) 832-2045; info@cgchamber.com; www.cgchamber.com*

Creswell • *Creswell C/C* • Don Amberg; Admin.; 104 S. Mill St., Ste. 102; P.O. Box 577; 97426; Lane; P 5,050; M 80; (541) 895-4398; Fax (541) 895-4398; creswellchamber@gmail.com; www.creswellchamber.com

Crooked River Ranch • *see Redmond*

Dallas • *Dallas Area C/C* • Chelsea Pope; Exec. Dir.; 168 S.W. Court St.; P.O. Box 377; 97338; Polk; P 15,000; M 200; (503) 623-2564; Fax (503) 623-8936; chamber@dallasoregon.org; www.dallasoregon.org*

Damascus • *see Happy Valley*

Deer Island • *see St. Helens*

Depoe Bay • *Depoe Bay C/C & Visitors Center* • Bill Johnson; Pres.; 223 S.W. Hwy. 101, Ste. B; P.O. Box 21; 97341; Lincoln; P 1,400; M 120; (541) 765-2889; (877) 485-8348; Fax (541) 765-2836; info@depoebaychamber.org; www.depoebaychamber.org

WHALE WATCHING CAPITOL OF OREGON. APRIL-WOODEN BOAT SHOW. SEPTEMBER-INDIAN SALMON BAKE. YEAR-ROUND STORMS AND SUNSETS.

Drain • *Drain C/C* • Georgia Richmond; Pres.; P.O. Box 885; 97435; Douglas; P 1,150; M 60; (541) 836-2417; drainchamber.com

Eagle Point • *Eagle Point Upper Rogue C/C* • Bob Pinnell; Pres.; P.O. Box 1539; 97524; Jackson; P 8,700; M 115; (541) 944-6925; info@eaglepointchamber.org; www.eaglepointchamber.org*

Elgin • *Elgin C/C* • Kathy Rysdam; Treas.; P.O. Box 1001; 97827; Union; P 1,700; M 40; (541) 786-1770; (541) 437-2253; elgincoc@gmail.com; www.visitelginoregon.com

Enterprise • *Wallowa County C/C* • Vicki Searles; Exec. Dir.; 309 S. River St., Ste. B; P.O. Box 427; 97828; Wallowa; P 7,000; M 400; (541) 426-4622; Fax (541) 426-2032; info@wallowacounty.org; www.wallowacountychamber.com

Estacada • *Estacada C/C* • Jordan Winthrop; Pres.; 475 S.E. Main; P.O. Box 298; 97023; Clackamas; P 2,855; M 143; (503) 630-3483; estacadachamber@cascadeaccess.com; www.estacadachamber.org

Eugene • *Eugene Area C/C* • David L. Hauser CCE; Pres./CEO; 1401 Willamette St.; P.O. Box 1107; 97440; Lane; P 160,561; M 1,200; (541) 484-1314; Fax (541) 484-4942; info@eugenechamber.com; www.eugenechamber.com*

Florence • *Florence Area C/C* • Cal Applebee; Exec. Dir.; 290 Hwy. 101; 97439; Lane; P 17,000; M 250; (541) 997-3128; Fax (541) 997-4101; cal@florencechamber.com; www.florencechamber.com*

Forest Grove • *Forest Grove/Cornelius C/C* • Howard Sullivan; Exec. Dir.; 2417 Pacific Ave.; 97116; Washington; P 23,000; M 213; (503) 357-3006; Fax (503) 357-2367; info@visitforestgrove.com; www.visitforestgrove.com

Gladstone • *see Happy Valley*

Gold Beach • *Gold Beach C/C* • Kathleen Root-Bunten; Exec. Dir.; 29692 Ellensburg Ave., Ste. 7; P.O. Box 489; 97444; Curry; P 8,000; M 300; (541) 247-0923; Fax (541) 247-4394; info@goldbeachchamber.com; www.goldbeachchamber.com

Grants Pass • *Grants Pass & Josephine County C/C* • Colene Martin; Pres./CEO; 1995 N.W. Vine St.; P.O. Box 970; 97528; Josephine; P 83,290; M 535; (541) 476-7717; Fax (541) 476-9574; gpcoc@grantspasschamber.org; www.grantspasschamber.org*

Gresham • *Gresham Area C/C & Visitors Center* • Bob McDonald; Exec. Dir.; 701 N.E. Hood Ave.; 97030; Multnomah; P 105,000; M 485; (503) 665-1131; Fax (503) 666-1041; gacc@greshamchamber.org; www.greshamchamber.org*

Happy Valley • *North Clackamas C/C* • Laura Edmonds; Pres./CEO; 8305 S.E. Monterey Ave., Ste. 104; 97086; Clackamas; P 197,000; M 500; (503) 654-7777; Fax (503) 653-9515; info@yourchamber.com; www.yourchamber.com*

Harney County • *see Burns*

Harrisburg • *see Junction City*

Hebo • *see Cloverdale*

Hemlock • *see Cloverdale*

Heppner • *Heppner C/C* • Sheryll Bates; Exec. Dir.; P.O. Box 1232; 97836; Morrow; P 1,300; M 125; (541) 676-5536; Fax (541) 676-9650; heppnerchamber@centurytel.net; www.heppnerchamber.com

Hermiston • *Greater Hermiston C/C* • Debbie Pedro; Exec. Dir.; 415 S. Hwy. 395; P.O. Box 185; 97838; Umatilla; P 16,000; M 450; (541) 567-6151; Fax (541) 564-9109; info@hermistonchamber.com; www.hermistonchamber.com*

Hillsboro • *Hillsboro C/C* • Deanna Palm; Pres.; 5193 N.E. Elam Young Pkwy., Ste. A; 97124; Washington; P 92,000; M 775; (503) 648-1102; Fax (503) 681-0535; info@hillchamber.org; www.hillchamber.org*

Hood River • *Hood River County C/C* • Kerry Cobb; Exec. Dir.; 720 E. Port Marina Dr.; 97031; Hood River; P 21,000; M 450; (541) 386-2000; (800) 366-3530; Fax (541) 386-2057; info@hoodriver.org; www.hoodriver.org*

Huntington • *Huntington C/C* • Elieen Driver; Pres.; P.O. Box 280; 97907; Baker; P 500; M 7; (541) 869-2529; huntingtonor@visithuntingtonor.org; www.visithuntingtonor.org

Illinois Valley • *see Cave Junction*

Jacksonville • *Jacksonville C of C & Visitors Info.* • Sandi Torrey; Dir. of Visitor Center; 185 N. Oregon St.; P.O. Box 33; 97530; Jackson; P 2,800; M 120; (541) 899-8118; Fax (541) 899-4462; chamber@jacksonvilleoregon.org; www.jacksonvilleoregon.org

John Day • *Grant County C/C & Visitors Center* • Jerry Franklin; Pres.; 301 W. Main St.; 97845; Grant; P 7,500; M 160; (541) 575-0547; (800) 769-5664; Fax (541) 575-1932; gcadmin@gcoregonlive.com; www.gcoregonlive.com

Johnson City • *see Happy Valley*

Joseph • *Joseph C/C* • Debbie Short; Ofc. Mgr.; 102 E. 1st St.; P.O. Box 1001; 97846; Wallowa; P 1,150; M 110; (541) 432-1015; cjdays@eoni.com; www.josephoregon.com

Junction City • *Tri-County C/C* • Rick Kissock; Exec. Dir.; 341 W. 6th Ave.; 97448; Lane; P 12,000; M 200; (541) 998-6154; Fax (541) 998-1037; rick@tri-countychamber.com; www.tri-countychamber.com

Keizer • *Keizer C/C* • Christine Dieker IOM; Exec. Dir.; 6150 Ulali Dr. N.E.; 97303; Marion; P 38,000; M 380; (503) 393-9111; (971) 703-2580; christine@keizerchamber.com; www.keizerchamber.com

Klamath Falls • *Klamath County C/C* • Heather Tramp; Interim Exec. Dir.; 205 Riverside Dr., Ste. A; 97601; Klamath; P 66,000; M 500; (541) 884-5193; (877) KLAMATH; inquiry@klamath.org; www.klamath.org*

La Grande • *Union County C/C & Visitors Info. Center* • 207 Depot St.; 97850; Union; P 25,000; M 310; (541) 963-8588; (800) 848-9969; Fax (541) 963-3936; info@unioncountychamber.org; www.unioncountychamber.org*

La Pine • *La Pine C/C & Visitor Center* • Ann Gawith; Exec. Dir.; 51429 Huntington Rd.; P.O. Box 616; 97739; Deschutes; P 22,000; M 290; (541) 536-9771; Fax (541) 536-8410; director@lapine.org; www.lapine.org*

Lake Oswego • *Lake Oswego C/C* • Lori Lauber; Mgr.; 459 Third St.; P.O. Box 368; 97034; Clackamas; P 35,000; M 600; (503) 636-3634; Fax (503) 636-7427; loril@lake-oswego.com; www.lake-oswego.com*

Lakeside • *Lakeside C/C* • Mrs. Cathy Reiss; Pres.; P.O. Box 333; 97449; Coos; P 1,200; M 50; (541) 759-3981; lkchamber@presys.com; www.lakesideoregonchambers.com

Lakeview • *Lake County C/C* • 126 North E St.; 97630; Lake; P 4,000; M 300; (541) 947-6040; Fax (541) 947-4892; info@lakecountychamber.org; www.lakecountychamber.org

Lebanon • *Lebanon Area C/C* • Shelley Garrett; Exec. Dir.; 1040 Park St.; 97355; Linn; P 15,850; M 346; (541) 258-7164; (877) 447-8873; Fax (541) 258-7166; shelley@lebanon-chamber.org; www.lebanon-chamber.org*

Lincoln City • *Lincoln City C/C* • Lori Arce-Torres; Exec. Dir.; 4039 N.W. Logan Rd.; 97367; Lincoln; P 8,400; M 310; (541) 994-3070; Fax (541) 994-8339; info@lcchamber.com; www.lcchamber.com*

Madras • *Madras-Jefferson County C/C* • Joe Krenowicz; Exec. Dir.; 274 S.W. 4th St.; P.O. Box 770; 97741; Jefferson; P 24,000; M 350; (541) 475-2350; (800) 967-3564; office@madraschamber.com; www.madraschamber.com

Manzanita • *see Wheeler*

McMinnville • *McMinnville Area C/C* • Gioia Goodrum; Pres./CEO; 417 N.W. Adams St.; 97128; Yamhill; P 33,000; M 445; (503) 472-6196; Fax (503) 472-6198; chamberinfo@mcminnville.org; www.mcminnville.org*

Medford • *The Chamber of Medford/Jackson County* • Brad S. Hicks CCE ACE IOM; Pres./CEO; 101 E. 8th St.; 97501; Jackson; P 203,300; M 1,282; (541) 779-4847; Fax (541) 776-4808; business@medfordchamber.com; www.medfordchamber.com*

Mill City • *North Santiam C/C* • Michelle Gates; Exec. Dir.; P.O. Box 222; 97360; Linn & Marion; P 7,500; M 325; (503) 897-5000; director@nschamber.org; www.nschamber.org

Milton-Freewater • *Milton-Freewater Area C/C* • Cheryl York; Exec. Dir.; 157 S. Columbia; 97862; Umatilla; P 7,050; M 179; (541) 938-5563; Fax (541) 938-5564; mfmdfrog@mfchamber.com; www.mfchamber.com*

Milwaukie • *see Happy Valley*

Molalla • *Molalla Area C/C* • Terri McConnachie; Ofc. Coord.; 107 E. Main St.; P.O. Box 472; 97038; Clackamas; P 8,500; M 200; (503) 829-6941; Fax (503) 829-7949; macc@molalla.net; www.molallachamber.com

Monmouth • *Monmouth-Independence C/C* • Jean Love; Exec. Dir.; 355 Pacific Ave. N., Ste. A; 97361; Polk; P 18,000; M 170; (503) 838-4268; Fax (503) 838-6658; micc@minetfiber.com; www.micc-or.org*

Mount Angel • *Mount Angel C/C* • Mary Kohler; P.O. Box 221; 97362; Marion; P 3,300; M 120; (503) 845-9440; machamber@mtangelchamber.org; www.mtangelchamber.org

Mount Hood • *see Welches*

Myrtle Creek • *Myrtle Creek - Tri City Area C/C* • Ted Romas; Pres.; P.O. Box 31; 97457; Douglas; P 8,000; M 100; (541) 863-3037; president@myrtlecreekchamber.com; www.myrtlecreekchamber.com

Nehalem • *see Wheeler*

Neskowin • *see Cloverdale*

Newberg • *Chehalem Valley C/C* • Sheryl Kelsh; Exec. Dir.; 115 N. College; 97132; Yamhill; P 20,500; M 460; (503) 538-2014; Fax (503) 538-2463; info@chehalemvalley.org; www.chehalemvalley.org*

Newport • *Greater Newport C/C* • Lorna Davis; Exec. Dir.; 555 S.W. Coast Hwy.; 97365; Lincoln; P 10,300; M 626; (541) 265-8801; (800) 262-7844; Fax (541) 265-5589; info@newportchamber.org; www.newportchamber.org*

North Bend • *see Coos Bay*

North Plains • *North Plains C/C* • Russ Sheldon; Pres.; P.O. Box 152; 97133; Washington; P 2,100; M 67; (503) 647-2207; (503) 647-4600; Fax (503) 647-5840; admin@northplainschamberofcommerce.org; www.northplainschamber.org

Nyssa • *Nyssa C/C & Ag.* • Susan Barton; Secy.; 105 Main St.; 97913; Malheur; P 3,200; M 95; (541) 372-3091; Fax (541) 372-9990; nyssachamber@nyssachamber.com; www.nyssachamber.com

Oakridge • *Oakridge-Westfir Area C/C* • Randy Dreiling; P.O. Box 217; 97463; Lane; P 5,000; M 75; (541) 782-4146; Fax (541) 782-1081; info@oakridgechamber.com; www.oakridgechamber.com

Ontario • *Ontario C/C* • John Breidenbach; Pres./CEO; 251 S.W. 9th St.; 97914; Malheur; P 12,000; M 345; (541) 889-8012; Fax (541) 889-8331; info@ontariochamber.com; www.ontariochamber.com*

Oregon City • *Oregon City C/C* • Amber Holveck; Exec. Dir.; 2895 S. Beavercreek Rd., Ste. 103; 97045; Clackamas; P 32,000; M 305; (503) 656-1619; Fax (503) 656-2274; chamberinfo@oregoncity.org; www.oregoncity.org*

Pacific City • *see Cloverdale*

Pendleton • *Pendleton C/C* • Gail Nelson; Exec. Dir.; 501 S. Main St.; 97801; Umatilla; P 17,000; M 450; (541) 276-7411; (800) 547-8911; Fax (541) 276-8849; info@pendletonchamber.com; www.pendletonchamber.com*

Philomath • *Philomath Area C/C* • Shelley Niemann; Dir.; P.O. Box 606; 97370; Benton; P 4,400; M 100; (541) 929-2454; director@philomathchamber.org; www.philomathchamber.org*

Phoenix • *Phoenix C/C* • Leone Holden; Pres.; P.O. Box 998; 97535; Jackson; P 5,000; M 100; (541) 535-6956; info@phoenixoregonchamber.org; www.phoenixoregonchamber.org

Port Orford • *Port Orford/North Curry County C/C* • David Smith; Pres.; P.O. Box 637; 97465; North Curry; P 1,100; M 60; (541) 332-8055; Fax (541) 332-8055; chamber@portorfordchamber.com; www.portorfordchamber.com

Portland • *Portland Bus. Alliance-Greater Portland's C/C* • Sandra McDonough; Pres./CEO; 200 S.W. Market St., Ste. 150; 97201; Multnomah; P 2,121,910; M 1,400; (503) 224-8684; Fax (503) 323-9186; info@portlandalliance.com; www.portlandalliance.com*

Portland • *African American C/C of Oregon* • Roy Jay; Exec. Dir.; 4300 N.E. Fremont St., Ste. 220; 97213; Clackamas, Multnomah & Washington; P 1,000,000; M 950; (503) 244-5794; Fax (503) 293-2094; roy@africanamericanchamberofcommerce.com; www.blackchamber.info

Prineville • *Prineville-Crook County C/C* • Casey Kaiser; Exec. Dir.; 185 N.E. 10th St.; 97754; Crook; P 25,000; M 350; (541) 447-6304; Fax (541) 447-6537; info@prinevillechamber.com; visitprineville.org*

Ranier • *Ranier C/C* • Florence Thomas; Pres.; P.O. Box 1085; 97048; Columbia; P 1,750; M 50; (503) 556-7212; Fax (503) 556-2199; rainierchamberofcommerce@gmail.com; www.rainierchamberofcommerce.com

Redmond • *Redmond C/C & CVB* • Eric Sande; Exec. Dir.; 446 S.W. 7th St.; 97756; Deschutes; P 27,000; M 807; (541) 923-5191; Fax (541) 923-6442; info@visitredmondoregon.com; www.visitredmondoregon.com*

Reedsport • *Reedsport/Winchester Bay C/C* • Amy Stauffer; Mgr.; 2741 Frontage Rd.; P.O. Box 11; 97467; Douglas; P 4,200; M 120; (541) 271-3495; Fax (541) 271-3496; amystauffer@frontier.com; www.reedsportcc.org*

Rockaway Beach • *Rockaway Beach C/C* • Christine Hayes; 103 S. 1st St.; P.O. Box 198; 97136; Tillamook; P 1,200; M 100; (503) 355-8108; rbccsec@gmail.com; www.rockawaybeach.net

Rogue River • *Rogue River Area C/C* • Dean Stirm; Pres.; 8898 Rogue River Hwy.; P.O. Box 457; 97537; Jackson; P 2,085; M 100; (541) 582-0242; info@rrchamber.cc; www.rrchamber.cc

Roseburg • *Roseburg Area C/C* • Debra L. Fromdahl; Pres./CEO; 410 S.E. Spruce St.; P.O. Box 1026; 97470; Douglas; P 60,000; M 500; (541) 672-2648; Fax (541) 673-7868; info@roseburgareachamber.org; www.roseburgareachamber.org*

Salem • *Salem Area C/C* • Jason Brandt; CEO; 1110 Commercial St. N.E.; 97301; Marion; P 165,000; M 1,270; (503) 581-1466; Fax (503) 581-0972; info@salemchamber.org; www.salemchamber.org*

Sandlake • *see Cloverdale*

Sandy • *Sandy Area C/C* • Khrys Jones; Exec. Dir.; 38979 Pioneer Blvd.; P.O. Box 536; 97055; Clackamas; P 10,900; M 320; (503) 668-4006; Fax (503) 668-3459; info@sandyoregonchamber.org; www.sandyoregonchamber.org*

Scappoose • *see St. Helens*

Seaside • *Seaside C/C* • Brian J. Owen; CEO; 7 N. Roosevelt; P.O. Box 7; 97138; Clatsop; P 6,700; M 325; (503) 738-6391; (800) 444-6740; Fax (503) 738-5732; director@seasidechamber.com; www.seasidechamber.com*

Sherwood • *Sherwood C/C* • Lana Painter; Exec. Dir.; P.O. Box 805; 97140; Washington; P 18,000; M 275; (503) 625-7800; Fax (503) 625-7550; chamber@sherwoodchamber.org; www.sherwoodchamber.org*

Silverton • *Silverton Area C/C* • Stacy Palmer; Exec. Dir.; 426 S. Water St.; P.O. Box 257; 97381; Marion; P 9,600; M 260; (503) 873-5615; Fax (503) 873-7144; info@silvertonchamber.org; www.silvertonchamber.org*

Sisters • *Sisters Area C/C* • Erin Borla; Exec. Dir.; 291 E. Main Ave.; P.O. Box 430; 97759; Deschutes; P 2,053; M 400; (541) 549-0251; Fax (541) 549-4253; info@sisterscountry.com; www.sisterscountry.com

Springfield • *Springfield Area C/C* • Vonnie Mikkelsen; Pres./CEO; 101 South A St.; P.O. Box 155; 97477; Lane; P 61,000; M 900; (541) 746-1651; Fax (541) 726-4727; info@springfield-chamber.org; www.springfield-chamber.org*

St. Helens • *South Columbia County C/C* • Natasha Parvey; Exec. Dir.; 2194 Columbia Blvd.; 97051; Columbia; P 25,000; M 250; (503) 397-0685; Fax (503) 397-7196; mgr@sccchamber.org; www.sccchamber.org

Stayton • *Stayton Sublimity C/C* • Kelly Schreiber; Pres./CEO; 175 E. High St.; P.O. Box 121; 97383; Marion; P 9,500; M 213; (503) 769-3464; Fax (503) 769-3463; sscoc@wvi.com; www.staytonsublimitychamber.org

Sunriver • *Sunriver Area C/C* • Kent Elliott; Exec. Dir.; 57195 Beaver Dr.; P.O. Box 3246; 97707; Deschutes; P 9,000; M 250; (541) 593-8149; Fax (541) 593-3581; info@sunriverchamber.com; www.sunriverchamber.com*

Sutherlin • *Sutherlin C/C & Visitors Center* • Greg Henderson; Exec. Dir.; 1310 W. Central Ave.; P.O. Box 1404; 97479; Douglas; P 7,300; M 120; (541) 459-3280; sutherlinareachamber@gmail.com; www.sutherlinchamber.com

Sweet Home • *Sweet Home C/C* • Andrea Culy; Exec. Mgr.; 1575 Main St.; 97386; Linn; P 8,300; M 150; (541) 367-6186; Fax (541) 367-6150; info@sweethomechamber.org; www.sweethomechamber.org*

The Dalles • *The Dalles Area C/C* • Lisa Farquharson; Pres./CEO; 404 W. 2nd St.; 97058; Wasco; P 15,000; M 500; (541) 296-2231; (800) 255-3385; Fax (541) 296-1688; info@thedalleschamber.com; www.thedalleschamber.com*

Tierra del Mar • *see Cloverdale*

Tigard • *Tigard Area C/C* • Debi Mollahan; CEO; 12345 S.W. Main St.; 97223; Washington; P 47,595; M 308; (503) 639-1656; Fax (503) 639-6302; info@tigardchamber.org; www.tigardchamber.org*

Tillamook • *Tillamook Area C/C* • Justin Aufdermauer; Exec. Dir.; 208 Main; 97141; Tillamook; P 26,000; M 280; (503) 842-7525; info@tillamookchamber.org; www.tillamookchamber.org

Toledo • *Toledo C/C* • Belinda Goody; Dir.; P.O. Box 249; 97391; Lincoln; P 3,580; M 100; (541) 336-3183; director@toledooregon.org; www.toledooregon.org

Troutdale • *West Columbia Gorge C/C* • Marcia Chiaudano; Office & Hospitality Mgr.; 107 E. Historic Columbia River Hwy.; P.O. Box 245; 97060; Multnomah; P 15,000; M 225; (503) 669-7473; Fax (503) 492-3613; info@westcolumbiagorgechamber.com; www.westcolumbiagorgechamber.com*

Tualatin • *Tualatin C/C* • Linda Moholt; CEO; 18791 S.W. Martinazzi Ave.; P.O. Box 701; 97062; Clackamas & Washington; P 28,000; M 425; (503) 692-0780; Fax (503) 692-6955; chamber@tualatinchamber.com; www.tualatinchamber.com*

Umatilla • *Umatilla C/C* • Karen Hutchinson-Talaski; Exec. Dir.; 100 Cline Ave.; P.O. Box 67; 97882; Umatilla; P 7,000; M 95; (541) 922-4825; Fax (541) 922-9551; karen@umatillachamber.net; www.umatillaoregonchamber.org

Vale • *Vale C/C* • Jessica Hale; Secy.; 252 B St. W.; 97918; Malheur; P 1,900; M 100; (541) 473-3800; Fax (541) 473-3895; director@valechamber.com; www.valechamber.com

Veneta • *Fern Ridge C/C* • Gina Haley-Morrell; Pres.; 24949 Hwy. 126; P.O. Box 335; 97487; Lane; P 4,700; M 140; (541) 935-8443; Fax (541) 935-1164; staff@fernridgechamber.com; www.fernridgechamber.com

Vernonia • *Vernonia Area C/C* • Pam Weller; Pres.; 1001 Bridge St.; 97064; Columbia; P 2,300; M 75; (503) 429-6081; Fax (503) 429-4232; info@vernoniachamber.org; www.vernoniachamber.org

Waldport • *Waldport C/C & Visitor Center* • Mark Campbell; Pres.; 320 N.W. Hwy. 101; P.O. Box 669; 97394; Lincoln; P 2,033; M 100; (541) 563-2133; Fax (541) 563-6326; chamber@peak.org; www.waldport-chamber.com

Warren • *see St. Helens*

Wedderburn • *see Gold Beach*

Welches • *Mount Hood Area C/C* • Coni Scott; Pres.; P.O. Box 819; 97067; Clackamas; P 8,000; M 138; (503) 622-3017; Fax (503) 622-4881; chamber@mthood.org; www.mthood.org

West Linn • *West Linn C/C* • Linda Neace; Pres.; 1745 Willamette Falls Dr.; 97068; Clackamas; P 24,482; M 200; (503) 655-6744; chamberinfo@westlinnchamber.com; www.westlinnchamber.com*

Westfir • *see Oakridge*

Wheeler • *Nehalem Bay Area C/C* • Donald H. Irvin; Dir.; 36005 7th St.; P.O. Box 601; 97147; Tillamook; P 1,413; M 80; (503) 368-5100; nehalem@nehalemtel.net; www.nehalembaychamber.com

Willamina • *Willamina Coastal Hills C/C* • Dennis Ulrich; V.P.; P.O. Box 411; 97396; Polk & Yamhill; P 2,050; M 45; (503) 876-4222; Fax (503) 876-4334

Wilsonville • *Wilsonville Area C/C* • Kevin Ferrasci O'Malley; CEO; 8565 S.W. Salish Ln, Ste. 150; 97070; Clackamas & Washington; P 20,000; M 420; (503) 682-0411; (800) 647-3843; Fax (503) 682-4189; info@wilsonvillechamber.com; www.wilsonvillechamber.com*

Winchester Bay • *see Reedsport*

Winston • *Winston Area C/C & Visitors Info. Center* • Michael Fernandez; Pres.; 30 N.W. Glenhart; P.O. Box 68; 97496; Douglas; P 10,000; M 100; (541) 679-0118; info@winstonchamber.org; www.winstonchamber.org

Woodburn • *Woodburn Area C/C & Tourism* • Brenda Shoup; Exec. Asst.; 979 Young St., Ste. A.; P.O. Box 194; 97071; Marion; P 25,000; M 260; (503) 982-8221; Fax (503) 982-8410; welcome@woodburnchamber.org; www.woodburnchamber.org*

Woods • *see Cloverdale*

Yachats • *Yachats Area C/C & Visitors Center* • David Locke; Pres.; 241 Hwy. 101; P.O. Box 728; 97498; Lincoln; P 670; M 205; (541) 547-3530; (800) 929-0477; info@yachats.org; www.yachats.org

Pennsylvania

The Pennsylvania Chamber of Bus. & Ind. • Gene Barr; Pres./CEO; 417 Walnut St.; Harrisburg; 17101; Cumberland, Dauphin & Perry; P 12,763,536; M 9,000; (717) 255-3252; (800) 225-7224; Fax (717) 255-3298; info@pachamber.org; www.pachamber.org

Adams County • *see Gettysburg*

Allegheny • *see Pittsburgh Area*

Allentown • *Greater Lehigh Valley C/C* • Tony Iannelli; Pres./CEO; 840 Hamilton St., Ste. 205; 18101; Lehigh; P 579,156; M 5,000; (610) 226-6323; Fax (610) 437-4907; miriamh@lehighvalleychamber.org; www.lehighvalleychamber.org*

Altoona • *Blair County C/C* • Joseph D. Hurd; Pres./CEO; 3900 Industrial Park Dr., Ste. 12; 16602; Blair; P 135,000; M 1,050; (814) 943-8151; Fax (814) 943-5239; chamber@blairchamber.com; www.blairchamber.com*

Ambridge • *Ambridge Area C/C* • Jenifer B. Watkins; Dir.; 562 Merchant St.; 15003; Beaver; P 8,000; M 160; (724) 266-3040; ambridgechamber@gmail.com; www.ambridgechamberofcommerce.com

Antrim • *see Greencastle*

Apollo • *see Kittanning*

Archbald • *see Carbondale*

Aspinwall • *Aspinwall C/C* • Gina Musser; Pres.; 217 Commercial Ave.; 15215; Allegheny; P 2,800; M 125; (412) 781-0213; chamber@aspinwallpa.com; www.aspinwallpa.com

Athens • *see Waverly, NY*

Audubon • *see Eagleville*

Baldwin • *see Pittsburgh-Brentwood Baldwin Whitehall C/C*

Bangor • *Slate Belt C/C* • Laura McLain; Exec. Dir.; 187 Blue Valley Dr.; (P.O. Box 5, Pen Argyl, 18072); 18013; Northampton; P 40,000; M 250; (610) 588-1000; Fax (610) 588-1000; info@slatebeltchamber.org; www.slatebeltchamber.org

Beaver • *Beaver County C/C* • Erica Wachtel; Pres.; 798 Turnpike St.; 15009; Beaver; P 170,539; M 600; (724) 775-3944; Fax (724) 728-9737; info@bcchamber.com; www.bcchamber.com*

Bedford • *Bedford County C/C* • Kellie Goodman Shaffer; Exec. Dir.; 125 S. Juliana St.; 15522; Bedford; P 50,000; M 575; (814) 623-2233; Fax (814) 623-6089; info@bedfordcountychamber.org; www.bedfordcountychamber.com*

Bellefonte • *Bellefonte Intervalley Area C/C* • Gary V. Hoover; Exec. Dir.; 320 W. High St.; Train Station; 16823; Centre; P 120,000; M 230; (814) 355-2917; Fax (814) 355-2761; bellefontecoc@aol.com; www.bellefontechamber.org

Bellevue • *North Suburban C/C* • 547 Lincoln Ave.; 15202; Allegheny; P 30,000; M 50; (412) 761-2113; Fax (412) 761-2113; info@northsuburbancoc.org; www.northsuburbancoc.org

Bensalem • *see Fairless Hills*

Berlin • *see Somerset*

Berwick • *see Bloomsburg*

Bethlehem • *Greater Lehigh Valley C/C* • Tony Iannelli; Pres./CEO; One E. Broad St., Ste. 560; 18018; Lehigh & Northampton; P 630,000; M 5,000; (610) 841-5800; (610) 841-5862; Fax (610) 758-9533; amandar@lehighvalleychamber.org; www.lehighvalleychamber.org*

Birdsboro • *see Pottstown*

Bloomsburg • *Columbia Montour C/C* • Fred Gaffney; Pres.; 238 Market St.; 17815; Columbia & Montour; P 85,600; M 600; (570) 784-2522; Fax (570) 784-2661; chamber@columbiamontourchamber.com; www.columbiamontourchamber.com*

Boyertown • *see Pottstown*

Brackenridge • *see Tarentum*

Bradford • *Bradford Area C/C* • Ron Orris; Exec. Dir.; 121 Main St.; 16701; McKean; P 20,000; M 410; (814) 368-7115; Fax (814) 368-6233; info@bradfordchamber.com; www.bradfordchamber.com

Brentwood • *see Pittsburgh-Brentwood Baldwin Whitehall C/C*

Bridgeport • *see Eagleville*

Bridgeville • *see Pittsburgh-South West Comm. C/C*

Brockway • *see DuBois*

Brookville • *Brookville Area C/C* • Jamie Barger; Exec. Dir.; 278 Main St.; 15825; Jefferson; P 4,000; M 185; (814) 849-8448; director@brookvillechamber.com; www.brookvillechamber.com

Brownsville • *Greater Brownsville Area C/C* • Scott Bowman; Exec. Dir.; 325 Market St.; 15417; Fayette; P 6,000; M 70; (724) 785-4160; Fax (724) 785-5631; www.brownsvillepa.org

Butler • *Butler County C/C* • Stan Kosciuszko; Pres.; 101 E. Diamond St., Ste. 116; P.O. Box 1082; 16003; Butler; P 184,000; M 550; (724) 283-2222; Fax (724) 283-0224; jennifer@butlercountychamber.com; www.butlercountychamber.com

California • *see Charleroi*

Camp Hill • *West Shore C/C* • George Book; Pres./CEO; 4211 Trindle Rd.; 17011; Cumberland; P 172,000; M 900; (717) 761-0702; Fax (717) 761-4315; wschamber@wschamber.org; www.wschamber.org

Canonsburg • *Washington County C/C* • Jeff M. Kotula; Pres.; 375 Southpointe Blvd., Ste. 240; 15317; Washington; P 208,000; M 1,000; (724) 225-3010; Fax (724) 228-7337; info@washcochamber.com; www.washcochamber.com

Canonsburg • *Greater Canonsburg C/C* • Anita Brecosky; Exec. Admin.; 169 E. Pike St.; 15317; Washington; P 12,000; M 200; (724) 745-1812; Fax (724) 745-5211; info@canonchamber.com; www.canonchamber.com

Canton • *Canton Area C/C* • Jodi Wesneski; Pres.; P.O. Box 153; 17724; Bradford; P 2,000; M 55; (570) 364-2600; cantonareachamberofcommerce@yahoo.com; www.cantonareachamberofcommerce.com

Carbondale • *Greater Carbondale C/C* • Laure E. Carlo; Exec. Dir.; 27 N. Main St.; 18407; Lackawanna; P 11,000; M 350; (570) 282-1690; Fax (570) 282-1206; info@carbondalechamber.org; www.carbondalechamber.org

Carlisle • *Greater Carlisle Area C/C* • Michelle Crowley; Pres.; 212 N. Hanover St.; 17013; Cumberland; P 72,000; M 670; (717) 243-4515; Fax (717) 243-4446; info@carlislechamber.org; www.carlislechamber.org*

Cecil • *see Canonsburg*

Chambersburg • *Greater Chambersburg C/C* • Noel Purdy; Pres.; 100 Lincoln Way East, Ste. A; 17201; Franklin; P 153,000; M 850; (717) 264-7101; Fax (717) 267-0399; receptionist@chambersburg.org; www.chambersburg.org*

Champion • *see Donegal*

Charleroi • *Mon Valley Reg. C/C* • Debra Keefer; Exec. Dir.; One Chamber Plaza; 15022; Washington; P 50,000; M 340; (724) 483-3507; Fax (724) 489-1045; members@mvrchamber.org; www.mvrchamber.org

Chester County • *see Malvern*

Childs • *see Carbondale*

Clairton • *see McKeesport*

Clarion • *Clarion Area Chamber of Bus. & Ind.* • Tracy J. Becker CFEE; Exec. Dir.; 650 Main St.; 16214; Clarion; P 39,500; M 350; (814) 226-9161; (814) 226-9632; Fax (814) 226-4903; tracy@clarionpa.com; www.clarionpa.com

Clearfield • *Clearfield C/C* • Kim McCullough; Exec. Dir.; 125 E. Market St.; 16830; Clearfield; P 18,000; M 380; (814) 765-7567; Fax (814) 765-6948; info@clearfieldchamber.com; www.clearfieldchamber.com

Clifford • *see Carbondale*

Coatesville • *Western Chester County C/C* • Donna Siter; Exec. Dir.; 50 S. First Ave.; 19320; Chester; P 12,000; M 275; (610) 384-9550; Fax (610) 384-9550; chamber@westernchestercounty.com; www.westernchestercounty.com

Collegeville • *Perkiomen Valley C/C* • Arlene Magargal; Dir. of Op.; 351 E. Main St.; 19426; Montgomery; P 65,000; M 500; (610) 489-6660; Fax (610) 454-1270; info@pvchamber.net; www.pvchamber.net*

Collier Twp. • *see Pittsburgh-South West Comm. C/C*

Columbia • *Susquehanna Valley C/C* • Kathleen Hohenadel; Exec. Dir.; 445 Linden St.; P.O. Box 510; 17512; Lancaster & York; P 20,000; M 260; (717) 684-5249; Fax (717) 684-5142; svcc@parivertowns.com; www.parivertowns.com

Confluence • *see Somerset*

Connellsville • *Greater Connellsville C/C* • Nancy Henry & Susan McCarthy; Ofc. Mgrs.; 100 S. Arch St.; 15425; Fayette; P 30,000; M 215; (724) 628-5500; Fax (724) 628-5676; info@greaterconnellsville.org; www.greaterconnellsville.org

Coraopolis • *see Pittsburgh-Pittsburgh Airport Area C/C*

Corry • *Corry Area C/C* • Chris Hornick; Exec. Dir.; 221 N. Center St.; 16407; Erie; P 7,500; M 130; (814) 665-9925; Fax (814) 665-9925; cacc@velocity.net; www.corrychamber.com

Coudersport • *Coudersport Area C/C* • Nancy Grupp; Asst. Mgr.; 227 N. Main St.; P.O. Box 261; 16915; Potter; P 5,500; M 124; (814) 274-8165; Fax (814) 274-8165; chamber@coudersport.org; www.coudersport.org

Cranberry Township • *see Wexford*

Crescent Twp. • *see Pittsburgh-Pittsburgh Airport Area C/C*

Cresson • *Borough of Cresson C/C* • Veronica Harkins; Secy.; P.O. Box 113; 16630; Cambria; P 5,000; M 65; (814) 886-8100; info@cressonarea.com; www.cressonarea.com

Cressona • *see Pottsville*

Danville • *see Bloomsburg*

Delmont • *see Greensburg*

Donegal • *Mountain Laurel C/C* • Kris Enberg; Exec. Dir.; 3682 State Rte. 31; P.O. Box 154; 15628; Westmoreland; P 15,000; M 180; (724) 593-8900; (888) 455-8900; Fax (724) 593-8900; mlcc@lhtot.com; www.mountainlaurelchamber.com

Donora • *Donora C/C* • Edie Jericho; V.P.; 638 McKean Ave.; 15033; Washington; P 4,745; M 30; (724) 823-0364; (724) 379-6600; donoraboro.org

Dormont • *see Pittsburgh-South Hills C/C*

Downingtown • *Downingtown-Thorndale Reg. C/C* • Steven J. Plaugher; Exec. Dir.; 216 E. Lancaster Ave.; 19335; Chester; P 10,000; M 140; (610) 269-1523; Fax (610) 269-6651; info@dtrcc.com; www.dtrcc.com

Doylestown • *Central Bucks C/C* • Dr. Vail P. Garvin; Exec. Dir.; Bailiwick, Ste. 23; 252 W. Swamp Rd.; 18901; Bucks; P 57,000; M 2,100; (215) 348-3913; (215) 345-7051; Fax (215) 348-7154; info@centralbuckschamber.com; www.centralbuckschamber.com

DuBois • *Greater DuBois C/C* • Jodi August; Exec. Dir.; 103 Beaver Dr.; 15801; Clearfield & Jefferson; P 25,000; M 500; (814) 371-5010; Fax (814) 371-5005; dacc@duboispachamber.com; www.duboispachamber.com

Duquesne • *see McKeesport*

Eagleville • *Montgomery County C/C* • Kathleen Brandon; Pres./CEO; The Historic King of Prussia Inn; P.O. Box 200; 19408; Montgomery; P 600,000; M 1,550; (610) 265-1776; Fax (610) 265-0473; info@montgomerycountychamber.org; www.montgomerycountychamber.org*

East Bangor • *see Bangor*

East Greenville • *Upper Perkiomen Valley C/C* • Luanne B. Stauffer; Exec. Dir.; 300 Main St.; 18041; Montgomery; P 18,638; M 300; (215) 679-3336; Fax (215) 679-2624; info@upvchamber.org; www.upvchamber.org*

Easton • *see Allentown*

Elizabethtown • *Elizabethtown Area C/C* • Ramon Escudero; Exec. Dir.; 50 S. Wilson Ave.; 17022; Lancaster; P 30,000; M 200; (717) 361-7188; Fax (717) 361-7186; info@elizabethtowncoc.com; www.elizabethtowncoc.com

Elizabethville • *Northern Dauphin Reg. C/C* • Mandy Carl; Secy.; P. O. Box 218; 17023; Dauphin; P 15,000; M 70; (717) 497-6003; (717) 692-5262; Fax (717) 896-8945; ndrcc@ndrcc.org; www.ndrcc.org

Ellwood City • *Ellwood City Area C/C* • Nikki Mars; Exec. Asst.; 806 Lawrence Ave.; 16117; Beaver & Lawrence; P 8,800; M 215; (724) 758-5501; Fax (724) 758-2143; info@ellwoodchamber.org; www.ellwoodchamber.org

Emmaus • *see Allentown*

Emporium • *Cameron County C/C* • Tina Solak; Exec. Dir.; 34 E. Fourth St.; 15834; Cameron; P 5,000; M 92; (814) 486-4314; cameroncountychamber@windstream.net; www.cameroncountychamber.org

Ephrata • *Ephrata Area C/C* • Andrea Glass; Exec. Dir.; 16 E. Main St., Ste. 1; 17522; Lancaster; P 30,000; M 264; (717) 738-9010; Fax (717) 738-9012; info@ephrataareachamber.org; www.ephrata-area.org*

Erie • *Erie Reg. Chamber & Growth Partnership* • Barbara Chaffee; Pres./CEO; 208 E. Bayfront Pkwy., Ste. 100; 16507; Erie; P 102,000; M 880; (814) 454-7191; Fax (814) 459-0241; bchaffee@eriepa.com; www.eriepa.com*

Export • *see Greensburg*

Exton • *Exton Region C/C* • Sara Capinski; Pres.; 185 Exton Sq. Pkwy.; 19341; Chester; P 50,000; M 550; (610) 363-7746; Fax (610) 594-3827; chamber@ercc.net; www.ercc.net

Eynon • *see Carbondale*

Fairless Hills • *Lower Bucks County C/C* • Amy M.B. McKenna; Pres./CEO; 409 Hood Blvd.; 19030; Bucks; P 650,000; M 1,400; (215) 943-7400; Fax (215) 943-7404; amckenna@lbccc.org; www.lbccc.org*

Falls Creek • *see DuBois*

Findlay Twp. • *see Pittsburgh-Pittsburgh Airport Area C/C*

Forest City • *see Carbondale*

Forest Hills • *see McKeesport*

Franklin • *Franklin Area C/C* • Lynn Cochran; Exec. Dir.; 1327 Liberty St.; 16323; Venango; P 25,000; M 547; (814) 432-5823; Fax (814) 437-2453; lynn@franklinareachamber.org; www.franklinareachamber.org

Frazer • *see Malvern-Great Valley Reg. C/C*

Galeton • *Galeton Area C/C* • Janet Green; P.O. Box 154; 16922; Potter; P 3,000; M 90; (814) 435-8737; visitgaleton@yahoo.com; www.visitgaleton.com

Gettysburg • *Gettysburg Adams C/C* • Carrie Stuart; Pres.; 1382 Biglerville Rd.; 17325; Adams; P 110,000; M 525; (717) 334-8151; info@gettysburg-chamber.org; www.gettysburg-chamber.org*

Gibsonia • *Twp. of Richland* • Herbert C. Dankmyer; Chrmn.; 4019 Dickey Rd.; 15044; Allegheny; P 11,100; (724) 443-5921; Fax (724) 443-8860; www.richland.pa.us

Girard • *Girard-Lake City C/C* • Nicole Haibach; 259 Main St. E.; 16417; Erie; P 6,200; M 60; (814) 774-3535; chamberbiz1@gmail.com; www.girardlakecity.org

Glenside • *Greater Glenside C/C* • Barbara Nye; Pres.; P.O. Box 180; 19038; Montgomery; P 44,000; M 370; (215) 500-4080; Fax (215) 885-7966; info@glensidechamber.org; www.glensidechamber.org

Gratz • *see Elizabethville*

Greencastle • *Greencastle-Antrim C/C* • Joel Fridgen; Exec. Dir.; 217 E. Baltimore St.; 17225; Franklin; P 17,500; M 350; (717) 597-4610; Fax (717) 597-0709; deanna@greencastlepachamber.org; www.greencastlepachamber.org

Greensburg • *Westmoreland County C/C* • Chad Amond; Pres.; 241 Tollgate Hill Rd.; 15601; Westmoreland; P 365,100; M 1,000; (724) 834-2900; Fax (724) 837-7635; info@westmorelandchamber.com; www.westmorelandchamber.com*

Greentown • *see Hamlin*

Greenville • *Greenville Area C/C* • Janice Schwanbeck; Ofc. Mgr.; 182 Main St.; P.O. Box 350; 16125; Mercer; P 19,120; M 280; (724) 588-7150; Fax (724) 588-2013; info@greenvillechamber-pa.com; www.greenvillechamber-pa.com

Grove City • *Grove City Area C/C* • Beth Black; Exec. Dir.; 119 S. Broad St.; 16127; Mercer; P 16,000; M 280; (724) 458-6410; Fax (724) 458-6841; execdir@shopgrovecity.com; www.shopgrovecity.com

Halifax • *see Elizabethville*

Hamlin • *Southern Wayne Reg. C/C* • Patty Blaum; Exec. Dir.; P.O. Box 296; 18427; Wayne; P 15,000; M 225; (570) 689-4199; Fax (570) 689-4391; info@southernwaynechamber.org; www.southernwaynechamber.org

Hanover • *Hanover Area C/C* • Gary Laird; Pres.; 146 Carlisle St.; 17331; York; P 50,000; M 650; (717) 637-6130; Fax (717) 637-9127; office@hanoverchamber.com; www.hanoverchamber.com*

Harmony • *see Zelienople*

Harrisburg • *Harrisburg Reg. Chamber & Capital Region Eco. Dev. Corp. (CREDC)* • David E. Black; Pres./CEO; 3211 N. Front St., Ste. 201; 17110; Dauphin; P 550,000; M 1,200; (717) 232-4099; (877) 883-8339; Fax (717) 232-5184; info@hbgrc.org; www.HarrisburgRegionalChamber.org*

Hatboro • *Greater Hatboro C/C* • Bill George; Pres.; 220 S. York Rd.; 19040; Montgomery; P 7,400; M 600; (215) 956-9540; Fax (215) 956-9635; office@hatborochamber.org; hatborochamber.org

Hatfield • *Hatfield C/C* • Larry Stevens; Exec. Dir.; P.O. Box 445; 19440; Montgomery; P 20,000; M 400; (215) 855-3335; Fax (215) 855-3335; admin@hatfieldchamber.com; www.hatfieldchamber.com

Hawley • *The Chamber of the Northern Poconos* • Debbie Gillette; Exec. Dir.; 2512 Rte. 6, Ste. 2; 18428; Pike & Wayne; P 100,000; M 600; (570) 226-3191; Fax (570) 226-9387; debbie@northernpoconoschamber.com; www.northernpoconoschamber.com

Hazleton • *Greater Hazleton C/C* • Mary Malone; Pres.; 20 W. Broad St.; 18201; Luzerne; P 80,000; M 700; (570) 455-1509; Fax (570) 450-2013; mmalone@hazletonchamber.org; www.hazletonchamber.org*

Hershey • *see Harrisburg*

Honesdale • *The Chamber of the Northern Poconos* • Debbie Gillette; Exec. Dir.; 32 Commercial St.; 18431; Pike & Wayne; P 52,800; M 675; (570) 253-1960; Fax (570) 253-1517; chamber@northernpoconoschamber.com; www.northernpoconoschamber.com

Horsham • *see Lansdale*

Houston • *see Canonsburg*

Hummelswharf • *see Milton*

Huntingdon • *Huntingdon County C/C* • Yvonne Martin; Pres./CEO; 500 Allegheny St.; 16652; Huntingdon; P 46,000; M 400; (814) 643-1110; Fax (814) 643-1115; mail@huntingdonchamber.com; www.huntingdonchamber.com

Indiana • *Indiana County C/C* • James B. Struzzi II; Pres.; 1019 Philadelphia St.; 15701; Indiana; P 90,000; M 663; (724) 465-2511; Fax (724) 465-3706; jstruzzi@indianacountychamber.com; indianacountychamber.com*

Irwin • *Norwin C/C* • Rosanne Barry Novotnak; Pres.; 321 Main St.; 15642; Westmoreland; P 34,000; M 350; (724) 863-0888; Fax (724) 863-5133; info@norwinchamber.com; www.norwinchamber.com*

Jeannette • *see Greensburg*

Jefferson Borough • *see McKeesport*

Jenkintown • *Eastern Montgomery County C/C* • Wendy Klinghoffer; Exec. Dir.; 436 Old York Rd.; 19046; Montgomery; P 100,000; M 500; (215) 887-5122; info@emccc.org; www.emccc.org*

Jermyn • *see Carbondale*

Jim Thorpe • *see Lehighton*

Johnsonburg • *see Ridgway*

Johnstown • *Greater Johnstown/Cambria County C/C* • Robert Layo; Pres./CEO; 245 Market St., Ste. 100; 15901; Cambria; P 143,679; M 677; (814) 536-5107; (800) 790-4522; Fax (814) 539-5800; chamber@johnstownchamber.com; www.johnstownchamber.com*

Jones Mills • *see Donegal*

Kane • *Kane C/C* • Pamela Miles; Exec. Dir.; 54 Fraley St.; 16735; McKean; P 4,000; M 145; (814) 837-6565; Fax (814) 837-8257; director@kanepa.com; www.kanepa.com

Kennett Square • *Southern Chester County C/C* • Cheryl Kuhn IOM; Exec. Dir.; 217 W. State St.; 19348; Chester; P 38,000; M 500; (610) 444-0774; Fax (610) 444-5105; info@scccc.com; www.scccc.com*

King of Prussia • *see Eagleville*

Kittanning • *see Tarentum*

Kutztown • *Northeast Berks C/C* • Lori B. Donofrio-Galley; Exec. Dir.; 110 W. Main St.; P.O. Box 209; 19530; Berks; P 25,000; M 250; (610) 683-8860; Fax (610) 683-8544; nbcc@ptd.net; www.northeastberkschamber.com*

Lake Ariel • *see Hamlin*

Lake Wallenpaupack • *see Hawley*

Lancaster • *The Lancaster C/C & Ind.* • Thomas T. Baldrige; Pres./CEO; 100 S. Queen St.; P.O. Box 1558; 17608; Lancaster; P 579,000; M 2,700; (717) 397-3531; Fax (717) 293-3159; info@lcci.com; www.lancasterchamber.com*

Lansdale • *PennSuburban Chamber of Greater Montgomery County* • Pamela A. Kelly; Pres./CEO; 34 Susquehanna Ave.; 19446; Montgomery; P 125,000; M 700; (215) 362-9200; Fax (215) 362-0393; info@pennsuburban.org; www.pennsuburban.org

Lansford • *see Lehighton*

Laporte • *see Muncy Valley*

Latrobe • *Greater Latrobe-Laurel Valley Comm. C/C* • David Martin; Pres.; P.O. Box 463; 15650; Westmoreland; P 50,000; M 400; (724) 537-2671; Fax (724) 537-2671; info@gllv.org; latrobelaurelvalley.org*

Lebanon • *Lebanon Valley C/C* • Greg Buckler IOM; Pres./CEO; 604 Cumberland St.; 17042; Lebanon; P 134,000; M 850; (717) 273-3727; Fax (717) 273-7940; info@lvchamber.org; www.lvchamber.org*

Lehighton • *Carbon Chamber & Eco. Dev. Corp.* • Marlyn Kissner; Exec. Dir.; 137 South St.; 18235; Carbon; P 65,200; M 350; (610) 379-5000; (610) 751-4932; Fax (610) 379-0130; mail@carboncountychamber.org; www.carboncountychamber.org*

Lewisburg • *see Shamokin Dam*

Lewistown • *Juniata Valley Area C/C* • Jim Tunall; Pres./Exec. Dir.; Historic Courthouse; One W. Market St.; 17044; Mifflin; P 68,463; M 505; (717) 248-6713; Fax (717) 248-6714; info@juniatarivervalley.org; www.juniatarivervalley.org

Ligonier • *Ligonier Valley C/C* • Susan Grunstra; Exec. Dir.; 120 E. Main St.; 15658; Westmoreland; P 3,500; M 350; (724) 238-4200; Fax (724) 238-4610; office@ligonierchamber.com; www.ligonier.com

Limerick • *Spring-Ford Chamber of Commerce* • Carla Haydt; Exec. Dir.; 313 W. Ridge Pike, 2nd Flr.; 19468; Montgomery; P 6,000; M 235; (610) 489-7200; Fax (610) 454-0059; carla@springfordchamber.com; www.springfordchamber.com

Linesville • *Linesville Area C/C* • Paula Heaney; Pres.; P.O. Box 651; 16424; Crawford; P 1,050; M 25; (412) 417-1706; (814) 720-6558; www.linesville.org

Littlestown • *see Gettysburg*

Lower Mount Bethel • *see Bangor*

Malvern • *Great Valley Reg. C/C* • Mary Ann Severance; Pres.; 5 Great Valley Pkwy.; 19355; Chester; P 30,000; M 240; (610) 889-2069; Fax (610) 889-2063; greatchamber@gvrcc.org; www.greatvalleyonline.com

Malvern • *Chester County Chamber of Bus. & Ind.* • Guy Ciarrocchi; Pres./CEO; 1600 Paoli Pike; 19355; Chester; P 500,182; M 1,000; (610) 725-9100; Fax (610) 725-8479; info@cccbi.org; www.cccbi.org

Manheim • *Manheim Area C/C* • Kelly Lauver; Admin. Coord.; 13 E. High St.; 17545; Lancaster; P 18,000; M 120; (717) 665-6330; Fax (717) 665-7656; info@manheimchamber.com; www.manheimchamber.com*

Mansfield • *Mansfield C/C* • Amy Farrer; Pres.; 51-B S. Main St.; 16933; Tioga; P 6,000; M 125; (570) 662-3442; Fax (570) 662-0259; info@mansfield.org; www.mansfield.org

Marietta • *see Columbia*

Mayfield • *see Carbondale*

McConnellsburg • *Fulton County C/C & Tourism* • Susan Cauffman; Exec. Dir.; 101 Lincoln Way W., Ste. 102; P.O. Box 141; 17233; Fulton; P 14,845; M 170; (717) 485-4064; Fax (717) 325-0023; info@fultoncountypa.com; www.fultoncountypa.com

McDonald • *see Canonsburg*

McKeesport • *Mon Yough Area C/C* • Maury Burgwin; Pres.; 201 Lysle Blvd.; 15132; Allegheny; P 180,000; M 290; (412) 678-2450; Fax (412) 678-2451; director@monyoughchamber.com; www.monyoughchamber.com

McMurray • *Peters Twp. C/C* • Brian L. Schill; Exec. Dir.; 3909 Washington Rd., Ste. 321; P.O. Box 991; 15317; Washington; P 21,000; M 400; (724) 941-6345; Fax (724) 942-2345; info@peterstownshipchamber.com; www.peterstownshipchamber.com

Meadowlands • *see Canonsburg*

Meadville • *Meadville-Western Crawford County C/C* • Christa Battin; Exec. Dir.; 908 Diamond Park; 16335; Crawford; P 13,900; M 525; (814) 337-8030; Fax (814) 337-8022; info@meadvillechamber.com; www.meadvillechamber.com

Mechanicsburg • *Mechanicsburg C/C* • Jeff Palm; Exec. Dir.; 6 W. Strawberry Ave.; 17055; Cumberland; P 10,000; M 400; (717) 796-0811; Fax (717) 796-1977; info@mechanicsburgchamber.org; www.mechanicsburgchamber.org*

Mercer • *Mercer Area C/C* • Dotty Pintar; Exec. Dir.; 143 N. Diamond St.; 16137; Mercer; P 2,500; M 160; (724) 662-4185; mercerchamber@zoominternet.net; www.mercerareachamber.com*

Mercersburg • *Tuscarora Area C/C* • Mary-Anne Gordon; Exec. Dir.; 3 S. Main St., Ste. 4; 17236; Franklin; P 1,100; M 172; (717) 328-5827; mgordon@tachamber.org; www.mercersburg.org

Meyersdale • *see Somerset*

Middleburg • *see Milton*

Middletown • *see Harrisburg*

Mifflinburg • *see Shamokin Dam*

Milford • *Pike County C/C* • 209 E. Harford St.; 18337; Pike; P 54,000; M 300; (570) 296-8700; Fax (570) 296-3921; info@pikechamber.com; www.pikechamber.com*

Millersburg • *see Elizabethville*

Milton • *Central PA C/C* • Bruce Smith; Pres./CEO; 30 Lawton Ln.; 17847; Northumberland; P 9,056; M 390; (570) 742-7341; (570) 768-4900; Fax (570) 742-2008; bsmith@centralpachamber.com; www.centralpachamber.com*

Monessen • *Greater Monessen C/C* • Gary W. Boatman; Pres.; Ste. 154, Eastgate 11; 15062; Westmoreland; P 8,500; M 100; (724) 684-3200; Fax (724) 684-8470; info@monessenchamberofcommerce.com; www.monessenchamberofcommerce.com

Monongahela • *Monongahela Area C/C* • Dorothea Pemberton; Exec. Dir.; 212 W. Main St.; 15063; Washington; P 13,310; M 135; (724) 258-5919; Fax (724) 258-5919; info@monongahelaareachamber.org; www.monongahelaareachamber.org

Monroeville • *Monroeville Area C/C* • Sean Logan; Pres./CEO; 2790 Mosside Blvd., Ste. 715; 15146; Allegheny; P 250,000; M 500; (412) 856-0622; Fax (412) 856-1030; macc@monroevillechamber.com; www.monroevillechamber.com*

Montrose • *Montrose Area C/C* • Marilyn Morgan; Secy.; P.O. Box 423; 18801; Susquehanna; P 1,700; M 110; (570) 278-1174; marilyn@montrosearea.com; www.montrosearea.com

Moon Twp. • *see Pittsburgh-Pittsburgh Airport Area C/C*

Mount Carmel • *see Shamokin*

Mount Joy • *Mount Joy C/C* • Kerry Meyers; Chamber Coord.; 62 E. Main, Ste. 1; 17552; Lancaster; P 7,300; M 230; (717) 653-0773; Fax (717) 653-0773; info@mountjoychamber.com; www.mountjoychamber.com

Mount Lebanon • *see Pittsburgh-South Hills C/C*

Mount Pleasant • *see Greensburg*

Muncy Valley • *Sullivan County C/C* • Florence Suarez; Admin. Dir.; 1240 Rte. 220, Ste. 3; P.O. Box 134; 17758; Sullivan; P 6,500; M 157; (570) 482-4088; office@sullivanpachamber.com; www.sullivanpachamber.com

Murrysville • *see Greensburg*

Nazareth • *Nazareth Area C/C* • Tina Smith; Pres.; 201 N. Main St.; 18064; Northampton; P 25,000; M 400; (610) 759-9188; Fax (610) 759-5262; tina@nazarethchamber.com; www.nazarethchamber.com

Nesquehoning • *see Lehighton*

Neville Island • *see Pittsburgh-Pittsburgh Airport Area C/C*

New Bethlehem • *Red Bank Valley C/C* • Richard McGarrity; Exec. Secy.; 309 Broad St., Ste. 2; 16242; Clarion; P 10,000; M 96; (814) 275-3929; Fax (814) 275-4269; nbchamber@windstream.net; www.newbethlehemarea.com

New Castle • *Lawrence County C/C* • Robert McCracken; Exec. V.P.; Shenango Street Station; 138 W. Washington St.; 16101; Lawrence; P 90,000; M 800; (724) 654-5593; Fax (724) 654-3330; info@lawrencecountychamber.org; www.lawrencecountychamber.org

New Hope • *Greater New Hope C/C* • Stephanie Nagy; Admin.; 10 Stockton Ave.; P.O. Box 633; 18938; Bucks; P 3,000; M 200; (215) 862-9990; info@VisitNewHope.com; www.newhopechamber.com

New Kensington • *New Kensington Area C/C* • 858 4th Ave.; 15068; Westmoreland; P 13,100; M 136; (724) 339-6616; Fax (724) 339-3346; admin@nkchamber.org; www.nkchamber.org

New Oxford • *New Oxford Area C/C* • Lorraine Nagy; Pres.; 27 Center Sq.; 17350; Adams & York; P 1,700; M 150; (717) 624-2800; info@newoxford.org; www.newoxford.org

New Stanton • *see Greensburg*

Newfoundland • *see Hamlin*

Norristown • *see Eagleville*

North East • *North East Area C/C* • Amy Vercant; Exec. Dir.; 17 E. Main St.; 16428; Erie; P 11,000; M 250; (814) 725-4262; Fax (814) 725-3994; info@nechamber.org; www.nechamber.org

North Fayette Twp. • *see Pittsburgh-Pittsburgh Airport Area C/C*

North Huntingdon • *see Irwin*

Northampton • *see Allentown*

Northern Allegheny County • *see Wexford*

Ohiopyle • *see Donegal*

Oil City • *Venango Area C/C* • Susan Williams; Exec. Dir.; 41 Main St.; P.O. Box 376; 16301; Venango; P 55,000; M 484; (814) 676-8521; Fax (814) 676-8185; chamber@venangochamber.org; www.venangochamber.org*

Oxford • *Oxford Area C/C* • Janis Walker; Exec. Dir.; P.O. Box 4; 19363; Chester; P 5,000; M 202; (610) 932-0740; oxfordchamber@zoominternet.net; www.oxfordpa.org

Palmerton • *Palmerton Area C/C* • Peter Kern; Pres.; 410 Delaware Ave.; 18071; Carbon; P 10,000; M 145; (610) 824-6954; www.palmertonpa.com/chamber

Paoli • *see Malvern-Great Valley Reg. C/C*

Pen Argyl • *see Bangor*

Penfield • *see DuBois*

Penn Twp. • *see Greensburg*

Perkasie • *Pennridge C/C* • Betty Graver; Exec. Dir.; 538 W. Market St.; 18944; Bucks; P 42,000; M 300; (215) 257-5390; Fax (267) 354-6924; pennridgecc@pennridge.com; www.pennridge.com*

Peters Twp. • *see McMurray*

Philadelphia Area

African American C/C of PA, NJ & DE • Shalimar Thomas; Exec. Dir.; One Penn Center; 1617 J.F.K. Blvd., Ste. 889; 19103; Philadelphia; M 400; (215) 751-9501; Fax (215) 751-9509; chamberadmin@aachamber.org; www.aachamber.org

Greater Northeast Philadelphia C/C • Pam Henshall; Pres.; 8025 Roosevelt Blvd., Ste. 200; 19152; Philadelphia; P 600,000; M 400; (215) 332-3400; Fax (215) 332-6050; info@nephilachamber.com; www.nephilachamber.com*

Greater Philadelphia C/C • Rob Wonderling; Pres./CEO; 200 S. Broad St., Ste. 700; 19102; Philadelphia; P 6,000,000; M 5,000; (215) 545-1234; Fax (215) 790-3600; lferry@greaterphilachamber.com; www.greaterphilachamber.com*

Philipsburg • *Moshannon Valley Eco. Dev. Partnership & Chamber Svcs.* • Stanley LaFuria; Exec. Dir.; 200 Shady Ln.; 16866; Centre; P 3,400; M 170; (814) 342-2260; Fax (814) 342-2878; sbeals@mvedp.org; www.mvedp.org

Phoenixville • *Phoenixville Reg. C/C* • Jessica Capistrant; Bus. Mgr.; 171 E. Bridge St.; 19460; Chester; P 20,000; M 500; (610) 933-3070; Fax (610) 917-0503; info@phoenixvillechamber.org; www.phoenixvillechamber.org

Pitcairn • *see McKeesport*

Pittsburgh Area

African American C/C of Western Pennsylvania • Doris Carson Williams; Pres./CEO; Koppers Bldg., Ste. 2220; 436 Seventh Ave.; 15219; Allegheny; M 504; (412) 392-0610; Fax (412) 392-0612; information@aaccwp.com; www.aaccwp.com

Brentwood Baldwin Whitehall C/C • Mary Dilla; Secy.; 3501 Brownsville Rd.; 15227; Allegheny; P 15,000; M 174; secretary@bbwchamber.com; www.bbwchamber.com

East Liberty Quarter C/C • Paul G. Brecht; Exec. Dir.; 5907 Penn Ave., Ste. 305; 15206; Allegheny; P 65,000; M 90; (412) 661-9660; Fax (412) 661-9661; pbrecht@eastlibertychamber.org; www.eastlibertychamber.org

Greater Pittsburgh C/C • Matt Smith; Pres.; 11 Stanwix St., 17th Flr.; 15222; Allegheny; P 2,356,285; M 1,200; (412) 392-4500; Fax (412) 392-4520; info@pittsburghchamber.com; www.pittsburghchamber.com

Northside Northshore C/C • Robin Rosemary Miller; Exec. Dir.; 809 Middle St.; 15212; Allegheny; P 54,600; M 215; (412) 231-6500; Fax (412) 321-6760; nsccrobin@hotmail.com; www.northsidechamberofcommerce.com*

Penn Hills C/C • Sara Werner; Co-Dir.; 12013 Frankstown Rd.; 15235; Allegheny; P 47,000; M 220; (412) 795-8741; Fax (412) 795-7993; s.werner@pennhillschamber.org; www.pennhillschamber.org

Pittsburgh Airport Area C/C • Bernadette Puzzuole; Pres./CEO; 850 Beaver Grade Rd.; Moon Twp.; 15108; Allegheny; P 170,000; M 1,100; (412) 264-6270; Fax (412) 264-1575; info@paacc.com; www.paacc.com*

South Hills C/C • 1910 Cochran Rd.; Manor Oak One, Ste. 140; 15220; Allegheny; P 225,000; M 574; (412) 306-8090; Fax (412) 306-8093; connie@shchamber.org; www.shchamber.org*

South Side C/C • Nancy Eshelman; 1505 E. Carson St.; P.O. Box 42380; 15203; Allegheny; P 15,000; M 150; (412) 431-3360; Fax (412) 481-2624; info@southsidechamber.aol; www.southsidechamber.org

South West Communities C/C • Emerald VanBuskirk; Exec. Dir.; 990 Washington Pike; Bridgeville; 15017; Allegheny; P 65,000; M 400; (412) 221-4100; Fax (412) 257-1210; info@swccoc.org; www.swccoc.org*

Wilkinsburg C/C • Vicki Cherney; Pres.; P.O. Box 86064; 15221; Allegheny; P 19,000; M 100; (412) 242-0234; info@wilkinsburgchamber.com; www.wilkinsburgchamber.com

---

Pittston • *Greater Pittston C/C* • Michelle Mikitish; Exec. V.P.; 104 Kennedy Blvd.; P.O. Box 704; 18640; Luzerne; P 50,000; M 400; (570) 655-1424; Fax (570) 655-0336; info@pittstonchamber.org; www.pittstonchamber.org

Plainfield • *see Bangor*

Pleasant Hills • *see McKeesport*

Plum Borough • *see Greensburg*

Pocono Mountains • *see Stroudsburg*

Portland • *see Bangor*

Pottstown • *TriCounty Area C/C* • Eileen Dautrich IOM; Pres.; 152 High St., Ste. 360; 19464; Montgomery; P 175,000; M 470; (610) 326-2900; Fax (610) 970-9705; eileen@tricountyareachamber.com; www.tricountyareachamber.com*

Pottsville • *Schuylkill C/C* • Robert S. Carl Jr.; Pres./CEO; Union Station; 1 Progress Cir., Ste. 201; 17901; Schuylkill; P 148,300; M 885; (570) 622-1942; (800) 755-1942; Fax (570) 622-1638; memberservices@schuylkillchamber.com; www.schuylkillchamber.com

Punxsutawney • *Punxsutawney Area C/C* • Patrick Fleckenstein; Dir.; 102 W. Mahoning St.; 15767; Jefferson; P 6,000; M 300; (814) 938-7700; (800) 752-PHIL; Fax (814) 938-4303; chamber@punxsutawney.com; www.punxsutawney.com

Quakertown • *Upper Bucks C/C* • Tara King; Exec. Dir.; 2170 Portzer Rd.; 18951; Bucks; P 50,000; M 700; (215) 536-3211; Fax (215) 536-7767; info@ubcc.org; www.ubcc.org

Quarryville • *Southern Lancaster County C/C* • BJ Abdo; Pres.; P.O. Box 24; 17566; Lancaster; P 8,000; M 230; (717) 786-1911; (717) 786-8361; president@southernlancasterchamber.com; www.southernlancasterchamber.com

Reading • *Greater Reading C/C & Ind.* • Karen Marsdale; Pres./CEO; 201 Penn St., Ste. 501; 19601; Berks; P 412,000; M 1,300; (610) 376-6766; Fax (610) 376-4135; info@greaterreadingchamber.org; www.greaterreadingchamber.org*

Richmondale • *see Carbondale*

Ridgway • *Ridgway-Elk County C/C* • Pete Terbovich; Bd. Pres.; 300 Main St.; 15853; Elk; P 34,000; M 150; (814) 776-1424; Fax (814) 772-2188; ridgwaychamber@ncentral.com; www.ridgwaychamber.com

Robinson Twp. • *see Pittsburgh-Pittsburgh Airport Area C/C*

Rochester • *Rochester C/C* • Michelle Long; Ofc. Mgr.; 350 Adams St.; 15074; Beaver; P 8,700; M 169; (724) 728-4998; info@rochesterpachamber.com; www.rochesterpachamber.com

Rockwood • *see Somerset*

Roseto • *see Bangor*

Saint Marys • *St. Marys Area C/C* • Ashley O'Dell; Comm. Outreach Coord.; 53 S. St. Marys St.; 15857; Elk; P 14,000; M 300; (814) 781-3804; Fax (814) 781-7302; aodell@stmaryschamber.org; www.stmaryschamber.org

Saltlick • *see Donegal*

Saxton • *Saxton Broad Top C/C* • Rodney Jenkins; Pres.; P.O. Box 121; 16678; Bedford; P 1,170; M 40; (814) 635-3861; www.saxtonbroadtopchamber.com

Sayre • *see Waverly, NY*

Scottdale • *Scottdale Area C/C* • David Mardis; Pres.; 318 Pittsburgh St.; 15683; Westmoreland; P 5,000; M 75; (724) 887-3611; scottdalechamber@gmail.com; www.scottdale.com

Scranton • *Greater Scranton C/C* • Robert F. Durkin; Pres.; 222 Mulberry St.; P.O. Box 431; 18501; Lackawanna; P 214,000; M 1,600; (570) 342-7711; Fax (570) 347-6262; info@scrantonchamber.com; www.scrantonchamber.com*

Scranton • *Greater Northeast C/C* • John Gleason; Chrmn.; P.O. Box 3893; 18505; Lackawanna; M 200; (570) 457-1130; Fax (570) 457-2495; secretary@gnecc.com; www.gnecc.com

Selinsgrove • *see Shamokin Dam*

Sellersville • *see Doylestown*

Shamokin • *Brush Valley Reg. C/C* • 2 E. Arch St., Ste. 313A; 17872; Northumberland; P 45,000; M 235; (570) 648-4675; info@brushvalleychamber.com; www.brushvalleychamber.com*

Shamokin Dam • *Greater Susquehanna Valley C/C* • Robert Garrett; Pres./CEO; 2859 N. Susquehanna Trl.; P.O. Box 10; 17876; Snyder; P 130,000; M 700; (570) 743-4100; (800) 410-2880; Fax (570) 743-1221; info@gsvcc.org; www.gsvcc.org*

Shanksville • *see Somerset*

Sharon • *Shenango Valley C/C* • Sherris Moreira; Exec. Dir.; 41 Chestnut Ave.; 16146; Mercer; P 52,000; M 400; (724) 981-5880; Fax (724) 981-5480; info@svchamber.com; www.svchamber.com*

U.S. Chambers of Commerce

Shenandoah • *see Pottsville*

Shippensburg • *Shippensburg Area C/C* • Scott Brown; Pres.; 53 W. King St.; 17257; Cumberland & Franklin; P 6,000; M 235; (717) 532-5509; Fax (717) 532-7501; chamber@shippensburg.org; www.shippensburg.org

Simpson • *see Carbondale*

Smethport • *Smethport Area C/C* • Nathan Muller; P.O. Box 84; 16749; McKean; P 1,700; M 60; (814) 887-4134; njmuller@smethportchamber.com; www.smethportchamber.com

Somerset • *Somerset County C/C* • Ron Aldom; Exec. Dir.; 601 N. Center Ave.; 15501; Somerset; P 77,405; M 700; (814) 445-6431; Fax (814) 443-4313; info@somersetcountychamber.com; www.somersetpa.net*

Souderton • *Indian Valley C/C* • Sharon L. Minninger; Exec. Dir.; 100 Penn Ave.; P.O. Box 64077; 18964; Montgomery; P 50,000; M 400; (215) 723-9472; Fax (215) 723-2490; ivchamber@indianvalleychamber.com; www.indianvalleychamber.com*

South Fayette Twp. • *see Pittsburgh-South West Comm. C/C*

South Sterling • *see Hamlin*

South Waverly • *see Waverly, NY*

Spring City • *see Pottstown*

Springfield • *Delaware County C/C* • Trish McFarland; Pres.; 1001 Baltimore Pike, Ste. 9LL; 19064; Delaware; P 559,000; M 1,200; (610) 565-3677; Fax (610) 565-1606; info@delcochamber.org; www.delcochamber.org*

Stahlstown • *see Donegal*

State College • *Chamber of Bus. & Ind. of Centre County* • Vern Squier; Pres./CEO; 131 S. Fraser St.; 16801; Centre; P 154,000; M 1,086; (814) 234-1829; Fax (814) 234-5555; cbicc@cbicc.org; www.cbicc.org*

Sterling • *see Hamlin*

Stroudsburg • *Greater Pocono C/C* • Robert Phillips IOM; Pres./CEO; 556 Main St.; 18360; Monroe; P 200,000; M 1,400; (570) 421-4433; Fax (570) 424-7281; rphillips@greaterpoconochamber.com; www.greaterpoconochamber.com*

Summit Hill • *see Lehighton*

Sunbury • *see Shamokin Dam*

Tamaqua • *Tamaqua Area C/C* • Linda Yulanavage; Exec. Dir.; 114 W. Broad St.; 18252; Schuylkill; P 7,000; M 200; (570) 668-1880; Fax (570) 668-0826; tamaquachamber@verizon.net; www.tamaqua.net

Tarentum • *Alle Kiski Strong C/C* • Colleen Felentzer; Exec. Dir.; 308 Pittsburgh Mills Cir.; 15084; Allegheny; P 200,000; M 600; (724) 224-3400; Fax (724) 224-3442; colleen@akstrong.com; www.allekiskistrong.com

Telford • *see Souderton*

Titusville • *Titusville Area C/C* • Emily Altomare; Exec. Dir.; 202 W. Central Ave.; 16354; Crawford; P 6,000; M 325; (814) 827-2941; Fax (814) 827-2914; emily@titusvillechamber.com; www.titusvillechamber.com

Towanda • *Central Bradford County C/C* • Jenny Marino; Exec. Dir.; 304 Main St., 3rd Flr.; P.O. Box 146; 18848; Bradford; P 7,000; M 170; (570) 268-2732; Fax (570) 265-2331; chamber@towandawysox.com; www.towandawysox.com

Trafford • *see McKeesport*

Trooper • *see Eagleville*

Tunkhannock • *Wyoming County C/C* • Maureen E. Dispenza; Exec. Dir.; 81 Warren St.; P.O. Box 568; 18657; Wyoming; P 29,000; M 440; (570) 836-7755; (570) 875-8325; Fax (570) 836-6049; maureen@wyccc.com; www.wyccc.com

Turtle Creek • *see McKeesport*

Tyrone • *Tyrone Area C/C* • Rose A. Black; Exec. Dir.; 1004 Logan Ave.; 16686; Blair; P 5,500; M 220; (814) 684-0736; Fax (814) 684-6070; rose@tyronechamber.com; www.tyronechamber.com

Uniontown • *Fayette C/C* • Muriel J. Nuttall; Exec. Dir.; 65 W. Main St.; 15401; Fayette; P 55,000; M 575; (724) 437-4571; (800) 916-9365; Fax (724) 438-3304; info@fayettechamber.com; www.fayettechamber.com

Upper Mount Bethel • *see Bangor*

Upper St. Clair • *see Pittsburgh-South West Comm. C/C*

Valley Forge • *see Eagleville*

Vandergrift • *see Tarentum*

Vandling • *see Carbondale*

Warminster • *The Greater BucksMont C/C* • Judy Doherty; Executive Director; P.O. Box 3014; 18974; Bucks; P 46,000; M 160; (215) 672-6633; Fax (215) 672-7637; admin@bucksmontchamber.com; www.bucksmontchamber.com

Warren • *Warren County Chamber of Bus. & Ind.* • James Decker; Pres./CEO; 308 Market St.; 16365; Warren; P 42,000; M 285; (814) 723-3050; Fax (814) 723-6024; info@wccbi.org; www.wccbi.org

Watsontown • *see Milton*

Wayne • *Main Line C/C* • Bernard Dagenais; Pres./CEO; 175 Strafford Ave., Ste. 130; 19087; Chester, Delaware & Montgomery; P 265,000; M 1,100; (610) 687-6232; Fax (610) 687-8085; bdagenais@mlcc.org; www.mlcc.org

Waynesboro • *Greater Waynesboro C/C* • Jackie Mowen; Exec. Dir.; 118 Walnut St., Ste. 111 ; 17268; Franklin; P 40,000; M 420; (717) 762-7123; Fax (717) 762-7124; director@waynesboro.org; www.waynesboro.org*

Waynesburg • *Waynesburg Area C/C* • Melody Longstreth; Exec. Dir.; 143 E. High St.; 15370; Greene; P 40,000; M 350; (724) 627-5926; Fax (724) 627-8017; info@waynesburgchamber.com; www.waynesburgchamber.com

Wellsboro • *Wellsboro Area C/C* • Julie VanNess; Exec. Dir.; 114 Main St.; P.O. Box 733; 16901; Tioga; P 3,500; M 300; (570) 724-1926; Fax (570) 724-5084; info@wellsboropa.com; www.wellsboropa.com

West Chester • *C/C of Greater West Chester Inc.* • Katie Doherty; Pres.; 119 N. High St.; 19380; Chester; P 81,000; M 800; (610) 696-4046; Fax (610) 696-9110; info@gwcc.org; www.greaterwestchester.com*

West Elizabeth • *see McKeesport*

West Mifflin • *see McKeesport*

Westfield • *see Galeton*

Westinghouse Valley • *see McKeesport*

Wexford • *Pittsburgh North Reg. C/C* • Jim Boltz; Exec. Dir.; 5000 Brooktree Rd., Ste. 100; 15090; Allegheny; P 25,000; M 1,100; (724) 934-9700; Fax (724) 934-9710; info@PghNorthChamber.com; www.thechamberinc.com*

White Oak • *see McKeesport*

Wilkes-Barre • *Greater Wilkes-Barre C/C* • Wico van Genderen; Pres./CEO; Two Public Square; 18701; Luzerne; P 321,000; M 800; (570) 823-2101; Fax (570) 822-5951; info@wilkes-barre.org; www.wilkes-barre.org*

Williamsport • *Williamsport/Lycoming C/C* • Vincent J. Matteo; Pres./CEO; 102 W. Fourth St.; 17701; Lycoming; P 120,000; M 945; (570) 326-1971; Fax (570) 321-1209; chamber@williamsport.org; www.williamsport.org

Willow Grove • *see Lansdale*

Wind Gap • *see Bangor*

Windber • *see Somerset*

Wrightsville • *see Columbia*

Wyalusing • *Greater Wyalusing C/C & IDC* • Carol Goodman; 20 Main St.; P.O. Box 55; 18853; Bradford; P 5,000; M 150; (570) 746-4922; wchamber@epix.net; www.wyalusing.net

Wysox • *see Bradford*

York • *York County Eco. Alliance* • Kevin Schreiber; Pres.; 144 Roosevelt Ave.; 17401; York; P 401,613; M 1,250; (717) 848-4000; Fax (717) 843-6737; info@ycea-pa.org; www.ycea-pa.org*

Zelienople • *Zelienople-Harmony Area C/C* • Jennifer Ackerman; Dir.; 111 W. New Castle St.; P.O. Box 464; 16063; Butler; P 8,000; M 200; (724) 452-5232; Fax (724) 452-5712; zhcc@zoominternet.net; www.zhchamber.com*

Puerto Rico

Puerto Rico C of C • Edgardo Bigas Valladares; Exec. V.P.; P.O. Box 9024033; San Juan; 00902; P 3,667,084; M 2,000; (787) 721-6060; Fax (787) 723-1891; camarapr@camarapr.net; www.camarapr.org

Mayaguez • *C/C of the West of Puerto Rico* • Elisamuel Rivera; Pres.; 101 Calle Méndez Vigo Oeste, Ste. 905; 00680; P 2,000,000; M 250; (787) 832-3749; Fax (787) 832-4287; info@ccopr.net; www.ccopr.com

Ponce • *Southern Puerto Rico C/C* • Hector E. Lopez; Exec. Dir.; P.O. Box 7455; 00732-7455; P 200,000; M 650; (787) 844-4400; Fax (787) 844-4705; contabilidad@camarasur.org; www.camarasur.com

Rhode Island

No State Chamber

Barrington • *see Warren*

Block Island • *Block Island C/C* • Kathleen Szabo; Exec. Dir.; P.O. Box D; 02807; Washington; P 1,000; M 250; (401) 466-2982; Fax (401) 466-2711; info@blockislandchamber.com; www.blockislandchamber.com

Bristol • *see Warren*

Burrillville • *see Lincoln*

Central Falls • *see Lincoln*

Centredale • *see Johnston*

Charlestown • *Charlestown C/C* • Heather Paliopta; Exec. Dir.; 4945 Old Post Rd.; P.O. Box 633; 02813; Washington; P 8,000; M 300; (401) 364-3878; Fax (401) 364-8794; charlestowncoc@earthlink.net; www.charlestownrichamber.com

Cranston • *Greater Cranston C/C* • Stephen C. Boyle; Pres.; 150 Midway Rd., Unit 178; 02920; Providence; P 81,500; M 300; (401) 785-3780; Fax (401) 785-3782; sboyle@cranstonchamber.com; www.cranstonchamber.com*

Cumberland • *see Lincoln*

East Greenwich • *East Greenwich C/C* • Stephen M. Lombardi; Exec. Dir.; 580 Main St.; P.O. Box 514; 02818; Kent; P 15,000; M 450; (401) 885-0020; Fax (401) 885-0048; steve@eastgreenwichchamber.com; www.eastgreenwichchamber.com*

East Providence • *East Providence Area C/C* • Laura A. McNamara; Exec. Dir.; 1011 Waterman Ave.; 02914; Providence; P 48,000; M 250; (401) 438-1212; Fax (401) 435-4581; office@eastprovidenceareachamber.com; www.eastprovidenceareachamber.com

Foster • *see Johnston*

Glocester • *see Johnston*

Jamestown • *Jamestown C/C* • John McCauley; Exec. Dir.; 53 Narragansett Ave.; P.O. Box 35; 02835; Newport; P 5,500; M 135; (401) 423-3650; info@jamestownrichamber.com; www.jamestownrichamber.com

Johnston • *North Central C/C* • Deborah Ramos; Pres.; 255 Greenville Ave.; 02919; Providence; P 150,000; M 250; (401) 349-4674; Fax (401) 349-4676; chamber@ncrichamber.com; www.ncrichamber.com*

Lincoln • *Northern Rhode Island C/C* • John C. Gregory; Pres./CEO; 6 Blackstone Valley Pl., Ste. 402; 02865; Providence; P 250,000; M 600; (401) 334-1000; Fax (401) 334-1009; general@nrichamber.com; www.nrichamber.com

Middletown • *Newport County C/C* • Erin Dovovan-Boyle; Exec. Dir.; 35 Valley Rd.; 02842; Newport; P 85,000; M 1,100; (401) 847-1600; Fax (401) 849-5848; info@newportchamber.com; www.newportchamber.com*

Narragansett • *Narragansett C/C* • Deborah Kelso; Exec. Dir.; P.O. Box 742; 02882; Washington; P 16,000; M 400; (401) 783-7121; (401) 788-0684; Fax (401) 789-0220; dkelso@narragansettcoc.com; www.narragansettcoc.com

Newport • *see Middletown*

North Kingstown • *North Kingstown C/C* • Martha M. Pughe; Exec. Dir.; 8045 Post Rd.; 02852; Washington; P 26,486; M 450; (401) 295-5566; Fax (401) 295-5582; info@northkingstown.com; www.northkingstown.com*

North Providence • *see Johnston*

North Smithfield • *see Lincoln*

Pawcatuck • *see Westerly*

Pawtucket • *see Lincoln*

Providence • *Greater Providence C/C* • Laurie L. White; Pres.; 30 Exchange Terrace; 02903; Providence; P 1,058,000; M 2,000; (401) 521-5000; Fax (401) 621-6109; chamber@provchamber.com; www.providencechamber.com*

Scituate • *see Johnston*

Smithfield • *see Johnston and Lincoln*

South Kingstown • *see Wakefield*

Wakefield • *Southern RI C/C* • Elizabeth Berman; Exec. Dir.; 230 Old Tower Hill Rd.; 02879; Washington; P 35,000; M 655; (401) 783-2801; Fax (401) 789-3120; info@srichamber.com; www.srichamber.com

Warren • *East Bay C/C* • Bette Walpole; Chrmn.; 16 Cutler St., Ste. 102; 02885; Bristol; P 50,000; M 350; (401) 245-0750; Fax (401) 245-0110; info@eastbaychamberri.org; www.eastbaychamberri.org*

Warwick • *Central Rhode Island C/C Inc.* • Lauren Slocum; Pres./CEO; 3288 Post Rd.; 02886; Kent; P 300,000; M 1,200; (401) 732-1100; Fax (401) 732-1107; admin@centralrichamber.com; www.centralrichamber.com*

West Warwick • *see Warwick*

Westerly • *Ocean Comm. C/C* • Lisa Konicki; Exec. Dir.; 1 Chamber Way; 02891; Washington; P 23,500; M 775; (401) 596-7761; Fax (401) 596-2190; info@oceanchamber.org; www.oceanchamber.org

Woonsocket • *see Lincoln*

South Carolina

South Carolina C of C • Otis Rawl; Pres./CEO; 1301 Gervais St., Ste. 1100; Columbia; 29201; Richland; P 4,723,723; M 2,000; (803) 799-4601; Fax (803) 779-6043; grassroots@scchamber.net; www.scchamber.net

Abbeville • *Greater Abbeville C/C* • Missy Wines; Exec. Dir.; 107 Court Sq.; 29620; Abbeville; P 26,000; M 200; (864) 366-4600; Fax (864) 366-4068; abvchamber@wctel.net; abbecc.publishpath.com*

Aiken • *Greater Aiken C/C* • J. David Jameson; Pres./CEO; 121 Richland Ave. E.; P.O. Box 892; 29802; Aiken; P 165,900; M 1,001; (803) 641-1111; Fax (803) 641-4174; chamber@aikenchamber.net; www.aikenchamber.net*

Anderson • *Anderson Area C/C* • Pamela Christopher; Pres./CEO; 907 N. Main St., Ste. 200; 29621; Anderson; P 191,500; M 850; (864) 226-3454; Fax (864) 226-3300; frontdesk@andersonscchamber.com; www.andersonscchamber.com*

Andrews • *see Georgetown*

Aynor • *Aynor C/C* • Jimmy Dyson; Chair; P.O. Box 175; 29511; Horry; P 640; M 75; (843) 358-4808; Info@aynorscchamber.org; www.townofaynor.net

Bamberg • *Bamberg County C/C* • Jerry Bell; Exec. Dir.; 604 Airport Rd.; 29003; Bamberg; P 16,000; M 94; (803) 245-4427; info@bambergcountychamber.org; www.bambergcountychamber.org

Barnwell • *Barnwell County C/C* • Angela Abstance; Exec. Dir.; 1750 Jackson St., Ste. 243; P. O. Box 898; 29812; Barnwell; P 23,000; M 200; (803) 259-7446; Fax (803) 259-0030; director@barnwellcountychamber.com; www.barnwellcountychamber.org

Batesburg-Leesville • *Batesburg-Leesville C/C & Visitors Center* • Mike Taylor; Pres./CEO; 350 E. Columbia Ave.; P.O. Box 2178; 29070; Lexington; P 5,400; M 154; (803) 532-4339; Fax (803) 532-3978; mike@batesburg-leesvillechamber.org; www.batesburg-leesvillechamber.org

Beaufort • *Beaufort Reg. C/C* • Blakely Williams; Pres./CEO; 701 Craven St.; P.O. Box 910; 29901; Beaufort; P 162,000; M 750; (843) 525-8500; Fax (843) 986-5405; info@beaufortsc.org; www.beaufortchamber.org*

Bennettsville • *Bennettsville C/C* • Rhonda Frazier; Dir.; 304 W. Main St.; P.O. Box 1036; 29512; Marlboro; P 30,000; M 200; (843) 479-3941; Fax (843) 479-4859; info@visitbennettsville.com; www.visitbennettsville.com

Bishopville • *Lee County C/C* • Pam Kelley; Exec. Dir.; 219 N. Main St.; P.O. Box 187; 29010; Lee; P 22,000; M 160; (803) 484-5145; Fax (803) 484-4270; kingcotton@ftc-i.net; www.leecountychambersc.com

Bluffton • *Greater Bluffton C/C* • Shellie West; Exec. Dir.; 217 Goethe Rd.; 29910; Beaufort; P 47,000; M 500; (843) 757-1010; Fax (843) 757-9984; info@blufftonchamberofcommerce.org; www.blufftonchamberofcommerce.org*

Bowman • *see Saint George*

Branchville • *see Saint George*

Camden • *Kershaw County C/C & Visitors Center* • Amy Kinard; Interim Exec. Dir.; 607 S. Broad St.; P.O. Box 605; 29021; Kershaw; P 62,000; M 500; (803) 432-2525; Fax (803) 432-4181; director@kershawcountychamber.org; www.kershawcountychamber.org*

Cayce • *Greater Cayce C/C & Visitors Center* • Gregg Pinner; Pres./CEO; 1006 12th St.; 29033; Lexington; P 35,000; M 390; (803) 794-6504; (866) 720-5400; Fax (803) 794-6505; cwcchambersc@gmail.com; www.cwcchamber.com*

Central • *see Clemson*

Chapin • *Greater Chapin C/C* • Risa Barnes; Exec. Dir.; 302 Columbia Ave.; P.O. Box 577; 29036; Lexington; P 50,000; M 321; (803) 345-1100; Fax (803) 345-0266; director@chapinchamber.com; www.chapinchamber.com

Cheraw • *Greater Cheraw C/C* • Roger Jones; Pres.; 221 Market St.; 29520; Chesterfield; P 5,900; M 300; (843) 537-7681; Fax (843) 537-5886; cherawchamber@cherawchamber.com; www.cherawchamber.com

Chester • *Chester County C/C* • Brooke Wilson; Pres.; 109 Gadsden St.; P.O. Box 489; 29706; Chester; P 34,000; M 300; (803) 581-4142; Fax (803) 581-2431; chestercountychamber@gmail.com; www.chesterchamber.com*

Chesterfield • *Greater Chesterfield C/C* • Monika Mucci; P.O. Box 708; 29709; Chesterfield; P 1,800; M 65; (843) 623-1590; (843) 623-2131; chesterfieldscchamber@gmail.com; www.chesterfieldscchamberofcommerce.com

Clemson • *Clemson Area C/C •* David Lane; Dir.; 1105 Tiger Blvd.; P.O. Box 1622; 29633; Pickens; P 12,000; M 400; (864) 654-1200; Fax (864) 654-5096; ruthie@clemsonareachamber.org; clemsonareachamber.org*

Clover • *Greater Clover C/C •* Jackie Robinson; Exec. Dir.; 118 Bethel St.; P.O. Box 162; 29710; York; P 5,200; M 150; (803) 222-3312; Fax (803) 222-8396; sccloverchamber@aol.com; www.cloverchamber.org*

Columbia • *Columbia Chamber •* Carl Blackstone; Pres./CEO; 930 Richland St.; P.O. Box 1360; 29202; Richland; P 767,500; M 1,200; (803) 733-1110; Fax (803) 733-1113; inquiries@columbiachamber.com; www.columbiachamber.com*

Conway • *Conway C/C •* Kelli James; Exec. Dir.; 203 Main St.; P.O. Box 831; 29526; Horry; P 14,000; M 550; (843) 248-2273; Fax (843) 248-0003; info@conwayscchamber.com; www.conwayscchamber.com*

Cross • *see Saint George*

Darlington • *Greater Darlington C/C •* John Isgett; Chair; 38 Public Sq.; 29532; Darlington; P 66,000; M 300; (843) 393-2641; Fax (843) 393-8059; info@darlingtonchamber.net; www.darlingtonchamber.net

Dillon • *Dillon County C/C •* Johnnie P. Luehrs; Pres./CEO; 100 N. MacArthur Ave.; P.O. Box 1304; 29536; Dillon; P 32,100; M 200; (843) 774-8551; (800) 444-6838; Fax (843) 774-0114; dillonchamber@bellsouth.net; www.dillonsc.gov*

Dorchester • *see Saint George*

Easley • *Greater Easley C/C •* Cindy B. Hopkins IOM; Pres.; 2001 E. Main St.; P.O. Box 241; 29641; Pickens; P 122,500; M 437; (864) 859-2693; Fax (864) 859-1941; ecc@easleychamber.org; www.easleychamber.org*

Edisto Island • *Edisto C/C •* Dan Carter; Exec. Dir.; P.O. Box 206; 29438; Colleton; P 3,500; M 180; (843) 869-3867; (888) 333-2781; eichamber@aol.com; www.edistochamber.com

Elloree • *see Orangeburg*

Eutawville • *see Saint George*

Florence • *Greater Florence C/C •* Mike Miller; Pres.; 100 W. Evans St.; 29501; Florence; P 149,000; M 600; (843) 665-0515; Fax (843) 662-2010; info@flochamber.com; www.flochamber.com*

Fort Mill • *see Rock Hill*

Fountain Inn • *Fountain Inn C/C •* John R. Hastings Sr.; Pres./CEO; 102 Depot St.; 29644; Greenville; P 8,500; M 265; (864) 862-2586; Fax (864) 862-1086; info@fountaininnchamber.org; www.FountainInnChamber.org*

Gaffney • *Cherokee County C/C •* Jonna Turner; Exec. Dir.; 225 S. Limestone St.; 29340; Cherokee; P 55,000; M 300; (864) 489-5721; Fax (864) 489-5722; info@cherokeechamber.org; www.cherokeechamber.org*

Garden City • *see Georgetown*

Georgetown • *Georgetown County C/C •* Beth Stedman; Pres./CEO; 531 Front St.; 29440; Georgetown; P 60,200; M 700; (843) 546-8436; (800) 777-7705; Fax (843) 520-4876; info@visitgeorge.com; www.visitgeorge.com*

Greeleyville • *see Kingstree*

Greenville • *Greenville C/C •* Ben Haskew; Pres./CEO; 24 Cleveland St.; 29601; Greenville; P 637,000; M 2,000; (864) 242-1050; (866) 485-5262; Fax (864) 282-8509; info@greenvillechamber.org; www.greenvillechamber.org*

Greenwood • *Greenwood Area C/C •* Angelle LaBorde; Pres./CEO; 110 Phoenix St.; P.O. Box 980; 29648; Greenwood; P 69,700; M 625; (864) 223-8431; Fax (864) 229-9785; info@greenwoodscchamber.org; www.greenwoodscchamber.org*

Greer • *Greater Greer C/C •* Mark Owens; Pres./CEO; 111 Trade St.; 29651; Greenville; P 50,000; M 658; (864) 877-3131; Fax (864) 877-0961; info@greerchamber.com; www.greerchamber.com*

Grover • *see Saint George*

Hampton • *Hampton County C/C •* Kevin Braddock; Pres.; 200 Jackson Ave. E.; P.O. Box 122; 29924; Hampton; P 22,000; M 120; (803) 914-2143; Fax (803) 943-2144; info@hamptoncountychamber.org; hamptoncountychamber.org

Hardeeville • *Greater Hardeeville C/C •* P.O. Box 307; 29927; Jasper; P 3,500; M 103; (843) 784-3606; Fax (843) 784-2781; info@hardeevillechamber.com; www.hardeevillechamber.com

Harleyville • *see Saint George*

Hartsville • *Greater Hartsville C/C •* Quinetta Buterbaugh; President; 214 N. Fifth St.; P.O. Box 578; 29550; Darlington; P 35,000; M 300; (843) 332-6401; Fax (843) 332-8017; president@hartsvillechamber.org; www.hartsvillechamber.org*

Hemingway • *see Kingstree*

Hilton Head Island • *Hilton Head Island-Bluffton C/C •* William G. Miles; Pres./CEO; 1 Chamber of Commerce Dr.; P.O. Box 5647; 29938; Beaufort; P 39,000; M 1,600; (843) 785-3673; Fax (843) 785-7110; info@hiltonheadisland.org; www.hiltonheadisland.org*

Holly Hill • *Tri-County Reg. C/C •* Teresa Hatchell; Exec. Dir.; 8603 Old State Rd.; P.O. Box 1012; 29059; Orangeburg; P 406,300; M 450; (803) 496-3831; Fax (803) 496-3831; tcrcc@bellsouth.net; www.tri-crcc.com*

Inman • *Greater Inman Area C/C •* David Grayshock; Pres.; P.O. Box 227; 29349; Spartanburg; P 2,500; M 115; (864) 472-3654; inmanchamber1@gmail.com; www.inmanscchamber.org

Irmo • *Greater Irmo C/C •* Tiffany Boyce; Pres./CEO; 1248 Lake Murray Blvd.; 29063; Lexington; P 90,000; M 380; (803) 749-9355; Fax (803) 732-7986; info@greaterirmochamber.com; www.greaterirmochamber.com

Jasper County • *see Ridgeland*

Johnston • *Edgefield County C/C •* Donna C. Livingston; Admin.; 416 Calhoun St.; 29832; Edgefield; P 27,000; M 175; (803) 275-0010; Fax (803) 275-0010; info@edgefieldcountychamber.org; www.edgefieldcountychamber.net

Kingstree • *Williamsburg HomeTown C/C •* Leslee Spivey; Exec. Dir.; 136 N. Academy St.; P.O. Box 696; 29556; Williamsburg; P 34,400; M 250; (843) 355-6431; Fax (843) 355-3343; whtc@FTC-i.net; www.williamsburgsc.org

Lake City • *Greater Lake City C/C •* Ava Baker; Exec. Dir.; 144 S. Acline Ave.; P.O. Box 669; 29560; Florence; P 7,500; M 225; (843) 374-8611; Fax (843) 374-7938; lccoc1@ftc-i.net; www.lakecitysc.org

Lake Wylie • *Lake Wylie C/C* • Susan Bromfield; Pres.; P.O. Box 5233; 29710; York; P 25,000; M 400; (803) 831-2827; Fax (803) 831-2460; info@lakewyliesc.com; www.lakewyliesc.com

Lancaster • *Lancaster County C/C* • Dean Faile IOM; Pres./CEO; 453 Colonial Ave.; P.O. Box 430; 29721; Lancaster; P 77,000; M 450; (803) 283-4105; brenda@lancasterchambersc.com; www.lancasterchambersc.org*

Lane • *see Kingstree*

Laurens • *Laurens County C/C* • Greg Alexander; Pres./CEO; P.O. Box 248; 29360; Laurens; P 69,700; M 500; (864) 833-2716; Fax (864) 833-6935; salexander@laurenscounty.org; www.laurenscounty.org*

Leesville • *see Batesburg-Leesville*

Lexington • *Greater Lexington Chamber & Visitors Center* • Randy Halfacre; Pres./CEO; 311 W. Main St.; P.O. Box 44; 29071; Lexington; P 256,000; M 950; (803) 359-6113; Fax (803) 359-0634; info@lexingtonsc.org; www.lexingtonsc.org*

Litchfield Beach • *see Georgetown*

Little River • *Little River C/C* • Jennifer Walters; Exec. Dir.; 1180 Hwy. 17 N., Ste. 1; P.O. Box 400; 29566; Horry; P 9,500; M 400; (843) 249-6604; (866) 817-8082; Fax (843) 249-9788; sandi@littleriverchamber.org; www.littleriverchamber.org*

Loris • *Loris Chamber and Visitors & Conv. Bur.* • Samantha Norris; Exec. Asst.; 4242 Main St.; P.O. Box 356; 29569; Horry; P 2,400; M 180; (843) 756-6030; Fax (843) 756-5661; loriscoc@sccoast.net; www.lorischambersc.com

Manning • *Clarendon County C/C* • Ericka Floyd; Exec. Dir.; 19 N. Brooks St.; 29102; Clarendon; P 35,412; M 320; (803) 435-4405; Fax (803) 435-4406; chamber@clarendoncounty.com; www.clarendoncounty.com*

Marion • *Marion C/C* • Judy J. Johnson; Exec. V.P.; 209 E. Bobby Gerald Pkwy.; P.O. Box 35; 29571; Marion; P 7,100; M 300; (843) 423-3561; Fax (843) 423-0963; marionsc@bellsouth.net; www.marionscchamber.com

Mauldin • *Greater Mauldin C/C* • Pat Pomeroy; Exec. Dir.; 101 E. Butler Rd.; P.O. Box 881; 29662; Greenville; P 20,000; M 390; (864) 297-1323; Fax (864) 297-5645; pat.pomeroy@mauldinchamber.org; www.mauldinchamber.org*

McCormick • *McCormick County C/C* • Anne Barron; Ofc. Mgr.; 100 S. Main St.; P.O. Box 938; 29835; McCormick; P 10,300; M 175; (864) 852-2835; Fax (864) 852-2382; info@mccormickscchamber.org; www.mccormickscchamber.org*

Moncks Corner • *Berkeley C/C* • Elaine Morgan; CEO; 1004 Old Hwy. 52; P.O. Box 968; 29461; Berkeley; P 210,000; M 450; (843) 761-8238; (800) 882-0337; Fax (843) 899-6491; info@berkeleysc.org; www.berkeleysc.org

Mullins • *Greater Mullins C/C* • Cindy L. Smith; Exec. Dir.; 100 N. Main St.; P.O. Box 595; 29574; Marion; P 5,500; M 250; (843) 464-6651; mullinschamber@bellsouth.net; www.mullinschamber.com*

Murrells Inlet • *see Georgetown*

Myrtle Beach • *Myrtle Beach Area C/C* • Brad Dean; Pres./CEO; 1200 N. Oak St.; P.O. Box 2115; 29578; Horry; P 269,300; M 3,000; (843) 626-7444; (800) 356-3016; Fax (843) 448-3010; info@visitmyrtlebeach.com; www.visitmyrtlebeach.com*

Newberry • *Newberry County C/C* • Ted Smith; Exec. Dir.; 1209 Caldwell St.; P.O. Box 396; 29108; Newberry; P 37,000; M 340; (803) 276-4274; Fax (803) 276-4373; ted@newberrycounty.org; www.newberrycounty.org

Ninety Six • *Ninety Six C/C* • Pamela Alford; Secy.; 97 Main St. E.; P.O. Box 8; 29666; Greenwood; P 1,975; M 80; (864) 543-2047; Fax (864) 543-4304; 96chamber@gmail.com; www.96chamberofcommerce.com

North Augusta • *North Augusta C/C* • Terra Carroll IOM; Pres./CEO; 406 West Ave.; 29841; Aiken; P 22,000; M 385; (803) 279-2323; Fax (803) 279-0003; terra@northaugustachamber.org; www.northaugustachamber.org*

North Charleston • *Charleston Metro C/C* • Bryan Derreberry; Pres./CEO; 4500 Leeds Ave., Ste. 100; 29405; Charleston; P 530,000; M 1,600; (843) 577-2510; (843) 723-1773; Fax (843) 723-4853; mail@charlestonchamber.org; www.charlestonchamber.net

North Myrtle Beach • *North Myrtle Beach C/C* • Marc Jordan; Pres./CEO; 1521 Hwy. 17 S.; 29582; Horry; P 16,200; M 1,200; (843) 281-2662; (877) 332-2662; Fax (843) 280-2930; info@northmyrtlebeachchamber.com; www.northmyrtlebeachchamber.com*

Orangeburg • *Orangeburg County C/C* • Melinda Jackson; Pres.; 155 Riverside Dr. S.W.; P.O. Box 328; 29116; Orangeburg; P 93,000; M 650; (803) 534-6821; (800) 545-6153; Fax (803) 531-9435; chamber@orangeburgsc.net; www.orangeburgchamber.com

Pageland • *Pageland C/C* • Sondra Price; 128 N. Pearl St.; P.O. Box 56; 29728; Chesterfield; P 3,000; M 100; (843) 672-6400; Fax (843) 672-6401; pagelandcham@shtc.net; www.pagelandcham.net

Pawleys Island • *see Georgetown*

Pickens • *Greater Pickens C/C* • Mike Parrott; Exec. Dir.; 222 W. Main St.; P.O. Box 153; 29671; Pickens; P 3,500; M 125; (864) 878-3258; Fax (864) 878-7317; info@pickenschamber.net; www.pickenschamber.net

Pine Ridge • *see Cayce*

Providence • *see Saint George*

Reevesville • *see Saint George*

Ridgeland • *Jasper County C/C* • Kendall Malphrus; Exec. Dir.; P.O. Box 1267; 29936; Jasper; P 24,700; M 275; (843) 726-8126; Fax (843) 726-6290; info@jaspercountychamber.com; www.jaspercountychamber.com

Ridgeville • *see Saint George*

Rock Hill • *York County Reg. C/C* • Rob Youngblood; Pres.; 116 E. Main St.; P.O. Box 590; 29731; York; P 226,100; M 1,050; (803) 324-7500; Fax (803) 324-1889; info@yorkcountychamber.com; www.yorkcountychamber.com*

Saint George • *Tri-County Reg. C/C* • Teresa Hatchell; Exec. Dir.; 225 Parler Ave.; 29477; Dorchester; P 406,300; M 450; (843) 563-9091; (800) 788-5646; Fax (843) 563-9091; tcrcc@bellsouth.net; www.tri-crcc.com*

Saluda • *Saluda County C/C* • Don Hancock; P.O. Box 246; 29138; Saluda; P 20,000; M 100; (864) 445-4100; saludacountychamber@embarqmail.com; www.saludacountychamber.com

Santee • *see Orangeburg and Saint George*

Seneca • *Greater Oconee County C/C •* Debbie Meinert; Interim Exec. Dir.; 135C Eagles Nest Dr.; P.O. Box 855; 29679; Oconee; P 75,000; M 365; (864) 882-2097; Fax (864) 882-2881; info@oconeechambersc.com; www.oconeechambersc.com*

Simpsonville • *Simpsonville Area C/C •* Hoyt Bynum; Pres./CEO; 211 N. Main St.; P.O. Box 605; 29681; Greenville; P 18,000; M 400; (864) 963-3781; Fax (864) 228-0003; hbynum@simpsonvillechamber.com; www.simpsonvillechamber.com*

South Congaree • *see Cayce*

Spartanburg • *Spartanburg Area C/C •* Allen Smith IOM CCE; Pres./CEO; 105 N. Pine St.; P.O. Box 1636; 29304; Spartanburg; P 284,300; M 1,200; (864) 594-5000; Fax (864) 594-5055; spartanburgchamber@spartanburgchamber.com; www.spartanburgchamber.com*

Springdale • *see Cayce*

Summerville • *Greater Summerville/Dorchester County C/C •* Rita Berry; Pres./CEO; 402 N. Main St.; P.O. Box 670; 29484-0670; Dorchester; P 148,000; M 827; (843) 873-2931; Fax (843) 875-4464; jbrooks@greatersummerville.org; www.greatersummerville.org

Sumter • *Greater Sumter C/C •* Chris Hardy CCE IOM; Pres./CEO; 32 E. Calhoun St.; 29150; Sumter; P 108,000; M 850; (803) 775-1231; Fax (803) 775-0915; chamber@sumterchamber.com; www.sumterchamber.com*

Tega Cay • *see Rock Hill*

Union • *Union County C/C •* Torance Inman; Exec. Dir.; 135 W. Main St.; 29379; Union; P 29,000; M 210; (864) 427-9039; (877) 202-8755; Fax (864) 427-9030; chamber@unionsc.com; www.unionsc.com

Vance • *see Saint George*

Walhalla • *Walhalla C/C •* Barbara Justus; Exec. Dir.; 105 West South Broad St.; 29691; Oconee; P 5,000; M 125; (864) 638-2727; Fax (864) 638-2727; walhallacoc@bellsouth.net; www.walhallachamber.com

Walterboro • *Walterboro-Colleton C/C •* Jeremy Ware; Pres.; 403 E. Washington St., Ste. A; P.O. Box 426; 29488; Colleton; P 40,000; M 300; (843) 549-9595; Fax (843) 549-5775; chamberadmin@colletoncounty.org; www.walterboro.org

Warrenville • *see Aiken*

West Columbia • *see Cayce*

Westminster • *Westminster C/C •* Sandra Powell; Dir.; 135 E. Main St.; P.O. Box 155; 29693; Oconee; P 3,000; M 125; (864) 647-5316; Fax (864) 647-5013; wcoc@nuvox.net; www.westminstersc.com

Winnsboro • *Fairfield County C/C •* Terry N. Vickers; Pres./CEO; 120 N. Congress St.; P.O. Box 297; 29180; Fairfield; P 26,400; M 203; (803) 635-4242; Fax (803) 635-7955; fchamber@truvista.net; www.fairfieldchamber.sc

Woodruff • *see Spartanburg*

York • *Greater York C/C •* Paul Boger; Exec. Dir.; 23 E. Liberty St.; P.O. Box 97; 29745; York; P 25,000; M 310; (803) 684-2590; (877) 684-2590; Fax (803) 684-2575; info@greateryorkchamber.com; www.greateryorkchamber.com

South Dakota

South Dakota C of C & Ind. • David Owen; Pres.; 222 E. Capital, Ste. 15; P.O. Box 190; Pierre; 57501; Hughes; P 883,354; M 450; (605) 224-6161; Fax (605) 224-7198; davido@sdchamber.biz; www.sdchamber.biz

Aberdeen • *Aberdeen Area C/C •* Gail Ochs; Pres.; 516 S. Main St.; P.O. Box 1179; 57402; Brown; P 27,000; M 605; (605) 225-2860; (800) 874-9038; Fax (605) 225-2437; gail@aberdeen-chamber.com; www.aberdeen-chamber.com*

Badlands • *see Wall*

Belle Fourche • *Belle Fourche C/C •* Gary Wood; Exec. Dir.; 620 State St.; 57717; Butte; P 5,300; M 210; (605) 892-2676; Fax (605) 892-4633; director@bellefourchechamber.org; www.bellefourchechamber.org*

Beresford • *Beresford C/C •* Jim Fedderson; P.O. Box 167; 57004; Lincoln & Union; P 2,250; M 75; (605) 763-2021; Fax (605) 763-2021; chamber@bmtc.net; www.bmtc.net

Brandon • *Brandon Valley Area C/C •* Kim Cerwick; Pres.; 109 N. Pipestone St.; 57005; Minnehaha; P 8,700; M 285; (605) 582-7400; Fax (605) 582-8941; admin_brancofc@alliancecom.net; www.brandonvalleychamber.com*

Britton • *Britton Area C/C •* Julie Zuehlke; Secy./Treas.; P.O. Box 96; 57430; Marshall; P 1,500; M 80; (605) 448-5323; brittonchamber@venturecomm.net; www.brittonsouthdakota.com

Brookings • *Brookings Area C/C •* David Merhib; Exec. Dir.; 414 Main Ave.; P.O. Box 431; 57006; Brookings; P 27,000; M 509; (605) 692-6125; Fax (605) 697-8109; info@brookingschamber.org; www.brookingschamber.org*

Buffalo • *Harding County C/C •* Jesse Glines; Pres.; P.O. Box 113; 57720; Harding; P 1,400; M 25; (605) 375-3345; (605) 375-3130; Fax (605) 375-3119

Canton • *Canton C/C •* Lisa Alden; Dir.; 600 W. 5th St.; P.O. Box 34; 57013; Lincoln; P 3,057; M 100; (605) 764-7864; cantonchamberdirector@gmail.com; www.cantonsouthdakota.org

Centerville • *Centerville C/C •* Kim Satter; Pres.; P.O. Box 266; 57014; Turner; P 910; M 60; (605) 563-2147; (605) 563-2302; www.centervillesd.org

Chamberlain • *Chamberlain-Oacoma Area C/C & CVB •* April Reis; Dir.; 115 W. Lawler; 57325; Brule; P 2,900; M 162; (605) 234-4416; Fax (605) 234-4418; chamber@chamberlainsd.org; www.chamberlainsd.org

Custer • *Custer Area C/C •* David Ressler; Exec. Dir.; 615 Washington St.; P.O. Box 5018; 57730; Custer; P 5,000; M 300; (605) 673-2244; (800) 992-9818; Fax (605) 673-3726; dressler@custersd.com; www.custersd.com

Deadwood • *Deadwood C/C & Visitors Bur. •* Lee Harstad; Exec. Dir.; 767 Main St.; 57732; Lawrence; P 1,300; M 400; (605) 578-1876; (800) 999-1876; Fax (605) 578-2429; visit@deadwood.org; www.deadwood.org

Dell Rapids • *Dell Rapids C/C •* Dan Ahlers; Coord.; P.O. Box 81; 57022; Minnehaha; P 3,650; M 75; (605) 428-4167; Fax (605) 428-4167; danahlers1973@gmail.com; www.dellrapids.org

DeSmet • *DeSmet C/C •* Chad Kruse; P.O. Box 105; 57231; Kingsbury; P 1,300; M 72; (605) 854-3731; www.desmetsd.com

Edgemont • *Edgemont C/C* • Kristy McElhaney; Ofc. Mgr.;
P.O. Box 797; 57735; Custer; P 700; M 70; (605) 662-5900;
edgemontchamber@gwtc.net; www.edgemont-sd.com

Eureka • *Eureka C/C* • Barb Billotto; Pres.; P.O. Box 272; 57437;
McPherson; P 900; M 42; (605) 284-5230; Fax (605) 284-2841;
ivybookkeep@yahoo.com; www.eurekasd.com

Flandreau • *Flandreau Dev. Corp.* • 1005 W. Elm Ave.; P.O. Box 343;
57028; Moody; P 2,400; M 65; (605) 997-2492; Fax (605) 997-2915;
chuck@cityofflandreau.com; www.cityofflandreau.com

Fort Pierre • *Fort Pierre C/C* • Dennis Booth; 320 S. Tibbs St.; P.O.
Box 426; 57532; Stanley; P 2,100; M 150; (605) 223-2178; (605) 222-
7123; www.fortpierre.com

Freeman • *Freeman Chamber/Comm. Dev.* • Carroll Vizecky;
City Admin./Eco. Developer; P.O. Box 43; 57029; Hutchinson;
P 1,306; M 100; (605) 925-4444; Fax (605) 925-7920;
freemandevcorp@gmail.com; www.freemansd.com

Garretson • *Garretson Commercial Club* • P.O. Box 297; 57030;
Minnehaha; P 1,165; M 60; (605) 594-6721; kvegas@alliancecom.net;
www.garretsonsd.com

Gettysburg • *Gettysburg C/C* • Molly McRoberts; Secy.; 110 S.
Exene St.; P.O. Box 33; 57442; Potter; P 1,300; M 60; (605) 765-2528;
gburgchamber@venturecomm.net; www.gettysburgsd.net

Gregory • *Gregory Dallas Area C/C* • Holly Glover; Exec. Dir.; 120
W. 6th St.; P.O. Box 283; 57533; Gregory; P 1,300; M 90; (605)
831-9773; (605) 835-8270; gregoryareachamber@gmail.com;
www.gregorydallassd.com

Hill City • *Hill City Area C/C* • Janet Wetovick-Bily; Exec. Dir.; 23935
Hwy. 385; P.O. Box 253; 57745; Pennington; P 950; M 230; (605) 574-
2368; (800) 888-1798; Fax (605) 574-2055; director@hillcitysd.com;
www.hillcitysd.com

Hot Springs • *Hot Springs Area C/C* • Scott Haden; Exec. Dir.; 801
S. 6th St.; P.O. Box 342; 57747; Fall River; P 4,000; M 250; (605) 745-
4140; (800) 325-6991; Fax (605) 745-5849; info@hotsprings-sd.com;
www.hotsprings-sd.com*

Huron • *Huron Area Chamber & Visitor Bur.* • Peggy Woolridge;
Exec. Dir.; 1725 Dakota Ave. S.; 57350; Beadle; P 12,100; M 400; (605)
352-0000; (800) 487-6673; Fax (605) 352-8321; cvb@huronsd.com;
www.huronsd.com*

Keystone • *Keystone C/C* • Dolsee Davenport; Exec. Dir.;
110 Swanzey St.; P.O. Box 653; 57751; Pennington; P 327;
M 104; (605) 666-4896; (800) 456-3345; Fax (605) 666-4896;
info@keystonechamber.com; www.keystonechamber.com

Kimball • *Kimball C/C* • Corinne Overweg; Secy.; P.O. Box 2; 57355;
Jerauld; P 700; M 100; (605) 680-1794; kimballsd@midstatesd.net;
www.kimballsd.org

Lead • *Lead Area C/C* • Melissa Johnson; Exec. Dir.; 160 W. Main;
57754; Lawrence; P 3,800; M 250; (605) 584-1100; Fax (605) 584-
2209; leadcoc@knology.net; www.leadmethere.org

Lemmon • *Lemmon Area C/C* • Stacy Daley; Coord.; 100 3rd St. W.;
57638; Perkins; P 1,350; M 120; (605) 374-5716; Fax (605) 374-5789;
lchamber@sdplains.com; www.lemmonsd.com

Lennox • *Lennox Commercial Club* • Brenda Sinning; Secy.; P.O. Box
181; 57039; Lincoln; P 2,200; M 35; (605) 647-2286; Fax (605) 647-
2281; brendasinning@cityoflennoxsd.com; www.cityoflennoxsd.com

Madison • *Madison Area C/C* • Rosie Jamison; Exec. Dir.; 315
S. Egan Ave.; P.O. Box 467; 57042; Lake; P 6,500; M 280; (605)
256-2454; Fax (605) 256-9606; director@chamberofmadisonsd.com;
www.chamberofmadisonsd.com

Milbank • *Milbank Area C/C* • Laura Kelly; Event Dir.; 1001 E. 4th
Ave., Ste. 101; 57252; Grant; P 3,500; M 160; (605) 432-6656; (800)
675-6656; Fax (605) 432-6507; eventdirector@milbanksd.com;
www.milbanksd.com

Miller • *Miller Civic & Commerce Assn.* • Greg Palmer; Pres.; 103 W.
3rd St.; 57362; Hand; P 3,500; M 100; (605) 853-3098; Fax (605) 853-
3276; Kecia@millersd.org; www.millersd.net

Mitchell • *Mitchell Area C/C* • Bryan Hisel; Exec. Dir.; 601 N.
Main St.; P.O. Box 1026; 57301; Davison; P 18,741; M 503; (605)
996-5567; Fax (605) 996-8273; info@mitchellchamber.com;
www.mitchellchamber.com*

Mobridge • *Mobridge Area C/C* • Lindsay Scott; Exec. Dir.; 212
N. Main St.; 57601; Walworth; P 4,200; M 200; (605) 845-2387;
(888) 614-3474; Fax (605) 845-3223; chamber@mobridge.org;
www.mobridge.org*

Murdo • *Murdo C/C* • Barb Hockenbary; Ofc. Mgr.; P.O. Box 242;
57559; Jones; P 500; M 80; (605) 669-3333; murdosd@gwtc.net;
www.murdosd.com

Oacoma • *see Chamberlain*

Philip • *Philip C/C* • Matt Reedy; P.O. Box 378; 57567;
Haakon; P 800; M 100; (605) 859-2175; Fax (605) 859-2622;
info@philipsouthdakota.com; www.philipsouthdakota.com

Pierre • *Pierre Area C/C* • Laura Schoen Carbonneau IOM; CEO;
800 W. Dakota Ave.; P.O. Box 548; 57501; Hughes; P 16,000;
M 425; (605) 224-7361; (800) 962-2034; Fax (605) 224-6485;
contactchamber@pierre.org; www.pierre.org*

Platte • *Platte Area C/C* • Laura Vanden Berge; Exec. Dir.; 521
Main St., Ste. A; P.O. Box 393; 57369; Charles Mix; P 1,300;
M 135; (605) 337-2275; (888) 297-8175; Fax (605) 337-3988;
plattechamber@midstatesd.net; www.plattesd.org

Presho • *Presho Area C/C* • Karen Willis; Dir.; P.O.
Box 415; 57568; Lyman; P 490; M 50; (605) 895-9445;
preshochamber@kennebectelephone.com; www.presho.net

Rapid City • *Rapid City Area C/C* • Linda Rabe IOM CCE;
Pres./CEO; 444 Mt. Rushmore Rd. N.; P.O. Box 747; 57709;
Pennington; P 70,000; M 1,400; (605) 343-1744; Fax (605) 343-6550;
info@rapidcitychamber.com; www.rapidcitychamber.com*

Redfield • *Redfield Area C/C* • Cathy Fink; Coord.; 626 Main St.;
57469; Spink; P 2,400; M 100; (605) 472-0965; Fax (605) 472-4553;
redfieldchamber@redfield-sd.com; www.redfield-sd.com

Sioux Falls • *Sioux Falls Area C/C* • Jason M. Ball; Pres./CEO; 200 N.
Phillips Ave., Ste. 200; P.O. Box 1425; 57101; Minnehaha; P 251,854;
M 2,250; (605) 336-1620; Fax (605) 336-6499; sfacc@siouxfalls.com;
www.siouxfallschamber.com*

*SOUTH DAKOTA'S LARGEST CITY. PROGRESSIVE
COMMUNITY, SEVERAL PUBLIC/PRIVATE
EDUCATION OPTIONS, RECREATION, LOW
UNEMPLOYMENT RATE.*

Sisseton • *Sisseton Area C/C & Visitors Bur.* • Sandi Jaspers; Exec. Dir.; 1608 SD Hwy. 10, Ste. A; 57262; Roberts; P 2,500; M 80; (605) 698-7261; (888) 512-1966; sissetonchamber@venturecomm.net; www.sisseton.com

Spearfish • *Spearfish Area C/C* • Melissa Barth IOM; Exec. Dir.; 106 W. Kansas St.; P.O. Box 550; 57783; Lawrence; P 15,000; M 596; (605) 642-2626; (800) 626-8013; Fax (605) 642-7310; director@spearfishchamber.org; www.spearfishchamber.org*

Sturgis • *Sturgis Area C/C & VB* • Heidi Kruse; Exec. Dir.; 2040 Junction Ave.; P.O. Box 504; 57785; Meade; P 6,700; M 350; (605) 347-2556; Fax (605) 347-6682; info@sturgis-sd.org; sturgis-sd.org

Tyndall • *Tyndall C/C* • Jane Sedlacek; P.O. Box 305; 57066; Bon Homme; P 1,200; M 50; (605) 589-9944; (605) 589-4050; www.tyndallsd.com

Vermillion • *Vermillion Area C/C & Dev. Co.* • Steve Howe; Exec. Dir.; 116 Market St.; 57069; Clay; P 13,000; M 300; (605) 624-5571; (800) 809-2071; Fax (605) 624-0094; vcdc@vermillionchamber.com; www.vermillionchamber.com*

Wagner • *Wagner C/C* • Kelsey Doom; Dir. of Eco. Dev.; P.O. Box 40; 57380; Charles Mix; P 2,000; M 65; (605) 491-4051; Fax (605) 384-5644; developwagner@hcinet.net; www.wagnerareagrowth.org

Wall • *Wall Badlands Area C/C* • Lindsey Hildebrand; Exec. Dir.; 501 Main St.; P.O. Box 527; 57790; Pennington; P 750; M 100; (605) 279-2665; Fax (605) 279-2067; wallchamber@gwtc.net; www.wall-badlands.com

Watertown • *Watertown Area C/C* • Megan Gruman IOM; Pres./CEO; 1 E. Kemp; P.O. Box 1113; 57201; Codington; P 25,000; M 715; (605) 886-5814; Fax (605) 886-5957; coc@watertownsd.com; www.watertownsd.com*

Webster • *Webster Area C/C* • Chris Vander Linden; Pres.; P.O. Box 123; 57274; Day; P 1,896; M 140; (605) 345-4668; wchamber@itctel.com; www.webstersd.com

Wessington Springs • *Wessington Springs Area C/C* • Scott Vaske; Pres.; P.O. Box 513; 57382; Jerauld; P 1,000; M 45; (605) 539-1929; wsprings@venturecomm.net; www.wessingtonsprings.com

White River • *Mellette County C/C* • Rose West; P.O. Box 223; 57579; Mellette; P 2,100; M 41; (605) 259-3651

Winner • *Winner C/C* • Karla Brozik; Exec. Dir.; 246 S. Main St.; P.O. Box 268; 57580; Tripp; P 5,000; M 150; (605) 842-1533; thechamber@gwtc.net; www.winnersd.org

Yankton • *Yankton Area C/C* • Carmen Schramm; Exec. Dir.; 803 E. 4th St.; 57078; Yankton; P 14,454; M 422; (605) 665-3636; (800) 888-1460; Fax (605) 665-7501; chamber@yanktonsd.com; www.yanktonsd.com*

Tennessee

Tennessee C of C & Ind. • Catherine Glover; Pres.; 414 Union St., Ste. 107; Nashville; 37219; Davidson; P 6,456,243; M 600; (615) 256-5141; Fax (615) 256-6726; info@tnchamber.org; www.tnchamber.org

Alamo • *Crockett County C/C* • Charlie Moore; Exec. Dir.; 25 N. Bells St.; 38001; Crockett; P 14,586; M 200; (731) 696-5120; Fax (731) 696-4855; cmoore@crockettchamber.com; www.crockettchamber.com*

Ardmore • *Ardmore AL/TN C/C* • 26314 Main St.; P.O. Box 845; 38449; Giles & Lincoln; P 2,500; M 124; (256) 278-5524; info@ardmorealtnchamber.org; www.ardmorealtnchamber.org

Arlington • *Arlington C/C* • Tonia Howell; Dir.; 12015 Walker St.; P.O. Box 545; 38002; Shelby; P 13,000; M 272; (901) 867-0545; Fax (901) 867-4066; info@arlingtontnchamber.com; arlingtontnchamber.com*

Ashland City • *Cheatham County C/C* • Brandi D. Ghergia; Exec. Dir.; 108 N. Main St.; P.O. Box 354; 37015; Cheatham; P 39,000; M 186; (615) 792-6722; Fax (615) 792-5001; info@cheathamchamber.org; www.cheathamchamber.org*

Athens • *Athens Area C/C* • Rob Preston; Pres./CEO; 13 N. Jackson St.; 37303; McMinn; P 15,000; M 600; (423) 745-0334; Fax (423) 745-0335; info@athenschamber.org; www.athenschamber.org

Bartlett • *Bartlett Area C/C* • John P. Threadgill; Pres./CEO; 2969 Elmore Park Rd.; 38134; Shelby; P 58,000; M 600; (901) 372-9457; Fax (901) 372-9488; info@bartlettchamber.org; www.bartlettchamber.org*

Benton • *Polk County C/C* • Adrian Lambert; Dir.; 1697 Hwy. 64; P.O. Box 560; 37307; Polk; P 18,000; M 200; (423) 338-5040; (800) 633-7655; Fax (423) 338-0056; westoffice@ocoeecountry.com; www.ocoeecountry.com

Big Sandy • *see Paris*

Bolivar • *Hardeman County C/C* • Rob Jensik; Exec. Dir.; 112 S. Main St.; P.O. Box 313; 38008; Hardeman; P 27,300; M 180; (731) 658-6554; Fax (731) 658-6874; hardemanchamber@aeneas.net; www.hardemancountytn.com

Brentwood • *see Franklin*

Bristol • *Bristol TN/VA C/C* • Joy Madison; Pres./CEO; 20 Volunteer Pkwy.; 37620; Sullivan; P 44,500; M 725; (423) 989-4850; (423) 989-4848; Fax (423) 989-4867; frontdesk@bristolchamber.org; www.bristolchamber.org*

Brownsville • *Brownsville-Haywood County C/C* • Reneé Moss; Exec. Dir.; 121 W. Main St.; 38012; Haywood; P 19,000; M 250; (731) 772-2193; Fax (731) 772-2195; info@brownsvillehaywoodcountychamber.com; www.brownsvillehaywoodcountychamber.com*

Bybee • *see Newport*

Byrdstown • *Byrdstown-Pickett County C/C* • Billy K. Robbins; Exec. Dir.; 1005 Livingston Hwy.; P.O. Box 447; 38549; Pickett; P 5,100; M 100; (931) 864-7195; (888) 406-4704; Fax (931) 864-7195; dalehollow@twlakes.net; www.dalehollow.com

Camden • *Benton County/Camden C/C* • Bill Kee; Exec. Dir.; 266 Hwy. 641 N.; 38320; Benton; P 16,328; M 209; (731) 584-8395; Fax (731) 584-5544; chamber1@usit.net; www.bentoncountycamden.com*

Carthage • *Smith County C/C* • Bill Woodard; Exec. Dir.; 939 Upper Ferry Rd.; 37030; Smith; P 19,166; M 150; (615) 735-2093; Fax (615) 735-2093; info@smithcountychamber.org; www.smithcountychamber.org

Celina • *Clay County C/C* • Ray Norris; Exec. Dir.; 424 Brown St.; 38551; Clay; P 8,000; M 75; (931) 243-3338; Fax (931) 243-6809; claychamber@twlakes.net; www.dalehollowlake.org

Centerville • *Hickman County C/C* • Nancy S. Roland; Exec. Dir.; 405 W. Public Sq.; P.O. Box 126; 37033; Hickman; P 25,000; M 190; (931) 729-5774; Fax (931) 729-0874; hickmancountycha@bellsouth.net; www.hickmanco.org

Chattanooga • *Chattanooga Area C/C* • William B. Kilbride; Pres./CEO; 811 Broad St., Ste. 100; 37402; Hamilton; P 547,000; M 1,960; (423) 756-2121; Fax (423) 267-7242; info@chattanoogachamber.com; www.chattanoogachamber.com*

Chester County • *see Henderson*

Church Hill • *see Rogersville*

Clarksville • *Clarksville Area C/C* • Melinda Shepard; Exec. Dir.; 25 Jefferson St., Ste. 300; P.O. Box 883; 37041; Montgomery; P 122,000; M 1,200; (931) 647-2331; (931) 245-4341; Fax (931) 645-1574; cacc@clarksville.tn.us; www.clarksvillechamber.com*

Cleveland • *Cleveland/Bradley C/C Inc.* • Gary Farlow; Pres./CEO; 225 Keith St. S.W.; P.O. Box 2275; 37320; Bradley; P 100,000; M 950; (423) 472-6587; Fax (423) 472-2019; info@clevelandchamber.com; www.clevelandchamber.com

Clinton • *Anderson County C/C* • Rick Meredith; Pres.; 245 N. Main St., Ste. 200; 37716; Anderson; P 77,156; M 494; (865) 457-2559; (865) 457-2977; Fax (865) 463-7480; accc@andersoncountychamber.org; www.andersoncountychamber.org*

Collierville • *Collierville C/C* • Fran Persechini; Pres.; 485 Halle Park Dr.; 38017; Shelby; P 43,000; M 683; (901) 853-1949; Fax (901) 853-2399; info@colliervillechamber.com; www.colliervillechamber.com*

Collinwood • *see Waynesboro*

Columbia • *Maury County C/C & Eco. Alliance* • Wil Evans; Pres.; 106 W. 6th St.; P.O. Box 1076; 38402; Maury; P 84,000; M 500; (931) 388-2155; Fax (931) 380-0335; wevans@mauryalliance.com; www.mauryalliance.com*

Cookeville • *Putnam County C/C* • George Halford; Pres./CEO; 1 W. First St.; 38501; Putnam; P 72,000; M 900; (931) 526-2211; (800) 264-5541; Fax (931) 526-4023; info@cookevillechamber.com; www.cookevillechamber.com*

Cool Springs • *see Franklin*

Copperhill • *Polk County C/C* • Adrian Lambert; Dir.; P.O. Box 960; 37317; Polk; P 18,000; M 200; (423) 496-9000; (877) 790-2157; Fax (423) 496-5415; eastoffice@ocoeecountry.com; www.ocoeecountry.com

Cosby • *see Newport*

Covington • *Covington-Tipton County C/C* • Lee Johnston; Exec. Dir.; 106 W. Liberty; P.O. Box 683; 38019; Tipton; P 61,000; M 349; (901) 476-9727; Fax (901) 476-0056; tiptoncounty_covingto@comcast.net; www.covington-tiptoncochamber.com

Cowan • *see Winchester*

Crossville • *Crossville-Cumberland County C/C* • J. Bradley Allamong; Pres./CEO; 34 S. Main St.; 38555; Cumberland; P 60,000; M 500; (931) 484-8444; (877) 465-3861; Fax (931) 484-7511; info@crossville-chamber.com; www.crossville-chamber.com*

Dandridge • *Jefferson County C/C* • Darrell Helton; Pres./CEO; 532 Patriot Dr.; P.O. Box 890; 37725; Jefferson; P 55,000; M 330; (865) 397-9642; Fax (865) 397-0164; info@jeffersoncountytennessee.com; www.jeffersoncountytennessee.com

Dayton • *Dayton C/C* • Cynthia Rodriguez; Admin. Asst.; 107 Main St.; 37321; Rhea; P 34,000; M 250; (423) 775-0361; Fax (423) 570-0105; chamber@volstate.net; www.daytontnchamber.org*

Decherd • *see Winchester*

Del Rio • *see Newport*

Dickson • *Dickson County C/C* • Joseph A. Graves; Pres./CEO; 119 Hwy. 70 E.; 37055; Dickson; P 49,666; M 448; (615) 446-2349; Fax (615) 441-3112; contactus@dicksoncountychamber.com; www.dicksoncountychamber.com*

Donelson • *see Nashville -- Donelson-Hermitage*

Dover • *Stewart County C/C* • Jenny L. Roecker; Dir.; 117 Visitors Center Ln.; P.O. Box 147; 37058; Stewart; P 14,000; M 85; (931) 232-8290; Fax (931) 232-4973; stewartcountychamber@gmail.com; www.stewartcountychamber.com

Dresden • *Weakley County C/C* • Barbara Virgin; Exec. Dir.; 114 W. Maple St.; P.O. Box 67; 38225; Weakley; P 35,000; M 425; (731) 364-3787; Fax (731) 364-2099; wccc@weakleycountychamber.com; www.weakleycountychamber.com

Dunlap • *Sequatchie County-Dunlap C/C* • Ms. Marlene Basham; Exec. Dir.; 15643 Rankin Ave. N.; P.O. Box 1653; 37327; Sequatchie; P 18,000; M 120; (423) 949-7608; Fax (423) 949-8052; sequatchie@bledsoe.net; www.sequatchie.com

Dyersburg • *Dyersburg/Dyer County C/C* • Allen Hester; Pres./CEO; 2000 Commerce Ave.; 38024; Dyer; P 20,000; M 500; (731) 285-3433; Fax (731) 286-4926; chamber@ecsis.net; www.dyerchamber.com

Eagleville • *see Murfreesboro*

Elizabethton • *Elizabethton/Carter County C/C* • Tonya Stevens; Exec. Dir.; 500 Veterans Memorial Pkwy.; P.O. Box 190; 37644; Carter; P 59,000; M 320; (423) 547-3850; Fax (423) 547-3854; director@elizabethtonchamber.com; www.elizabethtonchamber.com*

Erin • *Houston County C/C* • Melinda Conwell; Pres.; P.O. Box 603; 37061; Houston; P 8,500; M 110; (931) 289-5100; Fax (931) 289-5600; irish@peoplestel.net; www.houstoncochamber.com

Erwin • *Unicoi County C/C* • Amanda Delp; Exec. Dir.; 100 S. Main Ave.; P.O. Box 713; 37650; Unicoi; P 18,000; M 200; (423) 743-3000; Fax (423) 743-0942; amanda@unicoicounty.org; www.unicoicounty.org

Estill Springs • *see Winchester*

Etowah • *Etowah Area C/C* • Durant Tullock; Exec. Dir.; L & N Depot; P.O. Box 458; 37331; McMinn; P 52,200; M 200; (423) 263-2228; Fax (423) 263-1670; info@etowahcoc.org; www.etowahcoc.org

Fairview • *Fairview Area C/C* • Jon Cherry; Pres.; 7111 Bowie Lake Rd.; P.O. Box 711; 37062; Williamson; P 12,050; M 120; (615) 799-9290; Fax (615) 800-6233; fairviewchamber@bellsouth.net; www.fairviewchamber.org

Fayetteville • *Fayetteville-Lincoln County C/C* • Carolyn Denton; Exec. Dir.; 208 Elk Ave. S.; P.O. Box 515; 37334; Lincoln; P 37,000; M 360; (931) 433-1234; (888) 433-1238; Fax (931) 433-9087; flcchamber@fpunet.com; www.fayettevillelincolncountychamber.com

Franklin • *Williamson County C/C* • Matt Largen; Pres./CEO; 5005 Meridian Blvd., Ste. 150; 37067; Williamson; P 176,000; M 1,200; (615) 771-1912; matt@williamsonchamber.com; www.williamsonchamber.com*

Gainesboro • *Gainesboro-Jackson County C/C* • John Dennis; Pres./Dir.; P.O. Box 827; 38562; Jackson; P 11,000; M 100; (931) 268-0971; johndennis61@hotmail.com; www.gainesboro-jcchamber.com

Gallatin • *Gallatin Area C/C* • Kim Myers; Exec. Dir.; 118 W. Main St.; P.O. Box 26; 37066; Sumner; P 30,500; M 500; (615) 452-4000; (800) 452-5286; Fax (615) 452-4021; info@gallatintn.org; www.gallatintn.org

Gatlinburg • *Gatlinburg C/C* • Victoria Simms; Exec. Dir.; 811 E. Pkwy.; P.O. Box 527; 37738; Sevier; P 5,300; M 650; (865) 436-4178; (800) 568-4748; Fax (865) 430-3876; sherri@gatlinburg.com; www.gatlinburg.com*

Germantown • *Germantown Area C/C* • Janie Day; Exec. Dir.; 2195 S. Germantown Rd., Ste. 100; 38138; Shelby; P 42,000; M 700; (901) 755-1200; Fax (901) 755-9168; info@germantownchamber.com; www.germantownchamber.com*

Gleason • *see Dresden*

Goodlettsville • *Goodlettsville Area C/C* • Steve Shoulders; Exec. Dir.; 117 N. Main St.; 37072; Davidson; P 17,300; M 500; (615) 859-7979; Fax (615) 859-1480; steve@goodlettsvillechamber.com; www.goodlettsvillechamber.com*

Greeneville • *Greene County Partnership* • Matt Garland; Pres./CEO; 115 Academy St.; 37743; Greene; P 68,580; M 500; (423) 638-4111; Fax (423) 638-5345; gcp@greenecop.com; www.greenecountypartnership.com*

Greenfield • *see Dresden*

Gruetli • *see Monteagle*

Hartford • *see Newport*

Hartsville • *Hartsville-Trousdale County C/C* • Natalie Knudsen; Exec. Dir.; 240 Broadway; 37074; Trousdale; P 8,000; M 120; (615) 374-9243; chamber@hartsvilletrousdale.com; www.hartsvilletrousdale.com

Helenwood • *Scott County C/C* • Stacey Kidd; Exec. Dir.; 12025 Scott Hwy.; P.O. Box 766; 37755; Scott; P 22,000; M 150; (800) 645-6905; (423) 663-6900; Fax (423) 663-6906; scchamber@highland.net; www.scottcountychamber.com

Henderson • *Chester County-City of Henderson C/C* • Emily Shelton; Exec. Dir.; 130 E. Main St.; P.O. Box 1976; 38340; Chester; P 17,131; M 200; (731) 989-5222; Fax (731) 983-5518; info@chestercountychamber.com; www.chestercountychamber.com

Hendersonville • *Hendersonville Area C/C* • Kathleen Hawkins; Pres./CEO; 100 Country Club Dr., Ste. 104; 37075; Sumner; P 169,000; M 760; (615) 824-2818; Fax (615) 250-3637; info@hendersonchamber.com; www.hendersonvillechamber.com*

Hohenwald • *Hohenwald-Lewis County C/C* • Janet Johnson; Exec. Dir.; 106 N. Court St.; 38462; Lewis; P 12,461; M 145; (931) 796-4084; Fax (931) 796-6020; director@hohenwaldlewischamber.com; www.hohenwaldlewischamber.com

Humboldt • *Humboldt C/C* • Sherri McCarter; Exec. Dir.; 1200 Main St.; 38343; Gibson; P 9,000; M 250; (731) 784-1842; Fax (731) 784-1573; sherri@humboldttnchamber.org; www.humboldttnchamber.org*

Huntingdon • *Carroll County C/C* • Brad Hurley; Pres.; 20740 E. Main St.; P.O. Box 726; 38344; Carroll; P 28,500; M 320; (731) 986-4664; Fax (731) 986-2029; cchamber@earthlink.net; www.cchambertn.com

Huntland • *see Winchester*

Jacksboro • *Campbell County C/C* • John Branam; Exec. Dir.; 1016 Main St.; P.O. Box 305; 37757; Campbell; P 40,000; M 230; (423) 566-0329; info@campbellcountychamber.org; www.campbellcountychamber.com*

Jackson • *Jackson Chamber* • Kyle Spurgeon; Pres./CEO; 197 Auditorium St.; P.O. Box 1904; 38302; Madison; P 100,000; M 1,500; (731) 423-2200; Fax (731) 424-4860; chamber@jacksontn.com; www.jacksontn.com*

Jamestown • *Fentress County C/C* • Walter Page CTTP IOM; Exec. Dir.; 114 Central Ave. W.; P.O. Box 1294; 38556; Fentress; P 17,500; M 200; (931) 879-9948; Fax (931) 879-6767; wpage@jamestowntn.org; www.jamestowntn.org*

Jasper • *Marion County C/C* • Aimee Billingsley; Pres.; 302 Betsy Pack Dr.; 37347; Marion; P 29,000; M 125; (423) 942-5103; Fax (423) 942-0098; marioncoc@bellsouth.net; www.marioncountychamber.com

Jefferson City • *see Dandridge*

Johnson City • *The Chamber of Commerce* • Gary Mabrey; Pres./CEO; 603 E. Market St.; P.O. Box 180; 37605; Washington; P 126,000; M 640; (423) 461-8000; Fax (423) 461-8047; frontdesk@johnsoncitytnchamber.com; www.johnsoncitytnchamber.com*

Jonesborough • *see Johnson City*

Kingsport • *Kingsport Area C/C* • Miles Burdine; Pres./CEO; 400 Clinchfield St.; 37660; Sullivan; P 50,000; M 1,000; (423) 392-8800; Fax (423) 392-8834; kchamber@kingsportchamber.org; www.kingsportchamber.org*

Kingston • *Roane Alliance* • Wade Creswell; Pres./CEO; 1209 N. Kentucky St.; 37763; Roane; P 52,000; M 400; (865) 376-5572; Fax (865) 376-4978; chamber@roanealliance.org; www.roanechamber.com*

Knoxville • *Knoxville Chamber* • Mike Edwards; Pres./CEO; 17 Market Sq., Ste. 201; 37902; Knox; P 430,019; M 2,241; (865) 637-4550; Fax (865) 523-2071; medwards@knoxvillechamber.com; www.knoxvillechamber.com*

La Vergne • *Rutherford County C/C - La Vergne Branch* • Paul Latture IOM; Pres.; 5093 Murfreesboro Rd.; 37086; Rutherford; P 298,700; M 2,200; (615) 287-8668; Fax (615) 793-6025; dbalthrop@lavergnetn.gov; www.rutherfordchamber.org*

Lafayette • *Macon County C/C* • Lona Vinson; Exec. Secy.; 685 Hwy. 52 Bypass W.; 37083; Macon; P 22,300; M 178; (615) 666-5885; Fax (615) 666-6969; mchamber@nctc.com; www.maconcountytn.com

Lake City • *Rocky Top C/C* • Maria Hooks; Pres.; 506 S. Main St.; P.O. Box 1054; 37769; Anderson; P 2,007; M 100; (865) 426-9595; Fax (865) 457-4545; info@rockytoptnchamber.com; www.rockytoptnchamber.com

Lawrenceburg • *Lawrence County C/C* • Ethan Hadley; Pres./CEO; 25B Public Sq.; P.O. Box 86; 38464; Lawrence; P 42,600; M 316; (931) 762-4911; Fax (931) 762-3153; ethan@lawcotn.com; www.selectlawrence.com*

Lebanon • *Lebanon Wilson County C/C* • Melanie Minter; Pres./CEO; 149 Public Sq.; 37087; Wilson; P 113,900; M 960; (615) 444-5503; Fax (615) 443-0596; office@lebanonwilsonchamber.com; www.lebanonwilsonchamber.com*

Lenoir City • *see Loudon*

Lewisburg • *Marshall County C/C* • Ritaanne Wade-Weaver; Exec. Dir.; 227 Second Ave. N.; 37091; Marshall; P 30,000; M 205; (931) 359-3863; Fax (931) 359-3863; director@marshallchamber.org; www.marshallchamber.org*

Lexington • *Henderson C/C* • Vicki Bunch; Exec. Dir.; 149 Eastern Shores Dr.; 38351; Henderson; P 27,000; M 300; (731) 968-2126; Fax (731) 968-7006; vbunch@hctn.org; www.hctn.org

Livingston • *Livingston-Overton County C/C* • Greg McDonald; Exec. Dir.; 222 E. Main St.; P.O. Box 354; 38570; Overton; P 22,000; M 300; (931) 823-6421; Fax (931) 823-6422; chamber@twlakes.net; www.overtonco.com

Loudon • *Loudon County C/C* • Michael Bobo; Pres.; 318 Angel Row; P.O. Box 87; 37774; Loudon; P 51,200; M 500; (865) 458-2067; Fax (865) 458-1206; stacy@loudoncountychamber.com; www.loudoncountychamberofcommerce.com*

Lynchburg • *Lynchburg-Moore County C/C* • Ricky Lee; Pres.; P.O. Box 421; 37352; Moore; P 7,500; M 100; (931) 759-4111; info@lynchburgtn.com; www.lynchburgtn.com

Madison • *Madison-Rivergate Area C/C* • Debbie Pace; Exec. Dir.; P.O. Box 97; 37116; Davidson; P 36,000; M 350; (615) 865-5400; Fax (615) 865-0448; president@madisonrivergatechamber.com; www.madisonrivergatechamber.com

Madisonville • *Monroe County C/C* • Brandy Gentry; CEO; 520 Cook St., Ste. A; 37354; Monroe; P 40,000; M 300; (423) 442-4588; Fax (423) 442-9016; info@monroecountychamber.org; www.monroecountychamber.org*

Manchester • *Manchester Area C/C* • Terri Hudson; Exec. Dir.; 110 E. Main St.; 37355; Coffee; P 10,102; M 305; (931) 728-7635; Fax (931) 723-0736; manchesterchamberofcommerce@manchestertnchamber.org; www.manchestertnchamber.org

Martin • *see Dresden*

Maryville • *Blount Partnership* • Bryan T. Daniels CEcD CCE IOM; Pres./CEO; 201 S. Washington St.; 37804; Blount; P 126,339; M 1,100; (865) 983-2241; Fax (865) 984-1386; infodesk@blountpartnership.com; www.blountpartnership.com*

Maynardville • *Union County C/C* • Julie Graham; Pres./CEO; P.O. Box 848; 37807; Union; P 20,000; M 115; (865) 992-2811; Fax (865) 992-2812; info@comeherecomehome.com; www.comeherecomehome.com

McEwen • *see Waverly*

McMinnville • *McMinnville-Warren County C/C* • Alicea Weddington; Pres.; 110 S. Court Sq.; P.O. Box 574; 37111; Warren; P 40,000; M 325; (931) 473-6611; (931) 473-6612; Fax (931) 473-4741; warrencotn@blomand.net; www.warrentn.com

Memphis • *Greater Memphis Chamber* • Phil Trenary; Pres./CEO; 22 N. Front St., Ste. 200; P.O. Box 224; 38101; Shelby; P 1,345,345; M 2,300; (901) 543-3500; Fax (901) 543-3510; info@memphischamber.com; www.memphischamber.com*

Milan • *Milan C/C* • Julie Allen Burke; Exec. Dir.; 1069 S. Main St.; 38358; Gibson; P 8,000; M 219; (731) 686-7494; Fax (731) 686-7495; chamber@cityofmilantn.com; www.milantnchamber.com

Millington • *Millington Area C/C* • Teri Flannagan; Dlr. of Op.; 7965 Veterans Pkwy., Ste. 101; 38053; Shelby; P 10,500; M 300; (901) 872-1486; Fax (901) 872-0727; info@millingtonchamber.com; www.millingtonchamber.com*

Monteagle • *Monteagle Mountain C/C* • Rhonda Pilkington; Exec. Dir.; P.O. Box 353; 37356; Marion; P 5,000; M 200; (931) 924-5353; Fax (931) 924-5354; info@monteaglechamber.com; www.monteaglechamber.com

Morristown • *Morristown Area C/C* • Marshall Ramsey; Pres./CEO; 825 W. First N. St.; P.O. Box 9; 37815; Hamblen; P 63,000; M 726; (423) 586-6382; Fax (423) 586-6576; macc@morristownchamber.com; www.morristownchamber.com*

Mount Carmel • *see Rogersville*

Mount Juliet • *Mount Juliet C/C* • Mark Hinesley; Pres./CEO; 2055 N. Mt. Juliet Rd., Ste. 200; 37122; Wilson; P 30,000; M 625; (615) 758-3478; Fax (615) 754-8595; info@mtjulietchamber.com; www.mjchamber.org*

Mount Pleasant • *see Columbia*

Mountain City • *Johnson County C/C* • Tom Reece; Pres.; P.O. Box 66; 37683; Johnson; P 18,100; M 250; (423) 727-5800; Fax (423) 727-4943; info@johnsoncountychamber.org; www.johnsoncountychamber.org

Munford • *South Tipton County C/C* • Rosemary Bridges; Pres.; P.O. Box 1198; 38058; Tipton; P 59,000; M 300; (901) 837-4600; Fax (901) 837-4602; chamber@southtipton.com; www.southtipton.com

Murfreesboro • *Rutherford County C/C - Murfreesboro Branch* • Paul Latture IOM; Pres.; 3050 Medical Center Pkwy.; 37129; Rutherford; P 298,700; M 2,200; (615) 893-6565; (800) 716-7560; Fax (615) 890-7600; info@rutherfordchamber.org; www.rutherfordchamber.org*

Nashville Area

Bellevue Harpeth C/C • Amy Napoli; Admin. Liaison; 7041 Hwy. 70S., Ste. 100B; 37221; Davidson; P 43,000; M 190; (615) 662-2737; info@bellevueharpethchamber.com; www.thebellevuechamber.com*

Donelson Hermitage C/C • Leah Jack; Exec. Dir.; 125 Donelson Pike; P.O. Box 140200; 37214; Davidson; P 75,000; M 450; (615) 883-7896; Fax (615) 391-4880; admin@d-hchamber.com; www.d-hchamber.com*

Nashville Area C/C • Ralph Schulz; Pres./CEO; 211 Commerce St., Ste. 100; 37201; Davidson; P 550,000; M 2,200; (615) 743-3000; Fax (615) 743-3002; info@nashvillechamber.com; www.nashvillechamber.com

New Johnsonville • *see Waverly*

Newport • *Cocke County Partnership C/C* • Lynn Ramsey; Dir.; 433-B Prospect Ave.; 37821; Cocke; P 36,000; M 300; (423) 623-7201; (423) 623-7216; Fax (423) 625-1846; sball@cockecountypartnership.com; www.cockecountypartnership.com

Norris • *see Clinton*

Oak Ridge • *Oak Ridge C/C* • Parker Hardy CCE; Pres./CEO; 1400 Oak Ridge Tpk.; 37830; Anderson; P 29,000; M 550; (865) 483-1321; Fax (865) 325-0819; holt@orcc.org; www.orcc.org

Oliver Springs • *see Clinton*

Oneida • *see Helenwood*

Paris • *Paris-Henry County C/C* • Jennifer Wheatley; Exec. Dir.; 2508 E. Wood St.; 38242; Henry; P 31,115; M 400; (731) 642-3431; Fax (731) 642-3454; pariscoc@paristnchamber.com; www.paristnchamber.com*

Parrottsville • *see Newport*

Parsons • *Decatur County C/C* • Charles P. Taylor Sr.; Exec. Dir.; 139 Tennessee Ave. N.; P.O. Box 245; 38363; Decatur; P 12,000; M 165; (731) 847-4202; Fax (731) 847-4222; dccc@netease.net; www.decaturcountytennessee.org*

Pigeon Forge • *Pigeon Forge C/C* • Brandy Dominguez; Exec. Dir.; 231 Dollywood Ln.; 37863; Sevier; P 6,400; M 350; (865) 453-5700; (800) 221-9858; Fax (865) 453-6812; info@pigeonforgechamber.com; www.pigeonforgechamber.com*

Pigeon Forge • *City of Pigeon Forge Dept. of Tourism* • Leon Downey; Exec. Dir.; 2450 Pkwy.; P.O. Box 1390-I; 37868; Sevier; P 6,000; M 976; (865) 453-8574; (800) 251-9100; Fax (865) 429-7362; inquire@MyPigeonForge.com; www.mypigeonforge.com

Pikeville • *Pikeville-Bledsoe County C/C* • Roberta Smith; Secy.; P.O. Box 205; 37367; Bledsoe; P 12,800; M 50; (423) 447-2791; directors@pikeville-bledsoe.com; www.pikeville-bledsoe.com

Portland • *Portland C/C* • Sherri Ferguson; Exec. Dir.; 106 Main St.; 37148; Sumner; P 12,000; M 185; (615) 325-9032; Fax (615) 325-8399; info@portlandcofc.com; www.portlandcofc.com

Pulaski • *Giles County C/C* • Jessica Parker; CEO; 110 N. Second St.; 38478; Giles; P 30,000; M 320; (931) 363-3789; Fax (931) 363-7279; annbasinger@gilescountychamber.com; www.gilescountychamber.com*

Ripley • *Lauderdale Chamber/ECD* • Susan Todd; Exec. Dir.; 123 S. Jefferson St.; 38063; Lauderdale; P 27,815; M 254; (731) 635-9541; (731) 635-8463; Fax (731) 635-9064; stodd@lauderdalecountytn.org; www.lauderdalecountytn.org*

Rogersville • *Rogersville/Hawkins County C/C* • Nancy Barker; Exec. Dir.; 107 E. Main St., Ste. 100; 37857; Hawkins; P 58,000; M 380; (423) 272-2186; Fax (423) 272-2186**; hawkinschamber@gmail.com; www.rogersvillechamber.us*

Savannah • *Hardin County C/C* • Marilee Harrison; Exec. Dir.; 495 Main St.; P.O. Box 996; 38372; Hardin; P 30,000; M 300; (731) 925-2363; Fax (731) 925-6987; info@hardincountychamber.com; www.hardincountychamber.com

Selmer • *McNairy County C/C & EDC* • Russell Ingle; Exec. Dir.; 144 Cypress Ave.; P.O. Box 7; 38375; McNairy; P 26,000; M 300; (731) 645-6360; Fax (731) 645-7663; russell@mcnairy.com; www.mcnairy.com

Sevierville • *Sevierville C/C* • Brenda McCroskey; CEO; 110 Gary Wade Blvd.; 37862; Sevier; P 18,000; M 600; (865) 453-6411; Fax (865) 453-9649; amarr@scoc.org; www.scoc.org*

Sewanee • *see Winchester*

Sharon • *see Dresden*

Shelbyville • *Shelbyville-Bedford County C/C* • Allen Pitner; CEO; 100 N. Cannon Blvd.; 37160; Bedford; P 45,000; M 400; (931) 684-3482; (888) 662-2525; Fax (931) 684-3483; bedfordchamber@sbcchamber.com; www.shelbyvilletn.com*

Smithville • *Smithville-DeKalb County C/C* • Suzanne Williams; Exec. Dir.; 1 Public Sq., Rm. 201; P.O. Box 64; 37166; DeKalb; P 18,600; M 200; (615) 597-4163; Fax (615) 597-4164; swilliams@dekalbcountychamber.org; www.dekalbtn.org

Smyrna • *Rutherford County C/C - Smyrna Branch* • Paul Latture IOM; Pres.; 315 S. Lowry St.; 37167; Rutherford; P 298,700; M 2,200; (615) 355-6565; Fax (615) 355-5715; joy.galyon@townofsmyrna.org; www.rutherfordchamber.org*

Somerville • *Fayette County C/C* • Julie Perrine; Exec. Dir.; 120 E. Court Sq., Ste. 101; P.O. Box 411; 38068; Fayette; P 39,000; M 304; (901) 465-8690; Fax (901) 465-6497; director@fayettecountychamber.com; www.fayettecountychamber.com

South Fulton • *Twin Cities C/C* • Thea Vowell; Exec. Dir.; 700 Milton Counce Dr.; P.O. Box 5077; 38257; Obion; P 5,000; M 125; (731) 479-7029; Fax (731) 479-7029; twincitieschamber@bellsouth.net; www.fultonsouthfultonchamber.com

Sparta • *Sparta-White County C/C* • Jody Sliger; Dir.; 16 W. Bockman Way; 38583; White; P 26,000; M 250; (931) 836-3552; Fax (931) 836-2216; sparta-chamber@sparta-chamber.net; www.sparta-chamber.net*

Spencer • *Greater Van Buren County/Spencer C/C* • Marilyn H. Baker; Exec. Dir.; 66 Sparta St.; P.O. Box 814; 38585; Van Buren; P 5,500; M 60; (931) 946-7033; vbchamber@blomand.net; www.vanburenchamber.com

Spring City • *Spring City C/C* • Karen Valencie; Bus. Mgr.; 390 Front St.; P.O. Box 355; 37381; Rhea; P 2,100; M 140; (423) 365-5210; Fax (423) 365-9790; info@springcitychamberofcommerce.com; www.springcitychamberofcommerce.com

Spring Hill • *Spring Hill C/C* • Lauren Magli; Dir.; P.O. Box 1815; 37174; Maury; P 33,000; M 290; (931) 486-0625; Fax (931) 486-0516; info@springhillchamber.com; www.springhillchamber.com*

Springfield • *Robertson County C/C* • Margot Fosnes; Exec. Dir.; 503 W. Court Sq.; 37172; Robertson; P 66,283; M 545; (615) 384-3800; Fax (615) 384-1260; info@robertsonchamber.org; www.robertsonchamber.org*

Tazewell • *Claiborne County C/C* • Dennis Shipley; Exec. Dir./V.P.; 1732 Main St., Ste. 1; P.O. Box 649; 37879; Claiborne; P 32,200; M 220; (423) 626-4149; Fax (423) 626-1611; chamber@claibornecounty.com; www.claibornecounty.com

Tiptonville • *Reelfoot Area C/C* • Marcia Mills; Exec. Dir.; 130 S. Court St.; 38079; Lake; P 7,900; M 45; (731) 253-8144; Fax (731) 253-9923; info@reelfootareachamber.com; www.reelfootareachamber.com

Townsend • *see Maryville*

Tracy City • *see Monteagle*

Trenton • *Greater Gibson County Area C/C* • Libby Wickersham; Exec. Dir.; 111 W. Eaton St.; 38382; Gibson; P 49,600; M 275; (731) 855-0973; Fax (731) 855-0979; info@gibsoncountytn.com; www.gibsoncountytn.com*

Tullahoma • *Tullahoma Area C/C* • Diane Bryant; Exec. Dir.; 135 W. Lincoln St.; P.O. Box 1205; 37388; Coffee & Franklin; P 25,332; M 425; (931) 455-5497; tullahomachamber@tullahoma.org; www.tullahoma.org*

Union City • *Obion County C/C* • Lindsay Frilling; CEO; 214 E. Church St.; 38261; Obion; P 31,500; M 350; (731) 885-0211; Fax (731) 885-7155; lfrilling@obioncounty.org; www.obioncounty.org*

U.S. Chambers of Commerce

Wartburg • *Morgan County C/C* • Gigi Schooler; Exec. Dir.; 112 Hillcrest; P.O. Box 539; 37887; Morgan; P 21,000; M 105; (423) 346-5740; (423) 223-0980; morgancotn@yahoo.com; www.morgancountychamber.com

Wartrace • *Wartrace C/C* • Phillip D. Gentry; Pres.; 401 Blackman Blvd.; P.O. Box 543; 37183; Bedford; P 1,000; M 15; (931) 389-9999; wartracechamber@bellsouth.net; www.wartracechamber.org

Washington County • *see Johnson City*

Watertown • *Watertown-East Wilson County C/C* • Hunter Allen; Pres.; P.O. Box 5; 37184; Wilson; P 1,400; M 140; (615) 237-0270; info@watertowntn.com; www.watertowntn.com

Waverly • *Humphreys County Area C/C* • Daryl C. Mosley; Exec. Dir.; 124 E. Main St.; 37185; Humphreys; P 19,000; M 209; (931) 296-4865; info@humphreyscountychamberofcommerce.com; www.humphreyscountychamberofcommerce.com

Waynesboro • *Wayne County C/C* • Rena Purdy; Exec. Dir.; 100 Court Cir., Rm. 301; P.O. Box 574; 38485; Wayne; P 17,000; M 160; (931) 722-3575; chamber@netease.net; www.waynecountychamber.org*

Westmoreland • *Westmoreland Area C/C* • Jamie Thompson; Pres.; P.O. Box 536; 37186; Sumner; P 2,206; M 80; (615) 644-1531; (615) 644-5156; Fax (615) 644-1531; info@westmorelandchamber.org; www.westmorelandchamber.org

White House • *White House Area C/C* • Mandy Christenson; Exec. Dir.; 414 Hwy. 76; P.O. Box 521; 37188; Robertson & Sumner; P 10,255; M 265; (615) 672-3937; Fax (615) 672-2828; whcoc@bellsouth.net; www.whitehousechamber.org*

Winchester • *Franklin County C/C* • Judy D. Taylor IOM; Exec. Dir.; 44 Chamber Way; P.O. Box 280; 37398; Franklin; P 43,000; M 400; (931) 967-6788; (931) 308-6098; Fax (931) 967-9418; info@franklincountychamber.com; www.franklincountychamber.com*

Woodbury • *Historic Cannon County C/C* • Carolyn Motley; Svcs. Coord.; 1424 John Bragg Hwy.; P.O. Box 140; 37190; Cannon; P 13,700; M 101; (615) 563-2222; Fax (615) 563-1165; cannontn@dtccom.net; www.cannontn.com

Texas

Texas Assn. of Bus. • Bill Hammond; CEO; 1209 Nueces St.; Austin; 78701; Travis; P 26,059,203; M 5,000; (512) 477-6721; Fax (512) 477-0836; info@txbiz.org; www.txbiz.org

Abilene • *Abilene C/C* • Doug Peters IOM AP; Pres./CEO; 174 Cypress St., Ste. 200; 79601; Taylor; P 125,000; M 1,200; (325) 677-7241; info@abilenechamber.com; www.abilenechamber.com*

Alamo • *Alamo C/C & Visitors Bur.* • Jose R. Castilleja; Ofc. Mgr.; 803 Main St.; 78516; Hidalgo; P 18,353; M 120; (956) 787-2117; alamotx.chamber@gmail.com; www.alamochamber.com

Alamo Heights • *Alamo Heights C/C* • Geoffrey Elkins; Pres.; P.O. Box 6141; 78209; Bexar; P 10,000; M 150; (210) 822-7027; admin@alamoheightschamber.org; www.alamoheightschamber.org

Albany • *Albany C/C* • Diana Nail; Exec. Dir.; #2 Railroad; P.O. Box 2047; 76430; Shackelford; P 2,034; M 200; (325) 762-2525; Fax (325) 762-3125; chamber@albanytexas.com; www.albanytexas.com

Aldine • *see Houston-Houston Intercontinental C/C*

Aledo • *see Willow Park*

Alice • *Alice C/C & CVB* • Juan Navejar Jr.; Exec. Dir.; 612 E. Main St.; P.O. Box 1609; 78333; Jim Wells; P 19,000; M 411; (361) 664-3454; Fax (361) 664-2291; jnavejar@alicetx.org; www.alicetxchamber.org*

Allen • *Allen Fairview C/C* • Sharon Mayer; CEO; 210 W. McDermott; 75013; Collin; P 93,000; M 580; (972) 727-5585; Fax (972) 727-9000; sharon@allenfairviewchamber.com; www.allenfairviewchamber.com*

Alpine • *Alpine C/C* • Mark Hannan; Pres.; 106 N. 3rd St.; 79830; Brewster; P 6,300; M 218; (432) 837-2326; (800) 561-3712; Fax (432) 837-1259; info@alpinetexas.com; www.alpinetexas.com

Alvarado • *Alvarado C/C* • Jason Reynolds; Pres.; P.O. Box 712; 76009; Johnson; P 3,800; M 90; (817) 783-2233; email@welcometoalvarado.com; www.welcometoalvarado.com

Alvin • *Alvin-Manvel Area C/C* • Johanna G. McWilliams; Pres./CEO; 105 W. Willis; 77511; Brazoria; P 50,000; M 400; (281) 331-3944; chamber@amacc.org; www.alvinmanvelchamber.org*

Amarillo • *Amarillo C/C* • Gary Molberg; Pres./CEO; 1000 S. Polk St.; P.O. Box 9480; 79105; Potter; P 200,000; M 1,800; (806) 373-7800; Fax (806) 373-3909; chamber@amarillo-chamber.org; www.amarillo-chamber.org*

Anahuac • *Anahuac Area C/C* • Robbie King; Pres.; 603 Miller St.; P.O. Box R; 77514; Chambers; P 2,500; M 175; (409) 267-4190; Fax (409) 267-3907; anahuacchamber@windstream.net; www.anahuacchamber.com

Andrews • *Andrews C/C & CVB* • Julia Wallace; Exec. Dir.; 700 W. Broadway; 79714; Andrews; P 13,000; M 250; (432) 523-2695; Fax (432) 523-2375; achamber@andrewstx.com; www.andrewstx.com*

Angleton • *Angleton C/C* • Beth Journeay; Pres./CEO; 222 N. Velasco; 77515; Brazoria; P 19,000; M 500; (979) 849-6443; Fax (979) 849-4520; beth@angletonchamber.org; www.angletonchamber.org*

Annetta • *see Willow Park*

Anson • *Anson C/C* • Melissa Darnell; Mgr.; 1132 W. Court Plz.; P.O. Box 351; 79501; Jones; P 2,500; M 150; (325) 823-3259; Fax (325) 823-4326; ansoncofc@att.net; www.ansonchamber.com

Anthony • *see Anthony, NM*

Aransas Pass • *Aransas Pass C/C* • Rosemary Vega; CEO; 130 W. Goodnight; 78336; San Patricio; P 8,136; M 270; (361) 758-2750; (800) 633-3028; Fax (361) 758-8320; chamberasst@cableone.net; www.aransaspass.org

Argyle • *Argyle C/C* • Margie Sullivan; Exec. Dir.; 302 N. Hwy 377; 76226; Denton; P 3,300; M 150; (940) 464-9990; chamber@argylechamber.org; www.argylechamber.org*

Arlington • *Arlington C/C* • Wes Jurey; Pres./CEO; 505 E. Border St.; 76010; Tarrant; P 375,000; M 1,200; (817) 275-2613; Fax (817) 261-7389; wjurey@arlingtontx.com; www.arlingtontx.com*

Arp • *Arp Area C/C* • Jan Gibson; Pres.; P.O. Box 146; 75750; Smith; P 1,000; M 70; (972) 523-5278; (903) 859-6131; www.arptexaschamber.com

Aspermont • *Aspermont C/C* • Stephenia Mullen; Exec. Dir.; 701 Broadway; P.O. Box 556; 79502; Stonewall; P 1,200; M 75; (940) 988-2448; Fax (940) 989-2517; stephenia.coc@srcaccess.net

Athens • *Athens C/C* • Sarah Hueber; Pres.; 201 W. Corsicana, Ste. 1; 75751; Henderson; P 12,336; M 419; (903) 675-5181; (800) 755-7878; Fax (903) 675-4830; info@athenscc.org; www.athenscc.org*

Atlanta • *Atlanta Area C/C* • Lisa Thompson; Ofc. Mgr.; 101 N. East St.; 75551; Cass; P 5,745; M 165; (903) 796-3296; Fax (903) 796-5711; atlantaareacoc@sbcglobal.net; www.atlantatexas.net

Aubrey • *Aubrey 380 Area C/C* • Donna Sims; Exec. Dir.; 205 S. Main St.; 76227; Denton; P 3,000; M 190; (940) 365-9781; Fax (940) 365-9781; chamber@aubreycoc.org; www.aubreycoc.org

Austin Area

Greater Austin C/C • Michael W. Rollins CCE; Pres./CEO; 535 E. 5th St.; 78701; Travis; P 2,100,000; M 2,800; (512) 478-9383; Fax (512) 478-9615; memberinfo@austinchamber.com; www.austinchamber.com*

Greater Austin Hispanic C/C • Mark L. Madrid; Pres./CEO; 3601 Far West Blvd., Ste. 204; 78731; Travis; P 1,700,000; M 1,000; (512) 476-7502; Fax (512) 476-6417; mmadrid@gahcc.org; www.gahcc.org*

Lake Travis C/C • Laura Mitchell IOM; Pres.; 1415 Ranch Rd. 620 S., Ste. 202; 78734; Travis; P 24,000; M 430; (512) 263-5833; (877) 263-0073; jannine@laketravischamber.com; www.laketravischamber.com*

Women's C/C of Texas • Rose Batson; Pres.; P.O. Box 26051; 78755; Travis; M 500; (512) 338-0839; austin@womenschambertexas.com; www.womenschambertexas.com

Avinger • *Avinger C/C* • Janet Kenyan; V.P. of Mktg.; 181 C.R. 1537; 75630; Cass; P 434; M 50; (903) 562-1549; Fax (903) 562-1039; jkenyan@windstream.net; avingertxchamber.org

Azle • *Azle Area C/C* • Shelia Pippins; Exec. Dir.; 404 W. Main St., Ste. 102; 76020; Parker & Tarrant; P 12,000; M 300; (817) 444-1112; Fax (817) 444-1143; info@azlechamber.com; www.azlechamber.com

Bacliff • *see Dickinson*

Baird • *Baird C/C* • 328 Market St.; 79504; Callahan; P 1,651; M 75; (325) 854-2003; Fax (325) 854-2003; chamber@bairdtexas.com; www.bairdtexas.com

Balch Springs • *Balch Springs C/C* • Alvester Gibson Jr.; Pres.; 12400 Elam Rd.; 75180; Dallas; P 23,700; M 132; (972) 557-0988; Fax (972) 584-0320; ceo@balchspringschamber.org; www.balchspringschamber.org

Ballinger • *Ballinger C/C* • Tammie Virden; Exec. V.P.; 700 Railroad Ave.; P.O. Box 577; 76821; Runnels; P 4,200; M 160; (325) 365-2333; Fax (325) 365-3445; coc@ballingertx.org; www.ballingertx.org

Bandera • *Bandera County C/C* • Leslie Lester; Exec. Admin.; P.O. Box 2445; 78003; Bandera; P 22,000; M 325; (830) 796-3280; Fax (830) 796-3970; cowboy@banderatex.com; www.banderatex.com

Bartlett • *Bartlett Area C/C* • Barbara Sandobal; Pres.; P.O. Box 103; 76511; Bell & Williamson; P 1,675; M 50; (254) 527-0196; tina@steglich.net; www.bartletttexas.net

Bastrop • *Bastrop C/C* • Becki Womble IOM; Pres./CEO; 927 Main St.; 78602; Bastrop; P 7,800; M 725; (512) 303-0558; Fax (512) 303-0305; info@bastropchamber.com; www.bastropchamber.com*

Bay City • *Bay City C/C & Ag.* • Mitch Thames; Pres./CEO; 201 Seventh St.; P.O. Box 768; 77404; Matagorda; P 20,000; M 700; (979) 245-8333; (800) 806-8333; Fax (979) 245-1622; mitchthames@visitbaycity.org; www.baycitychamber.org*

Baytown • *Baytown C/C* • Tracey S. Wheeler; Pres./CEO; 1300 Rollingbrook St., Ste. 400; 77521; Harris; P 80,000; M 800; (281) 422-8359; Fax (281) 428-1758; info@baytownchamber.com; www.baytownchamber.com*

Baytown • *The Hispanic Chamber of Commerce of Greater Baytown* • Ruben F. de Hoyos; Pres.; 1300 Rollingbrook, Ste. 502; P.O. Box 815; 77522; Harris; P 80,000; M 115; (281) 422-6908; (281) 728-4221; Fax (281) 427-8988; hccgb@verizon.net; www.hccgb.org*

Bayview • *see Dickinson*

Beaumont • *Greater Beaumont C/C* • Jim Rich; Pres.; 1110 Park St.; 77704; Jefferson; P 115,000; M 1,500; (409) 838-6581; Fax (409) 833-6718; chamber@bmtcoc.org; www.bmtcoc.org*

Bedford • *Hurst-Euless-Bedford C/C* • Mary Martin Frazior IOM; Pres./CEO; 2109 Martin Dr.; P.O. Drawer 969; 76095; Tarrant; P 136,000; M 1,800; (817) 283-1521; Fax (817) 267-5111; chamber@heb.org; www.heb.org*

Beeville • *Bee County C/C* • Isabel Ramirez; Tourism Dir.; 1705 N. St. Marys St.; 78102; Bee; P 32,300; M 333; (361) 358-3267; Fax (361) 358-3966; iramirez@beecountychamber.org; www.beecountychamber.org

Bellmead • *Bellmead C/C* • Vivian Nowlin; Ofc. Mgr.; 3400 Bellmead Dr.; P.O. Box 154615; 76705; McLennan; P 10,500; M 200; (254) 799-1552; Fax (254) 799-9370; chamberoffice@clearwire.net; www.bellmeadchamber.com

Bellville • *Bellville C/C* • Tammy Hall; Exec. Dir.; 10 S. Holland St.; 77418; Austin; P 4,500; M 250; (979) 865-3407; bellvillechamber@sbcglobal.net; www.bellville.com*

Belton • *Belton Area C/C* • Mark Arrazola; Pres./CEO; 412 E. Central Ave.; P.O. Box 659; 76513; Bell; P 19,000; M 600; (254) 939-3551; Fax (254) 939-1061; info@beltonchamber.com; www.beltonchamber.com*

Benbrook • *Benbrook Area C/C* • Jamie Presley; Pres.; 8507 Benbrook Blvd.; P.O. Box 26745; 76126; Tarrant; P 21,000; M 278; (817) 249-4451; Fax (817) 249-3307; info@benbrookchamber.org; www.benbrookchamber.org*

Bertram • *Bertram C/C* • Marcie Masterson; Secy.; P.O. Box 508; 78605; Burnet; P 1,200; M 44; (512) 355-2197; www.bertramtx.org

Big Lake • *Big Lake C/C* • Nita Schubert; Dir./Mgr.; 120 N. Main St.; P.O. Box 905; 76932; Reagan; P 3,000; M 65; (325) 884-2980; Fax (325) 884-1416; blcoc@verizon.net; www.biglaketx.com*

Big Sandy • *Big Sandy C/C* • Travis Brewer; P.O. Box 175; 75755; Upshur; P 1,340; M 30; (903) 636-2238; info@bigsandytx.com; bigsandytx.net

Big Spring • *Big Spring Area C/C* • Debbye ValVerde IOM; Exec. Dir.; 215 W. 3rd St.; P.O. Box 1391; 79721; Howard; P 25,000; M 350; (432) 263-7641; (800) 734-7641; Fax (432) 264-9111; chamber@bigspringchamber.com; www.bigspringchamber.com

Bishop • *Bishop C/C* • Judy Gonzalez; Exec. Dir.; 213 E. Main St.; P.O. Box 426; 78343; Nueces; P 3,200; M 75; (361) 584-2214; Fax (361) 584-2214; bishopchamberofcomm@stx.rr.com; www.bishoptx.com

Blanco • *Blanco C/C* • Libbey Aly; Exec. Dir.; 300 Main St.; P.O. Box 626; 78606; Blanco; P 3,000; M 150; (830) 833-5101; Fax (830) 833-4381; info@blancochamber.com; www.blancochamber.com

Boerne • *Greater Boerne C/C* • Crisanne Zamponi; Pres.; 121 S. Main St.; P.O. Box 2328; 78006; Kendall; P 14,000; M 770; (830) 249-8000; Fax (830) 249-9639; crisanne@boerne.org; www.boerne.org*

Bonham • *Bonham Area C/C* • 119 E. 5th St.; 75418; Fannin; P 10,000; M 200; (903) 583-4811; Fax (903) 583-7972; bonhamchamber@cableone.net; www.bonhamchamber.com*

Borger • *Borger C/C* • Beverly Benton; Pres./CEO; 613 N. Main St.; P.O. Box 490; 79008; Hutchinson; P 13,525; M 250; (806) 274-2211; borgerchamber@amaonline.com; www.borgerchamber.org*

Bovina • *Bovina C/C* • Don Springs; Pres.; P.O. Box 627; 79009; Parmer; P 1,850; M 65; (806) 251-1116; (806) 251-1552; Fax (806) 251-1805; www.cityofbovina.net

Bowie • *Bowie C/C* • Diane Thomlinson; Exec. Dir.; 201-A Walnut St.; 76230; Montague; P 5,700; M 200; (940) 872-1173; Fax (940) 872-3291; info@bowietxchamber.org; www.bowietxchamber.org

Brackettville • *Kinney County C/C* • P.O. Box 986; 78832; Kinney; P 3,600; M 140; (830) 563-0514; (830) 563-2412; info@kinneycounty.org; www.kinneycounty.org*

Brady • *Brady/McCulloch County C/C* • Kathi Masonheimer; Dir.; 101 E. 1st St.; 76825; McCulloch; P 8,000; M 225; (325) 597-3491; (888) 577-5657; Fax (325) 792-9181; info@bradytx.com; www.bradytx.com*

Brazoria • *Brazoria C/C* • Erica M. Beaver; Exec. Dir.; 202 W. Smith St.; P.O. Box 992; 77422; Brazoria; P 14,720; M 220; (979) 798-6100; Fax (979) 798-6101; brazoriachamber@brazoriainet.com; www.brazoriachamber.net

Brazosport • *Brazosport Area C/C* • Sandra Shaw; Pres./CEO; 300 Abner Jackson Pkwy.; 77566; Brazoria; P 80,000; M 700; (979) 285-2501; Fax (979) 285-2505; chamber2@sbcglobal.net; www.brazosport.org*

Breckenridge • *Breckenridge C/C* • Sharon Mendoza; Exec. Dir.; 100 E. Elm St.; 76424; Stephens; P 6,000; M 300; (254) 559-2301; chamber@breckenridgetexas.com; www.breckenridgetexas.com

Bremond • *Bremond C/C* • Jeanne Wierzbicki; Treas.; P.O. Box 487; 76629; Roberston; P 930; M 40; (254) 746-7636; Fax (254) 746-7672; bremondchamber@yahoo.com; www.bremondtexas.org

Brenham • *Washington County C/C* • Page Michel; Pres./CEO; 314 S. Austin St.; 77833; Washington; P 33,000; M 770; (979) 836-3695; (888) BRENHAM; Fax (979) 836-2540; info@brenhamtexas.com; www.brenhamtexas.com*

Bridge City • *Bridge City C/C* • Randy Slaughter; Pres.; 150 W. Roundbunch; 77611; Orange; P 8,500; M 193; (409) 735-5671; Fax (409) 735-7017; bcchamber@sbcglobal.net; www.bridgecitychamber.com*

Bridgeport • *Bridgeport Area C/C* • Tiffany Evans; Exec. Dir.; 812 A Halsell St.; P.O. Box 1104; 76426; Wise; P 6,000; M 320; (940) 683-2076; Fax (940) 683-3969; tiffanyevans@bridgeportchamber.org; www.bridgeportchamber.org*

Bridgeport • *Greater Runaway Bay Alliance* • Jannie Tucknies; Pres.; 133 Lakeshore; P.O. Box 291; 76426; Wise; P 1,200; M 100; (940) 389-2016; tuckniesjannie@yahoo.com; www.greaterrunawaybayalliance.com

Brookshire • *see Pattison*

Brownfield • *Brownfield C/C & Visitor Info. Center* • Lorena Valencia; Exec. Dir.; 211 Lubbock Rd.; P.O. Box 152; 79316; Terry; P 9,500; M 185; (806) 637-2564; Fax (806) 637-2565; helpdesk@brownfieldchamber.com; www.brownfieldchamber.com*

Brownsboro • *see Chandler*

Brownsville • *Brownsville C/C* • Melinda Rodriguez; Pres./CEO; 1600 University Blvd.; 78520; Cameron; P 183,000; M 800; (956) 542-4341; Fax (956) 504-3348; info@brownsvillechamber.com; www.brownsvillechamber.com*

Brownwood • *Brownwood Area C/C* • Ray Tipton; Exec. Dir.; 600 E. Depot St.; P.O. Box 880; 76804; Brown; P 40,000; M 530; (325) 646-9535; Fax (325) 643-6686; director@brownwoodchamber.org; www.brownwoodchamber.org*

Bryan • *Bryan-College Station C/C* • Royce Hickman; Pres./CEO; 4001 E. 29th St., Ste. 175; P.O. Box 3579; 77802; Brazos; P 185,000; M 1,433; (979) 260-5200; Fax (979) 260-5208; receptionist@bcschamber.org; www.bcschamber.org*

Buchanan Dam • *Lake Buchanan-Inks Lake C/C & Tourist Center* • Ray McCasland; Pres.; 19611 Hwy. 29 at Buchanan Dam; P.O. Box 282; 78609; Llano; P 1,850; M 230; (512) 793-2803; Fax (512) 793-2112; buchinksoffice@gmail.com; www.buchanan-inks.com

Buda • *Buda Area C/C* • J.R. Gonzales; Managing Dir.; 203 N. Railroad St., Ste. 1C; P.O. Box 904; 78610; Hays; P 7,600; M 300; (512) 295-9999; Fax (512) 295-3569; jrgonzales@budachamber.com; www.budachamber.com*

Buffalo • *Buffalo C/C* • JoAnn Cockerell; Secy.; 1400 W. Commerce; P.O. Box 207; 75831; Leon; P 2,982; M 120; (903) 322-5810; chamber@buffalotex.com; www.buffalotxchamberofcommerce.org

Bullard • *Bullard Area C/C* • John Beasley; Pres.; 114 Phillips; P.O. Box 945; 75757; Cherokee & Smith; P 3,000; M 80; (903) 894-4238; bullardtxchamber@yahoo.com; www.bullardtexaschamber.com

Bulverde • *Bulverde-Spring Branch Area C/C* • Rhonda Zunker; Pres.; 121 Bulverde Crossing, Ste. 115; 78163; Comal; P 25,000; M 488; (830) 438-4285; Fax (830) 438-8572; office@bsbchamber.com; bulverdespringbranchchamber.com*

Buna • *Buna C/C* • Kathy Griffis; Ofc. Mgr.; 480 State Hwy. 62; P.O. Box 1782; 77612; Jasper; P 2,300; M 74; (409) 994-5586; Fax (409) 994-3855; bunatexas@att.net; www.bunatexas.net

Burkburnett • *Burkburnett C/C* • Dick Vallon; Dir.; 104 W. Third; 76354; Wichita; P 11,000; M 150; (940) 569-3304; Fax (940) 569-3306; president@burkburnettchamber.com; www.burkburnettchamber.com

Burleson • *Burleson Area C/C* • Belinda Alles; Pres.; 1044 S.W. Wilshire Blvd.; 76028; Johnson & Tarrant; P 43,000; M 550; (817) 295-6121; Fax (817) 295-6192; burlesonchamber@burleson.org; www.burleson.org*

Burnet • *Burnet C/C* • Kim Winkler; Exec. Dir.; 101 N. Pierce, Ste. 1; 78611; Burnet; P 5,000; M 350; (512) 756-4297; Fax (512) 756-2548; info@burnetchamber.org; www.burnetchamber.org*

Caldwell • *Burleson County C/C-Caldwell Office* • Angie Cruz; Ofc. Mgr.; 301 N. Main St.; 77836; Burleson; P 17,500; M 276; (979) 567-0000; info@burlesoncountytx.com; www.burlesoncountytx.com*

Calvert • *Calvert C/C* • Carla Barker; 300 S. Main St.; P.O. Box 132; 77837; Robertson; P 1,200; M 60; (979) 364-2559; (979) 364-2881; www.calverttx.com

Cameron • *Cameron Area C/C* • Charlotte Wyatt; Mgr.; 102 E. 1st St.; P.O. Drawer 432; 76520; Milam; P 5,629; M 161; (254) 697-4979; Fax (254) 697-2345; chamber@cameron-tx.com; www.cameron-tx.com

Camp Wood • *Nueces Canyon C/C* • Ben Cox; Pres.; P.O. Box 369; 78833; Real; P 1,300; M 50; (830) 597-6241; info@mycampwood.com; www.mycampwood.com

Canadian • *Canadian-Hemphill County C/C* • Shane Spencer; Dir.; 119 N. 2nd St.; 79014; Hemphill; P 3,800; M 130; (806) 323-6234; (806) 323-5397; Fax (806) 323-9243; chamber@canadiantx.com; www.canadiantx.org

Canton • *Canton C/C* • Julie Seymore; Pres.; 119 N. Buffalo; 75103; Van Zandt; P 3,800; M 300; (903) 567-2991; Fax (903) 567-1872; info@cantontexaschamber.com; www.cantontexaschamber.com*

Canyon • *Canyon C/C* • Roger Remlinger; Exec. Dir.; 1518 5th Ave.; 79015; Randall; P 13,000; M 375; (806) 655-7815; (800) 999-9481; Fax (806) 655-4608; director@canyonchamber.org; www.canyonchamber.org*

Canyon Lake • *Canyon Lake Area C/C & Visitor Center* • Richard Ferrell; Exec. Dir.; 3934 FM 2673; 78133; Comal; P 40,000; M 425; (830) 964-2223; (800) 528-2104; Fax (830) 964-3209; admin@canyonlakechamber.com; www.canyonlakechamber.com*

Carrizo Springs • *Dimmit County C/C* • Paula Seydel; Mgr.; 103 N. 6th St.; P.O. Box 699; 78834; Dimmit; P 12,000; M 90; (830) 876-5205; Fax (830) 876-5206; chamberofcommerce@the-i.net; www.dimmitcountychamber.org

Carrollton • *Metrocrest C/C* • Erin Carney IOM; Pres.; 2550 Midway Rd., Ste. 240; 75006; Dallas; P 158,000; M 438; (469) 587-0420; info@metrocrestchamber.com; www.metrocrestchamber.com*

Carthage • *Panola County C/C* • Tommie Ritter Smith; Pres.; 300 W. Panola St.; 75633; Panola; P 24,000; M 240; (903) 693-6634; Fax (903) 693-8578; tommie@carthagetexas.com; www.carthagetexas.com*

Castroville • *Castroville Area C/C* • Jeanie Haby; Exec. Dir. of Op.; 1115 Angelo St.; P.O. Box 572; 78009; Medina; P 4,500; M 335; (830) 538-3142; (800) 778-6775; Fax (830) 538-3295; chamber@castroville.com; www.castroville.com*

Cedar Creek Lake • *see Mabank*

Cedar Hill • *Cedar Hill C/C* • Amanda Skinner; Pres.; 300 Houston St.; 75104; Dallas; P 43,000; M 400; (972) 291-7817; Fax (972) 291-8101; info@cedarhillchamber.org; www.cedarhillchamber.org*

Cedar Park • *Cedar Park C/C* • Tony Moline IOM PCED; Pres./CEO; 1460 E. Whitestone Blvd., Ste. 180; 78613; Williamson; P 83,000; M 750; (512) 260-7800; Fax (512) 260-9269; info@cedarparkchamber.org; www.cedarparkchamber.org*

Celina • *Greater Celina C/C* • Melissa Cromwell; Pres.; 312 W. Walnut; P.O. Box 1476; 75009; Collin & Denton; P 8,500; M 160; (972) 382-3300; Fax (972) 382-3304; info@celinachamber.org; www.celinachamber.org

Center • *Shelby County C/C* • Pam Phelps; Exec. Dir.; 100 Courthouse Sq., Ste. A-101; 75935; Shelby; P 26,000; M 370; (936) 598-3682; Fax (936) 598-8163; info@shelbycountychamber.com; www.shelbycountychamber.com*

Centerville • *Centerville C/C* • Dennis Coffee; Pres.; P.O. Box 422; 75833; Leon; P 1,000; M 100; (903) 536-3318; centerville75833@yahoo.com; www.centervilletexas.com

Chandler • *Chandler C/C* • John Camper; Chrmn.; 811 Hwy. 31 E.; P.O. Box 1500; 75758; Henderson; P 30,000; M 105; (903) 849-5930; info@cbacc.net; www.cbacc.net

Channelview • *see Houston-North Channel Area C/C*

Childress • *Childress C/C* • Susan J. Leary; Exec. Dir.; 237 Commerce St.; P.O. Box 35; 79201; Childress; P 7,200; M 175; (940) 937-2567; Fax (940) 937-8836; c_commerce@att.net; www.childresschamber.com

Cibolo • *see Schertz*

Cisco • *Cisco C/C* • Bridget Flores; Exec. Dir.; 309 Conrad Hilton Blvd.; 76437; Eastland; P 3,851; M 195; (254) 442-2537; Fax (254) 442-2553; ciscoinfo@ciscotx.com; www.ciscochamber.com

Clarendon • *Clarendon C/C* • Bonnie Campbell; Ofc. Mgr.; P.O. Box 986; 79226; Donley; P 3,500; M 105; (806) 874-2421; Fax (806) 874-2911; contact@clarendonchamber.com; www.clarendonchamber.com

Clarksville • *Historic Red River County C/C* • Laura Dial; Ofc. Mgr.; 101 N. Locust St.; 75426; Red River County; P 3,879; M 169; (903) 427-2645; Fax (903) 427-5454; redrivercc@yahoo.com; www.redrivercoc.com*

Clear Lake City • *see Houston-Clear Lake Area C/C*

Clear Lake Shores • *also see Houston-Clear Lake Area C/C*

Clear Lake Shores • *see Dickinson*

Cleburne • *Cleburne C/C* • Cathy Marchel; Pres.; 1511 W. Henderson St.; P.O. Box 701; 76033; Johnson; P 30,000; M 947; (817) 645-2455; Fax (817) 641-3069; info@cleburnechamber.com; www.cleburnechamber.com*

Cleveland • *Greater Cleveland C/C* • Tracey Walters; CEO; 102 Hilltop Square; 77327; Liberty; P 7,275; M 250; (281) 592-8786; Fax (281) 592-6949; info@clevelandtxchamber.com; www.clevelandtxchamber.com*

Clifton • *Clifton C/C* • Paige Key; Exec. V.P.; 115 N. Ave. D; 76634; Bosque; P 3,600; M 200; (254) 675-3720; (800) 344-3720; paigekey@cliftontexas.org; www.cliftontexas.org*

Clyde • *Clyde C/C* • Jennifer Rector; Exec. Dir.; 614 N. 1st St.; P.O. Box 257; 79510; Callahan; P 4,500; M 120; (325) 893-4221; chamber@clydeamerica.com; clydechamber.webs.com

Coldspring • *Coldspring-San Jacinto County C/C* • Gayle Erwin; Pres.; P.O. Box 980; 77331; San Jacinto; P 22,500; M 155; (936) 653-2184; Fax (936) 653-2184; ccc@coldspringtexas.org; www.coldspringtexas.org

Coleman • *Coleman County C/C, Ag. & Tourist Bur.* • Mary Griffis; Exec. Dir.; 218 Commercial; P.O. Box 796; 76834; Coleman; P 8,798; M 215; (325) 625-2163; Fax (325) 625-2164; chamber@colemantexas.org; www.colemantexas.org

College Station • *see Bryan*

Colleyville • *Colleyville Area C/C* • Steve Johnson; Pres.; 6700 Colleyville Blvd.; 76034; Tarrant; P 24,000; M 750; (817) 488-7148; Fax (817) 488-4242; info@colleyvillechamber.org; www.colleyvillechamber.org*

Colorado City • *Colorado City Area C/C* • Amanda Ritchey; Dir.; 157 W. 2nd St.; 79512; Mitchell; P 4,200; M 94; (325) 728-3403; Fax (325) 728-2911; chamber@cityofcoloradocity.org; www.coloradocitychamberofcommerce.com

Columbus • *Columbus Area C/C* • Kim Dyer; Exec. Dir.; 425 Spring St.; 78934; Colorado; P 4,800; M 225; (979) 732-8385; Fax (979) 732-5881; contactus@columbuschamber.org; www.columbustexas.org

Comanche • *Comanche C/C* • Meagan Caffey; Exec. Dir.; 304 S. Austin St.; P.O. Box 65; 76442; Comanche; P 5,000; M 270; (325) 356-3233; Fax (325) 356-2940; comanchetxchamber@gmail.com; www.comanchechamber.org*

Comfort • *Comfort C/C* • Rose Burckhardt; Ofc. Mgr.; 630 Hwy. 27; P.O. Box 777; 78013; Kendall; P 2,500; M 250; (830) 995-3131; Fax (830) 995-5252; info@comfort-texas.com; www.comfortchamberofcommerce.com

Commerce • *Commerce C/C* • Paul Voss; Exec. Dir.; 1114 Main St.; P.O. Box 290; 75429; Hunt; P 8,800; M 300; (903) 886-3950; Fax (903) 886-8012; info@commerce-chamber.com; www.commerce-chamber.com

Conroe • *Greater Conroe/Lake Conroe Area C/C* • Scott Harper; Pres.; 505 W. Davis; 77301; Montgomery; P 49,000; M 1,300; (936) 756-6644; Fax (936) 756-6462; rsvp@conroe.org; www.conroe.org*

Converse • *see Universal City*

Cooper • *Delta County C/C* • Gracie Young; Ofc. Mgr.; 41 W. Side Sq.; P.O. Box 457; 75432; Delta; P 5,500; M 150; (903) 395-4314; Fax (903) 395-4318; deltacounty@neto.com; www.deltacounty.org

Coppell • *Coppell C/C* • Kristi Valentine; Pres./CEO; 708 Main St.; P.O. Box 452; 75019; Dallas; P 40,000; M 500; (972) 393-2829; Fax (972) 537-5581; chamber@coppellchamber.org; www.coppellchamber.org*

Copperas Cove • *Copperas Cove C/C* • Greg Solomon; Pres./CEO; 204 E. Robertson Ave.; 76522; Coryell; P 30,000; M 311; (254) 547-7571; Fax (254) 547-5015; chamber@copperascove.com; www.copperascove.com*

Corpus Christi • *Corpus Christi C/C* • Foster Edwards; Pres./CEO; 1501 N. Chaparral St.; 78401; Nueces; P 417,500; M 1,000; (361) 881-1800; Fax (361) 882-4256; foster@theccchamber.org; www.corpuschristichamber.org*

Corpus Christi • *Corpus Christi Hispanic C/C* • Rosie Collin; Exec. Dir.; 615 N. Upper Broadway, Ste. 410; P.O. Box 5523; 78465; Nueces; P 387,500; M 750; (361) 887-7408; Fax (361) 888-9473; rcollin@cchispanicchamber.org; www.cchispanicchamber.org*

Corsicana • *Corsicana & Navarro County C/C* • Paul Hooper; Pres.; 120 N. 12th St.; 75110; Navarro; P 47,735; M 425; (903) 874-4731; Fax (903) 874-4187; chamber@corsicana.org; www.corsicana.org*

Cotulla • *Cotulla-La Salle County C/C* • Melinda Rheinfeldt; Mgr.; 290 N. IH-35 Access Rd.; 78014; La Salle; P 5,100; M 150; (830) 879-2326; (800) 256-2326; Fax (830) 879-2326; coc.manager@cotulla-chamber.com; www.cotulla-chamber.com

Crandall • *Greater Crandall C/C* • Ken Godey; Pres.; P.O. Box 669; 75114; Kaufman; P 3,000; M 60; (972) 472-8663; coordinator@crandallchamber.net; www.crandallchamber.net

Crockett • *Crockett Area C/C* • Sheila Thomas; Exec. Dir.; 1100 Edmiston Dr.; P.O. Box 307; 75835; Houston; P 31,000; M 140; (936) 544-2359; (936) 544-9467; Fax (936) 544-4355; sheila@crockettareachamber.org; www.crockettareachamber.org*

Crosby • *Crosby-Huffman C/C* • Kim Harris; Pres.; 5317 First St.; P.O. Box 452; 77532; Harris; P 28,000; M 300; (281) 328-6984; Fax (281) 328-7296; chamber@crosbyhuffmancc.org; www.crosbyhuffmancc.org*

Crosbyton • *Crosbyton C/C* • Jacque James; Dir.; 124 S. Berkshire; P.O. Box 202; 79322; Crosby; P 1,741; M 60; (806) 675-2261; jjames@crosbyton.com; www.cityofcrosbyton.org

Cross Plains • *Cross Plains C/C* • Myleah McNutt; Admin. Asst.; 225 S.W. 5th St.; P.O. Box 233; 76443; Callahan; P 1,000; M 55; (254) 725-7251; Fax (254) 725-4184; crossplainschamber@yahoo.com; www.crossplainschamberofcommerce.com

Crowell • *Crowell C/C* • JoAnna Mills; P.O. Box 164; 79227; Foard; P 950; M 50; (940) 684-1722; (940) 684-1310; joannalmills@yahoo.com; www.crowelltex

Crowley • *Crowley Area C/C* • Terri Horn; Pres.; 201 N. Hampton Rd.; 76036; Johnson & Tarrant; P 11,000; M 364; (817) 297-4211; Fax (817) 297-7334; info@crowleyareachamber.org; www.crowleyareachamber.org

Crystal Beach • *Bolivar Peninsula C/C* • Mac McDonald; Pres.; 1750 Hwy. 87; P.O. Box 1170; 77650; Galveston; P 3,000; M 108; (409) 684-5940; Fax (409) 684-3123; info@bolivarchamber.org; www.bolivarchamber.org

Cuero • *Cuero C/C* • Sherry Esse; Exec. Dir.; 210 E. Main St., Ste. A; 77954; DeWitt; P 7,500; M 200; (361) 275-2112; cuerocc@cuero.org; www.cuero.org

Daingerfield • *Daingerfield C/C* • Sheri Kramer; Ofc. Mgr.; 102 Coffey St.; 75638; Morris; P 2,526; M 65; (903) 645-2646; Fax (903) 645-2646; daingerfieldchamberofcommerce@cebridge.net; www.daingerfieldtx.net

Dalhart • *Dalhart Area C/C* • Kristine Olsen; Pres.; 102 E. 7th St.; P.O. Box 967; 79022; Dallam & Hartley; P 9,000; M 265; (806) 244-5646; Fax (806) 244-4945; chamber@dalhart.org; www.dalhart.org*

Dallas Area

Dallas Black C/C • Wilton Munnings; Pres./COO; 2838 MLK Jr. Blvd.; 75215; Dallas; P 1,240,000; M 1,000; (214) 421-5200; Fax (214) 421-5510; info@dbcc.org; www.dbcc.org

Dallas Reg. Chamber • Dale Petroskey; Pres./CEO; 500 N. Akard St., Ste. 2600; 75201; Dallas; P 7,100,000; M 2,000; (214) 746-6600; Fax (214) 746-6799; information@dallaschamber.org; www.dallaschamber.org*

Frisco C/C • Tony Felker; Pres./CEO; 6843 Main St.; 75034; Collin & Denton; P 143,000; M 1,100; (972) 335-9522; Fax (972) 335-6654; info@friscochamber.com; www.friscochamber.com*

Greater East Dallas C/C • Darlene Ellison; Chair; 9543 Losa Dr., Ste. 118; 75218; Dallas; P 250,000; M 200; (214) 328-4100; Fax (214) 328-4124; president@eastdallaschamber.com; www.eastdallaschamber.com*

North Dallas C/C • Bruce R. Bradford; Pres./CEO; 10707 Preston Rd.; 75230; Dallas; P 500,000; M 900; (214) 368-6485; Fax (214) 368-6695; lwinkles@ndcc.org; www.ndcc.org*

Oak Cliff C/C • Kiyundra Gulley IOM; Pres.; 1001 N. Bishop Ave.; 75208; Dallas; P 330,000; M 650; (214) 943-4567; Fax (214) 943-4582; occ@oakcliffchamber.org; www.oakcliffchamber.org*

Southeast Dallas C/C • Susan Harris; Chrmn.; P.O. Box 170132; 75217; Dallas; P 300,000; M 300; (214) 398-9590; Fax (214) 398-9591; info@sedcc.org; www.sedcc.org

West Dallas C/C • Jamie Cornelius; Chrmn.; P.O. Box 225558; 75222; Dallas; P 25,000; M 120; (214) 930-5235; board@westdallaschamber.com; www.westdallaschamber.com

---

Dayton • *also see Liberty*

Dayton • *Dayton C/C* • Rhonda Dunn,; Exec. Dir.; 801 S. Cleveland; 77535; Liberty; P 30,000; M 270; (936) 257-2393; Fax (936) 257-2394; rdunn@daytontxchamber.com; www.daytontxchamber.com*

Dayton • *Liberty-Dayton Area C/C* • Mary Anne Campbell; Pres.; 109 S. Main St.; 77535; Liberty; P 35,000; M 450; (936) 257-8926; ldchamber@imsday.com; www.libertydaytonchamber.com

Decatur • *Decatur C/C* • Misty Hudson; Exec. Dir.; 308 W. Main; P.O. Box 474; 76234; Wise; P 6,250; M 350; (940) 627-3107; Fax (940) 627-3771; misty.hudson@netcommander.com; www.decaturtx.com

Deer Park • *Deer Park C/C* • Tim Culp; Pres./CEO; 110 Center St.; 77536; Harris; P 28,520; M 600; (281) 479-1559; Fax (281) 476-4041; info@deerpark.org; www.deerpark.org*

DeKalb • *DeKalb C/C* • Linda Wyse; Pres.; P.O. Box 219; 75559; Bowie; P 2,000; M 160; (903) 667-4120; info@dekalbtexas.org; www.dekalbtexas.org

Del Rio • *Del Rio C/C* • Blanca G. Larson; Exec. Dir.; 1915 Veterans Blvd.; 78840; Val Verde; P 45,000; M 500; (830) 775-3551; (800) 889-8149; Fax (830) 774-1813; blarson@drchamber.com; www.drchamber.com*

DeLeon • *DeLeon C/C & Ag.* • Teresa Baird; Exec. Dir.; 109 S. Texas St.; 76444; Comanche; P 2,500; M 143; (254) 893-2083; Fax (254) 893-7028; chamber@cctc.net; www.deleontexas.com

Dell City • *Dell Valley C/C* • Wilma Carpenter; P.O. Box 502; 79837; Hudspeth; P 413; M 40; (915) 964-2344; (915) 603-2787; www.dellcity.com

Denison • *Denison Area C/C* • Anna H. McKinney; Pres./CEO; 313 W. Woodard; P.O. Box 325; 75021; Grayson; P 24,000; M 546; (903) 465-1551; Fax (903) 465-8443; information@denisontexas.us; www.denisontexas.us*

Denton • *Denton C/C* • C.W. Carpenter; Pres.; 414 Pkwy. St.; 76201; Denton; P 120,000; M 878; (940) 382-9693; (940) 382-7895; Fax (940) 382-0040; info@denton-chamber.org; www.denton-chamber.org*

Denver City • *Denver City C of C & CVB* • Marilyn McCurley; Gen. Mgr.; 120 N. Main St.; 79323; Yoakum; P 4,500; M 120; (806) 592-5424; Fax (806) 592-7613; denvercitycofc@valornet.com; www.denvercitychamber.com*

DeSoto • *DeSoto C/C* • Laura Terhune; Pres.; 2010 N. Hampton, Ste. 200; 75115; Dallas; P 48,500; M 275; (972) 224-3565; Fax (972) 354-1022; admin@desotochamber.org; www.desotochamber.org*

Devine • *Greater Devine C/C* • Robyn Teague; Pres.; P.O. Box 443; 78016; Medina; P 4,500; M 55; (830) 663-2739; Fax (830) 663-2739; chamber@devinechamber.com; www.devinechamber.com

Dickinson • *North Galveston County C/C* • Theresa Graham; Pres.; 218 FM 517 W.; 77539; Galveston; P 120,000; M 315; (281) 534-4380; Fax (281) 534-4389; tgraham@northgalvestoncountychamber.com; www.northgalvestoncountychamber.com*

Dimmitt • *Dimmitt C/C* • Karron Smith; Exec. Dir.; 115 W. Bedford St.; 79027; Castro; P 4,000; M 170; (806) 647-2524; Fax (806) 647-2469; dimmittchamber@gmail.com; www.dimmittchamberofcommerce.com

Dripping Springs • *Dripping Springs C/C* • Sherrie Parks; Exec. Dir.; 509 W. Mercer St.; P.O. Box 206; 78620; Hays; P 1,800; M 460; (512) 858-7000; dschamber@drippingspringstx.org; www.drippingspringstx.org*

Dublin • *Dublin C/C* • Nancy Wooldridge; Exec. Dir.; 111 S. Patrick St.; 76446; Erath; P 3,800; M 125; (254) 445-3422; Fax (254) 445-0394; dublinnancy@aol.com; www.dublintxchamber.com

Dumas • *Dumas/Moore County C/C & Visitor Center* • Sam Cartwright; Pres./CEO; 1901 S. Dumas Ave.; P.O. Box 735; 79029; Moore; P 15,000; M 250; (806) 935-2123; (888) 840-8911; Fax (806) 935-2124; sam@dumaschamber.com; www.dumaschamber.com*

Duncanville • *Duncanville C/C* • Steve Martin; Pres.; 300 E. Wheatland Rd.; 75116; Dallas; P 36,500; M 400; (972) 780-4990; Fax (972) 298-9370; info@duncanvillechamber.org; www.duncanvillechamber.org*

Eagle Lake • *Eagle Lake C/C* • Mary Parr; Exec. Dir.; 303 E. Main; 77434; Colorado; P 3,664; M 150; (979) 234-2780; Fax (979) 234-2780; info@visiteaglelake.com; www.visiteaglelake.com

Eagle Pass • *Eagle Pass C/C* • Sandra Martinez; Exec. Dir.; 400 Garrison St.; P.O. Box 1188; 78853; Maverick; P 30,000; M 300; (830) 773-3224; (888) 355-3224; Fax (830) 773-8844; chamber@eaglepasstexas.com; www.eaglepasstexas.com

Early • *Early C/C* • Michelle Cortez; Mbrshp. Dir.; 104 E. Industrial Dr.; 76802; Brown; P 2,762; M 310; (325) 649-9317; (325) 642-3122; Fax (325) 643-4746; ecoc@earlytx.com; www.earlychamber.com*

East Bernard • *East Bernard C/C* • Ray Kerlick; Pres.; P.O. Box 567; 77435; Wharton; P 2,300; M 100; (979) 532-3871; rkerlick@wadleperches.com; www.ebchamber.com

East Tawakoni • *see West Tawakoni*

Eastland • *Eastland C/C* • Cecil Funderburgh; Exec. Dir.; 209 W. Main St., Ste. A; 76448; Eastland; P 4,000; M 200; (254) 629-2332; chamber@eastland.net; www.eastlandchamber.com

Eden • *Eden C/C* • Keith Hall; Pres.; P.O. Box 367; 76837; Concho; P 2,200; M 50; (325) 869-3336; edenchamber@verizon.net; www.edentexas.com

Edinburg • *Edinburg C/C* • Letty Gonzalez; Pres.; 602 W. University Dr.; P.O. Box 85; 78540; Hidalgo; P 72,424; M 450; (956) 383-4974; (800) 800-7214; Fax (956) 383-6942; chamber@edinburg.com; www.edinburg.com*

Edna • *Jackson County C/C & Ag.* • Kim Fojtik; Ofc. Mgr./Secy.; 317 W. Main St.; P.O. Box 788; 77957; Jackson; P 14,500; M 300; (361) 782-7146; Fax (361) 782-2811; j.chamber@att.net; www.jacksoncountytexas.com*

El Campo • *El Campo C/C* • Rebecca Munos; Pres.; 01 N. Mechanic St.; P.O. Box 1400; 77437; Wharton; P 11,062; M 500; (979) 543-2713; ecc@elcampochamber.com; www.elcampochamber.com*

El Lago • *see Houston-Clear Lake Area C/C*

El Paso • *Greater El Paso C/C* • Richard E. Dayoub; Pres./CEO; 10 Civic Center Plaza; 79901; El Paso; P 734,600; M 1,700; (915) 534-0500; (800) 651-8065; Fax (915) 534-0510; info@elpaso.org; www.elpaso.org

El Paso • *El Paso Hispanic C/C* • Cindy Ramos-Davidson; Pres./CEO; 2401 E. Missouri St.; 79903; El Paso; P 875,000; M 1,137; (915) 566-4066; Fax (915) 566-9714; jmontemayor@ephcc.org; www.ephcc.org*

Elbert • *see Throckmorton*

Electra • *Electra C/C* • Sherry Strange; Exec. Dir.; 112 W. Cleveland; 76360; Wichita; P 3,100; M 40; (940) 495-3577; Fax (940) 495-3022; electracoc@electratel.net; www.electratexas.org

Elgin • *Greater Elgin C/C* • Gena Carter; Pres.; 114 Central Ave.; P.O. Box 408; 78621; Bastrop & Travis; P 7,200; M 205; (512) 285-4515; Fax (512) 281-3393; info@elgintxchamber.com; www.elgintxchamber.com

Emory • *Rains County C/C* • Chris Downs; Pres.; 179 Doris Briggs Pkwy.; 75440; Rains; P 11,500; M 120; (903) 473-3913; Fax (903) 473-3913; rainschamber@verizon.net; www.rainscountychamberofcommerce.com

Ennis • *Ennis Area C/C* • Jeannette J. Patak; Pres.; 108 Chamber of Commerce Dr.; P.O. Box 1177; 75120; Ellis; P 20,000; M 450; (972) 878-2625; Fax (972) 875-1473; manager@ennis-chamber.com; www.ennis-chamber.com*

Euless • *see Bedford*

Eustace • *see Mabank*

Everman • *see Fort Worth-South Tarrant County C/C*

Fairfield • *Fairfield C/C* • Brenda Shultz; Exec. Admin.; 900 W. Commerce; P.O. Box 899; 75840; Freestone; P 3,306; M 165; (903) 389-5792; (903) 389-6122; Fax (903) 389-8382; chamber@fairfieldtx.com; www.fairfieldtexaschamber.com

Falfurrias • *Falfurrias C/C* • Gus Barrera; Exec. Dir.; 124 N. St. Mary St.; P.O. Box 476; 78355; Brooks; P 8,300; M 120; (361) 325-3333; Fax (361) 325-2956; c_of_commerce@yahoo.com

Farmers Branch • *Farmers Branch C/C* • Nanette Foght; Pres.; 2815 Valley View Ln., Ste. 118; 75234; Dallas; P 32,000; M 280; (972) 243-8966; nfoght@fbchamber.com; www.fbchamber.com*

Farmersville • *Farmersville C/C* • Lisa Eastman; Exec. Dir.; 201 S. Main; 75442; Collin; P 3,300; M 177; (972) 782-6533; Fax (972) 782-6603; lisa@farmersvillechamber.com; www.farmersvillechamber.com*

Farwell • *Farwell C/C* • Rob Pomper; P.O. Box 1005; 79325; Parmer; P 1,320; M 20; (806) 481-3681; (806) 481-3620

Fayetteville • *Fayetteville C/C* • Liz Cubage; V.P.; 123 N. Washington St.; P.O. Box 217; 78940; Fayette; P 258; M 100; (979) 378-4021; (979) 877-5290; info@fayettevilletxchamber.org; www.fayettevilletxchamber.org

Flatonia • *Flatonia C/C* • Beverly Z. Ponder; Exec. Dir.; 208 E. N. Main St.; P.O. Box 610; 78941; Fayette; P 1,400; M 125; (361) 865-3920; Fax (361) 865-2451; flatoniacofc@sbcglobal.net; www.flatoniachamber.com*

Florence • *Florence C/C* • Linda Nunn; Treas.; 210 Patterson; 76527; Williamson; P 1,400; M 50; (254) 793-4300; gnunnelectric@msn.com

Floresville • *Floresville C/C* • Crystal Anders; Pres.; P.O. Box 711; 78114; Wilson; P 7,500; M 300; (830) 216-3276; Fax (830) 393-9224; floresvillechamberofcommerce@yahoo.com; www.floresvillechamberofcommerce.com

Flower Mound • *Flower Mound C/C* • Lori Walker; Pres.; 700 Parker Sq., Ste. 100; 75028; Denton; P 65,000; M 700; (972) 539-0500; Fax (972) 539-4307; l.walker@flowermoundchamber.com; www.flowermoundchamber.com*

Floydada • *Floydada C/C & Ag.* • Darolyn Snell; Pres.; P.O. Box 147; 79235; Floyd; P 3,038; M 115; (806) 983-3434; floydadachamber@yahoo.com; www.floydadachamber.com

Forest Hill • *South Tarrant County C/C* • Gwen Barbee; Chrmn.; 5120 S.E. Loop 820; 76140; Tarrant; P 30,000; M 105; (817) 586-9092; info@southtarrantchamber.com; www.southtarrantchamber.com

Forney • *Forney C/C* • Laurie Barkham; Pres.; 100 U.S. Hwy. 80, Ste. 110; P.O. Box 570; 75126; Kaufman; P 18,000; M 250; (972) 564-2233; Fax (972) 564-3677; president@forneychamber.com; www.forneychamber.com

Fort Davis • *Fort Davis C/C* • Melissa Henderson; Exec. Dir.; P.O. Box 378; 79734; Jeff Davis; P 2,500; M 180; (432) 426-3015; (800) 524-3015; Fax (432) 426-3978; info@fortdavis.com; www.fortdavis.com

Fort Hood • *see Killeen*

Fort Stockton • *Fort Stockton C/C* • Arna McCorkle; Exec. V.P.; 1000 E. Railroad Ave.; 79735; Pecos; P 8,300; M 185; (432) 336-2264; (800) 336-2166; Fax (432) 336-6114; director@fortstockton.org; www.fortstockton.org*

Fort Worth • *Fort Worth C/C* • Bill Thornton; Pres./CEO; 777 Taylor, Ste. 900; 76102; Tarrant; P 618,600; M 3,500; (817) 336-2491; Fax (817) 877-4034; bthornton@fortworthchamber.com; www.fortworthchamber.com

Fort Worth • *Fort Worth Hispanic C/C* • Asusena Resendiz; Pres./CEO; 1327 N. Main St.; 76164; Tarrant; P 450,000; M 1,100; (817) 625-5411; Fax (817) 625-1405; asusena.resendiz@fwhcc.org; www.fwhcc.org*

Franklin • *Franklin C/C* • Peggy Baxter; Exec. Dir.; 351 Cooks Ln.; P.O. Box 126; 77856; Robertson; P 1,800; M 300; (979) 828-3276; Fax (979) 828-1816; franklincc@valornet.com; www.franklintexas.com

Fredericksburg • *Fredericksburg C/C* • Penny C. McBride; Pres./CEO; 306 E. Austin St.; 78624; Gillespie; P 11,111; M 800; (830) 997-5000; Fax (830) 997-8588; christie@fbgtxchamber.org; www.fredericksburg-texas.com*

Freer • *Freer C/C* • Brandy Benavides; Exec. Mgr.; P.O. Box 717; 78357; Duval; P 3,271; M 150; (361) 394-6891; Fax (361) 394-7055; freercofc@yahoo.com

Friendswood • *Friendswood C/C* • Carol Marcantel IOM; Pres.; 1100 S. Friendswood Dr.; P.O. Box 11; 77546; Galveston; P 35,000; M 550; (281) 482-3329; Fax (281) 482-3911; info@friendswoodchamber.com; www.friendswoodchamber.com*

Friona • *Friona C/C & Ag.* • Chris Alexander; Exec. V.P.; 621 Main St.; 79035; Parmer; P 4,100; M 200; (806) 250-3491; Fax (806) 250-2348; fedc@wtrt.net; www.frionachamber.com

Fulshear • *see Pattison*

Gainesville • *Gainesville Area C/C* • Lynette G. Pettigrew; Exec. Dir.; 311 S. Weaver St.; P.O. Box 518; 76241; Cooke; P 16,000; M 450; (940) 665-2831; Fax (940) 665-2833; lynette@gainesvillecofc.com; www.gainesvillecofc.com*

Galena Park • *see Houston-North Channel Area C/C*

Galveston • *Galveston Reg. C/C* • Gina M. Spagnola; Pres.; 2228 Mechanic St., Ste. 101; 77550; Galveston; P 55,000; M 900; (409) 763-5326; Fax (409) 763-8271; gspagnola@galvestonchamber.com; www.galvestonchamber.com*

Garden Oaks • *see Houston-Houston Intercontinental C/C*

Garden Ridge • *see Universal City*

Garland • *Garland C/C* • Paul Mayer; CEO; 520 N. Glenbrook Dr.; 75040; Dallas; P 235,000; M 480; (972) 272-7551; (469) 326-7444; Fax (972) 276-9261; paul.mayer@garlandchamber.com; www.garlandchamber.com

Gatesville • *Gatesville C/C* • Amanda Summers; Exec. Dir.; 2307 Hwy. 36 S.; 76528; Coryell; P 16,000; M 175; (254) 865-2617; Fax (800) 865-8508; chamber@gatesvilletx.info; www.gatesvillechamber.com*

George West • *George West C/C* • Rena McWilliams; Exec. Dir.; 400 N. Nueces; P.O. Box 359; 78022; Live Oak; P 12,000; M 110; (361) 449-2033; Fax (361) 449-2481; chamber@georgewest.org; www.georgewest.org

Georgetown • *Georgetown C/C* • Karen Sheldon; Pres.; 1 Chamber Way; P.O. Box 346; 78627; Williamson; P 58,700; M 1,050; (512) 930-3535; Fax (512) 930-3587; president@georgetownchamber.org; www.georgetownchamber.org*

Giddings • *Giddings Area C/C* • Denice Harlan; Exec. Dir.; 289 W. Railroad Ave.; 78942; Lee; P 6,500; M 275; (979) 542-3455; Fax (979) 540-2183; chambergiddings@gmail.com; www.giddingstx.com

Gilmer • *Gilmer Area C/C* • Linda Koudelka; Exec. Dir.; 106 Buffalo St.; P.O. Box 854; 75644; Upshur; P 10,000; M 210; (903) 843-2413; (903) 843-3981; Fax (903) 843-3759; gilmerareachamber@gmail.com; www.gilmerareachamber.com

Gladewater • *Gladewater C/C* • Marsha Valdetero; Mgr.; 215 N. Main St.; P.O. Box 1409; 75647; Gregg & Upshur; P 6,441; M 230; (903) 845-5501; (800) 627-0315; Fax (903) 845-6326; info@gladewaterchamber.org; www.gladewaterchamber.org*

Glen Rose • *Glen Rose-Somervell County C/C* • Rhonda Cagle; Pres.; 112 Walnut St.; P.O. Box 605; 76043; Somervell; P 6,800; M 300; (254) 897-2286; info@glenrosechamberofcommerce.com; www.glenrosechamberofcommerce.com

Goldthwaite • *Mills County C/C & Ag.* • Monica Vega; Exec. Dir.; 1001 Fisher St.; P.O. Box 308; 76844; Mills; P 1,800; M 129; (325) 648-3619; Fax (325) 648-3619; gcc@centex.net; www.goldthwaite.biz

Goliad • *Goliad C/C* • Mona Foust; Exec. Mgr.; 231 S. Market St.; P.O. Box 606; 77963; Goliad; P 9,200; M 100; (361) 645-3563; (800) 848-8674; Fax (361) 645-3579; goliadcc@goliad.net; www.goliadcc.org

Gonzales • *Gonzales C/C & Ag.* • Daisy Scheske; Exec. Dir.; 414 Saint Lawrence St.; 78629; Gonzales; P 7,300; M 389; (830) 672-6532; Fax (830) 672-6533; admin@gonzalestexas.com; www.gonzalestexas.com*

Gorman • *Gorman C/C* • Terry Treadway; Secy./Mgr.; P.O. Box 266; 76454; Eastland; P 1,500; M 40; (254) 639-2317; terry@cctc.net; www.gormantx.com

Graford • *Possum Kingdom Lake C/C* • Gayla Chambers; Exec. Dir.; 362 N. FM 2353; 76449; Palo Pinto; P 2,500; M 350; (940) 779-2424; pkchamber@possumkingdomlake.com; www.possumkingdomlake.com

Graham • *Graham C/C* • 608 Elm St.; P.O. Box 299; 76450; Young; P 10,000; M 360; (940) 549-3355; Fax (940) 549-6391; chamber@grahamtexas.org; www.grahamtexas.org*

Granbury • *Granbury C/C* • Mike Scott; CEO; 3408 E. Hwy. 377; 76049; Hood; P 58,000; M 900; (817) 573-1622; Fax (817) 573-0805; info@granburychamber.com; www.granburychamber.com*

Grand Prairie • *Grand Prairie C/C* • Lynn McGinley; Pres./CEO; 900 Conover Dr.; 75051; Dallas; P 170,000; M 600; (972) 264-1558; Fax (972) 264-3419; info@grandprairiechamber.org; www.grandprairiechamber.org*

Grand Saline • *Grand Saline C/C* • Janie Maxfield; Exec. Admin.; 203 N.E. Pacific; 75140; Van Zandt; P 3,262; M 66; (903) 962-7147; chamber@grandsaline.com; www.grandsalinechamber.com

Grandfalls • *Grandfalls-Royalty C/C* • Wanda Corrales; Pres.; P.O. Box 269; 79742; Ward; P 350; M 20; (432) 547-2331

Grandview • *Greater Grandview C/C* • Katherine Stewart; Pres.; P.O. Box 276; 76050; Johnson; P 5,100; M 50; (817) 866-4881; info@grandviewchamber.net; www.grandviewchamber.net

Grapevine • *Grapevine C/C* • RaDonna Hessel; CEO; 200 Vine St.; 76051; Tarrant; P 46,334; M 880; (817) 481-1522; Fax (817) 424-5208; info@grapevinechamber.org; www.grapevinechamber.org*

Greenspoint • *see Houston-Houston Intercontinental C/C*

Greenville • *Greenville C/C* • Jack Gray; Interim Pres./CEO; 2713 Stonewall St.; P.O. Box 1055; 75403; Hunt; P 26,500; M 560; (903) 455-1510; Fax (903) 455-1736; chamber@greenvillechamber.com; www.greenvillechamber.com*

Groesbeck • *Groesbeck C/C* • Sharon Fredriksson; Pres.; 106 E. Navasota St.; P.O. Box 326; 76642; Limestone; P 4,300; M 120; (254) 729-3894; info@groesbeckchamber.com; www.groesbeckchamber.com

Groves • *Groves C/C & Tourist Center* • Ronnie Boneau; Exec. Mgr.; 4399 Main Ave.; 77619; Jefferson; P 16,000; M 155; (409) 962-3631; (800) 876-3631; Fax (409) 963-0745; gchamberofcommer@gt.rr.com; www.grovescofc.com*

Groveton • *Trinity County C/C* • C. Snyder; Ofc. Mgr./Secy.; 227 W. First St.; P.O. Box 366; 75845; Trinity; P 6,000; M 65; (936) 642-1715; (936) 635-7583; Fax (936) 642-2144; tccoc@valornet.com; www.trinitycountychamber.org

Gruver • *Gruver C/C* • Lisa Johnson; Pres.; 201 E. Broadway; P.O. Box 947; 79040; Hansford; P 1,200; M 40; (806) 733-5114; Fax (806) 733-5038; www.gruvertexas.com

Gun Barrel City • *see Mabank*

Gunter • *Gunter Area C/C* • Lindsey Santee; Pres.; P.O. Box 830; 75058; Grayson; P 2,000; M 75; (903) 818-2877; chamberadmin@guntertxchamber.com; www.guntertxchamber.com

Hale Center • *Hale Center C/C* • Jimmy Cameron; Pres.; 703 N. Main St.; P.O. Box 487; 79041; Hale; P 2,200; M 106; (806) 839-2642; Fax (806) 839-2642; halecentercoc@hotmail.com; *

Hallettsville • *Hallettsville C/C & Ag.* • Sharee Rainosek; Exec. Dir.; 1614 N. Texana St.; 77964; Lavaca; P 2,531; M 280; (361) 798-2662; Fax (361) 798-1553; visit@hallettsville.com; www.hallettsville.com

Haltom City • *Northeast Tarrant C/C* • Jack Bradshaw; Pres./CEO; 5001 Denton Hwy.; 76117; Tarrant; P 135,000; M 600; (817) 281-9376; Fax (817) 281-9379; jbradshaw@netarrant.org; www.netarrant.org*

Hamilton • *Hamilton C/C* • Gayle Edwards; Mgr.; 103 1/2 N. Rice St.; P.O. Box 429; 76531; Hamilton; P 3,000; M 80; (254) 386-3216; Fax (254) 386-3563; hamiltonchambertx@gmail.com; www.hamiltontexas.com

Hamlin • *Hamlin C/C* • Elaine Lewis; Exec. Secy.; P.O. Box 402; 79520; Jones; P 2,000; M 100; (325) 576-3501; info@hamlincoc.com; www.hamlincoc.com

Harker Heights • *Harker Heights C/C* • Gina Pence; Pres./CEO; 552 E. FM 2410, Ste. B; 76548; Bell; P 29,000; M 850; (254) 699-4999; Fax (254) 699-5194; gina@hhchamber.com; www.hhchamber.com*

Harlingen • *Harlingen Area C/C & Visitor Bur.* • Chris Gonzales; Exec. Dir.; 311 E. Tyler St.; 78550; Cameron; P 84,832; M 1,020; (956) 423-5440; (800) 531-7346; Fax (956) 425-3870; thechamber@harlingen.com; www.harlingen.com*

Haskell • *Haskell C/C & Visitors Bur.* • Mynea Short; Gen. Mgr.; 510 S. 2nd St.; 79521; Haskell; P 3,300; M 90; (940) 864-2477; haskellcc@srcaccess.net; www.haskelltxchamber.com

Haslet • *see Roanoke*

Hawk Cove • *see West Tawakoni*

Hawkins • *Hawkins Area C/C* • Vic Niburgee; 109 Beaulah St.; P.O. Box 345; 75765; Wood; P 1,550; M 85; (903) 769-4482; hawkinsareachamberofcommerce@juno.com; www.hawkinschamberofcommerce.com

Hemphill • *Sabine County C/C* • Madelyn Flowers; Admin. Asst.; 1555 Worth St.; P.O. Box 717; 75948; Sabine; P 12,000; M 60; (409) 787-2732; Fax (409) 787-2158; sabinecounty1@windstream.net; www.sabinecountytexas.com

Hempstead • *Hempstead C/C* • Cheryl Carter; Pres.; P.O. Box 517; 77445; Waller; P 5,800; M 96; (979) 826-8217; info@hempsteadtxchamber.com; hempsteadtxchamber.com

Henderson • *Henderson Area C/C* • Bonnie Geddie; Exec. Dir.; 201 N. Main St.; 75652; Rusk; P 13,000; M 353; (903) 657-5528; Fax (903) 657-9454; info@hendersontx.com; www.hendersontx.com*

Henrietta • *Henrietta/Clay County C/C* • Randy Schaffner; Pres.; 202 W. Omega St.; P.O. Box 75; 76365; Clay; P 3,600; M 125; (940) 538-5261; claycountychamber@sbcglobal.net; www.hccchamber.org

Hereford • *Deaf Smith County C/C* • Sid Shaw; Exec. V.P.; 701 N. Main; P.O. Box 192; 79045; Deaf Smith; P 15,000; M 350; (806) 364-3333; Fax (806) 364-3342; deafs@wtrt.net; www.herefordtx.org

Hewitt • *Greater Hewitt C/C* • Alissa Cady; Exec. Dir.; 101 Third St.; P.O. Box 661; 76643; McLennan; P 14,000; M 334; (254) 666-1200; Fax (254) 666-3181; hewittdirector@grandecom.net; www.hewittchamber.com*

Hico • *Hico C/C* • Kenny Giessner; Pres.; P.O. Box 561; 76457; Hamilton; P 1,400; M 40; (254) 796-4727; (254) 796-4620; hicotxchamber@gmail.com; www.hicochamber.com

Hidalgo • *Hidalgo C/C* • Joe Vera; Pres.; 800 E. Coma Ave.; 78557; Hidalgo; P 13,000; M 570; (956) 843-2734; Fax (956) 843-2722; hidjoevera@aol.com; cityofhidalgo.net

Highlands • *Greater Highlands & Lynchburg C/C* • Reba Rachall; Exec. Admin.; 127 San Jacinto St.; 77562; Harris; P 12,500; M 100; (281) 426-7227; Fax (281) 426-7227; info@allabouthighlands.org; www.allabouthighlands.com

Hillje • *see Louise*

Hillsboro • *Hillsboro Area C/C* • Vicki Hidde; Pres.; 115 N. Covington St.; P.O. Box 358; 76645; Hill; P 8,500; M 360; (254) 582-2481; (800) 445-5726; Fax (254) 582-0465; director@hillsborochamber.org; www.hillsborochamber.org*

Hitchcock • *Hitchcock C/C* • Monica Cantrell; Exec. Dir.; 8300 Hwy. 6, Ste. A; P.O. Box 389; 77563; Galveston; P 7,186; M 300; (409) 986-9224; Fax (409) 986-6317; hcofc662@verizon.net; www.hitchcocktexaschamber.com

Hondo • *Hondo Area C/C* • Roxanne Carter; Exec. Dir.; 1113 17th St.; 78861; Medina; P 9,000; M 330; (830) 426-3037; hacc@hondochamber.com; www.hondochamber.org*

Honey Grove • *Honey Grove C/C* • Jason White; Pres.; P.O. Box 92; 75446; Fannin; P 1,940; M 74; (903) 378-7211; fanningraphics@sbcglobal.net; www.honeygrovechamber.com

Houston Area

***Clear Lake Area C/C* •** Cynthia Harreld; Pres./CEO; 1201 NASA Pkwy.; 77058; Harris; P 250,000; M 1,000; (281) 488-7676; (281) 488-7677; Fax (281) 488-8981; chamber@clearlakearea.com; www.clearlakearea.com

***Cy-Fair Houston C/C* •** Leslie Martone; Pres.; 8711 Hwy. 6 N., Ste. 120; 77095; Harris; P 750,000; M 700; (281) 373-1390; Fax (281) 373-1394; staff@cyfairchamber.com; www.cyfairchamber.com*

***Greater Heights Area C/C* •** Kenneth E. Stallman; Pres./CEO; 545 W. 19th St., 2nd Flr.; 77008; Harris; P 350,000; M 400; (713) 861-6735; Fax (713) 861-9310; president@heightschamber.com; www.heightschamber.com*

***Greater Houston Partnership* •** Bob Harvey; Pres./CEO; 701 Avenida de las Americas, Ste. 900; 77010; Harris; P 6,500,000; M 1,000; (713) 844-3600; ghp@houston.org; www.houston.org*

***Houston East End C/C* •** Frances Castaneda Dyess; Pres.; 550 Gulfgate Center; 77087; Harris; P 110,000; M 500; (713) 926-3305; Fax (713) 926-0960; frances@eecoc.org; www.eecoc.org*

***Houston Intercontinental C/C* •** Reggie Gray; Pres.; 12700 Northborough, Ste. 600; P.O. Box 670252; 77267; Harris; P 900,000; M 500; (281) 408-0866; (281) 408-3482; Fax (281) 248-4388; info@houstonicc.org; www.houstonicc.org*

***Houston Metropolitan Chamber* •** Peggy A. Wilson; Pres./CEO; 12 Greenway Plaza, Ste. 1100; 77046; Harris; P 2,250,000; M 300; (713) 666-1521; (713) 836-8405; Fax (713) 666-1523; info@houstonmetropolitanchamber.biz; www.houstonmetropolitanchamber.biz*

***Houston Northwest C/C* •** Barbara Thomason IOM PCED; Pres.; 3920 Cypress Creek Pkwy., Ste. 120; 77068; Harris; P 500,000; M 700; (281) 440-4160; chamberinfo@houstonnwchamber.org; www.houstonnwchamber.org*

***Houston West C/C* •** Jeannie Bollinger; Pres./CEO; 10370 Richmond Ave., Ste. 125; 77042; Harris; P 1,000,000; M 730; (713) 785-4922; Fax (713) 785-4944; info@hwcoc.org; www.hwcoc.org*

***North Channel Area C/C* •** Margie Buentello; Pres./CEO; 13301 I-10 E. Frwy., Ste. 100; P.O. Box 9759; 77213; Harris; P 210,000; M 700; (713) 450-3600; Fax (713) 450-0700; margie@ncachamber.com; www.northchannelarea.com*

***South Belt-Ellington C/C* •** Kay Barbour; Pres./CEO; 10500 Scarsdale Blvd.; 77089; Harris; P 81,000; M 250; (281) 481-5516; Fax (281) 922-7045; info@southbeltchamber.com; www.southbeltchamber.com*

Hubbard • *City of Hubbard C/C* • Margo Foster; V.P.; P.O. Box 221; 76648; Hill; P 1,600; M 100; (254) 576-2521; Fax (254) 576-2688; mfoster396@aol.com; www.hubbardchamber.com

Hudson Oaks • *see Willow Park*

Huffman • *see Crosby*

Hughes Springs • *Hughes Springs C/C* • Judi Howell; Exec. Dir.; 603 E. 1st St.; P.O. Box 218; 75656; Cass; P 2,000; M 100; (903) 639-2351; Fax (903) 639-3769; cofc@hughesspringstxusa.com; www.hughesspringstxusa.com*

Humble • *Lake Houston Area C/C* • Jenna Armstrong; Pres.; 110 W. Main St.; P.O. Box 3337; 77347; Harris; P 253,336; M 1,100; (281) 446-2128; Fax (281) 446-7483; jarmstrong@lakehouston.org; www.lakehoustonareachamber.org*

Huntsville • *Huntsville-Walker County C/C* • Carol Smith; Pres.; 1327 11th St.; P.O. Box 538; 77342; Walker; P 67,861; M 540; (936) 295-8113; (877) 646-8068; Fax (936) 295-0571; chamber@chamber.huntsville.tx.us; www.chamber.huntsville.tx.us*

Hurst • *see Bedford*

Hutto • *Hutto Area C/C* • John Darby; Pres./CEO; 122 East St.; P.O. Box 99; 78634; Williamson; P 21,200; M 330; (512) 759-4400; info@huttochamber.com; www.huttochamber.com*

Ingleside • *Ingleside C/C* • Jane Gimler; Pres./Dir.; 2867 Ave. J; P.O. Box 686; 78362; San Patricio; P 9,338; M 250; (361) 776-2906; Fax (361) 776-0678; inglesidetxchamber@gmail.com; www.inglesidetxchamber.com*

Ingram • *West Kerr County C/C* • Lucy Gould; Exec. Dir.; 3186 Junction Hwy.; P.O. Box 1006; 78025; Kerr; P 10,000; M 185; (830) 367-4322; Fax (830) 367-4375; wkccc1@ktc.com; www.wkcc.com

Iowa Park • *Iowa Park C/C* • David Owen; Dir. of Eco. Dev.; 102 N. Wall St.; 76367; Wichita; P 6,500; M 125; (940) 592-5441; dowen@iowapark.com; www.iowapark.com

Iraan • *Iraan-Sheffield C/C* • Dana St. Clair; Ofc. Mgr.; 501 W. 6th; P.O. Box 153; 79744; Pecos; P 1,535; M 60; (432) 639-2232; Fax (432) 639-2125; mail@iraantx.com; www.iraantx.com

Irving • *Irving-Las Colinas C/C* • Beth A. Bowman; Pres./CEO; 5201 N. O'Connor Blvd., Ste. 100; 75039; Dallas; P 236,000; M 1,900; (214) 217-8484; (214) 217-8471; Fax (214) 389-2513; bbowman@irvingchamber.com; www.irvingchamber.com*

Jacksboro • *Jacksboro C/C* • Redonna Pulis; Exec. Dir.; 302 S. Main St.; 76458; Jack; P 4,500; M 164; (940) 567-2602; Fax (940) 567-3161; office@jacksborochamber.com; www.jacksborochamber.com

Jacksonville • *Jacksonville C/C* • Peggy Renfro; Pres.; 526 E. Commerce St.; 75766; Cherokee; P 14,544; M 400; (903) 586-2217; Fax (903) 586-6944; chamber@jacksonvilletexas.com; www.jacksonvilletexas.com

Jasper • *Jasper-Lake Sam Rayburn Area C/C* • Liz Street; Exec. Dir.; 246 E. Milam St.; 75951; Jasper; P 8,500; M 395; (409) 384-2762; jaspercc@jaspercoc.org; www.jaspercoc.org

Jefferson • *Marion County C/C* • Kayann Hollomon; Dir.; 115 N. Polk St.; P. O. Box 967; 75657; Marion; P 2,100; M 195; (903) 665-2672; (888) 467-3529; Fax (903) 665-8233; jeffersontx1@att.net; www.jefferson-texas.com

Jewett • *Jewett Area C/C* • Scott Serafin; Pres.; 111 N. Robinson Rd.; P.O. Box 220; 75846; Leon; P 1,250; M 140; (903) 626-4202; Fax (903) 626-6599; contactus@jewetttexas.org; www.jewetttexas.org

Johnson City • *Johnson City Texas C/C & Visitors Center* • Frances Ann Giron; Dir./Pres.; 100 E. Main; P.O. Box 485; 78636; Blanco; P 1,350; M 250; (830) 868-7684; Fax (830) 868-5700; info@johnsoncitytexaschamber.com; www.johnsoncity-texas.com

Joshua • *Joshua Area C/C* • Kim Henderson; Pres.; 402 S. Main; P.O. Box 1292; 76058; Johnson; P 8,200; M 250; (817) 253-7233; (817) 556-2480; kim@joshuachamber.org; www.joshuachamber.org

Jourdanton • *Jourdanton C/C* • Rhonda Lem; Pres.; 1101 Campbell Ave.; P.O. Box 747; 78026; Atascosa; P 3,871; M 50; (830) 769-2866; (830) 769-3087; Fax (830) 769-4082; jourdlib@texun.net; www.jourdanton.net

Junction • *Kimble County C/C & Junction Visitor Info.* • Constance E. Booth; Exec. Dir.; 402 Main St.; 76849; Kimble; P 5,000; M 275; (325) 446-3190; (800) KIMBLE4; Fax (325) 446-2871; junctiontx@cebridge.net; www.junctiontexas.net

Karnack • *Caddo Lake Area C/C & Tourism* • Bill Dorsey; Pres.; P.O. Box 228; 75661; Harrison; P 2,200; M 25; info@caddolake.org; www.caddolake.org

Karnes City • *Karnes City Comm. C/C* • Amelia "Mely" Martinez; Exec. Dir.; 210 E. Calvert St.; 78118; Karnes; P 3,042; M 100; (830) 780-3112; karnescitychamber@att.net; www.karnescitychamber.net

Kashmere • *see Houston-Houston Intercontinental C/C*

Katy • *Katy Area C/C* • Ann Hodge; Pres./CEO; 23501 Cinco Ranch Blvd., Ste. B206; 77494; Fort Bend, Harris & Waller; P 219,348; M 800; (281) 391-5289; Fax (281) 391-7423; info@katychamber.com; www.katychamber.com*

Kaufman • *Greater Kaufman C/C* • Anne Glasscock; Pres./CEO; 2311 S. Washington, Ste. A; P.O. Box 146; 75142; Kaufman; P 7,120; M 240; (972) 932-3118; Fax (972) 932-8373; info@kaufmanchamber.com; www.kaufmantx.com

Keene • *Keene C/C* • Donnie Beeson; Pres.; P.O. Box 817; 76059; Johnson; P 6,258; M 125; (817) 556-2995; info@keenechamber.org; www.keenechamber.org

Keller • *Greater Keller C/C* • Rudy Martinez; Pres.; 420 Johnson Rd., Ste. 301; 76248; Tarrant; P 40,000; M 650; (817) 431-2169; Fax (817) 431-3789; keller@kellerchamber.com; www.kellerchamber.com*

Kemah • *also see Houston-Clear Lake Area C/C*

Kemah • *see Dickinson*

Kemp • *see Mabank*

Kenedy • *Kenedy C/C* • Hannah James; Exec. Dir.; 205 S. 2nd St.; P.O. Box 570; 78119; Karnes; P 3,500; M 200; (830) 583-3223; (830) 583-5929; Fax (830) 583-9166; kenedycc@outlook.com; www.kenedychamber.org*

Kennedale • *Kennedale C/C* • Jeremiah Wunneburger; Chrmn.; P.O. Box 1552; 76060; Tarrant; P 7,200; M 185; (817) 985-2109; Fax (817) 985-2119; info@kennedalechamber.com; www.kennedalechamber.com*

Kerens • *Kerens C/C* • Derinda Scott; Secy.; 101 S. Colket Ave.; P.O. Box 117; 75144; Navarro; P 1,835; M 100; (903) 396-2391; Fax (903) 396-2391; kerenschamber@txun.net; www.ci.kerens.tx.us

Kermit • *Kermit C/C* • Roni Martinez; Pres.; 112 N. Poplar St.; 79745; Winkler; P 5,500; M 85; (432) 586-2507; Fax (432) 586-2508; kermitchamber@cebridge.net; *

Kerrville • *Kerrville Area C/C* • 1700 Sidney Baker St., Ste. 100; 78028; Kerr; P 50,000; M 900; (830) 896-1155; Fax (830) 896-1175; shelly@kerrvilletx.com; www.kerrvilletx.com*

Kilgore • *Kilgore C/C* • Cindy Morris; Pres.; 813 N. Kilgore St.; P.O. Box 1582; 75663; Gregg; P 14,000; M 385; (903) 984-5022; (866) 984-0400; Fax (903) 984-4975; info@kilgorechamber.com; www.kilgorechamber.com*

Killeen • *Greater Killeen C/C* • John Crutchfield III; Pres./CEO; One Santa Fe Plaza; P.O. Box 548; 76540; Bell; P 132,000; M 700; (254) 526-9551; Fax (254) 526-6090; info@gkcc.com; www.killeenchamber.com*

Kingsland • *Kingsland/Lake LBJ C/C* • Letha Causey; Ofc. Mgr.; 2743 W. RR 1431; P.O. Box 465; 78639; Burnet & Llano; P 12,500; M 300; (325) 388-6211; Fax (325) 388-5391; kchamber@zeecon.com; www.kingslandchamber.org

Kingsville • *Kingsville C/C* • Alice L. Byers; Exec. Dir.; 635 E. King Ave.; P.O. Box 1030; 78364; Kleberg; P 27,000; M 324; (361) 592-6438; Fax (361) 592-0866; chamber@kingsville.org; www.kingsville.org*

Kirby • *see Universal City*

Kirbyville • *Kirbyville C/C* • Tim Menshac; Pres.; P.O. Box 793; 75956; Jasper; P 2,100; M 70; (409) 423-5827; Fax (409) 423-3353

Knox City • *Knox City C/C* • Emily Nelson; Ofc. Mgr.; 123 N. Central Ave.; P.O. Box 91; 79529; Knox; P 3,000; M 50; (940) 658-3442; Fax (940) 658-3442; kcchamber@srcaccess.net; www.knoxcitychamberofcommerce.com

Kountze • *Kountze C/C* • Ann Boyett; Pres.; P.O. Box 878; 77625; Hardin; P 2,123; M 88; (409) 246-3413; (866) 4-KOUNTZ; Fax (409) 246-4659; contact@kountzechamber.com; www.kountzechamber.com

Kyle • *Kyle Area C/C & Visitors Bur.* • Julie Snyder; CEO; 401 Center St.; P.O. Box 900; 78640; Hays; P 30,000; M 320; (512) 268-4220; Fax (800) 903-1564; julie@kylechamber.org; www.kylechamber.org*

La Grange • *La Grange Area C/C* • Paula Collins; Ofc. Mgr.; 220 W. Colorado St.; 78945; Fayette; P 4,000; M 305; (979) 968-5756; (800) LA-GRANGE; paulacollins@lagrangetx.org; www.lagrangetx.org

La Porte • *La Porte-Bayshore C/C* • Colleen Hicks; Pres.; 712 W. Fairmont Pkwy.; P.O. Box 996; 77572; Harris; P 38,000; M 450; (281) 471-1123; Fax (281) 471-1710; info-lpcc@laportechamber.org; www.laportechamber.org*

La Vernia • *Greater La Vernia C/C* • Wes Becknell; Pres.; 12 E. Chihuahua St.; P.O. Box 1055; 78121; Wilson; P 9,000; M 100; (830) 253-2100; staff@laverniachamber.com; www.laverniachamber.com

Ladonia • *Ladonia C/C* • Lavonne Duncan; Pres.; P.O. Box 44; 75449; Fannin; P 667; M 30; (903) 367-7011; chamber@cityofladonia.com; www.cityofladonia.com

Lago Vista • *Lago Vista & Jonestown Area C/C & CVB* • Sherri Campbell-Jander; Exec. Dir.; 20624 FM 1431, Ste. 8; P.O. Box 4946; 78645; Travis; P 6,500; M 225; (512) 267-7952; Fax (512) 267-2338; sandra@lagovista.org; www.lagovista.org*

Lake Conroe • *see Conroe*

Lake Dallas • *Lake Cities C/C* • Melissa Cox; Exec. Dir.; P.O. Box 1028; 75065; Denton; P 62,614; M 187; (940) 497-3097; Fax (972) 534-1375; lccc@lakecitieschamber.com; www.lakecitieschamber.com*

Lake Tawakoni • *see West Tawakoni*

Lake Worth • *Northwest Tarrant C/C* • Greg Fox; Dir.; 3918 Telephone Rd., Ste. 200; 76135; Tarrant; P 35,000; M 200; (817) 237-0060; Fax (817) 237-2365; chamberadmin@nwtcc.org; www.nwtcc.org*

Lakewood • *see Houston-Houston Intercontinental C/C*

Lamesa • *Lamesa Area C/C* • Sandra Adams; Pres.; 123 Main St.; P.O. Box 880; 79331; Dawson; P 9,950; M 250; (806) 872-2181; Fax (806) 872-5700; office@lamesachamber.org; www.lamesachamber.org

Lampasas • *Lampasas County C/C* • Jill Carroll; Exec. Dir.; 205 S. U.S. Hwy. 281; P.O. Box 627; 76550; Lampasas; P 18,500; M 310; (512) 556-5172; Fax (512) 556-2195; info@lampasaschamber.org; www.lampasaschamber.org*

Lancaster • *Lancaster Area C/C* • 100 N. Dallas Ave.; P.O. Box 1100; 75146; Dallas; P 38,000; M 450; (972) 227-2579; (972) 310-3311; Fax (972) 227-9555; chamber@lancastertexas.org; www.lancastertexas.org*

Laredo • *Laredo C/C* • Miguel Conchas; Pres./CEO; 2310 San Bernardo Ave.; P.O. Box 790; 78042; Webb; P 259,000; M 680; (956) 722-9895; Fax (956) 791-4503; chamber@laredochamber.com; www.laredochamber.com*

League City • *also see Houston-Clear Lake Area C/C*

League City • *League City Reg. C/C* • Steve Paterson; Pres./CEO; 217 E. Main St.; 77573; Galveston; P 99,000; M 525; (281) 338-7339; Fax (281) 554-8103; jane@leaguecitychamber.com; www.leaguecitychamber.com*

Leakey • *Frio Canyon C/C* • Bob Albright; Pres.; P.O. Box 743; 78873; Real; P 452; M 175; (830) 232-5222; friochamber@hctc.net; www.friocanyonchamber.com

Leander • *Greater Leander C/C* • Bridget L. Brandt; Pres./CEO; 100 N. Brushy St.; P.O. Box 556; 78646; Travis & Williamson; P 32,000; M 330; (512) 259-1907; Fax (512) 259-9114; contactus@leandercc.org; www.leandercc.org*

Leonard • *Leonard C/C* • Mark Blackerby; Pres.; P.O. Box 117; 75452; Fannin; P 1,900; M 60; (903) 587-3363; (903) 587-3334; leonardchamber.com

Levelland • *Levelland Area C/C* • Mary Siders; Pres.; 1101 Ave. H; 79336; Hockley; P 14,000; M 300; (806) 894-3157; msiders@levelland.com; www.levelland.com*

Lewisville • *Lewisville Area C/C* • Ray Hernandez IOM; Pres.; 551 N. Valley Pkwy.; 75067; Denton; P 200,000; M 765; (972) 436-9571; Fax (972) 436-5949; ray@lewisvillechamber.org; www.lewisvillechamber.org*

Liberty • *Liberty-Dayton Area C/C* • Mary Anne Campbell; Pres.; 1801 Trinity St.; P.O. Box 1270; 77575; Liberty; P 35,000; M 450; (936) 336-5736; Fax (936) 336-1159; chamber@imsday.com; www.libertydaytonchamber.com

Liberty Hill • *Liberty Hill C/C* • Steve Tatro; Chair; 155 Hillcrest Ave., Ste. A; P.O. Box 586; 78642; Williamson; P 967; M 112; (512) 548-6343; admin@libertyhillchamber.org; www.libertyhillchamber.org*

Lindale • *Lindale Area C/C* • Shelbie Glover; Exec. Dir.; 205 S. Main St.; P.O. Box 670; 75771; Smith; P 8,000; M 480; (903) 882-7181; Fax (903) 882-1790; info@lindalechamber.org; www.lindalechamber.org

Linden • *Linden Area C/C* • Carla Surratt; Pres.; 201 N. Main St.; P.O. Box 993; 75563; Cass; P 2,000; M 50; (903) 756-3106; Fax (903) 756-7842; www.lindentexas.org

Littlefield • *Littlefield C/C & Ag.* • Jim Jones; Exec. Dir.; 601 E. 4th St.; P.O. Box 507; 79339; Lamb; P 6,500; M 110; (806) 385-5331; Fax (806) 385-0801; littlefieldcc@gmail.com; littlefieldtexas.org

Live Oak • *see Universal City*

Livingston • *Polk County C/C* • Christi Sullivan; Exec. Dir.; 1001 U.S. Hwy. 59 Loop N.; P.O. Box 600; 77351; Polk; P 48,000; M 470; (936) 327-4929; (800) 918-1305; Fax (936) 327-2660; chamber@livingston.net; www.polkchamber.com*

Llano • *Llano C/C & Visitor Center* • Patti Zinsmeyer; Exec. Dir.; 100 Train Station Dr.; 78643; Llano; P 23,000; M 300; (325) 247-5354; Fax (325) 248-6917; info@llanochamber.org; www.llanochamber.org*

Lockhart • *Lockhart C/C & Visitors Center* • Wayne Bock; Pres./CEO; 631 S. Colorado St.; P.O. Box 840; 78644; Caldwell; P 12,698; M 330; (512) 398-2818; Fax (512) 376-2632; staff@lockhartchamber.com; www.lockhartchamber.com*

Lockney • *Lockney Area C/C* • Archie Jones; Pres.; P.O. Box 477; 79241; Floyd; P 1,800; M 33; (806) 652-3386; Fax (806) 652-2802

Lone Oak • *see West Tawakoni*

Longview • *Longview C/C* • Kelly Hall; Pres./CEO; 410 N. Center St.; 75601; Gregg; P 82,000; M 1,100; (903) 237-4000; Fax (903) 237-4049; info1@longviewtx.com; www.longviewchamber.com*

Los Fresnos • *Los Fresnos Area C/C* • Debra Badeaux & Alan Atherton; Co-Dirs.; 203 N. Arroyo Blvd., Ste. A; 78566; Cameron; P 6,000; M 85; (956) 233-4488; (956) 350-3000; losfresnoschamber@yahoo.com; www.losfresnoschamber.com

Louise • *Louise-Hillje C/C* • Darryl Chromcak; Pres.; P.O. Box 156; 77455; Wharton; P 1,000; M 75; (979) 648-2029; Fax (979) 648-2598; shellyfritz@yahoo.com; www.louisehilljechamber.org

Lubbock • *Lubbock C/C* • Eddie McBride IOM; Pres./CEO; 1500 Broadway, Ste. 101; 79401; Lubbock; P 289,000; M 2,100; (806) 761-7000; Fax (806) 761-7013; info@lubbockbiz.org; www.lubbockchamber.com*

Lufkin • *Lufkin/Angelina County C/C* • Jim Johnson; Pres./CEO; 1615 S. Chestnut; 75901; Angelina; P 85,000; M 1,400; (936) 634-6644; Fax (936) 634-8726; chamber@lufkintexas.org; www.lufkintexas.org*

Luling • *Luling Area C/C & Visitor Center* • Ashley Flores; Exec. Dir.; 421 E. Davis St.; P.O. Box 710; 78648; Caldwell; P 5,500; M 200; (830) 875-3214; Fax (830) 875-2082; info@lulingcc.org; www.lulingcc.org

Lumberton • *Lumberton C/C* • Brenda Erwin; Exec. Dir.; 826 N. Main; P.O. Box 8574; 77657; Hardin; P 20,000; M 200; (409) 755-0554; Fax (409) 755-2516; lcoc@lumbertoncoc.com; www.lumbertoncoc.com*

Lytle • *Greater Lytle C/C* • Brad Boyd; Pres.; P.O. Box 2131; 78052; Atascosa, Bexar & Medina; P 3,000; M 50; (830) 709-4304; lytlechamber@yahoo.com; www.lytlechamberofcommerce.com

Mabank • *Cedar Creek Lake Area C/C* • JoAnn Hanstrom; Pres.; 604 S. Third St., Ste. E; P.O. Box 581; 75147; Henderson & Kaufman; P 51,065; M 450; (903) 887-3152; Fax (903) 887-3695; info@cedarcreeklakechamber.com; www.cedarcreeklakechamber.com*

Madisonville • *Madison County C/C* • 113 W. Trinity; 77864; Madison; P 4,400; M 200; (936) 348-3591; Fax (936) 348-2212; director@madisoncountytxchamber.com; www.madisoncountytxchamber.com*

Magnolia • *Greater Magnolia C/C* • Terre Albert; Chair; 18935 FM 1488; P.O. Box 399; 77353; Montgomery; P 135,000; M 350; (281) 356-1488; Fax (281) 356-2552; gmcc@magnoliatexas.org; www.magnoliatexas.org*

Malakoff • *Malakoff Area C/C* • Kathy Roland; Pres.; P.O. Box 1042; 75148; Henderson; P 2,100; M 70; (903) 489-8118; Fax (903) 489-8118; malakoffchamber45@yahoo.com; www.malakoffchamber.org

Mansfield • *Mansfield Area C/C* • MK White-Ramsey; Pres./CEO; 114 N. Main St.; 76063; Ellis, Johnson & Tarrant; P 60,000; M 711; (817) 473-0507; Fax (817) 473-8687; membership@mansfieldchamber.org; www.mansfieldchamber.org*

Marathon • *Marathon C/C* • Daniel Self; Treas.; P.O. Box 163; 79842; Brewster; P 450; M 40; (432) 386-4522; (432) 386-4241; www.visitmarathontexas.com

Marble Falls • *Marble Falls/Lake LBJ C/C* • Bill Rives; Exec. Dir.; 916 Second St.; 78654; Burnet; P 30,000; M 800; (830) 693-2815; (800) 759-8178; Fax (830) 693-1620; info@marblefalls.org; www.marblefalls.org

Marfa • *Marfa C/C* • Andrew Peters; Pres.; P.O. Box 635; 79843; Presidio; P 2,000; M 134; info@marfachamber.org; marfachamber.org

Marion • *see Universal City*

Marlin • *Marlin C/C* • Cynthia Dees; Ofc. Mgr.; 245 Coleman St.; 76661; Falls; P 17,000; M 125; (254) 803-3301; Fax (254) 883-2171; marlintxchamber@aol.com; www.marlintexas.com

Marquez • *Marquez Area C/C & Visitor Center* • Winter Adams; Exec. Dir.; 318 S. Austin; 77865; Leon; P 260; M 60; (903) 529-1419; (979) 255-4436; Fax (903) 529-1419; marquezchamber@yahoo.com

Marshall • *Greater Marshall C/C* • Stormy Nickerson; Exec. Dir.; 208 E. Burleson St.; P.O. Box 520; 75671; Harrison; P 23,500; M 500; (903) 935-7868; Fax (903) 935-9982; info@marshalltexas.com; www.marshalltexas.com*

Mason • *Mason County C/C* • Nikki Sills; Exec. Dir.; 108 Ft. McKavitt; P.O. Box 156; 76856; Mason; P 2,300; M 230; (325) 347-5758; Fax (325) 347-5259; masontexas@hctc.net; www.masontxcoc.com

McAllen • *McAllen C/C* • Steve Ahlenius CEcD; Pres./CEO; 1200 Ash Ave.; P.O. Box 790; 78501; Hidalgo; P 137,000; M 2,000; (956) 682-2871; Fax (956) 687-2917; membership@mcallenchamber.com; www.mcallenchamber.com*

McCamey • *McCamey C/C & Visitors Center* • Velma Beasley; Dir.; 201 E. 6th St.; P.O. Box 906; 79752; Upton; P 1,846; M 58; (432) 652-8202; Fax (432) 652-8202; mccameychamber@sbcglobal.net; mccameychamber.com

McGregor • *McGregor C/C* • Jon Mark Smith; Dir.; 303 S. Main St.; 76657; Coryell & McLennan; P 5,000; M 125; (254) 840-2292; Fax (254) 840-2950; office@mcgregorchamber.com; www.mcgregorchamber.com

McKinney • *McKinney C/C* • Lisa Hermes IOM; Pres.; 400 W. Virginia St., Ste. 100; 75070; Collin; P 156,800; M 1,200; (972) 542-0163; Fax (972) 548-0876; limaidixon@mckinneychamber.com; www.mckinneychamber.com*

Melissa • *Melissa Area C/C* • Bill Jones; Exec. Dir.; 1501 W. Harrison St.; P.O. Box 121; 75454; Collin; P 8,200; M 140; (972) 837-4277; (903) 227-4538; Fax (972) 837-4277; melissaareachamber@gmail.com; www.melissatx.org

Memphis • *Memphis C/C* • Susan McQueen; Ofc. Mgr.; 515 W. Main; 79245; Hall; P 2,500; M 50; (806) 259-3144; Fax (806) 259-1133; memphistexaschamber@valornet.com

Menard • *Menard C/C* • Christy Eggleston; Ofc. Mgr.; 100 E. San Saba Ave.; P.O. Box 64; 76859; Menard; P 1,400; M 190; (325) 396-2365; Fax (325) 396-4646; menardcc@verizon.net; www.menardchamber.com

Mercedes • *Mercedes Area C/C* • Donna Jackson; Ofc. Mgr.; 417 S. Ohio; P.O. Box 37; 78570; Hidalgo; P 14,000; M 140; (956) 565-2221; Fax (956) 565-2221; donna@mercedeschamber.com; www.mercedeschamber.com*

Meridian • *Meridian C/C* • Kay Duke; Exec. Dir.; 107 N. Erath St., Ste. B; P.O. Box 758; 76665; Bosque; P 1,493; M 127; (254) 435-2966; Fax (254) 435-2806; meridian-chamber@sbcglobal.net; www.meridian-chamber.com

Merkel • *Merkel C/C & Eco. Dev. Corp.* • Kay Toombs; Bd. Member; Merkel City Hall; 100 Kent St.; 79536; Taylor; P 2,715; M 50; (325) 928-5722; (325) 794-2066; Fax (325) 928-5722; rmandm@gmail.com; www.merkeltexas.com

Mesquite • *Mesquite C of C & CVB* • Terry McCullar; Pres.; 617 N. Ebrite; 75149; Dallas; P 134,000; M 650; (972) 285-0211; (800) 541-2355; Fax (972) 285-3535; info@mesquitechamber.com; www.mesquitechamber.com*

Mexia • *Mexia Area C/C* • Linda Archibald; Pres.; 214 N. Sherman; 76667; Limestone; P 10,000; M 175; (254) 562-5569; (888) 535-5476; Fax (254) 562-7138; linda@mexiachamber.com; www.mexiachamber.com*

Miami • *Miami/Roberts County C/C* • Kathy Thompson; P.O. Box 355; 79059; Roberts; P 930; M 75; (806) 868-4791; info@miamitexas.org; www.miamitexas.org

Midland • *Midland C/C* • Robert Burns; Pres./CEO; 303 W. Wall, Ste. 200; 79701; Midland; P 163,000; M 1,200; (432) 683-3381; (800) 624-6435; Fax (432) 686-3556; info@midlandtxchamber.com; www.midlandtxchamber.com*

Midlothian • *Midlothian C/C* • Sara Garcia; Pres./CEO; 310 N. 9th St.; 76065; Ellis; P 16,000; M 425; (972) 723-8600; Fax (972) 723-9300; mcoc@midlothianchamber.org; www.midlothianchamber.org*

Mineola • *Mineola Area C/C* • Marianne Eubanks; Exec. Dir.; 101 E. Broad St.; P.O. Box 68; 75773; Wood; P 5,300; M 260; (903) 569-2087; Fax (903) 569-5510; chamber@mineola.com; www.mineolachamber.org

Mineral Wells • *Mineral Wells Area C/C* • Ryan Roach; Exec. Dir.; 511 E. Hubbard; P.O. Box 1408; 76068; Palo Pinto; P 27,960; M 430; (940) 325-2557; (800) 252-6989; Fax (940) 328-0850; info@mineralwellstx.com; www.mineralwellstx.com*

Mission • *Greater Mission C/C* • Josh Stockel; Pres./CEO; 202 W. Tom Landry; 78572; Hidalgo; P 82,000; M 400; (956) 585-2727; Fax (956) 585-3044; receptionist@missionchamber.com; www.missionchamber.com*

Monahans • *Monahans C/C* • Teresa Burnett; Exec. Dir.; 401 S. Dwight Ave.; 79756; Ward; P 10,000; M 350; (432) 943-2187; Fax (432) 943-6868; chamber@monahans.org; www.monahans.org*

Mont Belvieu • *West Chambers County C/C* • Melissa G. Malechek IOM; Pres./CEO; 11340 Eagle Dr., Ste. 4; P.O. Box 750; 77580; Chambers; P 5,984; M 341; (281) 576-5440; missy@thewccccc.com; www.thewccccc.com*

Moulton • *Moulton C/C* • Tammye McBride; Secy.; 405 S. Lavaca; P.O. Box 482; 77975; Lavaca; P 2,000; M 73; (361) 596-7205; Fax (361) 596-4384; chamber@moultontexas.com; www.moultontexas.com*

Mount Pleasant • *Mount Pleasant/Titus County C/C & Visitors Cncl.* • Katie A. Stedman; Pres./CEO; 1604 N. Jefferson; 75455; Titus; P 14,000; M 450; (903) 572-8567; Fax (903) 572-0613; info@mtpleasanttx.com; www.mtpleasanttx.com*

Mount Vernon • *Franklin County C/C* • Diane Newsom; Mgr.; 109 S. Kaufman St.; P.O. Box 554; 75457; Franklin; P 12,000; M 250; (903) 537-4365; Fax (903) 537-4160; chamber@mt-vernon.com; www.franklincountytx.com*

Muenster • *Muenster C/C* • John Broyles; Exec. Dir.; 1000 E. Division St., Ste. D; P.O. Box 714; 76252; Cook; P 2,000; M 135; (940) 759-2227; Fax (940) 759-2228; john.chamber@ntin.net; www.muensterchamber.com

Muleshoe • *Muleshoe C/C & Ag.* • Becky Hoksbergen; Exec. Asst.; 115 E. American Blvd.; P.O. Box 356; 79347; Bailey; P 5,100; M 100; (806) 272-4248; Fax (806) 272-4614; chamber@fivearea.com; www.muleshoechamber.com

Munday • *Munday C/C and Ag.* • Patricia A. Wild; Dir.; 121 E. B St.; P.O. Drawer L; 76371; Knox; P 1,550; M 110; (940) 422-4540; Fax (940) 421-3288; mundaychamber@gmail.com; www.mundaytexas.com

Nacogdoches • *Nacogdoches County C/C* • C. Wayne Mitchell; Pres./CEO; 2516 North St.; 75965; Nacogdoches; P 65,000; M 800; (936) 560-5533; Fax (936) 560-3920; chamber@nactx.com; www.nacogdoches.org*

Naples • *City of Naples* • Danny Mills; Mayor; P.O. Box 340; 75568; Morris; P 1,398; M 5; (903) 897-2271; Fax (903) 897-2913; cityofnaples@windstream.net; www.city-of-naples-texas.com

Nassau Bay • *see Houston-Clear Lake Area C/C*

Navasota • *Navasota/Grimes County C/C* • Johnny McNally; Exec. Dir.; 117 S. LaSalle; P.O. Box 530; 77868; Grimes; P 25,895; M 300; (936) 825-6600; Fax (936) 825-3699; assistant@navasotagrimeschamber.com; www.navasotagrimeschamber.com*

Nederland • *Nederland C/C & Tourist Bur.* • Diana LaBorde; Pres./CEO; 1515 Boston Ave.; P.O. Box 891; 77627; Jefferson; P 17,400; M 375; (409) 722-0279; Fax (409) 722-0615; nedcofc@nederlandtx.com; www.nederlandtx.com*

Needville • *Needville Area C/C* • Glenn Schmidt; P.O. Box 1200; 77461; Fort Bend; P 2,600; M 250; (979) 793-5700; needvillechamber@needville.org; www.needville.org

New Boston • *New Boston C/C* • Nancy Satterfield; Admin. Dir.; 100 N. Center St.; 75570; Bowie; P 4,808; M 202; (903) 628-2581; Fax (903) 628-6340; chamber@newbostontx.org; www.newbostontx.org*

New Braunfels • *Greater New Braunfels C/C Inc.* • Michael Meek CEcD; Pres./CEO; 390 S. Seguin Ave.; P.O. Box 311417; 78131; Comal; P 150,000; M 2,300; (830) 625-2385; (800) 572-2626; Fax (830) 625-7918; michael@innewbraunfels.com; www.innewbraunfels.com*

New Caney • *Greater East Montgomery County Chamber* • Rick Hatcher; Pres.; 21575 U.S. Hwy. 59 N., Ste. 100; 77357; Montgomery; P 74,000; M 440; (281) 354-0051; Fax (281) 354-0091; bobbi@gemcchamber.com; www.gemcchamber.com*

Newton • *Newton County C/C* • P.O. Box 66; 75966; Newton; P 15,000; M 100; (409) 379-5527; newtonchamber@hotmail.com; www.newton-texas.com

Nocona • *Nocona C/C* • Joni Coursey; Exec. Dir.; 1522 E. Hwy. 82; P.O. Box 27; 76255; Montague; P 8,000; M 120; (940) 825-3526; Fax (940) 825-5389; info@noconachamber.org; www.nocona.org*

Normangee • *Normangee Area C/C* • P.O. Box 436; 77871; Leon; P 690; M 30; (936) 396-1320; (936) 396-3691

North Richland Hills • *see Haltom City*

Northlake • *see Roanoke*

Northline • *see Houston-Houston Intercontinental C/C*

Odessa • *Odessa C/C* • Mike George; Pres./CEO; 700 N. Grant, Ste. 200; P.O. Box 3626; 79760; Ector; P 137,130; M 1,000; (432) 332-9111; Fax (432) 333-7858; comspec@odessachamber.com; www.odessachamber.com*

Olney • *Olney C/C* • Stacy Wade; Dir.; 108 E. Main St.; 76374; Young; P 3,000; M 110; (940) 564-5445; Fax (940) 564-3610; chamber@brazosnet.com; www.olneychamberofcommerce.com

Olton • *Olton C/C & Ag.* • Teresa Perez; Mgr.; 518 8th St.; P.O. Box 487; 79064; Lamb; P 2,215; M 49; (806) 285-2292; occa@oltonchamber.org; www.oltonchamber.org

Omaha • *Omaha C/C* • Cheryl Durrett; P.O. Box 816; 75571; Morris; P 1,021; M 50; (903) 884-3080; omahatxcc@gmail.com; omahatexas.org

Onalaska • *see Livingston*

Orange • *Greater Orange Area C/C* • Ida Schossow; Pres./CEO; 1012 Green Ave.; 77630; Orange; P 52,000; M 482; (409) 883-3536; Fax (409) 886-3247; thechamber@orangetexaschamber.org; www.orangetexaschamber.org*

Overton • *Overton-New London Area C/C* • Bobbie Guinn; Pres.; 121 E. Henderson St.; P.O. Box 6; 75684; Rusk & Smith; P 2,105; M 95; (903) 834-3542; Fax (903) 834-3063; onlchamber@gmail.com; www.onlchamber.com

Ozona • *Ozona C/C & Visitor Center* • Shanon Biggerstaff CTE; Pres; 505 15th St.; P.O. Box 1135; 76943; Crockett; P 4,000; M 200; (325) 392-3737; Fax (325) 392-3485; oztxcoc@aol.com; www.ozona.com*

Paducah • *Paducah C/C* • Ronnie Manley; P.O. Box 863; 79248; Cottle; P 1,500; M 57; (806) 492-2044; (806) 492-2167; info@paducahtx.com; www.paducahtx.com

Palacios • *Palacios C/C* • Patsy Gibson; Exec. Dir.; 420 Main St.; 77465; Matagorda; P 5,000; M 130; (361) 972-2615; (800) 611-4567; Fax (361) 972-9980; palcoc@warpspeed1.net; www.palacioschamber.com

Palestine • *Palestine Area C/C* • Marc C. Mitchell; Exec. Dir.; 401 W. Main St.; P.O. Box 1177; 75802; Anderson; P 55,000; M 460; (903) 729-6066; Fax (903) 729-2083; info@palestinechamber.org; www.palestinechamber.org*

Pampa • *Pampa C/C* • Pat Montoya; Exec. Dir.; 200 N. Ballard; 79065; Gray; P 19,000; M 320; (806) 669-3241; Fax (806) 669-3244; admin@pampachamber.com; www.pampachamber.com*

Panhandle • *Panhandle C/C* • Tammy Wendel; Pres.; P.O. Box 1021; 79068; Carson; P 2,400; M 74; (806) 537-4325; (806) 537-3517; www.panhandletx.govoffice2.com

Paris • *Lamar County C/C* • Ken Higdon; Pres./CEO; 8 W. Plaza; 75460; Lamar; P 63,000; M 512; (903) 784-2501; (800) PARIS-TX; Fax (903) 784-2158; ken@paristexas.com; www.paristexas.com*

Pasadena • *also see Houston-Clear Lake Area C/C*

Pasadena • *Pasadena C/C* • Cristina Womack; Pres./CEO; 4334 Fairmont Pkwy.; 77504; Harris; P 160,000; M 650; (281) 487-7871; Fax (281) 487-5530; info@pasadenachamber.org; www.pasadenachamber.org*

Pattison • *West I-10 C/C* • Corinne Vahalik; Pres.; 907 Bains St.; P.O. Box 100; 77466; Waller; P 5,000; M 100; (281) 375-8100; Fax (281) 934-2012; chamber@westi10chamber.org; www.westi10chamber.org*

Pearland • *Pearland C/C* • Carol Artz-Bucek CCE IOM; Pres./CEO; 6117 Broadway; 77581; Brazoria; P 242,240; M 750; (281) 485-3634; (281) 485-5983; Fax (281) 485-2420; cheryl.kepp@pearlandtexaschamber.us; www.pearlandtexaschamber.us*

Pearsall • *Pearsall C/C* • Janie Elizondo; 317 S. Oak St.; 78061; Frio; P 7,864; M 51; (830) 334-9414; info@pearsalltexas.com; www.pearsalltexas.com

Pecos • *Pecos Area C/C & CVB* • Ms. Lupe Davis; Exec. Dir.; 100 E. Dot Stafford St.; P.O. Box 27; 79772; Reeves; P 9,501; M 147; (432) 445-2406; Fax (432) 445-2407; infopecostx@gmail.com; www.pecostx.com

Perryton • *Perryton-Ochiltree C/C* • Marilyn Reiswig IOM; Pres.; 2000 S. Main; P.O. Drawer 789; 79070; Ochiltree; P 10,000; M 400; (806) 435-6575; Fax (806) 435-9821; pococ@ptsi.net; www.perryton.org*

Pflugerville • *Pflugerville C/C* • Patricia Gervan-Brown IOM; Pres./CEO; 101 S. 3rd St.; P.O. Box 483; 78691; Travis; P 70,000; M 500; (512) 251-7799; Fax (512) 251-7802; gpcc@sbcglobal.net; www.pfchamber.com*

Pilot Point • *Pilot Point C/C* • Michele L. Walling; Exec. Dir.; 300 S. Washington; P.O. Box 497; 76258; Denton; P 5,100; M 150; (940) 686-5385; (940) 597-2922; Fax (940) 686-5385; chamber@pilotpoint.org; www.pilotpoint.org

Pittsburg • *Pittsburg/Camp County C/C* • Allen Weatherford; Exec Dir.; 202 Jefferson St.; 75686; Camp; P 15,000; M 200; (903) 856-3442; Fax (903) 856-3570; info@pittsburgchamber.com; www.pittsburgchamber.com*

Plains • *Plains C/C* • Terry Howard; Pres.; P.O. Box 364; 79355; Yoakum; P 1,480; M 20; (806) 456-2288; www.plainstx.com

Plainview • *Plainview C/C* • Linda Morris; Exec. Dir.; 1906 W. 5th St.; 79072; Hale; P 21,400; M 350; (806) 296-7431; Fax (806) 296-0819; info@plainviewtexaschamber.com; www.plainviewtexaschamber.com

Plano • *Plano C/C* • Jamee Jolly; Pres./CEO; 5400 Independence Pkwy., Ste. 200; 75023; Collin; P 271,200; M 1,100; (972) 424-7547; Fax (972) 422-5182; info@planochamber.org; www.planochamber.org*

Pleasanton • *Pleasanton C/C* • Cindy Mumm; Exec. Dir.; 605 Second St.; 78064; Atascosa; P 9,500; M 180; (830) 569-2163; Fax (830) 569-8539; pleasantoncofc@att.net; www.pleasantoncofc.com

Point • *see West Tawakoni*

Port Aransas • *Port Aransas C/C* • Ann B. Vaughan; Pres./CEO; 403 W. Cotter; 78373; Nueces; P 3,480; M 373; (361) 749-5919; Fax (361) 749-4672; info@portaransas.org; www.portaransas.org

Port Arthur • *Greater Port Arthur C/C* • Bill McCoy; Pres.; 501 Procter St., Ste. 300; 77642; Jefferson; P 55,000; M 600; (409) 963-1107; portarthurchamber@portarthurtexas.com; www.portarthurtexas.com*

Port Isabel • *Port Isabel C/C* • Betty Wells; Pres.; 421 E. Queen Isabella Blvd.; 78578; Cameron; P 5,100; M 237; (956) 943-2262; (800) 527-6102; Fax (956) 943-4001; director@portisabel.org; www.portisabelchamber.com*

Port Lavaca • *Port Lavaca C/C* • Tina Crow; Exec. Dir.; 2300 Hwy. 35 N.; 77979; Calhoun; P 20,000; M 250; (361) 552-2959; (361) 552-1234; Fax (361) 552-1288; tina@portlavacatx.org; www.portlavacatx.org*

Port Mansfield • *Port Mansfield C/C* • Christine Simmons; Mgr.; 101 E. Port Dr.; 818 Mansfield Dr., Unit 75; 78598; Willacy; P 400; M 160; (956) 944-2354; Fax (956) 944-2515; pmft@granderiver.net; www.portmansfieldchamber.org

Port Neches • *Port Neches C/C* • Debbie Plaia; Exec. Dir.; 1110 Port Neches Ave.; P.O. Box 445; 77651; Jefferson; P 15,000; M 240; (409) 722-9154; Fax (409) 722-7380; pncoc@swbell.net; www.portnecheschamber.com*

Port O'Connor • *Port O'Connor C/C* • Leah Griffin; Pres.; 207 Trevor St.; P.O. Box 701; 77982; Calhoun; P 1,200; M 150; (361) 983-2898; Fax (361) 983-2898; poccc@tisd.net; www.portoconnorchamber.org

Portland • *Portland C/C* • Colette Walls; Pres./CEO; 904-B Memorial Pkwy.; P.O. Box 388; 78374; Nueces & San Patricio; P 19,000; M 300; (361) 643-2475; Fax (361) 643-7377; director@portlandtx.org; www.portlandtx.org*

Post • *Post Area C/C* • Janice Plummer; Mgr.; 1 Santa Fe Plz.; P.O. Box 610; 79356; Garza; P 6,000; M 100; (806) 495-3461; Fax (806) 495-0414; chamberofcommerce@postcitytexas.com; www.postcitytexas.com

Poteet • *Poteet C/C* • Diana Martinez; Pres.; 9199 N.S. Hwy. 16; P.O. Box 577; 78065; Atascosa; P 1,000; M 20; (830) 742-8144; (888) 742-8144; Fax (830) 742-3608; mdiana@yahoo.com

Pottsboro • *Pottsboro Area C/C* • Rosemary Hall; Mgr.; 615 Hwy. 120 E.; P.O. Box 995; 75076; Grayson; P 10,000; M 300; (903) 786-6371; Fax (903) 786-4965; info@pottsborochamber.com; pottsborochamber.com*

Prairie View • *Prairie View C/C* • George E. Higgs; Pres.; 224 University Dr.; P.O. Box 847; 77446; Waller; P 6,000; M 12; (936) 857-3226; prairieviewchamberofcommerce@gmail.com; prairieviewtexas.gov

Princeton • *Princeton Area C/C* • Kayla Anderson; Exec. Admin.; 275 W. Princeton Dr., Ste. 105; 75407; Collin; P 8,000; M 67; (972) 736-6462; Fax (972) 734-5276; info@princetontxchamber.com; www.princetontxchamber.com

Prosper • *Prosper C/C* • Susan Lane; Dir.; 100 N. Preston Rd.; P.O. Box 432; 75078; Collin & Denton; P 14,000; M 200; (972) 508-4200; director@prosperchamber.com; www.prosperchamber.com

Quanah • *Quanah C/C* • Bertha Woods; Dir.; 220 S. Main; P.O. Box 158; 79252; Hardeman; P 4,200; M 115; (940) 663-2222; Fax (940) 663-2222; quanahcoc@cebridge.net; *

Quinlan • *see West Tawakoni*

Quitaque • *Quitaque C/C* • Jack Johnson; Pres.; P.O. Box 487; 79255; Briscoe; P 411; M 5; (806) 455-1225; Fax (806) 455-1225; chamber@quitaque.org; www.quitaque.org

Quitman • *Greater Quitman Area C/C* • Sam Scroggins; Exec. Dir.; 100 Gov. Hogg Pkwy.; P.O. Box 426; 75783; Wood; P 1,809; M 100; (903) 763-4411; Fax ; qtmncoc@peoplescom.net; www.quitmancoc.com

Ralls • *Ralls C/C & Ag.* • Giselle Brock; Mgr.; 808 Ave. I; 79357; Crosby; P 2,500; M 30; (806) 253-2342; rallscofc@esc17.net; rallschamberofcommerce.com

Raymondville • *Raymondville C/C* • Elma Chavez; Mgr.; 700 FM 3168; P.O. Box 746; 78580; Willacy; P 20,000; M 175; (956) 689-1864; (888) 603-6994; Fax (956) 689-1863; chamber@granderiver.net; www.raymondvillechamber.com*

Red Oak • *Red Oak Area C/C* • Shelley Martinez IOM; Pres.; P.O. Box 2098; 75154; Ellis; P 12,000; M 165; (972) 617-0906; Fax (972) 576-3737; admin@redoakareachamber.org; www.redoakareachamber.com*

Refugio • *Refugio County C/C* • Jennifer Downen; Ofc. Mgr.; 301 N. Alamo; 78377; Refugio; P 7,383; M 99; (361) 526-2835; Fax (361) 526-1289; refugiochamber@sbcglobal.net; www.refugiocountytx.org

Richardson • *Richardson C/C* • Bill Sproull; Pres./CEO; 411 Belle Grove Dr.; 75080; Dallas; P 105,000; M 800; (972) 792-2800; Fax (972) 792-2825; jgrauel@richardsonchamber.com; www.richardsonchamber.com*

Richland Hills • *see Haltom City*

Richmond • *see Rosenberg*

River Oaks • *Tri-City Area C/C* • Nicki Matthews; Pres.; P.O. Box 10005; 76114; Tarrant; P 11,100; M 101; (817) 569-9098; (817) 999-9555; mayorjack@aol.com; www.tricityareachamber.org*

Roanoke • *Northwest Metroport C/C* • Sally Michalak; Pres./CEO; 600 E. Byron Nelson Blvd., Ste. 500; P.O. Box 74; 76262; Denton & Tarrant; P 18,000; M 300; (817) 837-1000; Fax (817) 837-1002; sally@nwmetroportchamber.org; www.nwmetroportchamber.org*

Robstown • *Robstown Area Dev. Comm.* • Josie Segura; Admin. Asst.; 1150 E. Main Ave.; P.O. Box 111; 78380; Nueces; P 14,000; M 100; (361) 387-3933; Fax (361) 387-7280; josie@robstownadc.com; www.robstownadc.com

Rockdale • *Rockdale C/C* • Deedra Jacob; Pres.; 1203 W. Cameron Ave.; 76567; Milam; P 5,595; M 290; (512) 446-2030; Fax (512) 446-5969; info@rockdalechamber.com; www.rockdalechamber.com*

Rockport • *Rockport-Fulton C/C* • Diane Probst IOM CCE; Pres./CEO; 319 Broadway; 78382; Aransas; P 24,000; M 720; (361) 729-6445; (800) 242-0071; Fax (361) 729-7681; president@1rockport.org; www.rockport-fulton.org*

Rocksprings • *Edwards County C/C* • Steve Haynes; P.O. Box 267; 78880; Edwards; P 2,000; M 100; (830) 683-6466; Fax (830) 683-3182; info@rockspringstexas.net

Rockwall • *Rockwall Area C/C* • Dana K. Macalik; Pres.; 697 E. I-30; 3021 Ridge Rd. #63; 75032; Rockwall; P 85,245; M 848; (972) 771-5733; dana@rockwallchamber.org; www.rockwallchamber.org*

Rosebud • *Rosebud C/C & Ag.* • Royce Spivey; Pres.; 402 W. Main; P.O. Box 369; 76570; Falls; P 1,500; M 100; (254) 583-7979; Fax (254) 583-2157; roycespivey@volornet.com; www.rosebudtx.org

Rosenberg • *Central Fort Bend Chamber Alliance* • Regina Morales; Pres./CEO; 4120 Ave. H; 77471; Fort Bend; P 250,000; M 800; (281) 342-5464; Fax (281) 342-2990; aschultz@cfbca.org; www.cfbca.org*

Round Rock • *Round Rock C/C* • Mike Odom; Pres./CEO; 212 E. Main St.; 78664; Travis & Williamson; P 150,000; M 1,250; (512) 255-5805; Fax (512) 255-3345; info@roundrockchamber.org; www.roundrockchamber.org*

Round Top • *Round Top Area C/C* • Laura Lee; Dir.; 110 Schumann Ln.; P.O. Box 216; 78954; Fayette; P 90; M 250; (979) 249-4042; Fax (979) 249-2085; info@roundtop.org; www.roundtop.org

Rowlett • *Rowlett C/C* • Diane Lemmons; Pres.; 4418 Main St.; 75088; Dallas & Rockwall; P 55,000; M 400; (972) 475-3200; diane@rowlettchamber.com; www.rowlettchamber.com*

Royse City • *Royse City C/C* • Julia Bryant; Exec. Dir.; 216 N. Arch St., Ste. A; P.O. Box 547; 75189; Rockwall; P 10,000; M 225; (972) 636-5000; Fax (972) 636-0051; info@roysecitychamber.com; www.roysecitychamber.com

Rule • *Rule C/C* • Orheana Greeson; Secy.; 701 Union Ave.; P.O. Box 58; 79547; Haskell; P 636; M 15; (940) 997-2141; (940) 997-2214

Runge • *Runge C/C* • Gloria Zapata; Pres.; P.O. Box 646; 78151; Karnes; P 1,000; M 36; (830) 200-8927; rungechamber@gmail.com; www.rungechamber.com

Rusk • *Rusk C/C* • Bob Goldsberry; Exec. Dir.; 184 S. Main St.; P.O. Box 67; 75785; Cherokee; P 5,325; M 200; (903) 683-4242; (800) 933-2381; Fax (903) 683-1054; cbrown@ruskchamber.com; www.ruskchamber.com

Sabinal • *Sabinal C/C* • P.O. Box 55; 78881; Uvalde; P 1,800; M 20; (830) 988-2010; sab@sabinalchamber.com; www.sabinalchamber.com

Sachse • *Sachse C/C* • Molly Hall; Pres.; 5560 Hwy. 78; 75048; Collin & Dallas; P 20,000; M 215; (972) 496-1212; info@sachsechamber.com; www.sachsechamber.com*

Saginaw • *Saginaw Area C/C* • Joyce Erwin; Exec. Dir.; 301 S. Saginaw Blvd.; 76179; Tarrant; P 100,000; M 320; (817) 232-0500; Fax (817) 232-2311; chamber@saginawtxchamber.org; www.saginawtxchamber.org*

Saint Jo • *Saint Jo C/C* • Maurine Cain; Pres.; 108 S. Broad St.; P.O. Box 130; 76265; Montague; P 1,000; M 40; (940) 995-2188; stjo@saintjochamber.com; www.saintjochamber.com

Salado • *Salado C/C* • Nicole Stairs; Pres.; 831 N. Main St.; P.O. Box 849; 76571; Bell; P 3,500; M 230; (254) 947-5040; Fax (254) 947-8388; chamber@salado.com; www.salado.com*

San Angelo • *San Angelo C/C* • Dan Koenig; Pres.; 418 W. Ave. B; 76903; Tom Green; P 100,000; M 1,200; (325) 655-4136; Fax (325) 658-1110; chamber@sanangelo.org; www.sanangelo.org*

San Antonio Area

***Alamo City Black C/C* •** Wayne Terry; Chrmn.; 126 Gonzales, Ste. 200; 78205; Bexar; P 1,000,000; M 375; (210) 226-9055; Fax (210) 226-0524; info@alamocitychamber.org; www.alamocitychamber.org

***Greater San Antonio C/C* •** Richard Perez; Pres.; 602 E. Commerce; 78205; Bexar; P 1,349,000; M 1,800; (210) 229-2100; Fax (210) 229-1600; info@sachamber.org; www.sachamber.org*

***North San Antonio C/C* •** E. Duane Wilson; Pres./CEO; 12930 Country Pkwy.; 78216; Bexar; P 1,500,000; M 1,300; (210) 344-4848; Fax (210) 525-8207; mwhite@northsachamber.com; www.northsachamber.com*

***San Antonio Hispanic C/C* •** Ramiro A. Cavazos; Pres./CEO; 200 E. Grayson, Ste. 203; 78212; Bexar; M 1,600; (210) 225-0462; Fax (210) 225-2485; jessicac@.sahcc.org; www.sahcc.org*

***South San Antonio C/C* •** Al Arreola; Pres./CEO; 7902 Challenger Dr.; 78235; Bexar; P 500,000; M 700; (210) 533-1600; Fax (210) 533-1611; events@southsachamber.com; www.southsachamber.org

San Augustine • *San Augustine County C/C* • Kelly Camp; Exec. Dir.; 611 W. Columbia St.; 75972; San Augustine; P 9,000; M 225; (936) 275-3610; Fax (936) 288-0380; sacc611@sbcglobal.net; www.sanaugustinetx.com*

San Benito • *San Benito C/C* • Zeke Padilla; Pres.; 400 N. Travis; 78586; Cameron; P 28,600; M 200; (956) 361-3800; Fax (956) 361-3810; zpadilla@cityofsanbenito.com; www.cityofsanbenito.com*

San Leon • *see Dickinson*

San Marcos • *San Marcos Area C/C* • Brian Bondy IOM; Pres.; 202 N. C.M. Allen Pkwy.; 78666; Hays; P 50,001; M 750; (512) 393-5900; Fax (512) 393-5912; chamber@sanmarcostexas.com; www.sanmarcostexas.com*

San Saba • *San Saba County C/C* • Dora Miller; Pres.; 120 S. Cherokee St.; P.O. Box 484; 76877; San Saba; P 3,000; M 160; (325) 372-5141; Fax (325) 372-4574; executive.director@sansabachamber.com; www.sansabachamber.com

Sanderson • *Sanderson C/C* • Lea Hawn; P.O. Box 734; 79848; Terrell; P 700; M 31; (432) 345-2509; Fax (432) 345-2509; chamber@sandersonchamberofcommerce.info; www.sandersonchamberofcommerce.info

Sanger • *Sanger Area C/C* • Debbie Reaves; Admin.; 300 Bolivar St.; P.O. Box 537; 76266; Denton; P 7,400; M 112; (940) 458-7702; sangerchamber@embarqmail.com; www.sangertexas.com

Sansom Park • *see River Oaks*

Santa Anna • *Santa Anna C/C* • P.O. Box 62; 76878; Coleman; P 1,000; M 35; (325) 348-3535; www.santaannatex.org

Santa Fe • *Santa Fe C/C Inc.* • Gina Bouvier; Pres.; 12425 Hwy. 6, Ste. 1; 77510; Galveston; P 12,000; M 286; (409) 925-8558; Fax (409) 925-8551; sfchamber@comcast.net; www.santafetexaschamber.com*

Schertz • *The Chamber* • Maggie Titterington; Pres.; 1730 Schertz Pkwy.; 78154; Bexar, Comal & Guadalupe,; P 73,000; M 430; (210) 619-1950; Fax (210) 619-1959; admin@schertzchamber.org; www.thechamber.info

Schulenburg • *Greater Schulenburg C/C* • Marcia Hrncir; Exec. Dir.; 618 N. Main St.; P.O. Box 65; 78956; Fayette; P 2,852; M 165; (979) 743-4514; (866) 504-5294; Fax (979) 743-9155; schulenburgchamber@cvctx.com; www.schulenburgchamber.org

Sea Brook • *see Houston-Clear Lake Area C/C*

Seadrift • *Seadrift C/C* • Jason Jones; Pres.; P.O. Box 3; 77983; Calhoun; P 1,352; M 60; (361) 237-0406; Fax (361) 785-2162; jason@seadriftchamber.com; www.seadriftchamber.com

Seagoville • *Seagoville C/C* • Phil Greenawalt; Exec. Dir.; 107 Hall Rd.; 75159; Dallas; P 12,600; M 195; (972) 287-5184; Fax (972) 287-5815; seagovillechamber@sbcglobal.net; www.seagovillecoc.org

Sealy • *Sealy C/C* • Lou Cox; Pres.; 309 Main St.; P.O. Box 586; 77474; Austin; P 6,000; M 300; (979) 885-3222; Fax (979) 885-7184; sealycoc@sbcglobal.net; www.sealychamber.com*

Seguin • *Seguin Area C/C* • Kendy Gravett; Pres.; 116 N. Camp St.; 78155; Guadalupe; P 30,000; M 650; (830) 379-6382; Fax (830) 379-6971; cofc@seguinchamber.com; www.seguinchamber.com*

Selma • *see Schertz*

Seminole • *Seminole Area C/C* • Shelby Concotelli; Pres./CEO; 119 S.E. Ave. B; P.O. Box 1198; 79360; Gaines; P 7,000; M 300; (432) 758-2352; Fax (432) 758-6698; president@seminoletxchamber.org; www.seminoletxchamber.org*

Seven Points • *see Mabank*

Seymour • *Seymour C/C* • Myra Busby; Exec. Dir.; 301 N. Washington; P.O. Box 1379; 76380; Baylor; P 2,900; M 80; (940) 889-2921; Fax (940) 889-8882; scoc@nts-online.net; www.seymourtxchamber.org

Shamrock • *Shamrock C/C* • David Rushing; Dir.; 105 E. 12th St.; 79079; Wheeler; P 2,000; M 65; (806) 256-2501; Fax (806) 256-2224; irishedb@hotmail.com; www.shamrocktx.net

Sheffield • *see Iraan*

Shepherd • *Greater Shepherd C/C* • Kay Martin; Exec. Dir.; 12231 W. Hwy. 150; P.O. Box 520; 77371; San Jacinto; P 3,000; M 45; (936) 628-3890; Fax (936) 628-3890; info@greatershepherdchamberofcommerce.org; www.greatershepherdchamberofcommerce.org

Sherman • *Sherman C/C* • Eddie Brown; Pres./CEO; 307 W. Washington St., Ste. 100; P.O. Box 1029; 75091; Grayson; P 40; M 550; (903) 893-1184; Fax (903) 893-4266; ebrown@shermanchamber.us; www.shermanchamber.us*

Shiner • *Shiner C/C* • Jeff Pesek; Pres.; P.O. Box 221; 77984; Lavaca; P 2,000; M 200; (361) 594-4180; shinerchamber@sbcglobal.net; www.shinertx.com

Silsbee • *Silsbee C/C* • Jim Willis; Exec. Dir.; 545 N. 5th St.; 77656; Hardin; P 10,000; M 350; (409) 385-5562; Fax (409) 385-5695; jim@silsbeechamber.com; www.silsbeechamber.com

Sinton • *Sinton C/C* • Anna Franklin; Dir.; 218 W. Sinton St.; 78387; San Patricio; P 7,000; M 100; (361) 364-2307; Fax (361) 364-3538; sintonchamber@sbcglobal.net; www.sintontexas.org

Slaton • *Slaton C/C* • Leslie Robinson; Ofc. Mgr.; 200 W. Garza St.; P.O. Box 400; 79364; Lubbock; P 6,200; M 80; (806) 828-6238; slatoncoc@sbcglobal.net; www.slatonchamberofcommerce.org

Smithville • *Smithville Area C/C* • Tina Smith; Pres.; 100 N.W. First St.; P.O. Box 716; 78957; Bastrop; P 5,000; M 360; (512) 237-2313; Fax (512) 237-2605; chamber@smithvilletx.org; www.smithvilletx.org

Snyder • *Snyder C/C* • Sandra Salinas; Interim Exec. Dir.; 2302 Ave. R; P.O. Box 840; 79550; Scurry; P 17,424; M 295; (325) 573-3558; Fax (325) 573-9721; events@snyderchamber.org; www.snyderchamber.org*

Somerville • *Burleson County C/C-Somerville Office* • Barbara Bray; Ofc. Mgr.; 131 7th St.; P.O. Box 596; 77879; Burleson; P 18,000; M 276; (979) 596-2383; Fax (979) 567-0818; info@burlesoncountytx.com; www.burlesoncountytx.com*

Sonora • *Sonora C/C* • Donna Garrett; Exec. Dir.; 205 Hwy. 277 N., Ste. B; P.O. Box 1172; 76950; Sutton; P 4,000; M 250; (325) 387-2880; (888) 387-2880; Fax (325) 387-5357; chamber@sonoratexas.org; www.sonoratexas.org

South Houston • *South Houston C/C* • JoAnn Parish; CEO; 58 Spencer Hwy.; 77587; Harris; P 17,000; M 200; (713) 943-0244; Fax (713) 943-3978; sohochamber@sbcglobal.net; www.southhoustonchamber.org

South Padre Island • *South Padre Island C/C* • Roxanne Guenzel; Pres.; 600 Padre Blvd.; 78597; Cameron; P 5,000; M 500; (956) 761-4412; Fax (956) 761-2739; info@spichamber.com; www.spichamber.com*

Southlake • *Southlake C/C* • Mark Guilbert; Pres./CEO; 1501 Corporate Circle, Ste. 100; 76092; Denton & Tarrant; P 28,000; M 600; (817) 481-8200; Fax (817) 749-8202; info@southlakechamber.com; www.southlakechamber.com*

Spearman • *Spearman C/C & Eco. Dev.* • 211 Main St.; P.O. Box 161; 79081; Hansford; P 3,370; M 150; (806) 659-5555; spearcc@hotmail.com; www.spearman.org

Spring Branch • *see Bulverde*

Springtown • *Springtown Area C/C* • Amy Walker; Exec. Dir.; 112 S. Main St.; P.O. Box 296; 76082; Parker; P 2,700; M 350; (817) 220-7828; (817) 220-7820; Fax (817) 523-3268; director@springtownchamber.org; www.springtownchamber.org*

Spur • *Spur Area C/C* • Joan Day; Secy.; P.O. Box 103; 79370; Dickens; P 1,093; M 48; (806) 271-3363; info@spurchamber.com; www.spurchamber.com

Stamford • *Stamford C/C* • Carolyn Smith; Exec. Dir.; 107 E. McHarg St.; 79553; Haskell & Jones; P 3,200; M 90; (325) 773-2411; Fax (325) 773-2851; chamber@stamfordcoc.org; www.stamfordcoc.org

Stanton • *Martin County C/C* • Heather Simpson; Dir.; 209 N. St. Peter; P.O. Box 615; 79782; Martin; P 4,800; M 100; (432) 756-3386; martincountychamber@msn.com; www.stantontex.com

Stephenville • *Stephenville C/C* • July Danley; Pres./CEO; 187 W. Washington St.; P.O. Box 306; 76401; Erath; P 17,000; M 600; (254) 965-5313; Fax (254) 965-3814; info@stephenvilletexas.org; www.stephenvilletexas.org*

Stockdale • *Stockdale C/C* • P.O. Box 446; 78160; Wilson; P 1,442; M 70; (830) 996-3128; www.stockdaletx.org

Stonewall • *Stonewall C/C* • Heather McCarver; Admin. Dir.; P.O. Box 1; 78671; Gillespie; P 330; M 100; (830) 644-2735; stonewallchamber@gmail.com; www.stonewalltexas.com

Sugar Land • *Fort Bend C/C* • Keri Schmidt; Pres./CEO; 445 Commerce Green Blvd.; 77478; Fort Bend; P 510,000; M 1,300; (281) 491-0800; Fax (281) 491-0112; keri@fortbendcc.org; www.fortbendchamber.com

Sulphur Springs • *Hopkins County C/C* • Lezley Brown; Pres./CEO; 300 W. Connally St.; P.O. Box 347; 75483; Hopkins; P 40,000; M 600; (903) 885-6515; Fax (903) 885-6516; WeTheChamber@gmail.com; www.sulphursprings-tx.com*

Sweeny • *Sweeny C/C* • Michelle Gonzalez; Exec. Dir.; 111 W. 3rd St.; 77480; Brazoria; P 3,900; M 130; (979) 548-3249; Fax (979) 548-3251; sweenychamber@windstream.net; www.sweenychamber.org

Sweetwater • *Sweetwater C/C* • Jacque McCoy; Exec. V.P.; 810 E. Broadway Ave.; P.O. Box 1148; 79556; Nolan; P 11,500; M 270; (325) 235-5488; (800) 658-6757; Fax (325) 235-1026; jacque@sweetwatertexas.org; www.sweetwatertexas.org*

Taft • *Taft C/C* • Mary Griffin; Exec. Dir.; 501 Green Ave.; P.O. Box 123; 78390; San Patricio; P 5,117; M 48; (361) 528-3230; Fax (361) 528-3515; mgriffin@cityoftaft.net; *

Taylor • *Greater Taylor C/C & Visitor Center* • Tia Rae Stone; Pres./CEO; 1519 N. Main St.; 76574; Williamson; P 16,500; M 360; (512) 352-6364; (512) 365-8485; Fax (512) 352-6366; info@taylorchamber.org; www.taylorchamber.org*

Taylor Lake Village • *see Houston-Clear Lake Area C/C*

Teague • *Teague C/C* • Rhonda Jones; Pres.; 316 Main St.; P.O. Box 484; 75860; Freestone; P 4,000; M 85; (254) 739-2061; Fax (254) 739-2061; teaguechamberofcommerce@gmail.com; www.teaguechamberofcommerce@gmail.com

Temple • *Temple C/C* • G. Roderick Henry CCE IOM; Pres./CEO; 2 N. 5th St.; P.O. Box 158; 76503; Bell; P 200,000; M 900; (254) 773-2105; Fax (254) 773-0661; temple@templetx.org; www.templetx.org*

Terrell • *Terrell C/C & CVB* • Carlton Tidwell; Pres.; 1314 W. Moore Ave.; P.O. Box 97; 75160; Kaufman; P 18,500; M 565; (972) 563-5703; (972) 524-5703; Fax (972) 563-2363; angie@terrelltexas.com; www.terrelltexas.com*

Texarkana • *Texarkana C/C* • Bill Cork; Pres./CEO; 819 N. State Line Ave.; P.O. Box 1468; 75504; Bowie; P 62,000; M 1,400; (903) 792-7191; Fax (903) 793-4304; chamber@texarkana.org; www.texarkana.org*

Texas City • *Texas City-La Marque C/C* • Jenny Senter; Pres.; 9702 Emmett F. Lowry Expy.; P.O. Box 1717; 77591; Galveston; P 46,300; M 800; (409) 935-1408; Fax (409) 316-0901; leanne@texascitychamber.com; www.texascitychamber.com*

The Colony • *The Colony C/C* • Scott Carpenter; Pres.; 4730 S.H. 121; P.O. Box 560006; 75056; Denton; P 40,000; M 300; (214) 705-3075; info@thecolonychamber.org; www.thecolonychamber.com*

The Woodlands • *The Woodlands Area C/C* • J.J. Hollie; Pres./CEO; 9320 Lakeside Blvd., Ste. 200; 77381; Montgomery; P 107,769; M 2,400; (281) 367-5777; Fax (281) 292-1655; jamie.sims@woodlandschamber.org; www.woodlandschamber.org*

Thorndale • *Thorndale Area C/C* • Brian Morton; Pres.; P.O. Box 668; 76577; Milam & Williamson; P 1,278; M 79; (512) 898-2121; (512) 898-2523; admin@txchamber.org; www.thorndaletx.com

Three Rivers • *Three Rivers C/C* • Virginia Herring; Exec. Dir.; 105 N. Harborth; P.O. Box 1648; 78071; Live Oak; P 1,848; M 100; (361) 786-4330; trchamber@threeriverstx.org; www.threeriverstx.org

Throckmorton • *Throckmorton County C/C & Ag.* • Brad Bellah; Pres.; P.O. Box 711; 76483; Throckmorton; P 1,650; M 40; (940) 849-4411; throckchamber@yahoo.com; www.throckmortontx.org

Timpson • *Timpson C/C* • Paul Smith; Pres.; 191 Bremond St.; P.O. Box 987; 75975; Shelby; P 1,100; M 70; (936) 254-3500; timpsgen@sbcglobal.net

Tomball • *Greater Tomball Area C/C* • Bruce E. Hillegeist; Pres.; 29201 Quinn Rd., Ste. B; P.O. Box 516; 77377; Harris; P 700,000; M 900; (281) 351-7222; (866) 670-7222; Fax (281) 351-7223; admin@tomballchamber.org; www.tomballchamber.org*

Tool • *see Mabank*

Trinity • *Trinity Peninsula C/C* • Rowan Ljungdahl; 702 S. Robb; P.O. Box 549; 75862; Trinity; P 14,600; M 105; (936) 594-3856; Fax (936) 594-0558; info@trinitychamber.org; www.trinitychamber.org*

Trophy Club • *see Roanoke*

Troup • *Troup C/C* • Gene Whitsell; Exec. V.P.; P.O. Box 336; 75789; Cherokee & Smith; P 1,949; M 50; (903) 842-4113; gwhitsell@embarqmail.com; www.trouptexas.org

Tulia • *Tulia C/C* • 127 S.W. 2nd; P.O. Box 267; 79088; Swisher; P 4,900; M 150; (806) 995-2296; Fax (806) 995-4426; exec@tuliachamber.com; www.tuliachamber.com

Tyler • *Tyler Area C/C* • Henry Bell; COO; 315 N. Broadway Ave.; 75702; Smith; P 107,000; M 2,500; (903) 592-1661; Fax (903) 592-1268; hbell@tylertexas.com; www.tylertexas.com*

Tyler • *Tyler Metro C/C* • Clyde Sanders; Exec. Dir.; 2000 W. Gentry Pkwy.; P.O. Box 4362; 75712; Smith; P 205,400; M 100; (903) 593-6026; Fax (903) 747-3952; tylermetrochamber@gmail.com; www.tylermetrochamber.com

Union Valley • *see West Tawakoni*

Universal City • *Texas Tri-County C/C* • Lisa Jubela; Dir.; P.O. Box 3122; 78148; Bexar, Comal & Guadalupe; P 200,000; M 400; (210) 658-8322; director@txtricountychamber.org; www.txtricountychamber.org*

Uvalde • *Uvalde Area C/C* • Olivia Rish; Exec. Dir.; 340 N. Getty; 78801; Uvalde; P 15,000; M 400; (830) 278-3361; Fax (830) 278-3363; director@uvalde.org; www.uvalde.org*

Van • *Van Area C/C* • Victoria Tankersley; Pres.; P.O. Box 55; 75790; Van Zandt; P 2,500; M 130; (903) 963-5051; vanchamber@vantexas.com; www.vantexas.com

Van Alstyne • *Van Alstyne Area C/C* • Connie Christianson; Mgr.; 228 E. Marshall; P.O. Box 698; 75495; Collin & Grayson; P 3,800; M 150; (903) 482-6066; Fax (903) 482-9687; vachamber@gcecisp.com; www.vanalstynechamber.org

Vega • *Oldham County C/C* • P.O. Box 538; 79092; Oldham; P 2,100; M 170; (806) 267-2828; Fax (806) 267-2645; oldhamco@arn.net; www.oldhamcofc.org

Vernon • *Vernon C/C* • Donna Moore; Pres.; 1614 Main St.; P.O. Box 1538; 76385; Wilbarger; P 10,000; M 200; (940) 552-2564; (800) 687-3137; Fax (940) 552-0654; vernonchamber@sbcglobal.net; www.vernontexas.net

Victoria • *Victoria C/C* • Randy Vivian; Pres./CEO; 3404 N. Ben Wilson; P.O. Box 2465; 77902; Victoria; P 65,000; M 1,132; (361) 573-5277; Fax (361) 573-5911; info@victoriachamber.org; www.victoriachamber.org*

Vidor • *Vidor C/C* • Brandi Leatherwood; Mgr.; 18635 IH 10, Ste. 200A; 77662; Orange; P 12,714; M 275; (409) 769-6339; Fax (409) 769-0227; vidorchamber@sbcglobal.net; www.vidorchamber.com*

Waco • *Greater Waco C/C* • Matthew T. Meadors IOM; Pres./CEO; 101 S. 3rd St.; P.O. Box 1220; 76703; McLennan; P 250,000; M 1,550; (254) 757-5600; Fax (254) 752-6618; mmeadors@wacochamber.com; www.wacochamber.com*

Waco • *CenTex Hispanic C/C* • Joe Rodriguez; Exec. Dir.; 915 LaSalle Ave.; 76706; McLennan; P 112,000; M 220; (254) 754-7111; Fax (254) 754-3456; joe@wacohispanicchamber.com; www.wacohispanicchamber.com

Waller • *Waller Area C/C* • Anthony Edmonds; Pres.; 1110 Farr St.; P.O. Box 53; 77484; Waller; P 15,000; M 167; (936) 372-5300; info@wallerchamber.com; www.wallerchamber.com

Watauga • *see Haltom City*

Waxahachie • *Waxahachie C/C* • Debra Wakeland; Pres./CEO; 102 YMCA Dr.; 75165; Ellis; P 30,000; M 800; (972) 937-2390; (972) 938-9617; Fax (972) 938-9827; dwakeland@waxahachiechamber.com; www.waxahachiechamber.com*

Weatherford • *Weatherford C/C* • Timmy Gazzola; Pres.; 401 Ft. Worth Hwy.; P.O. Box 310; 76086; Parker; P 27,000; M 900; (817) 594-3801; (888) 594-3801; Fax (817) 613-9216; info@weatherford-chamber.com; www.weatherford-chamber.com*

Webster • *see Houston-Clear Lake Area C/C*

Weimar • *Weimar Area C/C* • Sheemarie Besch; Exec. Secy.; 100 W. Grange; P.O. Box 90; 78962; Colorado; P 2,200; M 128; (979) 725-9511; Fax (979) 725-6890; weimarcc@weimartx.org; www.weimartx.org

Wellington • *Collingsworth County C/C* • P.O. Box 267; 79095; Collingsworth; P 3,100; M 35; (806) 447-5848; collingsworthchamber@windstream.net; www.wellingtontx.com

Weslaco • *Rio Grande Valley Partnership C/C* • Julian Alvarez; Pres./CEO; 322 S. Missouri; P.O. Box 1499; 78599; Hidalgo; P 1,100,000; M 850; (956) 968-3141; Fax (956) 968-0210; mail@valleychamber.com; www.valleychamber.com

Weslaco • *Weslaco Area C/C* • Martha Noell; Pres./CEO; 275 S. Kansas; P.O. Box 8398; 78599; Hidalgo; P 32,000; M 550; (956) 968-2102; Fax (956) 968-6451; chamber@weslaco.com; www.weslaco.com*

West • *West C/C* • David Pareya; Pres.; 308 N. Washington St.; P.O. Box 123; 76691; McLennan; P 2,800; M 110; (254) 826-3188; Fax (254) 826-3188; westchamber@sbcglobal.net; www.westchamberofcommerce.com

West Columbia • *West Columbia C/C* • 202 E. Brazos Ave.; P.O. Box 837; 77486; Brazoria; P 4,400; M 225; (979) 345-3921; Fax (979) 345-6526; westcolumbiachamber@gmail.com; *

West Tawakoni • *Lake Tawakoni Reg. C/C* • Kym French; Exec. Dir.; 100 Hwy. 276 W.; 75474; Hunt; P 20,000; M 175; (903) 447-3020; Fax (903) 447-3820; laketawakonichamber@yahoo.com; www.laketawakonichamber.org

Westlake • *see Roanoke*

Westworth Village • *see River Oaks*

Wharton • *Wharton C/C* • Ron Sanders; Exec. Dir.; 225 N. Richmond Rd.; 77488; Wharton; P 10,200; M 350; (979) 532-1862; Fax (979) 532-0102; admin@whartonchamber.com; www.whartontexas.com*

Wheeler • *Wheeler C/C & Eco. Dev.* • Kristen Moudy; Exec. Dir.; P.O. Box 221; 79096; Wheeler; P 1,700; M 50; (806) 826-3408; Fax (806) 826-5601; chamber@wheelertexas.org; www.wheelertexas.org

White Settlement • *White Settlement Area C/C* • Roger Chambers; Chamber Mgr.; 8211 White Settlement Rd.; 76108; Tarrant; P 16,830; M 161; (817) 246-1121; Fax (817) 246-1121; wsacc@whitesettlement-tx.com; www.whitesettlement-tx.com*

Whitehouse • *Whitehouse Area C/C* • Donny Green; Pres.; P.O. Box 1041; 75791; Smith; P 7,000; M 147; (903) 541-5221; info@whitehousetx.com; www.whitehousetx.com

Whitesboro • *Whitesboro Area C/C* • Barbara Bailey; Pres.; 2535 Hwy. 82 E., Ste. C; P.O. Box 522; 76273; Grayson; P 4,100; M 300; (903) 564-3331; Fax (903) 564-3397; chamber@whitesborotx.com; www.whitesborotx.com

Whitewright • *Whitewright Area C/C* • Cathy Pierce; Secy.; 113 W. Grand St.; P.O. Box 189; 75491; Grayson; P 1,760; M 94; (903) 364-2000; Fax (903) 364-1079; chamber@whitewright.org; www.whitewright.org

Whitney • *Lake Whitney C/C* • Diana Reed; Secy.; 102 W. Railroad Ave.; P.O. Box 604; 76692; Hill; P 20,000; M 205; (254) 694-2540; Fax (254) 694-3005; bluewater@lakewhitneychamber.com; www.lakewhitneychamber.com

Wichita Falls • *Wichita Falls C/C* • Henry Florsheim IOM; CEO; 900 8th St., Ste. 218; P.O. Box 1860; 76307; Wichita; P 105,000; M 775; (940) 723-2741; Fax (940) 723-8773; henry@wichitafallschamber.com; www.wichitafallschamber.com*

Willow Park • *East Parker County C/C* • Lisa Flowers IOM; Pres.; 100 Chuck Wagon Trl.; 76087; Parker; P 30,000; M 400; (817) 441-7844; Fax (817) 441-1544; lisa@eastparkerchamber.com; www.eastparkerchamber.com*

Wills Point • *Wills Point C/C* • Jennifer Ross; Pres.; 36671 State Hwy. 64; P.O. Box 178; 75169; Van Zandt; P 3,500; M 155; (903) 873-3111; (800) WP-BLUBIRD; Fax (903) 873-2199; contact@willspointchamber.com; www.willspointchamber.com

Wimberley • *Wimberley Valley Chamber & Visitor Center* • John Kimbrew; Pres.; P.O. Box 12; 78676; Hays; P 2,600; M 490; (512) 847-2201; info@wimberley.org; www.wimberley.org*

Windcrest • *see Universal City*

Wink • *Wink C/C* • Barbara Dudley; P.O. Box 401; 79789; Winkler; P 1,000; M 8; (432) 527-3365; Fax (432) 527-3949

Winnie • *Winnie Area C/C* • Rosie Hearn; Exec. Mgr.; 327 E. LeBlanc Rd.; P.O. Box 1715; 77665; Chambers; P 7,500; M 140; (409) 296-2231; Fax (409) 296-4213; winnie@winnietexas.com; www.winnietexas.com

Winnsboro • *Winnsboro Area C/C* • Sandy Thomas; Admin.; 100 E. Broadway St.; 75494; Franklin, Hopkins & Wood; P 3,584; M 275; (903) 342-3666; (903) 342-3667; Fax (903) 342-3667; info@winnsboro.com; www.winnsboro.com

Winters • *Winters Area C/C* • Tonia Boone; P.O. Box 662; 79567; Runnels; P 2,600; M 125; (325) 754-5210; wacc@wtxs.net; www.winters-texas.us

Wolfforth • *Wolfforth Area C/C & Ag.* • Terri Robinette; Pres.; P.O. Box 35; 79382; Lubbock; P 4,000; M 75; (806) 777-8971; wolfforthchamber@gmail.com; www.wolfforthtx.us

Woodson • *see Throckmorton*

Woodville • *Tyler County C/C* • Bryan Weatherford; Pres.; 717 W. Bluff St.; 75979; Tyler; P 20,000; M 210; (409) 283-2632; Fax (409) 283-6884; info@tylercountychamber.com; www.tylercountychamber.com

Wylie • *Wylie C/C* • Mike Agnew; Pres.; 307 N. Ballard Ave.; 75098; Collin; P 46,000; M 427; (972) 442-2804; info@wyliechamber.org; www.wyliechamber.org*

Yoakum • *Yoakum Area C/C* • Bill Lopez; Pres.; 105 Huck St.; 77995; DeWitt & Lavaca; P 6,000; M 125; (361) 293-2309; info@yoakumareachamber.com; www.yoakumareachamber.com

Yorktown • *Yorktown C/C* • Melissa Armstrong; Exec. Dir.; 141 S. Riedel St.; P.O. Box 488; 78164; DeWitt; P 2,106; M 150; (361) 564-2661; Fax (361) 564-2518; 4yorktowntx@sbcglobal.net; www.yorktowntx.com

Zapata • *Zapata County C/C* • Paco Mendoza Jr.; Pres./CEO; 601 N. Hwy. 83 S.; P.O. Box 1028; 78076; Zapata; P 16,000; M 209; (956) 765-4871; (800) 292-LAKE; Fax (956) 765-5434; customercare@zapatachamber.com; www.zapatausa.com

Utah

Utah State C of C • Heidi Walker; Exec. Admin.; 175 E. Univ. Blvd. (400 S.), Ste. 600; Salt Lake City; 84111; Salt Lake; P 2,855,287; M 15,500; (801) 328-5081; Fax (801) 328-5098; hwalker@slchamber.com; utahstatechamber.org

American Fork • *American Fork C/C* • Debby Lauret; Exec. Dir.; 51 E. Main St.; 84003; Utah; P 60,000; M 240; (801) 756-5110; chamber@afcity.net; www.afchamber.org

Beaver • *Beaver Valley C/C* • Ursula Carstensen; Pres.; P.O. Box 760; 84713; Beaver; P 2,500; M 50; (435) 438-5081; (888) 848-5081; chamber@beaverutchamber.com; www.beaverutchamber.com

Bluffdale • *see Riverton*

Bountiful • *see Kaysville*

Brian Head • *Brian Head C/C* • Emily Aaron Bradley; Co-Dir.; 56 N. Hwy. 143; P.O. Box 190325; 84719; Iron; P 80; M 50; (888) 677-2810; Fax (435) 677-2154; questions@brianheadchamber.com; www.brianheadchamber.com

Brigham City • *Brigham City Area C/C* • Monica Holdaway; Exec. Dir.; 6 N. Main; P.O. Box 458; 84302; Box Elder; P 18,000; M 345; (435) 723-3931; Fax (435) 723-5761; monica@brighamchamber.com; www.brighamchamber.com*

Cedar City • *Cedar City C/C* • Chris McCormick; CEO; 510 W. 800 S.; 84720; Iron; P 30,000; M 370; (435) 586-4484; Fax (435) 586-4310; cmccormick@cedarcitychamber.org; www.cedarcitychamber.org*

Centerville • *see Kaysville*

Clearfield • *see Kaysville*

Clinton • *see Kaysville*

Delta • *Delta Area C/C* • Tammy Bunker; Ofc. Mgr.; 75 W. Main St.; 84624; Millard; P 8,000; M 105; (435) 864-4316; Fax (435) 864-4313; daccinfo@deltautahchamber.com; www.deltautahchamber.com

Draper • *Draper Area C/C* • William E. Rappleye; Pres./CEO; 1160 E. Pioneer Rd.; P.O. Box 1002; 84020; Salt Lake & Utah; P 47,000; M 470; (801) 553-0928; wrappleye@integraonline.com; www.draperchamber.com*

Farmington • *see Kaysville*

Fillmore • *Fillmore Area C/C* • Molly Stevens; Pres.; P.O. Box 164; 84631; Millard; P 2,450; M 51; (435) 743-7803; (435) 743-5233; www.fillmoreutahchamber.com

Fruit Heights • *see Kaysville*

Garden City • *Bear Lake Rendezvous C/C* • Joey Stocking; Pres.; P.O. Box 55; 84028; Rich; P 650; M 95; (435) 946-2197; info@bearlakechamber.com; www.bearlakechamber.com

Heber City • *Heber Valley C/C* • Ryan Starks; Exec. Dir.; 475 N. Main St.; 84032; Wasatch; P 25,000; M 300; (435) 654-3666; (866) 994-3237; ryanstarks@gohebervalley.com; www.gohebervalley.com

Herriman • *see Riverton*

Hurricane • *Hurricane Valley C/C* • Pat Galvez; Pres.; 63 S. 100 W.; 84737; Washington; P 14,000; M 110; (435) 635-3402; Fax (435) 635-3402; office@hvchamber.com; www.hvchamber.com*

Kanab • *Kanab Area C/C* • Jeannie Hunt; Pres.; 78 S. 100 E.; P.O. Box 534; 84741; Kane; P 5,000; M 100; (435) 644-8276; soundroom@kanab.net; www.kanabchamber.com

Kaysville • *Davis C/C* • Jim Smith; Pres./CEO; 450 S. Simmons Way, Ste. 220; 84037; Davis; P 307,700; M 830; (801) 593-2200; daviscc@davischamberofcommerce.com; www.davischamberofcommerce.com*

Kearns • *see West Valley City*

Layton • *see Kaysville*

Lehi • *Lehi Area C/C* • Donna Milakovic; Pres.; 235 E. State St.; P.O. Box 154; 84043; Utah; P 80,000; M 150; (801) 766-9657; lehichamber@gmail.com; www.lehiareachamber.org

Logan • *Cache C/C* • Sandy Emile; Pres./CEO; 160 N. Main St.; 84321; Cache; P 117,000; M 590; (435) 752-2161; info@cachechamber.com; www.cachechamber.com*

Manila • *Flaming Gorge Area C/C* • P.O. Box 122; 84046; Daggett; P 1,000; M 42; (435) 277-0709; flaminggorge@live.com; www.flaminggorgecountry.com

Moab • *Moab Area C/C* • Kammy Wells; Exec. Dir.; 217 E. Center St., Ste. 250; 84532; Grand; P 9,000; M 250; (435) 259-7814; Fax (435) 259-8519; moabchamber@frontiernet.net; www.moabchamber.com

Monticello • *Monticello C/C* • Barbara Ford; Exec. Asst.; P.O. Box 217; 84535; San Juan; P 2,000; M 50; (435) 587-2992; bford1@frontiernet.net; www.monticelloutahchamber.com

Murray • *Murray Area C/C* • Scott Baker; Pres./CEO; 5250 S. Commerce Dr., Ste. 180; 84107; Salt Lake; P 48,000; M 300; (801) 263-2632; Fax (801) 263-8262; scott@murraychamber.net; www.murraychamber.org

Nephi • *Nephi City C/C* • Jamie John; Pres.; P.O. Box 219; 84648; Juab; P 5,000; M 60; (435) 623-1428; (800) 295-1784; nephichamber@gmail.com; nephichamberofcommerce.com

North Salt Lake • *see Kaysville*

Ogden • *Ogden/Weber C/C* • Chuck Leonhardt; Pres./CEO; 2380 Washington Blvd., Ste. 290; 84401; Weber; P 232,000; M 600; (801) 621-8300; (801) 814-3283; chamber@ogdenweberchamber.com; www.ogdenweberchamber.com*

Orem • *see Provo*

Park City • *Park City C/C* • William Malone; Pres./CEO; 1910 Prospector Ave., Ste. 103; P.O. Box 1630; 84060; Summit & Wasatch; P 24,500; M 1,075; (435) 649-6100; (800) 453-1360; Fax (435) 649-4132; info@parkcityinfo.com; www.parkcityinfo.com*

Payson • *Payson C/C* • Carolyn Bowman; Exec. Dir.; 20 S. Main; P.O. Box 176; 84651; Utah; P 18,000; M 100; (801) 465-2634; paysonchamber@yahoo.com; www.paysoncitychamber.org

Pleasant Grove • *Pleasant Grove C/C* • David Larson; Exec. Dir.; 70 S. 100 E.; 84062; Utah; P 35,000; M 1,000; (801) 922-4555; chamber@plgrovechamber.org; www.plgrovechamber.org

Price • *Carbon County C/C* • Jamill Tapia; Coord.; 81 N. 200 E., Ste. 3; 84501; Carbon; P 20,000; M 180; (435) 637-2788; Fax (435) 637-7010; cccc@carboncountychamber.net; www.carboncountychamber.net

Provo • *Utah Valley C/C* • Rona Rahlf; Pres.; 111 S. University Ave.; 84601; Utah; P 550,000; M 820; (801) 851-2555; Fax (801) 851-2557; info@thechamber.org; www.thechamber.org*

Richfield • *Richfield Area C/C* • Lorraine Gregerson; Exec. Dir.; 250 N. Main, Ste. B16; 84701; Sevier; P 7,200; M 145; (435) 896-4241; Fax (435) 896-4313; lorraine@richfieldareachamber.com; www.richfieldareachamber.com

Riverdale • *see Ogden*

Riverton • *Southwest Valley C/C* • Susan Schilling; Exec. Officer; 3600 W. 13001 S.; P.O. Box 330; 84065; Salt Lake; P 60,000; M 140; (801) 280-0595; susan@swvchamber.org; www.swvchamber.org

Roosevelt • *Duchesne County Area C/C* • Irene Hansen; Exec. Dir.; 50 E. 200 S.; P.O. Box 1417; 84066; Duchesne; P 12,000; M 300; (435) 722-4598; (435) 722-4597; Fax (435) 722-4579; dcac2@ubtanet.com; www.duchesne.net

Roy • *see Ogden*

Salem • *see Spanish Fork*

Salt Lake City • *Salt Lake C/C* • Lane Beattie; Pres./CEO; 175 E. University Blvd. (400 S.), Ste. 600; 84111; Salt Lake; P 3,000,000; M 7,700; (801) 364-3631; info@slchamber.com; www.slchamber.com*

Sandy • *Greater Sandy Area C/C* • Stan Parrish; Pres./CEO; 9350 S. 150 E., Ste. 980; 84070; Salt Lake; P 90,000; M 870; (801) 566-0344; Fax (801) 566-0346; sandychamber@sandychamber.com; www.sandychamber.com*

Smithfield • *Greater Smithfield C/C* • Stacey Dority; Secy.; P.O. Box 31; 84335; Cache; P 12,000; M 50; (435) 563-4104; (435) 563-3536; Stacey@SmithfieldChamber.com; www.smithfieldchamber.com

South Jordan • *South Jordan C/C* • Holly Heffron; Chair; 11565 S. District Main Dr., Ste. 600; 84095; Salt Lake; P 54,631; M 150; (801) 253-5200; Fax (801) 253-5201; mychamber@southjordanchamber.org; www.southjordanchamber.org*

South Salt Lake • *South Salt Lake C/C* • Gary Birdsall; Pres./CEO; 220 E. Morris Ave., Ste. 150; 84115; Salt Lake; P 24,000; M 250; (801) 466-3377; info@sslchamber.com; www.sslchamber.com*

South Weber • *see Kaysville*

Spanish Fork • *Spanish Fork/Salem Area C/C* • Ms. Cary Hanks; Exec. Dir.; 40 S. Main, Ste. 10; 84660; Utah; P 39,000; M 264; (801) 798-8352; office@spanishforkchamber.com; www.spanishforkchamber.com

Springville • *Springville Area C/C* • Shirlene Jordan; Exec Dir.; 110 S. Main St.; 84663; Utah; P 30,000; M 97; (801) 491-7830; info@springvilleutahchamber.org; www.springvilleutahchamber.org

St. George • *St. George Area C/C* • Pam Palermo; Pres.; 97 E. St. George Blvd.; 84770; Washington; P 138,115; M 700; (435) 628-1650; Fax (435) 673-1587; hotspot@stgeorgechamber.com; www.stgeorgechamber.com*

Sunset • *see Kaysville*

Syracuse • *see Kaysville*

Taylorsville • *see West Valley City*

Tooele • *Tooele County C/C* • Jared Hamner; Exec. Dir.; 154 S. Main St.; 84074; Tooele; P 59,000; M 430; (435) 882-0690; (800) 378-0690; Fax (435) 833-0946; chamber@tooelechamber.com; www.tooelechamber.com*

Tremonton • *Bear River Valley C/C* • Annette MacFarlane; Dir.; P.O. Box 311; 84337; Box Elder; P 20,000; M 120; (435) 279-7071; (435) 279-7076; bearriverchamber@gmail.com; www.brvcc.com

Vernal • *Vernal Area C/C* • Adam Massey; Exec. Dir.; 134 W. Main; 84078; Uintah; P 27,000; M 250; (435) 789-1352; Fax (435) 789-1355; vchambermgr@easilink.com; www.vernalchamber.com*

West Bountiful • *see Kaysville*

West Jordan • *West Jordan C/C* • N. Craig Dearing; Pres./CEO; 8000 S. Redwood Rd.; 84088; Salt Lake; P 105,000; M 350; (801) 569-5151; (801) 569-5150; Fax (801) 569-5153; info@westjordanchamber.com; www.westjordanchamber.com

West Point • *see Kaysville*

West Valley City • *ChamberWest* • Alan Anderson; Pres./CEO; 1241 Village Main Dr., Ste. B; 84119; Salt Lake; P 200,000; M 420; (801) 977-8755; Fax (801) 977-8329; chamber@chamberwest.org; www.chamberwest.org*

Woods Cross • *see Kaysville*

Vermont

Vermont C of C • Betsy Bishop; Pres.; P.O. Box 37; Montpelier; 05601; Washington; P 626,011; M 1,500; (802) 223-3443; Fax (802) 223-4257; info@vtchamber.com; www.vtchamber.com*

Andover • *see Ludlow*

Arlington • *see Manchester Center*

Ascutney • *see Windsor*

Athens • *see Bellows Falls*

Barre • *Central Vermont C/C* • George Malek; Pres.; 33 Stewart Rd., Berlin, VT; P.O. Box 336; 05641; Washington; P 60,000; M 350; (802) 229-5711; Fax (802) 229-5713; chamber@centralvt.com; www.central-vt.com

Barton • *Barton Area C/C* • Nancy Rodgers; P.O. Box 776; 05822; Orleans; P 5,000; M 130; (802) 239-4147; info@centerofthekingdom.com; www.centerofthekingdom.com

Bellows Falls • *Great Falls Reg. C/C* • Deborah Carbin; Exec. Dir.; 17 Depot St.; 05101; Windham; P 12,000; M 290; (802) 463-4280; Fax (802) 463-4280; info@gfrcc.org; www.gfrcc.org*

Bennington • *Bennington Area C/C* • Matt Harrington; Exec. Dir.; 100 Veterans Memorial Dr.; 05201; Bennington; P 15,500; M 400; (802) 447-3311; Fax (802) 447-1163; chamber@bennington.com; www.bennington.com*

Berlin • *see Barre*

Bethel • *see Randolph*

Bradford • *see Wells River*

Braintree • *see Randolph*

Brandon • *Brandon Area C/C* • Bernie Carr; Exec. Dir.; P.O. Box 267; 05733; Rutland; P 4,500; M 225; (802) 247-6401; info@brandon.org; www.brandon.org

Brattleboro • *Brattleboro Area C/C* • Kate O'Connor; Exec. Dir.; 180 Main St.; 05301; Windham; P 35,000; M 610; (802) 254-4565; (877) 254-4565; Fax (802) 254-5675; info@brattleborochamber.org; www.brattleborochamber.org

Bristol • *see Middlebury*

Brookfield • *see Randolph*

Burke Hollow • *see East Burke*

Burlington • *Lake Champlain Reg. C/C* • Tom Torti; Pres./CEO; 60 Main St., Ste. 100; 05401; Chittenden; P 200,000; M 2,500; (802) 863-3489; (877) 686-5253; Fax (802) 863-1538; vermont@vermont.org; www.vermont.org*

Cavendish • *see Ludlow*

Chelsea • *see Randolph*

Chester • *see Ludlow*

Dorset • *Dorset C/C* • P.O. Box 121; 05251; Bennington; P 2,000; M 65; chamber@dorsetvt.com; www.dorsetvt.com

East Burke • *Burke Area C/C* • Hannah Collins; P.O. Box 347; 05832; Caledonia; P 2,000; M 50; (802) 626-4124; burkechamber@burkevermont.com; www.burkevermont.com

Fair Haven • *Vermont Lakes Region C/C* • Pres.; P.O. Box 206; 05743; Rutland; P 8,000; M 86; (802) 265-8600; contact@fairhavenchambervt.com; www.fairhavenchambervt.com

Grafton • *see Bellows Falls*

Hancock • *see Randolph*

Hardwick • *Heart of Vermont* • Sandra Howard; Pres.; P.O. Box 111; 05843; Caledonia; P 7,000; M 125; (802) 472-5906; chamber@heartofvt.com; www.heartofvt.com

Hartford • *see Quechee*

Hartland • *see Windsor*

Island Pond • *Island Pond C/C* • Stephanie Nagle; P.O. Box 255; 05846; Essex; P 1,260; M 20; (802) 723-9889; chamber@islandpondchamber.org; www.islandpondchamber.org

Jeffersonville • *Smugglers Notch Area C/C* • Ray Saloomey; P.O. Box 364; 05464; Lamoille; P 3,000; M 98; (802) 644-8232; info@smugnotch.com; www.smugnotch.com

Killington • *Killington C/C* • Christopher Karr; Pres.; P.O. Box 114; 05751; Rutland; P 1,000; M 200; (802) 773-4181; (800) 337-1928; Fax (802) 775-7070; chamber@killingtonchamber.com; www.killingtonchamber.com

Lake Champlain Islands • *see North Hero*

Lincoln • *see Middlebury*

Londonderry • *Londonderry Area C/C* • James J. Lind; Exec. Dir.; P.O. Box 58; 05148; Windham; P 1,700; M 106; (802) 824-8178; londcham@aol.com

Ludlow • *Okemo Valley Reg. C/C* • Marji Graf; CEO; 57 Pond St., Clock Tower; P.O. Box 333; 05149; Rutland, Windham & Windsor; P 3,000; M 450; (802) 228-5830; Fax (802) 228-7642; mgraf@yourplaceinvermont.com; www.yourplaceinvermont.com*

Lyndonville • *Lyndon Area C/C* • Mary Marceau; Pres.; P.O. Box 886; 05851; Caledonia; P 5,981; M 150; (802) 626-9696; Fax (802) 626-1167; info@lyndonvermont.com; www.lyndonvermont.com

Manchester Center • *Manchester & The Mountains Reg. C/C* • Berta Maginniss; Exec. Dir.; 5046 Main St.; 05255; Bennington; P 3,800; M 730; (802) 362-2100; (800) 362-4144; Fax (802) 362-3451; visitor@manchesterchamber.net; visitmanchestervt.com*

Middlebury • *Addison County C/C* • Sue Hoxie; Pres.; 93 Court St.; 05753; Addison; P 37,600; M 450; (802) 388-7951; Fax (802) 388-8066; sue@addisoncounty.com; www.addisoncounty.com

Monkton • *see Middlebury*

Montpelier • *see Barre*

Morrisville • *Lamoille Region C/C* • Cindy Locke; Exec. Dir.; 34 Pleasant St., Ste. 1; 05661; Lamoille; P 21,225; M 390; (802) 888-7607; (800) 849-9985; Fax (802) 888-5006; marlene@lamoillechamber.com; www.lamoillechamber.com*

Mount Holly • *see Ludlow*

New Haven • *see Middlebury*

Newbury • *see Wells River*

Newport • *Vermont's North Country C/C* • Lynne Bertrand; Exec. Dir.; 246 The Causeway; 05855; Caledonia, Essex & Orleans; P 30,000; M 210; (802) 334-7782; Fax (802) 334-7238; chamber@vtnorthcountry.org; www.vtnorthcountry.org

North Hero • *Lake Champlain Reg. C/C - Islands Div.* • Sherri Potvin; Concierge; 3501 U.S. Rte. 2; P.O. Box 213; 05474; Grand Isle; P 7,000; M 200; (802) 372-8400; (800) 262-5226; Fax (802) 372-5107; info@champlainislands.com; www.champlainislands.com

Northfield • *see Barre*

Plymouth • *see Ludlow*

Poultney • *Poultney Area C/C* • 66 Beaman St., Stonebridge Bldg.; P.O. Box 151; 05764; Rutland; P 3,000; M 85; (802) 287-2010; poultneyvtchamber@gmail.com; www.poultneyvt

Putney • *see Bellows Falls*

Quechee • *Hartford Area C/C* • Patrick (P.J.) Skehan; Exec. Dir.; 5966 Quechee Rd.; P.O. Box 823; 05059; Windsor; P 11,000; M 250; (802) 295-7900; Fax (802) 296-8280; info@hartfordvtchamber.com; www.hartfordvtchamber.com

Randolph • *Randolph Area C/C* • Ben Merrill; Exec. Dir.; P.O. Box 9; 05060; Orange; P 30,000; M 188; (802) 728-9027; Fax (802) 728-4705; mail@randolph-chamber.com; www.randolph-chamber.com

Reading • *see Windsor*

Rochester • *see Randolph*

Rockingham • *see Bellows Falls*

Royalton • see Randolph

Rutland • Rutland Region C/C • Thomas L. Donahue; Exec. V.P.; 50 Merchants Row; 05701; Rutland; P 17,000; M 600; (802) 773-2747; (800) 756-8880; Fax (802) 773-2772; rrccvt@aol.com; www.rutlandvermont.com

Saint Albans • Franklin County Reg. C/C • Lisamarie Charlesworth; Asst. to the Dir.; 2 N. Main St., Ste. 101; 05478; Franklin; P 49,000; M 350; (802) 524-2444; info@fcrccvt.com; www.fcrccvt.com

Saxton's River • see Bellows Falls

Sharon • see Randolph

Smugglers Notch • see Jeffersonville

Springfield • Springfield Region • Caitlin Christiana; Exec. Dir.; 56 Main St., Ste. 2; 05156; Windsor; P 9,100; M 250; (802) 885-2779; Fax (802) 885-6826; springfieldrcoc@vermontel.net; www.springfieldvt.com

St. Johnsbury • Northeast Kingdom C/C • Darcie L. McCann; Exec. Dir.; 2000 Memorial Dr., Ste. 11; 05819; Caledonia, Essex & Orleans; P 65,000; M 375; (802) 748-3678; (800) 639-6379; Fax (802) 748-0731; nekinfo@nekchamber.com; www.nekchamber.com

Starksboro • see Middlebury

Stockbridge • see Randolph

Stowe • Stowe Area Assn. • Amy Morrison; Exec. Dir.; 51 Main St.; P.O. Box 1320; 05672; Lamoille; P 4,300; M 315; (802) 253-7321; (877) GO-STOWE; Fax (802) 253-6628; askus@gostowe.com; www.gostowe.com

Swanton • Swanton C/C • Adam Paxman; Pres.; P.O. Box 237; 05488; Franklin; P 6,000; M 62; (802) 868-7200; chamberoffice@swantonchamber.com; www.swantonchamber.com

Tunbridge • see Randolph

Vergennes • see Middlebury

Waitsfield • Mad River Valley C/C • Lisa Davis; Dir.; P.O. Box 173; 05673; Washington; P 4,000; M 240; (802) 496-3409; (800) 828-4748; Fax (802) 496-5420; info@madrivervalley.com; www.madrivervalley.com*

Waterbury • see Barre

Wells River • Lower Cohase Reg. C/C • Mark Nielsen; Exec. Dir.; P.O. Box 35; 05081; Orange; P 9,000; M 210; (802) 757-2549; info@cohase.org; www.cohase.org

West Burke • see East Burke

West Windsor • see Windsor

Westminster • see Bellows Falls

Weston • see Ludlow

White River Junction • see Quechee

Wilder • see Quechee

Wilmington • Southern Vermont Deerfield Valley C/C • Sharon Cunningham; Exec. Dir.; 21 W. Main St.; 05363; Windham; P 1,500; M 400; (802) 464-8092; info@visitvermont.com; www.visitvermont.com

Woodstock • Woodstock Area C/C • Elizabeth Finlayson; Dir.; P.O. Box 486; 05091; Windsor; P 3,232; M 305; (802) 457-3555; (888) 496-6378; Fax (802) 457-1601; info@woodstockvt.com; www.woodstockvt.com

Virgin Islands

Kingshill • St. Croix C/C • Kimberly McCollum; Pres.; P.O. Box 4355; 00851; P 50,600; M 325; (340) 773-1435; Fax (340) 773-8172; info@stxchamber.org; www.stxchamber.org

St. Thomas • St. Thomas-St. John C/C • Joseph S. Aubain; Exec. Dir.; 6-7 Dronningens Gade; P.O. Box 324; 00804; P 55,804; M 400; (340) 776-0100; Fax (340) 776-0588; chamber.vi@gmail.com; www.chamber.vi

Virginia

Virginia C of C • Barry E. DuVal; Pres./CEO; 919 E. Main St., Ste. 900; Richmond; 23219; Richmond City; P 8,185,867; M 1,000; (804) 644-1607; Fax (804) 783-6112; b.duval@vachamber.com; www.vachamber.com

Abingdon • Washington County C/C • Suzanne G. Lay; Exec. V.P.; 1 Government Ctr. Place, Ste. D; 24210; Washington; P 55,190; M 580; (276) 628-8141; Fax (276) 628-3984; chamber@bvu.net; www.washingtonvachamber.org

Alexandria • Mount Vernon Lee C/C • Holly Dougherty; Exec. Dir.; 6821 Richmond Hwy.; 22306; Fairfax; P 250,000; M 350; (703) 360-6925; Fax (703) 360-6928; info@MtVernon-LeeChamber.org; www.MtVernon-LeeChamber.org*

Alexandria • Alexandria C/C • Joe Haggerty; Pres./CEO; 2834 Duke St.; 22314; Alexandria City; P 153,500; M 850; (703) 549-1000; Fax (703) 739-3805; kgaines@alexchamber.com; www.alexchamber.com

Altavista • Altavista Area C/C • Heather Reynolds; Pres.; 414 Washington St.; P.O. Box 606; 24517; Campbell; P 3,500; M 170; (434) 369-6665; Fax (434) 369-0068; heatherreynolds@altavistachamber.com; www.altavistachamber.com

Amherst • Amherst County C/C • Linda Cocke; Pres.; 154 S. Main St.; P.O. Box 560; 24521; Amherst; P 32,384; M 200; (434) 946-0990; Fax (434) 946-0879; information@amherstvachamber.com; www.amherstvachamber.com

Annandale • Annandale C/C •; 7263 Maple Pl., Ste. 207; 22003; Fairfax; P 74,000; M 200; (703) 256-7232; Fax (703) 256-7233; info@annandalechamber.com; www.annandalechamber.com

Annandale • also see Tyson's Corner

Appomattox • Appomattox County C/C • John Redding; Pres.; 276 Court St.; P.O. Box 704; 24522; Appomattox; P 15,128; M 165; (434) 352-2621; Fax (434) 352-0294; chamber@appomattoxchamber.org; www.appomattoxchamber.org

Arlington • Arlington C/C • Kate Bates; Pres./CEO; 2009 14th St. N., Ste. 100; 22201; Arlington; P 221,045; M 700; (703) 525-2400; Fax (703) 522-5273; chamber@arlingtonchamber.org; www.arlingtonchamber.org*

Augusta County • see Fishersville

Baileys Crossroads • see Tyson's Corner

Bedford • *Bedford Area C/C* • Susan Martin IOM; Pres./CEO; 305 E. Main St.; 24523; Bedford City; P 68,600; M 725; (540) 586-9401; Fax (540) 587-6650; lmorck@bedfordareachamber.com; www.bedfordareachamber.com*

Berryville • *see Winchester*

Blacksburg • *see Christiansburg*

Blackstone • *Blackstone C/C* • Jane Barnes; Exec. Dir.; 121 N. Main St., Ste. A; P.O. Box 295; 23824; Nottoway; P 4,000; M 130; (434) 292-1677; (434) 294-0280; Fax (434) 292-1588; chamber@blackstoneva.com; www.blackstoneva.com*

Blairs • *Danville-Pittsylvania County C/C* • Laurie S. Moran CCE; Pres./CEO; 8653 U.S. Hwy. 29; P.O. Box 99; 24527; Pittsylvania; P 111,000; M 700; (434) 836-6990; Fax (434) 836-6955; chamber@dpchamber.org; www.dpchamber.org*

Bland County • *see Wytheville*

Botetourt County • *see Fincastle*

Bristol • *Bristol TN/VA C/C* • Joy Madison; Pres./CEO; P.O. Box 519; 24201; Washington; P 44,500; M 725; (423) 989-4850; (423) 989-4848; Fax (423) 989-4867; frontdesk@bristolchamber.org; www.bristolchamber.org*

Broadway • *see Timberville*

Brookneal • *Brookneal Area C/C* • Laura W. Shepherd; Pres.; P.O. Box 387; 24528; Campbell; P 3,300; M 25; (434) 376-3124; info@brooknealchamber.com; www.brooknealchamber.com

Buckingham County • *see Dillwyn*

Burke • *see Tyson's Corner*

Burkeville • *see Crewe*

Callao • *Northumberland County C/C* • Ann Lekander; Exec. Dir.; P.O. Box 149; 22435; Northumberland; P 12,400; M 160; (804) 529-5031; Fax (804) 529-5031; northumberlandcoc@verizon.net; www.northumberlandcoc.org

Cape Charles • *see Eastville*

Centreville • *see Tyson's Corner*

Chantilly • *Dulles Reg. C/C* • Eileen Curtis; Pres./CEO; 3901 Centerview Dr., Ste. S; 20151; Fairfax; P 64,300; M 930; (571) 323-5300; Fax (703) 787-8859; info@dullesregionalchamber.org; www.dullesregionalchamber.org*

Charlottesville • *Charlottesville Reg. C/C* • Timothy Hulbert; Pres./CEO; 209 5th St. N.E.; 22902; Charlottesville City; P 148,000; M 1,200; (434) 295-3141; Fax (434) 295-3144; desk@cvillechamber.com; www.cvillechamber.com*

Chase City • *Chase City C/C* • Braxton Rutledge; Exec. Dir.; 316 N. Main St.; 23924; Mecklenburg; P 2,400; M 100; (434) 372-0379; Fax (434) 372-4699; chasecityva@verizon.net; www.chasecitychamberofcomm.com

Chatham • *see Blairs*

Cheriton • *see Eastville*

Chesapeake • *see Norfolk*

Chesterfield • *Chesterfield County C/C* • Danna Geisler; Pres.; 9330 Iron Bridge Rd., Ste. B; 23832; Chesterfield; P 323,800; M 600; (804) 748-6364; Fax (804) 425-5669; danna@chesterfieldchamber.com; www.chesterfieldchamber.com*

Chincoteague Island • *Chincoteague C/C* • Evelyn Shotwell; Exec. Dir.; 6733 Maddox Blvd.; 23336; Accomack; P 2,941; M 300; (757) 336-6161; Fax (757) 336-1242; chincochamber@verizon.net; www.chincoteaguechamber.com

Christiansburg • *Montgomery County C/C* • Catherine Sutton CAE; Exec. Dir.; 1520 N. Franklin St.; 24073; Montgomery; P 95,600; M 1,100; (540) 382-3020; Fax (540) 381-1970; dlyons@montgomerycc.org; montgomerycc.org*

Clarksville • *Clarksville Lake Country C/C* • Sheila Cuykendall; Exec. Dir.; 105 2nd St.; P.O. Box 1017; 23927; Mecklenburg; P 5,500; M 180; (434) 374-2436; (800) 557-5582; Fax (434) 374-8174; chamber@clarksvilleva.com; www.clarksvilleva.com

Clifton • *see Tyson's Corner*

Clifton Forge • *see Covington*

Clintwood • *Dickenson County C/C* • Rita Surratt; Pres./CEO; 194 Clintwood Main St.; P.O. Box 1990; 24228; Dickenson; P 15,690; M 300; (276) 926-6074; Fax (276) 926-6074; chamberdickenson@yahoo.com; www.dickensonchamber.net

Colonial Beach • *Colonial Beach C/C* • Mattie Lillard; Mgr.; 106 Hawthorn St.; P.O. Box 475; 22443; Westmoreland; P 3,600; M 145; (804) 224-8145; Fax (804) 224-8147; info@colonialbeach.org; www.colonialbeach.org

Colonial Heights • *Colonial Heights C/C* • Roger M. Green; Exec. Dir.; 201 Temple Ave., Ste. E; 23834; Colonial Heights City; P 17,500; M 400; (804) 526-5872; Fax (804) 526-9637; roger.green@colonialheightschamber.com; www.colonialheightschamber.com

Covington • *Alleghany Highlands C/C* • Teresa A. Hammond; Exec. Dir.; 110 Mall Rd.; 24426; Covington City; P 22,357; M 280; (540) 962-2178; (888) 430-5786; Fax (540) 962-2179; info@ahchamber.com; www.ahchamber.com

Crewe • *Crewe-Burkeville C/C* • Eddie Higgins; Pres.; P.O. Box 305; 23930; Nottoway; P 2,760; M 40; (434) 645-8413; Fax (434) 645-8413; chamber@creweburkeville.org; www.creweburkeville.org

Culpeper • *Culpeper C/C* • Sandy Boone; Pres./CEO; 629 Sperryville Pike, Ste. 100; 22701; Culpeper; P 50,000; M 600; (540) 825-8628; (888) 285-7373; Fax (540) 825-1449; info@culpeperchamber.com; www.culpeperchamber.com*

Danville • *see Blairs*

Dillwyn • *Buckingham County C/C* • Janet Miller; Pres.; P.O. Box 951; 23936; Buckingham; P 17,100; M 165; (434) 983-2372; buckinghamchamberinfo@gmail.com; www.buckinghamchamber.org

Dublin • *Pulaski County C/C* • Peggy White; Exec. Dir.; 4440 Cleburne Blvd., Ste. B; 24084; Pulaski; P 35,000; M 500; (540) 674-1991; Fax (540) 674-4163; sheilanelson@pulaskichamber.info; www.pulaskichamber.info*

Eastville • *Northampton County C/C* • Renee Rice; Mgr.; 16429A Courthouse Rd.; P.O. Box 475; 23347; Northampton; P 12,500; M 250; (757) 678-0010; chamber@northamptoncountychamber.com; www.northamptoncountychamber.com

Edinburg • *see Woodstock*

Emporia • *Emporia-Greensville C/C* • LaVerne Jolly; Pres.; Emporia Train Depot; 400 Halifax St.; 23847; Emporia City; P 18,000; M 385; (434) 634-9441; Fax (434) 634-3485; ontrack@telpage.net; www.emporia-greensvillechamber.com

Exmore • *see Eastville*

Fairfax • *Central Fairfax C/C* • Doug Church; Chrmn.; 4031 University Dr., Ste. 100; P.O. Box 2912; 22031; Fairfax; P 200,000; M 200; (703) 591-2450; info@cfcc.org; www.cfcc.org

Falls Church • *Greater Falls Church C/C* • Sally Cole; Exec. Dir.; 417 W. Broad St., Ste. 205; 22046; Falls Church City; P 13,300; M 250; (703) 532-1050; Fax (703) 237-7904; andrea@fallschurchchamber.org; www.fallschurchchamber.org*

Falls Church • *also see Tyson's Corner*

Farmville • *Farmville Area C/C* • Lisa F. Tharpe; Exec. Dir.; 118A N. Main St.; P.O. Box 361; 23901; Prince Edward; P 8,200; M 280; (434) 392-3939; Fax (434) 392-3818; lisa@farmvilleareachamber.org; www.farmvilleareachamber.org

Fincastle • *Botetourt County C/C* • Doloris Vest; Exec. Dir.; 13 W. Main St.; P.O. Box 81; 24090; Botetourt; P 33,200; M 250; (540) 928-2017; (540) 526-6546; info@botetourtchamber.com; www.botetourtchamber.com

Fishersville • *Greater Augusta Reg. C/C* • Linda Hershey; Pres./CEO; 30 Ladd Rd.; P.O. Box 1107; 22939; Augusta; P 119,705; M 800; (540) 324-1133; Fax (540) 324-1136; officeadmin@augustava.com; www.augustava.com*

Floyd • *Floyd County C/C* • Melodie Pogue; Exec. Dir.; 201 E. Main St., Ste. 7; 24091; Floyd; P 15,400; M 200; (540) 745-4407; melodie@visitfloyd.org; www.visitfloyd.org

Forest • *Bedford Area C/C-Forest Satellite Ofc.* • Susan Martin IOM; Pres./CEO; 14805 Forest Rd., Ste. 107; 24551; Bedford; P 68,600; M 725; (434) 525-7860; Fax (434) 525-7862; lmorck@bedfordareachamber.com; www.bedfordareachamber.com*

Franklin • *Franklin-Southampton Area C/C* • Teresa Beale IOM; Exec. Dir.; 108 W. Third Ave.; P.O. Box 531; 23851; Franklin City; P 26,700; M 250; (757) 562-4900; Fax (757) 562-6138; join@fsachamber.com; www.fsachamber.com

Frederick County • *see Winchester*

Fredericksburg • *Fredericksburg Reg. C/C* • Susan Spears; Pres.; 2300 Fall Hill Ave., Ste. 240; P.O. Box 7476; 22404; Fredericksburg City; P 320,000; M 1,000; (540) 373-9400; Fax (540) 373-9570; stacey@fredericksburgchamber.org; www.fredericksburgchamber.org*

Front Royal • *Front Royal-Warren County C/C* • Niki Foster Cales IOM; Pres.; 106 Chester St.; 22630; Warren; P 39,000; M 605; (540) 635-3185; Fax (540) 635-9758; priffle@frontroyalchamber.com; www.frontroyalchamber.com*

Gainesville • *see Manassas*

Galax • *Twin County Reg. C/C* • Judy Brannock; Exec. Dir.; 405 N. Main St.; 24333; Galax City; P 55,000; M 400; (276) 236-2184; Fax (276) 236-1338; info@twincountychamber.com; www.twincountychamber.com*

Gate City • *Scott County C/C* • Penny Horton; Exec. Secy.; P.O. Box 609; 24251; Scott; P 23,000; M 110; (276) 386-6665; Fax (276) 386-6158; chamber@scottcountyva.com; www.scottcountyva.org

Giles County • *Giles County C/C* • Cathy Clark; Exec. Dir.; 101 S. Main St.; Pearisburg; 24134; Giles; P 17,000; M 150; (540) 921-5000; Fax (540) 921-3892; cathy@gileschamber.net; www.gileschamber.net

Gloucester • *Gloucester County C/C* • Makalia Records; Exec. Dir.; 3558 George Washington Memorial Hwy., Hayes, 23072; 6699 Fox Centre Pkwy., Ste. 609; 23061; Gloucester; P 36,900; M 300; (804) 693-2425; Fax (804) 693-7193; chamberexec@glocochamber.org; www.gloucestervachamber.org*

Goochland • *Goochland County C/C* • Bonnie Creasy; Exec. Dir.; 2913-D River Rd. W.; P.O. Box 123; 23063; Goochland; P 21,400; M 300; (804) 556-3811; Fax (804) 556-2131; director@goochlandchamber.org; www.goochlandchamber.org*

Gretna • *see Blairs*

Grundy • *Buchanan County C/C* • Mary M. Belcher; Exec. Dir.; 1025 Walnut St.; P.O. Box 2818; 24614; Buchanan; P 23,500; M 129; (276) 935-4147; bcchamber@bvu.net; www.buchanancofc.org

Hampton • *Virginia Peninsula C/C* • Mike Kuhns; Pres./CEO; 21 Enterprise Pkwy., Ste. 100; 23666; Hampton City; P 529,680; M 1,000; (757) 262-2000; Fax (757) 262-2009; vhurd@vpcc.org; www.vpcc.org*

Harrisonburg • *Harrisonburg-Rockingham C/C* • Frank M. Tamberrino; Pres./CEO; 800 Country Club Rd.; 22802; Harrisonburg City; P 128,400; M 880; (540) 434-3862; Fax (540) 434-4508; aschaefer@hrchamber.org; www.hrchamber.org*

Herndon • *see Chantilly*

Hillsville • *see Galax*

Hopewell • *Hopewell-Prince George C/C & Visitor Center* • Becky McDonough; CEO; 4100 Oaklawn Blvd.; P.O. Box 1297; 23860; Hopewell City; P 100,000; M 400; (804) 458-5536; (804) 458-5536; Fax (804) 458-0041; admin@hpgchamber.org; www.hpgchamber.org*

Hot Springs • *Bath County C/C* • Melinda Nichols; Exec. Dir.; 2696 Main St., Ste. 6; P.O. Box 718; 24445; Bath; P 4,800; M 140; (540) 839-5409; (800) 628-8092; Fax (540) 839-5409; bathco@tds.net; www.countyofbathchamber.org

Huntington • *see Tyson's Corner*

Hurt • *see Blairs*

Irvington • *see Kilmarnock*

Isle of Wight • *see Smithfield*

James City County • *see Hampton and Williamsburg*

Kenbridge • *see Lunenburg*

Kilmarnock • *Lancaster by the Bay C/C* • Anne Paparella; Exec. Dir.; 129 S. Main St.; P.O. Box 1868; 22482; Lancaster & Northumberland; P 12,000; M 300; (804) 435-6092; Fax (804) 435-2291; info@lancasterva.com; www.lancasterva.com*

King George • *King George County C/C* • Anita Churchill; Pres.; P.O. Box 164; 22485; King George; P 24,500; M 95; jherrink@journalpress,com; www.kinggeorgechamber.com

Ladysmith • *Caroline C/C* • Kimberly Hinneld; Exec. Dir.; P.O. Box 1125; 22427; Caroline; P 29,000; M 175; (804) 448-5264; chamber@bealenet.com; www.carolinecountychamber.com

Ladysmith • *see Bowling Green*

Lawrenceville • *Brunswick C/C* • Wendy Wright; Exec. Dir.; 400 N. Main St.; 23868; Brunswick; P 18,000; M 103; (434) 848-3154; Fax (434) 848-9356; brunschamber@lawrencevilleweb.com; www.brunswickchamber.com

Lebanon • *Russell County C/C* • Linda Marshall; Exec. Dir.; 331 W. Main St.; P.O. Box 926; 24266; Russell; P 29,000; M 200; (276) 889-8041; Fax (276) 889-8002; linda@russellcountyva.org; www.russellcountyva.org

Leesburg • *Loudoun County C/C* • Tony Howard; Pres./CEO; P.O. Box 1298; 20177; Loudoun; P 336,900; M 1,200; (703) 777-2176; Fax (703) 777-1392; kstethem@loudounchamber.org; www.loudounchamber.org*

Lexington • *The C/C serving Lexington, Buena Vista & Rockbridge County* • Tracy E. Lyons; Exec. Dir.; 18 E. Nelson St., Ste. 101; 24450; Lexington City; P 35,000; M 500; (540) 463-5375; Fax (540) 463-3567; info@lexrockchamber.com; www.lexrockchamber.com*

Loudoun County • *see Leesburg*

Louisa • *Louisa County C/C* • Keli Harold; Exec. Dir.; 214 Fredericksburg Ave.; P.O. Box 955; 23093; Louisa; P 33,430; M 160; (540) 967-0944; info@louisachamber.org; www.louisachamber.org

Lunenburg • *Lunenburg County C/C* • General Delivery; 23952; Lunenburg; P 13,000; M 100; (434) 696-2337; (434) 676-3555; glacrellc@earthlink.net; www.lunenburgchamber.org*

Luray • *Luray-Page County C/C* • John Robbins; Pres.; 18 Campbell St.; 22835; Page; P 24,100; M 400; (540) 743-3915; (888) 743-3915; Fax (540) 743-3944; gina.hilliard@luraypage.com; luraypage.com*

Lynchburg • *Lynchburg Reg. Bus. Alliance* • Megan Lucas; CEO; 2015 Memorial Ave.; 24501; Lynchburg City; P 252,600; M 850; (434) 845-5966; Fax (434) 522-9592; info@lynchburgregion.org; www.lynchburgregion.org*

Madison • *Madison C/C & Visitor Center* • Tracey Gardner; Exec. Dir.; 110A N. Main; P.O. Box 373; 22727; Madison; P 13,300; M 210; (540) 948-4455; Fax (540) 948-3174; chamber@madison-va.com; www.madison-va.com

Manassas • *Prince William C/C* • Debbie Jones; Pres./CEO; 9720 Capital Ct., Ste. 203; 20110; Prince William; P 438,600; M 1,600; (703) 368-6600; Fax (703) 368-4733; rward@pwchamber.org; www.pwchamber.org*

Marion • *C/C of Smyth County* • Sarah B. Gillespie; Exec. Dir.; 214 W. Main St.; P.O. Box 924; 24354; Smyth; P 32,300; M 400; (276) 783-3161; Fax (276) 783-8003; info@smythchamber.org; www.smythchamber.org

Martinsville • *Martinsville-Henry County C/C* • Amanda Witt; Pres.; 115 Broad St.; P.O. Box 709; 24114; Martinsville City; P 60,000; M 600; (276) 632-6401; (866) 632-3378; Fax (276) 632-5059; mhccoc@mhcchamber.com; www.martinsville.com*

Massaponax • *see Eastville*

McLean • *Greater McLean C/C* • Marcia Twomey; Pres.; 6649A Old Dominion Dr.; 22101; Fairfax; P 48,000; M 400; (703) 356-5424; Fax (703) 356-9244; mtwomey@mcleanchamber.org; www.mcleanchamber.org

Mechanicsville • *Hanover C/C* • Melissa Miller; Exec. Dir.; 9097 Atlee Station Rd., Ste. 117; 23116; Hanover; P 100,000; M 650; (804) 798-8130; Fax (804) 798-0014; melissa@hanoverchamberva.com; www.hanoverchamberva.com

Melfa • *Eastern Shore of Virginia C/C* • Jean Hungiville; Exec. Dir.; 19056 Pkwy.; P.O. Box 460; 23410; Accomack; P 53,000; M 550; (757) 787-2460; Fax (757) 787-8687; info@esvachamber.org; www.esvachamber.org

Merrifield • *see Tyson's Corner*

Moneta • *Smith Mountain Lake Reg. C/C* • Vicki Gardner; Exec. Dir.; 16430 Booker T. Washington Hwy., Ste. 2; Bridgewater Plaza; 24121; Franklin; P 25,000; M 680; (540) 721-1203; Fax (540) 721-7796; info@visitsmithmountainlake.com; www.visitsmithmountainlake.com*

Monterey • *Highland County C/C* • Tiffany White; Exec. Dir.; P.O. Box 223; 24465; Highland; P 2,400; M 196; (540) 468-2550; Fax (540) 468-2551; highcc@cfw.com; www.highlandcounty.org

Mount Jackson • *see Woodstock*

Mount Vernon Lee • *see Alexandria*

New Kent • *New Kent C/C* • Larry Ragsdale; Pres.; 7324 Vineyards Pkwy.; 23124; New Kent; P 18,500; M 120; (804) 966-8581; president@newkentchamber.org; www.newkentchamber.org

New Market • *New Market Area C/C* • Liz Gum; 9386 S. Congress St.; P.O. Box 57; 22844; Shenandoah; P 1,800; M 99; (540) 740-3212; (877) 740-3212; Fax (540) 740-4234; nmchambr@gmail.com; www.newmarketcoc.net

Newington • *see Tyson's Corner*

Newport News • *see Hampton*

Norfolk • *Hampton Roads C/C* • Bryan K. Stephens; Pres./CEO; 500 E. Main St., Ste. 700; 23510; Norfolk City; P 1,316,300; M 2,000; (757) 622-2312; Fax (757) 622-5563; info@hrccva.com; www.hamptonroadschamber.com*

Norton • *Wise County C/C* • Rick Colley; Exec. V.P.; 765 Park Ave.; P.O. Box 226; 24273; Norton City; P 43,000; M 300; (276) 679-0961; Fax (276) 679-2655; wisecountycoc@verizon.net; www.wisecountychamber.org*

Oakton • *see Tyson's Corner*

Orange • *Orange County C/C* • Amanda Settle; Exec. Dir.; 103 N. Madison Rd.; P.O. Box 146; 22960; Orange; P 36,000; M 250; (540) 672-5216; Fax (540) 672-2304; exec@orangevachamber.com; www.orangevachamber.com

Palmyra • *Fluvanna County C/C* • Trish Smith; Exec. Asst.; 177 Main St.; P.O. Box 93; 22963; Fluvanna; P 25,700; M 205; (434) 589-3262; Fax (434) 589-6212; fluvannacountycoc@embarqmail.com; www.fluvannachamber.org*

Pennington Gap • *Lee County Area C/C* • Robert Bost; Pres.; P.O. Box 417; 24277; Lee; P 26,000; M 100; (276) 337-9277; director@leecountyvachamber.org; www.leecountyvachamber.org

Petersburg • *Petersburg C/C* • Danielle Fitz-Hugh; Pres./CEO; 325 E. Washington St.; P.O. Box 928; 23804; Petersburg City; P 33,000; M 500; (804) 733-8131; Fax (804) 733-9891; info@petersburgvachamber.com; www.petersburgvachamber.com*

Poquoson • *see Hampton*

Portsmouth • *see Norfolk*

Powhatan • Powhatan C/C • Tina Bustos; Exec. Dir.; 3887 Old Buckingham Rd.; 23139; Powhatan; P 28,100; M 240; (804) 598-2636; Fax (804) 598-0023; info@powhatanchamber.org; www.powhatanchamber.org*

Prince William • see Manassas

Pulaski • see Dublin

Radford • Radford C/C • Keith Weltens; Pres.; 200 3rd Ave., Ste. C; 24141; Radford City; P 16,000; M 300; (540) 639-2202; Fax (540) 639-2228; info@radfordchamber.com; www.radfordchamber.com

Reston • Greater Reston C/C, Bus. & Visitors Center • Mark Ingrao CCP CAE; Pres./CEO; 1763 Fountain Dr.; 20190; Fairfax; P 67,910; M 1,000; (703) 707-9045; Fax (703) 707-9049; amym@restonchamber.org; www.restonchamber.org*

Reston • also see Tyson's Corner

Richlands • Richlands Area/Tazewell County C/C • Ginger H. Branton; Exec. Dir.; 1413 Front St.; 24641; Tazewell; P 45,100; M 250; (276) 963-3385; Fax (276) 963-4278; richlandschamber@roadrunner.com; richlandschamber.com*

Richmond • Greater Richmond C/C • Kim Scheeler; Pres./CEO; 600 E. Main St., Ste. 700; 23218; Richmond City; P 1,000,000; M 2,000; (804) 648-1234; Fax (804) 783-9366; denise.feys@grcc.com; www.grcc.com*

Roanoke • Roanoke Reg. C/C • Joyce Waugh; Pres./CEO; 210 S. Jefferson St.; 24011; Roanoke City; P 300,000; M 1,100; (540) 983-0700; Fax (540) 983-0723; business@roanokechamber.org; www.roanokechamber.org*

Rocky Mount • see Moneta

Salem • Salem-Roanoke County C/C • Caroline Goode; Exec. Dir.; 611 E. Main St.; P.O. Box 832; 24153; Roanoke; P 110,773; M 600; (540) 387-0267; Fax (540) 387-4110; chamber@s-rcchamber.org; www.s-rcchamber.org*

Scottsville • Scottsville Comm. C/C • Cynthia Bruce; Pres.; P.O. Box 11; 24590; Albemarle; P 560; M 90; (434) 286-6000; Fax (434) 286-9102; scccpresident@gmail.com; www.scottsville.org

Seven Corners • see Tyson's Corner

Smithfield • Isle of Wight-Smithfield-Windsor C/C • Andrew Cripps IOM; Pres./CEO; 100 Main St.; P.O. Box 38; 23431; Isle of Wight; P 35,000; M 450; (757) 357-3502; (888) 284-3475; Fax (757) 357-6884; chamber@theisle.org; www.theisle.org

South Boston • Halifax County C/C • Nancy Pool; Pres.; 515 S. Broad St.; P.O. Box 399; 24592; Halifax; P 37,000; M 415; (434) 572-3085; Fax (434) 572-1733; info@halifaxchamber.net; www.halifaxchamber.net

South Hill • South Hill C/C • Frank Malone; Exec. Dir.; 201 S. Mecklenburg Ave.; 23970; Chesapeake; P 5,000; M 300; (434) 447-4547; Fax (434) 447-4461; frank@southhillchamber.com; www.southhillchamber.com

Spotsylvania • see Fredericksburg

Springfield • Greater Springfield C/C • Nancy-jo Manney; Exec. Dir.; 6434 Brandon Ave., Ste. 208; 22150; Fairfax; P 32,000; M 250; (703) 866-3500; Fax (703) 866-3501; info@springfieldchamber.org; www.springfieldchamber.org*

Stafford • see Fredericksburg

Staunton • see Fishersville

Strasburg • Strasburg C/C • Angie Herman; Exec. Dir.; 132 W. King St.; P.O. Box 42; 22657; Shenandoah; P 6,000; M 165; (540) 465-3187; Fax (540) 465-2812; strasburgcoc@gmail.com; www.strasburgvachamber.com

Stuart • Patrick County C/C • Tom Bishop; Exec. Dir.; 20475 Jeb Stuart Hwy.; P.O. Box 577; 24171; Patrick; P 19,000; M 300; (276) 694-6012; Fax (276) 694-3582; patcchamber@embarqmail.com; www.patrickchamber.com

Suffolk • see Norfolk

Surry • Surry County C/C • Jason Wiedel; P.O. Box 353; 23883; Surry; P 7,100; M 47; (757) 294-0066; mail@surrychamber.org; www.surrychamber.org

Sussex • Sussex County C/C • Ellen Boone; Pres.; P.O. Box 1371; 23884; Sussex; P 10,000; M 30; (434) 246-1022; Fax (434) 246-4503; e.boone@sussexcountyva.gov

Tappahannock • Tappahannock-Essex County C/C • Dee Friel; P.O. Box 481; 22560; Essex; P 11,200; M 200; (804) 443-5241; Fax (804) 443-4157; www.tecoc.com

Tazewell • Tazewell Area C/C • Rebecca Duncan; Dir.; Tazewell Mall; Box 6; 24651; Tazewell; P 45,100; M 250; (276) 988-5091; Fax (276) 988-5093; info@tazewellchamber.org; www.tazewellchamber.com

Timberville • Broadway-Timberville C/C • Crystal Collins; Secy.; 233 McCauley Dr.; 22853; Rockingham; P 5,000; M 100; (540) 896-7413; Fax (540) 896-2825; secretary@btchamber.org; www.btchamber.com

Tysons • TysonsRegional C/C • Lori Lopez; Chrmn. of the Bd.; 7925 Jones Branch Dr., Ste. LL200; 22102; Fairfax; P 1,000,000; M 421; (703) 281-1333; Fax (703) 242-1482; info@tysonschamber.org; www.tysonschamber.org*

Tysons Corner • Fairfax County C/C • Jim Corcoran; Pres./CEO; 8230 Old Courthouse Rd., Ste. 350; 22182; Fairfax; P 1,000,000; M 650; (703) 749-0400; Fax (703) 749-9075; fccc@fairfaxchamber.org; www.fairfaxchamber.org

Victoria • see Lunenburg

Vinton • Vinton Area C/C • Angie Chewning Lewis; Exec. Dir.; 116 S. Poplar St., Ste. 1A; 24179; Roanoke; P 8,000; M 208; (540) 343-1364; info@vintonchamber.com; www.vintonchamber.com

Virginia Beach • see Norfolk

Warren County • see Front Royal

Warrenton • Fauquier County C/C • Joe Martin; Pres./CEO; 205-1 Keith St.; 20186; Fauquier; P 65,300; M 500; (540) 347-4414; Fax (540) 347-7510; mailbox@fauquierchamber.org; www.fauquierchamber.org*

Warsaw • Warsaw-Richmond County C/C • Sara Carroll; Pres.; P.O. Box 1141; 22572; Richmond; P 10,000; M 70; (804) 313-2252; warsawrcchamber@gmail.com; www.wrccoc.com

Waynesboro • see Fishersville

West Point • West Point/Tri-Rivers C/C • Janice McGowan; Ofc. Secy.; 621 Main St.; P.O. Box 1035; 23181; King William; P 3,300; M 60; (804) 843-4620; Fax (804) 843-2434; wpchamber@verizon.net; www.westpointvachamber.com

Williamsburg • *Greater Williamsburg C/C & Tourism Alliance* • Karen Riordan; Pres./CEO; 421 N. Boundary St.; 23185; Williamsburg City; P 200,000; M 967; (757) 229-6511; (800) 368-6511; Fax (757) 229-2047; wacc@williamsburgcc.com; www.williamsburgcc.com*

Winchester • *Top of Virginia Reg. Chamber* • Christine Kriz; CEO; 407 S. Loudoun St.; 22601; Winchester City; P 102,000; M 800; (540) 662-4118; Fax (540) 722-6365; cocinfo@regionalchamber.biz; www.regionalchamber.biz*

Windsor • *see Smithfield*

Wise County • *see Norton*

Woodbridge • *see Manassas*

Woodstock • *Shenandoah County C/C* • Cheri Wright; Exec. Dir.; 103 S. Main St.; P.O. Box 605; 22664; Shenandoah; P 42,600; M 300; (540) 459-2542; Fax (540) 459-2513; cwright@shenandoahcountychamber.com; www.shenandoahcountychamber.com

Wythe County • *see Wytheville*

Wytheville • *Wytheville-Wythe-Bland C/C* • Jennifer W. Atwell IOM; Exec. Director; 150 E. Monroe St.; 24382; Bland & Wythe; P 36,100; M 390; (276) 223-3365; (276) 223-3366; Fax (276) 223-3412; chamber@wytheville.org; www.wwbchamber.com

York County • *see Hampton and Williamsburg*

Yorktown • *York County C/C* • Karen E. Johnson; Assoc. Dir.; 5225 George Washington Memorial Hwy.; P.O. Box 1103; 23692; York; P 65,600; M 201; (757) 877-5920; karen@yorkcountycc.org; www.yorkcountycc.org

Washington

Assn. of Washington Bus. • Kristofer T. Johnson; Pres./CEO; 1414 Cherry St. S.E.; P.O. Box 658; Olympia; 98507; Thurston; P 700,000; M 7,000; (360) 943-1600; (800) 521-9325; Fax (360) 943-5811; krisj@awb.org; www.awb.org

Washington Chamber Executives • Robert Green; CEO; P.O. Box 1349; Enumclaw; 98022; King; P 6,897,012; M 125; (360) 802-4595; admin@wcce.org; www.wcce.org

Aberdeen • *Greater Grays Harbor Inc.* • Andre Garson; CEO; 506 Duffy St.; 98520; Grays Harbor; P 72,000; M 350; (360) 532-1924; (800) 321-1924; info@graysharbor.org; www.graysharbor.org*

Airway Heights • *see Cheney*

Allyn • *see Belfair*

Amboy • *see La Center*

Anacortes • *Anacortes C/C* • Stephanie Hamilton; Exec. Dir.; 819 Commercial Ave., Ste. F; 98221; Skagit; P 16,000; M 470; (360) 293-7911; (360) 293-3832; Fax (360) 293-1595; info@anacortes.org; www.anacortes.org*

Arlington • *Arlington-Smokey Point C/C* • 4126 B 172nd St. N.E.; 98223; Snohomish; P 17,000; M 200; (360) 659-5453; Fax (360) 657-2328; excutive@arlington-smokeypointchamber.com; *

Asotin • *Asotin C/C* • Wes Vaughn; Pres.; P.O. Box 574; 99402; Asotin; P 1,200; M 20; (509) 243-4242; Fax (509) 243-4243; asotin@cableone.net; www.cityofasotin.org

Auburn • *Auburn Area C/C* • Nancy E. Wyatt; Pres./CEO; 25 2nd St. N.W.; 98001; King & Pierce; P 85,000; M 402; (253) 833-0700; Fax (253) 735-4091; auburncc@auburnareawa.org; www.auburnareawa.org*

Bainbridge Island • *Bainbridge Island C/C* • Rex Oliver IOM; Pres./CEO; 395 Winslow Way E.; 98110; Kitsap; P 24,500; M 600; (206) 842-3700; Fax (206) 842-3713; roliver@bainbridgechamber.com; www.bainbridgechamber.com

Ballard • *see Seattle-Ballard C/C*

Battle Ground • *Battle Ground C/C* • Doug Quinn; Chair; 1419 W. Main St., Ste. 110; 98604; Clark; P 16,000; M 374; (360) 687-1510; Fax (360) 687-4505; info@battlegroundchamber.org; www.battlegroundchamber.org*

Belfair • *North Mason C/C* • Mark W. Costa; Pres./CEO; 30 N.E. Romance Hill Rd.; P.O. Box 416; 98528; Mason; P 22,000; M 450; (360) 275-4267; Fax (360) 275-0853; mark@northmasonchamber.com; www.northmasonchamber.com

Bellevue • *Bellevue C/C* • Betty Nokes; Pres./CEO; 302 Bellevue Sq.; 98004; King; P 120,000; M 1,100; (425) 454-2464; Fax (425) 462-4660; staffteam@bellevuechamber.org; www.bellevuechamber.org*

Bellingham • *Bellingham Whatcom C/C & Ind. Inc.* • Guy Occhiogrosso; Pres./CEO; 119 N. Commercial St., Ste. 110; P.O. Box 958; 98227; Whatcom; P 200,000; M 600; (360) 734-1330; Fax (360) 734-1332; guy@bellingham.com; bellingham.com*

Benton City • *Benton City C/C* • Tracy Berry; Pres.; 513 9th St.; P.O. Box 401; 99320; Benton; P 6,000; M 40; (509) 588-4984; info@bentoncitychamber.org; www.bentoncitychamber.org

Bingen • *see White Salmon*

Blaine • *Birch Bay C/C & Visitors Info. Center* • Dannita Schacht; Exec. Dir.; 7900 Birch Bay Dr.;; 98230; Whatcom; P 8,500; M 160; (360) 371-5004; info@birchbaychamber.com; www.birchbaychamber.com

Blaine • *Blaine C/C* • Carroll Solomon; Dir.; 728 Peace Portal Dr.; 98230; Whatcom; P 5,000; M 80; (800) 624-3555; (360) 332-6484; Fax (360) 332-4544; vic@cityofblaine.com; www.blainechamber.com

Bonney Lake • *Bonney Lake C/C* • Wendi Woodyard; Exec. Dir.; 20608 Hwy. 410 E.; P.O. Box 7171; 98391; Pierce; P 18,000; M 125; (253) 222-5945; Chamber@BonneyLake.com; www.bonneylake.com*

Bothell • *Greater Bothell C/C* • Lori Cadwell; Exec. Dir.; 10017 N.E. 185th St.; P.O. Box 1203; 98041; King & Snohomish; P 30,000; M 275; (425) 485-4353; Fax (425) 368-0396; lori@bothellchamber.com; www.bothellchamber.com*

Bremerton • *Bremerton C/C* • Gena Wales; Pres./CEO; 286 Fourth St.; 98337; Kitsap; P 40,000; M 400; (360) 479-3579; Fax (360) 479-1033; staff@bremertonchamber.org; www.bremertonchamber.org*

Brewster • *Brewster C/C* • 105 S. Third St.; P.O. Box 1087; 98812; Okanogan; P 2,195; M 66; (509) 689-3464; info@brewsterchamber.org; www.brewsterchamber.org

Brinnon • *see Quilcene*

Buckley • *Buckley C/C* • Ron Callis; Pres.; 769 Main St.; P.O. Box 168; 98321; Pierce; P 4,000; M 60; (360) 829-0975; Fax (360) 829-9201; information@buckleychamber.org; www.buckleychamber.org

Burien • *see Tukwila*

Burlington • *Burlington C/C* • Linda Fergusson; Pres./CEO; 520 E. Fairhaven Ave.; P.O. Box 1087; 98233; Skagit; P 122,000; M 400; (360) 757-0994; Fax (360) 757-0821; info@burlington-chamber.com; www.burlington-chamber.com*

Camano Island • *Camano Island C/C* • Karen Daum; Dir. of Tourism & Op.; 1992 S. Elger Bay Rd., PMB #416; 98282; Island; P 18,000; M 130; (360) 629-7136; Fax (360) 629-7136; chamber@camanoisland.org; www.camanoisland.org

Camas • *Camas-Washougal C/C* • Brent Erickson; Exec. Dir.; 422 N.E. 4th Ave.; 98607; Clark; P 39,000; M 265; (360) 834-2472; brent@cwchamber.com; www.cwchamber.com*

Carnation • *Carnation C/C* • Collienne Becker; P.O. Box 603; 98014; King; P 1,900; M 50; (425) 333-5556; (425) 333-5556; info@carnationchamber.com; www.carnationchamber.com

Cashmere • *Cashmere C/C* • Dawn Collings; Mgr.; 103 Cottage Ave.; P.O. Box 834; 98815; Chelan; P 3,200; M 150; (509) 782-7404; Fax ; info@cashmerechamber.org; www.cashmerechamber.org

Cathlamet • *Wahkiakum C/C* • Paige Lake; Dir.; 102 Main St, Ste. B52; P.O. Box 52; 98612; Wahkiakum; P 4,000; M 110; (360) 795-9996; wchamber@cni.net; www.wahkiakumchamber.com

Centralia • *see Chehalis*

Chehalis • *Centralia-Chehalis C/C* • Alicia N. Bull; Exec. Dir.; 500 N.W. Chamber Way; 98532; Lewis; P 25,000; M 525; (360) 748-8885; (800) 525-3323; Fax (360) 748-8763; thechamber@chamberway.com; www.chamberway.com*

Chelan • *Lake Chelan C/C* • Mike Steele; Exec. Dir.; 216 E. Woodin Ave.; P.O. Box 216; 98816; Chelan; P 10,000; M 500; (509) 682-3503; (800) 4-CHELAN; Fax (509) 682-3538; info@lakechelan.com; www.lakechelan.com

Cheney • *West Plains C/C* • Kathleen Zinke; Mgr.; 504 1st St.; 99004; Spokane; P 60,000; M 200; (509) 747-8480; Fax (509) 624-5244; chamberoffice@westplainschamber.org; www.westplainschamber.org

Chewelah • *Chewelah C/C* • 214 E. Main St.; P.O. Box 94; 99109; Stevens; P 2,500; M 120; (509) 935-8595; Fax (509) 935-8520; info@chewelah.org; www.chewelah.org*

Chimacum • *see Port Townsend*

Clallam Bay • *Clallam Bay-Sekiu C/C* • Patricia Hutson; Pres.; 16753 Hwy. 112; P.O. Box 355; 98326; Clallam; P 1,000; M 70; (360) 963-2339; (877) 694-9433; info@clallambay.com; www.clallambay.com

Clarkston • *Lewis Clark Valley C/C* • Kristin Kemak; Pres./CEO; 502 Bridge St.; 99403; Asotin & Nez Perce; P 59,624; M 733; (509) 758-7712; (800) 933-2128; Fax (509) 751-8767; info@lcvalleychamber.org; www.lcvalleychamber.org*

Cle Elum • *see Ellensburg*

Colfax • *Colfax C/C* • Kathy Clark; Secy.; 120 S. Main St.; 99111; Whitman; P 3,000; M 144; (509) 397-3712; Fax (509) 397-4458; colfaxchamber@gmail.com; www.visitcolfax.com

Colville • *Colville C/C* • Diane Connelly; Pres.; 986 S. Main St., Ste. B; 99114; Stevens; P 5,000; M 250; (509) 684-5973; Fax (509) 684-1344; colvillecoc@colville.com; www.colville.com

Conconully • *Town of Conconully C/C* • Janet Warner; Pres.; P.O. Box 309; 98819; Okanogan; P 210; M 58; (509) 826-9050; (877) 826-9050; www.conconully.com

Concrete • *Concrete C/C* • Valerie Stafford; Pres.; 45770 Main St.; P.O. Box 743; 98237; Skagit; P 1,000; M 45; (360) 853-8784; chamber@concrete-wa.com; concrete-wa.com

Connell • *Greater Connell Area C/C* • Kevin Besel; Pres.; P.O. Box 401; 99326; Franklin; P 5,300; M 70; (509) 234-2631; (509) 234-2701; kbesel@centurytel.net; www.cityofconnell.com

Cosmopolis • *see Aberdeen*

Coulee City • *Coulee City C/C* • Terri Zapone; Secy./Treas.; P.O. Box 896; 99115; Grant; P 600; M 50; (509) 681-2018; (509) 632-5331; tns@accima.com; www.couleecity.com

Coupeville • *Coupeville C/C* • Lynda Eccles; Exec. Dir.; 905 N.W. Alexander; P.O. Box 152; 98239; Island; P 1,900; M 198; (360) 678-5434; (360) 678-5664; director@coupevillechamber.com; www.coupevillechamber.com*

Crescent Bar • *see Quincy*

Dallesport • *see White Salmon*

Davenport • *Davenport C/C* • Kathryn Jump; Pres.; P.O. Box 869; 99122; Lincoln; P 1,780; M 90; (509) 725-6711; (509) 721-1459; chamberofcommercedavenport@gmail.com; www.davenportwa.org

Dayton • *Dayton C of C & Visitor Center* • Claudia Nysoe; Exec. Dir.; 166 E. Main; 99328; Columbia; P 4,100; M 196; (509) 382-4825; (800) 882-6299; Fax (509) 382-1969; chamber@historicdayton.com; www.historicdayton.com

Deer Park • *Deer Park C/C* • Rose Whapeles; Ofc. Mgr.; P.O. Box 518; 99006; Spokane; P 3,150; M 140; (509) 276-5900; Fax (509) 276-5900; info@deerparkchamber.com; www.deerparkchamber.com

Dungeness Valley • *see Sequim*

Duvall • *Duvall C/C* • NJ Shelsby; Pres.; 15619 Main St.; P.O. Box 581; 98019; King; P 7,500; M 206; (425) 788-9182; (425) 788-8384; info@duvallchamberofcommerce.com; www.duvallchamberofcommerce.com

East Wenatchee • *see Wenatchee*

Eastsound • *Orcas Island C/C* • Lance Evans; Exec. Dir.; 65 N. Beach Rd.; P.O. Box 252; 98245; San Juan; P 5,000; M 315; (360) 376-2273; info@orcasislandchamber.com; www.orcasislandchamber.com

Eatonville • *Greater Eatonville C/C* • Dawn Newkirk; P.O. Box 845; 98328; Pierce; P 2,100; M 97; (360) 832-4000; eatonville.wa.chamber@gmail.com; www.eatonvillechamber.com

Edmonds • *Edmonds C/C* • Greg Urban; Pres./CEO; 121 5th Ave. N.; P.O. Box 146; 98020; Snohomish; P 40,000; M 515; (425) 670-1496; (425) 332-7115; Fax (425) 712-1808; business@edmondswa.com; www.edmondswa.com*

Ellensburg • *Kittitas County C/C & EDC* • James Armstrong; CEO; 609 N. Main St.; 98926; Kittitas; P 40,000; M 500; (509) 925-2002; (888) 925-2204; Fax (509) 962-6148; info@kittitascountychamber.com; www.kittitascountychamber.com*

Elma • *Elma C/C* • Debbie Adolphsen; Dir.; P.O. Box 798; 98541; Grays Harbor; P 3,400; M 100; (360) 482-3055; info@elmachamber.org; www.elmachamber.org

Ephrata • *Ephrata C/C* • Amber Reynolds; Dir.; 112 Basin St. S.W.; P.O. Box 275; 98823; Grant; P 7,900; M 180; (509) 754-4656; Fax (509) 754-5788; info@ephratawachamber.com; www.ephratawachamber.com

Everson • *Everson Nooksack C/C* • Amy Ramstead; Pres.; 103 W. Main St.; P.O. Box 234; 98247; Whatcom; P 3,000; M 90; (360) 966-3407; info@eversonnooksackchamber.org; www.eversonnooksackchamber.org

Fairfield • *Hangman Creek C/C* • Linda A. Thomas; Pres.; P.O. Box 345; 99012; Spokane; P 1,719; M 43; (509) 291-3238; Fax (509) 291-4149; lthomas1012@hotmail.com; www.hangmancreekchamber.com

Fall City • *see North Bend*

Federal Way • *Federal Way C/C* • Rebecca Martin CCE; Pres./CEO; 31919 1st Ave. S., Ste. 202; P.O. Box 3440; 98003; King; P 85,000; M 600; (253) 838-2605; Fax (253) 661-9050; info@federalwaychamber.com; www.federalwaychamber.com*

Ferndale • *Ferndale C/C* • Ann Cline; Exec. Dir.; 2007 Cherry St.; P.O. Box 1264; 98248; Whatcom; P 13,700; M 280; (360) 384-3042; Fax (360) 384-3009; info@ferndale-chamber.com; www.ferndale-chamber.com*

Fife • *Fife Milton Edgewood C/C* • Lora Butterfield; Pres./CEO; 2018 54th Ave. E; 98424; Pierce; P 26,100; M 300; (253) 922-9320; Fax (253) 922-1638; officeadmin@fmechamber.org; www.fmechamber.org*

Forks • *Forks C/C* • Marcia Bingham; Dir.; 1411 S. Forks Ave.; P.O. Box 1249; 98331; Clallam; P 5,500; M 300; (360) 374-2531; (800) 44-FORKS; Fax (360) 374-9253; info@forkswa.com; www.forkswa.com

Frederickson • *see Puyallup*

Freeland • *Greater Freeland C/C* • Chet Ross; Pres.; 5575 Harbor Ave.; P.O. Box 361; 98249; Island; P 5,000; M 150; (360) 331-1980; freeland@whidbey.com; www.freeland-wa.org

Friday Harbor • *San Juan Island C/C* • Becki Day; Exec. Dir.; 135 Spring St.; P.O. Box 98; 98250; San Juan; P 7,600; M 300; (360) 378-5240; Fax ; chamber@sanjuanisland.org; www.sanjuanisland.org*

George • *see Quincy*

Gig Harbor • *Gig Harbor Peninsula Area C/C* • Warren Zimmerman; Pres./CEO; 3125 Judson St.; P.O. Box 102; 98335; Pierce; P 66,000; M 500; (253) 851-6865; (800) 359-8804; Fax (253) 851-6881; wzimmerman@gigharborchamber.com; www.gigharborchamber.com

Glenwood • *see White Salmon*

Goldendale • *Greater Goldendale Area C/C* • Earlene Sullivan; Exec. Dir.; 903 E. Broadway; 98620; Klickitat; P 4,000; M 180; (509) 773-3400; Fax (509) 773-3411; execdir@goldendalechamber.org; www.goldendalechamber.org*

Graham • *see Puyallup*

Grand Coulee • *Grand Coulee Dam Area C/C* • Peggy Nevsimal; Mgr.; 306 Midway; P.O. Box 760; 99133; Grant; P 5,000; M 85; (509) 633-3074; (800) 268-5332; Fax (509) 633-2366; peggy@grandcouleedam.org; www.grandcouleedam.org

Grandview • *Grandview C/C* • Kathy Viereck; Pres.; 303 W. Wine Country Rd.; P.O. Box 717; 98930; Yakima; P 10,000; M 90; (509) 882-2100; Fax (866) 308-4691; info@visitgrandview.org; www.visitgrandview.org

Granger • *Granger C/C* • Michelle F. Lee; Pres.; P.O. Box 250; 98932; Yakima; P 3,000; M 45; (509) 854-7304; grangerchamber@gmail.net; www.grangerchamber.org

Grapeview • *see Belfair*

Grays Harbor • *see Aberdeen*

Grays River • *see Cathlamet*

Greenbank • *see Coupeville*

Hockinson • *see La Center*

Hoquiam • *see Aberdeen*

Husum • *see White Salmon*

Irondale • *see Port Townsend*

Issaquah • *Greater Issaquah C/C* • Kathy McCorry; Exec. Dir.; 155 N.W. Gilman Blvd.; 98027; King; P 30,000; M 440; (425) 392-7024; Fax (425) 392-8101; info@issaquahchamber.com; www.issaquahchamber.com*

Kalama • *Kalama C/C* • Brad Whittaker; Pres.; P.O. Box 824; 98625; Cowlitz; P 3,000; M 80; (360) 673-6299; info@kalamachamber.com; www.kalamachamber.com

Kelso • *Kelso Longview C/C* • William G. Marcum Jr.; Pres./CEO; 105 N. Minor Rd.; 98626; Cowlitz; P 49,000; M 531; (360) 423-8400; Fax (360) 423-0432; ahallock@kelsolongviewchamber.org; www.kelsolongviewchamber.org*

Kelso • *see Longview*

Kenmore • *see Bothell*

Kennewick • *Tri-City Reg. C/C* • Lori Mattson; Pres./CEO; 7130 W. Grandridge Blvd., Ste. C; 99336; Benton; P 275,000; M 1,200; (509) 736-0510; Fax (509) 783-1733; info@tricityregionalchamber.com; www.tricityregionalchamber.com*

Kent • *Kent C/C* • Andrea Keikkala; Exec. Dir.; 524 W. Meeker St., Ste. 1; P.O. Box 128; 98035; King; P 86,660; M 500; (253) 854-1770; Fax (253) 854-8567; info@kentchamber.com; www.kentchamber.com*

Kettle Falls • *Kettle Falls Area C/C* • David Hudson; Pres.; P.O. Box 119; 99141; Stevens; P 1,611; M 80; (509) 738-2300; kettlefallscoc@dashwireless.com; www.kettle-falls.com

Kingston • *Greater Kingston C/C* • Colleen Carey; Exec. Dir.; 25923 Washington Blvd., Ste. 100; P.O. Box 78; 98346; Kitsap; P 10,000; M 240; (360) 297-3813; director@kingstonchamber.com; www.kingstonchamber.com

Kirkland • *Greater Kirkland C/C* • Bruce Wynn; Exec. Dir.; 328 Parkplace Center; 98033; King; P 82,000; M 325; (425) 822-7066; Fax (425) 827-4878; info@kirklandchamber.org; www.kirklandchamber.org*

Klickitat • *see White Salmon*

La Center • *La Center North Clark County C/C* • P.O. Box 83; 98629; Clark; P 6,000; M 50; (360) 263-4636; info@lacenternorthclarkcountychamber.com; www.lacenternorthclarkcountychamber.com

La Conner • *La Conner C/C* • Heather Carter; Exec. Dir.; 413 Morris St.; 98257; Skagit; P 900; M 160; (360) 466-4778; (888) 642-9284; Fax (360) 466-0204; director@laconnerchamber.com; www.laconnerchamber.com

Lacey • *Lacey South Sound Chamber* • Sierra Roundy; Exec. Dir.; 420 Golf Club Rd., Ste. 105; 98503; Thurston; P 42,680; M 445; (360) 491-4141; Fax (360) 491-9403; info@laceysschamber.com; www.laceysschamber.com*

Lake Stevens • *Lake Stevens C/C & Visitors Center* • Kim Daughtry; Pres.; 10020 Lundeen Park Way; P.O. Box 439; 98258; Snohomish; P 39,000; M 200; (425) 334-0433; info@lakestevenschamber.com; www.lakestevenschamber.com*

Lakewood • *Lakewood C/C* • Linda Smith; Pres./CEO; 6310 Mt. Tacoma Dr. S.W., Ste. B; 98499; Pierce; P 60,000; M 500; (253) 582-9400; Fax (253) 581-5241; scottj@lakewood-wa.com; www.lakewood-chamber.com*

Langley • *Langley C/C & Visitor Info. Center* • Marc Esterly; Exec. Dir.; 208 Anthes Ave.; P.O. Box 403; 98260; Island; P 5,700; M 209; (360) 221-6765; langley@whidbey.com; www.visitlangley.com

Latah • *see Fairfield*

Leavenworth • *Leavenworth C/C* • Nancy Smith; Exec. Dir.; 940 Hwy. 2; P.O. Box 327; 98826; Chelan; P 2,000; M 600; (509) 548-5807; Fax (509) 548-1014; info@leavenworth.org; www.leavenworth.org

Liberty Lake • *Greater Spokane Valley C/C* • Katherine Morgan; Pres./CEO; 1421 N. Meadowood Ln., Ste. 10; 99019; Spokane; P 104,000; M 600; (509) 924-4994; (866) 475-1436; Fax (509) 924-4992; info@spokanevalleychamber.org; www.spokanevalleychamber.org*

Lind • *Lind C/C* • Phil Kent; Pres.; P.O. Box 561; 99341; Adams; P 500; M 20; (509) 677-3655; lchamber@lindwa.com; www.lindwa.com

Longview • *see Kelso*

Lopez Island • *Lopez Island C/C* • Aaron Dye; Pres.; 265 Lopez Rd., Ste. F; P.O. Box 102; 98261; San Juan; P 2,200; M 147; (360) 468-4664; lopezchamber@lopezisland.com; www.lopezisland.com

Lyle • *see White Salmon*

Lynden • *Lynden C/C* • Gary Vis; Exec. Dir.; 518 Front St.; 98264; Whatcom; P 12,000; M 340; (360) 354-5995; Fax (360) 354-0401; lynden@lynden.org; www.lynden.org

Maple Valley • *Greater Maple Valley-Black Diamond C/C* • Sue VanRuff; CEO; 23745 225th Way S.E., Ste. 205; 98038; King; P 35,000; M 250; (425) 432-0222; Fax (888) 778-6823; suevanruff@maplevalleychamber.org; www.maplevalleychamber.org*

Marblemount • *North Cascades C/C* • Tim O'Mara; Exec. Dir.; 59831 State Rte. 20; P.O. Box 175; 98267; Skagit; P 1,000; M 25; (360) 873-4150; chamber@marblemount.com; www.marblemount.com

Marcus • *see Kettle Falls*

Marysville • *see Tulalip*

Maury Island • *see Vashon*

McCleary • *McCleary Comm. C/C* • Pauline Martin; Pres.; P.O. Box 53; 98557; Grays Harbor; P 1,653; M 52; (360) 495-7827; (360) 495-3667; mcclearychamber.com

McKenna • *see Yelm*

Medical Lake • *see Cheney*

Mercer Island • *Mercer Island C/C* • Terry Moreman; Exec. Dir.; 7605 S.E. 27th, Ste. 109; P.O. Box 108; 98040; King; P 23,000; M 200; (206) 232-3404; Fax (206) 232-8903; info@mercerislandchamberofcommerce.org; www.mercerislandchamberofcommerce.org.*

Metaline Falls • *North Pend Oreille C/C* • Jeanie Law; Pres.; P.O. Box 388; 99153; Pend Oreille; P 900; M 51; (509) 446-1721; npochamber@gmail.com; www.npochamber.org

Mica • *see Fairfield*

Mill Creek • *see Bothell*

Millwood • *see Liberty Lake*

Milton • *see Puyallup*

Monroe • *Monroe C of C & Visitor Info. Center* • Yvonne M. Gallardo-Van Ornam; Exec. Dir.; 125 S. Lewis St.; P.O. Box 69; 98272; Snohomish; P 18,000; M 200; (360) 794-5488; Fax (360) 794-2044; office@monroewachamber.org; www.ChooseMonroe.com*

Montesano • *Montesano C/C & Visitor Info. Center* • Tracy Travers; Pres.; P.O. Box 688; 98563; Grays Harbor; P 3,300; M 80; (360) 249-5522; info@montesanochamber.org; www.montesanochamber.org

Morton • *Morton C/C* • Kim Olive; Chamber Mgr.; 194 Main Ave.; P.O. Box 10; 98356; Lewis; P 1,200; M 50; (360) 496-6086; Fax (360) 496-6210; chamber@lewiscounty.com; mortonchamber.lewiscounty.com

Moses Lake • *Moses Lake C/C* • Debbie Doran-Martinez; Exec. Dir.; 324 S. Pioneer Way; 98837; Grant; P 45,000; M 482; (509) 765-7888; (800) 992-6234; Fax (866) 535-1246; information@moseslake.com; www.moseslake.com*

Mount St. Helens • *see Toutle*

Mount Vernon • *Mount Vernon C/C* • Andy Mayer; Pres./CEO; 301 W. Kincaid St.; P.O. Box 1007; 98273; Skagit; P 32,000; M 530; (360) 428-8547; Fax (360) 424-6237; info@mountvernonchamber.com; www.mountvernonchamber.com*

Naselle • *see Cathlamet*

Newhalem • *see Marblemount*

Newport • *Greater Newport Area C/C* • Valorie Hein; Exec. Dir.; 325 West 4th St.; 99156; Pend Oreille; P 2,500; M 143; (509) 447-5812; info@newportareachamber.com; www.newportareachamber.com

Nooksack • *see Everson*

Normandy Park • *see Tukwila*

North Bend • *Snoqualmie Valley C/C* • Susan Husa; Member Svcs. Mgr.; P.O. Box 357; 98045; King; P 39,000; M 350; (425) 888-6362; Fax (425) 888-4665; info@snovalley.org; www.snovalley.org*

North Creek Area • *see Bothell*

Oak Harbor • *Greater Oak Harbor C/C* • Christine Cribb; Exec. Dir.; 32630 S.R. 20; P.O. Box 883; 98277; Island; P 25,000; M 470; (360) 675-3755; Fax (360) 679-1624; info@oakharborchamber.com; www.oakharborchamber.com*

Oakville • *Oakville C/C* • Bill Scholl; P.O. Box 331; 98568; Grays Harbor; P 700; M 30; (360) 273-2702; info@oakville-wa.org; www.oakville-wa.org

Ocean Park • *Ocean Park Area C/C* • Karen Boardman; Ofc. Mgr.; 1715 Bay Ave., Ste. 1; P.O. Box 403; 98640; Pacific; P 7,000; M 97; (360) 665-4448; (888) 751-9354; opchamber@opwa.com; www.opwa.com

Ocean Shores • *Ocean Shores/North Beach C/C* • Douglas C. Orr; Exec. Dir.; 873 Pt. Brown Ave. N.W., Ste. 1; P.O. Box 382; 98569; Grays Harbor; P 5,500; M 218; (360) 289-2451; (888) 48-BEACH; Fax (360) 289-5005; chamber@oceanshores.org; www.oceanshores.org*

Odessa • *Odessa C/C* • Marlon Schafer; Pres.; P.O. Box 355; 99159; Lincoln; P 910; M 73; (509) 982-0049; (509) 988-0260; www.odessachamber.net

Okanogan • *Okanogan C/C* • P.O. Box 1125; 98840; Okanogan; P 2,500; M 36; (509) 422-1135; (888) 782-1134; Fax (509) 422-1541; okchamber@communitynet.org

Olympia • *Thurston County C/C* • David Schaffert; Pres./CEO; 809 Legion Way S.E.; P.O. Box 1427; 98507; Thurston; P 238,000; M 1,450; (360) 357-3362; Fax (360) 357-3376; info@thurstonchamber.com; www.thurstonchamber.com*

Omak • *Omak C/C* • Katherine MacKenzie; Ofc. Mgr.; 401 Omak Ave.; P.O. Box 3100; 98841; Okanogan; P 5,000; M 150; (509) 826-1880; (800) 225-6625; omakchamber@northcascades.net; www.omakchamber.com

Orcas Island • *see Eastsound*

Oroville • *Oroville C/C* • P.O. Box 2140; 98844; Okanogan; P 3,000; M 68; (509) 476-3602; orovillewashington@gmail.com; www.orovillewashington.com*

Orting • *see Puyallup*

Othello • *Greater Othello C/C* • Bianca Mendoza; Mgr.; 33 E. Larch St.; P.O. Box 2813; 99344; Adams; P 8,000; M 105; (509) 488-2683; manager@othellochamber.org; www.othellochamber.org

Palouse • *Palouse C/C* • Bev Pearce; Pres.; P.O. Box 174; 99161; Whitman; P 1,015; M 75; (509) 878-1811; palousechamber@visitpalouse.com; www.visitpalouse.com

Pasco • *Pasco C/C* • Colin Hastings; Exec. Dir.; 1110 Osprey Pointe Blvd., Ste. 101; 99301; Franklin; P 76,000; M 376; (509) 547-9755; admin@pascochamber.org; pascochamber.org

Pateros • *Pateros C/C* • P.O. Box 308; 98846; Okanogan; P 625; M 30; (509) 923-2571; info@pateros.com; www.pateros.com

Point Roberts • *Point Roberts C/C* • Heather McPhee; Secy.; P.O. Box 128; 98281; Whatcom; P 1,340; M 57; (360) 945-2313; info@pointrobertschamberofcommerce.com; www.pointrobertschamberofcommerce.com

Pomeroy • *Pomeroy C/C* • Stephanie Newberg; Exec. Dir.; P.O. Box 916; 99347; Garfield; P 1,515; M 65; (509) 843-5110; info@pomeroychamberofcommerce.com; www.pomeroychamberofcommerce.com

Port Angeles • *Port Angeles Reg. C/C & Visitor Center* • Russ Veenema; Exec. Dir.; 121 E. Railroad Ave.; 98362; Clallam; P 20,000; M 550; (360) 452-2363; Fax (360) 457-5380; russ@portangeles.org; www.portangeles.org*

Port Hadlock • *see Port Townsend*

Port Ludlow • *see Port Townsend*

Port Orchard • *Port Orchard C/C* • Christine Daniel; Exec. Dir.; 1014 Bay St., Ste. 3; 98366; Kitsap; P 11,680; M 337; (360) 876-3505; Fax (360) 895-1920; christine@portorchard.com; www.portorchard.com*

Port Townsend • *The Jefferson County C/C* • Teresa Verraes; Exec. Dir.; 440 12th St.; 98368; Jefferson; P 25,000; M 450; (360) 385-7869; Fax (360) 379-8204; admin@jeffcountychamber.org; jeffcountychamber.org*

Poulsbo • *Poulsbo C/C* • Sue Allison; Exec. Dir.; 19735 10th Ave. N.E. S100; P.O. Box 1063; 98370; Kitsap; P 10,210; M 400; (360) 779-4999; (877) 768-5726; Fax (360) 779-3115; director@poulsbochamber.com; www.poulsbochamber.com*

Prosser • *Prosser C/C & Visitor Info. Center* • Larelle Michener; Exec. Dir.; 1230 Bennett Ave.; 99350; Benton; P 5,600; M 250; (509) 786-3177; (800) 408-1517; Fax (509) 786-4545; info@prosserchamber.org; www.prosserchamber.org

Pullman • *Pullman C/C* • Marie Dymkoski; Exec. Dir.; 415 N. Grand Ave.; 99163; Whitman; P 30,000; M 500; (509) 334-3565; Fax (509) 332-3232; chamber@pullmanchamber.com; www.pullmanchamber.com*

Puyallup • *Puyallup/Sumner C/C* • Shelly Schlumpf; Exec. Dir.; 323 N. Meridian, Ste. A; P.O. Box 1298; 98371; Pierce; P 175,000; M 650; (253) 845-6755; Fax (253) 848-6164; admin@puyallupsumnerchamber.com; www.puyallupsumnerchamber.com*

Quilcene • *North Hood Canal C/C* • 295142 Hwy. 101; P.O. Box 774; 98376; Jefferson; P 2,600; M 50; (360) 765-4999; visitorscenter@embarqmail.com; www.emeraldtowns.com

Quincy • *Quincy Valley C/C* • Cari V. Mathews; Exec. Dir.; 119 F St. S.E.; P.O. Box 668; 98848; Grant; P 10,000; M 270; (509) 787-2140; Fax (509) 787-4500; qvcc@quincyvalley.org; www.quincyvalley.org

Rainier • *see Yelm*

Raymond • *Willapa Harbor C/C & Visitor Info.* • Michelle Layman; Dir.; 415 Commercial St.; P.O. Box 1249, South Bend; 98586; Pacific; P 3,500; M 200; (360) 942-5419; info@willapaharbor.org; www.willapaharbor.org

Redmond • *OneRedmond* • Bart Phillips; CEO; 8383 158th Ave. N.E., Ste. 225; 98052; King; P 55,000; M 450; (425) 885-4014; Fax (425) 882-0996; info@oneredmond.org; www.oneredmond.org*

Renton • *Renton C/C* • Lynn Wallace; Pres./CEO; 625 S. 4th St.; 98057; King; P 100,000; M 550; (425) 226-4560; Fax (425) 226-4287; info@gorenton.com; www.gorenton.com*

Republic • *Republic C/C* • Jim Milner; Pres.; 15-1 N. Kean St.; P.O. Box 502; 99166; Ferry; P 7,700; M 50; (509) 850-1427; info@republicchamber.org; www.republicchamber.org

Richfield • *see La Center*

Richland • *see Kennewick*

Ritzville • *Ritzville Area C/C* • Jennifer Saunders; Admin. Dir.; 111 W. Main; P.O. Box 122; 99169; Adams; P 1,800; M 115; (509) 659-1936; Fax (509) 659-0142; chamber@ritzville.com; www.visitritzville.com

Rockford • *see Fairfield*

Rockport • *see Marblemount*

Rosalia • *Rosalia C/C* • Pat Voge; Pres.; P.O. Box 132; 99170; Whitman; P 650; M 30; (509) 523-5962; Fax (509) 523-5962; rosalia.chamber@aol.com; www.rosaliachamber.com

Rosburg • *see Cathlamet*

Roslyn • *see Ellensburg*

Roy • *see Yelm*

Salmon Creek • *see La Center*

Sammamish • *Sammamish C/C* • Deborah Sogge; Exec. Dir.; 704 228th Ave. N.E., Ste. 123; 98074; King; P 51,000; M 268; (425) 681-4910; Fax (866) 868-6773; info@sammamishchamber.org; www.sammamishchamber.org*

San Juan Island • *see Friday Harbor*

Sauk Valley • *see Marblemount*

Sea Tac • *see Tukwila*

Seattle Area

Assn. of Washington State Hispanic C/C • Cris Guillén; Pres./CEO; 3305 E. Olive St.; 98122; Yakima; P 6,664,195; M 3,000; (206) 329-5534; (509) 452-0788; Fax (509) 452-0788; president@awshcc.com; www.awshcc.com*

Ballard C/C • Beth Williamson Miller; Exec. Dir.; 2208 N.W. Market St., Ste. 100; 98107; King; P 70,000; M 380; (206) 784-9705; Fax (206) 783-8154; info@ballardchamber.com; www.ballardchamber.com

Fremont C/C • Jessica Vets; Exec. Dir.; P.O. Box 31139; 98103; King; P 20,000; M 290; (206) 632-1500; Fax (206) 632-7156; director@fremont.com; www.fremont.com*

Greater Lake City C/C • Diane Haugen; Exec. Dir.; 12345 30th Ave. N.E., Ste. F-G; 98125; King; P 40,000; M 200; (206) 363-3287; Fax (206) 363-6456; lakecitychamberofcommerce@gmail.com; www.lakecitychamber.org*

The Greater Queen Anne C/C • Mrs. Charley Shore; Exec. Dir.; 2212 Queen Anne Ave., Ste. 809; 98109; King; P 36,000; M 180; (206) 412-5802; contact@queenannechamber.org; www.queenannechamber.org

Magnolia C/C • Nancy Callaghan; Exec. Dir.; 3214 W. McGraw St., Ste. 301B; 98199; King; P 22,000; M 140; (206) 284-5836; Fax (206) 352-7494; info@magnoliachamber.org; www.magnoliachamber.org

Northgate C/C • Tatyana Sineeva; Admin.; 9594 First Ave. N.E., Ste. 296; 98115; King; P 500,000; M 100; (206) 733-0115; info@northgatechamber.com; www.northgatechamber.com*

Seattle Metro C/C • Maud Daudon; Pres./CEO; 1301 5th Ave., Ste. 1500; 98101; King; P 500,000; M 2,400; (206) 389-7200; Fax (888) 392-2795; info@seattlechamber.com; www.seattlechamber.com*

The U Partnership • Erin Goodman; Events & Mbrshp. Mgr.; 4710 University Way, Ste. 114; 98105; King; P 70,000; M 170; (206) 547-4417; administrator@udistrictpartnership.org; http://udistrictpartnership.org

Wallingford C/C • Stephen Fickenscher; Ofc. Admin.; 4649 Sunnyside Ave. N., Ste. 140; 98103; King; P 20,000; M 140; (206) 632-0645; Fax (206) 632-4759; info@wallingfordchamber.org; www.wallingfordchamber.org

West Seattle C/C • 3614A California Ave. S.W.; 98116; King; P 125,000; M 286; (206) 932-5685; Fax (206) 938-7437; info@wschamber.com; www.wschamber.com

Sedro-Woolley • *Sedro-Woolley C/C* • Pola Kelley; Exec. Dir.; 810 Metcalf St.; 98284; Skagit; P 11,000; M 246; (360) 855-1841; Fax (360) 855-1582; director@sedro-woolley.com; www.sedro-woolley.com*

Selah • *Selah C/C* • Jean Brown; Pres.; 216 S. 1st St.; P.O. Box 415; 98942; Yakima; P 8,000; M 120; (509) 698-7303; Fax (509) 698-7309; selahchamber@fairpoint.net; www.selahchamber.org

Sequim • *Sequim-Dungeness Valley C/C & Visitor Info. Center* • Shelli Robb-Kahler; Exec. Dir.; 1192 E. Washington St.; P.O. Box 907; 98382; Clallam; P 26,000; M 450; (360) 683-6197; info@sequimchamber.com; www.sequimchamber.com*

Shelton • *Shelton-Mason County C/C* • Heidi McCutcheon; Exec. Dir.; 215 W. Railroad Ave; P.O. Box 2389; 98584; Mason; P 60,500; M 329; (360) 426-2021; Fax (360) 426-8678; info@sheltonchamber.org; www.sheltonchamber.org*

Shoreline • *Shoreline C/C* • Sharon Knight; Mgr.; 18560 1st Ave. N.E.; 98155; King; P 58,000; M 205; (206) 361-2260; Fax (206) 361-2268; info@shorelinechamber.com; www.shorelinechamber.com*

Silverdale • *Silverdale C/C & Visitors Info. Center* • Kathleen Gordon; Exec. Dir.; 3100 Bucklinn Hill Rd. N.W., Ste. 100; P.O. Box 1218; 98383; Kitsap; P 19,000; M 350; (360) 692-6800; Fax (360) 692-1379; kathleen@silverdalechamber.com; www.silverdalechamber.com*

Skamokawa • *see Cathlamet*

Smokey Point • *see Arlington*

Snohomish • *Snohomish C/C* • Pam Osborne; Ofc. Mgr.; 127 Ave. A; P.O. Box 135; 98291; Snohomish; P 9,800; M 200; (360) 568-2526; manager@cityofsnohomish.com; www.cityofsnohomish.com*

Snoqualmie • *see North Bend*

Snoqualmie Pass • *see North Bend*

Soap Lake • *Soap Lake C/C* • P.O. Box 433; 98851; Grant; P 1,733; M 52; (509) 246-1821; slcoc@soaplakecoc.org; www.soaplakecoc.org

South Bend • *see Raymond*

South Hill • *see Puyallup*

Spangle • *see Fairfield*

Spokane • *Greater Spokane Inc.* • Steve Stevens; Pres./CEO; 801 W. Riverside Ave., Ste. 100; 99201; Spokane; P 510,000; M 1,500; (509) 624-1393; (800) 776-5263; Fax (509) 747-0077; anaccarato@greaterspokane.org; www.greaterspokane.org*

Sprague • *Sprague C/C* • P.O. Box 17; 99032; Lincoln; P 500; M 30; (509) 979-3539; president@spraguechamber.org

Springdale • *Greater Springdale/Loon Lake C/C* • Lela Taylor; Pres.; 204 N. Second St.; P.O. Box 275; 99173; Stevens; P 300; M 37; (509) 258-7160; (509) 258-7258; gsllcoc@gmail.com; www.gllcoc

Stanwood • *Stanwood C/C* • Stacy Johnson; Exec. Dir.; 10101 270th St. N.W., Ste. 220; P.O. Box 641; 98292; Snohomish; P 40,000; M 150; (360) 629-0562; info@stanwoodchamber.org; www.stanwoodchamber.org

Steilacoom • *Steilacoom C/C* • Cynthia L. McKitrick; Pres.; P.O. Box 88584; 98388; Pierce; P 6,000; M 120; (253) 353-6982; steilacoomchamberofcommerce@comcast.net; www.steilacoomchamber.org

Stevenson • *Skamania County C/C* • Casey Roeder; Exec. Dir.; 167 N.W. Second St.; P.O. Box 1037; 98648; Skamania; P 12,000; M 280; (509) 427-8911; (800) 989-9178; Fax (509) 427-5122; casey@skamania.org; www.skamania.org

Sultan • *Sky Valley C/C* • Debbie Copple; Dir.; 320 Main St.; P.O. Box 46; 98294; Snohomish; P 20,000; M 140; (360) 793-0983; Fax (360) 793-3241; debbie@skyvalleyvic.net; www.skyvalleychamber.com

Sumas • *Sumas C/C* • Rod Fadden; Pres.; P.O. Box 268; 98295; Whatcom; P 1,200; M 30; (360) 988-2028; tony@kelleyinsurance.com; www.sumaschamber.com

Summit • *see Puyallup*

Sumner • *see Puyallup*

Sunland Estates • *see Quincy*

Sunnyside • *Sunnyside C/C* • Pam Turner; Exec. Dir.; 230 E. Edison; P.O. Box 360; 98944; Yakima; P 15,210; M 250; (509) 837-5939; (800) 457-8089; Fax (509) 837-8015; info@sunnysidechamber.com; www.sunnysidechamber.com

Tacoma • *Tacoma-Pierce County C/C* • Tom Pierson; Pres./CEO; 950 Pacific Ave., Ste. 300; P.O. Box 1933; 98401; Pierce; P 790,500; M 1,600; (253) 627-2175; Fax (253) 597-7305; info@tacomachamber.org; www.tacomachamber.org*

Tahuya • *see Belfair*

Tenino • *Tenino Area C/C* • Joyce Worrell; Pres.; P.O. Box 506; 98589; Thurston; P 1,695; M 55; (360) 264-5228; www.teninoacc.org

Toledo • *South Lewis County C/C* • Dan Godat; Chair; 408 Silver St.; P.O. Box 607; 98591; Lewis; P 5,000; M 90; (360) 864-8844; Fax (360) 864-8846; slccc@toledotel.com; www.thelewiscountychamber.com

Tonasket • *Tonasket C/C* • Julie Alley; Pres.; P.O. Box 523; 98855; Okanogan; P 1,025; M 80; (509) 486-4543; (866) 440-8828; president@tonasketchamber.com; www.tonasketchamber.com

Toppenish • *Toppenish C/C* • Zach Dorr; Exec. Dir./CEO; 504 S. Elm St.; P.O. Box 28; 98948; Yakima; P 9,000; M 75; (509) 865-3262; (800) 863-6375; Fax (509) 865-3549; toppenishchamber@gmail.com; www.visittoppenish.com

Toutle • *Mount St. Helens C/C* • Greg Drew; 5304 Spirit Lake Hwy.; 98649; Cowlitz; P 2,500; M 12; (360) 274-8920; www.mountsthelens.com

Trout Lake • *see White Salmon*

Tukwila • *Seattle Southside C/C* • Andrea Reay; Pres./CEO; 14220 Interurban Ave. S., Ste. 134; 98168; King; P 120,000; M 400; (206) 575-1633; Fax (206) 575-2007; staff@swkcc.org; www.sschamber.com*

Tulalip • *Greater Marysville Tulalip C/C* • Mary Jane Harmon; Dir. of Admin.; 8825 34th Ave. N.E., Ste. C; 98271; Snohomish; P 100,000; M 300; (360) 659-7700; Fax (360) 653-7539; admin@marysvilletulalipchamber.com; www.marysvilletulalipchamber.com*

Tumwater • *Tumwater Area C/C* • Marjorie Price; Exec. Dir.; 5304 Littlerock Rd. S.W.; 98512; Thurston; P 60,000; M 350; (360) 357-5153; Fax (360) 786-1685; office@tumwaterchamber.com; www.tumwaterchamber.com

Twisp • *Twisp C/C* • P.O. Box 686; 98856; Okanogan; P 1,000; M 85; (509) 997-2020; info@twispinfo.com; www.twispinfo.com

Valleyford • *see Fairfield*

Vancouver • *Greater Vancouver C/C* • John McDonagh; CEO; 1101 Broadway, Ste. 100; 98660; Clark; P 443,000; M 1,100; (360) 694-2588; Fax (360) 693-8279; yourchamber@vancouverusa.com; www.vancouverusa.com*

Vashon • *Vashon-Maury Island C/C* • Deborah Richards; Exec. Dir.; 17141 Vashon Hwy. S.W.; P.O. Box 1035; 98070; King; P 11,000; M 225; (206) 463-6217; Fax (206) 463-7590; discover@vashonchamber.com; www.vashonchamber.com

Victor • *see Belfair*

Walla Walla • *Walla Walla Valley C/C* • David Woolson; Pres./CEO; 29 E. Sumach St.; P.O. Box 644; 99362; Walla Walla; P 61,000; M 800; (509) 525-0850; Fax (509) 522-2038; info@wwvchamber.com; www.wwvchamber.com*

Washougal • *see Camas*

Waterville • *Waterville C/C* • P.O. Box 628; 98858; Douglas; P 1,180; M 20; (509) 745-8871; info@watervillewashington.org; www.watervillewashington.org

Waverly • *see Fairfield*

Wenatchee • *Wenatchee Valley C/C* • Craig Larsen; Exec. Dir.; 2 S. Mission St.; P.O. Box 850; 98807; Chelan; P 80,000; M 650; (509) 662-2116; Fax (509) 663-2022; info@wenatchee.org; www.wenatchee.org*

Wenatchee • *Northcentral Washington Hispanic C/C* • P.O. Box 2001; 98807; Chelan; M 63; (509) 665-9960; Fax (509) 663-2022; angelicao@nwi.net; www.ncwhcc.org*

West Richland • *West Richland Area C/C* • May Hays; Exec. Dir.; 6095 W. Van Giesen; P.O. Box 4023; 99353; Benton; P 15,000; M 300; (509) 967-0521; Fax (509) 967-2950; assistant@westrichlandchamber.org; www.westrichlandchamber.org

West Seattle • *see Seattle-West Seattle C/C*

West Spokane County • *see Cheney*

Westport • *Westport-Grayland C/C* • Leslie Eichner; Exec. Dir.; 2985 S. Montesano St.; P.O. Box 306; 98595; Grays Harbor; P 3,000; M 110; (360) 268-9422; (800) 345-6223; Fax (360) 268-1990; info@cometowestport.com; www.cometowestport.com*

Whidbey Island • *see Coupeville, Langley and Oak Harbor*

White Salmon • *Mt. Adams C/C* • Tammara Tippel; Exec. Dir.; 1 Heritage Plaza; P.O. Box 449; 98672; Klickitat; P 10,000; M 200; (509) 493-3630; info@mtadamschamber.com; www.mtadamschamber.com*

Wilbur • *Wilbur C/C* • Mel Novotney; Pres.; P.O. Box 111; 99185; Lincoln; P 950; M 60; (509) 977-1355; president@wilburwachamber.com; www.wilburwachamber.com

Winchester • *see Quincy*

Winthrop • *Winthrop C/C* • 202 Hwy. 20; P.O. Box 39; 98862; Okanogan; P 350; M 140; (509) 996-2125; (888) 463-8469; info@winthropwashington.com; www.winthropwashington.com

Woodinville • *Woodinville Chamber* • David H. Witt; Exec. Dir.; 17401 133rd Avenue N.E.; 98072; King; P 12,000; M 300; (425) 481-8300; Fax (425) 481-9743; info@woodinvillechamber.org; www.woodinvillechamber.org*

Woodland • *Woodland C/C & Visitors Info. Center* • John Burke; Exec. Dir.; 900 Goerig St.; P.O. Box 1012; 98674; Cowlitz; P 6,300; M 207; (360) 225-9552; Fax (360) 225-3490; jj@woodlandwachamber.com; www.woodlandwachamber.com*

Yakima • *Greater Yakima C/C* • Verlynn Best; Pres./CEO; 10 N. Ninth St.; P.O. Box 1490; 98907; Yakima; P 94,000; M 940; (509) 248-2021; Fax (509) 248-0601; chamber@yakima.org; www.yakima.org*

Yelm • *Yelm Area C/C* • Cecelia Jenkins; Exec. Dir.; 701 Prairie Park Lane S.E., Ste. A; P.O. Box 444; 98597; Thurston; P 12,000; M 450; (360) 458-6608; Fax (360) 458-6383; info@yelmchamber.com; www.yelmchamber.com*

Zillah • *Zillah C/C* • Sue Miller; Pres.; P.O. Box 1294; 98953; Yakima; P 2,720; M 50; (509) 829-5055; zillahchamber@zillahchamber.com; www.zillahchamber.com

West Virginia

West Virginia C of C • Steve Roberts; Pres.; 1624 Kanawha Blvd. E.; Charleston; 25311; Kanawha; P 1,855,413; M 1,850; (304) 342-1115; Fax (304) 342-1130; mhutchinson@wvchamber.com; www.wvchamber.com

Barrackville • *see Fairmont*

Beckley • *Beckley-Raleigh County C/C* • Ellen M. Taylor IOM; Pres./CEO; 245 N. Kanawha St.; 25801; Raleigh; P 17,000; M 690; (304) 252-7328; (877) 987-3847; Fax (304) 252-7373; ellenmtaylor@frontier.com; www.brccc.com*

Berkeley Springs • *Berkeley Springs-Morgan County C/C* • Andrea Curtin; Exec. Dir.; 127 Fairfax St.; 25411; Morgan; P 17,000; M 193; (304) 258-3738; chamber@berkeleysprings.com; www.berkeleyspringschamber.com

Bluefield • *Greater Bluefield C/C* • Marc Meachum; Pres./CEO; P.O. Box 4098; 24701; Mercer; P 11,000; M 450; (304) 327-7184; Fax (304) 325-3085; marc@bluefieldchamber.com; www.bluefieldchamber.com*

Buckhannon • *Buckhannon-Upshur C/C* • Tammy Reger; Exec. Dir.; 14 E. Main St.; P.O. Box 442; 26201; Upshur; P 25,000; M 220; (304) 472-1722; Fax (304) 472-4938; info@buchamber.com; www.buchamber.com

Charles Town • *Jefferson County C/C Inc.* • Heather Morgan McIntyre; Exec. Dir.; 201 E. Washington St.; 25414; Jefferson; P 53,500; M 450; (304) 725-2055; (800) 624-0577; Fax (855) 420-7009; chamber@jeffersoncountywvchamber.org; www.jeffersoncountywvchamber.org

Charleston • *Charleston Area Alliance* • Matthew G. Ballard; Pres./CEO; 1116 Smith St.; 25301; Kanawha; P 303,995; M 700; (304) 340-4253; Fax (304) 340-4275; eperry@charlestonareaalliance.org; www.charlestonareaalliance.org

Chester • *Chester-Newell Area C/C* • Marsha Nurmi; 326 5th St.; 26034; Hancock; P 4,000; M 50; (304) 387-2025; Fax (304) 387-2025; www.ci.chester.wv.us

Clarksburg • *Harrison County C/C* • Katherine Wagner PCED IOM; Pres.; 520 W. Main St.; 26301; Harrison; P 69,141; M 500; (304) 624-6331; Fax (304) 624-5190; marybeth@harrisoncountychamber.com; www.harrisoncountychamber.com*

Davis • *Tucker County C/C* • Bill Smith; Dir.; 410 William Ave. & 4th St.; P.O. Box 565; 26260; Tucker; P 7,000; M 60; (304) 259-5315; Fax (304) 259-4210; tuckerchamber@canaanvalley.org; www.canaanvalley.org

Delbarton • *see Williamson*

Elkins • *Elkins-Randolph County C/C* • Chelsey Jones; Exec. Dir.; 200 Executive Plaza; 26241; Randolph; P 29,200; M 303; (304) 636-2717; Fax (304) 636-8046; chamber@erccc.com; www.erccc.com*

Fairmont • *Marion County C/C* • Tina Shaw; Pres.; 110 Adams St.; 26554; Marion; P 56,600; M 500; (304) 363-0442; Fax (304) 363-0480; mccc@marionchamber.com; www.marionchamber.com

Fairview • *see Fairmont*

Farmington • *see Fairmont*

Follansbee • *Follansbee C/C* • Tony Paesano; Pres.; 1334 Main St.; 26037; Brooke; P 3,000; M 60; (304) 527-2668; Fax (304) 527-2615; www.cityoffollansbee.net

Gilbert • *see Williamson*

Grant Town • *see Fairmont*

Harrisville • *Ritchie County C/C* • David Scott; Pres.; 217 W. Main St.; P.O. Box 177; 26362; Ritchie; P 10,500; M 80; (304) 643-2500; Fax (304) 643-2502; ritchiechamber@zoominternet.net; www.ritchiechamber.com

Hinton • *Summers County C/C* • Mary Haley; Pres.; 238 Main St.; 25951; Summers; P 14,204; M 50; (304) 466-5332; Fax (304) 466-5332; mlhaley@yahoo.com

Huntington • *Huntington Reg. C/C* • Bill Bissett; Pres./CEO; 1108 Third Ave., Ste. 300; P.O. Box 1509; 25701; Cabell; P 51,000; M 550; (304) 525-5131; bill@huntingtonchamber.org; www.huntingtonchamber.org

Hurricane • *see Teays*

Keyser • *Mineral County C/C & CVB* • Anne Palmer; Exec. Dir.; 40 N. Main St.; 26726; Mineral; P 28,000; M 100; (304) 788-2513; Fax (304) 788-3887; office@mineralchamber.com; www.mineralchamber.com*

Kingwood • *Preston County C/C* • Jessica Lipscomb; Bd. Pres.; 200 W. Main St.; 26537; Preston; P 34,000; M 250; (304) 329-0576; Fax (304) 329-1407; info@prestonchamber.com; www.prestonchamber.com

Lewisburg • *Greater Greenbrier C/C* • Amber McHale; Exec. Dir.; 200 W. Washington St., Ste. C; 24901; Greenbrier; P 35,800; M 315; (304) 645-2818; Fax (304) 647-3001; director@greenbrierwvchamber.org; www.greenbrierwvchamber.org*

Logan • *Logan County C/C* • Debrina J. Williams; Exec. Dir.; P.O. Box 218; 25601; Logan; P 37,710; M 200; (304) 752-1324; Fax (304) 752-5988; logancountychamber@frontier.com; www.logancountychamberofcommerce.com

Mannington • *see Fairmont*

Marlinton • *Pocahontas County C/C* • Bill Jordan; Pres.; P.O. Box 272; 24954; Pocahontas; P 8,000; M 75; (304) 456-5466; info@pccocwv.com; www.pccocwv.com

Martinsburg • *Martinsburg-Berkeley County C/C* • Tina Combs; Pres./CEO; 198 Viking Way; 25401; Berkeley; P 109,000; M 530; (304) 267-4841; (800) 332-9007; Fax (304) 263-4695; chamber@berkeleycounty.org; www.berkeleycounty.org

Matewan • *see Williamson*

Monongah • *see Fairmont*

Morgantown • *Morgantown Area C/C* • Jason Pizatella; Pres./CEO; 1029 University Ave, Ste. 101; P.O. Box 658; 26507; Monongalia; P 97,000; M 450; (304) 292-3311; (800) 618-2525; Fax (304) 296-6619; sharon@morgantownchamber.org; www.morgantownchamber.org*

Moundsville • *Marshall County C/C* • David W. Knuth; Exec. Dir.; 609 Jefferson Ave.; 26041; Marshall; P 36,000; M 265; (304) 845-2773; Fax (304) 845-2773; dknuth@marshallcountychamber.com; www.marshallcountychamber.com

Mullens • *Mullens Area C/C* • Rhonda Stone; Pres.; P.O. Box 235; 25882; Wyoming; P 2,000; M 40; (304) 294-0700; mullenscoc@gmail.com; www.cityofmullens.com

New Martinsville • *Wetzel County C/C* • Don Riggenbach; Pres.; 201 Main St.; P.O. Box 271; 26155; Wetzel; P 15,000; M 150; (304) 455-3825; Fax (304) 455-3637; chamber@wetzelcountychamber.com; www.wetzelcountychamber.com*

Oak Hill • *Fayette County C/C* • Sharon P. Cruikshank; Exec. Dir.; 310 W. Oyler Ave.; 25901; Fayette; P 46,000; M 300; (304) 465-5617; Fax (304) 465-5618; sharon@fayettecounty.com; www.fayettecounty.com

Parkersburg • *C/C of the Mid-Ohio Valley* • Jill Parsons; Pres./CEO; 501 Avery St., 9th Flr.; 26101; Wood; P 140,000; M 400; (304) 422-3588; Fax (304) 485-5219; info@movchamber.org; www.movchamber.org*

Petersburg • *Grant County C/C* • Rachel Moyers; Ofc. Admin.; 126 S. Main St., Ste. 1; 26847; Grant; P 12,000; M 129; (304) 257-2722; gowv@gowv.com; www.gowv.com

Philippi • *Barbour County C/C* • Dr. Donald A. Smith; Exec. Dir.; 101 College Hill Dr.; Box 2124; 26416; Barbour; P 16,500; M 160; (304) 457-1958; Fax (304) 457-6239; info@barbourchamber.com; www.barbourchamber.com

Pineville • *Pineville Area C/C* • Dannette Parker; Treas.; P.O. Box 891 (Attn: Tammy Sammons); 24874; Wyoming; P 1,000; M 10; (304) 732-6255; www.local.wv.gov/Pineville

Point Pleasant • *Mason County Area C/C* • Hilda Austin; Exec. Dir.; 305 Main St.; 25550; Mason; P 27,300; M 90; (304) 675-1050; Fax (304) 675-1601; mccofc@pointpleasantwv.org; www.masoncountychamber.org

Princeton • *Princeton-Mercer County C/C* • Robert Farley; Pres./CEO; 1522 N. Walker St.; 24740; Mercer; P 63,000; M 300; (304) 487-1502; Fax (304) 425-0227; pmccc@frontiernet.net; www.pmccc.com

Ravenswood • *see Ripley*

Reedsville • *see Fairmont*

Richwood • *Richwood Area C/C* • Nancy L. Leffingwell; Exec. Dir.; 38 Edgewood Ave.; 26261; Nicholas; P 2,000; M 35; (304) 846-6790; rwdchamber@frontier.com; richwoodchamberofcommerce.org

Ripley • *Jackson County C/C* • Ron Gaskins; Pres./Mgr.; 167 Seneca Dr., Ste. C; 25271; Jackson; P 29,200; M 100; (304) 373-1117; Fax (304) 372-1153; manager@jacksonchamberwv.com; www.jacksonchamberwv.com

Romney • *Hampshire County C/C* • Melanie L. Milliken; Exec. Ofc.; 47-B E. Main St.; 26757; Hampshire; P 22,000; M 147; (304) 822-7221; Fax (304) 822-7221; hampshirechamberofcommerce@citlink.net; www.hampshirecountychamber.com

Saint Albans • *St. Albans Area C/C* • John C. Casto; Pres.; P.O. Box 675; 25177; Kanawha; P 13,000; M 50; (304) 727-7251; Fax (304) 727-7251; sachamber@frontier.com; www.stalbanswv.com

Salem • *Salem Area C/C* • Kevin Fluharty; P.O. Box 191; 26426; Harrison; P 1,500; M 40; (304) 782-1318; chamber@salemwv.com; www.salemwv.com

South Charleston • *South Charleston C/C* • Amanda Ream; Exec. Dir.; 401 D St.; P.O. Box 8595; 25303; Kanawha; P 6,000; M 150; (304) 744-0051; Fax (304) 744-1649; soccoc@wvdsl.net; www.southcharlestonchamber.org

Spencer • *Roane County C/C* • Kim Davis; Exec. Dir.; P.O. Box 1; 25276; Roane; P 15,446; M 74; (304) 927-1780; Fax (304) 927-5953; rchamber@commission.state.wv.us; www.roanechamberwv.org

Summersville • *Summersville Area C/C* • Mary Spencer; Exec. Dir.; 19 Memorial Park Dr.; P.O. Box 567; 26651; Nicholas; P 4,000; M 120; (304) 872-1588; Fax (304) 872-1588; info@summersvillechamber.com; www.summersvillechamber.com

Teays • *Putnam County C/C* • Marty Chapman; Pres.; P.O. Box 553; 25569; Putnam; P 55,000; M 470; (304) 757-6510; Fax (304) 757-6562; chamber@putnamcounty.org; putnamchamber.org

Weirton • *Weirton Area C/C* • Brenda Mull; Pres.; 3174 Pennsylvania Ave., Ste. 1; 26062; Hancock; P 19,000; M 400; (304) 748-7212; Fax (304) 748-0241; info@weirtonchamber.com; www.weirtonchamber.com*

Welch • *McDowell C/C* • Betty Jones; Secy.; 92 McDowell St., Ste. 100; 24801; McDowell; P 22,000; M 150; (304) 436-4260; Fax (304) 436-3837; betty.jones@mcdowelleda.com

Wellsburg • *Wellsburg C/C* • Jacie Ridgely; Chamber Coord.; P.O. Box 487; 26070; Brooke; P 3,500; M 100; (304) 479-2115; Fax (304) 737-1660; wellsburgchamber@gmail.com; www.wellsburgchamber.com

Weston • *Lewis County C/C* • Sherry Lambert; Exec. Dir.; 115 E. Second St.; 26452; Lewis; P 16,919; M 100; (304) 269-2608; Fax (304) 517-1608; lcinfo@lcchamber.org; www.lcchamber.org

Wheeling • *Wheeling Area C/C* • Erikka L. Storch; Pres.; 1100 Main St., 2nd Flr.; 26003; Ohio; P 154,000; M 700; (304) 233-2575; Fax (304) 233-1320; estorch@wheelingchamber.com; www.wheelingchamber.com*

White Sulphur Springs • *see Lewisburg*

Williamson • *Tug Valley C/C* • Natalie Young; Exec. Dir.; 73 E. 2nd St.; 25661; Mingo; P 42,000; M 150; (304) 235-5240; Fax (304) 235-4509; tvcc1@frontier.com; www.tugvalleychamber.com

Winfield • *see Teays*

Worthington • *see Fairmont*

Wisconsin

Wisconsin Manufacturers & Commerce • Kurt Bauer; Pres./CEO; 501 E. Washington Ave.; P.O. Box 352; Madison; 53701; Dane; P 5,726,398; M 3,500; (608) 258-3400; Fax (608) 258-3413; wmc@wmc.org; www.wmc.org

Abbotsford • **AbbyColby Crossings C/C** • Michelle Albrecht; Ofc. Coord.; 100 W. Spruce St.; P.O. Box 418; 54405; Clark & Marathon; P 5,000; M 115; (715) 223-8509; Fax (715) 316-0203; info@abbycolbyareachamber.org; www.abbycolbyareachamber.org*

Adams • **see Friendship**

Algoma • **Algoma Area C/C** • Joy Krieger; Exec. Dir.; 1226 Lake St.; 54201; Kewaunee; P 3,500; M 210; (920) 487-2041; (800) 498-4888; chamber@itol.com; www.algoma.org*

Antigo • **Antigo/Langlade County C/C** • Deena Grabowsky; Exec. Dir.; 1005 S. Superior St.; 54409; Langlade; P 19,575; M 210; (715) 623-4134; (888) 526-4523; Fax (715) 623-4135; info@antigochamber.com; www.antigochamber.com*

Appleton • **Fox Cities C/C & Ind.** • Shannon L. Full; Pres./CEO; 125 N. Superior St.; 54911; Outagamie; P 230,000; M 1,000; (920) 734-7101; Fax (920) 734-7161; info@foxcitieschamber.com; www.foxcitieschamber.com*

Arbor Vitae • **see Minocqua**

Ashland • **Ashland Area C/C** • Mary McPhetridge; Exec. Dir.; 1716 W. Lake Shore Dr.; P.O. Box 746; 54806; Ashland; P 8,700; M 300; (715) 682-2500; (800) 284-9484; Fax (715) 682-9404; ashchamb@centurytel.net; www.visitashland.com*

Baileys Harbor • **Baileys Harbor Comm. Assn.** • P.O. Box 31; 54202; Door; P 1,100; M 100; (920) 839-2366; info@baileysharbor.com; www.baileysharbor.com

Baldwin • **Baldwin-Woodville C/C & Visitor Bur.** • Bonnie Johnson; Pres.; 860 Main St.; P.O. Box 142; 54002; St. Croix; P 5,301; M 98; (715) 684-2221; bwchamber@baldwin-telecom.net; www.baldwin-woodvillechamber.org*

Bangor • **Bangor Bus. Club** • Sue Turnmire; P.O. Box 2; 54614; La Crosse; P 1,500; M 40; (608) 486-1420; (608) 486-4084; www.villageofbangor.com

Baraboo • **Baraboo Area C/C** • Bobbie Boettcher; Exec. Dir.; 600 W. Chestnut St.; P.O. Box 442; 53913; Sauk; P 12,100; M 400; (608) 356-8333; Fax (608) 356-8422; visitus@baraboo.com; www.baraboo.com*

Bayfield • **Bayfield C/C & Visitor Bur.** • David Eades; Exec. Dir.; 42 S. Broad St.; P.O. Box 138; 54814; Bayfield; P 487; M 400; (715) 779-3335; (800) 447-4094; Fax (715) 779-5080; chamber@bayfield.org; www.bayfield.org*

Beaver Dam • **Beaver Dam C/C** • Philip Fritsche; Pres.; 127 S. Spring St.; 53916; Dodge; P 18,000; M 300; (920) 887-8879; Fax (920) 887-9750; info@beaverdamchamber.com; www.beaverdamchamber.com*

Belgium • **Belgium Area C/C** • Jay Lauer; Pres.; P.O. Box 215; 53004; Ozaukee; P 2,500; M 55; (262) 285-3716; (262) 285-7654; bacced@yahoo.com; www.belgiumchamberofcommerce.com

Belleville • **Belleville C/C** • Brad Peterson; Exec. Dir.; P.O. Box 392; 53508; Dale & Green; P 2,000; M 72; (608) 438-4472; www.bellevillewi.org

Beloit • **Greater Beloit C/C** • Aimee Thurner; Interim Exec. Dir.; 635 3rd St.; 53511; Rock; P 37,110; M 335; (608) 365-8835; Fax (608) 365-6850; info@greaterbeloitchamber.org; www.greaterbeloitchamber.org*

Black River Falls • **Black River Area C/C** • Chris Hardie; Exec. Dir.; 120 N. Water St.; 54615; Jackson; P 5,000; M 250; (715) 284-4658; (800) 404-4008; Fax (715) 284-9476; chamber@blackrivercountry.net; www.blackrivercountry.net*

Blanchardville • **Blanchardville Comm. Pride** • Paul Saether; 208 Mason St.; P.O. Box 9; 53516; Iowa & Lafayette; P 825; M 20; (608) 523-4521; Fax (608) 523-4321; bcpi@tds.net; www.blanchardville.com

Bloomer • **Bloomer C/C** • 1731 17th Ave.; P.O. Box 273; 54724; Chippewa; P 3,400; M 145; (715) 568-3339; Fax (715) 568-3346; bchamber@bloomer.net; www.bloomerchamber.com

Boscobel • **Boscobel C/C** • Susie Fralick; Exec. Secy.; 800 Wisconsin Ave.; 53805; Grant; P 3,240; M 148; (608) 375-2672; chamber@boscobelwisconsin.com; www.boscobelwisconsin.com

Boulder Junction • **Boulder Junction C/C** • Theresa Smith; Exec. Dir.; P.O. Box 286; 54512; Vilas; P 1,000; M 130; (715) 385-2400; (800) GO-MUSKY; Fax (715) 385-2379; boulderjct@boulderjct.org; www.boulderjct.org

Brillion • **Brillion C/C** • P.O. Box 123; 54110; Calumet; P 3,000; M 75; (920) 875-0125; Fax (920) 756-2351; info@brillionchamber.com; www.brillionchamber.com

Brodhead • **Brodhead C/C** • Nancy Sutherland; Secy.; P.O Box 16; 53520; Green & Rock; P 4,000; M 60; (608) 897-8411; nancy@brodheadchamber.org; www.brodheadchamber.org

Brookfield • **Greater Brookfield C/C** • Carol White; Pres.; 17100 W. Bluemound Rd., Ste. 202; 53005; Waukesha; P 35,000; M 483; (262) 786-1886; Fax (262) 786-1959; carol@brookfieldchamber.com; www.brookfieldchamber.com*

Brooklyn • **Brooklyn Area C/C** • Sue McCallum; Pres.; P.O. Box 33; 53521; Green; P 1,200; M 18; (608) 455-1627; info@brooklynwisconsin.com; www.brooklynwisconsin.com

Bryant • **see Antigo**

Burlington • **Burlington Area C/C** • Janice Ludtke; Exec. Dir.; 113 E. Chestnut St., Ste. B; P.O. Box 156; 53105; Racine & Walworth; P 20,000; M 500; (262) 763-6044; Fax (262) 763-3631; info@burlingtonchamber.org; www.burlingtonchamber.org*

Butler • **Butler Area C/C** • Linda Ryfinski; Exec. Dir.; 12808 W. Hampton Ave.; 53007; Waukesha; P 1,900; M 100; (262) 781-5195; Fax (262) 781-7870; linda@butlerchamber.org; www.butlerchamber.org

Cable • **Cable Area Chamber** • James Bolen; Exec. Dir.; 13380 County Hwy. M; P.O. Box 217; 54821; Bayfield; P 2,000; M 190; (715) 798-3833; (800) 533-7454; Fax (715) 798-4456; info@cable4fun.com; www.cable4fun.com

Cadott • **Cadott Area C/C** • Huntz Geissler; Pres.; P.O. Box 84; 54727; Chippewa; P 1,400; M 100; (715) 289-3338; info@cadottchamber.org; www.cadottchamber.org

Cambria • **Cambria-Friesland Area C/C** • Sandy Witthun; Pres.; 106 W. Edgewater St.; P.O. Box 143; 53923; Columbia; P 1,100; M 50; (920) 348-6090; (920) 348-5641; floart2@hotmail.com; www.cambriafrieslandchamber.com

Cambridge • **Cambridge Area C/C** • Chair; 102 W. Main St.; P.O. Box 572; 53523; Dane; P 1,500; M 100; (608) 423-3780; office@cambridgewi.com; www.cambridgewi.com*

Campbellsport • *Campbellsport C/C* • Julie Roth; Treas.; P.O. Box 535; 53010; Fond du Lac; P 2,000; M 52; (920) 533-8386; editor@thecampbellsportnews.com; www.campbellsportchamber.org

Cedarburg • *Cedarburg C/C* • Kristine Hage; Exec. Dir.; W61 N480 Washington Ave.; P.O. Box 104; 53012; Ozaukee; P 11,500; M 300; (262) 377-5856; (262) 377-9620; Fax (262) 377-6470; cedarburgchamber@cedarburg.org; www.cedarburg.org

Chetek • *Chetek Area C/C* • P.O. Box 747; 54728; Barron; P 3,000; M 109; (715) 924-3200; (800) 317-1720; info@chetekwi.net; www.chetekwi.net

Chilton • *Chilton C/C* • Tammy Pethan; Exec. Secy.; P.O. Box 122; 53014; Calumet; P 4,000; M 150; (920) 418-1650; info@chiltonchamber.com; www.chiltonchamber.com

Chippewa Falls • *Chippewa Falls Area C/C* • Mike D. Jordan; Pres.; 1 N. Bridge St.; 54729; Chippewa; P 13,000; M 630; (715) 723-0331; (888) 723-0024; Fax (715) 723-0332; info@chippewachamber.org; www.chippewachamber.org*

Clam Lake • *see Cable*

Clear Lake • *Clear Lake Comm. Club* • TJ Buhr; Pres.; P.O. Box 266; 54005; Polk; P 1,070; M 40; (715) 263-2157; Fax (715) 263-2666; geriannemchristensen@gmail.com; clearlakewi.com

Cleveland • *Cleveland C/C* • Lacey Busse; c/o Cleveland State Bank; 1250 W. Washington Ave.; 53015; Manitowoc; P 1,500; M 40; (920) 693-8256; chamber@clevelandwi.net; www.clevelandwi.gov

Clintonville • *Clintonville Area C/C* • Sandy Yaeger; Exec. Dir.; 1 S. Main St.; 54929; Waupaca; P 4,700; M 150; (715) 823-4606; cvlchmbr@frontiernet.net; www.clintonvillewichamber.com

Colby • *see Abbotsford*

Columbus • *Columbus Area C/C* • Heather Whitman; Pres.; P.O. Box 362; 53925; Columbia & Dodge; P 5,000; M 80; (920) 623-3699; info@columbuswichamber.com; www.columbuswichamber.com*

Combined Locks • *see Kaukauna*

Conover • *Conover C/C* • P.O. Box 32; 54519; Vilas; P 1,265; M 70; (715) 479-4928; (866) 394-4386; Fax (715) 479-4928; conover.org@gmail.com; www.conover.org

Crandon • *Forest County C/C* • Melinda Otto; Exec. Dir.; 116 S. Lake Ave.; 54520; Forest; P 9,300; M 135; (715) 478-3450; (800) 334-3387; info@visitforestcounty.com; www.visitforestcounty.com*

Cross Plains • *Cross Plains Area C/C* • Amy Hansen; Exec. Dir.; P.O. Box 271; 53528; Dane; P 3,600; M 100; (608) 843-3166; amy.cpchamber@yahoo.com; www.crossplainschamber.net*

Cuba City • *Cuba City C/C* • Tim Gile; Pres.; 116 N. Main St.; P.O. Box 706; 53807; Grant & Lafayette; P 2,500; M 60; (608) 744-3456; Fax (608) 744-3457; tim@gilecheese.com; www.cubacity.org

Cudahy • *South Shore C/C* • Jerry Kotarak; Pres.; 4731 S. Packard Ave.; 53110; Milwaukee; P 18,500; M 150; (414) 483-8615; Fax (414) 486-9918; chamberpres@netzero.com; www.sscc.com

Cumberland • *Cumberland C/C* • P.O. Box 665; 54829; Barron; P 2,300; M 150; (715) 822-3378; bagafest@cumberland-wisconsin.com; www.cumberland-wisconsin.com

Darboy • *see Kaukauna*

Darlington • *Darlington Chamber/Main Street* • Suzi Osterday; Exec. Dir.; 447 Main St.; 53530; Lafayette; P 2,400; M 100; (608) 776-3067; Fax (608) 776-3067; mainstprogram@centurytel.net; www.darlingtonwi.org

Deer Park • *see New Richmond*

Deerbrook • *see Antigo*

DeForest • *DeForest Area C/C* • Lisa Beck; Exec. Dir.; 201 DeForest St.; 53532; Dane; P 16,000; M 200; (608) 846-2922; dacc1@centurytel.net; www.deforestarea.com*

Delafield • *Delafield Area C/C & Tourism* • Debra Smith; Exec. Dir.; 421 Main St.; P.O. Box 180171; 53018; Waukesha; P 7,100; M 250; (262) 646-8100; (888) 294-1082; Fax (262) 646-8237; info@visitdelafield.org; www.visitdelafield.org*

Delavan • *Delavan-Delavan Lake Area C/C* • Jackie Busch; Exec. Dir.; 52 E. Walworth Ave.; 53115; Walworth; P 12,000; M 230; (262) 728-5095; Fax (262) 728-9199; info@delavanwi.org; www.delavanwi.org*

Denmark • *Denmark Comm. Bus. Assn.* • Ryan Radue; Pres.; P.O. Box 97; 54208; Brown; P 2,130; M 50; (920) 371-0772; Fax (920) 863-3237; dcbawis@yahoo.com; www.dcbawis.com

Dodgeville • *Dodgeville Area C/C* • Lynn Price; Exec. Dir.; 338 N. Iowa St.; 53533; Iowa; P 6,500; M 200; (608) 935-9200; (877) 863-6343; Fax (608) 930-5324; projects@dodgeville.com; www.dodgeville.com

Dousman • *Dousman Area C/C* • Jane Pennycuff & Lynette Tyler; Co-Pres.; P.O. Box 2; 53118; Waukesha; P 2,300; M 100; (262) 719-0157; (262) 719-1506; ssarna@isb.com; www.dousmanchamber.org*

Drummond • *see Cable*

Dundas • *see Kaukauna*

Eagle River • *Vilas County Tourism & Publicity* • Cindy Burzinski; Dir.; 330 Court St.; 54521; Vilas; P 21,400; M 12; (715) 479-3649; (800) 236-3649; Fax (715) 479-3748; vilasadv@co.vilas.wi.us; www.vilas.org

Eagle River • *Eagle River C/C* • Kimberly L. Emerson; Exec. Dir.; 201 N. Railroad St.; P.O. Box 1917; 54521; Vilas; P 1,500; M 400; (715) 479-6400; (800) 359-6315; Fax (715) 479-1960; info@eagleriver.org; www.eagleriver.org*

East Troy • *East Troy Area C/C* • Katie Matteson; Exec. Dir.; 2096 Church St., Ste. A; P.O. Box 312; 53120; Walworth; P 8,000; M 188; (262) 642-3770; Fax (262) 642-8769; info@easttroywi.org; www.easttroywi.org*

Eau Claire • *Eau Claire Area C/C* • Bob McCoy CCE; Pres./CEO; 101 N. Farwell St., Ste. 101; P.O. Box 1107; 54702; Eau Claire; P 100,700; M 1,230; (715) 834-1204; Fax (715) 834-1956; information@eauclairechamber.org; www.eauclairechamber.org*

Edgerton • *Edgerton Area C/C* • Kathy Citta; Admin.; 20 S. Main St.; P.O. Box 5; 53534; Dane & Rock; P 5,300; M 100; (608) 884-4408; Fax (608) 884-4408; edgertonchamber@edgertonchamber.com; www.edgertonchamber.com*

Elcho • *see Antigo*

Elkhart Lake • *Elkhart Lake Area C/C* • Kari Wimmer; Exec. Dir.; 41 E. Rhine St.; P.O. Box 425; 53020; Sheboygan; P 961; M 138; (920) 876-2922; (877) 355-3554; Fax (920) 876-3659; chamber@elkhartlake.com; www.elkhartlake.com

Elkhorn • *Elkhorn Area C/C & Tourism Center* • Christine Clapper; Exec. Dir.; 203 E. Walworth St.; P.O. Box 41; 53121; Walworth; P 10,000; M 220; (262) 723-5788; Fax (262) 723-5784; elkchamber@elkhornchamber.com; www.elkhornchamber.com*

Ellsworth • *Ellsworth Area C/C* • Sarah Ries; Exec. Dir.; P.O. Box 927; 54011; Pierce; P 3,300; M 134; (715) 273-6442; info@ellsworthchamber.com; www.ellsworthchamber.com*

Elroy • *Elroy Area Advancement Corp.* • Kris Yager; P.O. Box 52; 53929; Juneau; P 1,623; M 50; (608) 462-5316; gyager000@centurytel.net; www.elroychamber.com

Elton • *see Antigo*

Evansville • *Evansville Area C/C & Tourism* • Christina Slaback; Exec. Dir.; 8 W. Main St.; 53536; Rock; P 5,000; M 82; (608) 882-5131; evansvillecoc@litewire.net; www.evansvillechamber.org*

Fennimore • *Fennimore C/C* • Linda Parrish; Promo. Coord.; 850 Lincoln Ave.; 53809; Grant; P 2,500; M 120; (608) 822-3599; Fax (608) 822-6007; promo@fennimore.com; www.fennimore.com*

Fish Creek • *Fish Creek Civic Assn.* • James DeGroot; Ofc. Mgr.; 4097 Main St.; P.O. Box 74; 54212; Door; P 1,000; M 140; (920) 868-2316; (800) 577-1880; manager@fishcreekinfo.com; www.visitfishcreek.com

Fitchburg • *Fitchburg C/C* • Angela Kinderman; Exec. Dir.; 5540 Research Park Dr.; 53711; Dane; P 25,300; M 315; (608) 288-8284; akinderman@fitchburgchamber.com; www.fitchburgchamber.com*

Florence • *Florence County C/C* • Rick Knepper; Pres.; P.O. Box 643; 54121; Florence; P 4,500; M 100; (715) 528-5999; web@florencecountychamber.org; www.florencecountychamber.org

Fond du Lac • *Fond du Lac Area Assn. of Commerce* • Joseph R. Reitemeier CCE; Pres./CEO; 207 N. Main St.; 54935; Fond du Lac; P 102,000; M 850; (920) 921-9500; Fax (920) 921-9559; info@fdlac.com; www.fdlac.com*

Fontana • *Geneva Lake West C/C* • Cherie Setteducate; Exec. Dir.; 175 Valley View Dr.; P.O. Box 118; 53125; Walworth; P 7,000; M 168; (877) 275-5102; (262) 275-5102; Fax (262) 275-0979; chamber@genevalakewest.com; www.genevalakewest.com*

Forest Junction • *see Kaukauna*

Fort Atkinson • *Fort Atkinson Area C/C* • Carrie Chisholm; Exec. Dir.; 244 N. Main St.; 53538; Jefferson; P 12,000; M 375; (920) 563-3210; (888) 733-3678; Fax (920) 563-8946; info@fortchamber.com; www.fortchamber.com*

Fox Lake • *Fox Lake Area C/C* • Keri Gossink; Pres.; P.O. Box 94; 53933; Dodge; P 1,700; M 75; (920) 928-3777; info@foxlakechamber.com; www.foxlakechamber.com

Franklin • *see Oak Creek*

Frederic • *Frederic Area C/C* • Rebecca Harlander; Secy./Treas.; P.O. Box 250; 54837; Polk; P 1,200; M 125; (715) 327-4836; Fax (715) 327-4294; www.fredericwi.com

Freedom • *see Kaukauna*

Fremont • *Fremont Area C/C* • Denny Fox; Pres.; P.O. Box 114; 54940; Waupaca; P 700; M 81; (920) 446-3838; denny@travelfremont.com; www.travelfremont.com

Friendship • *Adams County C/C & Tourism* • Laura Hook; Exec. Dir.; 500 Main St.; P.O. Box 295; 53934; Adams; P 20,800; M 160; (608) 339-6997; chamber@visitadamscountywi.com; www.visitadamscountywi.com

Friesland • *see Cambria*

Galesville • *Galesville Area C/C* • Pres.; P.O. Box 196; 54630; Trempealeau; P 1,481; M 70; (608) 582-2868; info@galesvillewi.com; www.galesvillewi.com

Germantown • *Germantown Area C/C* • Lynn Grgich; Exec. Dir.; W156 N11251 Pilgrim Rd., Lower Level; P.O. Box 12; 53022; Washington; P 20,000; M 185; (262) 255-1812; Fax (262) 255-9033; executivedirector@germantownchamber.org; www.germantownchamber.org*

Glendale • *Glendale C/C* • Dale Schmidt; Dir./Exec. V.P.; P.O. Box 170056; 53217; Milwaukee; P 13,000; M 220; (414) 332-0900; Fax (414) 332-0914; D.Schmidt@glendale-chamber.com; www.glendale-chamber.com

Grafton • *Grafton Area C/C* • Pam King; Exec. Dir.; 1624 Wisconsin Ave.; P.O. Box 132; 53024; Ozaukee; P 11,500; M 280; (262) 377-1650; Fax (262) 375-7087; chamber@grafton-wi.org; www.grafton-wi.org

Grand View • *see Cable*

Grantsburg • *Grantsburg C/C* • Nicki Peterson; Pres.; P.O. Box 451; 54840; Burnett; P 1,400; M 75; (715) 463-2405; Fax (715) 463-5555; info@grantsburgchamber.com; www.grantsburgchamber.com

Green Bay • *Greater Green Bay Chamber* • Laurie Radke; Pres.; 300 N. Broadway, Ste. 3A; 54303; Brown; P 306,000; M 1,100; (920) 437-8704; Fax (920) 593-3445; info@titletown.org; www.titletown.org*

Green Lake • *Green Lake Area C/C* • Todd Weir; Pres.; 550 Mill St.; P.O. Box 337; 54941; Green Lake; P 1,100; M 200; (920) 294-3231; (800) 253-7354; Fax (920) 294-3415; info@visitgreenlake.com; www.visitgreenlake.com

Greendale • *Greendale C/C* • Greg Turay; Pres.; P.O. Box 467; 53129; Milwaukee; P 14,200; M 75; (414) 423-3900; info@greendalechamber.com; www.greendalechamber.com

Greenfield • *Greenfield C/C* • Judy Baxter; 4818 S. 76th St., Ste. 129; 53220; Milwaukee; P 37,000; M 125; (414) 327-8500; Fax (877) 327-0084; gcc@thegreenfieldchamber.com; www.thegreenfieldchamber.com

Greenleaf • *see Kaukauna*

Greenwood • *Greenwood C/C* • Pat Linder; Pres.; P.O. Box D; 54437; Clark; P 1,024; M 50; (715) 267-6205; www.greenwoodwi.com

Hartford • *Hartford Area C/C* • Scott M. Henke; Exec. Dir.; 1246-A E. Sumner St.; P.O. Box 270305; 53027; Washington; P 14,500; M 250; (262) 673-7002; Fax (262) 673-7057; info@hartfordchamber.org; www.hartfordchamber.org*

Hartland • *Hartland C/C* • Lynn Minturn; Exec. Dir.; 116 W. Capitol Dr.; 53029; Waukesha; P 10,000; M 280; (262) 367-7059; Fax (262) 367-2980; chamberdirector@hartland-wi.org; www.hartland-wi.org*

Hayward • *Hayward Area C/C* • Doug Smith; Exec. Dir.; P.O. Box 726; 54843; Sawyer; P 4,000; M 339; (715) 634-8662; (800) 724-2992; Fax (715) 634-8498; doug@haywardareachamber.com; www.haywardareachamber.com

Holland • *see Kaukauna*

Holmen • *see Onalaska*

Horicon • *Horicon C/C* • Elena Backhaus; Secy./Treas.; 319 E. Lake St.; P.O. Box 23; 53032; Dodge; P 2,100; M 80; (920) 485-3200; Fax (920) 485-3200; writeus@horiconchamber.com; www.horiconchamber.com

Hudson • *Hudson Area C/C & Tourism Bur.* • Kim Heinemann; Pres.; 502 Second St.; 54016; St. Croix; P 30,000; M 575; (715) 386-8411; (800) 657-6775; Fax (715) 386-8432; andrea@hudsonwi.org; www.hudsonwi.org*

Hurley • *Hurley Area C/C* • Sharon Ofstad; Bd. Pres.; 316 Silver St.; 54534; Iron; P 1,565; M 165; (715) 561-4334; Fax (715) 561-3742; hurley@hurleywi.com; www.hurleywi.com

Iola • *Iola-Scandinavia Area C/C* • Greg Loescher; Pres.; P.O. Box 167; 54945; Waupaca; P 3,500; M 75; (715) 445-2456; onthelake2@tds.net; www.ischamber.com

Iron River • *Iron River Area C/C* • Geri Dresen; Dir.; 7515 U.S. Hwy. 2; P.O. Box 448; 54847; Bayfield; P 1,200; M 140; (715) 372-8558; (800) 345-0716; info@visitironriver.com; www.visitironriver.com

Janesville • *Forward Janesville Inc.* • John Beckord; Pres.; 14 S. Jackson St., Ste. 200; 53548; Rock; P 64,000; M 500; (608) 757-3160; Fax (608) 757-3170; forward@forwardjanesville.com; www.forwardjanesville.com*

Jefferson • *Jefferson C/C* • Janet M. Werner; Exec. Dir.; 623 W. Racine St.; 53549; Jefferson; P 7,900; M 180; (920) 674-4511; coc@jefnet.com; www.jeffersonchamberwi.com*

Johnson Creek • *Johnson Creek Area C/C* • Leigh Price; Exec. Dir.; 417 Union St.; P.O. Box 527; 53038; Jefferson; P 2,850; M 100; (920) 699-4949; johnsoncreekchamber@gmail.com; www.johnsoncreekchamber.com*

Juneau • *Juneau C/C* • Rita Zillmer; Pres.; P.O. Box 4; 53039; Dodge; P 2,500; M 70; (920) 386-3359; juneau@juneauwi.org; www.juneauwi.org

Kaukauna • *Heart of the Valley C/C* • Bobbie Beckman; Exec. Dir.; 101 E. Wisconsin Ave.; 54130; Outagamie; P 50,000; M 600; (920) 766-1616; Fax (920) 766-5504; bbeckman@heartofthevalleychamber.com; www.heartofthevalleychamber.com

Kempster • *see Antigo*

Kenosha • *Kenosha Area C/C* • Lou Molitor; Exec. Dir.; 600 52nd St., Ste. 130; 53140; Kenosha; P 102,000; M 659; (262) 654-1234; Fax (262) 654-4655; lou@kenoshaareachamber.com; www.kenoshaareachamber.com*

Kewaskum • *Kewaskum Area C/C* • Kristy Vogt; P.O. Box 300; 53040; Fond du Lac & Washington; P 4,035; M 85; (262) 626-3336; www.kewaskum.org

Kewaunee • *Kewaunee Area C/C* • Jessica Petersen; Pres.; 308 N. Main; P.O. Box 243; 54216; Kewaunee; P 3,000; M 120; (920) 388-4822; (800) 666-8214; davijl24@gmail.com; www.kewaunee.org

Kiel • *Kiel Area Assn. of Commerce* • P.O. Box 44; 53042; Calumet & Manitowoc; P 3,800; M 125; (920) 894-4638; info@kielwi.org; www.kielwi.org

Kimberly • *see Kaukauna*

La Crosse • *La Crosse Area C/C* • Vicki Markussen; Exec. Dir.; 601 7th Street N.; 54601; La Crosse; P 116,465; M 750; (608) 784-4880; (800) 889-0539; Fax (608) 784-4919; info@lacrossechamber.com; www.lacrossechamber.com*

Lac du Flambeau • *Lac du Flambeau C/C* • Brian Guthrie; 602 Peace Pipe Rd.; P.O. Box 456; 54538; Vilas; P 3,400; M 75; (715) 588-3346; (877) 588-3346; Fax (715) 588-9408; info@lacduflambeauchamber.com; www.lacduflambeauchamber.com

Ladysmith • *Greater Ladysmith Area C/C* • Arlene Knops; Ofc. Mgr.; 205 W. 9tn St. S.; 54848; Rusk; P 4,000; M 205; (715) 532-7328; Fax (715) 532-2649; ladysmithchamber@centurytel.net; www.ladysmithchamber.com

Lake Geneva • *Lake Geneva C/C* • Darien Schaefer; Pres.; 527 Center St.; 53147; Walworth; P 7,900; M 401; (262) 248-1000; (262) 248-4416; Fax (262) 661-7455; lgcc@lakegenevawi.com; www.visitlakegeneva.com*

Lake Mills • *Lake Mills Area C/C* • Kate Anderson; Exec. Dir.; 200 C. Water St.; 53551; Jefferson; P 5,700; M 125; (920) 648-3585; chamber@lakemills.org; www.lakemills.org

Lake Nebagamon • *Nebagamon Comm. Assn.* • P.O. Box 517; 54849; Douglas; P 1,069; M 50; (715) 374-3101; Fax (715) 374-3728; swan@gmail.com; www.lakenebagamonwi.com

Lakewood • *Lakewood Area C/C* • P.O. Box 87; 54138; Oconto; P 1,500; M 100; (715) 276-6500; info@lakewoodareachamber.com; www.lakewoodareachamber.com

Lancaster • *Lancaster Area C/C* • Heather Bontreger; Exec. Dir.; 206 S. Madison St.; P.O. Box 292; 53813; Grant; P 3,900; M 140; (608) 723-2820; (866) 876-2665; Fax (608) 723-7409; chamber@lancasterwisconsin.com; www.lancasterwisconsin.com*

Land O'Lakes • *Land O'Lakes C/C* • Sandy Wait; Exec. Secy.; 6484 Hwy. 45 N.; P.O. Box 599; 54540; Vilas; P 800; M 145; (715) 547-3432; (800) 236-3432; Fax (715) 547-8010; infolandolakes@gmail.com; www.landolakes-wi.org

LaPointe • *Madeline Island C/C* • Max Paap; Exec. Dir.; P.O. Box 274; 54850; Ashland; P 304; M 100; (715) 747-2801; (888) 475-3386; Fax (715) 747-2800; vacation@madelineisland.com; www.madelineisland.com

Little Chute • *see Kaukauna*

Lodi • *Lodi & Lake Wisconsin C/C* • Mandy Sitzman; Exec. Dir.; P.O. Box 43; 53555; Columbia; P 3,200; M 160; (608) 592-4412; info@lodilakewisconsin.org; www.lodilakewisconsin.org

Lomira • *Lomira Area C/C* • Dave Luedtke; P.O. Box 386; 53048; Dodge; P 2,450; M 80; (920) 933-4990; (920) 269-4112; www.lomirachamber.com

Luxemburg • *Luxemburg C/C* • Tom VandenAvond; Pres.; P.O. Box 141; 54217; Kewaunee; P 2,200; M 200; (920) 606-0311; (920) 845-1005; Fax (920) 845-1018; info@luxemburgchamber.com; luxemburgchamber.com

Madison • *Greater Madison C/C* • Zach Brandon; Pres.; 615 E. Washington Ave., 2nd Flr.; P.O. Box 71; 53701; Dane; P 300,000; M 2,500; (608) 256-8348; Fax (608) 256-0333; pfowler@greatermadisonchamber.com; www.greatermadisonchamber.com*

Manawa • *Manawa Area C/C* • Tom Squires; Pres.; P.O. Box 221; 54949; Waupaca; P 1,371; M 55; (920) 596-2495; manawachamberofcommerce@gmail.com; www.manawachamber.com

Manitowish Waters • *Manitowish Waters C/C* • Sarah Pischer; Exec. Dir.; 5733 Airport Rd.; P.O. Box 251; 54545; Vilas; P 740; M 100; (715) 543-8488; (888) 626-9877; chamber@manitowishwaters.org; www.manitowishwaters.org*

Manitowoc • *The Chamber of Manitowoc County* • Karen Szyman; Exec. Dir.; 1515 Memorial Dr.; 54220; Manitowoc; P 81,500; M 518; (920) 684-5575; (866) 727-5575; Fax (920) 684-1915; info@chambermanitowoccounty.org; www.chambermanitowoccounty.org*

Marinette • *Marinette Menominee Area C/C* • Jacqueline Boudreau IOM; Exec. Dir./CEO; 601 Marinette Ave.; 54143; Marinette; P 20,000; M 350; (715) 735-6681; Fax (715) 735-6682; jacqueline.boudreau@mandmchamber.com; www.mandmchamber.com*

Markesan • *Markesan Area C/C* • Clyde Olson; Pres.; P.O. Box 327; 53946; Green Lake; P 1,500; M 45; (920) 398-8023; (888) LT-GREEN; mail@markesanwi.com; www.markesanwi.com

Marshfield • *Marshfield Area C/C & Ind.* • Scott Larson; Exec. Dir.; 700 S. Central Ave.; 54449; Wood; P 50,000; M 500; (715) 384-3454; Fax (715) 387-8925; info@marshfieldchamber.com; www.marshfieldchamber.com*

Mauston • *Greater Mauston Area C/C* • Mary Hudack; Exec. Dir.; 503 State Hwy. 82 E.; P.O. Box 171; 53948; Juneau; P 4,500; M 198; (608) 847-4142; Fax (608) 847-5372; chamber@mauston.com; www.mauston.com/chamber

Mayville • *Mayville Area C/C* • Linda Turk; Ofc. Mgr.; 48 N. Main St.; P.O. Box 185; 53050; Dodge; P 5,000; M 100; (920) 387-5776; (800) 256-7670; Fax (920) 387-5776; info@mayvillechamber.com; www.mayvillechamber.com

Mazomanie • *Greater Mazomanie Area C/C* • Natalie Beil; Pres.; P.O. Box 84; 53560; Dane; P 1,650; M 30; (608) 795-9824; mazochamber@gmail.com; www.mazochamber.org

McFarland • *McFarland C/C* • Donna Manring; Exec. Dir.; 4869 Larson Beach Rd., Ste. B; P.O. Box 372; 53558; Dane; P 10,700; M 230; (608) 838-4011; Fax (608) 838-9463; info@mcfarlandchamber.com; www.mcfarlandchamber.com*

Medford • *Medford Area C/C* • Susan Emmerich; Exec. Dir.; 104 E. Perkins St.; P.O. Box 172; 54451; Taylor; P 4,350; M 325; (715) 748-4729; (888) 682-9567; Fax (715) 748-6899; medfordchamber1@gmail.com; www.medfordwis.com*

Menomonee Falls • *Menomonee Falls C/C Inc.* • Toni Gumina Yates; Exec. Dir.; N91 W17271 Appleton Ave., Ste. 2; 53051; Waukesha; P 33,000; M 340; (262) 251-2430; Fax (262) 251-0969; jane@fallschamber.com; www.fallschamber.com*

Menomonie • *Greater Menomonie Area C/C* • Michelle Dingwall; CEO; 342 E. Main St.; 54751; Dunn; P 16,300; M 500; (715) 235-9087; Fax (715) 235-2824; ceo@menomoniechamber.org; www.menomoniechamber.org*

Mequon • *Mequon-Thiensville Area C/C* • Tina Schwantes; Exec. Dir.; 6331 W. Mequon Rd.; 53092; Ozaukee; P 26,425; M 430; (262) 512-9358; Fax (262) 512-9359; info@mtchamber.org; www.mtchamber.org*

Mercer • *Mercer C/C* • Tina Brunell; Exec. Dir.; 5150 N. Hwy. 51; 54547; Iron; P 2,100; M 125; (715) 476-2389; Fax (715) 476-2389; info@mercercc.com; www.mercercc.com

Merrill • *Merrill Area C/C* • Debbe Kinsey; CEO; 705 N. Center Ave.; 54452; Lincoln; P 10,000; M 265; (715) 536-9474; (877) 90-PARKS; Fax (715) 539-2043; manager@merrillchamber.org; www.merrillchamber.org*

Middleton • *Middleton C/C* • Van Nutt; Exec. Dir.; 7427 Elmwood Ave.; 53562; Dane; P 18,000; M 700; (608) 827-5797; Fax (608) 831-7765; chamber@middletonchamber.com; www.middletonchamber.com*

Milltown • *Milltown Comm. Club* • P.O. Box 402; 54858; Polk; P 900; M 20; (715) 825-2222; (715) 825-3258; info@milltown-wi.com; www.milltown-wi.com

Milton • *Milton Area C/C* • JoLynn Burden; Exec. Dir.; 819 E. High St., Ste 4; P.O. Box 222; 53563; Rock; P 6,000; M 150; (608) 868-6222; execdir@maccit.com; www.maccit.com

Milwaukee • *Metro Milwaukee Assn. of Commerce* • Timothy Sheehy; Pres.; 756 N. Milwaukee St., Ste. 400; 53202; Milwaukee, Ozaukee, Washington, Waukesha; P 1,567,000; M 1,800; (414) 287-4100; Fax (414) 271-7753; kmclees@mmac.org; www.mmac.org

Milwaukee • *African American C/C of Wisconsin* • Dr. Eve Hall; Pres./CEO; 633 W. Wisconsin Ave., Ste. 603; 53203; Milwaukee; P 2,000,000; M 15; (414) 462-9450; Fax (414) 462-9452; info@aaccmke.org; aaccmke.org

Mineral Point • *Mineral Point C/C* • Joy Gieseke; Exec. Dir.; 225 High St.; 53565; Iowa; P 2,500; M 150; (608) 987-3201; (888) POINT-WI; info@mineralpoint.com; www.mineralpoint.com

Minocqua • *Minocqua Area C/C* • Krystal Westfahl; Exec. Dir.; 8216 Hwy. 51 S.; P.O. Box 1006; 54548; Oneida; P 5,000; M 490; (715) 356-5266; Fax (715) 358-2446; macc@minocqua.org; www.minocqua.org*

Mishicot • *MAGIC* • Kim E. Rezek; Coord.; 511 E Main St.; P.O. Box 237; 54228; Manitowoc; P 1,440; M 10; (920) 755-3411; Fax 920-755-2552; magic@mishicot.org; www.mishicot.org

Mondovi • *Mondovi Business Assn.* • Tessa Harmon; P.O. Box 25; 54755; Buffalo; P 2,800; M 50; (715) 926-3828; (715) 926-3866; www.mondovi.com

Monona • *Monona East Side Bus. Alliance* • Kristie Schilling; Exec. Dir.; 5708 Monona Dr., Ste. A; 53716; Dane; P 7,600; M 315; (608) 222-8565; Fax (608) 222-8596; connect@mononaeastside.com; www.mononaeastside.com*

Monroe • *Monroe C/C* • Cara Carper; Exec. Dir.; 1505 9th St.; 53566; Green; P 38,000; M 300; (608) 325-7648; Fax (608) 328-2241; contact@monroechamber.org; www.monroechamber.org*

Montello • *Marquette Now* • Laureen McHugh; P.O. Box 219; 53949; Marquette; P 14,000; M 264; (888) 318-0362; accentsbylaureen@aol.com; www.marquettenow.com

Mosinee • *Mosinee Area C/C* • Tammy Campo; Exec. Dir.; 201 Main St.; 54455; Marathon; P 3,900; M 158; (715) 693-4330; Fax (715) 693-9555; macoc@mtc.net; www.mosineechamber.org*

Mount Horeb • *Mount Horeb Area C/C* • Melissa Theisen; Exec. Dir.; 300 E. Main St.; 53572; Dane; P 8,000; M 200; (608) 437-5914; (88) TROLLWAY; Fax (608) 437-1427; info@trollway.com; www.trollway.com

Mountain • *see Lakewood*

Mukwonago • *Mukwonago Area C/C & Tourism Center* • April D. Reszka; Exec. Dir.; 100 Atkinson St.; 53149; Waukesha; P 14,800; M 300; (262) 363-7758; Fax (262) 363-7730; director@mukwonagochamber.org; www.mukwonagochamber.org*

Muscoda • *Muscoda Chamber & Ind. Dev. Corp.* • Dennis Brown; 802 N. Wisconsin; P.O. Box 587; 53573; Grant & Iowa; P 1,500; M 40; (608) 739-3616; dionjuly@yahoo.com; muscoda.com

Muskego • *Muskego Area C/C & Tourism* • Deb Skurulsky; Exec. Dir.; S74 W16894 Janesville Rd.; P.O. Box 234; 53150; Waukesha; P 24,000; M 340; (414) 422-1155; Fax (414) 422-1415; executivedirector@muskego.org; www.muskego.org*

Namakagon • *see Cable*

Necedah • *Necedah C/C* • Roger Herried; Admin.; 101 Center St.; P.O. Box 244; 54646; Juneau; P 888; M 61; (608) 565-2261; necedahadmin@necedah.us; www.necedah.us

Neenah • *see Appleton*

Neillsville • *Neillsville Area C/C* • Deanna Heiman; Exec. Dir.; 500 West St.; P.O. Box 52; 54456; Clark; P 2,500; M 142; (715) 743-6444; neillsvillechamber@gmail.com; www.neillsville.org*

New Berlin • *New Berlin Chamber & Visitors Bur.* • Edward Holpfer; Exec. Dir.; 13825 W. National Ave., Ste. 109A; 53151; Waukesha; P 39,000; M 210; (262) 786-5280; Fax (262) 786-9165; office@newberlinchamber.org; www.newberlinchamber.org

New Glarus • *New Glarus C/C* • Susie Weiss; Dir.; 418 Railroad St.; P.O. Box 713; 53574; Green; P 2,200; M 125; (608) 527-2095; (800) 527-6838; Fax (608) 527-4991; susie@swisstown.com; www.swisstown.com

New Holstein • *New Holstein Area C/C* • Robert Bosma; Pres.; P.O. Box 17; 53061; Calumet; P 3,400; M 91; (920) 898-5771; (920) 898-9095; nhchamber.newholsteinchamber@gmail.com; newholstein.org

New Lisbon • *New Lisbon Area C/C* • Nancy Cowan; Exec. Secy.; 218 E. Bridge St.; P.O. Box 79; 53950; Juneau; P 1,500; M 75; (608) 562-3555; Fax (608) 562-5625; nlchambr@mwt.net; www.newlisbonchamber.com

New London • *New London Area C/C* • Laurie Shaw; Exec. Dir.; 420 N. Shawano St.; 54961; Outagamie & Waupaca; P 7,000; M 250; (920) 982-5822; Fax (920) 982-6344; tracy@newlondonchamber.com; www.newlondonchamber.com*

New Richmond • *New Richmond Area C/C & Visitors Bur.* • Russ Korpela; Exec. Dir.; 245A S. Knowles Ave.; 54017; St. Croix; P 8,000; M 250; (715) 246-2900; (800) 654-6380; Fax (715) 246-7100; nrchamber@pressenter.com; www.newrichmondchamber.com*

Oak Creek • *South Suburban C/C* • Barbara Wesener CAE APR IOM; Exec. Dir.; 8040 S. 6th St.; 53154; Milwaukee; P 55,000; M 320; (414) 768-5845; Fax (414) 768-5848; info@southsuburbanchamber.com; www.southsuburbanchamber.com

Oconomowoc • *Oconomowoc Area C/C* • Katie Miller MSM; Exec. Dir.; 175 E. Wisconsin Ave., Ste. L; 53066; Waukesha; P 16,000; M 330; (262) 567-2666; Fax (262) 567-3477; chamber@oconomowoc.org; www.oconomowoc.org*

Oconto • *Oconto Area C/C* • Ron Hayes; Pres.; P.O. Box 174; 54153; Oconto; P 4,500; M 120; (920) 834-6254; (888) 626-6862; info@ocontoareachamber.com; www.ocontoareachamber.com

Oconto Falls • *Oconto Falls Area C/C* • Pam Lemorande; Pres.; P.O. Box 24; 54154; Oconto; P 2,800; M 90; (920) 846-8306; ofchamber@centurytel.net; www.ocontofallschamber.com

Omro • *Future Omro Chamber-Main Street* • Dana Racine; Comm. Dev. & Main Street Dir.; 130 W. Larrabee St.; 54963; Winnebago; P 3,500; M 82; (920) 685-6960; Fax (920) 685-0384; dracine@omro-wi.com; www.futureomro.org

Onalaska • *Onalaska Center for Commerce & Tourism* • Amy Gabay; Interim Dir.; 255 Riders Club Rd.; 54650; La Crosse; P 18,256; (608) 781-9570; (800) 873-1901; Fax (608) 781-9572; info@discoveronalaska.com; www.discoveronalaska.com

Oostburg • *Oostburg Area C/C* • Steve Klescewski; Pres.; P.O. Box 700433; 53070; Sheboygan; P 3,000; M 70; (920) 564-6500; www.oostburgchamber.com

Oregon • *Oregon Area C/C* • Judy Knutson; Exec. Dir.; 117 Spring St., 2nd Flr.; P.O. Box 123; 53575; Dane; P 8,000; M 206; (608) 835-3697; Fax (608) 835-2475; judy@oregonwi.com; www.oregonwi.com

Osceola • *Main Street/Chamber* • Courtney Sprecher; Dir.; P.O. Box 251; 54020; Polk; P 2,700; M 70; (715) 755-3300; (800) 947-0581; osceolachamber@centurytel.net; www.vil.osceola.wi.us

Oshkosh • *Oshkosh C/C* • John A. Casper; Pres./CEO; 120 Jackson St.; 54901; Winnebago; P 66,778; M 1,000; (920) 303-2266; Fax (920) 303-2263; info@oshkoshchamber.com; www.oshkoshchamber.com*

Owen • *Owen-Withee Area C/C* • Sid Borgeson; Pres.; P.O. Box 186; 54460; Clark; P 1,600; M 65; (715) 229-2697; info@owenwitheechamber.org; www.owenwitheechamber.org

Oxford • *see Montello*

Palmyra • *Palmyra Area C/C* • Rick Ball; Pres.; P.O. Box 139; 53156; Jefferson; P 1,774; M 45; (262) 495-8316; (414) 531-4357; tarawalters68@yahoo.com; www.palmyrawi.com

Pardeeville • *Pardeeville Area Bus. Assn.* • Bob Becker; Treas.; P.O. Box 337; 53954; Columbia; P 2,185; M 35; (608) 617-9201; (608) 429-3121; treasurer@pardeeville.biz; www.pardeeville.biz

Park Falls • *Park Falls Area C/C* • Sue Holm; Exec. Dir.; 400 4th Ave. S.; 54552; Price; P 2,500; M 220; (715) 762-2703; (877) 762-2703; Fax (715) 762-4130; chamber@parkfalls.com; www.parkfalls.com*

Parrish • *see Antigo*

Pearson • *see Antigo*

Pelican Lake • *Pelican Lake C/C* • Beth Reinemann; Comm. Dir.; P.O. Box 45; 54463; Oneida; P 1,000; M 74; (715) 487-5222; Fax (715) 487-4009; pelicanlakecc@frontiernet.net; www.pelicanlakewi.org

Peshtigo • *Peshtigo C/C* • Birdy McKenney; Secy.; 240 French St.; P.O. Box 36; 54157; Marinette; P 4,100; M 100; (715) 582-0327; Fax (715) 582-0327; peshtigochamber@centurytel.net; www.peshtigochamber.com

Pewaukee • *Pewaukee C/C* • Nancy Waters; Pres.; 1285 Sunnyridge Rd.; 53072; Waukesha; P 16,000; M 240; (262) 691-8851; Fax (262) 691-0922; info@pewaukeechamber.org; www.pewaukeechamber.org*

Phelps • *Phelps C/C* • Sheila Schmidt; Dir.; 2299 Hwy. 17; P.O. Box 217; 54554; Vilas; P 1,500; M 56; (715) 545-3800; (877) 669-7077; phelpschamber@gmail.com; www.phelpswi.us

Phillips • *Phillips Area C/C* • Judith Boers; Exec. Dir.; 305 S. Lake Ave.; 54555; Price; P 1,550; M 180; (715) 339-4100; (888) 408-4800; Fax (715) 339-4190; pacc@pctcnet.net; www.phillipswisconsin.net

Phlox • *see Antigo*

Pickerel • *see Antigo*

Platteville • *Platteville Reg. Chamber* • Kathy Kopp; Exec. Dir.; 275 Bus. Hwy. 151 W.; P.O. Box 724; 53818; Grant; P 11,000; M 330; (608) 348-8888; Fax (608) 348-8890; chamber@platteville.com; www.platteville.com*

Plover • *see Stevens Point*

Plymouth • *Plymouth C/C* • Mary Hauser; Exec. Dir.; 647 Walton Dr.; P.O. Box 584; 53073; Sheboygan; P 8,600; M 350; (920) 893-0079; (888) 693-8263; Fax (920) 893-8473; plymouthchamber@frontier.com; www.plymouthwisconsin.com*

Polar • *see Antigo*

Port Washington • *Port Washington C/C* • Lisa Crivello; Exec. Dir.; 126 E. Grand Ave.; P.O. Box 514; 53074; Ozaukee; P 11,500; M 200; (262) 284-0900; (800) 719-4881; Fax (262) 284-0591; pwcc@sbcglobal.net; www.visitportwashington.com

Portage • *Portage Area C/C* • Marianne Hanson; Exec. Dir.; 104 W. Cook St., Ste. A; 53901; Columbia; P 10,000; M 300; (608) 742-6242; pacc@portagewi.com; www.portagewi.com*

Potosi • *Potosi-Tennyson Area C/C* • Rosann Bausch; Pres.; P.O. Box 11; 53820; Grant; P 1,043; M 40; (608) 763-2300; potositennysoncc@tds.net; www.potosiwisconsin.com

Poynette • *Poynette Area C/C* • Brit Schoeneberg; Pres.; P.O. Box 625; 53955; Columbia; P 2,800; M 90; (608) 635-2425; britlivw@aol.com; www.poynettechamber.com

Prairie du Chien • *Prairie du Chien Area C/C* • Robert Moses; CEO; 211 S. Main St.; P.O. Box 326; 53821; Crawford; P 8,000; M 350; (608) 326-8555; (800) 732-1673; Fax (608) 326-7744; info@prairieduchien.org; www.prairieduchien.org*

Prairie du Sac • *see Sauk City*

Prescott • *Prescott Area C/C* • Trisha Huber; Coord.; 237 Broad St.; 54021; Pierce; P 4,000; M 115; (715) 262-3284; Fax (715) 262-5943; info@prescottwi.com; www.prescottwi.com

Presque Isle • *Presque Isle C/C* • Sarah Johnson; Dir.; P.O. Box 135; 54557; Vilas; P 600; M 80; (715) 686-2910; (888) 835-6508; presqueisle@centurytel.net; www.presqueisle.com

Princeton • *Greater Princeton Area C/C* • Karen Jacobi; Asst.; P.O. Box 45; 54968; Green Lake; P 1,500; M 150; (920) 295-3877; yesteryearantiques@centurytel.net; www.princetonwi.com*

Pulaski • *Pulaski Area C/C* • Gloria Morgan; Exec. Dir.; 159 W. Pulaski St.; P.O. Box 401; 54162; Brown, Oconto & Shawano; P 4,000; M 76; (920) 822-4400; Fax (920) 822-4455; pacc@netnet.net; www.pulaskichamber.org

Racine • *Racine Area Mfg. & Commerce* • Drew Abram; Interim Pres./CEO; 300 Fifth St.; 53403; Racine; P 194,800; M 750; (262) 634-1931; Fax (262) 634-7422; ramac@racinechamber.com; www.racinechamber.com*

Randolph • *Randolph C/C* • Peggy Potter; Pres.; P.O. Box 66; 53956; Columbia & Dodge; P 1,800; M 65; (920) 326-4769; (920) 326-4640; www.randolphwi.net

Reedsburg • *Reedsburg Area C/C* • Kristine Koenecke; Exec. Dir.; 240 Railroad St.; P.O. Box 142; 53959; Sauk; P 10,100; M 210; (608) 524-2850; Fax (608) 524-5392; reedsbrg@rucls.net; www.reedsburg.org*

Rhinelander • *Rhinelander Area C/C* • 450 W. Kemp St.; P.O. Box 795; 54501; Oneida; P 8,000; M 350; (715) 365-7464; (800) 236-4386; info@rhinelanderchamber.com; www.explorerhinelander.com *

Rice Lake • *Rice Lake Area C/C* • Karen Heram; Exec. Dir.; 37 S. Main St.; 54868; Barron; P 10,000; M 340; (715) 234-2126; Fax (715) 234-2085; chamber@rice-lake.com; www.ricelakechamber.org*

Ripon • *Ripon Area C/C* • Jason Mansmith; Mktg. & Events Coord.; 114 Scott St.; P.O. Box 305; 54971; Fond du Lac; P 8,000; M 300; (920) 748-6764; Fax (920) 748-6784; chamber@ripon-wi.com; www.ripon-wi.com

River Falls • *River Falls Area C/C & Tourism Bur.* • Chris Blasius; CEO; 215 W. Maple St.; 54022; Pierce & St. Croix; P 16,000; M 300; (715) 425-2533; Fax (715) 425-2305; info@rfchamber.com; www.rfchamber.com*

Saint Croix Falls • *Falls C/C* • Catherine Veith-Bruno; Exec. Dir.; 106 S. Washington; P.O. Box 178; 54024; Polk; P 3,000; M 165; (715) 483-3580; (800) 447-4958; Fax (715) 483-3580; director@fallschamber.org; www.fallschamber.org*

Saint Germain • *St. Germain C/C* • Penny Wiesmann; Dir.; 473 Hwy. 70 E.; P.O. Box 155; 54558; Vilas; P 2,000; M 160; (715) 477-2205; (800) 727-7203; sgexecutive@frontier.com; www.st-germain.com

Sauk City • *Sauk Prairie Area C/C* • Tywana German; Exec. Dir.; 109 Phillips Blvd.; 53583; Sauk; P 21,000; M 300; (608) 643-4168; (800) 683-2453; Fax (608) 643-3544; spacc@saukprairie.com; www.saukprairie.com*

Saukville • *Saukville C/C* • Sherri Yandry; Exec. Dir.; 101 N. Mill St., Ste. A; P.O. Box 80238; 53080; Ozaukee; P 4,400; M 110; (262) 268-1970; Fax (262) 268-1970; exec@saukvillechamber.org; www.saukvillechamber.org

Sayner • *Sayner-Starlake C/C* • P.O. Box 191; 54560; Vilas; P 500; M 50; (715) 542-3789; saynerstarlake@gmail.com; www.sayner-starlake.org

Sharon • *Sharon C/C* • Linda Dipiero; Pres.; P.O. Box 528; 53585; Walworth; P 1,605; M 63; (262) 736-1250; joann@sharontelephone.com; www.sharonchamberofcommerce.com

Shawano • *Shawano Country C/C* • Nancy Smith; Exec. Dir.; 1263 S. Main St.; P.O. Box 38; 54166; Shawano; P 42,000; M 430; (715) 524-2139; (800) 235-8528; Fax (715) 524-3127; nsmith@shawano.com; www.shawanocountry.com*

Sheboygan • *Sheboygan County C/C* • Betsy Alles; Exec. Dir.; 621 S. 8th St.; 53081; Sheboygan; P 115,000; M 975; (920) 457-9491; Fax (920) 457-6269; betsy@sheboygan.org; www.sheboygan.org*

Sheboygan Falls • *Sheboygan Falls Chamber-Main Street* • Shirl A. Breunig; Exec. Dir.; 504 Broadway; 53085; Sheboygan; P 7,775; M 207; (920) 467-6206; Fax (920) 467-9571; chambermnst@sheboyganfalls.org; www.sheboyganfalls.org*

Sherwood • *see Kaukauna*

Siren • *Siren C/C Inc.* • Christine Moeller; Exec. Dir.; 24049 1st Ave.; P.O. Box 57; 54872; Burnett; P 850; M 85; (715) 349-8399; (800) 788-3164; Fax (715) 349-2830; chamber@visitsiren.com; www.VisitSiren.com*

Slinger • *Slinger Advancement Assn.* • Dr. Don Crego; Pres.; P.O. Box 422; 53086; Washington; P 5,000; M 55; (262) 644-5866; saa@slingersaa.com; www.slingersaa.com

Somerset • *also see New Richmond*

Somerset • Somerset Area C/C • Casey Goessl; Pres.; P.O. Box 357; 54025; St. Croix; P 2,400; M 41; (715) 247-3366; schamber@somtel.net; www.somersetchamber.com

South Milwaukee • South Milwaukee C/C • Bryan Lorentzen; Pres.; 2424 15th Ave.; P.O. Box 207; 53172; Milwaukee; P 25,000; M 110; (414) 762-2222, X141; Fax (414) 768-9505; laurac@smaconline.com; www.smaconline.com

Sparta • Sparta Area C/C • Tim Hyma; CEO; 111 Milwaukee St.; 54656; Monroe; P 9,700; M 305; (608) 269-4123; (800) 354-2453; Fax (608) 269-3350; ceo@bikesparta.com; bikesparta.org*

Spencer • Spencer C/C • Dale Smith; Pres.; 105 Park St.; 54479; Marathon; P 1,941; M 50; (715) 659-5423; Fax (715) 659-5358; clerk@vil.spencer.wi.us; vil.spencer.wi.us

Spooner • Spooner Area C/C • Aaron Arf; Exec. Dir.; 122 N. River St.; 54801; Washburn; P 2,653; M 100; (715) 635-2168; (800) 367-3306; Fax (715) 635-5170; spoonerareachamber@spoonerchamber.org; www.spoonerchamber.org

Spring Green • Spring Green Area C/C • Kris Stoddard; Exec. Dir.; P.O. Box 3; 53588; Sauk; P 2,500; M 150; (608) 588-2054; (800) 588-2042; sgacc@springgreen.com; www.springgreen.com

Spring Valley • Spring Valley C/C • P.O. Box 351; 54767; Pierce & St. Croix; P 1,350; M 55; (715) 778-5015; tony@springvalleywisconsin.org; www.springvalleywisconsin.org

Stanley • Stanley Area C/C • Ryan Westaby; Pres.; P.O. Box 191; 54768; Chippewa & Clark; P 3,625; M 70; (715) 644-5933; stanleywisconsin.us

Star Prairie • see New Richmond

Starlake • see Sayner

Stevens Point • Portage County Bus. Cncl. • Lori Dehlinger; Exec. Dir.; 5501 Vern Holmes Dr.; 54482; Portage; P 70,400; M 500; (715) 344-1940; Fax (715) 344-4473; admin@portagecountybiz.com; www.portagecountybiz.com

Stone Lake • Stone Lake C/C • Susan Walker; P.O. Box 75; 54876; Washburn; P 300; M 20; (715) 865-3378; (715) 957-0055; www.stonelakewi.com

Stoughton • Stoughton C/C • Erica Dial; Exec. Dir.; 532 E. Main St.; 53589; Dane; P 13,000; M 250; (608) 873-7912; (888) 873-7912; Fax (608) 873-7743; administrator@stoughtonwi.com; www.stoughtonwi.com

Stratford • Stratford C/C • Beki Lemke; Pres.; P.O. Box 312; 54484; Marathon; P 1,600; M 100; (715) 687-4166; stratfordchamber@gmail.com; www.stratfordchamber.org

Summit Lake • see Antigo

Sun Prairie • Sun Prairie C/C • 109 E. Main St.; 53590; Dane; P 33,000; M 415; (608) 837-4547; Fax (608) 837-8765; spchamber@frontier.com; www.sunprairiechamber.com*

Superior • Superior-Douglas County C/C • David W. Minor; Pres./CEO; 205 Belknap St.; 54880; Douglas; P 44,100; M 415; (715) 394-7716; (800) 942-5313; Fax (715) 394-3810; chamber@superiorchamber.org; www.superiorchamber.org*

Sussex • Sussex Area C/C • Kathryn Wagner; Exec. Dir.; N64 W23760 Main St.; 53089; Waukesha; P 10,500; M 120; (262) 246-4940; Fax (262) 246-7350; info@sussexareachamber.org; www.sussexareachamber.org

Thiensville • see Mequon

Thorp • Thorp Area C/C • Justin J. Zoromski; Pres.; P.O. Box 16; 54771; Clark; P 1,650; M 90; (715) 669-5371; thorpchamber@yahoo.com; www.cityofthorp.com

Three Lakes • Three Lakes Area C/C • Skip Brunswick; Exec. Dir.; 1704 Superior St.; P.O. Box 268; 54562; Oneida; P 2,400; M 125; (715) 546-3344; (800) 972-6103; Fax (715) 545-2103; vacation@threelakes.com; www.threelakes.com

Tomah • Tomah Chamber & Visitor's Center • Tina Thompson; Pres./CEO; 901 Kilbourn Ave.; P.O. Box 625; 54660; Monroe; P 9,200; M 334; (608) 372-2166; Fax (608) 372-2167; info@tomahwisconsin.com; www.tomahwisconsin.com*

Tomahawk • Tomahawk Reg. C/C • Jesica Witte; Exec. Dir.; 208 N. 4th St.; P.O. Box 412; 54487; Lincoln; P 10,000; M 300; (715) 453-5334; (800) 569-2160; Fax (715) 453-1178; chambert@gototomahawk.com; www.gototomahawk.com*

Townsend • see Lakewood

Trempealeau • Trempealeau C/C • 24455 3rd St.; P.O. Box 242; 54661; Trempealeau; P 1,541; M 45; (608) 534-6780; chamber@trempealeau.net; www.trempealeau.net

Twin Lakes • Twin Lakes Area Chamber & Bus. Assn. Inc. • Marilyn Trongeau; Exec. Dir.; 349 E. Main St.; P.O. Box 64; 53181; Kenosha; P 6,041; M 80; (262) 877-2220; Fax (262) 877-9437; info@twinlakeschamber.com; www.twinlakeschamber.com

Two Rivers • see Manitowoc

Union Grove • Greater Union Grove Area C/C • Jennifer Ditscheit; Exec. Dir.; 925 15th Ave.; P.O. Box 44; 53182; Racine; P 5,000; M 250; (262) 878-4606; Fax (262) 878-9125; jennifer@uniongrovechamber.org; www.uniongrovechamber.org*

Verona • Verona Area C/C • Karl Curtis; Exec. Dir.; 120 W. Verona Ave.; P.O. Box 930003; 53593; Dane; P 10,600; M 309; (608) 845-5777; Fax (608) 845-2519; kcurtis@veronawi.com; www.veronawi.com

Viroqua • Viroqua C/C Main St. • Rebecca Eby; Exec. Dir.; 220 S. Main St.; 54665; Vernon; P 4,400; M 200; (608) 637-2575; infodesk@viroqua-wisconsin.com; www.viroqua-wisconsin.com

Wabeno • Wabeno C/C • Dawn Jakubiec; P.O. Box 105; 54566; Forest; P 1,500; M 30; (715) 473-2311; www.townofwabeno.org

Washburn • Washburn Area C/C • Nicole Then; Ofc. Mgr.; P.O. Box 74; 54891; Bayfield; P 2,200; M 135; (715) 373-5017; (800) 253-4495; Fax (715) 373-5017; info@washburnchamber.com; www.washburnchamber.com

Washington Island • Washington Island C/C • Mary Andersen; Pres.; 2206 W. Harbor Rd.; 54246; Door; P 700; M 100; (920) 847-2179; info@washingtonisland-wi.com; www.washingtonisland-wi.com

Waterford • Waterford Area C/C • Katy Engels; Exec. Dir.; 102 E. Main St.; P.O. Box 203; 53185; Racine; P 6,000; M 225; (262) 534-5911; Fax (262) 534-6507; chamber@waterford-wi.org; www.waterford-wi.org*

Waterloo • Waterloo C/C • William Hogan; Pres.; P.O. Box 1; 53594; Jefferson; P 3,000; M 65; (920) 478-2500; chamber@waterloowi.us; www.waterloowi.us

Watertown • *Watertown Area C/C* • Susan Dascenzo; Exec. Dir.; 519 E. Main St.; 53094; Dodge & Jefferson; P 29,000; M 300; (920) 261-6320; Fax (920) 261-6434; info@watertownchamber.com; www.watertownchamber.com*

Waukesha • *Waukesha County Bus. Alliance Inc.* • Suzanne Kelley; Pres.; 2717 N. Grandview Blvd., Ste. 300; 53188; Waukesha; P 390,000; M 900; (262) 542-4249; Fax (262) 542-8068; alliance@waukesha.org; www.waukesha.org*

Waunakee • *Waunakee Area C/C* • Ellen K. Schaaf; Exec. Dir.; 100 E. Main St.; P.O. Box 41; 53597; Dane; P 12,000; M 280; (608) 849-5977; Fax (608) 849-9825; office@waunakeechamber.com; www.waunakeechamber.com*

Waupaca • *Waupaca Area C/C Inc.* • Terri Schulz; Pres.; 221 S. Main St.; 54981; Waupaca; P 16,000; M 400; (715) 258-7343; (888) 417-4040; Fax (715) 258-7868; info@waupacaareachamber.com; www.waupacaareachamber.com*

Waupun • *Waupun Area C/C* • Charlene Becker; Exec. Dir.; 324 E. Main St.; 53963; Fond du Lac; P 11,300; M 160; (920) 324-3491; Fax (920) 324-4357; info@waupunchamber.com; www.waupunchamber.com

Wausau • *Wausau Region C/C* • Dave Eckmann; Pres./CEO; 200 Washington St., Ste. 120; 54403; Marathon; P 134,000; M 900; (715) 845-6231; Fax (715) 845-6235; info@wausauchamber.com; www.wausauchamber.com*

Wautoma • *Waushara Area C/C* • Deb Gabrilska; Exec. Dir.; 440 W. Main St.; P.O. Box 65; 54982; Waushara; P 24,000; M 240; (920) 787-3488; (877) 928-8662; wausharachamber@gmail.com; www.wausharachamber.com

Wauwatosa • *Wauwatosa C/C* • Terry Estness; Exec. Dir.; 10437 Innovation Dr., Ste. 130; 53226; Milwaukee; P 47,271; M 300; (414) 453-2330; Fax (414) 453-2336; info@tosachamber.org; www.tosachamber.org*

Webster • *Webster Area C/C* • Jim Olson; P.O. Box 48; 54893; Burnett; P 681; M 100; (715) 866-4298; websterchamber@yahoo.com; www.websterwisconsin.com

West Allis • *West Allis/West Milwaukee C/C* • Diane Brandt; Exec. Dir.; 7447 W. Greenfield Ave.; 53214; Milwaukee; P 70,000; M 400; (414) 302-9901; Fax (414) 302-9918; contact@wawmchamber.com; www.wawmchamber.com*

West Bend • *West Bend Area C/C* • Craig Farrell; Exec. Dir.; 304 S. Main St.; 53095; Washington; P 31,000; M 500; (262) 338-2666; Fax (262) 338-1771; linda@wbachamber.org; www.wbachamber.org*

West Milwaukee • *see West Allis*

West Salem • *see Onalaska*

Westby • *Westby Area C/C* • Trish Evenstad; Exec. Dir.; P.O. Box 94; 54667; Vernon; P 2,000; M 80; (608) 634-4011; (866) 493-7829; westbycoc@mwt.net; www.westbywi.com

Westport • *see Waunakee*

Weyauwega • *Weyauwega Area C/C* • Dan Knecht; Pres.; P.O. Box 531; 54983; Waupaca; P 1,900; M 61; (920) 867-2500; info@weyauwegachamber.com; www.weyauwegachamber.com

White Lake • *see Antigo*

Whitehall • *Whitehall Area C/C* • Betty Tulley; Pres.; P.O. Box 281; 54773; Trempealeau; P 1,600; M 45; (715) 538-1505; bjtulley@tcc.coop; www.whitehallwichamber.com

Whitewater • *Whitewater Area C/C* • Marie Koch; Exec. Dir.; 150 W. Main St.; 53190; Jefferson & Walworth; P 15,000; M 175; (262) 473-4005; (866) 4-WWTOUR; info@whitewaterchamber.com; www.whitewaterchamber.com

Williams Bay • *see Fontana*

Winneconne • *Winneconne Area C/C* • Donna Wicinsky; Pres.; 31 S. 2nd St.; P.O. Box 126; 54986; Winnebago; P 3,000; M 80; (920) 582-4775; Fax (920) 582-4801; chamber@winneconne.org; www.winneconne.org

Winter • *Winter Area C/C* • P.O. Box 245; 54896; Sawyer; P 1,500; M 90; (715) 266-2204; (800) 762-7179; mail@winterwi.com; www.winterwi.com

Wisconsin Rapids • *Heart of Wisconsin C/C* • Melissa Reichert; Pres.; 1120 Lincoln St.; 54494; Wood; P 40,000; M 400; (715) 423-1830; Fax (715) 423-1865; president@wisconsinrapidschamber.com; www.wisconsinrapidschamber.com*

Wittenberg • *Wittenberg Area C/C* • Anita Kostuch; Pres.; P.O. Box 284; 54499; Shawano; P 1,300; M 50; (715) 253-3525; chamber@wittenbergnet.net; www.wittenbergchamber.org

Woodruff • *see Minocqua*

Wrightstown • *see Kaukauna*

Wyoming

No State Chamber

Afton • *Star Valley C/C* • Melanie S. Wilkes; Pres./CEO; 150 S. Washington; P.O. Box 190; 83110; Lincoln; P 16,000; M 100; (307) 885-2759; (800) 426-8833; Fax (307) 885-2758; info@starvalleychamber.com; www.starvalleychamber.com

Basin • *Basin Area C/C* • Barbara Anne Greene; Pres.; 407 C. St.; P.O. Box 883; 82410; Big Horn; P 1,285; M 60; (307) 568-3055; basincc@tctwest.net; www.basincc

Buffalo • *Buffalo WY C/C* • Angela N. Fox IOM; CEO; 55 N. Main St.; 82834; Johnson; P 4,638; M 300; (307) 684-5544; (800) 227-5122; Fax (307) 684-0491; angela@buffalowyo.com; buffalowyo.com*

Casper • *Casper Area C/C* • Gilda Lara; Exec. Dir.; 500 N. Center St.; P.O. Box 399; 82602; Natrona; P 81,000; M 1,115; (307) 234-5311; Fax (307) 265-2643; information@casperwyoming.org; www.casperwyoming.org*

Cheyenne • *Greater Cheyenne C/C* • Dale G. Steenbergen IOM; Pres./CEO; 121 W. 15th St., Ste. 204; 82001; Laramie; P 96,000; M 1,000; (307) 638-3388; Fax (307) 778-1407; stephaniem@cheyennechamber.org; www.cheyennechamber.org*

Chugwater • *see Wheatland*

Cody • *Cody Country C/C* • Dennie Hammer; Interim Exec. Dir.; 836 Sheridan Ave.; 82414; Park; P 9,500; M 600; (307) 587-2777; Fax (307) 527-6228; exec@codychamber.org; www.codychamber.org*

Cokeville • *Cokeville C/C* • Carol Reed; Secy./Treas.; P.O. Box 358; 83114; Lincoln; P 528; M 15; (307) 459-4195; (307) 279-3386; www.cokevillewy.org

Diamondville • *see Kemmerer*

Douglas • *Douglas Area C/C* • Helga Bull; Exec. Dir.; 121 Brownfield Rd.; 82633; Converse; P 8,000; M 250; (307) 358-2950; (877) 937-4996; Fax (307) 358-2972; chamber@jackalope.org; www.jackalope.org

Dubois • *Dubois Area C/C* • Tylyn Hust; Exec. Dir.; 20 Stalnaker St.; P.O. Box 632; 82513; Fremont; P 1,200; M 220; (307) 455-2556; duboischamber@gmail.com; www.duboiswyomingchamber.org

Evanston • *Evanston C/C* • Dawn Darby IOM; Exec. Dir.; 1020 Front St.; P.O. Box 365; 82931; P 12,500; M 220; (307) 783-0370; (800) 328-9708; Fax (307) 789-4807; chamber@etownchamber.com; www.etownchamber.com*

Gillette • *Campbell County C/C* • Charlene Murdock; Exec. Dir.; 314 S. Gillette Ave.; 82716; Campbell; P 49,000; M 680; (307) 682-3673; Fax (307) 682-0538; frontoffice@gillettechamber.com; www.gillettechamber.com*

Glendo • *see Wheatland*

Glenrock • *Glenrock Area C/C* • Mary Kay Kindt; Dir.; 206 S. 4th St.; P.O. Box 411; 82637; Converse; P 2,500; M 102; (307) 436-5652; Fax (307) 436-5477; info@glenrockchamber.com; www.glenrockchamber.org

Green River • *Green River C/C* • Rebecca Briesmaster; Exec. Dir.; 1155 W. Flaming Gorge Way; 82935; Sweetwater; P 13,500; M 270; (307) 875-5711; (800) FL-GORGE; Fax (307) 872-6192; rebecca@grchamber.com; www.grchamber.com*

Greybull • *Greybull Area C/C* • Marilyn McCoy; Exec. Dir.; 521 Greybull Ave.; 82426; Big Horn; P 1,900; M 85; (307) 765-2100; chamber@greybull.com; www.greybull.com

Guernsey • *see Wheatland*

Hartville • *see Wheatland*

Hulett • *Hulett & Devils Tower Territory C/C* • John McPartland; Pres.; P.O. Box 421; 82720; Crook; P 383; M 45; (307) 467-5747; Fax (307) 467-5765; helen@hulett-wyoming.com; hulett-wyoming.com

Jackson • *Jackson Hole C/C* • Jeff Golightly; Exec. Dir.; 112 Center St.; P.O. Box 550; 83001; Teton; P 22,000; M 840; (307) 733-3316; Fax (307) 733-5585; casey@jacksonholechamber.com; www.jacksonholechamber.com

Kaycee • *Kaycee Area C/C* • Rhoni Stafford; Pres.; 100 Park Ave.; P.O. Box 147; 82639; Johnson; P 263; M 107; (307) 738-2444; Fax (307) 738-2444; kayceechamber@rtconnect.net; www.kayceewyoming.org

Kemmerer • *Kemmerer/Diamondville C/C* • Teri Picerno; Exec. Dir.; 921 Pine Ave.; 83101; Lincoln; P 3,000; M 80; (307) 877-9761; (888) 300-3413; Fax (307) 877-9762; chamber@hamsfork.net; www.kemmererchamber.org

Lander • *Lander Area C/C* • Scott Goetz; Exec. Dir.; 160 N. 1st St.; 82520; Fremont; P 7,500; M 356; (307) 332-3892; (800) 433-0662; Fax (307) 332-3893; director@landerchamber.org; www.landerchamber.com

Laramie • *Laramie Chamber Bus. Alliance* • Dan Furphy; Pres./CEO; 800 S. Third St.; 82070; Albany; P 32,000; M 500; (307) 745-7339; (866) 876-1012; Fax (307) 745-4624; jdavies@laramie.org; www.laramie.org*

Lovell • *Lovell Area C/C* • J. Heinert; 287 E. Main; 82431; Big Horn; P 2,500; M 90; (307) 548-7552; lovell@tctwest.net; www.lovellchamber.com

Lusk • *Niobrara C/C* • Jackie Bredthauer; Exec. Dir.; 224 S. Main; P.O. Box 457; 82225; Niobrara; P 2,500; M 120; (307) 334-2950; (800) 223-LUSK; Fax (307) 334-2951; luskchamberofcommerce@yahoo.com; www.luskwyoming.com

Lyman • *Greater Bridger Valley C/C* • Monica Streeter; Exec. Dir.; 100 E. Sage St.; P.O. Box 1506; 82937; Uinta; P 5,000; M 24; (307) 787-6738; bvchamber@bvea.net; www.bridgervalleychamber.com

Marbleton • *see Pinedale*

Moorcroft • *Moorcroft C/C* • Wanda Van Vleet; Pres.; P.O. Box 932; 82721; Crook; P 1,100; M 35; (307) 756-3473; publicrelations@moorcroftchamber.com; www.moorcroftchamber.com

Newcastle • *Newcastle Area C/C* • Susan Love; Exec. Dir.; 1323 Washington Blvd.; 82701; Weston; P 3,500; M 165; (307) 746-2739; Fax (307) 746-2739; nacoc@rtconnect.net; www.newcastlewyo.com

Pinedale • *Sublette County C/C* • Rachel Grimes; Exec. Dir.; 19 E. Pine St.; P.O. Box 176; 82941; Sublette; P 10,000; M 245; (307) 367-2242; (888) 285-7282; Fax (307) 367-2248; director@sublettechamber.com; www.sublettechamber.com*

Platte County • *see Wheatland*

Powell • *Powell Valley C/C* • Jaime Schmeiser; Exec. Dir.; 111 S. Day St.; P.O. Box 1258; 82435; Park; P 5,300; M 200; (307) 754-3494; (800) 325-4278; Fax (307) 754-3483; willie@powellchamber.org; www.powellchamber.org*

Rawlins • *Rawlins-Carbon County C/C* • Jessie Powell; Exec. Dir.; 519 W. Cedar St.; P.O. Box 1331; 82301; Carbon; P 12,000; M 140; (307) 324-4111; Fax (307) 324-5078; info@rawlinschamberofcommerce.org; www.rawlinschamberofcommerce.org

Riverton • *Riverton C/C* • Jim Davis; Exec. Dir.; 213 W. Main St., Ste.C; 82501; Fremont; P 10,000; M 330; (307) 856-4801; Fax (307) 857-0873; director@rivertonchamber.org; www.rivertonchamber.org

Rock Springs • *Rock Springs C/C* • Dave Hanks; CEO; 1897 Dewar Dr.; P.O. Box 398; 82901; Sweetwater; P 26,000; M 700; (307) 362-3771; (800) 46-DUNES; Fax (307) 362-3838; rschamber@sweetwaterhsa.com; www.rockspringschamber.com

Saratoga • *Saratoga/Platte Valley C/C* • Stacy Crimmins; Dir.; 210 W. Elm St.; P.O. Box 1095; 82331; Carbon; P 2,000; M 180; (307) 326-8855; Fax (307) 326-8850; info@saratogachamber.info; www.saratogachamber.info

Sheridan • *Sheridan County C/C* • Dixie Johnson; CEO; 171 N. Main St., Ste. D; P.O. Box 707; 82801; Sheridan; P 30,000; M 650; (307) 672-2485; (800) 453-3650; Fax (307) 672-7321; info@sheridanwyomingchamber.org; www.sheridanwyomingchamber.org*

Shoshoni • *Shoshoni C/C* • Dawn Marie Thacker; Secy./Treas.; P.O. Box 324; 82649; Fremont; P 640; M 100; (307) 851-1241; (307) 876-2515; shoshonichamber@outlook.com; www.shoshonichamber.com

Sundance • *Sundance Area C/C* • Jim Durfee; Treas.; P.O. Box 1004; 82729; Crook; P 1,300; M 100; (307) 283-1000; (800) 477-9340; chamber@sundancewyoming.com; www.sundancewyoming.com

Ten Sleep • *see Worland*

Thayne • *see Afton*

Thermopolis • *Thermopolis-Hot Springs C/C* • Meri Ann Rush; Exec. Dir.; 220 Park St.; P.O. Box 768; 82443; Hot Springs; P 3,019; M 208; (307) 864-3192; thermopolischamber@rtconnect.net; www.thermopolischamber.org*

Torrington • *Goshen County C/C* • 2042 Main St.; 82240; Goshen; P 13,300; M 275; (307) 532-3879; Fax (307) 534-2360; info@goshencountychamber.com; www.goshencountychamber.com

Upton • *Upton C/C* • Woody Gaughenbaugh; Pres.; P.O. Box 756, WY; 82730; Weston, P 1,100; M 60; (307) 468-2228; Fax (307) 468-2255; uptonchamberofcommerce@gmail.com

Wheatland • *Platte County C/C* • Ms. Kit Armour; Exec. Dir.; 65 16th St., WY; 82201; Platte, P 8800; M 225; (307) 322-2322; Fax (307) 322-3419; kit@plattechamber.com; http://www.plattechamber.com*

Worland • *Worland-Ten Sleep C/C* • Jenn Rasmussen; Exec. Dir.; P.O. Box 1772, WY; 82401; Washakie, P 5487; M 200; (307) 347-3226; Fax (307) 347-3025; wtschamber@rtconnect.net; http://www.wtschamber.org*

STATE BOARDS OF TOURISM

Alabama

Alabama Tourism Dept. • Lee Sentell; Dir.; 401 Adams Ave., Ste. 126; P.O. Box 4927; Montgomery; 36103; Montgomery; (334) 242-4169; (800) ALABAMA; Fax (334) 242-4554; info@tourism.alabama.gov; alabama.travel

Alaska

Alaska Travel Industry Assn. • Sarah Leonard; Pres./CEO; 610 E. 5th Ave., Ste. 200; Anchorage; 99501; (907) 929-2842; Fax (907) 561-5727; atia@alaskatia.org; www.travelalaska.com

Arizona

Arizona Office of Tourism • Debbie Johnson; Exec. Dir.; 1110 W. Washington St., Ste. 155; Phoenix; 85007; Maricopa; (602) 364-3700; (866) 275-5816; Fax (602) 364-3701; squerrero@tourism.az.gov; www.tourism.az.gov

Arkansas

Arkansas Dept. of Parks & Tourism • Joe David Rice; Dir. of Tourism; 1 Capitol Mall, Ste. 4A-900; Little Rock; 72201; Pulaski; (501) 682-7777; Fax (501) 682-2523; info@arkansas.com; www.arkansas.com

California

Visit California • Caroline Beteta; Pres./CEO; 555 Capitol Mall, Ste. 1100; Sacramento; 95814; Sacramento; (916) 444-4429; (877) 225-4367; Fax (916) 444-0410; info@visitcalifornia.com; www.visitcalifornia.com

Colorado

Colorado Tourism Office • Cathy Ritter; Exec. Dir.; 1625 Broadway, Ste. 2700; Denver; 80202; Denver; (303) 892-3840; (800) COLORADO; Fax (303) 892-3848; cathy.ritter@state.co.us; www.advancecolorado.com

Connecticut

Connecticut Office of Tourism • Randy Fiveash; Dir.; One Constitution Plaza, 2nd Flr.; Hartford; 06103; Hartford; (860) 256-2800; (888) CT-VISIT; Fax (860) 270-8077; ct.travelinfo@ct.gov; www.ctvisit.com

Delaware

Delaware Tourism Office • Linda Parkowski; Dir.; 99 Kings Hwy. S.W.; Dover; 19901; Kent; (302) 739-4271; (866) 284-7483; Fax (302) 736-9136; visit.delaware@state.de.us; www.visitdelaware.com

Florida

Visit Florida • Will Seccombe; Pres./CEO; 2540 W. Executive Center Cir., Ste. 200; Tallahassee; 32301; Leon; (850) 488-5607; Fax (850) 201-6908; ktorian@visitflorida.org; www.visitflorida.org

Georgia

Georgia Dept. of Eco. Dev. & Tourism • Kevin Langston; Deputy Commissioner; 75 Fifth St. N.W., Ste. 1200; Atlanta; 30308; Fulton; (404) 962-4000; Fax (404) 962-4093; travel@georgia.org; www.georgia.org

Hawaii

Hawaii Tourism Auth. • George Szigeti; Pres./CEO; 1801 Kalakaua Ave., 1st Flr.; Honolulu; 96815; Honolulu; (808) 973-2255; Fax (808) 973-2253; info@hawaiitourismauthority.org; www.hawaiitourismauthority.org

Idaho

Idaho State Tourism Ofc. • Diane Norton; Mgr.; 700 W. State St., 2nd Flr.; P.O. Box 83720; Boise; 83720; Ada; (208) 334-2470; (800) 847-4843; Fax (208) 334-2631; info@tourism.idaho.gov; www.visitidaho.org

Illinois

Illinois Office of Tourism • Cory Jobe; Deputy Dir.; 500 E. Monroe; Springfield; 62701; Sangamon; (217) 785-2007; Fax (217) 557-0829; cory.jobe@illinois.gov; www.enjoyillinois.com

Indiana

Indiana Office of Tourism Dev. • Mark Newman; Dir.; One N. Capitol, Ste. 600; Indianapolis; 46204; Marion; (317) 232-8860; (800) 677-9800; Fax (317) 233-6887; visitin@visitindiana.com; www.visitindiana.com

Iowa

Iowa Tourism Office • Shawna Lode; Mgr.; 200 E. Grand Ave.; Des Moines; 50309; Polk; (888) 472-6035; (800) 345-IOWA; Fax (515) 725-3010; shawna.lode@iowa.gov; www.traveliowa.com

Kansas

Kansas Dept. of Wildlife, Parks & Tourism • Pete Szabo; Fiscal Mgr.; 1020 S. Kansas Ave., Ste. 200; Topeka; 66612; Shawnee; (785) 296-2009; (800) 2-KANSAS; Fax (785) 296-6988; tourism@travelks.com; www.travelks.com

State Boards of Tourism

Kentucky

Kentucky Dept. of Travel & Tourism • Mike Mangeot; Commissioner; Capital Plaza Tower 22nd Flr.; 500 Mero St.; Frankfort; 40601; Franklin; (502) 564-4930; (800) 225-8747; Fax (502) 564-5695; info@kentuckytourism.com; www.kentuckytourism.com

Louisiana

Louisiana Office of Tourism • Kyle Edmiston; Asst. Secy. of Tourism; 1051 N. 3rd St.; P.O. Box 94291; Baton Rouge; 70804; E. Baton Rouge; (225) 342-8100; Fax (225) 342-1051; kedmiston@crt.la.gov; www.louisianatravel.com

Maine

Maine Office of Tourism • Carolann Ouellette; Dir.; 59 State House Station; Augusta; 04333; Kennebec; (207) 287-5711; (888) 624-6345; Fax (207) 287-8070; Carolann.Ouellette@maine.gov; www.visitmaine.com

Maryland

Maryland Office of Tourism Dev. • Liz Fitzsimmons; Exec. Dir.; 401 E. Pratt St., 14th Flr.; Baltimore; 21202; (410) 767-3400; (866) 639-3526; Fax (410) 333-6643; info@visitmaryland.org; www.visitmaryland.org

Massachusetts

Massachusetts Office of Travel & Tourism • 10 Park Plaza, Ste. 4510; Boston; 02116; Suffolk; (617) 973-8500; (800) 227-MASS; Fax (617) 973-8525; vacationinfo@state.ma.us; www.massvacation.com

Michigan

Travel Michigan • David Lorenz; V.P.; 300 N. Washington Sq.; Lansing; 48913; Ingham; (517) 335-4590; (888) 784-7328; Fax (517) 373-0059; munsona@michigan.org; www.michigan.org

Minnesota

Explore Minnesota Tourism • John Edman; Dir.; 121 7th Pl. E., Ste. 100; St. Paul; 55101; Ramsey; (651) 296-5029; (888) 868-7476; Fax (651) 296-7095; explore@state.mn.us; www.exploreminnesota.com

Mississippi

Mississippi Tourism • Daron Wilson; Dir.; P.O. Box 849; Jackson; 39205; Hinds; (601) 359-3297; Fax (601) 359-5757; tourdiv@mississippi.org; www.visitmississippi.org

Missouri

Missouri Div. of Tourism • Dan Lennon; Dir.; P.O. Box 1055; Jefferson City; 65102; Cole; (573) 751-4133; Fax (573) 751-5160; tourism@ded.mo.gov; www.visitmo.com

Montana

Montana Office of Tourism & Bus. Dev. • Sean Becker; Admin.; 301 S. Park Ave.; P.O. Box 200533; Helena; 59620; Lewis & Clark; (406) 841-2870; (800) 847-4868; Fax (406) 841-2871; seanbecker@mt.gov; www.visitmt.com

Nebraska

Nebraska Tourism Comm. • Kathy McKillip; Dir.; 301 Centennial Mall S.; P.O. Box 98907; Lincoln; 68509; Lancaster; (402) 471-3796; (877) 632-7275; Fax (402) 471-3026; tourism@visitnebraska.org; www.visitnebraska.com

Nevada

Nevada Dept. of Tourism & Cultural Affairs • Claudia Vecchio; Dir.; 401 N. Carson St.; Carson City; 89701; (775) 687-4322; (800) 237-0774; Fax (775) 687-6779; ncot@travelnevada.com; www.travelnevada.com

New Hampshire

New Hampshire Div. of Travel & Tourism Dev. • Victoria Cimino; Dir.; 172 Pembroke Rd.; P.O. Box 1856; Concord; 03302; Merrimack; (603) 271-2665; (800) FUN-IN-NH; Fax (603) 271-6870; travel@dred.nh.gov; www.visitnh.gov

New Jersey

New Jersey Div. of Travel & Tourism • Anthony Minick; Dir.; 225 W. State St. 5th Flr.; P.O. Box 460; Trenton; 08625; Mercer; (609) 599-6540; (800) VISIT-NJ; Fax (609) 633-7418; www.visitnj.org

New Mexico

New Mexico Tourism Dept. • Rebecca Latham; Cabinet Secy.; 491 Old Santa Fe Trl.; Santa Fe; 87501; Santa Fe; (505) 827-7400; (800) 545-2070; Fax (505) 827-7402; rebecca.latham@state.nm.us; www.newmexico.org

New York

New York State Div. of Tourism • Gavin Landry; Dir. of Tourism; 625 Broadway; P.O. Box 2603; Albany; 12245; Albany; (518) 292-5960; (800) CALL-NYS; Fax (518) 292-5893; info@iloveny.com; www.iloveny.com

North Carolina

North Carolina Div. of Tourism, Film & Sports Dev. • Wit Tuttell; Exec. Dir.; 301 N. Wilmington St.; Raleigh; 27601; Wake; (919) 447-7801; (800) VISIT-NC; Fax (919) 733-8582; www.visitnc.com

North Dakota

North Dakota Tourism Div. • Sara Otte Coleman; Dir.; 1600 E. Century Ave., Ste. 2; P.O. Box 2057; Bismarck; 58502; Burleigh; (701) 328-2525; (800) 435-5663; Fax (701) 328-4878; tourism@nd.gov; www.ndtourism.com

Ohio

TourismOhio • Mary Cusick; Tourism Dir.; 77 S. High St., 29th Flr.; P.O. Box 1001; Columbus; 43216; Delaware, Fairfield & Franklin; (614) 466-8844; (800) BUCKEYE; Fax (614) 466-6744; amy.summers@development.ohio.gov; www.discoverohio.com

Oklahoma

Oklahoma Tourism & Rec. Dept. • Dick Dutton; Exec. Dir.; 900 N. Stiles Ave.; P.O. Box 52002; Oklahoma City; 73152; Canadian, Cleveland, Oklahoma & Pottawatomie; (405) 230-8420; (800) 652-6552; info@travelok.com; www.travelok.com

Oregon

Travel Oregon • Todd Davidson; CEO; 250 Church St. S.E., Ste. 100; Salem; 97301; Marion; (800) 547-7842; Fax (503) 378-4574; info@traveloregon.com; www.traveloregon.com

Pennsylvania

Pennsylvania Tourism Office • Michael Chapaloney; Exec. Dir.; Commonwealth Keystone Bldg.; 400 North St., 4th Flr.; Harrisburg; 17120; Dauphin; (717) 787-5453; (800) VISITPA; Fax (717) 787-0687; mchapalone@pa.gov; www.visitpa.com

Rhode Island

Rhode Island Tourism • Mark Brodeur; Dir.; 315 Iron Horse Way., Ste. 101; Providence; 02908; Providence; (401) 278-9100; (800) 556-2484; Fax (401) 273-8270; mark.brodeur@commerceri.com; www.visitrhodeisland.com

South Carolina

South Carolina Dept. of Parks & Rec. & Tourism • Duane Parrish; Dir.; 1205 Pendleton St.; Columbia; 29201; Richland & Lexington; (803) 734-1700; Fax (803) 734-1409; aduffy@scprt.com; www.discoversouthcarolina.com

South Dakota

South Dakota Dept. of Tourism • James D. Hagen; Secy.; 711 E. Wells Ave.; Pierre; 57501; Hughes; (605) 773-3301; (800) S-DAKOTA; Fax (605) 773-5977; sdinfo@state.sd.us; www.travelsouthdakota.com

Tennessee

Tennessee Dept. of Tourist Dev. • Kevin Triplett; Commissioner; 312 Rosa L. Parks Ave., 13th Flr.; Nashville; 37243; Davidson; (615) 741-2159; (800) GO2-TENN; Fax (615) 741-9071; cindy.dupree@tn.gov; www.tnvacation.com

Texas

Office of Gov. Eco. Dev. & Tourism • Brad Smyth; Exec. Dir.; P.O. Box 12428; Austin; 78711; Travis; (512) 936-0100; Fax (512) 936-0450; brad.smyth@gov.texas.gov; www.traveltex.com

Utah

Utah Office of Tourism • Vicki Varela; Managing Dir.; Council Hall/Capitol Hill; 300 N. State St.; Salt Lake City; 84114; Salt Lake; (801) 538-1900; (800) 200-1160; Fax (801) 538-1399; info@visitutah.com; www.visitutah.com

Vermont

Vermont Dept. of Tourism & Mktg. • Megan Smith; Commissioner; 1 National Life Dr., 6th Flr.; Montpelier; 05620; Washington; (802) 828-3237; (800) VERMONT; info@vermontvacation.com; www.vermontvacation.com

Virginia

Virginia Tourism Corp. • Rita D. McClenny; Pres./CEO; 901 E. Byrd St.; Richmond; 23219; Richmond City; (804) 545-5500; (800) VISIT-VA; Fax (804) 545-5501; vainfo@helloinc.com; www.virginia.org

Washington

Washington Tourism Alliance • Louise Stanton-Masten; Exec. Dir.; P.O. Box 953; Seattle; 98111; King; (425) 478-5350; louise@watourismalliance.com; www.watourismalliance.com

West Virginia

West Virginia Div. of Tourism • Amy Goodwin; Commissioner; 90 MacCorkle Ave. S.W.; South Charleston; 25303; Kanawha; (304) 558-2200; Fax (304) 746-0010; tourism.info@wv.gov; gotowv.com

Wisconsin

Wisconsin Dept. of Tourism • Stephanie Klett; Secy.; 201 W. Washington Ave.; P.O. Box 8690; Madison; 53708; Dane; (608) 266-2161; (800) 432-8747; Fax (608) 266-3403; tourinfo@travelwisconsin.com; www.travelwisconsin.com

Wyoming

Wyoming Office of Tourism • Diane Shober; Exec. Dir.; 5611 High Plains Rd.; 82007; P 576412; (307) 777-7777; (800) 225-5996; Fax (307) 777-2877; info@wyomingtourism.org; www.wyomingtourism.org

State Boards of Tourism

CONVENTION AND VISITORS BUREAUS

Alabama

Anniston • *Calhoun County Chamber & Visitors Center* • Linda Hearn; Chamber Mgr.; 1330 Quintard Ave.; P.O. Box 1087; 36202; Calhoun; P 117,296; (256) 237-3536; (800) 489-1087; Fax (256) 237-0126; info@calhounchamber.com; www.calhounchamber.com

Auburn • *Auburn/Opelika Tourism Bur.* • John Wild; Pres.; 714 E. Glenn Ave.; 36830; Lee; P 81,000; (334) 887-8747; (866) 880-8747; Fax (334) 821-5500; info@aotourism.com; www.aotourism.com

Birmingham • *Greater Birmingham CVB* • James Smither; Pres.; 2200 9th Ave. N.; 35203; Jefferson; P 1,000,000; (205) 458-8000; (800) 458-8085; Fax (205) 458-8086; info@birminghamal.org; www.birminghamal.org

Decatur • *Decatur-Morgan County CVB* • Tami Reist; Pres.; 719 6th Ave. S.E.; P.O. Box 2349; 35602; Morgan; P 106,000; (256) 350-2028; (800) 524-6181; Fax (256) 350-2054; info@decaturcvb.org; www.decaturcvb.org

Dothan • *Dothan Area CVB* • Bob Hendrix; Exec. Dir.; 3311 Ross Clark Cir.; P.O. Box 8765; 36304; Houston; P 68,000; (334) 794-6622; (888) 449-0212; Fax (334) 712-2731; info@dothanalcvb.com; www.visitdothanal.com

Eufaula • *Eufaula/Barbour County Tourism Cncl.* • Ann Sparks; Tourism Dir.; 333 E. Broad St.; 36027; Barbour; P 28,000; (334) 687-7099; (800) 524-7529; Fax (334) 687-5240; info@eufaulachamber.com; www.eufaulachamber.com

Fort Payne • *DeKalb County Tourist Assn.* • John Dersham; Exec. Dir.; P.O. Box 681165; 35968; DeKalb; P 72,000; (256) 845-3957; (888) 805-4740; Fax (256) 845-3946; info@tourdekalb.com; www.tourdekalb.com

Gulf Shores • *Alabama Gulf Coast CVB* • Herbert Malone Jr.; Pres./CEO; 900 Commerce Loop; 36542; Baldwin; P 11,000; (251) 974-1510; (800) 745-7263; Fax (251) 974-1509; info@gulfshores.com; www.gulfshores.com

Guntersville • *Marshall County CVB* • Lisa Socha; Exec. Dir.; 200 Gunter Ave.; P.O. Box 711; 35976; Marshall; P 85,000; (256) 582-7015; (800) 582-6282; Fax (256) 582-3682; info@marshallcountycvb.com; www.marshallcountycvb.com

Huntsville • *Huntsville/Madison County CVB* • Judy S. Ryals; Pres./CEO; 500 Church St., Ste. 1; 35801; Madison; P 335,000; (256) 533-5723; (800) 772-2348; Fax (256) 518-6146; info@huntsville.org; www.huntsville.org

Mobile • *Mobile Bay CVB* • David Randel; Interim CEO; 1 S. Water St., 4th Flr.; P.O. Box 204; 36601; Mobile; P 413,000; (251) 208-2000; (800) 5-MOBILE; Fax (251) 208-2060; cecile-clark@mobile.org; www.mobilebay.org

Montgomery • *Montgomery Area CVB* • Dawn Hathcock; V.P.; 300 Water St., Ste. 200A; P.O. Box 79; 36101; Montgomery; P 230,000; (334) 261-1100; (800) 240-9452; Fax (334) 261-1111; tourism@montgomerychamber.com; www.visitingmontgomery.com

Orange Beach • *see Gulf Shores*

Scottsboro • *Jackson County Tourism* • J.P. Parsons; V.P. Destination Mktg.; 407 E. Willow St.; P.O. Box 973; 35768; Jackson; P 75,000; (800) 259-5508; (256) 259-5500; Fax (256) 259-4447; visitourcounty@scottsboro.org; www.discoverjacksoncountyalabama.com

Selma • *Selma CVB* • Candace Johnson; Pres.; 912 Selma Ave.; 36701; Dallas; P 47,000; (334) 875-7241; (800) 45-SELMA; Fax (334) 875-7142; info@SelmaAlabama.com; www.SelmaAlabama.com

Tuscaloosa • *Tuscaloosa Tourism & Sports* • Gina Simpson; CEO; P.O. Box 3167; 35403; Tuscaloosa; P 93,000; (205) 391-9200; (800) 538-8696; info@visittuscaloosa.com; www.visittuscaloosa.com

Tuscumbia • *Colbert County Tourism CVB* • Susann Hamlin; Exec. Dir.; P.O. Box 740425; 35674; Colbert; P 55,000; (256) 383-0783; (800) 344-0783; colberttourism@comcast.net; www.colbertcountytourism.org

Alaska

Anchorage • *Visit Anchorage* • Julie Saupe; CEO; 524 W 4th Ave.; 99501; Anchorage; (907) 276-4118; (800) 446-5352; Fax (907) 278-5559; hlewis@anchorage.net; www.anchorage.net

Fairbanks • *Explore Fairbanks* • Deb Hickok; Pres./CEO; 101 Dunkel St., Ste. 111; 99701; Fairbanks North Star; P 70,000; (907) 456-5774; (800) 327-5774; Fax (907) 459-3757; info@explorefairbanks.com; www.explorefairbanks.com

Gustavus • *Gustavus Visitors Assn.* • P.O. Box 167; 99826; Hoonah Angoon; P 420; (907) 697-2454; info@gustavusak.com; www.gustavusak.com

Haines • *Haines CVB* • Tanya Carlson; Dir.; 122 Second Ave.; P.O. Box 530; 99827; Haines; P 2,300; (907) 766-2234; Fax (907) 766-3155; hcvb@haines.ak.us; www.haines.ak.us

Homer • *Homer C/C & Visitor Center* • Karen Zak; Exec. Dir.; 201 Sterling Hwy.; 99603; Kenai Peninsula; P 5,000; (907) 235-7740; Fax (907) 235-8766; info@homeralaska.org; www.homeralaska.org

Iliamna • *Iliamna Cncl. Visitor Info.* • P.O. Box 286; 99606; Lak & Peninsula; P 150; (907) 571-1246; Fax (907) 571-1256; ilivc@aol.com

Juneau • *Juneau CVB* • Lorene Palmer; Pres./CEO; 800 Glacier Ave., Ste. 201; 99801; Juneau; P 31,300; (907) 586-1737; (800) 587-2201; Fax (907) 586-6304; info@traveljuneau.com; www.traveljuneau.com

Kenai • *Kenai C/C & Visitor Center* • Johna Beech; Pres./COO; 11471 Kenai Spur Hwy.; 99611; Kenai Peninsula; P 7,000; (907) 283-1991; Fax (907) 283-2230; visitorservices@visitkenai.com; www.visitkenai.com

Ketchikan • *Ketchikan Visitors Bur.* • Patricia Mackey; Exec. Dir.; 131 Front St.; 99901; Ketchikan Gateway; P 13,500; (907) 225-6166; (800) 770-3300; Fax (907) 225-4250; info@visit-ketchikan.com; www.visit-ketchikan.com

King Salmon • *King Salmon Visitor Center* • Debbie Tibbetts; Visitor Svcs.; King Salmon Airport; P.O. Box 298; 99613; Bristol Bay; P 350; (907) 246-4250; Fax (907) 246-8550; Deborah_Tibbetts@fws.gov

Kodiak • *Discover Kodiak* • Chastity McCarthy; Exec. Dir.; 100 Marine Way, Ste. 200; 99615; Kodiak Island; P 13,479; (907) 486-4782; (800) 789-4782; Fax (907) 486-6545; visit@kodiak.org; www.kodiak.org

Nome • *Nome CVB* • Mitch Erickson; Dir.; 301 Front St.; P.O. Box 240; 99762; Nome; P 3,800; (907) 443-6555; (907) 443-6566; Fax (907) 443-5832; visit@mynomealaska.com; www.visitnomealaska.com

Palmer • *Mat-Su CVB* • Bonnie Quill; Exec. Dir.; 7744 E. Visitors View Ct.; 99645; Matanuska Susitna; P 82,500; (907) 746-5000; Fax (907) 746-2688; info@alaskavisit.com; www.alaskavisit.com

Petersburg • *Petersburg Visitors Info. Center* • Sally Dwyer; Mgr.; P.O. Box 649; 99833; Petersburg; P 3,030; (907) 772-4636; (866) 484-4700; Fax (907) 772-2453; visitorinfo@petersburg.org; www.petersburg.org

Sitka • *Visit Sitka* • Rachel Roy; Exec. Dir.; 104 Lake St.; P.O. Box 1226; 99835; Sitka; P 8,900; (907) 747-8604; (800) 55-SITKA; Fax (907) 747-3739; tourism@sitka.org; www.sitka.org

Skagway • *Skagway CVB* • Cody Jennings; Tourism Dir.; 245 Broadway; P.O. Box 1029; 99840; Skagway; P 1,036; (907) 983-2854; (888) 762-1898; Fax (907) 983-3854; skagwayinfo@gmail.com; www.skagway.com

Soldotna • *Kenai Peninsula Tourism Mktg. Cncl.* • Shanon Hamrick; Exec. Dir.; 35571 Kenai Spur Hwy.; 99669; Kenai Peninsula; P 51,000; (907) 262-5229; (800) 535-3624; Fax (907) 262-5212; info@kenaipeninsula.org; www.kenaipeninsula.org

Tok • *Tok's 'Alaska Mainstreet' Visitor Center* • P.O. Box 389; 99780; Southeast Fairbanks; P 1,405; (907) 883-5775; info@TokAlaskaInfo.com; www.TokAlaskaInfo.com

Unalaska • *Unalaska/Port of Dutch Harbor CVB* • Cathy Jordan; Exec. Dir.; 5th & Broadway; P.O. Box 545; 99685; Aleutians West; P 8,500; (907) 581-2612; (866) 581-2612; Fax (907) 581-2613; unalaskacvb@gmail.com; www.unalaska.info

Valdez • *Valdez CVB* • Laurine Regan; Exec. Dir.; 399 Fairbanks Dr.; P.O. Box 1603; 99686; Valdez Cordova; P 4,000; (907) 835-2984; Fax (907) 835-4845; info@valdezalaska.org; www.valdezalaska.org

White Mountain • *White Mountain Visitor Info.* • c/o City Hall; P.O. Box 130; 99784; Nome; P 200; (907) 638-3411; Fax (907) 638-3421

Arizona

Arizona City • *Sunland Visitor Center Inc.* • Cindy Yates; Exec. Dir.; P.O. Box 280; 85123; Pinal; P 35,000; (520) 466-3007; (888) 786-3007; Fax (520) 466-3007; sunlandvisitorcenter@azci.net; sunlandvisitorcenter.org

Ash Fork • *Ash Fork Visitor's Center/Museum* • Fayrene Hume; Dir.; 901 W. Old Rte. 66; P.O. Box 1234; 86320; Yavapai; P 900; (928) 637-0204; (928) 637-8629; Fax (928) 637-0204; pjpopp.6@gmail.com; www.ashforkrt66museum.com

Flagstaff • *Flagstaff Visitor Center* • Heidi Hansen; Dir.; 1 E. Rte. 66; 86001; Coconino; P 68,000; (928) 213-2951; Fax (928) 556-1308; visitorcenter@flagstaffaz.gov; www.flagstaffarizona.org

Florence • *Florence Visitor Center* • Jennifer Evans; Dir.; 24 W. Ruggles St.; P.O. Box 2471; 85132; Pinal; P 9,433; (520) 868-4496; (866) 977-4496; info@visitflorenceaz.com; www.visitflorenceaz.com

Glendale • *Visit Glendale* • Lorraine Zomok; Mgr.; 5800 W. Glenn Dr., Ste. 140; 85301; Maricopa; P 248,000; (623) 930-4500; Fax (623) 463-2337; tourinfo@visitglendale.com; www.visitglendale.com

Kayenta • *Crawley's Monument Valley* • Bill Crawley; P.O. Box 187; 86033; Navajo; P 8,000; (928) 429-6833; crawleytours@citlink.net; www.crawleytours.com

Lake Havasu City • *Lake Havasu City CVB* • 314 London Bridge Rd.; 86403; Mohave; P 57,000; (928) 453-3444; (800) 242-8278; Fax (928) 453-3444; info@golakehavasu.com; www.golakehavasu.com

Mesa • *Visit Mesa* • Marc Garcia; Pres./CEO; 120 N. Center St.; 85201; Maricopa; P 460,000; (480) 827-4700; (800) 283-6372; Fax (480) 827-4704; info@visitmesa.com; www.visitmesa.com

Phoenix • *Greater Phoenix CVB* • J. Steven Moore; Pres./CEO; 400 E. Van Buren, Ste. 600; 85004; Maricopa; P 3,800,000; (602) 254-6500; (877) 225-5749; Fax (602) 253-4415; jmoore@visitphoenix.com; www.visitphoenix.com

Scottsdale • *Scottsdale CVB* • Rachel Sacco; Pres./CEO; 4343 N. Scottsdale Rd., Ste. 170; Galleria Corporate Center; 85251; Maricopa; P 250,000; (480) 421-1004; (800) 782-1117; Fax (480) 421-9733; visitorinformation@scottsdalecvb.com; www.scottsdalecvb.com

Sedona • *Sedona Chamber Tourism Bur.* • Donna Retegan; Dir. of Visitor Svcs.; 331 Forest Rd.; 86336; Coconino & Yavapai; P 18,000; (928) 282-7722; (800) 288-7336; Fax (928) 282-3916; info@sedonachamber.com; www.visitsedona.com

Sierra Vista • *Sierra Vista Visitors Center* • Kay Daggett; Dir.; 1011 N. Coronado Dr.; 85635; Cochise; P 44,000; (520) 417-6960; (800) 288-3861; Fax (520) 417-4890; info@visitsierravista.com; www.visitsierravista.com

Sun City • *Sun City Visitors Center* • Polly Corsino; Coord.; 16824 N. 99th Ave.; 85351; Maricopa; P 40,000; (623) 977-5000; (800) 437-8146; Fax (623) 977-4224; scvc@suncityaz.org; www.suncityaz.org

Tempe • *Tempe CVB* • Stephanie Nowack; Pres./CEO; 222 S. Mill Ave., Ste. 120; 85281; Maricopa; P 165,000; (480) 894-8158; (866) 914-1052; Fax (480) 968-8004; contact@tempetourism.com; www.tempetourism.com

Tombstone • *Bird Cage Theatre/Tombstone Ofc. of Tourism* • Bill Hunley; Chrmn.; P.O. Box 248; 85638; Cochise; P 1,000; (520) 457-3421; (800) 457-3423; Fax (520) 457-3189; tombstonebirdcage@gmail.com; www.tombstonebirdcage.com

Tucson • *Visit Tucson* • Brent DeRaad; Pres./CEO; 100 S. Church Ave.; 85701; Pima; P 1,000,000; (520) 624-1817; (800) 2-TUCSON; Fax (520) 884-7804; info@visittucson.org; www.visittucson.org

Williams • *Williams-Grand Canyon Visitors Center* • Gioia Goodrum; Pres./CEO; 200 W. Railroad Ave.; 86046; Coconino; P 5,000; (928) 635-0273; (800) 863-0546; Fax (928) 635-1417; ggoodrum@williamschamber.com; www.experiencewilliams.com

Yuma • *Yuma Visitors Bur.* • Linda Morgan; Exec. Dir.; 180 W. 1st St.; 85364; Yuma; P 120,000; (928) 783-0071; (800) 293-0071; Fax (928) 783-1897; info@visityuma.com; www.visityuma.com

Arkansas

Bentonville • *Bentonville CVB* • Kalene Griffith; Pres.; 104 E. Central; 72712; Benton; P 35,300; (479) 271-9153; (800) 410-2535; Fax (479) 464-4298; admin@bentonville.org; www.bentonville.org

Conway • *Conway CVB* • Brad Lacy; Dir.; 900 Oak St.; 72032; Faulkner; P 119,600; (501) 327-7788; (866) 726-6929; cvb@conwayarkansas.com; www.conwayark.com

C & VB

Fort Smith • *Fort Smith CVB* • Claude Legris; Exec. Dir.; 2 N. B St.; 72901; Crawford, Franklin & Sebastian; P 80,000; (479) 783-8888; (800) 637-1477; Fax (479) 784-2421; tourism@fortsmith.org; www.fortsmith.org

Harrison • *Harrison CVB* • Matt Bell; Exec. Dir.; 200 W. Stephenson Ave.; P.O. Box 940; 72601; Boone; P 12,943; (870) 741-1789; (888) 283-2163; Fax (870) 741-1159; mbell@harrisonarkansas.org; www.harrisonarkansas.org

Hot Springs • *Hot Springs CVB* • Steve Arrison; CEO; 134 Convention Blvd.; P.O. Box 6000; 71902; Garland; P 97,000; (501) 321-2277; (800) 543-2284; Fax (501) 321-2136; hscvb@hotsprings.org; www.hotsprings.org

Little Rock • *Little Rock CVB* • Gretchen Hall; Pres./CEO; 101 S. Spring St.; P.O. Box 3232; 72203; Pulaski; P 198,000; (501) 376-4781; (800) 844-4781; lrcvb@littlerock.com; www.littlerock.com

Pine Bluff • *Pine Bluff CVB* • Bob Purvis; Exec. Dir.; Pine Bluff Conv. Center; One Convention Center Plz.; 71601; Jefferson; P 54,000; (870) 536-7600; (800) 536-7660; Fax (870) 850-2105; pbinfo@pinebluff.com; www.pinebluffcvb.org

Rogers • *Rogers-Lowell CVB* • Allyson Twiggs Dyer; Dir.; 317 W. Walnut; 72756; Benton; P 63,000; (479) 636-1240; Fax (479) 636-5485; info@rogerslowell.com; www.rogerslowell.com

California

Anaheim • *Visit Anaheim* • Jay Burress CTA; Pres./CEO; 800 W. Katella Ave.; P.O. Box 4270; 92803; Orange; P 341,000; (714) 765-8888; (888) 598-3200; Fax (714) 991-8963; mdamon@visitanaheim.org; visitanaheim.org

Bakersfield • *Bakersfield CVB* • David Lyman; Mgr.; 515 Truxtun Ave.; 93301; Kern; P 500,000; (661) 852-7282; (866) 425-7353; Fax (661) 325-7074; cvb@visitbakersfield.com; www.visitbakersfield.com

Berkeley • *Visit Berkeley* • Barbara Hillman; CEO; 2030 Addison St., Ste. 102; 94704; Alameda; P 121,000; (510) 549-7040; (800) 847-4823; Fax (510) 644-2052; visitor@visitberkeley.com; www.visitberkeley.com

Beverly Hills • *Beverly Hills Conf. & Visitors Bur.* • Julie Wagner; CEO; 9400 S. Santa Monica Blvd., Ste. 102; 90210; Los Angeles; P 35,000; (310) 248-1015; (800) 345-2210; Fax (310) 461-1218; wagner@lovebeverlyhills.com; lovebeverlyhills.com

Bodega Bay • *Sonoma Coast Visitor Center* • Julie Ann Hill; Dir.; 850 Coast Hwy. 1; P.O. Box 518; 94923; Sonoma; P 1,250; (707) 875-3866; Fax (707) 875-3055; visitorcenter@innatthetides.com; www.bodegabay.com

Burlingame • *San Mateo County/Silicon Valley CVB* • Anne LeClair; Pres./CEO; 111 Anza Blvd., Ste. 410; 94010; San Mateo; P 722,762; (650) 348-7600; (800) 288-4748; Fax (650) 348-7687; info@smccvb.com; www.visitsanmateocounty.com

Carlsbad • *Visit Carlsbad* • Frankie Laney; Public Rel. Dir.; 400 Carlsbad Village Dr.; 92008; San Diego; P 100,000; (760) 434-6093; (800) 227-5722; Fax (760) 434-6056; info@visitcarlsbad.com; www.visitcarlsbad.com

Coronado • *Coronado Visitors Center* • Katherine Matlack; Mgr.; 1100 Orange Ave.; 92118; San Diego; P 25,000; (619) 437-8788; (866) 599-7242; vcmgr@coronadovisitorcenter.com; www.coronadovisitorcenter.com

Costa Mesa • *Costa Mesa Conf. & Visitor Bur.* • Paulette Lombardi-Fries; Pres.; 575 Anton Blvd., Ste. 880; 92626; Orange; P 123,955; (888) 588-9417; Fax (714) 668-9350; travel@travelcostamesa.com; www.travelcostamesa.com

Crescent City • *Crescent City/Del Norte County Visitors Bur.* • Jeff Parmer; Exec. Dir.; 1001 Front St.; 95531; Del Norte; P 28,000; (707) 464-3174; (800) 343-8300; chamber@delnorte.org; exploredelnorte.com

Davis • *Yolo County Visitors Bur.* • Alan Humason; Exec. Dir.; 604 2nd St.; 95616; Yolo; P 185,000; (530) 297-1900; (877) 713-2847; Fax (530) 297-1901; info@yolocvb.org; www.yolocvb.org

Desert Hot Springs • *Desert Hot Springs Visitors Hospitality Center* • Lorraine Becker; Pres.; 11-999 Palm Dr.; 92240; Riverside; P 22,000; (760) 329-7610; (866) 941-7610; info2@deserthotsprings.com; www.deserthotsprings.com

Eureka • *Humboldt County CVB* • Pete Oringer; 322 First St.; 95501; Humboldt; P 135,000; (707) 443-5097; (800) 346-3482; Fax (707) 443-5115; info@redwoods.info; www.redwoods.info

Fresno • *Fresno/Clovis CVB* • Layla Forstedt; Pres./CEO; 1550 E. Shaw Ave., Ste. 101; 93710; Fresno; P 500,000; (559) 981-5500; (800) 788-0836; Fax (559) 445-0122; info@fresnocvb.org; playfresno.org

Gilroy • *Gilroy Visitors Bur.* • Jane Howard; Exec. Dir.; 8155-6 Arroyo Cir., Ste. 6; 95020; Santa Clara; P 55,000; (408) 842-6436; (408) 842-6436; Fax (408) 842-6438; info@gilroywelcomecenter.org; www.visitgilroy.com

Hanford • *Hanford Conv. & Visitor Agency* • Mike Bertaina; Exec. Dir.; 113 Court St., Ste. 104; 93230; Kings; P 55,000; (559) 582-5024; Fax (559) 582-0960; visithanford@hanfordchamber.com; hanfordchamber.com

Huntington Beach • *Visit Huntington Beach* • Mr. Kelly Miller; Pres./CEO; 301 Main St., Ste. 212; 92648; Orange; P 200,000; (714) 969-3492; (800) 729-6232; Fax (714) 969-5592; info@surfcityusa.com; www.surfcityusa.com

Lee Vining • *Mono Lake Comm. Info. Center* • Geoff McQuilkin; Exec. Dir.; Hwy. 395 & Third St.; P.O. Box 29; 93541; Mono; P 398; (760) 647-6595; Fax (760) 647-6377; info@monolake.org; www.monolake.org

Lodi • *Lodi Conf. & Visitors Bur.* • Nancy Beckman; Exec. Dir.; 25 N. School St.; 95240; San Joaquin; P 65,000; (209) 365-1195; (800) 798-1810; Fax (209) 365-1191; info@visitlodi.com; www.visitlodi.com

Long Beach • *Long Beach Area CVB* • Iris A. Himert; Exec. V.P.; 301 E. Ocean Blvd., Ste. 1900; 90802; Los Angeles; P 470,000; (562) 436-3645; (800) 452-7829; Fax (562) 435-5653; info@longbeachcvb.org; www.visitlongbeach.com

Los Angeles • *Los Angeles CVB* • Ernie Wooden; Pres./CEO; 333 S. Hope St., 18th Flr.; 90071; Los Angeles; P 18,200,000; (213) 624-7300; (800) 228-2452; Fax (213) 624-9746; ewooden@latourism.org; www.discoverlosangeles.com

Lucerne • *Lake County Visitor Info. Center* • Melissa Fulton; CEO; 875 Lakeport Blvd.; P.O. Box 295; 95453; Lake; P 68,000; (707) 263-5092; (866) 525-3767; info@lakecochamber.com; www.lakecochamber.com

Mammoth Lakes • *Mammoth Lakes Tourism* • John Urdi; Exec. Dir.; 2520 Main St.; P.O. Box 48; 93546; Mono; P 8,234; (760) 934-2712; (888) GO-MAMMOTH; info@visitmammoth.com; www.visitmammoth.com

Marin County • *see San Rafael*

Marina del Rey • *Marina del Rey CVB* • Tiffani Miller; Op. Mgr.; 4701 Admiralty Way; 90292; Los Angeles; (310) 305-9545; info@visitmarinadelrey.com; www.visitmarinadelrey.com

Mariposa • *Mariposa County C/C & Visitor Center* • Dane Carlson; CEO; 5158 Hwy. 140; P.O. Box 425; 95338; Mariposa; P 20,000; (209) 966-7081; (800) 425-3366; Fax (209) 966-4193; admin@mariposachamber.org; www.mariposachamber.org

Mariposa • *Coulterville Visitor Center* • 5158 Hwy. 140; P.O. Box 425; 95338; Mariposa; P 1,800; (209) 878-3074; (209) 966-2456; Fax (209) 966-4193; coultervillevc@mariposachamber.org; www.mariposachamber.org

Modesto • *Modesto CVB* • Jennifer Mullen; Dir.; 1150 9th St., Ste. C; 95354; Stanislaus; P 246,000; (209) 526-5588; (888) 640-8467; Fax (209) 526-5586; info@visitmodesto.com; www.visitmodesto.com

Monterey • *Monterey County CVB* • Tammy Blount; Pres./CEO; 787 Munras Ave., Ste. 110; 93940; Monterey; P 386,000; (831) 657-6400; (888) 221-1010; Fax (831) 648-5373; info@seemonterey.com; www.seemonterey.com

Morro Bay • *Morro Bay Visitors Center* • Brent Haugen; Exec. Dir.; 695 Harbor St.; 93442; San Luis Obispo; P 11,000; (805) 225-1633; (800) 231-0592; Fax (805) 225-1636; visitor@seemorrobay.org; www.morrobay.org

Napa • *Visit Napa Valley* • Clay Gregory; CEO; 1001 Second St., Ste. 330; 94559; Napa; P 133,051; (707) 226-5813; Fax (707) 265-8154; info@visitnapavalley.com; www.visitnapavalley.com

Newport Beach • *Visit Newport Beach* • Alicia Snyder; Ofc. Mgr.; 1600 Newport Center Dr., Ste. 120; 92660; Orange; P 74,000; (949) 719-6100; (800) 94-COAST; Fax (949) 719-6101; info@visitnewportbeach.com; www.visitnewportbeach.com

Oakhurst • *Yosemite Sierra Visitors Bur.* • Dan Cunning; CEO; 40637 Hwy. 41; 93644; Madera; P 20,000; (559) 683-4636; Fax (559) 683-5697; ysvb@yosemitethisyear.com; www.yosemitethisyear.com

Oceanside • *Visit Oceanside Inc.* • Leslee Gaul; Pres./CEO; 928 N. Coast Hwy. Ste A; 92054; San Diego; P 183,095; (760) 721-1101; (800) 350-7873; Fax (760) 421-0106; visitorinfo@visitoceanside.org; www.visitoceanside.org

Ontario • *Ontario CVB* • Michael K. Krouse; Pres./CEO; 2000 E. Convention Center Way; 91764; San Bernardino; P 174,000; (909) 937-3000; (800) 455-5755; Fax (909) 937-3080; cdavis@ontariocvb.org; www.ontariocc.org

Oxnard • *Oxnard CVB* • Janet Sederquist; Pres./CEO; 1000 Town Center Dr., Ste. 130; 93036; Ventura; P 200,000; (805) 385-7545; (800) 2-OXNARD; Fax (805) 385-7571; info@visitoxnard.com; www.visitoxnard.com

Palm Desert • *Palm Desert Visitor Center* • Donna Gomez; Mgr.; 73-470 El Paseo, Ste. F-7; 92260; Riverside; P 50,000; (760) 568-1441; (800) 873-2428; Fax (760) 779-5271; vcenter@citypalm-desert.org; www.palm-desert.org

Pasadena • *Pasadena CVB* • Christine Susa; Dir. of Mktg. & Comm.; 300 E. Green St.; 91101; Los Angeles; P 140,000; (626) 795-9311; (800) 307-7977; Fax (626) 795-9656; travel@visitpasadena.com; www.visitpasadena.com

Pismo Beach • *Pismo Beach Conf. & Visitors Bur.* • Gordon Jackson; Exec. Dir.; 760 Mattie Rd.; 93449; San Luis Obispo; P 8,600; (805) 773-7034; (800) 443-7778; Fax (805) 779-1202; pbcity@pismobeach.org; www.classiccalifornia.com

Pleasanton • *Tri-Valley CVB* • G. Grant Raeside; Exec. Dir.; 5075 Hopyard Rd., Ste. 240; 94588; Alameda; P 190,000; (925) 846-8910; (888) 874-9253; Fax (925) 846-9502; info@trivalleycvb.com; www.trivalleycvb.com

Quincy • *Plumas County Tourism, Recreation & Hospitality Cncl.* • 550 Jackson St.; P.O. Box 1945; 95971; Plumas; P 20,000; info@plumascounty.org; www.plumascounty.org

Rancho Mirage • *Palm Springs-Desert Resort Communities CVA* • Scott White; Pres./CEO; 70-100 Hwy. 111; 92270; Riverside; P 300,000; (760) 770-9000; (800) 967-3767; Fax (760) 770-9001; swhite@palmspringsusa.com; www.palmspringsusa.com

Redding • *Redding CVB* • Laurie Baker; CEO; 1699 Hwy. 273; 96007; Shasta; P 110,000; (530) 225-4100; (800) 874-7562; Fax (530) 365-1258; laurie@shastacascade.org; www.visitredding.com

Redondo Beach • *Redondo Beach C/C & Visitors Bur.* • Marna Smeltzer; Pres./CEO; 119 W. Torrance Blvd., Ste. 2; 90277; Los Angeles; P 65,000; (310) 376-6911; (800) 282-0333; Fax (310) 374-7373; info@redondochamber.org; www.redondochamber.org

Ridgecrest • *Ridgecrest Area CVB & Film Commission* • Douglas Lueck; Exec. Dir.; 643 N. China Lake Blvd; P.O. Box 1838; 93555; Kern; P 25,000; (760) 375-8202; (800) 847-4830; Fax (760) 375-9850; racvb@filmdeserts.com; www.visitdeserts.com

Riverside • *Riverside CVB* • Debbi Guthrie; Senior V.P.; 3750 University Ave., Ste. 175; 92501; Riverside; P 300,000; (951) 222-4700; (888) 748-7733; Fax (951) 222-4712; dguthrie@riversidecvb.com; www.riversidecvb.com

Sacramento • *Sacramento CVB* • Steve Hammond; Pres./CEO; 1608 I St.; 95814; Sacramento; P 492,000; (916) 808-7777; (800) 292-2334; jvongeldern@visitsacramento.com; www.visitsacramento.com

San Diego • *San Diego Tourism Auth.* • Joe Terzi; Pres./CEO; 750 B St., Ste. 1500; 92101; San Diego; P 3,000,000; (619) 232-3101; Fax (619) 696-9371; sdinfo@sandiego.org; www.sandiego.org

San Francisco • *San Francisco Travel Assn.* • Joe D'Alessandro; Pres./CEO; One Front St., Ste. 2900; 94111; San Francisco; P 744,230; (415) 974-6900; Fax (415) 227-2602; administration@sftravel.com; www.sftravel.com

San Jose • *San Jose CVB* • Bill Sherry; Pres./CEO; 408 Almaden Blvd.; 95110; Santa Clara; P 1,000,000; (408) 295-9600; (800) SAN-JOSE; Fax (408) 295-3937; bsherry@sanjose.org; www.sanjose.org

San Luis Obispo • *Visit San Luis Obispo County* • Chuck Davison; Pres./CEO; 1334 Marsh St.; 93401; San Luis Obispo; P 281,200; (805) 541-8000; (800) 634-1414; brendan@visitsanluisobispocounty.com; www.visitsanluisobispocounty.com

San Rafael • *The Marin CVB* • Mark Essman; Pres.; 1 Mitchell Blvd., Ste. B; 94903; Marin; P 250,000; (415) 925-2060; (866) 925-2060; Fax (415) 925-2063; info@visitmarin.org; www.visitmarin.org

Santa Barbara • *Santa Barbara CVB & Film Commission* • Kathy Janega-Dykes; Pres./CEO; 500 E. Montecito St.; 93103; Santa Barbara; P 441,000; (805) 966-9222; (800) 676-1266; Fax (805) 966-1728; tourism@santabarbaraca.com; www.santabarbaraca.com

Santa Clara • *Santa Clara CVB* • Steve Van Dorn; Pres./CEO; 1850 Warburton Ave.; 95050; Santa Clara; P 110,000; (408) 244-9660; (800) 272-6822; Fax (408) 244-9202; steve.vandorn@santaclara.org; www.santaclara.org

C & VB

Santa Cruz • *Visit Santa Cruz County* • Maggie Ivy; CEO/Exec. V.P.; 303 Water St., Ste. 100; 95060; Santa Cruz; P 274,200; (831) 425-1234; (800) 833-3494; Fax (831) 425-1260; frontdesk@santacruz.org; www.santacruz.org

Santa Maria • *Santa Maria Valley Visitor & Conv. Bur.* • Jennifer Harrison; VCB Dir.; 614 S. Broadway; 93454; Santa Barbara; P 128,843; (805) 925-2403; (800) 331-3779; Fax (805)928-7559; jennifer@santamaria.com; www.santamaria.com

Santa Monica • *Santa Monica Travel & Tourism* • Misti Kerns; Pres./CEO; 2427 Main St.; 90405; Los Angeles; P 93,000; (310) 319-6263; (800) 771-2322; Fax (310) 319-6273; info@santamonica.com; www.santamonica.com

Santa Rosa • *Visit Santa Rosa* • Brad Calkins; Exec. Dir.; 9 Fourth St.; 95401; Sonoma; P 175,000; (707) 577-8674; (800) 404-7673; Fax (707) 571-5949; tanyar@visitsantarosa.com; www.visitsantarosa.com

Santa Rosa • *Sonoma County Tourism Bur.* • Ken Fischang; Pres./CEO; 400 Aviation Blvd., Ste. 500; 95403; Sonoma; P 450,000; (707) 522-5800; (800) 576-6662; Fax (707) 539-7252; info@sonomacounty.com; www.sonomacounty.com

Sherman Oaks • *The Valley Visitors Bur.* • Kenn Phillips; Pres./CEO; 5121 Van Nuys Blvd., Ste. 200; 91403; Los Angeles; P 2,000,000; (818) 379-7000; Fax (818) 379-7077; info@economicalliance.org; thevalley.net

Solvang • *Solvang Conf. & Visitors Bur* • Tracy Farhad; Exec. Dir.; 1639 Copenhagen Dr.; P.O. Box 70; 93464; Santa Barbara; P 5,500; (805) 688-6144; (800) 468-6765; Fax (805) 688-8620; info@solvangusa.com; www.solvangusa.com

Sonora • *Tuolumne County Visitors Bur.* • Lisa Mayo; Exec. Dir.; 542 W. Stockton Rd.; P.O. Box 4020; 95370; Tuolumne; P 59,500; (209) 533-4420; (800) 446-1333; Fax (209) 533-0956; tcvbinfo@mlode.com; www.tcvb.com

South Lake Tahoe • *see Stateline, NV*

Tahoe City • *North Lake Tahoe Visitor & Conv. Bur.* • Sandy Evans Hall; Exec. Dir./CEO; 100 N. Lake Blvd.; P.O. Box 5459; 96145; Placer; P 20,000; (888) 434-1262; (530) 583-3494; Fax (530) 581-1686; info@GoTahoeNorth.com; www.nltra.org

Temecula • *Temecula Valley CVB* • Kimberly Adams; Pres./CEO; 28690 Mercedes St., Ste. A; 92590; Riverside; P 108,000; (951) 491-6085; (888) 363-2852; Fax (951) 491-6089; info@visittemeculavalley.com; www.visittemeculavalley.com

Vallejo • *Vallejo CVB* • Mike Browne; Pres./CEO; 289 Mare Island Way, Ste. A; 94590; Solano; P 121,300; (707) 642-3653; (800) 482-5535; Fax (707) 644-2206; info@visitvallejo.com; www.visitvallejo.com

Ventura • *Ventura Visitors & Conv. Bur.* • Marlyss Auster; Exec. Dir.; 101 S. California St.; 93001; Ventura; P 109,000; (805) 648-2075; (800) 333-2989; Fax (805) 648-2150; chelsea@visitventuraca.com; www.visitventuraca.com

West Hollywood • *West Hollywood Mktg. & Visitors Bur.* • Bradley M. Burlingame; Pres./CEO; 8687 Melrose Ave., Ste. M-38; 90069; Los Angeles; P 39,000; (310) 289-2525; (800) 368-6020; Fax (310) 289-2529; info@visitwesthollywood.com; www.visitwesthollywood.com

Colorado

Boulder • *Boulder CVB* • Mary Ann Mahoney; Exec. Dir.; 2440 Pearl St.; 80302; Boulder; P 110,000; (303) 442-2911; (800) 444-0447; Fax (303) 938-2098; info@bouldercvb.com; www.bouldercoloradousa.com

Colorado Springs • *Colorado Springs CVB* • Doug Price; Pres./CEO; 515 S. Cascade Ave.; 80903; El Paso; P 604,500; (719) 635-7506; (800) 888-4748; Fax (719) 635-4968; gaby@visitcos.com; www.visitcos.com

Denver • *Visit Denver* • Richard Scharf; Pres./CEO; 1555 California St., Ste. 300; 80202; Denver; P 2,700,000; (303) 892-1112; (800) 233-6837; Fax (303) 892-1636; visitorinfo@visitdenver.com; www.denver.org

Empire • *see Idaho Springs*

Estes Park • *Estes Park CVB* • Peggy Campbell; Exec. Dir.; 500 Big Thompson Ave.; P.O. Box 1200; 80517; Larimer; P 6,500; (970) 577-9900; (800) 44-ESTES; Fax (970) 577-1677; cvbinfo@estes.org; www.estesparkcvb.com

Fort Collins • *Visit Fort Collins* • Cynthia Eichler; Pres./CEO; 19 Old Town Sq., Ste. 137; 80524; Larimer; P 155,000; (970) 232-3840; (800) 274-3678; Fax (970) 232-3841; information@ftcollins.com; www.visitftcollins.com

Grand Junction • *Grand Junction Visitor & Conv. Bur.* • Debbie Kovalik; Exec. Dir.; 740 Horizon Dr.; 81506; Mesa; P 137,879; (970) 244-1480; (800) 962-2547; Fax (970) 243-7393; info@visitgrandjunction.com; www.visitgrandjunction.com

Greeley • *Greeley CVB* • Sarah MacQuiddy; Pres.; 902 7th Ave.; 80631; Weld; P 100,000; (970) 352-3566; (800) 449-3866; Fax (970) 352-3572; smacquiddy@greeleychamber.com; www.greeleychamber.com

Idaho Springs • *Clear Creek County Tourism Bur.* • Cassandra Patton; Dir.; P.O. Box 100; 80452; Clear Creek; P 9,000; (303) 567-4660; Fax (303) 569-6296; info@clearcreekcounty.org; www.clearcreekcounty.org

Loveland • *Loveland Visitor Center* • Andrea Barry; Mgr.; 5400 Stone Creek Cir.; 80538; Larimer; P 67,000; (970) 667-5728; (800) 258-1278; Fax (970) 667-5211; vcmanager@loveland.org; www.loveland.org

Montrose • *Montrose Visitors & Conv. Bur.* • Jenni Sopsic; Mktg. & PR Dir.; 1519 E. Main St.; 81401; Montrose; P 41,000; (970) 252-0505; (800) 873-0244; Fax (970) 249-2907; jenni@montroseact.com; www.visitmontrose.com

Silver Plume • *see Idaho Springs*

South Fork • *South Fork Visitors Center* • Mark Teders; Dir.; 28 Silver Thread Ln.; 81154; Rio Grande; P 382; (719) 873-5512; Fax (719) 873-5693; marketingdirector@southfork.org; www.southfork.org

Steamboat Springs • *Steamboat Springs Chamber Resort Assn./Visitors Center* • Angela Sherwood; Mgr.; 125 Anglers Dr.; P.O. Box 774408; 80477; Routt; P 11,000; (970) 875-7000; Fax (970) 879-2543; info@steamboatchamber.com; www.steamboatchamber.com

Telluride • *Telluride Tourism Bd.* • Michael Martelon; Pres./CEO; 700 W. Colorado; P.O. Box 1009; 81435; San Miguel; P 3,000; (970) 728-3041; (888) 355-8743; Fax (970) 728-6475; info@visittelluride.com; www.visittelluride.com

Vail • **Vail Valley Partnership** • Michael Kurz; Pres./CEO; P.O. Box 1130; 81658; Eagle; P 48,000; (970) 476-1000; (800) 525-3875; Fax (970) 476-6008; info@visitvailvalley.com; www.visitvailvalley.com

Connecticut

Hartford • **Central Reg. Tourism Dist.** • Anne Orsene; Exec. Dir.; One Constitution Plz., 2nd Flr.; 06103; Hartford; P 1,100,000; (860) 787-9640; (800) 793-4480; Fax (860) 256-2811; anneo@centerofct.com; www.centerofct.com

Litchfield • **Western Connecticut CVB** • Janet L. Serra; Exec. Dir.; P.O. Box 968; 06759; Litchfield; P 8,000; (800) 663-1273; (860) 567-4506; Fax (860) 567-5214; info@northwestct.com; www.visitwesternct.com

Mystic • **Greater Mystic Visitors Bur.** • Karin Burgess; 27 Greenmanville Ave.; 06355; New London; P 350,000; (860) 701-9113; (860) 536-8822; Fax (860) 536-8855; greatermystic@gmail.com; www.mystic.org

New Haven • **Visit New Haven** • Ginny Kozlowski; Exec. Dir.; 545 Long Wharf Dr., 4th Flr.; 06511; New Haven; P 600,000; (203) 777-8550; (800) 332-STAY; Fax (203) 782-7755; barbaram@visitnewhaven.com; www.visitnewhaven.com

Norwalk • see Litchfield

Delaware

Dover • **Kent County Delaware CVB** • Wendie Vestfall; Exec. Dir.; 435 N. Dupont Hwy.; 19901; Kent; P 170,000; (302) 734-4888; (800) 233-5368; Fax (302) 734-0167; kctc@visitdover.com; www.visitdover.com

Wilmington • **Greater Wilmington CVB** • Sarah Willoughby; Exec. Dir.; 100 W. 10th St., Ste. 20; 19801; New Castle; P 538,500; (302) 295-2210; (800) 489-6664; Fax (302) 652-4726; lynlewis@visitwilmingtonde.com; www.visitwilmingtonde.com

District of Columbia

Washington • **Destination D.C.** • Elliott Ferguson; Pres./CEO; 901 7th St. N.W., 4th Flr.; 20001; District of Columbia; P 601,700; (202) 789-7000; (800) 422-8644; Fax (202) 789-7037; sales.rfp@washington.org; washington.org

Florida

Bradenton • **Bradenton Area CVB** • Elliot Falcione; Exec. Dir.; P.O. Box 1000; 34206; Manatee; P 300,000; (941) 729-9177; (800) 4-MANATEE; Fax (941) 729-1820; info@annamariaisland-longboatkey.com; www.annamariaisland-longboatkey.com

Brooksville • **Hernando County Tourism Bur.** • Tammy J. Heon; Tourism Dev. Mgr.; 31085 Cortez Blvd.; 34602; Hernando; P 174,000; (352) 754-4405; (800) 601-4580; Fax (352) 754-4406; info@hernandocounty.us; www.naturallyhernando.org

Cape Canaveral • see Cocoa

Clearwater • see Largo

Cocoa • **Florida's Space Coast Ofc. of Tourism** • Eric Garvey; Exec. Dir.; 430 Brevard Ave., Ste. 150; 32922; Brevard; P 550,000; (321) 433-4470; (877) 572-3224; Fax (321) 433-4476; info@visitspacecoast.com; www.visitspacecoast.com

Davenport • **Visit Central Florida** • Justin Laferriere; Visitor Svcs. Mgr.; 101 Adventure Ct.; 33837; Polk; P 500,000; (863) 420-2586; (800) 828-7655; Fax (863) 420-2593; info@visitcentralflorida.org; www.visitcentralflorida.org

Daytona Beach • **Daytona Beach Area CVB** • Jeffrey Hentz; Pres./CEO; 126 E. Orange Ave.; 32114; Volusia; P 61,000; (386) 255-0415; (800) 544-0415; Fax (386) 255-5478; tboyd@daytonabeachcvb.org; www.daytonabeach.com

Ecofina • see Perry

Fort Lauderdale • **Greater Ft. Lauderdale CVB** • Nicki E. Grossman; Pres.; 100 E. Broward Blvd., Ste. 200; 33301; Broward; P 166,000; (954) 765-4466; (800) 22-SUNNY; Fax (954) 765-4467; gflcvb@broward.org; www.sunny.org

Fort Myers • **Lee County Visitor & Conv. Bur.** • Tamara Pigott; Exec. Dir.; 2201 Second St., Ste. 600; 33901; Lee; P 619,000; (239) 338-3500; (800) 237-6444; Fax (239) 334-1106; vcb@leegov.com; www.fortmyers-sanibel.com

Fort Pierce • **St. Lucie County Tourist Dev. Cncl.** • Charlotte Bireley; Tourism & Venues Mgr.; 2300 Virginia Ave.; 34982; St. Lucie; P 278,000; (772) 462-1539; (800) 344-8443; Fax (772) 462-1128; bireleyc@stlucieco.org; www.visitstluciefla.com

Fort Walton Beach • **Emerald Coast CVB Inc.** • Mark Bellinger; Exec. Dir.; 1540 Miracle Strip Pkwy. S.E.; P.O. Box 609; 32549; Okaloosa; P 191,856; (850) 651-7131; (800) 322-3319; Fax (850) 651-7149; emeraldcoast@co.okaloosa.fl.us; www.emeraldcoastfl.com

Gainesville • **Alachua County Visitors & Conv. Bur.** • John Pricher; Dir.; 30 E. University Ave.; 32601; Alachua; P 253,000; (352) 374-5260; (866) 778-5002; Fax (352) 338-3213; info@visitgainesville.com; www.visitgainesville.com

Groveland • **Lake County Welcome Center** • Debi Dyer; Tourism Prog. Supervisor; 20763 U.S. Hwy. 27; 34736; Lake; P 312,000; (352) 429-3673; Fax (352) 429-4870; ddyer@lakecountyfl.gov; www.visitlakefl.com

Homosassa • **Citrus County Visitors & Conv. Bur.** • Marla Chancey; Dir. of Tourism; 9225 W. Fishbowl Dr.; 34448; Citrus; P 142,000; (352) 628-9305; (800) 587-6667; info@visitcitrus.com; www.visitcitrus.com

Jacksonville • **Visit Jacksonville** • Dan O'Byrne; Pres./CEO; 208 N. Laura St., Ste. 102; 32202; Duval; P 1,340,000; (904) 798-9111; (800) 733-2668; Fax (904) 798-9110; admin@visitjacksonville.com; www.visitjacksonville.com

Keaton Beach • see Perry

Key Largo • **Florida Keys Visitor Center** • Jackie Harder; Pres.; 106000 Overseas Hwy.; 33037; Monroe; P 18,000; (800) 822-1088; (305) 451-6266; Fax (305) 451-4726; info@keylargochamber.org; www.keylargo.org

Key West • **Monroe County Tourist Dev. Cncl.** • Harold Wheeler; Dir.; 1201 White St., Ste. 102; P.O. Box 866; 33040; Monroe; P 77,200; (305) 296-1552; Fax (305) 296-0788; officeasst@fla-keys.com; www.fla-keys.com

Kissimmee • **Experience Kissimmee** • DT Minich; Pres./CEO; 215 Celebration Place, Ste. 200; 34747; Osceola; P 160,000; (407) 847-5000; (800) 333-5477; Fax (407) 742-8226; dtminich@experiencekissimmee.com; www.experiencekissimmee.com

Lakeland • **Lakeland CVB** • Jacqueline Johnson; Senior V.P.; 35 Lake Morton Dr.; 33802; Polk; P 237,000; (863) 688-8551; Fax (863) 683-7454; awiggins@lakelandchamber.com; www.lakelandchamber.com

C & VB

Largo • *Visit St. Petersburg/Clearwater* • David Downing; Exec. Dir.; 8200 Bryan Dairy Road, Ste. 200; 33777; Pinellas; P 1,200,000; (727) 464-7200; (877) 352-3224; Fax (727) 464-7222; david@visitspc.com; www.visitstpeteclearwater.com

Melbourne • *The Melbourne Coast CVB* • Justin Anderson; COO; 1005 E. Strawbridge Ave.; 32901; Brevard; P 400,000; (321) 724-5400; (800) 771-9922; Fax (321) 725-2093; justin@melbourneregionalchamber.com; www.themelbournecoast.com

Miami • *Greater Miami CVB* • William D. Talbert III; Pres./CEO; 701 Brickell Ave., Ste. 2700; 33131; Miami-Dade; P 2,500,000; (305) 539-3000; (800) 933-8448; Fax (305) 539-3125; linda@gmcvb.com; www.miamiandbeaches.com

Naples • *Greater Naples VIC* • Lori Lou Waddell; Visitor Info. Center Coord.; 2390 Tamiami Trail N., Ste. 210; 34103; Collier; P 341,000; (239) 262-6141; (239) 298-7932; Fax (239) 692-9235; lorilou@napleschamber.org; www.napleschamber.org

New Port Richey • *Pasco County Ofc. of Tourism* • Eric Keaton; Pbl. Comm. Mgr.; 8731 Citizens Dr., Ste. 340; 34654; Pasco; P 465,000; (727) 847-8990; (800) 842-1873; Fax (727) 847-8168; ekeaton@pascocountyfl.net; www.visitpasco.net

Orlando • *Visit Orlando* • George Aguel; Pres./CEO; 6277 Sea Harbor Dr., Ste. 400; 32821; Orange; P 2,200,000; (407) 363-5800; (800) 972-3304; Fax (407) 370-5000; info@visitorlando.com; www.visitorlando.com

Panama City Beach • *Panama City Beach CVB* • Dan Rowe; Pres./CEO; 17001 Panama City Beach Pkwy.; 32417; Bay; P 13,300; (850) 233-5070; Fax (850) 233-5072; bainslie@visitpanamacitybeach.com; www.visitpanamacitybeach.com

Pensacola • *Pensacola Bay Area C/C - Conv. & Visitors Info. Center* • Steve Hayes; Pres.; 1401 E. Gregory St.; 32502; Escambia; P 53,100; (850) 434-1234; (800) 874-1234; Fax (850) 432-8211; jblack@visitpensacola.com; www.visitpensacola.com

Perry • *Taylor County Tourism Dev. Cncl.* • Dawn Taylor; Exec. Dir.; 428 N. Jefferson St.; P.O. Box 892; 32348; Taylor; P 23,000; (850) 584-5366; Fax (850) 584-8030; taylorchamber@fairpoint.net; www.taylorcountychamber.com

TOURIST CENTER FOR TAYLOR COUNTY WHICH INCLUDES STEINHATCHEE, PERRY, KEATON BEACH AND ECONFINA.

Port Charlotte • *Charlotte Harbor Visitor & Conv. Bur.* • Lorah Steiner; Dir. of Tourism; 18500 Murdock Cir., Ste. B104; 33948; Charlotte; P 55,000; (941) 743-1900; (800) 652-6090; Fax (941) 764-4932; visit@charlotteharbortravel.com; www.charlotteharbortravel.com

Saint Augustine • *St. Augustine, Ponte Vedra & The Beaches Visitors and Conv. Bur.* • Richard Goldman; Pres./CEO; 29 Old Mission Ave.; 32084; St. Johns; P 217,000; (904) 829-1711; (800) 653-2489; Fax (904) 829-6149; rgoldman@floridashistoriccoast.com; www.floridashistoriccoast.com

Saint Petersburg • *see Largo*

Santa Rosa Beach • *Walton County Tourist Dev. Cncl.* • 25777 U.S. 331 S.; 32459; Walton; P 55,100; (850) 267-1216; (800) 822-6877; Fax (850) 267-3943; www.visitsouthwalton.com

Sarasota • *Visit Sarasota County* • Virginia Haley; Pres.; 1777 Main St., Ste. 302; 34236; Sarasota; P 315,000; (941) 955-0991; (800) 522-9799; Fax (941) 955-1929; info@visitsarasota.org; www.visitsarasota.org

Sebring • *Highlands County Visitor & Conv. Bur.* • John Scherlacher; Tourism Dir.; 501 S. Commerce Ave., Ste. 3; 33870; Highlands; P 99,000; (863) 402-6909; Fax (863) 402-6795; tdc@highlandscvb.com; www.visithighlandscounty.com

Steinhatchee • *see Perry*

Tallahassee • *Tallahassee Area CVB* • Lee Daniel; Exec. Dir.; 106 E. Jefferson St.; 32301; Leon; P 265,000; (850) 606-2305; (800) 628-2866; Fax (850) 606-2301; vic@visittallahassee.com; www.visittallahassee.com

Tampa • *Visit Tampa Bay* • Santiago Corrada; Pres./CEO; 401 E. Jackson St., Ste. 2100; 33602; Hillsborough; P 1,140,000; (813) 223-1111; (800) 44-TAMPA; Fax (813) 229-6616; info@visittampabay.com; www.visittampabay.com

Tampa • *Ybor City Visitor Info. Center* • Lori Rosso; Exec. Dir.; 1600 E. 8th Ave., Ste. B104; 33605; Hillsborough; P 800,000; (813) 241-8838; Fax (813) 242-0398; lrosso@ybor.org; www.ybor.org

Weeki Wachee • *Hernando County Tourism Bur.* • Tammy J. Heon; Tourism Dev. Mgr.; Weeki Wachee Springs State Park; 6131 Commercial Way (U.S. 19); 34607; Hernando; P 174,000; (352) 754-4405; (800) 601-4580; Fax (352) 754-4406; info@hernandocounty.us; www.naturallyhernando.org

West Palm Beach • *Palm Beach County Tourist Dev. Cncl.* • Roger Amidon; Exec. Dir.; 1555 Palm Beach Lakes Blvd., Ste. 800; 33401; Palm Beach; P 1,300,000; (561) 233-3130; Fax (561) 233-3113; info@palmbeachfl.com; www.palmbeachfl.com

Ybor City • *see Tampa-Ybor City Visitor Info. Center*

Georgia

Albany • *Albany CVB* • Chris Hardy IOM CCE; Pres./CEO; 112 N. Front St.; 31701; Dougherty; P 94,000; (229) 317-4760; (866) 750-0840; Fax (229) 317-4765; chardy@albanyga.com; www.visitalbanyga.com

Alpharetta • *Alpharetta CVB* • Janet Rodgers; Pres./CEO; Park Plz.; 178 S. Main St., Ste. 200; 30009; Fulton; P 50,000; (678) 297-2811; (877) 202-5961; Fax (678) 297-9197; info@awesomealpharetta.com; www.awesomealpharetta.com

Athens • *Athens CVB* • Chuck Jones; Dir.; 300 N. Thomas St.; 30601; Athens & Clarke; P 116,000; (706) 357-4430; (800) 653-0603; Fax (706) 546-8040; askelton@visitathensga.com; www.visitathensga.com

Atlanta • *Atlanta CVB* • William Pate; Pres./CEO; 233 Peachtree St. N.E., Ste. 1400; 30303; Fulton; P 5,270,000; (404) 521-6600; (800) ATLANTA; Fax (404) 577-3293; hkirksey@atlanta.net; www.atlanta.net

Atlanta • *Cobb Travel & Tourism* • Holly Quinlan; CEO; One Galleria Pkwy.; 30339; Fulton; P 688,000; (678) 303-2622; (800) 451-3480; Fax (678) 303-2625; info@travelcobb.org; www.travelcobb.org

Augusta • *Augusta CVB* • Barry E. White; Exec. Dir.; 1450 Greene St., Ste. 110; P.O. Box 1331; 30903; Richmond; P 200,000; (706) 823-6600; (800) 726-0243; Fax (706) 823-6609; acvb@augustaga.org; www.augustaga.org

Brunswick • *Golden Isles CVB* • Scott McQuade; Pres./CEO; 1505 Richmond St., 2nd Flr.; 31520; Glynn; P 74,000; (912) 265-0620; (800) 933-COAST; Fax (912) 265-0629; info@goldenisles.com; www.goldenisles.com

Calhoun • *Calhoun/Gordon County CVB* • Sarah R. Husser; Dir.; 300 S. Wall St.; 30701; Gordon; P 56,000; (706) 625-3200; Fax (706) 625-5062; shusser@gordonchamber.org; www.exploregordoncounty.com

Carrollton • *Carrollton Area CVB* • Jonathan Dorsey; Exec. Dir.; 102 N. Lakeshore Dr.; 30117; Carroll; P 107,000; (770) 214-9746; (800) 292-0871; Fax (770) 830-1765; visit@carrollton-ga.gov; www.visitcarrollton.com

Cartersville • *Cartersville-Bartow County CVB* • Joe Frank Harris Jr.; Pres.; 5450 State Rte. 20; P.O. Box 307; 30120; Bartow; P 90,000; (770) 387-1357; (800) 733-2280; joe@notatlanta.org; www.notatlanta.org

Clayton • *Rabun County Tourism Dev. Auth.* • Teka Earnhardt; Exec. Dir.; P.O. Box 788; 30525; Rabun; P 16,300; (706) 212-0241; teka@explorerabun.com; www.explorerabun.com

Columbus • *Columbus CVB* • Peter Bowden; Pres./CEO; 900 Front Ave.; P.O. Box 2768; 31902; Muscogee; P 186,000; (706) 322-1613; (800) 999-1613; Fax (706) 322-0701; pbowden@visitcolumbusga.com; www.visitcolumbusga.com

Covington • *Covington-Newton County CVB* • Clara Deemer; Dir. of Tourism; 2101 Clark St.; P.O. Box 168; 30015; Newton; P 92,000; (770) 787-3868; (800) 616-8626; cdeemer@newtonchamber.com; www.newtonchamber.com

Dalton • *Dalton CVB* • Brett Huske; Exec. Dir.; P.O. Box 6177; 30722; Whitfield; P 100,000; (706) 270-9960; (800) 331-3258; Fax (706) 876-1561; info@visitdaltonga.com; www.daltoncvb.com

Douglas • *Douglas Area Welcome Center* • Pattie Merritt; Tourism Coord.; P.O. Box 470; 31533; Coffee; P 42,400; (912) 384-5161; (888) 426-3334; Fax (912) 383-6304; tourism@cityofdouglas.com; www.cityofdouglas.com

Duluth • *Gwinnett CVB* • Lisa Anders; Exec. Dir.; 6500 Sugarloaf Pkwy., Ste. 200; 30097; Gwinnett; P 805,300; (770) 623-3600; (888) 494-6638; Fax (770) 623-1667; info@gcvb.org; www.gcvb.org

Gainesville • *Lake Lanier CVB* • Millie Perez; Social Media Spec.; 2875 Browns Bridge Rd.; P.O. Box 2995; 30503; Hall; P 45,000; (770) 536-5209; (888) 536-0005; Fax (678) 866-2511; info@lakelaniercvb.com; www.lakelaniercvb.com

Hazlehurst • *Hazlehurst-Jeff Davis County Bd. of Tourism* • James Sewell; Exec. Dir.; 25 E. Coffee St.; P.O. Box 546; 31539; Jeff Davis; P 15,068; (912) 209-8805; (912) 240-0106; Fax (866) 570-8550; hjdtour@bellsouth.net; www.hazlehurst-jeffdavis.org

Helen • *Alpine Helen/White County CVB* • Debbie Gagliolo; 726 Bruckenstrasse; P.O. Box 730; 30545; White; P 25,300; (706) 878-2181; Fax (706) 878-4032; info@helenga.org; www.helenga.org

Homer • *Banks County Chamber CVB* • Brad Day; Exec. Dir.; P.O. Box 57; 30547; Banks; P 18,000; (706) 335-4866; (877) 389-2896; alicia@bankscountyga.info; www.bankscountyga.biz

Jekyll Island • *Jekyll Island Visitor Info. Center* • Eric Garvey; Dir.; 100 James Rd.; 31527; Glynn; P 1,200; (877) 453-5955; Fax (912) 635-4004; egarvey@jekyllisland.com; www.jekyllisland.com

Jonesboro • *Clayton County CVB* • Frenda Turner; V.P. of Finance & Admin.; 127 N. Main St.; 30236; Clayton; P 256,500; (678) 610-4242; frenda@visitscarlett.com; www.visitscarlett.com

Kingsland • *Kingsland CVB* • Tonya Rosado; Exec. Dir.; 1190 E. Boone Ave.; P.O. Box 1928; 31548; Camden; P 50,500; (912) 729-5999; (800) 433-0225; Fax (912) 729-7258; info@visitkingsland.com; www.visitkingsland.com

Macon • *Macon-Bibb County CVB* • Monica Smith; Pres./CEO; 450 Martin Luther King Jr. Blvd.; P.O. Box 6354; 31208; Bibb; P 125,000; (478) 743-3401; (800) 768-3401; Fax (478) 745-2022; maconcvb@maconga.org; www.visitmacon.org

Madison • *Madison-Morgan County CVB* • Ellen Ianelli Sims; Exec. Dir.; 115 E. Jefferson St.; 30650; Morgan; P 17,000; (706) 342-4454; (800) 709-7406; Fax (706) 342-4455; welcomecenter@madisonga.org; www.visitmadisonga.com

Milledgeville • *Milledgeville-Baldwin County CVB* • Jane Sowell; Dir.; 200 W. Hancock St.; P.O. Box 219; 31059; Baldwin; P 50,000; (478) 452-4687; (800) 653-1804; Fax (478) 453-4440; tourism@windstream.net; www.visitmilledgeville.com

Peachtree City • *Peachtree City CVB* • Nancy Price; Exec. Dir.; 201 McIntosh Trl.; 30269; Fayette; P 35,000; (678) 216-0282; Fax (770) 631-2575; mcamburn@visitpeachtreecity.com; www.visitpeachtreecity.com

Perry • *Perry Area CVB* • Sandi Smeltzer; Exec. Dir.; 101 Gen. Courtney Hodges Blvd.; 31069; Houston; P 12,000; (478) 988-8000; Fax (478) 988-8005; info@perryga.com; www.perryga.com

Pine Mountain • *Pine Mountain Tourism Assn.* • Hank Arnold; Exec. Dir.; 101 E. Broad St.; P.O. Box 177; 31822; Harris; P 32,000; (706) 663-4000; (800) 441-3502; Fax (706) 663-4726; hank@pinemountain.org; www.pinemountain.org

Rome • *Greater Rome CVB* • Lisa Smith; Exec. Dir.; 402 Civic Center Dr.; 30161; Floyd; P 95,000; (706) 295-5576; (800) 444-1834; Fax (706) 236-5029; lisa@romegeorgia.org; www.romegeorgia.org

Roswell • *Historic Roswell CVB* • Dotty Etris; Exec. Dir.; 617 Atlanta St.; 30075; Fulton; P 85,000; (770) 640-3253; (800) 776-7935; Fax (770) 640-3252; detris@roswellgov.com; www.visitroswellga.com

Saint Mary's • *St. Marys CVB* • Angela Wigger; Dir.; 400 Osborne St.; 31558; Camden; P 17,000; (912) 882-4000; (800) 868-8687; Fax (912) 882-6246; info@stmaryswelcome.com; www.VisitStMarys.com

Savannah • *Visit Savannah* • Joseph Marinelli; Pres.; 101 E. Bay St.; P.O. Box 1628; 31402; Chatham; P 372,700; (912) 644-6400; (877) SAVANNAH; Fax (912) 644-6499; www.visitsavannah.com

Statesboro • *Statesboro CVB* • Heidi Jeffers; Exec. Dir.; 332 S. Main St.; P.O. Box 1516; 30459; Bulloch; P 70,200; (912) 489-1869; (800) 568-3301; Fax (912) 489-2688; scvb@frontiernet.net; www.visitstatesboroga.com

Thomasville • *Thomasville Visitors Center* • Sherri Nix; 144 E. Jackson St.; 31792; Thomas; P 18,800; (229) 228-7977; (866) 577-3600; Fax (229) 228-4188; visit@thomasville.org; www.thomasvillega.com

Thomson • *Thomson-McDuffie Tourism CVB* • Elizabeth Vance; Exec. Dir.; 149 Main St.; 30824; McDuffie; P 22,000; (706) 597-1000; Fax (706) 595-2143; evance@thomson-mcduffie.net; www.exploremcduffiecounty.com

Tucker • *DeKalb CVB* • James Tsismanakis; Exec. Dir./CEO; 1957 Lakeside Pkwy., Ste. 510; 30084; DeKalb; P 700,000; (770) 492-5000; Fax (770) 492-5033; jamest@dcvb.org; www.visitatlantasdekalbcounty.com

C & VB

Tybee Island • *Tybee Island Visitor Info. Center* • Liz Hood; Supervisor; 802 1st St.; P.O. Box 491; 31328; Chatham; P 3,500; (912) 786-5444; (800) 868-2322; Fax (912) 786-5895; vc@VisitTybee.com; www.VisitTybee.com

Valdosta • *Valdosta-Lowndes County Conf. Center & Tourism Auth.* • Tim Riddle; Gen. Mgr.; 1 Meeeting Pl.; 31601; Lowndes; P 56,600; (229) 245-0513; (800) 569-TOUR; Fax (229) 245-5240; tyra@valdostatourism.com; www.visitvaldosta.org

Vidalia • *Vidalia CVB* • Alexa Carter Britton; Exec. Dir.; 100 Vidalia Sweet Onion Dr., Ste. A; 30474; Toombs; P 15,000; (912) 538-8687; Fax (912) 538-1466; abritton@vidaliaga.gov; www.vidaliaarea.com

Warner Robins • *Warner Robins CVB* • Marsha Buzzell; Dir.; 99 N. 1st St.; 31093; Houston; P 55,000; (478) 922-5100; Fax (478) 225-2631; cvb@wrga.gov; www.wrga.gov

Waycross • *Waycross Tourism Bur.* • Jan Harris Sanchez; Exec. Dir.; 315 Plant Ave., Stes. A-B; 31501; Ware; P 36,312; (912) 283-3742; Fax (912) 283-0121; waycrosstour@accessatc.net; www.swampgeorgia.com

Hawaii

Honolulu • *Hawaii Visitors & Conv. Bur.* • John Monahan; Pres./CEO; 2270 Kalakaua Ave., Ste. 801; 96815; Honolulu; P 1,400,000; (808) 923-1811; (800) 464-2924; Fax (808) 924-0290; info@hvcb.org; www.gohawaii.com

Kaunakakai • *Moloka'I Visitors Assn.* • Julie Bicoy; Dir.; P.O. Box 960; 96748; Maui; P 8,100; (808) 553-3876; (800) 800-6367; Fax (808) 553-5288; mvajulie@gmail.com; www.molokai-hawaii.com

Idaho

Boise • *Boise CVB* • Roberta Patterson; Exec. Dir.; 1199 Main St.; P.O. Box 2106; 83701; Ada; P 208,000; (208) 344-7777; (800) 635-5240; Fax (208) 344-6236; bpatters@boisecvb.org; www.boise.org

Coeur d'Alene • *Coeur d'Alene Visitors Bur.* • Steve Wilson; Pres./CEO; 105 N. 1st St., Ste. 100; 83814; Kootenai; P 45,900; (208) 664-3194; (877) 782-9232; Fax (208) 667-9338; info@coeurdalene.org; coeurdalene.org

Idaho Falls • *Idaho Falls CVB* • Michelle Holt; Exec. Dir.; 425 N. Capital Ave.; 83402; Bonneville; P 59,000; (208) 523-1010; (866) 365-6943; Fax (208) 523-2255; information@visitidahofalls.com; www.visitidahofalls.com

Ketchum • *Visit Sun Valley* • Aly Swindley; Mbrshp. & Visitor Svcs.; 491 Sun Valley Rd.; P.O. Box 4934; 83340; Blaine; P 10,000; (208) 726-3423; (800) 634-3347; Fax (208) 726-4533; info@visitsunvalley.com; www.visitsunvalley.com

McCall • *McCall Area Visitors Bur.* • 301 E. Lake St.; P.O. Box 350; 83638; Valley; P 3,500; (208) 634-7631; (800) 260-5130; Fax (208) 634-7752; info@mccallchamber.org; www.mccallchamber.org

Illinois

Alton • *Alton Reg. CVB* • Brett Stawar; Pres.; 200 Piasa St.; 62002; Madison; P 100,000; (618) 465-6676; (800) ALTON-IL; Fax (618) 465-6151; info@visitalton.com; www.visitalton.com

Anna • *Southernmost Illinois Tourism Bur.* • Cindy Cain; Dir.; P.O. Box 378; 62906; Union; P 71,500; (618) 833-9928; (800) 248-4373; Fax (618) 833-9928; sitb@frontier.com; www.southernmostillinois.com

Arlington Heights • *see Prospect Heights*

Aurora • *Aurora Area Conv. & Visitors Bur.* • Cort Carlson; Exec. Dir.; 43 W. Galena Blvd.; 60506-4129; Kane, Kendall, DuPage & Will; P 329,221; (630) 256-3190; (800) 477-4369; Fax (630) 256-3199; info@enjoyaurora.com; www.EnjoyAurora.com

Belleville • *Belleville Illinois Tourism* • Cathleen Lindauer; Dir.; 216 E. A St.; 62220; St. Clair; P 45,000; (618) 233-6769; (800) 677-9255; Fax (618) 233-2077; clindauer@bellevillechamber.org; www.bellevillechamber.org

Belvidere • *Chicago & Beyond Reg. Tourism Ofc.* • Bonnie Heimbach; Exec. Dir.; 8200 Fairgrounds Rd.; 61008; Boone; P 3,000,000; (815) 547-3740; Fax (815) 547-3740; bonnie@chicagoandbeyond.com; www.chicagoandbeyond.com

Bloomington • *Bloomington-Normal Area CVB* • Crystal Howard; Dir.; 3201 CIRA Dr., Ste. 201; 61704; McLean; P 132,000; (800) 433-8226; (309) 665-0033; Fax (309) 661-0743; brie@visitbn.org; www.visitbn.org

Carbondale • *Carbondale Conv. & Tourism Bur.* • Cinnamon Wheeles-Smith; Exec. Dir.; 126 S. Illinois Ave.; 62901; Jackson; P 26,400; (618) 529-4451; (800) 526-1500; Fax (618) 529-5590; jessica@carbondaletourism.org; www.carbondaletourism.org

Champaign • *Champaign County CVB* • Jayne DeLuce; Pres./CEO; 108 S. Neil St.; 61820; Champaign; P 190,000; (217) 351-4133; (800) 369-6151; Fax (217) 359-1809; lisab@champaigncounty.org; www.visitchampaigncounty.org

Chicago • *Choose Chicago* • David Whitaker; Pres./CEO; 301 E. Cermak Rd.; 60616; Cook; P 9,000,000; (312) 567-8500; (877) CHICAGO; Fax (312) 567-8535; cearner@choosechicago.com; www.choosechicago.com

Collinsville • *Gateway Center* • One Gateway Dr.; 62234; Madison; P 24,707; (618) 345-8998; (800) 289-2388; Fax (618) 345-9024; info@gatewaycenter.com; www.gatewaycenter.com

Danville • *Danville Area CVB* • D. Jeanie Cooke; Exec. Dir.; 100 W. Main St., Ste. 146; 61832; Vermilion; P 35,000; (217) 442-2096; (800) 383-4386; Fax (217) 442-2137; info@danvilleareainfo.com; www.danvilleareainfo.com

Decatur • *Decatur Area CVB* • Teri Hammel; Exec. Dir.; 202 E. North St.; 62523; Macon; P 80,000; (217) 423-7000; (800) 331-4479; Fax (217) 423-7455; tourism@decaturcvb.com; www.decaturcvb.com

Du Quoin • *Du Quoin Tourism Comm.* • Judy Smid; Pres.; 20 N. Chestnut St.; P.O. Box 1037; 62832; Perry; P 6,448; (618) 542-8338; (800) 455-9570; Fax (618) 542-2098; duquointourism@yahoo.com; www.duquointourism.org

Elgin • *Elgin Area CVB* • Kimberly Bless; Pres./CEO; 77 Riverside Dr.; 60120; Kane; P 285,000; (847) 695-7540; (800) 217-5362; Fax (847) 695-7668; kmurphy@northernfoxrivervalley.com; www.northernfoxrivervalley.com

Freeport • *Freeport/Stephenson County CVB* • Connie Sorn; Exec. Dir.; 4596 U.S. Rte. 20 E.; 61032; Stephenson; P 48,000; (815) 233-1357; (800) 369-2955; Fax (815) 233-1358; stephcvb@jcwifi.net; www.stephenson-county-il.org

Galena • *Galena/Jo Daviess County CVB* • Katherine Walker; Exec. Dir.; 720 Park Ave.; 61036; Jo Daviess; P 22,289; (815) 777-3557; (877) 464-2536; Fax (815) 777-3566; director@galena.org; www.galena.org

Galesburg • *Galesburg Area CVB* • Bill Morris; Exec. Dir.; 2163 E. Main St.; P.O. Box 60; 61402; Knox; P 34,500; (309) 343-2485; (800) 916-3330; Fax (309) 343-2521; visitors@visitgalesburg.com; www.visitgalesburg.com

Gurnee • *Visit Lake County* • Maureen Riedy; Pres.; 5465 W. Grand Ave., Ste. 100; 60031; Lake; P 703,462; (847) 662-2700; (800) LAKE-NOW; Fax (847) 662-2702; tourism@lakecounty.org; www.visitlakecounty.org

Jacksonville • *Jacksonville Area CVB* • Brittany Henry; Exec. Dir.; 310 E. State St.; 62650; Morgan; P 24,000; (217) 243-5678; (800) 593-5678; Fax (217) 243-5862; visitors@jacksonvilleil.org; www.jacksonvilleil.org

Kankakee • *Kankakee County CVB* • Larry Williams; Exec. Dir.; 1 Dearborn Sq., Ste. 1; 60901; Kankakee; P 105,000; (815) 935-7390; (800) 74-RIVER; Fax (815) 935-5169; larry@visitkankakeecounty.com; www.visitkankakeecounty.com

Lake County • *see Gurnee*

Lansing • *Chicago Southland CVB* • Jim Garrett CDME; Pres./CEO; 2304 173rd St.; 60438; Cook; P 871,138; (708) 895-8200; (888) 895-8233; Fax (708) 895-8288; info@visitchicagosouthland.com; www.visitchicagosouthland.com

Lincoln • *Logan County Tourism Bur.* • Sarah Wallick; Dir.; 1555 5th St.; 62656; Logan; P 35,000; (217) 732-8687; Fax (217) 735-9205; sarah.wallick@destinationlogancountyil.com; www.destinationlogancountyil.com

Lisle • *Lisle CVB* • Diane Homolka; Exec. Dir.; 4746 Main St.; 60532; DuPage; P 21,000; (630) 769-1000; (800) 733-9811; Fax (630) 769-1006; lislevisitor@stayinlisle.com; www.stayinlisle.com

Macomb • *Macomb Area CVB* • Tamara Parker; Interim Exec. Dir.; 201 S. Lafayette St.; 61455; McDonough; P 20,000; (309) 833-1315; Fax (309) 833-3575; macvb@macomb.com; www.makeitmacomb.com

Macomb • *Great Rivers Country Reg. Tourism Dev. Ofc.* • Roger Carmack; Exec. Dir.; 581 S. Deere Rd.; 61455; McDonough; (309) 837-7460; Fax (309) 833-4754; witdo@visitwesternillinois.info; www.greatriverscountry.info

Marion • *Williamson County CVB* • Shannon Johnson; Exec. Dir.; 1602 Sioux Dr.; 62959; Williamson; P 65,000; (618) 997-3690; (800) 433-7399; Fax (618) 997-1874; info@vistisi.com; www.visitsi.com

Moline • *Quad-Cities CVB* • Joe Taylor; Pres./CEO; 1601 River Dr., Ste. 110; 61265; Rock Island & Scott; P 400,000; (309) 277-0937; (800) 747-7800; Fax (309) 764-9443; cvb@visitquadcities.com; www.visitquadcities.com

Mount Vernon • *Mount Vernon CVB* • Angela Schrum; Dir.; 200 Potomac Blvd.; P.O. Box 1708; 62864; Jefferson; P 15,500; (618) 242-3151; (800) 252-5464; Fax (618) 242-6849; tourism@mtvernon.com; www.enjoymtvernon.com

Naperville • *Naperville Dev. Partnership & CVB* • Christine Jeffries; Pres.; 22 E. Chicago Ave., Ste. 205; 60540; DuPage & Will; P 147,000; (630) 305-7701; (877) 236-2737; Fax (630) 305-7793; ncvb@naper.org; www.visitnaperville.com

Oak Brook • *DuPage CVB* • Skip Strittmatter; Exec. Dir.; 915 Harger Rd., Ste. 240; 60523; DuPage; P 923; (630) 575-8070; (800) 232-0502; Fax (630) 575-8078; skip@discoverdupage.com; www.discoverdupage.com

Olney • *see Fairview Heights*

Pekin • *Pekin Visitors Bur.* • Leigh Ann Matthews; Coord.; 111 S. Capitol; 61554; Tazewell; P 35,000; (309) 477-2300; (877) 669-7741; Fax (309) 346-2095; tourism@ci.pekin.il.us; www.pekintourism.com

Peoria • *Peoria Area CVB* • Bob Marx; Pres./CEO; 456 Fulton St., Ste. 300; 61602; Peoria; P 344,000; (309) 676-0303; (800) 747-0302; Fax (309) 676-8470; bmarx@peoria.org; www.peoria.org

Polo • *Blackhawk Waterways CVB* • Diane Bausman; Exec. Dir.; 201 N. Franklin Ave.; 61064; Ogle; P 96,000; (815) 946-2108; (800) 678-2108; Fax (815) 946-2277; dbausman@bwcvb.com; www.bwcvb.com

Pontiac • *Pontiac Tourism* • Ellie Alexander; Tourism Dir.; 115 W. Howard St.; 61764; Livingston; P 12,000; (815) 844-5847; (800) 835-2055; Fax (815) 842-3885; tourism@pontiac.org; www.visitpontiac.org

Prospect Heights • *Chicago's North Suburbs CVB* • Brent Edwards; Exec. Dir.; 8 N. Elmhurst Rd., Ste. 100; 60070; Cook; P 17,000; (847) 577-3666; (800) 955-7259; Fax (847) 577-8306; info@chicagonorthsuburbs.com; www.chicagonorthsuburbs.com

Quincy • *Quincy Area CVB* • Holly Cain; Exec. Dir.; 532 Gardner Expy.; 62301; Adams; P 90,000; (217) 214-3700; (800) 978-4748; Fax (217) 214-2721; hcain@seequincy.com; www.seequincy.com

Rock Island • *see Moline*

Rockford • *Rockford Area CVB* • John Groh; Pres./CEO; 102 N. Main St.; 61101; Winnebago; P 295,300; (815) 963-8111; (800) 521-0849; Fax (815) 963-4298; info@gorockford.com; www.gorockford.com

Romeoville • *Heritage Corridor CVB* • Robert Navarro; Pres./CEO; 15701 S. Independence Blvd.; 60446; Kendall & Will; P 100,000; (815) 588-7940; (800) 926-2262; Fax (815) 588-7945; info@heritagecorridorcvb.com; www.heritagecorridorcvb.com

Rosemont • *Rosemont CVB* • William C. Anderson; Gen. Mgr.; 9301 W. Bryn Mawr Ave.; 60018; Cook; P 4,500; (847) 823-2100; Fax (847) 696-9700; rcb@rosemont.com; www.rosemont.com

Schaumburg • *Woodfield Chicago Northwest Conv. Bur.* • Dave Parulo; Pres.; 1375 E. Woodfield Rd., Ste. 120; 60173; Cook; P 640,000; (847) 490-1010; (800) 847-4849; Fax (847) 490-1212; info@chicagonorthwest.com; www.chicagonorthwest.com

Shelbyville • *Lake Shelbyville Area CVB/Shelby County Tourism* • Ms. Freddie Fry; Dir.; 315 E. Main St.; 62565; Shelby; P 20,000; (217) 774-2244; (800) 874-3529; info@lakeshelbyville.com; www.lakeshelbyville.com

Springfield • *Springfield CVB* • Gina Gemberling; Exec. Dir.; 109 N. 7th St.; 62701; Sangamon; P 117,000; (217) 789-2360; (800) 545-7300; Fax (217) 544-8711; pat.corcoran@springfield.il.us; www.visitspringfieldillinois.com

St. Charles • *Greater St. Charles CVB* • Amy Egolf; Exec. Dir.; 311 N. 2nd St., Ste. 100; 60174; Kane; P 33,000; (630) 377-6161; (800) 777-4373; Fax (630) 513-0566; info@visitstcharles.com; www.visitstcharles.com

Swansea • *Illinois South Tourism* • Dan Krankeola; Pres./CEO; 4387 N. Illinois St., Ste. 200; 62226; St. Clair; P 700,000; (618) 397-1488; (800) 442-1488; info@illinoisouth.org; illinoisouth.org

Indiana

Anderson • Anderson/Madison County Visitors Bur. • Matt Rust; Exec. Dir.; 6335 S. Scatterfield Rd.; 46013; Madison; P 132,000; (765) 643-5633; (800) 533-6569; Fax (765) 643-9083; ecleary@VisitAndersonMadisonCounty.com; www.VisitAndersonMadisonCounty.com

Angola • Steuben County Tourism Bur. • 430 N. Wayne St., Ste. 1B; 46703; Steuben; P 33,722; (260) 665-5386; (800) LAKE-101; info@lakes101.org; www.lakes101.org

Avon • see Danville

Bloomington • Visit Bloomington • Mike McAfee; Exec. Dir.; 2855 N. Walnut St.; 47404; Monroe; P 142,000; (812) 334-8900; (800) 800-0037; Fax (812) 334-2344; cvb@visitbloomington.com; www.visitbloomington.com

Carmel • Hamilton County Tourism Inc. • Brenda Myers; Pres./CEO; 37 E. Main St.; 46032; Hamilton; P 302,000; (317) 848-3181; (800) 776-TOUR; Fax (317) 848-3191; info@hamiltoncountytourism.com; www.VisitHamiltonCounty.com

Columbus • Columbus Area Visitors Center • Lynn Lucas; Exec. Dir.; 506 5th St.; 47201; Bartholomew; P 39,000; (812) 378-2622; (800) 468-6564; Fax (812) 372-7348; vgardner@columbus.in.us; www.columbus.in.us

Corydon • Harrison County CVB • Jeremy W. Yackle; Exec. Dir.; 310 N. Elm St.; 47112; Harrison; P 39,000; (812) 738-2138; (888) 738-2137; Fax (812) 738-3609; info@thisisindiana.org; www.thisisindiana.org

Crawfordsville • Montgomery County Visitors & Conv. Bur. • Heather Shirk; Exec. Dir.; 218 E. Pike St.; 47933; Montgomery; P 38,500; (765) 362-5200; (800) 866-3973; Fax (765) 362-5215; request@crawfordsville.org; www.visitmoco.com

Danville • Hendricks County CVB • Jaime Bohler Smith; Exec. Dir.; 8 W. Main St.; 46122; Hendricks; P 154,000; (317) 718-8750; (800) 321-9666; Fax (317) 718-9913; jaime@visithendrickscounty.com; www.visithendrickscounty.com

Elkhart • Elkhart County CVB • Diana Lawson; Exec. Dir.; 219 Caravan Dr.; 46514; Elkhart; P 195,362; (574) 262-8161; (800) 262-8161; Fax (574) 262-3925; ecconv@amishcountry.org; www.amishcountry.org

Evansville • Evansville CVB • Bob Warren; Exec. Dir.; 401 S.E. Riverside Dr.; 47713; Vanderburgh; P 170,000; (812) 421-2200; (800) 433-3025; Fax (812) 421-2207; info@evansvillecvb.org; www.evansvillecvb.org

Fort Wayne • Visit Fort Wayne • Dan O'Connell; Pres./CEO; 927 S. Harrison St.; 46802; Allen; P 370,000; (260) 424-3700; (800) 767-7752; Fax (260) 424-3914; info@visitfortwayne.com; www.visitfortwayne.com

Greencastle • Putnam County CVB • Nancy Mark; Exec. Dir.; 12 W. Washington St.; 46135; Putnam; P 38,000; (765) 653-8743; (800) 829-4639; Fax (765) 653-0851; pc@gmail.com; www.goputnam.com

Hammond • South Shore Conv. & Visitors Auth. • Speros Batistatos; Pres./CEO; 7770 Corinne Dr.; 46323; Lake; P 496,000; (219) 989-7770; (800) ALL-LAKE; Fax (219) 989-7777; info@southshorecva.com; www.southshorecva.com

Huntington • Huntington County Visitor & Conv. Bur. • Tina Bobilya; Exec. Dir.; 407 N. Jefferson St.; 46750; Huntington; P 38,000; (260) 359-8687; (800) 848-4282; info@visithuntington.org; visithuntington.org

Indianapolis • Indianapolis Conv. & Visitors Assn. • Leonard Hoops; Pres./CEO; 200 S. Capitol Ave., Ste. 300; 46225; Marion; P 865,000; (317) 639-4282; (800) 323-4639; Fax (317) 639-5273; icva@visitindy.com; www.visitindy.com

Jasper • Dubois County Visitors Center • Kevin Manley; Exec. Dir.; 2704 Newton St.; 47546; Dubois; P 38,000; (812) 482-9115; (800) 968-4578; Fax (812) 481-2809; info@visitduboiscounty.com; www.visitduboiscounty.com

Jeffersonville • Clark-Floyd Counties Conv. & Tourism Bur. • James P. Keith; Exec. Dir.; 315 Southern Indiana Ave.; 47130; Clark; P 200,000; (812) 282-6654; (800) 552-3842; Fax (812) 282-1904; tourism@sunnysideoflouisville.org; www.sunnysideoflouisville.org

Knox • Starke County Tourism Comm. • Deborah J. Mix; Exec. Dir.; 400 N. Heaton St.; 46534; Starke; P 25,000; (574) 772-0896; (877) 733-2736; Fax (574) 772-0867; travel@explorestarkecounty.com; www.explorestarkecounty.com

Kokomo • Kokomo Visitors Bur. • Sherry Matlock; Mgr.; 325 N. Main St.; 46901; Howard; P 82,000; (765) 457-6802; (800) 837-0971; Fax (765) 457-1572; information@visitkokomo.org; www.visitkokomo.org

Lafayette • Lafayette/West Lafayette CVB • Jo Wilson Wade; Pres./CEO; 301 Frontage Rd.; 47905; Tippecanoe; P 173,000; (765) 447-9999; (800) 872-6648; Fax (765) 447-5062; info@homeofpurdue.com; www.homeofpurdue.com

Lawrenceburg • Dearborn County Conv., Visitor & Tourism Bur. • Debbie Smith; Exec. Dir.; 320 Walnut St.; 47025; Dearborn; P 50,000; (800) 322-8198; (812) 537-0814; Fax (812) 537-0845; dearborn@visitsoutheastindiana.com; www.visitsoutheastindiana.com

Madison • VisitMadison • Linda Lytle; Exec. Dir.; 601 W. 1st St.; 47250; Jefferson; P 29,000; (812) 265-2956; (800) 559-2956; Fax (812) 273-3694; info@visitmadison.org; www.visitmadison.org

Marion • Marion/Grant County CVB • John Lightle; Exec. Dir.; P.O. Box 1327; 46952; Grant; P 70,000; (765) 668-5435; Fax (765) 668-5424; info@showmegrantcounty.com; showmegrantcounty.com

Michigan City • LaPorte County CVB • Jack Arnett; Exec. Dir.; Marquettte Mall, 4073 S. Franklin St.; 46360; LaPorte; P 120,000; (219) 326-8115; (800) 634-2650; Fax (219) 872-3660; jack@michigancitylaporte.com; www.michigancitylaporte.com

Mishawaka • see South Bend

Muncie • Muncie Visitors Bur. • James Mansfield; Exec. Dir.; 3700 S. Madison St.; 47302; Delaware; P 70,000; (765) 284-2700; (800) 568-6862; Fax (765) 284-3002; jim@visitmuncie.org; www.visitmuncie.org

Nashville • Brown County CVB • Jane Ellis; Exec. Dir.; 10 N. Van Buren St.; P.O. Box 840; 47448; Brown; P 14,950; (812) 988-7303; (800) 753-3255; Fax (812) 988-1070; info@browncounty.com; www.browncounty.com

New Castle • Henry County CVB • Lee Stacey; Ofc. Mgr.; 3205 S. Memorial Dr.; 47362; Henry; P 49,500; (765) 593-0764; (888) 676-4302; Fax (765) 593-0766; info@henrycountyin.org; www.henrycountyin.org

Plainfield • see Danville

Plymouth • Marshall County CVB • Mike Woolfington; Exec. Dir.; 220 N. Center; P.O. Box 669; 46563; Marshall; P 38,000; (574) 936-1882; (800) 626-5353; Fax (574) 936-9845; mcw@marshallcountytourism.org; www.marshallcountytourism.org

Porter • *Indiana Dunes Tourism* **•** Lorelei Weimer; Exec. Dir.; 1215 N. State Rd. 49; 46304; Porter; P 164,300; (219) 926-2255; (800) 283-TOUR; Fax (219) 929-5395; info@indianadunes.com; www.indianadunes.com

Portland • *Jay County Visitor & Tourism Bur.* **•** Gyneth Augsburger; Exec. Dir.; 118 S. Meridian St., Ste. C; 47371; Jay; P 22,000; (260) 726-3366; (877) 726-4481; Fax (260) 726-3372; infojc@visitjaycounty.com; www.visitjaycounty.com

Richmond • *Richmond-Wayne County Conv. & Tourism Bur.* **•** Mary T. Walker; Exec. Dir.; 5701 National Rd. E.; 47374; Wayne; P 70,000; (765) 935-8687; (800) 828-8414; Fax (765) 935-0440; askus@visitrichmond.org; www.visitrichmond.org

Rising Sun • *Rising Sun/Ohio County Tourism* **•** Brett Stowell; Interim Exec. Dir.; 120 Main St.; P.O. Box 112; 47040; Ohio; P 6,000; (812) 438-4933; (888) 776-4786; Fax (812) 438-4932; bstowell@enjoyrisingsun.com; www.enjoyrisingsun.com

Rockville • *Parke County Inc.* **•** Kelsey Canfield; Exec. Secy.; P.O. Box 165; 47872; Parke; P 15,000; (765) 569-5226; Fax (765) 569-3900; info@coveredbridges.com; www.coveredbridges.com

Rome City • *Noble County CVB* **•** Sheryl Prentice; Exec. Dir.; 8983 N. 350 E.; P.O. Box 325; 46784; Noble; P 14,363; (260) 854-2115; (877) 202-5761; Fax (260) 854-2115; info@visitnoblecounty.com; www.visitnoblecounty.com

Seymour • *Jackson County Visitor Center* **•** Tina Stark; Exec. Dir.; 100 N. Broadway St.; P.O. Box 607; 47274; Jackson; P 40,000; (812) 524-1914; (888) 524-1914; Fax (812) 524-1915; jacksoncountyin@frontier.com; www.jacksoncountyin.com

South Bend • *South Bend/Mishawaka CVB* **•** Rob DeCleene CDME; Exec. Dir.; 401 E. Colfax Ave., Ste. 310; 46617; St. Joseph; P 267,000; (574) 232-0231; (800) 519-0577; Fax (574) 289-0358; info@visitsouthbend.org; www.visitsouthbend.com

Tell City • *Perry County CVB* **•** Betty Cash; Exec. Dir.; 333 7th St.; P.O. Box 721; 47586; Perry; P 20,000; (812) 547-7933; (888) 343-6262; Fax (812) 547-8378; perrycountycvb@psci.net; www.perrycountyindiana.org

Terre Haute • *Terre Haute CVB* **•** David A. Patterson; Exec. Dir.; 5353 E. Margaret Dr.; 47803; Vigo; P 108,000; (812) 234-5555; (800) 366-3043; Fax (812) 234-6750; info@terrehaute.com; www.terrehaute.com

Vevay • *Switzerland County Tourism* **•** Kendal Miller; Exec. Dir.; 128 W. Main St.; 47043; Switzerland; P 11,000; (812) 427-3237; (800) 435-5688; visitsc@switzcotourism.com; www.switzcotourism.com

Vincennes • *Vincennes/Knox County VTB* **•** Shyla Beam; Exec. Dir.; 779 S. 6th St.; P.O. Box 602; 47591; Knox; P 38,500; (812) 886-0400; (800) 886-6443; Fax (812) 885-0033; info@visitvincennes.org; www.visitvincennes.org

Wabash • *Wabash County Tourism & Visitors Bur.* **•** Christine Flohr; Exec. Dir.; 221 S. Miami St.; 46992; Wabash; P 33,000; (260) 563-7171; (800) 563-1169; tourism@visitwabashcounty.com; www.visitwabashcounty.com

Warsaw • *Kosciusko County CVB* **•** Mary Kittrell; Dir.; 111 Capital Dr.; 46582; Kosciusko; P 75,667; (574) 269-6090; (800) 800-6090; Fax (574) 269-2405; info@koscvb.org; www.koscvb.org

Washington • *Daviess County Visitors Bur.* **•** Samantha Bobbitt; Exec. Dir.; One Train Depot St.; 47501; Daviess; P 32,000; (812) 254-5262; (800) 449-5262; Fax (812) 254-4003; sbobbitt@dcchamber.com; www.daviesscounty.net

Winchester • *Randolph County Visitor Info. Center* **•** Sandie Rowe; Exec. Dir.; 112 W. Washington St.; 47394; Randolph; P 27,066; (765) 584-3731; Fax (765) 584-5544; chamber@globalsite.net; www.winchesterareachamber.org

Iowa

Amana • *Amana Colonies CVB* **•** 622 46th Ave.; 52203; Iowa; P 1,500; (319) 622-7622; (800) 579-2294; Fax (319) 622-6395; info@amanacolonies.com; www.amanacolonies.com

Ames • *Ames CVB* **•** Julie Weeks; Dir.; 1601 Golden Aspen Dr., Ste. 110; 50010; Story; P 53,000; (515) 232-4032; (800) 288-7470; Fax (515) 232-6716; info@amescvb.com; www.visitames.com

Bettendorf • *see Moline, IL*

Boone • *Boone County CVB* **•** Kris Blocker; Mgr.; 903 Story St.; 50036; Boone; P 27,000; (515) 432-3342; (800) 266-6312; Fax (515) 432-3343; office@booneiowa.us; www.booneiowa.us

Burlington • *Greater Burlington Partnership* **•** Chelsea Tolle; Exec. Dir.; 610 N. 4th St., Ste. 200; 52601; Des Moines; P 42,000; (319) 752-6365; Fax (319) 752-6454; info@greaterburlington.com; www.visitburlingtoniowa.com

Cedar Falls • *Cedar Falls Tourism & Visitors Bur.* **•** Kim Manning; Exec. Dir.; 6510 Hudson Rd.; 50613; Black Hawk; P 39,300; (319) 268-4266; (800) 845-1955; Fax (319) 277-9707; visit@cedarfallstourism.org; www.cedarfallstourism.org

Cedar Rapids • *Cedar Rapids Area CVB* **•** Aaron McCreight; Pres./CEO; 87 16th Ave. S.W., Ste. 200; 52404; Linn; P 259,000; (319) 398-5009; (800) 735-5557; Fax (319) 398-5089; jennifer@gocedarrapids.com; www.gocedarrapids.com

Clear Lake • *Clear Lake Area CVB* **•** Libbey Patton; Tourism Dir.; 205 Main Ave.; P.O. Box 188; 50428; Cerro Gordo; P 8,200; (641) 357-2159; (800) 285-5338; Fax (641) 357-8141; info@clearlakeiowa.com; www.clearlakeiowa.com

Clinton • *Clinton CVB* **•** Carrie Donaire; Dir.; 721 S. 2nd St.; P.O. Box 1024; 52733; Clinton; P 28,293; (563) 242-5702; Fax (563) 242-5803; cvb@clintonia.com; www.clintoniowatourism.com

Coralville • *Iowa City/Coralville Area CVB* **•** Josh Schamberger; Pres.; 900 1st Ave.; 52241; Johnson; P 100,143; (319) 337-6592; (800) 283-6592; Fax (319) 337-9953; guest@iowacitycoralville.org; www.iowacitycoralville.org

Council Bluffs • *Council Bluffs CVB* **•** Mark Eckman; Exec. Dir.; 400 Willow Ave., Ste. 2C; 51503; Pottawattamie; P 62,000; (712) 3256-2577; (844) 271-6909; Fax (712) 322-5698; info@travelcouncilbluffs.com; www.travelcouncilbluffs.com

Cresco • *Howard County Bus. & Tourism* **•** Jason Passmore; Exec. Dir.; 101 2nd Ave. S.W.; P.O. Box 403; 52136; Howard; P 9,600; (563) 547-3434; Fax (563) 547-2056; crescochamber@yahoo.com; www.howard-county.com

Davenport • *see Moline, IL*

Decorah • *Winneshiek County CVB* **•** Charlene Selbee; Dir.; 507 W. Water St.; 52101; Winneshiek; P 8,700; (563) 382-2023; (800) 463-4692; Fax (563) 382-5515; info@visitdecorah.com; www.visitdecorah.com

Des Moines • *Greater Des Moines CVB* • Greg Edwards; Pres./CEO; 400 Locust St., Ste. 265; 50309; Polk & Warren; P 600,000; (515) 286-4960; (800) 451-2625; Fax (515) 244-9757; nancy@catchdesmoines.com; www.catchdesmoines.com

Fairfield • *Fairfield Iowa CVB* • Rustin Lippincott; Exec. Dir.; 200 N. Main; 52556; Jefferson; P 10,000; (641) 472-2828; rlippincott@travelfairfieldiowa.com; www.travelfairfieldiowa.com

Fort Madison • *Fort Madison Partners* • Tim Gobble; Exec. Dir.; 614 9th St.; P.O. Box 277; 52627; Lee; P 11,000; (319) 372-5472; (800) 210-TOUR; info@fortmadison.com; www.fortmadison.com

Keokuk • *Keokuk Area Conv. & Tourism Bur.* • Kirk Brandenberger; Exec. Dir.; 428 Main St.; 52632; Lee; P 10,531; (319) 524-5599; info@keokukiowatourism.org; www.keokukiowatourism.org

Marshalltown • *Marshalltown CVB* • Shannon Espenscheid; Exec. Dir.; 709 S. Center St.; P.O. Box 1000; 50158; Marshall; P 41,500; (641) 753-6645; (800) 697-3155; Fax (641) 752-8373; cvb@marshalltown.org; www.visitmarshalltown.com

Mason City • *Mason City CVB* • Sue Armour; Exec. Dir.; 2021 Fourth St. S.W., Hwy. 122 W.; 50401; Cerro Gordo; P 44,000; (641) 422-1663; (800) 423-5724; Fax (641) 423-5725; cvb@visitmasoncityiowa.com; www.visitmasoncityiowa.com

Muscatine • *Muscatine CVB* • Heather Shoppa; Mgr.; 102 Walnut St.; 52761; Muscatine; P 42,000; (563) 263-8895; info@muscatine.com; www.muscatine.com

Newton • *Newton CVB* • Annette West; Interim Exec. Dir.; 300 E. 17th St. S., Ste. 400; 50208; Jasper; P 15,000; (641) 792-0299; (800) 798-0299; Fax (641) 791-0879; info@visitnewton.com; www.visitnewton.com

Ottumwa • *Ottumwa Area CVB* • Mark Eckman; Dir.; 102 Church St.; 52501; Wapello; P 25,000; (641) 684-4303; Fax (641) 684-6305; meckman@exploreottumwa.com; www.exploreottumwa.com

Red Oak • *Western Iowa Tourism Region* • 103 N. Third St.; 51566; Montgomery; P 461,879; (712) 623-4232; (888) 623-4232; Fax (712) 623-9814; witr@traveliowa.org; www.visitwesterniowa.com

Sioux City • *Sioux City Conv. & Tourism Bur.* • Erika Newton; Exec. Dir.; 801 4th St.; P.O. Box 3183; 51102; Plymouth & Woodbury; P 82,700; (712) 279-4800; (800) 593-2228; Fax (712) 279-4900; enewton@sioux-city.org; www.visitsiouxcity.org

Walnut • *Walnut Welcome Center* • 607 Highland St.; P.O. Box 265; 51577; Pottawattamie; P 895; (712) 784-2100; (712) 784-3443; www.walnutiowa.org

Waterloo • *Waterloo CVB* • Aaron Buzza; Exec. Dir.; 500 Jefferson St.; 50701; Black Hawk; P 68,500; (319) 233-8350; (800) 728-8431; Fax (319) 233-2733; info@travelwaterloo.com; www.travelwaterloo.com

Kansas

Abilene • *Abilene CVB* • Glenda Purkis; Dir.; 201 N.W. 2nd St.; 67410; Dickinson; P 7,000; (785) 263-2231; (800) 569-5915; Fax (785) 263-4125; tourism@abilenecityhall.com; www.abilenekansas.org

Arkansas City • *Arkansas City CVB* • Pam Crain; Tour. Spec.; 106 S. Summit; 67005; Cowley; P 18,000; (620) 442-0236; Fax (620) 441-0048; cvb@arkcitychamber.org; www.arkcitychamber.org

Atchison • *Atchison Area Tourism Bur.* • Angie Cairo; Tourism Coord.; 200 S. 10th St.; P.O. Box 126; 66002; Atchison; P 20,000; (913) 367-2427; (800) 234-1854; Fax (913) 367-2485; tours@atchisonkansas.net; www.visitatchison.com

Augusta • *Augusta CVB* • 112 E. 6th Ave.; 67010; Butler; P 9,300; (316) 775-6339; Fax (316) 775-1307; augustacoc@sbcglobal.net; www.visitaugustaks.com

Colby • *Colby CVB* • Leilani Thomas; Dir.; 350 S. Range, Ste. 10; 67701; Thomas; P 5,500; (785) 460-7643; (800) 611-8835; Fax (785) 460-4509; cvb@thomascounty.com; www.oasisontheplains.com

Dodge City • *Dodge City CVB* • Jan Stevens; Dir.; 400 W. Wyatt Earp Blvd.; P.O. Box 1474; 67801; Ford; P 30,000; (620) 225-8186; (800) OLD-WEST; Fax (620) 225-8268; cvb@dodgecity.org; www.visitdodgecity.org

Emporia • *Emporia CVB* • Susan Rathke; Dir.; 719 Commercial; 66801; Lyon; P 25,000; (620) 342-1600; (800) 279-3730; Fax (620) 342-3223; visitors@emporiakschamber.org; www.visitemporia.com

Garden City • *Finney County CVB* • Roxanne Morgan; Exec. Dir.; 1513 E. Fulton Terrace; 67846; Finney; P 40,000; (620) 276-0607; (800) 879-9803; Fax (620) 276-6488; msowers@finneycountycvb.com; www.finneycountycvb.com

Goodland • *Sherman County CVB* • Donna Price; Exec. Dir.; P.O. Box 927; 67735; Sherman; P 7,400; (785) 890-3515; (888) 824-4222; Fax (785) 890-6980; cvb@goodlandnet.com; www.visitgoodland.com

Hays • *Hays CVB* • Melissa Dixon; Exec. Dir.; 2700 Vine St.; 67601; Ellis; P 21,000; (785) 628-8202; (800) 569-4505; tcrispin@haysusa.com; www.haysusa.net

Hutchinson • *Greater Hutchinson CVB* • LeAnn Cox; Dir.; 117 N. Walnut St.; P.O. Box 519; 67504; Reno; P 64,000; (620) 662-3391; (800) 691-4282; Fax (620) 662-2168; leannc@hutchchamber.com; www.visithutch.com

Independence • *Independence CVB* • Mike Flood; Tourism Dir.; 616 N. Pennsylvania Ave.; P.O. Box 386; 67301; Montgomery; P 9,400; (620) 331-1890; (800) 882-3606; Fax (620) 331-1899; tourism@indkschamber.org; www.indkschamber.org

Kansas City • *Kansas City Kansas CVB* • Bridgette Jobe; Exec. Dir.; 755 Minnesota Ave.; P.O. Box 171517; 66117; Wyandotte; P 160,000; (913) 321-5800; (800) 264-1563; Fax (913) 371-0204; info@visitkansascityks.com; www.visitkansascityks.com

Lawrence • *Lawrence Visitor Center* • Deborah White & Keith Manies; Mgrs.; 402 N. 2nd St.; P.O. Box 526; 66044; Douglas; P 111,000; (785) 856-3040; Fax (785) 865-5305; visinfo@explorelawrence.com; www.explorelawrence.com

Leavenworth • *Leavenworth CVB* • Connie Hachenberg; Dir.; 518 Shawnee St.; P.O. Box 44; 66048; Leavenworth; P 35,000; (913) 682-4113; Fax (913) 682-8170; connie.cvb@visitlvks.com; www.visitleavenworthks.com

Lenexa • *Lenexa CVB* • Julie Steiner; Dir.; 11180 Lackman Rd.; 66219; Johnson; P 48,000; (913) 888-1414; (800) 950-7867; Fax (913) 888-3770; jsteiner@lenexa.org; www.lenexa.org

Lindsborg • *Lindsborg CVB* • Holly Lofton; Dir.; 104 E. Lincoln St.; P.O. Box 70; 67456; McPherson; P 3,300; (785) 227-8687; (888) 227-2227; Fax (785) 227-4128; cvbdir@lindsborgcity.org; www.visitlindsborg.com

Manhattan • *Manhattan CVB* • Karen Hibbard; Dir.; 501 Poyntz Ave.; 66502; Riley; P 53,000; (785) 776-8829; (800) 759-0134; Fax (785) 776-0679; cvb@manhattan.org; www.manhattancvb.org

Newton • *Newton CVB* • Jennifer Mueller; Dir.; 500 N. Main, Ste. 101; 67114; Harvey; P 20,000; (316) 283-7555; (800) 899-0455; Fax (316) 283-8732; jennifer@thenewtonchamber.org; www.thenewtonchamber.org

Norton • *Norton C/C & Travel & Tourism* • Darla Beasley; Exec. Dir.; 205 S. State St.; 67654; Norton; P 3,000; (785) 877-2501; Fax (785) 877-3300; nortoncc@ruraltel.net; www.thenortonlocal.com

Oberlin • *Oberlin CVB* • Carol Hackney; Mgr.; 104 S. Penn Ave.; 67749; Decatur; P 4,000; (785) 475-3441; dcacc@eaglecom.net; www.oberlinks.com

Olathe • *Olathe Chamber CVB* • Ashley Arnold; V.P.; 18001 W. 106th St., Ste. 160; 66061; Johnson; P 130,000; (913) 764-1050; Fax (913) 782-4636; cvb@olathe.org; www.olathecvb.org

Ottawa • *Franklin County CVB* • Kristi Lee; Dir.; 2011 E. Logan; P.O. Box 203; 66067; Franklin; P 25,000; (785) 242-1411; Fax (785) 242-2238; director@visitottawakansas.com; www.visitottawakansas.com

Overland Park • *Overland Park CVB* • Jerry Cook; Pres.; 9001 W. 110th St., Ste. 100; 66210; Johnson; P 170,000; (913) 491-0123; (800) 262-PARK; Fax (913) 491-0015; jlcook@opcvb.org; www.visitoverlandpark.com

Parsons • *Labette County CVB* • Jim Zaleski; Tourism Dir.; 506 E. Main St.; 67357; Labette; P 21,600; (620) 421-6500; (800) 280-6401; Fax (620) 421-6501; tourism@parsonsks.com; www.visitlabette.com

Phillipsburg • *Phillips County CVB* • Jackie Swatzell; Dir.; 270 State St.; P.O. Box 326; 67661; Phillips; P 2,500; (785) 543-2321; Fax (785) 543-0038; cvbcham@ruraltel.net; www.phillipsburgks.us

Pittsburg • *Crawford County CVB* • 117 W. 4th St.; P.O. Box 1933; 66762; Crawford; P 38,242; (620) 231-1212; (800) 879-1112; Fax (620) 231-3178; chull@pittsburgareachamber.com; www.visitcrawfordcounty.com

Russell • *Russell County Eco. Dev. & CVB* • Janae Talbott; Dir.; 331 E. Wichita Ave.; 67665; Russell; P 8,000; (785) 483-4000; Fax (785) 483-2827; cvb2@russellks.org; www.russellcoks.org

Sedan • *Yellow Brick Road Visitors Center* • Nita Jones; Dir.; 102 E. Main; 67361; Chautauqua; P 1,300; (620) 725-3663; (620) 725-3663; Fax (620) 725-5707; jonesrealtyusa@yahoo.com; sedankansas.com

Shawnee • *Shawnee CVB* • Linda Leeper; Pres.; 15100 W. 67th St., Ste. 202; 66217; Johnson; P 62,200; (913) 631-6545; (888) 550-7282; Fax (913) 631-9628; info@shawneekscvb.com; www.shawneekscvb.com

Topeka • *Visit Topeka Inc.* • Terry Cook; Pres./CEO; 618 S. Kansas Ave; 66603; Shawnee; P 122,447; (785) 234-1030; (800) 235-1030; Fax (785) 234-8282; info@visittopeka.com; www.visittopeka.com

Wichita • *VisitWichita* • 515 S. Main St., Ste. 115; 67202; Sedgwick; P 600,000; (316) 265-2800; Fax (316) 265-0162; info@gowichita.com; www.gowichita.com

Winfield • *Winfield Conv. & Tourism* • Sarah Werner; Dir.; 123 E. 9th Ave.; P.O. Box 640; 67156; Cowley; P 12,000; (620) 221-2421; (877) 729-7440; Fax (620) 221-2958; tourism@winfieldpartners.org; VisitWinfield.com

Kentucky

Ashland • *Ashland Area CVB* • Sue G. Dowdy; Exec. Dir.; 1509 Winchester Ave.; 41101; Boyd; P 21,000; (606) 329-1007; (800) 377-6249; Fax (606) 329-1056; sue.dowdy@visitashlandky.com; www.visitashlandky.com

Bardstown • *Bardstown-Nelson County Visitors Bur.* • Dawn Ballard Przystal; V.P. of Tourism; One Court Sq.; 40004; Nelson; P 11,000; (502) 348-4877; (800) 638-4877; Fax (502) 349-0804; info@bardstowntourism.com; www.visitbardstown.com

Benton • *Marshall County Tourist Comm.* • Elena Blevins; Mktg. Asst.; 93 Carroll Rd.; 42025; Marshall; P 30,000; (270) 527-3128; (800) 467-7145; Fax (270) 527-9193; fun@kentuckylake.org; www.kentuckylake.org

Bowling Green • *Bowling Green Area CVB* • Vicki Fitch; Exec. Dir.; 352 Three Springs Rd.; 42104; Warren; P 118,000; (270) 782-0800; (800) 326-7465; Fax (270) 842-2104; info@visitbgky.com; visitbgky.com

Campbellsville • *Taylor County Tourist Comm.* • Marilyn Clarke; Exec. Dir.; 325 E. Main St.; P.O. Box 4021; 42719; Taylor; P 23,000; (270) 465-3786; (800) 738-4719; Fax (270) 465-3786; info@campbellsvilleky.com; www.campbellsvilleky.com

Cave City • *Cave City Tourist & Conv. Center* • Tim Riddle; Dir.; 502 Mammoth Cave St.; P.O. Box 518; 42127; Barren; P 2,000; (270) 773-3131; (800) 346-8908; Fax (270) 773-8834; cavecity@scrtc.com; www.cavecity.com

Covington • *meetNKY/Northern Kentucky CVB* • Eric Summe; Pres./CEO; 50 E. RiverCenter Blvd., Ste. 200; 41011; Carroll; P 300,000; (859) 261-4677; (877) 659-8474; Fax (859) 261-5135; information@meetnky.com; www.meetnky.com

Danville • *Danville-Boyle County CVB* • Jennifer Kirchner; Exec. Dir.; 105 E. Walnut St.; 40422; Boyle; P 30,000; (859) 236-7794; cvb@betterindanville.com; www.danvillekentucky.com

Elizabethtown • *Elizabethtown Tourism & Conv. Bur.* • Sherry Murphy; Exec. Dir.; 1030 N. Mulberry St.; 42701; Hardin; P 24,000; (270) 765-2175; (800) 437-0092; Fax (270) 737-6568; www.touretown.com

Frankfort • *Frankfort/Franklin County Tourist & Conv. Comm.* • Joy Jeffries; Exec. Dir.; 100 Capital Ave.; 40601; Franklin; P 47,000; (502) 875-8687; (800) 960-7200; Fax (502) 227-2604; inquire@visitfrankfort.com; www.visitfrankfort.com

Georgetown • *Georgetown/Scott County Tourism Comm.* • John Simpson; Exec. Dir.; 399 Outlet Center Dr.; P.O. Box 825; 40324; Scott; P 42,000; (502) 863-2547; (888) 863-8600; Fax (502) 863-2561; john@georgetownky.com; www.georgetownky.com

Harlan • *Harlan Tourist & Conv. Comm.* • Kim Collier; Exec. Dir.; 201 South Main Street; P.O. Box 489; 40831; Harlan; P 35,000; (606) 573-4156; Fax (606) 573-9485; htcc@harlanonline.net; www.harlantourism.com

Harrodsburg • *Harrodsburg/Mercer County Tour Comm.* • Karen P. Hackett; Exec. Dir.; 488 Price Ave.; P.O. Box 283; 40330; Mercer; P 21,300; (859) 734-2364; (800) 355-9192; Fax (859) 734-9938; tourism@harrodsburgky.com; www.harrodsburgky.com

Henderson • *Henderson County Tourist Comm.* • Kyle Hittner; Exec. Dir.; 101 N. Water St., Ste. B; 42420; Henderson; P 46,400; (270) 826-3128; (800) 648-3128; Fax (270) 826-0234; info@hendersonky.org; www.hendersonky.org

Hopkinsville • *Hopkinsville-Christian County CVB* • Cheryl Cook; Exec. Dir.; 2800 Fort Campbell Blvd.; 42240; Christian; P 73,000; (270) 885-9096; (800) 842-9959; Fax (270) 886-2059; tourism@visithopkinsville.com; www.visithopkinsville.com

Jamestown • *see Russell Springs*

Leitchfield • *Grayson County Tourist Comm.* • Ilsa Johnson; Exec. Dir.; 425 S. Main St.; 42754; Grayson; P 25,600; (270) 259-2735; (888) 624-9951; Fax (270) 230-0615; mail@graysoncountytourism.com; www.graysoncountytourism.com

Lexington • *Lexington CVB* • Jim Browder; Pres.; 250 W. Main St., Ste. 2120; 40507; Fayette; P 265,000; (859) 233-1221; (800) 845-3959; Fax (859) 254-4555; jbrowder@visitlex.com; www.visitlex.com

London • *London-Laurel County Tourist Comm.* • Ken Harvey; Exec. Dir.; 140 Faith Assembly Church Rd.; 40741; Laurel; P 56,000; (606) 878-6900; (800) 348-0095; Fax (606) 877-1689; tourism@lltc.net; www.laurelkytourism.com

Louisville • *Louisville CVB* • James Wood; Pres./CEO; One Riverfront Plz.; 401 W. Main St., Ste. 2300; 40202; Jefferson; P 2,000,000; (502) 584-2121; (800) 626-5646; Fax (502) 584-6697; jwood@gotolouisville.com; www.gotolouisville.com

Mayfield • *Mayfield Graves Tourism Comm.* • Kristin Woodward; Exec. Dir.; 201 E. College St.; 42066; Graves; P 47,000; (270) 247-6101; Fax (270) 247-6110; tourism@visitmayfieldgraves.com; www.visitmayfieldgraves.com

Maysville • *Maysville-Mason County CVB* • Suzie Pratt; Tourism Dir.; The Cox Bldg.; 2 E. Third St.; 41056; Mason; P 18,000; (606) 563-2596; (606) 564-9419; Fax (606) 564-9416; info@maysvilleky.net; www.cityofmaysville.com

Mount Sterling • *Mt. Sterling-Montgomery County Tourism Comm.* • 126 W. Main St.; 40353; Montgomery; P 26,500; (859) 498-8732; (866) 415-7439; Fax (859) 498-3947; mtourism@mis.net; www.mtsterlingtourism.com

Murray • *Murray CVB* • Erin Carrico; Exec. Dir.; 201 S. 4th St.; 42071; Calloway; P 15,000; (270) 759-2199; (800) 651-1603; Fax (270) 761-6793; erincarrico@tourmurray.com; www.tourmurray.com

Owensboro • *Owensboro Daviess County CVB* • Shannon Wetzel; Exec. Dir.; 215 E. 2nd St.; 42303; Daviess; P 100,000; (270) 926-1100; (800) 489-1131; Fax (270) 926-1161; info@visitowensboro.com; www.visitowensboro.com

Paducah • *Paducah CVB* • Mary Hammond; Exec. Dir.; 128 Broadway; 42001; McCracken; P 64,213; (270) 443-8783; (800) PADUCAH; Fax (270) 443-0122; mary@paducah.travel; www.paducah.travel

Paintsville • *Paintsville Tourism Comm.* • Cindy Wheat; Exec. Dir.; 100 Staves Branch Rd.; P.O. Box 809; 41240; Johnson; P 23,000; (606) 297-1469; (800) 542-5790; Fax (606) 297-1470; info@visitpaintsvilleky.com; www.visitpaintsvilleky.com

Radcliff • *Radcliff/Fort Knox Tourism & Conv. Comm.* • Kelly Barron; Exec. Dir.; 562 A1 N. Dixie; P.O. Box 845; 40159; Hardin; P 22,000; (270) 352-1204; (800) 334-7540; Fax (270) 352-2075; radclifftour@bbtel.com; www.radclifftourism.org

Richmond • *Richmond Tourism & Main Street Dept.* • Lori Murphy; Exec. Dir.; 345 Lancaster Ave.; 40475; Madison; P 32,000; (859) 626-8474; (800) 866-3705; Fax (859) 626-8121; tourism@richmond.ky.us; www.richmondkytourism.com

Russell Springs • *Russell County Tourist Comm.* • Lindsey Westerfield; Ofc. Mgr.; 650 S. Hwy. 127; P.O. Box 64; 42642; Russell; P 17,000; (270) 866-4333; lake@duo-county.com; www.lakecumberlandvacation.com

Russellville • *Logan County Tourism Ofc.* • Teresa Perkins; Ofc. Mgr.; P.O. Box 1678; 42276; Logan; P 27,100; (270) 726-1678; Fax (270) 726-2705; logancountytour@bellsouth.net; www.visitlogancounty.net

Shelbyville • *ShelbyKY Tourism Comm. & Visitors Bur.* • Katie Fussenegger CTP; Exec. Dir.; 1011 Main St.; P.O. Box 622; 40066; Shelby; P 43,000; (502) 633-6388; Fax (502) 633-7501; tours@shelbyvilleky.com; www.visitshelbyky.com

Shepherdsville • *Shepherdsville-Bullitt County Tourist & Conv. Comm* • Troy Beam; Exec. Dir.; 395 Paroquet Springs Dr.; 40165; Bullitt; P 74,300; (800) 526-2068; (502) 543-TOUR; Fax (502) 543-4889; tbeam@travelbullitt.org; www.travelbullitt.org

Williamsburg • *Williamsburg Tourism & Conv. Comm.* • Alvin Sharpe; Dir. of Tourism; P.O. Box 2; 40769; Whitley; P 5,600; (606) 549-0530; (800) 552-0530; Fax (606) 539-0095; wtour@bellsouth.net; www.williamsburgky.com

Winchester • *Winchester-Clark County Tourism Comm.* • Nancy Turner; Exec. Dir.; 2 S. Maple St.; 40391; Clark; P 36,000; (859) 744-0556; (800) 298-9105; Fax (859) 744-9229; info@tourwinchester.com; www.tourwinchester.com

Louisiana

Abbeville • *Vermilion Parish Tourist Comm.* • Ali Miller; Dir.; P.O. Box 1106; 70511; Vermilion; P 12,000; (337) 898-6600; Fax (337) 893-1807; director@vermilion.org; www.vermilion.org

Albany • *Livingston Parish CVB* • 30340 Catholic Hall Rd.; P.O. Box 1057; 70711; Livingston; P 111,863; (225) 567-7899; Fax (225) 567-7840; info@visitlivingstonparish.com; www.visitlivingstonparish.com

Alexandria • *Alexandria/Pineville Area CVB* • Sherry Ellington; Exec. Dir.; 707 Second St.; P.O. Box 1070; 71309; Rapides; P 133,937; (318) 442-9546; (800) 551-9546; Fax (318) 443-1617; cindyl@apacvb.org; www.alexandriapinevillela.com

Baton Rouge • *Visit Baton Rouge* • Paul Arrigo; Pres./CEO; 359 Third St.; P.O. Drawer 4149; 70821; East Baton Rouge; P 500,000; (225) 383-1825; (800) LAROUGE; Fax (225) 346-1253; paul@visitbatonrouge.com; www.visitbatonrouge.com

Crowley • *Acadia Parish Tourist, Conv. & Visitors Bur.* • Gwen Hanks; Exec. Dir.; 401 Tower Rd.; P.O. Box 1342; 70527; Acadia; P 56,000; (337) 783-2108; Fax (337) 783-2142; aptc@bellsouth.net; www.acadiatourism.org

Donaldsonville • *see Sorrento*

Grand Isle • *Grand Isle Tourist Comm.* • 2757 LA Hwy. 1; P.O. Box 817; 70358; Jefferson; P 1,500; (985) 787-2997; Fax (985) 787-2997; tourism@grand-isle.com; www.grand-isle.com

Gray • *Houma Area CVB* • Sharon Alford; Exec. Dir.; 114 Tourist Dr.; 70359; Terrebonne; P 33,000; (985) 868-2732; (800) 688-2732; Fax (985) 868-7170; info@houmatravel.com; www.houmatravel.com

Jackson • *East Feliciana Tourist Comm.* • Audrey Faciane; Exec. Dir.; 1752 High St.; P.O. Box 667; 70748; East Feliciana; P 22,000; (225) 634-7155; Fax (225) 634-7154; tourism1@bellsouth.net; www.felicianatourism.org

Lafayette • *Lafayette Conv. & Vistors Comm.* • Gerald P. Breaux; Exec. Dir.; 1400 N.W. Evangeline Thruway; 70501; Lafayette; P 206,976; (337) 232-3737; (800) 346-1958; Fax (337) 232-0161; info@lafayettetravel.com; www.lafayette.travel

Lake Charles • *Southwest Louisiana CVB* • Shelley Johnson; Exec. Dir.; 1205 N. Lakeshore Dr.; P.O. Box 1912; 70602; Calcasieu; P 172,200; (337) 436-9588; (800) 456-SWLA; Fax (337) 494-7952; touristinfo@visitlakecharles.org; www.visitlakecharles.org

Mandeville • *Louisiana Northshore* • Donna O'Daniels; Exec. Dir.; St. Tammany Tourist & Conv. Comm.; 68099 Hwy. 59; 70471; Saint Tammany; P 250,000; (985) 892-0520; (800) 634-9443; Fax (985) 892-1441; mail@louisiananorthshore.com; www.louisiananorthshore.com

Mansfield • *DeSoto Parish Tourist Bur.* • Edna Thornton; Dir.; 115 N. Washington Ave.; 71052; DeSoto; P 26,000; (318) 872-1177; Fax (318) 871-1875; touristb@bellsouth.net; www.desotoisdifferent.com

Many • *Sabine Parish Tourist Comm.* • Linda Curtis-Sparks; Tourism Dir.; 1601 Texas Hwy.; 71449; Sabine; P 24,000; (318) 256-5880; (800) 358-7802; Fax (318) 256-4137; staff@toledobendlakecountry.com; www.toledobendlakecountry.com

Minden • *Minden Webster Parish Tourist CVB* • Lynn Warnock-Dorsey; Exec. Dir.; 110 Sibley Rd.; P.O. Box 1528; 71058; Webster; P 42,000; (318) 377-4240; (888) 972-7474; Fax (318) 377-4215; lynn@visitwebster.com; www.visitwebster.com

Morgan City • *Cajun Coast Visitors & Conv. Bur.* • Carrie Gautreaux Stansbury; Exec. Dir.; P.O. Box 2332; 70381; Saint Mary; P 60,000; (985) 380-8224; (800) 256-2931; Fax (985) 380-2876; info@cajuncoast.com; www.cajuncoast.com

Natchitoches • *Natchitoches CVB* • Arlene Gould; Exec. Dir.; 780 Front St., Ste. 100; 71457; Natchitoches; P 40,000; (318) 352-8072; (800) 259-1714; Fax (318) 352-2415; director@natchitoches.com; www.natchitoches.com

New Iberia • *Iberia Parish CVB* • Fran Thibodeaux; Exec. Dir.; 2513 Hwy. 14; 70560; Iberia; P 72,000; (337) 365-1540; (888) 942-3742; Fax (337) 367-3791; info@iberiatravel.com; www.iberiatravel.com

New Orleans • *New Orleans Metropolitan CVB* • J. Stephen Perry; Pres./CEO; 2020 St. Charles Ave.; 70130; Orleans; P 1,200,000; (504) 566-5011; (800) 672-6124; Fax (504) 566-5046; tmicelle@neworleanscvb.com; www.neworleanscvb.com

Ruston • *Ruston/Lincoln CVB* • Kyle Edmiston CDME; Pres./CEO; 2111 N. Trenton St.; 71270; Lincoln; P 43,000; (318) 255-2031; (800) 392-9032; Fax (318) 255-3481; kedmiston@rustonlincoln.com; www.experienceruston.com

Saint Francisville • *West Feliciana Parish Tourist Comm.* • Laurie Walsh; Dir.; 11757 Ferdinand St.; P.O. Box 1548; 70775; West Feliciana; P 15,600; (225) 635-4224; (800) 789-4221; Fax (225) 635-6769; tourism@stfrancisville.us; stfrancisville.us

Saint Martinville • *St. Martinville Tourist Info. Center* • Michelle Johnson; Museum Dir.; 125 S. New Market; P.O. Box 379; 70582; Saint Martin; P 6,114; (337) 394-2233; Fax (337) 394-2260; info@acadianmemorial.org; www.stmartinville.org

Shreveport • *Shreveport-Bossier Conv. & Tourist Bur.* • Stacy Brown; Pres.; 629 Spring; P.O. Box 1761; 71166; Caddo; P 298,000; (318) 222-9391; (800) 551-8682; Fax (318) 222-0067; info2@sbctb.org; www.shreveport-bossier.org

Sorrento • *Ascension Parish Tourism Comm.* • 6967 Hwy. 22; 70778; Ascension; P 120,000; (225) 675-6550; (888) 775-7990; Fax (225) 675-6558; tour@ascensiontourism.com; www.ascensiontourism.com

West Monroe • *Monroe-West Monroe CVB* • Alana Cooper; Exec. Dir.; 601 Constitution Dr.; P.O. Box 1436; 71294; Ouachita; P 60,000; (318) 387-5691; (800) 843-1872; Fax (318) 324-1752; mwmcvb@monroe-westmonroe.org; www.monroe-westmonroe.org

Maine

Bangor • *Greater Bangor CVB* • Kerrie Tripp; Dir.; Intown Plz., 330 Harlow St.; 04401; Penobscot; P 33,000; (207) 947-5205; (800) 916-6673; kerrie@visitbangormaine.com; www.visitbangormaine.com

Portland • *Greater Portland CVB* • Lynn Tillotson; Pres./CEO; 94 Commercial St., Ste. 300; 04101; Cumberland; P 523,552; (207) 772-4994; (207) 772-5800; Fax (207) 874-9043; info@visitportland.com; www.visitportland.com

Maryland

Baltimore • *Visit Baltimore* • Ron Melton; Interim Pres./CEO; 100 Light St., 12th Flr.; 21202; Baltimore City; P 620,961; (877) BALTIMORE; Fax (443) 817-0613; members@baltimore.org; www.baltimore.org

Chester • *Queen Anne's County Ofc. of Tourism* • Faith Elliott-Rossing; Dir.; 425 Piney Narrows Rd.; 21619; Queen Anne's; P 47,800; (410) 604-2100; Fax (410) 604-2101; felliott-rossing@qac.org; www.discoverqueenannes.com

Denton • *Caroline County Ofc. of Tourism* • Kathy Mackel; Tourism Dir.; 10219 River Landing Rd.; 21629; Caroline; P 33,100; (410) 479-0655; Fax (410) 479-5563; info@tourcaroline.com; www.tourcaroline.com

Easton • *Talbot County Ofc. of Tourism* • Deborah Dodson; Exec. Dir.; 11 S. Harrison St.; 21601; Talbot; P 38,000; (410) 770-8000; Fax (410) 770-8057; ddodson@talbgov.org; www.tourtalbot.org

Frederick • *Tourism Cncl. of Frederick County Inc.* • John Fieseler; Exec. Dir.; 151 S. East St.; 21701; Frederick; P 233,400; (301) 600-2888; (800) 999-3613; Fax (301) 600-4044; tourism@fredco-md.net; www.fredericktourism.org

Hagerstown • *Hagerstown/Washington County CVB* • Daniel P. Spedden; Pres.; 16 Public Sq.; 21740; Washington; P 140,000; (301) 791-3246; (888) 257-2600; Fax (301) 791-2601; info@marylandmemories.com; www.marylandmemories.com

Ocean City • *Ocean City CVB* • Rick Hamilton; Exec. Dir.; 4001 Coastal Hwy.; 21842; Worcester; P 8,000; (410) 289-8181; (800) OC-OCEAN; Fax (410) 723-8655; dabbot@ococean.com; www.ococean.com

Rockville • *The Conf. & Visitors Bur. of Montgomery County* • Kelly Groff; Exec. Dir.; 111 Rockville Pike, Ste. 800; 20850; Montgomery; P 971,800; (240) 777-2060; (877) 789-6904; Fax (301) 777-2065; kgroff@visitmontgomery.com; www.visitmontgomery.com

Massachusetts

Boston • *Greater Boston CVB* • Patrick Moscaritolo; Pres./CEO; Two Copley Pl., Ste. 105; 02116; Suffolk; P 4,600,000; (617) 536-4100; (888) SEE-BOSTON; Fax (617) 424-7664; info@bostonusa.com; www.bostonusa.com

C & VB

Fitchburg • Johnny Appleseed Trail Assn. • Roy Nascimento IOM; Pres.; 860 South St.; 01420; P 225,000; (978) 353-7604; Fax (978) 353-4896; johnnyappleseedcountry@gmail.com; appleseed.org

New Bedford • Southeastern Mass. CVB • Roy Nascimento IOM; c/o New Bedford Area C/C; P.O. Box 8827; 02742; Bristol; P 548,300; (508) 999-5231; (800) 288-6263; Fax (508) 997-9090; info@visitsemass.com; www.visitsemass.com

Pittsfield • 1Berkshire • Jonathan Butler; Pres./CEO; 66 Allen St.; 01201; Berkshire; P 150,000; (413) 499-1600; (800) 237-5747; Fax (413) 743-4560; info@1berkshire.com; www.1berkshire.com

Provincetown • Provincetown Ofc. of Tourism • Anthony Fuccillo; Dir. of Tourism; 330 Commercial St.; 02657; Barnstable; P 3,000; (508) 487-3298; Fax (508) 487-7085; afuccillo@provincetown-ma.gov; www.provincetowntourismoffice.org

Salem • Destination Salem • Kate Fox; Exec. Dir.; P.O. Box 630; 01970; Essex; P 42,000; (978) 741-3252; salem@salem.org; www.salem.org

Salisbury • North of Boston CVB • Ann Marie Casey; Exec. Dir.; I-95 Southbound, Exit 60; P.O. Box 5193; 01952; Essex; P 736,457; (978) 465-6555; Fax (978) 465-6999; info@northofboston.org; www.northofboston.org

Somerville • Somerville CVB • Stephen V. Mackey; Pres./CEO; 2 Alpine St.; P.O. Box 440343; 02144; Middlesex; P 78,000; (617) 776-4100; Fax (617) 776-1157; info@somervillechamber.org; www.somervillechamber.org

Springfield • The Greater Springfield CVB • Mary Kay Wydra; Pres.; 1441 Main St.; 01103; Hampden; P 640,000; (413) 787-1548; (800) 723-1548; Fax (413) 781-4607; marykay@valleyvisitor.com; www.valleyvisitor.com

Worcester • Central MA CVB • Donna J. McCabe; Pres.; 91 Prescott St.; 01605; Worcester; P 700,000; (508) 755-7400; (866) 755-7439; Fax (508) 754-2703; dmccabe@worcester.org; www.worcester.org

Michigan

Allegan • Allegan County Parks, Rec. & Tourism • Rhonda Foreman; 3255 122nd Ave., Ste. 102; 49010; Allegan; P 111,400; (269) 686-9088; (888) 4-ALLEGAN; Fax (269) 673-0454; tourism@allegancounty.org; www.visitallegancounty.com

Alpena • Alpena Area CVB • Mary Beth Stutzman; Pres./CEO; 235 W. Chisholm St.; 49707; Alpena; P 30,000; (989) 354-4181; (800) 4-ALPENA; Fax (989) 356-3999; info@alpenacvb.com; www.visitalpena.com

Ann Arbor • Ann Arbor Area CVB • Mary A. Kerr; Pres.; 315 W. Huron, Ste. 340; 48103; Washtenaw; P 250,000; (734) 995-7281; (800) 888-9487; Fax (734) 995-7283; a2info@annarbor.org; www.visitannarbor.org

Battle Creek • Calhoun Co. CVB • Linda Freybler; CEO; 77 E. Michigan Ave., Ste. 100; 49017; Calhoun; P 93,000; (269) 962-2240; (800) 397-2240; Fax (269) 962-6917; info@battlecreekvisitors.org; www.battlecreekvisitors.org

Bay City • Great Lakes Bay Reg. CVB/Bay County CVB • Annette Rummel; Pres./CEO; One Wenonah Park Pl.; 48708; Bay; P 111,000; (989) 893-1222; (800) 444-9979; annette@gogreat.com; www.gogreat.com

Benton Harbor • Southwestern Michigan Tourist Cncl. • Millicent Huminsky; Exec. Dir.; 2300 Pipestone Rd.; 49022; Berrien; P 11,000; (269) 925-6301; info@swmichigan.org; www.swmichigan.org

Benzonia • Benzie County Visitors Bur. • Mary Carroll; Pres.; 826 Michigan Ave.; P.O. Box 204; 49616; Benzie; P 17,000; (231) 882-5801; (800) 882-5801; Fax (231) 882-9249; director@benzie.org; www.visitbenzie.com

Big Rapids • Mecosta County Area CVB • Connie Koepke; Exec. Dir.; 246 N. State St.; 49307; Mecosta; P 43,000; (231) 796-7640; Fax (231) 796-0832; director@bigrapids.org; www.bigrapids.org

Birch Run • see Saginaw

Cadillac • Cadillac Area Visitors Bur. • Joy VanDrie; Exec. Dir.; 201 N. Mitchell St., Ste. 102; 49601; Wexford; P 35,000; (231) 775-0657; (800) 22-LAKES; Fax (231) 779-5933; jvandrie@cadillacmichigan.com; www.cadillacmichigan.com

Calumet • Keweenaw CVB • 56638 Calumet Ave.; 49913; Houghton; P 37,000; (906) 337-4579; (800) 338-7982; Fax (906) 337-4285; info@keweenaw.info; www.keweenaw.info

Caro • Thumb Area Tourism Cncl. • Kris McArdle; Mktg. Dir.; 1111 W. Caro Rd., Ste. B; 48723; Tuscola; P 57,500; (810) 569-6856; kris@thumbtourism.org; www.thumbtourism.org

Charlevoix • Charlevoix Area CVB • Amanda Wilkin; Program Coord.; 109 Mason St.; 49720; Charlevoix; P 3,500; (800) 367-8557; Fax (231) 547-6633; info@charlevoixlodging.com; www.visitcharlevoix.com

Chesaning • see Saginaw

Clare • Clare County CVB • Lori Shoe; Mgr.; P.O. Box 226; 48617; Clare; P 31,000; (989) 386-6400; (800) 715-3550; lori@clarecounty.net; www.clarecounty.net

Coldwater • Coldwater Country CVB • Debra Yee; Exec. Dir.; 28 W. Chicago St., Ste. 1C; 49036; Branch; P 45,000; (517) 278-0241; dyee@discover-michigan.com; www.discover-michigan.com

Detroit • Detroit Metro CVB • Larry Alexander; Pres./CEO; 211 W. Fort St., Ste. 1000; 48226; Wayne; P 4,500,000; (313) 202-1800; (800) DETROIT; Fax (313) 202-1808; lalexander@visitdetroit.com; www.visitdetroit.com

Flint • Flint-Genesee County CVB • Jack Schripsema; Pres.; 502 Church St.; 48502; Genesee; P 431,000; (810) 232-8900; Fax (810) 232-1515; info@flint.travel; www.flint.travel

Frankenmuth • see Saginaw

Frankenmuth • Frankenmuth CVB • Jamie Furbush; Pres./CEO; 635 S. Main St.; 48734; Saginaw; P 4,400; (989) 652-6106; (800) 386-8696; Fax (989) 652-3841; chamber@frankenmuth.org; www.frankenmuth.org

Gaylord • Gaylord Area Conv. & Tourism Bur. • Paul Beachnau; Exec. Dir.; 319 W. Main St.; 49735; Otsego; P 26,000; (989) 732-4000; (800) 345-8621; Fax (989) 732-7990; info@gaylordmichigan.net; www.gaylordmichigan.net

Grand Haven • Grand Haven Area CVB • Marci Cisneros; Exec. Dir.; 225 Franklin Ave., Ste. A; 49417; Ottawa; P 35,000; (616) 842-4499; mcisneros@visitgrandhaven.com; www.visitgrandhaven.com

Grand Rapids • Experience Grand Rapids CVB • Douglas Small; Pres.; 171 Monroe Ave. N.W., Ste. 700; 49503; Kent; P 1,100,000; (616) 459-8287; (800) 678-9859; Fax (616) 459-7291; mailbox@experiencegr.com; www.experiencegr.com

Grand Rapids • West Michigan Tourist Assn. • Dan Sippel; CEO; 741 Kenmoor Ave., Ste. E; 49546; Kent; P 300,000; (616) 245-2217; (800) 442-2084; Fax (616) 954-3924; dan@wmta.org; www.wmta.org

Grayling • Grayling Visitors Bur. • Ilene Geiss-Wilson; Exec. Dir.; P.O. Box 217; 49738; Crawford; P 13,000; (989) 348-4945; (800) 937-8837; Fax (989) 348-9168; visitor@grayling-mi.com; www.grayling-mi.com

Holland • Holland Area CVB • Sally Laukitis; Exec. Dir.; 78 E. 8th St.; 49423; Ottawa; P 35,000; (800) 506-1299; (616) 394-0000; Fax (616) 394-0122; lucy@holland.org; www.holland.org

Howell • Livingston County CVB • 123 E. Washington St.; 48843; Livingston; P 105,000; (517) 548-1795; (800) 686-8474; Fax (517) 546-4115; info@lccvb.org; www.lccvb.org

Iron Mountain • Tourism Assn. of the Dickinson County Area • Chris LaVigne; Tourism Coord.; 333 S. Stephenson Ave., Ste. 202; 49801; Dickinson; P 26,000; (800) 236-2447; www.ironmountain.org

Iron Mountain • Upper Peninsula Travel & Rec. Assn. • P.O. Box 400; 49801; Dickinson; P 350,000; (906) 774-5480; (800) 562-7134; Fax (906) 774-5190; info@uptravel.com; www.uptravel.com

Ironwood • Western U.P. CVB • P.O. Box 706; 49938; Gogebic; P 35,000; (906) 932-4850; (800) 522-5657; Fax (906) 932-3455; bigsnow@westernup.info; www.westernup.info

Kalamazoo • Kalamazoo County CVB • Greg Ayers; Pres.; 141 E. Michigan Ave., Ste. 100; 49007; Kalamazoo; P 250,400; (269) 488-9000; (800) 888-0509; Fax (269) 488-0050; jbach@discoverkalamazoo.com; www.discoverkalamazoo.com

L'Anse • Baraga County CVB • Tracey E. Barrett; Exec. Dir.; 755 E. Broad St.; 49946; Baraga; P 8,000; (906) 524-7444; (800) 743-4908; Fax (906) 524-7454; bctra@up.net; www.baragacountytourism.org

Lansing • Greater Lansing CVB • Jack Schripsema CTA; Pres./CEO; 500 E. Michigan Ave., Ste. 180; 48912; Ingham; P 464,000; (517) 487-0077; (888) 487-0077; Fax (517) 487-5151; glcvb_info@lansing.org; www.lansing.org

Ludington • Ludington Area CVB • Brandy Henderson; Exec. Dir.; 5300 W. U.S. 10; 49431; Mason; P 30,000; (231) 845-5430; (800) 542-4600; Fax (231) 845-6857; brandyh@ludington.org; www.pureludington.com

Mackinac Island • Mackinac Island Tourism Bur. • P.O. Box 451; 49757; Mackinac; P 500; (906) 847-3783; (800) 454-5227; info@mackinacisland.org; www.mackinacisland.org

Mackinaw City • Mackinaw Area Visitors Bur. • Diane Klose; Admin. Asst.; 10800 W. U.S. 23 Hwy; 49701; Emmett; P 900; (231) 436-5664; (800) 666-0160; Fax (231) 436-5991; info@mackinawcity.com; www.mackinawcity.com

Marquette • Travel Marquette • Nicole Young; Exec. Dir.; 117 W. Washington St.; 49855; Marquette; P 74,000; (906) 228-7749; (800) 544-4321; Fax (906) 228-3642; director@travelmarquettemichigan.org; www.travelmarquettemichigan.org

Midland • Great Lakes Bay Reg. CVB • Annette Rummel; Pres./CEO; 215 E. Main St.; 48640; Midland; P 81,000; (989) 839-9775; (800) 444-9979; Fax (989) 498-9046; annette@gogreat.com; www.visitgreatlakesbay.org

Monroe • Monroe County Conv. & Tourism Bur. • John Patterson; Pres./CEO; 103 W. Front St.; 48161; Monroe; P 150,000; (734) 457-1030; Fax (734) 457-1097; thebureau@monroeinfo.com; www.monroeinfo.com

Mount Pleasant • Mount Pleasant Area CVB • Chris Rowley; Exec. Dir.; 113 W. Broadway, Ste. 180; 48858; Isabella; P 60,000; (989) 772-4433; Fax (989) 772-2909; visitor@mountpleasantwow.com; www.mountpleasantwow.com

Muskegon • Muskegon County CVB • Bob Lukens; Dir. of Comm. Dev.; 610 W. Western Ave.; 49440; Muskegon; P 173,000; (800) 250-9283; (231) 724-3100; Fax (231) 724-1398; bernadette@visitmuskegon.org; www.visitmuskegon.org

Newberry • Newberry Area Tourism Assn. • P.O. Box 308; 49868; Luce; P 8,000; (906) 293-5562; (800) 831-7292; Fax (906) 293-5739; newberry@lighthouse.net; www.newberrychamber.net

Niles • Four Flags Area Cncl. on Tourism • Melinda Michael; Exec. Dir.; 404 E. Main St.; P.O. Box 1300; 49120; Berrien; P 52,000; (269) 684-7444; Fax (269) 684-7477; info@fourflagsarea.org; www.fourflagsarea.org

Oscoda • Oscoda Area CVB • Debby Hearn; Admin. Asst.; P.O. Box 572; 48750; Iosco; P 7,000; (989) 739-0900; (877) 8-OSCODA; Fax (989) 739-0900; staff@oscoda.com; www.oscoda.com

Owosso • Shiawassee County CVB • Kimberly Springsdorf; Exec. Dir.; 215 N. Water St.; 48867; Shiawassee; P 70,880; (989) 723-1199; cvbshia@shiawassee.org; www.shiawassee.org

Paradise • Paradise Area Tourism Cncl. • P.O. Box 64; 49768; Chippewa; P 400; (906) 492-3927; info@paradisemi.org; www.paradisemi.org

Petoskey • Petoskey Area Visitors Bur. • Peter Fitzsimons; Exec. Dir.; 401 E. Mitchell St.; 49770; Emmet; P 20,000; (231) 348-2755; (800) 845-2828; Fax (231) 348-1810; info@petoskeyarea.com; www.petoskeyarea.com

Port Huron • Blue Water Area CVB • 405 Water St., Ste. 100; 48060; St. Clair; P 165,000; (810) 987-8687; (800) 852-4242; Fax (810) 987-1441; bluewater@bluewater.org; www.bluewater.org

Saginaw • Great Lakes Bay Reg. CVB • Annette Rummel; Pres./CEO; 515 N. Washington Ave., 2nd Flr.; 48607; Saginaw; P 210,039; (989) 752-7164; (800) 444-9979; Fax (989) 752-6642; annette@gogreat.com; www.gogreat.com

Saugatuck • Saugatuck/Douglas CVB • Felicia Fairchild; Exec. Dir.; 95 Blue Star Hwy.; P.O. Box 28; 49453; Allegan; P 1,000; (269) 857-1701; Fax (269) 857-2319; ffairchild@saugatuck.com; www.saugatuck.com

Sault Ste. Marie • Sault Ste. Marie CVB • Linda Hoath; Exec. Dir.; 225 E. Portage Ave.; P.O. Box 1000; 49783; Chippewa; P 15,000; (906) 632-3366; (800) MI-SAULT; Fax (906) 632-6161; info@saultstemarie.com; www.saultstemarie.com

South Haven • South Haven Visitors Bur. • Scott Reinart; Exec. Dir.; 546 Phoenix St.; 49090; Van Buren; P 5,000; (269) 637-5252; (800) SO-HAVEN; Fax (269) 637-8710; relax@southhaven.org; www.southhaven.org

St. Ignace • St. Ignace Visitors Bur. • 6 Spring St., Ste 100; 49781; Mackinac; P 2,700; (906) 643-6950; (800) 338-6660; Fax (906) 643-8067; info@stignace.com; www.stignace.com

Tawas City • Tawas Bay Tourist & Conv. Bur. • Heidi Dewald; Secy./Treas.; P.O. Box 10; 48764; Iosco; P 5,000; (989) 876-6018; (877) TO-TAWAS; Fax (989) 876-7472; info@tawas.com; www.tawasbay.com

C & VB

Three Rivers • *River Country Tourism Cncl.* • Sharon Zimont; Exec. Dir.; P.O. Box 214; 49093; St. Joseph; P 60,000; (269) 321-0640; (800) 447-2821; rivercountryinfo@gmail.com; www.rivercountry.com

Traverse City • *Traverse City CVB* • Joni McGuffin; Pres.; 101 W. Grandview Pkwy.; 49684; Grand Traverse; P 18,105; (231) 947-1120; (800) 940-1120; Fax (231) 947-2621; joni@traversecity.com; www.visittraversecity.com

West Branch • *West Branch Visitors Bur.* • Heather Johnson; Exec. Dir.; 422 W. Houghton Ave.; 48661; Ogemaw; P 30,000; (989) 345-2821; (800) 755-9091; Fax (989) 345-9075; info@visitwestbranch.com; www.visitwestbranch.com

Ypsilanti • *Ypsilanti Area CVB* • Debbie Locke-Daniel; Exec. Dir.; 106 W. Michigan Ave.; 48197; Washtenaw; P 71,000; (734) 483-4444; (800) 265-9045; Fax (734) 483-0400; dlocke@ypsilanti.org; www.ypsilanti.org

Minnesota

Albert Lea • *Albert Lea CVB* • Susie Petersen; Exec. Dir.; 102 W. Clark St.; 56007; Freeborn; P 18,500; (507) 373-2316; (800) 345-8414; Fax (507) 552-1248; susie@albertleatourism.org; www.albertleatourism.org

Alexandria • *Alexandria Lakes Area Visitors Center* • Tara Bitzan; Exec. Dir.; 206 Broadway St.; 56308; Douglas; P 25,000; (320) 763-3161; (800) 235-9441; Fax (320) 763-6857; info@alexandriamn.org; www.alexandriamn.org

Austin • *Austin CVB* • Nancy Schnable; Exec. Dir.; 104 11th Ave. N.W., Ste. D; 55912; Mower; P 24,000; (507) 437-4563; (800) 444-5713; Fax (507) 433-1052; visitor@austincvb.com; www.austincvb.com

Baudette • *Lake of the Woods Tourism* • Denelle Cauble; Exec. Dir.; 930 W. Main; P.O. Box 518; 56623; Lake of the Woods; P 4,000; (218) 634-1174; (800) 382-3474; Fax (218) 634-2915; info@lakeofthewoodsmn.com; www.lakeofthewoodsmn.com

Bemidji • *Visit Bemidji* • Susan Goudge; Exec. Dir.; 809 Paul Bunyan Dr. S.; P.O. Box 66; 56619; Beltrami; P 12,076; (218) 759-0164; (877) 250-5959; Fax (218) 759-0810; info@visitbemidji.com; www.visitbemidji.com

Bloomington • *Bloomington CVB* • 7900 International Dr., Ste. 990; 55425; Hennepin; P 86,400; (952) 858-8500; (800) 346-4289; Fax (952) 858-8854; info@bloomingtonmn.org; www.bloomingtonmn.org

Blue Earth • *Blue Earth Area C/C & CVB* • Cindy Lyon; Exec. Dir.; 113 S. Nicollet St.; 56013; Faribault; P 3,500; (507) 526-2916; Fax (507) 526-2244; chamber@bevcomm.net; www.blueearthchamber.com

Brooklyn Park • *Minneapolis Northwest Conv. & Visitors Bur.* • Dave Looby; Exec. Dir.; 7100 Northland Circle, Ste. 102; 55428; Hennepin; P 400,000; (763) 566-7722; (800) 541-4364; Fax (763) 566-6526; info@mplsnw.com; www.minneapolisnorthwest.com

Burnsville • *Burnsville CVB* • Amie Burrill; Exec. Dir.; 12600 Nicollet Ave., Ste. 100; 55337; Dakota; P 62,000; (952) 895-4690; (800) 521-6055; Fax (952) 487-1777; info@burnsvillemn.com; www.burnsvillemn.com

Caledonia • *see Rushford*

Crane Lake • *Crane Lake Visitors & Tourism Bur.* • 7238 Handberg Rd.; 55725; St. Louis; P 150; (218) 993-2901; (800) 362-7405; Fax (218) 993-2902; vacation@visitcranelake.com; www.visitcranelake.com

Crookston • *Crookston CVB* • Sandy Kegler; Tourism/Mktg. Coord.; 107 W. 2nd St.; P.O. Box 115; 56716; Polk; P 8,000; (218) 281-4320; (800) 809-5997; Fax (218) 281-4349; info@visitcrookston.com; www.visitcrookston.com

Detroit Lakes • *Detroit Lakes Tourism Bur.* • Cleone Stewart; Tourism Dir.; 700 Summit Ave.; P.O. Box 348; 56502; Becker; P 8,900; (218) 847-9202; (800) 542-3992; Fax (218) 847-9082; dlchamber@visitdetroitlakes.com; www.VisitDetroitLakes.com

Duluth • *Visit Duluth* • Terry Mattson; Pres.; 21 W. Superior St., Ste. 100; 55802; St. Louis; P 87,000; (218) 722-4011; (800) 4-DULUTH; Fax (218) 722-1322; cvb@visitduluth.com; www.visitduluth.com

Eagan • *Eagan CVB* • Brent Cory; Pres./CEO; 1501 Central Pkwy., Ste. E; 55121; Dakota; P 64,200; (651) 675-5546; (866) 324-2620; Fax (651) 675-5545; enjoyeagan@eaganmn.com; www.eaganmn.com

Eveleth • *Iron Range Tourism Bur.* • Cheyenne Draszt; Exec. Dir.; 111 Station 44 Rd.; 55734; St. Louis; (218) 749-8161; (800) 777-8497; Fax (218) 749-8055; cheyenne@ironrange.org; www.ironrange.org

Fairmont • *Fairmont CVB* • Stephanie Busiahn; Dir.; 323 E. Blue Earth Ave.; P.O. Box 976; 56031; Martin; P 10,889; (507) 235-8585; (800) 657-3280; Fax (507) 235-8411; director@fairmontcvb.com; www.visitfairmontmn.com

Faribault • *Faribault Area Tourism* • Todd Ginter; Dir.; 530 Wilson Ave.; P.O. Box 434; 55021; Rice; P 28,000; (507) 334-4381; (800) 658-2354; Fax (507) 334-1003; todd@faribaultmn.org; www.faribaultmn.org

Grand Rapids • *Visit Grand Rapids* • Megan Christianson; Exec. Dir.; Old Central School; 10 N.W. 5th St., Ste. 212; 55744; Itasca; P 11,000; (218) 326-9607; (800) 355-9740; Fax (218) 326-8219; info@visitgrandrapids.com; www.visitgrandrapids.com

Hutchinson • *Hutchinson Area Chamber of Commerce & Tourism* • Mary Hodson; Pres.; 2 Main St. S.; 55350; McLeod; P 14,600; (320) 587-5252; (800) 572-6689; Fax (320) 587-4752; info@explorehutchinson.com; www.explorehutchinson.com

Little Falls • *Little Falls CVB* • Kris Vonberge; Exec. Dir.; 606 S.E. First St.; 56345; Morrison; P 8,500; (320) 616-4959; (800) 325-5916; info@littlefallsmn.com; www.littlefallsmn.com

Mankato • *Visit Mankato* • Anna Thill; Pres.; Mankato Place Mall; 12 Civic Center Plz., Ste. 1645; 56001; Blue Earth, Le Sueur & Nicollet; P 50,000; (507) 385-6660; (800) 657-4733; Fax (507) 345-8376; visitors@greatermankato.com; www.visitgreatermankato.com

Marshall • *Marshall CVB* • Darin Rahm; Dir.; 118 W. College Dr.; 56258; Lyon; P 13,700; (507) 537-1865; Fax (507) 532-4485; info@visitmarshallmn.com; www.visitmarshallmn.com

Minneapolis • *Meet Minneapolis* • Melvin Tennant; Pres./CEO; 250 Marquette Ave. S., Ste. 1300; 55401; Hennepin; P 400,000; (612) 767-8000; (888) 676-6757; Fax (612) 767-8001; info@minneapolis; www.minneapolis.org

Moorhead • *see Fargo, ND*

Pipestone • *Pipestone CVB* • Erica Volkir; Exec. Dir.; 117 8th Ave. S.E.; P.O. Box 8; 56164; Pipestone; P 4,350; (507) 825-3316; (800) 336-6125; Fax (507) 825-3317; pipecham@pipestoneminnesota.com; www.pipestoneminnesota.com

Red Wing • *Red Wing Visitor & Conv. Bur.* • Arloa Bach; Exec. Dir.; 420 Levee St.; 55066; Goodhue; P 16,500; (651) 385-5934; (800) 498-3444; Fax (651) 388-3900; visitorscenter@redwing.org; www.redwing.org

Redwood Falls • *Redwood Area Chamber & Tourism •* Anne Johnson; Exec. Dir.; 200 S. Mill St.; 56283; Redwood; P 16,815; (507) 637-2828; (800) 657-7070; Fax (507) 637-5202; chamber@redwoodfalls.org; www.redwoodfalls.org

Rochester • *Rochester CVB •* Brad Jones; Exec. Dir.; 30 Civic Center Dr. S.E., Ste. 200; 55904; Olmsted; P 109,000; (507) 288-4331; (800) 634-8277; Fax (507) 288-9144; info@rochestercvb.org; www.visitrochestermn.com

Rushford • *Southeastern Minnesota Historic Bluff Country Inc. •* Bob Coe; Bd. Pres.; P.O. Box 489; 55971; Fillmore & Houston; P 15,000; (507) 421-2934; bobcoe27@gmail.com; www.bluffcountry.com

Saint Cloud • *Saint Cloud Area CVB •* Julie Lunning; Exec. Dir.; 1411 W. Saint Germain St., Ste. 104; 56301; Stearns; P 160,000; (320) 251-4170; (800) 264-2940; Fax (320) 656-0401; julie@granitecountry.com; www.granitecountry.com

Saint Paul • *Visit Saint Paul •* Terry Matson; Pres./CEO; 175 W. Kellogg Blvd., Ste. 502; 55102; Ramsey; P 300,900; (651) 265-4900; (800) 627-6101; Fax (651) 265-4999; info@visitsaintpaul.com; www.visitsaintpaul.com

Sauk Centre • *Sauk Centre CVB •* Pamela Borgmann; Mktg. Mgr.; 308 Oak St., Ste. 101; P.O. Box 222; 56378; Stearns; P 5,000; (320) 352-5201; (855) 444-SAUK; Fax (320) 351-5202; info@visitsaukcentre.com; www.visitsaukcentre.com

Shakopee • *Shakopee CVB •* Angie Whitcomb; Pres.; 1801 E. Cty. Rd. 101; 55379; Scott; P 36,000; (952) 445-1660; (800) 574-2150; Fax (952) 445-1669; awhitcomb@shakopee.org; www.shakopee.org

Thief River Falls • *Thief River Falls CVB •* Laura Anderson; Dir.; 2042 Hwy. 1 W.; P.O. Box 176; 56701; Pennington; P 8,600; (218) 686-9785; Fax (218) 683-5107; trfcvb@mncable.net; www.visittrf.com

Wadena • *Wadena Area CVB •* Shirley Uselman; Dir.; 5 Aldrich Ave. S.E.; P.O. Box 107; 56482; Wadena; P 4,100; (218) 632-7704; (877) 631-7704; Fax (218) 632-7705; www.wadena.org

Willmar • *Willmar Lakes Area CVB •* Beth Fischer; Exec. Dir.; 2104 E. Hwy. 12; 56201; Kandiyohi; P 20,000; (320) 231-0281; (800) 845-TRIP; Fax (320) 231-1948; bfischer@willmarlakesarea.com; www.willmarlakesarea.com

Winona • *Visit Winona •* Pat Mutter; Exec. Dir.; 160 Johnson St.; P.O. Box 1069; 55987; Winona; P 27,069; (507) 452-0735; (800) 657-4972; Fax (507) 454-0006; info@visitwinona.com; www.visitwinona.com

Worthington • *Worthington Area CVB •* Darlene Macklin; Exec. Dir.; 1121 Third Ave.; 56187; Nobles; P 12,724; (507) 372-2919; (800) 279-2919; Fax (507) 372-2827; wcofc@worthingtonmnchamber.com; www.worthingtonmnchamber.com

Mississippi

Aberdeen • *Aberdeen Visitors Bur. •* Tina Robbins; Dir.; 204 E. Commerce St.; P.O. Box 288; 39730; Monroe; P 6,500; (662) 369-9440; (800) 634-3538; Fax (662) 369-3436; info@aberdeenms.org; www.aberdeenms.org

Belzoni • *Catfish Capital Visitors Center •* Mark Bellipanni; Pres.; 111 Magnolia St.; P.O. Box 145; 39038; Humphreys; P 9,500; (662) 247-4838; (800) 408-4838; Fax (662) 247-4805; catfish@belzonicable.com; www.catfishcapitalonline.com

Canton • *Canton CVB •* JoAnn Gordon; Exec. Dir.; 147 N. Union St.; P.O. Box 53; 39046; Madison; P 13,000; (601) 859-1307; (800) 844-3369; Fax (601) 859-0346; canton@cantontourism.com; www.cantontourism.com

Columbus • *Columbus CVB •* Nancy Carpenter; Exec. Dir./CEO; 117 3rd St. S.; P.O. Box 789; 39703; Lowndes; P 64,000; (662) 329-1191; (800) 327-2686; Fax (662) 329-8969; nancy@visitcolumbusms.org; www.visitcolumbusms.org

Corinth • *Corinth Area CVB •* Kristy White; Exec. Dir.; 215 N. Filmore St.; 38834; Alcorn; P 15,000; (662) 287-8300; (800) 748-9048; Fax (662) 286-0102; tourism@corinth.net; www.corinth.net

Greenwood • *Greenwood CVB •* Danielle C. Morgan; Exec. Dir.; 225 Howard St.; P.O. Drawer 739; 38935; Leflore; P 15,200; (662) 453-9197; (800) 748-9064; danielle@visitgreenwood.com; visitgreenwood.com

Grenada • *Grenada Tourism Comm. •* Walter McCool; Exec. Dir.; 95 S.W. Frontage Rd.; 38902; Grenada; P 22,000; (662) 226-2571; (800) 373-2571; Fax (662) 226-9745; grenadamstourism@yahoo.com; www.grenadamississippi.com

Gulfport • *Mississippi Gulf Coast CVB •* Beth Carriere; Exec. Dir.; P.O. Box 6128; 39506; Harrison; P 250,000; (228) 896-6699; (888) 467-4853; Fax (228) 896-6788; tourism@gulfcoast.org; www.gulfcoast.org

Hattiesburg • *Visit Hattiesburg •* Rick Taylor; Exec. Dir.; 5 Convention Center Plz.; 39401; Lamar; P 142,842; (601) 296-7475; (866) 4-HATTIE; Fax (601) 296-7480; hellohattie@visithattie.com; www.hattiesburg.org

Holly Springs • *Holly Springs Tourism & Recreation Bur. •* Lakisha Mitchell-Buffington; Exec. Dir.; 195 E. Van Dorn Ave.; 38635; Marshall; P 8,000; (662) 252-2515; (888) 687-4765; Fax (662) 252-2696; info@visithollysprings.com; www.visithollysprings.com

Jackson • *Jackson CVB •* Wanda Collier-Wilson; Exec. Dir.; 111 E. Capitol St., Ste. 102; P.O. Box 1450; 39215; Hinds; P 200,000; (601) 960-1891; (800) 354-7695; Fax (601) 960-1827; wcwilson@visitjackson.com; www.visitjackson.com

Meridian • *Meridian/Lauderdale County Tourism Bur. •* DeDe Mogollon; Exec. Dir.; 212 Constitution Ave.; 39301; Lauderdale; P 80,300; (601) 482-8001; (888) 868-7720; Fax (601) 486-4988; tourism@visitmeridian.com; www.visitmeridian.com

Natchez • *Natchez CVB •* Connie Taunton; Dir. of Tourism; 640 S. Canal St.; 39120; Adams; P 35,000; (800) 647-6724; info@visitnatchez.org; www.visitnatchez.org

Oxford • *Oxford CVB •* Mary Allyn Roulhac; Tourism Mgr.; 107 Courthouse Sq.; 38655; Lafayette; P 15,000; (662) 234-4680; Fax (662) 232-8680; tourism@oxfordcvb.com; www.oxfordcvb.com

Ridgeland • *Ridgeland Tourism Comm. •* Doyle Warrington; Exec. Dir.; 1000 Highland Colony Pkwy., Ste. 6006; 39157; Madison; P 22,000; (601) 605-5252; (800) 468-6078; Fax (601) 605-5248; info@visitridgeland.com; www.visitridgeland.com

Starkville • *Greater Starkville Dev. Partnership/Welcome Center •* Brittney Young; Mgr.; 200 E. Main St.; 39759; Oktibbeha; P 50,000; (662) 323-3322; (800) 649-8687; Fax (662) 323-5815; byoung@starkville.org; www.starkville.org

Tunica Resorts • *Tunica CVB •* Webster Franklin; Pres./CEO; 13625 U.S. Hwy. 61 N.; 38664; Tunica; P 9,000; (662) 363-3800; (888) 4-TUNICA; Fax (662) 363-1493; tunicams@tunicatravel.com; www.tunicatravel.com

C & VB

Tupelo • *Tupelo CVB* • Neal McCoy; Exec. Dir.; P.O. Drawer 47; 38802; Lee; P 36,000; (662) 841-6521; (800) 533-0611; Fax (662) 841-6558; visittupelo@tupelo.net; www.tupelo.net

Vicksburg • *Vicksburg CVB* • William (Bill) Seratt, Jr; Exec. Dir.; 52 Old Hwy. 27; 1010 Levee St., Boxes B & C; 39183; Warren; P 48,800; (601) 636-9421; (800) 221-3536; Fax (601) 636-9475; debra@visitvicksburg.com; visitvicksburg.com

Yazoo City • *Yazoo County CVB* • Shanitra Finley; Exec. Dir.; 110 N. Jerry Clower Blvd., Ste. S; P.O. Box 186; 39194; Yazoo; P 28,100; (662) 746-1815; (800) 381-0662; Fax (662) 746-1816; info@visityazoo.org; www.visityazoo.org

Missouri

Branson • *Branson/Lakes Area CVB* • Leah Chandler CDME; Chief Mktg. Officer; 269 State Hwy. 248; P.O. Box 1897; 65615; P 35,000; (417) 334-4084; (800) 296-0463; lchandler@bransoncvb.com; www.explorebranson.com

Cape Girardeau • *Cape Girardeau CVB* • Chuck Martin; Exec. Dir.; 400 Broadway, Ste. 100; 63701; Cape Girardeau; P 36,000; (573) 335-1631; (800) 777-0068; Fax (573) 334-6702; info@visitcape.com; www.visitcape.com

Carthage • *Carthage CVB* • Wendi Douglas; Exec. Dir.; 402 S. Garrison Ave.; 64836; Jasper; P 14,055; (417) 359-8181; Fax (417) 359-9119; info@visit-carthage.com; www.visit-carthage.com

Columbia • *Columbia CVB* • Amy Schneider; Dir.; 300 S. Providence Rd.; 65203; Boone; P 115,000; (573) 441-5578; (573) 874-2489; Fax (573) 443-3986; info@gocolumbiamo.com; www.visitcolumbiamo.com

Independence • *Independence Tourism Dept.* • Cori Day; Dir.; 111 E. Maple; 64050; Jackson; P 116,000; (816) 325-7111; (800) 748-7323; Fax (816) 325-7932; cday@indepmo.org; www.visitindependence.com

Jefferson City • *Jefferson City CVB* • Diane Gillespie; Exec. Dir.; 100 E. High St.; P.O. Box 2227; 65102; Cole; P 43,000; (573) 632-2820; (800) 769-4183; Fax (573) 638-4892; info@visitjeffersoncity.com; www.visitjeffersoncity.com

Joplin • *Joplin CVB* • Vince Lindstrom; Dir.; 602 S. Main St.; 64801; Jasper; P 48,000; (417) 625-4789; (800) 657-2534; Fax (417) 624-7948; cvb@joplinmo.org; www.visitjoplinmo.com

Kansas City • *Visit KC* • Ronnie Burt; Pres./CEO; 1321 Baltimore Ave.; 64105; Jackson; P 1,900,000; (816) 221-5242; (800) 767-7700; tpreus@visitkc.com; www.visitkc.com

Maryland Heights • *Maryland Heights CVB* • Karen Krispin; Dir.; P.O. Box 2125; 63043; St. Louis; P 26,000; (888) 667-3236; karen@mhcvb.com; www.more2do.org

Nevada • *Nevada Tourism Center* • Gina Ensor; Exec. Dir.; 225 W. Austin Blvd., Ste. 200; 64772; Vernon; P 21,200; (417) 667-5300; Fax (417) 667-3492; visitors@nevada-mo.com; www.visitmo.com

Osage Beach • *Lake of the Ozarks CVB* • Tim Jacobsen; Exec. Dir.; 5815 Hwy. 54; P.O. Box 1498; 65065; Camden; P 7,000; (573) 348-1599; (800) 386-5253; Fax (573) 348-2293; info@funlake.com; www.funlake.com

Saint Charles • *Greater St. Charles CVB* • Joe Ward; Dir.; 230 S. Main St.; 63301; St. Charles; P 70,000; (636) 255-6103; (800) 366-2427; Fax (636) 949-3217; gsccvb@historicstcharles.com; www.historicstcharles.com

Saint Joseph • *St. Joseph CVB* • Marci Bennett; Exec. Dir.; 109 S. 4th; P.O. Box 445; 64502; Buchanan; P 77,000; (816) 233-6688; (800) 785-0360; Fax (816) 233-9120; stjosephcvb@stjomo.com; www.stjomo.com

Saint Louis • *St. Louis Conv. & Visitors Comm.* • Kathleen Ratcliffe; Pres.; 701 Convention Plz., Ste. 300; 63101; St. Louis; P 2,423,200; (314) 421-1023; (800) 325-7962; Fax (314) 421-0039; kratcliffe@explorestlouis.com; www.explorestlouis.com

Sikeston • *Sikeston CVB* • Linda Lowes; Exec. Dir.; 105 E. Center St.; 63801; Scott; P 17,000; (573) 471-2512; Fax (573) 471-1526; cvb@visitsikeston.com; www.visitsikeston.com

Springfield • *Springfield CVB* • Mr. Tracy Kimberlin; Pres./CEO; 815 E. Saint Louis St., Ste. 100; 65806; Greene; P 165,000; (417) 881-5300; (800) 678-8767; Fax (417) 881-2231; cvb@springfieldmo.org; www.springfieldmo.org

Washington • *Washington Area C/C & Div. of Tourism* • Mary Beth Rettke; Dir. of Tourism; 323 W. Main St.; 63090; Franklin; P 14,000; (636) 239-2715; (888) 7-WASH-MO; Fax (636) 239-1381; tourism@washmo.org; www.washmochamber.org

Montana

Billings • *Visit Billings* • Alex Tyson; Exec. Dir.; 815 S. 27th St.; P.O. Box 31177; 59107; Yellowstone; P 150,000; (406) 245-4111; Fax (406) 245-7333; info@billingschamber.com; www.visitbillings.com

Kalispell • *Kalispell CVB* • Diane Medler; Dir.; 15 Depot Park; 59901; Flathead; P 90,928; (406) 758-2808; (888) 888-2308; Fax (406) 758-2805; diane@discoverkalispell.com; www.discoverkalispell.com

Nebraska

Beatrice • *Gage County Tourism* • Lora Young; Exec. Dir.; 218 N. 5th St.; 68310; Gage; P 13,000; (402) 223-2338; Fax (402) 223-2339; lwiegand@visitbeatrice.com; www.visitbeatrice.com

Columbus • *Columbus/Platte County CVB* • Deb Loseke; Dir.; 764 33rd Ave.; P.O. Box 515; 68602; Platte; P 22,000; (402) 564-2769; Fax (402) 564-2026; dloseke@megavision.com; www.visitcolumbusne.com

Fairbury • *Jefferson County Visitors Comm.* • Sharon Priefert; Exec. Dir.; 518 E St.; P.O. Box 274; 68352; Jefferson; P 4,262; (402) 729-3000; Fax (402) 729-3076; jcvc@diodecom.net; www.visitoregontrail.org

Fremont • *Fremont & Dodge County CVB* • Leslie Carter; Exec. Dir.; 338 N. Main St.; 68025; Dodge; P 35,000; (402) 753-6414; (800) 727-8323; Fax (402) 721-9359; shannonm@fremontne.org; www.fremontne.org

Grand Island • *Grand Island/Hall County CVB* • Brad Mellema; Exec. Dir.; 2424 S. Locust St., Ste. C; 68801; Hall; P 51,000; (308) 382-4400; (800) 658-3178; Fax (308) 382-4908; info@visitgrandisland.com; www.visitgrandisland.com

Hastings • *Adams County CVB* • Kaleena Fong; Exec. Dir.; 100 North Shore Dr.; P.O. Box 941; 68902; Adams; P 33,000; (402) 461-2370; kaleena@visithastingsnebraska.com; www.visithastingsnebraska.com

Kearney • *Kearney Visitors Bur.* • Roger Jasnoch; Dir.; 1007 2nd Ave., P.O. Box 607; 68848; Buffalo; P 47,000; (308) 237-3178; (800) 652-9435; Fax (308) 236-9116; rjasnoch@visitkearney.org; www.visitkearney.org

Lincoln • *Lincoln CVB* • Jeff Maul; Exec. Dir.; 1135 M St., Ste. 300; P.O. Box 83737; 68501; Lancaster; P 250,000; (402) 434-5335; (800) 423-8212; Fax (402) 436-2360; info@lincoln.org; www.lincoln.org

McCook • *Red Willow County CVB* • Carol Schlegel; Coord.; 107 Norris Ave.; P.O. Box 337; 69001; Red Willow; P 11,450; (308) 345-3200; (800) 657-2179; Fax (308) 345-3201; bwchief@qwest.net; www.visitmccook.com

Norfolk • *Norfolk Area Visitors Bur.* • Traci Jeffrey; Exec. Dir.; 609 W. Norfolk Ave.; 68701; Madison; P 33,000; (402) 371-2932; (888) 371-2932; Fax (402) 316-3297; info@visitnorfolkne.com; www.visitnorfolkne.com

North Platte • *North Platte/Lincoln County CVB* • Lisa Burke; Exec. Dir.; 101 Halligan Dr.; 69101; Lincoln; P 37,000; (308) 532-4729; (800) 955-4528; Fax (308) 532-5914; info@visitnorthplatte.com; www.visitnorthplatte.com

Ogallala • *Ogallala/Keith County CVB* • Penny Seibert; Dir.; 418 N. Spruce; P.O. Box 628; 69153; Keith; P 8,877; (308) 284-4066; (800) 658-4390; Fax (308) 284-3126; lwortman@explorekeithcounty.com; www.explorekeithcounty.com

Omaha • *Greater Omaha CVB* • Dana Markel; Exec. Dir.; 1001 Farnam; 68102; Douglas; P 813,170; (402) 444-4660; (866) 937-6624; Fax (402) 444-4511; dmarkel@visitomaha.com; www.visitomaha.com

South Sioux City • *South Sioux City CVB* • Jim Steele; Pres.; 4401 Dakota Ave.; 68776; Dakota; P 13,500; (402) 494-1626; (866) 494-1307; Fax (402) 494-5010; info@visitsouthsiouxcity.com; www.visitsouthsiouxcity.com

York • *York County CVB* • Bob Sautter; Exec. Dir.; 601 N. Lincoln Ave.; 68467; York; P 14,500; (402) 362-4575; Fax (402) 362-3344; bobsautter@windstream.net; www.yorkvisitors.org

Nevada

Crystal Bay • *see Incline Village*

Incline Village • *Lake Tahoe-Incline Village Crystal Bay Visitor Bur.* • William Hoffman; Exec. Dir.; 969 Tahoe Blvd.; 89451; Washoe; P 9,143; (775) 832-1606; (800) GO-TAHOE; Fax (775) 832-1605; info@gotahoe.com; www.gotahoenorth.com

Las Vegas • *Las Vegas Conv. & Visitors Auth.* • Rossi Ralenkotter; Pres./CEO; 3150 Paradise Rd.; 89109; Clark; P 1,900,000; (702) 892-0711; (877) 847-4858; Fax (702) 892-2803; info@lvcva.com; www.lvcva.com

Reno • *Reno-Sparks Conv. & Visitors Auth.* • Ellen Oppenheim; Pres./CEO; 4001 S. Virginia St., Ste. G; P.O. Box 837; 89504; Washoe; P 323,670; (775) 827-7600; (800) 443-1482; Fax (775) 827-7666; info@rscva.com; www.visitrenotahoe.com

Stateline • *Lake Tahoe Visitors Auth.* • Carol Chaplin; Exec. Dir.; 169 U.S. Hwy. 50; P.O. Box 5878; 89449; Douglas; P 30,000; (775) 588-5900; (800) AT-TAHOE; Fax (775) 588-1941; info@ltva.org; www.tahoesouth.com

Tonopah • *Tonopah Conv. Center* • 301 Brougher Ave.; P.O. Box 408; 89049; Nye; P 3,000; (775) 482-3558; Fax (775) 482-3932; townoftonopah@frontiernet.net; www.tonopahnevada.com

New Jersey

Atlantic City • *Casino Reinvestment Dev. Auth.* • John F. Palmieri; Exec. Dir.; 2314 Pacific Ave.; 08401; Atlantic; P 380,000; (609) 449-7100; (888) 228-4748; Fax (609) 345-7287; visitors@accva.com; www.atlanticcitynj.com

Bridgewater • *Somerset County Bus. Partnership & Visitor Center* • Michael Kerwin; Pres./CEO; 360 Grove St.; 08807; Somerset; P 324,600; (908) 218-4300; Fax (908) 722-7823; info@scbp.org; www.scbp.org

Cape May County • *Cape May County Dept. of Tourism* • Diane Wieland; Dir. of Tourism; 4 Moore Rd.; P.O. Box 365, Cape May Court House; 08210; Cape May; P 97,300; (609) 463-6415; (800) 227-2297; Fax (609) 465-4639; tourism@co.cape-may.nj.us; www.thejerseycape.com

Red Bank • *Red Bank Visitors Center* • Margaret Mass; Exec. Dir.; 46 English Plz., Ste. 6; 07701; Monmouth; P 12,300; (732) 741-9211; (732) 842-4244; visitors@redbankrivercenter.org; www.visit.redbank.com

New Mexico

Albuquerque • *Albuquerque CVB* • Dale Lockett; Pres./CEO; 20 First Plz. N.W., Ste. 601; P.O. Box 26866; 87125; Bernalillo; P 700,000; (505) 842-9918; (800) 284-2282; Fax (505) 247-9101; info@itsatrip.org; www.itsatrip.org

Farmington • *Farmington CVB* • Debbie Dusenbery; Exec. Dir.; 3041 E. Main St.; 87402; San Juan; P 120,000; (505) 326-7602; (800) 448-1240; Fax (505) 327-0577; fmncvb@earthlink.net; www.farmingtonnm.org

Gallup • *Gallup Visitor Center* • Gretchen Herriman; Dir.; 106 W. Hwy. 66; 87301; McKinley; P 72,000; (505) 722-2228; (800) 380-4989; Fax (505) 863-2280; gretchen@thegallupchamber.com; www.thegallupchamber.com

Las Cruces • *Las Cruces CVB* • Philip San Filippo; Exec. Dir.; 211 N. Water St.; 88001; Dona Ana; P 95,000; (575) 541-2444; (800) FIESTAS; Fax (575) 541-2164; cvb@lascrucescvb.org; www.lascrucescvb.org

Los Alamos • *Los Alamos Mtg. & Visitor Bur.* • 109 Central Park Sq.; 87544; Los Alamos; P 18,000; (800) 444-0707; Fax (505) 662-8105; mvb@losalamos.org; www.locateinlosalamos.com

Rio Rancho • *Rio Rancho CVB* • Matt Geisel; Dir.; 3200 Civic Center Cir. N.E.; 87144; Sandoval; P 75,000; (505) 891-7258; (888) 746-7262; Fax (505) 892-8328; mgeisel@ci.rio-rancho.nm.us; www.rioranchonm.org

Roswell • *Roswell Visitors Bur.* • Suzy Wood; Dir.; 912 N. Main; 88201; Chaves; P 50,000; (575) 624-7704; Fax (575) 624-6863; suzyw@cableone.net; www.roswellmysteries.com

Roswell • *Roswell Civic Center* • Ruben Sanchez; Dir. of Civic Center; 912 N. Main; 88201; Chaves; P 50,000; (575) 624-6860; Fax (575) 624-6863; conventions@cableone.net; www.roswellmysteries.com

Ruidoso • *Ruidoso Conv. Center* • Gail Bailey; Dir. of Sales; 111 Sierra Blanca Dr.; 88345; Lincoln; P 10,500; (575) 258-5445; (877) 700-5445; Fax (575) 258-5040; sales@ruidosoconventioncenter.com; www.ruidosoconventioncenter.com

Santa Fe • *Tourism Santa Fe* • Randy Randall; Exec. Dir.; 201 W. Marcy St.; 87504; Santa Fe; P 70,000; (505) 955-6200; (800) 777-2489; Fax (505) 955-6222; info@santafe.org; www.santafe.org

Santa Rosa • *Santa Rosa Info. & Tourism Center* • Richard R. Delgado; Tourism Dir.; 244 S. 4th St.; 88435; Guadalupe; P 2,640; (575) 472-3763; Fax (575) 472-3848; rdelgado@srnm.org; www.santarosanm.org

Taos • *Taos Visitors Center* • Michelle Hammer; Supervisor; 1139 Paseo del Pueblo Sur.; 87571; Taos; P 31,800; (575) 758-3873; (800) 732-8267; Fax (575) 758-3872; information@taosvisitor.com; www.taosvisitor.com

New York

Albany • *Albany County CVB* • Michele Vennard; Pres./CEO; 25 Quackenbush Sq.; 12207; Albany; P 309,400; (518) 434-1217; (800) 258-3582; Fax (518) 434-0887; info@albany.org; www.albany.org

Binghamton • *Greater Binghamton CVB* • Jennifer Conway; Pres./CEO; 49 Court St.; P.O. Box 995; 13902; Broome; P 200,536; (607) 772-8860; (800) 836-6740; Fax (607) 722-4513; jconway@greaterbinghamtonchamber.com; www.visitbinghamton.org

Buffalo • *Buffalo/Niagara CVB* • Dottie Gallagher; Pres./CEO; 617 Main St., Ste. 200; 14203; Erie; P 985,000; (716) 852-0511; (800) 283-3256; Fax (716) 852-0131; info@visitbuffaloniagara.com; www.visitbuffaloniagara.com

Chautauqua • *Chautauqua County Visitors Bur.* • Andrew Nixon; Dir.; P.O. Box 1441; 14722; Chautauqua; P 135,000; (716) 357-4569; (800) 242-4569; Fax (716) 357-2284; info@tourchautauqua.com; www.tourchautauqua.com

Corning • *Steuben County Conf. & Visitors Bur.* • Jake Buganski; Pres.; 1 W. Market St., Ste. 201; 14830; Steuben; P 98,900; (607) 936-6544; (866) 946-3386; Fax (607) 936-6575; info@corningfingerlakes.com; www.corningfingerlakes.com

Goshen • *Orange County Tourism* • Susan H. Hawvermale; Dir.; 99 Main St.; 10924; Orange; P 372,813; (845) 615-3860; Fax (845) 360-7219; tourism@orangecountygov.com; www.orangetourism.org

Hauppauge • *Long Island CVB & Sports Commission* • Kristen Jarnagin; Pres.; 330 Motor Pkwy., Ste. 203; 11788; Suffolk; P 7,600,000; (631) 951-3900; (877) 386-6654; Fax (631) 951-3439; tourism@discoverlongisland.com; www.discoverlongisland.com

Ithaca • *Ithaca/Tompkins County CVB* • Peggy Coleman; Dir.; 904 E. Shore Dr.; 14850; Tompkins; P 105,000; (607) 272-1313; (800) 284-8422; Fax (607) 272-7617; peggy@visitithaca.com; www.visitithaca.com

Lake Placid • *Lake Placid-Essex County Visitors Bur.* • James McKenna; Pres./CEO; 2608 Main St.; P.O. Box 1570; 12946; Essex; P 39,370; (518) 523-2445; (800) 447-5224; Fax (518) 523-2605; info@lakeplacid.com; www.lakeplacid.com

Leeds • *Greene County Tourism Promotion* • Warren Hart; Dir.; 700 Rte. 23B; 12451; Greene; P 49,000; (518) 943-3223; (800) 355-CATS; Fax (518) 943-2296; tourism@discovergreene.com; www.greatnortherncatskills.com

Little Valley • *Cattaraugus County Tourism* • Debra Opferbeck; Tourism Spec.; 303 Court St.; 14755; Cattaraugus; P 80,300; (800) 331-0543; (716) 938-2307; Fax (716) 938-2779; info@enchantedmountains.com; www.enchantedmountains.info

Long Island • *see Hauppauge*

New York • *New York City & Co.* • Fred Dixon; Pres./CEO; 810 7th Ave., 3rd Flr.; Visitors Center; 10019; New York; P 11,685,650; (212) 484-1200; Fax (212) 245-5943; visitorinfo@nycgo.com; www.nycgo.com

Plattsburgh • *Adirondack Coast Visitors & Conv. Bur.* • Melanie Marr; Exec. Asst.; 7061 Rte. 9; P.O. Box 310; 12901; Clinton; P 200,000; (518) 563-1000; (877) 242-6752; Fax (518) 563-1028; info@goadirondack.com; www.goadirondack.com

Rochester • *Visit Rochester* • Greg Marshall; V.P.; 45 East Ave., Ste. 400; 14604; Monroe; P 211,000; (585) 279-8300; (800) 677-7282; Fax (585) 232-4822; info@visitrochester.com; www.visitrochester.com

Saratoga Springs • *Saratoga Conv. & Tourism Bur.* • Todd Garofano; Pres.; 60 Railroad Pl., Ste. 301; 12866; Saratoga; P 27,000; (518) 584-1531; (855) 424-6073; Fax (518) 584-2969; mail@discoversaratoga.org; www.discoversaratoga.org

Southampton • *Hamptons Visitors Cncl.* • 76 Main St.; 11968; P 50,000; (631) 283-0402; Fax (631) 283-8707; info@hamptonsvc.com; www.hamptonsvc.com

Syracuse • *Visit Syracuse* • David Holder; Pres.; 115 W. Fayette St.; 13202; Onondaga; P 460,000; (315) 470-1910; (800) 234-4797; Fax (315) 471-8545; info@visitsyracuse.com; www.visitsyracuse.com

Utica • *Oneida County Tourism* • Kelly Blazosky; Pres.; Exit 31, Off 1-90; P.O. Box 551; 13503; Oneida; P 100,000; (315) 724-7221; (800) 426-3132; Fax (315) 724-7335; info@oneidacountytourism.com; www.oneidacountytourism.com

White Plains • *Westchester County Ofc. of Tourism* • Natasa Caputo; Dir.; 148 Martine Ave., Ste. 104; 10601; Westchester; P 954,000; (914) 995-8500; (800) 833-9282; Fax (914) 995-8505; tourism@westchestergov.com; www.westchestertourism.com

Wilmington • *Whiteface Mountain Reg. Visitors Bur.* • Michelle Burns; Mgr.; 5753 NYS Rte. 86; P.O. Box 277; 12997; Essex; P 3,000; (518) 946-2255; (888) WHITE-FACE; Fax (518) 946-2683; info@whitefaceregion.com; www.whitefaceregion.com

North Carolina

Albemarle • *Stanly County CVB* • Chris Lambert; Exec. Dir.; 1000 N. 1st St., Ste. 11; 28001; Stanly; P 61,600; (704) 986-2583; (800) 650-1476; Fax (704) 983-5000; chris@stanlycvb.com; www.visitstanly.com

Alleghany County • *see Boone*

Ashe County • *see Boone*

Asheboro • *Randolph County Tourism Dev. Auth.* • Tammy O'Kelley; Dir. of Tourism; 145B Worth St.; 27203; Randolph; P 142,000; (336) 626-0364; vbloxham@heartofnorthcarolina.com; www.heartofnorthcarolina.com

Asheville • *Asheville CVB* • Mr. Kelly Miller; Exec. Dir./Exec. V.P.; 36 Montford Ave.; 28801; Buncombe; P 238,300; (828) 258-6102; (828) 258-6101; Fax (828) 254-6054; comments@exploreasheville.com; www.exploreasheville.com

Avery County • *see Boone*

Belmont • *Gaston County Travel & Tourism* • Walter Israel; Exec. Dir.; 620 N. Main St.; 28012; Gaston; P 210,500; (704) 825-4044; (800) 849-9994; Fax (704) 825-4029; walter.israel@co.gaston.nc.us; www.visitgaston.org

Boone • *North Carolina High Country Host & VIC* • Candice Cook; Exec. Dir.; 1700 Blowing Rock Rd.; 28607; Watauga; P 176,600; (828) 264-1299; (800) 438-7500; Fax (828) 265-0550; info@highcountryhost.com; www.mountainsofnc.com

Boone • *Boone Area Visitors Bur.* • Wright Tilley; Dir.; 815 W. King St., Ste. 10; 28607; Watauga; P 51,100; (828) 266-1345; Fax (828) 266-1346; michelle@exploreboonearea.com; www.exploreboonearea.com

Burlington • *Burlington/Alamance County CVB* • Grave Vandevisser; Exec. Dir.; 200 S. Main St.; P.O. Box 519; 27216; Alamance; P 140,000; (336) 570-1444; (800) 637-3804; Fax (336) 524-6528; info@visitalamance.com; www.visitalamance.com

Canton • *see Waynesville*

Chapel Hill • *Chapel Hill/Orange County Visitors Bur.* • Laurie Paolicelli; Exec. Dir.; 501 W. Franklin St.; 27516; Orange; P 141,500; (919) 245-4320; Fax (919) 968-2062; info@visitchapelhill.org; www.visitchapelhill.org

Charlotte • *Visit Charlotte* • Mike Butts; Exec. Dir.; 500 S. College St., Ste. 300; 28202; Mecklenburg; P 800,000; (704) 334-2282; (800) 722-1994; Fax (704) 342-3972; mike.butts@visitcharlotte.com; www.visitcharlotte.com

Cherokee • *Cherokee Welcome Center* • Josie Long; Coord.; 498 Tsali Blvd.; P.O. Box 460; 28719; Swain; P 15,000; (828) 359-6491; (800) 438-1601; Fax (828) 497-2505; travel@nc-cherokee.com; www.visitcherokeenc.com

Columbus • *Polk County Travel & Tourism* • Melinda Young; Dir.; 20 E. Mills St.; P.O. Box 308; 28722; Polk; P 20,500; (828) 894-2324; (800) 440-7848; Fax (828) 894-6142; visit@firstpeaknc.com; www.nc-mountains.org

Cornelius • *Visit Lake Norman* • Sally Ashworth; Exec. Dir.; 19900 W. Catawba Ave., Ste. 102; 28031; Mecklenburg; P 120,000; (704) 987-3300; (800) 305-2508; Fax (704) 892-5313; ashworth@lakenorman.org; www.visitlakenorman.org

Davidson • *see Cornelius*

Dunn • *Dunn Area Tourism Auth.* • Sharon Stevens; Mktg. Dir.; 103 E. Cumberland St.; P.O. Box 310; 28335; Harnett; P 10,000; (910) 892-3282; Fax (910) 892-5735; info@dunntourism.org; www.dunntourism.org

Durham • *Durham CVB* • Shelly Green; Pres./CEO; 212 W. Main St., Ste. 101; 27701; Durham; P 312,000; (919) 687-0288; (800) 446-8604; Fax (919) 680-8340; info@durham-cvb.com; www.durham-nc.com

Edenton • *Chowan County Tourism Dev. Auth.* • Nancy Nicholls; Tourism Dir.; 101 W. Water St.; P.O. Box 245; 27932; Chowan; P 14,800; (252) 482-0300; (800) 775-0111; Fax (252) 482-7093; nancy.nicholls@chowan.nc.gov; www.visitedenton.com

Elizabeth City • *Elizabeth City/Pasquotank County Tourism & Dev. Auth.* • Christina Rehklau; Dir.; 400 S. Water St., Ste. 101; 27909; Pasquotank; P 40,700; (252) 335-5330; (866) 324-8948; Fax (252) 335-1733; info@discoverelizabethcity.com; www.discoverelizabethcity.com

Fayetteville • *Fayetteville Area CVB* • John Meroski; Pres./CEO; 245 Person St.; 28301; Cumberland; P 320,000; (910) 483-5311; (800) 255-8217; Fax (910) 484-6632; facvb@visitfayettevillenc.com; www.visitfayettevillenc.com

Greensboro • *Greensboro Area CVB* • Henri Fourrier; Pres./CEO; 2411 W. Gate City Blvd.; 27403; Guilford; P 269,700; (336) 274-2282; (800) 344-2282; Fax (336) 230-1183; hfourrier@visitgreensboronc.com; www.visitgreensboronc.com

Greenville • *Greenville-Pitt County CVB* • Andrew Schmidt; Exec. Dir./CEO; 417 Cotanche St., Ste. 100; P.O. Box 8027; 27835; Pitt; P 169,000; (252) 329-4200; (800) 537-5564; Fax (252) 329-4205; info@visitgreenvillenc.com; www.visitgreenvillenc.com

Hendersonville • *Henderson County Tourism Dev. Auth.* • Elizabeth B. Carden; Exec. Dir.; 201 S. Main St.; 28792; Henderson; P 114,000; (828) 693-9708; (800) 828-4244; Fax (828) 697-4996; bcarden@visithendersonvillenc.org; visithendersonvillenc.org

Hickory • *Hickory Metro CVB* • Mandy Pitts; CEO; 1960-A 13th Ave. Dr. S.E.; 28602; Catawba; P 150,000; (828) 322-1335; (800) 509-2444; Fax (828) 345-0700; info@hickorymetro.com; www.hickorymetro.com

High Point • *High Point CVB* • Timothy C. Mabe; Pres./CEO; 1634 N. Main St., Ste. 102; P.O. Box 2273; 27261; Guilford; P 104,400; (336) 884-5255; (800) 720-5255; Fax (336) 884-4352; HPCVB@HighPoint.org; www.HighPoint.org

Highlands • *Highlands Visitor Center* • Jennifer Smathers-Cunningham; Dir.; 108 Main St.; P.O. Box 404; 28741; Macon; P 3,000; (828) 526-5841; Fax (828) 526-5803; visitor@highlandschamber.org; www.highlandschamber.org

Huntersville • *see Cornelius*

Jacksonville • *Onslow County Tourism* • Theresa Carter; Dir.; 1099 Gum Branch Rd.; 28540; Onslow; P 177,800; (910) 347-3141; (800) 932-2144; Fax (910) 347-4705; tourd@jacksonvilleonline.org; www.onlyinonslow.com

Kinston • *Kinston CVB* • Laura Lee Sylvester; Pres.; 301 N. Queen St.; P.O. Box 157; 28502; Lenoir; P 58,000; (252) 523-2500; (800) 869-0032; Fax (252) 527-1914; llsylvester@kinstonchamber.com; www.visitkinston.com

Lake Lure • *Hickory Nut Gorge Visitor Center* • Melissa Messer; Mgr.; 2926 Memorial Hwy.; P.O. Box 32, Chimney Rock, 28720; 28746; Rutherford; P 2,500; (828) 625-2725; (877) 625-2725; Fax (828) 625-9601; director@hickorynut.org; www.hickorynut.org

Lake Norman • *see Cornelius*

Maggie Valley • *see Waynesville*

Mitchell County • *see Boone*

Morehead City • *Crystal Coast Tourism Auth.* • Carol Lohr; Exec. Dir.; 3409 Arendell St.; 28557; Carteret; P 69,000; (252) 726-8148; (800) 786-6962; Fax (252) 726-0990; brochure@sunnync.com; www.crystalcoastnc.org

Morganton • *Burke County Travel & Tourism Comm.* • Ed Phillips; Exec. Dir.; 110 E. Meeting St.; 28655; Burke; P 90,000; (828) 433-6793; (888) 462-2921; Fax (828) 437-1613; director@discoverburkecounty.com; www.discoverburkecounty.com

New Bern • *New Bern-Craven County Convention & Visitor Center* • Mary Harris; Dir.; 203 S. Front St.; 28560; Craven; P 103,505; (252) 637-9400; (800) 437-5767; Fax (252) 637-0250; info@visitnewbern.com; www.visitnewbern.com

Pinehurst • *see Southern Pines*

Raleigh • *Greater Raleigh CVB* • Dennis Edwards; Pres./CEO; 421 Fayetteville St., Ste. 1505; 27601; Wake; P 405,000; (919) 834-5900; (800) 849-8499; Fax (919) 831-2887; visit@visitraleigh.com; www.visitraleigh.com

C & VB

Southern Pines • *CVB of Pinehurst, Southern Pines, Aberdeen Area* • Caleb Miles; Exec. Dir./CEO; 10677 Hwy. 15-501; 28387; Moore; P 84,000; (910) 692-3330; (800) 346-5362; Fax (910) 692-2493; cvb4golf@ncrrbiz.com; www.homeofgolf.com

Sparta • *Alleghany County C/C & Visitor Center* • Ashley Weaver; Exec. Dir.; 58 S. Main St.; P.O. Box 1237; 28675; Alleghany; P 11,000; (336) 372-5473; (800) 372-5473; Fax (336) 245-9601; info@sparta-nc.com; www.sparta-nc.com

Spruce Pine • *Mitchell County Visitor Center* • Patti Jensen; Travel/Tourism Dir.; P.O. Box 858; 28777; Mitchell; P 16,000; (828) 765-9483; (800) 227-3912; Fax (828) 765-9034; getinfo@mitchell-county.com; www.mitchell-county.com

Statesville • *Statesville CVB* • Donna Vanstory; Visitor Info. Spec.; 118 W. Broad St.; 28677; Iredell; P 25,000; (704) 878-3480; (877) 531-1819; Fax (704) 878-3489; info@visitstatesville.org; www.visitstatesville.org

Thomasville • *Thomasville Visitors Center* • Jarrod Dunbar; Dir.; 44 W. Main St.; 27360; Davidson; P 27,000; (336) 472-4422; visit@tvillenc.com; www.tvillenc.com

Watauga County • *see Boone*

Waynesville • *Haywood County Tourism Dev. Auth.* • Lynn Collins; Exec. Dir.; 44 N. Main St.; 28786; Haywood; P 57,000; (828) 452-0152; (800) 334-9036; Fax (828) 452-0153; hctda@smokeymountains.net; www.smokeymountains.net

Williamston • *Martin County Tourism Dev. Auth.* • Barney L. Conway; Exec. Dir.; 415 E. Blvd.; P.O. Box 382; 27892; Martin; P 24,000; (252) 792-6605; (800) 776-8566; Fax (252) 792-8710; tourism@visitmartincounty.com; www.visitmartincounty.com

Wilmington • *Wilmington & Beaches CVB* • Kim Hufham; Pres./CEO; 505 Nutt St., Unit A; 28401; New Hanover; P 206; (910) 341-4030; Fax (910) 341-4029; visit@wilmingtonandbeaches.com; www.WilmingtonAndBeaches.com

Wilson • *Wilson Visitors Center* • Sandra Homes; Exec. Dir.; 209 Broad St.; P.O. Box 2882; 27894; Wilson; P 81,300; (252) 243-8440; (800) 497-7398; Fax (252) 243-7550; info@wilson-nc.com; www.wilson-nc.com

Winston-Salem • *Winston-Salem CVB & Visitors Center* • Richard Geiger; Pres.; 200 Brookstown Ave.; 27101; Forsyth; P 241,300; (336) 728-4200; (866) 728-4200; Fax (336) 721-2202; info@visitwinstonsalem.com; www.visitwinstonsalem.com

North Dakota

Beulah • *Beulah CVB* • Steffanie Boeckel; Exec. Dir.; 120 Central Ave. N.; P.O. Box 730; 58523; Mercer; P 3,200; (701) 873-4585; (800) 441-2649; Fax (701) 873-5361; chamber@westriv.com; www.beulahnd.org

Bismarck • *Bismarck-Mandan CVB* • Sheri Grossman; CEO; 1600 Burnt Boat Dr.; 58503; Burleigh; P 117,000; (701) 222-4308; (800) 767-3555; visitnd@discoverbismarckmandan.com; www.bmcvb.com

Bottineau • *Bottineau CVB* • Clint Reinoehl; Coord.; 519 Main St.; 58318; Bottineau; P 2,400; (701) 228-3849; (800) 735-6932; Fax (701) 228-5130; bcc@utma.com; www.bottineau.com

Carrington • *Carrington CVB* • 871 Main St.; 58421; Foster; P 2,100; (701) 652-2524; (800) 641-9668; chambergal@daktel.com; www.carringtonnd.com

Devils Lake • *Devils Lake C/C & Tourism Ofc.* • Suzie Kenner; Exec. Dir.; 208 Hwy. 2 W.; P.O. Box 879; 58301; Ramsey; P 7,100; (701) 662-4903; (800) 233-8048; Fax (701) 662-2147; tourism@gondtc.com; www.devilslakend.com

Dickinson • *Dickinson CVB* • Terri Thiel; Exec. Dir.; 72 E. Museum Dr.; 58601; Stark; P 32,000; (701) 483-4988; (800) 279-7391; Fax (701) 483-9261; terri@visitdickinson.com; www.visitdickinson.com

Fargo • *Fargo-Moorhead CVB* • Charley Johnson; Pres./CEO; 2001 44th St. S.; 58103; Cass & Clay; P 233,000; (800) 235-7654; (701) 282-3653; Fax (701) 282-4366; danella@fargomoorhead.org; www.fargomoorhead.org

Grand Forks • *Greater Grand Forks CVB* • Julie Rygg; Exec. Dir.; 4251 Gateway Dr.; 58203; Grand Forks; P 60,000; (701) 746-0444; (800) 866-4566; info@visitgrandforks.com; www.visitgrandforks.com

Hettinger • *Dakota Buttes Visitors Cncl.* • Earleen Friez; Admin. Secy.; 120 S. Main St.; P.O. Box 1031; 58639; Adams; P 1,300; (701) 567-2531; hettingerchamber@ndsupernet.com; www.hettingernd.com

Jamestown • *Jamestown Civic Center/CVB* • 212 3rd Ave. N.E.; 58401; Stutsman; P 15,500; (701) 252-8088; Fax (701) 252-8089; director@jamestownciviccenter.com; www.jamestownciviccenter.com

Jamestown • *Buffalo City Tourism* • Nina Sneider; Dir.; 404 Louis L'Amour Ln.; P.O. Box 917; 58402; Stutsman; P 15,500; (701) 251-9145; (800) 222-4766; guestinfo@tourjamestown.com; www.tourjamestown.com

Minot • *Minot CVB* • Phyllis Burckhard; Exec. Dir.; 1020 S. Broadway; 58701; Ward; P 50,000; (701) 857-8206; (800) 264-2626; Fax (701) 857-8228; info@visitminot.org; www.visitminot.org

Rugby • *Rugby CVB* • Dondi Sobolik; Exec. Dir.; 224 Hwy. 2 S.W.; 58368; Pierce; P 2,950; (701) 776-5846; Fax (701) 776-6390; rugbychamber@stellarnet.com; www.rugbynorthdakota.com

Williston • *Williston CVB* • Amy Krueger; Exec. Dir.; 212 Airport Rd.; 58801; Williams; P 15,000; (701) 774-9041; (800) 615-9041; Fax (701) 774-0411; cvbsales@ci.williston.nd.us; www.visitwilliston.com

Ohio

Akron • *Akron/Summit CVB* • Susan Hamo; Pres./CEO; 77 E. Mill St.; 44308; Summit; P 515,000; (330) 374-7560; (800) 245-4254; Fax (330) 374-7626; information@visitakron-summit.org; www.visitakron-summit.org

Amherst • *Lorain County Visitors Bur.* • Barb Bickel; Exec. Dir.; 8025 Leavitt Rd.; 44001; Lorain; P 285,000; (440) 984-5282; (800) 334-1673; Fax (440) 984-7363; visitors@visitloraincounty.com; www.visitloraincounty.com

Ashland • *Ashland Area CVB* • Amy Daubenspeck; Exec. Dir.; 211 Claremont Ave.; 44805; Ashland; P 53,000; (419) 281-4584; (877) 581-2345; Fax (419) 281-4585; cvb@ashlandoh.com; www.visitashlandohio.com

Austinburg • *Ashtabula County CVB* • Mark Winchell; Exec. Dir.; 1850 Austinburg Rd.; 44010; Ashtabula; P 101,497; (440) 275-3202; (800) 337-6746; Fax (440) 275-3210; visitus@visitashtabulacounty.com; www.visitashtabulacounty.com

Batavia • *Clermont County CVB* • June Creager-Mason; Exec. Dir.; 410 E. Main St.; 45103; Clermont; P 200,000; (513) 732-3600; (800) 796-4282; Fax (513) 732-2244; info@visitclermontohio.com; www.visitclermontohio.com

Beavercreek • *Greene County CVB* • Kathleen Young; Exec. Dir.; 1221 Meadowbridge Dr., Ste. A; 45434; Greene; P 160,000; (937) 429-9100; (800) 733-9109; Fax (937) 429-7726; visitors@greenecountyohio.org; www.greenecountyohio.org

Bellefontaine • *Logan County CVB* • Paul Benedetti; Pres./CEO; 100 S. Main St.; 43311; Logan; P 46,000; (937) 599-5121; (888) LOGAN-CO; Fax (937) 599-2411; info@logancountyohio.com; www.logancountyohio.com

Bowling Green • *Bowling Green CVB* • Wendy Chambers; Exec. Dir.; Four Corners Center; 130 S. Main St.; 43402; Wood; P 30,000; (419) 353-9445; (800) 866-0046; Fax (419) 353-9446; wendychambers@visitbgohio.org; www.visitbgohio.org

Cambridge • *Cambridge/Guernsey County VCB* • Debbie Robinson; Exec. Dir.; 627 Wheeling Ave., Ste. 200; 43725; Guernsey; P 40,792; (740) 432-2022; (800) 933-5480; Fax (740) 432-5976; info@VisitGuernseyCounty.com; www.VisitGuernseyCounty.com

Canton • *Canton-Stark County CVB* • John Kiste; Exec. Dir.; 222 Market Ave. N.; 44702; Stark; P 379,000; (330) 454-1439; (800) 552-6051; Fax (330) 456-3600; events@visitcantonstark.com; www.visitcantonstark.com

Chillicothe • *Ross-Chillicothe CVB* • Kyrsten Vogel; Exec. Dir.; 45 E. Main St.; 45601; Ross; P 75,000; (740) 702-7677; (800) 413-4118; Fax (740) 702-2727; kyrsten@visitchillicotheohio.com; www.visitchillicotheohio.com

Cincinnati • *Cincinnati USA Conv. & Visitors Bur.* • Dan Lincoln; Pres./CEO; 525 Vine St., Ste. 1500; 45202; Hamilton; P 1,900,000; (513) 621-2142; (800) 543-2613; Fax (513) 621-5020; dlincoln@cincyusa.com; www.cincyusa.com

Circleville • *Pickaway County Welcome Center & Visitors Bur.* • Charlie Jackson; Exec. Dir.; 325 W. Main St.; 43113; Pickaway; P 52,000; (740) 474-3636; (888) 770-PICK; Fax (740) 477-6800; cjackson@pickaway.com; www.pickaway.com

Cleveland • *Destination Cleveland* • David Gilbert; Pres./CEO; 334 Euclid Ave.; 44114; Cuyahoga; P 4,000,000; (800) 321-1001; cleconcierge@destinationcle.org; www.thisiscleveland.com

Columbus • *Experience Columbus* • Paul D. Astleford; Pres./CEO; 277 W. Nationwide Blvd., Ste. 125; 43215; Franklin; P 1,600,000; (614) 221-6623; (800) 354-2657; Fax (614) 221-5618; visitorinfo@experiencecolumbus.com; www.experiencecolumbus.com

Coshocton • *Coshocton County CVB* • Jan Myers; Dir.; 432 N. Whitewoman St.; 43812; Coshocton; P 37,000; (740) 622-4877; (800) 338-4724; director@visitcoshocton.com; www.visitcoshocton.com

Dayton • *Dayton CVB* • Jacquelyn Y. Powell; Pres./CEO; 22 E. Fifth St., Chamber Plz., Ste. 100-A; 45402; Montgomery; P 780,000; (937) 226-8211; (800) 221-8235; Fax (937) 226-8294; jypowell@daytoncvb.net; www.daytoncvb.com

Delaware • *Delaware County CVB* • Debbie Shatzer; Exec. Dir.; 34 S. Sandusky; 43015; Delaware; P 174,200; (740) 368-4748; (888) DEL-OHIO; Fax (740) 369-9277; info@visitdelohio.com; www.visitdelohio.com

Findlay • *Hancock County CVB* • Angela Crist; Exec. Dir.; 123 E. Main Cross St.; 45840; Hancock; P 75,000; (419) 422-3315; (800) 424-3315; Fax (419) 422-9508; info@visitfindlay.com; www.visitfindlay.com

Fremont • *Fremont/Sandusky County CVB* • Peggy Courtney; Exec. Dir.; 712 North St., Ste. 102; 43420; Sandusky; P 61,000; (419) 332-4470; (800) 255-8070; Fax (419) 332-4359; info@sanduskycounty.org; www.sanduskycounty.org

Hamilton • *Hamilton Welcome Center* • Mark Hecquet; Exec. Dir.; One High St.; 45011; Butler; P 62,500; (513) 844-8080; (800) 311-5353; Fax (513) 844-8090; mhecquet@gettothebc.com; www.gettothebc.com

Heath • *Licking County CVB* • Susan Fryer; Exec. Dir.; 455 Hebron Rd.; 43056; Licking; P 135,800; (740) 345-8224; (800) 589-8224; Fax (740) 345-4403; sfryer@lccvb.com; www.lccvb.com

Hillsboro • *Visitors Bur. of Highland County* • Bob Lambert; Dir.; P.O. Box 1769; 45133; Highland; P 41,000; (937) 402-4347; Fax (937) 393-2697; visithighlandcounty@yahoo.com; www.highlandcounty.com

Lima • *Lima/Allen County CVB* • Christine Pleva; Exec. Dir.; 144 S. Main St., Ste. 101; 45801; Allen; P 106,000; (419) 222-6075; Fax (419) 222-0134; info@lima-allencvb.com; www.lima-allencvb.com

Mansfield • *Mansfield & Richland County CVB* • Lee M. Tasseff; Pres.; 124 N. Main St.; 44902; Richland; P 124,500; (419) 525-1300; (800) 642-8282; Fax (419) 524-7722; ltasseff@mansfieldtourism.com; www.mansfieldtourism.com

Marietta • *Marietta/Washington County CVB* • Jeri Knowlton; Exec. Dir.; 119 Greene St.; 45750; Washington; P 62,000; (740) 373-5178; (800) 288-2577; Fax (740) 376-2911; executivedirector@mariettaohio.org; www.mariettaohio.org

Marion • *Marion Area CVB* • Mark Holbrook; Exec. Dir.; 1713 Marion-Mount Gilead Rd., Ste. 110; 43302; Marion; P 67,000; (740) 389-9770; (800) 371-6688; Fax (740) 725-9295; info@visitmarionohio.com; www.visitmarionohio.com

Marysville • *Union County CVB* • Tina Knotts; Chamber & Tourism Dir.; 227 E. Fifth St.; 43040; Union; P 53,000; (937) 642-6279; (800) 642-0087; Fax (937) 644-0422; tknotts@unioncounty.org; www.unioncounty.org

McConnelsville • *Morgan County CVB* • Shayna Roberts; Dir.; 21 W. Main St.; 43756; Morgan; P 15,100; (740) 962-3200; Fax (740) 962-3516; visitmorgancounty@gmail.com; www.visitmorgancountyohio.com

Medina • *Medina County CVB* • Daniel D. Hostetler III; Exec. Dir.; 32 Public Sq.; 44256; Medina; P 175,000; (330) 722-5502; (800) 860-2943; Fax (330) 723-4713; info@visitmedinacounty.com; www.visitmedinacounty.com

Mount Vernon • *Knox County CVB* • Mr. Pat Crow; Dir.; 107 S. Main St.; 43050; Knox; P 55,000; (740) 392-6102; (800) 837-5282; Fax (740) 392-7840; pcrow@visitknoxohio.org; www.visitknoxohio.org

North Ridgeville • *North Ridgeville Visitors Bur.* • Dayle Noll; Pres./CEO; 34845 Lorain Rd.; 44039; Lorain; P 31,000; (440) 327-3737; Fax (440) 327-1474; nrvisbur@nrchamber.com; www.nrchamber.com

Norwalk • *Huron County Visitors Bur.* • Melissa James; Exec. Dir.; 10 W. Main St.; 44857; Huron; P 60,000; (419) 668-4155; (877) 668-4155; visit@huroncountyohio.com; www.VisitHuronCounty.com

Pomeroy • *Meigs County Tourism* • Luke Ortman; Tourism Dir.; 238 W. Main St.; 45769; Meigs; P 25,000; (740) 992-2239; (877) MEIGS-CO; Fax (740) 992-7942; luke@meigscountychamber.com; www.meigscountytourism.com

Port Clinton • *Lake Erie Shores & Islands Welcome Center - West* • Larry Fletcher; Exec. Dir.; 770 S.E. Catawba Rd.; 43452; Ottawa; P 40,000; (419) 734-4386; (800) 441-1271; Fax (419) 734-9798; tourism@lake-erie.com; www.shoresandislands.com

Saint Marys • *Auglaize & Mercer Counties CVB* • Donna Grube; Exec. Dir.; 900 Edgewater Dr.; 45885; Auglaize; P 85,000; (419) 394-1294; (800) 860-4726; Fax (419) 394-1642; info@seemore.org; www.seemore.org

C & VB

Sandusky • *Lake Erie Shores & Islands Welcome Center - East* • Larry Fletcher; Pres.; 4424 Milan Rd., Ste. A; 44870; Erie; P 77,000; (419) 625-2984; (800) 255-3743; Fax (419) 625-5009; info@shoresandislands.com; www.shoresandislands.com

Sidney • *Sidney Visitors Bur.* • Jeff Raible; Exec. Dir.; 101 South Ohio Ave., Flr. 2; 45365; Shelby; P 21,000; (937) 492-9122; (866) 892-9122; Fax (937) 498-2472; info@visitsidneyshelby.com; www.visitsidneyshelby.com

South Point • *Greater Lawrence County Area CVB* • Viviane Khounlavong-Vallance; Dir.; 216 Collins Ave.; P.O. Box 488; 45680; Lawrence; P 62,450; (740) 377-4550; (800) 408-1334; Fax (740) 377-2091; viviane@ledcorp.org; www.lawrencecountyohio.org

Springfield • *Greater Springfield CVB* • Christopher Schutte; Dir.; 20 S. Limestone St., Ste. 100; 45502; Clark; P 136,000; (937) 325-7621; cschutte@greaterspringfield.com; www.visitspringfieldohio.com

Tiffin • *Destination Seneca County* • John Detwiler; Exec. Dir.; 19 W. Market St., Ste. C; 44883; Seneca; P 57,000; (567) 220-6387; info@destinationsenecacounty.org; www.destinationsenecacounty.org

Toledo • *Destination Toledo Inc.* • Richard Nachazel; Pres.; 401 Jefferson Ave.; 43604; Lucas; P 300,000; (419) 321-6404; (800) 243-4667; Fax (419) 255-7731; rnachazel@doToledo.org; www.dotoledo.org

Upper Sandusky • *Wyandot County Visitors Bur.* • Sara Lou Binau; Exec. Dir.; 108 E. Wyandot Ave.; P.O. Box 357; 43351; Wyandot; P 22,000; (419) 294-3556; (419) 294-8401; wyandotcovb@udata.com; www.visitwyandotcounty.com

Van Wert • *Van Wert County CVB* • Larry Lee; Dir.; 136 E. Main St.; 45891; Van Wert; P 28,000; (419) 238-9378; (877) 989-2282; Fax (419) 238-4589; info@visitvanwert.org; www.visitvanwert.org

Washington Court House • *Fayette County Travel & Tourism Bur.* • Jolinda VanDyke; Exec. Dir.; 101 E. East St.; 43160; Fayette; P 32,000; (740) 335-8008; (800) 479-7797; jolinda@fayettecountyohio.com; www.fayettecountyohio.com

Waverly • *Pike County CVB* • Sharon Manson; Exec. Dir.; 126 W. Second St.; P.O. Box 134; 45690; Pike; P 27,695; (740) 947-9650; Fax (740) 947-7716; sharon@piketravel.com; www.piketravel.com

West Chester • *Butler County Visitors Bur.* • Mark Hecquet; Exec. Dir.; 8750 Union Centre Blvd.; 45069; Butler; P 369,000; (515) 860-4194; (888) 462-2282; Fax (515) 860-4195; mhecquet@gettothebc.com; www.gettothebc.com

West Union • *Adams County Travel & Visitors Bur.* • Tom Cross; Exec. Dir.; 509 E. Main St.; P.O. Box 577; 45693; Adams; P 28,500; (937) 544-5639; (877) 232-6764; info@adamscountytravel.org; www.adamscountytravel.org

Wooster • *Wayne County CVB* • Martha Starkey; Exec. Dir.; 428 W. Liberty St.; 44691; Wayne; P 111,564; (330) 264-1800; (800) 362-6474; Fax (330) 264-1141; info@wccvb.com; www.wccvb.com

Zanesville • *Zanesville-Muskingum County CVB* • Kelly Ashby; Dir.; 205 N. Fifth St.; 43701; Muskingum; P 83,388; (740) 455-8282; (800) 743-2303; Fax (740) 454-2963; kashby@zmchamber.com; www.visitzanesville.com

Oklahoma

Ardmore • *Ardmore Tourism Auth.* • Mita Bates; Pres.; 410 W. Main St.; 73401; Carter; P 35,000; (580) 223-7765; Fax (580) 223-7825; mbates@ardmore.org; www.ardmore.org

Bartlesville • *Bartlesville CVB* • Maria Gus; Exec. Dir.; 201 S.W. Keeler Ave.; 74003; Osage & Washington; P 36,000; (918) 336-8709; (800) 364-8708; Fax (918) 337-0216; cvbwebsite@bartlesville.com; www.visitbartlesville.com

Claremore • *Claremore CVB* • Tanya Andrews; Exec. Dir.; 400 Veterans Pkwy.; 74017; Rogers; P 17,500; (918) 341-8688; Fax (918) 341-7275; tanya@visitclaremore.org; www.visitclaremore.org

Duncan • *Duncan CVB* • Lois Dawn Jones; Exec. Dir.; 800 Chisholm Trail Pkwy.; P.O. Box 981; 73534; Stephens; P 25,000; (580) 252-2900; (800) 782-7167; Fax (580) 252-3799; tourism@simmonscenter.com; www.visitduncan.org

Edmond • *Edmond CVB* • Cathy Williams-White; Dir.; 1030 S. Bryant; P.O. Box 2970; 73083; Oklahoma; P 86,000; (405) 341-4344; (405) 216-7781; Fax (405) 216-7783; cwwhite@visitedmondok.com; www.visitedmondok.com

El Reno • *El Reno CVB* • Gene Stroman; Dir.; 110 S. Bickford Ave.; 73036; Canadian; P 16,212; (405) 262-8687; (888) 535-7366; Fax (405) 262-4637; gstroman@elrenotourism.com; www.elrenotourism.org

Guthrie • *Guthrie CVB* • Mary Coffin; Pres./CEO; 212 W. Oklahoma Ave.; 73044; Logan; P 38,000; (405) 282-1947; (800) 299-1889; Fax (405) 282-0061; info@guthrieok.com; www.guthrieok.com

Guymon • *Guymon Conv. & Tourism Dept.* • Miranda Gilbert; 219 N.W. 4th St.; 73942; Texas; P 14,000; (580) 338-5838; Fax (580) 338-0478; events@guymonok.org; www.guymonok.org

McAlester • *City of McAlester Tourism Dept.* • Jerry Lynn Wilson; Dir.; P.O. Box 578; 74502; Pittsburg; P 32,000; (918) 420-3976; Fax (918) 423-1092; tourism@cityofmcalester.com; www.cityofmcalester.com

Miami • *Miami CVB* • Amanda Davis; Exec. Dir.; 101 N. Main; 74355; Ottawa; P 14,000; (918) 542-4435; Fax (918) 542-4546; adavis@miamiokla.net; www.visitmiamiok.com

Muskogee • *Greater Muskogee Area C/C & Tourism* • Treasure McKenzie; Pres./CEO; 310 W. Broadway; P.O. Box 797; 74402; Muskogee; P 40,000; (918) 682-2401; (866) 381-6543; Fax (918) 682-2403; treasure@muskogeechamber.org; www.visitmuskogee.com

Norman • *Norman CVB* • Dan Schemm; Exec. Dir.; 309 E. Main St.; 73069; Cleveland; P 111,000; (405) 366-8095; (800) 767-7260; Fax (405) 366-8096; lacy@visitnorman.com; www.visitnorman.com

Oklahoma City • *Oklahoma City CVB* • Mike Carrier; Pres.; 123 Park Ave.; 73102; Oklahoma; P 1,300,000; (405) 297-8912; (800) 225-5652; Fax (405) 297-8888; contact@visitokc.com; www.visitokc.com

Okmulgee • *Okmulgee Tourism* • Nolan Crowley; Dir.; 112 N. Morton; 74447; Okmulgee; P 13,000; (918) 758-1015; Fax (918) 756-6441; okmulgeemainstreet@sbcglobal.net; www.okmulgeeonline.com

Ponca City • *Ponca City Tourism Bur.* • Crystal Vickford; Coord.; 420 E. Grand Ave.; P.O. Box 1109; 74602; Kay & Osage; P 26,000; (580) 763-8092; (866) 763-8092; Fax (580) 765-2798; info@poncacitytourism.com; www.poncacitytourism.com

Shawnee • *Greater Shawnee Area CVB* • Kinlee Farris; Exec. Dir.; 131 N. Bell; 74801; Pottawatomie; P 30,562; (405) 275-9780; (888) 404-9633; Fax (405) 275-9851; info@visitshawnee.com; www.visitshawnee.com

Stillwater • *Visit Stillwater* • Cristy Morrison; Pres./CEO; 2617 W. 6th Ave.; 74074; Payne; P 50,000; (405) 743-3697; Fax (405) 372-0765; cristy@visitstillwater.org; www.VisitStillwaterOK.org

Tahlequah • *Tahlequah Area CVB • Kate Kelly; Tourism Dir.; 123 E. Delaware St.; 74464; Cherokee; P 46,000; (918) 456-3742; (800) 456-4860; Fax (918) 456-3751; info@tahlequahchamber.com; www.tourtahlequah.com

Tulsa • *VisitTulsa • Ray Hoyt; Sr. V.P.; Williams Center Tower II; Two W. Second St., Ste. 150; 74103; Osage, Rogers, Tulsa & Wagoner; P 920,000; (918) 585-1201; Fax (918) 592-6244; paulasanders@tulsachamber.com; www.visittulsa.com

Oregon

Albany • *Albany Visitors Assn. • Jimmie Lucht; Exec. Dir.; 110 3rd Ave. S.E.; P.O. Box 965; 97321; Linn; P 50,000; (541) 928-0911; (800) 526-2256; Fax (541) 926-1500; info@albanyvisitors.com; www.albanyvisitors.com

Ashland • *Ashland CVB • Sandra Slattery; Exec. Dir.; 110 E. Main St.; P.O. Box 1360; 97520; Jackson; P 21,000; (541) 482-3486; Fax (541) 482-2350; katharine@ashlandchamber.com; www.ashlandchamber.com

Aurora • *Aurora Colony Visitors Assn. • Barbara Johnson; P.O. Box 86; 97002; Marion; P 702; (503) 939-0312; info@auroracolony.com; www.auroracolony.com

Beaverton • *Washington County Visitors Assn. • Carolyn McCormick; Pres./CEO; 12725 S.W. Millikan Way, Ste. 210; 97005; Washington; P 500,000; (503) 644-5555; (800) 537-3149; Fax (503) 644-9784; info@wcva.org; tualatinvalley.org

Bend • *Visit Bend • Valerie Warren; V.P. of Op.; 750 N.W. Lava Rd., Ste. 160; 97703; Deschutes; P 81,000; (541) 382-8048; (877) 245-8484; Fax (541) 382-8568; info@visitbend.com; www.visitbend.com

Charleston • *Charleston Visitor Center • 91141 Cape Arago Hwy.; 97420; Coos; P 5,000; (541) 888-2311

Corvallis • *Visit Corvallis • Mary Pat Parker; Exec. Dir.; 420 N.W. 2nd St.; 97330; Benton; P 54,800; (541) 757-1544; (800) 334-8118; Fax (541) 753-2664; info@visitcorvallis.com; www.visitcorvallis.com

Eugene • *Travel Lane County • Kari Westlund; Pres./CEO; 754 Olive St.; P.O. Box 10286; 97440; Lane; P 351,800; (541) 484-5307; (800) 547-5445; Fax (541) 343-6335; info@eugenecascadescoast.org; www.eugenecascadescoast.org

Gold Beach • *Gold Beach Visitors Center • Jodie Fritts; City Mgr.; 94080 Shirley Ln.; P.O. Box 375; 97444; Curry; P 2,200; (541) 247-7526; (800) 525-2334; Fax (541) 247-0187; visit@goldbeach.org; www.goldbeach.org

Grants Pass • *Grants Pass VCB • Kerrie Walters; Mktg. Coord.; 1995 N.W. Vine St.; 97526; Josephine; P 81,618; (541) 476-5510; Fax (541) 476-9574; vcb@visitgrantspass.org; www.visitgrantspass.org

Klamath Falls • *Discover Klamath • Jim Chadderdon; Exec. Dir.; 205 Riverside Dr., Ste. B; 97601; Klamath; P 42,000; (541) 882-1501; (800) 445-6728; Fax (541) 273-2017; visit@discoverklamath.com; www.meetmeinklamath.com

La Grande • *Union County C/C & Visitors Info. Center • 207 Depot St.; 97850; Union; P 25,000; (541) 963-8588; (800) 848-9969; Fax (541) 963-3936; info@unioncountychamber.org; www.unioncountychamber.org

Lincoln City • *Lincoln City Visitor & Conv. Bur. • Sandy Pfass; Exec. Dir.; 801 S.W. Hwy. 101, Ste. 401; 97367; Lincoln; P 7,500; (541) 996-1274; (800) 452-2151; Fax (541) 994-2408; events@lincolncity.org; www.oregoncoast.org

Medford • *Travel Medford • Anne Jenkins; Sr. V.P.; 101 E. 8th St.; 97501; Jackson; P 82,000; (541)779-4847; Fax (541) 776-4808; annj@travelmedford.org; www.travelmedford.orgg

North Bend • *North Bend Visitor Info. Center • Barbara Dunham; Mgr.; 1380 Sherman Ave. (Hwy. 101); 97459; Coos; P 10,000; (541) 756-4613; (800) 472-9176; Fax (541) 756-8527; bdunham@uci.net; www.northbendcity.org

Ontario • *Ontario Visitors & Conv. Bur. • John Breidenbach; Pres./CEO; 876 S.W. 4th Ave.; 97914; Malheur; P 12,000; (541) 889-8012; (866) 989-8012; Fax (541) 889-8331; info@ontariochamber.com; www.ontariochamber.com

Portland • *Travel Portland • Jeff Miller; Pres.; 100 S.W. Main St., Ste. 1100; 97204; Clackamas, Multnomah & Washington; P 1,950,000; (503) 275-9750; (800) 962-3700; Fax (503) 275-9284; visitorinfo@travelportland.com; www.travelportland.com

Portland • *African American Conv. & Tourism-A.C.T. • Roy Jay; Natl. Pres./CEO; P.O. Box 5488; 97228; Clackamas, Multnomah & Washington; (800) 909-2882; Fax (503) 698-2896; ACT.NOW@USA.NET; www.blackconventions.com

Roseburg • *Roseburg Area C/C & Roseburg Visitor Center • Debbie Fromdahl; Pres./CEO; 410 S.E. Spruce St.; P.O. Box 1262; 97470; Douglas; P 21,500; (541) 672-9731; (800) 440-9584; Fax (541) 673-7868; info@visitroseburg.com; www.visitroseburg.com

Salem • *Travel Salem • Angie Morris; CEO; 181 High St. N.E.; 97301; Marion; P 154,510; (503) 581-4325; (800) 874-7012; Fax (503) 581-4540; information@travelsalem.com; www.travelsalem.com

Seaside • *Seaside Civic & Conv. Center • Russell Vandenberg; Gen. Mgr.; 415 First Ave.; 97138; Clatsop; P 7,000; (503) 738-8585; (800) 394-3303; Fax (503) 738-0198; sales@seasideconvention.com; www.seasideconvention.com

Seaside • *Seaside Visitors Bur. • Jon Rahl; Dir. of Tourism Mktg.; 7 N. Roosevelt; 989 Broadway; 97138; Clatsop; P 6,500; (503) 738-3097; (888) 306-2326; Fax (503) 717-8299; info@seasideor.com; www.seasideor.com

Winston • *Winston-Dillard Area Visitors Bur. • Sherri Standley; Visitors Center Coord.; 30 N.W. Glenhart; P.O. Box 68; 97496; Douglas; P 10,000; (541) 679-0118; info@winstonchamber.org; www.winstonchamber.org

Pennsylvania

Allentown • *Discover Lehigh Valley • Michael Stershic; Pres.; 840 W. Hamilton St., Ste. 200; 18101; Northampton; P 600,000; (610) 882-9200; Fax (610) 882-0343; info@discoverlehighvalley.com; www.discoverlehighvalley.com

Altoona • *Allegheny Mountains CVB • Mark Ickes; Exec. Dir.; One Convention Center Dr.; 16602; Blair; P 54,000; (814) 943-4183; (800) 84-ALTOONA; Fax (814) 943-8094; info@amcvb.com; www.alleghenymountains.com

Beaver Falls • *Beaver County Rec. & Tourism Dept. • Tim Ishman; Dir.; 121 Bradys Run Rd.; 15010; Beaver; P 170,600; (800) 342-8192; Fax (724) 770-2063; klaurito@beavercountypa.gov; www.visitbeavercounty.com

Bedford • *Bedford County Visitors Bur. • Dennis Tice; Exec. Dir.; 131 S. Juliana St.; 15522; Bedford; P 49,800; (814) 623-1771; (800) 765-3331; bccvb@bedford.net; www.visitbedfordcounty.com

Bensalem • *Bucks County Conf. & Visitors Bur.* • Jerry Lepping; Exec. Dir.; 3207 Street Rd.; 19020; Bucks; P 625,300; (215) 639-0300; (800) 836-2825; Fax (215) 642-3277; visitorservices@visitbuckscounty.com; www.visitbuckscounty.com

Bloomsburg • *Columbia-Montour Visitors Bur.* • David Kurecian; Exec. Dir.; 121 Papermill Rd.; 17815; Columbia & Montour; P 85,600; (570) 784-8279; (800) 847-4810; Fax (570) 784-1166; itour@cmvb.com; www.itourcolumbiamontour.com

Bradford • *Allegheny Natl. Forest Visitors Bur.* • Linda Devlin; Exec. Dir.; 80 E. Corydon St.; P.O. Box 371; 16701; McKean; P 46,500; (800) 473-9370; Fax (814) 368-9370; info@visitanf.com; www.visitanf.com

Brookville • *NW PA Great Outdoors Visitors Bur.* • John Straitiff; Exec. Dir.; 2801 Maplevale Rd.; 15825; Jefferson; P 500,000; (814) 849-5197; (800) 348-9393; Fax (814) 849-1969; info@visitpago.com; www.visitpago.com

Canonsburg • *Washington County Tourism Promo. Agency* • Jeff Kotula; Dir.; 375 Southpointe Blvd., Ste. 240; 15317; Washington; P 208,000; (724) 225-3010; (866) WASH-WOW; Fax (724) 228-7337; info@visitwashingtoncountypa.com; www.visitwashingtoncountypa.com

Carlisle • *see Harrisburg*

Coudersport • *Potter County Visitors Assn.* • David Brooks; Exec. Dir.; P.O. Box 245; 16915; Potter; P 18,000; (814) 274-3365; (888) POTTER-2; Fax (814) 274-4334; potter@penn.com; www.visitpottercounty.com

Danville • *Columbia-Montour Visitors Bur.* • David Kurecian; Exec. Dir.; 316 Mill St., Ste. 2; 17821; Montour; P 90,000; (570) 284-4455; (800) 847-4810; Fax (570) 284-4456; itour@cmvb.com; www.itourcolumbiamontour.com

Erie • *VisitErie* • John F. Oliver; Pres.; 208 E. Bayfront Pkwy., Ste. 103; 16507; Erie; P 105,000; (814) 454-1000; (800) 524-ERIE; Fax (814) 459-0241; info@visiterie.com; www.visiterie.com

Gettysburg • *Destination Gettysburg* • Norris Flowers; Pres.; 571 W. Middle St.; 17325; Adams; P 101,400; (717) 334-6274; (800) 337-5015; Fax (717) 334-1166; info@destinationgettysburg.com; www.destinationgettysburg.com

Harrisburg • *Hershey-Harrisburg Reg. Visitors Bur.* • Mary Smith; Pres./CEO; 3211 N. Front St., Ste. 301A; 17110; Dauphin; (717) 231-7788; (877) 727-8573; Fax (717) 231-2808; allison@hersheyharrisburg.org; www.visithersheyharrisburg.org

Hershey • *see Harrisburg*

Hesston • *Raystown Lake Reg. & Huntingdon County Visitors Bur.* • Matthew Price; Exec. Dir.; 6993 Seven Points Rd., Ste. 2; 16647; Huntingdon; P 44,000; (814) 658-0060; (888) RAYSTOWN; Fax (814) 658-0068; info@raystown.org; www.raystown.org

Indiana • *Indiana County Tourist Bur.* • Denise Liggett; Exec. Dir.; 2334 Oakland Ave., Ste. 68; 15701; Indiana; P 88,900; (724) 463-7505; (877) 746-3426; Fax (724) 465-3819; info@visitindianacountypa.org; www.visitindianacountypa.org

Johnstown • *Greater Johnstown/Cambria County CVB* • Lisa M. Rager; Exec. Dir.; 111 Roosevelt Blvd., Ste. A; 15906; Cambria; P 143,679; (814) 536-7993; (800) 237-8590; Fax (814) 539-3370; jstcvb@visitjohnstownpa.com; www.visitjohnstownpa.com

Kennett Square • *Chester County Conf. & Visitors Bur.* • Susan Hamley; Exec. Dir.; 300 Greenwood Rd.; 19348; Chester; P 499,000; (484) 770-8550; (800) 566-0109; Fax (484) 770-8557; info@brandywinevalley.com; www.brandywinevalley.com

King of Prussia • *Valley Forge CVB* • Paul Decker; Pres.; 1000 1st Ave., Ste. 101; 19406; Montgomery; P 140,000; (610) 834-1550; (800) 441-3549; Fax (610) 834-0202; info@valleyforge.org; www.valleyforge.org

Kittanning • *Armstrong County Tourist Bur.* • Kevin S. Andrews; Dir. of Tourism; 125 Market St.; 16201; Armstrong; P 69,000; (724) 543-4003; (888) 265-9954; Fax (724) 545-3119; touristbur@co.armstrong.pa.us; www.armstrongcounty.com

Lancaster • *Pennsylvania Dutch CVB* • Christopher Barrett; Pres.; 501 Greenfield Rd.; 17601; Lancaster; P 579,000; (717) 299-8901; (800) PADUTCH; Fax (717) 299-0470; info@padutchcountry.com; www.padutchcountry.com

Lewisburg • *Susquehanna River Valley Visitors Bur.* • Andrew Miller; Exec. Dir.; 81 Hafer Rd.; 17837; Union; P 45,000; (570) 524-7234; (800) 525-7320; Fax (570) 524-7282; info@visitcentralpa.org; www.visitcentralpa.org

Lewistown • *Juniata River Valley Visitors Bur.* • Jim Tunall; Pres./Exec. Dir.; Historic Courthouse; One W. Market St., Ste. 103; 17044; Mifflin; P 68,463; (717) 248-6713; (877) 568-9739; Fax (717) 248-6714; jrvvb@juniatarivervalley.org; www.juniatarivervalley.org

Ligonier • *Laurel Highlands Visitors Bur.* • Ronald Virag; Exec. Dir.; 120 E. Main St., 2nd Flr.; 15658; Fayette, Somerset & Westmoreland; P 579,517; (724) 238-5661; (800) 333-5661; Fax (724) 238-3673; rroehrig@laurelhighlands.org; www.laurelhighlands.org

Lock Haven • *Clinton County Eco. Partnership* • Julie Brennan; Chamber/Tourism Dir.; 212 N. Jay St.; P.O. Box 506; 17745; Clinton; P 40,000; (570) 748-5782; (888) 388-6991; Fax (570) 893-0433; tourismdirector@kcnet.org; www.clintoncountyinfo.com

Meadville • *Crawford County CVB* • Juanita Hampton; Exec. Dir.; 16709 Conneaut Lake Rd.; 16335; Crawford; P 88,800; (814) 333-1258; (800) 332-2338; Fax (814) 333-9032; welcome@visitcrawford.org; www.visitcrawford.org

Media • *Brandywine Conf. & Visitors Bur.* • Tore Fiore; Exec. Dir.; 1501 N. Providence Rd.; 19063; Delaware; P 559,000; (610) 565-3679; (800) 343-3983; Fax (610) 361-0459; tfiore@brandywinecvb.org; www.brandywinecountry.org

Monroeville • *VisitMonroeville* • Donna Bower; Exec. Dir.; 209 Mall Blvd.; 15146; Allegheny; P 30,000; (412) 856-7422; Fax (412) 856-6979; info@visitmonroeville.com; www.visitmonroeville.com

Moosic • *Lackawanna County CVB* • Tracy Barone; Exec. Dir.; 99 Glenmaura National Blvd.; 18507; Lackawanna; P 214,400; (570) 963-6363; (800) 22-WELCOME; Fax (570) 963-6369; info@visitnepa.org; www.visitnepa.org

New Castle • *Lawrence County Tourist Promo. Agency* • JoAnn McBride; Exec. Dir.; 229 S. Jefferson St.; 16101; Lawrence; P 90,000; (724) 654-8408; Fax (724) 654-2044; info@visitlawrencecounty.com; www.visitlawrencecounty.com

Philadelphia • *Philadelphia CVB* • Jack Ferguson; Pres./CEO; 1700 Market St., Ste. 3000; 19103; Philadelphia; P 1,500,000; (215) 636-3300; Fax (215) 636-3327; info@philadelphiausa.travel; www.philadelphiausa.travel

Pittsburgh • *VisitPittsburgh* • Joseph McGrath; Pres./CEO; 120 Fifth Ave.; Fifth Ave. Pl., Ste. 2800; 15222; Allegheny; P 1,250,000; (412) 281-0482; (800) 359-0758; Fax (412) 644-5512; info@visitpittsburgh.com; www.visitpittsburgh.com

Plymouth Meeting • *see King of Prussia*

Pottsville • *Schuylkill County Visitors Bur.* • Regina Gargano; Exec. Dir.; Union Station Bldg.; One Progress Cir., Ste. 100; 17901; Schuylkill; P 148,300; (570) 622-7700; (800) 765-7282; Fax (570) 622-8035; tourism@schuylkill.org; www.schuylkill.org

Reading • *Greater Reading CVB* • Crystal Seitz; Pres.; 201 Washington St.; 19602; Berks; P 412,000; (610) 375-4085; (800) 443-6610; Fax (610) 375-9606; info@readingberkspa.com; www.readingberkspa.com

Sharon • *Mercer County CVB* • Peggy Mazyck; Exec. Dir.; 50 N. Water Ave.; 16146; Mercer; P 116,000; (724) 346-3771; Fax (724) 346-0575; mcpa@visitmercercountypa.com; www.visitmercercountypa.com

State College • *Central PA CVB* • Betsey Howell; Exec. Dir.; 800 E. Park Ave.; 16803; Centre; P 154,000; (814) 231-1400; (800) 358-5466; Fax (814) 231-8123; info@visitpennstate.org; www.visitpennstate.org

Stroudsburg • *Pocono Mountains Vacation Bur.* • Carl Wilgus; Exec. Dir.; 1004 Main St.; 18360; Monroe; P 172,000; (570) 421-5791; Fax (570) 421-6927; pocomts@poconos.org; www.800poconos.com

Tunkhannock • *Endless Mountains Visitors Bur.* • Jean Ruhf; Exec. Dir.; 5405 SR 6; 18657; Wyoming; P 145,091; (570) 836-5431; (800) 769-8999; Fax (570) 836-3927; jean@endlessmountains.org; www.endlessmountains.org

Warren • *Warren County Visitors Bur.* • Dave Sherman; Exec. Dir.; 22045 Rte. 6; 16365; Warren; P 40,000; (814) 726-1222; (800) 624-7802; Fax (814) 726-7266; info@wcvb.net; www.wcvb.net

Waynesburg • *Greene County Tourist Promomotion Agency* • JoAnne Marshall; Dir.; 19 S. Washington St.; Fort Jackson Bldg.; 15370; Greene; P 40,000; (724) 627-8687; (877) 280-TOUR; Fax (724) 627-8608; tourism@co.greene.pa.us; greenecountytourism.org

Wellsboro • *Tioga County Visitors Bur.* • Lori Copp; Exec. Dir.; 2053 Rte. 660; 16901; Tioga; P 40,000; (570) 724-0635; (888) TIOGA-28; Fax (570) 723-1016; tiogapa@epix.net; www.visittiogapa.com

Williamsport • *Lycoming County Visitors Bur.* • Jason Fink; Exec. Dir.; 102 W. Fourth St.; 17701; Lycoming; P 116,100; (570) 327-7700; (800) 358-9900; Fax (570) 321-1209; visitorinfo@williamsport.org; www.vacationpa.com

York • *York County CVB* • Anne Druck; Pres.; 60 East North St.; 17401; York; P 435,000; (717) 852-9675; (888) 858-9675; Fax (717) 854-5095; info@yorkpa.org; www.yorkpa.org

Zelienople • *Butler County Tourism & Conv. Bur.* • Jack Cohen; Exec. Dir.; 310 E. Grandview Ave.; 16063; Butler; P 184,000; (724) 234-4619; (866) 856-8444; Fax (724) 234-4643; visitors@visitbutlercounty.com; www.visitbutlercounty.com

Puerto Rico

San Juan • *Puerto Rico Conv. Bur.* • Edificio Ochoa; 500 Tanca, Ste. 402; 00902; P 4,000,000; (787) 725-2110; (800) 875-4765; Fax (787) 725-2133; info@meetpuertorico.com; www.meetpuertorico.com

Rhode Island

Newport • *Discover Newport* • Evan Smith; Pres./CEO; 23 America's Cup Ave.; 02840; Newport; P 25,000; (401) 849-8048; (800) 326-6030; Fax (401) 849-0291; info@gonewport.com; www.gonewport.com

Providence • *Providence Warwick CVB* • Martha Sheridan; Pres./CEO; 10 Memorial Blvd.; 02903; Providence; P 260,000; (401) 456-0200; (800) 233-1636; Fax (401) 351-2090; info@goprovidence.com; www.goprovidence.com

Warwick • *City of Warwick Dept. of Tourism, Culture & Dev.* • Warwick City Hall; 3275 Post Rd.; 02886; Kent; P 84,000; (401) 738-2000; (800) 492-7942; Fax (401) 732-7662; war.tour@warwickri.com; www.visitwarwickri.com

South Carolina

Charleston • *Charleston Area CVB* • Helen T. Hill; Exec. Dir.; 423 King St.; 29403; Charleston; P 350,200; (843) 853-8000; (800) 868-8118; Fax (843) 853-0444; info@explorecharleston.com; www.explorecharleston.com

Columbia • *Columbia Metropolitan CVB* • Ric Luber; Pres./CEO; 1101 Lincoln St.; P.O. Box 15; 29202; Richland; P 747,800; (803) 545-0000; (800) 264-4884; Fax (803) 545-0013; kjamieson@columbiaauthority.com; www.columbiacvb.com

Greenville • *VisitGreenvilleSC* • Chris Stone; Pres.; 148 River St., Ste. 222; 29601; Greenville; P 451,000; (864) 421-0000; (800) 351-7180; Fax (864) 421-0005; meet@visitgreenvillesc.com; www.visitgreenvillesc.com

Greenwood • *Greenwood Reg. Tourism & Visitors Bur.* • Kelly McWhorter; Exec. Dir.; 120 Main St., Federal Bldg.; P.O. Box 40; 29648; Greenwood; P 150,000; (864) 953-2466; (866) 493-8474; Fax (864) 953-2468; info@visitgreenwoodsc.com; www.visitgreenwoodsc.com

Hilton Head Island • *Hilton Head Island-Bluffton CVB* • William G. Miles; Pres./CEO; One Chamber Dr.; P.O. Box 5647; 29938; Beaufort; P 49,600; (843) 785-3673; Fax (843) 785-7110; info@hiltonheadisland.org; www.hiltonheadisland.org

Myrtle Beach • *Myrtle Beach Area CVB* • Dana Lilly; V.P.; 1200 N. Oak St.; P.O. Box 2115; 29578; Horry; P 269,300; (843) 626-7444; (800) 488-8998; Fax (843) 448-3010; info@visitmyrtlebeach.com; www.visitmyrtlebeach.com

North Myrtle Beach • *North Myrtle Beach CVB* • Marc Jordan; Pres./CEO; 1521 Hwy. 17 S.; P.O. Box 349; 29597; Horry; P 13,000; (843) 281-2662; Fax (843) 280-2930; info@northmyrtlebeachchamber.com; www.northmyrtlebeachchamber.com

Rock Hill • *Rock Hill/York County CVB* • Lisa Meadows; Exec. Dir.; 452 S. Anderson Rd.; P.O. Box 11377; 29731; York; P 226,100; (803) 329-5200; (888) 702-1320; Fax (803) 329-0145; lmeadows@visityorkcounty.com; www.visityorkcounty.com

Spartanburg • *Spartanburg CVB* • Chris Jennings; Exec. Dir.; 105 N. Pine St.; P.O. Box 1636; 29304; Spartanburg; P 284,300; (864) 594-5050; (800) 374-8326; Fax (864) 594-5052; aphillips@visitspartanburg.com; www.visitspartanburg.com

South Dakota

Aberdeen • *Aberdeen CVB* • Casey Weismantel; Exec. Dir.; 10 Railroad Ave. S.W.; P.O. Box 78; 57402; Brown; P 27,000; (605) 225-2414; (800) 645-3851; Fax (605) 225-3573; info@visitaberdeensd.com; www.visitaberdeensd.com

Brookings • *Brookings Area C/C & CVB* • Jennifer Johnson; Exec. Dir.; 414 Main Ave.; P.O. Box 431; 57006; Brookings; P 18,703; (605) 692-6125; (877) 750-7458; Fax (605) 697-8109; chamber@brookings.net; www.brookingssd.com

Huron • *Huron Chamber & Visitors Bur.* • Peggy Woolridge; Pres./CEO; 1725 Dakota Ave. S.; 57350; Beadle; P 13,000; (605) 352-0000; (800) 487-6673; Fax (605) 352-8321; cvb@huronsd.com; www.huronsd.com

Mitchell • *Mitchell CVB* • Katie Knutson; Dir.; 601 N. Main St.; P.O. Box 1026; 57301; Davison; P 18,741; (605) 996-6223; Fax (605) 996-8273; cvb@visitmitchell.com; www.visitmitchell.com

Pierre • *Pierre CVB* • Laura Schoen Carbonneau IOM; CEO; 800 W. Dakota Ave.; P.O. Box 548; 57501; Hughes; P 16,000; (605) 224-7361; (800) 962-2034; Fax (605) 224-6485; contactchamber@pierre.org; www.pierre.org

Rapid City • *Rapid City CVB* • Julie Schmitz Jensen; Exec. Dir./V.P.; 444 Mt. Rushmore Rd. N.; P. O. Box 747; 57709; Pennington; P 70,000; (605) 718-8484; (800) 487-3223; Fax (605) 348-9217; info@visitrapidcity.com; www.visitrapidcity.com

Sioux Falls • *Sioux Falls CVB* • Teri Schmidt; Exec. Dir.; 200 N. Phillips Ave., Ste. 102; 57104; Minnehaha; P 180,000; (605) 275-6060; (800) 333-2072; Fax (605) 338-0682; tschmidt@siouxfalls.com; www.visitsiouxfalls.com

Watertown • *Watertown CVB* • Julie Knutson; Exec. Dir.; 1 E. Kemp Ave.; P.O. Box 225; 57201; Codington; P 25,000; (605) 753-0282; Fax (605) 753-0394; cvb@visitwatertownsd.com; www.visitwatertownsd.com

Yankton • *Yankton CVB* • Kasi Haberman; Dir.; 803 E. 4th St.; 57078; Yankton; P 15,000; (800) 888-1460; (605) 665-3636; Fax (605) 665-7501; kasi@yanktonsd.com; www.visityanktonsd.com

Tennessee

Big Sandy • *Northwest Tennessee Tourism* • Gary Mason; Dir.; P.O. Box 127; 38221; Henry; P 250,000; (731) 593-0171; (866) 698-6386; Fax (731) 644-3051; info@kentuckylaketourism.com; www.kentuckylaketourism.com

Bristol • *see Bristol, VA*

Chattanooga • *Chattanooga Area CVB* • Bob Doak; Pres./CEO; 736 Market St., 18th Flr.; 37402; Hamilton; P 349,000; (423) 756-8687; (800) 322-3344; Fax (423) 265-1630; cindyd@chattanoogacvb.com; www.chattanoogafun.com

Clarksville • *Visit Clarksville* • Theresa Harrington; Exec. Dir.; 25 Jefferson St., Ste. 300; 37040; Montgomery; P 200,000; (931) 647-2331; (800) 530-2487; Fax (931) 645-1574; theresa@visitclarksvilletn.com; visitclarksvilletn.com

Cleveland • *Cleveland/Bradley CVB* • Melissa Woody; V.P.; 225 Keith St. S.W.; P.O. Box 2275; 37320; Bradley; P 99,000; (423) 472-6587; (800) 472-6588; Fax (423) 472-2019; info@clevelandchamber.com; www.visitclevelandtn.com

Columbia • *Maury County CVB* • Erin Jaggers; Exec. Dir.; 302 W. 7th St.; 38401; Maury; P 84,000; (931) 381-7176; (888) 852-1860; Fax (931) 375-4109; maurycvb@maurycounty-tn.gov; www.visitmaury.com

Cookeville • *Cookeville-Putnam County CVB* • Laura Canada; CVB Dir.; 1 W. First St.; 38501; Putnam; P 72,000; (931) 526-2211; (800) 264-5541; Fax (931) 526-4023; lcanada@cookevillechamber.com; www.mustseecookeville.com

Crossville • *Crossville-Cumberland County CVB* • Beth Alexander; Pres./CEO; 34 S. Main St.; 38555; Cumberland; P 60,000; (931) 484-8444; (877) 465-3861; Fax (931) 484-7511; thechamber@crossville-chamber.com; www.crossville-chamber.com

Eagleville • *see Murfreesboro*

Franklin • *Williamson County CVB* • Mark Shore; Exec. Dir.; 400 Main St., Ste. 200; 37064; Williamson; P 184,000; (615) 791-7554; (866) 253-9207; Fax (615) 550-2707; info@visitwilliamson.com; www.visitwilliamson.com

Gatlinburg • *Gatlinburg CVB* • Vicki Simms; Exec. Dir.; P.O. Box 527; 37738; Sevier; P 3,600; (865) 436-4178; Fax (865) 430-3876; info@gatlinburg.com; www.gatlinburg.com

Jackson • *Jackson Tennessee CVB* • Lori Nunnery CTTP TMP FEP; Exec. Dir.; 197 Auditorium St.; 38301; Madison; P 100,000; (731) 425-8333; (800) 498-4748; Fax (731) 424-4860; lnunnery@jacksontn.com; jacksontn.com/tourism/

Johnson City • *Johnson City CVB* • Brenda Whitson; Exec. Dir.; 603 E. Market St.; P.O. Box 180; 37605; Washington; P 126,000; (423) 461-8000; Fax (423) 461-8047; whitson@johnsoncitytnchamber.com; www.johnsoncitytnchamber.com

Kingsport • *Kingsport CVB* • Jud Teague; Exec. Dir.; 400 Clinchfield St., Ste. 100; 37660; Sullivan; P 50,000; (423) 392-8820; (800) 743-5282; Fax (423) 392-8833; jteague@visitkingsport.com; www.visitkingsport.com

Knoxville • *Knoxville Tourism & Sports Corp.* • Gloria Ray; Pres./CEO; 301 S. Gay St.; 37902; Knox; P 432,000; (865) 523-7263; (800) 727-8045; Fax (865) 522-3974; asebby@knoxville.org; www.knoxville.org

Lenoir City • *Loudon County Visitors Bur.* • Clayton Pangle; Dir.; 1075 Hwy. 321 N.; 37771; Loudon; P 49,000; (865) 986-6822; (888) 568-3662; Fax (865) 988-8959; cpangle@visitloudoncounty.com; www.visitloudoncounty.com

Memphis • *Memphis CVB* • Kevin Kane; Pres.; 47 Union Ave.; 38103; Shelby; P 1,100,000; (901) 543-5300; (800) 873-6282; Fax (901) 543-5350; kevinkane@memphistravel.com; www.memphistravel.com

Murfreesboro • *Rutherford County CVB* • Barbara Wolke; V.P.; 3050 Medical Center Pkwy.; 37129; Rutherford; P 298,700; (615) 278-2327; (615) 893-6565; Fax (615) 890-7600; info@rutherfordchamber.org; www.rutherfordchamber.org

Murfreesboro • *Rutherford County CVB* • Mona Herring; V.P.; 3050 Medical Center Pkwy.; 37129; Rutherford; P 298,700; (615) 893-6565; (800) 716-7560; Fax (615) 890-7600; info@rutherfordchamber.org; www.rutherfordchamber.org

Nashville • *Nashville CVB* • Butch Spyridon; Pres.; 1 Nashville Pl.; 150 4th Ave. N., Ste. G-250; 37219; Davidson; P 640,000; (615) 259-4730; (800) 657-6910; Fax (615) 259-4717; nashcvc@visitmusiccity.com; www.visitmusiccity.com

Oak Ridge • *Oak Ridge CVB* • 1400 Oak Ridge Tpk.; 37830; Anderson; P 29,000; (865) 482-7821; (800) 887-3429; Fax (865) 481-3543; info@oakridgevisitor.com; www.oakridgevisitor.com

Pigeon Forge • *City of Pigeon Forge Dept. of Tourism* • Leon Downey; Exec. Dir.; 135 Jake Thomas Rd.; P.O. Box 1390; 37868; Sevier; P 6,000; (865) 453-8574; (800) 251-9100; Fax (865) 429-7362; info@mypigeonforge.com; www.mypigeonforge.com

Pulaski • *Giles County Tourism* • Joyce Woodard; Dir.; 110 North 2nd St.; 38478; Giles; P 30,000; (931) 424-4044; Fax (931) 363-7279; tourism@gilescountychamber.com; www.gilescountychamber.com

Rugby • *Historic Rugby* • Cheryl Cribbet; Exec. Dir.; 5517 Rugby Hwy.; P.O. Box 8; 37733; Morgan; P 85; (423) 628-2441; (888) 214-3400; Fax (423) 628-2266; historicrugby@highland.net; www.historicrugby.org

Savannah • *Hardin County CVB* • Beth Pippin; Tourism Dir.; 495 Main St.; 38372; Hardin; P 30,000; (731) 925-8181; (800) 552-FUNN; Fax (731) 925-6987; info@tourhardincounty.org; www.tourhardincounty.org

Smyrna • *Rutherford County CVB* • Mona Herring; V.P.; 315 S. Lowry St.; 37167; Rutherford; P 298,700; (615) 893-6565; (800) 716-7560; Fax (615) 890-7600; info@rutherfordchamber.org; www.rutherfordchamber.org

Townsend • *Smoky Mountain Tourism Dev. Auth.* • Bryan T. Daniels CEcD CCE IOM; Pres./CEO; 7906 E. Lamar Alexander Pkwy.; 37882; Blount; P 126,339; (865) 448-6134; (800) 525-6834; Fax (865) 448-9806; info@smokymountains.org; www.smokymountains.org

Townsend • *see Maryville*

Texas

Abilene • *Abilene CVB* • Nanci M. Liles; Exec. Dir.; 1101 N. First; 79601; Taylor; P 125,000; (325) 676-2556; (800) 727-7704; Fax (325) 676-1630; info@abilenevisitors.com; www.abilenevisitors.com

Amarillo • *Amarillo Conv. & Visitor Cncl.* • Jerry Holt; V.P.; 1000 S. Polk St.; 79101; Potter; P 190,000; (806) 374-1497; (800) 692-1338; Fax (806) 373-3909; klynn@visitamarillotx.com; www.visitamarillotx.com

Arlington • *Arlington CVB* • Jay Burress; Pres./CEO; 1905 E. Randol Mill Rd.; 76011; Tarrant; P 370,000; (817) 265-7721; (800) 433-5374; Fax (817) 265-5640; visitinfo@arlington.org; www.arlington.org

Arlington • *Arlington CVB* • Mary German; Sr. Dir. of Bus. Svcs. & Prog.; 1905 E. Randol Mill Rd.; 76011; Tarrant; P 370,000; (817) 461-3888; (800) 433-5374; visitinfo@arlington.org; www.arlington.org

Austin • *Austin CVB* • Robert Lander; Pres./CEO; 111 Congress Ave., Ste. 700; 78701; Travis; P 1,000,000; (512) 474-5171; (800) 926-2282; Fax (512) 583-7282; rpalmertree@austintexas.org; www.austintexas.org

Bandera • *Bandera County CVB* • Patricia Moore; Exec. Dir.; 126 Hwy. 16 S.; P.O. Box 171; 78003; Bandera; P 21,000; (830) 796-3045; (800) 364-3833; Fax (830) 796-4121; cowpoke@banderacowboycapital.com; www.banderacowboycapital.com

Bay City • *Matagorda County CVB* • Mitch Thames; Pres./CEO; 201 Seventh St.; P.O. Box 768; 77404; Matagorda; P 38,000; (979) 245-8333; (800) 806-8333; Fax (979) 245-1622; mitchthames@visitbaycity.org; www.visitmatagorda.com

Beaumont • *Beaumont CVB* • Dean Conwell; Dir.; 505 Willow St.; P.O. Box 3827; 77704; Jefferson; P 115,000; (409) 880-3749; (800) 392-4401; Fax (409) 880-3750; sboutte@ci.beaumont.tx.us; www.beaumontcvb.com

Boerne • *Boerne CVB* • Larry Wood; Dir.; 1407 S. Main; 78006; Kendall; P 12,000; (830) 249-7277; (888) 842-8080; Fax (830) 249-9626; larry@visitboerne.org; www.visitboerne.org

Brady • *Brady Tourist & Conv. Bur.* • Kathi Masonheimer; Comm. Dev. Dir.; 101 E. 1st St.; 76825; McCulloch; P 8,000; (325) 597-3491; (888) 577-5657; Fax (325) 792-9181; info@bradytx.com; www.bradytx.com

Brenham • *Brenham/Washington County CVB* • Page Michel; Pres./CEO; 314 S. Austin St.; 77833; Washington; P 34,000; (979) 836-3695; (888) 273-6426; Fax (979) 836-2540; info@brenhamtexas.com; www.visitbrenhamtexas.com

Brownsville • *Brownsville CVB* • Mariano Ayala; Pres./CEO; 650 FM 802; P.O. Box 4697; 78523; Cameron; P 180,000; (956) 546-3721; (800) 626-2639; Fax (956) 546-3972; brownsvilleinfo@brownsville.org; www.brownsville.org

Brownwood • *Brownwood CVB* • Sunni Modawell; Tourism Dir.; 600 E. Depot St.; P.O. Box 880; 76804; Brown; P 40,000; (325) 646-9535; Fax (325) 643-6686; tourism@brownwoodchamber.org; www.brownwoodchamber.org

Bryan • *see College Station*

College Station • *Bryan/College Station CVB* • Shannon Overby; Exec. Dir.; 1101 University Dr. E., Ste. 108; 77840; Brazos; P 126,804; (979) 260-9898; (800) 777-8292; Fax (979) 260-9800; shannon@bcscvb.org; www.visitaggieland.com

Conroe • *Conroe CVB* • Harold Hutchison; Mgr.; 505 W. Davis St.; 77301; Montgomery; P 53,000; (936) 522-3500; (877) 426-6763; Fax (936) 756-6752; cvbinfo@cityofconroe.org; www.playinconroe.com

Corpus Christi • *Corpus Christi CVB* • Paulette Kluge; CEO; 101 N. Shoreline Blvd., Ste. 430; 78401; Nueces; P 320,400; (361) 881-1888; (800) 678-6232; Fax (361) 888-4998; tcarpenter@visitcorpuschristitx.org; www.visitcorpuschristitx.org

Dallas • *Dallas CVB* • Phillip Jones; Pres./CEO; 325 N. St. Paul St., Ste. 700; 75201; Dallas; P 1,189,000; (214) 571-1000; Fax (214) 571-1008; fwritesel@dallascvb.com; www.visitdallas.com

Del Rio • *Del Rio CVB* • Blanca G. Larson; Exec. Dir.; 1915 Veteran's Blvd.; 78840; Val Verde; P 45,000; (830) 775-3551; Fax (830) 774-1813; blarson@drchamber.com; www.drchamber.com

Denton • *Denton CVB* • Kim Phillips; V.P.; 414 W. Pkwy.; 76201; Denton; P 120,000; (940) 382-7895; (888) 381-1818; Fax (940) 382-6287; visitdenton@discoverdenton.com; www.discoverdenton.com

El Paso • *El Paso CVB* • William Blaziek; Gen. Mgr.; #1 Civic Center Plz.; 79901; El Paso; P 755,000; (915) 534-0600; Fax (915) 534-0687; info@elpasocvb.com; www.visitelpaso.com

Fort Stockton • *Fort Stockton CVB* • Doug May; Dir.; 1000 Railroad Ave.; 79735; Pecos; P 8,000; (432) 336-2264; (800) 336-2166; Fax (432) 336-6114; edc@fortstockton.org; www.cityfs.net

Fort Worth • *Fort Worth CVB* • Robert L. Jameson CTA; Pres./CEO; 111 W. 4th St., Ste. 200; 76102; Tarrant; P 816,000; (817) 336-8791; (800) 433-5747; Fax (817) 336-3282; francollins@fortworth.com; www.fortworth.com

Fredericksburg • *Fredericksburg CVB* • Ernest Loeffler; Pres.; 302 E. Austin St.; 78624; Gillespie; P 10,000; (830) 997-6523; (888) 997-3600; Fax (830) 997-8588; visitorinfo@fbgtx.org; www.visitfredericksburgtx.com

Galveston • *Galveston Island Visitors Center* • Stacy Gilbert; Dir.; 2328 Broadway; 77550; Galveston; P 65,000; (409) 763-4311; (888) GALISLE; Fax (409) 744-7873; sgilbert@galvestoncvb.com; www.galveston.com

Garland • *Garland CVB* • Lucia Arrant; Mgr.; 211 N. Fifth St.; 75040; Dallas; P 235,000; (972) 205-2749; (888) 879-0264; Fax (972) 205-3634; cvb@garlandtx.gov; www.visitgarlandtx.com

Georgetown • *Georgetown CVB* • Cari Miller; Tourism Mgr.; 103 W. 7th St.; P.O. Box 409; 78627; Williamson; P 58,700; (800) 436-8696; (512) 930-3545; Fax (512) 930-3697; cvb@georgetowntx.org; visit.georgetown.org

Granbury • *Granbury CVB* • Shanna Smith-Snyder; Mktg. Dir.; 116 W. Bridge; 76048; Hood; P 7,500; (817) 573-5548; (800) 950-2212; ssmithsnyder@granbury.org; www.granburytx.com

Grand Prairie • *City of Grand Prairie-Tourism* • Randy Sisson; Tourism Mgr.; 2170 N. Belt Line Rd.; 75050; Dallas; P 160,641; (972) 263-9588; (800) 288-8386; Fax (972) 642-4350; rsisson@gptx.org; www.gptexas.com

Grapevine • *Grapevine CVB* • Paul W. McCallum; Exec. Dir.; 636 S. Main St.; 76051; Tarrant; P 49,600; (817) 410-3185; (800) 457-6338; Fax (817) 410-3038; pmccallum@grapevinetexasusa.com; www.grapevinetexasusa.com

Houston • *Greater Houston CVB* • Mike Waterman; Pres.; 701 Avenida de las Americas; 77010; Harris; P 6,500,000; (713) 853-8100; dlewis@visithoustontexas.com; www.visithoustontexas.com

Huntsville • *Sam Houston Statue & Huntsville Tourism Dept.* • Kimm Thomas; Dir. of Tourism & Cultural Svcs.; 7600 Hwy. 75 S.; 77340; Walker; P 66,000; (936) 291-9726; 936-291-5932; Fax (936) 291-5936; kthomas@huntsvilletx.gov; www.huntsvilletexas.com

Irving • *Irving CVB* • Maura Gast; CEO; 500 W. Las Colinas Blvd.; 75039; Dallas; P 200,000; (972) 252-7476; (800) 2-IRVING; Fax (972) 401-7729; info@irvingtexas.com; www.irvingtexas.com

Kemah • *Kemah Visitors Center* • Carolyn Anderson; City Secy.; 604 Bradford Ave.; 77565; Galveston; P 1,800; (281) 334-1611; (281) 334-6583; Fax (281) 334-6583; citysecretary@kemah-tx.com; www.kemah-tx.com

Kerrville • *Kerrville CVB* • Charlie McIlvain; Pres./CEO; 2108 Sidney Baker; 78028; Kerr; P 24,000; (830) 792-3535; (800) 221-7958; Fax (830) 792-3230; julieland@ktc.com; www.kerrvilletexascvb.com

Killeen • *Killeen CVB* • Kathie Mulheron; Dir.; 3601 South W.S. Young Dr.; P.O. Box 1329; 76540; Bell; P 132,000; (254) 501-3888; (800) 221-7958; Fax (254) 501-6512; info@visitkilleen.com; www.visitkilleen.com

Kingsville • *Kingsville CVB* • Leo Alarcorn; Dir.; 1501 N. Hwy. 77; 78363; Kleberg; P 27,000; (361) 592-8516; (800) 333-5032; Fax (361) 592-3227; lalarcon@cityofkingsville.com; www.kingsvilletexas.com

Lake Jackson • *Brazosport Conv. & Visitors Cncl.* • Edith Fischer; Dir. of Tourism; 300 Abner Jackson Pkwy.; 77566; Brazoria; P 72,000; (979) 285-2501; (888) 477-2501; Fax (979) 285-2505; edithfischer@sbcglobal.net; www.visitbrazosport.com

Laredo • *Laredo CVB* • Blasita Lopez; Dir.; 501 San Agustin Ave.; 78040; Webb; P 250,000; (956) 795-2200; (800) 361-3360; Fax (956) 795-2185; blopez@ci.laredo.tx.us; www.visitlaredo.com

Longview • *Longview CVB* • Shawn Hara; Dir.; 300 W. Cotton St.; 75601; Gregg & Harrison; P 82,000; (903) 753-3281; Fax (903) 758-4791; cvb@longviewtexas.gov; www.longviewtexas.gov

Lubbock • *Lubbock CVB* • John Osborne; Pres./CEO; Wells Fargo Center; 1500 Broadway, 6th Flr.; 79401; Lubbock; P 289,000; (806) 747-5232; (800) 692-4035; Fax (806) 747-1419; amber@visitlubbock.org; www.visitlubbock.org

Lufkin • *Lufkin CVB* • Tara Watson-Watkins; Exec. Dir.; 1615 S. Chestnut; P.O. Box 190; 75902; Angelina; P 35,000; (936) 633-0349; (936) 633-0359; Fax (936) 634-8726; twatkins@cityoflufkin.com; www.visitlufkin.com

Marshall • *Marshall CVB* • Carolyn Howard; Tourism & Promotions Dir.; 301 N. Washington; 75670; Harrison; P 25,000; (903) 702-7777; cvb@visitmarshalltexas.org; marshalltxcvb.org

McAllen • *Visit McAllen* • Nancy S. Millar; V.P. & Dir.; 1200 Ash Ave.; P.O. Box 790; 78505; Hidalgo; P 150,000; (956) 682-2871; (877) MCALLEN; Fax (956) 631-8571; nmillar@visitmcallen.com; www.visitmcallen.com

McKinney • *McKinney CVB* • Dee-dee Guerra; Exec. Dir.; 200 W. Virginia; 75069; Collin; P 150,000; (214) 544-1407; (888) 649-8499; Fax (972) 542-6341; info@visitmckinney.com; www.visitmckinney.com

Midland • *VisitMidland* • Brad Barnett; Exec. V.P. Tourism & Facilities; 303 W. Wall, Ste. 200; 79701; Midland; P 132,950; (432) 683-3381; (800) 624-6435; Fax (432) 686-3556; crissy@visitmidland.com; www.visitmidland.com

Mineola • *Mineola Visitors Center* • Holly Herring; Comm. Dev. Dir.; P.O. Box 179; 75773; Wood; P 5,300; (903) 569-6983; (800) MINEOLA; Fax (903) 569-0856; ced@mineola.com; www.mineola.com

Mineral Wells • *Mineral Wells Area C/C* • Beth Watson; Exec. Dir.; 511 E. Hubbard; P.O. Box 1408; 76068; Palo Pinto; P 27,960; (940) 325-2557; (800) 252-MWTX; Fax (940) 328-0850; info@mineralwellstx.com; www.mineralwellstx.com

Nacogdoches • *Nacogdoches CVB* • Carl Watson; Exec. Dir.; 200 E. Main St.; 75961; Nacogdoches; P 30,000; (936) 564-7351; (888) 564-7351; Fax (936) 462-7688; info@visitnacogdoches.org; www.visitnacogdoches.org

New Braunfels • *New Braunfels CVB* • Judy Young; Dir.; 390 S. Seguin Ave.; P.O. Box 311417; 78131; Comal; P 150,000; (830) 625-2385; (800) 572-2626; Fax (830) 625-7918; judy@innewbraunfels.com; www.innewbraunfels.com

Odessa • *Odessa CVB* • Linda Sweatt; Dir.; 700 North Grant Ave., Ste. 200; 79761; Ector; P 137,130; (432) 333-7871; (800) 780-4678; Fax (432) 333-7858; info@odessacvb.com; www.odessacvb.com

Orange • *Orange CVB* • Ashley Mahana; Coord.; 803 W. Green Ave.; P.O. Box 520; 77631; Orange; P 18,643; (409) 883-1011; (800) 528-4906; Fax (409) 988-7321; cvb@orangetx.org; www.orangetexas.org

Palestine • *Palestine CVB* • 825 Spring St.; 75801; Anderson; P 19,000; (903) 723-3014; (800) 659-3484; Fax (903) 729-6067; palestinecvb@flash.net; www.visitpalestine.com

Paris • *Paris Visitors & Conv. Cncl.* • Becky Semple; Tourism Dir.; 8 W. Plaza; 75460; Lamar; P 26,000; (903) 784-2501; Fax (903) 784-2158; chamber@paristexas.com; www.paristexas.com

Plano • *Visit Plano* • Mark Thompson; Dir.; P.O. Box 860358; 75086; Collin; P 276,000; (972) 941-5843; (800) 81-PLANO; Fax (972) 424-0002; markth@plano.gov; www.visitpalno.com

Port Aransas • *Port Aransas CVB* • Ann B. Vaughan; Pres./CEO; 403 W. Cotter; 78373; Nueces; P 3,480; (361) 749-5919; (800) 452-6278; Fax (361) 749-4672; info@portaransas.org; www.portaransas.org

Port Arthur • *Port Arthur CVB •* Tammy Kotzur; Dir.; 3401 Cultural Center Dr.; 77642; Jefferson; P 58,000; (409) 985-7822; (800) 235-7822; Fax (409) 985-5584; tjhenderson@portarthurtexas.com; www.visitportarthurtx.com

Presidio • *Presidio CVB •* Brad Newton; Dir.; 507 W. O'Reilly St.; P.O. Box 1899; 79845; P 4,400; (432) 229-3517; tourism@cityofpresidio.com; www.cityofpresidio.com

Richardson • *Richardson CVB •* Geoff Wright; Dir.; 411 W. Arapaho Rd., Ste. 105; 75080; Dallas; P 105,000; (972) 744-4034; (888) 690-7287; Fax (972) 744-5834; conrad.castillo@cor.gov; www.richardsontexas.org

San Angelo • *San Angelo CVB •* Pamela Miller; V.P. of CVB; 418 W. Ave. B; 76903; Tom Green; P 100,000; (325) 655-4136; Fax (325) 658-1110; cvb@sanangelo.org; www.visitsanangelo.org

San Antonio • *San Antonio CVB •* Casandra Matej; Exec. Dir.; 203 S. St. Mary's, Ste. 200; 78205; Bexar; P 1,500,000; (210) 207-6700; (800) 447-3372; Fax (210) 207-6768; javiervasquez@visitsanantonio.com; visitsanantonio.com

San Marcos • *San Marcos CVB •* Rebecca Ybarra-Ramirez; Exec. Dir.; 617 IH 35 N.; 78666; Hays; P 50,000; (512) 393-5930; cvb@sanmarcostexas.com; www.toursanmarcos.com

Schulenburg • *Tourist Info. Center •* Marcia Hrncir; Exec. Dir.; 618 N. Main; P.O. Box 65; 78956; Fayette; P 2,852; (979) 743-4514; (866) 504-5294; Fax (979) 743-9155; schulenburgchamber@cvctx.com; www.schulenburgchamber.org

Seabrook • *Bay Area Houston CVB •* D'Anna Travis; Mgr.; 913 N. Meyer Rd.; 77586; Harris; P 550,000; (281) 474-9700; (866) 611-4688; Fax (281) 474-9701; info@bahcvb.org; www.visitbayareahouston.com

Seguin • *Seguin CVB •* Sherry Nefford-Esse; Exec. Dir.; 116 N. Camp St.; 78155; Guadalupe; P 25,090; (830) 379-6382; (800) 580-7322; Fax (830) 379-6971; cvb@seguinchamber.com; www.visitseguin.com

Sherman • *Sherman Dept. of Tourism •* April Patterson; Dir.; 405 N. Rusk St., 2nd Flr.; 75090; Grayson; P 40,000; (903) 957-0310; (888) 893-1188; Fax (903) 870-4045; tourism@ci.sherman.tx.us; www.shermantx.org

South Padre Island • *South Padre Island CVB •* Lacey Ekberg; Exec. Dir.; 7355 Padre Blvd.; 78597; Cameron; P 5,000; (956) 761-3000; (800) SOPADRE; Fax (956) 761-3024; info@sopadre.com; www.sopadre.com

Sweetwater • *Sweetwater CVB •* Jacque McCoy; Exec. Dir.; 810 E. Broadway; P.O. Box 1148; 79556; Nolan; P 11,500; (325) 235-5488; (800) 658-6757; Fax (325) 235-1026; chamber@sweetwatertexas.org; www.sweetwatertexas.org

Terrell • *Terrell C/C & CVB •* Donna Riley; Dir. of Tourism; 1314 W. Moore Ave.; P.O. Box 97; 75160; Kaufman; P 18,500; (972) 563-5703; (877) 837-7355; Fax (972) 563-2363; donna@terrelltexas.com; www.terrelltexas.com

Tyler • *Tyler CVB •* Shari Rickman; V.P.; 315 N. Broadway; 75710; Smith; P 100,000; (903) 592-1661; Fax (903) 592-1268; srickman@tylertexas.com; www.visittyler.com

Uvalde • *Uvalde CVB •* Debra Stifflemire; Exec. Dir.; 300 E. Main St.; 78801; Uvalde; P 17,817; (830) 278-4115; Fax (830) 278-3994; tourism@visituvalde.com; www.visituvalde.com

Van Horn • *Van Horn CVB •* Brenda Hinojos; Dir.; 1801 W. Broadway; P.O. Box 488; 79855; Culberson; P 2,400; (432) 283-2682; (866) 424-6939; Fax (432) 283-1413; info@vanhorntexas.org; www.vanhorntexas.org

Victoria • *Victoria CVB •* Anthony Cordo; Exec. Dir.; 700 N. Main St., Ste. 101; P.O. Box 1758; 77902; Victoria; P 91,000; (361) 485-3116; (800) 926-5774; Fax (361) 485-3108; acordo@victoriatx.org; www.visitvictoriatexas.com

Waco • *Waco CVB •* Elizabeth Taylor; Exec. Dir.; 100 Washington Ave.; P.O. Box 2570; 76702; McLennan; P 222,439; (254) 750-5810; (800) 321-9226; Fax (254) 750-5801; lizt@ci.waco.tx.us; www.wacocvb.com

Utah

Cedar City • *Cedar City/Brian Head Tourism Bur. •* Maria Twitchell; Exec. Dir.; 581 N. Main, Ste. A; 84721; Iron; P 30,000; (435) 586-5124; ccbhtourism@ironcounty.net; www.visitcedarcity.com

Farmington • *Davis County Tourism & Events •* Barbara Riddle; Pres./CEO; 61 S. Main St., Rm. 304; 84025; Davis; P 265,000; (801) 451-3237; (888) 777-9771; info@davisareacvb.com; www.davis.travel

Logan • *Cache Valley Visitors Bur. •* Julie Hollist; Dir.; 199 N. Main St.; 84321; Cache; P 117,000; (435) 755-1890; (800) 882-4433; Fax (435) 755-1993; julie@tourcachevalley.com; www.explorelogan.com

Moab • *Moab Area Travel Cncl. •* Marian DeLay; Exec. Dir.; P.O. Box 550; 84532; Grand; P 9,000; (435) 259-8825; (800) 635-6622; Fax (435) 259-1376; mdelay@discovermoab.com; www.discovermoab.com

Monticello • *San Juan County C/C •* Bayley Hedglin; Exec. Dir.; P.O. Box 217; 84535; San Juan; P 14,200; (435) 459-9700; (800) 574-4386; Fax (435) 587-2425; info@sanjuancountychamber.com; www.sanjuancountychamber.com

Nephi • *Juab Travel Cncl. •* 4 S. Main St.; P.O. Box 71; 84648; Juab; P 8,000; (435) 623-5203; (800) 748-4361; Fax (435) 623-4609; info@juabtravel.com; www.juabtravel.com

Ogden • *Ogden/Weber CVB •* Sara Toliver; Pres./CEO; 2438 Washington Blvd.; 84401; Weber; P 232,000; (800) 255-8824; (866) 867-8824; Fax (801) 399-0783; info@visitogden.com; www.visitogden.com

Panguitch • *Garfield County Ofc. of Tourism •* K. Bruce Fullmer; Exec. Dir.; 55 S. Main St.; P.O. Box 200; 84759; Garfield; P 4,600; (800) 444-6689; travgar@color-country.net; www.brycecanyoncountry.com

Park City • *Park City C/C & Visitor Bur. •* Bill Malone; Pres./CEO; 1850 Sidewinder Dr., Ste. 320; P.O. Box 1630; 84060; Summit; P 24,500; (435) 649-6100; (800) 453-1360; Fax (435) 649-4132; info@visitparkcity.com; www.visitparkcity.com

Saint George • *Saint George Area CVB •* 1835 Convention Center Dr.; 84790; Washington; P 125,000; (435) 634-5747; (800) 869-6635; Fax (435) 628-1619; info@utahstgeorge.com; www.utahstgeorge.com

Virgin Islands

Saint Croix • *Virgin Islands Dept. of Tourism •* Beverly Nicholson-Doty; Commissioner; P.O. Box 224538; Christiansted; 00822; P 51,000; (340) 773-0495; Fax (340) 773-5074; lawheatley@usvitourism.vi; www.visitusvi.com

C & VB

Saint Croix • *Virgin Islands Dept. of Tourism* • Beverly Nicholson-Doty; Commissioner; 321 King St., Ste. 7; Frederiksted; 00840; P 51,000; (340) 772-0357; Fax (340) 773-5074; lawheatley@usvitourism.vi; www.visitusvi.com

Saint John • *Virgin Islands Dept. of Tourism* • Beverly Nicholson-Doty; Commissioner; 6A Cruz Bay; P.O. Box 14; 00831; P 4,200; lawheatley@usvitourism.vi; www.visitusvi.com

Saint Thomas • *Virgin Islands Dept. of Tourism* • Beverly Nicholson-Doty; Commissioner; P.O. Box 6400; Charlotte Amalie; 00804; P 52,000; (340) 774-8784; (800) 372-8784; Fax (340) 774-4390; lawheatley@usvitourism.vi; www.visitusvi.com

Virginia

Abingdon • *Abingdon CVB* • Myra Cook; Dir. of Tourism; 335 Cummings St.; 24210; Washington; P 7,700; (276) 676-2282; (800) 435-3440; Fax (276) 676-3076; acvb@abingdon.com; www.abingdon.com

Alexandria • *Alexandria Conv. & Visitors Assn.* • Patricia Washington; Pres./CEO; 221 King St.; 22314; Alexandria City; P 153,500; (703) 746-3301; (800) 388-9119; mfallon@visitalexva.com; www.visitalexandriava.com

Arlington • *Arlington Conv. & Visitors Svcs.* • Emily Cassell; Dir.; 1100 N. Glebe Rd., Ste. 1500; 22201; Arlington; P 225,000; (703) 228-0874; (800) 296-7996; Fax (703) 228-0806; mcannon@arlingtonva.us; www.stayarlington.com

Ashland • *Ashland/Hanover Visitors Center* • Pamela Crisp; Mgr.; 112 N. Railroad Ave; 23005; Hanover; P 99,900; (804) 752-6766; (800) 897-1479; Fax (804) 752-2380; pcrisp@town.ashland.va.us; www.town.ashland.va.us

Bedford • *Bedford Welcome Center* • Jerry Craig; Dir.; 816 Burks Hill Rd.; 24523; Bedford City; P 66,300; (540) 587-5681; Fax (540) 587-5983; michelle@visitbedford.com; www.visitbedford.com

Bluefield • *Tazewell County Visitor Center* • David Woodard; Mgr.; 200 Sanders Ln.; 24605; Tazewell; P 45,100; (276) 322-1345; (800) 588-9401; Fax (276) 322-3908; visitorcenter@tazewellcounty.org; www.tazewellcounty.org

Bristol • *Bristol CVB* • Matt Bolas; Dir.; 20 Volunteer Pkwy.; P.O. Box 519; 24203; Bristol; P 47,000; (423) 989-4850; Fax (423) 989-4867; tourism@bristolchamber.org; www.bristolchamber.org

Charlottesville • *Charlottesville-Albemarle CVB* • Kurt Burkhart; Exec. Dir.; 610 E. Main St.; P.O. Box 178; 22902; Charlottesville City; P 148,000; (434) 293-6789; (877) 386-1103; Fax (434) 295-2176; troutmanl@charlottesville.org; www.visitcharlottesville.org

Chesapeake • *Chesapeake CVB* • Kimberly Murden; Dir.; 1224 Progressive Dr.; 23320; Chesapeake City; P 222,200; (757) 382-6411; (888) 889-5551; Fax (757) 502-8016; sdrewery@cityofchesapeake.net; www.visitchesapeake.com

Christiansburg • *Montgomery County Tourism Dev. Cncl.* • Lisa Bleakley; Dir.; 755 Roanoke St., Ste. 2E; 24073; Montgomery; P 97,300; (540) 394-2120; (540) 382-6954; Fax (540) 382-6943; bleakleyts@montgomerycountyva.gov; www.montva.com

Fairfax • *Visit Fairfax* • Barry H. Biggar CDME; Pres./CEO; 3702 Pender Dr., Ste. 420; 22030; Fairfax; P 1,100,000; (703) 790-0643; visitfairfax@fxva.com; www.fxva.com

Fredericksburg • *Fredericksburg Ofc. of Tourism & Eco. Dev.* • Bill Freehling; Dir. of Tourism & Eco. Dev.; 706 Caroline St.; 22401; Spotsylvania; P 24,200; (540) 372-1216; (800) 260-3646; Fax (540) 372-6587; jperry@fredericksburgva.gov; www.visitfred.com

Gloucester • *Gloucester Parks, Rec. & Tourism* • Hilton Snowdon; Tourism Coord.; 6489 Main St.; 23061; Gloucester; P 35,000; (804) 693-0014; Fax (804) 824-2450; tourism@gloucesterva.info; www.visitgloucesterva.org

Hampton • *Hampton CVB* • Mary Fugere CMP CTIS; Dir.; 1919 Commerce Dr., Ste. 290; 23666; Hampton City; P 137,000; (757) 722-1222; (800) 487-8778; Fax (757) 896-4600; vblackman@hamptoncvb.com; www.visithampton.com

Harrisonburg • *Harrisonburg Tourism & Visitor Svcs.* • Brenda Black; Tourism Dir.; 212 S. Main St.; 22801; Harrisonburg City; P 51,000; (540) 432-8935; Fax (540) 437-0631; tourism@harrisonburgva.gov; www.visitharrisonburgva.com

Hopewell • *Hopewell Ofc. of Tourism & Visitor Center* • Becky McDonough; Exec. Dir.; 4100 Oaklawn Blvd.; 23860; Hopewell City; P 23,000; (804) 541-2461; (800) 863-8687; Fax (804) 541-2459; info@hopewellva.gov; www.hopewellva.gov

Leesburg • *Loudon Conv. & Vistors Assn.* • Patrick Kaler; Pres.; 112 South St. S.E., Ste. G; 20175; Loudon; P 312,300; (703) 771-2170; (800) 752-6118; Fax (703) 771-4973; vchost@visitloudon.org; www.visitloudon.org

Lexington • *Lexington & the Rockbridge Area Tourism* • Jean Clark; Dir.; 106 E. Washington St.; 24450; Lexington City; P 34,000; (540) 463-3777; (877) 453-9822; Fax (540) 463-1105; director@lexingtonvirginia.com; www.lexingtonvirginia.com

Lovingston • *Nelson County Eco. Dev. & Tourism* • Maureen Kelley; Dir.; 8519 Thomas Nelson Hwy.; P.O. Box 636; 22949; Nelson; P 15,020; (434) 263-7015; (800) 282-8223; Fax (434) 263-6823; info@nelsoncounty.org; www.nelsoncounty-va.gov

Lynchburg • *Discover Lynchburg* • Beckie Nix; Dir.; Lynchburg Visitor Info. Center; 216 12th St.; 24504; Lynchburg City; (434) 845-5966; (800) 732-5821; Fax (434) 522-9592; tourism@discoverlynchburg.org; www.discoverlynchburg.org

Manassas • *Discover Prince William & Manassas CVB* • Ann Marie Maher; Pres./CEO; 10611 Balls Ford Rd., Ste. 110; 20109; Prince William; P 438,600; (703) 396-7130; (800) 432-1792; Fax (703) 396-7160; splattner@discoverpwm.com; www.discoverpwm.com

Mathews • *Mathews County Visitor & Info. Center* • Ann Miller; Exec. Dir.; 239 Main St.; P.O. Box 1456; 23109; Mathews; P 10,000; (804) 725-4229; mcvic@visitmathews.com; www.visitmathews.com

McLean • *Fairfax County Visitors Center* • Sue Porter; Dir. of Visitor Svcs.; 7927 Jones Branch Dr., South Wing 100; 22102; Fairfax; P 1,000,000; (703) 752-9500; (800) 732-4732; sporter@fxva.com; www.fxva.com

Newport News • *Newport News Visitor Center* • Janie Tross; Mgr.; 13560 Jefferson Ave.; 23603; Newport News City; P 181,000; (757) 886-7777; (888) 493-7386; Fax (757) 886-7920; jtross@nngov.com; www.newport-news.org

Norfolk • *VisitNorfolk* • Anthony DiFilippo; Pres./CEO; 232 E. Main St.; 23510; Norfolk City; P 245,000; (757) 664-6620; (800) 368-3097; Fax (757) 622-3663; info@visitnorfolktoday.com; www.visitnorfolktoday.com

Northern Neck • *see Warsaw-Northern Neck Tourism Comm.*

Orange • *Orange County Dept. of Tourism* • Leigh Mawyer; Tourism Mgr.; 122 E. Main St.; 22960; Orange; P 33,500; (540) 672-1653; (877) 222-8072; Fax (540) 672-1746; lmawyer@orangecountyva.gov; www.visitorangevirginia.com

Petersburg • *Petersburg Vistors Center* • Dawn Holmes; Supervisor; 19 Bollingbrook St.; 23803; Petersburg City; P 32,800; (804) 733-2400; (800) 368-3595; tourism@petersburg-va.org; www.petersburg-va.org

Portsmouth • *Portsmouth Visitor Center* • Dave Schulte; Tourism Mgr.; 6 Crawford Pkwy.; 23704; Portsmouth City; P 100,000; (757) 393-5111; (800) 767-8782; penneyc@portsmouthva.gov; www.visitportsva.com

Richmond • *Richmond Metro CVB* • Jack Berry; Pres./CEO; 401 N. 3rd St.; 23219; Richmond City; P 204,000; (804) 782-2777; (800) 370-9004; Fax (804) 780-2577; msemmeman@richmondva.org; www.visitrichmondva.com

Roanoke • *Roanoke Valley CVB* • Landon Howard; Exec. Dir.; 101 Shenandoah Ave. N.E.; 24016; Roanoke City; P 308,000; (540) 342-6025; (800) 635-5535; Fax (540) 342-7119; info@visitroanokeva.com; www.visitroanokeva.com

Smithfield • *Smithfield & Isle of Wight CVB* • Judy Winslow; Dir.; 319 Main St.; P.O. Box 37; 23431; Isle of Wight; P 43,000; (757) 357-5182; (800) 365-9339; Fax (757) 365-4360; kchapman@isleofwightus.net; www.smithfield-virginia.com

South Boston • *Halifax County Tourism Dept.* • Linda Shepperd; Dir.; 1180 Bill Tuck Hwy.; 24592; Halifax; P 36,200; (434) 572-2543; Fax (434) 572-2127; info@gohalifaxva.com; www.gohalifaxva.com

Spotsylvania • *Spotsylvania County Dept. of Tourism* • Debbie Aylor; Tourism Mgr.; 9019 Old Battlefield Blvd., Ste. 310; 22553; Spotsylvania; P 123,000; (540) 507-7210; (540) 507-7205; Fax (540) 507-7207; tourism@spotsylvania.va.us; www.visitspotsy.com

Staunton • *Staunton CVB* • Sheryl Wagner; Dir. of Tourism; 116 W. Beverly St., 3rd Flr.; P.O. Box 58; 24402; Staunton City; P 24,000; (540) 332-3865; (800) 342-7982; Fax (540) 851-4005; wagnerss@ci.staunton.va.us; www.visitstaunton.com

Suffolk • *Suffolk Div. of Tourism* • Lynette White; Dir. of Tourism; 524 N. Main St.; 23434; Suffolk City; P 84,600; (757) 923-3880; (866) 733-7835; Fax (757) 514-4145; VisitSuffolk@suffolkva.us.; www.suffolk-fun.com

Virginia Beach • *Virginia Beach CVB* • James Ricketts; Dir.; 2101 Parks Ave., Ste. 500; 23451; Virginia Beach City; P 438,000; (757) 385-4700; (800) 700-7702; Fax (757) 437-4747; vbgov@vbgov.com; www.visitvirginiabeach.com

Warrenton • *Warrenton-Fauquier County Visitor Center* • Becky Crouch; Mgr.; 33 N. Calhoun St.; 20186; Fauquier; P 68,000; (540) 341-0988; (800) 820-1021; Fax (540) 341-2126; visitorcenter@warrentonva.gov; www.visitfauquier.com

Warsaw • *Richmond County Museum & Visitors Center* • David Jett; Dir.; 5874 Richmond Rd.; P.O. Box 884; 22572; Richmond; P 9,100; (804) 333-3607; Fax (804) 333-3408; museum@co.richmond.va.us; www.co.richmond.va.us

Warsaw • *Northern Neck Tourism Comm.* • Lisa Hull; Tourism Coord.; 457 Main St.; P.O. Box 1707; 22572; Richmond; P 55,000; (804) 333-1919; Fax (804) 333-5274; nntc@northernneck.org; www.northernneck.org

Winchester • *Winchester-Frederick County CVB* • Sally Coates; Exec. Dir.; 1400 S. Pleasant Valley Rd.; 22601; Frederick; P 104,000; (540) 542-1326; (877) 871-1326; Fax (540) 450-0099; info@visitwinchesterva.com; www.visitwinchesterva.com

Woodstock • *Shenandoah County Tourism* • Jenna French; Dir. of Tourism; 600 N. Main St., Ste. 101; 22664; Shenandoah; P 43,000; (540) 459-6227; (888) 367-3965; Fax (540) 459-6228; tourism@shenandoahcountyva.us; www.shenandoahtravel.org

Wytheville Area

Blue Ridge Travel Assn. of VA • Felicia Hash; Pres.; P.O. Box 1395; 24382; Wythe; (800) 446-9670; info@virginiablueridge.org; www.virginiablueridge.org

Reg. Visitors Center • Rosa Lee Jude; Dir.; 975 Tazewell St.; 24382; Wythe; P 29,300; (276) 223-3441; (877) 347-8307; Fax (276) 223-3443; cvb@wytheville.org; visitwytheville.com

Wytheville CVB • Rosa Lee Jude; Dir. of Tourism; 975 Tazewell St.; P.O. Box 533; 24382; Wythe; P 30,000; (276) 223-3355; (877) 347-8307; Fax (276) 223-3443; cvb@wytheville.org; www.visitwytheville.com

Yorktown • *York County Tourism Dev.* • Kristi Olsen; Tourism Dev. Mgr.; P.O. Box 532; 23690; York; P 65,500; (757) 890-3500; (757) 890-3300; Fax (757) 890-3509; tourism@yorkcounty.gov; www.visityorktown.org

Washington

Clarkston • *Hells Canyon Visitor Bur.* • Michelle Peters; Pres./CEO; 847 Port Way; 99403; Asotin; P 60,000; (509) 758-7489; (877) 774-7248; Fax (509) 751-8767; info@hellscanyonvisitor.com; www.hellscanyonvisitor.com

Kelso • *see Longview*

Kennewick • *Visit TRI-CITIES* • Kris Watkins; Pres./CEO; 7130 W. Grandridge Blvd., Ste. B; 99336; Benton; P 242,000; (509) 735-8486; (800) 254-5824; Fax (509) 783-9005; info@VisitTri-Cities.com; www.VisitTri-Cities.com

Longview • *Mount St. Helens Tourism* • 1900 7th Ave.; 98632; Cowlitz; P 101,996; (360) 577-3137; Fax (360) 577-6254; tourism@visitmtsthelens.com; www.visitmtsthelens.com

Packwood • *Destination Packwood Assn.* • CJ Neer; Exec. Dir.; 12990 U.S. Hwy. 12; P.O. Box 64; 98361; Lewis; P 1,000; (360) 494-2223; Fax (360) 494-2216; info@destinationpackwood.com; www.destinationpackwood.com

Port Angeles • *Olympic Peninsula Visitors Bur.* • Diane Schostak; Exec. Dir.; 338 W. 1st St., Ste. 104; P.O. Box 670; 98362; Clallam; P 70,400; (360) 452-8552; (800) 942-4042; info@olympicpeninsula.org; www.olympicpeninsula.org

Seattle • *Seattle CVB* • Tom Norwalk; Pres./CEO; 701 Pike St., Ste. 800; 98101; King; P 608,606; (206) 461-5800; (866) 732-2695; Fax (206) 461-5855; visitorinfo@visitseattle.org; www.visitseattle.org

Seattle • *Seattle Southside Visitor Info.* • Katherine Kertzman; Exec. Dir.; 3100 S. 176th St.; 98188; King; P 157,830; (206) 575-2489; (877) 885-9452; Fax (206) 575-2529; kristina@seattlesouthside.com; www.seattlesouthside.com

Seaview • *Long Beach Peninsula VB* • Andi Day; Exec. Dir.; P.O. Box 562; 98644; Pacific; P 3,000; (360) 642-2400; (800) 451-2542; Fax (360) 642-3900; andi@funbeach.com; www.funbeach.com

Spokane • *Spokane Reg. CVB* • Cheryl Kilday; Pres./CEO; 801 W. Riverside, Ste. 301; 99201; Spokane; P 500,000; (509) 624-1341; (800) 662-0084; Fax (509) 623-1297; conventions@visitspokane.com; www.visitspokane.com

Tacoma • *Travel Tacoma & Pierce County* • Bennish Brown; Pres./CEO; 1119 Pacific Ave., Ste. 1400; 98402; Pierce; P 713,400; (253) 627-2836; (800) 272-2662; Fax (253) 627-8783; info@traveltacoma.com; www.traveltacoma.com

Vancouver • *Visit Vancouver USA* • Kim Bennett; Pres./CEO; 1220 Main St., Ste. 220; 98660; Clark; P 440,000; (360) 750-1553; (877) 600-0800; Fax (360) 750-1933; marcom@visitvancouverusa.com; www.visitvancouverusa.com

Wenatchee • *Wenatchee Valley Visitor Bur.* • Wendy LeSesne; Interim Exec. Dir.; 5 S. Wenatchee Ave., Ste. 100; 98801; Chelan; P 100,000; (509) 663-3723; (800) 572-7753; Fax (509) 663-3983; info@wenatcheevalley.org; www.wenatcheevalley.org

West Virginia

Beckley • *Southern West Virginia CVB* • Doug Maddy; Exec. Dir./CEO; 1406 Harper Rd.; 25801; Raleigh; P 225,000; (304) 252-2244; (800) VISIT-WV; Fax (304) 252-2252; travel@visitwv.com; www.visitwv.com

Bluefield • *Mercer County CVB* • Marie Blackwell; Exec. Dir.; 704 Bland St.; P.O. Box 4088; 24701; Tazewell; P 62,300; (304) 325-8438; (800) 221-3206; Fax (304) 324-8483; info@mccvb.com; www.mccvb.com

Bridgeport • *Greater Bridgeport CVB* • Michelle Duez; Exec. Dir.; 164 W. Main St.; 26330; Harrison; P 15,000; (304) 848-7200; info@connect-bridgeport.com; www.greater-bridgeport.com

Buckhannon • *Upshur County CVB* • Laura Meadows; Exec. Dir.; 16 S. Kanawha St.; P.O. Box 817; 26201; Upshur; P 25,000; (304) 473-1400; Fax (304) 473-1401; lmeadows@visitbuckhannon.org; www.visitupshur.org

Charleston • *Charleston CVB* • Patricia Bradley; Pres./CEO; 200 Civic Center Dr.; 25301; Kanawha; P 52,000; (304) 344-5075; (800) 733-5469; Fax (304) 344-1241; info@charlestonwv.com; www.charlestonwv.com

Elkins • *West Virginia Mountain Highlands Visitors Bur.* • Bonnie Branciaroli; Exec. Dir.; P.O. Box 1456; 26241; Randolph; P 100,000; (304) 636-8400; Fax (304) 637-9900; info@mountainhighlands.com; www.mountainhighlands.com

Hinton • *Summers County CVB* • 206 Temple St.; 25951; Summers; P 14,000; (304) 466-5420; info@threeriverswv.com; www.threeriverswv.com

Huntington • *Cabell-Huntington CVB* • Tyson Compton; Exec. Dir.; P.O. Box 347; 25701; Cabell; P 97,000; (304) 525-7333; (800) 635-6329; Fax (304) 525-7345; info@wvvisit.org; www.wvvisit.org

Hurricane • *Putnam County CVB* • Linda Bush; Exec. Dir.; #3 Valley Park Dr.; 25526; Putnam; P 55,500; (304) 562-0518; Fax (304) 562-0728; lindab@putnamcountycvb.com; www.putnamcountycvb.com

Keyser • *Mineral County CVB* • Anne Palmer; Exec. Dir.; 40 1/2 N. Main; 26726; Mineral; P 27,000; (304)788-3887; Fax (304)788-3887; apalmer@hereintown.net; visitmineraol.com

Lewisburg • *Greenbrier County CVB* • Kara Dense; Exec. Dir.; 200 W. Washington St.; P.O. Box 1107; 24901; Greenbrier; P 35,500; (304) 645-1000; (800) 833-2068; Fax (304) 647-3001; info@greenbrierwv.com; www.greenbrierwv.com

Morgantown • *Greater Morgantown CVB* • Peggy Myers-Smith; Exec. Dir.; 341 Chaplin Rd.; 26501; Monongalia; P 50,000; (304) 292-5081; (800) 458-7373; Fax (304) 291-1354; info@tourmorgantown.com; www.tourmorgantown.com

Oak Hill • *New River Gorge CVB* • Sharon Cruikshank; Exec. Dir.; 310 Oyler Ave.; 25901; Fayette; P 47,000; (304) 465-5617; (800) 927-0263; Fax (304) 465-5618; fayette@wvdsl.net; www.newrivergorgecvb.com

Parkersburg • *Greater Parkersburg CVB* • Steven W. Nicely; Pres.; 350 7th St.; 26101; Wood; P 87,000; (304) 428-1130; (800) 752-4982; Fax (304) 428-8117; info@parkersburgcvb.org; www.greaterparkersburg.com

Pleasant Valley • *CVB of Marion County* • Marianne Moran; Exec. Dir.; 1000 Cole St., Ste. A; 26554; Marion; P 57,000; (304) 368-1123; (800) 834-7365; Fax (304) 333-0155; cvb@marioncvb.com; www.marioncvb.com

Point Pleasant • *Mason County CVB* • Denny Bellamy; Exec. Dir.; 210 Viand St.; 25550; Mason; P 27,300; (304) 675-6788; Fax (304) 674-8005; tourism@masoncounty.org; www.masoncountytourism.org

South Charleston • *South Charleston CVB* • Bob T. Anderson Sr.; Exec. Dir.; 311 D St.; P.O. Box 8599; 25303; Kanawha; P 16,000; (304) 746-5552; (800) 238-9488; Fax (304) 746-2970; sochascvb@yahoo.com; www.southcharlestonwv.org

Summersville • *Summersville CVB, Arena & Conference Center* • Marianne Taylor; Exec. Dir.; 3 Armory Way; 26651; Nicholas; P 4,000; (304) 872-3722; Fax (304) 872-0901; marianne@summersvillecvb.com; www.summersvillecvb.com

Weston • *Lewis County CVB* • Mrs. Chris Richards; Dir.; 499 U.S. Hwy. 33 E., Ste. 2; 26452; Lewis; P 16,000; (304) 269-7328; (800) 296-7329; Fax (304) 269-3271; tour@stonewallcountry.com; www.stonewallcountry.com

Wheeling • *Wheeling CVB* • Frank O'Brien; Exec. Dir.; 1401 Main St.; 26003; Ohio; P 154,000; (304) 233-7709; (800) 828-3097; Fax (304) 233-1470; fobrien@wheelingcvb.com; www.visitwheelingwv.com

Wisconsin

Appleton • *Fox Cities CVB* • 3433 W. College Ave.; 54914; Calumet, Outagamie & Winnebago; P 227,708; (920) 734-3358; (800) 2DO-MORE; Fax (920) 734-1080; tourism@foxcities.org; www.foxcities.org

Beloit • *Beloit CVB* • Celestino Ruffini; Exec. Dir.; 500 Public Ave.; 53511; Rock; P 37,100; (608) 365-4838; Fax (608) 365-6850; info@visitbeloit.com; www.visitbeloit.com

Brookfield • *Brookfield CVB* • Nancy Justman; Exec. Dir.; 17100 W. Bluemound Rd., Ste. 203; 53005; Waukesha; P 46,000; (262) 789-0220; (800) 388-1835; Fax (262) 789-0221; nancy@visitbrookfield.com; www.visitbrookfield.com

Cedarburg • *Cedarburg Visitor Center* • Jennifer Andreas; Exec. Dir.; N58 W6194 Columbia Rd.; P.O. Box 104; 53012; Ozaukee; P 16,000; (262) 377-9620; (800) 237-2874; Fax (262) 377-6470; info@cedarburg.org; www.cedarburg.org

Door County • *see Sturgeon Bay*

Eagle River • *Vilas County Tourism & Publicity* • 330 Court St.; 54521; Vilas; P 21,430; (800) 236-3649; Fax (715) 479-3748; vilasadv@co.vilas.wi.us; www.vilas.org

Eau Claire • *Eau Claire Area CVB* • Linda John; Exec. Dir.; 4319 Jeffers Rd., Ste. 201; 54703; Eau Claire; P 63,214; (888) 523-3866; (715) 831-2345; Fax (715) 831-2340; betty@visiteauclaire.com; www.visiteauclaire.com

Fond du Lac • *Fond du Lac Area CVB* • Craig Molitor; Pres.; 171 S. Pioneer Rd.; 54935; Fond du Lac; P 47,000; (920) 923-3010; Fax (920) 929-6846; info@fdl.com; www.fdl.com

Green Bay • *Greater Green Bay CVB* • Brad Toll; Pres.; 1901 S. Oneida St.; P.O. Box 10596; 54307; Brown; P 256,908; (920) 494-9507; (888) 867-3342; Fax (920) 405-1271; visitorinfo@greenbay.com; www.greenbay.com

Holmen • *see Onalaska*

Janesville • *Janesville Area CVB* • Christine Rebout; Exec. Dir.; 20 S. Main St., Ste. 17; 53545; Rock; P 64,000; (608) 757-3171; (800) 48-PARKS; Fax (608) 754-2115; visit@janesvillecvb.com; www.janesvillecvb.com

Kenosha • *Kenosha Area CVB* • Dennis DuChene; Pres.; 812 56th St.; 53140; Kenosha; P 150,000; (262) 654-7307; (800) 654-7309; Fax (262) 654-0882; info@visitkenosha.com; www.visitkenosha.com

La Crosse • *La Crosse Area CVB* • Dave Clements; Exec. Dir.; 410 Veterans Memorial Dr.; 54601; La Crosse; P 52,000; (608) 782-2366; (800) 658-9424; Fax (608) 782-4082; info@explorelacrosse.com; www.explorelacrosse.com

Ladysmith • *Rusk County Tourism* • Andy Albarado; Dir.; 205 W. 9th St. S.; 54848; Rusk; P 15,000; (715) 532-2642; (800) 535-RUSK; Fax (715) 532-2649; aalbarado@ruskcountywi.us; www.ruskcounty.org

Lake Geneva • *Geneva Lake Area CVB* • Darien Schaefer; Pres./CEO; 527 Center St.; 53147; Walworth; P 7,900; (262) 248-1000; (800) 345-1020; Fax (262) 661-7455; info@lakegenevawi.com; www.visitlakegenevawi.com

Madison • *Greater Madison CVB* • Deb Archer; Pres.; 22 E. Mifflin St., Ste. 200; 53703; Dane; P 245,000; (608) 255-2537; (800) 373-6376; Fax (608) 258-4950; info@visitmadison.com; www.visitmadison.com

Manitowoc • *Manitowoc Area Visitor & Conv. Bur.* • Jason Ring; Pres.; 4221 Calumet Ave.; 54221; Manitowoc; P 35,000; (920) 686-3070; (800) 627-4896; Fax (920) 683-4876; visitmanitowoc@manitowoc.info; www.manitowoc.info

Marshfield • *Marshfield CVB* • Matt McLean; Dir.; 700 S. Central Ave.; P.O. Box 868; 54449; Marathon & Wood; P 20,000; (715) 384-4314; (800) 422-4541; Fax (715) 387-8925; matt@visitmarshfield.com; visitmarshfield.com

Mauston • *Castle Rock Petenwell Lakes/Juneau County Tourism* • Barbara Baker; Exec. Dir.; 807 Division St.; 53948; Juneau; P 26,000; (608) 847-1904; juneautourism@yahoo.com; www.castlerock-petenwell.com

Menomonee Falls • *Menomonee Falls Visitor Center* • Toni Gumina Yates; Exec. Dir.; N91 W17271 Appleton Ave., Ste. 2; 53051; Waukesha; P 33,000; (262) 251-2430; Fax (262) 251-0969; info@fallschamber.com; www.fallschamber.com

Milwaukee • *Visit Milwaukee* • Paul Upchurch; Pres./CEO; 648 N. Plankinton Ave., Ste, 425; 53203; Milwaukee, Washington & Waukesha; P 595,000; (414) 273-7222; (800) 554-1448; Fax (414) 273-5596; info@milwaukee.org; www.visitmilwaukee.org

Oconomowoc • *Oconomowoc CVB* • Bob Duffy; Dir.; 174 E. Wisconsin Ave.; P.O. Box 27; 53066; Waukesha; P 16,000; (262) 569-2186; (800) 524-3744; Fax (262) 569-3238; info@oconomowoc-wi.gov; www.oconomowoc-wi.gov

Onalaska • *Onalaska Center for Commerce & Tourism* • Amy Gabay; Interim Tourism Dir.; 255 Riders Club Rd.; 54650; La Crosse; P 18,256; (608) 781-9570; (800) 873-1901; Fax (608) 781-9572; info@discoveronalaska.com; www.discoveronalaska.com

Oshkosh • *Oshkosh CVB* • Wendy Hielsberg; Exec. Dir.; 100 N. Main St., Ste. 112; 54901; Winnebago; P 67,000; (920) 303-9200; (877) 303-9200; Fax (920) 303-9294; info@visitoshkosh.com; www.visitoshkosh.com

Pewaukee • *see Waukesha*

Phillips • *Price County Tourism Dept.* • Kathy Reinhard; Dir.; 126 Cherry St., Rm. 9; 54555; Price; P 14,159; (715) 339-4505; (800) 269-4505; Fax (715) 339-3089; tourism@co.price.wi.us; www.pricecountywi.net

Rice Lake • *Rice Lake Tourism Comm.* • Nicky Repka; Coord.; 2961 Decker Dr.; P.O. Box 507; 54868; Barron; P 10,000; (715) 234-8888; (800) 523-6318; info@ricelaketourism.com; www.ricelaketourism.com

Richland Center • *Richland Center Tourism* • 397 W. Seminary St.; 53581; Richland; P 5,147; (608) 649-3376; Fax (608) 647-8360; visitor.center@richlandcenter.com; richlandcentertourism.com

Stevens Point • *Stevens Point Area CVB* • Sara Brish; Exec. Dir.; 340 Division St. N.; 54481; Portage; P 67,000; (715) 344-2556; Fax (715) 344-5818; info@stevenspointarea.com; www.stevenspointarea.com

Sturgeon Bay • *Door County Visitor Bur.* • Jack Moneypenny; Pres./CEO; 1015 Green Bay Rd.; P.O. Box 406; 54235; Door; P 29,000; (920) 743-4456; (800) 52-RELAX; Fax (920) 743-7873; info@doorcounty.com; www.doorcounty.com

Sturtevant • *Real Racine* • Dave Blank; Pres./CEO; 14015 Washington Ave.; 53177; Racine; P 195,000; (262) 884-6400; Fax (262) 884-6404; infodesk@racine.org; www.racine.org

Superior • *Superior-Douglas County Visitors Bur.* • David W. Minor; Pres./CEO; 305 Harbor View Pkwy.; 54880; Douglas; P 44,100; (715) 392-2773; (800) 942-5313; vacation@superiorchamber.org; www.superiorchamber.org

Tomah • *Tomah CVB* • Tina Thompson; Pres./CEO; 901 Kilbourn Ave.; P.O. Box 625; 54660; Monroe; P 9,189; (800) 948-6624; (608) 372-2166; Fax (608) 372-2167; info@tomahwisconsin.com; www.tomahwisconsin.com

Waukesha • *Waukesha & Pewaukee CVB* • Tammy Tritz; Exec. Dir.; N14 W23755 Stone Ridge Dr., Ste. 225; 53188; Waukesha; P 77,000; (262) 542-0330; (800) 366-8474; Fax (262) 542-2237; info@visitwaukesha.org; www.visitwaukesha.org

Waupaca • *Waupaca Area CVB* • Terri Schulz; Pres.; 221 S. Main St.; 54981; Waupaca; P 16,000; (715) 258-7343; (888) 417-4040; Fax (715) 258-7868; terri@waupacaareachamber.com; www.WaupacaMemories.com

Wausau • *Wausau/Central Wisconsin CVB* • Richard Barrett; Exec. Dir.; 219 Jefferson St.; 54403; Marathon; P 84,000; (715) 355-8788; (888) 948-4748; Fax (715) 359-2306; info@visitwausau.com; www.visitwausau.com

West Salem • *see Onalaska*

C & VB

Wisconsin Dells • *Wisconsin Dells Visitor & Conv. Bur.* • P.O. Box 390; 53965; Columbia; P 3,787; (608) 254-8088; (800) 223-3557; Fax (608) 254-4293; info@wisdells.com; www.wisdells.com

Wisconsin Rapids • *Heart of Wisconsin C/C* • 1120 Lincoln St.; 54494; Wood; P 40,000; (715) 423-1830; Fax (715) 423-1865; info@heartofwi.com; www.heartofwi.com

Wyoming

Casper • *Casper Area CVB* • Brook Kreder; CEO; 139 W. 2nd St., Ste. 1B; 82601; Natrona; P 81,000; (307) 234-5362; (800) 852-1889; Fax (307) 261-9928; visitors@visitcasper.com; www.visitcasper.com

Cheyenne • *Visit Cheyenne* • Darren Rudloff; Pres./CEO; One Depot Sq.; 121 W. 15th St., Ste. 202; 82001; Laramie; P 96,000; (307) 778-3133; (800) 426-5009; Fax (307) 778-3190; info@cheyenne.org; www.cheyenne.org

Cody • *Park County Travel Cncl.* • Claudia Wade; Dir.; P.O. Box 2454; 82414; Park; P 25,000; (307) 587-2297; Fax (307) 527-6228; pctc2@codychamber.org; www.yellowstonecountry.org

Evanston • *Bear River Travel Info. Center & State Park* • Wade Henderson; Superintendent; 601 Bear River Dr.; 82930; Uinta; P 12,000; (307) 789-6547; (307) 789-6540; Fax (307) 789-2618; sphs@state.wy.us; wyoparks.state.wy.us

Laramie • *Laramie Area CVB* • Fred Ockers; Exec. Dir.; 210 E. Custer St.; 82070; Albany; P 35,000; (307) 745-4195; (800) 445-5303; Fax (307) 721-2926; director@visitlaramie.org; www.visitlaramie.org

Meeteetse • *Meeteetse Visitor Center* • Yvonne Renner; Ofc. Mgr.; 2005 Warren St.; P.O. Box 238; 82433; Park; P 327; (307) 868-2454; director@tctwest.net; www.meeteetsewy.com

Rawlins • **Carbon County Visitors Cncl.** • Leslie Jefferson; Exec. Dir.; 214 4th St., Ofc. 11; P.O. Box 1017; 82301; Carbon; (307) 324-3020; (800) 228-3547; Fax (307) 324-8440; info@wyomingcarboncounty.com; www.wyomingcarboncounty.com

Sheridan • **Sheridan Travel & Tourism** • Shawn Buckley; Exec. Dir.; 1517 E. Fifth St.; P.O. Box 7155; 82801; Sheridan; (307) 673-7120; Fax (307) 672-7321; stt@sheridanwyoming.org; www.sheridanwyoming.org

ECONOMIC DEVELOPMENT COUNCILS

If the area that interests you is not listed in this section, please refer to the **United States Chambers of Commerce** section. Many Chambers double as Economic Development Councils for their area.

Alabama

Federal

U.S. SBA, Alabama Dist. Ofc. • Tom Todt; Dist. Dir.; 801 Tom Martin Dr., Ste. 201; 35211; Jefferson; P 4,822,023; (205) 290-7101; Fax (205) 290-7404; thomas.todt@sba.gov; www.sba.gov/al

State

Alabama Dept. of Commerce • Ted Clem; Dir. of Bus. Dev.; 401 Adams Ave., 6th Flr.; P.O. Box 304106; Montgomery; 36130; Montgomery; P 4,822,023; (334) 242-0400; (800) 248-0033; Fax (334) 353-1330; contact@madeinalabama.com; www.madeinalabama.com

Communities

Alexander City • **Lake Martin Area Eco. Dev. Alliance** • Don McClellan; Exec. Dir.; 1675 Cherokee Rd.; P.O. Box 1105; 35011; Tallapoosa; P 41,616; (256) 215-4411; Fax (256) 215-4452; dmcclellan@lakemartineda.com; lakemartineda.com

Athens • **Limestone County Eco. Dev. Assn.** • Tom Hill; Pres.; P.O. Box 1346; 35612; Limestone; P 83,000; (256) 232-2386; Fax (256) 233-1034; tomhill@lceda.com; www.lceda.com

Atmore • **Escambia County Ind. Dev. Auth.** • Ms. Marshall Rogers; Exec. Dir.; P.O. Box 1266; 36504; Escambia; P 38,300; (251) 368-5404; Fax (251) 368-1328; info@escambiaida.com; www.escambiaida.com

Auburn • **Auburn EDC** • T. Phillip Dunlap; Dir.; City Hall; 144 Tichenor Ave., Ste. 2; 36830; Lee; P 53,400; (334) 501-7270; Fax (334) 501-7289; webecondev@auburnalabama.org; www.auburnalabama.org

Bessemer • **City of Bessemer** • Forest Davis; Dir. of Eco. Dev.; 1800 3rd Ave. N.; 35020; Jefferson; P 30,000; (205) 424-4060; Fax (205) 426-8374; economicdev@bessemeral.org; www.bessemeral.org

Birmingham • **City of Birmingham Ofc. of Eco. Dev.** • Lisa D. Cooper; Dir.; 710 N. 20th St., 3rd Flr.; 35203; Jefferson; P 212,200; (205) 254-2799; Fax (205) 254-7741; lisa.cooper@birminghamal.gov; www.birminghamal.gov

Birmingham • **Birmingham Bus. Alliance** • Brian Hilson; Pres./CEO; 505 20th St. N., Ste. 200; 35203; Jefferson; P 1,100,000; (205) 324-2100; Fax (205) 324-2560; nbaldwin@birminghambusinessalliance.com; www.birminghambusinessalliance.com

Cullman • **Cullman Comm. & Eco. Dev.** • Peggy Smith; Dir.; 200 First Ave. N.E.; P.O. Box 1009; 35056; Cullman; P 80,000; (256) 739-1891; Fax (256) 739-6721; cullmaneda@cullmaneda.org; www.cullmaneda.org

Decatur • **Morgan County Eco. Dev. Assn.** • Jeremy Nails; Pres./CEO; 300 Market St. N.E., Ste. 2; 35601; Morgan; P 117,000; (256) 353-1213; Fax (256) 353-0407; mceda@mceda.org; www.mceda.org

Decatur • **North Alabama Ind. Dev. Assn.** • Tate Godfrey CEcD; Pres./CEO; 410 Johnston St., Ste. A; P.O. Box 1668; 35602; Morgan; P 900,000; (256) 353-9450; Fax (256) 353-5982; naida@naida.com; www.northalabamausa.com

Enterprise • **Enterprise Coffee Geneva Eco. Dev. Corp.** • Frank Thompson CEcD; Exec. Dir.; P.O. Box 310130; 36331; Coffee; P 50,000; (334) 393-4769; Fax (334) 393-8127; fthompson@entercomp.com; www.ecgedc.org

Evergreen • **Evergreen-Conecuh Eco. Dev. Ofc.** • Robert E. Skipper; Dir.; 100 Depot Sq.; 36401; Conecuh; P 14,000; (251) 578-1000; Fax (251) 578-1044; bskipper@evergreenal.org; www.evergreenareachamber.com

Florence • **Shoals Eco. Dev. Auth.** • Forrest Wright CEcD; Pres.; 20 Hightower Pl., Ste. 1; 35630; Lauderdale; P 143,000; (256) 349-5632; Fax (256) 764-3850; shoalseda@seda-shoals.com; www.seda-shoals.com

Gadsden • **Gadsden-Etowah County Ind. Dev. Auth.** • Michael McCain; Exec. Dir.; P.O. Box 271; 35902; Etowah; P 103,059; (256) 543-9423; Fax (256) 547-2351; info@gadsdenida.org; www.gadsdenida.org

Greenville • **Butler County Comm. for Eco. Dev.** • David Hutchison; Exec. Dir.; 750 Greenville Bypass, Bldg. 1, Ste. A; P.O. Box 758; 36037; Butler; P 23,000; (334) 371-8400; Fax (334) 371-8402; dhutchison@bcced.com; www.bcced.com

Guntersville • **Marshall County Eco. Dev. Cncl.** • Matt Arnold; Pres./CEO; 2208 Ringold St., Ste. 1-A; 35976; Marshall; P 93,000; (256) 582-5100; Fax (256) 582-8700; mattarnold@marshallteam.org; www.marshallteam.org

Huntsville • **Madison County Comm., Intl. Trade Dev. Center** • Anne W. Burkett; Dir. of Planning & Eco. Dev.; 100 Northside Square; 35801; Madison; P 300,000; (256) 532-3505; Fax (256) 532-3704; naita@naita.org; www.naita.org

Lanett • **Chambers County Dev. Auth.** • Valerie G. Gray; Exec. Dir.; 2102 S. Broad Ave.; P.O. Box 269; 36863; Chambers; P 34,241; (334) 642-1412; (334) 642-1413; Fax (334) 642-6548; vgray@chambersida.com; www.chambersda.com

Madison • **City of Madison-Planning Dept.** • Mary Beth Broeren; Dir. of Planning & Eco. Dev.; 100 Hughes Rd.; 35758; Madison; P 45,000; (256) 772-2885; marybeth.broeren@madisonal.gov; www.madisonal.gov

Mobile • **Mobile Aeroplex at Brookley** • Roger Wehner; Exec. Dir.; 1891 9th St.; 36615; Mobile; P 470,000; (251) 438-7334; Fax (251) 694-7667; roger@mobairport.com; www.mobileaeroplex.org

Monroeville • **Coastal Gateway Reg. Eco. Dev. Alliance** • John A. Johnson Ph.D; Exec. Dir.; Trustmark Bank Bldg.; 60 Hines St., Ste. 200; 36460; Monroe; (251) 248-2143; jajohnson@coastalgatewayeda.com; www.coastalgatewayeda.com

Montgomery • *Montgomery Area C/C - Eco. Dev.* • Ellen McNair CeCD; Sr. V.P. of Corp. Dev.; 41 Commerce St.; P.O. Box 79; 36101; Montgomery; P 256,000; (334) 834-5200; Fax (334) 265-4745; emcnair@montgomerychamber.com; www.choosemontgomery.com

Montgomery • *Eco. Dev. Assn. of Alabama* • Jim Searcy; Exec. Dir.; 2 N. Jackson St., Ste. 302; 36104; P 4,822,023; (334) 676-2085; Fax (334) 676-2087; info@edaa.org; www.edaa.org

Moulton • *Lawrence County Ind. Dev. Bd.* • Tony Stockton; Exec. Dir.; 12001 Alabama Hwy. 157; P.O. Box 367; 35650; Lawrence; P 35,000; (256) 974-2899; Fax (256) 974-2816; tony.stockton@lawrenceidb.com; www.lawrenceidb.com

Opelika • *Opelika EDC* • Lori Huguley; Dir.; 204 Seventh St. S.; P.O. Box 390; 36803; Lee; P 25,000; (334) 705-5115; Fax (334) 705-5113; lhuguley@ci.opelika.al.us; www.opelika.org

Pelham • *Shelby County Eco. & Ind. Dev. Auth.* • James Dedes; Exec. Dir.; 1126 County Services Dr.; 35124; Shelby; P 195,085; (205) 620-6640; Fax (205) 620-6644; info@sceida.org; www.sceida.org

Pell City • *St. Clairn County Eco. Dev. Cncl.* • Don Smith; Exec. Dir.; 500 College Cir., Ste. 306; 35125; St. Clair; P 128,000; (205) 814-1440; Fax (205) 814-1441; chill@stclairedc.com; www.stclairedc.com

Robertsdale • *Baldwin County Eco. Dev. Alliance* • Lee Lawson; Pres./CEO; 22251 Palmer St.; P.O. Box 1340; 36567; Baldwin; P 175,000; (251) 970-4081; Fax (251) 970-4084; llawson@baldwineda.com; www.baldwineda.com

Russellville • *Franklin County Dev. Auth.* • Mitchell Mays; Exec. Dir.; 16109 Hwy. 43, Ste. C; 35653; Franklin; P 32,000; (256) 332-8726; Fax (256) 332-8728; business@franklineda.com; www.franklineda.com

Scottsboro • *Jackson County Eco. Dev. Auth.* • 817 S. Broad St.; 35768; Jackson; P 52,000; (256) 574-1331; Fax (256) 259-0873; grogers@scottsboro.org; www.jacksoncountyeda.org

Selma • *Selma & Dallas County Eco. Dev. Auth.* • M. Wayne Vardaman; Exec. Dir.; 912 Selma Ave.; 36701; Dallas; P 43,800; (334) 875-8365; (800) 335-1332; Fax (334) 875-8453; vardaman@selmaeda.com; www.selmaeda.com

Sylacauga • *Talladega County Eco. Dev. Auth.* • Calvin Miller; Exec. Dir.; P.O. Box 867; 35150; Talladega; P 82,300; (256) 245-8332; Fax (256) 245-8336; millercalv@tceda.com; www.tceda.com

Troy • *Pike County Eco. Dev. Corp.* • Marsha Gaylard; Pres.; 100 Industrial Blvd.; 36081; Pike; P 30,000; (334) 670-2274; Fax (334) 566-2298; marsha@pikecountyedc.net; www.troy-pike-edc.org

Tuscaloosa • *Tuscaloosa County Ind. Dev. Auth.* • Dara Longgrear; Exec. Dir.; P.O. Box 2667; 35403; Tuscaloosa; P 194,700; (205) 349-1414; Fax (205) 349-1416; info@tcida.com; www.tcida.com

Union Springs • *Bullock County Dev. Auth.* • Dr. Julian Cope; Admin.; 106 E. Conecuh Ave.; 36089; Bullock; P 11,000; (334) 738-5411; Fax (334) 738-5310; bcda@ustconline.net; www.unionspringsalabama.com

Wetumpka • *Elmore County EDA* • Leisa Finley; Exec. Dir.; P.O. Box 117; 36092; Elmore; P 80,000; (334) 514-5843; lfinley@elmoreeda.com; www.elmoreeda.com

Alaska

Federal

Eco. Dev. Admin. • Shirley Kelly; 510 L St., Ste. 444; 99501; P 731,449; (907) 271-2272; Fax (907) 271-2273; skelly2@eda.gov; www.eda.gov

U.S. SBA, Alaska Dist. Ofc. • Sam Dickey; Dist. Dir.; 420 L St., Ste. 300; 99501; P 731,449; (907) 271-4022; Fax (907) 271-4545; AKInfo@sba.gov; www.sba.gov/ak

State

Alaska Bus. Dev. Center Inc. • 840 K St., Ste. 202; Anchorage; 99501; P 731,449; (907) 562-0335; Fax (907) 562-6988; info@abdc.org; www.abdc.org

Communities

Anchorage Area

Anchorage Eco. Dev. Corp. • Bill Popp; Pres./CEO; 510 L St., Ste. 603; 99501; P 260,000; (907) 258-3700; Fax (907) 258-6646; info@aedcweb.com; www.aedcweb.com

Alaska Village Initiative • Charles Parker; Pres./CEO; 1577 C St., Ste. 304; 99501; Anchorage; P 50,000; (907) 274-5400; Fax (907) 263-9971; rweaver@akvillage.com; www.akvillage.com

Alaska Ind. Dev. & Export Auth. • Ted Leonard; Exec. Dir.; 813 W. Northern Lights Blvd.; 99503; Anchorage; P 700,000; (907) 771-3000; Fax (907) 771-3044; tleonard@aidea.org; www.aidea.org

Southwest Alaska Municipal Conf. • Erik OBrien; Interim Dir.; 3300 Arctic Blvd., Ste. 203; 99503; Anchorage; P 29,078; (907) 562-7380; Fax (888) 356-1206; eobrien@swamc.org; www.swamc.org

Fairbanks • *Fairbanks Eco. Dev. Corp.* • Jim Dodson; CEO; 330 Wendell Ave., Ste. E; 99701; Fairbanks North Star Borough; P 99,000; (907) 452-2185; Fax (907) 451-9534; info@investfairbanks.com; www.investfairbanks.com

Glennallen • *Copper Valley Dev. Assn.* • Jason Hoke; Exec. Dir.; P.O. Box 9; 99588; Valdez Cordova; P 2,997; (907) 822-5001; Fax (907) 822-5009; jhoke@coppervalley.org; www.coppervalley.org

Juneau • *Juneau Eco. Dev. Cncl.* • Brian Holst; Exec. Dir.; 612 W. Willoughby Ave., Ste. A; 99801; Juneau; P 30,000; (907) 523-2300; Fax (907) 463-3929; bholst@jedc.org; www.jedc.org

Kenai • *Kenai Peninsula Borough Eco. Dev. Dist.* • John Torgerson; Exec. Dir.; 14896 Kenai Spur Hwy., Ste. 103A; 99611; Kenai Peninsula; P 55,000; (907) 283-3335; Fax (907) 283-3913; jtorgerson@kpedd.org; www.kpedd.org

Kotzebue • *NW Arctic Borough Eco. Dev. Commission* • Lincoln Saito; Dir.; P.O. Box 1110; 99752; Northwest Arctic; P 7,200; (907) 442-2500; Fax (907) 442-2560; lsaito@nwabor.org; www.nwabor.org

Palmer • *Matanuska-Susitna Borough Planning & Land Use* • Christine Nelson; Dir.; 350 E. Dahlia Ave.; 99645; Matanuska Susitna; P 80,000; (907) 745-9850; cnelson@matsugov.us; www.matsugov.us

Sitka • *Sitka Eco. Dev. Comm.* • Wells Williams; Planning Dir.; 100 Lincoln St.; 99835; Sitka; P 8,947; (907) 747-1824; Fax (907) 747-6138; wells@cityofsitka.com; www.cityofsitka.com

Sitka • *Sitka Eco. Dev. Assn.* • Garry White; Exec. Dir.; 329 Harbor Dr., Ste. 212; 99835; Sitka; P 8,947; (907) 747-2660; inforequest@sitka.net; www.sitka.net

Skagway • *Skagway Dev. Corp.* • Juliene Miles; Exec. Dir.; 840 A State St.; P.O. Box 1236; 99840; Skagway; P 1,004; (907) 983-3414; Fax (907) 983-3414; skagdev@aptalaska.net; www.skagwaydevelopment.org

Wrangell • *Wrangell Eco. Dev. Dept.* • P.O. Box 531; 99929; Wrangell; P 2,200; (907) 874-2381; Fax (907) 874-3952; wrangell@wrangell.com; www.wrangell.com

Arizona

Federal

U.S. SBA, Arizona Dist. Ofc. • Robert J. Blaney; Dist. Dir.; 2828 N. Central Ave., Ste. 800; 85004; Maricopa; P 6,553,255; (602) 745-7200; Fax (602) 745-7210; robert.blaney@sba.gov; www.sba.gov/az

State

Arizona Commerce Auth. • Sandra Watson; Pres./CEO; 333 N. Central Ave., Ste. 1900; Phoenix; 85004; Maricopa; P 6,553,255; (602) 845-1200; Fax (602) 845-1201; nicolem@azcommerce.com; www.azcommerce.com

Communities

Apache Junction • *Apache Junction Eco. Dev. Ofc.* • Steve Filipowicz; Eco. Dev. Dir.; 300 E. Superstition Blvd., 2nd Flr.; 85219; Pinal; P 41,000; (480) 474-5064; Fax (480) 474-5110; econinfo@ajcity.net; www.ajcity.net

Ash Fork • *Ash Fork Dev. Assn.* • Fayrene Hume; Pres.; 518 W. Louis Ave.; P.O. Box 293; 86320; Yavapai; P 2,000; (928) 637-2774; Fax (928) 637-0394

Avondale • *Avondale Eco. Dev.* • Dina Mathias; Eco. Dev. Dir.; 11465 W. Civic Center Dr., Ste. 210; 85323; Maricopa; P 76,000; (623) 333-1400; Fax (623) 333-0140; emaileconomicdevelopment@avondale.org; www.avondale.org/econdev

Benson • *Southeast AZ Eco. Dev. Group* • George Scott; Exec. Dir.; 168 E. 4th St.; 85602; Cochise; P 130,000; (520) 265-6058; george@saedg.org; www.saedg.org

Buckeye • *Town of Buckeye, Eco. Dev. Dept.* • Cheryl Covert; Bus. Dev. Coord.; 530 E. Monroe Ave.; 85326; Maricopa; P 33,000; (623) 349-6970; Fax (623) 349-6099; ccovert@buckeyeaz.gov; www.buckeyeaz.gov

Bullhead City • *Bullhead Reg. Eco. Dev. Auth.* • Toby Cotter; City Mgr.; 2355 Trane Rd.; 86429; Mohave; P 40,000; (928) 763-9400; Fax (928) 704-6376; tcotter@bullheadcity.com; www.bullheadcity.com

Camp Verde • *Camp Verde Eco. Dev. Dept.* • Steve Ayers; 473 S. Main St., Ste. 102; 86322; Yavapai; P 11,000; (928) 554-0007; steve.ayers@campverde.az.gov; www.campverde.az.gov

Coolidge • *Growth Management Dept.* • C. Alton Bruce; Growth Mgmt. Dir.; 131 W. Pinkley Ave.; 85228; Pinal; P 11,000; (520) 723-6075; Fax (520) 723-6079; abruce@coolidgeaz.com; www.coolidgeaz.com

Cottonwood • *Cottonwood Eco. Dev. Cncl.* • Casey Rooney; Dir.; 827 N. Main St.; 86326; Yavapai; P 11,300; (928) 340-2741; crooney@cottonwoodaz.gov; www.cottonwoodedc.com

Eloy • *Eco. Dev. Group of Eloy* • Rick Miller; Exec. Dir.; 305 N. Stuart Blvd.; 85131; Pinal; P 11,000; (520) 466-3411; (888) 695-1695; info@edgeaz.org; www.edgeaz.org

Flagstaff • *Choose Flagstaff* • John Saltonstall; Bus. Retention & Expansion Mgr.; 211 W. Aspen Ave.; 86001; Coconino; P 68,800; (928) 213-2966; jsaltonstall@flagstaffaz.gov; www.chooseflagstaff.com

Gilbert • *Gilbert Eco. Dev. Advisory Bd.* • Dan Henderson CEcD; Eco. Dev. Mgr.; 90 E. Civic Center Dr.; 85296; Maricopa; P 203,500; (480) 503-6010; dan.henderson@gilbertaz.gov; www.ci.gilbert.az.us

Glendale • *Access Arizonaâ„¢* • Patricia King; Exec. Mgr.; 17235 N. 75th Ave., Ste. D145; 85308; Maricopa; P 74,250; (520) 836-6868; Fax (602) 789-9126; info@accessarizona.org; www.accessarizona.org

Glendale • *City of Glendale Eco. Dev. Dept.* • Brian Friedman; Dir.; 5850 W. Glendale Ave., Ste. 217; 85301; Maricopa; P 250,000; (623) 930-2983; Fax (623) 931-5730; bfriedman@glendaleaz.com; www.glendaleaz.com

Globe • *Gila County Comm. Dev. Ofc.* • Robert Gould; Dir.; 1400 E. Ash St.; 85501; Gila; P 51,000; (928) 425-3231; Fax (928) 425-0829; communitydevelopment@gilacountyaz.gov; www.gilacountyaz.gov

Goodyear • *Goodyear Eco. Dev. Dept.* • Michelle Lawrie; Eco. Dev. Dir.; 14455 W. Van Buren St., Ste. D102; 85338; Maricopa; P 77,000; (623) 932-3025; Fax (623) 932-3028; gyecdev@goodyearaz.gov; develop.goodyearaz.com

Kingman • *Mohave County Eco. Dev. Dept.* • Bennett R. Bratley; Dir.; 3250 E. Kino Ave, 2nd Flr.; 86409; Mohave; P 204,000; (928) 757-0960; Fax (928) 757-0934; bennett.bratley@mohavecounty.us; www.mohavedevelopment.org

Lake Havasu City • *Partnership for Eco. Dev.* • James Gray; Dir.; 314 London Bridge Rd.; 86403; Mohave; P 51,000; (928) 505-7333; jamesgray.lhc@gmail.com; www.lakehavasu.org

Maricopa • *Maricopa Eco. Dev. Dept.* • Micah Miranda; Dir.; 39700 W. Civic Center Plaza; 85138; Pinal; P 50,000; (520) 316-6812; Fax (520) 568-9120; micah.miranda@maricopa-az.gov; www.maricopamatters.com

Mesa • *City of Mesa* • William J. Jabjiniak; Dir. of Eco. Dev.; P.O. Box 1466; 85211; Maricopa; P 454,000; (480) 644-3561; Fax (480) 644-3458; william.jabjiniak@mesaaz.gov; www.mesaaz.gov

Peoria • *Peoria Eco. Dev. Dept.* • Scott Whyte; Dir.; 9875 N. 85th Ave.; 85345; Maricopa; P 162,600; (623) 773-7735; Fax (623) 773-7519; peoriaed@peoriaaz.gov; www.peoriaaz.gov

Phoenix • *City of Phoenix Comm. & Eco. Dev. Dept.* • Christine Mackay; Dir.; 200 W. Washington St., 20th Flr.; 85003; Maricopa; P 1,400,000; (602) 262-5040; Fax (602) 495-5097; phx.business@phoenix.gov; www.phoenix.gov/econdev/

Phoenix • *Greater Phoenix Eco. Cncl.* • Chris Camacho; Pres./CEO; 2 N. Central Ave., Ste. 2500; 85004; Maricopa; P 4,000,000; (602) 256-7700; (800) 421-4732; Fax (602) 256-7744; info@gpec.org; www.gpec.org

Prescott • *City of Prescott, Eco. Dev.* • Wendy Bridges; Tour. & Eco. Dev. Coord.; P.O. Box 2059; 86302; Yavapai; P 39,843; (928) 777-1100; Fax (928) 777-1255; citystaff@cityofprescott.net; www.cityofprescott.net

Sahuarita • *Sahuarita Eco. Dev.* • Kathy Ward; Eco. Dev. Mgr.; 375 W. Sahuarita Center Way; 85629; Pima; P 10,000; (520) 822-8815; kward@ci.sahuarita.az.us; www.ci.sahuarita.az.us

Scottsdale • *City of Scottsdale, Scottsdale Eco. Vitality Dept.* • Jim Mullin; Dir.; 4021 N. 75th St., Ste. 102; 85251; Maricopa; P 220,000; (480) 312-7989; Fax (480) 312-2672; jmullin@scottsdaleaz.gov; www.scottsdaleaz.gov

Sierra Vista • *Sierra Vista Eco. Dev. Found.* • Mignonne Hollis; Exec. Dir.; 750 E. Bartow Dr., Ste. 16; 85635; Cochise; P 45,303; (520) 458-6948; Fax (520) 458-7453; admin@svedf.org; www.svedf.org

Superior • *Eco. Dev. Advisory Bd.* • Melanie Oliver; Town Mgr.; 199 N. Lobb Ave.; 85173; Pinal; P 3,200; (520) 689-5752; Fax (520) 689-5822; townmanager@superior-arizona.com; www.superior-arizona.com

Tempe • *Tempe C/C Eco. Dev.* • Mary Ann Miller; Pres./CEO; 909 E. Apache Blvd.; P.O. Box 28500; 85285; Maricopa; P 166,840; (480) 967-7891; Fax (480) 966-5365; donna@tempechamber.org; www.tempechamber.org

Tolleson • *Tolleson Eco. Dev.* • Paul Magallanez; Eco. Dev. Dir.; 9555 W. Van Buren St.; 85353; Maricopa; P 6,500; (623) 474-4998; (623) 936-7111; Fax (623) 936-7117; pmagallanez@tollesonaz.org; www.tollesonaz.org

Tucson • *Sun Corridor Inc.* • Joe Snell; Pres./CEO; 1985 E. River Rd., Ste. 185; 85718; Pima; P 800,000; (520) 243-1900; (866) 600-0331; courtney.pulitzer@suncorridorinc.com; www.suncorridorinc.com

Wickenburg • *Wickenburg Eco. Dev. Comm.* • Joshua Wright; Town Mgr.; 155 N. Tegner St., Ste. A; 85390; Maricopa; P 6,363; (928) 684-5451; Fax (602) 506-1580; dables@wickenburgaz.org; www.ci.wickenburg.az.us

Willcox • *Willcox Eco. Dev.* • Telly Stanger; Mgr. of Eco. Dev.; 1500 N. Circle I Rd.; 85643; Cochise; P 4,000; (520) 384-5515; Fax (520) 384-0293; tstanger@ssvec.com; www.willcoxchamber.com

Winslow • *City of Winslow Eco. Dev.* • Jim Ferguson; City Mgr.; 21 N. Williamson Ave.; 86047; Navajo; P 9,800; (928) 289-2423; Fax (928) 289-2184; jim.ferguson@ci.winslow.az.us; www.ci.winslow.az.us

Yuma • *Greater Yuma Eco. Dev. Corp.* • Julie Engel; Pres./CEO; 899 E. Plaza Cir., Ste. 2; 85365; Yuma; P 196,000; (928) 782-7774; Fax (928) 782-7775; info@greateryuma.org; www.greateryuma.org

Arkansas

Federal

U.S. SBA, Arkansas Dist. Ofc. • Linda Nelson; Dist. Dir.; 2120 Riverfront Dr., Ste. 250; 72202; Pulaski; P 2,949,131; (501) 324-7379; Fax (501) 324-7394; linda.nelson@sba.gov; www.sba.gov/ar

State

Arkansas Eco. Dev. Comm. • Grant Tennille; Exec. Dir.; 900 W. Capitol Ave., Ste. 400; Little Rock; 72201; Pulaski; P 2,949,131; (501) 682-1121; (501) 682-7351; Fax (501) 682-7499; jsanderlin@arkansasedc.com; www.arkansasedc.com

Communities

Arkadelphia • *Arkadelphia Reg. Eco. Dev. Alliance & Area C/C* • Stephen Bell; Pres./CEO; 2401 Pine Street, Ste. B; 71923; Clark; P 22,750; (870) 246-1460; tiffany@arkadelphiaalliance.com; www.arkadelphiaalliance.com

Benton • *Benton Comm. & Eco. Dev.* • Brad Jordan; Dir.; P.O. Box 607; 72018; Saline; P 34,000; (501) 776-5938; Fax (501) 776-5910; brad@bentonar.org; www.bentonar.gov

Bentonville • *Bentonville Ind. Dev. Corp.* • Ed Clifford; Pres./CEO; 200 E. Central Ave.; P.O. Box 330; 72712; Benton; P 30,000; (479) 273-2841; Fax (479) 273-2180; eclifford@bbvchamber.com; www.bbvchamber.com

Booneville • *Booneville Dev. Corp.* • Trinity Damron; Exec. Dir.; 210 E. Main St.; P.O. Box 55; 72927; Logan; P 4,100; (479) 675-2666; Fax (479) 675-5158; information1@booneville.com; www.booneville.com

Camden • *Camden Area Ind. Dev. Corp.* • James Lee Silliman; Exec. Dir.; 314 Adams S.W.; P.O. Box 99; 71711; Ouachita; P 13,000; (870) 836-6426; Fax (870) 836-6400; caidcark@yahoo.com; www.teamcamden.com

Conway • *Conway Dev. Corp.* • Brad Lacy; Dir. of Eco. Dev.; 900 Oak St.; 72032; Faulkner; P 119,600; (501) 329-7788; Fax (501) 327-7790; brad@conwayarkansas.org; www.conwayarkansas.org

Crossett • *Crossett Eco. Dev. Found.* • Mike Smith; Exec. Dir.; 125 Main St.; 71635; Ashley; (870) 364-8745; Fax (870) 364-2358; mike@cityofcrossett.net; www.considercrossett.net

El Dorado • *El Dorado Dev. Corp.* • John Lowery Jr.; Pres.; 111 W. Main St.; 71730; Union; P 20,000; (870) 863-6113; Fax (870) 863-6115; jeremy@goeldorado.com; www.groweldorado.com

Heber Springs • *Cleburne County Ofc. of Eco. Dev.* • Jim Jackson; Dir.; 300 W. Main St.; 72543; Cleburne; P 26,000; (501) 362-8402; Fax (501) 362-4605; ccoed@cleburnecountyarkansas.com; www.cleburnecountyar.com

Helena • *Helena Harbor, Port & Industrial Park* • John C. Edwards; Eco. Dev. Dir.; Hwy. 20 & Helm Rd.; P.O. Box 407; 72342; Phillips; P 22,000; (870) 338-6444; (501) 680-5248; Fax (870) 338-6445; jedwards@helenaharbor.com; www.helenaharbor.com

Hope • *Hempstead County Eco. Dev. Corp.* • Wesley Woodard; Pres.; P.O. Box 971; 71802; Hempstead; P 22,600; (870) 777-8485; Fax (870) 777-5266; wesley@hopeusa.com; www.hopeusa.com

Hot Springs • *West Central AR Plan. & Dev. Dist. Inc.* • Dwayne Pratt; Exec. Dir.; 1000 Central Ave.; P.O. Box 6409; 71902; Garland; P 291,449; (501) 525-7577; Fax (501) 525-7677; dpratt@wcapdd.org; www.wcapdd.org

Little Rock • *Little Rock Port Auth.* • Bryan Day; Exec. Dir.; 10600 Industrial Harbor Dr.; 72206; Pulaski; P 198,000; (501) 490-1468; Fax (501) 490-1800; krobinson@lrportauthority.com; www.lrportauthority.com

Magnolia • *Magnolia Eco. Dev. Corp.* • Cammie Hambrice; Exec. Dir.; 211 W. Main St.; P.O. Box 866; 71754; Columbia; P 24,500; (870) 234-4352; Fax (870) 234-9291; ch@ccalliance.us; www.magnoliaedc.com

Marion • *Marion Eco. Dev.* • Kay Brockwell; Dir.; 13 Military Rd.; 72364; Crittenden; P 12,300; (870) 739-5414; Fax (870) 739-5448; kayb@marionarkansas.org; www.marionarkansas.org

Monticello • *Monticello Eco. Dev. Comm.* • Nita McDaniel; Exec. Dir.; 211 W. Gaines; P.O. Box 1890; 71657; Drew; P 18,900; (870) 367-3076; Fax (870) 367-3492; success@monticelloedc.org; www.monticelloedc.org

Morrilton • *Conway County Eco. Dev. Corp.* • John Gibson; Pres.; 120 N. Division St.; P.O. Box 589; 72110; Conway; P 6,700; (501) 354-2393; Fax (501) 354-8642; johngibson@suddenlinkmail.com; www.morrilton.com

Paragould • *Paragould EDC* • Sue McGowan; Dir./CEO; 300 W. Court St.; P.O. Box 124; 72451; Greene; P 26,500; (870) 236-7684; Fax (870) 236-7142; smcgowan@paragould.org; www.paragould.org

Pine Bluff • *Eco. Dev. Alliance for Jefferson County* • Lou Ann Nisbett; Pres./CEO; 510 Main St.; P.O. Box 5069; 71611; Jefferson; P 77,000; (870) 535-0110; Fax (870) 535-1643; lanisbett@sbcglobal.net; www.jeffersoncountyalliance.com

Prescott • *Prescott Eco. Dev. Ofc.* • Mary Godwin; Dir.; 116 E. 2nd St.; P.O. Box 307; 71857; Nevada; P 8,997; (870) 887-6208; Fax (870) 887-5317; mgodwin@pnpartnership.org; www.pnpartnership.org

Russellville • *Arkansas Valley Alliance for Eco. Dev.* • Stephanie Beerman; Interim Dir.; 708 W. Main St.; 72801; Pope; P 90,000; (479) 858-6555; Fax (479) 858-6496; sbeerman@arkansasvalleyalliance.org; arkansasvalleyalliance.org

Springdale • *Northwest Arkansas Cncl.* • Mike Malone; Pres./CEO; 4100 Corporate Center Dr., Ste. 205; 72762; Washington; P 73,500; (479) 582-2100; Fax (479) 582-1919; main@nwacouncil.org; www.nwacouncil.org

Wynne • *Wynne Eco. Dev. Corp.* • Chris Clifton CED IOM; Pres./CEO; 1790 N. Falls Blvd., Ste. 2; P.O. Box 234; 72396; Cross; P 17,800; (870) 238-9300; Fax (870) 238-7844; chrisc@crosscountychamber.com; www.crosscountychamber.com

California

Federal

U.S. SBA, Fresno Dist. Ofc. • Carlos G. Mendoza; Dist. Dir.; 801 R St., Ste. 201; 93721; Fresno; P 38,041,430; (559) 487-5791; Fax (559) 487-5636; carlos.mendoza@sba.gov; www.sba.gov/ca

U.S. SBA, Los Angeles Dist. Ofc. • Victor Parker; Dist. Dir.; 330 N. Brand, Ste. 1200; 91203; Los Angeles; P 38,041,430; (818) 552-3201; Fax (818) 552-3286; victor.parker@sba.gov; www.sba.gov/ca

U.S. SBA, Sacramento Dist. Ofc. • Joe McClure; Dist. Dir.; 6501 Sylvan Rd., Ste. 100; 95610; Sacramento; P 38,041,430; (916) 735-1700; Fax (916) 735-1719; joseph.mcclure@sba.gov; www.sba.gov/ca

U.S. SBA, San Diego Dist. Ofc. • Ruben Garcia; Dist. Dir.; 550 W. C St., Ste. 550; 92101; San Diego; P 38,041,430; (619) 557-7250; (619) 727-4883; Fax (619) 557-5894; kathleen.moran@sba.gov; www.sba.gov/ca

U.S. SBA, San Francisco Dist. Ofc. • Mark Quinn; Dist. Dir.; 455 Market St., Ste. 600; 94105; San Francisco; P 38,041,430; (415) 744-6820; john.quinn@sba.gov; www.sba.gov/ca

U.S. SBA, Santa Ana Dist. Ofc. • J. Adalberto Quijada; Dist. Dir.; 200 W. Santa Ana Blvd., Ste. 700; 92701; Orange; P 38,041,430; (714) 550-7420; Fax (714) 550-7409; adalberto.quijada@sba.gov; www.sba.gov/ca/santa

State

California Assn. for Local Eco. Dev. Prof. • Gurbax Sahota; Pres./CEO; 550 Bercut Dr., Ste. G; Sacramento; 95811; Sacramento; P 38,041,430; (916) 448-8252; Fax (916) 448-3811; gsahota@caled.org; www.caled.org

Communities

Anaheim • *City of Anaheim Comm. & Eco. Dev.* • John Woodhead; Dir.; City Hall East; 201 S. Anaheim Blvd., Ste. 1003; 92805; Orange; P 341,000; (714) 765-4300; Fax (714) 765-4313; cmorris@anaheim.net; www.anaheim.net

Apple Valley • *Apple Valley Eco. Dev.* • Frank W. Robinson; Town Mgr.; 14975 Dale Evans Pkwy.; 92307; San Bernardino; P 70,000; (760) 240-7000; Fax (760) 240-7910; applevalley@applevalley.org; www.applevalley.org

Auburn • *Placer County Ofc. of Eco. Dev.* • Paul Griffith; Mgr.; 175 Fulweiler Ave., Ste. 100; 95603; Placer; P 368,000; (530) 889-4058; Fax (530) 889-4095; jlsage@placer.ca.gov; www.placer.ca.gov

Bakersfield • *Kern Eco. Dev. Corp.* • Richard Chapman; Pres./CEO; 2700 M St., Ste. 200; 93301; Kern; (661) 862-5150; Fax (661) 862-5151; richard@kedc.com; www.kedc.com

Belmont • *San Mateo County Eco. Dev. Assn.* • Rosanne Foust; Pres./CEO; 1301 Shoreway Rd., Ste. 150; 94002; San Mateo; P 718,500; (650) 413-5600; Fax (650) 413-5909; cmadrigal@samceda.org; www.samceda.org

Berkeley • *Berkeley Eco. Dev.* • Felicia Graham; Bus. Asst.; 2180 Milvia St., 5th Flr.; 94704; Alameda; P 121,000; (510) 981-7530; Fax (510) 981-7099; fgraham@cityofberkeley.info; www.cityofberkeley.info

Brawley • *Brawley Eco. Dev. Comm.* • Katie B. Luna; Exec. Dir.; 204 S. Imperial Ave.; P.O. Box 218; 92227; Imperial; P 25,000; (760) 344-3160; (760) 344-3740; Fax (760) 344-7611; info@brawleychamber.com; www.brawleychamber.com

Brea • *Brea Eco. Dev.* • Eric Nicoll; Dir.; 1 Civic Center Circle, Level 2; 92821; Orange; P 39,200; (714) 671-4421; Fax (714) 671-4480; pamo@cityofbrea.net; www.ci.brea.ca.us

Burbank • *Burbank Eco. Dev.* • Mary Hamzoian; Eco. Dev. Mgr.; 150 N. Third St.; 91502; Los Angeles; P 105,400; (818) 238-5180; Fax (818) 238-5174; mhamzoian@burbankca.gov; econdev.burbankca.gov

Calexico • *Calexico Redev. Agency* • Oscar G. Rodriquez; Exec. Dir.; 608 Heber Ave.; 92231; Imperial; P 38,500; (760) 768-2177; Fax (760) 357-3831; orodriquez@calexico.ca.gov; www.calexico.ca.gov

California City • *California City Eco. Dev. Corp.* • Dr. Larry Adams; 8001 California City Blvd.; 93505; Kern; P 14,100; (760) 373-2007; Fax (760) 373-1414; californiacityedc@verizon.net; www.californiacityedc.org

Camarillo • *Ventura County Eco. Dev. Assn.* • Bill Buratto; Pres./CEO; 4219 Transport St.; 93003; Ventura; P 823,300; (805) 676-1332; Fax (805) 676-1362; info@vceda.org; www.vceda.org

Carson • *Carson Eco. Dev.* • Cliff Graves; Mgr.; 701 E. Carson St.; 90745; Los Angeles; P 91,714; (310) 233-4802; (310) 830-7600; cgraves@carson.ca.us; www.ci.carson.ca.us

Ceres • *City of Ceres Eco. Dev.* • Steven Hallam; Eco. Dev. Mgr.; 2720 2nd St.; 95307; Stanislaus; P 48,000; (209) 538-5756; Fax (209) 538-5650; steve.hallam@ci.ceres.ca.us; www.ci.ceres.ca.us

Chico • *3CORE* • Marc Nemanic; Exec. Dir.; 1430 East Ave., Ste. 4A; 95926; Butte; P 225,400; (530) 893-8732; Fax (530) 893-0820; mnemanic@3coreedc.org; www.3coreedc.org

Chula Vista • *South County Eco. Dev. Cncl.* • Cindy Gompper-Graves; Exec. Dir.; 1111 Bay Blvd., Ste. E; 91911; San Diego; P 800,000; (619) 424-5143; Fax (619) 424-5738; scedc@southcountyedc.com; www.southcountyedc.com

Colton • *Colton Eco. Dev. Div.* • Arthur W. Morgan; Eco. Dev. Mgr.; 650 N. La Cadena Dr.; 92324; San Bernardino; P 53,000; (909) 370-6170; Fax (909) 370-5196; amorgan@coltonca.gov; www.coltonca.gov

Colusa • *Colusa County Eco. Dev. Corp.* • Lynda Reynolds; 2963 Davison Ct.; P.O. Box 1077; 95932; Colusa; P 22,000; (530) 458-3028; lyndareynolds@colusacountyedc.com; www.colusacountyedc.com

Commerce • *Comm. Dev. Dept.* • Robert Zarrilli; Dir.; 2535 Commerce Way; 90040; Los Angeles; P 12,800; (323) 722-4805; Fax (323) 888-6537; robertz@ci.commerce.ca.us; www.ci.commerce.ca.us

Concord • *Contra Costa Cncl.* • Linda Best; Exec. Dir.; 1355 Willow Way, Ste. 253; 94520; Contra Costa; P 1,000,000; (925) 246-1880; Fax (925) 674-1654; info@contracostacouncil.com; www.contracostacouncil.com

Cypress • *City of Cypress Comm. Dev.* • Douglas Dancs P.E.; Comm. Dev. Dir.; 5275 Orange Ave.; P.O. Box 609; 90630; Orange; P 49,300; (714) 229-6720; Fax (714) 229-0154; cdd@cypressca.org; www.cypressca.org

El Cajon • *San Diego East County Eco. Dev. Cncl.* • Jo Marie Diamond; Pres./CEO; 1908 Friendship Dr., Ste. A; 92020; San Diego; P 480,500; (619) 258-3670; Fax (619) 258-3674; info@eastcountyedc.org; www.eastcountyedc.org

El Centro • *Imperial County Planning & Dev. Svcs.* • Jim Minnick; Dir.; 801 Main St.; 92243; Imperial; P 180,200; (442) 265-1736; Fax (442) 265-1735; planninginfo@co.imperial.ca.us; www.icpds.com

Escondido • *City of Escondido Eco. Dev. Div.* • Joyce Masterson; Dir.; 201 N. Broadway; 92025; San Diego; P 151,500; (760) 839-4587; (760) 839-4621; Fax (760) 839-4578; mgeller@escondido.org; www.escondido.org

Eureka • *Redwood Region Eco. Dev. Comm.* • Gregg Foster; Exec. Dir.; 520 E St.; 95501; Humboldt; P 129,000; (707) 445-9651; Fax (707) 445-9652; gregg@rredc.com; www.rredc.com

Eureka • *Arcata Eco. Dev. Corp.* • Ross Welch; Exec. Dir.; 707 K St.; 95501; Humboldt; P 228,700; (707) 798-6132; Fax (707) 798-6130; keif@aedc1.org; www.aedc1.org

Exeter • *Tulare County Eco. Dev. Corp.* • Paul Saldana CEcD; Pres./CEO; 506 N. Kaweah Ave., Ste. A; 93221; Tulare; P 460,000; (559) 592-1349; stradd@sequoiavalley.com; www.sequoiavalley.com

Fairfield • *Solano EDC* • Sandy Person; Pres.; 360 Campus Ln., Ste. 102; 94534; Solano; P 436,100; (707) 864-1855; (888) 864-1855; Fax (707) 864-6621; info@solanoedc.org; www.solanoedc.org

Fontana • *Fontana Eco. Dev.* • Jerry Edgett; Proj. Spec.; 8353 Sierra Ave.; 92335; San Bernardino; P 210,000; (909) 350-6741; Fax (909) 350-6616; jedgett@fontana.org; www.fontanabusiness.org

Fortuna • *Fortuna Bus. Improvement Dist.* • David Reed; Coord.; P.O. Box 1000; 95540; Humboldt; P 11,350; (707) 725-9261; Fax (707) 725-0806; info@fortunabusiness.com; www.fortunabusiness.com

Fountain Valley • *City of Fountain Valley, Planning Dept.* • Matt Mogensen; Dir.; 10200 Slater Ave.; 92708; Orange; P 58,000; (714) 593-4425; Fax (714) 593-4494; matt.mogensen@fountainvalley.org; www.fountainvalley.org

Fresno • *Eco. Dev. Corp. serving Fresno County* • Lee Ann Eager; Pres./CEO; 906 N St., Ste. 120; 93721; Fresno; (559) 476-2501; Fax (559) 233-2156; smoua@fresnoedc.com; www.fresnoedc.com

Fullerton • *City of Fullerton Eco. Dev. Div.* • Nicole Bernard; Mgr.; 303 W. Commonwealth; 92832; Orange; P 141,000; (714) 738-4102; nicoleb@ci.fullerton.ca.us; www.cityoffullerton.com

Garden Grove • *Garden Grove Eco. Dev.* • Greg Blodgett; Sr. Proj. Mgr.; 11222 Acacia Pkwy.; 92840; Orange; P 172,000; (714) 741-5130; econdev@ci.garden-grove.ca.us; www.ci.garden-grove.ca.us

Gilroy • *Gilroy Eco. Dev. Corp.* • Tammy Brownlow; Pres./CEO; 7471 Monterey St.; 95020; Santa Clara; P 57,000; (408) 847-7611; Fax (408) 842-6010; president@gilroyedc.org; www.gilroyedc.org

Glendale • *City of Glendale Comm. Redev. & Housing* • Ken Hitts; Eco. Dev. Mgr.; 633 E. Broadway, Ste. 201; 91206; Los Angeles; P 194,900; (818) 548-3155; Fax (818) 409-7239; khitts@ci.glendale.ca.us; www.thinkglendale.com

Grass Valley • *Nevada County Eco. Resource Cncl.* • Jon Gregory; Exec. Dir.; 104B New Mohawk Rd., Ste. 2; 95959; Nevada; P 99,000; (530) 274-8455; Fax (530) 274-3373; info@ncerc.org; www.ncerc.org

Hanford • *Kings County Eco. Dev. Corp.* • John S. Lehn; Pres./CEO; 120 N. Irwin St.; 93230; Kings; P 155,000; (559) 585-3576; Fax (559) 585-7398; info.kingsedc@co.kings.ca.us; www.kingsedc.org

Hesperia • *Hesperia Eco. Dev.* • Susie Flores; Admin. Secy.; 9700 7th Ave.; 92345; San Bernardino; P 91,000; (760) 947-1909; Fax (760) 947-1917; econdev@cityofhesperia.us; www.cityofhesperia.us

Huntington Beach • *Huntington Beach Bus. Dev.* • Kellee Fritzal; Dep. Dir.; 2000 Main St.; 92648; Orange; P 190,000; (714) 536-5582; (714) 536-5547; Fax (714) 375-5087; openhb@surfcity-hb.org; www.hbbiz.com

Irvine • *Orange County Bus. Cncl.* • Lucy Dunn; Pres./CEO; 2 Park Plz., Ste. 100; 92614; Orange; P 3,000,000; (949) 476-2242; Fax (949) 476-9240; bmoulthrop@ocbc.org; www.ocbc.org

Irwindale • *San Gabriel Valley Eco. Partnership* • Jeff Allred; Pres./CEO; 4900 Rivergrade Rd., Ste. B130; 91706; Los Angeles; P 1,800,000; (626) 856-3400; Fax (626) 856-5115; info@valleyconnect.com; www.sgvpartnership.org

Jackson • *Amador County Planning Dept.* • Susan Grijalva; Dir.; 810 Court St.; 95642; Amador; P 40,000; (209) 223-6380; planning@amadorgov.org; www.co.amador.ca.us/departments/planning

Lake Elsinore • *Lake Elsinore Eco. Dev.* • Cathy Barrozo; Eco. Dev./GIS Analyst; 130 S. Main St.; 92530; Riverside; P 42,000; (951) 674-3124; Fax (951) 674-1418; cbarrozo@lake-elsinore.org; www.lake-elsinore.org

Lancaster • *Greater Antelope Valley Eco. Alliance* • Kimberly Maevers; Pres./CEO; P.O. Box 5477; 93539; Los Angeles; P 580,000; (661) 722-6566; Fax (661) 722-6616; info@SoCalLeadingEdge.org; www.SoCalLeadingEdge.org

Lemon Grove • *Lemon Grove Eco. Dev.* • Kathi Henry; Interim City Mgr.; 3232 Main St.; 91945; San Diego; P 26,100; (619) 825-3800; Fax (619) 825-3804; khenry@lemongrove.ca.gov; www.lemongrove.ca.gov

Lompoc • *Lompoc Eco. Dev. Dept.* • Teresa Gallavan; Dir.; 100 Civic Center Plaza; P.O. Box 8001; 93438; Santa Barbara; P 43,500; (805) 875-8274; (805) 736-1261; t_gallavan@ci.lompoc.ca.us; www.cityoflompoc.com

Long Beach • *Long Beach Dev. Svcs.* • Amy J. Bodek AICP; Dir.; 333 W. Ocean Blvd., 3rd Flr.; 90802; Los Angeles; P 463,300; (562) 570-5237; Fax (562) 570-6205; lbds@longbeach.gov; www.lbds.info

Los Angeles • *LA County Eco. Dev. Corp.* • William C. Allen; Pres./CEO; 444 S. Flower St., 34th Flr.; 90071; Los Angeles; P 9,800,000; (213) 622-4300; Fax (213) 622-7100; bill.allen@laedc.org; www.laedc.org

Lynwood • *Eco. Resources Corp.* • Dutch Ross III; Pres./CEO; 2600 Industry Way; 90262; Los Angeles; P 85,000; (310) 537-4610; Fax (310) 762-6211; antonia.lopez@economicresources.org; www.economicresources.org

Madera • *Madera County Eco. Dev. Comm.* • Bobby Kahn; Exec. Dir.; 2425 W. Cleveland Ave., Ste. 101; 93637; Madera; P 135,000; (559) 675-7768; Fax (559) 675-3252; info@maderacountyedc.com; www.maderacountyedc.com

Martinez • *City of Martinez Eco. Dev.* • Brad Kilger; City Mgr.; 525 Henrietta St.; 94553; Contra Costa; P 36,000; (925) 372-3505; (925) 372-3512; economicdevelopment@cityofmartinez.org; www.cityofmartinez.org

Martinez • *Contra Costa County Dept. of Conservation & Dev.* • John Kopchik; Dir.; 30 Muir Rd.; 94553; Contra Costa; P 1,100,000; (925) 674-7200; Fax (925) 335-7201; john.kopchik@dcd.cccounty.us; www.dcd.cccounty.us

Merced • *City of Merced Eco. Dev. Ofc.* • Frank Quintero; Dir. of Eco. Dev.; 678 W. 18th St.; 95340; Merced; P 79,000; (209) 385-6827; (800) 723-4788; Fax (209) 723-1780; economicdevelopment@cityofmerced.org; www.cityofmerced.org

Merced • *Merced County Eco. Dev.* • Mark J. Hendrickson; Dir.; 2222 M St.; 95340; Merced; P 268,500; (209) 385-7654; Fax (209) 726-1710; mhendrickson@co.merced.ca.us; www.co.merced.ca.us

Mission Viejo • *South Orange County Eco. Coalition* • Nancy Tilove; Bus. Dev. Consultant; 27758 Santa Margarita Pkwy., Ste. 378; 92691; Orange; P 500,000; (949) 600-5470; info@economiccoalition.com; www.economiccoalition.com

Modesto • *Stanislaus Eco. Dev. & Workforce Alliance* • Bill Bassitt; Pres./CEO; 1010 10th St., Ste. 1400; 95354; Stanislaus; P 521,497; (209) 567-4985; Fax (209) 567-4944; bassittb@stanalliance.com; www.stanalliance.com

Montebello • *Dept. of Comm. Dev.* • Ben Kim; Eco. Dev. Div.; 1600 W. Beverly Blvd.; 90640; Los Angeles; P 63,000; (323) 887-1475; Fax (323) 887-1488; bkim@cityofmontebello.com; www.cityofmontebello.com

Moreno Valley • *City of Moreno Valley Eco. Dev. Dept.* • Mike Lee; Eco. Dev. Dir.; 14177 Frederick St.; P.O. Box 88005; 92552; Riverside; P 207,000; (951) 413-3460; Fax (951) 413-3478; edteam@moval.org; www.moval.org/edd

Morgan Hill • *Morgan Hill Eco. Dev.* • Edith Ramirez; Dir.; 17575 Peak Ave.; 95037; Santa Clara; P 43,000; (408) 310-4633; Fax (408) 779-7236; john.lang@morganhill.ca.gov; www.morganhill.ca.gov

Napa • *City of Napa, Eco. Dev. Div.* • Jennifer LaLiberte; Eco. Dev. Mgr.; 1600 First St.; P.O. Box 660; 94559-0660; Napa; P 79,068; (707) 257-9502; Fax (707) 258-7851; jlaliberte@cityofnapa.org; www.cityofnapa.org

Needles • *City of Needles Eco. & Comm. Dev.* • Cindy Semione; Dev. Asst.; 817 Third St.; 92363; San Bernardino; P 4,900; (760) 326-5740; Fax (760) 326-6765; ndlspldr@citlink.net; cityofneedles.com

Newport Beach • *Newport Beach Eco. Dev. Div.* • Leigh De Santis; Eco. Dev. Administrator; 3300 Newport Blvd.; 92663; Orange; P 86,000; (949) 644-3225; (949) 644-3207; Fax (949) 644-3229; ldesantis@city.newport-beach.ca.us; www.city.newport-beach.ca.us

North Fork • *North Fork Comm. Dev. Cncl.* • Dan Rosenberg; Bd. Member; P.O. Box 1484; 93643; Madera; P 3,500; (559) 877-2244; Fax (559) 877-4267; info@northforkcdc.org; www.northforkcdc.org

Oakland • *East Bay EDA* • Karen Engel; Exec. Dir.; 1221 Oak St., Ste. 555; 94612; Alameda; P 2,560,000; (510) 272-3885; Fax (510) 272-5007; info@eastbayeda.org; www.eastbayeda.org

Oakland • *City of Oakland Eco. & Workforce Dev.* • Aliza Gallo; Eco. Dev. Mgr.; 250 Frank H. Ogawa Plz., Ste. 3315; 94612; Alameda; P 419,300; (510) 238-3627; Fax (510) 238-2226; agallo@oaklandnet.com; www.oaklandnet.com

Oceanside • *City of Oceanside Eco. & Comm. Dev.* • Jane McVey; Eco. & Comm. Dev. Dir.; 300 N. Coast Hwy.; 92054; San Diego; P 176,644; (760) 435-3352; Fax (760) 722-1057; jmcvey@ci.oceanside.ca.us; www.ci.oceanside.ca.us

Ontario • *City of Ontario Eco. Dev.* • John Andrews; Dir.; 303 East B St.; 91764; San Bernardino; P 164,000; (909) 395-2005; Fax (909) 395-2102; kwakefield@ontarioca.gov; www.ontariothinksbusiness.com

Oxnard • *Eco. Dev. Corp. of Oxnard* • Elizabeth Callahan; Pres.; 400 E. Esplanade Dr., Ste. 301; 93036; Ventura; P 200,000; (805) 385-7444; (805) 377-0329; Fax (805) 385-7452; elizabeth@edco.us; www.edco.us

Palm Springs • *Coachella Valley Eco. Partnership* • Joe Wallace; Pres./CEO; 3111 E.Tahquitz Canyon Way; 92262; Riverside; P 242,000; (760) 340-1575; Fax (760) 548-0370; blueprint@cvep.com; www.cvep.com

Pasadena • *City of Pasadena Eco. Dev.* • Eric Duyshart; Mgr.; 100 N. Garfield, Rm. S116; 91109; Los Angeles; P 137,100; (626) 744-4660; awright@cityofpasadena.net; www.cityofpasadena.net

Pico Rivera • *Pico Rivera Comm. & Eco. Dev.* • Steve Carmona; Mgr.; 6615 Passons Blvd.; 90660; Los Angeles; P 63,000; (562) 801-4332; Fax (562) 949-0280; scarmona@pico-rivera.org; www.pico-rivera.org

Placerville • *El Dorado County Eco. Dev.* • Samuel Driggers; Dir.; 330 Fair Ln.; 95667; El Dorado; P 177,000; (530) 621-5570; samuel.driggers@edcgov.us; www.edcgov.us

Quincy • *Plumas Corp.* • Jim Wilcox; Exec. Dir.; 47 Trilogy Ln.; P.O. Box 3880; 95971; Plumas; P 20,000; (530) 283-3739; www.plumascorporation.org

Redding • *Superior Calif. Eco. Dev. Inc.* • Robert Nash; CEO; 350 Hartnell Ave., Ste. A; 96002; Shasta; P 177,223; (530) 225-2760; Fax (530) 225-2769; cheryl@scedd.org; www.scedd.org

Redding • *Shasta EDC* • Tony Giovaniello; Pres.; 4300 Caterpillar Rd.; 96003; Shasta; P 208,000; (530) 224-4920; (888) 618-0887; Fax (530) 224-4921; edc@shastaedc.org; www.shastaedc.org

Rialto • *Dev. Svcs. Dept.* • Robb Steel; Dir.; 150 South Palm Ave.; 92376; San Bernardino; P 99,200; (909) 421-7246; Fax (909) 873-4814; dsd@rialtoca.gov; www.yourrialto.com

Riverside • *Riverside County Eco. Dev. Agency* • Robert Field; Asst. CEO; 3403 10th St., Ste. 500; P.O. Box 1180; 92502; Riverside; P 2,190,000; (951) 955-8916; Fax (951) 955-6686; rfield@rivcoeda.org; www.rivcoeda.org

Sacramento • *Greater Sacramento Eco. Cncl.* • Barry Broome; Pres./CEO; 400 Capitol Mall, Ste. 2500; 95814; Sacramento; P 492,000; (916) 441-2144; Fax (916) 441-2312; info@selectsacramento.com; www.selectsacramento.com

Sacramento • *Valley Vision* • Bill Mueller; CEO; 2320 Broadway; 95818; Sacramento; P 492,000; (916) 325-1630; Fax (916) 325-1635; mail@valleyvision.org; www.valleyvision.org

San Bernadino • *Inland Empire Eco. Partnership* • Paul Granillo; Pres./CEO; 1601 E. Third St., Ste. 102; 92408; Riverside; (909) 382-6000; Fax (909) 888-9074; pgranillo@ieep.com; www.ieep.com

San Bernardino • *San Bernardino County Eco. Dev. Ag.* • Larry Vaupel; Admin.; 385 N. Arrowhead Ave., 3rd Flr.; 92415; San Bernardino; P 2,100,000; (909) 387-4700; Fax (909) 387-9855; info@sbcountyadvantage.com; www.sbcountyadvantage.com

San Diego • *San Diego Reg. Eco. Dev. Corp.* • Mark Cafferty; Pres./CEO; 530 B St., 7th Flr.; 92101; San Diego; P 3,500,000; (619) 234-8484; Fax (619) 234-1935; info@sandiegobusiness.org; www.sandiegobusiness.org

San Francisco • *San Francisco Center for Eco. Dev.* • Dennis Conaghan; Exec. Dir.; 235 Montgomery St., Ste. 760; 94104; San Francisco; P 805,300; (415) 352-8855; dconaghan@sfced.org; www.sfced.org

San Francisco • *Mission Eco. Dev. Agency* • Luis Granados; Exec. Dir.; 2301 Mission St., Ste. 301; 94110; San Francisco; P 805,000; (415) 282-3334; Fax (415) 282-3320; lgomez@medasf.org; www.medasf.org

San Jose • *City of San Jose Ofc. of Eco. Dev.* • Kim Walesh; Dir.; 200 E. Santa Clara St., 17th Flr.; 95113; Santa Clara; P 960,000; (408) 535-8181; Fax (408) 292-6719; economic.development@sanjoseca.gov; www.sjeconomy.com

San Juan Capistrano • *San Juan Capistrano Eco. Dev.* • Douglas Dumhart; Mgr.; 32400 Paseo Adelanto; 92675; Orange; P 35,000; (949) 493-1171; (949) 443-6316; Fax (949) 493-1053; ddumhart@sanjuancapistrano.org; www.sanjuancapistrano.org

San Luis Obispo • *San Luis Obispo Eco. Dev.* • Lee Johnson; Mgr.; 990 Palm St.; 93401; San Luis Obispo; P 47,000; (805) 781-7164; Fax (805) 781-7109; ljohnson@slocity.org; www.ci.san-luis-obispo.ca.us

Santa Ana • *Southland Eco. Dev. Corp.* • James Davis; Chrmn./CEO; 400 N. Tustin Ave., Ste. 125; 92705; Orange; P 4,000,000; (714) 868-0001; Fax (714) 868-0003; elopez@southlandedc.com; www.southlandedc.com

Santa Barbara • *Eco. Vitality Team of Santa Barbara County* • Zoe J. Taylor; Dir. of Eco. Dev.; 104 W. Anapamu St., Ste. A; 93101; Santa Barbara; P 435,697; (805) 965-3023; Fax (805) 966-5954; zoe@sbchamber.org; www.evtsb.com

Santa Cruz • *City of Santa Cruz Dept. of Eco. Dev.* • Bonnie Lipscomb; Dir.; 337 Locust St.; 95060; Santa Cruz; P 62,000; (831) 420-5150; Fax (831) 420-5101; economicdevelopment@cityofsantacruz.com; www.choosesantacruz.com

Santa Maria • *Santa Maria Valley Eco. Dev. Comm.* • Glenn D. Morris; Dir.; 614 S. Broadway; 93454; Santa Barbara; P 144,000; (805) 925-2403; (888) 768-6274; Fax (805) 928-7559; edc@santamaria.com; www.santamariaedc.com

Santa Monica • *Santa Monica Eco. Dev. Div.* • Jason Harris; Mgr.; 1901 Main St., Ste. E; 90405; Los Angeles; P 93,000; (310) 458-8906; Fax (310) 391-9996; econdev@smgov.net; www.smgov.net

Santa Rosa • *Sonoma County Eco. Dev. Bd.* • Ben Stone; Exec. Dir.; 141 Stony Cir., Ste. 110; 95401; Sonoma; P 502,200; (707) 565-7170; Fax (707) 565-7231; edb@sonoma-county.org; www.sonomaedb.org

Seaside • *City of Seaside Eco. Dev.* • Craig Malin; City Mgr.; 440 Harcourt Ave.; 93955; Monterey; P 34,000; (831) 899-6700; Fax (831) 899-6227; cmalin@ci.seaside.ca.us; www.ci.seaside.ca.us

Shasta Lake • *City of Shasta Lake* • Fred Castagna; Proj. Mgr.; 1650 Stanton Dr.; P.O. Box 777; 96019; Shasta; P 10,000; (530) 275-7400; Fax (530) 275-7414; fcastagna@cityofshastalake.org; www.cityofshastalake.org

Sherman Oaks • *Valley Eco. Dev. Center* • Robert Lopez; COO; 5121 Van Nuys Blvd., 3rd Flr.; 91403; Los Angeles; P 6,700,000; (818) 907-9977; (800) 304-1755; Fax (818) 907-9720; info@vedc.org; www.vedc.org

Simi Valley • *City of Simi Valley* • Brian Gablar; Dir. of Eco. Dev.; 2929 Tapo Canyon Rd.; 93063; Ventura; P 127,000; (805) 583-6701; Fax (805) 526-2489; bgabler@simivalley.org; www.simivalley.org

Sonora • *Sonora Grants & Redev. Dept.* • Rachelle Kellogg; Dir.; 94 N. Washington St.; 95370; Tuolumne; P 4,600; (209) 532-7725; Fax (209) 532-3511; rkellogg@sonoraca.com; www.sonoraca.com

Stockton • *San Joaquin Partnership* • Mike Ammann; Pres./CEO; 2800 W. March Ln., Ste. 470; 95219; San Joaquin; P 664,000; (209) 956-3380; (800) 570-5627; Fax (209) 956-1520; mammann@sanjoaquinusa.org; www.sanjoaquinusa.org

Temecula • *Temecula Eco. Dev.* • Christine Damko; Dev. Analyst; 41000 Main St.; 92590; Riverside; P 109,000; (951) 694-6444; (951) 693-3952; christine.damko@cityoftemecula.org; www.temeculaca.gov

Thousand Oaks • *Thousand Oaks Comm. Dev. Dept.* • Mark Towne; Interim Comm. Dev. Dir.; 2100 Thousand Oaks Blvd.; 91362; Ventura; P 128,200; (805) 449-2340; (805) 449-2323; communitydevelopment@toaks.org; www.toaks.org

Twentynine Palms • *City of Twentynine Palms* • Brenda Simmons; Associate Planner; 6136 Adobe Rd.; 92277; San Bernardino; P 26,000; (760) 367-6799; Fax (760) 367-4890; bsimmons@ci.twentynine-palms.ca.us; www.ci.twentynine-palms.ca.us

Vacaville • *City of Vacaville* • Michael Palombo; Eco. Dev. Mgr.; City Hall; 650 Merchant St.; 95688; Solano; P 93,800; (707) 449-5114; Fax (707) 449-5149; mpalombo@cityofvacaville.com; www.cityofvacaville.com

Vallejo • *City of Vallejo Eco. Dev. Div.* • Annette Taylor; Sr. Comm. Dev. Analyst; 555 Santa Clara St., 3rd Flr.; 94590; Solano; P 121,300; (707) 649-5452; Fax (707) 552-0163; angelina.abella@cityofvallejo.net; www.ci.vallejo.ca.us

Ventura • *City of Ventura Eco. Dev.* • Leigh A. Eisen; Eco. Dev. Mgr.; 501 Poli St.; P.O. Box 99; 93002; Ventura; P 109,000; (805) 677-3947; Fax (805) 654-7560; leisen@cityofventura.net; www.venturaventures.org

Victorville • *Victor Valley Eco. Dev. Dept.* • Sophie L. Smith; Dir.; 14343 Civic Dr.; 92392; San Bernardino; P 122,300; (760) 955-5032; (760) 955-5000; Fax (760) 269-0080; opportunities@victorvillecity.com; www.victorvillecity.com

Visalia • *Visalia Eco. Dev. Corp.* • Nancy Lockwood; Exec. Dir.; P.O. Box 2722; 93279; Tulare; P 130,100; (559) 733-3737; Fax (559) 733-8156; nlockwood@thelockwoodagency.net; www.visaliaedc.com

Vista • *City of Vista Eco. Dev. Dept.* • Kevin Ham; Dir.; 200 Civic Center Dr.; 92084; San Diego; P 98,100; (760) 639-6165; Fax (760) 724-3363; edinfo@cityofvista.com; www.cityofvista.com

Walnut • *City of Walnut Planning* • Justin Carlson; City Planner; 21201 La Puente Rd.; P.O. Box 682; 91789; Los Angeles; P 32,000; (909) 348-0739; Fax (909) 595-6095; jcarlson@ci.walnut.ca.us; www.cityofwalnut.org

Watsonville • *Watsonville Eco. Dev.* • Kurt Overmeyer; Eco. Dev. Mgr.; 250 Main St.; 95076; Santa Cruz; P 52,000; (831) 768-3087; Fax (831) 763-4114; kovermeyer@ci.watsonville.ca.us; growinwatsonville.com

West Sacramento • *City of West Sacramento/Eco. Dev.* • Aaron Laurel; Eco. Dev. Dir.; 1110 W. Capital Ave.; 95691; Yolo; P 50,000; (916) 617-4535; Fax (916) 372-8765; aaronl@cityofwestsacramento.org; www.cityofwestsacramento.org

Westminster • *Westminster Eco. Dev.* • Chet Simmons; Asst. City Mgr.; 8200 Westminster Blvd.; 92683; Orange; P 93,000; (714) 898-3311; Fax (714) 373-4684; csimmons@westminster-ca.gov; www.westminster-ca.gov

Woodland • *Yolo County Eco. Dev.* • Wes Ervin; Mgr.; 625 Court St.; 95695; Yolo; P 185,000; (530) 666-8066; Fax (530) 668-4029; wes.ervin@yolocounty.org; www.yolocounty.org

Yreka • *Siskiyou County EDC* • Tonya Dowse; Exec. Dir.; 1512 S. Oregon St.; 96097; Siskiyou; P 45,000; (530) 842-1638; Fax (530) 842-2685; scedc@siskiyoucounty.org; www.siskiyoucounty.org

Yuba City • *Yuba-Sutter Eco. Dev. Corp.* • Brynda Stranix; Pres./CEO; 950 Tharp Rd., Ste. 1303; 95993; Sutter; P 167,000; (530) 751-8555; Fax (530) 751-8515; ysedc@ysedc.org; www.ysedc.org

Colorado

Federal

***U.S. SBA, Colorado Dist. Ofc.* •** Greg Lopez; Dist. Dir.; 721 19th St., Ste. 426; 80202; Denver; P 5,187,582; (303) 844-2607; greg.lopez@sba.gov; www.sba.gov/co

State

***Colorado Ofc. of Eco. Dev. & Intl. Trade* •** Ken Lund; Exec. Dir.; 1625 Broadway, Ste. 2700; Denver; 80202; Denver; P 5,187,582; (303) 892-3840; Fax (303) 892-3848; ken.lund@state.co.us; www.advancecolorado.com

Communities

Alamosa • *San Luis Valley Dev. Resources Group* • Michael D. Wisdom; Exec. Dir.; 610 State St., Stes. 200 - 218; P.O. Box 300; 81101; Alamosa; P 48,506; (719) 589-6099; Fax (719) 589-6299; wisdom@slvdrg.org; www.slvdrg.org

Aurora • *Aurora Eco. Dev. Cncl.* • Wendy Mitchell; Pres./CEO; 12510 E. Iliff Ave., Ste. 115; 80014; Arapahoe; P 325,000; (303) 755-2223; Fax (303) 755-2224; hinson@auroraedc.com; www.auroraedc.com

Boulder • *Boulder Eco. Cncl.* • Clif Harald; Exec. Dir.; 2440 Pearl St.; P.O. Box 73; 80302; Boulder; P 103,000; (303) 442-1044; Fax (303) 938-8837; bec@bouldereconomiccouncil.org; www.bouldereconomiccouncil.org

Brighton • *Brighton Eco. Dev. Corp.* • Michael Martinez; Exec. Dir.; 22 S. 4th Ave., Ste. 305; 80601; Adams & Weld; P 36,000; (303) 655-2155; Fax (303) 655-2153; acoffey@brightonedc.org; www.brightonedc.org

Broomfield • *City & County of Broomfield Eco. Dev. Dept.* • Bo Martinez; Dir. of Eco. Dev.; One Descombes Dr.; 80020; Broomfield; P 65,000; (303) 464-5579; bmartinez@broomfield.org; investbroomfield.com

Canon City • *Fremont Eco. Dev. Corp.* • Robert Brown; Exec. Dir.; 402 Valley Rd.; Incubator Bldg.; 81212; Fremont; P 49,430; (719) 275-8601; Fax (719) 275-4400; armstrong@fedc.co; www.fedc.co

Castle Rock • *Castle Rock Eco. Dev. Cncl.* • Frank Gray; Pres./CEO; 18 S. Wilcox St., Ste. 202; 80104; Douglas; P 45,700; (303) 688-7488; angela@castlerockedc.com; www.credco.org

Colorado Springs • *Colorado Springs Reg. Bus. Alliance* • 102 S. Tejon St., Ste. 430; 80903; El Paso; P 676,597; (719) 471-8183; (887) 471-8183; Fax (719) 471-9733; info@springsbusinessalliance.com; www.coloradospringsbusinessalliance.com

Commerce City • *Commerce City Eco. Dev.* • Michelle Claymore; Eco. Dev. Dir.; 7887 E. 60th Ave.; 80022; Adams; P 50,000; (303) 289-3620; c3ed@c3gov.com; www.redefiningcommerce.com

Denver • *The Downtown Denver Partnership Inc.* • Tamara Door; Pres./CEO; 1515 Arapahoe St., Tower 2, Ste. 400; 80202; Denver; P 554,000; (303) 534-6161; Fax (303) 534-2803; info@downtowndenver.com; www.downtowndenver.com

Denver • *Denver Ofc. of Eco. Dev.* • Andre Pettigrew; Exec. Dir.; 201 W. Colfax; Dept. 204; 80202; Denver; P 554,000; (720) 913-1999; Fax (720) 913-1802; oed@denvergov.org; www.milehigh.com

Durango • *La Plata Eco. Dev. Alliance* • Roger Zalneraitis; Exec. Dir.; 1211 Main Ave., Ste. 1; 81301; La Plata; (970) 259-1700; info@yeslpc.com; www.yeslpc.com

Englewood • *City of Englewood* • Brad Power; Dir. of Comm. Dev.; 1000 Englewood Pkwy.; 80110; Arapahoe; P 30,225; (303) 762-2342; Fax (303) 783-6895; commdev@englewoodgov.org; www.englewoodgov.org

Englewood • *Southeast Bus. Partnership* • Mike Fitzgerald; Pres./CEO; 304 Inverness Way S., Ste. 315; 80112; Arapahoe; P 1,371,000; (303) 792-9447; Fax (303) 792-9452; mfitzgerald@sebp.org; www.sebp.org

Estes Park • *Estes Park Eco. Dev. Corp.* • 533 Big Thompson Ave., Ste. 103; 80517; Larimer; P 6,500; (970) 577-1031; info@estesparkedc.com; estesparkedc.com

Fort Collins • *see Loveland*

Fort Morgan • *Morgan County Eco. Dev. Corp.* • Cassandra Wilson; Exec. Dir.; 231 Ensign St., Rm. B102; 80701; Morgan; P 28,500; (970) 542-3527; (800) 522-4333; Fax (970) 542-3528; mcedc@morgancountyinfo.com; www.morgancountyinfo.com

Georgetown • *Clear Creek Eco. Dev. Corp.* • Peggy Stokstad; Pres./CEO; 502 6th St., 2nd Flr.; P.O. Box 2030; 80444; Clear Creek; P 10,000; (303) 569-2133; Fax (303) 569-3940; pstokstad@clearcreekedc.org; www.clearcreekedc.org

Georgetown • *Georgetown Promotion Comm.* • Marvin Geisness; 404 6th St.; P.O. Box 426; 80444; Clear Creek; P 1,000; (303) 569-2555; Fax (303) 569-2705; m.geisness@comcast.net; www.town.georgetown.co.us

Golden • *Jefferson County Eco. Dev. Corp.* • 1667 Cole Blvd., Ste. 400; 80401; Jefferson; P 530,000; (303) 202-2965; Fax (303) 202-2967; info@jeffcoedc.org; www.jeffcoedc.org

Grand Junction • *Grand Junction Eco. Partnership* • Kelly Flenniken; Exec. Dir.; 122 N. 6th St.; 81501; Mesa; P 146,000; (970) 245-4332; (800) 621-6683; Fax (970) 245-4346; kelly@gjep.org; www.gjep.org

Greeley • *Upstate Colorado Eco. Dev.* • Richard Werner; Pres./CEO; 822 7th St., Ste. 550; 80631; Weld; P 258,141; (970) 356-4565; Fax (970) 352-2436; info@upstatecolorado.org; www.upstatecolorado.org

Holyoke • *Phillips County Eco. Dev.* • Nici Bishop; Exec. Dir.; P.O. Box 424; 80734; Phillips; P 4,680; (970) 580-3614; Fax (970) 854-4387; pced@pctelcom.coop; www.phillipscountyco.org

Julesburg • *Sedgwick County Eco. Dev. Corp.* • 100 W. 2nd St.; 80737; Sedgwick; P 2,400; (970) 474-3504; (800) 226-0069; Fax (970) 474-4008; sced@kci.net; www.sedgwickcountycolorado.com

La Junta • *La Junta Eco. Dev.* • Ryan Stevens; Exec. Dir.; 1802 Colorado Ave., SCORE Center; 81050; Otero; P 7,100; (719) 671-9499; Fax (719) 384-6960; ryan.stevens@ojc.edu; www.lajuntaeconomicdevelopment.com

Lakewood • *City of Lakewood Eco. Dev.* • Nanette Neelan; Deputy City Mgr./Eco. Dev. Dir.; 480 S. Allison Pkwy.; Civic Center South; 80226; Jefferson; P 144,000; (303) 987-7730; Fax (303) 987-7063; ed@lakewood.org; www.lakewood.org/economicdevelopment/

Littleton • *Littleton Bus./Ind. Affairs Dept.* • Christian Gibbons; Dir.; 2255 W. Berry Ave.; 80120; Arapahoe; P 42,000; (303) 795-3760; Fax (303) 795-3749; cgibbons@littletongov.org; www.littletongov.org

Longmont • *Longmont Area Eco. Cncl.* • Jessica Erickson; Pres.; 630 15th Ave., Ste. 100A; 80501; Boulder; P 86,000; (303) 651-0128; Fax (303) 682-5446; laec@longmont.org; www.longmont.org

Loveland • *Northern Colorado Eco. Alliance* • Andy Montgomery; CEO; 1615 Foxtrail Dr., Ste. 130; 80538; Larimer; P 230,000; (970) 541-2118; mary@northerncolorado.com; www.northerncolorado.com

Montrose • *Montrose Eco. Dev. Corp.* • Sandy Head; Exec. Dir.; 1601 Oxbow Dr., Ste. 360B; 81401; Montrose; P 41,412; (970) 249-9438; (800) 270-0211; Fax (970) 249-9459; sandyh@montroseedc.org; www.montroseedc.org

Northglenn • *City of Northglenn Eco. Dev.* • Debbie Tuttle; Eco. Dev. Mgr.; 11701 Community Center Dr.; P.O. Box 330061; 80233; Adams; P 35,000; (303) 450-8743; Fax (303) 450-8798; dtuttle@northglenn.org; www.northglenn.org

Pagosa Springs • *Pagosa Springs Comm. Dev. Corp.* • Cindi Galabota; Exec. Dir.; P.O. Box 1183; 81147; Archuleta; P 12,100; (970) 264-2360; info@pagosaspringscdc.org; www.pagosaspringscdc.org

Parker • *Town of Parker Eco. Dev.* • John L. Hall; Eco. Dev. Dir.; 20120 E. Mainstreet; 80138; Douglas; P 42,000; (303) 805-3169; Fax (303) 805-3153; jhall@parkeronline.org; www.parkeronline.org

Pueblo • *Southern Colorado Eco. Dev. Dist.* • Douglas Dowler; Exec. Dir.; 1104 N. Main St.; 81003; Pueblo; P 306,000; (719) 545-8680; Fax (719) 545-9908; doug@scedd.com; www.scedd.com

Rifle • *Associated Governments of NW Colorado* • Jane Whitt; Admin. Asst.; P.O. Box 351; 81650; Garfield; P 382,600; (970) 625-1723; Fax (970) 625-1147; jane.whitt@agnc.org; www.agnc.org

Rocky Ford • *Rocky Ford Growth & Progress Inc.* • Julie Worley; Exec. Dir.; 408 N. Main St.; 81067; Otero; P 4,700; (719) 316-2753; jworley@ci.rocky-ford.co.us; www.rockyfordcolo.com

San Luis • *Costilla County Eco. Dev. Cncl.* • Robert Rael; P.O. Box 9; 81152; Costilla; P 3,500; (719) 672-0999; ccedc@centurytel.net

Silverthorne • *NW Colorado Cncl. of Govt.* • Pamela Caskie; Exec. Dir.; 249 Warren Ave.; P.O. Box 2308; 80498; Summit; P 111,400; (970) 468-0295; (800) 332-3669; Fax (970) 468-1208; pcaskie@nwccog.org; www.nwccog.org

Stratton • *The Prairie Dev. Corp.* • Mrs. Jo Downey; Exec. Dir.; 128 Colorado Ave.; P.O. Box 202; 80836; Kit Carson; P 38,000; (719) 348-5562; (800) 825-0208; Fax (719) 348-5887; jdowney@prairiedevelopment.com; www.prairiedevelopment.com

Thornton • *City of Thornton Dev. Dept.* • Jeff Coder; Dep. City Mgr.; 9500 Civic Center Dr.; 80229; Adams; P 121,000; (303) 538-7295; Fax (303) 538-7373; citydevelopment@cityofthornton.net; www.cityofthornton.net

Trinidad • *City of Trinidad - Eco. Dev. Dept.* • Jonathan Taylor; Dir.; 135 N. Animas St.; 81082; Las Animas; P 15,000; (719) 846-9843; Fax (719) 846-4550; jonathan.taylor@trinidad.co.gov; www.trinidad.co.gov

Wellington • *Wellington Area Eco. & Bus. Resource Comm.* • William Schneider; Chair; P.O. Box 1500; 80549; Larimer; P 6,000; (970) 568-4133; bill.schneider@wellingtoncoloradochamber.net; www.wellingtoncoloradochamber.net

Westminster • *City of Westminster Eco. Dev. Ofc.* • Susan F. Grafton CED; Eco. Dev. Dir.; 4800 W. 92nd Ave.; 80031; Adams & Jefferson; P 109,300; (303) 658-2400; Fax (303) 706-3922; sgrafton@cityofwestminster.us; www.cityofwestminster.us

Westminster • *Adams County Eco. Dev. Inc.* • Barry Gore; Pres./CEO; 12200 Pecos St., Ste. 100; 80234; Adams; P 449,000; (303) 453-8510; Fax (303) 453-8505; tallen@adamscountyed.com; www.adamscountyed.com

Wheat Ridge • *City of Wheat Ridge* • Steve Art; Eco. Dev. & Urban Renewal Mgr.; 7500 W. 29th Ave., 1st Flr.; 80033; Jefferson; P 31,000; (303) 235-2806; (720) 454-9040; Fax (303) 235-2806; sart@ci.wheatridge.co.us; www.ci.wheatridge.co.us

Yuma • *Yuma County Eco. Dev. Corp.* • Pat Duran; Exec. Dir.; P.O. Box 244; 80759; Yuma; P 10,000; (970) 630-4531; ycedc@ConsiderYumaCounty.com; www.ConsiderYumaCounty.com

Connecticut

Federal

U.S. SBA, Connecticut Dist. Ofc. • Robert H. Nelson; Dist. Dir.; 280 Trumbull St., 2nd Flr.; 06103; Hartford; P 3,600,000; (860) 240-4700; Fax (860) 240-4659; connecticut@sba.gov; www.sba.gov/ct

State

Connecticut Eco. Dev. Assn. • Elizabeth Stocker; Pres.; c/o CERC; 805 Brook St., Bldg. 4; Rocky Hill; 06067; Hartford; P 3,590,347; (860) 571-7136; Fax (860) 571-7150; elizabeth.stocker@newton-ct.gov; www.cedas.org

Communities

Bridgeport • *Ofc. of Planning & Eco. Dev.* • Thomas Gill; OPED Dir.; 999 Broad St.; 06604; Fairfield; P 145,000; (203) 576-7221; (203) 576-7200; Fax (203) 332-5611; thomas.gill@bridgeportct.gov; www.bridgeportct.gov

Cheshire • *Town of Cheshire Eco. Dev. Comm.* • Jerry Sitko; Coord.; 84 S. Main St.; 06410; New Haven; P 30,000; (203) 271-6670; Fax (203) 271-6688; cdonegan@cheshirect.org; www.cheshirect.org

Fairfield • *Town of Fairfield Comm. & Eco. Dev.* • Mark Barnhart; Dir.; 611 Old Post Rd.; 06824; Fairfield; P 59,400; (203) 256-3120; (203) 256-3000; Fax (203) 256-3114; mbarnhart@town.fairfield.ct.us; www.fairfieldct.org

Hartford • *MetroHartford Alliance* • John Shemo; V.P. & Dir. of Eco. Dev.; 31 Pratt Street, 5th Flr.; 06103; Hartford; P 1,200,000; (860) 525-4451; Fax (860) 293-2592; jshemo@metrohartford.com; www.metrohartford.com

Monroe • *Monroe Eco. Dev. Comm.* • 7 Fan Hill Rd.; 06468; Fairfield; P 20,000; (203) 452-2819; (203) 452-2800; Fax (203) 452-2253; monroemeansbusiness@monroect.org; www.monroect.org

New Britain • *New Britain C/C-Eco. Dev.* • Bill Carroll; Bus. Dev. Dir.; One Court St.; 06051; Hartford; P 74,000; (860) 229-1665; Fax (860) 223-8341; billcarroll@newbritainchamber.com; www.newbritainchamber.com

Old Saybrook • *Old Saybrook Eco. Dev. Comm.* • Wilma Asch; Exec. Dir.; 302 Main St., Town Hall; 06475; Middlesex; P 10,500; (860) 395-3139; Fax (860) 395-3125; wasch@town.old-saybrook.ct.us; www.oldsaybrookct.org

Waterbury • *Waterbury Dev. Corp.* • Todd M. Montello; CEO; 83 Bank St.; 06702; New Haven; P 109,000; (203) 346-2607; Fax (203) 346-3910; genovese@wdconline.org; www.wdconline.org

Windsor Locks • *Windsor Locks Eco. & Ind. Dev. Comm.* • Patrick McMahon; Coord.; 50 Church St.; 06096; Hartford; P 13,000; (860) 654-8923; (860) 627-1444; Fax (860) 292-1121; wleidc@sbcglobal.net; www.windsorlocksct.org

Delaware

Federal

***U.S. SBA, Delaware Dist. Ofc.* •** John F. Fleming; Dist. Dir.; 1007 N. Orange St., Ste. 1120; 19801; New Castle; P 917,092; (302) 573-6294; john.fleming@sba.gov; www.sba.gov/de

State

***Delaware Eco. Dev. Ofc.* •** Alan B. Levin; Dir.; 99 Kings Hwy.; Dover; 19901; Kent; P 917,092; (302) 739-4271; Fax (302) 739-5749; bernice.whaley@state.de.us; dedo.delaware.gov

Communities

Dover • *Kent Eco. Partnership* • James Waddington; Dir.; 555 Bay Rd.; 19901; Kent; P 170,000; (302) 678-3028; Fax (302) 736-2279; james.waddington@co.kent.de.us; www.kentpartnership.org

Wilmington • *Wilmington Ofc. of Eco. Dev.* • Jeffrey C. Flynn; Dir.; 800 N. French St., 3rd Flr.; 19801; New Castle; P 80,000; (302) 576-2120; (302) 576-2123; Fax (302) 571-4326; alance@wilmingtonde.gov; www.wilmingtonde.gov

Wilmington • *Wilmington Eco. Dev. Corp.* • David A. Daniels; Exec. Dir.; 100 W. 10th St., Ste. 214; 19801; New Castle; P 80,000; (302) 571-9088; Fax (302) 652-5679; info@wedco.org; www.wedco.org

District of Columbia

Federal

***Eco. Dev. Admin.* •** Jay Williams; Asst. Secy.; 1401 Constitution Ave. N.W., Ste. 71014; 20230; District of Columbia; P 632,323; (202) 482-5081; pamela.bell@eda.gov; www.eda.gov

***Ofc. of Natl. Ombudsman* •** Brian Castro; Natl. Ombudsman; 409 3rd St. S.W., Ste. 7125; 20416; District of Columbia; P 632,323; (888) 734-3247; Fax (202) 481-5719; brian.castro@sba.gov; www.sba.gov/ombudsman

***U.S. SBA, Washington D.C. Dist. Ofc.* •** Antonio Doss; Dist. Dir.; 409 3rd St. S.W., 2nd Flr.; 20416; District of Columbia; P 632,323; (202) 205-8800; antonio.doss@sba.gov; www.sba.gov/dc

State

***Ofc. of the Deputy Mayor for Planning & Eco. Dev.* •** Brian T. Kenner; Deputy Mayor; 1350 Pennsylvania Ave. N.W., Ste. 317; Washington; 20004; District of Columbia; P 632,323; (202) 727-6365; Fax (202) 727-6703; dmped.eom@dc.gov; www.dcbiz.dc.gov

Communities

Washington • *Dept. of Housing & Comm. Dev.* • Michael P. Kelly; Dir.; 1800 Martin Luther King Jr. Ave. S.E.; 20020; District of Columbia; (202) 442-7200; Fax (202) 645-6727; dhcd@dc.gov; www.dhcd.dc.gov

Washington • *Greater Washington Bd. of Trade* • Jim Dinegar; Pres./CEO; 1725 I St. N.W., Ste. 200; 20006; District of Columbia; (202) 857-5900; Fax (202) 223-2648; info@bot.org; www.bot.org

Florida

Federal

***U.S. SBA, Jacksonville Dist. Ofc.* •** Wilfredo J. Gonzalez; Dist. Dir.; 7825 Baymeadows Way, Ste.100B; 32256; Duval; P 19,317,568; (904) 443-1970; wilfredo.gonzalez@sba.gov; www.sba.gov/fl

***U.S. SBA, Miami Dist. Ofc.* •** Francisco A. Marrero; Dist. Dir.; 100 S. Biscayne Blvd., 7th Flr.; 33131; Miami-Dade; P 19,317,568; (305) 536-5521; Fax (305) 536-5058; francisco.marrero@sba.gov; www.sba.gov/fl

State

***Enterprise Florida* •** Gray Swoope; Pres./CEO; 800 N. Magnolia Ave., Ste. 1100; Orlando; 32803; Orange; P 19,317,568; (407) 956-5600; Fax (407) 956-5599; alatimer@eflorida.com; www.eflorida.com

Communities

Auburndale • *Central Florida Dev. Cncl.* • Jim Bell; Exec. Dir.; 2701 Lake Myrtle Park Rd.; 33823; Polk; P 602,000; (863) 551-4760; Fax (863) 551-4739; brandy@cfdc.org; www.cfdc.org

Avon Park • *see Sebring*

Bonifay • *Holmes County Dev. Comm.* • Raymon Thomas; Exec. Dir.; 106 E. Byrd Ave.; 32425; Holmes; P 19,900; (850) 547-4682; hcdc1978@gmail.com; www.holmescountyonline.com

Boynton Beach • *City of Boynton Beach Eco. Dev.* • Andrew Mack; Dir. of Dev.; 100 E. Boynton Beach Blvd.; P.O. Box 310; 33435; Palm Beach; P 68,300; (561) 742-6350; Fax (561) 742-6357; macka@bbfl.us; www.boynton-beach.org

Bradenton • *Bradenton Downtown Dev. Auth.* • Karen Kyser; Exec. Dir.; 101 Old Main St.; 34205; Manatee; P 53,800; (941) 932-9440; kkyser@ddabradenton.com; www.ddabradenton.com

Bradenton • *Bradenton Area Eco. Dev. Cncl.* • Sharon Hillstrom; Pres./CEO; 4215 Concept Ct.; 34211; Manatee; P 350,774; (941) 803-9030; Fax (941) 803-9039; info@thinkbradentonarea.com; www.thinkbradentonarea.com

EDC

Brooksville • *Hernando County Ofc. of Bus. Dev.* • Valerie Pianta; Eco. Dev. Mgr.; 15800 Flight Path Dr.; 34604; Hernando; P 178,439; (352) 540-6400; Fax (352) 754-5361; vpianta@henandocounty.us; www.hernandobusiness.com

Bunnell • *Flagler County EDC* • Helga van Eckert; Exec. Dir.; 1769 E. Moody Blvd., Bldg. 2; 32110; Flagler; P 105,000; (386) 313-4071; Fax (386) 313-4101; hvaneckert@flaglercountyedc.com; www.flaglercountyedc.com

Clearwater • *City of Clearwater* • Denise Sanderson; Eco. Dev. Dir.; 112 S. Osceola Ave.; P.O. Box 4748; 33758; Pinellas; P 110,000; (727) 562-4040; Fax (727) 562-4052; denise.sanderson@myclearwater.com; www.myclearwater.com

Coral Gables • *Florida East Cost Ind. LLC* • Vincent Signorello; Pres./CEO; 2855 Le Jeune Rd., 4th Flr.; 33134; Duval; P 864,200; (305) 520-2300; Fax (904) 565-4144; vincent.signorello@feci.com; www.feci.com

Crystal River • *Eco. Dev. Auth. for Citrus County* • Don Taylor; Exec. Dir.; 915 N. Suncoast Blvd.; 34429; Citrus; P 138,000; (352) 795-2000; Fax (352) 6376498; info@edacitrus.com; www.edacitrus.com

Daytona Beach • *County of Volusia Eco. Dev.* • Rob Ehrhardt; Mgr.; 700 Catalina Dr., Ste. 200; 32114; Volusia; P 494,500; (386) 248-8048; (800) 554-3801; Fax (386) 238-4761; rehrhardt@volusia.org; www.floridabusiness.org

Fleming Island • *Clay County Eco. Dev. Corp.* • Bill Garrison; Pres./Exec. Dir.; 1845 Town Center Blvd., Ste. 110 B; 32003; Clay; P 200,000; (904) 375-9394; bgarrison@chooseclay.com; www.chooseclay.com

Fort Lauderdale • *Greater Fort Lauderdale Alliance* • Bob Swindell; Pres./CEO; 110 E. Broward Blvd., Ste. 1990; 33301; Broward; P 1,000,500; (954) 524-3113; (800) 741-1420; Fax (954) 524-3167; info@gflalliance.org; www.gflalliance.org

Fort Myers • *Lee County Eco. Dev. Ofc.* • John Boland; Dir.; 2201 Second St., Ste. 500; 33901; Lee; P 650,000; (239) 338-3161; (800) 330-3161; Fax (239) 338-3227; aforbes@leegov.com; www.leecountybusiness.com

Fort Walton Beach • *Eco. Dev. Cncl. of Okaloosa County* • Nathan Sparks CEcD; Exec. Dir.; P.O. Box 4097; 32549; Okaloosa; P 193,900; (850) 362-6467; (800) 995-7374; Fax (850) 362-6471; info@florida-edc.org; www.florida-edc.org

Gainesville • *Gainesville Cncl. for Eco. Outreach* • Susan Davenport; Pres./CEO; 300 E. University Ave., Ste. 100; 32601; Alachua; P 250,000; (352) 334-7100; Fax (352) 334-7141; susan@gainsvillechamber.com; www.gceo.com

Hialeah • *Hialeah-Dade Dev. Inc.* • Mario Arus; Exec. Dir.; 501 Palm Ave.; 33010; Miami-Dade; P 254,000; (305) 884-1219; Fax (305) 884-1740; hddi@bellsouth.net; www.hddi.org

Hollywood • *South FL Reg. Planning Cncl.* • James F. Murley; Exec. Dir.; 3440 Hollywood Blvd., Ste. 140; 33021; Broward; (954) 985-4416; Fax (954) 985-4417; sfadmin@sfrpc.com; www.sfrpc.com

Jacksonville • *Jacksonville Port Auth.* • Bryan Taylor; CEO; 2831 Talleyrand Ave.; P.O. Box 3005; 32206; Duval; P 821,800; (904) 357-3360; Fax (904) 357-3060; nancy.rubin@jaxport.com; www.jaxport.com

Jacksonville Beach • *Jacksonville Beach Planning & Dev. Dept.* • William C. Mann; Dir.; 11 N. 3rd St.; 32250; Duval; P 22,805; (904) 247-6231; Fax (904) 247-6107; planning@jaxbchfl.net; www.jacksonvillebeach.org

Lake City • *Columbia County Eco. Dev. Dept.* • Glenn Hunter; Exec. Dir.; 259 N.E. Franklin St., Ste. 101; 32055; Columbia; P 70,000; (386) 758-1033; Fax (386) 758-1167; ghunter@columbiacountyfla.com; www.ccfledd.com

Lakeland • *Lakeland Downtown Dev. Auth.* • Julie Townsend; Exec. Dir.; 228 S. Massachusetts Ave.; 33801; Polk; P 101,000; (863) 687-8910; julie.townsend@lakelandgov.net; www.ldda.org

Lakeland • *Lakeland Eco. Dev. Cncl.* • Steven J. Scruggs; Exec. Dir.; 226 N. Kentucky Ave.; 33801; Polk; P 101,000; (863) 687-3788; Fax (863) 688-2941; sscruggs@lakelandedc.com; www.lakelandedc.com

Live Oak • *Suwannee County Dev. Auth.* • Tim Alcorn; Chrmn.; 212 N. Ohio Ave.; P.O. Drawer C; 32064; Suwannee; P 41,500; (386) 362-3071; Fax (386) 362-4758; www.suwanneechamber.com

Lutz • *Pasco Eco. Dev. Cncl.* • Bill Kronin; Pres./CEO; 16506 Pointe Village Dr., Ste. 101; 33558; Pasco; P 470,000; (813) 926-0827; (800) 607-2726; Fax (813) 926-0829; suzanne@pascoedc.com; www.pascoedc.com

Macclenny • *Baker County Dev. Comm.* • Darryl Register; Exec. Dir.; 20 E. Macclenny Ave.; 32063; Baker; P 27,000; (904) 259-6433; Fax (904) 259-2737; dregister@bakerchamberfl.com; www.bakerchamberfl.com

Mexico Beach • *Mexico Beach Comm. Dev. Cncl.* • Kimberly Shoaf; Dir.; P.O. Box 13382; 32410; Bay; P 1,072; (850) 648-8196; (888) 723-2546; Fax (850) 648-9403; kimberly@mexico-beach.com; www.mexicobeach.com/cdc

Miami Area

***The Beacon Council* •** Larry K. Williams; Pres./CEO; 80 S.W. 8th St., Ste. 2400; 33130; Dade; P 2,500,000; (305) 579-1300; Fax (305) 375-0271; info@beaconcouncil.com; www.beaconcouncil.com

***Dade County Ind. Dev. Auth.* •** James Wagner Jr.; Exec. Dir.; 80 S.W. 8th St., Ste. 2801; 33130; Miami-Dade; P 2,500,000; (305) 579-0070; Fax (305) 579-0225; info@mdcida.org; www.mdcida.org

***Dept. of Small Bus. Dev.* •** Penelope Townsley; Dir.; 111 N.W. 1st St., 19th Flr.; 33128; Miami-Dade; P 2,500,000; (305) 375-3111; Fax (305) 375-3160; coop2@miamidade.gov; www.miamidade.gov/sba

***Downtown Dev. Auth. of Miami* •** Alyce Robertson; Exec. Dir.; 200 S. Biscayne Blvd., Ste. 2929; 33131; Miami-Dade; P 300,000; (305) 579-6675; Fax (305) 371-2423; robertson@miamidda.com; www.miamidda.com

Milton • *Santa Rosa County EDO* • Shannon Ogletree; Exec. Dir.; 6491 Caroline St., Ste. 4; 32570; Santa Rosa; P 158,912; (850) 623-0174; edo@santarosa.fl.gov; www.santarosaedo.com

Milton • *City of Milton Eco. Dev. Comm.* • Randy Jorgenson; Planning Mgr.; City Hall; P.O. Box 909; 32572; Santa Rosa; P 8,600; (850) 983-5440; Fax (850) 983-5415; landplan@aol.com; www.ci.milton.fl.us

Naples • *Collier County Ofc. of Bus. & Eco. Dev.* • Jace Kentner; Interim Dir.; 2660 N. Horseshoe Dr., Ste. 105; 34104; Collier; P 321,500; (239) 252-8990; jacekentner@colliergov.net; www.colliergov.net

Ocala • *Ocala-Marion County Chamber & Eco. Partnership •* Kevin Sheilley; Pres./CEO; 310 S.E. 3rd St.; 34471; Marion; P 331,298; (352) 291-4410; Fax (352) 629-8051; kevin@ocalacep.com; www.ocalacep.com

Orlando • *Metro Orlando Eco. Dev. Comm. •* Rick Weddle; Pres./CEO; 301 E. Pine St., Ste. 900; 32801; Orange; P 2,000,000; (407) 422-7159; Fax (407) 425-6428; info@orlandoedc.com; www.orlandoedc.com

Palatka • *Putnam County Dev. Auth. •* Brian Bergen; V.P. of Eco. Dev.; 1100 Reid St.; 32177; Putnam; P 73,000; (386) 328-1503; Fax (386) 328-7076; brian@chamberpc.com; putnamcountydevelopmentauthority.com

Panama City • *Bay County Eco. Dev. Alliance •* Becca Hardin; Pres.; 5230 W. Hwy. 98; 32401; Bay; P 179,000; (850) 215-9965; (888) 229-7483; Fax (850) 215-9962; polly@bayeda.com; www.bayeda.com

Pensacola • *FloridaWest Eco. Dev. Alliance •* Scott Luth; CEO; 117 W. Garden St.; 32502; Escambia & Pensacola; P 483,494; (850) 898-2201; inquiries@floridawesteda.com; www.choosegreaterpensacola.com

Perry • *Taylor County Dev. Auth. •* Scott Frederick; Dir. of Eco. Dev.; 103 E. Ellis St.; 32347; Taylor; P 23,000; (850) 584-5627; Fax (850) 223-0161; tcda@fairpoint.net; www.floridasrisingstar.com

Plant City • *Plant City Eco. Dev. Corp. •* Jake Austin; Exec. Dir.; 118 W. Reynolds St.; 33563; Hillsborough; P 37,000; (813) 756-7140; jaustin@plantcityedc.com; www.plantcityedc.com

Pompano Beach • *Pompano Beach Eco. Dev. Cncl. •* Chris Clemens; Eco. Dev. Mgr.; 100 W. Atlantic Blvd.; 33062; Broward; P 106,060; (954) 786-4048; Fax (954) 786-4044; chris.clemens@copbfl.com; www.pompanobeachfl.gov

Port Charlotte • *Charlotte County EDO •* Lucienne Pears; Dir.; 18501 Murdock Cir., Ste. 302; 33948; Charlotte; P 160,000; (941) 764-4941; (800) 729-5836; Fax (941) 764-4947; FloridaEDO@charlottecountyfl.gov; www.FloridasInnovationCoast.com

Riviera Beach • *Riviera Beach Comm. Redev. Agency •* Tony Brown; Chair; 2001 Broadway, Ste. 300; 33404; Palm Beach; P 35,000; (561) 844-3408; Fax (561) 881-8043; tbrown@rbcra.com; www.rbcra.com

Rockledge • *Eco. Dev. Comm. of Florida's Space Coast •* Lynda Weatherman; Pres./CEO; 6525 3rd St., Ste. 305; 32955; Brevard; P 505,000; (321) 638-2000; (800) 535-0203; Fax (321) 633-4200; info@spacecoastedc.org; www.spacecoastedc.org

Saint Petersburg • *St. Petersburg Downtown Partnership •* Joni James; CEO; 244 2nd Ave. N., Ste. 201; 33701; Pinellas; P 245,000; (727) 821-5166; Fax (727) 896-6302; joni@stpetepartnership.org; www.stpetepartnership.org

Saint Petersburg • *Eco. Dev. Dept., City of St. Petersburg •* Dave Goodwin; Dir. of Eco. Dev.; P.O. Box 2842; 33731; Pinellas; P 256,681; (727) 893-7100; (800) 874-9026; Fax (727) 892-5465; business@stpete.org; www.stpete.org

Sarasota • *Eco. Dev. Corp. of Sarasota County •* Mark Huey; Pres./CEO; 1680 Fruitville Rd., Ste. 402; 34236; Sarasota; P 375,000; (941) 309-1200; Fax (941) 309-1209; mhuey@edcsarasotacounty.com; www.edcsarasotacounty.com

Sebring • *Highlands County Ofc. of Eco. Dev. •* Taylor Benson; Coord.; 501 S. Commerce Ave.; 33870; Highlands; P 98,786; (863) 402-6924; Fax (863) 402-6561; tbenson@hcbcc.net; www.hcbcc.net

Starke • *Bradford Co. Eco. Dev. Auth. •* Virgil Berry; Chrmn.; 100 E. Call St.; 32091; Bradford; P 28,500; (904) 964-5278; Fax (904) 964-2863; chair@choosebradfordcounty.com; www.choosebradfordcounty.com

Stuart • *Eco. Cncl. of Martin County •* Charles Gerardi; Pres./CEO; 1002 S.E. Monterey Commons Blvd., Ste. 201; The Rubicon Bldg.; 34996; Martin; P 151,000; (772) 288-1225; cgerardi@mceconomy.org; www.mceconomy.org

Sunrise • *City of Sunrise, Ofc. of Eco. Dev. •* Mr. Lou Sandora; Eco. Dev. Dir.; 10770 W. Oakland Park Blvd.; 33351; Broward; P 84,400; (954) 746-3430; Fax (954) 746-3439; lsandora@sunrisefl.gov; www.sunrisefl.gov

Tampa Area

Greater Tampa C/C • Bob Rohrlack CEcD; Pres./CEO; 201 N. Franklin St., Ste. 201; P.O. Box 420; 33601; Hillsborough; P 1,118,988; (813) 228-7777; Fax (813) 223-7899; info@tampachamber.com; www.tampachamber.com

Port Tampa Bay • Paul Anderson; Pres./CEO; 1101 Channelside Dr.; 33602; Hillsborough; P 336,000; (813) 905-7678; (800) 741-2297; Fax (813) 905-5109; klw@tampaport.com; www.tampaport.com

Tampa Bay Partnership • Stuart Rogel; Pres./CEO; 4300 W. Cypress St., Ste. 700; 33607; Hillsborough; P 4,200,000; (813) 878-2208; Fax (813) 872-9356; srogel@tampabay.org; www.tampabay.org

Tavares • *Lake County Eco. Growth •* Robert Chandler; Dir.; 315 W. Main St., Ste. 520; 32778; Lake; P 320,000; (352) 742-3918; Fax (352) 742-3906; rchandler@lakecountyfl.gov; www.visitlakefl.com

Titusville • *Space Coast Eco. Dev. Comm. •* Jennifer Giddens; SEDC Liaison; 2000 S. Washington Ave.; 32780; Brevard; P 70,000; (321) 267-3036; Fax (321) 264-0127; giddens@titusville.org; titusville.org

Titusville • *City of Titusville Eco. Dev. Dept. •* Edyie McCall; Eco. Dev. Dir.; 555 S. Washington Ave.; 32796; Brevard; P 70,000; (321) 567-3774; edyie.mccall@titusville.com; titusville.com

West Palm Beach • *West Palm Beach Downtown Dev. Auth. •* Raphael Clemente; Exec. Dir.; 301 Clematis St., Ste. 200; 33401; Palm Beach; P 102,436; (561) 833-8873; Fax (561) 833-5870; rclemente@westpalmbeachdda.com; www.downtownwpb..com

West Palm Beach • *Bus. Dev. Bd. of Palm Beach County Inc. •* Kelly Smallridge; Pres./CEO; 310 Evernia St.; 33401; Palm Beach County; P 1,300,000; (561) 835-1008; Fax (561) 835-1160; ssemon@bdb.org; www.bdb.org

Winter Haven • *Winter Haven Eco. Dev. Cncl. •* Bruce Lyon; Pres.; 401 Ave. B N.W.; 33881; Polk; P 75,000; (863) 837-5280; Fax (877) 252-8389; contact@whedc.com; www.whedc.com

Georgia

Federal

U.S. SBA, Georgia Dist. Ofc. • Terri L. Denison; Dist. Dir.; 233 Peachtree St. N.E., Ste. 1900; 30303; Fulton; P 9,919,945; (404) 331-0100; terri.denison@sba.gov; www.sba.gov/ga

EDC

State

Georgia Dept. of Eco. Dev. • Chris Carr; Comm.; 75 Fifth St. N.W., Ste. 1200; Atlanta; 30308; Fulton; P 9,919,945; (404) 962-4000; business@georgia.org; www.georgia.org

Communities

Albany • *Albany/Dougherty Eco. Dev. Comm.* • Justin Strickland; Pres.; 125 Pine Ave., Ste. 200; 31701; Dougherty; P 96,000; (229) 434-0044; Fax (229) 434-1310; jstrickland@choosealbany.com; www.choosealbany.com

Athens • *East Athens Dev. Corp.* • Winston Heard; Dir.; 410 McKinley Dr.; 30601; Clarke; P 20,000; (706) 208-0048; Fax (706) 208-0015; wheard0822@aol.com; www.eadcinc.com

Atlanta • *Atlanta BeltLine Inc.* • Jerald Mitchell; Dir. of Eco. Dev.; 86 Pryor St. S.W., Ste. 300; 30303; Fulton; P 347,600; (404) 477-3537; (404) 477-3003; Fax (404) 477-3606; jmitchell@atlbeltline.org; beltline.org

Atlanta • *Fulton County Eco. Div.* • Kenneth Dobson; Admin.; 141 Pryor St., 5th Flr.; 30303; Fulton; P 984,300; (404) 612-1021; (404) 612-8338; erika.smith@fultoncountyga.gov; www.fultoncondev.org

Blackshear • *Pierce County Ind. Dev. Auth.* • Matt Carter; Exec. Dir.; 200 S.W. Central Ave.; P.O. Box 47; 31516; Pierce; P 18,800; (912) 807-7432; Fax (912) 449-7045; matt.carter@piercecountyga.gov; pcgeorgia.com

Brunswick • *Brunswick & Glynn County Dev. Auth.* • Mel Baxter; Pres.; 1505 Richmond St., 2nd Flr.; 31520; Glynn; P 79,600; (912) 265-6629; Fax (912) 265-9460; melbaxter@bwkeda.com; www.georgiasgoldenopportunity.com

Camilla • *SW Georgia Reg. Comm.* • Robert McDaniel; Exec. Dir.; 181 E. Broad St.; P.O. Box 346; 31730; Mitchell; P 365,000; (229) 522-3552; Fax (229) 522-3558; rmcdaniel@swgrc.org; www.swgrc.org

Carnesville • *Franklin County Ind. Bldg. Auth.* • Frank Ginn; Dir. of Eco. Dev.; 961 Hall Ave.; P.O. Box 151; 30521; Franklin; P 24,000; (706) 384-5112; Fax (706) 384-3204; frank@franklin-county.com; www.franklincountyga.com

Carrollton • *Carroll Tomorrow* • Andy Camp; V.P. of Eco. Dev.; 200 Northside Dr.; 30117; Carroll; P 115,000; (678) 890-2354; andy@carroll-ga.org; www.carrolltomorrow.com

Claxton • *Claxton-Evans County Ind. Dev. Auth.* • Randy Mayfield; Chrmn.; 4 N. Duval St.; 30417; Evans; P 11,000; (912) 739-1391; Fax (912) 739-3827; info@claxtonevanschamber.com; www.claxtonevanschamber.com

Cordele • *Cordele/Crisp Ind. Dev. Cncl.* • Grant C. Buckley Esq.; Exec. Dir.; 202 S. 7th St.; P.O. Box 38; 31010; Crisp; P 24,000; (229) 273-9570; Fax (229) 273-9571; gcbuckley@crispidc.com; www.crispidc.com

Cumming • *Forsyth County Planning & Comm. Dev.* • Tom Brown; Dir.; 110 E. Main St., Ste. 100; 30040; Forsyth; P 175,500; (770) 781-2115; Fax (770) 781-2197; lakyle@forsythco.com; forsythco.com

Dallas • *Paulding County Eco. Dev.* • P.O. Box 2836; 30132; Paulding; P 150,000; (770) 505-7700; Fax (770) 505-8877; yolanda.newell@pauldingairport.com; www.pauldingdevelopment.org

Dalton • *North Georgia CDC Inc.* • Jennifer Whorton; Officer; 503 W. Waugh St.; 30720; Whitfield; P 209,000; (706) 226-1110; Fax (706) 272-2253; ngcdc@ngcdc.org; www.ngcdc.org

Darien • *McIntosh County Dev. Auth.* • Wally Orrel; Dir.; 105 Fort King George Dr.; P.O. Box 896; 31305; McIntosh; P 12,000; (912) 437-6659; Fax (912) 437-3505; mcda@darientel.net; www.georgiascoast2success.com

Dublin • *Dublin-Laurens County Dev. Auth.* • Brad Lofton; Pres.; 1200 Bellevue Ave.; P.O. Box 818; 31040; Laurens; P 48,000; (478) 272-3118; (478) 272-3128; Fax (478) 275-0811; blofton@dlcda.com; www.dlcda.com

Eatonton • *Putnam Dev. Auth.* • Terry Schwindler; Eco. Dev. Dir.; 117 Putnam Dr.; 31024; Putnam; P 21,000; (706) 816-8099; tschwindler@putnamdevelopmentauthority.com; www.putnamdevelopmentauthority.com

Fitzgerald • *Fitzgerald/Ben Hill County Dev. Auth.* • Jason Dunn; Exec. Dir.; 121 E. Pine St.; 31750; Ben Hill; P 17,500; (229) 423-9357; Fax (229) 423-1052; derinda@developfitzgeraldbenhill.com; www.developfitzgeraldbenhill.com

Fort Gaines • *Clay County Eco. Dev. Cncl.* • Bill Kenyon; Vice Chair; P.O. Box 825; 39851; Clay; P 3,500; (229) 768-3238; Fax (229) 768-3672; chairman@claycountyga.org; www.claycountyga.org

Fort Oglethorpe • *see Rock Spring*

Fort Valley • *Dev. Auth. of Peach County* • BJ Walker; Exec. Dir.; 425 James E. Khoury Dr., Ste. B; P.O. Box 935; 31030; Peach; P 27,000; (478) 825-3826; peachcountydevelopment@ymail.com; www.peachcountydevelopment.com

Greenville • *Meriwether Ind. Dev. Auth.* • Jane Fryer; Pres.; 17234 Roosevelt Hwy., Bldg. B; 30222; Meriwether; P 22,000; (706) 672-3467; (702) 672-3464; Fax (706) 672-4465; j.fryer@meriwethercountyga.gov; www.meriwetherida.com

Hazlehurst • *Joint Dev. Auth. of Jeff Davis County, Hazlehurst & Denton, GA* • Illya S. Copeland; Exec. Dir.; 95 E. Jarman St.; P.O. Box 546; 31539; Jeff Davis; P 15,068; (912) 375-4543; Fax (912) 375-7948; devauthjd@bellsouth.net; www.hazlehurst-jeffdavis.org

Hinesville • *Liberty County Dev. Auth.* • Ronald E. Tolley CEcD; CEO; 425 W. Oglethorpe Hwy.; 31313; Liberty; P 63,000; (912) 368-3356; Fax (912) 368-5585; ron.tolley@lcda.com; www.lcda.com

Irwinton • *Dev. Auth. of Wilkinson County* • Jonathan Jackson; Exec. Dir.; 100A Bacon St.; P.O. Box 413; 31042; Wilkinson; P 10,000; (478) 946-1122; Fax (478) 946-4394; jjackson@wilkinsoncounty.net; www.wilcodevauthority.com

Jackson • *Butts County Ind. Dev. Auth.* • Laura Hale Sistrunk; Exec. Dir.; 625 W. Third St., Ste. 6; 30233; Butts; P 26,000; (770) 775-4851; Fax (770) 775-3118; buttscountyida@buttscountyida.com; www.buttscountyida.com

Jasper • *Pickens-Jasper Eco. Dev.* • Gerald Nechvatal; Dir.; 500 Stegall Dr.; 30143; Pickens; P 30,000; (706) 692-5600; economicdevelopment@pickenschamber.com; www.pickenschamber.com

Jonesboro • *Clayton County Dept. of Eco. Dev.* • Grant Wainscott; Dir.; 112 Smith St.; 30236; Clayton; P 259,400; (770) 477-4450; econ.dev@co.clayton.ga.us; www.claytoncountyga.us

Macon • *Middle Georgia Reg. Commission* • Laura Mathis; Exec. Dir.; 175 Emery Hwy., Ste. C; 31217; Bibb; P 441,000; (478) 751-6160; Fax (478) 751-6517; admin@mg-rc.org; www.middlegeorgiarc.org

Madison • *Madison-Morgan C/C & EDC* • Bob Hughes; Pres./Eco. Dev. Dir.; 118 N. Main St.; P.O. Box 826; 30650; Morgan; P 17,000; (706) 438-3120; bhughes@madisonga.org; www.madisonga.org

McDonough • *Henry County Dev. Auth.* • Charles Moseley; Exec. Dir.; 125 Westridge Industrial Blvd.; 30253; Henry; P 206,000; (770) 288-8000; Fax (770) 288-8008; cmoseley@choosehenry.com; www.choosehenry.com

Moultrie • *Moultrie Colquitt County Dev. Auth.* • Darrell Moore; Pres.; 116 First Ave. S.E.; P.O. Box 487; 31776; Colquitt; P 48,000; (229) 985-2131; Fax (229) 890-2638; contact@moultriechamber.com; www.selectmoultrie.com

Rabun County • *see Rabun Gap*

Rabun Gap • *Dev. Auth. of Rabun County* • Ray Coulombe; Exec. Dir.; 400 Kelly's Creek Rd, Ste. 201; P.O. Box 126; 30568; Rabun; P 16,812; (706) 746-9975; rcoulombe@darcga.com; www.darcga.com

Reidsville • *Tattnall County Dev. Auth.* • Wayne Dasher; Chrmn.; 108 Brazell; P.O. Box 759; 30453; Tattnall; P 25,500; (912) 557-6323; Fax (912) 557-3046; davidavery61@yahoo.com; www.tattnall.com

Rock Spring • *NW Georgia Joint Dev. Auth.* • Jeff Mullis; Exec. Dir.; 10052 N. Hwy. 27; P.O. Box 220; 30739; Walker; P 180,000; (706) 375-5793; (800) 966-8092; Fax (706) 375-5795; info@northwestgeorgia.us; www.northwestgeorgia.us

Rockmart • *Dev. Auth. of Polk County* • Rachel Rowell; Pres.; 133 S. Marble St.; 30153; Polk; P 44,000; (678) 971-3095; Fax (678) 971-3095; president@polkgeorgia.com; www.polkgeorgia.com

Rome • *Northwest Georgia Reg. Comm.* • William Steiner; Exec. Dir.; 1 Jackson Hill Dr.; P.O. Box 1798; 30162; Floyd; P 556,207; (706) 295-6485; Fax (706) 295-6665; wsteiner@nwgrc.org; www.nwgrc.org

Savannah • *Savannah Eco. Dev. Auth.* • Trip Tollison; Pres./CEO; 131 Hutchinson Island Rd., 4th Flr.; P.O. Box 128; 31402; Chatham; P 366,000; (912) 447-8450; Fax (912) 447-8455; cdriggers@seda.org; www.seda.org

Springfield • *Effingham County Ind. Dev. Auth.* • John A. Henry; CEO; 520 W. Third St.; P.O. Box 1078; 31329; Effingham; P 56,000; (912) 754-3301; Fax (912) 754-1236; effingham@effinghamcounty.com; www.effinghamcounty.com

Statesboro • *Dev. Auth. of Bulloch County* • Benjy Thompson; CEO; 102 S. Main St.; P.O. Box 303; 30459; Bulloch; P 70,000; (912) 489-9115; Fax (912) 489-3108; benjy.thompson@advantagebulloch.com; www.advantagebulloch.com

Sylvania • *Screven County Dev. Auth.* • Dorie Bacon; Exec. Dir.; 101 S. Main St.; 30467; Screven; P 14,600; (912) 564-7850; Fax (912) 564-0081; dorie@screvencountydevelopmentauthority.com; www.screvencountydevelopmentauthority.com

Sylvester • *Worth County Eco. Dev. Auth.* • Karen M. Rackley; Exec. Dir.; 122 N. Main St.; 31791; Worth; P 22,000; (229) 776-7599; (229) 349-7703; Fax (229) 776-7719; worthcoeda@bellsouth.net; www.worthcountyeda.com

Thomasville • *Thomasville-Thomas County Eco. Dev.* • Shelley Zorn; Exec. Dir.; 401 S. Broad St.; P.O. Box 560; 31799; Thomas; P 45,000; (229) 225-1422; Fax (229) 226-9603; szorn@rose.net; developthomas.com

Thomson • *Forward McDuffie* • Matt Morris; Exec. Dir.; 149 Main St.; 30824; McDuffie; P 22,000; (706) 597-1000; Fax (706) 595-2143; matt.morris@thomson-mcduffie.net; www.thomson-mcduffie.com

Valdosta • *Valdosta-Lowndes Dev. Auth.* • Andrea Schruijer; Exec. Dir.; 103 Roosevelt Dr.; P.O. Box 1963; 31603; Lowndes; P 109,200; (229) 259-9972; Fax (229) 259-9973; info@buildlowndes.com; www.buildlowndes.com

Vienna • *Dooly County Eco. Dev. Cncl.* • Robert Jeter; Exec. Dir.; 402 Hawkinsville Rd.; 31092; Dooly; P 12,000; (229) 268-4554; Fax (229) 268-4500; bobjeter@sowega.net; www.doolyedc.org

Villa Rica • *Villa Rica Downtown Dev. Auth.* • Christopher G. Pike; Dir. of Downtown Dev. & Tour.; 571 W. Bankhead Hwy.; 30180; Carroll; P 14,000; (678) 840-1441; (404) 273-3878; Fax (770) 459-7003; cpike@villarica.org; www.downtownvillarica.com

Warner Robins • *Houston County Dev. Auth.* • Angie Gheesling; Exec. Dir.; 200 Carl Vinson Pkwy.; 31088; Houston; P 135,000; (478) 923-5470; Fax (478) 923-5472; gheesling@houstoncountyga.net; www.houstoncountyga.net

Waynesboro • *Dev. Auth. of Burke County* • Jessica Hood; Exec. Dir.; 241 E. Sixth St.; 30830; Burke; P 25,500; (706) 554-2923; Fax (706) 554-7091; jhood@selectburke.com; selectburke.com

Hawaii

Federal

U.S. SBA, Hawaii Dist. Ofc. • Jane A. Sawyer; Dist. Dir.; 500 Ala Moana Blvd., Ste. 1-306; 96850; Honolulu; P 1,392,313; (808) 541-2990; Fax (808) 541-2976; jane.sawyer@sba.gov; www.sba.gov/hi

State

State of Hawaii Dept. of Bus., Eco. Dev. & Tourism • Richard C. Lim; Dir.; 250 S. Hotel St.; P.O. Box 2359; Honolulu; 96804; Honolulu; P 1,392,313; (808) 586-2355; Fax (808) 586-2377; director@dbedt.hawaii.gov; dbedt.hawaii.gov

Communities

Hilo • *County of Hawaii, Dept. of Research & Dev.* • John DeFries; Dir.; 25 Aupuni St., Rm. 1301; 96720; Hawaii; P 186,100; (808) 961-8366; Fax (808) 935-1205; chresdev@hawaiicounty.gov; www.hawaiicounty.gov

Hilo • *Hawaii Island Eco. Dev. Bd.* • Jacqui Hoover; Exec. Dir./COO; 117 Keawe St., Ste. 107; 96720; Hawaii; P 168,000; (808) 935-2180; Fax (808) 935-2187; hiedb@hiedb.org; www.hiedb.org

Honolulu • *City & County of Honolulu* • Linda Chu-Takayama; Exec. Dir.; Ofc. of Eco. Dev.; 530 S. King St., Rm. 306; 96813; Honolulu; P 1,000,000; (808) 768-5764; Fax (808) 768-4242; ltakayama@honolulu.gov; www.honolulu.gov

Honolulu • *Enterprise Honolulu* • Pono Shim; Pres./CEO; 735 Bishop St., Ste. 424; 96813; Honolulu; P 1,276,000; (808) 521-3611; Fax (808) 536-2281; info@enterprisehonolulu.com; www.enterprisehonolulu.com

Lihue • *Kauai Eco. Dev. Bd.* • Susan Tai Kaneko; Pres.; 4290 Rice St.; 96766; Kauai; P 67,100; (808) 245-6692; Fax (808) 246-1089; info@kedb.com; www.kedb.com

Lihue • *County of Kauai Ofc. of Eco. Dev.* • George Costa; Dir.; 4444 Rice St., Ste. 200; 96766; Kauai; P 67,100; (808) 241-4946; Fax (808) 241-6399; gcosta@kauai.gov; www.kauai.gov/oed

Maui • *Maui Economic Dev. Board Inc.* • Jeanne Skog; Pres./CEO; 1305 N. Holopono St., Ste. 1; Kihei; 96753; Maui; P 155,000; (808) 875-2300; Fax (808) 879-0011; info@medb.org; www.medb.org

Wailuku • *County of Maui Eco. Dev.* • Teena Rasmussen; Dir.; 2200 Main St., Ste. 305; 96793; Maui; P 155,000; (808) 270-7710; Fax (808) 270-7995; economic.development@mauicounty.gov; www.mauicounty.gov

Idaho

Federal

U.S. SBA, Boise Dist. Ofc. • Rodney Grzadzieleski; Dist. Dir.; 380 E. Parkcenter Blvd., Ste. 330; 83706; Ada; P 1,595,728; (208) 334-9004; Fax (208) 334-9353; rodney.grzadzieleski@sba.gov; www.sba.gov/id

State

Idaho Dept. of Comm. • Jeffrey Sayer; Dir.; 700 W. State St.; P.O. Box 83720; Boise; 83720; Ada; P 1,595,728; (208) 334-2470; Fax (208) 334-2631; jeffrey.sayer@commerce.idaho.gov; commerce.idaho.gov

Communities

Boise • ***Boise Valley Eco. Partnership*** • Clark Krause; Exec. Dir.; 250 S. 5th St., Ste. 300; 83702; Ada; P 562,932; (208) 472-5229; Fax (208) 472-5201; lholland@bvep.org; www.bvep.org

Caldwell • ***Caldwell Eco. Dev. Dept.*** • Steve Fultz; Exec. Dir.; 4814 E. Linden St.; P.O. Box 1179; 83606; Canyon; P 51,000; (208) 615-6135; sfultz@cityofcaldwell.org; www.cityofcaldwell.org

Heyburn • ***Southern Idaho Comm.*** • Kyla Sawyer; Pres./CEO; 1177 7th St.; P.O. Box 638; 83336; Minidoka; P 80,000; (208) 679-4793; Fax (208) 679-4794; president@minicassiachamber.com; www.minicassiachamber.com

Idaho Falls • ***Regional Eco. Dev. Corp. for East Idaho*** • Jan Rogers; CEO; 901 Pier View Dr., Ste. 204; P.O. Box 51564; 83405; Bonneville; P 140,000; (208) 534-1318; (800) 900-2014; info@easternidaho.org; www.easternidaho.org

Jerome • ***Jerome Eco. & Comm. Dev.*** • Mike Williams; City Admin.; 152 East Ave., Ste. A; 83338; Jerome; P 18,342; (208) 324-8189; Fax (208) 324-8204; mwilliams@ci.jerome.id.us; www.ci.jerome.id.us

Pocatello • ***Bannock Dev. Corp.*** • John Regetz; Exec. Dir.; 1651 Alvin Ricken Dr.; 83201; Bannock; P 83,000; (208) 233-3500; Fax (208) 233-0268; angie@bdcidaho.org; www.bdcidaho.org

Pocatello • ***SE Idaho Cncl. of Govts. Inc.*** • Kathleen Lewis; Exec. Dir.; 214 E. Center; P.O. Box 6079; 83205; Bannock; P 154,000; (208) 233-4032; Fax (208) 233-4841; kathleenl@sicog.org; www.sicog.org

Rexburg • ***Madison Eco. Partners Inc.*** • 35 N. 1 E., Ste. 4; 83440; Madison; P 38,300; (208) 372-2129; info@madisoneconomicpartners.org; www.madisoneconomicpartners.org

Twin Falls • ***Region IV Dev. Assn.*** • Joe Herring; Pres.; 315 Falls Ave.,; Evergreen Bldg., SIDC Wing, Ste. C77; 83301; Twin Falls; P 200,000; (208) 732-5727; Fax (208) 732-5454; brenda@rivda.org; www.rivda.org

Wallace • ***Silver Valley Eco. Dev. Corp.*** • Vince Rinaldi; Exec. Dir.; 703 Cedar St.; 83873; Shoshone; P 12,827; (208) 752-5511; (800) 523-7889; Fax (208) 556-2351; vern@silvervalleyedc.com; www.silvervalleyedc.com

Illinois

Federal

U.S. SBA, Illinois Dist. Ofc. • Dorothy A. Overal; Interim Dist. Dir.; 500 W. Madison St., Ste. 1150; 60661; Cook; P 12,875,255; (312) 353-4528; Fax (312) 886-5688; luz.rodriguez@sba.gov; www.sba.gov/il

State

Illinois Dept. of Comm. & Eco. Opportunity • Sean McCarthy; Interim Dir.; 500 E. Monroe; Springfield; 62701; Sangamon; P 12,831,000; (217) 782-7500; (800) 252-2923; ceo.edoutreach@illinois.gov; www.ildceo.net

Communities

Aurora • ***Invest Aurora*** • David A. Hulseberg; Pres./CEO; 43 W. Galena Blvd.; 60506; DuPage, Kane, Kendall & Will; P 200,700; (630) 256-3160; info@investinaurora.org; www.investaurora.org

Berwyn • ***Berwyn Dev. Corp.*** • Anthony Griffin; Exec. Dir.; 3322 S. Oak Park Ave., 2nd Flr.; 60402; Cook; P 56,600; (708) 788-8100; Fax (708) 788-0966; info@berwyn.net; www.berwyn.net

Carbondale • ***Carbondale Eco. Dev. Ofc.*** • Gary Williams; Asst. City Mgr. of EDC; 200 S. Illinois Ave.; P.O. Box 2047; 62901; Jackson; P 25,000; (618) 549-5302; gwilliams@ci.carbondale.il.us; www.explorecarbondale.com

Champaign • ***Champaign County Eco. Dev. Corp.*** • John Dimit; Pres./CEO; 1817 S. Neil St., Ste. 201; 61820; Champaign; P 178,591; (217) 359-6261; john@champaigncountyedc.org; www.champaigncountyedc.org

Charleston • ***see Mattoon***

Chester • ***Randolph County Eco. Dev.*** • Chris Martin; Coord.; 1 Taylor St.; 62233; Randolph; P 33,900; (618) 826-5000; Fax (618) 826-3363; econdev@randolphco.org; www.randolphco.org

Chicago Area

Calumet Area Ind. Comm. • Ted Stalnos; Pres.; 1000 E. 111th St., 7th Flr.; 60628; Cook; P 250,000; (773) 928-6000; Fax (773) 928-6016; beth@calumetareaindustrial.com; www.calumetareaindustrial.com

Mount Greenwood Comm. & Bus. Assn. • Mary Gill; Exec. Dir.; 3400 W. 111th St., Ste. 496; 60655; Cook; P 19,000; (773) 881-0622; (773) 881-0622; Fax (773) 881-4622; mgcba2013@gmail.com; www.mgcba.org

Planning & Dev. Comm. of the City of Chicago • Arnold Randall; Comm.; 121 N. LaSalle, Ste. 1000; 60602; Cook; P 3,000,000; (312) 744-9476; Fax (312) 742-9899; communitydevelopment2@cityofchicago.org; www.cityofchicago.org

Clinton • ***DeWitt County Cncl.*** • 1060 Rte. 54 W.; 61727; DeWitt; P 16,500; (217) 935-0500; info@dcdc-illinois.net; www.dcdc-illinois.org

Crystal Lake • ***McHenry County Eco. Dev. Corp.*** • Pam Cumpata; Pres.; 620 Dakota St., Ste. 244; 60012; McHenry; P 307,000; (815) 893-0895; info@mcedc.com; www.mchenrycountyedc.com

Danville • ***Vermilion Advantage-EDC Div.*** • Vicki Haugen; Pres./CEO; 15 N. Walnut St.; 61832; Vermilion; P 80,000; (217) 442-6201; Fax (217) 442-6228; tshade@vermilionadvantage.com; www.vermilionadvantage.com

Decatur • ***Eco. Dev. Corp. of Decatur & Macon County*** • Craig Coil; Pres.; 101 S. Main St., Ste. LL5; 62523; Macon; P 114,500; (217) 422-9520; Fax (217) 422-9307; ccoil@decaturedc.com; www.decaturedc.com

Des Plaines • *Des Plaines Comm. & Eco. Dev.* • Alex Dambach; Dir.; 1420 Miner St., Ste. 301; 60016; Cook; P 57,000; (847) 391-5545; Fax (847) 827-2196; adambach@desplaines.org; www.desplaines.org

Dixon • *Lee County Ind. Dev. Assn.* • John R. Thompson; Pres./CEO; 101 W. Second St., Ste. 301; 61021; Lee; P 36,100; (815) 284-3361; Fax (815) 284-3675; dchamber@essex1.com; www.dixonillinoischamber.com

Dolton • *Village of Dolton* • Bert Herzog; Village Admin.; 14014 Park Ave.; 60419; Cook; P 25,614; (708) 201-3348; bherzog@vodolton.org; www.vodolton.org

Elgin • *Elgin Dev. Group* • Tony Lucenko; Dir. Eco. Dev.; 31 S. Grove Ave.; 60120; Cook & Kane; P 120,000; (847) 741-5660; Fax (847) 741-5677; info@elgindevelopment.com; elgindevelopment.com

Fairfield • *Fairfield-Wayne County Area Dev. Comm.* • Flo Simpson; Exec. Dir.; 121 E. Main St.; 62837; Wayne; P 5,421; (618) 842-4802; Fax (618) 842-4802; adc@fairfieldwireless.net; www.fairfield-il.com

Flora • *Flora Ind. Comm.* • Dan Sulsberger; Dir.; 131 E. 2nd; P.O. Box 249; 62839; Clay; P 5,000; (618) 662-7111; (618) 662-2312; Fax (618) 662-7204; cityadmin@florail.us; www.florail.us

Freeport • *Northwest IL Dev. Alliance* • David Young; Exec. Dir.; 27 W. Stephenson St.; 61032; Stephenson; P 46,800; (815) 233-1356; Fax (815) 235-4038; dave.young@nidaworks.com; www.nidaworks.com

Godfrey • *River Bend Growth Assn.* • Monica Bristow; Pres.; 6722 Godfrey Rd. (Physical); 5800 Godfrey Rd. (Mailing); 62035; Madison; P 90,000; (618) 467-2280; Fax (618) 466-8289; info@growthassociation.com; www.growthassociation.com

Granite City • *America's Central Port* • Dennis Wilmsmeyer; Exec. Dir.; 1635 W. 1st St.; 62040; Madison; P 60,000; (618) 877-8444; Fax (618) 452-3402; dwilmsmeyer@americascentralport.com; www.americascentralport.com

Jacksonville • *Jacksonville Reg. EDC* • Paul Ellis; Pres.; 221 E. State St.; 62650; Morgan; P 40,000; (217) 479-4627; Fax (217) 479-4629; paul@jredc.org; www.jredc.org

Joliet • *Will County Center for Eco. Dev.* • John E. Greuling; Pres./CEO; 116 N. Chicago St., Ste. 101; 60432; Kendall & Will; P 690,000; (815) 723-1800; Fax (815) 723-6972; info@willcountyced.com; www.willcountyced.com

Kankakee • *Eco. Alliance of Kankakee County* • Michael Van Mill; Pres./CEO; 200 E. Ct., Ste. 507; 60901; Kankakee; P 113,500; (815) 935-1177; Fax (815) 935-1181; mvanmill@kankakeecountyed.org; www.kankakeecountyed.org

Lawrenceville • *Lawrence County Ind. Dev. Cncl.* • Ann Emken; Exec. Dir.; 600 Cherry Ln.; 62439; Lawrence; P 15,545; (618) 943-5219; (888) 943-5305; Fax (618) 943-5910; lcidc@lawrencecountyillinois.com; www.lawrencecountyillinois.com

Lincoln • *Logan County Eco. Dev. Partnership* • Christel Huff; Exec. Dir.; 120 S. McLean St.; 62656; Logan; P 30,000; (217) 732-8739

Lincolnshire • *Lake County Partners* • Michael Stevens; Pres./CEO; 100 Tri-State International Dr., Ste. 122; 60069; Lake; P 617,000; (847) 597-1220; Fax (847) 597-1235; rlumadue@lakecountypartners.com; www.lakecountypartners.com

Lisle • *Choose DuPage* • Greg Bedalov; Pres./CEO; 2525 Cabot Dr., Ste. 303; 60532; DuPage; P 916,900; (630) 955-2090; info@choosedupage.com; choosedupage.com

Lockport • *City of Lockport* • Pamela Hirth; Eco. Dev. Coord.; Ofc. of Eco. Dev.; 921 S. State St.; 60441; Will; P 25,000; (815) 838-0549; Fax (815) 588-0111; kbown@lockport.org; www.cityoflockport.net

Loves Park • *City of Loves Park EDC* • Daniel Jacobson; Dir. of Dev.; 100 Heart Blvd.; 61111; Winnebago; P 24,000; (815) 654-5033; Fax (815) 654-5004; danjacobson@loves-park.il.us; www.loves-park.il.us

Macomb • *Macomb Area Eco. Dev. Corp.* • Kim Pierce; Exec. Dir.; 510 N. Pearl St., Ste. 300; 61455; McDonough; P 21,500; (309) 837-4684; Fax (309) 837-4688; maedco@wiu.edu; www.maedco.org

Mattoon • *Coles Together* • Angela Griffin; Pres.; 400 Airport Rd.; 61938; Coles; P 52,600; (217) 258-5627; angela@colestogether.com; www.colestogether.com

Milan • *University of Illinois Ext.* • Jenny Garner; Educator; 321 W. 2nd Ave.; 61264; Rock Island; (309) 756-9978; Fax (309) 756-9987; jsgarnr@illinois.edu; www.merceredp.org

Mount Vernon • *Jefferson County Dev. Corp.* • Jonathon D. Hallberg; Exec. Dir.; 200 Potomac Blvd., Ste. 3; 62864; Jefferson; P 38,800; (618) 244-3554; (888) 708-6088; Fax (618) 244-7533; admin@jeffcodev.org; www.jeffcodev.org

Naperville • *Naperville Dev. Partnership & CVB* • Christine Jeffries; Pres.; 22 E Chicago Ave., Ste. 205; 60540; DuPage & Will; P 147,000; (630) 305-7701; (877) 236-2737; Fax (630) 305-7793; ncvb@naper.org; www.visitnaperville.com

Normal • *Eco. Dev. Cncl. of the Bloomington-Normal Area* • Kyle Ham; CEO; 200 W. College Ave., Ste. 402; 61761; McLean; P 132,000; (309) 452-8437; becky@bnbiz.org; www.bnbiz.org

Oak Forest • *City of Oak Forest* • Adam Dotson; Comm. Dev. Dir.; 15440 S. Central Ave.; 60452; Cook; P 28,000; (708) 687-4050; Fax (708) 687-8817; adotson@oak-forest.org; www.oak-forest.org

Oak Lawn • *Village of Oak Lawn* • Steve Radice; Dir. of Eco. Dev.; 9446 S. Raymond Ave.; 60453; Cook; P 57,100; (708) 499-7068; Fax (708) 499-7823; sradice@oaklawn-il.gov; www.oaklawn-il.gov

Oakland • *see Mattoon*

Olney • *Richland County Dev. Corp.* • Courtney Yockey; Exec. Dir.; 315 W. Main St.; 62450; Richland; P 16,100; (618) 392-2305; Fax (618) 392-2405; cyockey@rcdc.com; www.rcdc.com

Orland Park • *Orland Park Bus. & Dev.* • Karie Friling; Dir.; 14700 S. Ravinia Ave.; 60462; Cook; P 56,876; (708) 403-5300; Fax (708) 403-6215; developmentservices@orland-park.il.us; www.orland-park.il.us

Ottawa • *Ottawa Eco. Dev. Task Force* • Boyd Palmer; Exec. Dir.; 633 LaSalle St., Ste. 401; 61350; LaSalle; P 24,000; (815) 433-0084; Fax (815) 433-2405; info@ottawachamberillinois.com; www.ottawachamberillinois.com

Pana • *Pana Ind. Dev. Corp.* • Jim Deere; Exec. Dir.; 120 E. 3rd St.; City Hall; 62557; Christian; P 7,100; (217) 562-3109; Fax (217) 562-3823; panail@consolidated.net; www.panaindustrial.com

Park Forest • *Park Forest Eco. Dev. & Planning* • Hildy Kingma; Dir.; 350 Victory Dr.; 60466; Cook; P 22,000; (708) 283-5622; Fax (708) 748-4355; hkingma@vopf.com; www.villageofparkforest.com

Peoria • *Eco. Dev. Cncl. for Central IL* • Jim McConoughey; CEO; 100 S.W. Water St.; 61602; Peoria; P 370,000; (309) 676-0755; Fax (309) 676-7534; jmcconoughey@h-p.org; www.edc.centralillinois.org

Pittsfield • *City of Pittsfield - Eco. Dev. Ofc.* • William W. McCartney; Dir.; 215 N. Monroe; 62363; Pike; P 4,614; (217) 285-4484; Fax (217) 285-4485; pittsed@pittsfieldil.org; www.pittsfieldil.org

Plano • *Plano Eco. Dev. Corp.* • Rich Healy; Exec. Dir.; 7050 Burroughs Ave.; 60545; Kendall; P 8,300; (630) 552-9119; Fax (630) 552-0165; director@planoedc.org; www.planoedc.org

Quincy • *Great River Eco. Dev. Found.* • Marcel Wagner; Pres.; 300 Civic Center Plz., Ste. 256; 62301; Adams; P 42,202; (217) 223-4313; Fax (217) 231-2030; gredf@gredf.org; www.gredf.org

Rockford • *Rockford Dept. of Comm. & Eco. Dev.* • Mark Williams; Eco. Dev. Div. Head; 425 E. State St.; 61104; Winnebago; P 153,000; (779) 348-7449; (779) 348-7418; mark.williams@rockfordil.gov; www.rockfordil.gov

Springfield • *Ofc. of Planning & Eco. Dev.* • Karen Davis; Dir.; 800 E. Monroe, Rm. 107; 62701; Sangamon; P 116,300; (217) 789-2377; (800) 357-2379; Fax (217) 789-2380; karen.davis@springfield.il.us; www.springfield.il.us

Sterling • *Greater Sterling Dev. Corp.* • Heather Sotelo; Exec. Dir.; 1741 Industrial Dr.; 61081; Whiteside; P 16,000; (815) 625-5255; Fax (815) 625-5094; hsotelo@sterlingdevelopment.org; www.sterlingdevelopment.org

Taylorville • *Taylorville/Christian County EDC* • Mary Renner; Exec. Dir.; 108 W. Market St., 2nd Flr.; 62568; Christian; P 12,000; (217) 287-2580; Fax (217) 824-6689; tccedc1@consolidated.net; www.christiancountyedc.com

Washington • *Washington Eco. Dev. Comm.* • Candy Liggin; Ofc. Mgr.; 114 Washington Sq.; 61571; Tazewell; P 13,500; (309) 444-8909; Fax (309) 444-9225; wcoc@mtco.com; www.washingtoncoc.com

Waukegan • *Waukegan Port Dist.* • Duncan C. Henderson; Exec. Dir.; 55 S. Harbor Pl.; P.O. Box 620; 60079; Lake; (847) 244-3133; Fax (847) 244-1348; wkgnport@waukeganport.com; www.waukeganport.com

Woodridge • *Village of Woodridge Comm. Dev. Dept.* • Michael Mays; Dir.; Five Plaza Dr.; 60517; Cook, DuPage & Will; P 33,000; (630) 719-4766; mmays@vil.woodridge.il.us; www.vil.woodridge.il.us

Yorkville • *Eco. Dev. of Kendall Co.* • 111 W. Fox St., Rm. 316; 60560; Kendall; P 118,200; (630) 385-3000; kendalledc@co.kendall.il.us; www.co.kendall.il.us

Zion • *City of Zion Planning & Eco. Dev.* • Sonolito Bronson; Coord.; 2828 Sheridan Rd.; 60099; Lake; P 25,000; (847) 746-4056; Fax (847) 746-4017; sonolitob@zion.il.us; www.cityofzion.com

Indiana

Federal

U.S. SBA, Indiana Dist. Ofc. • Gail Gesell; Dist. Dir.; 8500 Keystone Crossing, Ste. 400; 46240; Marion; P 6,537,334; (317) 226-7272; g.gesell@sba.gov; www.sba.gov/in

State

Indiana Eco. Dev. Corp. • Jim Schellinger; Pres.; One N. Capitol Ave., Ste. 700; Indianapolis; 46204; Marion; P 6,571,000; (317) 232-8800; (800) 463-8081; Fax (317) 232-4146; iedc@iedc.in.gov; www.iedc.in.gov

Communities

Anderson • *Corp. for Eco. Dev. [CED]* • Rob Sparks; Exec. Dir.; 2705 Enterprise Dr., Ste. 161; 46013; Madison; P 132,000; (765) 642-1860; Fax (765) 642-0266; jackharter@cedanderson.com; www.cedanderson.com

Avon • *Hendricks County Eco. Dev. Partnership* • Jeff Pipkin; Interim Exec. Dir.; 5250 E. U.S. Hwy. 36, Ste. 1101; 46123; Hendricks; P 154,000; (317) 745-2400; Fax (317) 745-0757; jeff@hcedp.org; www.hcedp.org

Bedford • *Lawrence County Eco. Growth Cncl.* • Gene McCracken; Exec. Dir.; 1116 16th St.; 47421; Lawrence; P 47,000; (812) 275-5123; (812) 275-4493; Fax (812) 279-5998; gene@lawrencecountygrowth.com; www.lawrencecountygrowth.com

Bloomfield • *Greene County Eco. Dev. Corp.* • Brianne Jerrels; Exec. Dir.; 4513 W. State Rd. 54, Ste. 105; 47424; Greene; P 33,100; (812) 659-2109; Fax (812) 847-0937; info@insidegreenecounty.com; www.insidegreenecounty.com

Bloomington • *Bloomington Eco. Dev. Corp.* • Lynn Coyne; Pres.; 1720 N. Kinser Pike, Ste. 001; 47404; Monroe; P 142,000; (812) 335-7346; Fax (812) 335-7348; amccombe@bloomingtonedc.com; www.bloomingtonedc.com

Bluffton • *Wells County Eco. Dev.* • Mike Row; Dir.; 211 W. Water St.; 46714; Wells; P 27,600; (260) 824-0510; Fax (260) 824-5871; mrow@wellsedc.com; www.wellsedc.com

Bremen • *Town of Bremen Dept. of Eco. Dev.* • Trend Weldy; Dir.; 104 S. Center St.; 46506; Marshall; P 5,000; (574) 546-2044; Fax (574) 546-5487; townbremenin@mchsi.com; www.townofbremen.com

Cayuga • *Vermillion County Eco. Dev. Cncl.* • Dylan Riggen; Exec. Dir.; 703 W. Park St.; 47928; Vermillion; P 16,212; (765) 492-9153; (765) 832-1899; Fax (765) 492-9178; susie@vermillioncountyedc.com; www.vermillioncountyedc.com

Columbus • *Columbus Eco. Dev. Bd.* • Jason Hester CEcD; Exec. Dir.; 500 Franklin St.; 47201; Bartholomew; P 40,000; (812) 378-7300; Fax (812) 372-6756; patwilson@columbusin.org; www.columbusin.org

Corydon • *Harrison County Eco. Dev. Corp.* • Darrell Voelker; Dir.; 111 W. Walnut St.; 47112; Harrison; P 39,200; (812) 738-0120; Fax (812) 738-0500; dvoelker@hcedcindiana.org; www.hcedcindiana.org

Crawfordsville • *Indiana West Advantage* • Tom Utley; Exec. Dir.; 200 S. Washington St., Ste. 305; 47933; Montgomery; P 38,500; (765) 362-6851; Fax (765) 362-6900; indianawestadvantage@gmail.com; www.indianawest.com

Decatur • *Adams County Eco. Dev. Corp.* • Larry D. Macklin; Exec. Dir.; 313 W. Jefferson St.; P.O. Box 492; 46733; Adams; P 34,000; (260) 724-2588; lmacklin@adamscountyedc.com; www.adamscountyedc.com

Elkhart • *Center of Business Excellence* • Merritt Dilts; V.P. Business Resources; 418 S. Main St.; P.O. Box 2586; 46515; Elkhart; P 320,000; (574) 293-3209; Fax (574) 294-1859; mdilts@elkhart.org; www.elkhart.org

Elkhart • *Eco. Dev. Corp. of Elkhart County* • Mark Dobson; Pres./CEO; 300 NIBCO Pkwy., Ste. 201; 46516; Elkhart; P 201,971; (574) 293-JOBS; (877) 535-1002; Fax (574) 343-2951; edc@elkhartcountybiz.com; www.elkhartcountybiz.com

Evansville • *Eco. Dev. Coalition of Southwest Indiana •* Greg Wathen; Pres./CEO; 318 Main St., Ste. 400; P.O. Box 20127; 47708; Vanderburgh; P 314,000; (812) 423-2020; (800) 401-7683; Fax (812) 423-2080; info@southwestindiana.org; www.southwestindiana.org

Fort Wayne • *Greater Fort Wayne Inc. •* Eric Doden; CEO; 200 E. Main St., Ste. 800; 46802; Allen; P 370,000; (260) 420-6945; Fax (260) 426-0837; info@greaterfortwayneinc.com; www.greaterfortwayneinc.com

Fowler • *Benton County Eco. Dev. •* Paul Jackson; Dir.; 706 E. 5th St., Ste. 11; 47944; Benton; P 8,700; (765) 884-2080; pjackson@bentoncounty.in.gov; www.benton4biz.com

Franklin • *Johnson County Dev. Corp. •* Cheryl Morphew; Pres./CEO; 2797 N. Morton St., Ste. F; 46131; Johnson; P 147,538; (317) 736-4300; Fax (317) 736-7220; cmorphew@jcdc.org; www.jcdc.org

Greencastle • *Greencastle/Putnam County Dev. Center Inc. •* Kristin Clary; Exec. Dir.; 2 S. Jackson St.; 46135; Putnam; P 38,000; (765) 653-2474; Fax (765) 653-6385; tami@gcpcdc.com; www.gcpcdc.com

Greenfield • *Hancock Eco. Dev. Cncl. •* Dennis Maloy; Dir.; One Courthouse Plz.; 46140; Hancock; P 70,000; (317) 477-7241; Fax (317) 477-2353; dmaloy@hancockedc.org; www.hancockedc.org

Greenwood • *see Franklin*

Hartford City • *Blackford County Eco. Dev. Corp. •* Jacob Everett; Exec. Dir.; 121 N. High St.; 47348; Blackford; P 13,000; (765) 348-4944; Fax (765) 348-4945; jeverett@blackfordcoedc.org; www.blackfordcoedc.org

Huntington • *Huntington County Eco. Dev. Corp. •* Mark A. Whickersham; Exec. Dir.; 8 W. Market St.; 46750; Huntington; P 38,000; (260) 356-5688; Fax (260) 358-5692; helen@hcued.com; www.hcued.com

Indianapolis • *Indy Partnership •* 111 Monument Cir., Ste. 1950; 46204; Marion; P 1,905,981; (317) 464-2204; Fax (317) 464-2217; pgalloway@indypartnership.com; www.indychamber.com/economic-development/why-indy-region

Kendallville • *Eco. Dev. Steering Comm. •* Michael Walton; Coord.; 122 S. Main St.; 46755; Noble; P 10,000; (260) 347-1554; (877) 347-1554; Fax (260) 347-1575; info@kendallchamber.com; www.kendallvillechamber.com

Knox • *Starke County Eco. Dev. Found. •* Charles W. Weaver JD; Exec. Dir.; 1915 S Heaton St.; 46534; Starke; P 24,000; (574) 772-5627; (574) 806-8030; Fax (574) 772-5912; execdir@scedf.biz; www.scedf.biz

Kokomo • *Greater Kokomo Eco. Dev. Alliance •* Chris Hamm; Pres./CEO; 325 N. Main St.; 46901; Howard; P 85,000; (765) 457-5301; (765) 457-2000; Fax (765) 452-4564; chamm@greaterkokomo.com; www.greaterkokomo.com

Lafayette • *Greater Lafayette Commerce •* Scott Walker; Pres./CEO; 337 Columbia St.; P.O. Box 348; 47902; Tippecanoe; P 173,000; (765) 742-4044; Fax (765) 742-6276; info@greaterlafayettecommerce.com; www.greaterlafayettecommerce.com

Leavenworth • *Crawford County Eco. Dev. Comm. •* Don DuBois; Exec. Dir.; 6225 E. Industrial Ln., Ste. B; 47137; Crawford; P 11,076; (812) 739-2248; Fax (812) 739-4180; don@selectcrawfordcounty.com; www.selectcc.com

Lebanon • *Boone County Eco. Dev. Corp. •* Molly Whitehead; Exec. Dir.; 218 E. Washington St.; 46052; Boone; P 60,500; (765) 482-5761; (317) 995-3207; Fax (765) 482-5782; asamson@booneedc.org; www.booneedc.org

Liberty • *Union County Dev. Corp. •* Melissa Browning; Exec. Dir.; 5 W. High St.; 47353; Union; P 7,200; (765) 458-5976; Fax (765) 458-5976; unioncodc@frontier.com; www.ucdc.us

Logansport • *Cass-Logansport County Eco. Dev. Organization •* Bill Cuppy; Exec. Dir.; 311 S. 5th St.; 46947; Cass; P 39,000; (574) 722-5988; (800) 686-1067; Fax (574) 735-0909; admin@connectincass.com; www.connectincass.com

Marion • *Grant County Eco. Growth Cncl. •* Timothy K. Eckerle; Exec. Dir.; 301 S. Adams St.; 46952; Grant; P 70,000; (888) 668-3203; Fax (765) 662-8340; info@grantcounty.com; www.grantcounty.com

Monticello • *White County Eco. Dev. •* Randall R. Mitchell; Pres.; 124 N. Main St.; P.O. Box 1031; 47960; White; P 25,000; (574) 583-6557; Fax (574) 583-6230; dconover@whiced.com; www.whitecountyin.org

Mooresville • *Morgan County Eco. Dev. Corp. •* Mike Dellinger; Exec. Dir.; 4 E. Harrison St.; P.O. Box 606; 46158; Morgan; P 69,000; (317) 831-9544; Fax (317) 831-9548; mcedc@morgancoed.com; www.morgancoed.com

Mount Comfort • *see Greenfield*

New Castle • *New Castle/Henry County Eco. Dev. Corp. •* Corey Murphy; Dir.; 100 S. Main St., Ste. 203; 47362; Henry; P 49,500; (765) 521-7402; Fax (765) 521-7404; info@nchcedc.org; www.nchcedc.org

Newburgh • *Success Warrick County •* Larry Taylor; Exec. Dir.; 4763 Rosebud Ln., Ste. C; 47630; Warrick; P 60,000; (812) 858-3555; Fax (812) 858-3558; barb.beachler@warrickcounty.gov; www.successwarrickcounty.com

Noblesville • *City of Noblesville Eco. Dev. •* Judi Johnson; Eco. Dev. Dir.; 16 S. 10th St., Ste. 275, 46060; Hamilton; P 58,000; (317) 776-6345; Fax (317) 776-6363; jjohnson@noblesville.in.us; www.choosenoblesville.com

North Vernon • *Jennings County Eco. Dev. Comm. •* Kathy Ertel; Exec. Dir.; 1865 W. U.S. Hwy. 50; P.O. Box 15; 47265; Jennings; P 28,300; (812) 346-2388; Fax (812) 346-7992; kertel@jenningsedc.com; www.jenningsedc.com

Peru • *Miami County Eco. Dev. Auth. •* James Tidd; Exec. Dir.; 1525 W. Hoosier Blvd., Ste. 201; 46970; Miami; P 36,082; (765) 689-0159; (800) 472-0449; Fax (765) 689-0168; info@miamicountyeda.com; www.miamicountyeda.com

Petersburg • *Pike County Eco. Dev. Corp. •* Ashley P. Willis; Exec. Dir.; 1592 N. State Rd. 61; P.O. Box 204; 47567; Pike; P 13,000; (812) 354-2271; Fax (812) 354-7196; pikegrowth@frontier.com; www.pikegrowth.com

Plymouth • *Marshall County Eco. Dev. Corp. •* Jerry Chavez; Pres./CEO; 2864 Miller Dr.; 46563; Marshall; P 47,051; (574) 935-8499; Fax (547) 936-2645; mail@marshallcountyedc.org; www.marshallcountyedc.org

Portage • *Northwest IN Forum Inc. •* Heather Ennis; Pres./CEO; 6100 Southport Rd.; 46368; Porter; P 787,000; (219) 763-6303; (800) 693-6786; Fax (219) 763-2653; msaltanovitz@nwiforum.org; www.nwiforum.org

Portland • *Jay County Dev. Corp. •* Bill Bradley; Exec. Dir.; 118 S. Meridian St., Ste. B; 47371; Jay; P 22,000; (260) 726-9311; Fax (260) 726-4477; info@jaycodev.org; www.jaycountydevelopment.org

Richmond • *EDC of Wayne County* • Tim Rogers; Pres./CEO; 500 S. A St., Ste. 2; P.O. Box 1919; 47375; Wayne; P 72,000; (765) 983-4769; Fax (765) 966-0882; info@edcwc.com; www.edcwc.com

Rochester • *Fulton Eco. Dev. Corp.* • Terry Lee; Exec. Dir.; 822 Main St.; 46975; Fulton; P 21,000; (574) 223-3326; tlee@fultondevelopment.org; www.fultondevelopment.org

Rockport • *Lincolnland Eco. Dev. Corp.* • Tom Utter; Exec. Dir.; 2792 N. U.S. Hwy. 231; P.O. Box 276; 47635; Spencer; P 21,000; (812) 649-2119; Fax (812) 649-2236; specialproject@ledc.org; www.ledc.org

Rushville • *Rush County Eco. & Comm. Dev. Corp.* • John McCane; Exec. Dir.; 210 E. U.S. 52, Ste. C; 46173; Rush; P 18,000; (765) 938-3232; Fax (765) 932-4355; johnmccane@rushecdc.org; www.rushecdc.org

Salem • *Washington County Eco. Growth Partnership* • Sabrina Burdine; Exec. Dir.; 1707 N. Shelby St., Ste. 109; 47167; Washington; P 28,000; (812) 883-8803; Fax (812) 883-8739; info@wcegp.org; www.wcegp.org

Scottsburg • *Scott County Eco. Dev. Corp.* • Robert Peacock; Exec. Dir.; 821 S. Lake Rd. S.; P.O. Box 156; 47170; Scott; P 24,000; (812) 752-7268; (812) 752-7270; Fax (812) 752-7272; info@scottcountyin.com; www.scottcountyin.com

Seymour • *Jackson County Ind. Dev. Corp.* • James Plump; Exec. Dir.; 301 N. Chestnut St.; P.O. Box 783; 47274; Jackson; P 43,000; (812) 522-4951; Fax (812) 522-1235; jimplump@jcidc.com; www.jcidc.com

Shelbyville • *Shelby County Dev. Corp.* • Brian Asher; Exec. Dir.; 16 Public Sq., Ste. A; 46176; Shelby; P 45,000; (317) 398-8903; Fax (317) 398-8915; b.asher@shelbydevelopment.com; www.shelbydevelopment.com

Tell City • *Perry County Dev. Corp.* • Alvin Evans; Pres./CEO; 601 Main St., Ste. A; P.O. Box 731; 47586; Perry; P 20,000; (812) 547-8377; Fax (812) 547-8378; carol@pickperry.com; www.pickperry.com

Terre Haute • *Terre Haute Eco. Dev. Corp.* • Steve Witt; Pres.; 630 Wabash Ave., Ste. 101; 47807; Vigo; P 108,000; (812) 234-2524; Fax (812) 232-6054; info@terrehauteedc.com; www.terrehauteedc.com

Tipton • *Tipton County Eco. Dev.* • Jeff Sheridan; Dir.; 114 S. Main St.; 46072; Tipton; P 16,000; (765) 675-7417; djeffreysheridan@gmail.com; www.tiptonedc.com

Vincennes • *Knox County Dev. Corp.* • Ken Utt & Becky Litherland; 1101 N. 3rd St.; P.O. Box 701; 47591; Knox; P 38,500; (812) 886-6993; Fax (812) 886-0888; info@kcdc.com; www.kcdc.com

Wabash • *Eco. Dev. Group of Wabash County* • William Konyha; Pres./CEO; 214 S. Wabash St.; 46992; Wabash; P 32,300; (260) 563-5258; (877) 509-9919; info@edgwc.com; www.edgwc.com

Walkerton • *Walkerton Area Eco. Dev. Corp.* • Phil Buckmaster; Exec. Dir.; 301 Michigan St.; 46574; St. Joseph; P 2,300; (574) 910-0820; Fax (574) 586-2248; waedc@walkerton.org; www.walkerton.org

Warsaw • *Kosciusko Eco. Dev. Corp.* • Kim Nance; Coord.; 121 N. Lake St.; 46580; Kosciusko; P 77,300; (574) 265-2601; knance@kosciuskoedc.com; www.kosciuskoedc.com

Zanesville • *see Lebanon*

Iowa

Federal

U.S. SBA, Cedar Rapids Branch Ofc. • Dennis Larkin; Branch Mgr.; 2750 1st Ave. N.E., Ste. 350; 52402; Linn; P 3,074,186; (319) 362-6405; Fax (319) 362-7861; g.d.larkin@sba.gov; www.sba.gov/ia

U.S. SBA, Des Moines Dist. Ofc. • Joseph Folsom; Dist. Dir.; 210 Walnut St., Rm. 749; 50309; Polk; P 3,074,186; (515) 284-4422; Fax (515) 284-4572; j.folsom@sba.gov; www.sba.gov/ia

State

Iowa Eco. Dev. Auth. • Deborah V. Durham; Dir.; 200 E. Grand Ave.; Des Moines; 50309; Polk; P 3,000,000; (515) 725-3000; Fax (515)725-3010; director@iowa.gov; www.iowaeconomicdevelopment.com

Communities

Ackley • *Ackley Eco. Dev. Comm.* • Michael Nuss; Eco. Dev. Dir.; City Hall; 208 State St.; 50601; Hardin; P 1,589; (641) 847-2214; Fax (641) 847-3204; ackley@mchsi.com; www.ackleyiowa.net

Albia • *Albia Ind. Dev. Corp.* • Dave Johnson; Pres.; Bates Bldg.; 1 Benton Ave. W.; 52531; Monroe; P 8,016; (641) 932-7233; Fax (641) 932-3044; aidc@iowatelecom.net; www.albiaindustrial.com

Algona • *Kossuth County EDC* • Maureen Elbert; Exec. Dir.; 106 S. Dodge St., Ste. 210; 50511; Kossuth; P 25,000; (515) 295-7979; Fax (515) 295-8873; kcedc@kossuthia.com; www.kossuth-edc.com

Altoona • *see Pleasant Hill*

Ames • *Ames Eco. Dev. Comm.* • Dan Culhane; Pres./CEO; 304 Main St.; 50010; Story; P 61,000; (515) 232-2310; Fax (515) 233-3203; dan@ameschamber.com; www.amesedc.com

Ankeny • *Ankeny Eco. Dev. Corp.* • Joey Beech; Exec. Dir.; 210 S. Ankeny Blvd.; 50023; Polk; P 50,000; (515) 964-0747; Fax (515) 964-0487; jbeech@ankeny.org; www.ankenyedc.com

Arnolds Park • *Iowa Great Lakes Ind. Dev. Bd.* • Tom Kuhlman; Exec. Dir.; 243 W. Broadway; P.O. Box 9; 51331; Dickinson; P 16,424; (712) 332-2107; Fax (712) 332-7714; tom@okobojichamber.com; www.vacationokoboji.com

Atlantic • *Southwest Iowa Planning Cncl.* • John P. McCurdy AICP; Exec. Dir.; 1501 S.W. 7th St.; 50022; Cass; P 182,531; (712) 243-4196; (866) 279-4720; Fax (712) 243-3458; swipco@swipco.org; www.swipco.org

Audubon • *Audubon County Eco. Dev. Corp.* • Chad Schreck; Exec. Dir.; 800 Market St.; 50025; Audubon; P 6,119; (712) 563-2742; Fax (712) 563-2742; aced@iowatelecom.net; www.auduboncounty.com

Avoca • *Western Iowa Dev. Assn.* • Lori Holste; Exec. Dir.; 1911 N. LaVista Height Rd., Ste. 102; P.O. Box 579; 51521; Pottawattamie; P 11,000; (712) 343-6368; Fax (712) 343-2136; lori@wida.org; www.wida.org

Bedford • *Bedford Area Dev. Center* • Tracy Sleep; Pres.; 601 Madison Ave.; 50833; Taylor; P 2,600; (712) 523-3637; Fax (712) 523-3384; bedfordareadc@frontiernet.net; www.bedford-iowa.com

Belle Plaine • *Belle Plaine Comm. Dev. Corp.* • Sheila Hlas; Exec. Dir.; 826 12th St.; P.O. Box 163; 52208; Benton; P 2,800; (319) 434-6481; Fax (319) 434-6026; bpcdc@netins.net; www.belleplainecommunitydevelopment.net

Belmond • *BIDCO Org.* • Brad Robson; 235 E. Main St.; 50421; Wright; P 3,000; (641) 444-3937; Fax (641) 444-3944; bacoc@frontiernet.net; www.belmond.com

Bettendorf • *Bettendorf Dev. Corp.* • Jeff Reiter; Dir.; 1609 State St.; 52722; Scott; P 33,300; (563) 344-4060; Fax (563) 344-4012; jreiter@bettendorf.org; www.bettendorf.org

Bloomfield • *Davis County Dev. Corp.* • John Schroeder; Exec. Dir.; 111 S. Washington St.; 52537; Davis; P 8,753; (641) 664-2300; Fax (206) 202-1334; info@daviscounty.org; www.daviscounty.org

Bondurant • *see Altoona*

Boone • *Boone County Eco. Growth Corp.* • Robert Fisher; Exec. Dir.; 903 Story St.; 50036; Boone; P 27,000; (515) 432-7868; Fax (515) 432-3343; boonesfuture@booneiowa.us; www.booneiowa.us

Burlington • *Greater Burlington Partnership* • Jason Hutcheson; Pres./CEO; 610 N. 4th St., Ste. 200; 52601; Des Moines; P 42,000; (319) 208-0043; Fax (319) 752-6454; jhutcheson@greaterburlington.com; www.greaterburlington.com

Carroll • *Carroll Area Dev. Corp.* • Shannon Landauer; Exec. Dir.; 407 W. 5th St.; P.O. Box 307; 51401; Carroll; P 21,000; (712) 792-4383; Fax (712) 792-4384; cadc@carrolliowa.com; www.carrollareadev.com

Cascade • *Cascade Eco. Dev. Corp.* • Fred Kremer; Pres.; P.O. Box 695; 52033; Dubuque; P 2,240; (563) 852-3020; (563) 852-7214; Fax (563) 852-7554; cascadecity@netins.net; www.cityofcascade.org

Cedar Falls • *Cedar Falls Dept. of Eco. Dev.* • Bob Seymour; Comm. Svcs. Mgr.; 220 Clay St.; 50613; Black Hawk; P 39,300; (319) 273-8606; Fax (319) 273-8610; bob.seymour@cedarfalls.com; www.50613.com

Cedar Rapids • *Cedar Rapids Metro Eco. Alliance* • Doug Neumann; Interim Pres./CEO; 501 First St. S.E.; 52401; Linn; P 259,000; (319) 398-5317; Fax (319) 398-5228; economicalliance@cedarrapids.org; www.priority1.com

Centerville • *Appanoose Eco. Dev. Corp.* • Tod Faris; Exec. Dir.; 101 W. Van Buren St., Ste. 1; 52544; Appanoose; P 12,800; (641) 856-3388; Fax (641) 856-6046; aedcdirector@iowatelecom.net; www.appanoosecounty.org

Chariton • *Lucas County Dev. Corp.* • Kris Patrick; Exec. Dir.; 104 N. Grand St.; P.O. Box 735; 50049; Lucas; P 8,860; (641) 774-4059; (641) 774-4059; Fax (641) 774-2801; kris@charitonareachambermainstreet.com; www.charitonareachambermainstreet.com

Charles City • *Charles City Area Dev. Corp.* • Timothy S. Fox CEcD; Exec. Dir.; 401 N. Main St.; 50616; Floyd; P 20,000; (641) 228-3020; Fax (641) 228-4744; ccadc@charlescityia.com; www.charlescityia.com

Cherokee • *Cherokee Area Eco. Dev. Corp.* • Mark Buschkamp; Exec. Dir.; 201 W. Main St.; 51012; Cherokee; P 12,000; (712) 225-5739; Fax (712) 225-1991; mark@cherokeeia.com; www.cherokeeia.com

Clinton • *Clinton Reg. Dev. Corp.* • Mike Kirchhoff CEcD; Pres./CEO; 721 S. 2nd St.; 52732; Clinton; P 250,000; (563) 242-4536; Fax (563) 242-4554; mkirchhoff@clintondevelopment.com; www.clintondevelopment.com

Columbus Junction • *Columbus Comm. Dev.* • Kirsten Shellabarger; Pres.; 232 2nd St.; 52738; Louisa; P 1,900; (319) 728-2414; Fax (319) 728-7502; cdc@columbusjunctioniowa.org; www.columbusjunctioniowa.org

Conrad • *Conrad Chamber-Main Street* • Darla Ubben; Prog. Dir.; P.O. Box 414; 50621; Grundy; P 1,108; (641) 366-2108; Fax (641) 366-2109; cmspd@heartofiowa.net; www.conrad.govoffice.com

Coon Rapids • *Coon Rapids Dev. Group* • Mark Thomas; Pres.; P.O. Box 226; 50058; Carroll; P 1,310; (712) 999-2734; crdg@longlines.com; www.coonrapidsiowa.com

Corning • *Adams Comm. Eco. Dev. Corp.* • Derek Lumsden; Exec. Dir.; 710 Davis Ave.; 50841; Adams; P 1,800; (641) 322-5229; Fax (641) 322-4387; adamschamber@frontiernet.net; www.adamscountyiowa.com

Council Bluffs • *City of Council Bluffs Comm. Dev. Dept.* • Donald Gross; Dir.; 209 Pearl St.; 51503; Pottawattamie; P 62,200; (712) 328-4629; Fax (712) 328-4915; dgross@councilbluffs-ia.gov; www.communitydev.councilbluffs-ia.gov

Cresco • *Howard County Eco. Dev.* • Jason Passmore; Exec. Dir.; 101 2nd Ave. S.W.; 52136; Howard; P 9,600; (563) 547-3434; Fax (563) 547-2056; jason@howard-county.com; www.howard-county.com

Davenport • *Quad Cities First* • Paul Rumler; Exec. V.P.; 331 W. 3rd St.; 52801; Scott County, IA; Henry, Mercer & Rock Island, IL; P 360,000; (563) 322-1706; prumler@quadcitieschamber.com; www.quadcitiesfirst.com

Des Moines • *Iowa Area Dev. Group* • Rand M. Fisher; Pres.; 2600 Grand Ave., Ste. 430; 50312; Polk & Warren; P 611,600; (515) 223-4817; (800) 888-4743; Fax (515) 223-5719; rfisher@iadg.com; www.iadg.com

Des Moines • *City of Des Moines - Ofc. of Eco. Dev.* • Ryan Moffatt; Eco. Dev. Proj. Mgr.; City Hall; 400 Robert D. Ray Dr., 1st Flr.; 50309; Polk & Warren; P 204,000; (515) 283-4004; Fax (515) 237-1667; oed@dmgov.org; www.dmgov.org

DeWitt • *DeWitt Dev. Co.* • Tami Petsche; Exec. Dir.; 1010 6th Ave.; 52742; Clinton; P 5,200; (563) 659-8508; Fax (563) 659-2410; ddc.ceo@dewitt.org; www.dewittdevelopmentcompany.com

Dubuque • *Greater Dubuque Dev. Corp.* • Rick Dickinson; Pres./CEO; 900 Jackson St., Ste. 109; 52001; Dubuque; P 60,000; (563) 557-9049; gddc@greaterdubuque.org; www.greaterdubuque.org

Dysart • *Dysart Dev. Corp.* • Dwayne Luze; Pres.; P.O. Box 223; 52224; Tama; P 1,380; (319) 476-4949; (319) 269-5762; Fax (319) 476-4948; luzere@fctc.coop; www.dysartiowa.com

Eldora • *City of Eldora Eco. Dev.* • Deb Crosser; Exec. Dir.; 1442 Washington St.; 50627; Hardin; P 2,835; (641) 939-3241; Fax (641) 939-7555; eldoraecondev@heartofiowa.net; www.eldoraiowa.com

Elkader • *Main Street Elkader/Eco. Dev.* • Roger Thomas; Dir.; 207 N. Main St.; P.O. Box 125; 52043; Clayton; P 1,300; (563) 245-2770; Fax (563) 245-1033; mse@alpinecom.net; www.elkader-iowa.com

Fairfield • *Fairfield Eco. Dev. Assn.* • Joshua Laraby; Exec. Dir.; 605 S. 23rd St., Ste. 102; 52556; Jefferson; P 16,900; (641) 472-3436; Fax (641) 209-3508; joshua.laraby@growfairfield.com; www.growfairfield.com

Forest City • *Forest City Dev. Inc.* • David Kingland; Pres.; 145 E. K St.; 50436; Winnebago; P 4,500; (641) 585-5560; Fax (641) 585-2687; info@forestcityia.com; www.forestcityia.com

Fort Dodge • *Greater Fort Dodge Growth Alliance* • Kelly Halsted; Eco. Dev. Dir.; 24 N. 9th St., Ste. A; 50501; Webster; P 39,000; (515) 955-8909; (515) 227-7121; Fax (515) 955-3245; info@greaterfortdodge.com; www.greaterfortdodge.com

Garner • *Garner Area Comm. Betterment Assn.* • Howard Parrott; Secy./Treas.; 265 E. Lyon St.; 50438; Hancock; P 2,922; (641) 923-2739; hmparrot@ncn.net; www.garneriowa.org

Greenfield • *Greenfield Main Street Dev. Corp.* • Ginny Kuhfus; Dir.; 215 S. First St.; P.O. Box 61; 50849; Adair; P 2,100; (641) 743-8444; Fax (641) 743-8205; grfld_cc_ms_dev@iowatelecom.net; www.greenfieldiowa.com

Grinnell • *Poweshiek Area Dev.* • Deb Collum-Calderwood; Exec. Dir.; 927 4th Ave.; 50112; Poweshiek; P 9,100; (641) 236-1626; Fax (641) 236-2626; deb@powi80.com; www.powi80.com

Hampton • *Franklin County Dev. Assn.* • Karen Mitchell; Exec. Dir.; 5 First St. S.W.; 50441; Franklin; P 10,700; (641) 430-2578; Fax (641) 456-5660; fcda_director@mchsi.com; www.franklincountyiowa.com

Harlan • *Shelby County DevelopSource* • 1901 Hawkeye Ave., Ste. 101; 51537; Shelby; P 12,200; (712) 755-3569; Fax (712) 733-8921; info@developsource.com; www.developsource.com

Hartley • *see Primghar*

Hull • *Hull Ind. Dev. Corp.* • Les VanRoekel; City Admin.; City Hall; P.O. Box 816; 51239; Sioux; P 2,600; (712) 439-1521; Fax (712) 439-2512; hullcity@hickorytech.net; www.cityofhull.org

Ida Grove • *Ida Grove Eco. Dev. Corp.* • Clay Miller; 501 Second St.; P.O. Box 111; 51445; Ida; P 2,142; (712) 364-3393; (712) 364-2428; Fax (712) 364-3293; www.idagroveia.com

Independence • *Independence Enterprises Inc.* • Steve Ohl; Pres.; 115 First St. E.; 50644; Buchanan; P 6,500; (319) 334-4329; (319) 334-7497; Fax (319) 334-6335; steveohl@indytel.com

Independence • *Buchanan County Eco. Dev. Comm.* • George K. Lake; Dir.; 112 First St. E.; P.O. Box 109; 50644; Buchanan; P 21,000; (319) 334-7497; Fax (319) 334-5982; director@growbuchanan.com; www.growbuchanan.com

Indianola • *Warren County Eco. Dev. Corp.* • Hollie Askey; Exec. Dir.; 111 N. Buxton St.; 50125; Warren; P 47,400; (515) 961-1067; Fax (515) 961-1156; info@wcedc.com; www.wcedc.com

Inwood • *Inwood Dev. Corp.* • Carol VanderKolk; City Clerk; P.O. Box 298; 51240; Lyon; P 875; (712) 753-4833; Fax (712) 753-2538; cityhall@inwoodiowa.com; www.inwoodiowa.com

Iowa City • *Iowa City Area Dev. Group* • Mark Nolte; Pres.; 136 S. Dubuque St.; 52240; Johnson; P 131,000; (319) 354-3939; Fax (319) 338-9958; sjelinek@icadgroup.com; www.iowacityareadevelopment.com

Iowa Falls • *Iowa Falls Area Dev. Corp.* • Cindy Litwiller; Exec. Dir.; 520 Rocksylvania Ave.; 50126; Hardin; P 5,200; (641) 648-5604; Fax (641) 648-3702; director@iowafallsdevelopment.com; www.iowafallsdevelopment.com

Jefferson • *Greene County Dev. Corp.* • Ken Paxton; Exec. Dir.; 220 N. Chestnut St.; 50129; Greene; P 9,800; (515) 386-8255; (515) 386-2155; Fax (515) 386-2156; information@greenecountyiowadevelopment.org; www.greenecountyiowadevelopment.org

Johnston • *Iowa Bus. Growth Co.* • Daniel T. Robeson; Pres.; 5409 N.W. 88th St., Ste. 100; 50131; Polk; P 3,000,000; (515) 223-4511; Fax (515) 223-5017; iabusgrowth@iowabusinessgrowth.com; www.iowabusinessgrowth.com

Knoxville • *Knoxville Eco. Dev.* • Harold Stewart; City Mgr.; 305 S. 3rd St.; 50138; Marion; P 8,000; (641) 828-0550; Fax (641) 828-0511; citymanager@discoverknoxville.com; www.discoverknoxville.com

Lake Mills • *Winn-Worth BETCO* • Teresa Nicholson; Exec. Dir.; 203a N. 1st Ave. W.; P.O. Box 93; 50450; Winnebago; P 18,500; (641) 592-0800; Fax (641) 592-0801; wwb@wctatel.net; www.winnworthbetco.com

Le Mars • *Le Mars Bus. Initiative Corp.* • Neal Adler; Exec. Dir.; 50 Central Ave. S.E.; 51031; Plymouth; P 10,000; (712) 546-8821; Fax (712) 546-7218; neal@lemarschamber.org; www.lemarsiowa.com

Lenox • *Lenox Dev. Corp.* • Gary Zabel; Dir.; P.O. Box 8; 50851; Adams & Taylor; P 1,407; (641) 333-2255; (641) 333-2228; www.lenoxia.com

Logan • *Harrison County Dev. Corp.* • Renea Anderson; Exec. Dir.; 109 N. 4th Ave., Ste. 2; 51546; Harrison; P 15,000; (712) 644-3081; Fax (712) 644-3107; hcdc@iowatelecom.net; www.hcdconline.com

Lorimor • *Lorimor Comm. Dev. Corp.* • F. Dennis Orwan; Pres.; P.O. Box 63; 50149; Union; P 427; (641) 763-2334; fdorwan@grm.net; www.lorimor.org

Manchester • *Delaware County Eco. Dev. Comm.* • Donna Boss; Exec. Dir.; 200 E. Main St.; 52057; Delaware; P 17,800; (563) 927-3325; (563) 927-2958; dboss@delawarecountyia.com; www.delawarecountyia

Marcus • *MEDCO* • Ed Sand; Dir.; P.O. Box 56; 51035; Cherokee; P 1,200; (712) 376-2707; Fax (712) 376-4140; tower@evertek.net; www.marcusiowa.com

Marshalltown • *Marshalltown Reg. Partnership* • David Barajas Jr.; CEO; 709 S. Center St.; P.O. Box 1000; 50158; Marshall; P 41,500; (641) 753-6645; (800) 725-5301; Fax (641) 752-8373; dbarajas@marshalltown.org; www.marshalltownworks.com

Mason City • *North Iowa Corridor Eco. Dev. Corp.* • Brent Willett; Exec. Dir.; 9 N. Federal Ave.; 50401; Cerro Gordo; P 44,000; (641) 423-0315; (800) 944-1708; bwillett@northiowacorridor.com; www.northiowacorridor.com

Mitchellville • *see Altoona*

Monticello • *Monticello Dev. Corp.* • Bob Goodyear; P.O. Box 191; 52310; Jones; P 3,800; (319) 480-0171; (319) 465-3577; Fax (319) 465-4611; www.ci.monticello.ia.us

Mount Ayr • *Ringgold County Dev. Corp.* • Karen Bender; Coord.; 117 S. Fillmore; 50854; Ringgold; P 5,200; (641) 464-3704; Fax (641) 464-3704; rdevco@iowatelecom.net; www.mountayriowa.org

Nevada • *Nevada, IA Eco. Dev. Corp.* • LaVon Schiltz; Exec. Dir.; 516 K Ave., Ste. 100; P.O. Box 157; 50201; Story; P 7,000; (515) 382-1430; nedc@iowatelecom.net; www.nevadaiowaedc.com

New Hampton • *New Hampton Eco. Dev.* • Bob Soukup; Dir. of Eco. Dev.; 112 E. Spring St.; 50659; Chickasaw; P 4,000; (641) 394-2437; Fax (641) 394-4514; nhampton@iowatelecom.net; www.newhamptonia.com

Newton • *Newton Dev. Corp.* • Frank Liebl; Exec. Dir.; 600 N. 2nd Ave. W., Ste. P; 50208; Jasper; P 15,400; (641) 787-8209; (641) 521-1868; frankliebl.ndc@gmail.com; www.newtondevelopmentcorporation.com

Oakland • *Golden Hills Resource Conservation & Dev.* • Michelle Wodtke Franks; Exec. Dir.; 712 S. Hwy. 6; P.O. Box 189; 51560; Pottawattamie; P 200,000; (712) 482-3029; Fax (712) 482-5590; becky@goldenhillsrcd.org; www.goldenhillsrcd.org

Osceola • *Clarke County Dev. Corp.* • William Trickey; Exec. Dir.; P.O. Box 426; 50213; Clarke; P 9,200; (641) 342-2944; Fax (641) 342-6353; info@clarkecountyiowa.com; www.clarkecountyiowa.com

Ottumwa • *Ottumwa Eco. Dev. Corp.* • Sharon Stroh; Exec. Dir.; 217 E. Main St.; P.O. Box 1288; 52501; Wapello; P 35,700; (641) 682-3465; Fax (641) 682-3466; info@ottumwaiowa.com; www.ottumwadevelopment.org

Panora • *Panora Reg. Ind. Dev. Enterprise [PRIDE]* • John Rutledge; P.O. Box 141; 50216; Guthrie; P 3,000; (641) 755-2131; (641) 755-2301; pride@panora.org; panora.org

Pleasant Hill • *Eastern Polk Reg. Dev. Inc.* • Alex Lynch; Dir.; 5160 Maple Dr., Ste. C; 50327; Polk; P 30,000; (515) 957-0088; Fax (515) 957-0089; alex.lynch@eprd.org; www.eprd.org

Pleasant Hill • *see Altoona*

Primghar • *O'Brien County Eco. Dev. Corp.* • Kiana L. Johnson; Exec. Dir.; 160 S. Hayes; P.O. Box 616; 51245; O'Brien; P 14,100; (712) 957-1313; (712) 261-1313; Fax (712) 957-3015; ocedc@tcaexpress.net; www.obriencounty.com

Remsen • *Remsen Dev. Corp.* • Angela Waldschmitt; Eco. Dev. Coord.; 008 W. 2nd St.; P.O. Box 510; 51050; Plymouth; P 1,663; (712) 540-0277; (712) 786-2136; angelawaldschmitt@gmail.com; www.remseniowa.org

Rock Valley • *Rock Valley Dev. Corp.* • James Vander Velde; Dev. Dir.; 1507 Main St.; 51247; Sioux; P 4,700; (712) 476-2576; Fax (712) 476-2576; jvv@cityofrockvalley.com; www.cityofrockvalley.com

Rockwell City • *Calhoun County Eco. Dev. Corp.* • Pamela Meeder; Dir.; P.O. Box 47; 50579; Calhoun; P 10,000; (712) 297-5601; Fax (712) 297-5481; ccedc@iowatelecom.net; www.calhoundev.com

Roland • *Roland Area Dev. Corp.* • Lyn Schultz; Pres.; P.O. Box 288; 50236; Story; P 1,284; (515) 388-4861; Fax (515) 388-5595; cityhall@cityofroland.org; www.cityofroland.org

Saint Ansgar • *St. Ansgar Eco. Dev. Corp.* • Ivan Wold; Pres.; P.O. Box 224; 50472; Mitchell; P 1,100; (641) 713-4501; (641) 713-4921; www.stansgar.org

Shenandoah • *Shenandoah Chamber & Ind. Org.* • Gregg Connell; Exec. Dir.; 619 W. Sheridan Ave.; 51601; Page; P 5,500; (712) 246-3455; Fax (712) 246-3456; gconnell@shenandoahiowa.net; www.shenandoahiowa.net

Sigourney • *Sigourney Area Dev. Corp.* • Jim Dickinson; Exec. Dir.; 112 E. Washington St.; 52591; Keokuk; P 2,000; (641) 622-2288; Fax (641) 622-2396; sadc@sigourney.com; www.sigourney.com

Sioux Center • *Sioux Center Eco. Dev.* • Dennis Dokter; Eco. Dev. Dir.; 335 1st Ave. N.W.; 51250; Sioux; P 6,000; (712) 722-0761; Fax (712) 722-0760; ddokter@siouxcenter.org; www.siouxcenter.org

Sioux City • *The Siouxland Chamber/Eco. Dev.* • Christopher McGowan; Pres.; 101 Pierce St.; 51101; Plymouth & Woodbury; P 130,000; (712) 255-7903; Fax (712) 258-7578; mkoster@siouxlandchamber.com; www.siouxlandchamber.com

Sioux City • *Siouxland Eco. Dev. Corp.* • Ken Beekley; Exec. V.P.; 617 Pierce St.; 51102; Woodbury; P 168,000; (712) 279-6430; Fax (712) 224-2510; ken@siouxlandedc.com; www.siouxlandedc.com

Spencer • *Iowa Lakes Corridor Dev. Corp.* • Kathy Evert CEcD; Pres./CEO; 520 2nd Ave E, Ste. 2; 51301; Clay; P 64,000; (712) 264-3474; (800) 765-1428; Fax (712) 580-3472; hpearson@lakescorridor.com; www.lakescorridor.com

Story City • *Story City Dev. Corp.* • Mark Jackson; City Admin.; 504 Broad St.; 50248; Story; P 3,500; (515) 733-2121; Fax (515) 733-2460; mainstreet@storycity.com; www.storycity.net

Strawberry Point • *Strawberry Point Eco. Dev. & C/C* • Carrie Weaver; Dir.; 105 W. Mission; P.O. Box 85; 52076; Clayton; P 1,270; (563) 933-4417; Fax (563) 933-4417; econdev@strawberrypt.com; www.strawberrychamber.com

Stuart • *Midwest Partnership Dev. Corp.* • Sarah Gomez; Exec. Dir.; 615 S. Division; P.O. Box 537; 50250; Adair, Audubon, Greene, Guthrie; P 30,000; (515) 523-1262; Fax (515) 523-1397; sgomez@midwestpartnership.com; www.midwestpartnership.com

Sumner • *Sumner's Future Inc.* • Rick Rath; Pres.; 104 Catalina Dr.; P.O. Box 207; 50674; Bremer; P 2,200; (563) 578-5963; rath@iowatelecom.net; www.sumnerfuture.org

Tama • *Tama County Eco. Dev. Comm.* • Linda Roelofse; Exec. Dir.; 1007 Prospect Dr.; P.O. Box 22; 52339; Tama; P 2,800; (641) 484-3108; info@tamacountyiowa.org; www.tamacountyiowa.org

Tipton • *Cedar County Eco. Dev. Comm.* • Rod Ness; Exec. Dir.; 107 Cedar St.; 52772; Cedar; P 18,500; (563) 886-3761; here@cedarcountyia.org; www.growcedar.org

Urbandale • *City of Urbandale Comm. Dev.* • Paul Dekker; Dir.; 3600 86th St.; 50322; Dallas & Polk; P 39,463; (515) 278-3935; Fax (515) 278-3927; pdekker@urbandale.org; www.urbandale.org

Wall Lake • *SacCounty Eco. & Tourism Dev.* • 108 Boyer St.; P.O. Box 327; 51466; Sac; P 10,400; (712) 664-2940; (712) 664-2216; info@saccountyiowa.com; www.saccountyiowa.com

Wapello • *Wapello Dev. Corp.* • Roger Huddle; Secy.; P.O. Box 226; 52653; Louisa; P 2,050; (319) 523-4221; Fax (319) 523-5603; huddle@louisacomm.net; www.cityofwapello.com

Washington • *Washington Eco. Dev. Group* • Ed Raber; Exec. Dir.; 205 W. Main St.; 52353; Washington; P 22,000; (319) 653-3942; wedg@washingtoniowa.org; www.washingtoniowa.org

Waterloo • *Greater Cedar Valley Alliance* • Steve Dust; CEO; 10 W. Fourth St., Ste. 310; 50701; Black Hawk; P 236,000; (319) 232-1156; Fax (319) 233-4580; info@cedarvalleyalliance.com; www.cedarvalleyalliance.com

Waterloo • *Black Hawk Eco. Dev. Inc.* • Steve Brustkern; Dir.; 3835 W. 9th St.; 50702; Black Hawk; P 131,100; (319) 235-2960; Fax (319) 235-9171; bhed@bhed.org; www.bhed.org

Waukon • *Allamakee County Eco. Dev.* • Mike Kruckenberg; Pres.; 101 W. Main St.; 52172; Allamakee; P 14,000; (563) 568-2624; Fax (563) 568-6990; neiatourism@mchsi.com; www.allamakeecounty.com

Waverly • *Waverly Eco. Dev. Dept.* • W.D. Werger; Eco. Dev. Dir.; 200 1st St. N.E.; P.O. Box 616; 50677; Bremer; P 10,000; (319) 352-9210; Fax (319) 352-5772; wdwerger@ci.waverly.ia.us; www.waverlyia.com

Webster City • *Webster City Area Dev. & C/C* • Carrie Fitzgerald; Exec. Dir.; 628 2nd St.; P.O. Box 310; 50595; Hamilton; P 8,000; (515) 832-2564; Fax (515) 832-5130; info@webstercity-iowa.com; www.visitwebstercityiowa.com

West Des Moines • *West Des Moines Comm. & Eco. Dev.* • Clyde E. Evans AICP; Dir. of Comm. & Eco. Dev.; 4200 Mills Civic Pkwy., Ste. E-200; P.O. Box 65320; 50265; Polk; P 61,000; (515) 273-0770; Fax (515) 273-0603; clyde.evans@wdm.iowa.gov; www.wdm.iowa.gov

EDC

West Union • *Fayette County Eco. Dev. Comm.* • 101 N. Vine St.; 52175; Fayette; P 2,000; (563) 422-5073; Fax (563) 422-6322; fced@alpinecom.net; www.fayettecountyia.com

Wilton • *Wilton Dev. Corp.* • Becky Allgood; 210 W. 4th St.; P.O. Box 443; 52778; Muscatine; P 3,000; (563) 732-5002; (877) 477-5002; Fax (563) 732-5002; wiltondev@netwtc.net; www.wiltoniowa.org

Woodbine • *Woodbine Betterment Dev. Corp.* • Noel Sherer; Pres.; 501 Normal St.; 51579; Harrison; P 1,460; (712) 647-2010; (712) 647-2550; woodbinemainstreet@windstream.net; www.woodbineia.org

Kansas

Federal

U.S. SBA, Wichita Dist. Ofc. • Wayne Bell; Dist. Dir.; 220 W. Douglas Ave., Ste. 4505; 67202; Sedgwick; P 2,885,905; (316) 269-6566; wayne.bell@sba.gov; www.sba.gov/ks

State

Kansas Dept. of Commerce • Barbara Hake; Bus. Recruitment Mgr.; 1000 S.W. Jackson St., Ste. 100; Topeka; 66612; Shawnee; P 2,885,905; (913) 307-7379; bhake@kansascommerce.com; www.kansascommerce.com

Communities

Abilene • *Abilene Eco. Dev. Cncl.* • Daniel J. Shea MRCP; Comm. Dev. Dir.; 419 N. Broadway; P.O. Box 519; 67410; Dickinson; P 7,000; (785) 263-2550; Fax (785) 263-2552; development@abilenecityhall.com; www.abilenecityhall.com

Atchison • *City of Atchison Eco. Dev.* • Becky Berger; Asst. City Mgr.; 515 Kansas Ave.; 66002; Atchison; P 20,000; (913) 367-5506; beckyb@cityofatchison.com; www.cityofatchison.com

Burlington • *Coffey County Eco. Dev.* • Jon Hotaling; Dir.; 110 S. 6th St.; 66839; Coffey; P 8,600; (620) 364-8780; Fax (620) 364-2045; jhotaling@coffeycountyks.org; www.coffeycountyks.org

Clay Center • *Clay County Eco. Dev. Group* • Lori Huber; Exec. Dir.; 517 Court; 67432; Clay; P 8,600; (785) 632-5974; clayks@eaglecom.net; www.claycountykansas.org

Colby • *Thomas County Eco. Dev. Alliance* • Rick Patrick; Exec. Dir.; 350 S. Range, Ste. 12; 67701; Thomas; P 7,200; (785) 460-4511; Fax (785) 460-4509; ecodev@thomascounty.com; www.thomascounty.com

Columbus • *Columbus Eco. Dev. Corp.* • Trish Tarroll; 224 S. Kansas; 66725; Cherokee; P 3,500; (620) 429-3132; (620) 429-1492; Fax (620) 429-1704; coltelco@columbus-ks.com; www.columbus-ks.com

Concordia • *CloudCorp* • Kirk G. Lowell; Exec. Dir.; 606 Washington St.; 66901; Cloud; P 5,714; (785) 243-2010; Fax (785) 243-2014; kirk.lowell@cloudcorp.net

Council Grove • *Greater Morris County Dev. Corp.* • C. Kay Hutchinson; Exec. Dir.; P.O. Box 276; 66846; Morris; P 6,000; (620) 767-7355; Fax (785) 466-2270; kayhutch@tctelco.net; www.morriscountydevelopment.com

Derby • *City of Derby* • Marcia Hartman; Dev. Mgr.; 611 Mulberry Rd., Ste. 300; 67037; Sedgwick; P 24,000; (316) 788-3081; Fax (316) 788-6067; marciahartman@derbyweb.com; www.derbyweb.com

Dodge City • *Dodge City/Ford County Dev. Corp.* • Joann Knight; Exec. Dir.; 311 W. Spruce St.; P.O. Box 818; 67801; Ford; P 30,000; (620) 227-9501; (800) 381-3690; Fax (620) 338-8734; jknight@dodgedev.org; www.dodgedev.org

El Dorado • *Butler County Eco. Dev.* • David A. Alfaro; Dir.; 121 S. Gordy; 67042; Butler; P 66,800; (316) 322-4325; Fax (316) 322-4264; economicdevelopment@bucoks.com; www.bucoks.com

Emporia • *Reg. Dev. Assn. of East Central Kansas* • Kent Heermann CEcD; Pres.; 719 Commercial St.; 66801; Lyon; P 30,000; (620) 342-1600; Fax (620) 342-3223; kheermann@emporiarda.org; www.emporiarda.org

Garden City • *Finney County Eco. Dev. Corp.* • Lona DuVall; Pres.; 114 W. Pine St.; 67846; Finney; P 40,000; (620) 271-0388; Fax (620) 271-0588; fcedc@ficoedc.com; www.ficoedc.com

Goodland • *Sherman County Eco. Dev.* • Michael Solomon; Dir.; 204 W. 11th; P.O. Box 59; 67735; Sherman; P 5,000; (785) 890-3743; Fax (785) 890-4532; edev@goodlandks.us; www.shermancountyed.org

Hays • *Ellis County Coalition for Eco. Dev.* • Aaron White; Exec. Dir.; 2700 Vine St.; 67601; Ellis; P 29,100; (785) 628-3102; ernee@haysamerica.net; www.ellisco.org

Hiawatha • *Hiawatha Found. for Eco. Dev.* • Don Nigus; Dir.; 105 S. 6th St.; 66434; Brown; P 3,500; (785) 740-4333; Fax (785) 742-7951; don.nigus@gmail.com

Hill City • *NW Kansas Planning & Dev. Comm.* • Randall Hrabe; Exec. Dir.; 319 N. Pomeroy; P.O. Box 248; 67642; Graham; P 106,625; (785) 421-2151; Fax (785) 421-3496; nwkpdc@ruraltel.net

Hillsboro • *Hillsboro Dev. Corp.* • Clint Seibel; Exec. Dir.; 116 E. Grand; 67063; Marion; P 3,000; (620) 947-3458; Fax (620) 947-2585; cseibel@cityofhillsboro.net; www.cityofhillsboro.net

Horton • *Horton Ind. Dev. Corp.* • 205 E. 8th St.; 66439; Brown; P 1,900; (785) 486-2681; cityofhorton@hortonkansas.net; www.hortonkansas.net

Hugoton • *Stevens County Eco. Dev. Bd.* • Neal R. Gillespie; Dir.; 630 S. Main; 67951; Stevens; P 5,700; (620) 544-4440; ecodevo@pld.com; stevenscountyks.com

Hutchinson • *Reno County Eco. Dev.* • Abby Stockebrand; Eco. Dev. Coord.; 117 N. Walnut St.; P.O. Box 519; 67504; Reno; P 64,000; (620) 662-3391; Fax (620) 662-2168; abbys@hutchchamber.com; www.hutchchamber.com

Independence • *Montgomery County Action Cncl.* • Aaron Heckman; Exec. Dir.; 115 S. 6th St.; P.O. Box 588; 67301; Montgomery; P 34,000; (620) 331-3830; Fax (620) 331-3834; pbenson@actioncouncil.com; www.actioncouncil.com

Jewell • *Jewell County Comm. Dev. Assn.* • Martha Matthews; Coord.; 606 Broadway St.; 66949; Jewell; P 3,000; (785) 428-3634; jewell7jccda@aol.com; www.jewellcountyks.com

Junction City • *Junction City/Geary County EDC* • Dennis Beson; Dir.; 222 W. 6th St.; P.O. Box 26; 66441; Geary; P 22,000; (785) 762-2632; dennis.beson@jcacc.org; www.jcgced.com

Kansas City • *Eco. Dev. Div.* • George Brajkovic; Dir.; 701 N. 7th St., Ste. 421; 66101; Wyandotte; P 160,000; (913) 573-5730; Fax (913) 573-5745; gbrajkovic@wycokck.org; www.wycokck.org

Kingman • *Kingman County Eco. Dev.* • Tom Winters; Exec. Dir.; 324 N. Main; 67068; Kingman; P 7,800; (620) 532-3694; kcedc@terraworld.net; www.kingmanks.com

Kinsley • *Edwards County Eco. Dev. Corp.* • Linette Miller; Exec. Dir.; 108 E. 6th St.; P.O. Box 161; 67547; Edwards; P 2,900; (620) 659-2711; (877) 464-3929; Fax (620) 659-2711; ecedc@sbcglobal.net; www.edwardscounty.org

Larned • *Pawnee County Eco. Dev. Comm.* • Courtland Holman; Exec. Dir.; 502 Broadway; 67550; Pawnee; P 7,600; (620) 285-6916; (800) 747-6919; Fax (620) 285-6917; larnedcofc@gbta.net; www.larnedks.org

Leavenworth • *Leavenworth County Dev. Corp.* • Steve Jack; Exec. Dir.; 1294 Eisenhower Rd.; 66048; Leavenworth; P 79,000; (913) 727-6111; Fax (913) 727-5515; sjack@lvcountyed.org; www.lvcountyed.org

Lenexa • *Lenexa Eco. Dev. Cncl.* • Blake Schreck; Pres.; 11180 Lackman Rd.; 66219; Johnson; P 50,000; (913) 888-1414; Fax (913) 888-3770; staff@lenexa.org; www.lenexa.org

Liberal • *Liberal/Seward County Eco. Dev.* • Jeff Parsons; Dir.; P.O. Box 2199; 67905; Seward; P 23,000; (620) 626-2255; Fax (620) 626-0589; chooseliberal@gmail.com; www.chooseliberal.com

Lincoln • *Lincoln County Eco. Dev. Found.* • Kelly Larson; Exec. Dir.; 216 E. Lincoln Ave.; 67455; Lincoln; P 3,200; (785) 524-8954; Fax (785) 524-5206; lcedf@lincolncoks.org; www.lincolncoks.com

McPherson • *McPherson Ind. Dev. Co.* • Bradley Eilts; Exec. Dir.; 401 W. Kansas Ave.; P.O. Box 768; 67460; McPherson; P 14,000; (620) 245-2521; Fax (620) 245-2529; midc@mcpbpu.com; www.mcphersonindustry.com

Mound City • *Linn County Eco. Dev.* • Dennis Arnold; Dir.; 306 Main St.; P.O. Box 350; 66056; Linn; P 9,700; (913) 795-2274; Fax (913) 795-2016; darnold@linncountyks.com; www.linncountyksed.com

Newton • *Harvey County Eco. Dev.* • Beth Shelton; Exec. Dir.; 500 N. Main St., Ste. 109; 67114; Harvey; P 35,100; (316) 283-6033; (800) 648-7759; Fax (316) 283-8732; charity@harveycoedc.org; www.harveycoedc.org

Norton • *Norton City/County Eco. Dev.* • Scott Sproul; Exec. Dir.; 205 S. State St.; 67654; Norton; P 5,560; (785) 874-4816; Fax (785) 874-4817; nortoneda@ruraltel.net; www.discovernorton.com

Olathe • *Olathe Chamber EDC* • Tim McKee; CEO; 18001 W. 106th St., Ste. 160; 66061; Johnson; P 130,000; (913) 764-1050; Fax (913) 782-4636; edc@olathe.org; www.olathe.org

Osborne • *Osborne Eco. Dev. Ofc.* • Kenny Ubelaker; Dir.; 130 N. First St.; 67473; Osborne; P 1,500; (785) 346-2670; (866) 346-2670; Fax (785) 346-2522; osborneed@ruraltel.net; www.discoverosborne.com

Ottawa • *Ottawa/Franklin County Eco. Dev.* • Blaine Finch; Pres.; 109 E. 2nd; P.O. Box 580; 66067; Franklin; P 28,000; (785) 242-1000; Fax (785) 242-4792; chambertw@ottawakansas.org; www.ottawakansas.org

Overland Park • *Overland Park Eco. Dev. Cncl.* • Beth Johnson CEcD; Sr. V.P.; 9001 W. 110th St., Ste. 150; 66210; Johnson; P 175,000; (913) 491-7605; (913) 491-3600; Fax (913) 491-0393; mkelley@opchamber.org; www.opchamber.org

Pittsburg • *City of Pittsburg Eco. Dev. Corp.* • Blake Benson; Dir.; 201 W. 4th St.; P.O. Box 688; 66762; Crawford; P 20,300; (620) 231-4100; (620) 231-1000; Fax (620) 231-0964; bbenson@pittsburgareachamber.com; www.pittks.org

Russell • *Russell County EDC* • Janae Talbott; Dir.; 331 E. Wichita Ave.; 67665; Russell; P 8,000; (785) 483-4000; (877) 830-3737; Fax (785) 483-2827; rced@russellks.org; www.visitrussellcoks.com

Sabetha • *Sabetha Ind. Dev. Corp.* • Doug Allen; City Admin.; 805 Main St.; P.O. Box 187; 66534; Nemaha; P 2,600; (785) 284-2158; Fax (785) 284-2112; CofS09@rainbowtel.net; www.cityofsabetha.com

Saint Francis • *Cheyenne County Dev. Corp.* • Helen Norman Dobbs; Dir.; 107 W. Washington; P.O. Box 255; 67756; Cheyenne; P 2,500; (785) 332-3508; director@ccdcks.com; www.ccdcks.com

Shawnee • *Shawnee Eco. Dev. Cncl.* • Linda Leeper; Exec. Dir.; 15100 W. 67th St., Ste. 202; 66217; Johnson; P 65,000; (913) 631-6545; Fax (913) 631-9628; lleeper@shawnee-edc.com; www.shawnee-edc.com

Stockton • *Rooks County Eco. Dev. Comm.* • Roger Hrabe; Dir.; 115 N. Walnut; 67669; Rooks; P 5,200; (785) 425-6881; (800) 496-9930; Fax (785) 425-6881; rooksed@ruraltel.net; www.rookscounty.net

Topeka • *City of Topeka Housing & Comm. Dev.* • Bill Fiander; Dir.; 620 S.E. Madison, 1st Flr.; 66607; Shawnee; P 127,700; (785) 368-3711; Fax (785) 368-2546; rfaulkner@topeka.org; www.topeka.org

Tribune • *Greeley County Comm. Dev.* • Christy Hopkins; Dir.; P.O. Box 656; 67879; Greeley; P 1,200; (620) 376-2548; greeleyc@fairpoint.net; www.greeleycounty.org

Ulysses • *Grant County Eco. Dev. Inc.* • Bob Dale; Dir.; 113 S. Main St., Ste. B; 67880; Grant; P 6,900; (620) 356-2171; Fax (620) 424-2437; gced@pld.com

WaKeeney • *Trego County Eco. Dev.* • Jody Zeman; Dir.; 216 N. Main; 67672; Trego; P 2,900; (785) 743-5785; tregocoed@ruraltel.net; www.tregocountyks.com

Wamego • *Pottawatomie County Eco. Dev. Corp.* • Jack Allston; Exec. Dir.; 1004 Lincoln; P.O. Box 288; 66547; Pottawatomie; P 22,000; (785) 456-9776; Fax (785) 456-9775; jessica@ecodevo.com; www.ecodevo.com

Wellington • *Sumner County Eco. Dev.* • Stacy Davis; Exec. Dir.; P.O. Box 279; 67152; Sumner; P 24,000; (620) 326-8779; Fax (620) 326-6544; scedc@co.sumner.ks.us; www.gosumner.com

Wichita • *Greater Wichita Eco. Dev. Coalition* • Tim Chase CEcD FM; Pres.; 350 W. Douglas Ave.; 67202; Sedgwick; P 636,105; (316) 268-1128; tnolan@gwedc.org; www.gwedc.org

Wichita • *South Central KS Eco. Dev. Dist. Inc.* • Bill Bolin; Exec. Dir.; 200 W. Douglas Ave., Ste. 710; 67202; Sedgwick; P 685,000; (316) 262-7035; (800) 326-8353; Fax (316) 262-7062; bill@sckedd.org; www.sckedd.org

Winfield • *Cowley First - Cowley County Eco. Dev. Partnership* • Kerri Falletti; Dir. of Comm. & Eco. Dev.; 22193 Tupper St.; 67156; Cowley; P 37,000; (620) 221-9951; Fax (620) 221-7782; kfalletti@cowleycounty.org; www.cowleyfirst.com

Kentucky

Federal

U.S. SBA, Kentucky Dist. Ofc. • Ralph Ross; Dist. Dir.; 600 M.L. King Jr. Pl., Rm. 188; 40202; Jefferson; P 4,380,415; (502) 582-5971; Fax (502) 582-5819; ralph.ross@sba.gov; www.sba.gov/ky

State

Kentucky Cabinet for Eco. Dev. • Larry Hayes; Secy.; Old Capital Annex; 300 W. Broadway St.; Frankfort; 40601; Franklin; P 4,380,415; (502) 564-7670; (800) 626-2930; Fax (502) 564-1535; econdev@ky.gov; www.thinkkentucky.com

Communities

Ashland • *City of Ashland Eco. Dev. Dept.* • Chris Pullem; Dir.; 1700 Greenup Ave.; 41101; Boyd; P 22,000; (606) 327-2005; Fax (606) 325-8412; cpullem@ashlandky.org; www.ashlandky.gov

Bowling Green • *South CentralKentucky* • Ron Bunch CEcD; Pres./CEO; 710 College St.; 42101; Warren; P 10,000; (866) 330-2422; Fax (270) 432-7199; info@southcentralky.com; www.southcentralky.com

Calhoun • *see Henderson - Northwest Kentucky Forward*

Carrollton • *Carroll County Comm. Dev. Corp.* • Joan Moore; Exec. Dir.; 511 Highland Ave.; P.O. Box 334; 41008; Carroll; P 10,634; (502) 732-7035; Fax (502) 732-7028; development@carrollcountyky.com; www.carrollcountyky.com

Central City • *Muhlenberg Alliance for Progress* • Kenneth Robinson; Pres./CEO; 50 Career Way; 42330; Muhlenberg; P 32,000; (270) 338-4102; Fax (270) 338-4106; ken@mafp.us; www.mafp.us

Corbin • *Corbin Eco. Dev. Agency* • Bruce Carpenter; Exec. Dir.; 101 N. Depot St.; 40701; Whitley; P 8,000; (606) 528-6390; Fax (606) 523-6538; becarpenter@corbinky.org; www.corbinky.org

Danville • *Danville-Boyle County Eco. Dev. Partnership* • Jody Lassiter; Pres./CEO; 105 E. Walnut St.; 40422; Boyle; P 30,000; (859) 236-2361; Fax (859) 236-2361; info@betterindanville.com; www.betterindanville.com

Florence • *Northern KY Area Dev. Dist.* • Lisa Cooper; Exec. Dir.; 22 Spiral Dr.; 41042; Boone; P 370,000; (859) 283-1885; Fax (859) 283-8178; info@nkadd.org; www.nkadd.org

Fort Mitchell • *Northern KY Tri-ED* • Dan Tobergte; Pres./CEO; 300 Buttermilk Pike, Ste. 332; P.O. Box 17246; 41017; Carroll; P 300,000; (859) 344-0040; (888) 874-3365; Fax (859) 344-8130; mlh@northernkentuckyusa.com; www.northernkentuckyusa.com

Franklin • *Franklin/Simpson Ind. Auth.* • Dennis Griffin; Dir.; 109 S. Main St.; P.O. Box 876; 42135; Simpson; P 18,000; (270) 586-4477; Fax (270) 586-3685; info@f-sindustry.com; www.f-sindustry.com

Fulton • *Fulton County Eco. Dev. Partnership* • Eddie Crittendon; Exec. Dir.; P.O. Box 1413; 42041; Fulton; P 7,500; (270) 472-2125; Fax (270) 472-1944; fultoneconomic@bellsouth.net; www.westkyeconomic.com

Greensburg • *Green County Ind. Found.* • Ivy Stanley; Comm. Dev. Coord.; 110 W. Court St.; 42743; Green; P 11,200; (270) 932-4298; Fax (270) 932-7778; i.stanley@greensburgonline.com; www.greensburgonline.com

Harrodsburg • *Harrodsburg-Mercer County Ind. Dev. Auth.* • Dick Webb; Exec. Dir.; 488 Price Ave., Ste. 3; P.O. Box 283; 40330; Mercer; P 22,000; (859) 734-0063; Fax (859) 734-0587; hmcida@mercerky.com; www.hmcida.com

Hartford • *Ohio County Ind. Found.* • Hayward Spinks; Pres.; P.O. Box 3; 42347; Ohio; P 23,000; (270) 298-3551; Fax (270) 298-3331; ocif@ohiocounty.com; www.ohiocountyindustrialfoundation.com

Hazard • *Kentucky River Area Dev. Dist.* • Mike Miller; Exec. Dir.; 941 N. Main; 41701; Perry; P 122,000; (606) 436-3158; Fax (606) 436-2144; gladys@kradd.org; www.kradd.org

Henderson • *Northwest Kentucky Forward* • Kevin Sheilley; Pres./CEO; P.O. Box 674; 42419; Henderson; P 46,000; (270) 826-7505; Fax (270) 827-2969; kevin@northwestky.com; www.northwestky.com

Henderson • *Kyndle* • Tony Iriti; CEO; 136 2nd St., Ste. 500; 42420; Henderson; P 46,400; (270) 826-7505; Fax (270) 826-4471; info@kyndle.us; www.kyndle.us

Hopkinsville • *Pennyrile Area Dev. Dist.* • Jason Vincent; Exec. Dir.; 300 Hammond Dr.; 42240; Christian; P 206,000; (270) 886-9484; (800) 928-7233; Fax (270) 886-3211; kim.meredith@ky.gov; www.peadd.org

Hopkinsville • *Hopkinsville-Christian County Eco. Dev. Cncl.* • Lee Conrad; Dir.; 2800 Fort Campbell Blvd.; 42240; Christian; P 74,000; (270) 885-1499; Fax (270) 886-2059; info@hopkinsvilleindustry.com; www.hopkinsvilleindustry.com

Irvine • *Estill County Dev. Alliance* • Joe Crawford; Exec. Dir.; 177 Broadway; P.O. Box 421; 40336; Estill; P 15,000; (606) 723-2450; info@estillcountyky.net; www.estillcountyky.net

Kevil • *Ballard County Eco. & Ind. Dev.* • Terry Simmons; Pres./CEO; 101 Liberty Dr., Ste. 4; 42053; McCracken; P 8,300; (270) 744-3232; Fax (270) 744-3308; tls@sei-us.net

Lebanon • *Marion County Eco. Dev.* • Tom Lund; Exec. Dir.; 223 N. Spaulding Ave., Ste. 300; 40033; Marion; P 19,820; (270) 692-6002; (877) 692-6002; Fax (270) 692-0510; tlund@marioncountyky.com; www.marioncountyky.com

Lexington • *Lexington-Fayette Urban County Govt.* • Kevin Atkins; Chief Dev. Ofc.; Mayor's Ofc. of Eco. Dev.; 200 E. Main St.; 40507; Fayette; P 314,500; (859) 258-3100; Fax (859) 258-3194; katkins@lexingtonky.gov; www.lexingtonky.gov

Lexington • *Bluegrass Area Dev. Dist.* • David Duttlinger; Exec. Dir.; 699 Perimeter Dr.; 40517; Fayette; P 600,000; (859) 269-8021; Fax (859) 269-7917; cclark@bgadd.org; www.bgadd.org

London • *Cumberland Valley Area Dev. Dist.* • Mike Patrick; Exec. Dir.; P.O. Box 1740; 40743; Laurel; P 240,000; (606) 864-7391; Fax (606) 878-7361; cvadd@cvadd.org; www.cvadd.org

London • *Laurel County Ind. Dev. Auth.* • Paula Thompson; Exec. Dir.; 4598 Old Whitley Rd.; 40744; Laurel; P 58,800; (606) 864-8115; Fax (606) 878-7107; llcida@windstream.net; www.llcida.com

Louisville • *Eco. Dev. Dept. of Metro Louisville* • Ted Smith; Dir.; Metro Dev. Center; 444 S. 5th St., Ste. 600; 40202; Jefferson; P 1,240,000; (502) 574-4140; Fax (502) 574-4143; ted.smith@louisvilleky.gov; www.louisvilleky.gov

Louisville • *Jefferson Riverport Intl.* • Larry McFall; Pres.; 6900 Riverport Dr.; P.O. Box 58010; 40268; Jefferson; P 741,000; (502) 935-6024; Fax (502) 935-6050; Larry.McFall@jeffersonriverport.com; www.jeffersonriverport.com

Madisonville • *Madisonville/Hopkins County Eco. Dev. Corp.* • Ray Hagerman; Pres.; 755 Industrial Rd.; 42431; Hopkins; P 47,000; (270) 821-1939; Fax (270) 821-1945; rpadgett@KentuckyEDC.com; www.kentuckyedc.com

Mayfield • *Graves Growth Alliance* • Ryan Drane; Pres.; 201 E. College St.; 42066; Graves; P 37,500; (270) 247-0626; Fax (270) 247-6781; ryan@gravescountyed.com; www.gravescountyed.com

Maysville • *Buffalo Trace Area Dev. Dist.* • Amy Kennedy; Exec. Dir.; 201 Govt. St., Ste. 300; P.O. Box 460; 41056; Mason; P 55,229; (606) 564-6894; (800) 998-4347; Fax (606) 564-0955; cpadgett@btadd.com; www.btadd.com

Middlesboro • *Bell County Eco. Dev. Found.* • Ed Harris; Exec. Dir.; N. 20th St.; P.O. Box 788; 40965; Bell; P 30,000; (606) 248-1075; Fax (606) 248-8851; info@bcedf.com; www.bcedf.com

Morganfield • *Union County First* • Garrick Thompson; Comm. Dev. Dir.; 100 W. Main St.; P.O. Box 374; 42437; Union; P 15,000; (270) 389-9600; lindsay.jenkins@unioncountyky.org; www.ucfirst.org

Mount Sterling • *Mt. Sterling-Montgomery County Ind. Auth.* • Sandy Romenesko; Exec. Dir.; 126 W. Main St.; 40353; Montgomery; P 26,902; (859) 498-5400; Fax (859) 498-3947; sandy@mtsterlingchamber.com; www.mtsterlingchamber.com

Owensboro • *Green River Area Dev. Dist.* • Mr. Jiten Shah; Exec. Dir.; 300 Gradd Way; 42301; Daviess; P 200,000; (270) 926-4433; (800) 648-6056; Fax (270) 684-0714; carlsims@gradd.com; www.gradd.com

Owensboro • *Greater Owensboro Eco. Dev. Corp.* • Madison Silvert; Pres./CEO; 200 E. 3rd St.; 42303; Daviess; P 100,000; (270) 926-4339; mlanham@owensboro.com; edc.owensboro.com

Paducah • *Greater Paducah Eco. Dev. Cncl.* • Scott Darnell; Pres./CEO; 300 S. 3rd St.; P.O. Box 1155; 42002; McCracken; P 66,000; (270) 575-6633; Fax (270) 575-6648; info@epaducah.com; www.epaducah.com

Prestonsburg • *Big Sandy Area Dev. Dist.* • Sandy Runyon; Exec. Dir.; 110 Resource Ct.; 41653; Floyd; P 161,000; (606) 886-2374; Fax (606) 886-3382; terry.trimble@bigsandy.org; www.bigsandy.org

Richmond • *Richmond Ind. Dev. Corp.* • Dave Stipes; Exec. Dir.; 239 W. Main St.; 40476; Madison; P 35,000; (859) 623-1000; Fax (859) 623-7618; dstipes@richmond.ky.us; www.richmondkyindustrial.com

Shelbyville • *Shelby County Ind. & Dev. Found.* • Libby Adams; Exec. Dir.; 316 Main St.; P.O. Box 335; 40066; Shelby; P 43,000; (502) 633-5068; Fax (502) 633-7501; libby@scidf.com; www.scidf.com

Somerset • *Center for Rural Dev.* • Lonnie Lawson; Pres./CEO; 2292 S. Hwy. 27, Ste. 300; 42501; Pulaski; P 500,000; (606) 677-6000; Fax (606) 677-6010; lglover@centertech.com; www.centertech.com

Versailles • *Woodford County Eco. Dev. Auth.* • Brad McLean; Chrmn.; 103 S. Main St., Ste. 204; 40383; Woodford; P 24,000; (859) 873-1845; Fax (859) 873-6006; thmclean500@yahoo.com; www.woodfordcountyinfo.com

Williamsburg • *see Corbin*

Winchester • *Winchester-Clark County Ind. Dev. Auth.* • Todd Denham; Dir. of Eco. Dev.; 2 S. Maple St.; 40391; Clark; P 36,000; (859) 744-5627; Fax (859) 744-9229; todd@winchesterindustry.com; www.winchesterindustry.com

Louisiana

Federal

***U.S. SBA, Louisiana Dist. Ofc.* •** Michael Ricks; Dist. Dir.; 365 Canal St., Ste. 2820; 70130; Orleans; P 4,601,893; (504) 589-6685; michael.ricks@sba.gov; www.sba.gov/la

State

***Louisiana Dept. of Eco. Dev.* •** Stephen Moret; Secy. of Eco. Dev.; 1051 N. 3rd St.; Baton Rouge; 70802; East Baton Rouge; P 4,601,893; (225) 342-3000; (800) 450-8115; Fax (225) 342-9095; jenny.waites@la.gov; www.opportunitylouisiana.com

Communities

Alexandria • *Kisatchie-Delta Reg. Planning & Dev. Dist.* • Heather Smoak Urena; Exec. Dir.; 3516 Parliament Ct.; 71303; Rapides; P 312,026; (318) 487-5454; Fax (318) 487-5451; kdbiz@kricket.net; www.kdelta.org

Bastrop • *Morehouse Eco. Dev. Corp.* • Kay King; CEO; Capital One Bank Bldg.; 101 Franklin St., Ste. A; 71220; Morehouse; P 30,000; (318) 283-4000; Fax (318) 283-0651; medc@morehouseedc.org; www.morehouseedc.org

Baton Rouge • *Capital Region Planning Comm.* • Huey P. Dugas; Exec. Dir.; 333 N. 19th St.; P.O. Box 3355; 70821; East Baton Rouge; (225) 383-5203; Fax (225) 383-3804; hdugas@brgov.com; www.crpc-la.org

Baton Rouge • *Cncl. for a Better Louisiana* • Gregory N. Rattler Sr.; Chrmn.; P.O. Box 4308; 70821; East Baton Rouge; (225) 344-2225; Fax (225) 338-9470; info@cabl.org; www.cabl.org

Bogalusa • *Washington Eco. Dev. Found.* • Ryan Seal; Exec. Dir.; 526 Georgia Ave.; P.O. Box 668; 70429; Washington; P 47,200; (985) 735-7565; Fax (985) 730-2500; rseal@wedf.com; i12alliance.com

Hammond • *Tangipahoa Eco. Dev. Found.* • Stacey Neal; Exec. Dir.; 1514 Martens Dr., Ste. 130; 70401; Tangipahoa; P 128,800; (985) 549-3170; Fax (985) 549-2127; info@tangipahoa.org; www.tedf.org

Lafayette • *Lafayette Eco. Dev. Auth.* • Gregg Gothreaux; Pres./CEO; 211 E. Devalcourt St.; 70506; Lafayette; P 230,847; (337) 593-1400; Fax (337) 234-3009; information@lafayette.org; www.lafayette.org

Lake Charles • *Southwest Louisiana Eco. Dev. Alliance* • George Swift; Pres./CEO; 4310 Ryan St., 3rd Flr.; P.O. Box 3110; 70602; Calcasieu; P 287,001; (337) 433-3632; Fax (337) 436-3727; gswift@allianceswla.org; www.allianceswla.org

Livingston • *Livingston Eco. Dev. Cncl. Inc.* • David Bennett; CEO; 20355 Government Blvd., Ste. E; P.O. Box 809; 70754; Livingston; P 128,000; (225) 686-3982; Fax (225) 686-3983; kaylynn@ledc.net; www.ledc.net

Mandeville • *St. Tammany Eco. Dev. Found.* • Brenda Bertus; CEO; 21489 Koop Dr., Ste. 7; 70471; St. Tammany; P 248,604; (985) 809-7874; stedfinfo@stedf.org; www.stedf.org

Mansfield • *DeSoto Parish Ind. Dist.* • Kari Boudreaux; Admin. Asst.; 115 N. Washington Ave.; 71052; DeSoto; P 27,100; (318) 872-1310; Fax (318) 871-1875; chamber75@bellsouth.net; www.desotoparishchamber.net

Minden • *Minden EDC* • James Graham; Eco. Dev. Dir.; 520 Broadway; P.O. Box 580; 71055; Webster; P 13,100; (318) 377-2144; Fax (318) 371-4200; economicdevelopment@mindenusa.com; www.developminden.com

Monroe • *North Louisiana Eco. Partnership* • 1900 N. 18th St., Ste. 440; 71201; Ouachita; P 740,000; (318) 387-0787; Fax (318) 387-8529; lpierre@nlep.org; www.nlep.org

Monroe • *North Delta Reg. Planning & Dev. Dist.* • David Creed; Exec. Dir.; 1913 Stubbs Ave.; 71201; Ouachita; (318) 387-2572; Fax (318) 387-9054; david@northdelta.org; www.northdelta.org

New Iberia • *Iberia Ind. Dev. Found.* • Mike Tarantino; Exec. Dir.; 101 Burke St.; 70560; Iberia; P 74,100; (337) 367-0834; (888) 879-9669; Fax (337) 367-7421; info@iberiabiz.org; www.iberiabiz.org

New Orleans • *Reg. Planning Comm.* • Walter Brooks; Exec. Dir.; 10 Veterans Memorial Blvd.; 70124; Orleans; (504) 483-8500; Fax (504) 483-8526; rpc@norpc.org; www.norpc.org

New Orleans • *Greater New Orleans Inc.* • Michael Hecht; Pres./CEO; 365 Canal St., Ste. 2300; 70130; Orleans; P 1,151,000; (504) 527-6900; Fax (504) 527-6970; csmith@gnoinc.org; www.gnoinc.org

Oakdale • *Ind. Dev. Bd. of Elizabeth-Oakdale Inc.* • Gene Paul; Mayor; P.O. Box 728; 71463; Allen; P 8,137; (318) 335-1111; Fax (318) 335-3638; ericasmith2166@att.net

Opelousas • *St. Landry Parish Eco. Ind. Dev. Dist.* • Bill Rodier; Exec. Dir.; 5367 I-49 S. Svc. Rd.; 70570; St. Landry; P 84,000; (337) 948-1391; Fax (337) 407-2283; opportunitystlandry@stlandryed.com; www.sleidd.com

Ruston • *Ruston-Lincoln Ind. Dev. Corp.* • Scott C. Terry; Exec. Dir.; 2111 N. Trenton St.; P.O. Box 1383; 71272; Lincoln; P 43,000; (318) 255-2031; (800) 392-9032; Fax (318) 255-3481; sterry@rustonlincoln.org; www.rustonlincoln.org

Shreveport • *North Louisiana Eco. Partnership* • 415 Texas St., Ste. 320; 71101; Caddo; P 740,000; (318) 677-2536; (318) 387-0787; Fax (318) 677-2548; tmiles@nlep.org; www.nlep.org

Shreveport • *The Coord. & Dev. Corp.* • Knox Ross; Pres./CEO; 5210 Hollywood Ave.; P.O. Box 37005; 71133; Caddo; P 378,000; (318) 632-2022; Fax (318) 632-2099; info@cdconline.org; www.cdconline.org

Springhill • *North Webster Parish Ind. Dist.* • Mitch Stubblefield; Mgr.; P.O. Box 176; 71075; Webster; P 12,000; (318) 539-5058; Fax (318) 994-2753; websterboard@centurytel.net; www.nwpid.com

Tallulah • *Madison Eco. Dev. Found.* • Thomas Joe Williams; Pres.; P.O. Box 562; 71284; Madison; P 12,100; (318) 574-2716; Fax (318) 574-0506; medf_tallulah@bellsouth.net

Vidalia • *Vidalia Eco. Dev.* • Hyram Copeland; Mayor; P.O. Box 2010; 71373; Concordia; P 6,500; (318) 336-5206; Fax (318) 336-6253; cityofvidalia@bellsouth.net; www.seevidalia.com

Maine

Federal

***U.S. SBA, Maine Dist. Ofc.* •** Marilyn Geroux; Dist. Dir.; 68 Sewall St., Rm. 512; 04330; Kennebec; P 1,329,192; (207) 622-8382; Fax (207) 622-8277; marilyn.geroux@sba.gov; www.sba.gov/me

State

***Maine Dept. of Eco. & Comm. Dev.* •** George C. Gervais; Comm.; 111 Sewall St.; 59 State House Station; Augusta; 04333; Kennebec; P 1,329,192; (207) 624-9800; Fax (207) 287-2861; biz.growth@maine.gov; www.maine.gov/decd

Communities

Auburn • *Auburn Eco. Dev.* • Michael Chammings; Dir.; 60 Court St.; 04210; Androscoggin; P 23,000; (207) 333-6601; Fax (207) 333-6621; mchammings@auburnmaine.gov; www.auburnmaine.gov

Augusta • *Econ. & Comm. Dev. of Augusta* • Matt Nazar; Dir.; 16 Cony St.; City Center Plz.; 04330; Kennebec; P 19,000; (207) 626-2336; Fax (207) 626-2520; matt.nazar@augustamaine.gov; www.augustamaine.gov

Bangor • *Eastern Maine Dev. Corp.* • Michael Aube; Pres./CEO; 40 Harlow St.; 04401; Penobscot; P 257,400; (207) 942-6389; (800) 339-6389; Fax (207) 942-3548; info@emdc.org; www.emdc.org

Belfast • *City of Belfast* • Joseph Slocum; City Mgr.; 131 Church St.; City Hall; 04915; Waldo; P 6,500; (207) 338-3370; Fax (207) 338-2419; cityclerk@cityofbelfast.org; www.cityofbelfast.org

Berwick • *Town of Berwick* • Susie Scott; Planning Coord.; 11 Sullivan St.; P.O. Box 696; 03901; York; P 7,000; (207) 698-1101; Fax (207) 698-5181; townmanager@berwickmaine.org; www.berwickmaine.org

Brewer • *Ofc. of Eco. Dev.* • Darcy Main-Boyington; Dir. of Eco. Dev.; 80 N. Main St.; 04412; Penobscot; P 9,100; (207) 989-7500; Fax (207) 989-8425; dmain-boyington@brewerme.org; www.brewerme.org

Farmington • *Greater Franklin Dev. Corp.* • Alison Hagerstrom; Exec. Dir.; 165 Front St.; P.O. Box 107; 04938; Franklin; P 31,000; (207) 778-5887; Fax (207) 778-3442; mspencer@greaterfranklin.com; www.greaterfranklin.com

Fort Kent • *Ofc. of Planning & Eco. Dev.* • 416 W. Main St.; 04743; Aroostook; P 4,097; (207) 834-3507; Fax (207) 834-3126; fkecondev@fortkent.org; www.fortkent.org

Gardiner • *Gardiner Eco. Dev. Dept.* • Nate Rudy; Dir.; City Hall; 6 Church St.; 04345; Kennebec; P 6,746; (207) 582-6888; Fax (207) 582-6895; econdev@gardinermaine.com; www.gardinermaine.com

Gorham • *Gorham Eco. Dev. Corp.* • Thomas Ellsworth; Pres.; 286 New Portland Rd.; 04038; Cumberland; P 16,381; (207) 854-5077; Fax (207) 856-1300; gedc@gorhammeusa.org; www.gorhammeusa.org

Greenville • *Ofc. of Eco. Dev.-Town of Greenville* • Gary Lamb; Town Mgr.; 7 Minden St.; P.O. Box 1109; 04441; Piscataquis; P 1,800; (207) 695-2421; Fax (207) 695-4611; townmanager@greenvilleme.com; www.greenvilleme.com

Houlton • *Houlton Comm. Dev.* • Douglas Hazlett; Town Mgr.; 21 Water St.; 04730; Aroostook; P 6,400; (207) 532-7113; Fax (207) 532-1304; town.manager@houlton-maine.com; www.houlton-maine.com

Jay • *Town of Jay* • Ruth Cushman; Town Mgr.; 340 Main St.; 04239; Franklin; P 5,000; (207) 897-6785; Fax (207) 897-9420; jmanager@jay-maine.org; www.jay-maine.org

Lewiston • *Lewiston-Auburn Eco. Growth Cncl.* • Scott Benson; Eco. & Bus. Dev. Dir.; 415 Lisbon St., Ste. 400; 04240; Androscoggin; P 110,000; (207) 784-0161; Fax (207) 786-4412; laegc@economicgrowth.org; laegc.org

Limestone • *Loring Dev. Auth. of Maine* • Carl Flora; Pres./CEO; 154 Development Dr., Ste. F; 04750; Aroostook; P 2,400; (207) 328-7005; Fax (207) 328-6811; LDA@Loring.org; www.loring.org

Lubec • *Lubec Eco. & Comm. Dev. Ofc.* • John Sutherland; Town Admin.; 40 School St.; 04652; Washington; P 1,650; (207) 733-2341; Fax (207) 733-4737; lubecadmin@wwsisp.com; www.lubecme.govoffice2.com

Old Town • *Old Town Ind. Dev. Comm.* • Dave Wight; 256 Main St.; 04468; Penobscot; P 8,100; (207) 827-3965; Fax (207) 827-3966; dwhite@old-town.org; www.old-town.org

Portland • *City of Portland, Econ. Dev. Div.* • Gregory Mitchell; Dir.; 389 Congress St., Rm. 308; 04101; Cumberland; P 67,000; (207) 874-8683; Fax (207) 756-8217; edc@portlandmaine.gov; www.portlandmaine.gov

Skowhegan • *Town of Skowhegan-Eco./Comm. Dev.* • Jeff Hewett; Dir.; 225 Water St.; 04976; Somerset; P 9,000; (207) 474-6905; (207) 474-6900; Fax (207) 474-9413; jhewett@skowhegan.org; www.skowhegan.org

Waterville • *Central Maine Growth Cncl.* • Kimberly Lindlof; Interim Exec. Dir.; 50 Elm St.; 04901; Kennebec; P 16,000; (207) 680-7300; gdonegan@centralmaine.org; centralmaine.org

Winslow • *Town of Winslow EDA* • Michael Heavener; Town Mgr.; 114 Benton Ave.; 04901; Kennebec; P 8,000; (207) 872-2776; Fax (207) 872-1999; jbouchard@winslow-me.gov; www.winslow-me.gov

Maryland

Federal

U.S. SBA, Maryland Dist. Ofc. • Stephen D. Umberger; Dist. Dir.; City Crescent Bldg., 6th Flr.; 10 S. Howard St.; 21201; Baltimore City; P 5,884,563; (410) 962-6195; stephen.umberger@sba.gov; www.sba.gov/md

State

Maryland Dept. of Bus. & Eco. Dev. • Robert Walker; Deputy Secy.; 401 E. Pratt St.; Baltimore; 21202; Baltimore City; P 5,884,563; (888) CHOOSE-MD; Fax (410) 333-6609; communications@choosemaryland.org; www.choosemaryland.org

Communities

Annapolis • *Anne Arundel Eco. Dev. Corp.* • Mark Hartzell; Interim Pres./CEO; 2660 Riva Rd., Ste. 200; 21401; Anne Arundel; P 537,600; (410) 222-7410; Fax (410) 222-7415; info@aaedc.org; www.aaedc.org

Baltimore • *City of Baltimore Dev. Corp.* • William H. Cole IV; Pres.; 36 S. Charles St., Ste. 1600; 21201; Baltimore; P 620,900; (410) 837-9305; Fax (410) 837-6363; info@baltimoredevelopment.com; www.baltimoredevelopment.com

Baltimore • *Dept. of Bus. & Eco. Dev.* • Robert Walker; Asst. Secy.; 401 E. Pratt St.; 21202; Baltimore; P 5,700,000; (410) 767-6300; Fax (410) 333-8628; rwalker@choosemaryland.org; www.choosemaryland.org

Cambridge • *Dorchester County Eco. Dev. Ofc.* • Keasha Haythe CEcD; Dir.; 5263 Bucktown Rd.; 21613; Dorchester; P 32,000; (410) 228-0155; Fax (410) 228-9518; khaythe@choosedorchester.org; www.choosedorchester.org

Chestertown • *Kent County Eco. Dev.* • Jamie Williams; Coord.; 400 High St.; 21620; Kent; P 20,200; (410) 810-2168; Fax (410) 778-7482; jwilliams@kentgov.org; www.kentcounty.com

Cumberland • *Allegany County Dept. of Eco. Dev.* • Matthew Diaz CEcD; Dir.; 701 Kelly Rd., Ste. 400; 21502; Allegany; P 75,000; (301) 777-5967; (800) 555-4080; Fax (301) 777-2194; mdiaz@allconet.org; www.alleganyworks.org

Federalsburg • *Federalsburg Eco. Dev. Comm.* • John Phillips; Pres.; 118 N. Main St.; P.O. Box 471; 21632; Caroline; P 2,755; (410) 754-8173; Fax (410) 754-9269; grantmainstreet@hotmail.com; www.federalsburg.org

Frederick • *Frederick County Ofc. of Eco. Dev.* • Helen Propheter; Dir.; 118 North Market St.; 21701; Frederick; P 245,000; (301) 600-1058; (800) 248-2296; Fax (301) 600-2340; info@discoverfrederickmd.com; www.discoverfrederickmd.com

Hagerstown • *Hagerstown-Washington County Eco. Dev. Comm.* • Timothy R. Troxell CEcD; Exec. Dir.; 100 W. Washington St., Rm. 103; 21740; Washington; P 147,400; (240) 313-2280; Fax (240) 313-2281; edcinfo@hagerstownedc.org; www.hagerstownedc.org

Havre De Grace • *Harford County Ofc. of Eco. Dev.* • Karen Holt; Dir.; 2021 Pulaski Hwy., Ste. D; 21078; Harford; P 251,000; (410) 638-3059; (888) I95-SITE; oed@harfordcountymd.gov; www.harfordcountymd.gov

Indian Head • *Indian Head Eco. Dev. Comm.* • Ryan L. Hicks; Town Mgr.; 4195 Indian Head Hwy.; 20640; Charles; P 3,500; (301) 743-5511; Fax (301) 743-9008; info@townofindianhead.org; www.townofindianhead.org

Largo • *Prince George's County Eco. Dev. Corp.* • James Coleman; Pres./CEO; 1801 McCormick Dr., Ste. 350; 20774; Prince George's; P 863,420; (301) 583-4650; Fax (301) 772-8540; www.pgcedc.com

Oakland • *Garrett County Eco. Dev. Dept.* • Alex McCoy; Dir.; 203 S. Fourth St., Ste. 208; 21550; Garrett; P 30,000; (301) 334-1921; Fax (301) 334-7469; economicdevelopment@garrettcounty.org; www.gcedonline.com

Prince Frederick • *Calvert County Dept. of Eco. Dev.* • Linda Vassallo; Dir.; 205 Main St.; 20678; Calvert; P 90,000; (410) 535-4583; 301-855-1880; Fax (410) 535-4585; info@ecalvert.com; www.ecalvert.com

Princess Anne • *Somerset County Eco. Dev. Comm.* • Danny Thompson; Exec. Dir.; 11916 Somerset Ave., Rm. 202; 21853; Somerset; P 26,400; (410) 651-0500; (888) 651-0500; Fax (410) 651-3836; edc@somersetmd.us; www.somersetcountyedc.org

Rockville • *Montgomery County - Dept. of Eco. Dev.* • Steve Silverman; Dir.; 111 Rockville Pike, Ste. 800; 20850; Montgomery; P 971,700; (240) 777-2000; Fax (240) 777-2001; steve.silverman@montgomerycountymd.gov; www.choosemontgomerymd.com

Salisbury • *Salisbury-Wicomico Eco. Dev. Inc.* • David Ryan; Exec. Dir.; One Plaza East Ste. 501; P.O. Box 4700; 21803; Wicomico; P 100,000; (410) 749-1251; Fax (410) 749-1252; info@swed.org; www.swed.org

Takoma Park • *Takoma Park Housing & Comm. Dev.* • Sara Anne Daines; Dir. of Eco. & Comm. Dev.; 7500 Maple Ave.; Community Center, 3rd Flr.; 20912; Montgomery; P 18,000; (301) 891-7119; Fax (301) 270-4568; sarad@takomaparkmd.gov; www.takomaparkmd.gov

Towson • *Baltimore County Dept. of Eco. & Workforce Dev.* • Will Anderson; 400 Washington Ave., Ste. 100; 21204; Baltimore; P 806,000; (410) 887-8000; Fax (410) 887-8017; businesshelp@baltimorecountymd.gov; www.baltimorecountymd.gov

Westminster • *Carroll County Dept. of Eco. Dev.* • John T. "Jack" Lyburn; Dir.; 225 N. Center St., Ste. 101; 21157; Carroll; P 168,000; (410) 386-2070; (410) 876-2450; Fax (410) 876-8471; info@carrollbiz.org; www.carrollbiz.org

Massachusetts

Federal

U.S. SBA, Massachusetts Dist. Ofc. • Robert H. Nelson; Dist. Dir.; 10 Causeway St., Rm. 265; 02222; Essex, Middlesex, Norfolk, Plymouth, Suffolk & Worcester; P 6,646,144; (617) 565-5590; robert.nelson@sba.gov; www.sba.gov/ma

State

Massachusetts Ofc. of Bus. Dev. • Nam Pham; Asst. Secy. of Bus. Dev.; 10 Park Plaza, Ste. 3730; Boston; 02116; Suffolk; P 6,547,629; (617) 973-8600; Fax (617) 973-8554; camille.passatempo@state.ma.us; www.mass.gov/mobd

Communities

Chicopee • *see Springfield*

Easthampton • *Eco. Dev. Comm.* • Jessica Allan AICP; City Planner; 50 Payson Ave.; 01027; Hampshire; P 17,000; (413) 529-1406; (413) 529-1460; Fax (413) 529-1433; allanj@easthampton.org; www.easthampton.org

Fitchburg • *Fitchburg (City of) - Eco. Dev. Div.* • Mary Jo Bohart; Dir.; 166 Boulder Dr.; 01420; Worcester; P 41,000; (978) 829-1896; Fax (978) 345-9553; mbohart@fitchburgma.gov; www.fitchburgma.gov

Fitchburg • *North Central Massachusetts Dev. Corp.* • Roy Nascimento IOM; Pres./CEO; 860 South St.; 01420; Worcester; P 225,000; (978) 353-7607; (978) 353-7600; Fax (978) 353-4896; info@massweb.org; www.ncmedc.com

Holyoke • *Holyoke Ofc. of Planning & Eco. Dev.* • Marcos A. Marrero; Dir.; City Hall Annex, Rm. 406; 20 Korean Veterans Plaza; 01040; Hampden; P 50,000; (413) 322-5575; (413) 322-5655; Fax (413) 322-5576; oped@ci.holyoke.ma.us; www.holyoke.org

Lynn • *Eco. Dev. & Ind. Corp. of Lynn* • James Cowdell; Exec. Dir.; Lynn City Hall, Rm. 307; 3 City Hall Sq.; 01901; Essex; P 90,000; (781) 581-9399; Fax (781) 581-9731; info@ediclynn.org; www.ediclynn.org

Orange • *Orange EDIC* • Wendy Johnson; Admin. Asst.; c/o Town Hall; 6 Prospect St.; 01364; Franklin; P 7,500; (978) 544-1100; Fax (978) 544-1101; commdev@townoforange.org; www.townoforange.org

Plymouth • *Plymouth Reg. Eco. Dev. Foundation Inc.* • Denis Hanks; Exec. Dir.; 134 Court St.; 02360; Plymouth; P 580,000; (508) 830-1620; dhanks@townhall.plymouth.ma.us; www.plymouthbusiness.org

Springfield • *Eco. Dev. Cncl. of Western Mass.* • Rick Sullivan; Pres./CEO; 1441 Main St.; 01103; Hampden; P 640,000; (413) 755-1368; Fax (413) 755-1371; a.burke@westernmassedc.com; www.WesternMassedc.com

Winchendon • *Winchendon Planning & Dev. Ofc.* • James Kreidler; Town Mgr.; 109 Front St.; 01475; Worcester; P 10,000; (978) 297-0085; (978) 297-3308; Fax (978) 297-5411; planning@town.winchendon.ma.us; www.townofwinchendon.com

Michigan

Federal

U.S. SBA, Michigan Dist. Ofc. • Gerald L. Moore; Dist. Dir.; 477 Michigan Ave., Ste. 515; McNamara Bldg.; 48226; Wayne; P 9,883,360; (313) 226-6075; gerald.moore@sba.gov; www.sba.gov/mi

State

Michigan Eco. Developers Assn. • John Avery; Exec. Dir.; P.O. Box 15096; Lansing; 48901; Ingham; P 9,883,360; (517) 241-0011; Fax (517) 241-0089; tschooley@medaweb.org; www.medaweb.org

Communities

Adrian • *Lenawee Eco. Dev. Corp.* • James Gartin; Pres./CEO; 5285 W. U.S. 223, Ste. A; 49221; Lenawee; P 100,000; (517) 265-5141; Fax (517) 263-6065; cjackson@theledc.org; www.onelenawee.com

Alpena • *Target Alpena Eco. Dev. Corp.* • Jim Klarich; Dir.; 235 W. Chisolm St.; 49707; Alpena; P 30,000; (989) 354-2666; Fax (989) 356-3999; info@alpenachamber.com; www.alpenachamber.com

Ann Arbor • *Ann Arbor Spark* • Paul Krutko; Pres./CEO; 201 S. Division St., Ste. 430; 48104; Washtenaw; P 359,000; (734) 761-9317; (888) SPARK-01; Fax (734) 761-9062; info@annarborusa.org; www.annarborusa.org

Bad Axe • *Huron County EDC* • Carl J. Osentoski; Exec. Dir.; 250 E. Huron Ave., Rm. 303; 48413; Huron; P 32,000; (989) 269-6431; (800) 35-THUMB; Fax (989) 269-8209; info@huroncounty.com; www.huroncounty.com

Battle Creek • *Battle Creek Unlimited Inc.* • Karl Dehn; Pres./CEO; 4950 W. Dickman Rd., Ste. A1; 49037; Calhoun; P 52,300; (269) 962-7526; Fax (269) 962-8096; dehn@bcunlimited.org; www.bcunlimited.org

Bay City • *Bay Future Inc.* • Mark D. Litten; Pres./CEO; 721 Washington Ave., Ste. 309; 48708; Bay; P 107,700; (989) 892-1400; Fax (989) 892-1402; tkeyes@bayfuture.com; www.bayfuture.com

Bay City • *Bay County Growth Alliance* • Andrea Hales; Pres.; 721 Washington Ave., Ste. 309; 48708; Bay; P 107,700; (989) 893-5596; Fax (989) 893-8420; bcgaccv@gmail.com; www.baycounty-mi.gov

Benton Harbor • *Cornerstone Alliance* • Rob Cleveland; Pres./CEO; 38 W. Wall St.; 49022; Berrien; P 157,000; (269) 925-6100; Fax (269) 925-4471; pflourry@cstonealliance.org; www.cstonealliance.org

Big Rapids • *Mecosta County Dev. Corp.* • Jim Sandy; Pres.; 14330 Northland Dr.; 49307; Mecosta; P 43,000; (231) 592-3403; (231) 250-9226; jsandy@co.mecosta.mi.us; www.mecostaedc.com

Boyne City • *Northern Lakes Eco. Alliance* • Andy Hayes; Pres.; P.O. Box 8; 49712; Charlevoix; P 70,000; (231) 582-6482; Fax (231) 582-3213; info@northernlakes.net; www.northernlakes.net

Detroit Area

Detroit Eco. Growth Corp. • Rodrick Miller; Pres./CEO; 500 Griswold, Ste. 2200; 48226; Wayne; P 688,700; (313) 963-2940; Fax (313) 963-8839; jjosaitis@degc.org; www.degc.org

Detroit Reg. Eco. Dev. • Ben Erulkar; Sr. V.P.; One Woodward Ave., Ste. 1900; P.O. Box 33840; 48232; Wayne; P 5,200,000; (313) 964-4000; Fax (313) 964-0183; berulkar@detroitchamber.com; www.detroitchamber.com

Wayne County Eco. Dev. • Dave Tyler; Dep. Dir.; 500 Griswold, 30th Flr.; 48226; Wayne; P 1,800,000; (313) 224-0410; Fax (313) 224-8458; dtyler@co.wayne.mi.us; www.waynecounty.com

Eastpointe • *City of Eastpointe* • Mary Van Haaren; Comm. & Eco. Dev. Dir.; 23200 Gratiot Ave.; 48021; Macomb; P 35,000; (586) 445-3661; Fax (586) 445-5195; mvanhaaren@eastpointecity.org; www.cityofeastpointe.net

Escanaba • *Central Upper Peninsula Plan. & Dev. Reg. Comm. [CUPPAD]* • Joel Schultz; Exec. Dir.; 2950 College Ave.; 49829; Delta; P 180,000; (906) 786-9234; Fax (906) 786-4442; cuppad@cuppad.org; www.cuppad.org

Flint • *Genesee County Metro Planning Comm.* • Derek Bradshaw; Dir./Coord.; 1101 Beach St., Rm. 223; 48502; Genesee; P 411,000; (810) 257-3010; Fax (810) 257-3185; gcmpc@co.genesee.mi.us; www.gcmpc.org

Gaylord • *Northeast Michigan Cncl. of Govts.* • Diane Rekowski; Exec. Dir.; 80 Livingston Blvd., Ste. 8; P.O. Box 457; 49734; Otsego; P 141,199; (989) 705-3730; Fax (989) 705-3729; ppapendic@nemcog.org; www.nemcog.org

Grand Rapids Area

Eco. Dev. Found. • Julie Parker; Pres.; 1345 Monroe Ave. N.W., Ste. 132; 49505; Kent; P 600,000; (616) 459-4825; (888) 330-1776; Fax (616) 458-5736; info@growmichigan.com; www.growmichigan.com

The Right Place Inc. • Birgit Klohs; Pres.; 161 Ottawa Ave. N.W., Ste. 400; 49503; Kent; P 1,302,000; (616) 771-0325; Fax (616) 771-0555; thomasr@rightplace.org; www.rightplace.org

West MI Reg. Planning Comm. • Dave Bee; Dir.; 1345 Monroe N.W., Ste. 255; 49505; Kent; P 1,100,000; (616) 774-8400; Fax (616) 774-0808; dbee@wmrpc.org; www.wmrpc.org

Howell • *Eco. Dev. Cncl. of Livingston County* • Fred Dillingham; Exec. Dir.; 1240 Packard Dr., Ste. 101; 48843; Livingston; P 180,900; (517) 546-0822; Fax (517) 546-4084; information@livingstonedc.com; www.livingstonedc.com

Ionia • *Ionia Downtown Dev. Auth.* • Linda Curtis; Dir.; 203 W. Main St.; P.O. Box 496; 48846; Ionia; P 11,500; (616) 527-1420; Fax (616) 527-0810; lcurtis@ci.ionia.mi.us; www.ci.ionia.mi.us

Iron Mountain • *Dickinson Area Partnership* • Bruce Orttenburger; Pres./CEO; 600 S. Stephenson Ave.; 49801; Dickinson; P 27,500; (906) 774-2202; Fax (906) 774-2004; ortennburger@dickinsonchamber.com; www.dickinsonchamber.com

Ironwood • *Downtown Ironwood Dev. Auth.* • Michael J. D. Brown; Comm. Dev. Dir.; 213 S. Marquette St.; 49938; Gogebic; P 5,400; (906) 932-5050; Fax (906) 932-5745; brownm@cityofironwood.org; www.cityofironwood.org

Ithaca • *Greater Gratiot Dev. Inc.* • Donald C. Schurr; Pres.; 136 S. Main St.; 48847; Gratiot; P 46,000; (989) 875-2083; Fax (989) 875-2990; don.schurr@gratiot.org; www.gratiot.org

Jackson • *Enterprise Group of Jackson Inc.* • Tim Rogers; Pres./CEO; 100 E. Michigan Ave., Ste. 1100; 49201; Jackson; P 160,200; (517) 788-4455; Fax (517) 782-0061; atorres@enterprisegroup.org; www.enterprisegroup.org

Jonesville • *Eco. Dev. Partnership of Hillsdale County* • Susan Smith; Exec. Dir.; 859 Olds Rd.; 49250; Hillsdale; P 46,600; (517) 437-3200; Fax (517) 437-3735; angie@hillsdaleedp.org; www.hillsdaleedp.org

Kalamazoo • *Southwest Michigan First* • Ron Kitchens; CEO; 241 E. Michigan Ave.; P.O. Box 50827; 49005; Kalamazoo; P 250,400; (269) 553-9588; Fax (269) 553-6897; hburnett@southwestmichiganfirst.com; www.southwestmichiganfirst.com

Kalamazoo • *City of Kalamazoo Eco. Dev. & Bus. Assistance* • Jerome Kisscorni; Dir.; 241 W. South St.; 49007; Kalamazoo; P 75,000; (269) 337-8082; Fax (269) 337-8182; cokeconomicdevelopment@kalamazoocity.org; www.kalamazoocity.org

Kincheloe • *Eco. Dev. Corp. of Chippewa County* • Tom Ewing; Pres.; 5019 W. Airport Dr.; 49788; Chippewa; P 38,500; (906) 495-5631; Fax (906) 495-5714; tomewing@charter.net; chippewacountyedc.com

Lansing • *Michigan Eco. Dev. Corp.* • Steve Arwood; CEO; 300 N. Washington Sq.; 48913; Ingham; P 9,910,000; (888) 522-0103; arwoods1@michigan.org; www.michiganbusiness.org

Ludington • *Mason County Growth Alliance* • Spence Riggs; Eco. Dev. Coord.; 5300 W. U.S. 10; 49431; Mason; P 30,000; (231) 845-6646; Fax (231) 845-6857; spencer@ludington.org; www.masoncountygrowth.com

Marquette • *Lake Superior Comm. Partnership-Marquette Area C/C* • Amy Clickner; Exec. Dir.; 501 S. Front St.; 49855; Marquette; P 311,361; (906) 226-6591; (888) 578-6489; Fax (906) 226-2099; lscp@marquette.org; www.marquette.org

Mason • *Ingham County Eco. Dev. Corp.* • Sandy Gower; Eco. Dev. Dir.; 121 E. Maple St.; 48854; Ingham; P 280,000; (517) 676-7285; Fax (517) 676-7358; sgower@ingham.org; www.ingham.org

Midland • *Midland Tomorrow* • Kate Julius; Eco. Dev. Mgr.; 300 Rodd St., Ste. 201; 48640; Midland; P 84,000; (989) 839-0340; Fax (989) 839-7372; info@midlandtomorrow.org; www.midlandtomorrow.org

Monroe • *Monroe County Bus. Dev. Corp.* • Tim C. Lake; Pres./CEO; 102 E. Front St.; 48161; Monroe; P 150,000; (734) 241-8081; bdc@monroecountybdc.org; www.monroecountybdc.org

Mount Clemens • *Macomb County Planning & Eco. Dev. Dept.* • Robert Tess; Program Mgr.; 1 S. Main, 7th Flr.; 48043; Macomb; P 831,100; (586) 469-5285; Fax (586) 469-6787; planning@macombcountymi.gov; www.macombcountymi.gov

Mount Pleasant • *Middle MI Dev. Corp.* • Brian Anderson; Pres./CEO; 200 E. Broadway; 48858; Isabella; P 98,000; (989) 772-2858; Fax (989) 773-2115; info@mmdc.org; www.mmdc.org

Muskegon • *Muskegon Area First* • Ed Garner; Pres./CEO; 380 W. Western, Ste. 202; 49440; Muskegon; P 173,000; (231) 722-3751; Fax (231) 728-7251; info@muskegonareafirst.org; www.muskegonareafirst.org

Newberry • *Eco. Dev. Corp. of Luce County* • Carmen Pittenger; Exec. Dir.; 401 W. Harrie St.; 49868; Luce; P 6,700; (906) 293-5982; Fax (906) 293-2904; pittenger@lighthouse.net; www.edc.lucecountymi.org

Niles • *Southwestern Michigan Eco. Growth Alliance Inc.* • Joe Sobieralski; Exec. Dir.; 333 N. 2nd St., Ste. 302; 49120; Berrien; P 819,000; (269) 683-1833; Fax (269) 683-7515; southwesternalliance@gmail.com; www.southwesternalliance.org

Novi • *Novi Comm. Dev. Dept.* • Larry Butler; Deputy Dir.; 45175 W. Ten Mile Rd.; 48375; Oakland; P 55,200; (248) 347-0415; Fax (248) 735-5600; lbutler@cityofnovi.org; www.cityofnovi.org

Port Huron • *Eco. Dev. Alliance of St. Clair County* • Dan Casey; CEO; 100 McMorran Blvd., 4th Flr.; Exec. Ste. B; 48060; St. Clair; P 163,100; (810) 982-9511; Fax (810) 982-9531; dhorvath@edascc.com; www.edascc.com

Saginaw • *Saginaw Future Inc.* • JoAnn Crary CEcD; Pres.; 515 N. Washington, 3rd Flr.; 48607; Saginaw; P 200,100; (989) 754-8222; Fax (989) 754-1715; sgray@saginawfuture.com; www.saginawfuture.com

Sault Ste. Marie • *Sault Ste. Marie Eco. Dev. Corp.* • Jeff Holt; Dir.; 2345 Meridian St.; 49783; Chippewa; P 15,000; (906) 635-9131; Fax (906) 635-1999; tlaitinen@saultcity.com; www.saultedc.com

Southgate • *Downriver Comm. Conf.-Eco. Dev. Dept.* • Paula Boase; Eco. Dev. Dir.; 15100 Northline Rd.; 48195; Wayne; P 500,000; (734) 362-3442; (734) 362-3469; Fax (734) 281-6661; cari.eggleton@dccwf.org; www.dccwf.org

St. Joseph • *Berrien County Comm. Dev. Dept.* • Dan Fette; Dir.; 701 Main St.; 49085; Berrien; P 156,800; (269) 983-7111; Fax (269) 982-8611; dfette@berriencounty.org; www.berriencounty.org

Tecumseh • *City of Tecumseh Eco. Dev. Dept.* • Paula Holtz; Dir.; 309 E. Chicago Blvd.; 49286; Lenawee; P 8,500; (517) 424-6003; Fax (517) 423-3610; pholtz@tecumseh.mi.us; www.downtowntecumseh.com

Waterford • *Oakland County Eco. Dev. Dept.* • Dan Hunter; Mgr.; 2100 Pontiac Lake Rd., Bldg. 41W; 48328; Oakland; P 1,200,000; (248) 858-0720; Fax (248) 975-9555; hunterd@oakgov.com/peds; www.oakgov.com/peds

Wayne • *Comm. Dev. for the City of Wayne* • Lori Gouin; Comm. Dev. Dir.; 3355 S. Wayne Rd.; 48184; Wayne; P 17,600; (734) 722-2002; Fax (734) 722-5052; commdev@ci.wayne.mi.us; www.ci.wayne.mi.us

West Branch • *Ogemaw County EDC* • Mandi Chasey; Dir.; Michigan Works! Bldg.; 2389 S. M-76; 48661; Ogemaw; P 21,700; (989) 345-1090; mchasey@michworks4u.org; www.everythingogemaw.com

West Olive • *Ottawa County Eco. Dev. Ofc.* • Paul Sachs; Dir.; 12220 Fillmore St., Rm. 260; 49460; Ottawa; P 280,000; (616) 738-4852; Fax (616) 738-4625; plan@miottawa.org; www.miottawa.org

Minnesota

Federal

U.S. SBA, Minnesota Dist. Ofc. • Nancy Libersky; Dist. Dir.; 330 2nd Ave. S., Ste. 430; 55401; Hennepin; P 5,379,139; (612) 370-2324; Fax (202) 481-0139; nancy.libersky@sba.gov; www.sba.gov/mn

State

Dept. of Employment & Eco. Dev. • Katie Clark Sieben; Comm.; 1st Natl. Bank Bldg.; 332 Minnesota St., Ste. E200; Saint Paul; 55101; Ramsey; P 5,379,139; (651) 259-7114; Fax (651) 215-3841; deed.customerservice@state.mn.us; www.PositivelyMinnesota.com

Communities

Ada • *Ada Eco. Dev. Auth.* • Shelley Kappes; Clerk; 15 E. 4th Ave.; 56510; Norman; P 1,700; (218) 784-5524; Fax (218) 784-2711; adaclerk@loretel.net; www.adamn.gov

Alexandria • *Alexandria Area Eco. Dev. Comm.* • Nicole Fernholz; Exec. Dir.; 324 Broadway, Ste. 101; 56308; Douglas; P 37,100; (320) 763-4545; Fax (320) 763-5320; sgraf@alexmn.org; www.livingalexarea.org

Anoka • *Anoka Eco. Dev. Comm.* • Doug Borglund; Deputy Comm. Dev. Dir.; 2015 1st Ave. N.; 55303; Anoka; P 18,000; (763) 576-2720; Fax (763) 576-2727; dborglund@ci.anoka.mn.us; www.ci.anoka.mn.us

Austin • *Dev. Corp. of Austin* • John Garry; Pres./CEO; 329 N. Main St., Ste. 106 L; 55912; Mower; P 24,000; (507) 433-9495; Fax (507) 433-9470; austindca@austindca.org; www.austindca.org

Barnum • *Barnum Eco. Dev.* • Bernadine Reed; City Admin.; 3741 Front St.; 55707; Carlton; P 600; (218) 389-6814; Fax (218) 389-3235; breed@scicable.com; www.barnummn.us

Bemidji • *Headwaters Reg. Dev. Comm.* • Tim Flathers; Exec. Dir.; 403 4th St. N.W., Ste. 310; P.O. Box 906; 56619; Beltrami; P 80,000; (218) 444-4732; (218) 333-6541; Fax (218) 444-4722; hrdc@hrdc.org; www.hrdc.org

Blue Earth • *Blue Earth EDA* • Linsey Preuss; EDA Dir.; 125 W. 6th St.; P.O. Box 38; 56013; Faribault; P 3,244; (507) 526-7336; Fax (507) 526-7352; linsey@fcdcorp.net; www.becity.org

Brainerd • *Brainerd Lakes Area Eco. Dev. Corp.* • Sheila Haverkamp; Exec. Dir.; 224 W. Washington St.; 56401; Crow Wing; P 67,000; (218) 828-0096; (888) 322-5232; Fax (218) 829-8199; megan@growbrainerdlakes.org; www.growbrainerdlakes.org

Brooklyn Park • *Eco. Dev. Auth.* • Kimberly Berggren; Exec. Dir.; 5200 85th Ave. N.; 55443; Hennepin; P 76,000; (763) 493-8059; (763) 493-8050; Fax (763) 493-8391; kim.berggren@brooklynpark.org; www.brooklynpark.org

Champlin • *City of Champlin Comm. Dev. Dept.* • John Cox; Dev. Dir.; 11955 Champlin Dr.; 55316; Hennepin; P 23,900; (763) 421-8100; (763) 923-7104; Fax (763) 421-5256; jcox@ci.champlin.mn.us; www.ci.champlin.mn.us

Chaska • *City of Chaska Eco. Dev. Dept.* • Matthew Podhradsky; Exec. Dir.; 1 City Hall Plaza; 55318; Carver; P 24,000; (952) 448-9200; Fax (952) 448-9300; matt@chaskamn.com; www.chaskamn.com

Coon Rapids • *City of Coon Rapids Eco. Dev.* • Grant Fernelius; Dev. Spec.; 11155 Robinson Dr.; 55433; Anoka; P 62,100; (763) 767-6430; Fax (763) 767-6573; econdev@coonrapidsmn.gov; www.coonrapidsmn.gov

Cottage Grove • *Cottage Grove Eco. Dev. Auth.* • Christine Costello; Eco. Dev. Dir.; 12800 Ravine Pkwy.; 55016; Washington; P 35,000; (651) 458-2824; (651) 458-2890; Fax (651) 458-2800; mwolf@cottage-grove.org; www.cottage-grove.org

Crookston • *Crookston Housing & Eco. Dev. Auth.* • Craig Hoiseth; Exec. Dir.; 510 County Rd. 71, Ste. 1; 56716; Polk; P 8,000; (218) 470-2000; Fax (218) 470-2005; choiseth@crookstonheda.com; www.crookstonheda.com

Detroit Lakes Area

Becker County Eco. Dev. Auth. • Guy Fischer; Eco. Dev. Coord.; 915 Lake Ave.; 56501; Becker; P 33,400; (218) 846-7316; Fax (218) 846-7329; ghfisch@co.becker.mn.us; www.co.becker.mn.us

Becker Lakes Comm. Dev. • Larry Remmen AICP; Comm. Dev. Dir.; 1025 Roosevelt Ave.; 56501; Becker; P 9,000; (218) 846-7125; Fax (218) 847-8969; lremmen@ci.detroit-lakes.mn.us; www.cityofdetroitlakes.com

Comm. Dev. of Detroit Lakes • Larry Remmen; Dir.; 1025 Roosevelt Ave.; P.O. Box 647; 56502; Becker; P 8,600; (218) 847-5658; Fax (218) 847-8969; lremmen@lakesnet.net; www.ci.detroit-lakes.mn.us

Detroit Lakes Dev. Auth. • Larry Remmen AICP; Comm. Dev. Dir.; 1025 Roosevelt Ave.; P.O. Box 647; 56502; Becker; P 8,300; (218) 847-5658; Fax (218) 847-8969; lremmen@lakesnet.net; www.ci.detroit-lakes.mn.us

Midwest Minnesota Comm. Dev. Corp. • Arlen Kangas; Pres.; 119 Graystone Plz., Ste. 100; 56501; Becker; P 7,500; (218) 847-3191; Fax (218) 844-6345; info@mmcdc.com; www.mmcdc.com

Duluth • *Duluth Bus. & Eco. Dev.* • Heather Rand; Dir. of Bus. & Eco. Dev.; City Hall, Rm. 402; 411 W. 1st St.; 55802; St. Louis; P 87,000; (218) 730-5322; Fax (218) 730-5904; hrand@duluthmn.gov; www.duluthmn.gov

Fairmont • *Fairmont Eco. Dev. Auth.* • Michael Humpal; Asst. City Admin.; 100 Downtown Plz.; P.O. Box 751; 56031; Martin; P 12,000; (507) 238-9461; Fax (507) 238-9469; ecodevo@fairmont.org; www.fairmont.org

Fridley • *City of Fridley Comm. Dev.* • Scott Hickok; Comm. Dev. Dir.; 6431 University Ave. N.E.; 55432; Anoka; P 27,300; (763) 572-3590; Fax (763) 571-1287; Scott.Hickok@FridleyMN.gov; www.ci.fridley.mn.us

Grand Marais • *Cook County/Grand Marais Joint Eco. Dev. Auth.* • Matt Geretschlaeger; Dir.; P.O. Box 597; 55604; Cook; P 5,200; (218) 387-3067; Fax (218) 387-3018; edamatt@boreal.org

Grand Rapids • *Itasca EDC* • Mark Zimmerman; Pres./CEO; 12 N.W. 3rd St.; 55744; Itasca; P 45,500; (218) 326-9411; (888) 890-5627; info@itascadv.org; www.itascadv.org

Granite Falls • *Granite Falls Eco. Dev. Auth.* • Dennis VanHoof; Exec. Dir.; 641 Prentice St.; 56241; Yellow Medicine; P 2,900; (320) 564-2255; Fax (320) 564-3210; eda@granitefalls.com; www.granitefalls.com

Hibbing • *Hibbing Eco. Dev. Auth.* • Michael Egan; Pres.; 401 E. 21st St.; 55746; St. Louis; P 16,400; (218) 362-5930; tdicklich@ci.hibbing.mn.us; www.hibbing.mn.us

International Falls • *Koochiching Eco. Dev. Auth.* • Paul Nevanen; Dir.; 405 3rd St.; P.O. Box 138; 56649; Koochiching; P 13,300; (218) 283-8585; Fax (218) 283-4688; keda@businessupnorth.com; www.businessupnorth.com

Jackson • *Jackson Eco. Dev. Corp.* • Susan Pirsig; Coord.; 80 W. Ashley St.; 56143; Jackson; P 3,300; (507) 847-4423; info@cityofjacksonmn.com; www.cityofjacksonmn.com

Lake City • *Lake City Eco. Dev. Auth.* • Erin Sparks; Exec. Dir.; 205 W. Center St.; 55041; Wabasha; P 5,350; (651) 345-6808; Fax (651) 345-3208; esparks@lakecityeda.com; www.lakecityeda.com

Le Center • *Le Center Area Eco. Dev. Auth.* • Don Hayden; Mgr.; 10 W. Tyrone St.; 56057; Le Sueur; P 2,500; (507) 357-6737; Fax (507) 357-6888; info@cityoflecenter.com; www.cityoflecenter.com

Luverne • *Luverne Eco. Dev. Auth.* • Ted LaFrance; Eco. Dev. Dir.; 305 E. Luverne St.; P.O. Box 659; 56156; Rock; P 4,600; (507) 449-5033; Fax (507) 449-5034; tlafrance@cityofluverne.org; www.cityofluverne.org

Mankato • *Greater Mankato Growth* • Jonathan Zierdt; Pres./CEO; 1961 Premier Dr., Ste. 100; 56001; Blue Earth; P 99,000; (507) 385-6640; (800) 697-0652; Fax (507) 345-4451; info@greatermankato.com; www.greatermankato.com

Marshall • *Marshall Eco. Dev. Auth.* • Nick Johnson; Exec. Dir.; 344 W. Main St.; 56258; Lyon; P 13,700; (507) 537-6760; nick.johnson@ci.marshall.mn.us; www.ci.marshall.mn.us

Minneapolis • *Minneapolis Comm. Planning & Eco. Dev.* • D. Craig Taylor; Dir.; 105 5th Ave. S., Ste. 200; Crown Roller Mill Bldg.; 55401; Hennepin; P 411,000; (612) 673-5095; Fax (612) 673-5100; dorothea.martti@minneapolismn.gov; www.minneapolismn.gov

Montevideo • *Montevideo Eco. Dev. Auth.* • Nick Haggenmiller; Dir.; 103 Canton Ave.; P.O. Box 517; 56265; Chippewa; P 5,500; (320) 269-6575; Fax (320) 269-9340; cdd@montevideomn.org; www.montechamber.com

Monticello • *City of Monticello Eco. Dev.* • James Thares; Eco. Dev. Mgr.; 505 Walnut St., Ste. 1; 55362; Wright; P 13,125; (763) 271-3254; (763) 295-2711; Fax (763) 295-4404; info@ci.monticello.mn.us; www.ci.monticello.mn.us

Morris • *Stevens County Eco. Imp. Comm.* • 215 Atlantic Ave.; 56267; Stevens; P 9,700; (320) 585-2609; sceic@hometownsolutions.net; www.sceic.org

Ortonville • *Ortonville Eco. Dev. Auth.* • Vicki Oakes; Secy.; 987 U.S. Hwy. 12; 56278; Big Stone; P 1,916; (320) 839-3284; eda@ortonville.net; www.ortonville.net

Osakis • *Osakis Eco. Dev. Auth.* • Angela Jacobson; Admin.; P.O. Box 486; 56360; Douglas & Todd; P 1,740; (320) 859-2150; Fax (320) 859-3978; cityhall@cityofosakis.com; www.cityofosakis.com

Pipestone • *Pipestone Eco. Dev. Auth.* • Jeff Jones; City Admin.; 119 2nd Ave. S.W.; 56164; Pipestone; P 4,300; (507) 825-3324; Fax (507) 825-5353; dnelson@cityofpipestone.com; www.progressivepipestone.com

Red Lake Falls • *Red Lake Falls Comm. Dev. Corp.* • Allen Bertilrud; Chair; 108 2nd St. S.W.; P.O. Box 37; 56750; Red Lake; P 1,427; (218) 253-2684; Fax (218) 253-4431; info@redlakefalls.com; www.redlakefalls.com

Redwood Falls • *Redwood Area Dev. Corp.* • Julie Rath; Eco. Dev. Spec.; 200 S. Mill St.; P.O. Box 481; 56283; Redwood; P 16,000; (507) 637-4004; (507) 637-4003; julie@radc.org; www.radc.org

Rochester • *Rochester Area Eco. Dev.* • Gary Smith; Pres.; 220 S. Broadway, Ste. 100; 55904; Olmsted; P 106,800; (507) 288-0208; tbernard@raedi.com; www.raedi.com

Saint Charles • *St. Charles Eco. Dev. Auth.* • Nick Koverman; City Admin.; 830 Whitewater Ave.; 55972; Winona; P 3,700; (507) 932-3020; Fax (507) 932-5301; nkoverman@stcharlesmn.org; www.stcharlesmn.org

Saint Cloud • *Greater St. Cloud Dev. Corp.* • John Kramer; CEO; P.O. Box 1662; 56302; Stearns; P 189,000; (320) 252-2177; jkramer@greaterstcloud.com

Saint Paul Area

City of St. Paul • Kit Hadley; Interim Dir.; Dept. of Plan. & Eco. Dev.; 25 W. 4th, 1300 City Hall Annex; 55102; Ramsey; P 278,700; (651) 266-6565; Fax (651) 228-3261; kit.hadley@ci.stpaul.mn.us; www.ci.stpaul.mn.us

Grand Avenue Bus. Assn. • Sue Evens; Exec. Dir.; 752 Grand Ave.; 55105; Ramsey; (651) 699-0029; Fax (651) 699-7775; info@grandave.com; www.grandave.com

Saint Paul Port Auth. • Lee Krueger; Pres.; 380 St. Peter St., Ste. 850; 55102; Ramsey; P 300,900; (651) 224-5686; (800) 328-8417; Fax (651) 223-5198; amk@sppa.com; www.sppa.com

Saint Peter • *Dept. of Comm. Dev.* • Russ Wille; Dir.; 227 S. Front St.; 56082; Nicollet; P 11,196; (507) 934-0661; Fax (507) 934-4917; cindym@saintpetermn.gov; www.saintpetermn.gov

Slayton • *Southwest Reg. Dev. Comm.* • Jay Trusty; Exec. Dir.; 2401 Broadway Ave., Ste. 1; 56172; Murray; P 130,000; (507) 836-8547; Fax (507) 836-8866; srdc@swrdc.org; www.swrdc.org

Spicer • *Spicer Eco. Dev. Auth.* • P.O. Box 656; 56288; Kandiyohi; P 1,200; (320) 796-5562; Fax (320) 796-2044; lvaliant@cityofspicer.org; spicer.govoffice.com

Vadnais Heights • *Vadnais Heights Eco. Dev. Corp.* • Keith Warner; Exec. Dir.; 800 E. County Rd. E; 55127; Ramsey; P 12,300; (651) 426-0299; (651) 204-6000; Fax (651) 204-6111; warner1955@comcast.net; www.vhedc.com

Virginia • *Virginia Eco. Dev. Auth.* • John Tourville; Op. Dir.; 327 1st St. S.; City Hall; 55792; St. Louis; P 8,407; (218) 748-7535; Fax (218) 749-3580; veda@virginiamn.us; www.virginia-mn.com

White Bear Lake • *White Bear Lake Area Comm. Dev. Dept.* • Anne Kane; Comm. Dev. Dir.; 4701 Hwy. 61; 55110; Ramsey; P 25,000; (651) 429-8562; Fax (651) 429-8503; akane@whitebearlake.org; www.whitebearlake.org

Willmar • *Mid-Minnesota Dev. Comm.* • Les Nelson; Eco. Dev. Dir.; 333 6th St. S.W., Ste. 2; 56201; Kandiyohi; P 120,000; (320) 235-8504; (800) 450-8608; Fax (320) 235-4329; mmrdc@mmrdc.org; www.mmrdc.org

Worthington • *Worthington Reg. Eco. Dev. Corp.* • Nicole Frodermann; Admin. Asst.; 1121 Third Ave.; 56187; Nobles; P 12,000; (507) 372-5515; Fax (507) 372-7165; wredc@frontiernet.net; www.wgtn.net

Mississippi

Federal

U.S. SBA, Mississippi Dist. Ofc. • Janita R. Stewart; Dist. Dir.; 210 E. Capital St., Ste. 900; 39201; Hinds; P 2,984,926; (601) 965-4378; Fax (601) 965-5629; janita.r.stewart@sba.gov; www.sba.gov/ms

State

Mississippi Dev. Auth. • Brent Christensen; Exec. Dir.; 501 N. West St.; P.O. Box 849; Jackson; 39205; Hinds; P 2,984,926; (601) 359-3449; Fax (601) 359-2832; mmcphillips@mississippi.org; www.mississippi.org

Communities

Belzoni • *Belzoni-Humphreys Dev. Found.* • Mark Bellipanni; Pres.; 111 Magnolia St.; P.O. Box 145; 39038; Humphreys; P 9,500; (662) 247-4838; Fax (662) 247-4805; catfish@belzonicable.com; www.belzonims.com

Booneville • *Prentiss County Dev. Assn.* • Leon N. Hays; Exec. Dir.; 401 W. Parker Dr.; P.O. Box 672; 38829; Prentiss; P 25,500; (662) 728-3505; Fax (662) 728-0086; slpcda@bellsouth.net; www.goprentiss.com

Brandon • *Rankin First Eco. Dev. Auth.* • Tom Troxler; Exec. Dir.; P.O. Box 129; 39043; Rankin; P 149,000; (601) 825-5335; Fax (601) 825-1977; ttroxler@rankinfirst.com; www.rankinfirst.com

Brookhaven • *Lincoln County Ind. Dev. Found.* • Cliff Brumfield; Exec. V.P.; 230 S. Whitworth Ave.; P.O. Box 978; 39602; Lincoln; P 35,000; (601) 833-1411; (800) 613-4667; Fax (601) 833-1412; chb@brookhavenchamber.com; www.brookhavenchamber.com

Canton • *Madison County Eco. Dev. Auth.* • Ken Oilschlager; Interim Exec. Dir.; 135 Mississippi Pkwy.; 39046; Madison; P 103,500; (601) 605-0368; Fax (601) 407-2835; christy@madisoncountyeda.com; www.madisoncountyeda.com

Cleveland • *Cleveland-Bolivar County Ind. Dev. Found.* • Judson Thigpen III; Exec. Dir.; 101 S. Bayou Ave.; P.O. Box 490; 38732; Bolivar; P 40,000; (662) 843-2712; (800) 295-7473; Fax (662) 843-2718; info@clevelandmschamber.com; www.clevelandmschamber.com

Columbus • *Golden Triangle Dev. LINK* • Joe Max Higgins Jr.; CEO; 1102 Main St.; P.O. Box 1328; 39703; Lowndes; P 63,000; (662) 328-8369; (800) 748-8882; Fax (662) 327-3417; info@gtrlink.org; www.gtrlink.org

Corinth • *The Alliance* • Clayton Stanley; Pres./COO; 810 Tate St.; 38834; Alcorn; P 15,000; (662) 287-5269; alliance@corinthalliance.com; www.corinthalliance.com

DeKalb • *Kemper County Eco. Dev. Auth.* • Cindy Cumberland; Exec. Dir.; 102 Industrial Park Dr.; 39328; Kemper; P 10,500; (601) 743-2754; Fax (601) 743-2760; kceda@bellsouth.net; www.kempercounty.com

Fulton • *Itawamba County Dev. Cncl.* • Vaunita Martin; Exec. Dir.; 107 W. Wiygul St.; 38843; Itawamba; P 23,600; (662) 862-4571; (800) 371-8642; Fax (662) 862-5637; icdc@itawamba.com; www.itawamba.com

Greenwood • *Greenwood LeFlore/Carroll Eco. Dev. Found.* • Angela Curry; Exec. Dir.; 402 Hwy. 82 Bypass; P.O. Box 26; 38935; Leflore; P 42,000; (662) 453-5321; (800) 844-SITE; Fax (662) 453-8003; angcur@bellsouth.net; www.glcedf.com

Gulfport • *Southern Miss. Planning & Dev. Dist.* • Leonard Bentz; Exec. Dir.; 9229 Hwy. 49; 39503; Harrison; P 731,620; (228) 868-2311; (800) 444-8014; Fax (228) 868-2550; lbentz@smpdd.com; www.smpdd.com

Gulfport • *Harrison Co. Dev. Comm.* • Bill Hessell; Exec. Dir.; 12281 Intraplex Pkwy.; 39503; Harrison; (228) 896-5020; Fax (228) 896-6020; hcdc@mscoast.org; www.mscoast.org

Hattiesburg • *Area Dev. Partnership* • Chad Newell; Pres.; One Convention Center Plaza; 39401; Lamar; P 156,000; (601) 296-7500; Fax (601) 296-7505; receptionist@theadp.com; www.theadp.com

Hernando • *DeSoto County Eco. Dev. Cncl.* • Jim Flanagan; Pres./CEO; 316 W. Commerce St.; 38632; DeSoto; P 173,500; (662) 429-4414; Fax (662) 429-0952; dmorgan@desotocounty.com; www.desotocounty.com

Houston • *Chickasaw Dev. Found.* • Joyce East; Exec. Dir.; 635 Starkville Rd.; P.O. Box 505; 38851; Chickasaw; P 18,000; (662) 456-2321; (662) 456-5134; Fax (662) 456-2595; jeastcdf@bellsouth.net; www.houstonms.org

Jackson • *Mississippi Eco. Dev. Cncl.* • Mary Swoope; Exec. Dir. & CEO; 1675 Lakeland Dr., Ste. 502; 39216; Hinds; P 2,985,000; (601) 352-1909; Fax (855) 443-2828; info@medc.ms; www.medc.ms

Kosciusko • *Kosciusko-Attala Dev. Corp.* • Steve Zea; Pres.; 101 N. Natchez St.; 39090; Attala; P 20,000; (662) 289-2981; Fax (662) 289-2986; szea@kadcorp.org; www.kadcorp.org

Laurel • *Eco. Dev. Auth. of Jones County* • Ross Tucker; Pres.; 153 Base Dr., Ste. 3; P.O. Box 527; 39441; Jones; P 67,761; (601) 649-3031; Fax (601) 428-2047; info@edajones.com; www.jonescounty.com

Louisville • *Winston County Eco. Dev. Dist.* • Gerald Mills; Exec. Dir.; 311 W. Park St.; P.O. Box 551; 39339; Winston; P 20,160; (662) 773-8719; Fax (662) 773-8909; gmills@winstoncounty.com; winstoncountyms.com

McComb • *Pike County Eco. Dev. Dist.* • J. Britt Herrin; Exec. Dir.; 112 N. Railroad Blvd.; P.O. Box 83; 39649; Pike; P 38,000; (601) 684-2291; (800) 399-4404; Fax (601) 684-4899; pcedd@pikeinfo.com; www.pikeinfo.com

Meridian • *East Mississippi Bus. Dev. Corp.* • Bill Hannah; Pres./CEO; 1901 Front St., Ste. A; P.O. Box 790; 39302; Lauderdale; P 93,551; (601) 693-1306; Fax (601) 693-5638; info@embdc.org; www.embdc.org

Monticello • *Lawrence County Comm. Dev. Assn.* • Bob Smira; Pres./CEO; 517 Broad St. E.; P.O. Box 996; 39654; Lawrence; P 13,000; (601) 587-3007; Fax (601) 587-0765; bsmira@lccda.org; www.lccda.org

Natchez • *Natchez Inc.* • Chandler Russ; Exec. Dir.; 100 S. Pearl St.; P.O. Box 700; 39121; Adams; P 33,000; (601) 445-0288; info@natchezinc.com; www.natchezinc.com

New Albany • *Union County Dev. Assn.* • Phil Nanney; Exec. Dir.; P.O. Box 125; 38652; Union; P 28,500; (662) 534-4354; (662) 539-3903; Fax (662) 538-4107; info@ucda-newalbany.com; www.ucda-newalbany.com

Oxford • *Oxford-Lafayette Eco. Dev. Found.* • Jon Maynard; Pres./CEO; 299 W. Jackson Ave.; P.O. Box 108; 38655; Lafayette; P 47,400; (662) 234-4651; (800) 880-6967; Fax (662) 234-4655; info@oxfordms.com; www.oxfordms.com

Pascagoula • *Jackson County Port Auth.* • Mark McAndrews; Port Dir.; P.O. Box 70; 39568; Jackson; P 140,000; (228) 762-4041; info@portofpascagoula.com; www.portofpascagoula.com

Pascagoula • *Jackson County Eco. Dev. Found.* • George Freeland Jr.; Exec. Dir.; 3033 Pascagoula St.; P.O. Drawer 1558; 39568; Jackson; P 140,000; (228) 769-6263; (800) 362-0103; Fax (228) 762-8431; prussell@jcedf.org; www.jcedf.org

Philadelphia • *Community Dev. Partnership* • David Vowell; Pres.; 256 W. Beacon St.; 39350; Neshoba; P 30,000; (601) 656-1000; (877) 752-2643; Fax (601) 656-1066; dvowell@neshoba.org; www.neshoba.org

Picayune • *Partners for Pearl River County* • P.O. Box 278; 39466; Pearl River; P 55,000; (601) 749-4919; partners@partners.ms; www.partners.ms

Purvis • *Lamar County Planning Dept.* • Michael Hershman; Sr. Planner; 144 Shelby Speights Dr.; P.O. Box 1240; 39475; Lamar; P 60,600; (601) 794-1024; Fax (601) 794-3900; www.lamarcountyms.gov

Ripley • *Tippah County Dev. Found.* • Matthew Harrison; Exec. Dir./COO; 201 Union St.; 38663; Tippah; P 23,000; (662) 837-3353; (662) 837-6592; Fax (662) 837-3006; tcdf@dixie-net.com; www.tippahcounty.ripley.ms

Senatobia • *Tate County Eco. Dev. Found.* • J.E. Mortimer; Exec. Dir.; 135 N. Front St.; 38668; Tate; P 27,000; (662) 562-8715; Fax (662) 562-5786; jemortimer@cityofsenatobia.com; www.tate-county.com

Starkville • *Greater Starkville Dev. Partnership* • Jennifer Prather; Comm. Mktg. Mgr.; 200 E. Main St.; 39759; Oktibbeha; P 50,000; (662) 323-3322; Fax (662) 323-5815; jprather@starkville.org; www.starkville.org

Tupelo • *Comm. Dev. Found.* • David Rumbarger; Pres./CEO; 398 E. Main St.; 38804; Lee; P 85,300; (662) 842-4521; Fax (662) 841-0693; info@cdfms.org; www.cdfms.org

Vicksburg • *Vicksburg-Warren County Eco. Dev. Found.* • Beverly Steward; Proj. Mgr.; P.O. Box 820363; 39182; Warren; P 48,800; (601) 631-0555; Fax (601) 631-6953; beverlys@co.warren.ms.us; www.vicksburgedf.org

Waynesboro • *Wayne County Eco. Dev. District* • Sean Dunlap; Exec. Dir.; 610 Azalea Dr.; 39367; Wayne; P 20,747; (601) 735-6056; Fax (601) 735-6246; j.dunlap@cmaaccess.com; www.waynecounty.ms

West Point • *North Mississippi Ind. Dev. Assn.* • Joseph Geddie; Exec. Dir.; 757 E. Main St.; P.O. Box 718; 39773; Clay; (662) 494-4633; Fax (662) 494-3231; krichardson@nmida.com; www.nmida.com

West Point • *Growth Alliance* • Lisa Klutts; Dir.; 746 E. Main St.; 39773; Clay; P 22,000; (662) 494-5121; (866) 494-5127; Fax (662) 494-6396; info@westpointms.org; www.westpointms.org

Winona • *Montgomery County Eco. Dev. Partnership* • Sue Stidham; Exec. Dir.; P.O. Box 248; 38967; Montgomery; P 11,000; (662) 283-4828; Fax (662) 283-5986; info@mcedp.ms; www.mcedp.ms

Missouri

Federal

***U.S. SBA, Kansas City Dist. Ofc.* •** Roderick M. Cox; Dist. Dir.; 1000 Walnut St., Ste. 500; 64106; Jackson; P 6,021,988; (816) 426-4900; Fax (816) 426-4939; roderick.cox@sba.gov; www.sba.gov/mo

***U.S. SBA, St. Louis Dist. Ofc.* •** Dennis S. Melton; Dist. Dir.; 1222 Spruce St., Ste. 10.103; 63103; St. Louis; P 6,021,988; (314) 539-6600; dennis.melton@sba.gov; www.sba.gov/mo

State

***Missouri Dept. of Eco. Dev.* •** Mike Downing; Dept. Dir.; 301 W. High St., Rm. 680; P.O. Box 1157; Jefferson City; 65102; Cole; P 6,021,988; (573) 751-4962; Fax (573) 526-7700; ecodev@ded.mo.gov; www.ded.mo.gov

Communities

Belton • *Belton Eco. Dev. Dept.* • Jay Leipzig; Dir.; 520 Main St.; 64012; Cass; P 28,000; (816) 331-4331; Fax (816) 331-6973; cyatsook@belton.org; www.belton.org

Branson • *City of Branson Eco. Dev.* • Garrett Anderson; Eco. Dev. Dir.; 110 W. Maddux; 65616; Taney; P 10,500; (417) 337-8589; (417) 337-8548; Fax (417) 334-6095; ganderson@bransonmo.gov; www.cityofbranson.org

Cape Girardeau • *Cape Girardeau Area C/C & Eco. Dev.* • John E. Mehner; Pres./CEO; 1267 N. Mount Auburn Rd.; 63701; Cape Girardeau; P 75,000; (573) 335-3312; Fax (573) 335-4686; info@capechamber.com; www.capechamber.com

Chillicothe • *Chillicothe Ind. Dev. Corp.* • Steve Franke; Pres.; 514 Washington; P.O. Box 1022; 64601; Livingston; P 9,500; (660) 646-4071; Fax (660) 646-5571; cdc@chillicothemo.com; www.chillicothemo.com

Clayton • *City of Clayton, Eco. Dev. Div.* • Gary Carter; Eco. Developer; 10 N. Bemiston; 63105; St. Louis; P 16,000; (314) 290-8453; Fax (314) 863-0296; gcarter@ci.clayton.mo.us; www.claytonmo.gov

Clinton • *City of Clinton Eco. Dev. Dept.* • Christy Maggi; City Admin.; 105 E. Ohio; 64735; Henry; P 10,000; (660) 885-6121; Fax (660) 885-2023; cmaggi@cityofclintonmo.com; www.clintonmo.com

Columbia • *Reg. Eco. Dev. Inc.* • J. Michael Brooks; Pres.; 302 Campusview Dr., Ste. 208; P.O. Box 6015; 65205; Boone; P 146,626; (573) 442-8303; Fax (573) 443-8834; jmbrooks@gocolumbiamo.com; www.columbiaredi.com

Ferguson • *City of Ferguson Bus. & Dev. Dept.* • Dan Bish; Comm. Dev. Coord.; 110 Church St.; 63135; St. Louis; P 21,300; (314) 524-5196; Fax (314) 524-5173; dbish@fergusoncity.com; www.fergusoncity.com

Fulton • *Fulton Area Dev. Corp.* • Bruce Hackmann; Pres.; 510 Market St.; 65251; Callaway; P 44,000; (573) 642-4841; (877) 642-5964; Fax (573) 642-5964; hackmann@fadc.org; www.fadc.org

Grandview • *Grandview Area Eco. Dev. Cncl.* • Kim Curtis; Pres.; 12500 S. 71 Hwy., Ste. 100; 64030; Jackson; P 26,000; (816) 761-6505; Fax (816) 763-8460; ksc@grandview.org; www.grandview.org

Hannibal • *Northeast Missouri Eco. Dev. Cncl.* • George Walley; Exec. Dir.; 201 N. Third, Ste. 220; 63401; Marion; P 28,400; (573) 221-1033; Fax (573) 221-1084; gwalley@nemodev.org; www.nemodev.org

Harrisonville • *City of Harrisonville Comm. Dev. Dept.* • Rick DeLuca; Comm. Dev. Dir.; 300 E. Pearl St.; 64701; Cass; P 9,700; (816) 380-8912; Fax (816) 380-8910; developdir@ci.harrisonville.mo.us; www.ci.harrisonville.mo.us

Independence • *Independence EDC* • Tom Lesnak; Pres.; 201 N. Forest Ave., Ste. 120; 64050; Jackson; P 116,800; (816) 252-5777; Fax (816) 252-5777; jmann@inedc.biz; www.inedc.biz

Joplin • *Joplin Bus. & Ind. Dev. Corp.* • Rob O'Brian CEcD; Pres.; 320 E. 4th St.; 64801; Jasper; P 118,600; (417) 624-4150; Fax (417) 624-4303; info@joplincc.com; www.joplinregionalpartnership.com

Kansas City Area

Clay County Eco. Dev. Cncl. • Jim Hampton; Exec. Dir.; 1251 NW Briarcliff Pkwy., Ste. 25; 64116; Clay; P 230,473; (816) 468-4989; Fax (816) 587-1996; info@clayedc.com; www.clayedc.com

Kansas City Area Dev. Cncl. • Robert J. Marcusse; Pres./CEO; 30 W. Pershing Rd., Ste. 200; 64108; Jackson; P 2,000,000; (816) 221-2121; (888) 99KC-ADC; Fax (816) 842-2865; kcadc@thinkKC.com; www.thinkKC.com

Platte County Eco. Dev. Cncl. Inc. • Burdette Fullerton; Exec. Dir.; 11724 N.W. Plz. Cir., Ste. 400; 64153; Platte; P 89,332; (816) 270-2119; Fax (816) 270-2135; pfullerton@plattecountyedc.com; www.plattecountyedc.com

Kearney • *Kearney Area Dev. Cncl.* • Jim Eldridge; Secy.; 100 E. Washington; P.O. Box 291; 64060; Clay; P 8,381; (816) 628-3343; jeldridge@ci.kearney.mo.us; www.kearneyadc.com

Lamar • *Barton County Comm. Dev. Corp.* • Robert Harrington; Eco. Dev. Dir.; 128 W. 10th St., Ste. 9; 64759; Barton; P 12,400; (417) 681-2500; Fax (417) 681-2501; rob@bartoncountycdc.org; www.bartoncountycdc.org

Lee's Summit • *Lee's Summit Eco. Dev. Cncl.* • Rick McDowell; Pres./CEO; 218 S.E. Main St.; 64063; Jackson; P 90,000; (816) 525-6617; Fax (816) 524-8851; tchace@leessummit.org; www.leessummit.org

Mexico • *City of Mexico Dept. of Eco. Dev.* • Russell Runge; Dir.; 300 N. Coal; 65265; Audrain; P 11,300; (573) 581-2100; Fax (573) 581-2305; rrunge@mexicomissouri.org; www.mexicomissouri.net

Moberly • *Moberly Area Eco. Dev. Corp.* • Corey J. Mehaffy; Pres.; 115 N. Williams; P.O. Box 549; 65270; Randolph; P 25,400; (660) 263-8811; (660) 998-0097; Fax (660) 263-8883; info@moberly-edc.com; www.moberly-edc.com

Nevada • *Eco. Dev. of City of Nevada* • Johnna Williams; Dir.; 110 S. Ash; 64772; Vernon; P 8,300; (417) 448-2700; Fax (417) 448-2707; jwilliams@nevadamo.org; www.nevadamo.org

Perryville • *Perry County Eco. Dev. Auth.* • Scott Sattler; Exec. Dir.; 112 W. Ste. Maries St.; P.O. Box 109; 63775; Perry; P 19,000; (573) 547-1097; Fax (573) 547-7327; perryida@perrycountymo.org; www.perrycountymo.org

Saint Charles • *Eco. Dev. Center of St. Charles County* • Gregory Prestemon; Pres./CEO; 5988 Mid Rivers Mall Dr.; 63304; St. Charles; P 385,600; (636) 441-6880; Fax (636) 441-6881; agordon@edcscc.com; www.edcscc.com

Saint Louis • *St. Louis Eco. Dev. Partnership* • Sheila M. Sweeney; CEO; 7733 Forsyth Blvd., Ste. 2300; 63105; St. Louis; P 1,000,000; (314) 615-7663; Fax (314) 615-7666; etriplett@stlpartnership.com; www.stlpartnership.com

Sikeston • *Sikeston Dept. of Eco. Dev.* • Ed Dust; Dir.; 128 N. New Madrid St.; 63801; New Madrid & Scott; P 28,200; (573) 471-2780; (800) 494-6476; Fax (573) 471-7564; ded@sikeston.org; www.sikeston.org

Springfield • *Dept. of Eco. Dev.* • Mary Lilly Smith; Dir.; 840 Boonville Ave.; 65802; Greene; P 167,000; (417) 864-1094; Fax (417) 864-1030; mlsmith@springfieldmo.gov; www.springfieldmo.gov

Springfield • *Springfield Reg. Eco. Partnership* • Ryan Mooney; Sr. V.P. of Eco. Dev.; 202 S. John Q. Hammons Pkwy.; P.O. Box 1687; 65801; Greene; P 456,500; (417) 862-5567; Fax (417) 862-1611; ryan@springfieldchamber.com; www.springfieldregion.com

Washington • *City of Washington* • Darren Lamb; Comm. & Eco. Dev. Dir.; 405 Jefferson St.; 63090; Franklin; P 14,000; (636) 390-1004; (636) 667-1000; Fax (636) 239-8945; dlamb@ci.washington.mo.us; www.washmoworks.com

Wright City • *Wright City Eco. Dev. Dept.* • Karen Girondo; Eco. Developer; P.O. Box 436; 63390; Warren; P 3,119; (636) 745-3101; Fax (636) 745-3119; econdevelop@wrightcity.org; www.wrightcity.org

Montana

Federal

U.S. SBA, Montana Dist. Ofc. • Wayne Gardella; Dist. Dir.; 10 W. 15th St., Ste. 1100; 59626; Lewis & Clark; P 1,005,141; (406) 441-1081; Fax (406) 441-1090; wayne.gardella@sba.gov; www.sba.gov/mt

State

Montana Ofc. of Eco. Dev. • John Rogers; Chief of Eco. Dev.; P.O. Box 200801; Helena; 59620; Lewis & Clark; P 1,005,141; (406) 444-5634; business@mt.gov; business.mt.gov

Communities

Colstrip • *Southeastern Montana Dev. Corp./Small Bus. Dev.* • Jim Atchison; Exec. Dir.; 6200 Main St.; P.O. Box 1935; 59323; Rosebud; P 14,000; (406) 748-2990; Fax (406) 748-2990; jatchison@semdc.org; www.semdc.org

Havre • *Bear Paw Dev. Corp.* • Paul Tuss; Exec. Dir.; 48 2nd Ave.; P.O. Box 170; 59501; Hill; P 16,600; (406) 265-9226; (888) 528-2327; Fax (406) 265-5602; mburchard@bearpaw.org; www.bearpaw.org

Kalispell • *Montana West Eco. Dev.* • Kellie Danielson; Pres./CEO; 314 Main St.; 59901; Flathead; P 90,900; (406) 257-7711; (888) 870-5440; Fax (406) 257-7772; info@dobusinessinmontana.com; www.dobusinessinmontana.com

Nebraska

Federal

U.S. SBA, Nebraska Dist. Ofc. • Leon J. Milobar; Dist. Dir.; 10675 Bedford Ave., Ste. 100; 68134; Douglas; P 1,855,525; (402) 221-4691; Fax (402) 221-3680; leon.milobar@sba.gov; www.sba.gov/ne

State

Nebraska Dept. of Eco. Dev. • Catherine Lang; Dir.; 301 Centennial Mall S.; P.O. Box 94666; Lincoln; 68509; Lancaster; P 1,855,525; (800) 426-6505; Fax (402) 471-3778; gary.hamer@nebraska.gov; www.neded.org

Communities

Alliance • *Box Butte Dev. Corp.* • Chelsie Herian; Exec. Dir.; 305 Box Butte Ave.; 69301; Box Butte; P 11,374; (308) 762-1800; Fax (308) 762-4919; info@boxbuttedevelopment.com; www.boxbuttedevelopment.com

Arnold • *Arnold EDC* • Sandy Hicks; Dir.; P.O. Box 376; 69120; Custer; P 680; (308) 848-2211; Fax (308) 848-2211; aedc@gpcom.net; www.arnoldne.org

Atkinson • *Atkinson Eco. Dev.* • Lou Ann Tooker; Dir. of Eco. Dev.; P.O. Box 519; 68713; Holt; P 1,245; (402) 925-5313; Fax (402) 925-5780; louann.tooker@atkinsonne.com; www.atkinsonne.com

Bassett • *Bassett Eco. Dev. Comm.* • Kristine Gale; Dir.; P.O. Box 383; 68714; Rock; P 700; (402) 684-3319; bassettcda@bassettnebr.com; www.bassettnebr.com

Cambridge • *Cambridge Eco. Dev. Bd.* • Ashley Rice-Gerlach; Dir.; 722 Patterson St.; P.O Box Q; 69022; Furnas; P 1,100; (308) 697-3711; Fax (308) 697-3253; edcity@swnebr.net; www.cambridgene.org

Center • *Knox County Dev. Ag.* • Matt Cerny; Dir.; P.O. Box 165; 68724; Knox; P 8,500; (402) 288-5619; (402) 358-0211; Fax (402) 288-5605; knoxcodevelopment@gpcom.net; www.knoxcountyeconomicdevelopment.com

Central City • *Merrick County Dev. Corp.* • Miles McGinnis; Dir.; City Hall; P.O. Box 418; 68826; Merrick; P 8,000; (308) 946-3806; Fax (308) 946-3334; CCEcDev@gmail.com; www.cc-ne.com

Chadron • *Nebraska Northwest Dev. Corp.* • Deb Cottier; Exec. Dir.; 706 W. 3rd St.; 69337; Dawes; (308) 432-4023; Fax (308) 432-6740; dcottier@gpcom.net; www.nndc.chadron-nebraska.com

Curtis • *Medicine Valley Eco. Dev. Corp.* • Doug Schultz; Pres.; 201 Garlick Ave.; P.O. Box 437; 69025; Frontier; P 800; (308) 367-4122; Fax (308) 367-4125; curtis@curtis-ne.com; www.medicinevalleyedc.com

Falls City • *Falls City Eco. Dev.* • Becki Cromer; Exec. Dir.; 1705 Stone St.; P.O. Box 574; 68355; Richardson; P 5,000; (402) 245-2105; Fax (402) 245-2106; info@fallscityedge.com; www.fallscityedge.com

Fremont • *Greater Fremont Dev. Cncl.* • Cecilia Harry CEcD; Exec. Dir.; 1005 E. 23rd St., Ste. 2; 68026; Dodge; P 26,400; (402) 753-8126; Fax (402) 727-2667; therese.hoyle@fremontecodev.org; www.fremontecodev.org

Geneva • *Fillmore County Dev. Corp.* • Patt Lentfer; Exec. Dir.; 1032 G St.; 68361; Fillmore; P 6,000; (402) 759-4910; Fax (402) 759-4455; lentfer.fcdc@genevamail.com; www.fillmorecountydevelopment.org

Gothenburg • *Gothenburg Comm. Dev. Ofc.* • Anne Anderson; Exec. Dir.; 1001 Lake Ave.; 69138; Dawson; P 4,000; (308) 537-3505; Fax (308) 537-2541; anne@gothenburgdelivers.com; www.gothenburgdelivers.com

Grand Island • *Grand Island Area Eco. Dev. Corp.* • Marlan Ferguson; Pres.; 308 N. Locust St., Ste. 400; P.O. Box 1151; 68802; Hall; P 50,000; (308) 381-7500; (800) 658-4283; Fax (308) 398-7205; giaedc@grandisland.org; www.grandisland.org

Hartington • *Hartington Comm. Dev. Corp.* • Carla Becker; Coord.; 107 W. State St.; P.O. Box 427; 68739; Cedar; P 1,640; (402) 254-6357; Fax (402) 254-6391; devcoor@hartel.net; www.ci.hartington.ne.us

Hastings • *Hastings Eco. Dev. Corp.* • Dave Rippe; Exec. Dir.; P.O. Box 1104; 68902; Adams; P 25,300; (402) 461-8403; Fax (402) 461-4400; drippe@hastingsedc.com; www.hastingsedc.com

Holdrege • *Phelps County Dev. Corp.* • Ron Tillery; Exec. Dir.; 502 East Ave., Ste. 201; P.O. Box 522; 68949; Phelps; P 9,000; (308) 995-4148; Fax (308) 995-4158; pcdc@phelpscountyne.com; www.phelpscountyne.com

Kearney • *Buffalo County Eco. Dev. Cncl.* • Darren Robinson; Pres.; 1007 2nd Ave.; P.O. Box 607; 68848; Buffalo; P 47,000; (308) 237-9346; info@edcbc.com; www.edcbc.com

Kimball • *City of Kimball Eco. Dev. Assn.* • 223 S. Chestnut; 69145; Kimball; P 2,400; (308) 235-3639; (888) 274-6004; Fax (308) 235-2971; econdev@megavision.com; www.kimballne.org

Lexington • *Dawson Area Dev.* • Jennifer McKeone; Exec. Dir.; 1501 Plum Creek Pkwy., Ste. 2B; 68850; Dawson; P 25,000; (308) 217-0008; (308) 217-0004; jen@dawsonareadevelopment.com; www.dawsonareadevelopment.com

Lincoln • *USDA Rural Dev. State Ofc.* • Joan Scheel; Bus. & Cooperative Programs Dir.; Ste. 308, Fed. Bldg.; 100 Centennial Mall N.; 68508; Lancaster; P 1,827,000; (402) 437-5594; (402) 437-5575; Fax (402) 437-5408; joan.scheel@ne.usda.gov; www.rd.usda.gov/ne

McCook • *McCook Eco. Dev. Corp.* • Kirk W. Dixon; Exec. Dir.; 402 Norris Ave., Ste. 301; 69001; Red Willow; P 8,000; (308) 345-1200; (800) 658-4213; Fax (308) 345-2152; angela@mccookne.org; www.mccookne.org

Nebraska City • *Nebraska City Area Eco. Dev. Corp.* • Dan Mauk; Exec. Dir.; 123 S. 8th Ave., Ste. 7; 68410; Otoe; P 7,200; (402) 873-4293; Fax (402) 873-4924; director@nebraskacityareaedc.org; www.nebraskacityareaedc.com

Norfolk • *Northeast Nebraska Eco. Dev. Dist.* • Tom Higginbotham Jr.; Exec. Dir.; 111 S. 1st; 68701; Madison; P 220,000; (402) 379-1150; Fax (402) 379-9207; thomash@nenedd.org; www.nenedd.org

North Platte • *North Platte Area Chamber & Dev. Corp.* • Megan McGown; V.P. of Eco. Dev.; 502 S. Dewey St.; 69101; Lincoln; P 30,000; (308) 532-4966; Fax (308) 532-4827; megan@nparea.com; www.nparea.com

Ogallala • *Keith County Area Dev.* • Travis Haggard; Exec. Dir.; 10 N. Spruce St., Ste. C; 69153; Keith; P 8,850; (308) 284-6623; Fax (308) 284-7057; travis.haggard@kcad.org; www.kcad.org

Ogallala • *West Central Neb. Dev. Dist.* • Karl Elmshaeuser; Exec. Dir.; 333 E. 2nd St.; P.O. Box 599; 69153; Keith; P 103,000; (308) 284-6077; Fax (308) 284-6070; info@west-central-nebraska.com; www.west-central-nebraska.com

Omaha • *Greater Omaha Eco. Dev. Partnership* • Rod Moseman; V.P. of Eco. Dev.; 1301 Harney St.; 68102; Douglas; P 840,000; (402) 346-5000; Fax (402) 346-7050; rmoseman@selectgreateromaha.com; www.selectgreateromaha.com

Omaha • *Sarpy County Eco. Dev. Corp.* • Toby Churchill; Exec. Dir.; 1301 Harney St.; 68102; Douglas; P 158,800; (402) 346-5000; Fax (402) 346-7050; tchurchill@selectgreateromaha.com; www.selectgreateromaha.com

Ord • *Valley County Eco. Dev.* • Kristina Foth; Dir.; 1514 K St.; 68862; Valley; P 4,200; (308) 728-7875; (877) 728-7875; Fax (308) 728-7691; kristinafoth@ordnebraska.com; www.ordnebraska.com

Randolph • *Randolph Comm. Club* • Vonnie Arens; Secy./Treas.; P.O. Box 624; 68771; Cedar; P 960; (402) 337-1234; va5a@yahoo.com; www.ci.randolph.ne.us

Ravenna • *Ravenna Eco. Dev.* • Dana Dennison; Exec. Dir.; 318 Grand Ave.; 68869; Buffalo; P 1,400; (308) 452-3133; economicdevelopment@myravenna.com; www.myravenna.com

Scottsbluff • *Twin Cities Dev. Assn. Inc.* • Rawnda Pierce; Exec. Dir.; 1620 Broadway; 69361; Scotts Bluff; P 37,000; (308) 632-2833; Fax (308) 633-2854; twincitiesinfo@tcdne.org; www.tcdne.org

Sidney • *Sidney/Cheyenne County Eco. Dev.* • Tina Hochwender; Eco. Dev. Dir.; 1115 13th Ave.; P.O. Box 79; 69162; Cheyenne; P 10,000; (308) 254-8455; (308) 254-4444; Fax (308) 254-3164; development@cityofsidney.org; www.cityofsidney.org

Wahoo • *Wahoo Area Eco. Dev.* • Doug Watts; Exec. Dir.; 640 N. Broadway; 68066; Saunders; P 4,500; (402) 443-4001; Fax (402) 443-3077; watts@wahoo.ne.us; www.wahoo.ne.us

Wayne • *Wayne Area Eco. Dev./Chamber/Main Street* • Wes Blecke; Exec. Dir.; 108 W. 3rd St.; P.O. Box 275; 68787; Wayne; P 5,000; (402) 375-2240; (866) 929-6363; Fax (402) 375-2246; info@wayneworks.org; www.wayneworks.org

West Point • *West Point Dev. Corp.* • Glen Prinz; Secy./Treas.; P.O. Box 265; 68788; Cuming; P 3,600; (402) 372-2495; drprinz@hotmail.com; www.ci.westpoint.ne.us

York • *York County Dev. Corp.* • Cassie Seagren; Exec. Dir.; 601 N. Lincoln Ave.; 68467; York; P 13,600; (402) 362-3333; (888) 733-9675; Fax (402) 362-3344; info@yorkdevco.com; www.yorkdevco.com

Nevada

Federal

U.S. SBA, *Nevada Dist. Ofc.* • Edward J. Cadena; Dist. Dir.; 300 S. 4th St., Ste. 400; 89101; Clark; P 2,758,931; (702) 388-6611; Fax (702) 388-6469; edward.cadena@sba.gov; www.sba.gov/nv

State

Nevada Governor's *Ofc. of Eco. Dev.* • Cory Hunt; Deputy Dir.; 808 W. Nye Ln.; Carson City; 89703; Carson City; P 2,839,000; (775) 687-9900; (800) 336-1600; Fax (775) 687-9924; success@diversifynevada.com; www.diversifynevada.com

Communities

Carson City • *Northern Nevada Dev. Auth.* • Robert C. Hooper; Exec. Dir.; 704 W. Nye Ln., Ste. 201; 89703; Carson City; P 150,000; (775) 883-4413; Fax (775) 883-0494; nnda@nnda.org; www.nnda.org

Elko • *Northeastern Nevada Reg. Dev. Auth.* • Pam Borda; Exec. Dir.; 1500 College Pkwy.; McMullen Hall #103; 89801; Elko; P 54,000; (775) 738-2100; (866) 937-3556; Fax (775) 738-7978; pam@nnrda.com; www.nnrda.com

Ely • *White Pine County Comm. & Econ. Dev.* • Elaine Blackham; 801 Clark St., Ste. 5; 89301; Clark; P 10,030; (775) 293-6592; Fax (775) 289-8860; edcoffice@whitepinecountynv.gov; www.whitepinecounty.net

Fallon • *Churchill Eco. Dev. Auth.* • Eric Grimes; Exec. Dir.; 448 W. Williams Ave., Ste. 103; P.O. Box 1236; 89407; Churchill; P 30,000; (775) 423-8587; Fax (775) 423-1759; kmaffi@ceda-nv.org; www.ceda-nv.org

Henderson • *Henderson Dev. Assoc.* • Scott Muelrath; Pres./CEO; 590 S. Boulder Hwy.; 89015; Clark; P 260,000; (702) 565-8951; Fax (702) 565-3115; info@hendersonchamber.com; www.hendersonchamber.com

Las Vegas • *City of Las Vegas, Eco. & Urban Dev. Dept.* • Bill Arent; Dir.; 495 S. Main St.; 89101; Clark; P 583,800; (702) 229-6551; Fax (702) 385-3128; edinfo@lasvegasnevada.gov; www.lasvegasnevada.gov

Las Vegas • *Nevada Dev. Auth.* • A. Somer Hollingsworth; Pres./CEO; 6700 Via Austi Pkwy., Ste. B; 89119; Clark; (702) 791-0000; (888) 466-8293; Fax (702) 796-6483; info@nevadadevelopment.org; www.nevadadevelopment.org

North Las Vegas • *City of North Las Vegas Eco. Dev. Div.* • Terri Sheridan; Admin.; 2250 Las Vegas Blvd. N., Ste. 910; 89030; Clark; P 190,000; (702) 633-1523; Fax (702) 633-7164; sheridant@cityofnorthlasvegas.com; www.cityofnorthlasvegas.com

Reno • *Eco. Dev. Auth. of Western Nevada* • Mike Kazmierski; Pres./CEO; 5190 Neil Rd., Ste. 110; 89502; Washoe; P 330,000; (775) 829-3700; (800) 256-9761; Fax (775) 829-3710; matteoni@edawn.org; www.edawn.org

New Hampshire

Federal

U.S. SBA, *New Hampshire Dist. Ofc.* • Greta Johansson; Dist. Dir.; 55 Pleasant St., Ste. 3101; 03301; Merrimack; P 1,320,718; (603) 225-1400; Fax (603) 225-1409; greta.johansson@sba.gov; www.sba.gov/nh

State

New Hampshire *Dept. of Resources & Eco. Dev.* • Carmen Lorentz; Dir.; 172 Pembroke Rd.; Concord; 03301; Merrimack; P 1; (603) 271-2341; Fax (603) 271-6784; lorna.colquhoun@dred.nh.gov; www.nheconomy.com

Communities

Concord • *City of Concord Comm. Dev. Dept.* • Carlos P.
Baia; Deputy City Mgr. - Dev.; City Hall; 41 Green St.; 03301;
Merrimack; P 43,000; (603) 225-8595; Fax (603) 228-2701;
communitydevelopment@concordnh.gov; www.concordnh.gov

Concord • *Capital Reg. Dev. Cncl.* • Stephen Heavener; Exec. Dir.;
91 N. State St., Ste. 101; P.O. Box 664; 03302; Merrimack; P 200,000;
(603) 496-1875; Fax (603) 226-3588; sheavener@crdc-nh.com;
www.crdc-nh.com

Dover • *City of Dover* • Daniel J. Barufaldi; Eco. Dev. Dir.; Eco. Dev.
Dept.; 288 Central Ave.; 03820; Strafford; P 30,000; (603) 516-6043;
(603) 516-1560; Fax (603) 516-6049; d.barufaldi@dover.nh.gov;
www.dover.nh.gov

Exeter • *Exeter Dev. Comm.* • Sylvia von Aulock; Town Planner; 10
Front St.; 03833; Rockingham; P 14,500; (603) 773-6114; Fax (603)
772-4709; svonaulock@town.exeter.nh.us; www.town.exeter.nh.us

Keene • *Monadnock Eco. Dev. Corp.* • John G. Dugan; Pres./CEO;
51 Railroad St., Ste. 101; 03431; Cheshire; P 23,000; (603) 352-
4939; Fax (603) 357-4917; info@monadnock-development.org;
www.monadnock-development.org

Manchester • *Manchester Eco. Dev. Ofc.* • Jay Minkarah; Dir.; 1 City
Hall Plz.; 03101; Hillsborough; P 109,500; (603) 624-6505; Fax (603)
624-6308; econdev@manchesternh.gov; www.yourmanchesternh.com

Peterborough • *see Keene*

Portsmouth • *Granite State Dev. Corp.* • Alan Abraham; Pres.; One
Cate St., 3rd Flr.; P.O. Box 1491; 03802; Rockingham; P 1,300,000;
(603) 436-0009; Fax (603) 436-5547; lpowers@granitestatedev.com;
www.granitestatedev.com

Rochester • *City of Rochester* • Kenneth Ortmann; Planning
& Dev. Dir.; 31 Wakefield St.; 03867; Strafford; P 30,000; (603)
335-1338; Fax (603) 335-7585; kenn.ortmann@rochesternh.net;
www.rochesternh.net

Wilton • *Wilton Main Street Assoc.* • Bart Hunter; Mgr.; P.O. Box
333; 03086; Hillsborough; P 3,900; (603) 654-3020; wmsa@tds.net;
www.mainstreet.wilton.nh.us

New Jersey

Federal

***U.S. SBA, New Jersey Dist. Ofc.* •** Alfred Titone; Dist. Dir.; Two
Gateway Center, Ste. 1501; 07102; Essex; P 8,864,590; (973) 645-
2434; Fax (973) 645-6265; alfred.titone@sba.gov; www.sba.gov/nj

State

***New Jersey Eco. Dev. Auth.* •** Michele Brown; CEO; 36 W. State St.;
P.O. Box 990; Trenton; 08625; Mercer; P 8,864,590; (609) 858-6700;
customercare@njeda.com; www.njeda.com

Communities

Absecon • *Eco. Dev. Comm. of City Cncl.* • Lynn Caterson; Cncl.
Pres.; Municipal Complex; 500 Mill Rd.; 08201; Atlantic; P 7,800;
(609) 641-0663; Fax (609) 645-5098; info@absecon-newjersey.org;
www.absecon-newjersey.org

Asbury Park • *Asbury Park Ofc. of Eco. Dev.* • Michael Capabianco;
Town Mgr.; 1 Municipal Plaza; 07712; Monmouth; P 16,200; (732) 775-
2100; Fax (732) 775-1483; michael.capabianco@cityofasburypark.com;
www.cityofasburypark.com

Atlantic City • *Atlantic City Div. of Planning* • Elizabeth Terenik;
Dir.; City Hall, Rm. 506; 1301 Bacharach Blvd.; 08401; Atlantic;
P 40,000; (609) 347-5404; (609) 347-5300; Fax (609) 347-5345;
eterenik@cityofatlanticcity.org; www.cityofatlanticcity.org

Atlantic City • *Metropolitan Bus. & Citizens Assoc.* • Mr. Gary Hill;
Exec. Dir.; 1616 Pacific Ave., 6th Flr.; 08401; Atlantic; P 275,000;
(609) 348-1903; Fax (609) 344-5244; comments@acmetbiz.com;
www.mbcanj.com

Bayville • *Berkeley Twp. Eco. Dev. Comm.* • Berkeley Municipal
Bldg.; P.O. Box B; 08721; Ocean; P 41,700; (732) 244-7400; Fax (732)
505-0145; administrator@twp.berkeley.nj.us; www.twp.berkeley.nj.us

Belvidere • *Warren County Eco. Dev. Comm.* • Betty Schultheis;
Chair; 165 County Rte. 519 S.; 07823; Warren; P 108,700; (908)
475-6580; Fax (908) 475-6577; publicinfo@co.warren.nj.us;
www.warrenecdev.com

Bridgeton • *City of Bridgeton Dept. of Dev. & Planning* • Kevin
Rabago; Dir.; 50 E. Broad St.; 181 E. Commerce St.; 08302;
Cumberland; P 19,000; (856) 451-3407; Fax (856) 455-7421;
rabagok@cityofbridgeton.com; www.cityofbridgeton.com

Bridgeton • *Cumberland Dev. Corp.* • Anthony M. Stanzione; Exec.
Dir.; P.O. Box 1021; 08302; Cumberland; P 157,000; (856) 451-4200;
(609) 364-5528; Fax (856) 453-9795; cdc@cdcnj.com; www.cdcnj.com

Bridgewater • *Somerset County Bus. Partnership* • Michael
Kerwin; Pres./CEO; 360 Grove St. at Rte. 22 E.; 08807; Somerset;
P 324,600; (908) 218-4300; Fax (908) 722-7823; jmaddocks@scbp.org;
www.scbp.org

Buena Vista • *Buena Vista Eco. Dev.* • Chuck Chiarello; Mayor;
890 Harding Hwy.; P.O. Box 605; 08310; Atlantic; P 7,600; (856)
697-2100; Fax (856) 697-8651; mayor@buenavistanj.com;
www.buenavistatownship.org

Camden • *Camden Redev. Agency* • Saundra Ross Johnson;
Exec. Dir.; 520 Market St., Ste. 1300; City Hall; P.O. Box 95120;
08101; Camden; P 87,000; (856) 757-7600; Fax (856) 964-2262;
CRAInfo@ci.camden.nj.us; www.camdenredevelopment.com

Camden • *South Jersey Port Corp.* • Kevin Castagnola; Exec.
Dir./CEO; 101 Joseph A. Balzano Blvd.; 08103; Camden; (856)
757-4969; Fax (856) 757-4903; kcastagnola@southjerseyport.com;
www.southjerseyport.com

Cape May Court House • *Cape May County Planning Dept.* •
Leslie Gimeno; Dir.; 4 Moore Rd.; 08210; Cape May; P 97,300; (609)
465-1080; Fax (609) 463-0347; planningbd@co.cape-may.nj.us;
www.capemaycountynj.gov

Cherry Hill • *Cherry Hill Twp. Community Dev.* • Paul Stridick
AIA; Dir.; 820 Mercer St., Rm. 202; 08002; Camden; P 71,000;
(856) 488-7870; Fax (856) 661-4746; pstridick@chtownship.com;
www.cherryhill-nj.com

Clifton • *Clifton Eco. Dev.* • Harry Swanson; Eco. Dev. Dir.; City Hall;
900 Clifton Ave.; 07013; Passaic; P 84,200; (973) 470-5200; Fax (973)
470-9456; hswanson@cliftonnj.org; www.cliftonnj.org

Columbia • *Knowlton Twp. Eco. Dev.* • Municipal Bldg.; 628 Rte.
94; 07832; Warren; P 3,055; (908) 496-4816; Fax (908) 496-8144;
deputyclerk@knowlton-nj.com; www.knowlton-nj.com

Cranford • *Union County Eco. Dev. Corp. [UCEDC]* • Maureen Tinen; Pres.; 75 Chestnut St.; 07016; Union; P 536,500; (908) 527-1166; Fax (908) 527-1207; info@ucedc.com; www.ucedc.com

Deptford • *Deptford Twp. Planning & Zoning* • Donald Banks; Dir. of Comm. Dev.; 1011 Cooper St.; 08096; Gloucester; P 31,000; (856) 686-2218; (856) 845-5300; Fax (856) 848-8227; dbanks@deptford-nj.org; www.deptford-nj.org

East Orange • *East Orange Div. of Eco. Dev.* • Valerie Jackson; Dir.; 44 City Hall Plz.; Lower Level; 07018; Essex; P 65,000; (973) 266-5141; Fax (862) 930-7804; valerie.jackson@eastorange-nj.gov; www.eastorange-nj.gov

East Orange • *Dept. of Eco. Dev., Training & Employment* • Anibal Ramos; Dir.; 50 S. Clinton St.; 07018; Essex; P 784,000; (973) 395-8400; Fax (973) 395-8493; mcollins@dedte.essexcountynj.org; www.essex-countynj.org

Edgewater Park • *Edgewater Park Redev. Comm.* • 400 Delanco Rd.; 08010; Burlington; P 7,800; (609) 877-2050; Fax (609) 877-2308; mpeak@edgewaterpark-nj.com; www.edgewaterpark-nj.com

Edison • *New Jersey Alliance for Action* • Lynn Schwalje; Ofc. Mgr.; Raritan Center Plz. II; 91 Fieldcrest Ave., Ste. A24; 08837; Middlesex; P 8,792,000; (732) 225-1180; Fax (732) 225-4694; lschwalje@allianceforaction.com; www.allianceforaction.com

Egg Harbor City • *Egg Harbor City Planning, Zoning & Bldg. Depts.* • Tim Michel; City Planner; 500 London Ave.; 08215; Atlantic; P 4,300; (609) 965-1616; (609) 965-0081; Fax (609) 965-0715; donnah@eggharborcity.org; www.eggharborcity.org

Elizabeth • *Planning & Comm. Dev. Dept.* • Phyllis Reich; Dir. of Planning; City Hall; 50 Winfield Scott Plaza; 07201; Union; P 126,000; (908) 820-4000; Fax (908) 820-8624; preich@elizabethnj.org; www.elizabethnj.org

Elizabeth • *Elizabeth Dev. Co.* • Bill O'Dea; Exec. Dir.; 205 First St., Ste. 114; 07206; Union; P 126,000; (908) 289-0262; Fax (908) 558-1142; rluciano@edcnj.org; www.edcnj.org

Florence • *Florence Twp. Eco. Dev. Cncl.* • Tom McCue; Chair; Municipal Complex; 711 Broad St.; 08518; Burlington; P 11,000; (609) 499-2525; Fax (609) 499-1186; economicdevelopment@florence-nj.gov; www.florence-nj.gov

Florham Park • *Morris County Eco. Dev. Corp.* • James D. Jones; Exec. Dir.; 325 Columbia Tpke., Ste. 101; 07932; Morris; P 492,200; (973) 539-8270; Fax (973) 377-0859; jjones@morriscountyedc.org; www.morriscountyedc.org

Forked River • *Lacey Twp. Dept. of Comm. Dev.* • Chris Reid; Dir.; 818 W. Lacey Rd.; Municipal Bldg.; 08731; Ocean; P 27,700; (609) 693-1100; Fax (609) 693-8466; lacey.commdev@laceytownship.org; www.laceytownship.org

Freehold • *Monmouth County Dept. of Eco. Dev. & Tourism* • John Ciufo & Amy Fitzgerald; Co-Dirs.; 1 E. Main St.; 07728; Monmouth; P 655,000; (732) 431-7470; Fax (732) 294-5930; john.ciufo@co.monmouth.nj.us; www.visitmonmouth.com

Galloway • *Galloway Twp. Eco. Dev. Advisory Comm.* • Tiffany Cuviello; Twp. Planner; 300 E. Jimmie Leeds Rd.; 08205; Atlantic; P 37,200; (609) 652-3700; Fax (609) 652-1967; tcuviello@gtnj.org; www.gtnj.org

Hamilton • *Twp. of Hamilton Dept. of Tech. & Eco. Dev.* • Martin Flynn; Dir.; 2090 Greenwood Ave.; 08650; Mercer; P 88,500; (609) 890-3519; Fax (609) 890-3876; mflynn@hamiltonnj.com; www.hamiltonnj.com

Hillsborough • *Hillsborough Twp. Eco. & Bus. Dev. Comm.* • Gene Strupinsky; Bus. Advocate; 379 S. Branch Rd.; 08844; Somerset; P 36,600; (908) 369-4313; Fax (908) 369-3954; ebdc@hillsborough-nj.org; www.hillsboroughbusiness.org

Jersey City • *Jersey City Eco. Dev. Corp.* • Steve Lipski; CEO; 30 Montgomery St., Rm. 820; 07302; Hudson; P 248,000; (201) 333-7797; Fax (201) 333-9323; bwilson@jcedc.org; www.jcedc.org

Jersey City • *Hudson County Eco. Dev. Corp.* • Elizabeth Spinelli; Exec. Dir.; 257 Cornelison Ave., 7th Flr.; 07302; Hudson; P 634,000; (201) 369-4370; Fax (201) 369-4371; director@hudsonedc.org; www.hudsonedc.org

Kearny • *Kearny Enterprise Zone/Dev. Corp.* • John Peneda; Dept. Head; Town Hall Annex; 410 Kearny Ave.; 07032; Hudson; P 41,700; (201) 955-7905; (201) 955-7981; Fax (201) 998-5171; jpeneda@kearnynj.org; www.kearnynj.org

Lakewood • *Lakewood Dev. Corp.* • Patricia Komsa; Exec. Dir.; 231 3rd St.; 08701; Ocean; P 54,000; (732) 364-2500; Fax (732) 994-4574; pkomsa@lakewoodnj.gov; www.lakewoodnj.gov

Long Branch • *Long Branch Ofc. of Comm. & Eco. Dev.* • Jacob Jones; Dir.; 228 Broadway, 2nd Flr.; 07740; Monmouth; P 31,000; (732) 923-2040; (732) 923-2043; Fax (732) 263-0218; jjones@longbranch.org; www.visitlongbranch.com

Manalapan • *Manalapan Twp. Eco. Dev. Comm.* • Tara Lovrich; Admin.; 120 Rte. 522; Municipal Complex; 07726; Monmouth; P 39,000; (732) 446-8305; Fax (732) 446-9615; admin2@twp.manalapan.nj.us; www.mtnj.org

Mays Landing • *Hamilton Twp. Planning & Eco. Dev.* • Phil Sartorio; Dir.; 6101 13th St.; 08330; Atlantic; P 26,000; (609) 625-4762; (609) 625-1511; Fax (609) 909-1348; psartorio@townshipofhamilton.com; www.townshipofhamilton.com

Mickleton • *East Greenwich Twp. Enterprise Comm.* • James Watson; Dir.; 159 Democrat Rd.; 08056; Gloucester; P 5,430; (856) 423-0654; Fax (856) 224-0296; jameswatson@eastgreenwichnj.com; www.eastgreenwichnj.com

Millville • *Cumberland County Improvement Auth.* • Gerard Velazquez III; Exec. Dir.; 2 N. High St.; 08332; Cumberland; P 156,900; (856) 825-3700; Fax (856) 776-5391; jvelazquez@ccia-net.com; www.cumberlandyes.com

Millville • *Millville Comm. Dev.* • Samantha Silvers; Admin.; City Hall, 12 S. High St.; P.O. Box 609; 08332; Cumberland; P 28,000; (856) 825-7000; samantha.silvers@millvillenj.gov; www.millvillenj.gov

Monmouth Junction • *South Brunswick Eco. Dev. Committee* • Dan Frankel; Chrmn.; Planning Dept.; 540 Ridge Rd.; 08852; Middlesex; P 42,000; (732) 329-4000; Fax (732) 274-2084; www.sbtnj.net

Moorestown • *Moorestown Dept. of Comm. Dev.* • Raymond C. Holshue; Dir.; 111 W. Second St.; 08057; Burlington; P 19,000; (856) 914-3021; Fax (856) 914-3081; rholshue@moorestown.nj.us; www.moorestown.nj.us

New Brunswick • *New Brunswick Dev. Corp.* • Christopher Paladino; Pres.; 120 Albany St. Tower 1, 7th Flr.; 08901; Middlesex; P 55,200; (732) 249-2220; Fax (732) 249-4671; mluongo@devco.org; www.devco.org

New Brunswick • *Middlesex County Ofc. of Eco. & Bus. Dev.* • Kathaleen Shaw; Dept. Dir.; 75 Bayard St.; 08901; Middlesex; P 836,000; (732) 745-4379; Fax (732) 745-2568; economicdevelopment@co.middlesex.nj.us; www.co.middlesex.nj.us

Northfield • *Atlantic County Ofc. of Planning & Reg. Dev.* • John Peterson; Dept. Head; Rte. 9 & Dolphin Ave.; P.O. Box 719; 08225; Atlantic; P 276,000; (609) 645-5898; (609) 343-2313; Fax (609) 645-5836; gilmore_linda@aclink.org; www.aclink.org

Old Bridge • *Old Bridge Twp./Mayor's Ofc. of Eco. Dev.* • Steve Mamakas; Dir.; 1 Old Bridge Plz.; 08857; Middlesex; P 66,000; (732) 607-7920; Fax (732) 607-7957; obdeo@oldbridge.com; www.oldbridge.com

Palmyra • *Burlington County Eco. Dev. & Reg. Planning* • Mark Remsa; Dir.; P.O. Box 6; 08065; Burlington; P 423,394; (609) 265-5055; Fax (609) 265-5006; economicdevelopment@bcbridges.org; www.co.burlington.nj.us

Paramus • *Commerce & Ind. Assn. of N. J.* • John Galandak; Pres.; S. 61 Paramus Rd.; 07652; Bergen; P 8,700,000; (201) 368-2100; Fax (201) 368-3438; info@cianj.org; www.cianj.org

Paterson • *City of Paterson Dept. of Eco. Dev.* • Ruben Gomez; Dir. of Eco. Dev.; 125 Ellison St.; 07505; Passaic; P 146,200; (973) 321-1220; Fax (973) 321-1202; rgomez@patersonnj.gov; www.patersonnj.gov

Perth Amboy • *Ofc. of Eco. Dev./Enterprise Zone* • Roxana Troche; Coord.; 260 High St.; 08861; Middlesex; P 52,000; (732) 442-6421; Fax (732) 826-1160; rtroche@perthamboy.nj.us; www.ci.perthamboy.nj.us

Plainfield • *Plainfield Ofc. of Eco. Dev.* • Carlos N. Sanchez; Deputy City Admin.; 515 Watchung Ave.; City Hall, 2nd Flr.; 07060; Union; P 51,000; (908) 226-2513; (908) 753-3602; Fax (908) 753-3679; jeannette.aparicio@plainfieldnj.gov; www.plainfieldnj.gov

Rahway • *Rahway Comm. Dev./Eco. Dev.* • Jacqueline Foushee; Dir.; 1 City Hall Plz.; 07065; Union; P 28,000; (732) 827-2176; Fax (732) 680-1375; jfoushee@cityofrahway.com; www.cityofrahway.com

Rutherford • *Rutherford Eco. Dev. Comm.* • Jack Manzo; 176 Park Ave.; 07070; Bergen; P 18,400; (201) 460-3001; Fax (201) 460-3003; jmanzo@rutherford-nj.com; www.rutherford-nj.com

Swedesboro • *Pureland Ind. Complex* • Charles J. Walters; V.P.; 545 Beckett Rd., Ste. 204; 08085; Gloucester; P 7,000; (856) 467-2333; Fax (856) 467-5552; cwalters@pureland.com; www.purelandindustrialcomplex.com

Totowa • *Passaic County Dept. of Planning & Eco. Dev.* • Michael La Place; Dir.; 930 Riverview Dr., Ste. 250; 07512; Passaic; P 508,900; (973) 569-4040; Fax (973) 812-3450; ecodev@passaiccountynj.org; www.passaiccountynj.org

Trenton • *Div. of Eco. Dev.* • Diana Rogers; Dir.; City of Trenton; 319 E. State St.; 08608; Mercer; P 84,900; (609) 989-3512; (609) 989-3518; Fax (609) 989-4243; crobinson@trentonnj.org; www.trentonnj.org

Trenton • *Mercer County Ofc. of Eco. Opportunity* • Elizabeth Maher Muoio; Dir.; Mercer County Admin. Bldg., 640 S. Broad St.; P.O. Box 8068; 08650; Mercer; P 366,500; (609) 989-6555; Fax (609) 695-4943; elizabethm@mercercounty.org; www.mercercounty.org

Union City • *Union City Comm. Dev. Agency* • Erin Knoedler; Dir.; 3715 Palisade Ave.; 07087; Hudson; P 66,500; (201) 348-2765; (201) 348-5733; Fax (201) 348-9069; eknoedler@ucnj.com; www.ucnj.com

Vineland • *Vineland Eco. Dev.* • Sandra Forosisky; Dir.; City Hall; 640 E. Wood St., 4th Flr.; 08360; Cumberland; P 61,000; (856) 794-4100; economicdevelopment@vinelandcity.org; www.vinelandbusiness.com

Voorhees • *Voorhees Twp. Eco. Dev.* • Mario DiNatale; Dir. of Comm. & Eco. Dev.; 2400 Voorhees Town Center; 08043; Camden; P 30,390; (856) 882-5263; (856) 882-5263; Fax (856) 882-5263; mdinatale@voorheesnj.com; www.voorheesprospector.com

Wayne • *Wayne Township Eco. Dev. Comm.* • Linda Lutz; Twshp. Planner; 475 Valley Rd.; 07470; Passaic; P 55,000; (973) 694-1800; Fax (973) 694-8136; llutz@waynetownship.com; www.waynetownship.com

West Deptford • *Gloucester County Eco. Dev.* • Tom Bianco; Dir.; 115 Budd Blvd.; 08096; Gloucester; P 288,300; (856) 384-6930; (856) 384-6963; Fax (856) 384-6938; tbianco@co.gloucester.nj.us; www.gloucestercountynj.gov

West Milford • *West Milford Planning Dept.* • 1480 Union Valley Rd.; 07480; Passaic; P 27,000; (973) 728-2796; Fax (973) 728-2843; planningboard@westmilford.org; www.westmilford.org

West Orange • *Downtown West Orange Alliance* • Megan Brill; Exec. Dir.; 66 Main St.; 07052; Essex; P 45,000; (973) 325-4109; Fax (973) 325-6359; downtown@westorange.org; www.downtownwo.com

Westfield • *Downtown Westfield Corp.* • Shery Cronin; Exec. Dir.; 105 Elm St.; 07090; Union; P 31,000; (908) 789-9444; Fax (908) 789-7550; s.cronin@westfieldtoday.com; www.westfieldtoday.com

Woodbridge • *WEDCO* • Marta Lefsky; Dir.; 1 Main St., 3rd Flr.; 07095; Middlesex; P 100,000; (732) 602-6029; Fax (732) 602-6038; planninganddevelopment@twp.woodbridge.nj.us; www.twp.woodbridge.nj.us

New Mexico

Federal

U.S. SBA, New Mexico Dist. Ofc. • John C. Woosley; Dist. Dir.; P.O. Box 2206; 87103; Bernalillo; P 2,085,538; (505) 248-8225; Fax (505) 248-8245; john.woosley@sba.gov; www.sba.gov/nm

State

State of New Mexico Eco. Dev. Dept. • Jon Barela; Cabinet Secy.; 1100 S. St. Francis Dr.; Santa Fe; 87505; Santa Fe; P 2,085,538; (505) 827-0300; (800) 374-3061; Fax (505) 827-0328; edd.info@state.nm.us; www.gonm.biz

Communities

Albuquerque • *Albuquerque Eco. Dev. Inc.* • Gary Tonjes; Pres.; 851 University Blvd. S.E., Ste. 203; 87106; Bernalillo; P 801,000; (505) 246-6200; (800) 451-2933; Fax (505) 246-6219; info@abq.org; www.abq.org

Belen • *Belen Eco. Dev. Corp.* • Andrew Camillo; Dir.; 100 S. Main St.; 87002; Valencia; P 7,100; (505) 966-2745; Fax (505) 966-2745; andrew.camillo@belen-nm.gov; www.belen-nm.gov

Carlsbad • *Carlsbad Dept. of Dev.* • John Waters; Exec. Dir.; 400-2 Cascades Ave., Ste. 201; 88220; Eddy; P 55,000; (575) 887-6562; Fax (575) 885-0818; jwaters@developcarlsbad.org; www.developcarlsbad.org

Farmington • *San Juan Eco. Dev. Svc.* • Margaret McDaniel; Dir.; 5101 College Blvd.; 87402; San Juan; P 126,208; (505) 566-3720; (800) 854-5053; Fax (505) 566-3698; sjeds@sanjuaneds.com; www.sanjuaneds.com

Gallup • *NW New Mexico Cncl. of Governments* • Jeff Kiely; Exec. Dir.; 106 W. Aztec Ave.; 87301; McKinley; P 236,000; (505) 722-4327; Fax (505) 722-9211; jkiely@nwnmcog.org; www.nwnmcog.com

EDC

Grants • *Cibola Communities Eco. Dev. Found.* • Eileen Chavez Yarborough; Exec. Dir.; 701 E. Roosevelt Ave.; P.O. Box 277; 87020; Cibola; P 27,000; (505) 287-6685; Fax (505) 287-2125; eileen@cibolaedc.com; www.cibolaedc.com

Hobbs • *Eco. Dev. Corp. of Lea County* • Steve Vierck; Pres./CEO; 200 E. Broadway, Ste. A201; P.O. Box 1376; 88241; Lea; P 65,000; (575) 397-2039; (800) 443-2236; Fax (575) 392-2300; svierck@edclc.org; www.edclc.org

Las Cruces • *MVEDA* • Davin Lopez; Pres./CEO; 277 E. Amador, Ste. 304; P.O. Box 1299; 88004; P 189,000; (505) 525-2852; (800) 523-6833; Fax (505) 523-5707; info@mveda.com; www.mveda.com

Los Alamos • *Los Alamos Commerce & Dev. Corp.* • Don Wright; Team Leader; 190 Central Park Sq.; P.O. Box 1206; 87544; Los Alamos; P 18,000; (505) 661-4854; Fax (505) 662-0099; donw@losalamos.org; www.locateinlosalamos.com

Portales • *Roosevelt County Comm. Dev. Corp.* • Greg Fisher CEcD; Exec. Dir.; 100 S. Ave. A; 88130; Roosevelt; P 18,500; (505) 356-5354; (800) 635-8036; Fax (505) 356-8542; economicdevelopment@portalesnm.org; www.goportales.com

Raton • *Raton Eco. Dev. Cncl.* • 100 Clayton Rd.; 87740; Colfax; P 6,600; (505) 445-3689; ratonchamber@bacavalley.com; www.raton.info

Rio Rancho • *AMREP Southwest Inc.* • Louie Maldonado; V.P.; 333 Rio Rancho Blvd. N.E., Ste. 400; 87124; Sandoval; P 94,000; (505) 892-9200; Fax (505) 896-9180; amrepsales@aswinc.com; www.amrepsw.com

Rio Rancho • *Sandoval Eco. Alliance* • Jami Grindatto; Pres./CEO; 1201 Rio Rancho Blvd., Ste. C; 87124; Sandoval; P 137,600; (505) 891-4305; info@innovatesandoval.com; sandovaleconomicalliance.org

Roswell • *Roswell-Chaves County EDC* • Bob Donnell; Exec. Dir.; 131 W. Second St.; P.O. Box 849; 88202; Chaves; P 61,382; (505) 622-1975; Fax (505) 624-6870; rdonnell1@chavescounty.net; www.chavescounty.net

Santa Fe • *Santa Fe Eco. Dev. Div.* • Fabian Trujillo; Dir.; 120 S Federal Place, Rm. 314; 87501; Santa Fe; P 148,700; (505) 955-6912; selectsantafe@santafenm.gov; santafebiz.org

Silver City • *Silver City Comm. Dev. Dept.* • Peter Russell; Dir.; 1203 N. Hudson St.; P.O. Box 1188; 88061; Grant; P 11,000; (575) 534-6392; tsccomdevdir@qwestoffice.net; www.townofsilvercity.org

Tucumcari • *Greater Tucumcari Eco. Dev. Corp.* • Patrick Vanderpool; Exec. Dir.; 1500 W. Tucumcari Blvd.; P.O. Box 1392; 88401; Quay; P 6,000; (575) 461-4079; Fax (575) 461-1838; patv@tucumcari.biz; www.tucumcari.biz

New York

Federal

U.S. SBA, Buffalo Dist. Ofc. • Franklin J. Sciortino; Dist. Dir.; 130 S. Elmwood Ave., Ste. 540; 14202; Erie; P 19,570,261; (716) 551-4301; Fax (716) 551-4418; franklin.sciortino@sba.gov; www.sba.gov/ny

U.S. SBA, New York Dist. Ofc. • 26 Federal Plaza, Ste. 3100; 10278; New York; P 19,570,261; (212) 264-4354; Fax (212) 264-4963; nydo@sba.gov; www.sba.gov/ny

U.S. SBA, Syracuse Dist. Ofc. • Bernard Paprocki; Dist. Dir.; 224 Harrison St., 5th Flr.; 13202; Onondaga; P 19,570,261; (315) 471-9393; Fax (315) 471-9288; bernard.paprocki@sba.gov; www.sba.gov/ny/syracuse

State

Empire State Dev. • Kenneth Adams; Pres./CEO; 625 Broadway; Albany; 12245; Albany; P 19,570,261; (518) 292-5100; cmccann@esd.ny.gov; www.empire.state.ny.us

Communities

Albany • *Center for Eco. Growth Inc.* • Andrew Kennedy; Pres./CEO; 39 N. Pearl St., Ste. 100; 12207; Albany; P 309,400; (518) 465-8975; Fax (518) 465-6681; ceg@ceg.org; www.ceg.org

Albany • *NYS Eco. Dev. Cncl.* • Brian McMahon; Exec. Dir.; 111 Washington Ave., 6th Flr.; 12210; Albany; P 19,600,000; (518) 426-4058; Fax (518) 426-4059; eaton@nysedc.org; www.nysedc.org

Amsterdam • *Amsterdam Ind. Dev. Agency* • Jody Zakrevsky; Exec. Dir.; 61 Church St.; 12010; Montgomery; P 18,600; (518) 842-5011; Fax (518) 843-2862; syutes@amsterdamny.gov; www.amsterdamny.gov

Auburn • *City of Auburn Ofc. of Plan. & Eco. Dev.* • Jennifer Haines; Dir.; Memorial City Hall; 24 South St.; 13021; Cayuga; P 27,700; (315) 255-4115; Fax (315) 253-0282; jhaines@auburnny.gov; www.auburnny.gov

Babylon • *Town of Babylon/Ind. Dev. Ag.* • Matt McDonough; CEO; 47 W. Main, Ste. 3; 11702; Suffolk; P 250,000; (631) 587-3679; Fax (631) 587-3675; info@babylonida.org; www.babylonida.org

Batavia • *Genessee County Eco. Dev. Center* • Steven G. Hyde; Pres./CEO; 99 MedTech Dr., Ste. 106; 14020; Genesee; P 60,000; (585) 343-4866; Fax (585) 343-0848; gcedc@gcedc.com; www.gcedc.com

Bath • *Steuben County Ind. Dev. Agency* • James Johnson; Exec. Dir.; 7234 Rte. 54 N.; P.O. Box 393; 14810; Steuben; P 98,900; (607) 776-3316; Fax (607) 776-5039; scida@steubencountyida.com; www.steubencountyida.com

Belmont • *Allegany County Ofc. of Dev.* • H. Kier Dirlam; Planner; Crossroad Commerce Conf. Center; 6087 State Rte. 19 N., Ste. 100; 14813; Allegany; P 49,000; (585) 268-7472; (800) 893-9484; Fax (585) 268-7473; dirlamhk@alleganyco.com; www.alleganyco.com

Binghamton Area

Broome County Ind. Dev. Agency • Richard D'Attilio; Exec. Dir.; 60 Hawley St., 5th Flr.; P.O. Box 1510; 13902; Broome; P 200,600; (607) 584-9000; Fax (607) 584-9009; pjd@bcida.com; www.bcida.com

Empire State Dev.-Southern Tier • 44 Hawley St., Ste. 1508; State Office Bldg.; 13901; Broome; P 653,000; (607) 721-8605; Fax (607) 721-8613; nys-southerntier@esd.ny.gov; www.empire.state.ny.us

NYS Trade Adjust. Asst. Ctr. • Louis G. McKeage; Dir.; 81 State St., Ste. 4; 13901; Broome; (607) 771-0875; Fax (607) 724-2404; information@nystaac.org; www.nystaac.org

Buffalo Area

Empire State Dev.-Western NY Region • Christopher Schoepflin; Reg. Dir.; 95 Perry St., Ste. 500; 14203; Erie; P 2,500,000; (716) 846-8200; Fax (716) 846-8260; nys-westernny@esd.ny.gov; www.empire.state.ny.us

Erie County Ofc. of Eco. Dev. • Dan Barry; Dep. Commissioner of Eco. Dev.; Edward A. Rath County Ofc. Bldg.; 95 Franklin St., 10th Flr.; 14202; Erie; P 952,000; (716) 858-8390; Fax (716) 858-7248; daniel.barry@erie.gov; www.erie.gov

Invest Buffalo Niagara • Thomas Kucharski; Pres./CEO; 257 W. Genesee St., Ste. 600; 14202; Erie; P 1,300,000; (716) 842-1330; (800) 916-9073; Fax (716) 842-1724; tkucharski@buffaloniagara.org; www.buffaloniagara.org

Canandaigua • *Ontario County Eco. Dev.* • Michael J. Manikowski; Eco. Developer; 20 Ontario St., Ste. 106-B; 14424; Ontario; P 108,000; (585) 396-4460; Fax (585) 396-4594; diane.foster@co.ontario.ny.us; www.ontariocountydev.org

Canastota • *Madison County Ind. Dev. Agency* • Kipp Hicks; Exec. Dir.; 3215 Seneca Tpk.; 13032; Madison; P 73,400; (315) 697-9817; Fax (315) 697-8169; director@madisoncountyida.com; www.madisoncountyida.com

Canton • *St. Lawrence County Ofc. of Eco. Dev.* • Patrick J. Kelly; CEO; 19 Commerce Ln., Ste. 1; 13617; St. Lawrence; P 111,944; (315) 379-9806; Fax (315) 386-2573; info@slcida.com; www.slcida.com

Carmel • *Putnam County Eco. Dev. Corp.* • Jill Varricchio; Pres.; 40 Gleneida Ave.; 10512; Putnam; P 99,100; (845) 808-1021; Fax (845) 808-1958; info@putnamedc.org; www.putnamedc.org

Cooperstown • *Otsego County Eco. Dev. Dept.* • Karen Sullivan; Dir.; 140 County Hwy. 33 W.; 197 Main St.; 13326; Otsego; P 62,300; (607) 547-4225; Fax (607) 547-4285; sullivank@otsegocounty.com; www.otsegocounty.com

Corning • *Three Rivers Dev. Corp.* • Betsey Hale; Pres.; 19 E. Market St., Ste. 201; 14830; Steuben; P 30,000; (607) 962-4693; Fax (607) 936-9132; emarino@3riverscorp.com; www.3riverscorp.com

Coxsackie • *Greene County Ind. Dev. Agency* • Rene VanSchaack; Exec. Dir.; 270 Mansion St.; 12051; Greene; P 50,000; (518) 731-5500; Fax (518) 731-5520; snyder@greeneida.com; www.greeneida.com

Dutchess • *see New Windsor*

Elmira • *Chemung County Ind. Dev. Agency* • George Miner; Pres.; 400 E. Church St.; 14901; Chemung; P 88,000; (607) 733-6513; Fax (607) 734-2698; smgeary@steg.com; www.steg.com

Endwell • *Eco. Dev. for Town of Union* • Joseph Moody; Eco. Dev. Dir.; 3111 E. Main St.; 13760; Broome; P 55,000; (607) 786-2945; Fax (607) 786-2321; jmoody@townofunion.com; www.townofunion.com

Farmingville • *Town of Brookhaven Eco. Dev.* • Lisa Mulligan; Dir.; 1 Independence Hill; 11738; Suffolk; P 486,000; (631) 451-6563; (631) 451-8696; lmulligan@brookhaven.org; www.brookhavenny.gov

Fonda • *Montgomery County Eco. Dev. & Planning* • Kenneth Rose; CEO; Bus. Dev. Center, 9 Park St.; P.O. Box 1500; 12068; Montgomery; P 49,700; (518) 853-8334; Fax (518) 853-8336; krose@co.montgomery.ny.us; www.co.montgomery.ny.us

Fort Edward • *Washington County Local Dev. Corp.* • Deanna Derway; Pres./Exec. Dir.; County Municipal Center; 383 Broadway; 12828; Washington; P 62,200; (518) 746-2292; Fax (518) 746-2293; ldarfler@co.washington.ny.us; www.wcldc.org

Geneseo • *Livingston County Dev. Corp.* • William Bacon; Dir.; 6 Court St., Rm. 306; 14454; Livingston; P 65,000; (585) 243-7124; Fax (585) 243-7126; maureenwheeler@co.livingston.ny.us; www.livingstoncountydevelopment.com

Goshen • *Orange County Partnership* • Maureen Halahan; Pres./CEO; 40 Matthews St., Ste. 108; 10924; Orange; P 372,813; (845) 294-2323; Fax (845) 294-8023; info@ocpartnership.org; www.ocpartnership.org

Hauppauge • *Suffolk County Dept. of Eco. Dev.* • Joanne Minieri; Commissioner; H. Lee Dennison Bldg.; 100 Veterans Hwy., 11th Flr.; 11788; Suffolk; P 1,503,000; (631) 853-4800; Fax (631) 853-4888; ecodev@suffolkcountyny.gov; www.suffolkcountyny.gov

Hauppauge • *Empire State Dev.-Long Island Reg.* • 150 Motor Pkwy., Ste. 311; 11788; Suffolk; P 7,500,000; (631) 435-0717; Fax (631) 435-3399; nys-longisland@esd.ny.gov; www.empire.state.ny.us

Hempstead • *Planning & Eco. Dev. Agency of Hempstead* • George Bakich; Commissioner; 200 N. Franklin Ave.; 11550; Nassau; P 760,000; (516) 538-7100; Fax (516) 393-0080; www.townofhempstead.org

Hempstead • *Incorporated Village of Hempstead Comm. Dev. Agency* • Claude Gooding; Commissioner; 75 Clinton St.; 11550; Nassau; P 54,000; (516) 485-5737; Fax (516) 485-1667; clerksoffice@villageofhempsteadny.gov; www.villageofhempstead.org

Herkimer • *Herkimer County Ind. Dev. Agency* • Mark D. Feane; Exec. Dir.; 320 N. Prospect St.; P.O. Box 390; 13350; Herkimer; P 64,500; (315) 867-1373; Fax (315) 867-1515; ida@herkimercounty.org; www.herkimercountyida.com

Hornell • *Hornell Ind. Dev. Agency* • James W. Griffin; Exec. Dir.; 40 Main St.; 14843; Steuben; P 11,000; (607) 324-0310; Fax (607) 324-3776; griff@hornellny.com; www.hornellny.com

Hudson • *Columbia County Planning, Eco. Dev. & Tourism Dept.* • Kenneth Flood; Dir.; 401 State St.; 12534; Columbia; P 62,000; (518) 828-3375; Fax (518) 828-2825; kenneth.flood@columbiacountyny.com; www.columbiacountyny.com

Islip • *Town of Islip Eco. Dev. Div.* • William G. Mannix; Dir.; 40 Nassau Ave.; 11751; Suffolk; P 335,000; (631) 224-5512; Fax (631) 224-5532; ecodev@islipny.gov; townofislip-ny.gov

Ithaca • *Tompkins County Area Dev., Inc.* • Martha Armstrong; V.P. & Dir. of Eco. Dev. Planning; 401 E. State St., Ste. 402B; 14850; Tompkins; P 105,000; (607) 273-0005; Fax (607) 273-8964; info@tcad.org; www.tcad.org

Jamestown • *County of Chautauqua Ind. Dev. Agency [IDA]* • Kevin M. Sanvidge; CEO; 201 W. Third St., Ste. 115; 14701; Chautauqua; P 135,000; (716) 661-8900; (716) 661-8903; Fax (716) 664-4515; casels@co.chautauqua.ny.us; www.ccida.com

Johnstown • *Fulton County Planning Dept.* • James Mraz; Dir.; 1 E. Montgomery St.; 12095; Fulton; P 54,000; (518) 736-5660; Fax (518) 762-4597; planning@co.fulton.ny.us; www.fultoncountyny.gov

Kingston • *Ulster County Eco. Dev. Alliance* • Suzanne Holt; Dir.; 244 Fair St., 6th Flr.; 12401; Ulster; P 180,200; (845) 340-3556; oed@co.ulster.ny.us; www.ulstercountyny.gov

EDC

Little Valley • *Cattaraugus County Dept. of Eco. Dev. & Tourism* • Crystal Abers; Dir.; 303 Court St.; 14755; Cattaraugus; P 80,300; (716) 938-2310; (800) 331-0543; Fax (716) 938-2779; planning@cattco.org; www.cattco.org

Lockport • *Lockport Eco. Dev. Agency* • Marc Smith; Admin. Dir.; Town Hall; 6560 Dysinger Rd.; 14094; Niagara; P 22,200; (716) 478-0608; (716) 478-0625; Fax (716) 439-9715; led@elockport.com; www.lockporteconomicdevelopment.com

Lyons • *Wayne Eco. Dev. Corp.* • Peg Churchill; Exec. Dir.; 9 Pearl St.; 14489; Wayne; P 94,000; (315) 946-5917; Fax (315) 946-5918; wedcny@co.wayne.ny.us; www.wedcny.com

Malone • *County of Franklin Ind. Dev. Agency* • John Tubbs; Exec. Dir.; 10 Elm St., Ste. 2; 12953; Franklin; P 51,500; (518) 483-9472; Fax (518) 483-2900; rhiscock@franklinida.org; www.franklinida.org

Mineola • *Nassau County Ind. Dev. Agency* • Joseph J. Kearney; Exec. Dir.; 1550 Franklin Ave., Ste. 235; 11501; Nassau; P 1,360,000; (516) 571-1945; Fax (516) 571-1076; cpereira@nassauida.org; www.nassauida.org

Mohawk • *Mohawk Valley Eco. Dev. Dist.* • Joseph Caruso; Exec. Dir.; 26 W. Main St.; P.O. Box 69; 13407; Herkimer; P 622,000; (315) 866-4671; Fax (315) 866-9862; info@mvedd.org; mvedd.org

Monticello • *Partnership for Eco. Dev. for Sullivan County* • Allan Scott; Pres.; 198 Bridgeville Rd.; 12701; Sullivan; P 77,500; (845) 794-1110; Fax (845) 794-2324; allan@scpartnership.com; www.scpartnership.com

New Windsor • *Empire State Dev.-Mid-Hudson Reg. Ofc.* • Meghan Taylor; Exec. Dir.; 33 Airport Center Dr., Ste. 201; 12553; Orange; P 2,229,000; (845) 567-4882; Fax (845) 567-6085; nys-midhudson@esd.ny.gov; www.empire.state.ny.us

New Windsor • *Hudson Valley Eco. Dev. Corp.* • Laurence Gottlieb; Pres./CEO; 4 Crotty Ln., Ste. 100; 12553; Orange; P 2,000,000; (845) 220-2244; Fax (845) 220-2247; lgottlieb@hvedc.com; www.hvedc.com

New York • *Empire State Dev.-NYC* • Kenneth Adams; Pres./CEO; 633 3rd Ave., 36th Flr.; 10017; New York; P 19,400,000; (212) 803-3100; Fax (212) 803-3131; nys-nyc@esd.ny.gov; www.empire.state.ny.us

New York • *New York City Eco. Dev. Corp.* • Maria Torres-Springer; Pres.; 110 Williams St.; 10038; New York; P 8,176,000; (212) 619-5000; (212) 619-3600; Fax (212) 312-3909; www.nycedc.com

Newburgh • *Hudson Valley Reg. Cncl.* • John F. Crews; Exec. Dir.; 3 Washington Center, 2nd Flr.; 12550; Orange; P 2,000,000; (845) 564-4075; Fax (845) 565-4918; hvrc@hvi.net; www.hudsonvalleyregionalcouncil.com

Ontario • *Town of Onatario Ofc. of Eco. Dev.* • William Riddell; Dir.; 6551 Knickerbocker Rd.; 14519; Wayne; P 11,000; (315) 524-5908; Fax (315) 524-7465; riddell@ontariotown.org; www.ontariotown.org

Orange • *see New Windsor*

Oswego • *Operation Oswego County Inc.* • L. Michael Treadwell CEcD; Exec. Dir.; 44 W. Bridge St.; 13126; Oswego; P 122,000; (315) 343-1545; Fax (315) 343-1546; ooc@oswegocounty.org; www.oswegocounty.org

Owego • *Tioga County Ind. Dev. Agency* • Bryant Myers; Exec. Admin.; 56 Main St., Ste. 205; 13827; Tioga; P 51,100; (607) 687-8259; Fax (607) 223-7125; sampsonl@co.tioga.ny.us; www.TiogaCountyNY.com

Pearl River • *Rockland Eco. Dev. Corp.* • Richard M. Struck; Pres./CEO; One Blue Hill Plaza; P.O. Box 1575; 10965; Rockland; P 311,700; (845) 735-7040; Fax (845) 735-5736; jaynen@redc.org; www.redc.org

Penn Yan • *Finger Lakes Eco. Dev. Center* • Steve Griffin; CEO; 1 Keuka Business Park; 14527; Yates; P 25,000; (315) 536-7328; Fax (315) 272-4208; info@fingerlakesedc.com; www.fingerlakesedc.com

Plattsburgh • *The Development Corp.* • Paul A. Grasso Jr.; Pres./CEO; 190 Banker Rd., Ste. 500; 12901; Clinton; P 81,800; (518) 563-3100; (888) 699-6757; Fax (518) 562-2232; tdc@thedevelopcorp.com; www.thedevelopcorp.com

Putnam • *see New Windsor*

Rochester • *Empire State Dev.-Finger Lakes* • Vincent Esposito; Reg. Dir.; 400 Andrews St., Ste. 300; 14604; Monroe; P 1,100,000; (585) 399-7050; Fax (585) 423-7570; nys-fingerlakes@esd.ny.gov; www.esd.ny.gov

Rochester • *County of Monroe Ind. Dev. Agency* • 50 W. Main St., Ste. 8100; 14614; Monroe; P 749,857; (585) 753-2000; Fax (585) 753-2028; dgeorge@monroecounty.gov; www.monroecounty.gov

Rockland • *see New Windsor*

Rome • *Mohawk Valley Edge* • Steven DiMeo; Pres.; 584 Phoenix Dr.; 13441; Oneida; P 300,000; (315) 338-0393; Fax (315) 338-5694; sjdimeo@mvedge.org; www.mvedge.org

Salamanca • *Salamanca Ind. Dev. Agency* • Matt Bull; Exec. Dir.; 225 Wildwood Ave.; 14779; Cattaraugus; P 6,100; (716) 945-3230; Fax (716) 945-8289; mbull@salmun.com; www.salmun.com

Saranac Lake • *Adirondack Eco. Dev. Corp.* • James Murphy; Exec. Dir.; 67 Main St., Ste. 300; 12983; Essex & Franklin; P 132,000; (518) 891-5523; (888) 243-2332; Fax (518) 891-9820; jamesmurphy52@me.com; www.aedconline.com

Saratoga Springs • *Saratoga Eco. Dev. Corp.* • Dennis Brobston; Pres.; 28 Clinton St.; 12866; Saratoga; P 226,300; (518) 587-0945; Fax (518) 587-5855; dbrobston@saratogaedc.com; www.saratogaedc.com

Schenectady • *Schenectady County Eco. Dev. & Planning Dept.* • Ray Gillen; Commissioner; 107 Nott Terrace, Ste. 303; 12308; Schenectady; P 155,400; (518) 386-2225; Fax (518) 382-5539; contact-us@schenectadycounty.com; www.schenectadycounty.com

Sullivan • *see New Windsor*

Syracuse • *Onondaga County IDA* • Julie A. Cerio; Exec. Dir.; 333 W. Washington St., Ste. 130; 13202; Onondaga; P 468,500; (315) 435-3770; (877) 797-8222; Fax (315) 435-3669; christophercox@ongov.net; www.syracusecentral.com

Syracuse • *Empire State Dev.-Central New York* • James Fayle; Reg. Dir.; 620 Erie Blvd. W., Ste. 112; 13204; Onondaga; P 742,600; (315) 425-9110; Fax (315) 425-7156; nys-centralny@esd.ny.gov; www.empire.state.ny.us

Ulster • *see New Windsor*

Utica • *Empire State Dev.-Mohawk Valley Reg. Ofc.* • Michael Reese; Reg. Dir.; 207 Genesee St.; 13501; Herkimer, Madison & Oneida; P 500,000; (315) 793-2366; Fax (315) 793-2705; nys-mohawkval@esd.ny.gov; www.esd.ny.gov

Watkins Glen • *Schuyler County IDA* • Judy McKinney Cherry CEcD; Exec. Dir.; 910 S. Decatur St.; 14891; Schuyler; P 18,000; (607) 535-4341; Fax (607) 535-7221; anne@flxgateway.com; www.flxgateway.com

West Amherst • *Amherst Ind. Dev. Agency* • David S. Mingoia; Interim Exec. Dir.; 4287 Main St.; 14226; Erie; P 125,000; (716) 688-9000; Fax (716) 688-0205; laure@amherstida.com; www.amherstida.com

Westbury • *Greater NY Dev. Co./Long Island Dev. Corp.* • Roslyn D. Goldmacher; Pres./CEO; 400 Post Ave., Ste. 201A; 11590; Nassau; P 2,700,000; (516) 433-5000; (866) 433-5432; Fax (516) 433-5046; info@lidc.org; www.lidc.org

Westchester • *see New Windsor*

Westfield • *Westfield Dev. Corp.* • Aaron J. Resnick; Exec. Dir.; 31 E. Main St.; 14787; Chautauqua; P 3,200; (716) 326-2200; aresnick@westfieldny.com; www.westfieldny.com

White Plains • *Westchester County Ofc. of Eco. Dev.* • Laurence Gottlieb; Dir.; 148 Martine Ave., Rm. 903; 10601; Westchester; (914) 995-2963; Fax (914) 995-3044; lpg2@westchestergov.com; www.westchestergov.com

Yonkers • *Yonkers Ofc. of Eco. Dev.* • Louis Kirven; Commissioner; City Hall; 40 S. Broadway, Ste. 416; 10701; Westchester; P 200,000; (914) 377-6797; Fax (914) 377-6003; Louis.Kirven@YonkersNY.Gov; www.yonkersny.gov

North Carolina

Federal

***U.S. SBA, North Carolina Dist. Ofc.* •** Lynn Douthett; Dist. Dir.; 6302 Fairview Rd., Ste. 300; 28210; Mecklenburg; P 9,752,073; (704) 344-6563; Fax (704) 344-6769; lynn.douthett@sba.gov; www.sba.gov/nc

State

***North Carolina Dept. of Commerce* •** John E. Skvarla III; Secy. of Commerce; 301 N. Wilmington St.; 4301 Mail Service Center; Raleigh; 27699; Wake; P 9,752,073; (919) 814-4600; Fax (919) 733-4563; info@nccommerce.com; www.nccommerce.com

Communities

Albemarle • *Stanly County Eco. Dev. Comm.* • Paul Stratos; Dir.; 1000 N. 1st St., Ste. 11; 28001; Stanly; P 61,600; (704) 986-3682; Fax (704) 986-3685; edc@stanlyedc.org; www.stanlyedc.org

Asheboro • *Randolph County Eco. Dev. Corp.* • Bonnie Renfro; Pres.; 145-A Worth St.; P.O. Box 2001; 27204; Randolph; P 143,000; (336) 626-2233; Fax (336) 626-0777; brenfro@rcedc.com; www.rcedc.com

Asheville • *Asheville Area C/C-Eco. Dev. Dept.* • Ben Teague; Sr. V.P. Eco. Dev.; 36 Montford Ave.; P.O. Box 1010; 28802; Buncombe; P 413,600; (828) 258-6137; Fax (828) 251-0926; ljohnson@ashevillechamber.org; www.ashevillechamber.org

Bakersville • *Mitchell County Eco. Dev. Comm.* • Jack Dobson; Dir.; 26 Crimson Laurel Cir.; 28705; Mitchell; P 15,600; (828) 688-2139; becky@mitchelledc.org; www.mitchelledc.org

Beech Mountain • *see Boone*

Black Mountain • *see Asheville*

Blowing Rock • *see Boone*

Boone • *Watauga County Ofc. of Eco. Dev.* • Joe Furman AICP; Dir.; 331 Queen St., Ste. A; P.O. Box 404; 28607; Watauga; P 51,000; (828) 264-3082; Fax (828) 265-8080; joe.furman@watgov.org; www.wataugaedc.org

Brevard • *Transylvania County Planning & Comm. Dev.* • Mark Burrows; Dir.; 98 E. Morgan St.; 28712; Transylvania; P 33,100; (828) 884-3205; Fax (828) 884-3275; kalen.lawson@transylvaniacounty.org; planning.transylvaniacounty.org

Canton • *see Waynesville*

Cary • *Eco. Dev. Partnership of NC* • Christopher Chung; CEO; 15000 Weston Pkwy.; 27513; Chatham & Wake; P 9,535,483; (919) 447-7777; tiffany.mcneill@edpnc.com; www.thrivenc.com

Clyde • *see Waynesville*

Danbury • *Stokes County Eco. Dev.* • David Sudderth; Interim Dir.; 1014 Main St.; 27016; Stokes; P 47,400; (336) 593-2496; Fax (336) 593-2346; stokesecd@co.stokes.nc.us; www.stokesedc.org

Edenton • *Edenton-Chowan Eco. Dev.* • Richard Bunch; Exec. Dir.; 116 E. King St.; P.O. Box 245; 27932; Chowan; P 14,800; (252) 482-3400; Fax (252) 482-7093; richard.bunch@ncmail.net; www.visitedenton.com

Elizabeth City • *Elizabeth City/Pasquotank County Eco. Dev. Comm.* • Wayne Harris; Dir.; 405 E. Main St., Ste. 4; 27907; Pasquotank; P 40,700; (252) 338-0169; (888) 338-1678; Fax (252) 338-0160; director@elizabethcitypasquotankedc.com; www.elizabethcitypasquotankedc.com

Elizabeth City • *Elizabeth City Comm. Dev. Div.* • Wade Nichols; Mgr.; 302 E. Colonial Ave., Ste. 307; P.O. Box 347; 27907; Pasquotank; P 18,300; (252) 337-6672; Fax (252) 331-1291; wnichols@cityofec.com; www.cityofec.com

Elizabethtown • *Bladen County Eco. Dev. Comm.* • Chuck Heustess; Dir.; 218A Aviation Pkwy.; 28337; Bladen; P 35,200; (910) 645-2292; Fax (910) 645-2293; edc@bladenco.org; www.bladeninfo.org

Farmville • *Farmville Dev. Partnership* • Jan Greene; Admin. Asst.; P.O. Box 150; 27828; Pitt; P 4,650; (252) 753-4670; Fax (252) 753-7313; jhgreenefdp@embarqmail.com; www.farmville-nc.com

Forest City • *Rutherford County Eco. Dev. Comm.* • Mary Taylor; Eco. Dev. Specialist; 142 E. Main St., Ste. 100; 28043; Rutherford; P 67,000; (828) 287-6200; Fax (828) 287-6201; info@rutherfordncedc.com; www.rutherfordncedc.com

Gastonia • *Gaston County Eco. Dev. Comm.* • Gary D. Hicks Jr. CEcD; Exec. Dir.; 620 N. Main St.; P.O. Box 2339; 28053; Gaston; P 213,000; (704) 825-4046; Fax (704) 825-4066; donny.hicks@gastongov.com; www.gaston.org

Goldsboro • *Wayne County Dev. Alliance* • Crystal Gettys; Pres.; P.O. Box 1280; 27533; Wayne; P 124,000; (919) 731-7700; Fax (919) 580-9147; waynealliance@waynegov.com; www.waynealliance.org

Greensboro • *Greensboro Eco. Dev.* • Brent Christenson; Pres./CEO; 111 W. February One Place; 27401; Guilford; P 269,700; (336) 387-8301; Fax (336) 275-9299; info@greensboro.org; www.greensboropartnership.com

Greenville • *Pitt County Dev. Comm.* • Wanda E. Yuhas; Exec. Dir.; 111 S. Washington St.; P.O. Box 837; 27853; Pitt; P 169,000; (252) 902-2075; pittedc@pittcountync.gov; www.locateincarolina.com

Greenville • *NCEast Alliance* • John D. Chaffee; Pres./CEO; 1020 Red Banks Rd., Ste. 202; 27858; Pitt; P 1,000,000; (252) 689-6496; Fax (252) 689-6498; howard@nceast.org; www.nceast.org

Hazelwood • *see Waynesville*

Henderson • *Henderson-Vance County EDC* • P.O. Box 2017; 27536; Vance; P 45,400; (252) 492-2094; Fax (252) 492-4428; info@vancecountyedc.com; www.vancecountyedc.com

Hickory • *Catawba County Eco. Dev. Corp.* • Scott L. Millar; Pres.; 1960-B 13th Ave. Dr. S.E.; P.O. Box 3388; 28603; Catawba; P 154,400; (828) 267-1564; Fax (828) 267-1884; edc@catawbacountync.gov; www.catawbaedc.org

High Point • *High Point Eco. Dev. Corp.* • Loren Hill; Pres.; 211 S. Hamilton St., Ste. 200; 27260; Guilford; P 104,400; (336) 883-3116; Fax (336) 883-3057; hpedc@highpointnc.gov; www.highpointnc.gov

Hillsborough • *Orange County Eco. Dev. Comm.* • Steve Brantley; Dir.; 131 W. Margaret Ln.; 27278; Orange; P 134,000; (919) 245-2325; sbrantley@orangecountync.gov; www.orangecountync.gov

Jacksonville • *Jacksonville Onslow Eco. Dev. [JOED]* • Sheila Pierce Knight; Exec. Dir.; 1099 Gum Branch Rd.; 28540; Onslow; P 195,000; (910) 347-3141; Fax (910) 347-2842; sknight@JOEDNC.com; www.JOEDNC.com

Jefferson • *Ashe County Eco. Dev. Comm.* • Dr. Patricia Mitchell; Dir.; 150 Government Cir., Ste. 2500; 28640; Ashe; P 27,200; (336) 846-5502; Fax (336) 846-5516; director@ashencedc.com; www.ashencedc.com

Kenansville • *Duplin County EDC* • 260 Airport Rd.; 28349; Duplin; P 58,500; (910) 296-2180; Fax (910) 296-2184; heather.beard@duplinedc.com; www.duplinedc.com

Kinston • *Lenoir County Eco. Dev. Dept.* • D. Mark Pope; Exec. Dir.; 101 N. Queen St.; 28501; Lenoir; P 59,500; (252) 527-1963; Fax (252) 527-1914; info@lenoiredc.com; www.lenoiredc.com

Lenoir • *Eco. Dev. Comm. of Caldwell County* • Deborah Murray; Exec. Dir.; 1909 Hickory Blvd. S.E.; P.O. Box 2888; 28645; Caldwell; P 83,100; (828) 728-0768; Fax (828) 726-8926; pteague@caldwelledc.org; www.caldwelledc.org

Lexington • *Davidson County Eco. Dev.* • Steve Googe; Exec. Dir.; 1900 S. Main St.; P.O. Box 1287; 27293; Davidson; P 163,500; (336) 243-1900; Fax (336) 243-3027; slgooge@davidsoncountyedc.com; www.co.davidson.nc.us/dcedc

Lincolnton • *Lincoln Eco. Dev. Assn.* • Cliff Brumfield; Exec. Dir.; 502 E. Main St.; 28092; Lincoln; P 70,000; (704) 732-1511; Fax (704) 736-8451; leda@lincolneda.org; www.lincolneda.org

Marion • *McDowell Eco. Dev. Assn. Inc.* • Charles Abernathy; Dir.; 634 College Dr.; 28752; McDowell; P 45,000; (828) 652-9391; Fax (828) 652-8775; meda@mcdowelleda.com; www.mcdowelleda.org

Mocksville • *Davie County Eco. Dev. Comm.* • Terry Bralley; Pres.; 135 S. Salisbury St.; 27028; Davie; P 41,300; (336) 751-2714; (336) 909-1403; Fax (336) 751-5697; terry.bralley@daviecounty.com; www.daviecountyedc.com

Monroe • *Monroe-Union County Eco. Dev.* • R. Christopher Platé; Exec. Dir.; 3509 Old Charlotte Hwy.; 28110; Union; P 203,000; (704) 282-5780; jball@monroenc.org; www.developunion.com

Morehead City • *Carteret Eco. Dev. Cncl.* • Greg Lewis; Interim Exec. Dir.; Commerce Dev. Center; 3615 Arendell St.; 28557; Carteret; P 66,500; (252) 222-6122; Fax (252) 222-6124; edc@carteret.edu; www.carteretedc.com

Mt. Airy • *Surry County Eco. Dev. Partnership Inc.* • Todd Tucker; Pres.; 1218 State St.; P.O. Box 7128; 27030; Surry; P 73,000; (336) 401-9900; Fax (336) 401-9901; surryedp@surry.net; www.surryedp.com

New Bern • *Craven County Eco. Dev. Dept.* • Timothy Downs; Dir.; 406 Craven St.; 28560; Craven; P 104,000; (252) 633-5300; Fax (252) 637-0526; economicdev@cravencountync.gov; www.cravenbusiness.com

North Wilkesboro • *Wilkes Eco. Dev. Corp.* • Jeff Garstka CEcD; Pres.; 213 Ninth St.; 28659; Wilkes; P 69,300; (336) 838-1501; Fax (336) 838-1693; jgarstka@wilkesedc.com; www.wilkesedc.com

Oxford • *Granville Eco. Dev. Comm.* • Jay Tilley; Exec. Dir.; 310 Williamsboro St.; P.O. Box 26; 27565; Granville; P 59,900; (919) 693-5911; Fax (919) 693-1952; jay.tilley@granvillecounty.com; www.granvillecounty.com

Pinehurst • *Moore County Partners in Progress* • Pat Corso; Exec. Dir.; P.O. Box 5885; 28374; Moore; P 94,500; (910) 246-0311; (800) 461-3755; Fax (910) 246-0312; econdev@moorebusiness.org; www.moorebusiness.org

Roanoke Rapids • *Halifax Dev. Comm.* • Cathy A. Scott; Exec. Dir.; 260 Premier Blvd.; 27870; Halifax; P 54,000; (252) 519-2630; Fax (252) 519-2632; cathyscott@halifaxdevelopment.com; www.halifaxdevelopment.com

Rocky Mount • *Carolinas Gateway Partnership* • Norris Tolson; Pres./CEO; 427 Falls Rd.; 27804; Nash; P 151,000; (252) 442-0114; (800) 550-6151; Fax (252) 442-7315; cgp@econdev.org; www.econdev.org

Salisbury • *Salisbury-Rowan Eco. Dev. Comm.* • Robert Van Geons; Exec. Dir.; 204 E. Innes St., Ste. 220; 28144; Rowan; P 138,400; (704) 637-5526; Fax (704) 637-0173; robert@rowanworks.com; www.rowanworks.com

Sparta • *Alleghany County Eco. Dev. Corp.* • Don Adams; County Mgr.; 348 S. Main St.; P.O. Box 366; 28675; Alleghany; P 11,100; (336) 372-4179; Fax (336) 372-5969; manageralc@skybest.com; www.alleghanycounty-nc.gov

Spruce Pine • *see Bakersville*

Statesville • *Statesville Reg. Dev.* • Russ Rogerson; Exec. Dir.; 116 N. Center St.; 28677; Iredell; P 70,000; (704) 871-0062; Fax (704) 871-0223; lisa@statesvilleregion.com; www.statesvilleregion.com

Troy • *Montgomery County Eco. Dev.* • Amanda Whitaker; Dir.; 102 E. Spring St.; 27371; Montgomery; P 28,000; (910) 576-4221; Fax (910) 576-4566; amanda.whitaker@montgomerycountync.com; www.montgomerycountync.com

Wadesboro • *Anson County Eco. Dev. Dept.* • Misty Harris; Dir. of Eco. Dev.; 101 S. Greene St., Ste. 211; P.O. Box 339; 28170; Anson; P 26,900; (704) 994-3229; Fax (704) 994-3239; mharris@co.anson.nc.us; www.ansonedc.org

Warrenton • *Warren County EDC* • Ken Bowman; Dir.; 501 U.S. Hwy. 158 Bus. East; P.O. Box 804; 27589; Warren; P 20,300; (252) 257-3114; Fax (252) 257-2277; edc@warrencountync.gov; www.warrencountync.org

Washington • *Beaufort County Eco. Dev. Comm.* • Tom Thompson; Exec. Dir.; 705 Page Rd.; 27889; Beaufort; P 47,700; (252) 946-3970; Fax (252) 946-0849; info@beaufortedc.com; www.beaufortedc.com

Waynesville • *Haywood Eco. Dev. Cncl.* • Mark B. Clasby; Exec. Dir.; 28 Walnut St., Ste. 4; 28786; Haywood; P 60,000; (828) 456-3737; Fax (828) 452-1352; mclasby@haywoodchamber.com; www.haywoodedc.org

Weaverville • *see Asheville*

Williamston • *Martin County Eco. Dev. Corp.* • Jason Semple; Pres./CEO; 415 East Blvd.; 27892; Martin; P 24,000; (252) 789-4904; Fax (252) 792-0993; gperry@martincountyedc.com; www.martincountyedc.com

Wilson • *Wilson Eco. Dev. Cncl.* • Jennifer Lantz; Exec. Dir.; 405 W. Nash St., Ste. 210; P.O. Box 728; 27894; Wilson; P 81,300; (252) 237-1115; Fax (252) 237-1116; kfarris@wilsonedc.com; www.wilsonedc.com

Winston-Salem • *Winston-Salem Bus. Inc.* • Robert E. Leak Jr. CEcD; Pres.; 1080 W. 4th St.; 27101; Forsyth; P 351,000; (336) 723-8955; Fax (336) 761-1069; khess@wsbusinessinc.com; www.wsbusinessinc.com

Winton • *Hertford County Eco. Dev. Comm.* • William S. Early; Dir.; 115 Justice Dr., Ste. 2; 27986; Hertford; P 24,669; (252) 358-7801; Fax (252) 358-0198; hertford.county@hertfordcountync.gov; www.hertfordcounty.com

Youngsville • *Franklin County Eco. Dev. Comm.* • Richie Duncan; Dir.; 228 Park Ave.; 27596; Franklin; P 63,700; (919) 554-1863; Fax (919) 554-1781; lduke@franklincountync.us; www.franklincountync.us

North Dakota

Federal

***U.S. SBA, North Dakota Dist. Ofc.* •** Michael J. Gallagher; Dist. Dir.; 657 2nd Ave. N., Rm. 218; 58108; Cass; P 699,628; (701) 239-5131; Fax (701) 239-5645; michael.gallagher@sba.gov; www.sba.gov/nd

State

***North Dakota Dept. of Commerce* •** Al Anderson; Comm.; 1600 E. Century Ave., Ste. 2; Bismarck; 58503; Burleigh; P 699,628; (701) 328-5312; Fax (701) 328-5320; alranderson@nd.gov; www.commerce.nd.gov

Communities

Beach • *Prairie West Dev. Found.* • Debra Walworth; Exec. Dir.; 55 1st St. S.E.; P.O. Box 784; 58621; Golden Valley; P 1,300; (701) 872-3121; Fax (701) 872-3125; prairiewestdeputy@yahoo.com; www.prairiewestdev.com

Bismarck • *Bismarck-Mandan Dev. Assn.* • Brian Ritter; Pres./CEO; 400 E. Broadway Ave., Ste. 417; 58501; Burleigh; P 81,400; (701) 222-5530; (888) 222-5497; Fax (701) 222-3843; info@bmda.org; www.bmda.org

Bottineau • *Bottineau County Eco. Dev. Corp.* • Diane Olson; EDC Dir.; 519 Main St.; 58318; Bottineau; P 2,400; (701) 228-3922; Fax (701) 228-5130; edc@utma.com; www.bottineau.com

Carrington • *Carrington Eco. Dev. Corp.* • Lucinda Grandalen; Dir.; 103 10th Ave. N.; P.O. Box 501; 58421; Foster; P 2,100; (701) 652-3919; cedd@daktel.com; www.carringtonnd.com

Colfax • *Colfax Dev. Corp.* • Gordon Olson; 16420 67th Ave. S.E.; 58018; Richland; P 121; (701) 372-3877

Cooperstown • *Cooperstown/Griggs County Eco. Dev. Corp.* • Becky Meidinger; Dev. Spec.; P.O. Box 553; 58425; Griggs; P 2,420; (701) 797-3712; Fax (701) 797-3713; cooperedc@invisimax.com; ww.growingcooperstown.com

Devils Lake • *FORWARD Devils Lake Dev. Corp.* • Rachel Lindstrom; Exec. Dir.; P.O. Box 879; 58301; Ramsey; P 7,231; (701) 662-4933; Fax (701) 662-2147; rachel@devilslakend.com; development.devilslakend.com

Dickinson • *Roosevelt-Custer Reg. Cncl. for Dev.* • Gene Buresh; Exec. Dir.; 300 13th Ave. W., Ste. 3; 58601; Stark; P 40,000; (701) 483-1241; Fax (701) 483-1243; info@rooseveltcuster.com; www.rooseveltcuster.com

Fargo • *Greater Fargo Moorhead Eco. Dev. Corp.* • James Gartin; Pres.; 51 Broadway, Ste. 500; 58102; Cass; P 224,000; (701) 364-1900; (877) 243-0821; info@gfmedc.com; gfmedc.com

Fargo • *Lake Agassiz Dev. Group* • Amber Metz; Exec. Dir.; 417 Main Ave.; 58103; Cass; P 160,000; (701) 235-1197; Fax (701) 235-6706; amber@lakeagassiz.com; www.lakeagassiz.com

Grand Forks • *Grand Forks Reg. Eco. Dev. Corp.* • Klaus Thiessen; Pres./CEO; 120 N. 4th St.; 58203; Grand Forks; P 67,000; (701) 746-2720; Fax (701) 746-2725; dorisc@grandforks.org; www.grandforks.org

Grand Forks • *Grand Forks Comm. Dev. Div.* • Brad Gengler; Dir.; 255 N. 4th St.; P.O. Box 5200; 58203; Grand Forks; P 60,000; (701) 746-2661; (701) 746-4636; bgengler@grandforksgov.com; www.grandforksgov.com

Harvey • *Harvey Area Eco. Dev. Inc.* • Nicki Weissman; Dir.; 120 8th St. W.; 58341; Wells; P 1,850; (701) 324-2490; (701) 324-2000; Fax (701) 324-2674; harveyJDA@harveynd.com; www.harveynd.com

Hazen • *Hazen Comm. Dev.* • Buster Langowski; Exec. Dir.; 146 Main St. E.; P.O. Box 717; 58545; Mercer; P 2,457; (701) 748-6886; (701) 870-2253; Fax (701) 748-2559; hcd@westriv.com; www.hazennd.org

Hettinger • *Adams County Dev. Corp.* • Jim Goplin; Exec. Dir.; 120 S. Main; P.O. Box 1323; 58639; Adams; P 2,300; (701) 567-2531; Fax (701) 567-2690; adamscdc@ndsupernet.com; www.hettingernd.com

Hillsboro • *Hillsboro Eco. Dev. Corp.* • Sheila Geray; Exec. Dir.; 521 First Ave. N.E.; 58045; Traill; P 1,610; (701) 636-2338; (701) 636-4620; visit@acupofcoffeeaway.com; acupofcoffeeaway.com

Hillsboro • *Traill County Eco. Dev.* • Melissa Beach; Exec. Dir.; 102 1st St. S.W.; P.O. Box 856; 58045; Traill; P 8,200; (701) 636-4746; Fax (701) 636-4744; director@traillcountyedc.com; www.traillcountyedc.com

Linton • *Linton Ind. Dev. Corp.* • P.O. Box 433; 58552; Emmons; P 1,321; (701) 254-4267; Fax (701) 254-4382; lidcbek@bektel.com; www.lintonnd.org

Minnewaukan • *Minnewaukan Eco. Dev. Corp.* • Tom Lang; Pres.; P.O. Box 192; 58351; Benson; P 224; (701) 473-5735; Fax (701) 473-5377; www.minnewaukan.com

Minot • *Minot Area Dev. Corp.* • Stephanie Hoffart; Pres./CEO; 1020 20th Ave. S.W.; 58701; Ward; P 50,000; (701) 852-1075; Fax (701) 857-8234; madc@minotusa.com; www.minotusa.com

Oakes • *Oakes Enhancement Inc.* • Audrey O'Brien; Secy.; P.O. Box 365; 58474; Dickey; P 4,000; (701) 742-2137; aobrien@drtel.net; www.oakesnd.com

Rugby • *Rugby Job Dev. Auth.* • SyAnn Graber; Dir.; P.O. Box 136; 58368; Pierce; P 3,000; (701) 776-7655; Fax (701) 776-5281; admin@rugbyjda.com; www.rugbyjda.com

Underwood • *Underwood Area Eco. Dev. Corp.* • Wendy Spencer; Dir.; 88 Lincoln Ave.; P.O. Box 368; 58576; McLean; P 1,000; (701) 442-9455; Fax (701) 442-5482; wendy@cedc.coop; www.underwoodnd.net

Valley City • *Valley City-Barnes County Dev. Corp.* • Jennifer Feist; Dir. of Dev.; 250 W. Main St.; P.O. Box 724; 58072; Barnes; P 7,000; (701) 840-7820; Fax (701) 845-1892; vdg@hellovalley.com; www.hellovalley.com

Wahpeton • *City of Wahpeton Eco. Dev. Dept.* • Jane Priebe CEcD; Dir.; 1900 4th St. N.; 58075; Richland; P 8,000; (701) 642-8559; (888) 850-9544; Fax (701) 642-1428; janep@wahpeton.com; www.wahpeton.com

Washburn • *Washburn Area Eco. Dev. Assn.* • Karen Hanson; 907 M Main Ave.; 58577; McLean; P 1,400; (701) 462-3801; Fax (701) 462-8598; waeda@westriv.com; www.washburnnd.com

Williston • *Williston Eco. Dev.* • Shawn Wenko; Exec. Dir.; 113 4th St. E.; P.O. Box 1306; 58802; Williams; P 21,000; (701) 577-8110; (800) 735-6959; Fax (701) 713-3837; shawnw@ci.williston.nd.us; www.willistondevelopment.com

Ohio

Federal

U.S. SBA, Cleveland Dist. Ofc. • Gil Goldberg; Dist. Dir.; 1350 Euclid Ave., Ste. 211; 44115; Cuyahoga; P 11,544,225; (216) 522-4180; Fax (216) 522-2038; gilbert.goldberg@sba.gov; www.sba.gov/oh

U.S. SBA, Columbus Dist. Ofc. • Martin D. Golden; Dist. Dir.; 401 N. Front St., Ste. 200; 43215; Franklin; P 11,544,225; (614) 469-6860; martin.golden@sba.gov; www.sba.gov/oh

State

Ohio Dev. Svcs. Agency • David Goodman; Dir.; 77 S. High St., 29th Flr.; Columbus; 43215; Franklin; P 11,544,225; (614) 466-3379; (800) 848-1300; Fax (614) 644-0745; david.goodman@development.ohio.gov; www.development.ohio.gov

Communities

Alliance • *Alliance Area Dev. Found.* • Thomas Pukys; Pres.; 2500 W. State St., Ste. E11; 44601; Stark; P 23,000; (330) 823-0700; Fax (330) 823-2660; aadf@allianceadf.com; www.allianceadf.com

Ashtabula • *see Jefferson*

Athens • *Athens County Eco. Dev. Cncl.* • Sara Marrs-Maxfield; Exec. Dir.; 340 W. State St., Unit 26; 45701; Athens; P 64,700; (740) 597-1420; Fax (740) 597-1548; admin@businessremixed.com; www.businessremixed.com

Bellefontaine • *Logan County Eco. Dev.* • Paul Benedetti; Pres./CEO; 100 S. Main St.; 43311; Logan; P 46,000; (937) 599-5121; Fax (937) 599-2411; ceo@logancountyohio.com; www.logancountyohio.com

Brook Park • *City of Brook Park Dev. Dept.* • Mike Dolan; Eco. Dev. Commissioner; 6161 Engle Rd.; 44142; Cuyahoga; P 19,200; (216) 433-1300; Fax (216) 433-1511; mdolan@cityofbrookpark.com; www.cityofbrookpark.com

Bryan • *Williams County Eco. Dev. Corp. [WEDCO]* • Matthew Davis; Exec. Dir.; 1425 E. High St.; 43506; Williams; P 38,000; (419) 636-8727; Fax (419) 636-5589; economic@wedco.info; www.wedco.info

Bucyrus • *Crawford County Partnership* • Gary Frankhouse; Exec. Dir.; 117 E. Mansfield St.; 44820; Crawford; P 43,800; (419) 563-1809; Fax (419) 563-1813; partnership@crawford-co.org; www.crawford2020.com

Cambridge • *Cambridge-Guernsey County Comm. Improvement Corp.* • Norman Blanchard; Eco. Dev. Dir.; 806 Cochran Ave.; 43725; Guernsey; P 40,000; (740) 432-1881; Fax (740) 432-1990; cgccic@frontier.com; www.cgccic.org

Cambridge • *Ohio Mid-Eastern Govts. Assn.* • Jeannette Wierzbicki P.E.; Exec. Dir.; 326 Highland Ave., Ste. B; 43725; Guernsey; P 590,200; (740) 439-4471; Fax (740) 439-7783; cindim@omegadistrict.org; www.omegadistrict.org

Canton • *Stark Dev. Bd.* • Stephen L. Paquette; Pres./CEO; 116 Cleveland Ave. N.W.; 44702; Stark; P 375,600; (330) 453-5900; Fax (330) 453-1793; sdbfc@starkcoohio.com; www.starkcoohio.com

Carlisle • *Carlisle Area Eco. Dev.* • Mayor Randy Winkler; 760 W. Central Ave.; 45005; Montgomery & Warren; P 5,000; (937) 746-0555; Fax (937) 743-8178; festes@carlisleoh.org; www.carlisleoh.org

Chillicothe • *Eco. Dev. Alliance of Southern Ohio* • Christopher M. Manegold CEcD; CEO; 45 E. Main St.; 45601; Ross; P 80,000; (740) 772-5100; (877) 70-EDASO; Fax (740) 702-2727; cmanegold@edaso.org; www.edaso.org

Cincinnati • *Dept. of Comm. & Eco. Dev.* • Bill Fischer; Eco. Dev. Mgr.; Two Centennial Plaza; 805 Central Ave., Ste. 700; 45202; Hamilton; P 331,300; (513) 352-6146; Fax (513) 352-6113; edinfo@cincinnati-oh.gov; www.choosecincy.com

Cincinnati • *Hamilton County Dev. Co.* • David K. Main; Pres.; 1776 Mentor Ave., Ste. 100; 45212; Hamilton; P 802,300; (513) 631-8292; Fax (513) 631-4887; maind@hcdc.com; www.hcdc.com

Cleveland • *City of Cleveland Dept. of Eco. Dev.* • Tracey A. Nichols; Dir.; 601 Lakeside Ave., Rm. 210; 44114; Cuyahoga; P 400,000; (216) 664-2406; Fax (216) 664-3681; tnichols2@city.cleveland.oh.us; rethinkcleveland.org/home.aspx

Columbus • *Mid-Ohio Reg. Planning Comm.* • William Murdock; Exec. Dir.; 111 Liberty St., Ste. 100; 43215; Franklin; P 1,400,000; (614) 228-2663; Fax (614) 228-1904; cklein@morpc.org; www.morpc.org

Conneaut • *see Jefferson*

Dayton Area

City of Dayton, Ofc. of Eco. Dev. • Shelley Dickstein; Dir.; 101 W. 3rd St., City Mgr. Ofc.; 45402; Montgomery; P 150,000; (937) 333-3600; Fax (937) 333-4298; shelley.dickstein@daytonohio.gov; www.daytonohio.gov

CityWide Dev. Corp. • Brian Heitkamp; Dir.; 8 N. Main St.; 45402; Montgomery; P 841,500; (937) 226-0457; Fax (937) 222-7035; bheitkamp@citywidedev.com; www.citywidedev.com

Dayton Eco. Dev. • Ford P. Weber; Dir.; 101 W. Third St., Ste. 430; P.O. Box 22; 45401; Montgomery; P 142,000; (937) 333-3634; jeffrey.bankston@daytonohio.gov; www.daytonohiobusiness.com

Elyria • Lorain County Comm. Dev. • Donald Romancak; Dir.; 226 Middle Ave., 5th Flr.; 44035; Lorain; P 301,400; (440) 328-2322; Fax (440) 328-2349; dromancak@loraincounty.us; www.loraincounty.us

Euclid • Euclid Planning & Dev. • Jonathan Holody; Dir.; 585 E. 222nd St.; 44123; Cuyahoga; P 49,000; (216) 289-2830; Fax (216) 289-8366; amiller@cityofeuclid.com; www.cityofeuclid.com

Fairfield • Fairfield Dev. Svcs. • Greg Kathman; Dir.; 5350 Pleasant Ave.; 45014; Butler; P 42,600; (513) 867-5345; development@fairfield-city.org; www.fairfield-city.org

Findlay • Findlay-Hancock County Eco. Dev. • Anthony P. Iriti; Dir.; 123 E. Main Cross St.; 45840; Hancock; P 75,000; (419) 422-3313; Fax (419) 422-9508; airiti@findlayhancocked.com; www.findlayhancocked.com

Forest Park • City of Forest Park Eco. Dev. • Paul Brehm; Dir.; 1201 W. Kemper Rd.; 45240; Hamilton; P 18,800; (513) 595-5207; Fax (513) 595-5285; pbrehm@forestpark.org; www.forestpark.org

Fostoria • Fostoria Eco. Dev. Corp. • Joan M. Nye-Reinhard; Exec. Dir.; 121 N. Main St.; 44830; Seneca; P 13,000; (419) 435-7789; Fax (419) 435-0936; fostoriaed@aol.com; www.fostoriaohio.org

Fremont • Sandusky County Eco. Dev. Corp. • Kay E. Reiter; Exec. Dir.; 2511 Countryside Dr.; 43420; Sandusky; P 61,000; (419) 332-2882; Fax (419) 332-3347; director@sanduskycountyedc.org; www.sanduskycountyedc.org

Geneva • see Jefferson

Hamilton • Butler County Dept. of Eco. Dev. • David Fehr; Dir.; 130 High St.; 45011; Butler; P 369,000; (513) 887-3413; Fax (513) 785-5723; fehrd@butlercountyohio.org; development.butlercountyohio.org

Jefferson • Growth Partnership for Ashtabula County • Brian M. Anderson; Exec. Dir; 17 N. Market St.; 44047; Ashtabula; P 101,400; (440) 576-9126; (800) 487-4769; Fax (440) 576-5003; brian@ashtabulagrowth.com; www.ashtabulagrowth.com

Lima • Allen Eco. Dev. Group • Marcel Wagner Jr.; Pres./CEO; 144 S. Main, Ste. 200; 45801; Allen; P 106,300; (419) 222-7706; (877) 222-7706; Fax (419) 222-7916; holbrookb@aedg.org; www.aedg.org

Lorain • Lorain Dev. Corp. • Leon Mason; Exec. Dir.; 200 W. Erie Ave.; 44052; Lorain; P 64,100; (440) 204-2020; Fax (440) 204-2080; leon_mason@cityoflorain.org; www.cityoflorain.org

Loudonville • Mohican Area Growth Found. Inc. • Kathy Goon; Exec. Dir.; 131 W. Main St.; 44842; Ashland & Holmes; P 3,000; (419) 289-3200; Fax (419) 289-3233; kathygoon@ashlanded.com; www.mohicanareagrowthfoundation.org

Mansfield • City of Mansfield Eco. Dev. • Tim Bowersock; Dir.; 30 N. Diamond St.; 44902; Richland; P 47,900; (419) 755-9794; Fax (419) 755-9465; tbowersock@ci.mansfield.oh.us; www.ci.mansfield.oh.us

Marion • Marion CAN DO Inc. • Gus Comstock; Dir.; 222 W. Center St.; 43302; Marion; P 67,000; (740) 387-2267; (800) 841-7302; Fax (740) 387-5522; info@marioncando.com; www.marioncando.com

Marysville • Union County Eco. Dev. • Eric S. Phillips; Exec. Dir.; 227 E. Fifth St.; 43040; Union; P 53,000; (937) 642-6279; (800) 642-0087; Fax (937) 644-0422; ephillips@unioncounty.org; www.unioncounty.org

Massillon • Massillon Dev. Found. • 137 Lincoln Way E.; 44646; Stark; P 32,000; (330) 833-3146; Fax (330) 833-8944; info@massillondevelopment.com; www.massillondevelopment.com

Mentor • City of Mentor Eco. & Comm. Dev. • Ronald Traub; Dir.; 8500 Civic Center Blvd.; 44060; Lake; P 47,200; (440) 974-5740; Fax (440) 205-3605; thielman@cityofmentor.com; www.cityofmentor.com

Mount Vernon • Area Dev. Found. of Knox County • Steve Waers; Pres.; 110 E. High St.; 43050; Knox; P 60,900; (740) 393-3806; (888) 411-4233; Fax (740) 397-5762; steve@knoxadf.com; www.knoxadf.com

Napoleon • Henry County Comm. Improvement Corp. • Denise Dahl; Exec. Dir.; 104 E. Washington, Ste. 301; 43545; Henry; P 28,200; (419) 592-4637; jhoren@hencoed.com; www.hencoed.com

New London • New London Comm. Improvement Corp. • Yvonne Von Baron; Pres.; 115 E. Main St.; 44851; Huron; P 2,400; (419) 929-4091; Fax (419) 929-0738; nlvillage@newlondonohio.com; www.newlondonohio.com

New Philadelphia • Comm. Improvement Corp. of Tuscarawas County • Gary D. Little; Exec. Dir.; 1776 Tech Park Dr. N.E., Ste. 102; 44663; Tuscarawas; P 92,500; (330) 308-7524; Fax (330) 308-5879; garylittle@tusccic.com; www.tusccic.com

Norwood • City of Norwood Eco. Dev. Dept. • Gerry Stoker; Dir.; 4645 Montgomery Rd., Rm. 101; 45212; Hamilton; P 19,207; (513) 458-4596; Fax (513) 458-4511; gstoker@norwood-ohio.com; www.norwood-ohio.com

Oak Harbor • Ottawa County Improvement Corp. • Jamie Beier Grant; Dir.; 8043 W. State Rte. 163, Ste. 100; 43449; Ottawa; P 41,000; (419) 898-6242; (866) 734-6789; Fax (419) 898-6244; jkowalski@ocic.biz; www.ocic.biz

Orrville • Orrville Area Dev. Found. • Jennifer Reusser; Pres.; 132 S. Main St.; 44667; Wayne; P 8,500; (330) 682-8881; Fax (330) 682-8383; jenni@orrvillechamber.com; www.orrvillechamber.com

Painesville • Lake County Port Auth. • John Loftus; Exec. Dir.; One Victoria Pl., Ste. 265A; 44077; Lake; P 230,000; (440) 357-2290; Fax (440) 357-2296; jloftus@lcport.org; www.lcport.org

Piqua • City of Piqua Eco. Dev. • Justin Sommer; Dir.; 201 W. Water; 45356; Miami; P 20,600; (937) 778-8198; (800) 251-1742; jsommer@piquaoh.org; www.piquaoh.org

Pomeroy • Meigs County EDC • Perry Varnadoe; Dev. Dir.; 238 W. Main St.; 45769; Meigs; P 23,300; (740) 992-3034; Fax (740) 992-7942; director@meigscountyohio.com; www.meigscountyohio.com

Reno • Buckeye Hills-Hocking Valley Reg. Dev. Dist. • Misty Casto; Exec. Dir.; 1400 Pike St.; 45750; Washington; P 259,600; (740) 374-9436; Fax (740) 374-8038; info@buckeyehills.org; www.buckeyehills.org

Saint Clairsville • Dept. of Dev. of Belmont County • Sue Douglass; Exec. Dev. Dir.; 117 E. Main St.; 43950; Belmont; P 70,400; (740) 695-9678; Fax (740) 695-1536; suedouglass.belmontcounty@comcast.net; www.belmontdod.com

Saint Marys • City of St. Marys Dev. Dept. • Susan Crotty CEcD; Mgr of Ind. & Eco. Dev.; 101 E. Spring St.; 45885; Auglaize; P 8,332; (419) 394-3303; Fax (419) 394-2452; scrotty@cityofstmarys.net; www.stmarysdevelops.com

Sandusky • Erie County Eco. Dev. Corp. • Abbey Bemis; Exec. Dir.; 247 Columbus Ave., Ste. 126; 44870; Erie; P 76,000; (419) 627-7791; Fax (419) 627-7595; kevin@eriecountyedc.org; www.eriecountyedc.org

EDC

Sidney • *Sidney-Shelby Partnership* • Mike Dodds; Exec. Dir.; 101 S. Ohio Ave., 2nd Flr.; 45365; Shelby; P 49,000; (937) 498-9554; Fax (937) 498-2191; info@choosesidneyshelby.com; choosesidneyshelby.com

South Point • *Lawrence Eco. Dev. Corp.* • Bill Dingus; Exec. Dir.; 216 Collins Ave.; P.O. Box 488; 45680; Lawrence; P 61,200; (740) 377-4550; Fax (740) 377-2091; dingus@ohio.edu; www.ledcorp.org

Springfield • *Comm. Improvement Corp. of Springfied & Clark County* • Horton Hobbs IV; V.P.; 20 S. Limestone St., Ste. 100; 45502; Clark; P 136,000; (937) 325-7621; (800) 803-1553; Fax (937) 325-8765; hhobbs@greaterspringfield.com; www.greaterspringfield.com

Struthers • *CASTLO Comm. Improvement Corp.* • Michael L. Hoza; Exec. Dir.; 100 S. Bridge St.; 44471; Mahoning; P 36,513; (330) 750-1363; denise@castlo.com; www.castlo.com

Tiffin • *Seneca Ind. & Eco. Dev. Corp.* • Richard Focht Jr.; Pres./CEO; 19 W. Market St., Ste. C; 44883; Seneca; P 56,700; (419) 447-3831; Fax (419) 447-5141; siedc@bpsom.com; www.seneca-edc.com

Toledo • *Reg. Growth Partnership* • Dean Monske; Pres./CEO; 300 Madison Ave., Ste. 270; 43604; Lucas; P 1,000,000; (419) 252-2700; Fax (419) 252-2724; mcwilliams@rgp.org; www.rgp.org

Troy • *Troy Dev. Cncl.* • J.C. Wallace; Pres.; 405 S.W. Public Sq., Ste. 330; 45373; Miami; P 26,000; (937) 339-7809; Fax (937) 339-4944; tdc@troyohiochamber.com; www.troyeconomicdevelopment.com

Urbana • *Champaign County Eco. Partnership* • Marcia Bailey; Dir.; 3 Monument Sq.; 43078; Champaign; P 40,100; (937) 653-7200; info@cepohio.com; www.cepohio.com

Van Wert • *Van Wert Area Eco. Dev. Corp.* • Sue Gerker; Interim Dir.; 114 E. Main St., Ste. 200; 45891; Van Wert; P 28,000; (419) 238-6159; Fax (419) 238-4528; sgerker@vanwertcounty.org; www.vanwertcounty.org

Wauseon • *Fulton County Eco. Dev.* • Matt Gilroy; Exec. Dir.; 123 Courthouse Plaza, Ste. 2; 43567; Fulton; P 43,000; (419) 337-9270; Fax (419) 337-9295; shannon@fcedc-ohio.com; www.fcedc-ohio.com

Wintersville • *Jefferson County Port Auth.* • Evan Scurti; Dir. of Eco. Dev.; 600 Airpark Dr.; 43953; Jefferson; P 70,000; (740) 283-2476; Fax (740) 283-2607; evan@jcport.com; www.jcport.com

Wooster • *Wayne Eco. Dev. Cncl.* • Rod Crider; Pres.; 542 E. Liberty St.; 44691; Wayne; P 114,600; (330) 264-2411; Fax (330) 264-2412; info@waynecountyedc.com; www.waynecountyedc.com

Youngstown Area

City of Youngstown Eco. Dev. • T. Sharon Woodberry; Dev. Dir.; 20 W. Federal St., Ste. 602; 44503; Mahoning; P 67,000; (330) 744-1708; Fax (330) 744-7522; developmentinfo@youngstownohio.gov; www.youngstownohio.gov

Mahoning Valley Eco. Dev. Corp. • Mike Conway; Exec. Dir.; 4319 Belmont Ave.; 44505; Mahoning; P 557,000; (330) 759-3668; Fax (330) 759-3686; wendy@mvedc.com; www.mvedc.com

Youngstown/Warren Reg. C/C • Sarah Boyarko; Sr. V.P. of Eco. Dev.; 11 Central Sq., Ste. 1600; 44503; Mahoning; P 459,000; (330) 744-2131; Fax (330) 746-0330; anthony@regionalchamber.com; www.regionalchamber.com

Zanesville • *Zanesville-Muskingum County Port Auth.* • Mike Jacoby; Exec. Dir.; 205 N. 5th St.; 43701; Muskingum; P 86,000; (740) 455-0742; (800) 988-4388; Fax (740) 452-9703; stacy.hazen@zmcport.com; www.zmcport.com

Oklahoma

Federal

U.S. SBA, Oklahoma Dist. Ofc. • Dorothy Overal; Dist. Dir.; 301 N.W. 6th St., Ste. 116; 73102; Oklahoma; P 3,814,820; (405) 609-8000; Fax (405) 609-8990; dorothy.overal@sba.gov; www.sba.gov/ok

State

Oklahoma Dept. of Commerce • Larry Parman; Secy. of Commerce; 900 N. Stiles Ave.; Oklahoma City; 73104; Oklahoma; P 3,814,820; (405) 815-6552; Fax (405) 815-5290; martin_roberts@okcommerce.gov; www.okcommerce.gov

Communities

Altus • *Altus/Southwest Area Eco. Dev. Corp.* • David C. Webb; Mayor; 509 S. Main St.; 73521; Jackson; P 20,000; (580) 481-2202; Fax (580) 481-2203; davidcwebb@sbcglobal.net; www.altusok.gov

Ardmore • *Ardmore Dev. Auth.* • Mita Bates; Pres./CEO; 410 W. Main St.; P.O. Box 1585; 73402; Carter; P 35,000; (580) 223-6162; (580) 223-7765; Fax (580) 223-7825; aanderson@ardmore.org; www.ardmoredevelopment.com

Atoka • *Atoka County Ind. Auth.* • Joe Hill; Dir.; P.O. Box 900; 74525; Atoka; P 15,000; (580) 889-3341; (580) 889-6575; Fax (580) 889-7584; joe.hill@atokaok.org; www.atokaok.org

Bartlesville • *Bartlesville Dev. Auth.* • David Wood; Pres./CEO; 201 S.W. Keeler Ave.; 74003; Washington; P 36,000; (918) 337-8086; Fax (918) 337-0216; lclark@bdaok.org; www.bdaok.org

Blackwell • *Blackwell Ind. Auth.* • Jeff Seymour; Exec. Dir.; 120 S. Main; P.O. Box 150; 74631; Kay; P 7,600; (580) 363-2934; Fax (580) 363-1704; jseymour@blackwellindustrialauthority.com; www.blackwellindustrialauthority.com

Buffalo • *Buffalo Eco. Dev.* • James Leonard; Dir.; P.O. Box 439; 73834; Harper; P 1,300; (580) 735-2521; Fax (580) 735-2253; buffalo@pldi.net; www.BuffaloOklahoma.com

Claremore • *Rogers County Dev.* • Debi Ward; Exec. Dir.; 1503 N. Lynn Riggs Blvd., Ste. D; 74017; Rogers; P 91,000; (918) 343-8959; Fax (918) 343-2907; DebWard@RCDOklahoma.com; RogersCountyDevelopment.com

Duncan • *Duncan Area Eco. Dev. Found.* • Lyle Roggow; Pres.; 8100 N. Hwy. 81, Ste. 31; 73533; Stephens; P 45,000; (580) 255-9675; (888) 254-9675; Fax (580) 255-2647; info@ok-duncan.com; www.ok-duncan.com

Durant • *Durant Ind. Auth.* • Tommy Kramer; Exec. Dir.; 215 N. 4th Ave.; 74701; Bryan; P 43,000; (580) 924-7254; Fax (580) 924-0348; tkramer@durant.org; www.ok-durant.org

Grove • *Grove Eco. Dev.* • Debbie Bottoroff; Asst. City Mgr.; 104 W. Third; 74344; Delaware; P 6,623; (918) 786-6107; Fax (918) 786-8939; dbottoroff@cityofgroveok.gov; www.cityofgroveok.gov

Guthrie • *Logan County Eco. Dev. Cncl.* • Kay Wade; Dir.; 212 W. Oklahoma Ave.; 73044; Logan; P 44,000; (405) 282-0060; Fax (405) 282-0061; kaywade@logancountyedc.com; www.logancountyedc.com

Idabel • *Idabel Ind. Dev. Auth.* • Walter Frey; Chrmn.; 7 S.W. Texas St.; 74745; McCurtain; P 7,000; (580) 286-3305; Fax (580) 286-6708; iida@idabelok.net

Lawton • *Lawton-Fort Sill Eco. Dev. Corp.* • Tom E. Thomas III; Pres./CEO; 302 W. Gore Blvd.; 73501; Comanche; P 100,000; (580) 355-3541; (800) 872-4540; Fax (580) 357-3642; marketing@lawtonedc.com; www.lawtonedc.com

Miami • *Miami Reg. C/C - EDC* • Steve Gilbert; Pres.; 111 N. Main St.; 74354; Ottawa; P 30,000; (918) 542-4481; Fax (918) 540-1260; info@miamiokchamber.com; www.miamiokchamber.com

Midwest City • *MWC Comm. & Eco. Dev.* • David Burnett CEcD; Dir. of Econ. Dev.; 5905 Trosper Rd.; P.O. Box 10980; 73140; Oklahoma; P 55,000; (405) 733-3801; Fax (405) 733-5633; david.burnett@midwestcityok.com; www.mwcok.com

Muskogee • *Port of Muskogee Bus. Dev.* • Leisha Haworth; Dir. of Bus. & Eco. Dev.; 216 W. Okmulgee; 74401; Muskogee; P 40,000; (918) 682-7887; Fax (918) 683-2110; brien@muskogeeport.com; www.muskogeedevelopment.org

Norman • *Norman Eco. Dev. Coalition* • Jason P. Smith; Pres./CEO; 710 Asp Ave., Ste. 100; 73069; Cleveland; P 111,000; (405) 573-1900; Fax (405) 573-1999; mhammond@nedcok.com; www.nedcok.com

Oklahoma City • *Greater Oklahoma City Partnership* • Kurt Foreman; Exec. V.P.; 123 Park Ave.; 73102; Oklahoma; P 1,240,000; (405) 297-8945; Fax (405) 297-8845; kforeman@okcchamber.com; www.greateroklahomacity.com

Perry • *Perry Eco. Dev. Auth.* • Jim Davis; City Mgr.; 622 Cedar St.; P.O. Drawer 798; 73077; Noble; P 5,200; (580) 336-4241; Fax (580) 336-4065; vicki.hagerman@sbcglobal.net; www.cityofperryok.com

Tulsa • *Eco. Dev. Div., Tulsa Metro C/C* • Jim Fram; Sr. V.P.; Two W. 2nd St., Ste. 150; 74103; Osage, Rogers, Tulsa & Wagoner; P 920,000; (918) 560-0231; (918) 585-1201; Fax (918) 585-6126; angiemoore@tulsachamber.com; www.growmetrotulsa.com

Wewoka • *Eco. Dev. City of Wewoka* • Mark Mosley; City Mgr.; P.O. Box 1497; 74884; Seminole; P 3,560; (405) 257-2413; Fax (405) 257-7020; citymanager@cityofwewoka.com; www.cityofwewoka.com

Oregon

Federal

U.S. SBA, Portland Dist. Ofc. • Camron Doss; Dist. Dir.; 601 S.W. 2nd Ave., Ste. 950; 97204; Multnomah; P 3,899,353; (503) 326-2682; Fax (503) 326-2808; camron.doss@sba.gov; www.sba.gov/or

State

Business Oregon • Tim McCabe; Dir.; 775 Summer St. N.E., Ste. 200; Salem; 97301; Marion; P 3,899,353; (503) 986-0123; (866) 467-3466; Fax (503) 581-5115; biz.info@state.or.us; www.oregon4biz.com

Communities

Albany • *Albany-Millersburg Eco. Dev. Corp.* • John Pascone; Pres.; 435 1st Ave. W.; P.O. Box 548; 97321; Linn; P 52,000; (541) 926-1519; Fax (541) 926-7064; pasconj@peak.org; www.albany-millersburg.com

Albany • *Cascade West Comm. & Eco. Dev.* • Phil Warnock; Comm. & Eco. Dev. Dir.; 1400 Queen Ave., Ste. 205A; 97322; Linn; P 209,400; (541) 967-8551; Fax (541) 967-4651; pwarnock@ocwcog.org; www.ocwcog.org

Baker City • *Baker County Eco. Dev.* • Greg Smith; Dir.; 1705 Main St., Ste. 500-A; 97814; Baker; P 10,500; (541) 523-5460; Fax (541) 523-2306; bakercountyedc@gmail.com; www.bakercountyeconomicdevelopment.com

Bend • *Eco. Dev. for Central Oregon* • Roger Lee; Exec. Dir.; 705 S.W. Bonnett Way, Ste. 1000; 97702; Deschutes; P 185,230; (541) 388-3236; Fax (541) 388-6705; tom@edcoinfo.com; www.edcoinfo.com

Coos Bay • *Port of Coos Bay* • David Koch; CEO; 125 Central Ave., Ste. 300; P.O. Box 1215; 97420; Coos; P 62,000; (541) 267-7678; Fax (541) 269-1475; portcoos@portofcoosbay.com; www.portofcoosbay.com

Dallas • *Dallas Eco. Dev. Comm.* • Jerry Wyatt; City Mgr.; 187 S.E. Court St.; 97338; Polk; P 15,000; (503) 623-2338; Fax (503) 623-2339; jerry.wyatt@ci.dallas.or.us; www.ci.dallas.or.us

Enterprise • *Northeast Oregon Eco. Dev. Dist.* • Lisa Dawson; Exec. Dir.; 101 N.E. First St., Ste. 100; 97828; Wallowa; P 45,000; (541) 426-3598; (800) 645-9454; Fax (541) 426-9058; lisadawson@neoedd.org; www.neoedd.org

Eugene Area

City of Eugene - Bus. & Eco. Dev. • Sarah Medary; Exec. Dir.; 99 W. 10th Ave.; 97401; Lane; P 156,200; (541) 682-5086; (541) 682-5010; www.eugene-or.gov

Greater Eugene Inc. • Ward Wimbish; Dir.; 859 Willamette St., Ste. 350; 97441; Lane; P 170,000; (541) 686-2741; Fax (541) 686-2325; melissam@greatereugeneinc.com

Lane Cncl. of Govts. • Brenda Wilson; Exec. Dir.; 859 Willamette St., Ste. 500; 97401; Lane; P 351,800; (541) 682-4283; Fax (541) 682-4099; bwilson@lcog.org; www.lcog.org

Oregon Small Bus. Dev. Center • Mark Gregory; Dir.; 1445 Willamette St., Ste. 5; 97401; Lane; P 3,970,000; (541) 463-5250; gregorym@lanecc.com; www.bizcenter.org

Klamath Falls • *Klamath County Eco. Dev. Assn.* • Greg O'Sullivan; Dir.; 205 Riverside Dr., Ste. E; 97601; Klamath; P 66,000; (541) 882-9600; Fax (541) 882-7648; info@teamklamath.com; www.chooseklamath.com

La Grande • *Union County Eco. Dev. Corp.* • Dan Stark; Exec. Dir.; P.O. Box 1208; 97850; Union; P 26,000; (541) 963-0926; (800) 806-7278; Fax (541) 963-0689; ucedc@eoni.com; www.ucedc.org

McMinnville • *Yamhill County Dept. of Plan. & Dev.* • Ken Friday; Dir.; 525 N.E. 4th St.; 97128; Yamhill; P 100,000; (503) 434-7516; Fax (503) 434-7544; planning@co.yamhill.or.us; www.co.yamhill.or.us/plan

McMinnville • *McMinnville Eco. Dev. Partnership* • Jody Christensen; Exec. Dir.; 417 N.W. Adams St.; 97128; Yamhill; P 33,000; (503) 550-8504; Fax (503) 550-8504; info@mcminnvillebusiness.com; www.mcminnvillebusiness.com

Medford • *Southern Oregon Reg. Eco. Dev. Inc. [SOREDI]* • Colleen Padilla; Exec. Dir.; 100 E. Main St., Ste. A; 97501; Jackson; P 280,000; (541) 773-8946; Fax (541) 779-0953; kathy@soredi.org; www.soredi.org

EDC

Moro • *County Comm. Dev. Ofc.* • Georgia Macnab; Planning Dir.; 110 Main St., Ste. 2; 97039; Sherman; P 1,900; (541) 565-3601; Fax (541) 565-3078; georgiamac@embarqmail.com; www.co.sherman.or.us

Ontario • *Malheur County Eco. Dev.* • Greg Smith; Dir.; 522 S.W. 4th St.; 97914; Malheur; P 32,000; (541) 889-6216; Fax (541) 889-6398; malheurcountyedc@gmail.com; www.malheurcountyeconomicdevelopment.com

Oregon City • *Clackamas County Bus. & Eco. Dev.* • Catherine Grubowski-Johnson; Mgr.; 150 Beavercreek Rd.; 97045; Clackamas; P 376,000; (503) 742-4249; Fax (503) 742-4349; 4biz@clackamas.us; www.clackamas.us

Portland • *Portland Dev. Comm.* • Patrick Quinton; Exec. Dir.; 222 N.W. 5th Ave.; 97209; Clackamas, Multnomah & Washington; P 610,000; (503) 823-3200; Fax (503) 823-3368; mangana@pdc.us; www.pdc.us

Redmond • *Redmond Eco. Dev. Inc.* • John Stark; Sr. Mgr.; 446 S.W. 7th St.; 97756; Deschutes; P 27,000; (541) 923-5223; Fax (541) 923-6442; redi@rediinfo.com; www.rediinfo.com

Redmond • *City of Redmond Comm. Dev.* • 716 S.W. Evergreen Ave.; 97756; Deschutes; P 27,500; (541) 923-7710; Fax (541) 548-0706; www.ci.redmond.or.us

Roseburg • *CCD Bus. Dev.* • Wayne Luzier; Exec. Dir.; 522 S.E. Washington Ave., Ste. 111A; 97470; Douglas; P 200,000; (541) 672-6728; Fax (541) 672-7011; w.luzier@ccdbusiness.com; ccdbusiness.org

Salem • *Strategic Eco. Dev. Corp. [SEDCOR]* • Ray Burstedt; Pres.; 626 High St. N.E., Ste. 200; 97301; Marion; P 388,000; (503) 588-6225; Fax (503) 588-6240; rburstedt@sedcor.com; www.sedcor.com

Springfield • *City of Springfield Eco. Dev.* • Courtney Griesel; Eco. Dev. Mgr.; 225 5th St.; 97477; Lane; P 60,000; (541) 736-7132; Fax (541) 726-2363; cgriesel@springfield-or.gov; www.springfield-or.gov

Sweet Home • *Sweet Home Eco. Dev. Group* • Brian Hoffman; Exec. Dir.; 1331 Main St., Ste. B; 97386; Linn; P 8,300; (541) 367-3061; c.erickson@centurytel.net; www.sweethomeoregon.org

The Dalles • *Mid-Columbia Eco. Dev. Dist.* • Amanda Hoey; Exec. Dir.; 515 E. 2nd St.; 97058; Wasco; P 77,000; (541) 296-2266; Fax (541) 296-3283; sbohn@mcedd.org; www.mcedd.org

Tillamook • *Eco. Dev. Cncl. of Tillamook County* • Mike Cohen; Dir.; 4301 Third St.; 97141; Tillamook; P 25,300; (503) 842-8222; Fax (503) 842-8334; mikecohen@tillamookbaycc.edu; www.edctc.com

Umatilla • *Port of Umatilla* • Mr. Kim Puzey; Gen. Mgr.; 500 Willamette Ave.; P.O. Box 879; 97882; Umatilla; P 62,000; (541) 922-3224; Fax (541) 922-5609; portinfo@uci.net; www.portofumatilla.com

Pennsylvania

Federal

U.S. SBA, Philadelphia Dist. Ofc. • Michael Wilk; Deputy Dist. Dir.; 1150 First Ave., Ste. 1001; 19406; Philadelphia; P 12,763,536; (610) 382-3062; Fax (220) 481-1925; michael.wilk@sba.gov; www.sba.gov/pa

U.S. SBA, Pittsburgh Dist. Ofc. • Kelly A. Hunt; Dist. Dir.; 411 7th Ave., Ste. 1450; 15219; Allegheny; P 12,763,536; (412) 395-6560; Fax (412) 395-6562; kelly.hunt@sba.gov; www.sba.gov/pa

State

Pennsylvania Dept. of Comm. & Eco. Dev. • C. Alan Walker; Secy.; Commonwealth Keystone Bldg.; 400 North St., 4th Flr.; Harrisburg; 17120; Dauphin; P 12,763,536; (717) 787-3003; (866) 466-3972; Fax (717) 787-6866; ra-dcedcs@pa.gov; www.newpa.com

Pennsylvania Eco. Dev. Assn. • Joshua Skopp; Exec. Dir.; 908 N. Second St.; Harrisburg; 17102; Dauphin; P 12,763,536; (717) 441-6047; Fax (717) 236-2046; jskopp@wannerassoc.com; www.peda.org

Communities

Altoona • *Altoona-Blair County Dev. Corp.* • Stephen J. McKnight; Pres./CEO; 3900 Industrial Park Dr.; 16602; Blair; P 127,000; (814) 944-6113; Fax (814) 946-0157; abcd@abcdcorp.org; www.abcdcorp.org

Bedford • *Bedford County Dev. Assn.* • Bette Slayton; Pres.; 1 Corporate Dr., Ste. 101; 15522; Bedford; P 49,000; (814) 623-4816; (800) 634-8610; Fax (814) 623-6455; info@bcda.org; www.bcda.org

Berwick • *Berwick Ind. Dev. Assn.* • Stephen Phillips; Exec. Dir.; 107 S. Market St., Ste. 5; 18603; Columbia; P 22,000; (570) 752-3612; Fax (570) 752-2334; info@bida.com; www.bida.com

Bethlehem • *Lehigh Valley Ind. Park Inc.* • Kerry A. Wrobel; Pres.; 1720 Spillman Dr., Ste. 150; 18015; Northampton; P 821,000; (610) 866-4600; Fax (610) 867-9154; mfrable@lvip.org; www.lvip.org

Bethlehem • *Lehigh Valley Eco. Dev. Corp.* • Don Cunningham; Pres./CEO; 2158 Ave. C, Ste. 200; 18017; Northampton; P 821,000; (610) 266-6775; Fax (610) 266-7623; lvedc@lehighvalley.org; www.lehighvalley.org

Bloomsburg • *Columbia Alliance for Eco. Growth* • Marty Bowman; 4999 Columbia Blvd.; 17815; Columbia; P 85,600; (570) 784-9188; choosecolumbiamontour.com

Brookville • *Jefferson County Dept. of Dev.* • Craig Coon; Dir. of Comm. & Eco. Dev.; Jefferson Pl.; 155 Main St., 2nd Flr.; 15825; Jefferson; P 45,200; (814) 849-1603; Fax (814) 849-5049; cwcoon@jeffersoncountypa.com; www.jeffersoncountypa.com

Butler • *Comm. Dev. Corp. of Butler County* • Ken Raybuck; Exec. Dir.; 112 Hollywood Dr., Ste. 102; 16001; Butler; P 184,000; (724) 283-1961; (800) 283-0021; Fax (724) 283-3599; kraybuck@butlercountycdc.com; www.butlercountycdc.com

Carbondale • *Carbondale Comm. Dev.* • Nancy Perri; 10 Enterprise Dr.; 18407; Lackawanna; P 9,804; (570) 282-1255; Fax (570) 282-1426; nperri@echoes.net

Chambersburg • *Franklin County Area Dev. Corp.* • L. Michael Ross; Pres.; 1900 Wayne Rd.; 17202; Franklin; P 153,000; (717) 263-8282; Fax (717) 263-0662; info@fcadc.com; www.fcadc.com

Charleroi • *Middle Monongahela Ind. Dev. Assn.* • Lue Ann Pawlick; Exec. Dir.; P.O. Box 145; 15022; Washington; P 50,000; (724) 565-5636; Fax (724) 565-5642; lpawlick@mmida.com; mmida.com

Clearfield • *Clearfield County Eco. Dev. Corp.* • Rob Swales; CEO; 511 Spruce St., Ste. 5; 16830; Clearfield; P 82,000; (814) 768-7838; (877) 768-7838; Fax (814) 768-7338; info@clearlyahead.com; www.clearlyahead.com

Doylestown • *Bucks County Eco. Dev. Corp.* • Robert F. Cormack; Exec. Dir.; 2 E. Court St.; 18901; Bucks; P 625,000; (215) 348-9031; Fax (215) 348-8829; rfc@bcedc.com; www.bcedc.com

Easton • *Easton Comm. & Eco. Dev.* • Gretchen Longenbach; Dir.; 1 S. 3rd St.; 18042; Northampton; P 26,200; (610) 250-6721; Fax (610) 250-6607; glongenbach@easton-pa.gov; www.easton-pa.gov

Erie • *DevelopErie* • Katrina J. Vincent; Pres./CEO; 5240 Knowledge Pkwy.; 16510; Erie; P 280,000; (814) 899-6022; Fax (814) 899-0250; info@developerie.com; www.developerie.com

Exton • *Chester County Eco. Dev. Cncl.* • Gary Smith; Pres./CEO; 737 Constitution Dr.; 19341; Chester; P 498,000; (610) 458-5700; Fax (610) 458-7770; tconnor@cceconomicdevelopment.com; www.cceconomicdevelopment.com

Freeport • *Armstrong County Ind. Dev. Cncl.* • Michael P. Coonley AICP; Exec. Dir.; Northpointe Technology Center II; 187 Northpointe Blvd.; 16229; Armstrong; P 69,000; (724) 548-1500; Fax (724) 545-6055; economicdevelopment@co.armstrong.pa.us; www.armstrongidc.org

Greensburg • *Eco. Growth Connection of Westmoreland* • James Smith; Pres./CEO; 40 N. Pennsylvania Ave., Ste. 510; 15601; Westmoreland; P 365,100; (724) 830-3604; Fax (724) 850-3974; egc@egcw.org; www.egcw.org

Greenville • *Greenville Area Eco. Dev. Center* • James Lowry; Exec. Dir.; 12 N. Diamond St.; 16125; Mercer; P 19,120; (724) 588-1161; Fax (724) 588-9881; jim.lowry@gaedc.org; www.gaedc.org

Grove City • *79-80 Interstate Dev. Corp.* • Beth Black; Admin.; 119 S. Broad St.; 16127; Mercer; P 16,000; (724) 458-6410; Fax (724) 458-6841; info@79-80idc.com; www.79-80idc.com

Harrisburg • *Dauphin County Ofc. of Eco. Dev.* • August Memmi; Dir.; 112 Market St., 7th Flr.; 17101; Dauphin; P 268,100; (717) 780-6250; Fax (717) 257-1513; amemmi@dauphinc.org; www.dauphincounty.org

Hazleton • *CAN DO Inc. [Eco. Dev. Corp.]* • Kevin O'Donnell; Pres./CEO; 1 S. Church St., Ste. 200; 18201; Luzerne; P 80,000; (570) 455-1508; Fax (570) 454-7787; cando@hazletoncando.com; www.hazletoncando.com

Huntingdon • *Huntingdon County Bus. & Ind. Inc.* • Amy Wise; Exec. Dir.; 9136 William Penn Hwy.; 16652; Huntingdon; P 46,000; (814) 506-8287; staff@hcbi.com; www.hcbi.com

Indiana • *Indiana County Center for Eco. Operations* • Byron G. Stauffer Jr.; Exec. Dir.; 801 Water St.; 15701; Indiana; P 90,000; (724) 465-2662; Fax (724) 465-3150; info@indianacountyceo.com; www.indianacountyceo.com

Johnstown • *Cambria County Eco. Dev. Auth.* • Nick Felice; Exec. Dir.; 479 Airport Rd., Ste. 2; 15904; Cambria; P 14,100; (814) 792-2759; info@cambriaeda.org; www.cambriaeda.org

Johnstown • *Johnstown Ind. Dev. Corp.* • Linda Thomson; Pres.; 245 Market St., Ste. 200; 15901; Cambria; P 143,600; (814) 535-8675; Fax (814) 535-8677; mclapper@jari.com; www.jari.com

Lancaster • *Eco. Dev. Co. of Lancaster County* • David Nikoloff; Pres.; 100 S. Queen St.; P.O. Box 1558; 17608; Lancaster; P 519,400; (717) 397-4046; Fax (717) 293-3159; edc@edclancaster.com; www.edclancaster.com

Lebanon • *Lebanon Valley Eco. Dev. Corp.* • Charles Blankenship; Pres.; 16 Lebanon Valley Pkwy.; 17042; Lebanon; P 120,000; (717) 274-3180; Fax (717) 274-1367; cblankenship@lvedc.org; www.lvedc.org

Lehighton • *Carbon Chamber & Eco. Dev. Corp.* • Kathy Henderson; Dir. of Eco. Dev.; 137 South St.; 18235; Carbon; P 65,200; (610) 379-5000; Fax (610) 379-0130; info@carboncountychamber.org; www.carboncountychamber.org

Lemont Furnace • *Fay-Penn Eco. Dev. Cncl.* • Bob Shark; Exec. Dir.; 1040 Eberly Way, Ste. 200; 15456; Fayette; P 148,644; (724) 437-7913; Fax (724) 437-7315; bobs@faypenn.org; www.faypenn.org

Lewisburg • *Union County Eco. Dev. Ofc.* • Shawn McLaughlin; Planning Dir.; 155 N. 15th St.; 17837; Union; P 45,000; (570) 524-3845; smclaughlin@unionco.org; www.uncoedc.org

Lewistown • *Mifflin County Ind. Dev. Corp.* • Robert P. Postal; Pres.; 6395 S.R. 103 N.; 17044; Mifflin; P 46,600; (717) 242-0393; Fax (717) 242-1842; mcidc@mcidc.org; www.mcidc.org

Lock Haven • *Clinton County Eco. Partnership* • Michael K. Flanagan; Pres./CEO; 212 N. Jay St.; P.O. Box 506; 17745; Clinton; P 40,000; (570) 748-5782; Fax (570) 893-0433; flanagan@kcnet.org; www.clintoncountyinfo.com

McKeesport • *McKeesport Ind. Dev.* • Dennis Pittman; Admin.; 500 5th Ave.; 15132; Allegheny; P 24,040; (412) 675-5020; Fax (412) 675-5049; dennis.pittman@mckeesport.org; www.mckeesport.org

Meadville • *Redev. Auth. of the City of Meadville* • Jill Withey; Exec. Dir.; 984 Water St., Ste. 2; 16335; Crawford; P 13,600; (814) 337-8200; Fax (814) 337-7257; twhite2@redevelopmeadville.com; www.redevelopmeadville.com

Media • *Delaware County Eco. Dev. Oversight Bd.* • J. Patrick Killian; Dir.; 100 W. 6th St., Ste. 100; 19063; Delaware; P 570,000; (610) 566-2225; Fax (610) 566-7337; info@delcopa.org; www.delcopa.org

Mercer • *Penn-Northwest Dev. Corp.* • Larry D. Reichard; Exec. Dir.; 749 Greenville Rd.; 16137; Mercer; P 120,000; (724) 662-3705; Fax (724) 662-0283; lreichard@penn-northwest.com; www.penn-northwest.com

Milford • *Pike County Ind. Dev. Auth.* • Michael J. Sullivan; Exec. Dir.; 209 E. Harford St.; 18337; Pike; P 58,000; (570) 296-7332; Fax (570) 296-3921; tammy@edapikepa.org; www.edapikepa.org

New Castle • *Lawrence County Eco. Dev. Corp.* • Linda D. Nitch; Exec. Dir.; 100 E. Reynolds St., Ste. 100; 16101; Lawrence; P 90,160; (724) 658-1488; Fax (724) 658-0313; info@lawrencecounty.com; www.lawrencecounty.com

Norristown • *Montgomery County Dev. Corp.* • 104 W. Main St., Ste. 2; 19401; Montgomery; P 813,000; (610) 272-5000; Fax (610) 272-6235; mcdc@montcopa.org; www.montcodc.org

Norristown • *Montgomery County Dept. of Eco. & Workforce Dev.* • Marisol Lezcano; Exec. Dir.; 1430 Dekalb St., 5th Flr.; P.O. Box 311; 19404; Montgomery; P 799,800; (610) 278-5950; Fax (610) 278-1100; mlezcano@montcopa.org; www.montcopa.org

Oil City • *Oil Region Alliance of Bus., Ind. & Tourism* • John R. Phillips II; Pres./CEO; 217 Elm St.; 16301; Venango; P 55,000; (814) 677-3152; (800) 483-6264; Fax (814) 677-5206; jphillips@oilregion.org; www.oilregion.org

Oil City • *Northwest Commission* • Jill Foys; Exec. Dir.; 395 Seneca St.; 16301; Venango; P 721,200; (814) 677-4800; Fax (814) 677-7663; vondac@northwestpa.org; www.northwestpa.org

Philadelphia • *Philadelphia Ind. Dev. Corp.* • John Grady; Pres.; 1500 Market St., Ste. 2600 W.; 19102; Philadelphia; P 1,560,000; (215) 496-8020; Fax (215) 977-9618; info@pidcphila.com; www.pidcphila.com

EDC

Philadelphia • *Delaware Valley Reg. Planning Comm.* • Barry Seymour; Exec. Dir.; 190 N. Independence Mall West; 19106; Philadelphia; P 5,000,000; (215) 592-1800; Fax (215) 592-9125; bseymour@dvrpc.org; www.dvrpc.org

Philipsburg • *Moshannon Valley Eco. Dev. Partnership* • Stanley LaFuria; Exec. Dir.; 200 Shady Ln.; 16866; Centre; P 3,400; (814) 342-2260; Fax (814) 342-2878; info@mvedp.org; www.mvedp.org

Pittsburgh • *Allegheny County Dept. of Eco. Dev.* • Dennis M. Davin; Dir.; 425 Sixth Ave., Ste. 800; 15219; Allegheny; P 1,200,000; (412) 350-1000; Fax (412) 642-2217; michele.capuano@alleghenycounty.us; economic.alleghenycounty.us

Pittsburgh • *Reg. Ind. Dev. Corp. of Southwestern PA [RIDC]* • Tim White; Asst. V.P.; 210 Sixth Ave., Ste. 3620; 15222; Allegheny; P 2,100,000; (412) 315-6447; Fax (412) 471-1740; twhite@ridc.org; www.ridc.org

Pittston • *Northeastern Pennsylvania Alliance* • Jeffrey Box; Pres./CEO; 1151 Oak St.; 18640; Luzerne; (570) 655-5581; Fax (570) 654-5137; info@nepa-alliance.org; www.nepa-alliance.org

Pottsville • *Schuylkill EDC* • Frank J. Zukas; Pres.; Union Station; One Progress Cir., Ste. 200; 17901; Schuylkill; P 148,300; (570) 622-1943; Fax (570) 622-2903; lreiser@sed-co.com; www.sed-co.com

Quakertown • *Nockamixon-Bucks Ind. & Comm. Dev. Auth.* • Stephen Shelly; Solicitor; 525 W. Broad St.; 18951; Bucks; P 12,700,000; (215) 538-1400; Fax (215) 538-9033; shelly@enter.net

Reading • *Greater Berks Dev. Fund* • Debra Millman; Dir. of Bus. Dev.; P.O. Box 8621; 19603; Berks; P 411,400; (610) 376-6739; Fax (610) 478-9553; greaterberks@readingpa.com; www.readingpa.com

Saint Marys • *St. Marys Area Eco. Dev. Corp.* • Val Weis; Exec. Dir.; 32 S. St. Marys St.; 15857; Elk; P 14,000; (814) 834-2125; Fax (814) 834-2126; stmarysedc@windstream.net

Scranton • *Lackawanna County Dept. of Eco. Dev.* • Mary Ellen Clark; Secy.; 200 Adams Ave., 5th Flr.; 18503; Lackawanna; P 214,400; (570) 963-6862; (570) 963-6830; Fax (570) 342-4088; clark@lackawannacounty.org; www.lackawannacounty.org

Shippensburg • *Shippensburg Area Dev. Corp.* • Mickey Nye; Pres.; 53 W. King St.; 17257; Cumberland & Franklin; P 28,000; (717) 532-5509; Fax (717) 532-7501; chamber@shippensburg.org; www.shippensburg.org

Somerset • *Somerset County Eco. Dev. Cncl.* • Gary DuFour; Exec. Dir.; 125 N. Center Ave.; P.O. Box 48; 15501; Somerset; P 78,000; (814) 445-9655; Fax (814) 443-4610; contact@scedc.net; www.scedc.net

State College • *Chamber of Bus. & Ind. of Centre County* • Vern Squier; Pres./CEO; 131 S. Fraser St.; 16801; Centre; P 154,000; (814) 234-1829; Fax (814) 234-5869; cbicc@cbicc.org; www.cbicc.org

Sunbury • *Northumberland County Ind. Dev. Auth.* • Patrick Mack; Dir.; 399 S. Fifth St.; 17801; Northumberland; P 94,000; (570) 988-4343; (570) 988-4100; Fax (570) 988-4436; pat.mack@norrycopa.net; www.norrycopa.net

Titusville • *Titusville Ind. Fund* • P.O. Box 425; 16354; Crawford; P 6,000; (814) 827-3668; Fax (814) 827-1234; rlh@tcda.org; www.tcda.org

Tobyhanna • *Pocono Mountains Eco. Dev. Corp.* • Chuck Leonard; Exec. Dir.; 300 Community Dr., Ste. D; 18466; Monroe; P 163,000; (570) 839-1992; (877) 736-7700; Fax (570) 839-6681; cleonard@pmedc.com; www.pmedc.com

Washington • *Redev. Auth. of WA County* • William McGowen; Exec. Dir.; 100 W. Beau St., Ste. 603; 15301; Washington; P 209,000; (724) 228-6875; Fax (724) 228-6829; redevelopment@racw.net; www.racw.net

Waynesburg • *Greene County Ind. Dev. Auth.* • Crystal Simmons; Dir.; 49 S. Washington St.; 15370; Greene; P 40,000; (724) 627-9259; Fax (724) 627-6569; csimmons@co.greene.pa.us; www.co.greene.pa.us

Wilkes-Barre • *Luzerne County Ofc. of Comm. Dev.* • Andrew Reilly; Exec. Dir.; 54 W. Union St.; 18702; Luzerne; P 321,000; (570) 824-7214; Fax (570) 829-2910; andy.reilly@luzernecounty.org; www.luzernecounty.org

Wilkes-Barre • *Greater Wilkes-Barre Dev. Corp.* • Joseph Boylan; V.P. of Eco. Dev.; Two Public Square; 18701; Luzerne; P 321,000; (570) 823-2101; Fax (570) 822-5951; wbcofc@wilkes-barre.org; wilkes-barre.org

York • *York County Eco. Alliance* • Loren Kroh; Interim Pres.; 144 Roosevelt Ave.; 17401; York; P 401,613; (717) 848-4000; Fax (717) 843-8837; info@ycea-pa.org; www.ycea-pa.org

Puerto Rico

Federal

U.S. SBA, Puerto Rico Dist. Ofc. • Yvette T. Collazo; Dist. Dir.; 273 Ponce de Leon Ave.; Plz. 273, Ste. 510; 00917; P 3,500,000; (787) 766-5572; Fax (787) 766-5309; yvette.collazo@sba.gov; www.sba.gov/pr

Communities

Hato Rey • *Puerto Rico Ind. Dev. Co.* • José R. Pérez Riera; Exec. Dir.; #355 FD Roosevelt Ave., Ste. 404; 00918; P 3,920,000; (787) 758-4747; Fax (787) 764-1415; nparkhurst@ddecpr.com; www.pridco.com

Rhode Island

Federal

U.S. SBA, Rhode Island Dist. Ofc. • Mark S. Hayward; Dist. Dir.; 380 Westminster St., Rm. 511; 02903; Providence; P 1,050,292; (401) 528-4561; Fax (401) 528-4539; mark.hayward@sba.gov; www.sba.gov/ri

State

Rhode Island Eco. Dev. Corp. • Marcel Valois; Exec. Dir.; 315 Iron Horse Way, Ste. 101; Providence; 02908; Providence; P 1,050,292; (401) 278-9100; Fax (401) 273-8270; info@riedc.com; www.riedc.com

Communities

Bristol • *Bristol Eco. Dev. Comm.* • Diane Williamson; Dir. of Comm. Dev.; 9 Court St.; 02809; Bristol; P 24,000; (401) 253-7000; Fax (401) 396-5466; dianew@bristolri.us; www.bristolri.us

Cranston • *City of Cranston-Dept. of Eco. Dev.* • Lawrence DiBoni; Dir.; City Hall; 869 Park Ave.; 02910; Providence; P 81,500; (401) 780-3166; (401) 780-3168; Fax (401) 780-3179; ldiboni@cranstonri.org; www.cranstonri.com

Cumberland • *New England Eco. Dev. Svcs. Inc.* • Scott A. Gibbs; Pres.; 1300 Highland Corporate Dr., Ste. 202; 02864; Providence; P 14,700,000; (401) 658-0665; Fax (401) 658-0630; sgibbs@needsinc.com; www.needsinc.com

Cumberland • *Eco. Dev. Found. of Rhode Island Inc.* • Scott A. Gibbs; Pres.; 1300 Highland Corporate Dr., Ste. 202; 02864; Providence; P 1,600,000; (401) 658-1050; Fax (401) 658-1064; sgibbs@edf-ri.com; www.edf-ri.com

East Providence • *East Providence Planning Dept.* • Jeanne Boyle; Planning Dir.; 145 Taunton Ave.; City Hall; 02914; Providence; P 48,000; (401) 435-7500; (401) 435-7531; jboyle@cityofeastprov.com; www.eastprovidenceri.net

Lincoln • *Lincoln Town Planning Dept.* • Albert Ranaldi Jr. AICP; Planner; 100 Old River Rd.; P.O. Box 100; 02865; Providence; P 21,200; (401) 333-8433; (401) 333-1100; Fax (401) 333-3648; aranaldi@lincolnri.org; www.lincolnri.org

Pawtucket • *Dept. of Planning & Redev. - City of Pawtucket* • Susan Mara; Interim Dir.; 137 Roosevelt Ave.; 02860; Providence; P 73,000; (401) 728-0500; Fax (401) 726-6237; smara@pawtucketri.com; www.pawtucketri.com

Warwick • *Warwick Eco. Dev. Dept.* • Karen Jedson; Eco. Dev. Dir.; Warwick City Hall; 3275 Post Rd.; 02886; Kent; P 84,000; (401) 738-2000; Fax (401) 738-6639; econ.dir@warwickri.com; www.movetowarwickri.com

West Warwick • *West Warwick Eco. Dev.* • Mark Carruolo; Town Planner/Eco. Dev. Coord.; 1170 Main St.; 02893; Kent; P 30,000; (401) 827-9025; (401) 822-9200; Fax (401) 822-9266; mcarruolo@westwarwickri.org; www.westwarwickri.org

Westerly • *Town of Westerly* • Amy Grzybowski; Dir. of Dev. Svcs.; 45 Broad St.; 02891; Washington; P 23,000; (401) 348-2617; Fax (401) 348-2513; agrzybowski@westerly.org; westerly.govoffice.com

South Carolina

Federal

U.S. SBA, South Carolina Dist. Ofc. • Elliott O. Cooper; Dist. Dir.; 1835 Assembly St., Ste. 1425; 29201; Richland; P 4,723,723; (803) 765-5377; Fax (803) 765-5962; elliott.cooper@sba.gov; www.sba.gov/sc

State

South Carolina Dept. of Commerce • Robert M. Hitt III; Secy. of Commerce; 1201 Main St., Ste.1600; Columbia; 29201; Richland; P 4,723,723; (803) 737-0400; (800) 868-7232; Fax (803) 737-0418; info@sccommerce.com; www.sccommerce.com

Communities

Abbeville • *Abbeville County Dev. Bd.* • Stephen Taylor; Dev. Svcs. Dir.; 901 W. Greenwood St., Ste. 2600; 29620; Abbeville; P 25,000; (864) 366-2181; Fax (864) 366-9266; jhannah@abbevillecountysc.com; www.investabbevillecounty.com

Aiken • *Eco. Dev. Partnership* • Will Williams; Pres./CEO; P.O. Box 1708; 29802; Aiken; P 165,900; (803) 641-3300; Fax (803) 641-3369; wwilliams@edpsc.org; www.edpsc.org

Allendale • *Allendale County Dev. Bd.* • Timothy Bennett; County Admin.; P.O. Box 190; 29810; Allendale; P 11,200; (803) 584-3438; Fax (803) 584-7042; tbennett@allendalecounty.com; www.allendalecounty.com

Anderson • *Anderson County Eco. Dev.* • Burriss Nelson; Dir.; 126 N. McDuffie St.; 29621; Anderson; P 191,000; (864) 260-4386; Fax (864) 260-4369; bnelson@andersoncountysc.org; www.andersoncountytoday.com

Barnwell • *Barnwell County Eco. Dev. Comm.* • Marshall Martin; Exec. Dir.; P.O. Box 898; 29812; Barnwell; P 22,600; (803) 259-1263; Fax (803) 259-0030; mmartin@discoverbarnwellcounty.com; www.discoverbarnwellcounty.com

Barnwell • *SouthernCarolina Reg. Dev. Alliance* • Danny Black; Pres./CEO; 1750 Jackson St., Ste. 100; 29812; Barnwell; P 70,000; (803) 541-0023; Fax (803) 541-3322; sca@southerncarolina.org; www.southerncarolina.org

Beaufort • *Lowcountry Eco. Alliance* • Kim D. Statler; Exec. Dir.; 1911 Boundary St.; P.O. Box 2025; 29901; Beaufort; P 120,937; (843) 379-3955; Fax (843) 379-3954; info@lowcountryalliance.com; www.lowcountryalliance.com

Bennettsville • *Marlboro County Eco. Dev. Partnership* • Jim Haynes; Interim Exec. Dir.; 214 E. Market St.; P.O. Box 653; 29512; Marlboro; P 28,813; (843) 479-5626; (843) 862-3868; Fax (843) 479-2663; mcecodev@marlborocounty.sc.gov; www.marlborocountysc.org

Bishopville • *see Sumter*

Camden • *Kershaw County Eco. Dev. Ofc.* • Peggy McLean; Dir.; 80 Campus Dr.; P.O. Box 763; 29021; Kershaw; P 62,000; (803) 425-7685; Fax (803) 425-7687; econ.develop@kershaw.sc.gov; www.kershawcountysc.org

Cheraw • *see Chesterfield*

Chesterfield • *Chesterfield County Eco. Dev. Bd.* • Kim Burch; Exec. Dir.; 105 Green St.; 29709; Chesterfield; P 46,800; (843) 623-6500; Fax (843) 623-3167; cchambers@shtc.net; www.chesterfieldcountysc.org

Columbia • *SC Power Team* • Ralph U. Thomas; Pres.; 1201 Main St., Ste. 1710; 29201; Richland; P 800,000; (803) 254-9211; Fax (803) 771-0233; mail@scpowerteam.com; www.scpowerteam.com

Columbia • *Central SC Alliance* • G. Michael Briggs; Pres./CEO; 1201 Main St., Ste. 100; 29201; Richland; P 986,276; (803) 733-1131; Fax (803) 733-1125; kcoffey@centralsc.org; www.centralsc.org

Conway • *Myrtle Beach Reg. Eco. Dev. Corp.* • Josh Kay; Pres./CEO; 2050 Hwy. 501 E., Bldg. 900; 29526; Horry; P 175,000; (843) 347-4604; (800) 844-4983; info@mbredc.org; mbredc.org

Dillon • *Dillon County Dev. Partnership* • Tonny McNeil; Dir.; 101 E. Main St.; P.O. Box 911; 29536; Dillon; P 32,100; (843) 774-1402; Fax (843) 841-3872; dilloncoecondev@bellsouth.net; www.dilloncounty.org

Fort Mill • *York County Eco. Dev.* • David Swenson; Dir.; 1830 Second Baxter Crossing; 29708; York; P 245,000; (803) 802-4300; Fax (803) 802-4299; david.swenson@yorkcountygov.com; www.ycedb.com

Fountain Inn • *Fountain Inn Eco. Dev.* • Van Broad; Eco. Dev. Dir.; 315 N. Main; 29644; Laurens; P 6,000; (864) 862-0042; van.broad@fountaininn.org; www.fountaininn.org

Gaffney • *Cherokee County Eco. Dev. Bd.* • Jim Cook; Exec. Dir.; 101 Campus Dr.; 29341; Cherokee; P 56,000; (864) 206-2804; Fax (864) 206-2801; cookj@sccsc.edu; www.cherokeecountydevelopmentboard.com

EDC

Georgetown • *Georgetown County Eco. Dev.* • Brian Tucker; Dir. of Eco. Dev.; 716 Prince St.; 29440; Georgetown; P 62,000; (843) 545-3163; (843) 545-3006; Fax (843) 545-3259; info@seegeorgetown.com; www.seegeorgetown.com

Greenwood • *Greenwood Partnership Alliance* • Heather Simmons Jones; CEO; P.O. Box 366; 29648; Greenwood; P 69,700; (864) 388-1250; Fax (864) 388-1253; info@partnershipalliance.com; www.partnershipalliance.com

Hampton • *Hampton County Eco. Dev. Comm.* • Jo Ann Lamprecht; Admin. Asst.; 200 Jackson Ave. E.; 29924; Hampton; P 22,000; (803) 914-2140; Fax (803) 914-2144; jlamprecht@hamptoncountysc.org; www.hamptoncountysc.org

Kingstree • *Williamsburg County Dev. Bd.* • Frank Hilton McGill Jr.; Exec. Dir.; P.O. Box 1132; 29556; Williamsburg; P 37,217; (843) 382-9393; Fax (843) 382-5353; hmcgill@ftc-i.net; www.williamsburgcountydevelopment.com

Lancaster • *Lancaster County Eco. Dev. Dept.* • Jamie Gilbert; Dir.; 101 N. Main St.; P.O. Box 1809; 29721; Lancaster; P 77,000; (803) 286-3633; Fax (803) 416-9497; econdev@lancastercountysc.net; www.mylancastersc.org

Liberty • *Alliance Pickens* • A. Ray Farley II CEcD; Exec. Dir.; 1390 Smith Grove Rd.; P.O. Box 149; 29657; Pickens; P 120,000; (864) 898-1500; Fax (864) 843-5790; rfarley@alliancepickens.com; www.alliancepickens.com

Manning • *Clarendon County Dev. Bd.* • George Kosinski; Exec. Dir.; 411 Sunset Dr.; 29102; Clarendon; P 35,412; (803) 435-8813; (800) 729-0973; Fax (803) 435-4925; gkosinski@clarendoncountygov.org; www.clarendoncountyusa.com

Marion • *Marion County Eco. Dev. Comm.* • Rodney Berry; Exec. Dir.; P.O. Box 840; 29571; Marion; P 35,000; (843) 423-8235; Fax (843) 423-8233; rberry@marionsc.org; www.marioncountysc.com

McCall • *see Bennettsville*

McCormick • *McCormick County Dev. Bd.* • George Woodsby; Eco. Dev. Dir.; 610 S. Mine St.; 29835; McCormick; P 10,000; (864) 852-2231; Fax (864) 852-2783; gwoodsby@mccormickcountysc.org; www.mccormickcountysc.org

Moncks Corner • *Berkeley County Eco. Dev. Dept.*
• Gene Butler; Eco. Dev. Dir.; P.O. Box 6122; 29461; Berkeley; P 160,000; (843) 719-4096; Fax (843) 719-4381; Web_EconomicDevelopment@berkeleycountysc.gov; www.berkeleycountysc.gov

North Charleston • *Charleston Reg. Dev. Alliance* • David Ginn; Pres./CEO; 4401 Belle Oaks Dr., Ste. 420; 29405; Berkeley, Charleston & Dorchester; P 712,220; (843) 767-9300; alliance@crda.org; www.crda.org

Orangeburg • *Orangeburg County Dev. Comm.* • C. Gregory Robinson; Exec. Dir.; 125 Regional Pkwy., Ste. 100; 29118; Orangeburg; P 93,000; (803) 536-3333; Fax (803) 534-1165; grobinson@ocdc.com; www.ocdc.com

Pageland • *see Chesterfield*

Rock Hill • *Rock Hill Eco. Dev. Corp.* • Stephen Turner; Exec. Dir.; 155 Johnston St.; P.O. Box 11706; 29731; York; P 66,200; (803) 329-7090; Fax (803) 329-7007; stephenturner@cityofrockhill.com; www.rockhillusa.com

Seneca • *Oconee Eco. Alliance* • Richard K. Blackwell; Exec. Dir.; 528 Bypass 123, Ste. G; 29678; Oconee; P 75,000; (864) 638-4210; rblackwell@oconeesc.com; www.oconeescedc.com

Spartanburg • *Upstate Employers Network* • Don Woodward; Pres.; 1004 S. Pine St.; 29302; Spartanburg; P 284,300; (864) 585-1007; Fax (864) 573-6534; info@employersnet.com; www.employersnet.com

Summerville • *Dorchester County Eco. Dev. Dept.* • John Truluck; Dir.; 402 N. Main St., Ste. C; 29483; Dorchester; P 148,000; (843) 875-9109; Fax (843) 821-9994; info@dorchesterforbusiness.com; www.dorchesterforbusiness.com

Sumter • *Sumter Eco. Dev.* • Jay Schwedler; Pres./CEO; 32 E. Calhoun St.; 29150; Sumter; P 107,500; (803) 418-0700; (800) 888-7926; Fax (803) 775-0915; ebuxton@sumter-sc.com; www.sumteredge.com

Union • *Union County Dev. Bd.* • Joe Nichols; Chrmn.; 207 S. Herndon St.; 29379; Union; P 29,000; (864) 319-1097; Fax (864) 319-1099; jtrammell@uniondevelopmentboard.com; www.uniondevelopmentboard.com

South Dakota

Federal

***U.S. SBA, South Dakota Dist. Ofc.* •** John L. Brown II; Dist. Dir.; 2329 N. Career Ave., Ste. 105; 57107; Minnehaha; P 883,354; (605) 330-4243; Fax (605) 330-4215; john.l.brown@sba.gov; www.sba.gov/sd

State

***South Dakota Governor's Ofc. of Eco. Dev.* •** Aaron Scheibe; Interim Commissioner; 711 E. Wells Ave.; Pierre; 57501; Hughes; P 854,000; (605) 773-3301; Fax (605) 773-3256; goed.info@state.sd.us; www.sdreadytowork.com

Communities

Aberdeen • *Aberdeen Dev. Corp.* • Michael Bockorny; CEO; 416 Production St. N.; 57401; Brown; P 27,000; (605) 229-5335; Fax (605) 229-6839; contact@adcsd.com; www.adcsd.com

Aberdeen • *NE Cncl. of Govts.* • Eric Senger; Exec. Dir.; 416 Production St. N., Ste. 1; 57401; Brown; (605) 626-2595; Fax (605) 626-2975; jennifer@necog.org; www.necog.org

Belle Fourche • *Belle Fourche Dev. Corp.* • 511 6th Ave.; 57717; Butte; P 5,700; (605) 892-2494; city@bellefourche.org; bellefourche.org

Beresford • *Beresford Ind. Dev.* • Jerry Zeimetz; City Admin.; 101 N. 3rd; 57004; Lincoln & Union; P 2,100; (605) 763-2008; Fax (605) 763-2329; jerry@bmtc.net; www.beresfordsd.com

Brandon • *Brandon Dev. Found. Inc.* • Joel Jorgenson; Dir.; 304 Main Ave.; P.O. Box 95; 57005; Minnehaha; P 8,785; (605) 582-6515; Fax (605) 582-6831; dolson@cityofbrandon.org; www.brandonsd.com

Britton • *Britton Dev. Corp.* • Tom Farber; Pres.; P.O. Box 413; 57430; Marshall; P 1,241; (605) 448-5150; Fax (605) 448-2810; www.brittonsouthdakota.com

Centerville • *Centerville Dev. Corp.* • Jared Hybertson; Eco. Dev. Coord.; 741 Main St.; 57014; Turner; P 900; (605) 563-2302; jhybertson@hotmail.com; centervillesd.com

Chamberlain • *Lake Francis Case Dev.* • April Reis; Exec. Dir.; 115 W. Lawler Ave.; 57325; Brule; P 2,600; (605) 234-4419; Fax (605) 234-4418; lfcdc@midstatesd.net; www.dakotadevelopment.com

Dakota Dunes • *Dakota Dunes Dev. Co.* • Dennis Melstad; Pres.; 335 Sioux Point Rd., Ste. 100; 57049; Union; P 2,700; (605) 232-5990; Fax (605) 232-5995; tim@dakotadunes.com; www.dakotadunes.com

Dell Rapids • *Dell Rapids Eco. Dev. Corp.* • Doug Hainje; Pres.; 306 N. Ladelle; 57022; Minnehaha; P 3,633; (605) 428-5645; www.cityofdellrapids.org

Estelline • *Estelline Area Eco. Dev. Corp.* • Tammy Krein; Pres.; P.O. Box 198; 57234; Hamlin; P 770; www.estellinesd.com

Faith • *Faith Country Dev. Corp.* • Randy Thomas; Pres.; P.O. Box 341; 57626; Meade; P 421; (605) 967-2242; (605) 967-2261; www.faith.govoffice.com

Gregory • *Gregory Bus. & Ind. Dev.* • Ron Kyburz; Pres.; c/o City of Gregory; P.O. Box 436; 57533; Gregory; P 1,295; (605) 835-8270; Fax (605) 835-8422; gregcity@gwtc.net; www.cityofgregory.com

Herreid • *Herreid Eco. Dev. Corp.* • Dean Schwartz; Pres.; 110 S. Main; P.O. Box 275; 57632; Campbell; P 438; (605) 437-2294; Fax (605) 437-2278; cityofherreid@valleytel.net; www.herreidsd.com

Hosmer • *Eco. Dev. Corp.* • John Eisenberisz; Treas.; 33920 127th St.; 57448; Edmunds; P 208; (605) 283-2639; (605) 283-2748; Fax (605) 283-2605

Howard • *Howard Industries* • Dave Callies; Secy.; P.O. Box 187; 57349; Miner; P 900; (605) 772-4380; (605) 772-4391; Fax (605) 772-5492; www.cityofhoward.com

Huron • *Greater Huron Dev. Corp.* • Jim Borszich; Exec. Dir.; 1705 Dakota Ave. S.; 57350; Beadle; P 12,100; (605) 352-0363; (800) 487-6673; Fax (605) 352-8321; ghdc@huronsd.com; www.huronsd.com

Lennox • *Lennox Area Dev. Corp.* • Rob Huber; Pres.; 107 S. Main; 57039; Lincoln; P 2,200; (605) 359-5364; (605) 647-2286; Fax (605) 647-2281; www.cityoflennoxsd.com

Mitchell • *Mitchell Area Dev. Corp.* • Bryan Hisel; Exec. Dir.; 601 N. Main; P.O. Box 1087; 57301; Davison; P 18,741; (605) 996-1140; Fax (605) 996-8273; bhisel@mitchellsd.org; www.mitchellsd.org

Pierre • *Pierre Eco. Dev. Corp.* • Jim Protexter; COO; 800 W. Dakota; 57501; Hughes; P 17,500; (605) 224-6610; (800) 962-2034; Fax (605) 224-6485; jim@pedco.biz; www.pedco.biz

Rapid City • *Rapid City Area Eco. Dev. Partnership* • Benjamin Snow; Pres.; 525 University Loop, Ste. 101; 57701; Pennington; P 105,000; (605) 343-1880; Fax (605) 343-1916; info@rapiddevelopment.com; www.rapiddevelopment.com

Redfield • *Grow Spink Inc.* • Craig Johnson; Exec. Dir.; 701 Main St.; 57469; Spink; P 6,470; (605) 472-5011; (605) 450-0565; Fax (605) 472-1280; craigj@growspink.com; www.growspink.com

Scotland • *Scotland Area Dev. Corp.* • Greg Gemar; Pres.; P.O. Box 274; 57059; Bon Homme; P 900; (605) 583-4234; (605) 583-2570; scotnews@gwtc.net; www.scotlandsd.org

Sioux Falls • *Sioux Falls Dev. Found.* • Slater R. Barr; Pres.; 200 N. Phillips Ave., Ste. 101; 57104; Minnehaha; P 180,000; (605) 339-0103; (800) 658-3373; Fax (605) 339-0055; marya@siouxfalls.com; www.siouxfallsdevelopment.com

Spearfish • *Spearfish Eco. Dev. Corp.* • Stephanie Salazar CEcD; Exec. Dir.; 106 W. Kansas; P.O. Box 550; 57783; Lawrence; P 15,000; (605) 642-3832; (605) 641-1406; Fax (605) 642-7310; director@spearfishdevelopment.com; www.spearfishdevelopment.com

Sturgis • *Black Hills Comm. Eco. Dev. Inc.* • Blaise Emerson; Exec. Dir.; 2885 Dickson Dr.; P.O. Box 218; 57785; Meade; P 130,000; (605) 347-5837; Fax (605) 347-5223; bemerson@tie.net; www.bhced.org

Sturgis • *Sturgis Eco. Dev. Corp.* • Pat Kurtenbach; Pres.; 2885 Dickson Dr.; P.O. Box 218; 57785; Meade; P 6,000; (605) 347-4906; Fax (605) 347-5223; info@sturgisdevelopment.com; www.sturgisdevelopment.com

Tripp • *Tripp Dev. Corp.* • Bob Just; Bd. Member; P.O. Box 105; 57376; Hutchinson; P 650; (605) 935-6661; (605) 935-6332; www.trippsd.com

Tyndall • *Tyndall Dev. Co.* • Ron Wagner; Pres.; P.O. Box 454; 57066; Bon Homme; P 1,200; (605) 464-1085; Fax (605) 589-4109; www.tyndallsd.com

Wakonda • *Wakonda Dev. Corp.* • Ron Peterson; Treas.; 29714 455th Ave.; 57073; Clay; P 321; (605) 263-3526; (605) 267-3118; townofwakonda.org

Watertown • *Watertown Dev. Co.* • Craig Atkins; Pres.; 1 E. Kemp Ave.; P.O. Box 332; 57201; Codington; P 22,000; (605) 884-0340; (888) 898-6767; Fax (605) 882-0199; michelle@watertownworks.com; www.watertownworks.com

Webster • *Webster Area Dev. Corp.* • Melissa Waldner; Exec. Dir.; P.O. Box 6; 57274; Day; P 1,900; (605) 345-3159; (605) 345-3639; Fax (605) 345-3509; wadc@itctel.com; www.webstersd.com

Wessington Springs • *Wessington Springs Area Dev. Corp.* • Laura Kieser; Coord.; 101 Wallace Ave. S.; P.O. Box 132; 57382; Jerauld; P 956; (605) 539-1929; Fax (605) 539-0249; wsprings@venturecomm.net; www.wessingtonsprings.com

Winner • *South Central Dev. Corp.* • Tovi Cox Bartels; Exec. Dir.; 201 Monroe; P.O. Box 624; 57580; Tripp; P 3,400; (605) 842-1551; develop@winnersd.org; www.winnersd.org

Yankton • *Yankton Area Progressive Growth, Inc.* • John Kramer; Pres.; 803 E. 4th St.; 57078; Yankton; P 14,454; (888) 926-5866; (605) 665-9011; Fax (605) 665-7501; ecodev@yanktonsd.com; www.yanktonedc.com

Tennessee

Federal

U.S. SBA, Tennessee Dist. Ofc. • Walter N. Perry III; Dist. Dir.; 2 International Plaza Dr., Ste. 500; 37217; Davidson; P 6,456,243; (615) 736-5881; Fax (615) 736-7232; walter.perry@sba.gov; www.sba.gov/tn

State

Tennessee Dept. of Eco. & Comm. Dev. • Leslee T. Alexander; Intl. Dir.; 312 Rosa L. Parks Ave., 27th Flr.; Nashville; 37243; Davidson; P 7,000,000; (615) 483-7293; leslee.alexander@tn.gov; www.tnecd.com

Communities

Athens • *McMinn County Eco. Dev. Auth.* • Kathy Price CEcD; Exec. Dir.; 5 S. Hill St., Ste. C; 37303; McMinn; P 52,200; (423) 745-1506; (865) 271-8228; Fax (423) 745-1507; kathy@makeitinmcminn.org; makeitinmcminn.org

Chattanooga • *Chattanooga Area C/C-Eco. Dev. Dept.* • Charles Wood; V.P. Eco. Dev.; 811 Broad St., Ste. 100; 37402; Hamilton; P 349,000; (423) 756-4369; (423) 756-2121; Fax (423) 267-7242; info@chattanoogachamber.com; www.chattanoogachamber.com

Columbia • *Maury County C/C & Eco. Alliance* • Travis Groth; Dir.; 106 W. 6th St.; P.O. Box 1076; 38402; Maury; P 84,000; (931) 388-2155; Fax (931) 380-0335; tcasimier@mauryalliance.com; www.mauryalliance.com

Dayton • *Rhea Eco. & Tourism Cncl.* • Dennis Tumlin; Exec. Dir.; 107 Main St.; 37321; Rhea; P 34,000; (423) 775-6171; Fax (423) 775-7653; director@rheacountyetc.com; www.rheacountyetc.com

Gallatin • *Gallatin Eco. Dev. Agency* • James Fenton; Exec. Dir.; 132 W. Main St.; 37066; Sumner; P 34,000; (615) 451-5940; (615) 428-8179; Fax (615) 451-5941; james.fenton@gallatin-tn.gov; www.gallatingetsit.com

Hendersonville • *Eco. & Comm. Dev. of Hendersonville* • Scott Foster; Dir.; 101 Maple Dr. N.; 37075; Sumner; P 52,000; (615) 822-1000; Fax (615) 264-5327; sfoster@hvilletn.org; www.hvilletn.org

Jackson • *West Tennessee Ind. Assn.* • Michael M. Philpot; Exec. Dir.; 26 Conrad Dr.; 38305; Madison; (731) 668-4300; (800) 336-2036; Fax (731) 668-7554; westtn@wtia.org; www.wtia.org

Jasper • *Marion County Partnership for Eco. Dev.* • David Abbott; Chrmn.; 302 Betsy Pack Dr.; 37347; Marion; P 28,247; (423) 942-5103; Fax (423) 942-0098; mcexec@bellsouth.net; www.marioncountychamber.com

Johnson City • *Washington County Eco. Dev. Cncl.* • Mitch Miller; CEO; 300 E. Main St., Ste. 406; 37601; Washington; P 126,000; (423) 202-3510; (855) 885-3685; Fax (423) 928-2425; miller@thewcedc.com; www.thewcedc.com

La Vergne • *see Murfreesboro*

Lebanon • *Wilson County Joint Eco. & Comm. Dev. Bd.* • G.C. Hixson; Exec. Dir.; 115 Castle Heights Ave. N., Ste. 102; 37087; Wilson; P 113,900; (615) 443-1210; Fax (615) 443-0277; info@doingbiz.org; www.doingbiz.org

Lewisburg • *Lewisburg Eco. Dev.* • Greg Lowe; Dir.; P.O. Box 1968; 37091; Marshall; P 10,422; (931) 359-1544; Fax (931) 359-7055; glowe@ctyoflew.com; www.lewisburgtn.com

Loudon • *Loudon County Eco. Dev. Agency* • Jack Qualls; Exec. Dir.; 274 Blair Bend Dr.; 37774; Loudon; P 51,200; (865) 458-8889; Fax (865) 458-3792; lceda@loudoncountyeda.org; www.loudoncountyeda.org

Manchester • *Ind. Bd. of Coffee County* • Ted Hackney; Exec. Dir.; 1329 McArthur, Ste. 4; 37355; Coffee; P 53,000; (931) 723-5120; Fax (931) 723-5121; ib@coffeetn.com; www.coffeetn.com

Maryville • *Blount Partnership* • Bryan T. Daniels CEcD CCE IOM; Pres./CEO; 201 S. Washington St.; 37804; Blount; P 126,339; (865) 983-7715; (855) 257-3964; Fax (865) 984-1386; rbuchanan@blountpartnership.com; www.blountindustry.com

Memphis • *Mid-South Minority Bus. Cncl. Continuum* • Luke Yancy III; Pres./CEO; 158 Madison Ave., Ste. 300; 38103; Shelby; (901) 525-6512; Fax (901) 525-5204; lyancy@mmbc-memphis.org; www.mmbc-memphis.org

Mount Juliet • *see Lebanon*

Murfreesboro • *Rutherford County C/C* • Brian Hercules; V.P. of Eco. Dev.; 3050 Medical Center Pkwy.; 37129; Rutherford; P 298,700; (615) 278-2393; Fax (615) 278-2013; bhercules@rutherfordchamber.org; www.rutherfordchamber.org

Newport • *Cocke County Partnership* • Sherry Butler; V.P. of Op.; 433 Prospect Ave.; 37821; Cocke; P 35,662; (423) 623-3008; Fax (423) 625-1846; sbutler@cockecountypartnership.com; www.cockecountypartnership.com

Pigeon Forge • *Pigeon Forge Comm. Dev.* • David Taylor; Dir.; 225 Pine Mountain Rd.; P.O. Box 1350; 37868; Sevier; P 6,100; (865) 429-7312; Fax (865) 429-7322; dtaylor@cityofpigeonforge.com; www.cityofpigeonforge.com

Pulaski • *Pulaski-Giles County Eco. Dev. Comm.* • Dan Speer; Exec. Dir.; 203 S. First St., Ste. 5; 38478; Giles; P 30,000; (931) 363-9138; Fax (931) 424-4460; dan@gilescountyedc.com; www.gilescountyedc.com

Savannah • *Savannah Ind. Dev. Corp.* • Steve Bunnell; CEO; 495 Main St.; 38372; Hardin; P 30,000; (731) 925-8181; Fax (731) 925-6987; sbunnell@tourhardincounty.org; www.tourhardincounty.org

Sevierville • *Sevier County Eco. Dev. Cncl.* • Allen Newton; Exec. Dir.; 321 Court Ave.; 37862; Sevier; P 81,000; (865) 428-2212; shelton@seviercountytn.org; www.scedc.com

Smyrna • *see Murfreesboro*

Union City • *Obion County Joint Eco. Dev. Cncl.* • Lindsay Frilling; CEO; 214 E. Church St.; 38261; Obion; P 31,500; (731) 885-0211; Fax (731) 885-7155; lfrilling@obioncounty.org; www.obioncounty.org

Vonore • *Tellico Reservoir Dev. Agency* • Ron Hammontree; Exec. Dir.; 165 Deer Crossing; 37885; Monroe; P 15,000; (423) 884-6868; (800) 562-8732; Fax (423) 884-6869; trda@tds.net; www.tellico.com

Watertown • *see Lebanon*

Waverly • *Humphreys County Eco. Dev. Cncl.* • Ted Moore; Exec. Dir.; 301 N. Church St.; P.O. Box 218; 37185; Humphreys; P 19,000; (931) 296-5199; Fax (931) 296-2135; humpco_edc@waverly.net; www.humphreystn.com

Texas

Federal

U.S. SBA, Dallas/Fort Worth Dist. Ofc. • Herbert Austin; Dist. Dir.; 4300 Amon Carter Blvd., Ste. 114; 76155; Tarrant; P 26,059,203; (817) 684-5500; Fax (817) 684-5516; herbert.austin@sba.gov; www.sba.gov/tx

U.S. SBA, El Paso Dist. Ofc. • Phillip C. Silva; Dist. Dir.; 211 N. Florence St., Ste. 201; 79901; El Paso; P 26,059,203; (915) 834-4600; Fax (915) 834-4689; phillip.silva@sba.gov; www.sba.gov/tx

U.S. SBA, Houston Dist. Ofc. • Manuel R. Gonzalez; Dist. Dir.; 8701 S. Gessner Dr., Ste. 1200; 77074; Harris; P 26,059,203; (713) 773-6500; Fax (713) 773-6550; manuel.gonzalez@sba.gov; www.sba.gov/tx

U.S. SBA, Lower Rio Grande Valley Dist. Ofc. • Sylvia G. Zamponi; Dist. Dir.; 2422 E. Tyler Ave., Ste. E; 78550; Cameron; P 26,059,203; (956) 427-8533; Fax (956) 427-8537; sylvia.zamponi@sba.gov; www.sba.gov/tx

U.S. SBA, Lubbock Dist. Ofc. • Calvin O. Davis; Dist. Dir.; 1205 Texas Ave., Rm. 408; 79401; Lubbock; P 26,059,203; (806) 472-7462; Fax (806) 472-7487; calvin.davis@sba.gov; www.sba.gov/tx

U.S. SBA, San Antonio Dist. Ofc. • Pamela Sapia; Dist. Dir.; 615 E. Houston St., Ste. 298; 78205; Bexar, Comal & Medina; P 26,059,203; (210) 403-5900; Fax (210) 403-5936; pamela.sapia@sba.gov; www.sba.gov/tx

State

Texas Eco. Dev. Cncl. • Carlton Schwab; Pres./CEO; 1601 Rio Grande St., Ste. 455; Austin; 78701; Travis; P 26,059,203; (512) 480-8432; Fax (512) 472-7907; crystal@texasedc.org; www.texasedc.org

Communities

Abilene • ***Abilene Ind. Found.*** • Justin Jaworski; Pres.; 174 Cypress St., Ste. 300; P.O. Box 2281; 79604; Taylor; P 176,937; (325) 673-7349; (800) 299-0005; Fax (325) 673-9193; info@abileneind.com; www.developabilene.com

Alice • ***Alice-Jim Wells County EDC*** • Juan Navejar Jr.; Dir.; 612 E. Main St.; P.O. Box 1609; 78333; Jim Wells; P 43,000; (361) 664-3454; Fax (361) 664-2291; jnavejar@alicetx.org; www.alicetx.org

Angleton • ***Eco. Dev. Alliance for Brazoria County*** • Sean Stockard; Pres./CEO; 4005 Technology Dr., Ste. 1010; 77515; Brazoria; P 342,677; (979) 848-0560; Fax (979) 848-0403; seans@eda-bc.com; www.eda-bc.com

Aransas County • *see Corpus Christi*

Bay City • ***Matagorda County Eco. Dev. Corp.*** • Heather Menzies; Dir. of Comm.; 2200 7th St., Ste. 302; 77414; Matagorda; P 38,800; (979) 245-8913; Fax (979) 245-5661; hmenzies@mcedc.net; www.mcedc.net

Baytown • ***Baytown West Chambers County Eco. Dev. Found.*** • Michael Shields; Exec. Dir.; 1300 Rollingbrook, Ste. 505; 77521; Harris; P 138,000; (281) 420-2961; Fax (281) 422-7682; baytownedf@baytownedf.org; www.baytownedf.org

Bedford • ***Hurst-Euless-Bedford Eco. Dev. Found.*** • Mary Martin Frazior; Pres./CEO; 2109 Martin Dr.; P.O. Drawer 969; 76095; Tarrant; P 136,000; (817) 540-1053; Fax (817) 267-5111; chamber@heb.org; www.heb.org

Bee County • *see Corpus Christi*

Bellville • ***Bellville EDC*** • Mr. Monte Byrd; Pres.; 30 S. Holland St.; 77418; Austin; P 4,500; (979) 865-3136; Fax (979) 865-9760; bedc@sbcglobal.net; www.bellvilleedc.com

Belton • ***Belton Eco. Dev. Corp.*** • Cynthia Hernandez; Exec. Dir.; 2180 N. Main St., Ste. C1; 76513; Bell; P 19,000; (254) 770-2270; chernandez@beltonedc.org; www.beltonedc.org

Belton • ***Dev. Dist. of Central Texas*** • Beth Correa; Reg. Planner; P.O. Box 729; 76513; Bell; (254) 770-2200; Fax (254) 770-2360; ddoctinfo@ddoct.org; www.ddoct.org

Brady • ***McCulloch County Ind. Found.*** • Kathi Masonheimer; Dir.; 101 E. 1st St.; 76825; McCulloch; P 8,000; (325) 597-3491; Fax (325) 792-9181; info@bradytx.com; www.bradytx.com

Brazoria County • *see Angleton*

Breckenridge • ***Breckenridge Eco. Dev.*** • Virgil Moore; Exec. Dir.; 100 E. Elm St.; P.O. Box 1466; 76424; Stephens; P 10,000; (254) 559-6228; Fax (254) 559-7104; vmoore@breckenridgetexas.com; www.breckenridgetexas.com

Brenham • ***Brenham Eco. Dev. Found.*** • Page Michel; Pres./CEO; 314 S. Austin St.; 77833; Washington; P 16,579; (979) 836-8927; Fax (979) 836-2540; page@brenhamtexas.com; www.brenhamEDF.com

Brownsville • ***Brownsville Eco. Dev. Cncl.*** • Jason Hilts; Pres./CEO; 301 Mexico Blvd., Ste. F-1; 78520; Cameron; P 200,000; (956) 541-1183; (800) 552-5352; Fax (956) 546-3938; jvelasquez@bedc.com; www.bedc.com

Brownwood • ***Brownwood Municipal Dev. Dist.*** • Guy Andrews; Exec. Dir.; 501 Center Ave.; P.O. Box 1389; 76804; Brown; P 20,000; (325) 646-6751; Fax (325) 641-3769; gandrews@brownwoodtexas.gov; www.brownwoodtexas.gov

Bryan • *see College Station*

Buffalo • ***Buffalo EDC*** • Ken Jones; Exec. Dir.; P.O. Box 1186; 75831; Leon; P 3,000; (903) 388-1881; bedc@buffalotex.com; www.buffalotxedc.com

Caldwell • ***Burleson County Eco. Dev. Cncl.*** • Sal Zaccagnino; 301 N. Main; 77836; Burleson; P 17,500; (979) 777-5708; Fax (979) 567-7147; salzacc@aol.com; www.burlesoncountytx.com

Canadian • ***Canadian EDC*** • Shane Spencer; Exec. Dir.; 119 N. 2nd St.; 79014; Hemphill; P 2,649; (806) 323-6234; Fax (806) 323-9243; chamber@canadiantx.com; www.canadiantx.com

Carrollton • ***Carrollton Eco. Dev.*** • Tom Latchem; Dir.; P.O. Box 110535; 75011; Collin, Dallas & Denton; P 122,000; (972) 466-3299; (972) 466-5741; Fax (972) 466-4882; andrea.roy@cityofcarrollton.com; www.cityofcarrollton.com

Childress • ***Childress Eco. Dev. Corp.*** • Russell Graves; Exec. Dir.; 1902 Ave. G N.W.; P.O. Box 10; 79201; Childress; P 7,600; (940) 937-8629; Fax (940) 937-2520; info@childresstexas.com; www.childresstexas.com

Clarendon • ***Clarendon Eco. Dev. Corp.*** • Roger Estlack; Secy./Treas.; 110 S. Kearney St.; P.O. Box 826; 79226; Donley; P 3,522; (806) 874-2421; (806) 874-3438; Fax (806) 874-2911; cedcsecretary@gmail.com; www.clarendonedc.org

Cleveland • ***Cleveland Eco. Dev. Corp.*** • Dion Miller; City Mgr.; 907 E. Houston St.; 77327; Liberty; P 7,605; (281) 592-2667; Fax (281) 592-6624; dmiller@clevelandtexas.com; www.clevelandtexas.com

College Station • ***Research Valley Partnership*** • Todd McDaniel CEcD; Pres./CEO; 1500 Research Pkwy., Ste. 270; 77845; Brazos; P 306,000; (979) 260-1755; (800) 449-4012; Fax (979) 260-5252; kschreiber@researchvalley.org; www.researchvalley.org

Comanche • ***Comanche Texas Eco. Dev. Corp.*** • Jacci Stewart CCD; Dir.; 115 W. Grand Ave.; P.O. Box 144; 76442; Comanche; P 4,400; (325) 356-2032; www.cityofcomanchetexas.net

Conroe • ***Greater Conroe Eco. Dev. Cncl.*** • Fred Welch; Exec. Dir.; 505 W. Davis St.; 77301; Montgomery; P 68,700; (936) 538-7118; Fax (936) 756-6162; info@gcedc.org; www.gcedc.org

Coppell • ***City of Coppell Eco. Dev. Dept.*** • Mindi Hurley; Eco. Dev. Coord.; 255 E. Parkway Blvd.; 75019; Denton; P 40,000; (972) 304-3677; Fax (972) 304-7092; mhurley@coppelltx.gov; www.coppelltx.gov

Corpus Christi • ***Corpus Christi Reg. Eco. Dev. Corp.*** • Iain Vasey; Pres./CEO; 800 N. Shoreline, Ste. 1300S; 78401; Nueces; P 417,000; (361) 882-7448; Fax (361) 882-9930; plago@ccredc.com; www.ccredc.com

Corpus Christi • ***Coastal Bend Cncl. of Govts.*** • John Buckner; Exec. Dir.; 2910 Leopard St.; 78408; Nueces; P 572,000; (361) 883-5743; Fax (361) 883-5749; yazmin@fin.cbcog98.org; www.cbcog98.org

Crockett • ***Crockett Eco. & Ind. Dev. Corp.*** • Thom Lambert; Exec. Dir.; 1117 Edmiston Blvd.; P.O. Box 307; 75835; Houston; P 7,400; (936) 546-5636; Fax (936) 544-4355; suzanne@crockett.org; www.crockett.org

Crowell • ***Crowell Ind. Dev.*** • Stacy Henry; Pres.; P.O. Box 848; 79227; Foard; P 950; (940) 684-1531; www.crowelltex.com

Crystal City • *Crystal City Eco. Dev.* • 101 E. Dimmit; 78839; Zavala; P 7,200; (830) 374-3477; Fax (830) 374-2123; info@cityofcc.org; www.cityofcc.org

Dallas • *City of Dallas Dept. of Eco. Dev.* • Karl Zavitkovsky; Dir.; City Hall; 1500 Marilla, Rm. 5C South; 75201; Dallas; P 1,200,000; (214) 670-1685; Fax (214) 670-0158; www.dallas-ecodev.org

Dallas • *Dallas Reg. Chamber Eco. Dev. Group* • Mike Rosa; Senior V.P. of Eco. Dev.; 500 N. Akard St., Ste. 2600; 75201; Dallas; P 6,500,000; (214) 746-6735; Fax (214) 746-6669; information@dallaschamber.com; www.dallaschamber.org

Del Rio • *Del Rio Area Dev. Found.* • Mike Wrob; Pres.; 1915 Veteran's Blvd.; 78840; Val Verde; P 45,000; (830) 775-3551; Fax (830) 774-1813; blarson@drchamber.com; www.drchamber.com

DFW Airport • *North Texas Comm.* • Mabrie Jackson; CEO; 8445 Freeport Pkwy., Ste. 640, Irving, 75063; P.O. Box 610246; 75261; Dallas; P 6,400,000; (972) 621-0400; info@ntc-dfw.org; www.ntc-dfw.org

Dumas • *Dumas Eco. Dev. Corp.* • Mike Running; Exec. Dir.; 900 N. Dumas Ave.; P.O. Box 595; 79029; Moore; P 16,000; (806) 934-3332; Fax (806) 934-0180; running@dumasedc.org; www.dumasedc.org

Eagle Pass • *Maverick County Dev. Corp.* • Raul E. Perez; Exec. Dir.; 1828 Industrial Blvd.; 78852; Maverick; P 58,000; (830) 773-6166; Fax (830) 773-6287; mcdc@hotmail.com; www.mcdcportofeaglepass.com

Early • *Early Eco. Dev. Corp. Small Bus. Incubator* • Shawn Russell; CDC; 104 E. Industrial Dr.; 76802; Brown; P 2,762; (325) 649-9300; Fax (325) 643-4746; shawn@earlytx.com; www.earlychamber.com

El Paso • *El Paso Reg. Eco. Dev.* • Rolando Pablos; CEO; 123 Mills St., Ste. 111; 79901; El Paso; P 2,000,000; (915) 298-1000; rpablos@borderplexalliance.org; www.borderplexalliance.org

Euless • *see Bedford*

Farmers Branch • *Farmers Branch Eco. Dev.* • Allison Cook; Eco. Dev. Mgr.; 13000 William Dodson Pkwy.; 75234; Dallas; P 32,000; (972) 919-2509; allison.cook@farmersbranchtx.gov; www.farmersbranchtx.gov

Flower Mound • *Town of Flower Mound Eco. Dev.* • Mark Wood; Dir. of Eco. Dev.; 2121 Cross Timbers Rd.; 75028; Denton & Tarrant; P 65,000; (972) 874-6044; mark.wood@flower-mound.com; www.flower-mound.com/econdev

Floydada • *Floydada Eco. Dev. Corp.* • Erica Johnston; Exec. Asst.; 105 S. 5th St.; 79235; Floyd; P 3,038; (806) 983-3318; (806) 983-2834; Fax (806) 983-6017; info@floydadaedc.com; www.floydadaedc.com

Fort Stockton • *Fort Stockton EDC* • Doug May; Exec. Dir.; 1000 Railroad Ave.; 79735; Pecos; P 8,000; (432) 336-2264; (423) 290-1963; Fax (432) 336-6114; edc@fortstockton.org; www.fortstockton.org

Fredericksburg • *Gillespie County EDC* • Tim Lehmberg; Exec. Dir.; 302 E. Austin St.; 78624; Gillespie; P 26,000; (830) 997-6523; Fax (830) 997-8588; edc@fbgtx.org; www.gillespiecountyedc.com

Friona • *Friona Eco. Dev. Corp.* • Bill Stovell; Pres.; 621 Main St.; 79035; Parmer; P 4,100; (806) 250-3491; Fax (806) 250-2348; fedc@wtrt.net; www.frionachamber.com

Garland • *Garland Eco. Dev. Dept.* • David Gwin; Dir. of Eco. Dev.; 217 N. 5th St., 3rd Flr.; 75040; Dallas; P 235,000; (972) 205-3800; economicdevelopment@garlandtx.gov; www.garlandtx.gov

Georgetown • *City of Georgetown Eco. Dev. Dept.* • Michaela Dollar; Dir.; 809 Martin Luther King Jr. St.; 78626; Williamson; P 58,700; (512) 930-3546; ed@georgetown.org; invest.georgetown.org

Giddings • *Giddings Eco. Dev. Corp.* • Joyce M. Bise; Dir.; 289 W. Railroad Ave.; 78942; Lee; P 5,400; (979) 542-2067; Fax (979) 540-2183; jmbise@giddings.net; www.giddingsedc.com

Gladewater • *Gladewater Eco. Dev. Corp.* • Robert Johnson; Exec. Dir.; 213 N. Main St.; 75647; Gregg & Upshur; P 6,500; (903) 845-5441; Fax (903) 845-1282; gedco@suddenlinkmail.com; www.gladewateredc.com

Gonzales • *Gonzales Eco. Dev. Corp.* • Genora C. Young; Pres./CEO; 820 St. Joseph St.; P.O. Drawer 547; 78629; Gonzales; P 21,000; (830) 263-9327; gyoung@cityofgonzales.org; www.gonzalesedc.org

Gorman • *Gorman Eco. Dev. Corp.* • Cliffa Vaughn; Dir.; 118 S. Kent; P.O. Box 236; 76454; Eastland; P 1,000; (254) 734-3933; Fax (254) 734-2270; cliffa.gormanedc.vaughn@gmail.com; www.gormantx.com

Graham • *Graham Eco. Dev.* • Neal Blanton; Exec. Dir.; P.O. Box 1465; 76450; Young; P 9,000; (940) 549-6006; Fax (940) 549-5030; nblanton@grahamtexas.net; www.grahamtexas.net

Grand Prairie • *Grand Prairie Eco. Dev. Dept.* • Bob O'Neal; Eco. Dev. Dir.; 317 W. College St.; 75050; Dallas, Ellis & Tarrant; P 184,000; (972) 237-8160; Fax (972) 237-8161; boneal@gptx.org; www.gptx.org

Groesbeck • *Groesbeck Eco. Dev. Corp.* • Chris Henson; City Admin.; 402 W. Navasota; 76642; Limestone; P 4,300; (254) 729-3293; Fax (254) 729-8155; info@groesbeckedc.org; www.groesbeckedc.com

Hamilton • *Hamilton Eco. Dev. Corp.* • Jane Crouch; Exec. Dir.; 204 E. Main St.; P.O. Box 224; 76531; Hamilton; P 3,095; (254) 386-5954; Fax (254) 386-3563; hamiltonedc@htcomp.net; www.hamiltontexas.com

Henderson • *Henderson Eco. Dev. Corp.* • Sue Henderson; Gen. Mgr.; 400 W. Main St.; 75652; Rusk; P 13,700; (903) 657-9146; Fax (903) 655-1296; hedco@hendersontx.us; www.hendersontx.us

Houston • *Greater Houston Partnership* • Bob Pertierra; Sr. V.P. & Chief Eco. Dev. Officer; Eco. Dev. Div.; 701 Avenida de las Americas, Ste. 900; 77010; Harris; P 6,500,000; (713) 844-3647; Fax (713) 844-0212; bpertierra@houston.org;; www.houston.org

Houston • *Bay Area Houston Eco. Partnership* • Bob Mitchell; Pres.; P.O. Box 58724; 77258; Harris; P 2,300,000; (832) 536-3255; Fax (832) 536-3258; elaine@bayareahouston.com; www.bayareahouston.com

Huntsville • *Huntsville Eco. Dev. Cncl.* • Aaron Kulhavy; Eco. Dev. Dir.; 448 S.H. 75 North; 77320; Walker; P 40,000; (936) 294-5793; (936) 291-5400; Fax (936) 291-5409; akulhavy@huntsvilletx.gov; www.huntsvilletx.gov

Hurst • *see Bedford*

Jacksonville • *Jacksonville Dev. Corp.* • Marc Farmer; Pres.; 309 E. Commerce; P.O. Box 1604; 75766; Cherokee; P 14,000; (903) 586-2102; (800) 376-2217; Fax (903) 586-2193; mfarmer@jacksonvilleedc.com; www.jacksonvilleedc.com

Jasper • *Jasper Eco. Dev. Corp.* • Kari Ellis; Exec. Dir.; 246 E. Milam; 75951; Jasper; P 8,300; (409) 383-6120; Fax (409) 383-6122; info@jasperedc.com; www.jasperedc.com

Jim Wells County • *see Corpus Christi*

Keller • *City of Keller Eco. Dev.* • Trina Zais; Dir. of Public Svcs. & Eco. Dev.; 1100 Bear Creek Pkwy.; P.O. Box 770; 76244; Tarrant; P 44,050; (817) 743-4020; economicdevelopment@cityofkeller.com; www.cityofkeller.com/ed

Kemah • *Kemah Comm. Dev. Corp.* • Carl Joiner; Pres.; 1401 Hwy. 146; 77565; Galveston; P 2,204; (281) 334-1611; Fax (281) 334-6583; broberts@kemah-tx.com; www.kemah-tx.gov

Kerrville • *Kerrville Eco. Dev. Corp.* • Jonas Titas; Exec. Dir.; 1700 Sidney Baker St., Ste. 100; 78028; Kerr; P 50,000; (830) 896-1157; Fax (830) 896-1175; jtitas@kerr-edc.com; www.kerr-edc.com

Killeen • *Killeen Eco. Dev.* • Phyllis Gogue; V.P. of Eco. Dev.; One Santa Fe Plz.; P.O. Box 548; 76540; Bell; P 132,000; (254) 526-9551; Fax (254) 526-6090; phyllis@killeenchamber.com; www.killeenchamber.com

Kingsville • *Kingsville Eco. Dev. Cncl.* • Manny Salazar; Exec. Dir.; 635 E. King St.; P.O. Box 5032; 78364; Kleberg; P 27,000; (361) 592-6438; Fax (361) 592-0866; edcdirector@kingsville.org; www.kingsville.org

Kleberg County • *see Corpus Christi*

Lancaster • *Lancaster Eco. Dev. Dept.* • Ed Brady; Dir.; 211 N. Henry St.; 75146; Dallas; P 38,000; (972) 218-1310; ebrady@lancaster-tx.com; www.lancaster-tx.com

Laredo • *Laredo Dev. Found.* • Olivia Varela; Exec. Dir.; 616 Leal St.; P.O. Box 2682; 78044; Webb; P 250,000; (956) 722-0563; Fax (956) 722-6247; ldfinfo@ldfonline.org; www.ldfonline.org

Live Oak County • *see Corpus Christi*

Longview • *Longview Eco. Dev. Corp.* • Wayne Mansfield; Pres./CEO; 410 N. Center St.; 75601; Gregg & Harrison; P 82,000; (903) 753-7878; (800) 952-2613; Fax (903) 753-3646; Info@longviewusa.com; www.longviewusa.com

Lubbock • *Lubbock Eco. Dev. Alliance* • John Osborne; Pres./CEO; 1500 Broadway, 6th Flr.; 79401; Lubbock; P 289,000; (806) 749-4500; Fax (806) 749-4501; john.osborne@lubbockeda.org; www.lubbockeda.org

Madisonville • *Madison County Eco. Dev. Corp.* • Duane Standley; Pres.; 113 W. Trinity St.; P.O. Box 1392; 77864; Madison; P 13,500; (936) 349-0163; Fax (936) 348-2212; mcedc@rodzoo.com; www.madisoncountyedc.com

McAllen • *McAllen Eco. Dev. Corp.* • Keith Patridge; Pres./CEO; 6401 S. 33rd St.; 78503; Hidalgo; P 137,000; (956) 682-2875; Fax (956) 682-3077; mluna@mcallenedc.org; www.mcallenedc.org

McKinney • *McKinney Eco. Dev. Corp.* • Darrell W. Auterson; Pres.; 5900 S. Lake Forest Dr., Ste. 110; 75070; Collin; P 161,000; (972) 547-7651; (800) 839-6259; Fax (972) 542-0926; info@mckinneyedc.com; www.mckinneyedc.com

Midland • *Midland Dev. Corp.* • Pamela Welch; Exec. Dir.; 109 N. Main, 2nd Flr.; 79701; Midland; P 124,000; (432) 686-3579; (800) 624-6435; Fax (432) 687-8214; pwelch@midlandtxedc.com; www.midlandtxedc.com

Mineola • *Mineola Dev. Inc.* • Mercy Rushing; Exec. Dir.; 300 Greenville Ave.; P.O. Box 179; 75773; Wood; P 5,611; (903) 569-6183; (800) MINEOLA; Fax (903) 569-0856; mrushing@mineola.com; www.mineola.com

Monahans • *Monahans Eco. Dev. Corp.* • Morse Haynes; Eco. Dev. Dir.; 303 S. Allen, Ste. 5; P.O. Box 61; 79756; Ward; P 6,400; (432) 943-2062; Fax (432) 943-2062; monahansedc@monahans.org; www.monahans.org

Mount Pleasant • *Mount Pleasant Eco. Dev. Corp.* • Charles L. Smith CEcD; Exec. Dir.; 1604 N. Jefferson; 75455; Titus; P 36,000; (903) 572-6602; Fax (903) 572-0613; csmith@mpedc.org; www.mpedc.org

New Braunfels • *New Braunfels EDC* • Rusty Brockman; Dir. of EDC; 390 S. Seguin Ave.; P.O. Box 311417; 78131; Comal; P 150,000; (830) 625-2385; (866) 927-0905; Fax (830) 625-7918; rusty@innewbraunfels.com; www.newbraunfelsedc.com

Nueces County • *see Corpus Christi*

Odessa • *Grow Odessa* • Tracy Jones; Asst. Secy.; 700 N. Grant, Ste. 200; P.O. Box 3626; 79760; Ector; P 137,130; (432) 333-7886; Fax (432) 333-7858; info@odessaecodev.com; www.growodessa.net

Pampa • *Pampa Eco. Dev. Corp.* • Clay Rice; Exec. Dir.; 107 E. Foster; P.O. Box 2398; 79065; Gray; P 18,700; (806) 665-0800; pampaedc@sbcglobal.net; www.pampaedc.com

Pearland • *Pearland Eco. Dev. Corp.* • Matt Buchanan; Pres.; 11233 Shadow Creek Pkwy., Ste. 235; 77584; Brazoria, Fort Bend & Harris; P 242,240; (281) 997-3000; info@pearlandedc.com; www.pearlandedc.com

Pharr • *Pharr Eco. Dev. Corp. II* • Sergio Contreras; Exec. Dir.; 1215 S. Cage Blvd.; P.O. Box 1729; 78577; Hidalgo; P 70,400; (956) 402-4332; Fax (956) 475-3449; sergio.contreras@pharr-tx.gov; pharredc.com

Plainview • *Plainview/Hale County Eco. Dev. Corp.* • Michael Fox; Exec. Dir.; 1906 W. 5th St.; 79072; Hale; P 38,000; (806) 293-8536; Fax (806) 296-0819; michael.fox@plainviewedc.org; www.plainviewedc.org

Plano • *Plano Eco. Dev. Dept.* • Sally Bane; Exec. Dir.; 5601 Granite Pkwy., Ste. 310; 75024; Collin; P 275,000; (972) 208-8300; Fax (972) 208-8305; sallyb@plano.gov; www.planotexas.org

Port Neches • *Port Neches Eco. Dev. Corp.* • Amy Guidroz; Exec. Dir.; 1110 Port Neches Ave.; P.O. Box 758; 77651; Jefferson; P 13,000; (409) 719-4211; aguidroz@pnedc.com; www.ci.port-neches.tx.us

Quanah • *Quanah Eco. Dev. Corp.* • Eugene Johnson; Exec. Dir.; P.O. Box 327; 79252; Hardeman; P 3,022; (940) 663-2690; Fax (940) 663-6791; qedc@speednet.com; www.quanahnet.com/qedc

Quitman • *Wood County Ind. Comm.* • Kiki Bettis; Exec. Dir.; Wood County Airport Terminal Bldg.; P.O. Box 578; 75783; Wood; P 43,000; (903) 768-2402; (888) 506-3458; Fax (903) 768-2403; woodcic@peoplescom.net; www.woodcountytx.com

Richardson • *Richardson Eco. Dev. Partnership* • Bill Sproull; Pres./CEO; 411 Belle Grove Dr.; 75080; Dallas; P 105,000; (972) 792-2800; Fax (972) 792-2825; john@telecomcorridor.com; www.telecomcorridor.com

Robstown • *Robstown Area Dev. Comm.* • Josie Segura; Admin. Asst.; 1150 E. Main Ave.; P.O. Box 111; 78380; Nueces; P 14,000; (361) 387-3933; Fax (361) 387-7280; josie@robstownadc.com; www.robstownadc.com

Rockwall • *Rockwall Eco. Dev. Corp.* • Sheri Franza; Pres./CEO; 2610 Observation Trl.; 75032; Rockwall; P 41,000; (972) 772-0025; sbell@rockwalledc.com; www.rockwalledc.com

EDC

Rosenberg • *Rosenberg Dev. Corp.* • Randall D. Malik; Eco. Dev. Dir.; 3825 Texas 36; 77471; Fort Bend; P 34,000; (832) 595-3330; (800) 530-3389; Fax (832) 595-3311; randallm@ci.rosenberg.tx.us; www.rosenbergecodev.com

San Antonio • *San Antonio Eco. Dev. Found.* • Mario Hernandez; Pres.; 602 E. Commerce St.; P.O. Box 1628; 78296; Bexar; P 2,140,000; (210) 226-1394; Fax (210) 223-3386; edf@sanantonioedf.com; www.sanantonioedf.com

San Juan • *San Juan Eco. Dev. Corp.* • Benjamin Arjona; Interim Dir.; 4810 N. Raul Longoria Ste. 5; 78589; Hidalgo; P 36,000; (956) 783-3448; Fax (956) 783-5413; barjona@cityofsanjuantexas.com; www.sjedc.com

Seminole • *Seminole Eco. Dev. Corp.* • Donna Johnson; Exec. Dir.; 302 S. Main St.; 79360; Gaines; P 6,505; (432) 758-8803; (432) 758-8804; Fax (432) 758-2349; director@mywdo.com; www.seminoleedc.org

South Padre Island • *Eco. Dev. Corp.* • Darla Lapeyre; Exec. V.P.; 6801 Padre Blvd.; 78597; Cameron; P 2,820; (956) 761-6805; spiedc@aol.com; www.myspi.org

Southlake • *City of Southlake Eco. Dev. & Tourism* • Alison Ortowski; Interim Eco. Dev. & Tourism Dir.; 1400 Main St., Ste. 300; 76092; Tarrant; P 29,000; (817) 748-8039; (817) 748-8400; Fax (817) 748-8040; dartho@ci.southlake.tx.us; www.cityofsouthlake.com

Stamford • *Dev. Corp. of Stamford* • Fareed Hassen; Exec. Dir.; P.O. Box 669; 79553; Jones; P 3,000; (325) 773-2495; Fax (325) 773-2851; eddirector@stamfordtx.com; www.stamfordtx.com

Stratford • *Sherman County Dev. Comm.* • Kathy Allen; Exec. Dir.; 301 N. Main St.; P.O. Box 652; 79084; Sherman; P 2,000; (806) 366-2897; Fax (806) 366-3025; scdc@xit.net; www.shermancountytx.org

Sudan • *Sudan Eco. Dev. Corp.* • Clay Carr; Pres.; P.O. Box 59; 79371; Lamb; P 953; (806) 227-2112; Fax (806) 227-2164; sudancityhall@yahoo.com; www.cityofsudantx.com

Sulphur Springs • *Sulphur Springs/Hopkins County Eco. Dev. Corp.* • Roger Feagley; Exec. Dir.; 1200 Enterprise Dr.; 75482; Hopkins; P 40,000; (903) 439-0101; Fax (903) 439-6396; mitzi@ss-edc.com; www.ss-edc.com

Sweetwater • *Sweetwater Enterprise for Eco. Dev.* • Ken Becker; Exec. Dir.; 810 E. Broadway; P.O. Box 785; 79556; Nolan; P 10,906; (325) 235-0555; (877) 301-SEED; Fax (325) 235-1026; ken@sweetwatertexas.net; www.sweetwatertexas.net

Temple • *Temple Eco. Dev. Corp.* • David Blackburn; Pres.; One S. First St.; 76501; Bell; P 71,000; (254) 773-8332; Fax (254) 773-8856; info@choosetemple.com; www.choosetemple.com

Terrell • *Terrell Eco. Dev. Corp.* • Danny Booth; Pres.; P.O. Box 97; 75160; Kaufman; P 18,500; (972) 524-5703; Fax (972) 563-2363; dawn@terrelltexas.com; www.terrelltexasedc.com

Weatherford • *Weatherford Eco. Dev. - City of Weatherford* • Dennis Clayton CEcD AIA; Dir. of Eco. Dev.; 202 W. Oak St.; P.O. Box 255; 76086; Parker; P 27,600; (817) 594-9429; (817) 598-4302; Fax (817) 594-4786; dclayton@weatherfordtx.gov; www.weatherfordtxeda.org

Weslaco • *Lower Rio Grande Valley Dev. Cncl.* • Kenneth N. Jones; Exec. Dir.; 301 W. Railroad St.; 78596; Hidalgo; P 1,200,000; (956) 682-3481; Fax (956) 631-4670; knjones@lrgvdc.org; www.lrgvdc.org

White Settlement • *White Settlement Eco. Dev. Corp.* • Kyle Reeves; Eco. Dev. Dir.; Eco. Dev. Dept.; 214 Meadow Park Dr.; 76108; Tarrant; P 16,000; (817) 246-4971; Fax (817) 246-8761; kreeves@wstx.us; www.wstx.us

Whitesboro • *Whitesboro Eco. Dev. Corp.* • Lynda Anderson; Dir.; 111 W. Main; P.O. Box 340; 76273; Grayson; P 3,800; (903) 564-4000; Fax (903) 564-6105; landerson@whitesborotexas.com; www.whitesborotexas.com

Wichita Falls • *Wichita Falls C/C & Ind.* • Kevin M. Pearson; Exec. V.P.; 900 8th St., Ste. 218; P.O. Box 1860; 76307; Wichita; P 105,000; (940) 723-2741; Fax (940) 723-8773; kevin@wichitafallschamber.com; www.wichitafallscommerce.com

Wills Point • *Wills Point EDC* • Pam Pearson; Admin.; 36671 State Hwy. 64; P.O. Box 217; 75169; Van Zandt; P 4,000; (903) 873-3381; Fax (903) 873-3081; WPEDC@sbcglobal.net; www.willspointedc.com

Yoakum • *Yoakum Eco. Dev. Corp.* • Patrick J. Kennedy; Dir.; 808 U.S. Hwy. 77A S.; P.O. Box 738; 77995; DeWitt & Lavaca; P 6,000; (361) 293-6321; Fax (361) 293-3318; pkennedy@cityofyoakum.org; www.yoakumusa.com

Utah

Federal

***U.S. SBA, Utah Dist. Ofc.* •** Stan Nakano; Dist. Dir.; 125 S. State St., Rm. 2227; 84138; Salt Lake; P 2,855,287; (801) 524-3209; Fax (801) 524-4160; stanley.nakano@sba.gov; www.sba.gov/ut

State

***Eco. Dev. Corp. of Utah* •** Jeffrey Edwards; Pres./CEO; 201 S. Main St., Ste. 2150; Salt Lake City; 84111; Salt Lake; P 2,855,287; (801) 328-8824; (800) 574-8824; Fax (801) 531-1460; jedwards@edcutah.org; www.edcutah.org

***Labor Comm. of Utah* •** Jaceson R. Maughan; Interim Commissioner; 160 E. 300 S., Ste. 300; P.O. Box 146600; Salt Lake City; 84114; Salt Lake; P 1; (801) 530-6800; Fax (801) 530-6390; laborcom@utah.gov; www.laborcommission.utah.gov

Communities

Cedar City • *Cedar City/Iron County Eco. Dev.* • Danny Stewart; Eco. Dev. Dir.; 10 N. Main St.; 84720; Iron; P 47,000; (435) 855-5115; (435) 586-2770; Fax (435) 586-2949; cameronc@cedarcity.org; www.cedarcity.org

Fillmore • *Fillmore City Redev. Agency* • Kevin Orton; City Recorder; 75 W. Center St.; 84631; Millard; P 2,300; (435) 743-5233; Fax (435) 743-5195; recorder@fillmorecity.org; www.fillmorecity.org

Heber City • *Heber Valley Eco. Dev.* • Ryan Starks; Dir.; 475 N. Main St.; 84032; Wasatch; P 25,000; (435) 654-3666; (866) 994-3237; rachel@gohebervalley.com; www.gohebervalley.com

Logan • *Cache Eco. Dev.* • Sandra Emile; Pres./CEO; 160 N. Main St.; 84321; Cache; P 117,000; (435) 752-2161; semile@cachechamber.com; www.cachechamber.com

Moab • *Moab Area Eco. Dev. Ofc.* • Ken Davey; Eco. Dev. Spec.; 217 E. Center St.; 84532; Grand; P 8,500; (435) 259-5121; Fax (435) 259-4135; ken@moabcity.org; www.moabcity.org

Nephi • *Juab County Eco. Dev. Ag.* • Byron Woodland; Dir.; 160 N. Main St., Rm. 102; 84648; Juab; P 10,246; (435) 623-3415; byronw@co.juab.ut.us; www.co.juab.ut.us

Ogden Area

Ogden City Bus. Dev. • Tom T. Christopulos; Dir.; 2549 Washington Blvd., Ste. 420; 84401; Weber; P 84,300; (801) 629-8910; oppportunity@ogdencity.com; www.ogdenbusiness.com

Weber County Comm. • Matthew Bell; Chrmn.; 2380 Washington Blvd., Ste. 360; 84401; Weber; P 232,000; (801) 399-8590; Fax (801) 399-8305; mbell@co.weber.ut.us; www.co.weber.ut.us

Weber Eco. Dev. Partnership • Douglas S. Larsen; Exec. Dir.; 2380 Washington Blvd., Ste. 250; 84401; Weber; P 230,000; (801) 399-8586; weberedp@co.weber.ut.us; webercountyutah.gov

Orem • **City of Orem Eco. Dev.** • Ryan L. Clark; Div. Mgr.; 56 N. State St., Rm. 101; 84057; Utah; P 89,000; (801) 229-7172; Fax (801) 229-7178; rlclark@orem.org; www.orem.org

Panguitch • **Garfield County Eco. Dev.** • Justin Fischer; Dir.; 55 S. Main St.; P.O. Box 77; 84759; Garfield; P 5,100; (435) 676-1157; Fax (435) 676-8239; justin.fischer@garfield.utah.gov; garfield.utah.gov

Price • **Carbon County Eco. Dev.** • Delynn Fielding; Dir.; 120 E. Main St.; 84501; Carbon; P 23,000; (435) 636-3295; Fax (435) 636-3210; delynn.fielding@carbon.utah.gov; www.carbon-county.com

Provo • also see Orem

Provo • **Mayor's Ofc. of Eco. Dev.** • Dixon Holmes; Deputy Mayor; 351 W. Center St.; 84601; Utah; P 113,000; (801) 852-6166; Fax (801) 375-1469; dixon@provo.org; www.provo.org

Tooele • **Tooele County Eco. Dev.** • Shawn Milne; Commissioner; 47 S. Main; 84074; Tooele; P 59,000; (435) 843-3150; Fax (435) 843-3400; smilne.tooelecounty@gmail.com; www.tooeleeconomicdevelopment.com

Vermont

Federal

U.S. SBA, Vermont Dist. Ofc. • Darcy Carter; Dist. Dir.; 87 State St., Rm. 205; P.O. Box 605; 05601; Washington; P 626,011; (802) 828-4422; Fax (802) 828-4485; darcy.carter@sba.gov; www.sba.gov/vt

State

Vermont Agency of Commerce & Comm. Dev. • Lawrence Miller; Secy.; 1 National Life Dr., 6th Flr.; Montpelier; 05620; Washington; P 626,011; (802) 828-3211; lawrence.miller@state.vt.us; www.thinkvermont.com

Communities

Burlington • **Greater Burlington Ind. Corp. [GBIC]** • Frank Cioffi; Pres.; 60 Main St.; P.O. Box 786; 05402; Chittenden; P 213,700; (802) 862-5726; Fax (802) 860-1899; info@gbicvt.org; www.gbicvt.org

Middlebury • **Addison County Eco. Dev. Corp.** • Robin Scheu; Exec. Dir.; 1590 Rte. 7 S., Ste. 8; 05753; Addison; P 36,800; (802) 388-7953; Fax (802) 388-0119; nackland@addisoncountyedc.org; www.addisoncountyedc.org

Montpelier • **Central Vermont Eco. Dev. Corp.** • James 'Jamie' Stewart; Exec. Dir.; 1 National Life Dr.; P.O. Box 1439; 05601; Washington; P 63,200; (802) 223-4654; (888) 769-2957; Fax (802) 223-4655; cvedc@sover.net; www.cvedc.org

Morrisville • **Lamoille Eco. Dev. Corp.** • John Mandeville; Exec. Dir.; P.O. Box 455; 05661; Lamoille; P 25,000; (802) 888-5640; Fax (802) 851-1136; john@lamoilleeconomy.org; www.lamoilleeconomy.org

N. Bennington • **Bennington County Ind. Corp.** • Peter Odierna; Exec. Dir.; 215 South St., 2nd Flr.; P.O. Box 923; 05201; Bennington; P 36,800; (802) 442-8975; Fax (802) 447-1101; peter@bcic.org; www.bcic.org

Rutland • **Rutland Eco. Dev. Corp.** • Lyle P. Jepson; Exec. Dir.; 67 Merchants Row; City Center, Ste. 6; 05701; Rutland; P 63,000; (802) 773-9147; Fax (802) 770-7089; lyle@rutlandeconomy.com; www.rutlandeconomy.com

Saint Albans • **Franklin County Ind. Dev. Corp.** • Timothy Smith; Exec. Dir.; 2 N. Main St., 4th Flr.; P.O. Box 1099; 05478; Franklin; P 49,000; (802) 524-2194; Fax (802) 524-6793; info@fcidc.com; www.fcidc.com

Saint Johnsbury • **Northeastern Vermont Dev. Assn.** • Steven Patterson; Exec. Dir.; 36 Eastern Ave.; P.O. Box 630; 05819; Caledonia, Essex & Orleans; P 62,438; (802) 748-5181; Fax (802) 748-1223; spatterson@nvda.net; www.nvda.net

Springfield • **Springfield Reg. Dev. Corp.** • Bob Flint; Exec. Dir.; 14 Clinton St., Ste. 7; 05156; Windsor; P 10,000; (802) 885-3061; Fax (802) 885-3027; bobf@springfielddevelopment.org; www.springfielddevelopment.org

White River Junction • **Green Mountain Eco. Dev. Corp.** • Robert Haynes; Exec. Dir.; 35 Railroad Row, Ste. 101; 05001; Windsor; P 90,000; (802) 295-3710; Fax (802) 295-3779; gmedc@gmedc.com; www.gmedc.com

Windsor • **Connecticut River Dev. Corp.** • Don Griswold; Mgr.; One Railroad Ave.; P.O. Box 88; 05089; Windsor; P 56,000; (802) 674-9202; (802) 236-9434; Fax (802) 674-2999; wintownsend@yahoo.com; www.connriverdevcorp.org

Windsor • **Windsor Eco. Dev.** • Tom Marsh; Town Mgr.; Windsor Town Hall; 29 Union St.; 05089; Windsor; P 3,500; (802) 674-6786; tmarsh@windsorvt.org; www.windsorvt.org

Virgin Islands

Communities

St. Croix • **Virgin Islands Eco. Dev. Auth.** • Wayne L. Biggs Jr.; Asst. CEO; 116 King St. Frederiksted; 00840; P 119,000; (340) 773-6499; wbiggs@usvieda.org; www.usvieda.org

St. Thomas • **Virgin Islands Eco. Dev. Auth.** • Wayne L. Biggs Jr.; Asst. CEO; 8000 Nisky Shopping Center, Ste. 620; P.O. Box 305038; 00802; P 119,000; (340) 714-1700; wbiggs@usvieda.org; www.usvieda.org

Virginia

Federal

U.S. SBA, Richmond Dist. Ofc. • Jayne E. Armstrong; Dist. Dir.; The Federal Bldg.; 400 N. 8th St., Ste. 1150; 23219; Richmond City; P 8,185,867; (804) 771-2400; Fax (804) 771-2764; jayne.armstrong@sba.gov; www.sba.gov/va

State

Virginia Eco. Dev. Partnership • Martin Briley; Pres./CEO; 901 E. Cary St.; P.O. Box 798; Richmond; 23219; Richmond City; P 8,185,867; (804) 545-5600; Fax (804) 545-5611; info@yesvirginia.org; www.yesvirginia.org

Communities

Alexandria • *Alexandria Eco. Dev. Partnership* • Stephanie Landrum; Pres./CEO; 625 N. Washington St., Ste. 400; 22314; Alexandria City; P 153,500; (703) 739-3820; Fax (703) 739-1384; info@alexecon.org; www.alexecon.org

Arlington • *Arlington Eco. Dev.* • Victor L. Hoskins; Dir.; 1100 N. Glebe Rd., Ste. 1500; 22201; Arlington; P 225,000; (703) 228-0808; Fax (703) 228-0805; mleonzo@arlingtonva.us; www.arlingtoneconomicdevelopment.com

Ashburn • *Loudoun County Dept. of Eco. Dev.* • Buddy Rizer; Exec. Dir.; 43777 Central Station Dr., Ste. 300; P.O. Box 7000; 20147; Loudoun; P 360,000; (703) 777-0426; (800) LOUDOUN; Fax (703) 771-5363; ded@loudoun.gov; biz.loudoun.gov

Charles City • *Charles City County Eco. Dev.* • Rachel Chieppa; Dir. of Planning/Eco. Dev.; 10900 Courthouse Rd.; P.O. Box 66; 23030; Charles City; P 7,256; (804) 652-4707; Fax (804) 829-5819; rchieppa@co.charles-city.va.us; www.co.charles-city.va.us

Charlottesville • *City of Charlottesville Eco. Dev. Dept.* • Chris Engel; Dir.; P.O. Box 911; 22902; Charlottesville City; P 45,000; (434) 970-3110; Fax (434) 970-3299; nessj@charlottesville.org; www.charlottesville.org

Chatham • *Pittsylvania County Eco. Dev.* • Kenneth Bowman; Dir.; P.O. Box 426; 24531; Pittsylvania; P 63,500; (434) 432-1669; (800) 491-2842; Fax (434) 432-1709; patsy.thompson@pittgov.org; www.pittced.com

Chesapeake • *see Norfolk*

Chesterfield • *Chesterfield County Eco. Dev.* • Garrett Hart; Dir.; 9401 Courthouse Rd., Ste. B; 23832; Chesterfield; P 337,000; (804) 318-8550; Fax (804) 796-3638; info@chesterfieldbusiness.com; www.chesterfieldbusiness.com

Christiansburg • *Montgomery County Dept. of Eco. Dev.* • Brian Hamilton; Dir.; 755 Roanoke St., Ste. 2H; 24073; Montgomery; P 94,400; (540) 382-5732; (866) 270-9185; Fax (540) 381-6888; www.yesmontgomeryva.org

Culpeper • *Culpeper County Dept. of Eco. Dev.* • Carl Sachs; Dir.; 803 S. Main St.; 22701; Culpeper; P 50,000; (540) 727-3410; (800) 793-0631; csachs@culpepercounty.gov; www.culpeperusa.com

Danville • *City of Danville, Ofc. of Eco. Dev.* • Telly D. Tucker; Dir.; 427 Patton St., Rm. 203; P.O. Box 3300; 24543; Danville City; P 43,000; (434) 793-1753; Fax (434) 797-9606; econdev@discoverdanville.com; www.discoverdanville.com

Emporia • *Greensville County Eco. Dev. Dept.* • Natalie B. Slate; Dir.; 1781 Greensville County Cir.; 23847; Emporia City; P 12,000; (434) 348-4205; Fax (434) 348-4113; admin@greensvillecountyva.gov; www.greensvillecountyva.gov

Falls Church • *City of Falls Church Ofc. of Eco. Dev.* • Rick Goff; Exec. Dir.; 300 Park Ave.; 22046; Falls Church City; P 12,300; (703) 248-5491; Fax (703) 248-5103; rickgoff@fallschurchva.gov; www.fallschurchva.gov

Fincastle • *Botetourt County Dept. of Eco. Dev.* • Ken McFadyen; Dir.; 5 W. Back St.; 24090; Botetourt; P 33,200; (540) 928-2140; Fax (540) 473-8225; economicdevelopment@botetourtva.gov; www.botetourt.org

Fredericksburg • *Fredericksburg Ofc. of Tourism & Eco. Dev.* • Bill Frehling; Interim Dir.; 706 Caroline St.; 22401; Spotsylvania; P 29,000; (540) 372-1216; (800) 260-3646; Fax (540) 372-6587; aperegoy@fredericksburgva.gov; www.fredericksburgva.gov

Fredericksburg • *Spotsylvania County Dept. of Eco. Dev. & Tourism* • Tom Rumora; Dir.; 9019 Old Battlefield Blvd., Ste. 310; 22553; Spotsylvania; P 122,397; (540) 507-7210; Fax (540) 507-7207; economicdevelopment@spotsylvania.va.us; www.spotsylvania.org

Front Royal • *Eco. Dev. Auth. of Front Royal & Warren County* • Jennifer McDonald; Exec. Dir.; 400 D Kendrick Ln.; P.O. Box 445; 22630; Warren; P 39,000; (540) 635-2182; Fax (540) 635-1853; mcdonald@wceda.com; www.wceda.com

Gainesville • *Prince William County Dept. of Eco. Dev.* • Tom Flynn; Dir.; 13575 Heathcote Blvd., Ste. 240; 20155; Prince William; P 438,600; (703) 792-5517; (703) 792-5500; Fax (703) 792-5502; econdev@pwcgov.org; www.pwcecondev.org

Galax • *City of Galax Eco. Dev.* • Keith Barker; City Mgr.; 111 E. Grayson St.; 24333; Galax City; P 7,042; (276) 236-5773; Fax (276) 236-2889; kbarker@galaxva.com; www.galaxva.com

Gate City • *Scott County Eco. Dev. Auth.* • John Kilgore; Dir.; 180 W. Jackson St.; 24251; Scott; P 24,200; (276) 386-2525; Fax (276) 386-6158; jkilgore@scottcountyva.org; www.scottcountyva.org

Gloucester • *Dept. of Eco. Dev.* • Douglas Meredith; Dir.; 6467 Main St.; P.O. Box 915; 23061; Gloucester; P 37,262; (804) 693-1415; Fax (804) 693-6004; dmeredit@gloucesterva.info; www.gloucesterva.info

Henrico • *Eco. Dev. Auth. of Henrico County* • Gary McLaren; Exec. Dir.; 4300 E. Parham Rd.; 23228; Henrico; P 319,000; (804) 501-7654; Fax (804) 501-7890; wendy@henrico.com; www.henrico.com

Hopewell • *City of Hopewell Dept. of Dev.* • March Altman; Comm. Dev. Dir.; 300 N. Main St., Rm. 321; 23860; Hopewell City; P 23,590; (804) 541-2220; Fax (804) 541-2318; maltman@hopewellva.gov; www.hopewellva.gov

Lawrenceville • *Brunswick County IDA* • Joan Moore; Exec. Dir.; 116 W. Hicks St.; P.O. Box 48; 23868; Brunswick; P 17,400; (434) 848-0248; Fax (434) 848-0202; jvmoore@bcida.org; www.bcida.org

Lovingston • *Nelson County Eco. Dev. & Tourism Bur.* • Maureen Kelley; Dir.; 8519 Thomas Nelson Hwy.; P.O. Box 636; 22949; Nelson; P 15,020; (434) 263-7015; (888) 662-9400; Fax (434) 263-6823; info@nelsoncounty.org; www.nelsoncounty-va.gov

Lynchburg • *City of Lynchburg Ofc. of Eco. Dev.* • Marjette G. Upshur; Dir.; 900 Church St., 2nd Flr.; 24504; Lynchburg City; P 75,500; (434) 455-4490; Fax (434) 847-2067; marjette.upshur@lynchburgva.gov; www.opportunitylynchburg.com

Mechanicsville • *Hanover County Dept. of Eco. Dev.* • Edwin Gaskin; Dir.; 8200 Center Path Ln., Ste. E; 23116; Hanover; P 100,000; (804) 365-6464; (800) 936-6168; Fax (804) 365-6463; tjmiller@co.hanover.va.us; www.hanovercounty.biz

Newport News • *Peninsula Cncl. for Workforce Dev.* • Matthew James; Pres./CEO; 11820 Fountain Way, Ste. 301; 23606; Newport News City; P 460,000; (757) 826-3327; Fax (757) 826-6706; info@pcfwd.org; www.pcfwd.org

Norfolk • *Hampton Roads Eco. Dev. Alliance* • Darryl Gosnell; Pres.; 500 E. Main St., Ste. 1300; 23510; Norfolk City; P 1,700,000; (757) 627-2315; Fax (757) 623-3081; info@hreda.com; www.hreda.com

Portsmouth • *also see Norfolk*

Portsmouth • *Portsmouth Dept. of Eco. Dev.* • Mallory C. Butler CEcD; Dir.; 801 Crawford St., 5th Flr.; 23704; Portsmouth City; P 97,000; (757) 393-8804; Fax (757) 393-8293; porteco@portsmouthva.gov; www.portsmouthvaed.com

Radford • *New River Valley Eco. Dev. Alliance* • Charlie Jewell; Exec. Dir.; 6226 University Park Dr., Ste. 2200; 24141; Radford City; P 180,000; (540) 267-0007; (800) 678-1734; Fax (540) 267-0013; thodge@nrvalliance.org; www.nrvalliance.org

Richmond • *Greater Richmond Partnership Inc.* • Gregory H. Wingfield; Pres.; 901 E. Byrd St., Ste. 801; West Tower; 23219; Richmond City; P 1,000,000; (804) 643-3227; (800) 229-6332; Fax (804) 343-7167; asaunders@grpva.com; www.grpva.com

Richmond • *Dept. of Eco. Dev. & Comm. Dev.* • Lee Downey; Dir.; 1500 E. Main St., Ste. 400; 23219; Richmond City; P 200,000; (804) 646-5633; Fax (804) 646-6793; econdev@richmondgov.com; www.richmondgov.com

Roanoke • *Dept. of Eco. Dev., City of Roanoke* • Wayne Bowers; Dir.; 117 Church Ave. S.W.; 24011; Roanoke City; P 99,400; (540) 853-2715; Fax (540) 853-1213; econdevl@roanokeva.gov; www.bizroanoke.com

South Boston • *Ind. Dev. Auth. of Halifax County* • Mike Sexton; Exec. Dir.; 1100 Confroy Dr., Ste. 1; 24592; Halifax; P 36,200; (434) 572-1734; Fax (434) 572-1762; meades@halifaxvirginia.com; www.halifaxvirginia.com

Staunton • *Staunton Dept. of Eco. Dev.* • William Vaughn; Dir.; 116 W. Beverley St.; P.O. Box 58; 24402; Staunton City; P 25,000; (540) 332-3869; Fax (540) 851-4008; vaughnwl@ci.staunton.va.us; www.stauntonbusiness.com

Suffolk • *City of Suffolk Eco. Dev. Auth.* • Kevin Hughes; Dir.; 442 W. Washington St.; P.O. Box 1858; 23439; Suffolk City; P 87,000; (757) 514-4040; Fax (757) 514-4054; dholt@suffolkva.us; www.suffolkva.us

Suffolk • *also see Norfolk*

Tysons Corner • *Fairfax County Eco. Dev. Auth.* • Gerald L. Gordon; Pres./CEO; 8300 Boone Blvd., Ste. 450; 22182; Fairfax; P 1,100,000; (703) 790-0600; Fax (703) 893-1269; cmartelli@fceda.org; www.fairfaxcountyeda.org

Virginia Beach • *Virginia Beach Dept. of Eco. Dev.* • Warren D. Harris; Dir.; 4525 Main St., Ste. 700; 23462; Virginia Beach City; P 449,500; (757) 385-6464; Fax (757) 499-9894; ecdev@vbgov.com; www.yesvirginiabeach.com

Warm Springs • *Bath County Eco. Dev. Auth.* • J. Wayne Anderson; Chrmn.; P.O. Box 13; 24484; Bath; P 5,000; (540) 839-7221; Fax (540) 839-7222; janetbryan@bathcountyva.org.; www.bathcountyva.org

Winchester • *Frederick County Eco. Dev. Auth.* • Patrick Barker CEcD; Exec. Dir.; 45 E. Boscawen St.; 22601; Frederick; P 109,000; (540) 665-0973; Fax (540) 722-0604; info@YesFrederickVA.com; www.YesFrederickVA.com

Woodstock • *Shenandoah County Eco. Dev.* • Vince Poling; Eco. Dev. Prog. Mgr.; 600 N. Main St., Ste. 101; 22664; Shenandoah; P 42,000; (540) 459-6220; Fax (540) 459-6228; vpoling@shenandoahcountyva.us; www.shenandoah-ed.org

Wytheville • *Joint Ind. Dev. Auth. of Wythe County, Wytheville & Rural Retreat* • David Manley; Exec. Dir.; 190 S. First St.; 24382; Wythe; P 30,000; (276) 223-3370; Fax (276) 258-0779; office@wytheida.org; www.wytheida.org

Washington

Federal

U.S. SBA, Washington Dist. Ofc. • Nancy Porzio; Dist. Dir.; 2401 4th Ave., Ste. 450; 98121; King; P 6,897,012; (206) 553-7310; Fax (206) 553-0194; nancy.porzio@sba.gov; www.sba.gov/wa

State

State Dept. of Comm. • Brian Bonlender; Dir.; 1011 Plum St. S.E.; P.O. Box 42525; Olympia; 98504; Thurston; P 6,897,012; (360) 725-4000; Fax (360) 586-8440; connie.robins@commerce.wa.gov; www.commerce.wa.gov

Communities

Aberdeen • *Greater Grays Harbor Inc.* • Andre Garson; CEO; 506 Duffy St.; 98520; Grays Harbor; P 72,000; (360) 532-7888; info@graysharbor.org; graysharbor.org

Bainbridge Island • *see Silverdale*

Bellingham • *Port of Bellingham* • Rob Fix; Exec. Dir.; 1801 Roeder Ave.; 98225; Whatcom; P 208,400; (360) 676-2500; Fax (360) 671-6400; johnmi@portofbellingham.com; www.portofbellingham.com

Benton City • *Benton City Eco. Dev. Cncl.* • Larry D. Howell; Pres.; 513 9th St.; P.O. Box 1038; 99320; Benton; P 5,000; (509) 588-4984; bcedc@bentoncityedc.org; www.bentoncityedc.org

Bremerton • *see Silverdale*

Cathlamet • *Lower Columbia Eco. Dev. Cncl.* • David Goodroe; Exec. Dir.; P.O. Box 52; 98612; Wahkiakum; P 4,000; (360) 795-3996; Fax (360) 795-3944; davidg.lcedc@cni.net; www.lowercolumbiaedc.org

Chehalis • *Lewis County Eco. Dev. Cncl.* • Dick Larman; Exec. Dir.; 1611 N. National Ave.; P.O. Box 916; 98532; Lewis; P 67,000; (360) 748-0114; Fax (360) 748-1238; dlarman@lewisedc.com; www.lewisedc.com

College Place • *see Walla Walla*

Colville • *Tri-County Eco. Dev. Dist.* • Jeff Koffel; Exec. Dir.; 986 S. Main St., Ste. A; 99114; Stevens; P 41,000; (509) 684-4571; (800) 776-7318; Fax (509) 684-4788; admin@teddonline.com; www.tricountyedd.com

Coupeville • *Island County Eco. Dev. Cncl.* • Ron Nelson; Exec. Dir.; 180 N.W. Coveland; P.O. Box 279; 98239; Island; P 79,000; (360) 678-6889; icedc@whidbey.net; www.iscoedc.com

Everett • *Eco. Alliance of Snohomish County* • Patrick Pierce; Pres./CEO; 808 134th St. S.W., Ste. 101; 98204; Snohomish; P 593,500; (425) 743-4567; johnm@economicalliancesc.org; www.economicalliancesc.org

Ferry County • *see Colville*

Longview • *Cowlitz Eco. Dev. Cncl.* • Ted Sprague; Pres.; 1452 Hudson, Ste. 208; P.O. Box 1278; 98632; Cowlitz; P 102,000; (360) 423-9921; sprague@cowlitzedc.com; www.cowlitzedc.com

Moses Lake • *Grant County Eco. Dev. Cncl.* • Terry Brewer CEcD; Exec. Dir.; 6594 Patton Blvd. N.E.; 98837; Grant; P 89,100; (509) 764-6579; Fax (509) 764-8591; jonathan@grantedc.com; www.grantedc.com

Palouse • *Palouse Eco. Dev. Cncl.* • Mike Milano; Dir.; P.O. Box 174; 99161; Whitman; P 1,015; (509) 878-1811; palousechamber@visitpalouse.com; www.liveinpalouse.com

Pend Orielle County • *see Colville*

Port Angeles • *Clallam County EDC* • Bill Greenwood; Exec. Dir.; 905 W. 9th St.; P.O. Box 1085; 98362; Clallam; P 67,000; (360) 457-7793; info@clallam.org; www.clallam.org

Port Orchard • *see Silverdale*

Poulsbo • *see Silverdale*

Prescott • *see Walla Walla*

Prosser • *Prosser Eco. Dev. Assn.* • Deb Heintz; Exec. Dir.; 1230 Bennett Ave.; 99350; Benton; P 5,600; (509) 786-3600; Fax (509) 786-2399; info@prosser.org; www.prosser.org

Raymond • *Pacific County Eco. Dev. Cncl.* • Paul Philpot; Exec. Dir.; 600 Washington Ave.; 98577; Pacific; P 21,800; (360) 875-9330; director@pacificedc.org; www.pacificedc.org

Seattle • *Eco. Dev. Cncl. of Seattle & King County* • Suzanne Dale Estey; Pres./CEO; 1301 Fifth Ave., Ste. 1500; 98101; King; P 2,000,000; (206) 389-8650; frobertson@edc-seaking.org; edc-seaking.org

Silverdale • *Kitsap Eco. Dev. Alliance* • John Powers; Exec. Dir.; Cavalon Place II; 2021 N.W. Mhyre Rd., Ste. 100; 98383; Kitsap; P 254,500; (360) 377-9499; Fax (360) 479-4653; info@kitsapeda.org; www.kitsapeda.org

Stevens County • *see Colville*

Stevenson • *Skamania County Eco. Dev. Cncl.* • Robert Waymire; Exec. Dir.; 167 N.W. Second St.; P.O. Box 436; 98648; Skamania; P 10,800; (509) 427-5110; Fax (509) 427-5122; scedc@skamania-edc.org; www.skamania-edc.org

Tacoma • *Eco. Dev. Bd. for Tacoma-Pierce County* • Bruce Kendall; Pres./CEO; 950 Pacific Ave., Ste. 410; 98402; Pierce; P 733,700; (253) 383-4726; Fax (253) 383-4676; info@edbtacomapierce.org; www.edbtacomapierce.org

Tacoma • *Pierce County Dept. of Comm. Svcs.* • Helen Howell; Dir.; 3602 Pacific Ave., Ste. 200; 98418; Pierce; P 725,000; (253) 798-7205; Fax (253) 798-6604; hhowell@co.pierce.wa.us; www.co.pierce.wa.us

Vancouver • *Columbia River Eco. Dev. Cncl.* • Mike Bomar; Pres.; 805 Broadway, Ste. 412; 98660; Clark; P 443,000; (360) 694-5006; info@credc.org; www.credc.org

Waitsburg • *see Walla Walla*

Walla Walla • *Port of Walla Walla* • Patrick Reay; Exec. Dir.; 310 A St.; Walla Walla Reg. Airport; 99362; Walla Walla; P 61,000; (509) 525-3100; Fax (509) 525-3101; pr@portwallawalla.com; www.portwallawalla.com

Winslow • *see Silverdale*

Yakima • *Yakima County Dev. Assn.* • Jonathan Smith; Pres./CEO; 10 N. 9th St.; P.O. Box 1387; 98907; Yakima; P 248,000; (509) 575-1140; Fax (509) 575-1508; newvision@ycda.com; www.ycda.com

West Virginia

Federal

***U.S. SBA, West Virginia Dist. Ofc.* •** Judy McCauley; Dist. Dir.; 320 W. Pike St., Ste. 330; 26301; Harrison; (304) 623-5631; Fax (304) 623-0023; wvinfo@sba.gov; www.sba.gov/wv

State

***West Virginia Eco. Dev. Auth.* •** David Warner; Exec. Dir.; Northgate Bus. Park; 160 Association Dr.; Charleston; 25311; Kanawha; (304) 558-3650; Fax (304) 558-0206; caren.d.wilcher@wv.gov; www.wveda.org

Communities

Beckley • *New River Gorge Reg. Dev. Auth.* • Judy Radford; Exec. Dir.; 116 N. Heber St., Ste. B; 25801; Raleigh; P 188,685; (304) 254-8115; Fax (304) 254-8112; nrgrda@nrgrda.org; www.nrgrda.org

Berkeley Springs • *Morgan County Eco. Dev. Auth.* • William Clark; Exec. Dir.; 77 Fairfax St., Rm. 106; 25411; Morgan; P 17,500; (304) 258-8546; Fax (304) 258-7305; bclark@morgancountywv.gov; www.morgancountywv.gov

Buckhannon • *Upshur County Dev. Auth.* • Robert R. Hinton; Exec. Dir.; 30 E. Main St.; P.O. Box 2377; 26201; Upshur; P 25,000; (304) 472-1757; Fax (304) 472-4998; info@upshurda.com; www.upshurda.com

Charleston • *West Virginia Dev. Ofc.* • Keith Burdette; Exec. Dir.; State Capitol Complex; Bldg. 6, Rm. 525; 25305; Kanawha; P 1,850,000; (304) 558-2234; Fax (304) 558-1189; kim.l.harbour@wv.gov; www.wvdo.org

Clarksburg • *Harrison County Dev. Auth.* • Jacqui Tennant; Admin. Asst.; 301 W. Main St., 6th Flr.; 26301; Harrison; P 69,088; (304) 326-0213; Fax (304) 626-1070; hcda@westvirginia.com; www.hcdawv.com

Elkins • *Randolph County Dev. Auth.* • Robbie Morris; Exec. Dir.; 10 Eleventh St.; 26241; Randolph; P 29,500; (304) 637-0803; Fax (304) 637-4902; info@rcdawv.org; www.rcdawv.org

Keyser • *Mineral County Dev. Auth.* • Kevin R. Clark; Exec. Dir.; 87 N. Main St., Ste. 1; 26726; Mineral; P 28,200; (304) 788-2233; Fax (304) 788-2998; Kclark@mineralEDA.com; www.mineralcountydevelopmentauthority.com

Marshall • *see Wheeling*

Martinsburg • *Berkeley County Dev. Auth.* • Stephen L. Christian; Exec. Dir.; 300 Foxcroft Ave., Ste. 201; 25401; Berkeley; P 104,100; (304) 267-4144; Fax (304) 267-2283; info@developmentauthority.com; www.developmentauthority.com

Maxwelton • *Greenbrier Valley EDC* • Tom Cross; Interim Exec. Dir.; 804 Industrial Park Rd., Ste. 5; 24957; Greenbrier; P 56,000; (304) 497-4300; Fax (304) 497-4330; info@gvedc.com; www.gvedc.com

Moorefield • *Hardy County Rural Dev. Auth.* • Mallie J. Combs; Exec. Dir.; P.O. Box 209; 26836; Hardy; P 14,025; (304) 530-3047; Fax (304) 530-6995; hardyrda@hardynet.com; www.hardycountywv.com

Ohio • *see Wheeling*

Petersburg • *Grant County Dev. Auth.* • Tammy Kitzmiller; Exec. Dir.; P.O. Box 114; 26847; Grant; P 12,000; (304) 257-2168; Fax (304) 257-5454; tkitzmiller@grantcounty-wv.com; www.grantcounty-wv.com

Point Pleasant • *Mason County Dev. Auth.* • John Musgrave; Exec. Dir.; 305 Main St.; 25550; Mason; P 27,300; (304) 675-1497; Fax (304) 675-1601; mcdaadm@masoncounty.org; www.masoncounty.org

Princeton • *Dev. Auth. of Mercer County* • Janet E. Bailey; Exec. Dir.; 1500 W. Main St.; 24740; Mercer; P 62,000; (304) 431-8521; (304) 431-8523; Fax (304) 487-5616; mercercounty@citlink.net; www.mercercoeda.com

Ripley • *Jackson County Dev. Auth.* • Mark Whitley; Exec. Dir.; 167 Seneca Dr.; 25271; Jackson; P 29,200; (304) 372-1151; Fax (304) 372-1153; info@jcda.org; www.jcda.org

Scott Depot • *Putnam County Dev. Auth.* • Andrew Dunlap; Exec. Dir.; 5664 State Rte. 34, Winfield, WV 25213; P.O. Box 167; 25213; Putnam; P 57,000; (304) 757-0318; Fax (304) 757-7748; adunlap@pcda.org; www.pcda.org

Spencer • *Roane County Eco. Dev. Auth.* • Mark Whitley; Eco. Dev. Dir.; P.O. Box 1; 25276; Roane; P 15,446; (304) 927-5189; Fax (304) 927-5953; director@roanecountyeda.org; www.roanecountyeda.org

Summersville • *Nicholas County Comm. Ofc.* • Patty Neff; Admin. Asst.; 700 Main St., Ste. 1; 26651; Nicholas; P 26,200; (304) 872-7830; Fax (304) 872-9602; ncc_pattyneff@yahoo.com; www.nicholascountywv.org

Webster Springs • *Webster County Eco. Dev. Auth.* • Geary Weir; Exec. Dir.; 139 Baker St.; 26288; Webster; P 9,100; (304) 847-2145; Fax (304) 847-5198; wcda@websterwv.com; www.websterwv.com

Welch • *McDowell County Eco. Dev. Auth.* • Stephanie Addair; Exec. Dir.; 92 McDowell St., Ste. 100; 24801; McDowell; P 22,000; (304) 436-3833; Fax (304) 436-3837; stephanie.addair@mcdowelleda.com; www.mcdowelleda.com

Wheeling • *Reg. Eco. Dev. Partnership* • Don Rigby; Exec. Dir.; P.O. Box 1029; 26003; Ohio; P 154,000; (304) 232-7722; Fax (304) 232-7727; info@redp.org; www.redp.org

Whitehall • *Region VI Planning & Dev. Cncl.* • James L. Hall; Exec. Dir.; 34 Mountain Park Dr.; 26554; Marion; P 253,304; (304) 366-5693; Fax (304) 367-0804; regionvi@regionvi.com; www.regionvi.com

Wisconsin

Federal

U.S. SBA, Wisconsin Dist. Ofc. • Eric Ness; Dist. Dir.; 740 Regent St., Ste. 100; 53715; Dane; P 5,742,713; (608) 441-5261; (608) 441-5263; Fax (608) 441-5541; wisconsin@sba.gov; www.sba.gov/wi

State

Wisconsin Eco. Dev. Corp. • Ryan Murray; COO; 201 W. Washington Ave.; P.O. Box 1687; Madison; 53701; Dane; P 5,726,398; (608) 210-6700; brenda.hickssorensen@wedc.org; www.wedc.org

Communities

Algoma • *Community Dev. Comm.* • Bruce Charles; Chrmn.; 416 Fremont St.; 54201; Kewaunee; P 3,162; (920) 487-5203; Fax (920) 487-3499; algoma@algomacity.org; www.algomacity.org

Almena • *Impact Seven Inc.* • William Bay; Pres.; 147 Lake Almena Dr.; 54805; Barron; P 5,300,000; (715) 357-3334; Fax (715) 357-6233; impact@impactseven.org; www.impactseven.org

Antigo • *Langlade County Eco. Dev. Corp.* • Angie Close; Exec. Dir.; 312 Forrest Ave.; 54409; Langlade; P 20,000; (715) 623-5123; (715) 623-2085; aclose@co.langlade.wi.us; www.langladecounty.org

Ashland • *Ashland Area Dev. Corp.* • Dale Kupczyk; Exec. Dir.; 422 3rd St. W., Ste. 101; 54806; Ashland; P 16,200; (715) 682-8344; Fax (715) 682-8415; info@ashlandareadevelopment.org; www.ashlandareadevelopment.org

Athens • *Athens Area Dev. Corp.* • Randy Decker; Pres.; P.O. Box A; 54411; Marathon; P 1,200; (715) 257-7531; randyd@deckerlumber.com; www.athenswis.com

Baraboo • *Baraboo Eco. Dev. Comm.* • Ed Geick; City Admin.; 135 4th St.; 53913; Sauk; P 12,100; (608) 355-2715; Fax (608) 355-2719; egeick@cityofbaraboo.com; www.cityofbaraboo.com

Baraboo • *Sauk County Dev. Corp.* • Keri Olson; Organizational Facilitator; 505 Broadway; P.O. Box 33; 53913; Sauk; P 63,700; (608) 355-4870; (608) 393-7419; Fax (608)355-2083; kerijolson@gmail.com; www.scdc.com

Beaver Dam • *Beaver Dam Area Dev. Corp.* • Trent Campbell; Exec. V.P.; 203 Corporate Dr.; P.O. Box 492; 53916; Dodge; P 17,000; (920) 887-4661; Fax (920) 885-5008; bdadc@cityofbeaverdam.com; www.cityofbeaverdam.com

Beloit • *Greater Beloit Eco. Dev. Corp.* • Andrew Janke CPM; Exec. Dir.; 500 Public Ave.; 53511; Rock; P 37,110; (608) 364-6748; Fax (608) 364-6756; jankea@beloitwi.gov; www.greaterbeloitworks.com

Berlin • *Berlin Comm. Dev. Corp.* • Mary Neubauer; 108 N. Capron; P.O. Box 272; 54923; Green Lake; P 5,600; (920) 361-5403; Fax (920) 361-5405; mneubauer@cityofberlin.net; www.1berlin.com

Boscobel • *City of Boscobel Eco. Dev.* • Arlie Harris; City Admin.; 1006 Wisconsin Ave.; 53805; Grant; P 3,308; (608) 375-4400; Fax (608) 375-4750; contact@boscobelwisconsin.com; www.boscobelwisconsin.com

Cashton • *Cashton Dev. Corp.* • Scot Wall; Pres.; 723 Main St.; P.O. Box 70; 54619; Monroe; P 1,102; (608) 654-5121; villageofcashton@centurytel.net; www.cashton.com

Chippewa Falls • *Chippewa County Eco. Dev. Corp.* • Charlie Walker CEcD; Pres./CEO; 770 Technology Way; 54729; Chippewa; P 65,000; (715) 723-7150; Fax (715) 723-7140; ccedc@chippewa-wi.com; www.chippewa-wi.com

Clear Lake • *Clear Lake Ind. Dev. Corp.* • Al Bannink; Clerk/Treas.; 350 4th Ave.; P.O. Box 48; 54005; Polk; P 1,100; (715) 263-2157; Fax (715) 263-2666; vilofcl@cltcomm.net; www.clearlakewi.com

Cottage Grove • *Cottage Grove Eco. Dev. Comm.* • Diane Wiedenbeck, Chair; Village Pres.; 221 E. Cottage Grove Rd.; 53527; Dane; P 6,200; (608) 839-4704; Fax (608) 839-4698; dwiedenbeck@village.cottage-grove.wi.us; www.village.cottage-grove.wi.us

Cuba City • *Cuba City Comm. Dev. Corp.* • Richard Brown; 108 N. Main St.; 53807; Grant & Lafayette; P 2,100; (608) 744-2152; Fax (608) 744-2151; gdroessler@wppienergy.org; www.cubacitywi.com

Delafield • *Delafield Plan Comm.* • Michele DeYoe; Mayor; City Hall; 500 Genesee St.; 53018; Waukesha; P 7,085; (262) 646-6220; Fax (262) 646-6223; www.cityofdelafield.com

Delavan • *Delavan Dev. Corp.* • Denise Pieroni; City Admin.; 123 S. Second St.; P.O. Box 465; 53115; Walworth; P 8,500; (262) 728-5585; Fax (262) 728-4566; cityadmin@ci.delavan.wi.us; www.ci.delavan.wi.us

Dodgeville • *Iowa County Area Eco. Dev. Corp.* • Rick Terrien; Exec. Dir.; 222 N. Iowa St.; 53533; Iowa; P 2,400; (608) 553-7575; rickt@iowacountyedc.org; www.iowacountyedc.org

Eau Claire • *City of Eau Claire Comm. Dev.* • Michael Schatz; Eco. Dev. Dir.; 203 S. Farwell St.; P.O. Box 5148; 54702; Eau Claire; P 65,800; (715) 839-4914; Fax (715) 839-4939; mike.schatz@eauclairewi.gov; www.eauclairedevelopment.com

Eau Claire • *Eau Claire Area Eco. Dev. Corp.* • Luke Hanson; Exec. Dir.; 7 S. Dewey St.; P.O. Box 1108; 54702; Eau Claire; P 100,000; (715) 834-0070; (800) 944-2449; Fax (715) 834-1956; ec.info@eauclaire-wi.com; www.eauclaire-wi.com

Edgerton • *Edgerton Eco. Dev. Corp.* • Ramona Flanigan; City Admin.; 12 Albion St.; 53534; Dane & Rock; P 5,300; (608) 884-3341; Fax (608) 884-8892; rflanigan@cityofedgerton.com; www.cityofedgerton.com

Elkhorn • *City of Elkhorn* • Sam Tapson; City Admin.; 9 S. Broad St.; 53121; Walworth; P 9,956; (262) 723-2219; Fax (262) 741-5131; info@cityofelkhorn.org; www.cityofelkhorn.org

Fennimore • *Grant County Eco. Dev. Corp.* • Ron Brisbois; Exec. Dir.; 1800 Bronson Blvd.; 53809; Grant; P 52,300; (608) 822-3501; Fax (608) 822-6019; gcedc@grantcounty.org; www.grantcounty.org

Fennimore • *Fennimore Ind. & Eco. Dev. Corp.* • Linda Parrish; Promo. Coord.; 850 Lincoln Ave.; 53809; Grant; P 2,400; (608) 822-3599; Fax (608) 822-6007; promo@fennimore.com; www.fennimore.com

Florence • *Florence County Eco. Dev.* • Wendy Gehlhoff; Dir.; 501 Lake Ave.; P.O. Box 88; 54121; Florence; P 4,500; (715) 528-3294; Fax (715) 528-5071; wgehlhoff@co.florence.wi.us; www.exploreflorencecounty.com

Fond du Lac • *Fond du Lac County Eco. Dev. Corp.* • Steve Jenkins CEcD; Pres.; 116 N. Main St.; P.O. Box 1303; 54936; Fond du Lac; P 102,000; (920) 929-2928; Fax (920) 929-7126; hello@futurefc.com; www.fcedc.com

Fort Atkinson • *Fort Atkinson Ind. Dev. Corp.* • Randall Knox; V.P.; 244 N. Main St.; 53538; Jefferson; P 12,000; (920) 563-3210; Fax (920) 563-8946; idc@fortchamber.com; www.fortchamber.com/businessdevelopment

Friendship • *Adams County Rural & Ind. Dev. Comm.* • Daric Smith; Exec. Dir.; P.O. Box 236; 53934; Adams; P 20,800; (608) 339-6945; Fax (608) 339-0052; economicdevelopment@adamscountywi.com; www.adamscountywi.com

Germantown • *Germantown Comm. Dev.* • Jeff Retzlaff AICP; Dir.; N112 W17001 Mequon Rd.; 53022; Washington; P 20,000; (262) 250-4735; Fax (262) 253-8255; jretzlaff@village.germantown.wi.us; www.village.germantown.wi.us

Grantsburg • *Grantsburg Ind. Dev. Corp.* • Gordy Lewis; Pres.; P.O. Box 365; 54840; Burnett; P 1,400; (715) 463-2405; info@grantsburgidc.com; www.grantsburgidc.com

Green Bay • *Advance Bus. Dev. Center* • Fred Monique; V.P. Eco. Dev.; 2701 Larsen Rd.; 54303; Brown; P 306,000; (920) 496-9010; Fax (920) 496-6009; monique@titletown.org; www.titletown.org

Hartford • *City of Hartford Eco. Dev. Dept.* • Gary Koppelberger; Coord.; 109 N. Main St.; 53027; Washington; P 14,253; (262) 673-8202; Fax (262) 673-8218; jhanrahan@ci.hartford.wi.us; www.ci.hartford.wi.us

Hurley • *Iron County Dev. Zone* • Mr. Kelly Klein; Coord.; 100 Cary Rd.; 54534; Iron; P 6,000; (715) 561-2922; Fax (715) 561-3103; kelly@ironcountywi.com; www.ironcountywi.com

Janesville • *City of Janesville Eco. Dev. Agency* • Vic Grassman; Econ. Dev. Dir.; 18 N. Jackson St., 3rd Flr.; P.O. Box 5005; 53547; Rock; P 63,000; (608) 755-3181; Fax (608) 755-3189; grassmanv@ci.janesville.wi.us; www.growjanesville.com

Janesville • *Forward Janesville Inc.* • John Beckord; Pres.; 14 S. Jackson St., Ste. 200; 53548; Rock; P 64,000; (608) 757-3160; Fax (608) 757-3170; forward@forwardjanesville.com; www.forwardjanesville.com

Juneau • *Juneau Comm. Dev. Auth.* • Ron Bosak; Mayor; 150 Miller St.; P.O. Box 163; 53039; Dodge; P 2,500; (920) 386-4800; Fax (920) 386-4802; cda@cityofjuneau.net; www.cityofjuneau.net

Kenosha • *Kenosha Area Bus. Alliance* • Todd Battle; Pres.; 5500 6th Ave., Ste. 200; 53140; Kenosha; P 166,000; (262) 605-1100; Fax (262) 605-1111; info@kaba.org; www.kaba.org

La Crosse • *La Crosse Area Dev. Corp.* • James P. Hill; Exec. Dir.; 601 7th St. North; 54601; La Crosse; P 115,600; (608) 784-5488; (888) 208-0698; Fax (608) 784-5408; ladco@centurytel.net; www.ladcoweb.org

Ladysmith • *Ladysmith Comm. Ind. Dev. Corp.* • Al Christianson; City Admin.; 120 W. Miner Ave.; P.O. Box 431; 54848; Rusk; P 3,200; (715) 532-2600; Fax (715) 532-2620; achristianson@cityofladysmithwi.com; www.cityofladysmithwi.com

Lancaster • *Lancaster Eco. Dev. Comm.* • Steve Winger; City Admin.; 206 S. Madison St.; 53813; Grant; P 4,000; (608) 723-4246; Fax (608) 723-4789; cityhall@lancasterwisconsin.com; www.lancasterwisconsin.com

Loyal • *Clark County Eco. Dev. Corp. & Tourism Bur.* • Sheila Nyberg; Exec. Dir.; 301 N. Main St.; P.O. Box 236; 54446; Clark; P 35,000; (715) 255-9100; Fax (715) 255-9153; sheila@clark-cty-wi.org; www.clark-cty-wi.org

Manitowoc • *Manitowoc Ind. Dev. Corp.* • David Less; City Planner; 900 Quay St.; 54220; Manitowoc; P 35,000; (920) 686-6930; Fax (920) 686-6939; dless@manitowoc.org; www.manitowoc.org

Manitowoc • *Progress Lakeshore* • Peter Wills; Exec. Dir.; 202 N. 8th St., Ste. 101; 54220; Manitowoc; P 81,500; (920) 482-0540; Fax (920) 682-6816; info@progresslakeshore.org; www.progresslakeshore.org

Marinette • *Marinette County Assn. for Bus. & Ind.* • Ann Hartnell; Exec. Dir.; 1926 Hall Ave.; 54143; Marinette; P 43,713; (715) 732-7421; Fax (715) 854-7002; info@mcabi.com; www.mcabi.com

Marion • *Marion Eco. Dev. Corp.* • Mary S. Rogers; Clerk; 217 N. Main St.; P.O. Box 127; 54950; Shawano & Waupaca; P 1,250; (715) 754-2124; comarion@frontiernet.net; www.marion.govoffice2.com

Marshfield • *Marshfield Area C/C & Ind.* • Scott Larson; Exec. Dir.; 700 S. Central Ave.; P.O. Box 868; 54449; Wood; P 20,000; (715) 384-3454; Fax (715) 387-8925; macci@marshfieldchamber.com; www.marshfieldchamber.com

Mauston • *Greater Mauston Area Dev. Corp.* • Barb Martin; Exec. Dir.; 103 Division St.; 53948; Juneau; P 10,000; (608) 847-7483; Fax (608) 847-5814; gmadc@mwt.net; www.mauston.com

Medford • *Medford Area Eco. Dev.* • Mark Hoffman; Pres.; 104 E. Perkins St.; P.O. Box 172; 54451; Taylor; P 4,324; (715) 748-4729; Fax (715) 748-6899; medfordchamber@tds.net; www.medfordwis.com

EDC

Menomonie • *Dunn County Eco. Dev. Corp.* • Eric S. Turner; Exec. Dir.; 800 Wilson Ave., Ste. 219; 54751; Dunn; P 40,315; (715) 232-4009; Fax (715) 232-4034; director@dunnedc.com; www.dunnedc.com

Milwaukee • *Metro Milwaukee Assn. of Commerce* • Timothy Sheehy; Pres.; 756 N. Milwaukee St., Ste. 400; 53202; Milwaukee, Ozaukee, Washington & Waukesha; P 1,567,000; (414) 287-4126; Fax (414) 271-7753; myoshida@mmac.org; www.mmac.org

Milwaukee • *Milwaukee County Eco.& Comm. Dev.* • Robert Dennik; Dir.; 2711 W. Wells St., 5th Flr.; 53208; Milwaukee, Washington & Waukesha; P 970,000; (414) 278-4905; Fax (414) 223-1917; econdevelop@milwcnty.com; www.co.mil.wi.us

Monroe • *Green County Dev. Corp.* • Michael Johnson AICP; Exec. Dir.; Green County Courthouse, 2nd Flr.; 1016 16th Ave.; 53566; Green; P 37,100; (608) 328-9452; Fax (608) 328-9460; mike.gcdc@tds.net; www.greencountyedc.com

Neenah • *Future Neenah Inc.* • Amy Barker; Exec. Dir.; 135 W. Wisconsin Ave.; 54956; Winnebago; P 25,500; (920) 722-1920; info@neenah.org; www.neenah.org

Neillsville • *Neillsville Dept. of Eco. Dev.* • Steve Mabie; Mayor; City Hall; 118 W. 5th St.; 54456; Clark; P 2,463; (715) 743-2105; Fax (715) 743-2727; clerk@neillsville-wi.com; www.neillsville-wi.com

Neshkoro • *Tri-County Reg. Eco. Dev. Corp.* • Bill Wheeler; Exec. Dir.; 126 S. Main St.; P.O. Box 120; 54960; Green Lake, Marquette & Waushara; P 59,200; (920) 382-0963; bwheeler@tcredc.org; www.tcredc.org

New Glarus • *New Glarus Comm. Dev. Auth.* • Nicholas Owen; Village Admin.; 319 2nd St.; P.O. Box 399; 53574; Green; P 2,165; (608) 527-2510; Fax (608) 527-6630; nowen@newglarusvillage.com; www.newglarusvillage.com

New Holstein • *New Holstein Ind. Dev. Corp.* • Lee Watson; Dir.; 2110 Washington St.; 53061; Calumet; P 4,000; (920) 898-5766; Fax (920) 898-5879; lwatson@myfrontiermail.com; www.ci.new-holstein.wi.us

New London • *New London Eco. Dev.* • Kent Hager; City Admin.; 215 N. Shawano St.; 54961; Outagamie & Waupaca; P 7,300; (920) 982-8500; Fax (920) 982-8665; khager@newlondonwi.org; www.newlondonwi.org

New London • *Waupaca County Eco. Dev. Corp.* • David Thiel; Exec. Dir.; N. 3512 Dawn Dr.; 54961; Outagamie & Waupaca; P 52,400; (920) 982-1582; Fax (920) 982-9047; wcedc@charter.net; www.wcedc.org

New Richmond • *Comm. Dev. of New Richmond* • Beth Thompson; Dir.; 156 E. 1st St.; 54017; St. Croix; P 8,600; (715) 246-4268; Fax (715) 246-7129; bthompson@newrichmondwi.gov; www.newrichmondwi.gov

Oak Creek • *Oak Creek Dept. of Comm. Dev.* • Doug Seymour; Dir.; 8040 S. 6th St.; 53154; Milwaukee; P 34,451; (414) 766-7000; Fax (414) 768-9587; dseymour@oakcreekwi.org; www.oakcreekwi.org

Oconomowoc • *Oconomowoc Bur. of Eco. Dev. & Tour.* • Robert Duffy; Dir.; 174 E. Wisconsin Ave.; 53066; Waukesha; P 16,000; (262) 569-2185; Fax (262) 569-3238; info@oconomowoc-wi.gov; www.oconomowoc-wi.gov

Omro • *Future Omro Chamber Main Street* • Dana Racine; Dir. of Comm. & Eco. Dev.; 130 W. Larrabee St.; 54963; Winnebago; P 3,500; (920) 685-6960; Fax (920) 685-0384; dracine@omro-wi.com; www.FutureOmro.org

Park Falls • *Park Falls Area Comm. Dev. Corp.* • Frank Kempf; Admin.; 1224 S. 4th Ave.; P.O. Box 408; 54552; Price; P 2,800; (715) 744-4700; pfacdc@pctcnet.net; www.pfacdc.org

Pewaukee • *Waukesha County Eco. Dev. Corp.* • Bill Mitchell; Exec. Dir.; 892 Main St., Ste. D; 53072; Waukesha; P 389,800; (262) 695-7900; Fax (262) 695-7902; bmitchell@wctc.edu; www.understandingbusiness.org

Phillips • *Phillips Ind. Dev. Corp.* • Tom Boers; Pres.; 174 S. Eyder Ave.; 54555; Price; P 1,500; (715) 339-3223; Fax (715) 339-6564; clerk@cityofphillips.com; www.cityofphillips.com

Platteville • *Platteville Area Ind. Dev. Corp.* • George Krueger; Exec. Dir.; 52 Means Dr., Ste. 104; 53818; Grant; P 10,300; (608) 348-3050; Fax (608) 348-3426; plattevilleindustry@centurytel.net; www.plattevilleindustry.com

Prairie du Chien • *Prairie du Chien Eco. Dev. Corp.* • William Adamany; Pres.; 211 S. Main St.; P.O. Box 326; 53821; Crawford; P 8,000; (608) 326-8555; (800) 732-1673; Fax (608) 326-7744; bill.adamany@gmail.com; www.prairieduchienedc.com

Prentice • *Prentice Ind. Dev. Corp.* • Dale Heikkinen; Pres.; P.O. Box 78; 54556; Price; P 660; (715) 428-2124; Fax (715) 428-2120; daleh@pctcnet.net; www.vil.prentice.wi.gov

Reedsburg • *Reedsburg Ind. Dev. Comm.* • Don Lichte; Chrmn.; P.O. Box 490; 53959; Sauk; P 9,301; (608) 524-6404; Fax (608) 524-8458; lichteins@rucls.net; www.reedsburgwi.gov

Rhinelander • *Oneida County Eco. Dev. Corp.* • Roger Luce; Exec. Dir.; 3375 Airport Rd.; P.O. Box 682; 54501; Oneida; P 36,000; (715) 369-9110; (715) 356-5590; info@ocedc.org; www.ocedc.org

Rice Lake • *Rice Lake Eco. Dev. Corp.* • Bruce Markgren; Pres.; P.O. Box 526; 54868; Barron; P 8,438; (715) 234-2126; (715) 234-7008; Fax (715) 234-1025; ricelakeedc@gmail.com; www.rled.org

Shawano • *Shawano County Eco. Progress Inc.* • Dennis L. Heling; Chief Eco. Dev. Officer; 1263 S. Main St.; 54166; Shawano; P 42,000; (715) 526-5839; Fax (715) 526-2125; scepi@frontiernet.net; www.shawanoecondev.org

Sheboygan • *Sheboygan Dev. Corp.* • Patrick Drinan; Exec. Dir.; 508 New York Ave., Rm. 209; 53081; Sheboygan; P 115,500; (920) 452-2350; drinan@sheboygancountyedc.com; www.sheboygancountyedc.com

Shullsburg • *Shullsburg Comm. Dev. Corp.* • Cheryl Fink; Pres.; P.O. Box 3; 53586; Lafayette; P 1,247; (608) 965-4579; (608) 965-4424; cdc@mhtc.net; www.shullsburgwisconsin.org

Siren • *Burnett County Dev. Assn.* • Michael Kornmann; Advisor; 7410 County Rd. K #129; 54872; Burnett; P 16,000; (715) 349-2979; Fax (715) 349-2102; mkornmann@burnettcounty.org; www.burnettcounty.com

Soldiers Grove • *Soldiers Grove Comm. Dev.* • Vicki Campbell; Treas.; P.O. Box 121; 54655; Crawford; P 1,714; (608) 624-3264; Fax (608) 624-5209; sgrove@mwt.net; www.soldiersgrove.com

Sparta • *City of Sparta Eco. Dev.* • Todd Fahning; Dir. of Comm. Dev.; 201 W. Oak St.; 54656; Monroe; P 9,600; (608) 269-4340; bldg@spartawisconsin.org; www.spartawisconsin.org

Sturgeon Bay • *Door County Eco. Dev. Corp.* • William D. Chaudoir; Exec. Dir.; 185 E. Walnut St.; 54235; Door; P 29,000; (920) 743-3113; Fax (920) 743-3811; sam@doorcountybusiness.com; www.doorcountybusiness.com

Sturtevant • *Racine County Eco. Dev. Corp.* • Jenny Trick; Exec. Dir.; 2320 Renaissance Blvd.; 53177; Racine; P 196,360; (262) 898-7400; Fax (262) 898-7401; rcedc@racinecountyedc.org; www.racinecountyedc.org

Superior • *The Dev. Assn. Inc.* • Jim Caesar; Exec. Dir.; 205 Belknap St.; 54880; Douglas; P 44,100; (715) 392-4749; jim@wegrowbiz.org; www.wegrowbiz.org

Tomah • *Forward Tomah Dev. Inc.* • Tina Thompson; Pres./CEO; P.O. Box 625; 54660; Monroe; P 9,189; (608) 372-2166; (800) 94-TOMAH; Fax (608) 372-2167; info@tomahwisconsin.com; www.tomahwisconsin.com

Viroqua • *Viroqua Dev. Assn.* • Jeff Gohlke; Dir.; 202 N. Main St.; 54665; Vernon; P 5,100; (608) 637-3251; Fax (608) 637-3108; cityadmin@mwt.net; www.viroqua-wisconsin.com

Waupun • *Waupun Ind. Dev. Corp.* • Kyle Clark; City Admin.; 201 E. Main St.; 53963; Fond du Lac; P 11,000; (920) 324-7919; Fax (920) 324-7939; admin@cityofwaupun.org; www.cityofwaupun.org

Wausau • *Wausau Comm. & Eco. Dev.* • Christian Schock; Interim Dir.; 407 Grant St.; 54403; Marathon; P 39,200; (715) 261-6680; (800) 692-8728; comdev@ci.wausau.wi.us; www.wausaudevelopment.com

Wauwatosa • *Wauwatosa Eco. Dev. Corp.* • Jennifer Ferguson; Mgr.; 7725 W. North Ave.; 53213; Milwaukee; P 47,271; (414) 479-5639; (414) 479-3520; Fax (414) 479-8986; jferguson@wauwatosa.net; www.wauwatosa.net

West Allis • *City of West Allis Dept. of Dev.* • Patrick Schloss; Mgr.; 7525 W. Greenfield Ave., Rm. 220; 53214; Milwaukee; P 60,411; (414) 302-8460; Fax (414) 302-8401; pschloss@westalliswi.gov; www.westalliswi.gov

Winneconne • *Winneconne Dev. Corp.* • Steve Volkert; Village Admin.; 30 S. 1st St.; P.O. Box 488; 54986; Winnebago; P 2,400; (920) 582-4381; Fax (920) 582-0660; svolkert@winneconnewi.gov; www.winneconniewi.gov

Wisconsin Rapids • *Heart of Wisconsin C/C* • Melissa Reichert; Pres.; 1120 Lincoln St.; 54494; Wood; P 40,000; (715) 423-1830; Fax (715) 423-1865; president@wisconsinrapidschamber.com; www.wisconsinrapidschamber.com

Wyoming

State

Wyoming Eco. Dev. Assn. [WEDA] • Brittany Ashby; Coord.; 1401 Airport Pkwy., Ste 300; Cheyenne; 2001; Laramie; P 576,412; (307) 772-9146; Fax (307) 778-3943; info@wyomingeda.org; www.wyomingeda.org

Communities

Buffalo • *JOCO First* • Dave Simonsen; CEO; 63 N. Burritt Ave.; P.O. Box 490; 82834; Johnson; P 8,600; (307) 425-1007; (307) 620-1260; dave@jocofirst.com; www.jocofirst.com

Casper • *Casper Area Eco. Dev. Alliance Inc.* • Bill Edwards; Pres./CEO; 300 S. Wolcott, Ste. 300; 82601; Natrona; P 81,000; (307) 577-7011; (800) 634-5012; Fax (307) 577-7014; lacy@caeda.net; www.caeda.net

Cheyenne Leads • Randy Bruns; CEO; 121 W. 15th St., Ste. 304; 82001; Laramie; P 96,000; (307) 638-6000; (800) 255-0742; Fax (307) 638-7728; kareng@cheyenneleads.org; www.cheyenneleads.org

Wyoming Bus. Cncl. • Shawn Reese; CEO; 214 W. 15th St.; 82002; Laramie; P 563,626; (307) 777-2800; Fax (307) 777-2837; info.wbc@wyo.gov; www.wyomingbusiness.org

Cody • *Cody Country Eco. Dev.* • 836 Sheridan Ave.; 82414; Park; P 9,500; (307) 587-2777; exec@codychamber.org; www.codychamber.org

Diamondville • *South Lincoln County Eco. Dev. Corp.* • Mark Ramsperger; Exec. Dir.; P.O. Box 495; 83116; Lincoln; P 3,500; (307) 877-9781; Fax (307) 877-6709; director@southlincolnedc.org; www.southlincolnedc.org

Evanston • *Uinta County Eco. Dev. Comm.* • Gary Welling; Eco. Dev. Dir.; 225 9th St.; 82930; Uinta; P 20,872; (307) 783-0378; Fax (307) 783-0379; gawelling@uintacounty.com; www.uintacounty.com

Evanston • *City of Evanston Eco. Dev.* • Jim Davis; Clerk; City Hall; 1200 Main St.; 82930; Uinta; P 13,000; (307) 783-6300; Fax (307) 783-6390; jdavis@evanstonwy.org; www.evanstonwy.org

Gillette • *Energy Capital Eco. Dev.* • Phil Christopherson; CEO; 2001 W. Lakeway Rd., Ste. C; 82718; Campbell; P 49,000; (307) 686-2603; Fax (307) 686-7268; mary@energycapitaled.com; www.energycapitaled.com

Gillette • *North East Wyoming Eco. Dev. Coalition (NEWEDC)* • Dell Atkinson; Exec. Dir.; 2001 W. Lakeway Rd., Ste. D; 82718; Campbell; P 84,000; (307) 686-3672; Fax (307) 686-3673; dell@newedc.com; www.newedc.com

Laramie • *Laramie Chamber Bus. Alliance* • JJ Harris; Pres./CEO; 800 S. Third St.; 82070; Albany; P 35,000; (307) 745-7339; (307) 760-9905; Fax (307) 742-8200; jharris@laramie.org; www.laramie.org

Rawlins • *Carbon County Eco. Dev. Corp.* • Cindy Wallace; Exec. Dir.; 215 W. Buffalo St., Rm. 304; 82301; Carbon; P 16,000; (307) 324-3836; (307) 710-5432; Fax (307) 324-3820; info@ccwyed.net; www.ccwyed.net

Riverton • *IDEA Inc.* • Phillip Christopherson; 213 W. Main St., Ste. C; 82501; Fremont; P 10,000; (307) 856-0952; philc@wyoming.com; www.rivertonidea.com

Sheridan • *Forward Sheridan Inc.* • Jay Stender; Exec. Dir.; 224 S. Main St., Ste. 107; 82802; Sheridan; P 30,000; (307) 673-8004; Fax (307) 673-8006; info@forwardsheridan.com; www.forwardsheridan.com

Thermopolis • *Thermopolis-Hot Springs Eco. Dev. Co.* • Amanda Moeller; Exec. Dir.; 420 Broadway St.; 82443; Hot Springs; P 4,900; (307) 864-2348; Fax (307) 864-9353; thermopolisedc@rtconnect.net; www.thermopolisedc.com

Torrington • *Goshen County Eco. Dev. Corp.* • Lisa Johnson; Exec. Dir.; 110 W. 22nd Ave.; P.O. Box 580; 82240; Goshen; P 13,000; (307) 532-5162; Fax (307) 532-7641; progress@goshenwyo.com; www.goshenwyo.com

Wheatland • *Platte County Eco. Dev. Corp.* • Daphanie Taylor; Exec. Dir.; 851 Gilchrist St.; P.O. Box 988; 82201; Platte; P 8,700; (307) 322-4232; Fax (307) 322-1629; info@pcedwyo.org; www.pcedwyo.org

Worland • *Washakie Dev. Assn.* • LeAnn Baker Chenoweth; Exec. Dir.; 101 Rodeo Dr.; P.O. Box 228; 82401; Washakie; P 8,500; (307) 347-8900; wda@rtconnect.net; www.washakiedevelopment.com

THE CANADIAN CHAMBER OF COMMERCE

Head Office

360 Albert Street, Suite 420
Ottawa, Ontario K1R 7X7
Telephone: (613) 238-4000
FAX: (613) 238-7643
Email: info@chamber.ca
Website: www.chamber.ca

Calgary Office

P.O. Box 38057
Calgary, Alberta T3K 5G9
Telephone: (403) 271-0595
FAX: (403) 226-6930
Email: info@chamber.ca
Website: www.chamber.ca

Montreal Office

999 Boulevard de Maisonneuve Ouest, Ste. 560
Montreal, Quebec H3A 3L4
Telephone: (514) 866-4334
FAX: (514) 866-7296
Email: info@chamber.ca
Website: www.chamber.ca

Toronto Office

55 University Avenue, Suite 901
Toronto, Ontario M5J 2H7
Telephone: (416) 868-6415
FAX: (416) 868-0189
Email: info@chamber.ca
Website: www.chamber.ca

Senior Officers

Chair of the Board
(September 2016-September 2017)
Duncan Wilson, V.P., Corporate Social Responsibility,
Vancouver Fraser Port Authority (c/o Head Office)

President & Chief Executive Officer
Honourable Perrin Beatty (c/o Head Office)
pbeatty@chamber.ca

Chief Operating Officer
Guy Legault (c/o Head Office)
glegault@chamber.ca

Senior Vice President, Policy
Warren Everson (c/o Head Office)
weverson@chamber.ca

Director, Public Affairs & Media Relations
Guillaum (Will) Dubreuil (c/o Head Office)
gdubreuil@chamber.ca

Vice President and Chief Financial Officer
Adéle Laronde, CA (c/o Head Office)
alaronde@chamber.ca

Canadian C/C

CANADIAN CHAMBERS OF COMMERCE

Alberta

Alberta C/C • Ken Kobly; Pres./CEO; 1808, 10025 - 102A Ave. 1808; Edmonton; T5J 2Z2; P 3,700,000; M 24,000; (780) 425-4180; Fax (780) 429-1061; tacorn@abchamber.ca; www.abchamber.ca

Airdrie • *Airdrie C/C* • Lorna Hunt; Exec. Dir.; #102, 150 Edwards Way N.W.; Box 3661; T4B 4B9; P 60,000; M 500; (403) 948-4412; Fax (403) 948-3141; info@airdriechamber.ab.ca; www.airdriechamber.ab.ca

Alix • *Alix C/C* • Clarence Verveda; P.O. Box 145; T0C 0B0; P 825; M 20; (403) 747-2405; Fax (403) 747-2403; www.villageofalix.ca

Athabasca • *Athabasca Dist. C/C* • Nigel Satchwell; Pres.; P.O. Box 3074; T9S 2B9; P 12,000; M 65; (780) 213-0433; chamber@athabascachamber.ca; www.athabascachamber.ca

Barrhead • *Barrhead & Dist. C/C* • Elize Zuk; P.O. Box 4524; T7N 1A4; P 4,500; M 87; (780) 674-6100; info@barrheadchamber.ca; www.barrheadchamber.ca

Beaverlodge • *Beaverlodge & Dist. C/C* • Judy Olson; Exec. Dir.; P.O. Box 303; T0H 0C0; P 2,100; M 65; (780) 354-8785; Fax (780) 354-2101; rjolson@telus.net; www.beaverlodge.ca

Berwyn • *Berwyn & Dist. C/C* • P.O. Box 144; T0H 0E0; P 606; M 15; (780) 338-3922; berwynchamber@gmail.com; www.berwyn.govoffice.com

Blairmore • *Crowsnest Pass C/C* • Crystal Husch; Ofc. Mgr.; 12707 20th Ave.; P.O. Box 706; T0K 0E0; P 5,500; M 125; (403) 562-7108; (888) 562-7108; Fax (406) 562-7493; cnpchamber@telus.net; www.cnpchamber.ca

Breton • *Breton & Dist. C/C* • P.O. Box 850; T0C 0P0; P 500; M 25; bretonchamber@gmail.com; www.village.breton.ab.ca

Brooks • *Brooks & Dist. C/C* • Karen Vogelaar; Exec. Dir.; 4-4-2nd Ave.; T1R 0S3; P 15,000; M 200; (403) 362-7641; Fax (403) 362-6893; manager@brookschamber.ab.ca; www.opportunitynewell.com

Calgary • *Calgary Chamber* • Adam Legge; Pres./CEO; 600, 237 8th Ave. S.E.; T2G 5C3; P 1,100,000; M 2,000; (403) 750-0400; Fax (403) 266-3413; info@calgarychamber.com; www.calgarychamber.com*

Camrose • *Camrose C/C* • Sharon Anderson; Exec. Dir.; 5402 - 48 Ave.; T4V 0J7; P 17,300; M 386; (780) 672-4217; (780) 679-0064; Fax (780) 672-1059; camcham@telus.net; www.camrosechamber.ca

Canmore • *Canmore Eco. Dev.* • Teresa Mullen; Exec. Dir.; 202, 600 9th St.; T1W 2T2; P 18,000; (403) 678-6902; (866) CAN-MORE; Fax (403) 678-5730; tmullen@tourismcanmore.com; www.canmorebusiness.com

Cardston • *Cardston & Dist. C/C* • Zenith Gaynor; Pres.; P.O. Box 1212; T0K 0K0; P 4,000; M 100; (403) 795-1032; Fax (403) 653-2644; info@cardstonchamber.com; www.cardstonchamber.com

Coaldale • *Coaldale & Dist. C/C* • Dixie McCarley; Ofc. Mgr.; 1401 20 Ave.; P.O. Box 1117; T1M 1M9; P 6,000; M 150; (403) 345-2358; Fax (403) 345-2339; info@coaldalechamber.com; www.coaldalechamber.com

Cochrane • *Cochrane & Dist. C/C* • Bill Popplewell; Pres.; P.O. Box 996; T4C 1B1; P 21,000; M 270; (403) 932-0320; Fax (403) 541-0915; c.business@cochranechamber.ca; www.cochranechamber.ca

Cold Lake • *Cold Lake Reg. C/C* • Sherri Bohme; Exec. Dir.; 4009 50th St.; P.O. Box 454; T9M 1P1; P 16,000; M 305; (780) 594-4747; info@coldlakechamber.ca; www.coldlakechamber.ca

Consort • *Consort & Dist. C/C* • Dave Bruha; Pres.; P.O. Box 335; T0C 1B0; P 2,300; M 40; (403) 577-7907; Fax (403) 577-3570; psdahl@xplorenet.com; www.village.consort.ab.ca

Devon • *Devon & Dist. C/C* • Barry Breau; Ofc. Mgr.; 32 Athabasca Ave., Ste. 104; T9G 1G2; P 6,500; M 82; (780) 987-5177; Fax (780) 987-3303; devoncc@telus.net; www.devon.ca

Didsbury • *Didsbury & Dist. C/C* • Sandi Clark; Mgr.; P.O. Box 981; T0M 0W0; P 4,900; M 80; (403) 335-3265; Fax (403) 335-3265; info@didsburychamber.ca; www.didsburychamber.ca

Drayton Valley • *Drayton Valley & Dist. C/C* • Tom Campbell; Pres.; P.O. Box 5318; T7A 1R5; P 7,050; M 130; (780) 542-7578; Fax (780) 542-2688; dvchamberpresident@gmail.com; www.dvchamber.com

Drumheller • *Drumheller & District C/C* • Heather Bitz; Exec. Dir.; 60 - 1st Ave. W.; Box 999; T0J 0Y0; P 8,000; M 230; (403) 823-8100; Fax (403) 823-4469; h.bitz@drumhellerchamber.com; www.drumhellerchamber.com

Edgerton • *Edgerton & C/C* • 5017-50th Ave.; T0B 1K0; P 403; (780) 755-3933; info@edgerton-oasis.ca; www.edgerton-oasis.ca

Edmonton • *Edmonton C/C* • James Cumming; Pres./CEO; #700 - 9990 Jasper Ave.; T5J 1P7; P 1,034,945; M 3,000; (780) 426-4620; Fax (780) 424-7946; info@edmontonchamber.com; www.edmontonchamber.com

Edson • *Edson & Dist. C/C* • Heather Kelly; Mgr.; 211-55th St.; T7E 1L5; P 8,500; M 320; (780) 723-4918; Fax (780) 723-5545; manageredsonchamber@gmail.com; www.edsonchamber.com

Elk Point • *Elk Point C/C* • Jonny Neilson; Pres.; Box 639; T0A 1A0; P 1,643; M 60; (780) 724-3810; www.elkpoint.ca

Evansburg • *Evansburg & Entwistle C/C* • Al Hagman; P.O. Box 598; T0E 0T0; P 2,000; M 80; (780) 727-3643; info@partnersonthepembina.com; www.partnersonthepembina.com

Fairview • *Fairview & Dist. C/C* • Debie Knudsen; Exec. Dir.; 10308 - 110 St., Bay 4,; P.O. Box 1034; T0H 1L0; P 3,500; M 131; (780) 835-5999; Fax (780) 835-5991; director@fairviewchamber.com; www.fairviewchamber.com

Falher • *Smoky River Reg. Eco. Dev. Bd.* • Diane Chiasson; Eco. Dev. Officer; P.O. Box 210; T0H 1M0; P 5,000; (780) 837-2364; Fax (780) 837-2453; ecdev@mdsmokyriver.com; www.smokyriverregion.com

Foremost • *Foremost & Dist. C/C* • Samantha Bodin; Pres.; P.O. Box 272; T0K 0X0; P 500; M 50; (403) 867-3077; Fax (403) 867-2700; cofc4mst@shockware.com; www.foremostalberta.com

Fort Macleod • *Fort Macleod & Dist. C/C* • Domiec Holwerda; Pres.; P.O. Box 178; T0L 0Z0; P 3,200; M 90; (587) 220-5335; (877) 622-5366; Fax (403) 553-2426; fmchamber1888@gmail.com; fort-macleod-chamber.com

Fort McMurray • *Fort McMurray C/C* • Diane Slater; CAO; 304 - 9612 Franklin Ave.; T9H 2J9; P 61,400; M 500; (780) 743-3100; Fax (780) 790-9757; fmcoc@telus.net; www.fortmcmurraychamber.ca

Fort McMurray • *Fort McMurray Tourism Assn.* • Denise Barrow; Ofc. Mgr.; 400 Sakitaww Trl.; T9H 4Z3; P 61,400; M 150; (780) 791-4336; (800) 565-3947; Fax (780) 790-9509; info@fortmcmurraytourism.com; www.fortmcmurraytourism.com

Fort Saskatchewan • *Fort Saskatchewan C/C* • Dione Chambers; Exec. Dir.; 10030 - 99 Ave.; P.O. Box 3072; T8L 2T1; P 24,000; M 420; (780) 998-4355; Fax (780) 998-1515; chamber@fortsaskchamber.com; www.fortsaskchamber.com

Grande Cache • *Grande Cache C/C* • Rick Bambrick; Pres.; P.O. Box 1342; T0E 0Y0; P 4,000; M 60; (780) 501-4461; gcc@grandecachechamber.com; www.grandecachechamber.com

Grande Prairie • *Grande Prairie & Dist. C/C* • Dan Pearcy; CEO; #217-11330 106th St.; T8V 7X9; P 55,000; M 1,100; (780) 532-5340; Fax (780) 532-2926; info@gpchamber.com; www.grandeprairiechamber.com

Grimshaw • *Grimshaw & Dist. C/C* • P.O. Box 919; T0H 1W0; P 2,500; M 67; (780) 561-0030; (780) 332-4370; Fax (780) 332-1299; info@grimshawchamber.com; www.grimshawchamber.com

High Level • *High Level & Dist. C/C* • Cheryl Ernst; Co-Pres.; 10803 96th St.; T0H 1Z0; P 3,600; M 110; (780) 926-2470; Fax (780) 926-4017; info@highlevelchamber.com; www.highlevelchamber.com

High River • *High River & Dist. C/C* • Lynette McCracken; Exec. Dir.; P.O. Box 5244; T1V 1M4; P 13,000; M 125; (403) 652-3336; Fax (403) 652-7677; hrdccxtra@gmail.com; www.hrchamber.ca

Hinton • *Hinton & Dist. C/C* • George Higgerty; Exec. Dir.; 309 Gregg Ave.; T7V 2A7; P 9,700; M 140; (780) 865-2777; (877) 446-8666; Fax (780) 865-1062; hintoncc@telus.net; www.hintonchamber.com

Jasper • *Jasper Park C/C* • Pattie Pavlov; Gen. Mgr.; 409 Patrica St.; P.O. Box 98; T0E 1E0; P 5,000; M 192; (780) 852-4621; Fax (780) 852-4932; admin@jpcc.ca; www.jasperparkchamber.ca*

Killam • *Killam & Dist. C/C* • Dan Fee; Pres.; P.O. Box 189; T0B 2L0; P 5,000; M 31; (780) 385-7050; www.town.killam.ab.ca

Lacombe • *Lacombe & Dist. C/C* • Angela Law; Bd. Pres.; 6005-50 Ave.; T4L 1K7; P 12,800; M 240; (403) 782-4300; Fax (403) 782-4302; info@lacombechamber.ca; www.lacombechamber.ca

Leduc • *Wetaskiwin Reg. C/C* • Jennifer Garries; Exec. Dir.; 6420 - 50 St.; T9E 7K9; P 12,525; M 233; (780) 312-0657; Fax (780) 986-8108; info@wetaskiwinchamber.ca; www.wetaskiwinchamber.com

Leduc • *Leduc Reg. C/C* • Jennifer Garries; Exec. Dir.; 6420-50 St.; T9E 7K9; P 28,500; M 750; (780) 986-5454; Fax (780) 986-8108; info@leduc-chamber.com; www.leduc-chamber.com

Lethbridge • *Lethbridge C/C* • Karla Pyrch; Exec. Dir.; 200 Commerce House; 529 - 6th St. S.; T1J 2E1; P 97,000; M 770; (403) 327-1586; Fax (403) 327-1001; office@lethbridgechamber.com; www.lethbridgechamber.com*

Lloydminster • *Lloydminster C/C* • Pat Tenney; Exec. Dir.; 4419 - 52nd Ave.; T9V 0Y8; P 27,800; M 520; (780) 875-9013; Fax (780) 875-0755; contactllc@lloydminsterchamber.com; www.lloydminsterchamber.com

Marwayne • *Marwayne & Dist. C/C* • Sharon Kneen; Pres.; P.O. Box 183; T0B 2X0; P 600; M 20; (780) 847-2538; 780-872-0011; Fax (780) 847-2538; marwayne@mcsnet.ca; www.marwayne.ca

Medicine Hat • *Medicine Hat & Dist. C/C* • Lisa Kowalchuk; Exec. Dir.; 413 6 Ave. S.E.; T1A 2S7; P 63,000; M 700; (403) 527-5214; Fax (403) 527-5182; info@medicinehatchamber.com; www.medicinehatchamber.com

Nanton • *Nanton & Dist. C/C* • Pam Woodall; Pres.; P.O. Box 711; T0L 1R0; P 2,155; M 80; (403) 646-2111; (403) 646-2029; president@nantonchamber.com; www.nantonchamber.com

Okotoks • *Okotoks & Dist. C/C* • Carol Quinn; Exec. Asst.; 14 McRae St.; P.O. Box 1053; T1S 1B1; P 24,500; M 320; (403) 938-2848; Fax (403) 938-6649; okotokschamber@telus.net; www.okotokschamber.ca

Onoway • *Onoway & Dist. C/C* • Ed Gahleger; Pres.; P.O. Box 723; T0E 1V0; P 1,100; M 46; (780) 967-2550; info@onowaychamber.ca; www.onowaychamber.ca

Oyen • *Oyen & Dist. C/C* • Kari Kuzmiski; Pres.; P.O. Box 718; T0J 2J0; P 1,000; M 20; (403) 664-2339; (403) 664-3511; stitchworx@telus.net; www.townofoyen.com

Peace River • *Peace River C/C* • Michele Snyder; Gen. Mgr.; 9309 100 St.; P.O. Box 6599; T8S 1S4; P 6,744; M 207; (780) 624-4166; Fax (780) 624-4663; programs@peaceriverchamber.com; www.peaceriverchamber.com

Picture Butte • *Picture Butte & Dist. C/C* • Gus Buytels; Pres.; P.O. Box 517; T0K 1V0; P 1,700; M 71; (403) 732-4302; (403) 732-4555; chamber@picturebutte.ca; www.picturebutte.ca

Pincher Creek • *Pincher Creek & Dist. C/C* • Lieve Parisis; Ofc. Admin.; P.O. Box 2287; T0K 1W0; P 3,500; M 125; (403) 627-5199; info@pincher-creek.com; www.pincher-creek.com

Ponoka • *Ponoka & Dist. C/C* • Andrew Middleton; Pres.; 4205 Hwy. 2A; P.O. Box 4188; T4J 1R6; P 12,000; M 165; (403) 783-3888; Fax (403) 783-3886; chamberp@telus.net; www.ponokalive.ca

Provost • *Provost & Dist. C/C* • Kim Halushka; Secy./Treas.; P.O. Box 637; T0B 3S0; P 2,045; M 70; (780) 753-6145; provostchamberofcommerce@gmail.com; www.provost.ca

Red Deer • *Red Deer & Dist. C/C* • Tim Creedon; CEO; 3017 Gaetz Ave.; T4N 5Y6; P 100,000; M 900; (403) 347-4491; Fax (403) 343-6188; rdchamber@reddeerchamber.com; www.reddeerchamber.com*

Rimbey • *Rimbey & Dist. C/C* • Carrie Vaartstra; Exec. Dir.; 4937 - 50 Ave.; Box 87; T0C 2J0; P 2,496; M 68; (403) 392-6521; rimbeychamber@gmail.com; www.rimbeychamberofcommcerce.com

Rocky Mountain House • *Rocky Mountain House & Dist. C/C* • Cindy Taschuk; Exec. Dir.; 5406 - 48th St.; Box 1374; T4T 1B1; P 21,000; M 350; (403) 845-5450; Fax (403) 845-7764; rmhcofc@rockychamber.org; www.rockychamber.org

Saint Paul • *St. Paul & Dist. C/C* • Rhea Labrie; Exec. Dir.; 4802 - 50 Ave.; P.O. Box 887; T0A 3A0; P 5,000; M 160; (780) 645-5820; Fax (780) 645-5820; admin@stpaulchamber.ca; www.stpaulchamber.ca

Sexsmith • *Sexsmith C/C* • Freda King; P.O. Box 146; T0H 3C0; P 2,300; M 46; (780) 568-4663; info@sexsmithchamber.com; www.sexsmith.ca

Sherwood Park • *Sherwood Park & Dist. C/C* • Todd Banks; Exec. Dir.; 100 Ordze Ave.; T8B 1M6; P 66,000; M 1,200; (780) 464-0801; (866) 464-0801; Fax (780) 449-3581; admin@sherwoodparkchamber.com; www.sherwoodparkchamber.com

Smoky Lake • *Smoky Lake & Dist. C/C* • Wayne Taylor; Pres.; P.O. Box 635; T0A 3C0; P 4,500; M 50; (780) 656-3842; Fax (780) 451-3321; wayne@ethicaladvisor.com; www.smokylakeregion.ca

Spruce Grove • *Spruce Grove & Dist. C/C* • Brenda Johnson; Exec. Dir.; 99 Campsite Rd.; Box 4210; T7X 3B4; P 26,200; M 550; (780) 962-2561; Fax (780) 962-4417; info@sprucegrovechamber.com; www.sprucegrovechamber.com

St. Albert • *St. Albert & Dist. C/C* • Lynda Moffat; Pres./CEO; 71 St. Albert Trl.; T8N 6L5; P 61,500; M 930; (780) 458-2833; Fax (780) 458-6515; chamber@stalbertchamber.com; www.stalbertchamber.com

Stettler • *Stettler Reg. Bd. of Trade & Comm. Dev.* • Stacey Benjamin; Mgr.; 6606 50th Ave.; T0C 2L2; P 5,800; M 150; (403) 742-3181; (877) 742-9499; Fax (403) 742-3123; s.benjamin@stettlerboardoftrade.com; www.stettlerboardoftrade.com

Stony Plain • *Stony Plain & Dist. C/C* • John Gilchrist; Pres.; 4815 - 44 Ave.; T7Z 1V5; P 15,100; M 545; (780) 963-4545; Fax (780) 963-4542; office@stonyplainchamber.ca; www.stonyplainchamber.ca

Swan Hills • *Swan Hills C/C* • Daniel Goselin; Pres.; P.O. Box 149; T0G 2C0; P 1,500; M 50; (780) 333-4477; info@townofswanhills.com; www.townofswanhills.com

Sylvan Lake • *Sylvan Lake C/C* • Dwayne Stoesz; Pres.; P.O. Box 9119; T4S 1S6; P 12,400; M 150; (403) 887-3048; Fax (403) 887-3048; info@sylvanlakechamber.com; www.sylvanlakechamber.com

Taber • *Taber & Dist. C/C* • Bruce Warkentin; Pres.; 4702 - 50 St.; T1G 2B6; P 6,900; M 260; (403) 223-2265; Fax (403) 223-2291; taberchamber.president@telus.net; www.taberchamber.com

Thorhild • *Thorhild C/C* • Christopher Lloyd; P.O. Box 384; T0A 3J0; P 3,000; M 40; (780) 307-6031; thorhildchamber@telus.net; www.thorhild.com

Vegreville • *Vegreville & Dist. C/C* • Elaine Kucher; Gen. Mgr.; 5009 50th Ave.; P.O. Box 877; T9C 1R9; P 5,700; M 155; (780) 632-2771; Fax (780) 632-6958; vegchamb@telusplanet.net; www.vegrevillechamber.com

Vermilion • *Vermilion & Dist. C/C* • Robert Ernst; Pres.; 4606 52 St.; T9X 0A1; P 4,545; M 170; (780) 853-6593; Fax (780) 853-1740; vermilionchamber@gmail.com; www.vermilionchamber.ca

Vulcan • *Vulcan & Dist. C/C* • Trish Standing; V.P.; P.O. Box 1161; T0L 2B0; P 2,000; M 70; (403) 485-2657; (403) 485-2417; pstandg@telus.net; www.vulcanchamber.com

Westerose • *Pigeon Lake Regional C/C* • Rodger Cole; Pres.; 6C Village Dr., Village at Pigeon Lake; R.R. #2, Site 6, Box 6; T0C 2V0; M 97; (780) 586-3667; Fax (780) 586-3667; info@pigeonlakechamber.ca; www.pigeonlakechamber.ca

Whitecourt • *Whitecourt & District C/C* • Michelle Jones; Chief Admin. Officer; Box 1011; 4907 - 52 Avenue; T7S 1N9; P 9,600; M 250; (780) 778-5363; Fax (780) 778-2351; manager@whitecourtchamber.com; www.whitecourtchamber.com

British Columbia

British Columbia C/C • John Winter; Pres./CEO; 1201-750 W. Pender St.; Vancouver; V6C 2T8; P 4,530,000; (604) 683-0700; Fax (604) 683-0416; bccc@bcchamber.org; www.bcchamber.org

100 Mile House • *South Cariboo C/C* • Shelly Morton; Exec. Dir.; 2-385 Birch Ave.; P.O. Box 2312; V0K 2E0; P 15,600; M 150; (250) 395-6124; Fax (250) 395-8974; manager@southcariboochamber.org; www.southcariboochamber.org

Abbotsford • *Abbotsford C/C* • Allan Asaph; Exec. Dir.; 32900 S. Fraser Way, Unit 207; V2S 5A1; P 190,000; M 750; (604) 859-9651; Fax (604) 850-6880; acoclavonne@telus.net; www.abbotsfordchamber.com

Armstrong • *Armstrong-Spallumcheen C/C* • Patti Noonan; Mgr.; P.O. Box 118; V0E 1B0; P 9,600; M 201; (250) 546-8155; Fax (250) 546-8868; manager@aschamber.com; www.aschamber.com

Bamfield • *Bamfield C/C* • Phil Lavoie; Pres.; General Delivery; V0R 1B0; P 165; M 30; (250) 728-3351; info@bamfieldchamber.com; www.bamfieldchamber.com

Barriere • *Barriere & Dist. C/C* • Marie Downing; Mgr.; #3-4353 Conner Rd.; P.O. Box 1190; V0E 1E0; P 3,500; M 69; (250) 672-9221; Fax (260) 672-1866; bcoc@telus.net; www.barrierechamber.com

Bowen Island • *Bowen Island C/C* • Rod Marsh; Pres./Chair; P.O. Box 199; V0N 1G0; P 4,200; M 150; (604) 947-9024; chamber@bowenisland.org; www.bowenchamber.com

Burnaby • *Burnaby Bd. of Trade* • Paul Holden; Pres./CEO; 4555 Kingsway, Unit 201; V5H 4T8; P 233,200; M 1,200; (604) 412-0100; Fax (604) 412-0102; admin@bbot.ca; www.bbot.ca*

Burns Lake • *Burns Lake & Dist. C/C* • P.O. Box 339; V0J 1E0; P 13,000; M 63; (250) 692-3773; Fax (250) 692-3493; bldcoc@telus.net; www.bldchamber.ca

Cache Creek • *Cache Creek C/C* • Ben Roy; Secy.; P.O. Box 460; V0K 1H0; P 1,100; M 30; (250) 457-7157; Fax (250) 457-7662; benroy@telus.net

Campbell River • *Campbell River & Dist. C/C* • Colleen Evans; Exec. Dir.; 900 Alder St.; Enterprise Centre; V9W 2P6; P 36,000; M 450; (250) 287-4636; colleen.evans@campbellriverchamber.ca; www.campbellriverchamber.ca

Castlegar • *Castlegar & Dist. C/C* • Tammy Verigin-Burk; Exec. Dir.; 1995 6th Ave.; V1N 4B7; P 18,000; M 250; (250) 365-6313; (877) 365-6313; Fax (250) 365-5778; cdcoced@castlegar.com; www.castlegar.com

Chase • *Chase & Dist. C/C* • Elena Markin; Mgr.; 400 Shuswap Ave.; P.O. Box 592; V0E 1M0; P 2,600; M 100; (250) 679-8432; Fax (250) 679-3120; admin@chasechamber.com; www.chasechamber.com

Chemainus • *Chemainus & Dist. C/C* • George Gates; Pres.; 102-9799 Waterwheel Cresc.; P.O. Box 575; V0R 1K0; P 3,500; M 100; (250) 246-3944; Fax (250) 246-3251; chamber@chemainus.bc.ca; www.chemainus.bc.ca*

Chetwynd • *Chetwynd & Dist. C/C* • Tonia Richter; Mgr.; 5217 N. Access Rd.; P.O. Box 870; V0C 1J0; P 5,000; M 125; (250) 788-3345; (250) 788-1943; Fax (250) 788-3655; manager@chetwyndchamber.ca; www.chetwyndchamber.ca

Chilliwack • *Chilliwack C/C* • Fieny van den Boom; Exec. Dir.; 46093 Yale Rd., Unit 201; V2P 2L8; P 80,000; M 503; (604) 793-4323; Fax (604) 793-4303; info@chilliwackchamber.com; www.chilliwackchamber.com

Christina Lake • *Christina Lake C/C* • Sheldon Weigel; Pres.; 1675 Hwy. 3; V0H 1E2; P 1,500; M 54; (250) 447-6161; Fax Fax Same; cltourism@live.ca; www.christinalake.com

Clearwater • *Clearwater & Dist. C/C* • Bill Cairns; Mgr.; 201-416 Eden Rd.; V0E 1N1; P 5,000; M 100; (250) 674-3530; Fax (250) 674-3693; info@clearwaterbcchamber.com; www.clearwaterbcchamber.com

Cloverdale • *Cloverdale Dist. C/C* • Natasha Taylor; Ofc. Mgr.; 5748 176th St.; V3S 4C8; P 50,000; M 360; (604) 574-9802; Fax (604) 576-3145; info@cloverdalechamber.ca; www.cloverdalechamber.ca

Coquitlam • *Tri-Cities C/C* • Michael Hind; Exec. Dir.; 1209 Pinetree Way; V3B 7Y3; P 200,000; M 830; (604) 464-2716; Fax (604) 464-6796; info@tricitieschamber.com; www.tricitieschamber.com

Courtenay • *Comox Valley C/C* • Dianne Hawkins; Pres./CEO; 2040 Cliffe Ave.; V9N 2L3; P 65,000; M 700; (250) 334-3234; Fax (250) 334-4908; admin@comoxvalleychamber.com; www.comoxvalleychamber.com

Cranbrook • *Cranbrook C/C* • David Hull; Exec. Dir.; 2279 Cranbrook St. N.; P.O. Box 84; V1C 4H6; P 20,000; M 500; (250) 426-5914; Fax (250) 426-3873; info@cranbrookchamber.com; www.cranbrookchamber.com*

Crawford Bay • *Kootenay Lake C/C* • Gina Medhurst; Pres.; P.O. Box 120; V0B 1E0; P 1,200; M 75; (250) 227-9466; Fax (250)227-9535; info@kootenaylake.bc.ca; www.kootenaylake.bc.ca

Creston • *Creston C/C* • Jim Jacobsen; Exec. Dir.; 121 N.W. Blvd.; P.O. Box 268; V0B 1G0; P 15,000; M 200; (250) 428-4342; Fax (250) 428-9411; manager@crestonvalleychamber.com; crestonvalleychamber.com

Cumberland • *Cumberland C/C & Visitors Center* • Meaghan Cursons; Pres.; 2680 Dunsmuir Ave.; P.O. Box 250; V0R 1S0; P 3,800; M 70; (250) 336-8313; Fax (250) 336-2455; chamber@cumberlandbc.org; www.cumberlandbc.org

Dawson Creek • *Dawson Creek & Dist. C/C* • Kathleen Connolly; Mgr.; 10201 10th St.; V1G 3T5; P 12,500; M 300; (250) 782-4868; Fax (250) 782-2371; info@dawsoncreekchamber.ca; www.dawsoncreekchamber.ca

Delta • *Delta C/C* • Peter Roaf; Exec. Dir.; 6201 - 60th Ave.; V4K 4E2; P 100,000; M 400; (604) 946-4232; Fax (604) 946-5285; execdirector@deltachamber.ca; www.deltachamber.ca

Duncan • *Duncan-Cowichan C/C* • Sonja Nagel; Exec. Dir.; 2896 Drinkwater Rd.; V9L 6C2; P 80,000; M 400; (250) 748-1111; Fax (250) 746-8222; chamber@duncancc.bc.ca; www.duncancc.bc.ca

Elkford • *Elkford C/C* • Melody Anderson; Mgr.; P.O. Box 220; V0B 1H0; P 2,800; M 70; (250) 865-4614; Fax (250) 865-2442; info@tourismelkford.ca; www.tourismelkford.ca

Enderby • *Enderby & Dist. C/C* • Corinne Van De Crommenacker; Gen. Mgr.; 700 Railway St.; P.O. Box 1000; V0E 1V0; P 7,000; M 146; (250) 838-6727; Fax (250) 838-0123; info@enderbychamber.com; www.enderbychamber.com

Esquimalt • *Esquimalt C/C* • A. Adrian Andrew; Exec. Dir.; #103-1249 Esquimalt Rd.; Box 36019 - 1153 Esquimalt Rd.; V9A 2C5; P 16,151; M 160; (250) 590-2125; Fax (250) 590-1849; admin@esquimaltchamber.ca; esquimaltchamber.ca

Falkland • *Falkland & Dist. C/C* • Pres.; Hwy. 97; P.O. Box 92; V0E 1W0; P 700; M 10; falklandchamber@yahoo.ca; www.falklandbc.ca

Fernie • *Fernie C/C* • Patty Vadnais; Exec. Dir.; 102 Hwy. 3; V0B 1M5; P 4,900; M 270; (250) 423-6868; Fax (250) 423-3811; ed@ferniechamber.com; www.ferniechamber.com

Fort Langley • *see Langley*

Fort Nelson • *Fort Nelson & District C/C* • P.O. Box 196; V0C 1R0; P 5,000; M 325; (250) 774-2956; Fax (250) 774-2958; info@fortnelsonchamber.com; www.fortnelsonchamber.com

Fort St. James • *Fort St. James C/C* • Rosa Anne Howell; Mgr.; 115 Douglas Ave.; P.O. Box 1164; V0J 1P0; P 5,000; M 110; (250) 996-7023; Fax (250) 996-7047; fsjchamb@fsjames.com; www.fortstjameschamber.ca

Fort St. John • *Fort St. John & Dist. C/C* • Lilia Hansen; Exec. Dir.; 9907 - 99th Ave., Unit 100; V1J 1V1; P 21,000; M 400; (250) 785-6037; Fax (250) 785-6050; info@fsjchamber.com; www.fsjchamber.com

Fraser Lake • *Fraser Lake & Dist. C/C* • Maureen Olson; Pres.; P.O. Box 1059; V0J 1S0; P 1,300; M 32; (250) 699-6257; info@fraserlakechamber.com

Gabriola Island • *Gabriola Island C/C* • Carol Ramsay; Mgr.; 377 Berry Point Rd., Unit 5; P.O. Box 249; V0R 1X0; P 5,000; M 110; (250) 247-9332; Fax (250) 247-9332; giccmanager@shaw.ca; www.gabriolaisland.org

Galiano Island • *Galiano Island C/C* • Conny Nordin; Pres.; P.O. Box 73; V0N 1P0; P 1,260; (250) 539-2233; info@galianoisland.com; www.galianoisland.com

Gibsons • *Gibsons & Dist. C/C* • Chris Nicholls; Exec. Dir.; P.O. Box 1190; V0N 1V0; P 14,000; M 200; (604) 886-2325; Fax (604) 886-2379; exec@gibsonschamber.com; www.gibsonschamber.com

Gillies Bay • *Texada Island C/C* • Elayne Boloten; Secy.; P.O. Box 249; V0N 1W0; P 1,000; M 95; (604) 486-7457; Fax (604) 486-6703; brakes@telus.net; www.texada.org

Gold River • *Gold River C/C* • Peggy Sheehan; Pres.; Nootka Plaza - The Vault; P.O. Box 39; V0P 1G0; P 1,400; M 39; goldriverchamber@gmail.com; www.goldriver.ca

Golden • *Kicking Horse Country C/C* • Ruth Kowalski; Mgr.; P.O. Box 1320; V0A 1H0; P 8,800; M 221; (250) 344-7125; Fax (250) 344-6688; info@goldenchamber.bc.ca; www.goldenchamber.bc.ca

Greenwood • *Greenwood Bd. of Trade* • Dave Evans; Pres.; P.O. Box 430; V0H 1J0; P 700; M 30; gbtic@direct.ca; www.greenwoodcity.com

Harrison Hot Springs • *Harrison Agassiz C/C* • Robert Reyerse; Pres.; P.O. Box 429; V0M 1K0; P 7,500; M 103; Fax (604) 796-3694; info@harrison.ca; www.harrison.ca

Hope • *Hope & Dist. C/C* • Shanon Fischer; Admin. Asst.; P.O. Box 588; V0X 1L0; P 10,000; M 100; (604) 869-3111; Fax (604) 869-8208; info@hopechamber.net; www.hopechamber.net

Houston • *Houston & Dist. C/C* • Maureen Czirfusz; Mgr.; P.O. Box 396; V0J 1Z0; P 3,200; M 102; (250) 845-7640; Fax (250) 845-3682; info@houstonchamber.ca; www.houstonchamber.ca

Inveremere • *Columbia Valley C/C* • Susan Clovechok; Exec. Dir.; P.O. Box 1019; V0A 1K0; P 10,000; M 275; (250) 342-2844; Fax (250) 342-3261; info@cvchamber.ca; www.cvchamber.ca

Kamloops • *Kamloops C/C* • Deb McClelland; Exec. Dir.; 615 Victoria St.; V2C 2B3; P 85,000; M 850; (250) 372-7722; (800) 662-1994; Fax (250) 828-9500; mail@kamloopschamber.ca; www.kamloopschamber.ca

Kaslo • *Kaslo & Dist. C/C* • Steve Hoffart; Pres.; P.O. Box 329; V0G 1M0; P 1,026; M 82; (866) 276-3212; info@kaslochamber.com; www.kaslochamber.com

Kelowna • *Kelowna C/C* • Caroline Grover; CEO; 544 Harvey Ave.; V1Y 6C9; P 117,300; M 1,450; (250) 861-3627; Fax (250) 861-3624; info@kelownachamber.org; www.kelownachamber.org*

Keremeos • *Similkameen Country Dev. Assoc.* • Jan McMurray; Pres.; P.O. Box 490; V0X 1N0; P 5,000; M 156; (250) 499-5225; Fax (250) 499-5225; siminfo@nethop.net; www.similkameencountry.org

Kimberley • *Kimberley & Dist. C/C & Visitors Center* • Sioban Staplin; Exec. Dir.; 270 Kimberley Ave.; V1A 3N3; P 7,000; M 200; (250) 427-3666; info@kimberleychamber.com; www.kimberleychamber.com

Kitimat • *Kitimat C/C* • Trish Parsons; Exec. Dir.; 2109 Forest Ave.; P.O. Box 214; V8C 2G7; P 9,000; M 190; (250) 632-6294; Fax (250) 632-4685; kitimatchamber@telus.net; www.kitimatchamber.ca

Ladysmith • *Ladysmith C/C* • Mark Drysdale; Mgr.; 33 Roberts St.; P.O. Box 598; V9G 1A4; P 8,300; M 120; (250) 245-2112; Fax (250) 245-2124; mark@ladysmithcofc.com; www.ladysmithcofc.com

Lake Country • *Lake Country C/C & Visitors Center* • Linda Wilson; Mgr.; 9522 Main St., Unit 40; V4V 2L9; P 10,000; M 245; (250) 766-5670; (888) 766-5670; Fax (250) 766-0170; admin@lakecountrychamber.com; www.lakecountrychamber.com

Lake Cowichan • *Cowichan Lake Dist. C/C* • Jim Humphrey; Pres.; 125C S. Shore Rd.; P.O. Box 824; V0R 2G0; P 6,000; M 97; (250) 749-3244; Fax (250) 749-0187; lcchamber@shaw.ca; www.cowichanlake.ca

Langley • *Greater Langley C/C* • Lynn Whitehouse; Exec. Dir.; 5761 Glover Rd., Unit 1; V3A 8M8; P 125,000; M 1,100; (604) 530-6656; Fax (604) 530-7066; info@langleychamber.com; www.langleychamber.com

Likely • *Likely & Dist. C/C* • P.O. Box 29; V0L 1N0; P 350; M 45; (250) 790-2127; chamber@likely-bc.ca; www.likely-bc.ca

Lillooet • *Lillooet & Dist. C/C* • Scott Hutchinson; Pres.; P.O. Box 650; V0K 1V0; P 10,000; M 50; (250) 256-3578; info@lillooetchamberofcommerce.com; www.lillooetchamberofcommerce.com

Lumby • *Lumby & Dist. C/C* • Stephanie Sexsmith; Exec. Dir.; P.O. Box 534; V0E 2G0; P 5,400; M 100; (250) 547-2300; Fax (250) 547-2390; lumbychamber@shaw.ca; www.monasheetourism.com*

Lytton • *Lytton & Dist. C/C* • Terry Raymond; Pres.; 400 Fraser St.; P.O. Box 460; V0K 1Z0; P 3,000; M 35; (250) 455-2523; lyttoncofc@lyttonbc.net; www.lyttonchamber.com

Mackenzie • *Mackenzie C/C* • Kelly McEachnie; Mgr.; 88 Centennial Dr.; P.O. Box 880; V0J 2C0; P 3,000; M 70; (250) 997-5459; Fax (250) 997-6117; office@mackenziechamber.bc.ca; www.mackenziechamber.bc.ca

Madeira Park • *Pender Harbour & Dist. C/C* • Kerry Milligan; Exec. Dir.; P.O. Box 265; V0N 2H0; P 2,600; M 86; (604) 883-2561; (604) 740-2712; Fax (604) 883-2561; chamber@penderharbour.ca; www.penderharbour.ca

Maple Ridge • *Maple Ridge-Pitt Meadows C/C* • Jesse Sidhu; Exec. Dir.; 22238 Lougheed Hwy.; V2X 2T2; P 90,000; M 400; (604) 463-3366; admin@ridgemeadowschamber.com; www.ridgemeadowschamber.com

Mayne Island • *Mayne Island Comm. C/C* • Millie Leathers; Chair; P.O. Box 2; V0N 2J0; P 1,100; M 60; executiveofficer@mayneislandchamber.ca; www.mayneislandchamber.ca

McBride • *McBride & Dist. C/C* • Allen Fredrick; Pres.; P.O. Box 2; V0J 2E0; P 2,500; M 65; (250) 569-3366; (866) 569-3366; come2mcbride@telus.net; www.mcbridebc.info

Merritt • *Merritt & Dist. C/C* • Etelka Gillespie; Mgr.; P.O. Box 1649; V1K 1B8; P 7,500; M 150; (250) 378-5634; manager@merrittchamber.com; www.merrittchamber.com

Midway • *Boundary Country Reg. C/C* • Kathy Wright; Exec. Dir.; 907 Hwy. 3; P.O. Box 379; V0H 1M0; P 10,000; M 115; (250) 442-7263; Fax (250) 442-5311; info@boundarychamber.com; www.boundarychamber.com

Mission • *Mission Reg. C/C* • Michelle Favero; Mgr.; 34033 Lougheed Hwy.; V2V 5X8; P 37,500; M 435; (604) 826-6914; (877) 826-6914; Fax (604) 826-5916; manager@missionchamber.bc.ca; www.missionchamber.bc.ca

Nakusp • *Nakusp & Dist. C/C* • Cedra Eichenauer; Mgr.; 92 6th Ave. N.W.; P.O. Box 387; V0G 1R0; P 3,000; M 135; (250) 265-4234; (800) 909-8819; Fax (250) 265-3808; nakusp@telus.net; www.nakusparrowlakes.com

Nanaimo • *Greater Nanaimo C/C* • Kim Smythe; CEO; 2133 Bowen Rd.; V9S 1H8; P 85,000; M 800; (250) 756-1191; Fax (250) 756-1584; info@nanaimochamber.bc.ca; www.nanaimochamber.bc.ca*

Nelson • *Nelson & Dist. C/C & Visitors Center* • Tom Thomson; Exec. Dir.; 91 Baker St.; V1L 4G8; P 10,230; M 530; (250) 352-3433; (877) 663-5706; Fax (250) 352-6355; info@discovernelson.com; www.discovernelson.com

New Denver • *Slocan Dist. C/C* • P.O. Box 448; V0G 1S0; P 2,000; M 90; chamber@slocanlake.com; www.slocanlake.com

New Westminster • *New Westminster C/C* • Cori Lynn Germiquet; Exec. Dir.; 601 Queens Ave.; V3M 1L1; P 58,000; M 340; (604) 521-7781; Fax (604) 521-0057; nwcc@newwestchamber.com; www.newwestchamber.com

North Vancouver • *North Vancouver C/C* • Louise Ranger; Pres./Gen. Mgr.; 102-124 W. 1st St.; V7M 3N3; P 130,000; M 700; (604) 987-4488; Fax (604) 987-8272; admin@nvchamber.ca; www.nvchamber.ca

Okanagan Falls • *see Oliver*

Oliver • *South Okanagan C/C* • Bonnie Dancey; CEO; 36205 93rd Street; P.O. Box 460; V0H 1T0; P 35,000; M 345; (250) 498-6321; (866) 498-6321; Fax (250) 498-3156; manager@sochamber.ca; www.sochamber.ca

Osoyoos • *see Oliver*

Parksville • *Parksville & Dist. C/C* • Mr. Kim Burden; Exec. Dir.; 1275 E. Island Hwy.; P.O. Box 99; V9P 2G3; P 39,000; M 430; (250) 248-3613; Fax (250) 248-5210; info@parksvillechamber.com; www.parksvillechamber.com

Peachland • *Peachland C/C* • 5812 Beach Ave.; V0H 1X7; P 5,300; M 150; (250) 767-2455; Fax (250) 767-2420; peachlandchamber@shawcable.com; www.peachlandchamber.bc.ca

Pemberton • *Pemberton & Dist. C/C* • Shirley Henry; Secy./Treas.; P.O. Box 370; V0N 2L0; P 7,000; M 143; (604) 894-6477; Fax (604) 894-5571; info@pembertonchamber.com; www.pembertonchamber.com

Pender Island • *Pender Island C/C* • Carol Budnyk; Pres.; P.O. Box 164; V0N 2M0; P 2,500; M 100; travel@penderislandchamber.com; www.penderislandchamber.com

Penticton • *Penticton & Wine Country C/C* • Erin Hanson; Gen Mgr.; 553 Vees; V2A 5A4; P 44,000; M 700; (250) 492-4103; Fax (250) 492-6119; admin@penticton.org; www.penticton.org*

Pitt Meadows • *see Maple Ridge*

Port Hardy • *Port Hardy & Dist. C/C* • Angela Smith; Exec. Dir.; 7250 Market St.; P.O. Box 249; V0N 2P0; P 5,000; M 200; (250) 949-7622; Fax (250) 949-6653; phcc@cablerocket.com; www.ph-chamber.bc.ca*

Port McNeill • *Port McNeill & Dist. C/C* • C. Jorgenson; Exec. Dir.; 1594 Beach Dr.; P.O. Box 129; V0N 2R0; P 2,800; M 120; (250) 956-3131; (888) 956-3131; Fax (250) 956-3132; pmccc@island.net; www.portmcneill.net

Port Renfrew • *Port Renfrew C/C* • Rose Betsworth; Pres.; P.O. Box 39; V0S 1K0; P 300; M 56; (250) 647-0175; rosieb1@telus.net; www.portrenfrewcommunity.com

Powell River • *Powell River C/C* • Kim Miller; Mgr.; 6807 Wharf St.; V8A 1T9; P 20,000; M 300; (604) 485-4051; office@powellriverchamber.com; www.powellriverchamber.com

Prince George • *Prince George C/C* • Christie Rae; CEO; 890 Vancouver St.; V2L 2P5; P 80,000; M 1,000; (250) 562-2454; Fax (250) 562-6510; chamber@pgchamber.bc.ca; www.pgchamber.bc.ca

Prince Rupert • *Prince Rupert & Dist. C/C* • Simone Clark; Mgr.; 100-515 3rd Ave W.; V8J 1L9; P 13,500; M 272; (250) 624-2296; Fax (250) 622-2334; info@princerupertchamber.ca; www.princerupertchamber.ca

Princeton • *Princeton & Dist. C/C* • Lori Thomas; Mgr.; 105 Hwy #3 E.; P.O. Box 540; V0X 1W0; P 5,000; M 80; (250) 295-3103; Fax (250) 295-3255; chamber@nethop.net; www.princeton.ca

Qualicum Beach • *Qualicum Beach C/C* • Peter Doukakis; Pres./CEO; 124 W. 2nd Ave.; P.O. Box 159; V9K 1S7; P 8,502; M 275; (250) 752-0960; Fax (250) 752-2923; chamber@qualicum.bc.ca; www.qualicum.bc.ca

Quathiaski Cove • *Discovery Islands C/C* • Michael Lynch; Pres.; P.O. Box 790; V0P 1N0; P 3,800; M 130; (250) 285-2234; Fax (250) 285-2236; dichamberofcommerce@yahoo.ca; www.discoveryislands.ca/chamber

Quesnel • *Quesnel & Dist. C/C* • Amber Gregg; Mgr.; 335 E. Vaughan St.; V2J 2T1; P 25,000; M 245; (250) 992-7262; qchamber@quesnelbc.com; www.quesnelchamber.com

Radium Hot Springs • *Radium Hot Springs C/C* • Kent G. Kebe; Mgr.; 7556 Main St. E.; P.O. Box 225; V0A 1M0; P 800; M 100; (250) 347-9331; (888) 347-9331; Fax (250) 347-9127; chamber@radiumhotsprings.com; www.radiumhotsprings.com

Revelstoke • *Revelstoke C/C* • Judy Goodman; Exec. Dir.; P.O. Box 490; V0E 2S0; P 7,400; M 315; (250) 837-5345; Fax (250) 837-4223; info@revelstokechamber.com; www.revelstokechamber.com

Richmond • *Richmond C/C* • Matt Pitcairn; Pres./CEO; Ste. 202, North Tower; 5811 Cooney Rd.; V6X 3M1; P 200,000; M 1,200; (604) 278-2822; Fax (604) 278-2972; rcc@richmondchamber.ca; www.richmondchamber.ca*

Rossland • *Rossland C/C* • Renee Clark; Exec. Dir.; 204-2012 Washington; P.O. Box 1385; V0G 1Y0; P 3,500; M 160; (250) 362-5666; Fax (250) 362-5399; commerce@rossland.com; www.rossland.com

Saanich Peninsula • *see Sidney*

Salmo • *Salmo & Dist. C/C* • Heather Street; Mgr.; P.O. Box 400; V0G 1Z0; P 3,300; M 30; (250) 357-2596; Fax (250) 357-2596; salmoch@telus.net; www.salmo.net

Salmon Arm • *Salmon Arm & Dist. C/C* • Corryn Grayston; Gen. Mgr.; 20 Hudson Ave. N.E., Unit 101; P.O. Box 999; V1E 4P2; P 18,000; M 395; (250) 832-6247; admin@sachamber.bc.ca; www.sachamber.bc.ca

Salt Spring Island • *Salt Spring Island Chamber & Salt Spring Tourism* • Janet Clouston; Exec. Dir.; 121 Lower Ganges Rd.; V8K 2T1; P 10,500; M 300; (250) 537-4223; (250) 537-8320; Fax (250) 537-4276; chamber@saltspringchamber.com; www.saltspringchamber.com

Sandspit • *Sandspit Community Ofc.* • #1 Airport Rd.; P.O. Box 33; V0T 1T0; P 362; (250) 637-2466

Scotch Creek • *North Shuswap C/C* • Dave Cunliffe; Pres.; 1-3871 Squilax-Anglemont Rd.; V0E 1M5; P 3,000; M 100; (250) 955-2113; Fax (250) 955-2113; requests@northshuswapbc.com; www.northshuswapbc.com

Sechelt • *Sechelt & Dist. C/C* • Colleen Clark; Exec. Dir.; 102 5700 Cowrie St.; P.O. Box 360; V0N 3A0; P 10,000; M 200; (604) 885-0662; Fax (604) 885-0691; sdcoc9@telus.net; www.secheltchamber.bc.ca

Sicamous • *Sicamous & Dist. C/C* • Michelle Wolff; Exec. Dir.; #3, 446 Main St.; P.O. Box 346; V0E 2V0; P 3,776; M 126; (250) 836-0002; Fax (250) 836-4368; info@sicamouschamber.bc.ca; www.sicamouschamber.bc.ca

Sidney • *Saanich Peninsula C/C* • Denny Warner; Exec. Dir.; 10382 Pat Bay Hwy.; V8L 5S8; P 40,000; M 450; (250) 656-3616; Fax (250) 656-7111; info@peninsulachamber.ca; www.peninsulachamber.ca

Smithers • *Smithers Dist. C/C* • Heather Gallagher; Mgr.; P.O. Box 2379; V0J 2N0; P 5,404; M 225; (250) 847-5072; Fax (250) 847-3337; info@smitherschamber.com; www.smitherschamber.com

Sooke • *Sooke Region C/C* • Aline Doiron; Ofc. Mgr.; #201-2015 Shields Rd.; P.O. Box 18; V9Z 0E4; P 12,000; M 150; (250) 642-6112; Fax (250) 642-6127; info@sookeregionchamber.com; www.sookeregionchamber.com

Sorrento • *South Shuswap C/C* • Judy Smith; Pres.; P.O. Box 7; V0E 2W0; P 8,000; M 105; (250) 835-4669; sorrentochamber@telus.net; www.southshuswapchamberofcommerce.org

Sparwood • *Sparwood & Dist. C/C* • John Himel; Mgr.; P.O. Box 1448; V0B 2G0; P 4,211; M 110; (250) 425-2423; (877) 485-8185; Fax (250) 425-7130; manager@sparwoodchamber.bc.ca; www.sparwoodchamber.bc.ca

Squamish • *Squamish C/C* • Elliot Moses; Mgr.; 38551 Loggers Ln., Ste. 102; V8B 0H2; P 17,150; M 500; (604) 815-4990; (604) 815-4991; admin@squamishchamber.com; www.squamishchamber.com

Stewart • *Stewart-Hyder Intl. C/C* • Gwen McKay; Mgr.; P.O. Box 306; V0T 1W0; P 100; M 70; (250) 636-9224; Fax (250) 636-2199; stewartchamber@gmail.com

Summerland • *Summerland C/C* • Christine Petkau; Executive Director; 15600 Hwy. 97; P.O. Box 130; V0H 1Z0; P 11,000; M 750; (250) 494-2686; Fax (250) 494-4039; visitors@summerlandchamber.com; summerlandchamber.com

Surrey • *Surrey Bd. of Trade* • Anita Huberman; CEO; 101-14439 104th Ave.; V3R 1M1; P 525,000; M 2,200; (604) 581-7130; Fax (604) 588-7549; info@businessinsurrey.com; businessinsurrey.com

Tahsis • *Tahsis C/C* • Tony Ellis; P.O. Box 278; V0P 1X0; P 600; M 20; (250) 934-6425; info@tahsischamber.com; www.tahsischamber.com

Terrace • *Terrace & Dist. C/C* • Carol Fielding; Exec. Dir.; 4511 Keith Ave.; V8G 1K1; P 20,000; M 350; (250) 635-2063; (250) 641-4342; Fax (250) 635-2573; terracechamber@telus.net; www.terracechamber.com

Tofino • *Tofino-Long Beach C/C* • Jen Dart; Exec. Dir.; 341 Main St.; P.O. Box 249; V0R 2Z0; P 1,876; M 300; (250) 725-3153; info@tofinochamber.org; tofinochamber.org*

Trail • *Trail & Dist. C/C* • Audry Durham; Exec. Dir.; 200-1199 Bay Ave.; V1R 4A4; P 7,000; M 250; (250) 368-3144; Fax (250) 368-6427; executivedirector@trailchamber.bc.ca; www.trailchamber.bc.ca*

Ucluelet • *Ucluelet C/C* • Marny Saunders; Gen. Mgr.; P.O. Box 428; V0R 3A0; P 1,800; M 140; (250) 726-4641; Fax (250) 726-4611; marny@uclueletinfo.com; www.uclueletinfo.com

Valemount • *Valemount & Area C/C* • Marie Birkeck; Exec. Dir./Mgr.; P.O. Box 690; V0E 2Z0; P 900; M 45; (250) 566-0061; Fax (250) 566-0061; chamber@valemount.com; www.valemountchamber.com

Vancouver Area

Kitsilano C/C • Cheryl Ziola; Exec. Dir.; 1681 Chestnut St., Ste. 400; V6J 4M6; P 75,000; M 395; (604) 731-4454; (877) 312-1898; Fax (604) 681-4545; office@kitsilanochamber.com; www.kitsilanochamber.com

Tourism Vancouver-Tourist Info. Centre • Rick Antonson; Pres./CEO; Plaza Level; 200 Burrard St.; V6C 3L6; P 2,300,000; M 1,200; (604) 683-2000; Fax (604) 682-6839; info@tourismvancouver.com; www.tourismvancouver.com

Vancouver Bd. of Trade • Iain Black; Pres./CEO; 400 - 999 Canada Pl.; V6C 3E1; P 2,300,000; M 5,300; (604) 681-2111; Fax (604) 681-0437; contactus@boardoftrade.com; www.boardoftrade.com

Vanderhoof • *Vanderhoof & Dist. C/C* • Spencer Siemens; Exec. Dir.; P.O. Box 126; V0J 3A0; P 4,800; M 175; (250) 567-2124; Fax (250) 567-3316; manager@vanderhoofchamber.com; www.vanderhoofchamber.com

Vernon • *Greater Vernon C/C* • Dan Rogers; Mgr.; 2901 32nd St., Ste. 102; V1T 5M2; P 50,000; M 650; (250) 545-0771; Fax (250) 545-3114; info@vernonchamber.ca; www.vernonchamber.ca

Victoria • *Greater Victoria C/C* • Catherine Holt; CEO; 100-852 Fort St.; V8W 1H8; P 344,600; M 1,450; (250) 383-7191; Fax (250) 385-3552; chamber@gvcc.org; www.victoriachamber.ca*

Victoria • *WestShore C/C* • Dan Spinner; CEO; 2830 Aldwynd Rd.; V9B 3S7; P 57,000; M 567; (250) 478-1130; Fax (250) 478-1584; chamber@westshore.bc.ca; www.westshore.bc.ca

Wells • *Wells & Dist. C/C* • P.O. Box 123; V0K 2R0; P 250; M 50; (250) 994-3330; Fax (250) 994-3331; info@wellsbc.com; www.wellsbc.com

West Kelowna • *Greater Westside Bd. of Trade* • Karen Beaubier; Exec. Dir.; 2372 Dobbin Rd.; V4T 2H9; P 31,000; M 350; (250) 768-3378; Fax (250) 768-3465; admin@gwboardoftrade.com; www.gwboardoftrade.com

West Vancouver • *West Vancouver C/C* • Leagh Gabriel; Exec. Dir.; 100 Park Royal, Ste. 401; V7T 1A2; P 43,000; M 300; (604) 926-6614; Fax (604) 926-6647; info@westvanchamber.com; www.westvanchamber.com

Whistler • *Whistler C/C* • Fiona Famulak; Pres./CEO; 4230 Gateway Dr., Unit 201; V0N 1B4; P 10,000; M 830; (604) 932-5922; Fax (604) 932-3755; chamber@whistlerchamber.com; www.whistlerchamber.com

White Rock • *South Surrey & White Rock C/C* • Cliff Annable; Exec. Dir.; 100 - 15261 Russell Ave.; V4B 2P7; P 80,000; M 700; (604) 536-6844; Fax (604) 536-4994; admin@whiterockchamber.com; www.whiterockchamber.com

Williams Lake • *Williams Lake & Dist. C/C* • Claudia Blair; Exec. Dir.; P.O. Box 4878; V2G 2V8; P 12,000; M 300; (250) 392-5025; Fax (250) 392-4214; visitors@telus.net; www.williamslakechamber.com

Manitoba

Manitoba C/C • Graham S. Starmer; Pres./CEO; 227 Portage Ave.; Winnipeg; R3B 2A6; P 1,210,000; M 10,000; (204) 948-0100; Fax (204) 948-0110; mbchamber@mbchamber.mb.ca; www.mbchamber.mb.ca

Altona • *Altona & Dist. C/C* • Kathy Klassen; Pres.; P.O. Box 329; R0G 0B0; P 4,000; M 150; (204) 324-8793; Fax (204) 324-1314; chamber@shopaltona.com; www.shopaltona.com

Arborg • *Arborg & Dist. C/C* • Owen Eyolfson; Pres.; P.O. Box 415; R0C 0A0; P 5,000; M 47; (204) 376-5453; arborgchamber@gmail.com; www.townofarborg.com

Ashern • *Ashern & Dist. C/C* • Edith Peterson; Pres.; Box 582; R0C 0E0; P 1,000; M 57; president@ashern.ca; www.ashern.ca*

Beausejour • *Beausejour & Dist. C/C* • Carol Boychuk; Exec. Dir.; Box 224; R0E 0C0; P 3,000; M 80; (204) 268-3502; chamber@mybeausejour.com/chamber; www.mybeausejour.com/chamber

Boissevain • *Boissevain & Dist. C/C* • Stacey Teetaert; Pres.; P.O. Box 734; R0K 0E0; P 2,000; M 50; (204) 534-2411; b.dougall@boundarycoop.ca; www.boissevain.ca

Brandon • *Brandon C/C* • Carolynn Cancade; Gen. Mgr.; 1043 Rosser Ave.; R7A 0L5; P 53,000; M 600; (204) 571-5340; gm@brandonchamber.ca; www.brandonchamber.ca

Carberry • *Carberry & Dist. C/C* • Sharon Biehn; Pres.; Box 101; R0K 0H0; P 1,700; M 50; (204) 834-2790; Fax (204) 834-3764; sharon@biehnneufeldcga.com; www.townofcarberry.ca

Carman • *Carman & Comm. C/C* • Paul Clark; Pres.; P.O. Box 249; R0G 0J0; P 8,000; M 143; (204) 750-3050; ccchamber@gmail.com; www.carmanchamberofcommerce.com

Churchill • *Churchill C/C* • Dave Daley; Pres.; 211 Kelsey Blvd.; P.O. Box 176; R0B 0E0; P 900; M 50; (204) 675-2022; Fax (204) 675-2021; churchillchamber@mymts.net; www.churchillchamberofcommerce.ca

Crystal City • *Crystal City & Dist. C/C* • Doug Treble; Box 56; R0K 0N0; P 750; M 36; (204) 873-2427; Fax (204) 873-2656; doug_treble@mts.net; www.crystalcitymb.ca

Cypress River • *Cypress River C/C* • Jim Cassels; Pres.; P.O. Box 261; R0K 0P0; P 240; M 22; (204) 743-2119; Fax (204) 743-2339; cypressmotorinnone@hotmail.com; www.cypressriver.ca

Dauphin • *Dauphin & District C/C* • Tamara Wills; Coord./Mgr.; 100 Main St. S.; R7N 1K3; P 8,300; M 187; (204) 622-3140; Fax (204) 622-3141; info@dauphinchamber.ca; www.dauphinchamber.ca

Deloraine • *Deloraine & Dist. C/C* • Deb Calverley; Pres.; P.O. Box 748; R0M 0M0; P 1,500; M 50; (204) 747-2842; Fax (204) 747-2856; debcalv@mts.net; www.deloraine.org

Elkhorn • *Elkhorn Dist. C/C* • Mark Humpheries; Chair; Box 141; R0M 0N0; P 1,000; M 40; (204) 845-2455; Fax (204) 845-4232; triden@mts.net; www.elkhornchamberofcommerce.ca

Eriksdale • *Eriksdale & Dist. C/C* • Jason Watson; Secy./Treas.; P.O. Box 434; R0C 0W0; P 920; M 20; (204) 739-2641; jcwatson@xplornet.com; www.areyouonline.biz/chamber

Falcon Lake • *Falcon-West Hawk C/C* • Mike Valks; Pres.; Box 187; R0E 0N0; P 400; M 60; (204) 349-2214; Fax (204) 349-3008; info@falconwesthawkchamber.com; www.falconwesthawkchamber.com

Fisher Branch • *Fisher Branch C/C* • Wayne Smith; Box 566; R0C 0Z0; P 1,500; M 36; (204) 372-8585; Fax (204) 372-6504; smtech.smith@gmail.com; www.rmoffisher.com

Flin Flon • *Flin Flon & Dist. C/C* • Michelle Reid; Ofc. Mgr.; 235-35 Main St.; R8A 1J7; P 5,000; M 100; (204) 687-4518; Fax (204) 687-4456; flinflonchamber@mymts.net; www.flinflondistrictchamber.com

Gillam • *Gillam C/C* • Ken Hill; Pres.; P.O. Box 366; R0B 0L0; P 1,200; M 29; (204) 652-3133; chamber@townofgillam.com; www.townofgillam.com

Glenboro • *Glenboro Comm. Dev. Corp.* • Christine Tanasichuk; Dev. Officer; Box 296; R0K 0X0; P 1,500; M 200; (204) 827-2575; Fax (204) 827-2575; gcdc@glenboro.com; www.glenboro.com

Grandview • *Grandview & Dist. C/C* • Pierce Cairnes; Pres.; P.O. Box 28; R0L 0Y0; P 1,500; M 35; (204) 546-5250; (204) 546-2626; www.grandviewmanitoba.com

Grunthal • *Grunthal & Dist. C/C* • Leonard Hiebert; Pres.; P.O. Box 451; R0A 0R0; P 3,000; M 26; (204) 434-6750; Fax (204) 434-9353; leonard@emergencyvehicles.ca; www.grunthal.ca

Hamiota • *Hamiota C/C* • Karen Bell; Pres.; P.O. Box 310; R0M 0T0; P 1,000; M 45; (204) 764-2487; (204) 764-3050; Fax (204) 764-3055; midwestrec@hamiota.com; www.hamiota.com

Headingley • *Headingley Reg. C/C* • Graham Hawryluk; Pres.; 126 Bridge Rd., Unit 1; R4H 1J9; P 2,700; M 90; (204) 889-3132; Fax (204) 831-0816; dwhitermofheadingley@mts.net; www.headingleychamber.ca

Ile-des-Chênes • *Ritchot Reg. C/C* • Marc Palud; VP; Box 1059, 1 Rivard St., Rm. 205; R0A 0T0; P 5,478; M 70; (204) 471-5680; (204) 881-2350; Marc@RitchotChamber.com; www.RitchotChamber.com

La Salle • *La Salle & Area C/C* • Allyson Demski; Ofc. Mgr.; P.O. Box 66; R0G 1B0; P 3,000; M 60; (855) 273-3278; (204) 801-3492; Fax (866) 234-6272; info@lasalleonline.ca; www.lasalleonline.ca

Lac du Bonnet • *Lac Du Bonnet & Dist. C/C* • Jennifer Hudson Stewart; Admin.; P.O. Box 598; R0E 1A0; P 4,500; M 100; (204) 340-0497; ldbchamberofcommerce@gmail.com; www.lacdubonnetchamber.com

Macgregor • *MacGregor & Dist. C/C* • Elaine Taylorson; P.O. Box 685; R0H 0R0; P 1,100; M 25; (204) 685-2484; Fax (204) 685-2484; larrysfurniture@mymts.net; www.macgregorchamber.com

Melita • *Melita & Dist. C/C* • Bill Warren; Pres.; P.O. Box 666; R0M 1L0; P 1,200; M 45; (204) 522-8184; wjwarren52@hotmail.com; www.melitamb.ca

Minnedosa • *Minnedosa & Dist. C/C* • Beth McNabb; Box 857; R0J 1E0; P 2,500; M 103; (204) 867-2951; minnedosachamber@gmail.com; www.discoverminnedosa.com

Morden • *Morden & Dist. C/C* • Candace Olafson; Exec. Dir.; 100-379 Stephen St.; R6M 1V1; P 7,500; M 240; (204) 822-5630; Fax ; execdirector@mordenchamber.com; www.mordenchamber.com

Morris • *Morris & Dist. C/C* • Pat Schmitke; Pres.; 141 Main St. S.; P.O. Box 98; R0G 1K0; P 1,600; M 70; (855) 333-9323; president@morrischamberofcommerce.com; morrischamberofcommerce.com

Neepawa • *Neepawa & Dist. C/C* • Barb Harris; Ofc. Admin.; P.O. Box 726; R0J 1H0; P 5,000; M 100; (204) 476-5292; Fax (204) 476-5231; info@neepawachamber.com; www.neepawachamber.com

Niverville • *Niverville C/C* • Leighton Reimer; P.O. Box 157; R0A 1E0; P 3,500; M 90; (204) 388-4600; chamber@niverville.com; www.niverville.com

Oak Lake • *Oak Lake C/C* • Greg Vincent; Pres.; P.O. Box 23; R0M 1P0; (204) 855-3287; Fax (204) 855-3287; gvincent@mts.net

Oakville • *Oakville & Dist. C/C* • Sian Taris; Pres.; P.O. Box 263; R0H 0Y0; P 600; M 50; (204) 267-2792; (204) 267-2112; Fax (204) 267-7015; bingram@mymts.net

Pilot Mound • *Pilot Mound & Dist. C/C* • John Darracott; Pres.; P.O. Box 356; R0G 1P0; P 1,000; M 50; (204) 825-2432; chamberofcommerce@pilotmound.com; www.pilotmound.com

Pinawa • *Pinawa C/C* • Jeff Simpson; Pres.; P.O. Box 544; R0E 1L0; P 1,500; M 40; (204) 753-2747; Fax (204) 753-8478; president@pinawachamber.com; www.pinawachamber.com

Plum Coulee • *Plum Coulee & Dist. C/C* • Moira Porte; Pres.; Box 392; R0G 1R0; P 900; M 40; (204) 362-4195; brewstr@mymts.net; www.townofplumcoulee.com

Portage la Prairie • *Portage la Prairie & Dist. C/C* • Cindy McDonald; Exec. Dir.; 56 Royal Rd. N.; R1N 1V1; P 14,000; M 215; (204) 857-7778; Fax (204) 239-0176; info@portagechamber.com; www.portagechamber.com

Rivers • *Rivers & Dist. C/C* • Jean Young; Secy./Treas.; P.O. Box 795; R0K 1X0; P 1,200; M 50; (204) 328-7316; Fax (204) 328-4460; bonnierivers@mymts.net; www.riversdaly.ca

Riverton • *Riverton & Dist. C/C* • Susie Eyolfson; Pres.; P.O. Box 238; R0C 2R0; P 600; M 60; (204) 376-5023; susie@giftwares.ca; www.rivertoncanada.com

Roblin • *Roblin & Dist. C/C* • Kevin Arthur; Pres.; 147 Main St. N.W.; P.O. Box 160; R0L 1P0; P 3,400; M 80; (204) 937-3194; Fax (204) 937-3817; rdcoc@mymts.net; www.roblinmanitoba.com

Rosenort • *Rosenort C/C* • Frank Peters; P.O. Box 222; R0G 1W0; (204) 746-4217; Fax (204) 746-8878; rosenortchamber@yahoo.caalvdia@mts.net

Rossburn • *Rossburn & Dist. C/C* • Tony White; Pres.; P.O. Box 579; R0J 1V0; P 1,500; M 35; (204) 859-3313; rossburn.chamber@live.ca; www.town.rossburn.mb.ca

Russell • *Russell & Dist. C/C* • Sherry Fraser; Ofc. Mgr.; P.O. Box 579; R0J 1W0; P 2,000; M 100; (204) 773-2456; Fax (204) 773-3525; chamber@russellmb.com; www.russellmb.com

Saint-Boniface • *Chambre de commerce francophone de Saint-Boniface* • Paulette Desaulniers; Exec. Dir.; P.O. Box 204; R2H 3B4; P 70,000; M 200; (204) 235-1406; info@ccfsb.mb.ca; www.ccfsb.mb.ca

Selkirk • *Selkirk & Dist. C/C* • Sherry Skalesky; Ofc. Mgr.; 200 Eaton Ave.; R1A 0W6; P 25,000; M 130; (204) 482-7176; Fax (204) 482-5448; info@selkirkanddistrictchamber.ca; www.selkirkanddistrictchamber.ca

Shoal Lake • *Shoal Lake C/C Inc.* • Lasha Watson; Pres.; General Delivery; R0J 1Z0; P 1,200; M 70; (204) 365-0963; Fax (204) 759-2740; tcp@live.ca; www.shoallake.ca

Souris • *Souris & Glenwood C/C* • Sandy Denbow; Pres.; P.O. Box 939; R0K 2C0; P 1,683; M 65; (204) 483-2070; sourischamber@gmail.com; www.sourismanitoba.com

St-Pierre-Jolys • *St. Pierre-Jolys C/C* • Marcel Mulaire; Pres.; Box 71; R0A 1V0; P 1,000; M 70; (204) 433-7501; Fax (204) 433-3015; marcel@delowater.ca; www.stpierrejolys.com

Steinbach • *Steinbach C/C* • Linda Peters; Exec. Dir.; D4-284 Reimer Ave.; R5G 0R5; P 25,000; M 292; (204) 326-9566; Fax (204) 346-3638; info@steinbachchamberofcommerce.com; www.steinbachchamberofcommerce.com

Stonewall • *Stonewall & Dist. C/C* • Deborah Jensen; Pres.; Box 762; R0C 2Z0; P 5,000; M 76; (204) 467-8377; (204) 467-7125; djensen@mts.net; www.stonewallchamber.com

Swan River • *Swan Valley C/C* • Erin Brown; Exec. Coord.; P.O. Box 1540; R0L 1Z0; P 13,000; M 160; (204) 734-3102; Fax (204) 734-4342; chamberofcommerce@chamber8.ca

Teulon • *Teulon & Dist. C/C* • Jan Lambourne; Pres.; P.O. Box 235; R0C 1H0; P 1,200; M 50; (204) 886-3910; president@teulonchamber.ca; www.teulon.ca

The Pas • *The Pas & Dist. C/C* • Shirley Barbeau; Ofc. Mgr.; Box 996; R9A 1L1; P 10,318; M 120; (204) 623-7256; Fax (204) 623-2589; tpchamber@mailme.ca; www.thepaschamber.com

Thompson • *Thompson C/C* • P.O. Box 363; R8N 1N2; P 13,000; M 185; (204) 677-4155; Fax (204) 677-3434; commerce@mymts.net; www.thompsonchamber.ca

Treherne • *Treherne & Dist. C/C* • Keith Sparling; P.O. Box 344; R0G 2V0; P 1,200; (204) 723-2774; (204) 723-2044; Fax (204) 723-2719; psparling@treherne.ca; www.treherne.ca

Virden • Virden Comm. C/C • Amanda Isaac; Mgr.; 425 6th Ave. S.; Box 899; R0M 2C0; P 3,500; M 85; (204) 851-1551; virdencc@mymts.net; www.virdenchamber.ca

Waskada • Waskada & Dist. C/C • Audrey Dickinson; Secy.; P.O. Box 239; R0M 2E0; P 250; M 20; (204) 673-2465; (204) 673-2774; Fax (204) 673-2210; abhdick@goinet.ca; www.waskada.ca

Winkler • Winkler & Dist. C/C • Tanya Chateauneuf; Exec. Dir.; 185 Main St.; R6W 1B4; P 12,000; M 365; (204) 325-9758; Fax (204) 325-8290; admin@winklerchamber.com; www.winklerchamber.com

Winnipeg Area

Aboriginal C/C • Karl Zadnik; Pres.; 227 Portage Ave.; R3C 0C3; P 730,000; M 50; (204) 237-9359; Fax (204) 947-0145; accadmin@mts.net; www.aboriginalchamber.ca

Assiniboia C/C • Richard Halliday; Pres./CEO; 1867 Portage Ave.; P.O. Box 42122, RPO Ferry Rd.; R3J 3X7; P 100,000; M 425; (204) 774-4154; (204) 899-1939; Fax (204) 774-4201; info@assiniboiacc.mb.ca; www.assiniboiachamber.ca

The Winnipeg C/C • Loren Remillard; Pres./CEO; 100 - 259 Portage Ave.; R3B 2A9; P 684,100; M 2,000; (204) 944-8484; Fax (204) 944-8492; info@winnipeg-chamber.com; www.winnipeg-chamber.com

New Brunswick

New Brunswick C/C • Judith Murray; Chair; 1 Canada Rd.; Edmundston; E3V 1T6; P 751,200; M 2,000; (506) 737-1868; Fax (506) 737-1862; info@nbchamber.ca; www.nbchamber.ca

Bathurst • Greater Bathurst C/C • Danielle Goyette; Gen. Mgr.; 270 av. Douglas Ave., Ste. 500; E2A 1M9; P 32,000; M 305; (506) 548-8498; Fax (506) 548-2200; info@bathurstchamber.ca; www.bathurstchamber.ca

Bouctouche • Bouctouche C/C • Claude LeBlanc; Pres.; P.O. Box 2104; E4S 2J2; P 2,000; M 120; (506) 743-2411; chambouc@nb.aibn.com; www.bouctouche.ca

Campbellton • Campbellton Reg. C/C • Johanne L. Martin; Dir.; 64 Water St., 2nd Flr.; E3N 1B1; P 8,000; M 172; (506) 759-7856; Fax (506) 759-7557; crcc@nbnet.nb.ca; www.campbelltonregionalchamber.ca

Caraquet • La Chambre de commerce du Grand Caraquet • 39-1 boul. St-Pierre W.; E1W 1B7; P 4,200; M 300; (506) 727-2931; Fax (506) 727-3191; info@chambregrandcaraquet.com; www.chambregrandcaraquet.com

Centreville • Centreville C/C • Kathleen Simonson; Secy.; 836 Central St.; E7K 2E7; P 550; M 45; (506) 276-3674; centreville.chamber@aernet.ca; www.villageofcentreville.ca

Edmundston • Edmundston Reg. C/C • Mme Marie-Eve Castonguay; Gen. Dir.; 1 Canada Rd.; E3V 1T6; P 21,400; M 400; (506) 737-1866; Fax (506) 737-1862; info@ccedmundston.com; www.ccedmundston.com

Florenceville-Bristol • Florenceville-Bristol & Dist. C/C • Pam Brennan; Pres.; P.O. Box 601; E7L 1Y7; P 1,640; M 60; (506) 392-0900; Fax (506) 392-5211; chamber@florencevillebristol.ca; www.florencevillebristol.ca

Fredericton • Fredericton C/C • Krista Ross; CEO; 270 Rookwood Ave.; P.O. Box 275; E3B 4Y9; P 56,200; M 920; (506) 458-8006; Fax (506) 451-1119; fchamber@frederictonchamber.ca; www.frederictonchamber.ca

Fredericton • Enterprise Fredericton • Doug Motty; Exec. Dir.; 10 Knowledge Park Dr., Ste. 110; E3C 2M7; P 125,000; (506) 444-4686; Fax (506) 444-4649; info@ent-fredericton.ca; www.enterprisefredericton.ca

Grand Bay - Westfield • see Saint John

Grand Falls • Valley Chamber of Commerce • Luc Theriault; Gen. Mgr.; 131 rue Pleasant St., Ste. 200; E3Z 1G6; P 30,000; M 244; (506) 473-1905; Fax (506) 475-7779; info@destinationdelavallee.com; destinationdelavallee.com

Grand Manan • Grand Manan C/C • Peter Wilcox; Pres.; Box 1310; E5G 4E9; P 2,400; M 80; (506) 662-3442; (888) 525-1655; info@grandmanannb.com; www.grandmanannb.com

Hampton • Hampton Area C/C • Sara Barnett; Ofc. Admin.; 27 Centennial Rd., Unit 7; E5N 6N3; P 4,000; M 80; (506) 832-2559; hacc@nbnet.nb.ca; www.hamptonareachamber.ca

Miramichi • Miramichi C/C • Joyce Buckley BA LLB; Exec. Dir.; 120 Newcastle Blvd.; P.O. Box 342; E1N 3A7; P 18,000; M 230; (506) 622-5522; Fax (506) 622-5959; mirchamber@nb.aibn.com; www.miramichichamber.com

Moncton • Greater Moncton C/C • Carol O'Reilly; CEO; 1273 Main St., Ste. 200; E1C 0P4; P 138,644; M 825; (506) 857-2883; Fax (506) 857-9209; services@gmcc.nb.ca; www.gmcc.nb.ca

Oromocto • Oromocto & Area C/C • Mrs. Beth Crowell; Pres.; P.O. Box 20124; E2V 2R6; P 25,500; M 100; (506) 446-6043; Fax (506) 446-6925; oromoctochamber@nb.aibn.com; www.oromoctochamber.nb.ca

Richibucto • Kent-Centre C/C • Jody Pratt; Pres.; 9235 Main St., Ste. 1; E4W 4B4; P 1,209; M 80; (506) 523-7870; melanie.savoie@richibucto.org; www.richibucto.org

Rogersville • Rogersville C/C • Lise McCeie; Pres.; 11085 Rue Principale; E4Y 2L9; P 3,500; M 90; (506) 775-1013; (506) 775-6600; lmceie@hotmail.com; www.rogersvillenb.com

Rogersville • Rogersville C/C • Alain Lamerre; Pres.; 11033 Principal St.; E4Y 2L7; P 3,500; M 90; (506) 775-2728; www.rogersville.info

Sackville • Greater Sackville C/C • Gwen Zwicker; Exec. Dir.; 87 Main St., Unit 8; E4L 4A9; P 5,600; M 65; (506) 364-8911; Fax (506) 364-8082; gscc@eastlink.ca; www.greatersackvillechamber.com

Saint Andrews • St. Andrews C/C • Brad Henderson; Pres.; 252C Water Street; E5B 1B5; P 1,800; M 100; (506) 529-3555; stachamb@nbnet.nb.ca; www.standrewsbythesea.ca

Saint Francois • Chambre de Commerce Haut-Madawaska • Cathy Pelletier; Mgr.; P.O. Box 378; E7A 1G4; P 1,300; M 125; (506) 992-6067; (506) 992-5610; cdecstf@nb.aibn.com

Saint John • The Saint John Region C/C • David Duplisea; CEO; 40 King St.; E2L 1G3ï»¿; P 130,000; M 800; (506) 634-8111; Fax (506) 632-2008; info@thechambersj.com; www.thechambersj.com

Saint-Simon • Saint-Simon C/C • Ecole des Peches; E0B 1L0; P 760; M 30; (506) 727-6531

Shippagan • Shippagan C/C • Marie-Lou Noelq; Coord.; 227 blvd. J.D. Gauthier; E8S 1N2; P 4,000; M 130; (506) 336-3993; chambredecommercedeshippagan@nb.aibn.com; www.shippagan.ca

St. Stephen • *St. Stephen Area C/C* • David Archambault; Pres.; 123 Milltown Blvd., Ste. 207; Box 131; E3L 2X1; P 5,000; M 150; (506) 466-7703; Fax (506) 466-7701; chamber.ststephen@nb.aibn.com; www.ststepehenchamber.com

Sussex • *Sussex and Dist. C/C* • Ivan Graham; Pres.; 66 Broad St., Unit 2; P.O. Box 4963; E4E 5L2; P 35,000; M 145; (506) 433-1845; Fax (506) 433-1886; sdcc@nb.aibn.com; www.sdccinc.org*

Woodstock • *Greater Woodstock C/C* • Lance Minard; Pres.; 220 King St., Unit 2; E7M 1Z8; P 5,300; M 134; (506) 325-9049; Fax (506) 328-4683; info@gwcc.ca; www.gwcc.ca

Newfoundland & Labrador

Bonavista • *Bonavista Area C/C* • Rodney Gray; Pres.; P.O. Box 280; A0C 1B0; P 6,500; M 55; Fax (709) 468-2495; info@bacc.ca; www.bacc.ca

Clarenville • *Clarenville Area C/C* • Ina Marsh; Ofc. Mgr.; 263 Memorial Dr., Ste. 203; A5A 1R5; P 6,100; M 127; (709) 466-5800; Fax (709) 466-5803; info@clarenvilleareachamber.com; www.clarenvilleareachamber.com

Conception Bay South • *Conception Bay Area C/C* • Margo Murphy; Pres.; 24 Cherry Ln., Unit 1; A1W 3B3; P 50,000; M 100; (709) 834-5670; Fax (709) 834-5760; info@cbachamber.com; www.cbachamber.com

Corner Brook • *Greater Corner Brook Bd. of Trade* • Keith Goulding; Pres.; 61 Riverside Dr.; P.O. Box 475; A2H 6E6; P 20,000; M 200; (709) 634-5831; Fax (709) 639-9710; sherry@gcbbt.com; www.gcbbt.com

Deer Lake • *Deer Lake C/C* • Terrilynn Robbins; Exec. Dir.; 9A Church St.; A8A 1C9; P 5,000; M 183; (709) 636-4735; Fax (709) 635-5857; info@deerlakechamber.com; www.deerlakechamber.com

Grand Falls-Windsor • *Exploits Reg. C/C* • Gerald Thomson; Exec. Dir.; 2B Mill Rd.; P.O. Box 272; A2A 2J7; P 35,000; M 200; (709) 489-7512; Fax (709) 489-7532; info@exploitschamber.com; www.exploitschamber.com

Happy Valley • *Labrador North C/C* • Brian Fowlow; CEO; 169 Hamilton River Rd.; P.O. Box 460, Station B; A0P 1E0; P 8,500; M 150; (709) 896-8787; Fax (709) 896-8039; ceo@chamberlabrador.com; www.chamberlabrador.com

Labrador City • *Labrador West C/C* • Patsy Ralph; Bus. Mgr.; 118 Humphrey Rd.; P.O. Box 273; A2V 2K5; P 12,000; M 87; (709) 944-3723; Fax (709) 944-4699; lwc@crrstv.net; www.labradorwestchamber.ca

Lewisporte • *Lewisporte & Area C/C* • Brian Pike; Pres.; P.O. Box 953; A0G 3A0; P 3,000; M 58; (709) 535-2500; Fax (709) 535-2482; lacc@easlewisporte.ca; www.lewisporteareachamberofcommerce.ca

Mount Pearl • *Mount Pearl Paradise C/C* • Tammy Clarke; Pres.; 365 Old Placentia Rd.; A1N 0G7; P 26,000; M 230; (709) 364-8513; (709) 364-2130; Fax (709) 364-8500; info@mtpearlparadisechamber.com; ww.mtpearlchamber.com*

Port-Aux-Basques • *Port-Aux-Basques & Area C/C* • Natashua Osmond; Managing Coord.; P.O. Box 1389; A0M 1C0; P 9,000; M 102; (709) 695-3688; Fax (709) 695-5898; pabchamber@nf.aibn.com; www.pabchamber.com

Springdale • *Springdale & Area C/C* • Glenn Seabright; Treas.; P.O. Box 37; A0J 1T0; P 2,900; M 50; (709) 673-3837; Fax (709) 673-3897; www.townofspringdale.ca

St. Anthony • *St. Anthony & Area C/C* • Desmond McDonald; Pres.; P.O. Box 650; A0K 4S0; P 2,500; M 75; (709) 454-5147; stanthonyandareachamber@yahoo.ca; www.town.stanthony.nf.ca

St. John's • *St. John's Bd. of Trade* • Nancy Healey; CEO; 34 Harvey Rd., 3rd Flr.; P.O. Box 5127; A1C 5V5; P 180,000; M 900; (709) 726-2961; Fax (709) 726-2003; nhealey@bot.nf.ca; www.bot.nf.ca*

Stephenville • *Bay St. George C/C* • Debbie Brake-Patten; Pres.; 35 Carolina Ave.; A2N 3P4; P 8,000; M 100; (709) 643-5854; Fax (709) 643-6398; bsgcoc@wec-center.nl.ca; www.bsgchamber.com

Northwest Territories

Northwest Territories C/C • Hughie Graham; Pres.; 4802 50th Ave., Unit 13; Yellowknife; X1A 1C4; P 48,000; M 250; (867) 920-9505; Fax (867) 873-4174; admin@nwtchamber.com; www.nwtchamber.com

Fort Simpson • *Fort Simpson C/C* • Angela Fiebelkorn; Pres.; P.O. Box 244; X0E 0N0; P 2,500; M 22; (867) 695-6538; fscofc@gmail.com; www.fortsimpsonchamber.ca

Fort Smith • *Fort Smith C/C* • Jane Hobart; Pres.; P.O. Box 628; X0E 0P0; P 2,500; M 25; (867) 872-0931; (867) 872-8400; www.fortsmith.ca

Hay River • *Hay River C/C* • Joe Melanson; Pres.; 10K Gagnier St.; X0E 1G1; P 3,800; M 110; (867) 874-2565; Fax (867) 874-3631; info@hayriverchamber.com; www.hayriverchamber.com

Norman Wells • *Norman Wells & Dist. C/C* • Chris Buist; Pres.; P.O. Box 400; X0E 0V0; P 727; M 30; (867) 587-2416; www.normanwellschamber.ca

Yellowknife • *Yellowknife C/C* • Deneen Everett; Exec. Dir.; #21, 4802 50 Ave.; X1A 1C4; P 20,000; M 300; (867) 920-4944; Fax (867) 920-4640; executivedirector@ykchamber.com; www.ykchamber.com

Nova Scotia

Nova Scotia C/C • Wayne Fiander; Exec. Dir.; 605 Prince St.; P.O. Box 54; Truro; B2N 5B6; P 934,000; M 33; (902) 895-6329; Fax (902) 897-6641; wayne@nschamber.ca; www.nschamber.ca

Annapolis • *Annapolis & Dist. Bd. of Trade* • P.O. Box 2; B0S 1A0; P 21,000; M 98; (902) 532-5454; (902) 526-0944; info@tradeannapolis.com; www.tradeannapolis

Antigonish • *Antigonish C/C* • Dan Fougere; Pres.; 188 Main St.; B2G 2B9; P 19,000; M 165; (902) 863-6308; Fax (902) 863-2656; contact@antigonishchamber.com; www.antigonishchamber.com

Berwick • *Berwick & Dist. Bd. of Trade* • Jill Eason; P.O. Box 664; B0P 1E0; P 2,500; M 85; (902) 538-5633; www.town.berwick.ns.ca

Bridgewater • *Bridgewater & Area C/C* • Ann O'Connell; Exec. Dir.; 373 King St.; B4V 1B1; P 10,000; M 170; (902) 543-4263; Fax (902) 543-1156; bacc@eastlink.ca; www.bridgewaterchamber.com

Chester • *Chester Municipal C/C* • Ben Wiper; Pres.; 4171 Hwy. 3 RR 2; B0J 1J0; P 10,750; M 200; (902) 275-4709; Fax (902) 275-4629; admin@chesterareans.com; www.chesterareans.com

Church Point • *Clare C/C* • Marcel Saulnier; Pres.; P.O. Box 35; B0W 1M0; P 10,000; M 100; (902) 769-5312; Fax (902) 769-5500; contact@commercedeclare.ca; www.commercedeclare.ca

Dartmouth • *Halifax C/C* • Valerie Payn; Pres.; 656 Windmill Rd., Ste. 200; B3B 1B8; P 390,000; M 1,500; (902) 468-7111; Fax (902) 468-7333; dianna@halifaxchamber.com; www.halifaxchamber.com

Digby • *Digby & Area Bd. of Trade* • Linda Weir; Secy.; P.O. Box 641; B0V 1A0; P 3,000; M 40; info@digbytrade.ca; www.digbytrade.ca

Enfield • *East Hants & Dist. C/C* • Richard Ramsay; Pres.; 8 Old Enfield Rd., Unit 13; B2T 1C9; P 21,400; M 165; (902) 883-1010; Fax (902) 883-7862; info@ehcc.ca; www.ehcc.ca

Kentville • *Eastern Kings C/C* • Judy Rafuse; Exec. Dir.; 325 Main St.; P.O. Box 314; B4N 3X1; P 27,500; M 375; (902) 678-4634; Fax (902) 678-5448; executivedirector@ekcc.ca; www.ekcc.ca

Kentville • *Atlantic Provinces C/C* • 57 Webster St.; B4N 4H8; P 2,000,000; M 16,000; (902) 678-6284; contact@apcc.ca; www.apcc.ca

Liverpool • *South Queens C/C* • Barry Tomalin; Pres.; P.O. Box 1378; B0T 1K0; P 12,500; M 85; (902) 350-1826; secretary@southqueenschamber.com; www.southqueenschamber.com

New Glasgow • *Pictou County C/C* • Faus Johnson; Exec. Dir.; 980 E. River Rd.; B2H 3S8; P 47,000; M 230; (902) 755-3463; Fax (902) 755-2848; heather.macculloch@pictouchamber.com; www.pictouchamber.com

Parrsboro • *Parrsboro C/C & Bd. of Trade* • Karen Dickinson; Pres.; P.O. Box 297; B0M 1S0; P 1,500; M 75; (902) 546-2342; www.town.parrsboro.ns.ca

Pictou County • *see New Glasgow*

Port Hawkesbury • *Strait Area C/C* • Damian MacInnis; CEO; 609 Church St., Ste. 205; B9A 3K5; P 35,000; M 308; (902) 625-1588; Fax (902) 625-5985; info@straitareachamber.ca; www.straitareachamber.ca

Riverport • *Riverport Dist. Bd. of Trade* • John Bryson; Pres.; P.O. Box 28; B0J 2W0; P 1,000; M 30; (902) 766-0382; boardoftrade@riverport.org; www.riverport.org

Springhill • *Springhill C/C* • Rev. Frank Likely; Pres.; P.O. Box 1030; B0M 1X0; P 4,000; M 60; (902) 597-3026; amcentre@eastlink.ca; www.town.springhill.ns.ca

Sydney • *Sydney & Area C/C* • Adrian White; CEO; 275 Charlotte St.; P.O. Box 131; B1P 1C6; P 100,000; M 390; (902) 564-6453; Fax (902) 539-7487; info@sydneyareachamber.ca; www.sydneyareachamber.ca

Tatamagouche • *North Shore Comm. Dev. Assn.* • Paul Brinkhurst; Chair; P.O. Box 152; B0K 1V0; P 1,000; M 15; (902) 657-3811; www.tatamagouchetoday.com

Truro • *Truro & Dist. C/C* • Tim Tucker; Exec. Dir.; 605 Prince St.; B2N 4V8; P 46,000; M 430; (902) 895-6328; Fax (902) 897-6641; tim@trurochamber.com; www.trurochamber.com

Windsor • *West Hants C/C* • Scott Geddes; Pres.; P.O. Box 2188; B0N 2T0; P 14,000; M 70; (902) 798-5106; info@whcc.ca; www.whcc.ca

Yarmouth • *Yarmouth & Area C/C* • Matthew Trask; Exec. Dir.; 368 Main St.; P.O. Box 532; B5A 4B4; P 28,000; M 200; (902) 742-3074; Fax (902) 749-1383; info@yarmouthchamberofcommerce.com; www.yarmouthchamberofcommerce.com

Nunavut

Baker Lake • *Baker Lake C/C & EDC* • Trevor Attungala; Dev. Officer; P.O. Box 149; X0C 0A0; P 1,700; (867) 793-2874; Fax (867) 793-2509; bledo@bakerlake.ca; www.bakerlake.ca

Iqaluit • *Baffin Reg. C/C* • Hal Timer; Exec. Dir.; Box 59, Bldg. 607; X0A 0H0; P 15,000; M 120; (867) 979-4654; (867) 979-4656; Fax (867) 979-2929; execdir@baffinchamber.ca; www.baffinchamber.ca

Rankin Inlet • *Kivalliq C/C* • Ellie Cansfield; Pres.; P.O. Box 146; X0C 0G0; P 7,500; M 150; (867) 645-2817; Fax (867) 645-2483; krmanson@artic.ca

Ontario

Ontario C/C • Allan O'Dette; Pres./CEO; 180 Dundas St. W., Ste. 505; Toronto; M5G 1Z8; P 12,850,000; M 65,000; (416) 482-5222; Fax (416) 482-5879; info@occ.on.ca; www.occ.on.ca

---

Alliston • *Alliston & Dist. C/C* • Sarah Stewart; Exec. Dir.; 60B Victoria St. W.; P.O. Box 32; L9R 1T9; P 16,000; M 230; (705) 435-7921; Fax (705) 435-0289; info@adcc.ca; www.adcc.ca

Amherstburg • *Amherstburg C/C* • Karen Girard; Admin. Asst.; 268 Dalhousie St.; P.O. Box 101; N9V 2Z3; P 21,748; M 190; (519) 736-2001; acoc@mnsi.net; www.amherstburgchamberofcommerce.ca

Apsley • *see Lakefield*

Aurora • *Aurora C/C* • Judy Marshall; CEO; 6-14845 Yonge St., Ste. 321; L4G 6H8; P 57,000; M 700; (905) 727-7262; Fax (905) 841-6217; info@aurorachamber.on.ca; www.aurorachamber.on.ca

Bancroft • *Bancroft & Dist. C/C* • Greg Webb; Gen. Mgr.; 8 Hastings Heritage Way; P.O. Box 539; K0L 1C0; P 3,700; M 300; (613) 332-1513; (888) 443-9999; Fax (613) 332-2119; chamber@bancroftdistrict.com; www.bancroftdistrict.com

Barrie • *Greater Barrie C/C* • Rod Jackson; CEO; 97 Toronto St.; L4N 1V1; P 150,000; M 1,000; (705) 721-5000; Fax (705) 726-0973; admin@barriechamber.com; www.barriechamber.com

Belleville • *Belleville C/C* • Bill Saunders; CEO; 5 Moira St. E.; P.O. Box 726; K8N 5B3; P 50,000; M 600; (613) 962-4597; Fax (613) 962-3911; info@bellevillechamber.ca; www.bellevillechamber.ca

Blenheim • *Blenheim & Dist. C/C* • Frank Vercouteren; P.O. Box 1353; N0P 1A0; P 4,600; M 60; (519) 676-8090; (519) 676-6555; www.blenheimontario.com

Blind River • *Blind River C/C* • Louise Demers; Pres.; 243 Causley St.; P.O. Box 998; P0R 1B0; P 3,600; M 100; (705) 356-5715; Fax (705) 356-5715; chamber@blindriver.com; www.brchamber.ca

Bobcaygeon • *Bobcaygeon & Area C/C* • Ruthann Wilson; Ofc. Mgr.; 21 E. Canal St.; P.O. Box 388; K0M 1A0; P 2,000; M 222; (705) 738-2202; (800) 318-6173; Fax (705) 738-1534; chamber@bobcaygeon.org; www.bobcaygeon.org

Bolton • *Caledon C/C* • Kelly Darnley; Exec. Dir.; 12598 Hwy. 50 S.; P.O. Box 626; L7E 5T5; P 59,500; M 275; (905) 857-7393; (888) 599-9967; Fax (905) 857-7405; Info@caledonchamber.com; www.caledonchamber.com*

Bracebridge • *Bracebridge C/C* • Brenda Rhodes; Exec. Dir.; 1 Manitoba St., Ste.1, 2nd Flr.; P1L 1S4; P 15,500; M 330; (705) 645-5231; Fax None; chamber@bracebridgechamber.com; www.bracebridgechamber.com

Brampton • *Brampton Bd. of Trade* • Steve Sheils; CEO; 36 Queen St. E., Ste. 101; L6V 1A2; P 524,000; M 1,100; (905) 451-1122; Fax (905) 450-0295; admin@bramptonbot.com; www.bramptonbot.com

Brantford • *Chamber of Commerce Brantford Brant* • Charlene Nicholson; CEO; 77 Charlotte St.; N3T 2W8; P 136,000; M 750; (519) 753-2617; Fax (519) 753-0921; nancy@brcc.ca; www.brantfordbrantchamber.com

Brockville • *Brockville & Dist. C/C* • Pamela Robertson; Exec. Dir.; 3 Market St. W., Ste. 1; K6V 7L2; P 22,000; M 400; (613) 342-6553; Fax (613) 342-6849; info@brockvillechamber.com; www.brockvillechamber.com

Buckhorn • *see Lakefield*

Burleigh Falls • *see Lakefield*

Burlington • *Burlington C/C* • Keith Hoey; Pres.; 414 Locust St., Ste. 201; L7S 1T7; P 175,800; M 1,057; (905) 639-0174; Fax (905) 333-3956; info@burlingtonchamber.com; www.burlingtonchamber.com

Cambridge • *Cambridge C/C* • Greg Durocher; Pres./CEO; 750 Hespeler Rd.; N3H 5L8; P 126,700; M 1,900; (519) 622-6543; (519) 622-2221; Fax (519) 622-0177; greg@cambridgechamber.com; www.cambridgechamber.com

Campbellford • *Trent Hills C/C* • Nancy Allanson; Exec. Dir.; 51 Grand Rd.; P.O. Box 376; K0L 1L0; P 12,500; M 250; (705) 653-1551; Fax (705) 653-1629; info@trenthillschamber.ca; www.trenthillschamber.ca

Carleton Place • *Carleton Place & Dist. C/C* • Tracy Lamb; Pres.; 132 Coleman St.; K7C 4M7; P 10,000; M 184; (613) 257-1976; Fax (613) 257-4148; manager@cpchamber.com; www.cpchamber.com

Chatham • *Chatham-Kent C/C* • Gail Hundt; Pres./CEO; 54 Fourth St.; N7M 2G2; P 44,000; M 400; (519) 352-7540; Fax (519) 352-8741; gail@chatham-kentchamber.ca; www.chatham-kentchamber.ca

Cobourg • *Northumberland Central C/C* • Kevin Ward; Pres./CEO; The Chamber Bldg.; 278 George St.; K9A 3L8; P 35,000; M 425; (905) 372-5831; Fax (905) 372-2411; info@nccofc.ca; www.nccofc.ca

Collingwood • *Collingwood C/C* • Trish Irwin; Gen. Mgr.; 25 Second St.; L9Y 1E4; P 19,300; M 525; (705) 445-0221; Fax (705) 445-6858; info@collingwoodchamber.com; www.collingwoodchamber.com

Concord • *see Vaughan*

Cornwall • *Cornwall C/C* • Lezlie Strasser; Exec. Mgr.; 113 2nd St. E., Ste. 100; K6H 1Y5; P 46,400; M 550; (613) 933-4004; Fax (613) 933-8466; strasser@cornwallchamber.com; www.cornwallchamber.com

Dryden • *Dryden Dist. C/C* • Mgr.; 284 Government St.; P8N 2P3; P 35,000; M 150; (807) 223-2622; (800) 667-0935; Fax (807) 223-2626; chamber@drytel.net; www.drydenchamber.ca

Dunnville • *Dunnville C/C* • Sandy Passmore; Ofc. Mgr.; 231 Chestnut St.; P.O. Box 124; N1A 2X1; P 6,000; M 80; (905) 774-3183; (905) 774-5203; Fax (905) 774-9281; dunnvillecoc@shaw.ca; www.dunnvillechamberofcommerce.ca

Durham • *West Grey C/C* • Greta Kennedy; Secy./Treas.; P.O. Box 800; N0G 1R0; P 2,640; M 50; (519) 369-5750; Fax (519) 369-5750; info@westgreychamber.com; www.westgreychamber.ca

Dutton • *Dutton & Dunwich C/C* • Brian Girard; Pres.; P.O. Box 547; N0L 1J0; P 3,820; M 77; (519) 762-6550; jbgirard@live.ca; www.ddchamber.ca

Elliot Lake • *Elliot Lake & Dist. C/C* • Todd Stencill; Gen. Mgr.; 1 Horne Walk, Ste. 102; P.O. Box 81; P5A 2J6; P 11,400; M 130; (705) 848-3974; Fax (705) 461-8039; elchamber@onlink.net; www.elliotlakechamber.com

Embrun • *Prescott-Russell C/C* • Sylvie GuÃƒÂ©nette; Exec. Dir.; 923 Notre Dame; C.P. 734; K0A 1W0; P 8,000; M 80; (613) 443-7606; Fax (866) 638-5910; info@ccprcc.com; www.ccprcc.com

Englehart • *Englehart & Dist. C/C* • Wayne Stratton; Pres.; P.O. Box 171; P0J 1H0; P 1,500; M 44; (705) 544-8916; (705) 544-8916; englehartchamber@weebly.com; englehartchamber.weebly.com

Fenelon Falls • *Fenelon Falls & Dist. C/C* • 15 Oak St.; P.O. Box 28; K0M 1N0; P 2,000; M 130; (705) 887-3409; Fax (705) 887-6912; info@fenelonfallschamber.com; www.fenelonfallschamber.com

Fergus • *Centre Wellington C/C* • Roberta Scarrow; Gen. Mgr.; 400 Tower St. S.; N1M 2P7; P 29,000; M 340; (519) 843-5140; (877) 242-6353; Fax (519) 787-0983; chamber@cwchamber.ca; www.cwchamber.ca

Fort Erie • *Greater Fort Erie C/C* • Karen Audet; Op. Mgr.; 660 Garrison Rd., Unit 1; L2A 6E2; P 32,000; M 400; (905) 871-3803; Fax (905) 871-1561; info@forteriechamber.com; www.forteriechamber.com

Fort Frances • *Fort Frances C/C* • Jennifer Soderholm; Exec. Dir.; 102-240 First St. E.; P9A 1K5; P 8,000; M 160; (807) 274-5773; (800) 820-3678; Fax (807) 274-8706; thefort@fortfranceschamber.com; www.fortfranceschamber.com

Grand Bend • *Grand Bend & Area C/C* • Susan Mills; Ofc. Mgr.; 1-81 Crescent; P.O. Box 248; N0M 1T0; P 10,000; M 208; (519) 238-2001; (888) 338-2001; Fax (519) 238-5201; info@grandbendchamber.ca; www.grandbendchamber.ca

Grimsby • *Grimsby & Dist. C/C* • Jinny Day; Exec. Dir.; 33 Main St. West, 2nd Flr.; L3M 1R3; P 22,000; M 240; (905) 945-8319; Fax (905) 945-1615; info@grimsbychamber.com; grimsbychamber.com

Guelph • *Guelph C/C* • Lloyd Longfield; Pres./CAO; 111 Farquhar St., 2nd Flr.; N1H 3N4; P 121,700; M 840; (519) 822-8081; Fax (519) 822-8451; chamber@guelphchamber.com; www.guelphchamber.com

Hagersville • *Hagersville & Dist. C/C* • Rob Phillips; Pres.; P.O. Box 1090; N0A 1H0; P 2,600; M 70; (905) 768-0422; Fax (289) 282-0105; rphillips@heaslipford.com; www.hagersvillechamber.ca

Haliburton • *Haliburton Highlands C/C* • Autumn Smith; Mgr.; 195 Highland St., Ste. L1; P.O. Box 670; K0M 1S0; P 18,000; M 300; (705) 457-4700; (877) 811-6111; Fax (705) 457-4702; admin@haliburtonchamber.com; www.haliburtonchamber.com*

Halton Hills • *Halton Hills C/C* • Kathleen Dills; Gen. Mgr.; 8 James St.; L7G 2H3; P 59,000; M 500; (905) 877-7119; Fax (905) 877-5117; info@haltonhillschamber.on.ca; www.haltonhillschamber.on.ca

Hamilton • *Hamilton C/C* • David Adames; Pres./CEO; 555 Bay St. N.; L8L 1H1; P 500,000; M 1,200; (905) 522-1151; Fax (905) 522-1154; hdcc@hamiltonchamber.on.ca; www.hamiltonchamber.on.ca

Hastings • *see Campbellford*

Hawkesbury • *Hawkesbury C/C* • Roxanne Courcy; Pres.; P.O. Box 36; K6A 2R4; P 11,000; M 125; (613) 632-8066; info@hawkesburychamberofcommerce.ca; www.hawkesburychamberofcommerce.ca

Hearst • *Hearst, Mattice-Val Cote & Area C/C* • Luc Pepin; Pres.; P.O. Box 987; P0L 1N0; P 7,000; M 125; (705) 362-5880; Fax (705) 362-5880; info@hearstcoc.com; www.hearstcoc.com

Huntsville • *Huntsville/Lake of Bays C/C* • Kelly Haywood; Exec. Dir.; 8 West St. N.; P1H 2B6; P 22,000; M 621; (705) 789-4771; Fax (705) 789-6191; chamber@huntsvillelakeofbays.on.ca; www.huntsvillelakeofbays.on.ca

Ingersoll • *Ingersoll Dist. C/C* • Ann Campbell; Gen. Mgr.; 118 Oxford St.; N5C 2V5; P 12,500; M 220; (519) 485-7333; Fax (519) 485-6606; anncampbell@ingersollchamber.com; www.ingersollchamber.com

Ingleside • *South Stormont C/C* • J.R. (Bob) Copeland; Pres.; P.O. Box 489; K0C 1M0; P 1,800; M 62; (613) 537-4427; info@sscc.on.ca; sscc.on.ca

Innisfil • *Greater Innisfil C/C* • Tami Smith; Mgr.; 8034 Yonge St, Unit 3; L9S 1L6; P 34,000; M 254; (705) 431-4199; Fax (705) 431-6628; info@innisfilchamber.com; www.innisfilchamber.com

Iroquois Falls • *Iroquois Falls & Dist. C/C* • Lola Brousseau; Ofc. Mgr.; 727 Synagogue Ave.; P.O. Box 840; P0K 1G0; P 5,000; M 50; (705) 232-4656; Fax (705) 232-4656; ifchamber@hotmail.com; www.iroquoisfallschamber.com

Kemptville • *North Grenville C/C* • Melissa D. White; Chair; 509 Kernahan St.; P.O. Box 1047; K0G 1J0; P 15,100; M 160; (613) 258-4838; Fax (613) 258-3801; info@northgrenvillechamber.com; www.northgrenvillechamber.com*

Kenora • *Kenora & Dist. C/C* • Andy Scribilo; Pres.; 103-115 Chipman St.; P.O. Box 471; P9N 3X5; P 15,400; M 200; (807) 467-4646; Fax (807) 468-3056; kenorachamber@kmts.ca; www.kenorachamber.com

Keswick • *Georgina C/C* • Monique Dixon; Exec. Dir.; 430 The Queensway S.; L4P 2E1; P 44,000; M 278; (905) 476-7870; Fax (905) 476-6700; admin@georginachamber.com; www.georginachamber.com

Kincardine • *Kincardine & Dist. C/C* • Colleen Dostle; Exec. Dir.; 777B Queen St.; P.O. Box 115; N2Z 2Y6; P 12,000; M 150; (519) 396-9333; Fax (519) 396-5529; kincardine.cofc@bmts.com; www.kincardinechamber.com

Kingston • *Greater Kingston C/C* • Martin Sherris; CEO; Innovation Park; 945 Princess St.; K7L 3N6; P 140,000; M 875; (613) 548-4453; (888) 855-4555; Fax (613) 548-4743; info@kingstonchamber.ca; www.kingstonchamber.ca

Kirkland Lake • *Kirkland Lake Dist. C/C* • Jennifer Verge; Ofc. Coord.; 400 Government Rd. W.; P.O. Box 966; P2N 3L1; P 8,500; M 125; (705) 567-5444; Fax (705) 567-1666; klcofc@ntl.sympatico.ca; www.kirklandlakechamberofcommerce.com

Kitchener • *Greater Kitchener Waterloo C/C* • Ian McLean; Pres./CEO; 80 Queen St. N.; P.O. Box 2367; N2H 6L4; P 400,000; M 18,000; (519) 576-5000; (888) 672-4760; Fax (519) 742-4760; admin@greaterkwchamber.com; www.greaterkwchamber.com

Kleinburg • *see Vaughan*

Lakefield • *Kawartha Lakes C/C - Eastern Region* • Sherry Boyce-Found; Gen. Mgr.; 12 Queen St.; P.O. Box 537; K0L 2H0; P 15,000; M 370; (705) 652-6963; (888) 565-8888; Fax (705) 652-9140; info@kawarthachamber.ca; www.kawarthachamber.ca

Leamington • *Leamington & Dist. C/C* • Sally McDonald; Gen. Mgr.; 21 Talbot St. E.; P.O. Box 321; N8H 3W3; P 35,000; M 400; (519) 326-2721; (800) 250-3336; Fax (519) 326-3204; sally@leamingtonchamber.com; www.leamingtonchamber.com

Lindsay • *Lindsay & Dist. C/C* • Christine Baily; Gen. Mgr.; 20 Lindsay St. S.; K9V 2L6; P 21,000; M 400; (705) 324-2393; Fax (705) 324-2473; info@lindsaychamber.com; www.lindsaychamber.com

Listowel • *North Perth C/C* • Sharon D'Arcey; Gen. Mgr.; 580 Main St. W.; N4W 1A8; P 14,000; M 200; (519) 291-1551; Fax (519) 291-4151; info@npchamber.com; npchamber.com

London • *London C/C* • Gerry Macartney; CEO/Gen. Mgr.; 101-244 Pall Mall St.; N6A 5P6; P 366,100; M 1,030; (519) 432-7551; Fax (519) 432-8063; info@londonchamber.com; www.londonchamber.com

Manotick • *Rideau C/C* • Salima Ismail; Pres.; P.O. Box 247; K4M 1A3; P 5,000; M 60; (613) 692-6262; drsalima@doctor.com; www.rideauchamber.com

Maple • *see Vaughan*

Markdale • *Grey Highlands C/C* • Doug Crawford; Pres.; 13 Toronto St. S.; P.O. Box 177; N0C 1H0; P 15,000; M 150; (519) 986-4612; info@greyhighlandschamber.com; www.greyhighlandschamber.com

Markham • *Markham Bd. of Trade* • Richard Cunningham; Pres./CEO; 3600 Steeles Ave. E., C-1, Ste. 105; L3R 9Z7; P 301,700; M 750; (905) 474-0730; Fax (905) 474-0685; info@markhamboard.com; www.markhamboard.com

Merrickville • *Merrickville & Dist. C/C* • Katherine Miller; P.O. Box 571; K0G 1N0; P 2,850; M 150; (613) 269-2229; Fax (613) 269-2229; info@realmerrickville.ca; www.realmerrickville.ca

Midland • *Southern Georgian Bay C/C* • Denise Hayes; Bus. Mgr.; 208 King St.; L4R 3L9; P 43,000; M 530; (705) 526-7884; Fax (705) 526-1744; info@sgbchamber.ca; www.southerngeorgianbay.on.ca

Milton • *Milton C/C* • Sandy Martin; Exec. Dir.; 251 Main St. E., Ste. 104; L9T 1P1; P 101,000; M 770; (905) 878-0581; Fax (905) 878-4972; info@miltonchamber.ca; www.miltonchamber.ca

Mindemoya • *Manitoulin C/C* • Owen Legge; Pres.; P.O. Box 307; P0P 1S0; P 12,600; M 150; (705) 377-7501; office@manitoulinchamber.com; www.manitoulinchamber.com

Mississauga • *Mississauga Bd. of Trade* • David Wojcik; Pres./CEO; 77 City Center Dr., Ste. 701; L5B 1M5; P 713,400; M 1,500; (905) 273-6151; Fax (905) 273-4937; info@mbot.com; www.mbot.com

Mono • *Greater Dufferin Area C/C* • Theresa Sauren; Exec. Dir.; 246372 Hockley Rd.; P.O. Box 101; L9W 6K4; P 56,881; M 415; (519) 941-0490; Fax (519) 941-0492; info@gdacc.ca; www.gdacc.ca

Morrisburg • *South Dundas C/C* • Geraldine Fitzsimmons; Ofc. Mgr.; P.O. Box 288; K0C 1X0; P 12,000; M 100; (613) 662-2653; Fax (613) 652-4120; manager@southdundaschamber.ca; www.southdundaschamber.ca

Mount Forest • *Mount Forest & Dist. C/C* • Trish Wake; Admin.; 514 Main St. N.; N0G 2L2; P 5,000; M 130; (519) 323-4480; Fax (519) 323-1557; chamber@mountforest.ca; www.mountforest.ca

New Hamburg • *New Hamburg Bd. of Trade* • Joe Figliomeni; Pres.; 121 Huron St.; N3A 1K1; P 8,000; M 100; (226) 791-2672; newhamburgboardoftrade@hotmail.com; www.nhbot.ca

Newmarket • *Newmarket C/C* • Debra Scott; Pres./CEO; 470 Davis Dr.; L3Y 2P3; P 80,000; M 850; (905) 898-5900; Fax (905) 853-7271; info@newmarketchamber.ca; www.newmarketchamber.ca

Niagara Falls • *The Chamber of Commerce at Niagara Falls Canada C/C* • Dolores Fabiano; Pres.; 4056 Dorchester Rd.; L2E 6M9; P 82,000; M 700; (905) 374-3666; Fax (905) 374-2972; info@niagarafallschamber.com; www.niagarafallschamber.com

Niagara-on-the-Lake • *Niagara-on-the-Lake C/C & Visitors Bur.* • Janice Thomson; Exec. Dir.; 26 Queen St.; P.O. Box 1043; L0S 1J0; P 15,000; M 515; (905) 468-1950; Fax (905) 468-4930; admin@niagaraonthelake.com; www.niagaraonthelake.com

Nipigon • *Top of Lake Superior C/C* • Brigitte Tremblay; Coord.; P.O. Box 760; P0T 2J0; P 2,000; M 37; (807) 887-0740; Fax (807) 887-0741; nipigonchamber@vianet.ca; www.loncoc.ca

Nipigon • *North of Superior Tourism Assn.* • Dan Bevilacqua; Exec. Dir.; 425 Hwy. 11/17; R.R. 1 Box, 1 Maatas Rd.; P0T 2J0; P 200,000; M 300; (807) 887-3188; Fax (807) 887-3189; info@northofsuperior.org; www.nosta.on.ca

North Bay • *North Bay & Dist. C/C* • Patti Carr; Exec. Dir.; 1375 Seymour St.; P1B 9V6; P 64,000; M 895; (705) 472-8480; Fax (705) 472-8027; nbcc@northbaychamber.com; www.northbaychamber.com

Norwich • *Twp. of Norwich C/C* • Darren Dayman; Pres.; 41 Main St. W.; N0J 1P0; P 10,000; M 120; (519) 805-2825; darren@specialtyforging.com; www.norwichchamberofcommerce.ca

Oakville • *Oakville C/C* • John Sawyer; Pres.; 700 Kerr St., Ste. 200; L6K 3W5; P 185,000; M 1,175; (905) 845-6613; Fax (905) 845-6475; info@oakvillechamber.com; www.oakvillechamber.com

Oshawa • *Greater Oshawa C/C* • Nancy Shaw; Gen. Mgr./CEO; 44 Richmond St. W., Ste. 100; L1G 1C7; P 150,000; M 800; (905) 728-1683; (905) 725-4523; Fax (905) 432-1259; info@oshawachamber.com; www.oshawachamber.com*

Ottawa • *Ottawa C/C* • Erin Kelly; Exec. Dir.; 328 Somerset St. W.; K2P 0J9; P 1,236,000; M 900; (613) 236-3631; Fax (613) 236-7498; info@ottawachamber.ca; www.ottawachamber.ca*

Owen Sound • *Owen Sound & Dist. C/C* • Peter Reesor; CEO; 1051 2nd Ave E., Ste. 226; P. O. Box 811; N4K 6K6; P 32,300; M 460; (519) 376-6261; Fax (519) 376-5647; peggy@oschamber.com; www.oschamber.com

Parry Sound • *Parry Sound Area C/C* • Heather Murch; Mgr. of Member Svcs.; 21 William St.; P2A 1V2; P 16,000; M 275; (705) 746-4213; info@psachamber.ca; www.psachamber.ca

Pembroke • *Upper Ottawa Valley C/C* • Lorraine MacKenzie; Exec. Dir.; 224 Pembroke St. W.; P.O. Box 1010; K8A 5N2; P 30,000; M 300; (613) 732-1492; Fax (613) 732-5793; manager@uovchamber.com; www.uovchamber.com

Perth • *Perth & Dist. C/C* • Amber M. Hall; Gen. Mgr.; 66 Craig St.; K7H 1Y5; P 6,500; M 280; (613) 267-3200; welcome@perthchamber.com; www.perthchamber.com

Peterborough • *Greater Peterborough C/C* • Stuart Harrison; Pres./CEO; 175 George St. N.; K9J 3G6; P 130,000; M 980; (705) 748-9771; Fax (705) 743-2331; stuart@peterboroughchamber.ca; www.peterboroughchamber.ca*

Picton • *Prince Edward County C/C* • Emily Cowan; Exec. Dir.; 116 Main St.; K0K 2T0; P 24,000; M 250; (613) 476-2421; (800) 640-4717; Fax (613) 476-7461; contactus@pecchamber.com; www.pecchamber.com

Pointe au Baril • *Pointe au Baril C/C* • Lillian White; Ofc. Admin.; 1650 Hwy. 69; P.O. Box 67; P0G 1K0; P 6,000; M 137; (705) 366-2331; Fax (705) 366-2331; info@pointeaubarilchamber.com; www.pointeaubarilchamber.com

Port Colborne • *Port Colborne-Wainfleet C/C* • Dolores Fabiano; Exec. Dir.; 76 Main St. W.; L3K 3V2; P 26,000; M 231; (905) 834-9765; Fax (905) 834-9765; katie@pcwchamber.com; www.pcwchamber.com

Port Dover • *Port Dover Bd. of Trade* • Adam Veri; Pres.; 19 Market St. W.; P.O. Box 239; N0A 1N0; P 6,400; M 250; (519) 583-1314; Fax (519) 583-3275; info@portdover.ca; www.portdover.ca

Port Elgin • *Saugeen Shores C/C* • Joanne Robbins; Gen. Mgr.; 559 Goderich St.; N0H 2C4; P 12,500; M 430; (519) 832-2332; (800) 387-3456; Fax (519) 389-3725; portelgininfo@saugeenshores.ca; www.saugeenshoreschamber.ca

Port Hope • *Port Hope & Dist. C/C* • Bree Nixon; CEO; 58 Queen St.; L1A 3Z9; P 17,000; M 205; (905) 885-5519; Fax (905) 885-1142; thechamber@porthope.ca; www.porthopechamber.com

Port Perry • *Scugog C/C* • Kenna Kozak; Exec. Dir./Gen. Mgr.; 237 Queen St.; P.O. Box 1282; L9L 1A0; P 22,500; M 230; (905) 985-4971; (877-820-3595; Fax (905) 985-7698; info@scugogchamber.ca; www.scugogchamber.ca

Port Rowan • *Long Point Country C/C* • Jane Thomson; Pres.; P.O. Box 357; N0E 1M0; P 4,000; M 100; (519) 586-8888; info@portrowan-longpoint.org; www.portrowan-longpoint.org

Prescott • *South Grenville C/C* • Jen Wyman; Pres.; 107 King St. W.; P.O. Box 2000; K0E 1T0; P 4,200; M 150; (613) 213-1043; secretary@southgrenvillechamber.ca; www.southgrenvillechamber.ca

Red Lake • *Red Lake Dist. C/C* • Colin Knudsen; Pres.; P.O. Box 430; P0V 2M0; P 6,000; M 65; (807) 727-3722; Fax (807) 727-3285; redlakechamber@shaw.ca

Renfrew • *Renfrew & Area C/C* • Tammy Logan; Mgr.; 161 Raglan St. S.; K7V 1R2; P 8,700; M 200; (613) 432-7015; Fax (613) 432-8645; info@renfrewareachamber.ca; www.renfrewareachamber.ca

Richmond Hill • *Richmond Hill Bd. of Trade* • Elio Furlan; Exec. Dir.; 376 Church St. S.; L4C 9V8; P 202,000; M 600; (905) 884-1961; Fax (905) 884-1962; info@rhbot.ca; www.rhbot.ca*

Ridgetown • *Ridgetown & S.E. Kent C/C* • Charlie Mitton; Pres.; P.O. Box 522; N0P 2C0; P 3,450; M 90; (519) 674-5554; ridgetownchamber@gmail.com; www.ridgetown.com

Sarnia • *Sarnia/Lambton C/C* • Rory Ring; Pres.; 556 N. Christina St.; N7T 5W6; P 126,200; M 975; (519) 336-2400; Fax (519) 336-2085; info@sarnialambtonchamber.com; www.sarnialambtonchamber.com

Sauble Beach • *Sauble Beach C/C* • Trevor Dykstra; Pres.; 627 Main St.; N0H 2G0; P 3,000; M 120; (519) 422-1262; admin@saublebeach.com; www.saublebeach.com

Sault Ste. Marie • *Sault Ste. Marie C/C* • Rory Ring; CEO; 369 Queen Street E., Ste. 1; P6A 1Z4; P 75,000; M 700; (705) 949-7152; Fax (705) 759-8166; info@ssmcoc.com; www.ssmcoc.com

Scarborough • *see Toronto*

Schomberg • *King C/C* • Helen Neville; Admin.; P.O. Box 381; L0G 1T0; P 5,000; M 200; (905) 717-7199; Fax (416) 981-7174; info@kingchamber.ca; www.kingchamber.ca

Selwyn • *see Lakefield*

Simcoe • *Simcoe & Dist. C/C* • Yvonne Di Pietro; Gen. Mgr.; 95 Queensway W.; Chamber Plaza; N3Y 2M8; P 63,000; M 350; (519) 426-5867; Fax (519) 428-7718; chamber@simcoechamber.on.ca; www.simcoechamber.on.ca

Sioux Lookout • *Sioux Lookout C/C* • Tiana Korobanik; Exec. Asst.; 11 First Ave. S.; P.O. Box 577; P8T 1A8; P 5,500; M 155; (807) 737-1937; Fax (807) 737-1778; chamber@siouxlookout.com; www.siouxlookout.com

Smiths Falls • *Smiths Falls & Dist. C/C* • Heather Whiting; Mktg. Coord.; 77 Beckwith St. N.; K7A 2B8; P 9,100; M 300; (613) 283-1334; Fax (613) 283-4764; info@smithsfallschamber.ca; www.smithsfallschamber.com

Smithville • *West Lincoln C/C* • Pamela Haire; Ofc. Mgr.; 288 Station St.; P.O. Box 555; L0R 2A0; P 13,500; M 105; (905) 957-1606; Fax (905) 957-4628; westlincolnchamber@bellnet.ca; www.westlincolnchamber.com

St. Catharines • *Greater Niagara C/C* • Mishka Balsom; Pres./CEO; One St. Paul St., Ste. 103; P.O. Box 940; L2R 6Z4; P 400,000; M 1,580; (905) 684-2361; Fax (905) 684-2100; info@gncc.ca; www.gncc.ca

St. Thomas • *St. Thomas & Dist. C/C* • Robert (Bob) Hammersley; Pres./CEO; 115 - 300 S. Edgeware Rd.; N5P 4L1; P 68,000; M 620; (519) 631-1981; Fax (519) 631-0466; mail@stthomaschamber.ca; www.stthomaschamber.on.ca

Stoney Creek • *Stoney Creek C/C* • Dave Cage; Exec. Dir.; 21 Mountain Ave. S.; L8G 2V5; P 58,000; M 435; (905) 664-4000; Fax (905) 664-7228; admin@chamberstoneycreek.com; www.chamberstoneycreek.com

Stony Lake • *see Lakefield*

Stratford • *Stratford & Dist. C/C* • Brad Beatty; Gen. Mgr.; 55 Lorne Ave. E.; N5A 6S4; P 32,000; M 320; (519) 273-5250; Fax (519) 273-2229; manager@stratfordchamber.com; www.stratfordchamber.com

Sturgeon Falls • *West Nipissing C/C* • Jolene Greer; Proj. Mgr.; 173 King St.; P2B 1R6; P 14,200; M 110; (705) 753-5672; Fax (705) 580-5672; info@westnipissingchamber.ca; www.westnipissingchamber.ca

Sudbury • *Greater Sudbury C/C* • Debbi M. Nicholson; Pres./CEO; 40 Elm St., Ste. 100; P3C 1S8; P 160,300; M 1,800; (705) 673-7133; Fax (705) 673-1951; cofc@sudburychamber.ca; www.sudburychamber.ca

Tavistock • *Tavistock C/C* • Andrew Raymer; Pres.; P.O. Box 670; N0B 2R0; P 2,800; M 30; (519) 655-2700; www.tavistock.on.ca

Thornhill • *see Vaughan*

Thorold • *see St. Catharines*

Thunder Bay • *Thunder Bay C/C* • Charla Robinson; Pres.; 200 Syndicate Ave. S., Ste. 102; P7E 1C9; P 110,000; M 910; (807) 624-2626; Fax (807) 622-7752; chamber@tbchamber.ca; www.tbchamber.ca*

Tilbury • *Tilbury Bus. Improvement Area* • Natalie Whittal; Exec. Dir.; P.O. Box 1299; N0P 2L0; P 4,500; M 120; (519) 682-3040; bia@tilburyontario.com; www.tilburyontario.com

Tillsonburg • *Tillsonburg Dist. C/C* • Suzanne Renken; CEO; 20 Oxford St.; N4G 2G1; P 45,000; M 220; (519) 688-3737; suzanne@tillsonburgchamber.ca; www.tillsonburgchamber.ca

Timmins • *Timmins C/C* • Keitha Robson; Chief Admin. Ofc.; 76 McIntyre Rd., Schumacher P0N 1G0; P.O. Box 985; P4N 7H6; P 45,000; M 830; (705) 360-1900; Fax (705) 360-1193; admin@timminschamber.on.ca; www.timminschamber.on.ca*

Tobermory • *Tobermory C/C* • Kathy Rehorek; Coord.; 7420 Hwy. 6; P.O. Box 250; N0H 2R0; P 1,000; M 75; (519) 596-2452; Fax (519) 596-2452; chamber@tobermory.org; www.tobermory.com

Toronto • *Toronto Region Bd. of Trade* • Janet De Silva; Pres./CEO; 77 Adelaide St. W.; P.O. Box 60; M5X 1C1; P 2,600,000; M 10,000; (416) 366-6811; Fax (416) 366-8406; contactus@bot.com; www.bot.com*

Tottenham • *Tottenham Beeton & Dist. C/C* • Linda Spurr; Ofc. Admin.; 54 Queen St. S.; P.O. Box 922; L0G 1W0; P 10,000; M 100; (905) 936-4100; Fax (905) 936-4664; tottenhamchamberofcommerce@bellnet.ca; www.tottenhamchamber.on.ca

Trenton • *Quinte West C/C* • Suzanne Andrews; Gen. Mgr.; 97 Front St.; K8V 4N6; P 43,000; M 420; (613) 392-7635; (800) 930-3255; Fax (613) 392-8400; info@quintewestchamber.ca; www.quintewestchamber.ca

Uxbridge • *Uxbridge C/C* • Terry Barrett; Pres.; 2 Campbell Dr.; P.O. Box 810; L9P 0A3; P 19,200; M 120; (905) 852-7683; Fax (905) 852-2632; info@uxcc.ca; www.uxcc.ca*

Vaughan • *Vaughan C/C* • Deborah Bonk-Greenwood; Pres./CEO; 25 Edilcan Dr., Unit 2; L4K 3S4; P 288,300; M 976; (905) 761-1366; Fax (905) 761-1918; info@vaughanchamber.ca; www.vaughanchamber.ca

Walkerton • *Walkerton & Dist. C/C* • Tracey Cassidy; Mgr.; P.O. Box 1344; N0G 2V0; P 10,000; M 280; (519) 881-3413; Fax (519) 881-4009; chamberinfo@wightman.ca; www.brockton.ca

Wasaga Beach • *Wasaga Beach C/C* • Trudie McCrea; Ofc. Mgr.; 550 River Rd. W.; P.O. Box 394; L9Z 1A4; P 18,500; M 250; (705) 429-2247; (866) 292-7242; Fax (705) 429-1407; info@wasagainfo.com; www.wasagainfo.com

Waterdown • *Flamborough C/C* • Arend Kersten; Exec. Dir.; 227 - 7 Innovation Dr.; P.O. Box 1030; L9H 7H9; P 39,000; M 250; (905) 689-7650; Fax (905) 689-1313; admin@flamboroughchamber.ca; www.flamboroughchamber.ca

Waterloo • *see Kitchener*

Wawa • *Wawa Tourist Info. Center* • Lori Johnson; Dir. of Comm. Svcs. & Tourism; P.O. Box 500; P0S 1K0; P 2,600; (705) 856-2244; Fax (705) 856-2120; info@wawa.cc; www.wawa.cc

Welland • *Welland/Pelham C/C* • Dolores Fabiano; Exec. Dir.; 32 E. Main St.; L3B 3W3; P 56,000; M 500; (905) 732-7515; Fax (905) 732-7175; karen@wellandpelhamchamber.com; www.wellandpelhamchamber.com

Westport • *Westport & Rideau Lakes C/C* • 1 Spring St.; P.O. Box 157; K0G 1X0; P 9,000; M 115; (613) 273-2929; therideaucalls@gmail.com; www.therideaucalls.com

Whitby • *Whitby C/C* • Gordon Mackey CSP CAE; CEO; 128 Brock St. S.; L1N 4J8; P 120,000; M 1,000; (905) 668-4506; Fax (905) 668-1894; info@whitbychamber.org; www.whitbychamber.org

Windsor • *Windsor-Essex Reg. C/C* • Matt Marchand; Pres./CEO; 2575 Ouellette Pl.; N8X 1L9; P 323,000; M 1,300; (519) 966-3696; Fax (519) 966-0603; info@windsorchamber.org; www.windsorchamber.org

Woodbridge • *see Vaughan*

Woodstock • *Woodstock Dist. C/C •* Deb Masters; Gen. Mgr.; 476 Peel St., 3rd Flr.; N4S 1K1; P 37,700; M 375; (519) 539-9411; (519) 536-3309; Fax (519) 456-1611; info@woodstockchamber.ca; www.woodstockchamber.on.ca

Young's Point • *see Lakefield*

Prince Edward

Alberton • *West Prince C/C •* John Lane; 455 Main St.; P.O. Box 220; C0B 1B0; P 1,100; M 50; (902) 853-4555; Fax (902) 853-3298; chamber@resourceswest.pe.ca; www.resourceswest.pe.ca

Charlottetown • *Greater Charlottetown Area C/C •* Kathy Hambly; Exec. Dir.; 134 Kent St., Ste. 230; P.O. Box 67; C1A 7K2; P 140,000; M 1,000; (902) 628-2000; Fax (902) 368-3570; chamber@charlottetownchamber.com; www.charlottetownchamber.com*

Crapaud • *South Shore C/C •* Cathie Thomas; Secy.; P.O. Box 127; C0A 1J0; P 10,000; M 60; (902) 437-2510

Kensington • *Kensington & Area C/C •* Glenna Lohnes; Mgr.; P.O. Box 234; C0B 1M0; P 6,000; M 100; (902) 836-3209; kacc@pei.aibn.com; www.kensington.ca/chamber

Montague • *Eastern Prince Edward Island C/C •* Joan Gleadall; P.O. Box 1593; C0A 1R0; P 137,000; M 1,300; (902) 838-4791; (800) 274-3825; Fax (902) 836-4427; info@peibwa.org; www.peibwa.org

Summerside • *Greater Summerside C/C •* Jane Sharpe; Exec. Dir.; 263 Heather Moyse Dr., Ste. 10; C1N 5P1; P 15,000; M 400; (902) 436-9651; Fax (902) 436-8320; info@summersidechamber.com; www.summersidechamber.com

Quebec

Federation des chambres de commerce du Quebec • Francoise Bertrand; CEO; 555 Rene-Levesque Blvd. W., 11th Flr.; Montreal; H2Z 1B1; P 8,000,000; M 60,000; (514) 844-9571; Fax (514) 844-0226; info@fccq.ca; www.fccq.ca

Alma • *Chambre de Commerce Lac-Sainte-Jean-Est •* 625, rue Bergeron ouest; G8B 1V3; P 31,000; (418) 662-2734; Fax (418) 669-2220; cca@qc.aira.com

Amos • *Chambre de Commerce D'Amos-Region •* Donald Blanchet; Pres.; C.P. 93; J9T 3X4; P 17,100; (819) 732-8100; Fax (819) 732-8101; ccar@ccar.qc.ca; www.ccar.qc.ca

Baie-Comeau • *Chambre de Commerce de Manicouagan •* Genevieve Parent; 67 LaSalle Place, Local #302; G4Z 1K1; P 28,800; (418) 296-2010; Fax (418) 296-5397; info@ccmanic.qc.ca; www.ccmanic.qc.ca

Becancour • *Chambre de Commerce de Becancour •* Jean-Denis Girard; Pres.; 1045 ave. Nicolas Perrot; G9H 3B7; P 12,000; M 519; (819) 294-6010; Fax (819) 294-6020; info@ccicq.ca; www.ccicq.ca

Beloeil • *Vallee du Richelieu C/C •* Christine Richer; Pres.; 230, rue Brebeuf, bureau 102; J3G 5P3; P 51,000; (450) 464-3733; Fax (450) 446-4163; chambre@ccvr.qc.ca; www.ccvr.qc.ca

Chicoutimi • *Promotion Saguenay •* Ghislain Harvey; Pres.; 295, rue Racine Est.; C.P. 8266; G7H 5B7; P 145,000; (418) 698-3157; Fax (418) 698-3279; marie-josee.boudreault@saguenay.ca; www.ville.saguenay.qc.ca

Coaticook • *Chambre de Commerce et d'industrie de la Region de Coaticook •* Caroline Thibeault; Pres.; 150, rue Child; J1A 2B3; P 9,000; M 200; (819) 849-4733; info@ccircoaticook.ca; www.ccircoaticook.ca

Drummondville • *Chambre de Commerce de Drummond •* Alain Cote; Dir. Gen.; 234 Saint Marcel St.; C.P. 188; J2B 6V7; P 67,000; M 1,263; (819) 477-7822; Fax (819) 477-2823; info@ccid.qc.ca; www.ccid.qc.ca

East-Angus • *Chambre de Commerce de East Angus et Region •* 221 St. Jean St. West; J0B 1R0; P 4,000; M 100; (819) 832-4950; ccea@bellnet.ca

Ile d'Orleans • *Chambre de Commerce de L'Ile d'Orleans •* Sylvie Ann Tremblay; Gen. Dir.; 490, Cote du Pont; St-Pierre; G0A 4E0; P 8,000; M 116; (418) 828-0880; Fax (418) 828-2335; ccio@videotron.ca; www.cciledorleans.com

Joliette • *Chambre de Commerce du Grand Joliette •* 500, rue Dollard; J6E 4M4; P 47,000; M 200; (450) 759-6363; Fax (450) 759-5012; info@ccgj.qc.ca; www.ccgj.qc.ca

Jonquiere • *see Chicoutimi*

Laval • *Chambre de Commerce et D'Industrie de Laval •* 1555, boul. Chomedey, bureau 200; H7V 3Z1; P 286,000; M 2,300; (450) 682-5255; Fax (450) 682-5735; info@ccilaval.qc.ca; www.ccilaval.qc.ca

Levis • *Chambre de Commerce de Levis •* Christian Guay; Pres.; 5700, JB-Michaud St., Ofc. 225; G6V 0B1; P 130,000; M 1,000; (418) 837-3411; Fax (418) 837-8497; cclevis@cclevis.ca; www.cclevis.ca*

Longueuil • *Chambre de Commerce et d'Industrie de la Rive-Sud •* HélÃ¨ne Bergeron & Stéphanie Brodeur; Co-Directors; 85, rue Saint-Charles Ouest, bureau 101; J4H 1C5; P 400,000; M 1,900; (450) 463-2121; Fax (450) 463-1858; info@ccirs.qc.ca; www.ccirs.qc.ca

Louiseville • *Chambre de Commerce et d' Industrie de la MRC de Maskinonge •* Josee Lessard; Gen. Mgr.; 396, Ste-Elizabeth; J5V 1M8; P 17,000; M 300; (819) 228-8582; Fax (819) 228-8989; dg@cci-maskinonge.ca; www.cci-maskinonge.ca*

Maniwaki • *Chambre de Commerce et d'Industrie de Maniwaki •* Denis Bonhomme; Pres.; 186, rue King; Local 174; J9E 3N6; P 5,500; M 200; (819) 449-6627; Fax (819) 449-7667; info@ccimaniwaki.com; www.ccimki.ca

Mascouche • *Chambre de Commerce de Mascouche •* Vicky Marchand; Dir. Gen.; 760 Montée Masson bur. 204; J7K 3B6; P 42,400; M 306; (450) 966-1536; Fax (450) 966-1531; info@ccmascouche.com; www.ccmascouche.com

Montreal • *Board of Trade of Metropolitan Montreal •* Michel Leblanc; Pres./CEO; 380 St. Antoine St. W. #6000; H2Y 3X7; P 3,000,000; M 7,000; (514) 871-4000; Fax (514) 871-1255; info@ccmm.qc.ca; www.btmm.qc.ca

Normandin • *Chambre de Commerce du Secteur de Normandin •* 1048, rue St-Cyrille; G8M 4R9; P 3,300; (418) 274-2004; Fax (418) 274-7171; ccnormandin@hotmail.com

Pointe-Calumet • *Chambre de Commerce du Lac Des Deux-Montagnes •* 190, 41st Avenue #400; J0N 1G2; P 31,000; (450) 472-7535; Fax (450) 472-0229; c.c.lac2montagnes@videotron.ca; www.cclac2montagnes.com

Pointe-Claire • *West Island of Montreal C/C* • Joseph Huza; Pres./Exec. Dir.; 1870 Blvd. des Sources, Ste. 106; H9R 5N4; P 350,000; M 850; (514) 697-4228; Fax (514) 697-2562; info@ccoim.ca; www.ccoim.ca

Quebec • *Chambre de Commerce et d'industrie de Quebec* • Mr. Alain Aubut; Pres./CEO; 17, rue St-Louis; G1R 3Y8; P 766,000; M 4,600; (418) 692-3853; Fax (418) 694-2286; info@cciquebec.ca; www.cciquebec.ca

Rimouski • *Chambre de Commerce de Rimouski-Neigette* • Annie St-Laurent; Coord.; 23, rue de l'Eveche Ouest; CP 1296; G5L 8M2; P 40,000; M 350; (418) 722-4494; Fax (418) 722-8402; ccriki@ccrimouski.com; www.ccrimouski.com

Roberval • *Chambre de Commerce et d'industrie de Roberval* • Pascal Gagnon; Gen. Mgr.; P.O. Box 115; G8H 2N4; P 15,000; M 140; (418) 275-3504; Fax (418) 275-0851; info@ccisr.qc.ca; www.ccisr.qc.ca

Rouyn-Noranda • *Chambre de Commerce du Rouyn-Noranda Regional* • M. Jean-Claude Loranger; Pres.; 70 Avenue du lac; J9X 4N4; P 41,800; M 1,100; (819) 797-2000; Fax (819) 762-3091; reseau@ccirn.qc.ca; www.ccirn.qc.ca

Saint-Jean-de-Matha • *Chambre de Commerce St-Jean-de-Matha* • Bernard Chasse; Pres.; 1159 route Louis-Cyr; J0K 2S0; P 3,030; M 52; (450) 886-0599; Fax (450) 886-3123; info@chambrematha.com; www.chambrematha.com

Saint-Martin-de-Beauce • *Chambre de Commerce de St-Martin de Beauce* • Diane Bilton; Admin. Secy.; C.P. 2022; G0M 1B0; P 2,500; M 65; (418) 382-5549; Fax (418) 382-5512; chambre@st-martin.qc.ca; www.st-martin.qc.ca

Salaberry-de-Valleyfield • *Chambre de Comm. Reg. de Salaberry-de-Valleyfield* • Sylvie Villemure; Dir. Gen.; 100, rue Ste-Cecile, bureau 400; J6T 1M1; P 40,000; (450) 373-8789; Fax (450) 373-8642; info@ccrsv.com; www.ccrsv.com

Sept Iles • *Chambre de Commerce de Sept-Iles* • Ginette Le-houx; Gen. Mgr.; 700, Boul Laure, bureau 237; G4R 1Y1; P 28,500; M 450; (418) 968-3488; Fax (418) 968-3432; ccsi@globetrotter.net; www.ccseptiles.com

Sept-Iles • *Corporation Touristique de Sept-Iles, Inc.* • Marie-Eve Cyr; Gen. Mgr.; 1401 Blvd. Laure Quest; G4R 4K1; P 28,500; (418) 962-1238; Fax (418) 968-0022; info@tourismeseptiles.ca; www.tourismeseptiles.ca

Sorel-Tracy • *Chambre de Commerce Sorel-Tracy Metropolitan* • Marie-France Carra; Pres.; 67 George St., bureau 112; J3P 1C2; P 35,000; M 430; (450) 742-0018; Fax (450) 742-7442; ccstm@ccstm.qc.ca; www.ccstm.qc.ca

St-Donat • *Tourist Info. Office de St-Donat* • Sophie Charpentier; Dir.; 536, rue Principale; J0T 2C0; P 4,300; (819) 424-2833; (888) 783-6628; Fax (819) 424-3809; tourisme@saint-donat.com; www.saint-donat.com

St-Georges • *Chambre de Commerce de St-Georges* • Nathalie Roy; Dir. Gen.; 8585, boul Lacroix, bureau 310; G5Y 5L6; P 26,000; (418) 228-7879; Fax (418) 228-8074; reception@ccstgeorges.com; www.ccstgeorges.com

St-Jerome • *Chambre de Commerce St-Jerome* • 309, rue De Villemure; J7Z 5J5; P 58,000; (450) 431-4339; Fax (450) 431-1677; chambre@ccisj.qc.ca; www.ccisj.qc.ca

St-Laurent • *Chambre de Commerce de St-Laurent* • Sylvie Sequin; Gen. Mgr.; 935 Decarie #204; H4L 3M3; P 85,000; M 840; (514) 333-5222; Fax (514) 333-0937; info@ccstl.qc.ca; www.ccstl.qc.ca

St-Raymond • *Chambre de Commerce de St-Raymond* • Charlotte Cote; 100, rue St-Jacques Bureau 1; G3L 3Y1; P 10,000; M 185; (418) 337-4049; Fax (418) 337-8017; ccrsr@cige.com; www.ccrsr

Ste-Agathe-des-Monts • *Sainte-Agathe-des-Monts C/C* • Daniel Desjardins; Dir. Gen.; 24, rue St-Paul-Est; C.P. 323; J8C 3C6; P 10,000; M 340; (819) 326-3731; (888) 326-0457; Fax (819) 326-3936; info@sainte-agathe.org; www.sainte-agathe.org

Ste-Justine • *Chambre de Commerce de Ste-Justine* • 167, Rte. 204; G0R 1Y0; P 2,000; (418) 383-3207; sjustine@sogetel.net; www.stejustine.net

Temiscaming • *Chambre de Commerce de Temiscaming-Kipawa* • Nathalie Labrosse Lebel; Coord.; C.P. 442; J0Z 3R0; P 4,500; M 60; (819) 627-6160; Fax (819) 627-3390; cctk@temiscaming.net; www.temiscaming.net

Terrebonne • *Chambre de Commerce de Terrebonne* • Robert Lalancette; Dir. Gen./CEO; 1025, montee Masson, #301; J6W 5H9; P 106,000; M 600; (450) 471-8779; Fax (450) 471-5610; admin@ccterrebonne.qc.ca; www.ccterrebonne.qc.ca

Trois-Rivieres • *Ofc de Tourisme et des Congres de Trois Rivieres* • Yolaine Masse; Dir.; 370, rue des Forges, bur. 100; G9A 2H1; P 125,000; M 150; (819) 374-4061; Fax (819) 373-6511; coordination@tourismetroisrivieres.com; www.v3r.net

Trois-Rivieres • *Chambre de commerce et d'industries de Trois-Rivieres* • Marie-Pier Matteau; Gen. Dir.; 225, rue des Forges, bur. 200; P.O. Box 1045; G9A 5K4; P 126,000; M 900; (819) 375-9628; Fax (819) 375-9083; info@ccitr.net; www.ccitr.net

Val-d'Or • *Chambre de Commerce de Val-d'Or* • 921,3e Ave. - Bureau 200; J9P 1T4; P 33,300; M 1,000; (819) 825-3703; Fax (819) 825-8599; info@ccvd.qc.ca; www.ccvd.qc.ca

Weedon • *Chambre de Commerce de la Region de Weedon* • 280 9th Ave.; J0B 3J0; P 1,200; M 60; (819) 560-8555; admin@ccweedon.com; www.ccweedon.com

Saskatchewan

Saskatchewan C/C • Steve McLellan; CEO; 1630 Chateau Tower; 1920 Broad St.; Regina; S4P 3V2; P 1,000,000; M 1,500; (306) 352-2671; Fax (306) 781-7084; info@saskchamber.com; www.saskchamber.com

Aylsham • *Aylsham & Dist. Bd. of Trade* • Glen Gray; Pres.; P.O. Box 21; S0E 0C0; P 200; M 30; (306) 862-3822; Fax (306) 862-4384; b.ander@sasktel.net

Broadview • *Broadview C/C* • Donna Brown; P.O. Box 119; S0G 0K0; P 800; M 12; (306) 696-7689; www.broadview.ca

Coronach • *Coronach Comm. C/C* • Jackie Marshall; Pres.; P.O. Box 577; S0H 0Z0; P 950; M 26; (306) 267-5734; (306) 267-2077; Fax (306) 267-2047; marshalljackie@hotmail.com; www.townofcoronach.com

Eastend • *Eastend & Dist. C/C* • Matthew Johnston; Chair; P.O. Box 534; S0N 0T0; P 560; M 50; (306) 295-7480; Fax (306) 295-3883; matthew.johnston@innovationcu.ca; www.townofeastend.com

Esterhazy • *Esterhazy & Dist. C/C* • General Delivery; S0A 0X0; P 2,800; M 45; (306) 745-5405; Fax (306) 745-6797; esterhazy.ed@sasktel.net; www.townofesterhazy.com

Estevan • *Estevan C/C* • Jackie Wall; Exec. Dir.; 2-322 4th St.; S4A 0T8; P 13,000; M 325; (306) 634-2828; Fax (306) 634-6729; admin@estevanchamber.ca; www.estevanchamber.ca

Foam Lake • *Foam Lake C/C* • Jinnie Johnson; Pres.; P.O. Box 238; S0A 1A0; P 1,400; M 75; (306) 272-4443; flchamberofcommerce@sasktel.net; www.foamlake.com

Fort Qu'Appelle • *Fort Qu'Appelle & Dist. C/C* • Michelle Johns; Treas.; 203 Broadway St.; P.O. Box 1273; S0G 1S0; P 10,000; M 60; (306) 332-5717; fqchamber@hotmail.com; www.fortquappelle.com

Fox Valley • *Fox Valley C/C* • Delia Hughes; Secy.; Railway Box 72; S0N 0V0; P 350; M 45; (306) 666-2139

Herbert • *Herbert & Dist. C/C* • Doreen Shroeder; Box 370; S0H 2A0; P 840; M 25; (306) 784-2400; t.o.herbert@sasktel.net

Humboldt • *Humboldt & Dist. C/C* • Crystal Young; Exec. Dir.; 640 - 9th St.; Box 1440; S0K 2A0; P 6,800; M 263; (306) 682-4990; Fax (306) 682-5203; humboldtchamber@sasktel.net; www.humboldtchamber.ca

Kenaston • *Kenaston & Dist. C/C* • ML Whittles; Pres.; P.O. Box 253; S0G 2N0; P 320; M 32; (306) 252-2236; r.m.whittles@sasktel.net; www.kenaston.ca

Kerrobert • *Kerrobert C/C* • Phyllis M. Barth; Admin. Asst.; P.O. Box 408; S0L 1R0; P 1,250; M 45; (306) 834-5423; kerrobertchamber@sasktel.net; www.kerrobertsk.com

Kindersley • *Kindersley C/C* • Heather Wall; Ofc. Mgr.; 605 Main St.; Box 1537; S0L 1S0; P 5,500; M 120; (306) 463-2320; Fax (306) 463-2312; kindersleychamber@sasktel.net; www.kindersleychamber.com

La Ronge • *La Ronge & Dist. C/C* • Betty Hutchinson; Pres.; P.O. Box 1493; S0J 1L0; P 2,750; M 100; (306) 425-4744; (306) 425-2195; chamber@laclarongechamber.ca; laclarongechamber.ca

Maple Creek • *Maple Creek C/C* • Blaine Filthaut; Pres.; P.O. Box 1776; S0N 1N0; P 3,000; M 45; (306) 661-8119; info@maplecreekchamber.ca; www.maplecreekchamber.ca

Meadow Lake • *Meadow Lake & Dist. C/C* • Adriane Ouellette; Admin.; 902 - Hwy. 4 S.; P.O. Box 847; S9X 1Y6; P 6,000; M 130; (306) 236-4061; Fax (306) 236-4031; mlchamberofcommerce@sasktel.net; www.meadowlakechamber.ca

Melfort • *Melfort & Dist. C/C* • Nicole Gagne; Exec. Dir.; P.O. Box 2002; S0E 1A0; P 7,000; M 145; (306) 752-4636; Fax (306) 752-9505; melfortchamber@sasktel.net; www.melfortchamber.com

Melville • *Melville & Dist. C/C* • Joanne Kirwan; Exec. Dir.; 76 Halifax Ave.; P.O. Box 429; S0A 2P0; P 4,700; M 62; (306) 728-4177; Fax (306) 728-5911; melvillechamber@sasktel.net; www.melvillechamber.com

Moose Jaw • *Moose Jaw & Dist. C/C* • Brian Martynook; CEO; 88 Saskatchewan St. E.; S6H 0V4; P 35,000; M 525; (306) 692-6414; Fax (306) 694-6463; chamber@mjchamber.com; www.mjchamber.com

Moosomin • *Moosomin C/C* • Ed Hilderbrandt; Pres.; P.O. Box 819; S0G 3N0; P 2,500; M 100; (306) 435-3175; Fax (306) 435-2540; world_spectator@sasktel.net

Nipawin • *Nipawin & Dist. C/C* • Shellan Baranieski; Exec. Dir.; 308 Nipawin Rd. E.; P.O. Box 177; S0E 1E0; P 5,000; M 140; (306) 862-5252; Fax (306) 862-5350; nipawin.chamber@sasktel.net; www.nipawinchamber.ca

Norquay • *Norquay & Dist. C/C* • Kevin Ebert; Pres.; P.O. Box 457; S0A 2V0; P 435; M 32; (306) 594-2101; Fax (306) 594-2347; norquay@sasktel.net; www.norquay.ca

North Battleford • *Battlefords C/C* • Linda Machniak; Exec. Dir.; Jct. of Hwy. 16 & 40 E.; P.O. Box 1000; S9A 3E6; P 20,000; M 380; (306) 445-6226; Fax (306) 445-6633; b.chamber@sasktel.net; www.battlefordschamber.com

Outlook • *Outlook & Dist. C/C* • Justin Turton; Pres.; P.O. Box 431; S0L 2N0; P 5,000; M 50; (306) 867-9944; outlookchamber@gmail.com; outlookchamber.webs.com

Prince Albert • *Prince Albert & Dist. C/C* • Merle Lacert; CEO; 3700 2nd Ave. W.; S6W 1A2; P 36,000; M 520; (306) 764-6222; Fax (306) 922-4727; admin.pachamber@sasktel.net; www.princealbertchamber.com

Redvers • *Redvers C/C* • P.O. Box 249; S0C 2H0; P 975; M 47; (306) 452-3255; Fax (306) 452-3155; redverschamberofcommerce@gmail.com

Regina • *Regina & Dist. C/C* • John Hopkins; CEO; 2145 Albert St.; S4P 2V1; P 199,974; M 1,300; (306) 757-4658; Fax (306) 757-4668; info@reginachamber.com; www.reginachamber.com*

Saskatoon • *Greater Saskatoon C/C* • Kent Smith-Windsor; Exec. Dir.; 104-202 4th Ave. N.; S7K 0K1; P 258,000; M 1,900; (306) 244-2151; Fax (306) 244-8366; chamber@saskatoonchamber.com; www.saskatoonchamber.com

Shaunavon • *Shaunavon C/C* • Joanne Gregoire; Pres.; 299 Center St.; P.O. Box 1048; S0N 2M0; P 2,500; M 87; (306) 297-2134; shaunavonchamber@hotmail.com; www.shaunavon.com

Spiritwood • *Spiritwood & Dist. C/C* • George Pretly; Pres.; P.O. Box 267; S0J 2M0; P 918; M 116; (306) 883-2426; Fax (306) 883-2427; www.townofspiritwood.ca

Swift Current • *Swift Current & Dist. C/C* • Clayton Wicks; CEO; Swift Current Bus. Centre; 145 1st Ave. N.E.; S9H 2B1; P 17,500; M 343; (306) 773-7268; Fax (306) 773-5686; info@swiftcurrentchamber.ca; www.swiftcurrentchamber.ca

Tisdale • *Tisdale & District C/C* • Rachelle Casavant; P.O. Box 219; S0E 1T0; P 3,500; M 150; (306) 873-4257; Fax (306) 873-4241; tisdalechamber@sasktel.net; www.tisdalechamber.com

Turtleford • *Turtleford C/C* • Charlene Marcs; Pres.; P.O. Box 177; S0M 2Y0; P 550; M 20; (306) 845-3021

Watson • *Watson & Dist. C/C* • Debbie Schwartz; Treas.; P.O. Box 686; S0K 4V0; P 800; M 50; (306) 287-3636; www.townofwatson.ca

Weyburn • *Weyburn C/C* • Rochelle Wendt; Mgr.; 11 Third St. N.E.; S4H 0W5; P 12,000; M 210; (306) 842-4738; Fax (306) 842-0520; info@weyburnchamber.com; www.weyburnchamber.com

Yorkton • *Yorkton C/C* • Juanita Polegi; Exec. Dir.; P.O. Box 1051; S3N 2X3; P 20,000; M 450; (306) 783-4368; Fax (306) 786-6978; yorktonchamber@sasktel.net; www.yorktonchamber.com

Yukon

Dawson City • *Dawson City C/C* • Coralee Rudachyk; Gen. Mgr.; P.O. Box 1006; Y0B 1G0; P 2,000; (867) 993-5274; Fax (867) 993-6817; office@dawsoncitychamberofcommerce.ca; www.dawsoncitychamberofcommerce.ca

Whitehorse • *Whitehorse C/C* • Rick Karp; Pres.; 101 - 302 Steele St.; Y1A 2C5; P 28,000; (867) 667-7545; Fax (867) 667-4507; business@whitehorsechamber.ca; www.whitehorsechamber.ca

AMERICAN CHAMBERS OF COMMERCE ABROAD

American Chambers of Commerce Abroad are voluntary associations of American enterprises and individuals doing business in a particular country, as well as firms and individuals of that country who operate in the U.S.

Along with pursuing trade policy initiatives, AmChams make available publications and services and sponsor a variety of business development programs. The AmChams represent the concerns and interests of the business community at the highest levels of government and business in trade policy development.

AmChams also:

• Develop mutually prosperous and amicable economic, social and commercial relations between U.S. businesses and service industries and those of the host country.

• Represent members' views on policy and regulatory matters to both U.S. and host country governments and interpret the point of view of other countries to the American business public.

• Promote local economic and social contributions for the benefit of host countries.

Albania

Tirana • *American Chamber of Commerce in Albania* • Rr. Deshmoret e 4 shkurtit; Sky Tower, kati 11 Ap 3; P 3,204,284; 355-22-59779; Fax 355-22-35350; info@amcham.com.al; www.amcham.com.al

Argentina

Buenos Aires • *American Chamber of Commerce in Argentina* • Alejandro Diaz; CEO; Viamonte 1133 Piso 8; C1053ABW; P 40,412,376; 5411-4371-4500; Fax 5411-4371-8400; amcham@amchamar.com.ar; www.amchamar.com.ar

Armenia

Yerevan • *American Chamber of Commerce in Armenia* • Irina Chobanyan; Interim Exec. Dir.; 1 Amiryan street, Armenia Marriott Hotel, 3th Flr., Rm. 315, 317; 0010; P 3,000,000; 374-10-599-187; Fax 374-10-587-651; amcham@arminco.com; www.amcham.am

Asia

Ho Chi Minh City • *Asia-Pacific Cncl. of American Chambers of Commerce* • Chris Twomey; Chrmn.; % Car Rental Svcs. Joint Stock Co.; 21 Phung Khac Khoan St., Dist. 1; 84-8-3930-1118; Fax 84-8-3941-5445; www.apcac.org

Australia

Sydney • *American Chamber of Commerce in Australia* • Niels Marquardt; CEO; Ste. 9, Ground Level; 88 Cumberland St.; 2000; P 22,328,800; 02-8031-9000; Fax 02-9251-5220; receptionnsw@amcham.com.au; www.amcham.com.au

Austria

Vienna • *American Chamber of Commerce in Austria* • Mag. Daniela Homan; Exec. Dir.; Porzellangasse 39/7; 1090; P 8,384,745; 43-1-319-57-51; Fax 43-1-319-57-51-15; office@amcham.at; www.amcham.at

Bahrain

Manama • *American Chamber of Commerce in Bahrain* • Hamid Al Zayani; V.P. of Programs; Ministry of Ind. & Commerce, Ground Flr.; Bldg. 240, Rd. 1704, Block 317; P 1,261,835; 973-17-522-777; Fax 973-17-522-737; info@amcham-bahrain.org; www.amcham-bahrain.org

Bangladesh

Dhaka • *American Chamber of Commerce in Bangladesh* • A. Gafur; Exec. Dir.; Rm No. 319, Ruposhi Bangla Hotel; 1000; P 148,692,130; 880-2-8330001; Fax 880-2-9349217; amcham@amchambd.org; www.amchambd.org

Belgium

Brussels • *American Chamber of Commerce in Belgium* • Marcel Claes; Chief Exec.; rue du TrÃ´ne 60/6 Troonstraat; 1050; P 11,000,000; 32-(0)2-513-67-70; Fax 32-(0)2-513-35-90; info@amcham.be; www.amcham.be

Bolivia

La Paz • *American Chamber of Commerce of Bolivia* • Claribel Aparicio Ferreira; Gen. Mgr.; Av. 6 de Agosto N; Edif. Hilda - Piso 2 Of. 204; P 9,929,849; 591-2-2443939; Fax 591-2-2443972; gerencia@amchambolivia.com; www.amchambolivia.com

Brazil

Rio de Janeiro • *American Chamber of Commerce for Brazil - Rio de Janiero* • Steven Bipes; Managing Dir.; Praca Pio X, 15/5th Flr., Centro; 20040-020; 55-21-3213-9200; 55-21-3213-9205; Fax 55-21-3213-9201; amchamrio@amchamrio.com; www.amchamrio.com

Sao Paulo, S.P. • *American Chamber of Commerce for Brazil-Sao Paulo* • Eduardo Wanick; Pres.; Rua da Paz, no. 1431; 04713-001; P 194,946,470; 55-11-3324-0194; Fax 55-11-5180-3777; ombudsman@amchambrasil.com.br; www.amcham.com.br

Bulgaria

Sofia • *American Chamber of Commerce in Bulgaria* • Valentin Georgiev; Exec. Dir.; Business Park Sofia, Mladost 4 Area; Bldg. 2, Flr. 6; 1766; P 7,543,325; 359-2-9742-743; Fax 359-2-9742-741; amcham@amcham.bg; www.amcham.bg

Cambodia

Phnom Penh • *American Cambodian Bus. Cncl.* • James Swander; Exec. Dir.; P.O. Box 1153; P 14,138,255; 855-15-333-715; 855-17-666-529; amcham@sa-cambodia.com; www.amchamcambodia.net

Canada

Manotick • *American Chamber of Commerce in Canada* • Rick Tachuk; National Chair; P.O. Box 492; K4M 1A5; P 34,108,752; info@amchamcanada.ca; www.amchamcanada.ca

Chile

Santiago • *Chilean-American Chamber of Commerce* • Jaime Bazan; Gen. Mgr.; Av. Kennedy 5735, Of. 201; Torre Poniente, Las Condes; P 17,113,688; 56-2-290-97-00; Fax 56-2-212-05-15; amcham@amchamchile.cl; www.amchamchile.cl

China

Beijing • *American Chamber of Commerce PRC Beijing* • Mark Duval; Pres.; The Office Park, Tower AB, 6th Flr.; No. 10 Jintongxi Rd.; 100020; P 133,829,9500; 86-10-8519-0800; Fax 86-10-8519-1910; amcham@amchamchina.org; www.amchamchina.org

Guangzhou • *American Chamber of Commerce in South China* • Harley Seyedin; Pres.; Ste. 1801, Guangzhou Sourcing Center; No.8 E. Pa Zhou Ave.; 510335; P 133,829,9500; 86-20-8335-1476; Fax 86-20-8332-1642; amcham@amcham-southchina.org; www.amcham-southchina.org

Macau • *American Chamber of Commerce in Macau* • Paul Tse; Chrmn.; Alameda Dr. Carlos d' Assumpcao, No. 263; Edif. China Civil Plaza, 20 Andar; P 138,829,9500; 853-2857-5059; Fax 853-2857-5060; info@amcham.org.mo; www.amcham.org.mo

Shanghai • *American Chamber of Commerce in Shanghai* • Mr. Kenneth Jarrett; Pres.; Shanghai Centre, Ste. 568; 1376 Nanjing Rd. W.; 200040; P 133,829,9500; 86-21-6279-7119; Fax 86-21-6279-7643; amcham@amcham-shanghai.org; www.amcham-shanghai.org

Colombia

Bogota • *Colombian-American Chamber of Commerce* • Camilo Reyes Rodriguez; Exec. Dir.; Calle 98 #22-64 Of. 1209; P 46,294,841; 571-587-78-28; Fax 571-587-78-28-2; direct@amchamcolombia.com.co; www.amchamcolombia.com.co

Costa Rica

San Jose • *Costa Rican-American Chamber of Commerce* • Catherine Reuben; Exec. Dir.; P.O. Box 4946; 1000; P 4,658,887; 506-2220-2200; Fax 506-2220-2300; chamber@amcham.co.cr; www.amcham.co.cr

Cote D'Ivoire

Abidjan • *American Chamber of Commerce of Cote d'Ivoire* • Deborah Gray; Pres.; Riviera Attoban 06; BP 2282; 6; P 21,504,162; 225-22-42-68-66; Fax 225-22-42-30-64; amchamci@ameritechafr.com; www.amchamci.org

Croatia

Zagreb • *American Chamber of Commerce in Croatia* • Mrs. Andrea Doko Jelusic; Exec. Dir.; Strojarska cesta 22; 10000; P 4,400,000; 385-1-4836-777; 385-1-4836-778; Fax 385-1-4836-776; info@amcham.hr; www.amcham.hr

Cyprus

Nicosia • *Cyprus-American Bus. Assn.* • Mr. Chris Christodoulou; Pres.; P.O. Box 21455; CY-1509; P 1,103,647; 357-22-889830; Fax 357-22-668630; cyaba@cyaba.com.cy; www.cyaba.com.cy

Czech Republic

Prague • *American Chamber of Commerce in the Czech Republic* • Weston Stacey; Exec. Dir.; Dusni 10; 110 00; P 10,512,400; 420-222-329-430; Fax 420-222-329-433; amcham@amcham.cz; www.amcham.cz

Denmark

Copenhagen • *American Chamber of Commerce in Denmark* • Stephen Brugger; Exec. Dir.; Christians Brygge 26; 1559; P 5,544,139; 45-33-932-932; Fax 45-33-932-938; mail@amcham.dk; www.amcham.dk

Dominican Republic

Santo Domingo • *American Chamber of Commerce of the Dominican Republic* • William M. Malamud; Exec. V.P.; Avenida Sarasota No. 20; Torre Empresearial 6to. Piso; P 9,927,320; 809-381-0777; Fax 809-381-0286; amcham@amcham.org.do; www.amcham.org.do

Ecuador

Guayaquil • *Ecuadorian-American Chamber of Commerce-Guayaquil* • Maria Antonieta Reyes De Luca; Exec. Dir.; Cdla. Kennedy Norte, Ave. Francisco de Orellana; Edificio Centrum, Piso 6, Oficina 5; P 14,464,739; 593-4-269-3470; Fax 593-4-269-3465; camara@amchamecuador.org; www.amchamecuador.org

Quito • *Ecuadorian-American Chamber of Commerce-Quito* • Felipe Espinosa; Exec. Dir.; Edificio Multicentro, Piso 4; La Nina y Avda. 6 de Diciembre; P 14,464,739; 593-2-2507450; Fax 593-2-2504571; info@ecamcham.com; www.ecamcham.com

Egypt

Cairo • *American Chamber of Commerce in Egypt* • Hisham A. Fahmy; CEO; 33 Soliman Abaza St.; Dokki-Giza; 12311; P 81,121,077; 20-2-3338-1050; Fax 20-2-3338-1060; infocenter@amcham.org.eg; www.amcham.org.eg

El Salvador

San Salvador • *American Chamber of Commerce of El Salvador* • Carmen Aida Mu; Exec. Dir.; Edificio World Trade Center, Torre II, Nivel 3, Local 308; 89 Avenida Norte, Colonia Escalon; P 6,058,580; 503-2263-9494; Fax 503-2263-9393; amchamsal@amchamsal.com; www.amchamsal.com

European Union

Brussels • *American Chamber of Commerce to the European Union* • Susan Danger; Managing Dir.; ave. des Arts/Kunstlaan 53; 1000; P 492,387,344; 32-2-513-68-92; Fax 32-2-513-79-28; info@amchameu.eu; www.amchameu.eu

Finland

Helsinki • *Amcham Finland* • Kristiina Helenius; CEO; Etelaranta 6 A 8; 130; P 5,500,000; 358-40-466-4576; info@amcham.fi; www.amcham.fi

France

Paris • *American Chamber of Commerce in France* • Caroline Ryan; Managing Dir.; 77 Rue de Miromesnil; 75008; P 64,876,618; 33-(0)1-5643-4567; Fax 33-(0)1-5643-4560; amchamfrance@amchamfrance.org; www.amchamfrance.org

Georgia

Tbilisi • *American Chamber of Commerce in Georgia* • George Welton; Exec. Dir.; 36a Lado Asatiani St.; 105; P 4,700,000; 995-32-2226907; Fax 995-32-226792; amcham@amcham.ge; www.amcham.ge

Germany

Frankfurt • *American Chamber of Commerce in Germany* • Dr. Dierk M; Gen. Mgr.; Borsenplatz 7-11; 60313; P 81,702,329; 49-69-929-104-0; Fax 49-69-929-104-11; amcham@amcham.de; www.amcham.de

Ghana

Cantonments-Accra • *American Chamber of Commerce in Ghana* • Mr. Simon Madjie; Exec. Secy.; 5th Crescent St., Asylum Down; P.O. Box CT2869; P 24,391,823; 233-030-224-7562; Fax 233-030-224-7562; info@amchamghana.org; www.amchamghana.org

Greece

Athens • *American-Hellenic Chamber of Commerce* • Elias Spirtounias; Exec. Dir.; 109-111 Messoghion Ave.; Politia Business Center; GR-115 26; P 11,319,048; 30-210-699-3559; Fax 30-210-698-5686; info@amcham.gr; www.amcham.gr

Guatemala

Ciudad • *American Chamber of Commerce in Guatemala* • Carolina Castellanos; Exec. Dir.; 5a Ave. 5-55, Zona 14 Edif. Europlaza WBC Torre I, Niv. 5; 1014; P 14,388,929; 502-2417-0800; Fax 502-2417-0777; recepcion@amchamguate.com; www.amchamguate.com

Haiti

Petion-Ville • *American Chamber of Commerce in Haiti* • Guy-Olivier Jeanty; Exec. Dir.; 18 Rue Moise; P 9,993,247; 509-2940-3024; gojeanty@amchamhaiti.com; amchamhaiti.com

Honduras

Tegucigalpa • *Honduran-American Chamber of Commerce* • Aracely Batres; Exec. Dir.; Edificio Torre Alianza I; P 7,600,524; 504-2271-0094; 504-2271-0095; Fax 504-271-0097; amcham@amchamhonduras.org; www.amchamhonduras.org

Hong Kong (China)

Central • *American Chamber of Commerce in Hong Kong* • Dr. Richard Vuylsteke; Pres.; 1904 Bank of America Tower; 12 Harcourt Rd.; P 7,067,800; 852-2530-6900; Fax 852-2810-1289; amcham@amcham.org.hk; www.amcham.org.hk

Hungary

Budapest • *American Chamber of Commerce in Hungary* • Ã risz Lippai-Nagy; CEO; Szent Istvan ter 11; 1051; P 90,000,000; 36-1-266-9880; Fax 36-1-266-9888; laszlo.metzing@amcham.hu; www.amcham.hu

India

New Delhi • *American Chamber of Commerce in India* • Mr. Ajay Singha; Exec. Dir.; PHD House, 4th Flr.; 4/2, Siri Institutional Area, August Kranti Marg; 110016; P 117,093,8000; 91-11-2652-5201; 91-11-2652-5202; Fax 91-11-2652-5203; amcham@amchamindia.com; www.amchamindia.com

Indonesia

Jakarta • *American Chamber of Commerce in Indonesia* • Lin Neumann; Managing Dir.; World Trade Center, 11th Flr.; Jl. Jend. Sudirman Kav. 29-31; 12920; P 239,870,940; 62-21-526-2860; Fax 62-21-526-2861; info@amcham.or.id; www.amcham.or.id

Ireland

Dublin • *American Chamber of Commerce in Ireland* • Joanne Richardson; CEO; 6 Wilton Pl.; 2; P 4,481,430; 353-1-6616201; Fax 353-1-6616217; info@amcham.ie; www.amcham.ie

Israel

Tel Aviv • *Israel-America Chamber of Commerce* • Oded Rose; CEO; 35 Shaul Hamelech Blvd.; P.O. Box 33174; 61333; P 7,624,600; 972-3-6952341; Fax 972-3-6951272; amcham@amcham.co.il; www.amcham.co.il

Italy

Milano • *American Chamber of Commerce in Italy* • Simone Crolla; Managing Dir.; Via Cesare Cant; 20123; P 60,000,000; 39-02-87-212-103; 39-02-86-90-661; Fax 39-02-87-212-103; amcham@amcham.it; www.amcham.it

Ivory Coast

See Cote d'Ivoire

Jamaica

Kingston • *American Chamber of Commerce of Jamaica* • Mrs. Gail Abrahams; CEO; The Jamaica Pegasus Hotel; 81 Knutsford Blvd., Ste. 106; 5; P 2,700,000; 876-929-7866-7; 876-968-2090; Fax 876-929-8597; amcham.ja@gmail.com; www.amchamjamaica.org

Japan

Okinawa City • *American Chamber of Commerce in Okinawa* • Mr. Tony Sakuda; Pres.; P.O. Box 235; 904-8591; P 127,450,460; 81-98-898-5401; Fax 81-98-898-5411; chamber@amchamokinawa.org; www.amchamokinawa.org

Tokyo • *American Chamber of Commerce in Japan* • Laurence W. Bates; Pres.; Masonic 39, MT Bldg. 10F; 2-4-5 Azabudai, Minato-ku; 106-0041; P 127,450,460; 03-3433-5381; 03-3433-7304; Fax 03-3436-8454; info@accj.or.jp; www.accj.or.jp

Jordan

Amman • *American Chamber of Commerce in Jordan* • Ahmad Tawfiq; Bus. Dev. Officer; P.O. Box 840817; 11184; P 8,047,000; 962-7-987-78708; Fax 962-6-565-1862; amcham@amcham.jo; www.amcham.jo

Kenya

Nairobi • *American Chamber of Commerce of Kenya* • Ms. Ferial Nathoo; CEO; Coca-Cola Central, East & West Africa Ltd., Kilimanjaro Rd., Upperhill; P. O. Box 9746; 100; P 40,512,682; 254-733-880458; 254-020-325 3350; Fax 254-20-3750448; info@amcham.co.ke; www.amcham.co.ke

Korea

Seoul • *American Chamber of Commerce in Korea* • Amy Jackson; Pres.; #4501, Trade Tower, 159-1; Samsung-dong, Kangnam-gu; 135-729; P 48,875,000; 82-2-6201-2200; Fax 82-2-564-2050; amchamrsvp@amchamkorea.org; www.amchamkorea.org

Kosovo

Prishtina • *American Chamber of Commerce in Kosovo* • Arian Zeka; Exec. Dir.; Perandori Justinian Nr. 16; 10000; P 1,805,000; 381-38-609-013; 381-38-609-012; Fax 381-38-609-012; arian.zeka@amchamksv.org; www.amchamksv.org

Kuwait

Salwa • *American Bus. Cncl. of Kuwait* • Ms. Muna Al Fuzai; Exec. Dir.; Salwa, Blk. 11, St. 7, Bld. 15, Pillars Apt. 2; P 2,736,732; 2-563-4051; Fax 2-563-4051; muna@abckw.org; www.abckw.org

Kyrgyz Republic

Bishkek • *American Chamber of Commerce in the Kyrgyz Republic* • Zarina Chekirbaeva; Exec. Dir.; 191 Abdrakhmanova Str., off. #123; 720011; P 5,000,000; 996-312-62-33-89; 996-312-62-34-06; Fax 996-312-62-34-06; memberservices@amcham.kg; www.amcham.kg

Latvia

Riga • *American Chamber of Commerce in Latvia* • Liga Smildzina-Bertulsone; Exec. Dir.; Torna iela 4, IIA, 301; LV-1050; P 2,000,000; 371-6721-2204; Fax 371-6732-3521; amcham@amcham.lv; www.amcham.lv

Lebanon

Beruit • *American Lebanese Chamber of Commerce* • Ms. Paola Chakhtoura; Exec. Dir.; 1153 Foch St., Beirut Central Dist.; P.O. Box 175093; P 4,223,553; 961-1-98-5330; Fax 961-1-98-5331; info@amcham.org.lb; www.amcham.org.lb

Lithuania

Vilnius • *American Chamber of Commerce in Lithuania* • Zivile Sabaliauskaite; Exec. Dir.; Konstitucijos 26 (1st Flr.); LT-08105; P 2,921,262; 370-5-261-1181; Fax 370-5-212-6128; info@amcham.lt; www.amcham.lt

Luxembourg

Luxembourg • *American Chamber of Commerce in Luxembourg* • Paul-Michael Schonenberg; Chrmn./CEO; 6, rue Antoine de St-Exup; L-1432; P 505,831; 352-43-1756; Fax 352-26-09-4704; info@amcham.lu; www.amcham.lu

Malaysia

Kuala Lumpur • *American Malaysian Chamber of Commerce* • Anne Marie Brooks; Exec. Dir.; Ste. 6 - 1A, Level 6; Menara CIMB, Jalan Stesen, Sentral 2; 55100; P 28,401,017; 603-2148-2407; Fax 603-2142-8540; info@amcham.com.my; www.amcham.com.my

Mexico

Garza Garcia, N.L. • *American Chamber of Commerce of Mexico - Monterrey* • Rio Manzanares 434 Oriente; Col. Del Valle; 66220; P 113,423,050; 52-81-8114-2000; Fax 52-81-8114-2100; socios_mty@amcham.org.mx; www.amcham.org.mx

Mexico City • *American Chamber of Commerce of Mexico* • Guillermo Wolf; Exec. V.P./Gen. Dir.; Blas Pascal 205, 3.er piso; Col. Los Morales; 11510; P 113,423,050; 52-55-5141-3800; Fax 52-55-5141-3835; amchammx@amcham.org.mx; www.amcham.com.mx

Zapopan, Jal. • *American Chamber of Commerce of Mexico - Guadalajara* • Av. Moctezuma 442; Col. Jardines del Sol; 45050; P 113,423,050; 52-33-3634-6606; Fax 52-33-3634-7374; gbricio@amcham.org.mx; www.amcham.com.mx

Montenegro

Podgorica • *American Chamber of Commerce in Montenegro* • Milica DragojeviÄ‡; Interim Exec. Dir.; Rimski trg 4/V; 81000; P 625,000; 382-20-621-328; Fax 382-20-621-628; info@amcham.me; www.amcham.me

Netherlands

Amsterdam • *American Chamber of Commerce in the Netherlands* • Patrick Mikkelsen; Exec. Dir.; Vijzelstraat 68-78; Schiphol Blvd. 171; 1017 HL; P 16,612,213; 31-20-795-1840; Fax 31-20-795-1850; office@amcham.nl; www.amcham.nl

New Zealand

Auckland • *American Chamber of Commerce in New Zealand Inc.* • Mike Hearn; Exec. Dir.; P.O. Box 106 002 Auckland Central; 1143; P 4,471,000; 64-9-309-9140; Fax 64-9-309-1090; amcham@amcham.co.nz; www.amcham.co.nz

Nicaragua

Managua • *American Chamber of Commerce of Nicaragua* • Avil Ramirez; Exec. Dir.; P.O. Box 2720; P 5,788,163; 505-2266-2758; Fax 505-2266-2758; publicrelations@amcham.org.ni; www.amcham.org.ni

Norway

Oslo • *American Chamber of Commerce in Norway* • Jason Turflinger; Managing Dir.; Lille Grensen 5; 159; P 5,033,675; 47-22-41-50-10; Fax 47-22-41-50-11; amcham@amcham.no; www.amcham.no

Pakistan

Karachi • *American Bus. Cncl. of Pakistan* • Ms. Amna Daudi; Secy. Gen.; F-30, Block-7, K.D.A. Scheme No. 5; Kehkashan Clifton; P 173,593,380; 021-35877351-52; Fax 021-35877391; abcpak@cyber.net.pk; www.abcpk.org.pk

Panama

Marbella • *American Chamber of Commerce & Ind. of Panama* • C.E. Maurice Belanger; Exec. Dir.; Ocean Business Plaza, Suite 1709; Ave. Aquilino de la Guardia & 47 St.; P 3,608,431; 507-301-3881; Fax 507-301-3882; executivedirector@panamcham.com; www.panamcham.com

Paraguay

Asuncion • *Paraguayan American Chamber of Commerce* • Jose Luis Salomon; Gen. Mgr.; 25 de Mayo 2090 & Mayor Bullo; 1535; P 7,000,000; 595-21-222-160; Fax 595-21-222-160; pamcham@pamcham.com.py; www.pamcham.com.py

Peru

Lima • *American Chamber of Commerce of Peru* • Aldo R. Defilippi; Exec. Dir.; Av. Victor Andres Belaunde 177; San Isidro; 27; P 29,076,512; 511-705-8000; Fax 511-705-8026; amcham@amcham.org.pe; www.amcham.org.pe

Philippines

Manila • *American Chamber of Commerce of the Philippines* • Ebb Hinchliffe; Exec. Dir.; 2nd Flr., Corinthian Plaza Bldg.; Paseo de Roxas, Makati City; 1229; P 93,260,798; 63-2-818-7911; Fax 63-2-811-3081; amcham@amchamphilippines.com; www.amchamphilippines.com

Poland

Warsaw • *American Chamber of Commerce in Poland* • Dorota Dabrowski; Exec. Dir.; Warsaw Financial Center; ul. E. Plater 53; PL-00-113; P 38,187,488; 48-22-520-5999; Fax 48-22-520-5998; office@amcham.com.pl; www.amcham.com.pl

Portugal

Lisbon • *American Chamber of Commerce in Portugal* • Graca Didier; Exec. Dir.; Rua D. Estefania nº155-5 5 Esq1000-1541000-154; P 10,642,841; 351-213-572-561; Fax 351-213-572-580; amchamportugal@mail.telepac.pt; www.amcham.org.pt

Republic of Macedonia

Skopje • *American Chamber of Commerce in Macedonia* • Michelle Osmanli; Exec. Dir.; Vasil Gjorgov 20A, 2nd Flr.; 1000; P 2,060,563; 389-2-3216-714; Fax 389-2-3246-950; info@amcham.com.mk; amcham.com.mk

Romania

Bucharest • *American Chamber of Commerce in Romania* • Anca Harasim; Exec. Dir.; 11 Ion Campineanu St.; Union International Center, 4th Flr.; 10031; P 19,043,767; 40-21-312-48-34; Fax 40-21-312-48-51; amcham@amcham.ro; www.amcham.ro

American C/C Abroad

Russia

Moscow • *American Chamber of Commerce in Russia* • Andrew B. Somers; Pres./CEO; Ulitsa Dolgorukovskaya 7, 14th Flr.; 127006; P 141,750,000; 7-495-961-2141; Fax 7-495-961-2142; asomers@amcham.ru; www.amcham.ru

Saudi Arabia

Al-Khobar • *American Bus. Assn., Eastern Province* • David Cantrell; Pres.; P.O. Box 3672; 31952; P 27,448,086; 966-3-882-5288 x1253; Fax 966-3-882-5288 x1497; abaep@abaksa.org; www.abaksa.org

Jeddah, KSA • *American Business Group of Jeddah (ABJ)* • Forrest Young Jr.; Pres.; InterContinental Hotel Jeddah; P.O. Box 41855; 21534; P 27,448,086; 966-050-701-4504; Fax 966-2-663-4674; manager@abj-sa.com; www.abj-sa.com

Serbia

Belgrade • *American Chamber of Commerce in Serbia* • Vera Nikolić Dimić; Exec. Dir.; Smiljaniceva 24/I; 11000; P 7,292,574; 381-11-30-88-132; Fax 381-11-30-88-922; info@amcham.rs; www.amcham.rs

Singapore

Singapore • *American Chamber of Commerce in Singapore* • Judith Fergin; Exec. Dir.; 1 Scotts Rd., Shaw Centre; #23-03/04/05; 228208; P 5,076,700; 65-6597-5730; Fax 65-6732-5917; contact@amcham.org.sg; www.amcham.org.sg

Slovak Republic

Bratislava • *American Chamber of Commerce in Slovakia* • Jake Slegers; Exec. Dir.; Hotel Crowne Plaza, 1st Flr.; Hodzovo nam 2; 811 06; P 5,433,456; 421-2-5464-0534; Fax 421-2-5464-0535; director@amcham.sk; www.amcham.sk

Slovenia

Ljubljana • *American Chamber of Commerce in Slovenia* • Ajsa Vodnik; Exec. Dir.; Dunajska cesta 156; 1000; P 2,052,821; 386-8-205-13-51; Fax 386-1-564-72-04; ajsa.vodnik@amcham.si; www.amcham.si

South Africa

Johannesburg • *American Chamber of Commerce in South Africa* • Carol O'Brien; Exec. Dir.; P.O. Box 1132, Houghton; 2041; P 49,991,300; 27-11-788-0265; Fax 27-11-880-1632; amcham@amcham.co.za; www.amcham.co.za

Spain

Barcelona • *American Chamber of Commerce in Spain* • Aida Casamitjana; Exec. Dir.; Calle Tuset 10, Piso 1; 8006; P 46,081,574; 34-93-415-99-63; Fax 34-93-415-11-98; amcham@amchamspain.com; www.amchamspain.com

Sri Lanka

Colombo • *American Chamber of Commerce in Sri Lanka* • Asanka Ratnayake; Pres.; 3rd. Flr., Aitken Spence Tower 1; 305, Vauxhall St.; 2; P 20,859,949; 94-11-2300116; Fax 94-11-2300118; info@amcham.lk; www.amcham.lk

Sweden

Stockholm • *American Chamber of Commerce in Sweden* • Peter R. Dahlen; Managing Dir.; Klarabergsviadukten 63; SE-111 64; P 9,804,082; 46-8-506-126-10; info@amcham.se; www.amcham.se

Switzerland

Zurich • *Swiss-American Chamber of Commerce* • Martin Senn; Chrmn.; Talacker 41; 8001; P 7,825,243; 41-43-443-72-00; Fax 41-43-497-22-70; info@amcham.ch; www.amcham.ch

Taiwan, Roc

Taipei • *American Chamber of Commerce in Taipei* • Andrea Wu; Pres.; 129 MinSheng E. Road, Sec. 3, 7F, Ste. 706; 10596; P 22,974,347; 886-2-2718-8226; Fax 886-2-2718-8182; amcham@amcham.com.tw; www.amcham.com.tw

Thailand

Bangkok • *American Chamber of Commerce in Thailand* • Judy Benn; Exec. Dir.; 7th Flr., GPF Witthayu Tower A; 93/1 Wireless Rd., Lumpini, Pathumwan; 10330; P 69,122,234; 66-0-2254-1041; Fax 66-0-2251-1605; execdirector@amchamthailand.com; www.amchamthailand.com

Trinidad & Tobago

Port of Spain • *American Chamber of Commerce of Trinidad & Tobago* • Mr. Nirad Tewarie; CEO; 62 Maraval Rd.; P.O. Bag 150, Newtown; P 1,341,465; 868-622-4466; Fax 868-628-9428; niradtewarie@amchamtt.com; www.amchamtt.com

Turkey

Istanbul • *Turkish-American Bus. Assn.* • Asude Yade Akdeniz; Exec. Mgr.; Cemiltopuzlu Caddesi, Bank of Turkey; Bloklari F24, blok, d:20 Fenerbahce Kadikoy; 34360; P 72,752,325; 9-0216-355-50-50; Fax 9-0216-355-78-92; asudeyesilbas@amcham.org; www.amcham.org

Ukraine

Kyiv • *American Chamber of Commerce in Ukraine* • Mr. Andy Hunder; Pres.; 12 Amosova St., 15th Flr.; 3680; P 42,000,000; 380-44-490-5800; Fax 380-44-490-5801; chamber@chamber.ua; www.chamber.ua

United Arab Emirates

Dubai • *American Bus. Cncl. of Dubai & the Northern Emirates* • Cara Nazari; Exec. Dir.; P.O. Box 37068; P 7,511,690; 971-4-3791414; Fax 971-4-3791515; director@abcdubai.com; www.abcdubai.com

United Kingdom

London • *BritishAmerican Bus.* • Jeffries Briginshaw; Managing Dir.; 75 Brook St.; W1K 4AD; P 62,218,761; 44-20-7290-9888; ukinfo@babinc.org; www.babinc.org

Uruguay

Montevideo • *Chamber of Commerce Uruguay-USA* • Magdalena Aonzo; Mgr.; Pza. Independencia 831, Ofc. 209; 11000; P 3,356,584; 598-2-9089186; Fax 598-2-9089187; info@ccuruguayusa.com; www.ccuruguayusa.com

Uzbekistan

Tashkent • *American Chamber of Commerce in Uzbekistan* • Nazi Aripdjanova; Exec. Dir.; Afrosiab St. 4B; 100031; P 28,160,361; 998-871-140-0877; Fax 998-871-140-0977; amcham.director@amcham.uz; www.amcham.uz

Venezuela

Caracas • *Venezuelan-American Chamber of Commerce & Ind.* • Carlos Tejera; Gen. Mgr.; Torre Credival, Piso 10; 2da Av. de Campo Alegre; 1010-A; P 28,834,000; 58-212-2630833; Fax 58-212-2631829; ctejera@venamcham.org; www.venamcham.org

Vietnam

Hanoi • *American Chamber of Commerce-Hanoi* • Adam Sitkoff; Exec. Dir.; M Flr., Hilton Hanoi Opera; No. 1 Le Thanh Tong St.; P 86,936,464; 84-4-3934-2790; Fax 84-4-3934-2787; info@amchamhanoi.com; www.amchamhanoi.com

Ho Chi Minh City • *American Chamber of Commerce in Vietnam* • Herb Cochran; Exec. Dir.; New World Saigon Hotel, Ste. 323; 76 Le Lai St., Dist. 1; P 86,936,464; 84-8-3824-3562; Fax 84-8-3824-3572; contact@amchamvietnam.com; www.amchamvietnam.com

FOREIGN & ETHNIC CHAMBERS OF COMMERCE IN THE UNITED STATES

Africa

African Chamber of Commerce • Sanmi Akinmulero; Pres./CEO; 2639 Walnut Hill Ln., Ste. 125; Dallas; TX; 75229; (214) 628-2569; info@africanchamberdfw.org; www.africanchamberdfw.org

Angola

U.S.-Angola Chamber of Commerce • Maria da Cruz; Exec. Dir.; 1100 17th St. N.W., Ste. 1000; Washington; DC; 20036; (202) 857-0789; Fax (202) 223-0551; mdacruz@us-angola.org; www.us-angola.org

Argentina

Argentine-American Chamber of Commerce • Claudia Schaefer-Farre; Exec. Dir.; 150 E. 58th St., 20th Flr.; New York; NY; 10155; (212) 698-2238; argentinechamber@argentinechamber.org; www.argentinechamber.org

Australia

Australian American Chamber of Commerce • Ms. Lynn Ellis; Exec. Dir.; 1300 McGowen, Ste. 120; Houston; TX; 77004; (713) 527-9688; Fax (832) 415-0545; info@aacc-houston.org; www.aacc-houston.org

Austria

Austrian Trade Comm. in Chicago • Franz Roessler; Trade Comm.; 500 N. Michigan Ave., Ste. 1950; Chicago; IL; 60611; (312) 644-5556; Fax (312) 644-6526; chicago@advantageaustria.org; www.advantageaustria.org

Austrian Trade Comm. in Los Angeles • Rudolf Thaler; Trade Comm.; 11601 Wilshire Blvd., Ste. 2420; Los Angeles; CA; 90025; (310) 477-9988; Fax (310) 477-1643; losangeles@advantageaustria.org; www.advantageaustria.org/US

Austrian Trade Comm. in New York • Christian Kesberg; Trade Comm.; 120 W. 45th St., 9th Flr.; New York; NY; 10036; (212) 421-5250; Fax (212) 421-5251; newyork@advantageaustria.org; www.advantageaustria.org

U.S.-Austrian Chamber of Commerce • Johannes P. Hofer; Pres.; 165 W. 46th St., Ste. 1113; New York; NY; 10036; (212) 819-0117; office@usaustrianchamber.org; www.usaustrianchamber.com

Azerbaijan

U.S.-Azerbaijan Chamber of Commerce • Susan Sadigova; Prog. Mgr.; 1212 Potomac St. N.W.; Washington; DC; 20007; (202) 333-8702; Fax (202) 333-8703; chamber@usacc.org; www.usacc.org

Barbados

Barbados Investment & Dev. Corp. • Leslie Gittens; Bus. Dev. Officer; 820 2nd Ave., 5th Flr.; New York; NY; 10017; (212) 551-4375; (800) 841-7860; Fax (212) 682-5496; newyork@investbarbados.org; investbarbados.org

Belgium

Belgian-American Chamber of Commerce • c/o KBC Bank; 1177 Ave. of the Americas, 8th Flr.; New York; NY; 10036; (212) 541-0779; info@belcham.org; www.belcham.org

Brazil

Brazilian-American Chamber of Commerce Inc. • 509 Madison Ave., Ste. 304; New York; NY; 10022; (212) 751-4691; Fax (212) 751-7692; info@brazilcham.com; www.brazilcham.com

Brazilian-American Chamber of Commerce of Florida • Mary Arnaud; Exec. Dir.; P.O. Box 310038; Miami; FL; 33231; (305) 579-9030; Fax (305) 579-9756; baccf@brazilchamber.org; www.brazilchamber.org

Brazil-U.S. Bus. Cncl. • Monique Fridell; Exec. Dir.; 1615 H St. N.W.; Washington; DC; 20062; (202) 463-5898; brazilcouncil@uschamber.com; www.brazilcouncil.org

Chile

North American-Chilean Chamber • Mario J. Paredes; Pres.; 866 United Nations Plaza, Ste. 4019; New York; NY; 10017; (212) 317-1959; Fax (212) 758-8598; info@nacchamber.com; www.nacchamber.com

China

U.S.-China Chamber of Commerce • Siva Yam; Pres.; 55 W. Monroe St., Ste. 630; Chicago; IL; 60603; (312) 368-9911; Fax (312) 368-9922; info@usccc.org; www.usccc.org

Colombia

Colombian-American Chamber of Commerce • Jesus Riano; Pres.; P.O. Box 82; Bay Shore; NY; 11706; (716) 222-2541; secretary@caccli.org; www.caccli.org

Proexport Colombia • Luis German Restrepo; Dir.; 601 Brickell Key Dr., Ste. 608; Miami; FL; 33131; (305) 374-3144; Fax (212) 922-9115; miami@proexport.com.co; www.proexport.com.co

Cyprus

Cyprus-U.S. Chamber of Commerce • Despina Axiotakis; Exec. Dir.; c/o Peter Kakoyiannis, Esq.; 805 Third Ave.,10th Flr.; New York; NY; 10017; (201) 981-5764; Fax (201) 444-0445; director@cyprususchamber.com; www.cyprususchamber.com

Denmark

Danish American Chamber of Commerce • Anders Lindskov Jensen; Gen. Mgr.; 885 Second Ave., 18th Flr.; New York; NY; 10017; (646) 790-7169; Fax (212) 754-1904; daccny@daccny.com; www.daccny.com

Ecuador

Ecuadorian-American Chamber of Commerce • 3403 N.W. 82nd Ave., Ste. 310; Miami; FL; 33122; (305) 539-0010; Fax (305) 591-0868; ecuacham@bellsouth.net; www.ecuachamber.com

Europe

Trans-Atlantic Bus. Cncl. • Tim Bennett; Dir. Gen./CEO; 919 18th St. N.W., Ste. 220; Washington; DC; 20006; (202) 828-9104; Fax (202) 828-9106; dnunnery@transatlanticbusiness.org; www.transatlanticbusiness.org

Finland

Finnish American Chamber of Commerce • Kerstin Nordin; Exex. Dir.; 20 W. 20 St., Ste. 212; New York; NY; 10011; (212) 821-0225; Fax (212) 750-4418; faccnyc@verizon.net; facc-ny.com

Finnish American Chamber of Commerce-Pacific Coast • Michael S. Berlin; Pres.; c/o Michael S. Berlin; Glaucoma Institute Beverly Hills, 8733 Beverly Blvd., Ste. 301; Los Angeles; CA; 90048; (310) 855-1112; Fax (310) 855-1211; berlin@ucla.edu; faccpacific.com

France

French-American Chamber of Commerce • 1350 Broadway, Ste. 2101; New York; NY; 10018; (212) 867-0123; Fax (212) 867-9050; info@faccnyc.org; www.faccnyc.org

French-American Chamber of Commerce • Sophie Woodville; Exec. Dir.; 26 O'Farrell St., Ste. 500; San Francisco; CA; 94108; (415) 442-4717; Fax (415) 442-4621; info@faccsf.com; www.faccsf.com

Germany

German-American Chamber of Commerce • Dietmar Rieg; Pres./CEO; 75 Broad St., 21st Flr.; New York; NY; 10004; (212) 974-8830; Fax (212) 974-8867; info@gaccny.com; www.gaccny.com

German-American Chamber of Commerce • Lindi von Mutius; Exec. Dir.; 2 Penn Center; 1500 JFK Blvd., Ste. 200; Philadelphia; PA; 19102; (215) 665-1585; Fax (215) 864-7288; admin@gaccphiladelphia.com; www.gaccphiladelphia.com

German-American Chamber of the Midwest • Mark Tomkins; Pres./CEO; 321 N. Clark St.; Chicago; IL; 60654; (312) 644-2662; (312) 494-2162; Fax (312) 644-0738; info@gaccmidwest.org; www.gaccmidwest.org

German American Chamber of Commerce of the Southern U.S. Inc. • Martina Stellmaszek; Pres./CEO; 1170 Howell Mill Rd., Ste. 300; Atlanta; GA; 30318; (404) 586-6800; Fax (404) 586-6820; info@gaccsouth.com; www.gaccsouth.com

Greece

Hellenic-American Chamber of Commerce • 370 Lexington Ave., 27th Flr.; New York; NY; 10017; (212) 629-6380; Fax (212) 564-9281; hellenicchamber-nyc@att.net; www.hellenicamerican.cc

Haiti

Haitian-American Chamber of Commerce • Paola Pierre; Exec. Dir.; 1510 N.E. 162nd St.; North Miami; FL; 33162; (305) 733-9066; info@haccof.com; www.haccof.com

Hungary

Hungarian-American Chamber of Commerce • Katalin Csorba; 3910 Shoemaker St. N.W.; Washington; DC; 20008; (202) 362-7169; Fax (202) 686-6412; kcsorba@mfa.gov.hu; washington.kormany.hu

Iceland

Icelandic-American Chamber of Commerce • 800 Third Ave., 36th Flr.; New York; NY; 10022; (646) 282-9360; Fax (646) 282-9369; www.iceland.is

Indonesia

American-Indonesian Chamber of Commerce • Wayne Forrest; Pres.; 317 Madison Ave., Ste. 1619; New York; NY; 10017; (212) 687-4505; Fax (212) 687-5844; wayne@aiccusa.org; www.aiccusa.org

Iran

US-Iran Chamber of Commerce • Hadi Sadeghi; Pres.; 1300 Pennsylvania Ave. N.W., Ste. 700; Washington; DC; 20004; (888) 300-1682; info@usircc.org; www.usircc.org

Ireland

Ireland Chamber of Commerce in the U.S. • Brian O'Dwyer; Chrmn.; 556 Central Ave.; New Providence; NJ; 07974; (908) 286-1300; Fax (908) 286-1200; info@iccusa.org; www.iccusa.org

Israel

American-Israel Chamber of Commerce-Chicago • Michael Schmitt; Exec. Dir.; 203 N. LaSalle St., Ste. 2100; Chicago; IL; 60601; (312) 558-1346; (847) 597-7069; Fax (312) 346-9603; m.schmitt@americaisrael.org; www.americaisrael.org

America-Israel Chamber of Commerce & Ind. • Ronny Bassan; Exec. V.P.; c/o Ansonia Post Office; P.O. Box 237205; New York; NY; 10023; (212) 819-0430; info@aicci.net; www.aicci.net

Conexx:America Israel Business Connector • Shai Robkin; Pres./CEO; 400 Northridge Rd., Ste. 250; Atlanta; GA; 30350; (404) 843-9426; Fax (404) 843-1416; srobkin@conexx.org; www.conexx.org

Ohio-Israel Chamber of Commerce • Howard Gudell; Pres.; 815 Superior Ave., Ste. 2025; P.O. Box 39007; Cleveland; OH; 44139; (216) 965-4474; (216) 589-0693; Fax (440) 248-4888; ohioisraelchamber@ameritech.net; www.ohioisraelchamber.com

Italy

Italian American Chamber of Commerce Midwest • Mauro Galli; Pres.; 500 N. Michigan Ave., Ste. 506; Chicago; IL; 60611; (312) 553-9137; Fax (312) 553-9142; info@iacc-chicago.com; www.iacc-chicago.com

Italy-America Chamber of Commerce West • 10537 Santa Monica Blvd., Ste. 210; Los Angeles; CA; 90025; (310) 557-3017; Fax (310) 470-2200; info@iaccw.net; www.iaccw.net

Italy-America Chamber of Commerce Inc. • Claudio Bozzo; Pres.; 730 Fifth Ave., Ste. 600; New York; NY; 10019; (212) 459-0044; Fax (212) 459-0090; info@italchamber.org; www.italchamber.org

Japan

Japan Bus. Assn. of Southern California • Yuji Takahashi; Exec. Dir.; 1411 W. 190th St., Ste. 220; Gardena; CA; 90248; (310) 515-9522; Fax (310) 515-9722; jba@jba.org; www.jba.org

Japan Bus. Assn. of Houston • 12651 Briar Forest Dr., Ste. 105; Houston; TX; 77077; (281) 493-1512; Fax (281) 531-6730; sansuikai@jbahouston.org; www.jbahouston.org

Japanese Chamber of Commerce-Southern California • 244 San Pedro St., Ste. 504; Los Angeles; CA; 90012; (213) 626-3067; Fax (213) 626-3070; office@jccsc.com; www.jccsc.com

Japanese Chamber of Commerce & Ind. of NY • Seiei Ono; Pres.; 145 W. 57th St.; New York; NY; 10019; (212) 246-8001; Fax (212) 246-8002; info@jcciny.org; www.jcciny.org

Korea

Korean American Chamber of Commerce of LA • 3435 Wilshire Blvd., Ste. 2450; Los Angeles; CA; 90010; (213) 480-1115; Fax (866) 936-4497; office@kaccla.com; kaccla.com

Korea Chamber of Commerce & Ind. in the USA • 460 Park Ave., Ste. 410; New York; NY; 10022; (212) 644-0140; Fax (212) 644-9106; admin@kocham.org; www.kocham.org

Latin America

Cncl. of the Americas • Susan Segal; Pres./CEO; 680 Park Ave.; New York; NY; 10065; (212) 249-8950; Fax (212) 249-5868; ssegal@as-coa.org; counciloftheamericas.org

Latin American Chamber of Commerce • 3512 W. Fullerton Ave.; Chicago; IL; 60647; (773) 252-5211; Fax (773) 252-7065; lacc@latinamericanchamberofcommerce.com; www.latinamericanchamberofcommerce.com

Latin-American Chamber of Commerce • Juan M. Ruiz; Pres.; 1405 S. Main St.; Salt Lake City; UT; 84115; (801) 649-5465; Fax (888) 534-2230; info@laccutah.org; www.camaralatinoamericana.org

Latin Chamber of Commerce of USA • Luciano Garcia; Exec. Dir.; 1401 W. Flagler St.; Miami; FL; 33135; (305) 642-3870; Fax (305) 642-0653; lgarcia@camacol.org; www.camacol.org

Luxembourg

Luxembourg American Chamber of Commerce • Tatjana Schaefer; Exec. Dir.; 17 Beekman Pl.; New York; NY; 10022; (212) 888-6701; Fax (212) 935-5896; info@laccny.com; laccny.com

Luxembourg Trade & Investment Ofc. • Georges Schmit; Exec. Dir.; One Sansome St., Ste. 830; San Francisco; CA; 94104; (415) 788-0816; Fax (415) 788-0985; sanfrancisco@investinluxembourg.us; www.investinluxembourg.us

Malaysia

Malaysia Trade Comm. (MATRADE) • Muhd Shahrulmiza Zakaria; Trade Commissioner; 313 E. 43rd St., 3rd Flr.; New York; NY; 10017; (212) 682-0232; Fax (212) 983-1987; newyork@matrade.gov.my; www.matrade.gov.my

Mexico

Mexican Intl. Chamber of Commerce & Ind. • P.O. Box 4422; Rancho del Rey; CA; 91909; (213) 261-3979;; info@mexchamber.com; www.mexchamber.com

U.S.-Mexico Chamber of Commerce • Albert Zapanta; Pres./CEO; 6800 Versar Center, Ste. 450; Springfield; VA; 22151; (703) 752-4751; (703) 752-4752; Fax (703) 642-1088; news-hq@usmcoc.org; www.usmcoc.org

Middle East

Arab American Chamber of Commerce • 1050 17th St. N.W., Ste. 600; Washington; DC; 20036; (202) 347-5800; (888) 939-ARAB; Fax (202) 521-4050; aacc@arabchamber.org; www.arabchamber.org

National U.S.-Arab Chamber of Commerce • Rim Elbayar Aly; 350 S. Bixel St., Ste. 200; Los Angeles; CA; 90017; (213) 482-5111; Fax (213) 482-5110; raly@nusacc.org; www.nusacc.org

National U.S.-Arab Chamber of Commerce • Janine Colon; 369 Lexington Ave., Ste. 213; New York; NY; 10017; (212) 986-8024; Fax (212) 986-0216; jcolon@nusacc.org; www.nusacc.org

National U.S.-Arab Chamber of Commerce • 1023 15th St. N.W., Ste. 400; Washington; DC; 20005; (202) 289-5920; Fax (202) 289-5938; info@nusacc.org; www.nusacc.org

Norway

Norwegian-American Chamber of Commerce • 655 Third Ave., Ste. 1810; New York; NY; 10017; (212) 885-9737; nacc@naccusa.org; www.naccusa.org

Peru

Peruvian American Chamber of Commerce • 1948 N.W. 82nd Ave.; Doral; FL; 33126; (305) 599-1057; info@peruvianchamber.org; www.peruvianchamber.org

Philippines

Philippine American Chamber of Illinois • Joseph Cana; Exec. Dir.; 5850 N. Lincoln Ave., Ste. 208; Chicago; IL; 60659; (800) 850-2632; Fax (800) 505-8753; info@paccil.org; www.paccil.org

Portugal

Portugal-U.S. Chamber of Commerce • 590 Fifth Ave., 4th Flr.; New York; NY; 10036; (212) 354-4627; Fax (212) 575-4737; chamber@portugal-us.com; www.portugal-us.com

Puerto Rico

Puerto Rican Chamber of Commerce • 3550 Biscayne Blvd., Ste. 306; Miami; FL; 33137; (305) 571-8006; Fax (305) 571-8007; mdw@puertoricanchamber.com; www.puertoricanchamber.com

Russia

Russian-American Chamber of Commerce • Aventira; FL; (786) 252-6616; www.rasouthflorida.com

Saudi Arabia

Royal Embassy of Saudi Arabia, Commercial Ofc. • 601 New Hampshire Ave. N.W.; Washington; DC; 20037; (202) 337-4088; Fax (202) 342-0271; info@saudicommercialoffice.com; www.saudicommercialoffice.com

Singapore

Intl. Enterprise Singapore • Amreeta Eng; Dir.; 55 E. 59th St., Ste. 21A; New York; NY; 10022; (212) 421-2207; Fax (212) 888-2897; newyork@iesingapore.gov.sg; www.iesingapore.gov.sg

Spain

Spain-U.S. Chamber of Commerce • 1221 Brickell Ave., Ste. 1540; Miami; FL; 33131; (305) 358-5988; Fax (305) 358-6844; info@spainchamber.org; www.spain-uschamber.com

Spain-U.S. Chamber of Commerce • Carlos Pujol; Pres.; 350 5th Ave., Ste. 2600; New York; NY; 10118; (212) 967-2170; Fax (212) 564-1415; events@spainuscc.org; www.spainuscc.org

Sweden

Swedish-American Chamber of Commerce • Renee Lundholm; Pres.; 570 Lexington Ave., 20th Flr.; New York; NY; 10022; (212) 838-5530; Fax (212) 755-7953; renee.lundholm@saccny.org; www.saccny.org

Swedish-American Chamber of Commerce • Jonna Augustsson; Bus. Relations; 350 Townsend St., Ste. 409B; San Francisco; CA; 94107; (415) 781-4188; info@sacc-sf.org; www.sacc-sf.org

Switzerland

Swiss-American Chamber of Commerce • Tina Rudolf; New York Chapter; 500 Fifth Ave., Rm. 1800; New York; NY; 10110; (212) 246-7789; Fax (212) 246-1366; newyork@amcham.ch; www.amcham.ch

Swiss American Chamber of Commerce • San Francisco Chapter; P.O. Box 26007; San Francisco; CA; 94126; (415) 433-6679; swissamericanchamber@saccsf.com; www.saccsf.com

Thailand

Thai Trade Center • 630 Fifth Ave., Ste. 1915; New York; NY; 10111; (212) 482-0077; Fax (212) 482-1177; info@thaitradeny.com; www.thaitradeusa.com

United Kingdom

British American Bus. Cncl.-Orange County • Valerie Blackholly; Exec. Dir.; 25422 Trabuco Rd., Ste. 105-266; Lake Forest; CA; 92630; (949) 472-2221; info@babcoc.org; www.babcoc.org

British American Business • Wendy Mendenhall; Managing Dir.; 52 Vanderbilt Ave., 20th Flr.; New York; NY; 10017; (212) 661-4060; Fax (212) 661-4074; nyinfo@babinc.org; www.babinc.org

British American Bus. Cncl. • Jo Healey; Exec. Dir.; 703 Market St., Ste. 1214; San Francisco; CA; 94103; (415) 296-8645; Fax (415) 296-9649; info@babcsf.org; www.babcsf.org

British American Bus. Cncl. • Paul Wright; Pres.; c/o Krycler, Ervin, Taubman & Walheim; 15303 Ventura Blvd., Ste. 1040; Sherman Oaks; CA; 91403; (310) 312-1962; info@babcla.org; www.babcla.org

Uzbekistan

American-Uzbekistan Chamber of Commerce • Timothy Y. McGraw; Pres.; 1300 I St. N.W., Ste. 720; Washington; DC; 20005; (202) 509-3744; info@aucconline.com; www.aucconline.com

Venezuela

Venezuelan-American Chamber of Commerce • E. Adriana Kostencki; Pres.; 1600 Ponce de Leon Blvd., 10th Flr., Ste. 1033; Coral Gables; FL; 33134; (786) 350-1190; Fax (786) 350-1191; info@venezuelanchamber.org; www.venezuelanchamber.org

Foreign C/C in US

FOREIGN CHAMBERS OF COMMERCE

ALBANIA

Tirana • *Chamber of Commerce & Ind. of Tirana* • Rr. Kavajes No. 6; P 3,204,284; 355-4-2232446; Fax 355-4-2227997; info@cci.al; www.cci.al

ALGERIA

Alger • *Algerian Chamber of Commerce & Ind.* • Hamiti Boukhalfa; Dir. of Publications; Palais Consulaire 6. boulevard Amilcar Cabral; 16003; P 35,468,208; 021-96-77-77; Fax 021-96-70-70; dpd@caci.dz; www.caci.dz

ANTIGUA & BARBUDA

Saint John's • *Antigua & Barbuda Chamber of Commerce & Ind.* • P.O. Box 774; P 88,710; 268-462-0743; Fax 268-462-4575; chamcom@candw.ag

ARGENTINA

Buenos Aires • *Argentina Chamber of Commerce* • Av. Leandro N. Alem 36; 1003; P 40,412,376; 54-11-5300-9000; Fax 54-11-5300-9058; difusion2@cac.com.ar; www.cac.com.ar

Buenos Aires • *Argentine Chamber of Exporters* • Av. Roque Saenz Pena 740; Piso 1; 1035; P 40,412,376; 54-11-4394-4482; Fax 54-11-4394-4482; contacto@cera.org.ar; www.cera.org.ar

Camara Argentina de Comercio Electronico • Calle 25 de Mayo 611 Piso 2; 1005; P 40,412,376; 54-11-5917-7435; contacto@cace.org.ar; www.cace.org.ar

Rosario • *Foreign Trade Chamber of Commerce of Rosario* • Silvana Pendín; Tech,; Córdoba 1868 1ºF, Office 114 - 115, St; 2000; P 40,412,376; 54-341-425-7147; 54-341-425-7486; Fax 54-341-425-7147; ccer@commerce.com.ar; www.commerce.com.ar

ARUBA

Oranjestad • *Aruba Chamber of Commerce & Ind.* • Mrs. Sofia J. Velthuizen; Interim Dir.; J.E. Irausquin Boulevard 10; P.O. Box 140; P 107,488; 297-582-1566; Fax 297-583-3962; info@arubachamber.com; www.arubachamber.com

AUSTRALIA

Albany WA • *Albany Chamber of Commerce & Ind.* • Russ Clark; CEO; 76 Collie St.; P.O. Box 5273; 6332; P 35,000; 61-8-9845-7888; Fax 61-8-9845-7877; ceo@albanycci.com.au; www.albanycci.com.au

Barton • *Australian Chamber of Commerce & Ind.* • James Pearson; CEO; Commerce House; Level 3 24 Brisbane Ave.; 2600; P 25,000,000; 61-2-6270-8000; Fax 61-2-6273-3286; info@acci.asn.au; www.acci.asn.au

Brisbane QLD • *Queensland Chamber of Commerce & Ind.* • Stephen Tait; CEO; 375 Wickham Terrace; 4000; P 22,328,800; 61-7-3842-2244; Fax 61-7-3832-3195; contact@cciq.com.au; www.cciq.com.au

Cairns QLD • *Cairns Chamber of Commerce* • Deb Hancock; CEO; P.O. Box 2336; 4870; P 22,328,800; 61-7-4031-1838; Fax 61-7-4031-0883; info@cairnschamber.com.au; www.cairnschamber.com.au

Darwin NT • *Northern Territory Chamber of Commerce & Ind.* • Greg Bicknell; CEO; Ste. 5/4 Shepherd St.; GPO Box 1825; 801; P 22,328,800; 61-8-8982-8100; Fax 61-8-8981-1405; darwin@chambernt.com.au; www.chambernt.com.au

East Perth WA • *Chamber of Commerce & Ind. of Western Australia* • Deidre Willmott; CEO; 180 Hay St.; P.O. Box 6209; 6892; P 22,328,800; 61-8-9365-7555; Fax 61-8-9365-7550; info@cciwa.com; www.cciwa.com

Hobart TAS • *Tasmanian Chamber of Commerce & Ind.* • Michael Bailey; CEO; GPO Box 793; 7001; P 22,328,800; 61-3-6236-3600; Fax 61-3-6231-1278; kristen.finnigan@tcci.com.au; www.tcci.com.au

Melbourne VIC • *Australian Chamber of Commerce & Ind.* • James Pearson; CEO; Level 2 150 Collins St.; P.O. Box 18008; 8003; P 22,328,800; 61-2-6270-8000; Fax 61-3-9668-9958; info@acci.asn.au; www.acci.asn.au

North Sydney NSW • *NSW Business Chamber* • Stephen Cartwright; Exec. Dir.; Level 15 140 Arthur St.; Locked Bag 938; 2059; P 22,328,800; 61-2-13-26-96; Fax 61-2-1300-655-277; ann.quach@australianbusiness.com.au; www.nswbusinesschamber.com.au

AUSTRIA

Feldkirch • *Wirtschaftskammer Vorarlberg* • Wichnergasse 9; A-6800; P 8,384,745; 43-5522-305-0; Fax 43-5522-305-14; office@wkvlbg.at; wko.at/vlbg

Graz • *Economic Chamber of Styria* • P.O. Box 1038; A-8021; P 8,384,745; 43-316-601-0; Fax 43-316-601-361; office@wkstmk.at; wko.at/stmk

Innsbruck • *Tyrolean Chamber of Commerce* • Meinhardstrasse 14; A-6020; P 8,384,745; 43-5-90-9050; Fax 43-5-90-905-1467; offfice@wktirol.at; wko.at/tirol

Vienna • *Federal Economic Chamber of Commerce* • Wiedner Hauptstrasse 63; 1045; P 8,384,745; 43-1-50105-4503; Fax 43-1-50206-255

Vienna • *International Congress Vienna* • Börsegasse 9/8A-1010; P 8,384,745; 43-1-532-1000-14; Fax 43-1-532-1000-30; office@icon-vienna.net; www.icon-vienna.net

Vienna Chamber of Commerce & Ind. • Stubenring 8-10; A-1010; P 8,384,745; 43-1-514-50; Fax 43-1-514-50-3740; postbox@wkw.at; wko.at/wien

AZERBAIJAN

Baku • *The Azerbaijan Republic Chamber of Commerce & Ind.* • Mr. Niyaz Ali-zada; Pres.; 47 (31) Istiglaliyyat str.; 1001; P 9,047,932; 994-12-492 8912; Fax 994-12-4971997; expo@chamber.az; www.chamber.az

BAHAMAS

Grand Bahama • *Grand Bahama Chamber of Commerce* • PO Box F-40808 Freeport; P 342,877; 242-352-8329; Fax 242-352-3280; gbchamber@batelnet.bs

Nassau • *Bahamas Chamber of Commerce & Employers' Confederation* • Edison Sumner; CEO; Shirley St. & Collins Ave.; P.O. Box N-665; P 342,877; 242-322-2145; Fax 242-322-4649; info@thebahamaschamber.com; www.thebahamaschamber.com

BAHRAIN

Manama • *Bahrain Chamber of Commerce & Ind.* • P.O. Box 248; P 1,261,835; 973-17-380000; Fax 973-17-380123; bcci@bcci.bh; www.bcci.bh

BANGLADESH

Chittagong • *Chittagong Chamber of Commerce & Ind.* • Chamber House 38 Agrabad C/A; 4100; P 148,692,130; 880-31-713366; Fax 880-31-710183; info@chittagongchamber.com; www.chittagongchamber.com

Dhaka • *The Federation of Bangladesh Chambers of Commerce & Ind.* • Mr. Abdul Matlub Ahmad; Pres.; Federation Bhaban 60 Motijheel C/A; 1000; P 165,000,000; 880-2-9560102-3; 880-2-9560456 9561714; Fax 880-2-9576261; fbcci@bol-online.com; www.fbcci-bd.org

Khulna • *Khulna Chamber of Commerce & Ind.* • Chamber Mansion 5 KDA C/A; 9100; P 148,692,130; 880-41-721695; Fax 880-41-725365; khulnachamber@gmail.com; www.khulnachamber.com

BARBADOS

Bridgetown • *Barbados Investment & Dev. Corp.* • P.O. Box 1250; 11000; P 273,331; 246-427-5350; Fax 246-426-7802; bidc@bidc.org; www.bidc.org

St. Michael • *Barbados Chamber of Commerce & Ind.* • Mr. Andy Armstrong; Pres.; Braemer Ct. Deighton Rd.; P 273,331; 246-434-4750; Fax 246-228-2907; bcci@bdscham.com; www.barbadoschamberofcommerce.com

BELGIUM

Antwerp • *Chamber of Commerce & Ind. of Antwerp* • Markgravestraat 12; 2000; P 10,879,159; 32-3-2322219; Fax 32-3-2336442; info.antwerpen@voka.be; www.voka.be/antwerpen-waasland

Brussels • *Federation of Belgian Chambers of Commerce* • Wouter Van Gulck; Gen. Mgr.; Avenue Louise 500; B-1050; P 10,879,159; 32-2-209-05-50; Fax 32-2-209-05-68; info@belgianchambers.be; www.belgianchambers.be

Ghent • *Chamber of Commerce & Ind. of Ghent* • Martelaarslaan 49; 9000; P 10,879,159; 32-9-2661440; Fax 32-9-2661441; kkngent@cci.be

Kortrijk • *Chamber of Commerce West Flanders* • Casinoplein 10; B-8500; P 10,879,159; 32-56-235051; Fax 32-56-218564; kortrijk@voka.be

Leuven • *Chamber of Commerce & Ind. of Leuven* • Tiensevest 61; 3010; P 10,879,159; 32-16-222689; Fax 32-16-237828; info@ccileuven.be; www.cci.be/leuven

BELIZE

Belize City • *Belize Chamber of Commerce & Ind.* • Mrs. Kim Aikman; CEO; 4792 Coney Dr. 1st Flr. WithField Tower; P.O. Box 291; P 368,000; 501-223-5330; Fax 501-223-5333; bcci@belize.org; http://www.belize.org

BERMUDA

Hamilton • *Bermuda Chamber of Commerce* • Kendaree Burgess; Exec. Dir.; 1 Point Pleasant Rd.;; HM 11; P 64,600; (441) 295-4201; (441) 295-8930; Fax (441) 292-5779; info@bcc.bm; www.bermudachamber.bm

BOLIVIA

La Paz • *Chamber of Commerce of Bolivia* • Av. Mariscal Santa Cruz No. 1392; P 9,929,849; 591-2-378606; Fax 591-2-391004; cnc@boliviacomercio.org.bo; www.boliviacomercio.org.bo

Santa Cruz • *Chamber of Commerce & Ind. Of Santa Cruz* • Av. Las Americas Ste. 7; Casilla 180; P 9,929,849; 591-3-3334555; Fax 591-3-3342353; cainco@cainco.org.bo; cainco.org.bo

BOSNIA AND HERZEGOVINA

Sarajevo • *Chamber of Eco. of the Federation of Bosnia and Herzegovina* • Mr. Mirsad Jasarspahic; Pres.; Branislava Djurdjeva 10; 71000; P 387-33-217-782; Fax 387-33-217-783; info@kfbih.com; www.kfbih.com

BRAZIL

Rio de Janeiro • *National Confederaton of Ind.* • Av. General Justo 307; 20021-130; P 194,946,470; 55-21-3804920; Fax 55-21-3804920; sgr@cnc.com.br; www.cnc.com.br

Sao Paulo • *Federation of Industries of Sao Paulo* • Paulista Avenue 1313; 01311-923; P 194,946,470; 55-11-3549-4499; Fax 55-11-2531-972; relacionamento@fiesp.org.br; www.fiesp.com.br

BULGARIA

Sofia • *Bulgarian Chamber of Commerce & Ind.* • Tsvetan Simeonov; Pres.; 9 Iskar Str.; 1058; P 7,543,325; 359-2-811-74-00; Fax 359-2-987-32-09; bcci@bcci.bg; www.bcci.bg

BURKINA FASO

Ouagadougou • *Chamber of Commerce & Ind.* • Ave. de Lyon; 502; P 15,757,000; 226-50-30-61-14; Fax 226-50-30-61-16; www.ccia.bf

CAMEROON

Douala • *Chamber of Commerce Ind. & Mines of Cameroon* • P.O. Box 4011; P 19,598,889; 237-342-98-81; Fax 237-342-55-96

CAPE VERDE

Mindelo SV • *Camara de Comercio Industria y Servicos* • P.O. Box 728; P 495,999; 238-32-8495; Fax 238-32-8496; camara.com@mail.cvtelecom.cv

CAYMAN ISLANDS

Grand Cayman • *Cayman Islands C/C & Visitors Centre* • Wil Pineau CCE; CEO; 23 Lime Tree Bay Ave. West Bay Rd.; P.O. Box 1000; KY1-1101; P 60,000; 345-949-8090; 345-743-9122; Fax 345-949-0220; info@caymanchamber.ky; www.caymanchamber.ky

CHILE

Santiago • *Camara de Comercio De Santiago* • Monjitas 392; P 17,113,688; 56-2-360-7000; cpn@ccs.cl; www.ccs.cl

CHINA

Beijing • *China Cncl. for the Promotion of Intl. Trade* • 1 Fuxingmenwai St.; 100860; P 133,829,9500; 86-10-8807-5769; Fax 86-10-6803-0747; BCNweb@ccpit.org; www.ccpit.org

Qingdao • *China Chamber of Intl. Commerce* • 121 Yanan Sanlu Rd. Ste. 403; 266071; P 133,829,9500; 86-532-8389-7605; Fax 86-532-8389-8251; project@82invest.com; www.82invest.com/en_index.htm

COLOMBIA

Barranquilla • *Camara de Comercio de Barranquilla* • Via 40 #36-135; P 46,294,841; 57-53-361-7555; comunica@camarabaq.org.co; www.camarabaq.org.co

Buenaventura • *Camara de Comercio de Buenaventura* • Alexander Micolta Sabid; CEO; Calle 1 No. 1A-88; P 392,054; 57-2-2424508; 57-3-185309746; Fax 57-2-2434202; presidencia@ccbun.org; www.ccbun.org

Cartagena • *Camara de Comercio de Cartagena* • Santa Teresa St. No 32-41; 2117; P 46,294,841; 57-56-501110; Fax 57-56-501126; camaradecomercio@cccartagena.org.co; www.cccartagena.org.co

COSTA RICA

San Jose • *Chamber of Commerce of Costa Rica* • P.O. Box 1114; 1000; P 4,658,887; 506-2221-0005; Fax 506-2256-9680; camara@camara-comercio.com; www.camara-comercio.com

COTE d'IVOIRE

Abidjan • *Chambre de Commerce et d'Industrie* • P.O. Box 1399; 01; P 21,504,162; 225-20-33-16-00; Fax 225-20-32-39-42; info@chamco-ci.org; www.chamco-ci.org

CROATIA

Zagreb • *Croatian Chamber of Eco.* • Rooseveltov trg 2; P.O. Box 630; 10000; P 4,400,000; 385-1-4561555; Fax 385-1-4828380; hgk@hgk.hr; www.hgk.hr

CUBA

Havana • *Chamber of Commerce of the Republic of Cuba* • 21 No. 661 esq.A Vedado; P.O. Box 370; 10 400; P 11,193,192; 53-833-8040; Fax 53-838-1321; camaracuba@camara.com.cu; www.camaracuba.cu

CYPRUS

Limassol • *Famagusta Chamber of Commerce & Ind.* • Mr. Iacovos Hadjivarnavas; Mgr.; Ayiou Andreou 339 flat 201; P.O. Box 53124; 3300; P 1,103,647; 357-25-370165; Fax 357-25-370291; info@famagustachamber.org.cy; www.famagustachamber.org.cy

Nicosia • *Cyprus Chamber of Commerce & Ind.* • P.O. Box 21455; 1509; P 1,103,647; 357-2-288-9800; Fax 357-2-266-9048; chamber@ccci.org.cy; www.ccci.org.cy

DOMINICAN REPUBLIC

Santo Domingo • *C/C & Production of Santo Domingo* • Pedro Perez Gonzalez; Pres.; Av. 27 de Febrero No. 228 esq. Av. Tiradentes Torre Friusa La Esperilla; P 10,000,000; (809) 682-2688; mgmorales@camarasantodomingo.do; www.camarasantodomingo.do

ECUADOR

Guayaquil • *Guayaquil Chamber of Commerce* • Av. Francisco de Orellana y Miguel H Alcivar; Edif. Las Camaras P.3; P 14,464,739; 593-4-2596100; Fax 593-4-2682725; info@lacamara.org; www.lacamara.org

Quito • *Camara de Industrias y Produccion* • Richard Martinez Alvarado; Chrmn.; Avenidas Amazonas y Republica Edificio Las Camaras Piso 10 y 11; P.O. Box 17-01-2438; 170515; P 14,464,739; 593-2-2452-500; Fax 593-2-244-8118; camara@cip.org.ec; www.cip.org.ec

EGYPT

Cairo • *Federation of Egyptian Chambers of Commerce* • 4 El Falaki Sq.; P 81,121,077; 20-2-3551164; Fax 20-2-3557940

Cairo • *Cairo Chamber of Commerce* • 4 Midan El Falaki; P 81,121,077; 20-2-354-2943; Fax 20-2-355-7940; www.cairochamber.org.eg

EL SALVADOR

San Salvador • *Camara De Comercio E Industria De El Salvador* • 9a Av. Norte y 5a C. Pte.; P 6,058,580; 503-2231-3000; Fax 503-2271-4461; camara@camarasal.com; www.camarasal.com

ESTONIA

Tallinn • *Estonian Chamber of Commerce & Ind. •* Toom-Kooli 17; 10130; P 1,315,819; 372-604-0060; Fax 372-604-0061; koda@koda.ee; www.koda.ee

FINLAND

Helsinki • *Finland Chamber of Commerce •* Dr. Risto E.J. Penttila; Pres./CEO; P.O. Box 1000; 00101; P 5,439,000; 358-9-4242-6200; Fax 358-9-650-303; anne.hatanpaa@chamber.fi; www.chamber.fi

Jyvaskyla • *Central Finland Chamber of Commerce •* Mr. Uljas Valkeinen; Managing Dir.; Sepankatu 4; 40100; P 5,338,395; 358-10-322-2380; Fax 358-10-322-2389; info@centralfinlandchamber.fi; www.centralfinlandchamber.fi

Kuopio • *Kuopio Chamber of Commerce •* Kasarmikatu 2; 70110; P 5,338,395; 358-17-266-3800; Fax 358-17-282-3304; kauppakamari@kuopiochamber.fi; www.kuopiochamber.fi

Lahti • *Hame Chamber of Commerce •* Ruahankatu 10; 15110; P 5,338,395; 358-75-7566-700; Fax 358-75-7566-701; kirsi.aaltio@hamechamber.fi; www.hamechamber.fi

Tampere • *Tampere Chamber of Commerce & Ind. •* Kalevantie 2 B; 33100; P 500,166; 358-3-230-0555; Fax 358-3-230-0550; info@tampere.chamber.fi; www.tampere.chamber.fi

Turku • *Turku Chamber of Commerce •* Jari Lahteenmaki; CEO; Puolalankatu 1; 20100; P 5,468,609; 358-2-274-3400; Fax 358-2-251-8569; kauppakamari@turku.chamber.fi; www.turku.chamber.fi

FRANCE

Marseille • *Chamber of Commerce & Ind. of Marseille Provence •* 35 rue Sainte-Victoire; 13292; P 64,876,618; 33-491-395889; Fax 33-491-395600; www.ccimp.com

Paris • *Chamber of Commerce & Ind. of France •* 46 Ave. de la Grande Armee; 75858; P 64,876,618; 33-1-40693700; Fax 33-1-47206128; service.courrier@acfci.cci.fr; www.acfci.cci.fr

Paris • *Chamber de Commerce et D'Industrie de Paris •* 27 Av. Friedland; 75382; P 64,876,618; 33-105657069; cpdp@ccip.fr; www.ccip.fr

GAMBIA

Serekunda • *Gambia Chamber of Commerce & Ind. •* P.O. Box 3382; P 1,728,394; 220-437-8929; Fax 220-437-8936; gcci@gambiachamber.com; www.gambiachamber.com

GERMANY, FEDERAL REP. OF

Berlin • *Deutscher Industrie und Handelstag •* Breite Strasse 29; 10178; P 81,702,329; 49-30-20308-0; Fax 49-30-20308-1000; infocenter@dihk.de; www.dihk.de

Bremen • *Bremen Chamber of Commerce •* P.O. Box 105107; 28051; P 81,702,329; 49-421-36370; Fax 49-421-3637299; service@handelskammer-bremen.de; www.handelskammer-bremen.de

Dusseldorf • *Dusseldorf Chamber of Ind. & Commerce •* Ernst-Schneider-Platz 1; 40212; P 81,702,329; 49-211-3557-0; Fax 49-211-3557-400; ihkdus@duesseldorf.ihk.de; www.duesseldorf.ihk.de

Hannover • *Hannover Chamber of Ind. & Commerce •* Schiffgraben 49; 30175; P 81,702,329; 49-511-3107-0; Fax 49-511-3107-333; info@hannover.ihk.de; www.hannover.ihk.de

GHANA

Accra • *Reg. Chamber of Commerce & Ind. •* P.O. Box 2325; P 24,391,823; 233-302-769125; accra@ghanachamber.org; www.ghanachamber.org

Accra North • *Assn. of Ghana Industries •* P. O. Box AN-8624; P 24,391,823; 233-302-779023; Fax 233-302-773143; agi@agighana.org; www.agighana.org

Takoradi • *Sekondi Takoradi C/C & Ind. •* Vincent Annan; CEO; 33/8 Liberation Rd.; P.O. Box 45; 00233; P 24,391,823; 233-3120-22385; 233-433-3882; Fax 233-3120-31625; info@sekonditakoradichamber.org; www.sekonditakoradichamber.org

GREECE

Athens • *Athens Chamber of Commerce & Ind. •* 7 Academias St.; 10671; P 11,319,048; 30-210-360-4815; Fax 30-210-361-6408; info@acci.gr; www.acci.gr

Heraklion • *Heraklion Chamber of Commerce & Ind. •* 9 Koroneou Str.; P.O. Box 1154; 71110; P 11,319,048; 30-81-247010; Fax 30-81-222914; info@ebeh.gr; www.ebeh.gr

Patras • *Patras Chamber of Commerce & Ind. •* 58 Michalakopoulou St.; P.O. Box 1048; 26110; P 11,319,048; 30-61-277779; Fax 30-61-276519; www.patrascc.gr

Piraeus • *Piraeus Chamber of Commerce & Ind. •* 1 Loudovikou str. Odissos sq.; 18531; P 11,319,048; 30-210-417-7241; 30-210-417-7245; Fax 30-210-417-8680; evep@pcci.gr; www.pcci.gr

Thessaloniki • *Thessaloniki Chamber of Commerce & Ind. •* 29 Tsimiski Str.; 54624; P 11,319,048; 30-23-10370100; Fax 30-23-10370166; root@ebeth.gr; www.ebeth.gr

GRENADA

Saint George's • *Grenada Chamber of Ind. & Commerce •* P.O. Box 129; P 104,487; 473-440-2937; Fax 473-440-6621; info@grenadachamber.org; www.grenadachamber.org

GUAM

Hagatna • *Guam Chamber of Commerce •* Reina A. Leddy; Pres.; 173 Aspinall Ave. Ste. 101; Ada Plaza Center Bldg.; 96910; P 179,896; 671-472-6311; Fax 671-472-6202; gchamber@guamchamber.com.gu; www.guamchamber.com.gu

GUATEMALA

Guatemala City • *Camara de Comercio de Guatemala •* 10a. Calle 3-80 zona 1; 1001; P 14,388,929; 502-2417-2700; Fax 502-2-2291897; info@camaradecomercio.org.gt; www.negociosenguatemala.com

Guatemala City • *Camara de Industria de Guatemala* • Ruta 6 9-21 zona 4; nivel 12 Edificio; 214; P 14,388,929; 502-2-3809000; Fax 502-2-809110; info@industriaguate.com; www.industriaguate.com

GUYANA

Georgetown • *Georgetown Chamber of Commerce & Ind.* • 156 Waterloo Street; P 754,493; 592-227-6441; Fax 592-226-3519; gtchambe@networksgy.com; www.georgetownchamberofcommerce.org

HONDURAS

Tegucigalpa • *Tegucigalpa Chamber of Commerce & Ind.* • P.O. Box 3444; P 7,600,524; 504-2232-4200; Fax 504-2232-5764; asuservicio@ccit.hn; www.ccit.hn

HONG KONG (CHINA)

Hong Kong • *Hong Kong General Chamber of Commerce* • 22/F United Centre; 95 Queensway; P 7,067,800; 852-25299229; Fax 852-25279843; chamber@chamber.org.hk; www.chamber.org.hk

Hong Kong • *Hong Kong Trade Dev. Cncl.* • 38th Flr. Ofc. Tower Convention Plaza; 1 Harbour Rd. Wanchai; P 7,067,800; 852-1830-668; Fax 852-2824-0249; hktdc@hktdc.org; www.hktdc.com

HUNGARY

Budapest • *Hungarian Chamber of Commerce & Ind.* • Mr. Péter Dunai; Secy. General; Szabadság tér 7..; 1054; P 10,022,302; 36-1-474-5100; 36-1-474-5141; Fax 36-1-474-5105; mkik@mkik.hu; www.mkik.hu

Budapest • *Budapest Chamber of Commerce & Ind.* • Krisztina Krt. 99; 1016; P 10,022,302; 36-1-488-2111; Fax 36-1-488-2145; ugyfelszolgalat@bkik.hu; www.bkik.hu

Zalaegerszeg • *Chamber of Commerce & Ind. of Zala County* • Petofi u. 24; 8900; P 10,022,302; 36-92-550514; Fax 36-92-550525; zmkik@zmkik.hu; www.zmkik.hu

ICELAND

Reykjavik • *Iceland Chamber of Commerce* • Kringlan 7; 103; P 317,398; 354-5107100; Fax 354-5686564; info@chamber.is; www.vi.is

INDIA

Mubai • *Bombay Industries Assn.* • Sahakar Bhavan; LBS Marg Ghatkopar; 400086; P 117,093,8000; 91-22-2516-53-03; Fax 91-22-2516-53-03; biaoffice@biaindia.org; www.biaindia.org

Mumbai • *Indo-American Chamber of Commerce* • 1-C Vulcan Insurance Bldg Veer Nariman Rd.; Churchgate; 400 020; P 117,093,8000; 91-22-2821413; Fax 91-22-2046141; ho@iaccindia.com; www.iaccindia.com

New Delhi • *Federation of Indian Chambers of Commerce & Ind.* • Federation House; Tansen Marg; 110 001; P 117,093,8000; 91-011-23738760-70; Fax 91-011-23320714; ficci@ficci.com; www.ficci.com

IRAN

Tehran • *Iran Chamber of Commerce Industries & Mines* • 175 Taleghani Ave.; P.O. Box 15875-4671; 15814; P 73,973,630; 98-21-88825111; info@iccim.ir; www.iccim.ir

IRELAND

Cork • *Cork Chamber of Commerce* • Conor Healy; CEO; Fitzgerald House; Summerhill North; P 4,481,430; 353-21-4509044; naoimh@corkchamber.ie; www.corkchamber.ie

Drogheda • *Drogheda & Dist. Chamber of Commerce* • Patricia White; Ofc. Mgr.; Broughton House Dublin Rd.; P 7,800,000; 353-41-9833544; Fax 353-41-9841609; manager@droghedachamber.com; www.droghedachamber.com

Dublin • *Chambers Ireland* • Ian Talbot; CEO; 3rd Flr. Newmount House; Lower Mount St.; 2; P 4,481,430; 353-1-4004300; Fax 353-1-6612811; info@chambers.ie; www.chambers.ie

Dublin • *Dublin Chamber of Commerce* • Mary Rose Burke; CEO; 7 Clare St.; 2; P 4,481,430; 353-1-644-7200; Fax 353-1-676-6043; info@dubchamber.ie; www.dubchamber.ie

Galway • *Galway Chamber of Commerce & Ind.* • Maeve Joyce-Crehan; Gen. Mgr.; Commerce House; Merchant's Rd.; P 4,481,430; 353-91-563536; Fax 353-91-561963; maeve@galwaychamber.com; www.galwaychamber.com

Limerick • *Limerick Chamber* • Dr. James Ring; CEO; 96 O'Connell St.; P 4,481,430; 353-61-415180; Fax 353-61-415785; info@limerickchamber.ie; www.limerickchamber.ie

Sligo • *Sligo Chamber of Commerce* • Paul Keyes; CEO; 16 Quay Street; P 4,481,430; 353-71-61274; Fax 353-71-60912; pkeyes@sligochamber.ie; www.sligochamber.ie

Waterford • *Waterford Chamber of Commerce* • Nick Donnelly; CEO; 2 George's St.; X91 AH9K; P 4,481,430; 353-51-872639; Fax 353-51-876002; info@waterfordchamber.ie; www.waterfordchamber.ie

Wexford • *Wexford Chamber of Ind. & Commerce* • Madeleine Quirke; CEO; Chamber Offices; Hill Street; P 4,481,430; 353-053-912-2226; Fax 353-053-912-1478; traceymorgan@wexfordchamber.ie; www.wexfordchamber.ie

IRELAND, NORTHERN

Londonderry • *Londonderry Chamber of Commerce* • Sinead McLaughlin; Chief Exec.; 1a Hawkin St.; BT48 6RD; P 1,799,000; 28-71-262-379; Fax 28-71-286-789; info@londonderrychamber.co.uk; www.londonderrychamber.co.uk

ISRAEL

Haifa • *Chamber of Commerce & Ind. of Haifa & The North* • 53 Haatzmaut Rd.; P.O. Box 33176; 31331; P 7,624,600; 972-04-864-5428; Fax 972-04-830-2100; main@haifachamber.org.il; www.haifachamber.org.il

Jerusalem • *Jerusalem Chamber of Commerce* • P.O. Box 2083; 91020; P 7,624,600; 972-2-6254333; Fax 972-2-6254335; chamber@chamber.org.il; www.chamber.org.il

Tel Aviv • *Federation of Israeli Chambers of Commerce* • Uriel Lynn; 84 Hahashmonaim St.; P.O. Box 20027; 61200; P 7,624,600; 972-3-5631020; Fax 972-3-5619027; chamber@chamber.org.il; www.chamber.org.il

ITALY

Alessandria • *Alessandria Chamber of Commerce* • via Vochieri 58; 15100; P 60,000,000; 39-131-3131; Fax 39-131-43186; info@al.camcom.it; www.al.camcom.it

Bologna • *Camera di Commercio Ind Art E Ag di Bologna* • Piazza Affari; Piazza Costituzione 8; 40128; P 60,000,000; 39-51-6093111; Fax 39-51-6093452; info@bo.camcom.it; www.bo.camcom.it

Genova • *Genova Chamber of Commerce* • via Garibaldi 4; 16124; P 60,000,000; 39-10-27041; Fax 39-10-2704300; camera.genova@ge.camcom.it; www.ge.camcom.it

Milano • *Milano Chamber of Commerce* • via Meravigli 9/B; 20123; P 60,000,000; 39-2-85151; Fax 39-2-85154232; urp@mi.camcom.it; www.mi.camcom.it

Rome • *Chamber of Commerce & Ind. of Italy* • Piazza Sallustio 21; I-00187; P 60,000,000; 39-6-47041; Fax 39-6-470-4240; unioncamere@unioncamere.it; www.unioncamere.it

Rome • *Rome Chamber of Commerce* • v. de Burro 147; 186; P 60,000,000; 39-6-520821; Fax 39-6-6790547; callcenter-cciaa-roma@infocamere.it; www.rm.camcom.it

Trieste • *Trieste Chamber of Commerce* • Piazza Della Borsa 14; 34121; P 60,000,000; 39-40-67011; Fax 39-40-6701321; urp@ts.camcom.it; www.ts.camcom.it

IVORY COAST

See Cote d'Ivoire

JAMAICA

Kingston • *Jamaica Chamber of Commerce* • Ste. 13-15 UDC Office Centre Bldg.; 12 Ocean Blvd.; P 2,700,000; 876-922-0150; Fax 876-924-9056; info@jamaicachamber.org.jm; www.jamaicachamber.org.jm

JAPAN

Hiroshima • *Higashi-Hiroshima Chamber of Commerce & Ind.* • 44 Matomachi 5-chome; Naka-ku; 739-0025; P 127,450,460; 81-082-420-0301; Fax 81-082-420-0309; kaigisho@hhcci.or.jp; www.hhcci.or.jp

Hokkaido • *Sapporo Chamber of Commerce & Ind.* • Kita-1 Nishi-2; Chuo-ku Sapporo; 060-8610; P 127,450,460; 81-11-231-1122; Fax 81-11-231-1078; kokusai@sapporo-cci.or.jp; www.sapporo-cci.or.jp

Kawasaki • *Kawasaki Chamber of Commerce & Ind.* • 11-2 Ekimaehoncho; Kawasaki-ku; 210-0007; P 127,450,460; 81-044-540-3901; Fax 81-044-540-3900; kokusai@kawasaki-cci.or.jp; www.kawasaki-cci.or.jp

Kobe • *Kobe Chamber of Commerce & Ind.* • 1 Minatojima-Nakamachi; 6-chome Chuo-ku; 650-8543; P 1,540,000; 81-783035806; Fax 81-783062348; info@kobe-cci.or.jp; www.kobe-cci.or.jp

Osaka • *Osaka Chamber of Commerce & Ind.* • 2-8 Hommachi-Bashi; Chuo-ku; 540-0029; P 127,450,460; 81-6-69446400; Fax 81-6-69446293; intl@osaka.cci.or.jp; www.osaka.cci.or.jp

Tokyo • *Japan Chamber of Commerce & Ind.* • 3-2-2 Marunouchi; Chiyoda-ku; 100-0005; P 127,450,460; 81-3-32837500; Fax 81-3-32166497; info@jcci.or.jp; www.jcci.or.jp

JORDAN

Amman • *Jordan Chamber of Commerce* • P.O. Box 7029; 11118; P 6,047,000; 962-6-590-2040; Fax 962-6-590-2051; info@jocc.org.jo; www.jocc.org.jo

Amman • *Amman Chamber of Commerce* • P.O. Box 287; 11118; P 6,047,000; 962-6-5666151-4; Fax 962-6-5666155; info@ammanchamber.org.jo; www.ammanchamber.org

KAZAKHSTAN

Almaty • *Chamber of Commerce & Ind. of Kazakhstan* • 26 Masanche St.; 480091; P 16,316,050; 7-327267-7823; Fax 7-327250-7029; akmcci@dan.kz; www.chamber.kz

KENYA

Mombosa • *Kenya Natl. Chamber of Commerce & Ind.* • James Kitavi; Exec. Officer; P.O. Box 90271; 80100; P 40,512,682; 254-41-231-6161; Fax 254-721-373343; info@kenyachamber.co.ke; www.kenyachamber.co.ke

KOREA, REPUBLIC OF

Busan • *Busan Chamber of Commerce & Ind.* • 853-1 Bumchun-Dong Busanjin-Ku; 614-721; P 48,875,000; 82-51-990-7085; Fax 82-51-990-7099; julyjang@pcci.or.kr; www.pcci.or.kr

Seoul • *Korea Chamber of Commerce & Ind.* • 45 4ga Namdaemunro Jung-gu; 100-743; P 48,875,000; 82-2-6050-3114; Fax 82-2-6050-3400; trade@kccioa.kcci.or.kr; english.korcham.net

KUWAIT

Kuwait City • *Kuwait Chamber of Commerce & Ind.* • Commercial Area #9 Al-Shuhadaa St.; P.O. Box 775 Safat; 13008; P 3,800,000; 965-1805580; Fax 965-22300074; kcci@kcci.org.kw; www.kuwaitchamber.org.kw

KYRGYZ REPUBLIC

Bishkek • *Chamber of Commerce of the Kyrgyz Republic* • Mr. Marat Sharshekeev; Pres.; 107 Kievskaya str.; 720001; P 57,200,000; 996-312-61-38-74; Fax 996-312-61-38-75; info@cci.kg; www.cci.kg

LATVIA

Riga • *Latvian Chamber of Commerce & Ind.* • Mr. Aigars Rostovskis; Pres.; Valdemara str. 35; 1010; P 2,242,916; 371-6225595; Fax 371-678-20092; info@chamber.lv; www.chamber.lv

LEBANON

Beirut • *Chamber of Commerce & Ind. of Beirut & Mt. Lebanon*
• P.O. Box 11-1801; P 4,223,553; 961-1485461; info@ccib.org.lb;
www.ccib.org.lb

LITHUANIA

Kaunas • *Kaunas Reg. Chamber of Commerce Ind. & Crafts* • K.
Donelaicio str. 8; LT-44213; P 3,320,656; 370-37-229212; Fax 370-7-
208330; chamber@chamber.lt; www.chamber.lt

Panevezys • *Panevezys Reg. Chamber of Commerce Ind. & Crafts*
• Respublikos g. 34; 35173; P 3,320,656; 370-45-463687; Fax 370-45-
500309; panevezys@chambers.lt; www.ccic.lt

Siauliai • *Siauliai Reg. Chamber of Commerce Ind. & Crafts* •
Vilniaus str. 88; LT-76285; P 3,320,656; 370-41-523224; Fax 370-41-
523903; siauliai@chambers.lt; www.rumai.lt

Vilnius • *Assn. of Lithuania Chambers of Commerce Ind. & Crafts*
• Vasingtono sq. 1-63A; LT-01108; P 3,320,656; 370-52-612102;
Fax 370-52-612112; info@chambers.lt; www.chambers.lt

LUXEMBOURG

Luxembourg-City • *Grand Duchy of Luxembourg Chamber of
Commerce* • 7 rue Alcide Gasperi; L-2981; P 505,831; 352-4239391;
Fax 352-438326; chamcom@cc.lu; www.cc.lu

MADAGASCAR

Antananarivo • *Chamber of Commerce & Ind. In Antananarivo* •
20 rue Henry Razanatseheno Antaninarenina; BP 166; P 20,713,819;
261-20-2220211; email@cci.mg; www.cci.mg

MALAWI

Blantyre • *Malawi Confederation of Chambers of Commerce &
Ind.* • P.O. Box 258; P 14,900,841; 265-1-871988; Fax 265-1-871147;
mcci@mccci.org; www.mccci.org

MALAYSIA

Kuala Lumpur • *Malaysian International Chamber of Commerce
and Industry* • C-08-08 8th Flr. Block C Plaza Mont' Kiara; 50480;
P 28,401,017; 60-3-6201-7708; Fax 60-3-6201-7705; micci@micci.com;
www.micci.com

MALTA

Valletta • *Malta Chamber of Commerce Enterprise & Ind.* •
The Exchange Buildings; Republic Street; VLT 1117; P 412,961;
356-2123-3873; Fax 356-2124-5223; info@maltachamber.org.mt;
www.maltachamber.org.mt

MARSHALL ISLANDS

Majuro MH • *Marshall Islands Chamber of Commerce* • P.O.
Box 1226; 96960; P 54,038; 692-625-3177; Fax 692-625-3330;
commerce@ntamar.net; www.marshallislandschamber.net

MAURITIUS

Port-Louis • *Mauritius Chamber of Commerce & Ind.* • 3 Royal St.;
P 1,281,214; 230-208-3301; Fax 230-208-0076; www.mcci.org

MEXICO

La Paz • *La Paz Chamber of Commerce* • Mexico 1970 E/
Bravo y Allende; 23040; P 113,423,050; 52-612-122-75-11;
correo@canacolapaz.com; www.canacolapaz.com

Mexico City • *Mexico City Chamber of Commerce* • Paseo de
la Reforma Ste. 42; Col. Centro; 6040; P 113,423,050; 52-55-
3685-2269; Fax 52-55-3685-2269; crflores@ccmexico.com.mx;
www.camaradecomerciodemexico.com.mx

Puebla • *Puebla Chamber of Commerce* • Ave. Reforma Ste. 2704
7 Piso; 72140; P 113,423,050; 52-222-2480800; Fax 52-222-2310655;
canaco@canacopuebla.org.mx; www.canacopuebla.org.mx

Saltillo • *Saltillo Chamber of Commerce* • Av. Universidad Ste.
514; 25260; P 113,423,050; 52-841-55611; Fax 52-841-52903;
conasalt@mcsa.net.mx

Tijuana • *Tijuana Chamber of Commerce* • Xavier Villaurritia 1271
Zona Rio; 22320; P 113,423,050; 52-664-6828488; Fax 52-554-
6828486; web@canacotijuana.com; www.canacotijuana.com

Zapopan • *National Chamber of Commerce of Guadalajara* • Av.
Vallarta Ste. 4095; 45000; P 113,423,050; 52-3-1229020; Fax 52-3-
1217950; comexca@vianet.com.mx

MICRONESIA

Colonia • *Yap State Govt. Commerce & Ind.* • P.O. Box 336;
96943; P 111,064; 691-350-2182; 691-350-2184; Fax 691-350-2571;
yapci@mail.fm; yapdevelopments.org

Tofol • *Kosrae State Chamber of Commerce* • P.O. Box 600;
96944; P 111,064; 691-370-3044; Fax 691-370-2066; drea@mail.fm;
fsminvest.fm/kosrae

Weno • *Chuuk State Chamber of Commerce* • P.O. Box 280; 96942;
P 111,064; 691-330-2552; Fax 691-330-2233; www.fsminvest.fm/chuuk

MOLDOVA

Chisinau • *Chamber of Commerce & Ind. of the Rep. of Moldova* •
28 M Eminescu Str.; 2012; P 3,562,062; 373-22-22-15-52; Fax 373-22-
23-44-25; foreign@chamber.md; www.chamber.md

MONGOLIA

Ulaanbaatar • *Mongolian Natl. Chamber of Commerce & Ind.* •
Magvan Oyunchimeg; CEO; Mahatma Gandhi Street Khan Uul Dist.;
UB Post 101011001; 17011; P 3,000,000; 976-11-327176; 976-11-
312501; Fax 976-11-324620; oyunchimeg.m@mongolchamber.mn;
www.mongolchamber.mn

MOZAMBIQUE

Maputo • *Mozambique Chamber of Commerce* • P.O. Box 1836;
P 23,390,765; 258-1-491970; Fax 258-1-490428; cacomo@teledata.mz;
www.teledata.mz/cacomo/index.htm

NAMIBIA

Windhoek • *Namibia Natl. Chamber of Commerce & Ind.* • P.O. Box 20783; P 2,283,289; 264-61-279-600; Fax 264-61-279-602; windhoek@ncci.org.na; www.namibian.com.na

NEPAL

Kathmandu • *Federation of Nepalese Chambers of Commerce & Ind. (FNCCI)* • Mr. Dharanidhar Khatiwada; Dir. Gen.; Teku; P.O. Box 269; 44600; P 29,959,364; 977-1-426-2061; 977-1-426-6889; Fax 977-1-426-1022; fncci@mos.com.np; www.fncci.org

NETHERLANDS, THE

Almere • *Chamber of Commerce for Gooi- & Eemland* • P.O. Box 10318; 1301 AH; P 16,600,000; 036-524-86-00; Fax 036-524-87-00; gef@kvk.nl; www.kvk.nl

Amsterdam • *Chamber of Commerce & Ind. for Amsterdam* • PO Box 2852; 1000 CW; P 16,612,213; 31-20-531-40-00; Fax 31-20-531-47-99; info@amsterdam.kvk.nl; www.amsterdam.kvk.nl

Arnhem • *Chamber of Commerce & Ind. for Central Gelderland* • P.O. Box 9292; 6800 KZ; P 16,612,213; 31-26-3538888; Fax 31-26-3538999; gelderland@kvk.nl; www.kvk.nl

Eindhoven • *Kamer van Koophandel Oost-Brabant* • P.O. Box 735; 5600 AS; P 16,612,213; 31-40-232-39-11; Fax 31-40-244-95-05; info@brabant.kvk.nl; www.eindhoven.kvk.nl

Gouda • *Central Holland Chamber of Commerce & Ind.* • P.O. Box 57; 2803 PA; P 16,612,213; 31-182-569111; Fax 31-182-571050; info@gouda.kvk.nl; www.kvk.nl

Groningen • *Kamer van Koophandel Friesland* • P.O. Box 134; 9700 AC; P 16,612,213; 31-58-88-585-10-00; Fax 31-58-88-585-10-20; info-leeuwarden@kvk.nl; www.leeuwarden.kvk.nl

The Hague • *Chamber of Commerce & Ind. The Hague* • P.O. Box 29718; 2502 LS; P 16,612,613; 31-70-88-588-80-00; denhaag@kvk.nl; www.denhaag.kuk.nl

Tilburg • *Midden-Brabant Chamber of Commerce & Ind.* • P.O. Box 90154; 5000 LG; P 16,612,613; 31-13-5944122; Fax 31-13-468215; info@tilburg.kvk.nl; www.tilburg.kvk.nl

Utrecht • *Chamber of Commerce Utrecht* • P.O. Box 48; 3500 AA; P 16,612,213; 31-30-239-66-00; Fax 31-30-231-28-04; servicecenter-midden@kvk.nl; www.utrecht.kvk.nl

Woerden • *Chamber of Commerce of the Netherlands* • Watermolenlaan 1; P.O. Box 265; 3440 AG; P 16,612,213; 31-348-426-911; Fax 31-348-426-216; site@vvk.kvk.nl; www.kvk.nl

NETHERLANDS-ANTILLES

Willemstad • *Curacao Chamber of Commerce & Ind.* • John H. Jacobs; Exec. Dir.; Kaya Junior Salas 1; P.O. Box 10; P 160,000; 599-9-461-3918; Fax 599-9-461-5652; businessinfo@curacao-chamber.cw; www.curacao-chamber.cw

NEW ZEALAND

Auckland • *Auckland Reg. Chamber of Commerce & Ind.* • 100 Mayoral Drive Level 3; P.O. Box 47; 1140; P 4,638,414; 64-9-309-6100; Fax 64-9-309-0081; marketing@chamber.co.nz; www.aucklandchamber.co.nz

Dunedin • *Otago Chamber of Commerce* • Dougal McGowan; CEO; P.O. Box 5713; 9058; P 4,367,800; 64-3-479-0181; Fax 64-3-477-0341; office@otagochamber.co.nz; www.otagochamber.co.nz

Hamilton • *Waikato Chamber of Commerce & Ind. Inc.* • William Durning; CEO; Level 2 Wintec House Cnr Nisbet & Angelsea St.; P.O. Box 1122; 3240; P 4,548,009; 64-7-839-5895; Fax 64-7-839-4581; william.durning@waikatochamber.co.nz; www.waikatochamber.co.nz

Lower Hutt • *Hutt Valley Chamber of Commerce & Ind. Inc.* • Mark Futter; CEO; Level 3 15 Daly St.; P.O. Box 30-653; 5040; P 4,367,800; 64-4-939-9821; Fax 64-4-939-9824; info@hvcci.org.nz; www.hutt-chamber.org.nz

Rotorua • *Rotorua Chamber of Commerce* • 1081 Hinemoa St.; P.O. Box 385; 3040; P 4,367,800; 64-7-346-3657; Fax 64-7-349-1388; admin@rotoruachamber.co.nz; www.rotoruachamber.co.nz

Tauranga • *Chamber of Commerce Tauranga Region* • Stan Gregec; CEO; 65 Chapel St.; P.O. Box 414; 3140; P 4,367,800; 64-07-577-9823; 64-07-577-8958; Fax 64-07-577-0364; chamber@tauranga.org.nz; www.tauranga.org.nz

Wellington • *New Zealand Chambers of Commerce & Ind.* • Level 2 3 - 11 Hunter St.; P.O. Box 1590; 6140; P 4,367,800; 64-4-4722725; Fax 64-4-4171767; info@wecc.org.nz ; www.newzealandchambers.co.nz

Wellington • *Wellington Reg. Chamber of Commerce* • John Milford; CEO; Level 2 3 - 11 Hunter St.; P.O. Box 1590; 6140; P 4,367,800; 64-4-473-7224; Fax 64-4-473-4501; www.wecc.org.nz

Whangarei • *Northland Chamber of Commerce* • Tony Collins; CEO; P.O. Box 1703; P 4,367,800; 64-9-4384771; Fax 64-9-4384770; info@northchamber.co.nz; www.northchamber.co.nz

NIGER

Niamey • *Chamber of Commerce Ag. & Ind.* • P.O. Box 209; P 15,511,953; 227-20-73-22-10; Fax 227-20-73-87-64; ccaian@intnet.ne

NIGERIA

Lagos • *Nigerian Assn. of Chambers of Commerce* • P.M.B. 12816; P 158,423,180; 234-01-4964727; Fax 234-01-4964737; naccima30@yahoo.co.uk; www.fewacci.org

Lagos • *The Lagos Chamber of Commerce & Ind.* • P.O. Box 109; P 158,423,180; 234-1-7746617; Fax 234-1-2705145; lcci@lagoschamber.com; www.lagoschamber.com

NORWAY

Kristiansand • *Kristiansand Chamber of Commerce* • Ostre Strandgate 56 Postboks 269; 4663; P 4,885,240; 47-99-23-80-00; Fax 47-38-12-39-79; post@kristiansand-chamber.no; www.kristiansand-chamber.no

Oslo • *Assn. of Norwegian Chambers of Commerce •* Camilla Forgaard Andreassen; CEO; P.O. Box 2900 Solli; 230; P 4,885,240; 47-22-541-779; Fax 47-22-561-700; camilla.forgaard.andreassen@hsh-org.no; www.chamber.no

Oslo • *Oslo Chamber of Commerce •* Mr. Lars KÃ¥re Legernes; Managing Dir.; Henrik Ibsensgt. 100; P.O. Box 2874 Solli; 0230; P 600,000; 47-22-129400; 47-9962-1568; Fax 47-22-129401; mail@chamber.no; www.chamber.no

Stavanger • *Stavanger Chamber of Commerce •* Jostein Soland; CEO; P.O. Box 182; N-4001; P 4,885,240; 47-51-51-08-80; Fax 47-51-51-08-81; post@stavanger-chamber.no; www.stavanger-chamber.no

Trondheim • *Mid Norway Chamber of Commerce & Ind. •* P.O. Box 778; 7408; P 4,885,240; 47-73-88-31-10; Fax 47-73-883111; firmapost@trondheim-chamber.no; www.trondheim-chamber.no

OMAN

Ruwi • *Oman Chamber of Commerce & Ind. •* P.O. Box 1400; 112; P 2,782,435; 968-24707674; Fax 968-24708497; occi@omanchamber.com; www.omanchamber.com

PAKISTAN

Faisalabad • *Faisalabad Chamber of Commerce & Ind. •* East Canal Road Canal Park; 38000; P 173,593,380; 92-41-9230265; Fax 92-41-9230270; info@fcci.com.pk; www.fcci.com.pk

Gujranwala • *Gujranwala Chamber of Commerce & Ind. •* Aiwan-e-Tijarat Rd. Trust Plaza; 52250; P 173,593,380; 92-55-3256701; Fax 92-55-3254440; info@gcci.org.pk; gcci.org.pk

Karachi • *Overseas Investors Chamber of Commerce & Ind. •* P.O. Box 4833; 74000; P 173,593,380; 92-21-2410814; Fax 92-21-2427315; info@oicci.org; www.oicci.org

Karachi • *Federation of Pakistan Chambers of Commerce •* P.O. Box 13875; 75600; P 173,593,380; 92-21-5873691; Fax 92-21-5874332; info@fpcci.com.pk; www.fpcci.com.pk

Lahore • *The Lahore Chamber of Commerce & Ind. •* Mr. Ijaz Ahmad Mumtaz; Pres.; 11-Shahrah-e-Aiwan-e-Sanat-o-Tijarat; 54000; P 173,593,380; 92-42-111222499; 92-42-36305538; Fax 92-42-36368854; president@lcci.org.pk; www.lcci.com.pk

Rawalpindi • *Rawalpindi Chamber of Commerce & Ind. •* Irfan Manan Khan; Secy. Gen.; 39 Mayo Road Civil Lines; P.O. Box 323; 46000; P 173,593,380; 92-51-111722475; 92-51-5111051; Fax 92-51-5111055; rcci@rcci.org.pk; www.rcci.org.pk

Sialkot • *Sialkot Chamber of Commerce & Ind. •* Tariq Mehmood Malik; Gen Secy.; Shahrah-e-Aiwan-e-Sanat-o-Tijarat; P.O. Box 1870; 51310; P 185,000,000; 92-52-4261881; Fax 92-52-4268835; sialkot@scci.com.pk; www.scci.com.pk

PANAMA

Panama • *Camara de Comercio Industrias & Ag de Panama •* Cuba and Ecuador Ave. 33A St.; 1; P 3,516,820; 507-207-3400; Fax 507-207-3422; arbitraje@panacamara.org; www.panacamara.com

PAPUA NEW GUINEA

Port Moresby • *Papua New Guinea Chamber of Commerce & Ind.* • Mr. John Leahy; Pres.; P.O. Box 1621; 121; P 6,858,266; 675-321-3057; Fax 675-321-0566; pngcci@global.net.pg; www.pngcci.org.pg

PERU

Cusco • *Camara de Comercio de Cusco •* Jr. Julio C. tello C-11 - Urb. Santa Monica; 2010; P 29,076,512; 51-84-240090; camcusco@camaralima.org.pe; www.camaracusco.org

PORTUGAL

Lega Da Palmeria • *Bus. Assn. of Portugal •* Av. Dr. Antonio Macedo; 4450-617; P 10,642,841; 351-229-981-500; Fax 351-229-981-616; aep@aeportugal.pt; www.aeportugal.pt

Lisboa • *Chamber of Commerce & Ind. of Portugal •* Rua Portas de Santo Antao 89; 1169-022; P 10,642,841; 351-213-224-050; Fax 351-213-224-051; mm@acl.org.pt; www.en.acl.org.pt

Lisbon • *Investment Trade & Tourism of Portugal •* Av. 5 de Outubro 101; 1050; P 10,642,841; 351-21-790-9500; Fax 351-21-793-8028

Ponta Delgada • *Chamber of Commerce & Ind. of the Azores •* Rua Ernesto do Canto 13; 9504-531; P 10,600,000; 351-296-305-000; Fax 351-296-305-040; ccipd@ccipd.pt; www.ccipd.pt

Porto • *Chamber of Commerce & Ind. of Porto •* Palacio da Bolsa; Rua Ferreira Borges; 4050-253; P 10,642,841; 351-22-3399000; Fax 351-22-3399090; correio@cciporto.pt; www.cciporto.com

QATAR

Doha • *Qatar Chamber of Commerce & Ind. •* P.O. Box 402; P 1,758,793; 974-4559111; Fax 974-4661693; info@qcci.org; www.qatarchamber.com

ROMANIA

Bucharest • *Chamber of Commerce of Romania & Bucharest Muni.* • 2 Octavian Goga Blvd.; Sector 3; 030982; P 21,442,012; 40-21-319-01-14-18; ccir@ccir.ro; www.ccir.ro

RUSSIAN FEDERATION

Moscow • *Chamber of Commerce & Ind. of the Russian Fed. •* 6 Ilyinka Str.; 109012; P 141,750,000; 7-495-6200009; Fax 7-495-6200360; tpprf@tpprf.ru; www.tpprf.ru

RWANDA, REPUBLIC OF

Kigali • *Chamber of Commerce & Ind. of Rwanda •* P.O. Box 319; P 10,624,005; 250-252-583541; Fax 250-252-583532; frsp@rwanda1.com

SAINT KITTS & NEVIS

Basseterre • *St. Kitts & Nevis Chamber of Ind. & Commerce* • P.O. Box 332; P 52,402; 869-465-2980; Fax 869-465-4490; sknchamber@caribsurf.com; www.stkittsnevischamber.org

SAINT LUCIA

Castries • *St. Lucia Chamber of Commerce Ind. & Ag.* • Mr. Brian Louisy; Exec. Dir.; Vide Boutielle; P.O. Box 482; P 174,000; 758-4523165; 758-4531540; Fax 758-4536907; info@stluciachamber.org; www.stluciachamber.org

SAINT VINCENT & THE GRENADINES

Kingstown • *St. Vincent & the Grenadines Chamber of Ind. & Commerce* • Anthony Regisford; Exec. Dir.; Criuse Ship Terminal; P.O. Box 134; VC100; P 104,574; (784) 457-1464; (784) 493 9133; Fax (784) 456-2944; svgchamber@svg-cic.org; www.svg-cic.org

SAMOA

Apia • *Samoa Chamber of Commerce & Ind.* • Ane L. Moananu; CEO; 1st Flr. Le Sanalele Complex Saleufi; P.O. Box 2014; P 183,081; 685-31090; Fax 685-31089; samoachamber@samoachamber.ws; www.samoachamber.ws

Apia • *Dept. of Trade Commerce & Ind.* • P.O. Box 862; 98682; P 183,081; 685-20471; Fax 685-21646

SAUDI ARABIA

Dammam • *Chamber of Commerce & Ind. Eastern Province* • P.O. Box 719; 31421; P 27,448,086; 966-3-8571111; Fax 966-3-8570607; info@chamber.org.sa; www.chamber.org.sa

Dammam • *Federation of GCC Chambers of Commerce & Ind.* • Abulrahim Hasan Naqi; Secy. Gen.; P.O. Box 2198; 31451; P 27,448,086; 966-13-8993749; 966-564-852442; Fax 966-13-8994638; fgccc@fgccc.org; www.fgccc.org

Riyadh • *Cncl. of Saudi Chambers of Commerce & Ind.* • P.O. Box 16683; 11474; P 27,448,086; 966-1-218-2222; Fax 966-1-218-2111; council@saudichambers.org.sa; www.saudichambers.org.sa

Riyadh • *Riyadh Chamber of Commerce & Ind.* • P.O. Box 596; 11421; P 27,448,086; 966-1-404-3812; Fax 966-1-402-1103; www.riyadhchamber.com

SCOTLAND

Glasgow • *Glasgow Chamber of Commerce* • Mr. Stuart Patrick; CEO; 30 George Sq.; G2 1EQ; P 5,094,800; 44-141-204-2121; Fax 44-141-221-2336; chamber@glasgowchamber.org; www.glasgowchamber.org

SENEGAL

Dakar • *Chamber of Commerce Ind. & Ag.* • P.O. Box 118; P 12,433,728; 221-823-71-89; Fax 221-823-93-63; cciad@orange.sn; www.cciad.sn

SERBIA

Belgrade • *Chamber of Commerce & Ind. of Serbia* • Resavska st. 13-15; P.O. Box 959; 11000; P 7,292,574; 381-11-3300900; Fax 381-11-3239009; www.pks.rs

Belgrade • *Belgrade Chamber of Commerce* • Kneza Milosa 12; 11000; P 7,292,574; 381-11-2641355; Fax 381-11-2642029; mmj@kombeg.org.rs; www.kombeg.org.rs

SINGAPORE

Singapore • *Singapore Intl. Chamber of Commerce* • Victor Mills; CEO; 6 Raffles Quay #10-01; 48580; P 5,000,000; 65-65000988; Fax 65-62242785; general@sicc.com.sg; www.sicc.com.sg

SLOVAK REPUBLIC

Bratislava • *Slovak Chamber of Commerce & Ind.* • Gorkeho 9; 81603; P 5,443,456; 421-7-54433291; Fax 421-7-54131159; sopkurad@scci.sk; www.scci.sk

SLOVENIA

Ljubljana • *Chamber of Commerce & Ind. of Slovenia* • Dimiceva 13; 1000; P 2,052,821; 386-1-5898000; Fax 386-1-5898100; info@gzs.si; www.gzs.si/eng

SOUTH AFRICA

Cape Town • *Cape C/C & Ind.* • Ms. Janine Myburgh; Pres.; 4th flr. 33 Martin Hammerschlag Way Foreshore; P. O. Box 204; 8000; P 49,991,300; 27-21-402-4300; Fax 27-21-402-4302; info@capechamber.co.za; www.capechamber.co.za

Durban • *Durban Chamber of Commerce & Ind.* • Dumile Cele; CEO; Lion Match office Park Chamber Square 892 Umgeni Rd.; P.O. Box 1506; 4000; P 49,991,300; 27-31-335-1000; Fax 27-31-309-1149; chamber@durbanchamber.co.za; www.durbanchamber.co.za

East London • *Border-Kei Chamber of Bus.* • Mr Les Holbrook; Exec. Dir.; Chamber House The Hub; Bonza Bay Rd. Beacon Bay; 5214; P 60,000,000; 27-43-743-8438; Fax 27-43-743-2249; info@bkcob.co.za; www.bkcob.co.za

Johannesburg • *Johannesburg Chamber of Commerce & Ind.* • Joan Warburton-McBride; CEO; Private Bag 34; Auckland Park; 2006; P 49,991,300; 27-11-726-5300; Fax 27-11-482-2000; joan@jcci.co.za; www.jcci.co.za

Saxonwold • *South African Chamber of Commerce & Ind.* • Mr. Vusi Khumalo; Pres.; P.O. Box 213; 2132; P 49,991,300; 27-11-446-3800; 27-82-430-1584; Fax 27-865491102; corporate@sacci.org.za; www.sacci.org.za

SPAIN

Barcelona • *Barcelona Chamber of Commerce* • Avda. Diagonal 452-454; 8006; P 46,081,574; 34-93-902-448-448; cambra@cambrabcn.org; www.cambrabcn.org

Bilbao • *Chamber of Commerce & Ind. of Bilbao* • Alda. Recalde 50; 48008; P 46,081,574; 34-944706500; Fax 34-94-4436171; atencionaclientes@camarabilbao.com; www.camarabilbao.com

Cordoba • *Chamber of Commerce of Cordoba* • Ignacio Fernandez de Mesa Delgado; Pres.; Perez de Castro 1; 14003; P 805,000; 34-957-296199; Fax 34-957-202106; info@camaracordoba.com; www.camaracordoba.com

Madrid • *Madrid Chamber of Commerce & Ind.* • Plaza de la Independencia 1; 28001; P 46,081,574; 34-91-538-3500; Fax 34-1-5383677; camara@camaramadrid.es; www.camaramadrid.es

Valencia • *Valencia Chamber of Commerce & Ind.* • c/. Jesus 19; 46007; P 46,081,574; 34-963-103-900; Fax 34-963-531-742; info@camaravalencia.com; www.camaravalencia.com

SRI LANKA

Colombo • *The Ceylon Chamber of Commerce* • Mr. Mangala P.B. Yapa; Secy. Gen./CEO; 50 Nawam Mawatha; 2; P 20,859,949; 94-11-5588888; 94-11-2421745-7; Fax 94-11-2449352; info@chamber.lk; www.chamber.lk

SUDAN

Khartoum • *Union of Sudanese Chambers of Commerce* • P.O. Box 81; 11123; P 43,551,941; 249-11-772346; Fax 249-11-780748; ashrafmutuakil@yahoo.com; www.sudanchamber.org

SURINAME

Paramaribo • *Chamber of Commerce & Ind.* • Mrs. Joanne Pancham; Secy.; P.O. Box 149; P 524,636; 597-530-511; Fax 597-437-971; chamber@sr.net; www.surinamechamber.com

SWAZILAND

Mbabane • *Federation of Swaziland Employers & C/C* • Ms. Zodwa Mabuza; CEO; Emafini Business Center Malagwane Hill; P.O.Box 72; H100; P 1,186,056; 268-404-0768; 268-404-4408; Fax 268-409-0051; fsecc@business-swaziland.com; www.business-swaziland.com

SWEDEN

Gavle • *Chamber of Commerce of Central Sweden* • P.O. Box 296; 801 04; P 9,379,116; 46-26-662080; Fax 46-26-662099; chamber@mhk.cci.se; www.mhk.cci.se

Gothenburg • *Western Sweden Chamber of Commerce* • Massans Gata 18; P.O. Box 5253; S-402 25; P 9,379,116; 46-31-835900; Fax 46-31-835936; info@handelskammaren.net; www.handelskammaren.net

Jonkoping • *Jonkoping Chamber of Commerce* • Jonas Ekeroth; CEO; Elmiavagen 13; 554 54; P 9,379,116; 46-36-301430; Fax 46-36-129579; info@handelskammarenjonkoping.se; www.handelskammarenjonkoping.se

Karlstad • *Wermland Chamber of Commerce* • S. Kyrkogatan 6; 652 24; P 9,379,116; 46-54-221480; Fax 46-54-221490; info@handelskammarenvarmland.se; www.handelskammarenvarmland.se

Lulea • *Norrbotten Chamber of Commerce* • Kyrkogatan 13; 972 32; P 9,379,116; 46-920-455660; Fax 46-920-455666; info@north.cci.se; www.north.cci.se

Malmo • *Chamber of Commerce and Ind. of Southern Sweden* • Stephan Müchler; CEO; Skeppsbron 2; SE-211 20; P 9,379,116; 46-40-6902400; Fax 46-40-6902490; info@handelskammaren.com; www.handelskammaren.com

Orebro • *Chamber of Commerce Malardalen* • Christina Hedberg; Managing Dir.; Box 8044; 70008; P 9,379,116; 46-19-689-35-00; Fax 46-19-611-77-50; info@handelskammarenmalardalen.se; www.handelskammarenmalardalen.se

Skelleftea • *Vesterbotten Chamber of Commerce* • Expolaris Center; 93178; P 9,379,116; 46-910-77-08-90; Fax 46-910-77-08-99; handelskammaren@ac.cci.se; www.ac.cci.se

Stockholm • *Stockholm Chamber of Commerce* • P.O. Box 16050; SE-103 21; P 9,379,116; 46-8-555-100-00; Fax 46-8-566-316-00; info@chamber.se; www.chamber.se

SWITZERLAND

Geneva • *Geneva Chamber of Commerce & Ind.* • 4 boulevard du Theatre; PO Box 5039; 1211; P 7,825,243; 41-22-8199111; Fax 41-22-8199100; ccig@cci.ch; www.ccig.ch

Zurich • *Swiss Business Federation* • Hegibachstrasse 47; CH-8032; P 7,825,243; 41-1-4213535; Fax 41-1-4213434; info@economiesuisse.ch; www.economiesuisse.ch

SYRIA

Aleppo • *Aleppo Chamber of Commerce* • P.O. Box 1261; P 20,446,609; 963-21-2238236; Fax 963-21-2213493; alepchmb@mail.sy; www.aleppochamber.net

Damascus • *Federation of Syrian Chambers of Commerce* • Mr. Mhd Ghassan Al-Qallaa; Pres.; Mousa Bin Nosair St.; P.O. Box 5909; P 20,446,609; 963-11-3311504; Fax 963-11-3331127; syr-trade@mail.sy; fedcommsyr.sy

Damascus • *Damascus Chamber of Commerce* • P.O. Box 1040; P 20,446,609; 963-11-2211339; Fax 963-11-2225874; dcc@net.sy; www.dcc-sy.com

Federation of Syrian Chambers of Commerce • Mousa Bin Nosair St.; P.O. Box 5909; P 20,446,609; 963-11-3311504; Fax 963-11-3331127; syr-trade@mail.sy; fedcommsyr.org

TAIWAN

Taipei • *World Taiwanese Chambers of Commerce* • 7G06 No 5; Hsin-Yi Road Sec 5; 110; P 22,974,347; 886-2-87881466; Fax 886-2-87881533; wtccmail@ms67.hinet.net; www.tccseattle.org

TANZANIA

Dar es Salaam • *Tanzania Chamber of Commerce Ind. & Ag.* • Daniel Machemba; Exec. Dir.; 21 Ghana Ave.; 9713 DSM; P 44,841,226; 255-22-211-9436; Fax 255-22-211-9437; info@tccia.com; www.tccia.com

THAILAND

Bangkok • *Bd. of Trade of Thailand* • 150/2 Rajbopit Rd.; 10200; P 69,122,234; 66-2-622-1111; Fax 66-2-225-5475; bot@thaichamber.org; www.thaichamber.org

Bangkok • *The Thai Chamber of Commerce* • 150/2 Rajbopit Rd.; 10200; P 69,122,234; 660-2-6221860; Fax 660-2-2253372; tcc@thaichamber.org; www.thaichamber.org

TONGA, SOUTH PACIFIC

Nuku'alofa • *Tonga Chamber of Commerce & Ind.* • P.O. Box 1704; P 104,058; 676-25-168; Fax 676-26-039; admin@tongachamber.org; www.tongachamber.org

TRINIDAD & TOBAGO

Point Lisas • *The Energy Chamber of Trinidad & Tobago* • Dr. Thackwray Driver; Pres./CEO; Unit B2.03 Atlantic Plaza Atlantic Ave.; P 1,341,465; 868-679-6623; Fax 868-679-4242; execoffice@energy.tt; www.energy.tt

Port of Spain • *Trinidad & Tobago Chamber of Ind. & Commerce* • P.O. Box 499; P 1,341,465; 868-637-6966; Fax 868-637-7425; chamber@chamber.org.tt; www.chamber.org.tt

TURKEY

Ankara • *Union of Chambers & Commodity Exchanges* • Dumlupinar Bulvari No. 252; Bakanliklar; 06530; P 72,752,325; 90-312-218-2000; Fax 90-312-219-4090; info@tobb.org.tr; www.tobb.org.tr

Ankara • *Ankara Chamber of Commerce* • Sogutozu Mh. Eskisehir Yolu 2 Cd.; 06520; P 72,752,325; 90-312-201-81-00; Fax 90-312-201-81-87; info@atoankaraexport.org; www.atoankaraexport.org

Izmir • *Izmir Chamber of Commerce* • Ataturk cad. No:126 Pasaport; 35210; P 72,752,325; 90-232-498-4266; Fax 90-232-445-3861; info@izto.org.tr; www.izto.org.tr

UGANDA

Kampala • *Uganda Natl. Chamber of Commerce & Ind.* • Plot 1A Kiira Rd.; P.O. Box 3809; P 33,424,683; 256-75350-3035; Fax 256-41-4230310; info@chamberuganda.com; www.chamberuganda.com

UKRAINE

Ivano-Frankivsk • *Ivano-Frankivsk Chamber of Commerce & Ind.* • 9 Teodor Tsiokler str.; 76014; P 45,870,700; 380-342523347; Fax 380-342523347; office@cci.if.ua; www.cci.if.ua

Sumy • *Sumy Chamber of Commerce & Ind.* • 7a. Chervonogvardijska Str.; 40030; P 45,870,700; 380-542-600390; Fax 380-542-210041; chamber@cci.sumy.ua; www.cci.sumy.ua

UNITED ARAB EMIRATES

Abu Dhabi • *Abu Dhabi Chamber of Commerce & Ind.* • P.O. Box 662; P 7,511,690; 971-2-6214000; Fax 971-2-6215867; services@adcci.gov.ae; www.abudhabichamber.ae

Abu Dhabi • *Federation of UAE Chambers of Commerce & Ind.* • H.E. Abdulla Sultan Abdulla; Secy. Gen.; P.O. Box 3014; P 7,511,690; 971-2-6214144; Fax 971-2-6339210; info@fcciuae.ae; www.fcciuae.ae

Ajman • *Ajman Chamber of Commerce & Ind.* • P.O. Box 662; P 7,511,690; 971-67422177; Fax 971-67471222; fatima.alsuwaidi@ajcci.gov.ae; www.ajcci.gov.ae

Dubai • *Dubai Chamber of Commerce & Ind.* • P.O. Box 1457; P 7,511,690; 971-4-2280000; 800-242-6237; Fax 971-4-2028888; customercare@dubaichamber.com; www.dubaichamber.com

Sharjah • *Sharjah Chamber of Commerce & Ind.* • P.O. Box 580; P 7,511,690; 971-65-30-2222; Fax 971-65-30-2226; scci@sharjah.gov.ae; www.sharjah.gov.ae

UNITED KINGDOM

Birmingham • *Greater Birmingham Chambers of Commerce* • Paul Faulkner; CEO; 75 Harborne Rd.; B15 3DH; P 62,218,761; 44-121-454-6171; Fax 44-121-455-8670; info@birmingham-chamber.com; www.birmingham-chamber.com

Bristol • *Business West - Leigh Ct.* • Phil Smith; Managing Dir.; Leigh Court Abbots Leigh; BS8 3RA; P 62,218,761; 44-01275-373-373; phil.smith@businesswest.co.uk; www.businesswest.co.uk

London • *Intl. Chamber of Commerce-United Kingdom* • Chris Southworth; Secy. General; First Flr. 1-3 Staple Inn; WC1V 7QH; P 62,218,761; 44-20-78389363; Fax 44-20-72355447; info@iccwbo.uk; www.iccwbo.uk

London • *London Chamber of Commerce & Ind.* • 33 Queen St.; EC4R 1AP; P 62,218,761; 44-20-7248-4444; Fax 44-20-7489-0391; lc@londonchamber.co.uk; www.londonchamber.co.uk

Manchester • *Greater Manchester Chamber of Commerce* • Clive Memmott; CEO; Elliot House; 151 Deansgate; M3 3WD; P 62,218,761; 44-161-2374102; Fax 44-161-2364160; info@gmchamber.co.uk; www.gmchamber.co.uk

Staffordshire • *Staffordshire Chambers of Commerce* • Commerce House Festival Park; Stoke-on-Trent; ST1 5BE; P 62,218,761; 44-1-782-202222; Fax 44-1-782-202448; info@staffordshirechambers.co.uk; staffordshirechambers.co.uk

URUGUAY

Montevideo • *Camara Nacional de Comercio* • Rincón 454 P.2; 11000; P 3,356,584; 598-2-916-1277; Fax 598-2-916-1243; gerencia@cncs.com.uy; www.cncs.com.uy

VIETNAM

Hanoi • *Vietnam Chamber of Commerce & Ind.* • 9 Dao Duy Anh St.; Dong Da District; P 86,936,464; 84-4-5742187; Fax 84-4-5742622; vbfhn@hn.vnn.vn; vcocaiv.en.china.cn

WALES

Newport • *South Wales Chamber of Commerce* • Gemma Bafico; Head of Op.; Enterprise Way; East Tyndall St.; NP20 2AQ; P 3,004,600; 44-29-20-481532; 44-1633-222664; info@southwaleschamber.co.uk; www.southwaleschamber.co.uk

ZAMBIA

Kitwe • *Kitwe & Dist. Chamber of Commerce & Ind.* • Engineers House 8 Kantanta Street; P.O. Box 20672; 10101; P 12,926,409; 260-21-2225345; Fax 260-21-2221681; info@kitwechamber.com; kitwechamber.com

Lusaka • *Zambia Chamber of Commerce & Ind.* • Ms. Prisca M. Chikwashi; CEO; Plot no. 2374 Financial Lane Showgrounds; P.O. Box 30844; 10101; P 12,926,409; 260-211-252483; 260 211 253007; Fax 260-211-253020; secretariat@zacci.co.zm; zambiachamber.org

Ndola • *Ndola & District Chamber of Commerce & Ind.* • Kevin Shone; P.O. Box 71346; 10101; P 12,926,409; 260-212-650130; Fax 260-212-651135; kevin_shone@kasembo.com; zambiachambers.org

ZIMBABWE

Harare • *Confederation of Zimbabwe Industries* • 31 J. Chinamano Ave; P 12,571,454; 263-4-251490-6; Fax 263-4-252424; info@czi.co.zw; www.czi.co.zw

Harare • *Zimbabwe Natl. Chamber of Commerce* • P.O. Box 1934; P 12,571,454; 263-2936818; lindah@zncc.co.zw; www.zncc.co.zw

THE ONE HUNDRED AND FIFTEENTH CONGRESS - FIRST SESSION

U.S. Capitol Switchboard   (202) 224-3121

Addressing Correspondence
To a Senator:
The Honorable (last name)
United States **Senate**
Washington DC 20510

Dear Senator (last name):

To a Representative:
The Honorable (last name)
United States House of **Representatives**
Washington DC 20515

Dear Representative (last name):

Key Websites
White House   http://www.whitehouse.gov
Senate Home Page   http://www.**senate**.gov
House Home Page   http://www.house.gov

Alabama

State Capitol • Montgomery, AL 36130 (334) 242-7100

Governor • Robert J. Bentley (R) 2019

Senate • Jeff Sessions (R) 2021, Richard C. Shelby (R) 2023

Representatives • Bradley Byrne (R), Martha Roby (R), Mike Rogers (R), Robert Aderholt (R), Mo Brooks (R), Gary Palmer (R), Terri Sewell (D)

Alaska

State Capitol • Juneau, AK 99811-0001 (907) 465-3500

Governor • Bill Walker (I) 2018

Senate • Daniel Sullivan (R) 2021, Lisa Murkowski (R) 2023

Representative • Don Young (R)

Arizona

State Capitol • Phoenix, AZ 85007 (602) 542-4331

Governor • Doug Ducey (R) 2019

Senate • Jeff Flake (R) 2019, John McCain (R) 2023

Representatives • Tom O'Halleran (D), Martha McSally (R), Raul Grijalva (D), Paul A. Gosar (R), Andy Biggs (R), David Schweikert (R), Ruben Gallego (D), Trent Franks (R), Kyrsten Sinema (D)

Arkansas

State Capitol • Little Rock AR 72201 (501) 682-2345

Governor • Asa Hutchinson (R) 2019

Senate • Tom Cotton (R) 2021, John Boozman (R) 2023

Representatives • Rick Crawford (R), French Hill (R), Steve Womack (R), Bruce Westerman (R)

California

State Capitol • Sacramento CA 95814 (916) 445-2841

Governor • Jerry Brown (D) 2019

Senate • Dianne Feinstein (D) 2019, Kamala Harris (D) 2023

Representatives • Doug LaMalfa (R), Jared Huffman (D), John Garamendi (D), Tom McClintock (R), Mike Thompson (D), Doris Matsui (D), Ami Bera (D), Paul Cook (R), Jerry McNerney (D), Jeff Denham (R), Mark DeSaulnier (D), Nancy Pelosi (D), Barbara Lee (D), Jackie Speier (D), Eric Swalwell (D), Jim Costa (D), Ro Khanna (D), Anna Eshoo (D), Zoe Lofgren (D), Jimmy Panetta (D), David Valadao (R), Devin Nunes (R), Kevin McCarthy (R), Salud Carbajai (D), Steve Knight (R), Julia Brownley (D), Judy Chu (D), Adam Schiff (D), Tony Cardenas (D), Brad Sherman (D), Pete Aguilar (D), Grace Napolitano (D), Ted Lieu (D), Xavier Becerra (D), Norma Torres (D), Raul Ruiz (D), Karen Bass (D), Linda Sanchez (D), Ed Royce (R), Lucille Roybal-Allard (D), Mark Takano (D), Ken Calvert (R), Maxine Waters (D), Nanette Barragan (D), Mimi Walters (R), Lou Correa (D), Alan Lowenthal (D), Dana Rohrabacher (R), Darrell Issa (R), Duncan D. Hunter (R), Juan Vargas (D), Scott Peters (D), Susan Davis (D)

Colorado

State Capitol • Denver CO 80203 (303) 866-2471

Governor • John Hickenlooper (D) 2019

Senate • Cory Gardner (R) 2021, Michael Bennet (D) 2023

Representatives • Diana DeGette (D), Jared Polis (D), Scott Tipton (R), Ken Buck (R), Doug Lamborn (R), Mike Coffman (R), Ed Perlmutter (D)

Connecticut

State Capitol • Hartford CT 06106 (860) 566-4840

Governor • Dan Malloy (D) 2019

Senate • Christopher Murphy (D) 2019, Richard Blumenthal (D) 2023

Representatives • John Larson (D), Joe Courtney (D), Rosa DeLauro (D), Jim Himes (D), Elizabeth Esty (D)

U.S. Congress

Delaware

State Capitol • Dover DE 19901 (302) 739-4101

Governor • John Carney (D) 2021

Senate • Thomas Carper (D) 2019, Christopher A. Coons (D) 2021

Representative • Lisa Blunt Rochester (D)

District of Columbia

District Building • Washington D.C. 20002 (202) 727-1000

Representative • Eleanor Holmes Norton (D)

Florida

State Capitol • Tallahassee FL 32399 (850) 488-2272

Governor • Rick Scott (R) 2015

Senate • Bill Nelson (D) 2019, Marco Rubio (R) 2023

Representatives • Matt Gaetz (R), Neal Dunn (R), Ted Yoho (R), John Rutherford (R), Al Lawson (D), Ron DeSantis (R), Stephanie Murphy (D), Bill Posey (R), Darren Soto (D), Val Demings (D), Daniel Webster (R), Gus M. Bilirakis (R), Charlie Crist (D), Kathy Castor (D), Dennis Ross (R), Vern Buchanan (R), Tom Rooney (R), Brian Mast (R), Francis Rooney (R), Alcee Hastings (D), Lois Frankel (D), Ted Deutch (D), Debbie Wasserman Schultz (D), Frederica Wilson (D), Mario Diaz-Balart (R), Carlos Curbelo (R), Ileana Ros-Lehtinen (R)

Georgia

State Capitol • Atlanta GA 30334 (404) 656-1776

Governor • Nathan Deal (R) 2019

Senate • David Perdue (R) 2021, Johnny Isakson (R) 2023

Representatives • Buddy Carter (R), Sanford Bishop Jr. (D), Drew Ferguson (R), Henry C. "Hank" Johnson Jr. (D), John Lewis (D), Tom Price (R), Robert Woodall (R), Austin Scott (R), Doug Collins (R), Jody Hice (R), Barry Loudermilk (R), Rick W. Allen (R), David Scott (D), Tom Graves (R)

Hawaii

State Capitol • Honolulu HI 96801 (808) 586-0013

Governor • David Ige (D) 2018

Senate • Mazie Hirono (D) 2019, Brian Schatz (D) 2023

Representatives • Colleen Hanabusa (D), Tulsi Gabbard (D)

Idaho

State Capitol • Boise ID 83720 (208) 334-2100

Governor • Butch Otter (R) 2019

Senate • James E. Risch (R) 2021, Michael Crapo (R) 2023

Representatives • Raul Labrador (R), Mike Simpson (R)

Illinois

State Capitol • Springfield IL 62706 (217) 782-6830

Governor • Bruce Rauner (R) 2019

Senate • Richard Durbin (D) 2021, Tammy Duckworth (D) 2023

Representatives • Bobby Rush (D), Robin Kelly (D), Daniel Lipinski (D), Luis Gutierrez (D), Mike Quigley (D), Peter J. Roskam (R), Danny K. Davis (D), Raja Krishnamoorthi (D), Jan Schakowsky (D), Brad Schneider (D), Bill Foster (D), Mike Bost (R), Rodney Davis (R), Randy Hultgren (R), John Shimkus (R), Adam Kinzinger (R), Cheri Bustos (D), Darin LaHood (R)

Indiana

State Capitol • Indianapolis IN 46204 (317) 232-4567

Governor • Eric Holcomb (R) 2021

Senate • Joe Donnelly (D) 2019, Todd Young (R) 2023

Representatives • Peter J. Visclosky (D), Jackie Walroski (R), Jim Banks (R), Todd Rokita (R), Susan Brooks (R), Luke Messer (R), Andre Carson (D), Larry Bucshon (R), Trey Hollingsworth (R)

Iowa

State Capitol • Des Moines IA 50319 (515) 281-5211

Governor • Terry Branstad (R) 2019

Senate • Joni Ernst (R) 2021, Charles E. Grassley (R) 2023

Representatives • Rod Blum (R), David Loebsack (D), David Young (R), Steve King (R)

Kansas

State Capitol • Topeka KS 66612 (785) 296-3232

Governor • Sam Brownback (R) 2019

Senate • Pat Roberts (R) 2021 , Jerry Moran (R) 2023

Representatives • Roger Marshall (R), Lynn Jenkins (R), Kevin Yoder (R), Mike Pompeo (R)

Kentucky

State Capitol • Frankfort KY 40601 (502) 564-2611

Governor • Matt Bevin (R) 2019

Senate • Mitch McConnell (R) 2021, Rand Paul (R) 2023

Representatives • James Corner (R), Brett S. Guthrie (R), John A.Yarmuth (D), Thomas Massie (R), Harold Rogers (R), Andy Barr (R)

Louisiana

State Capitol • Baton Rouge LA 70804 (225) 342-7015

Governor • John Bel Edwards (D) 2020

Senate • Bill Cassidy (R) 2021, John Neely Kennedy (R) 2023

Representatives • Steve Scalise (R), Cedric Richmond (D), Clay Higgins (R), Mike Johnson (R), Ralph Abraham (R), Garett Graves (R)

Maine

State Capitol • Augusta ME 04333 (207) 287-3531

Governor • Paul LePage (R) 2019

Senate • Angus S. King Jr. (I) 2019, Susan Collins (R) 2021

Representatives • Chellie Pingree (D), Bruce Poliquin (R)

Maryland

State Capitol • Annapolis MD 21401 (410) 974-3901

Governor • Larry Hogan (R) 2019

Senate • Benjamin Cardin (D) 2019, Chris Van Hollen (D) 2023

Representatives • Andy Harris (R), Dutch Ruppersberger (D), John P. Sarbanes (D), Anthony G. Brown (D), Steny H. Hoyer (D), John K. Delaney (D), Elijah Cummings (D), Jamie Raskin (D)

Massachusetts

State House • Boston MA 02133 (617) 725-4000

Governor • Charlie Baker (R) 2019

Senate • Elizabeth Warren (D) 2019, Edward J. Markey (D) 2021

Representatives • Richard Neal (D), James McGovern (D), Niki Tsongas (D), Joseph Kennedy III (D), Katherine Clark (D), Seth Moulton (D), Michael Capuano (D), Stephen F. Lynch (D), William Keating (D)

Michigan

State Capitol • Lansing MI 48909 (517) 373-3400

Governor • Rick Snyder (R) 2015

Senate • Debbie Stabenow (D) 2019, Gary Peters (D) 2021

Representatives • Jack Bergman (R) , Bill Huizenga (R), Justin Amash (R), John Moolenaar (R), Daniel Kildee (D), Fred Upton (R), Tim Walberg (R), Mike Bishop (R), Sander Levin (D), Paul Mitchell (R), David Trott (R), Debbie Dingell (D), John Conyers Jr. (D), Brenda Lawrence (D)

Minnesota

State Capitol • Saint Paul MN 55155 (651) 296-3391

Governor • Mark Dayton (D) 2019

Senate • Amy Klobuchar (D) 2019, Al Franken (D) 2021

Representatives • Timothy Walz (D), Jason Lewis (R), Erik Paulsen (R), Betty McCollum (D), Keith Ellison (D), Tom Emmer (R), Collin Peterson (D), Rick Nolan (D)

Mississippi

State Capitol • Jackson MS 39205 (601) 359-3100

Governor • Phil Bryant (R) 2020

Senate • Roger Wicker (R) 2019, Thad Cochran (R) 2021

Representatives • Trent Kelly (R), Bennie Thompson (D), Gregg Harper (R), Steven Palazzo (R)

Missouri

State Capitol • Jefferson City MO 65102 (573) 751-3222

Governor • Eric Greitens (R) 2021

Senate • Claire McCaskill (D) 2019, Roy Blunt (R) 2023

Representatives • William "Lacy" Clay Jr. (D), Ann Wagner (R), Blaine Luetkemeyer (R), Vicky Hartzler (R), Emanuel Cleaver (D), Sam Graves (R), Billy Long (R), Jason Smith (R)

Montana

State Capitol • State Capitol • Helena MT 59620 (406) 444-3111

Governor • Steve Bullock (D) 2021

Senate • Jon Tester (D) 2019, Steve Daines (R) 2021

Representatives • Ryan Zinke (R)

Nebraska

State Capitol • Lincoln NE 68509 (402) 471-2244

Governor • Pete Ricketts (R) 2019

Senate • Deb Fischer (R) 2019, Ben Sasse (R) 2021

Representatives • Jeff Fortenberry (R), Don Bacon (R), Adrian Smith (R)

Nevada

State Capitol • Carson City NV 89701 (775) 684-5670

Governor • Brian Sandoval (R) 2019

Senate • Dean Heller (R) 2019, Catherine Cortez Masto (D) 2023

Representatives • Dina Titus (D), Mark Amodei (R), Jacky Rosen (D), Ruben Kihuen (D)

New Hampshire

State Capitol • Concord NH 03301 (603) 271-2121

Governor • Chris Sununu (R) 2019

Senate • Jeanne Shaheen (D) 2021, Maggie Hassan (D) 2023

Representatives • Carol Shea-Porter (D), Ann McLane Kuster (D)

New Jersey

State Capitol • Trenton NJ 08625 (609) 292-6000

Governor • Chris Christie (R) 2018

Senate • Robert Menendez (D) 2019, Cory A. Booker (D) 2021

Representatives • Donald Norcross (D), Frank LoBiondo (R), Tom MacArthur (R), Chris Smith (R), Josh Gottheimer (D), Frank Pallone Jr. (D), Leonard Lance (R), Albio Sires (D), Bill Pascrell Jr. (D), Donald Payne Jr. (D), Rodney Frelinghuysen (R), Bonnie Watson Coleman (D)

New Mexico

State Capitol • Santa Fe NM 87501 (505) 476-2200

Governor • Susana Martinez (R) 2019

Senate • Martin T. Heinrich (D) 2019, Tom Udall (D) 2021

Representatives • Michelle Lujan Grisham (D), Steve Pearce (R), Ben R. Lujan (D)

New York

State Capitol • Albany NY 12224 (518) 474-7516

Governor • Andrew Cuomo (D) 2019

Senate • Kirsten E. Gillibrand (D) 2019, Charles Schumer (D) 2023

Representatives • Lee Zeldin (R), Peter King (R), Thomas Suozzi (D), Kathleen Rice (D), Gregory Meeks (D), Grace Meng (D), Nydia Velazquez (D), Hakeem Jeffries (D), Yvette Clarke (D), Jerrold Nadler (D), Daniel Donovan (R), Carolyn Maloney (D), Adriano Espaillat (D), Joseph Crowley (D), José E. Serrano (D), Eliot Engel (D), Nita Lowey (D), Sean Patrick Maloney (D), John Faso (R), Paul D. Tonko (D), Elise Stefanik (R), Claudia Tenney (R), Tom Reed (R), John Katko (R), Louise Slaughter (D), Brian Higgins (D), Chris Collins (R)

North Carolina

State Capitol • Raleigh NC 27603 (919) 733-5811

Governor • Roy Cooper (D) 2021

Senate • Thom Tillis (R) 2021, Richard Burr (R) 2023

Representatives • G.K. Butterfield (D), George Holding (R), Walter Jones (R), David Price (D), Virginia Foxx (R), Mark Walker (R), David Rouzer (R), Richard Hudson (R), Robert Pittenger (R), Patrick T. McHenry (R), Mark Meadows (R), Alma Adams (D), Ted Budd (R)

North Dakota

State Capitol • Bismarck ND 58505 (701) 328-2200

Governor • Doug Burgum (R) 2020

Senate • Heidi Heitkamp (D) 2019, John Hoeven (R) 2023

Representative • Kevin Cramer (R)

Ohio

State Capitol • Columbus OH 43266 (614) 466-3555

Governor • John Kasich (R) 2019

Senate • Sherrod Brown (D) 2019, Rob Portman (R) 2023

Representatives • Steve Chabot (R), Brad Wenstrup (R), Joyce Beatty (D), Jim Jordan (R), Robert Latta (R), Bill Johnson (R), Bob Gibbs (R), Warren Davidson (R) , Marcy Kaptur (D), Michael Turner (R), Marcia L. Fudge (D), Patrick Tiberi (R), Tim Ryan (D), David Joyce (R), Steve Stivers (R), Jim Renacci (R)

Oklahoma

State Capitol • Oklahoma City OK 73105 (405) 521-2342

Governor • Mary Fallin (R) 2019

Senate • James M. Inhofe (R) 2021, James Lankford (R) 2023

Representatives • Jim Bridenstine (R), Markwayne Mullin (R), Frank Lucas (R), Tom Cole (R), Steve Russell (R)

Oregon

State Capitol • Salem OR 97310 (503) 378-3111

Governor • Kate Brown (D) 2019

Senate • Jeff Merkley (D) 2021, Ron Wyden (D) 2023

Representatives • Susan Bonamici (D), Greg Walden (R), Earl Blumenauer (D), Peter DeFazio (D), Kurt Schrader (D)

Pennsylvania

State Capitol • Harrisburg PA 17120 (717) 787-2500

Governor • Tom Wolf (D) 2019

Senate • Robert P. Casey Jr. (D) 2019, Patrick J. Toomey (R) 2023

Representatives • Robert Brady (D), Dwight Evans (D), Mike Kelly (R), Scott Perry (R), Glen Thompson (R), Ryan Costello (R), Pat Meehan (R), Brian Fitzpatrick (R), Bill Shuster (R), Tom Marino (R), Lou Barletta (R), Keith Rothfus (R), Brendan Boyle (D), Mike Doyle (D), Charles W. Dent (R), Lloyd Smucker (R), Matthew Cartwright (D), Tim Murphy (R)

Rhode Island

State Capitol • Providence RI 02903 (401) 222-2080

Governor • Gina Raimondo (D) 2019

Senate • Sheldon Whitehouse (D) 2019, Jack Reed (D) 2021

Representatives • David Cicilline (D), Jim Langevin (D)

South Carolina

State Capitol • Columbia SC 29211 (803) 734-2100

Governor • Nikki Haley (R) 2019

Senate • Lindsey Graham (R) 2021, Tim Scott (R) 2023

Representatives • Mark Sanford (R), Joe Wilson (R), Jeff Duncan (R), Trey Gowdy (R), Mick Mulvaney (R), James Clyburn (D), Tom Rice (R)

South Dakota

State Capitol • Pierre SD 57501 (605) 773-3212

Governor • Dennis Daugaard (R) 2019

Senate • Mike Rounds (R) 2021, John Thune (R) 2023

Representative • Kristi Noem (R)

Tennessee

State Capitol • Nashville TN 37423

Governor • Bill Haslam (R) 2019

Senate • Bob Corker (R) 2019, Lamar Alexander (R) 2021

Representatives • Phil Roe (R), John James "Jimmy" Duncan Jr. (R), Chuck Fleischmann (R), Scott DesJarlais (R), Jim Cooper (D), Diane Black (R), Marsha Blackburn (R), David Kustoff (R), Steve Cohen (D)

Texas

State Capitol • Austin TX 78711 (512) 463-2000

Governor • Greg Abbott (R) 2019

Senate • Ted Cruz (R) 2019, John Cornyn (R) 2021

Representatives • Louie Gohmert (R), Ted Poe (R), Sam Johnson (R), John Ratcliffe (R), Jeb Hensarling (R), Joe Barton (R), John Culberson (R), Kevin Brady (R), Al Green (D), Michael McCaul (R), K. Michael Conaway (R), Kay Granger (R), Mac Thornberry (R), Randy Weber (R), Vicente Gonzalez (D), Beto O'Rourke (D), Bill Flores (R), Sheila Jackson-Lee (D), Jodey Arrington (R), Joaquin Castro (D), Lamar Smith (R), Pete Olson (R), Will Hurd (R), Kenny Marchant (R), Roger Williams (R), Michael Burgess (R), Blake Farenthold (R), Henry Cuellar (D), Gene Green (D), Eddie Bernice Johnson (D), John Carter (R), Pete Sessions (R), Mark Veasey (D), Filemon Vela Jr. (D), Lloyd Doggett (D), Brian Babin (R)

Utah

State Capitol • Salt Lake City UT 84114 (801) 538-1000

Governor • Gary Herbert (R) 2021

Senate • Orrin G. Hatch (R) 2019, Mike Lee (R) 2023

Representatives • Rob Bishop (R), Chris Stewart (R), Jason Chaffetz (R), Mia Love (R)

Vermont

State Capitol • Montpelier VT 05609 (802) 828-3333

Governor • Phil Scott (R) 2019

Senate • Bernard Sanders (I) 2019, Patrick J. Leahy (D) 2023

Representative • Peter Welch (D)

Virginia

State Capitol • Richmond VA 23219 (804) 786-2211

Governor • Terry McAuliffe (D) 2018

Senate • Tim Kaine (D) 2019, Mark R. Warner (D) 2021

Representatives • Robert Wittman (R), Scott Taylor (R), Robert Scott (D), Donald McEachin (D), Thomas Garrett, Jr. (R), Bob Goodlatte (R), Dave Brat (R), Don Beyer (D), Morgan Griffith (R), Barbara Comstock (R), Gerald E. "Gerry" Connolly (D)

Washington

State Capitol • Olympia WA 98504 (360) 902-4111

Governor • Jay Inslee (D) 2021

Senate • Maria Cantwell (D) 2019, Patty Murray (D) 2023

Representatives • Suzan DelBene (D), Rick Larsen (D), Jamie Herrera Beutler (R), Dan Newhouse (R), Cathy McMorris Rodgers (R), Derek Kilmer (D), Pramila Jayapal (D), David Reichert (R), Adam Smith (D), Denny Heck (D)

West Virginia

State Capitol • Charleston WV 25305 (304) 558-2000

Governor • Jim Justice (D) 2021

Senate • Joe Manchin III (D) 2019, Shelley Moore Capito (R) 2021

Representatives • David McKinley (R), Alex X. Mooney (R), Evan Jenkins (R)

Wisconsin

State Capitol • Madison WI 53707 (608) 266-1212

Governor • Scott Walker (R) 2019

Senate • Tammy Baldwin (D) 2019, Ron Johnson (R) 2023

Representatives • Paul Ryan (R), Mark Pocan (D), Ron Kind (D), Gwen Moore (D), F. James Sensenbrenner Jr. (R), Glen Grothman (R), Sean P. Duffy (R), Mike Gallagher (R)

Wyoming

State Capitol • Cheyenne WY 82002 (307) 777-7434

Governor • Matt Mead (R) 2019

Senate • John Barrasso (R) 2019, Michael Enzi (R) 2021

Representative • Liz Cheney (R)

U.S. Congress

NOTES